ISBN 978-1-330-13332-3
PIBN 10033945

This book is a reproduction of an important historical work. Forgotten Books uses
state-of-the-art technology to digitally reconstruct the work, preserving the original format
whilst repairing imperfections present in the aged copy. In rare cases, an imperfection in
the original, such as a blemish or missing page, may be replicated in our edition. We do,
however, repair the vast majority of imperfections successfully; any imperfections that
remain are intentionally left to preserve the state of such historical works.

English
Français
Deutsche
Italiano
Español
Português

www.forgottenbooks.com

Mythology Photography **Fiction** Fishing Christianity **Art** Cooking Essays Buddhism Freemasonry Medicine **Biology** Music **Ancient Egypt** Evolution Carpentry Physics Dance Geology **Mathematics** Fitness Shakespeare **Folklore** Yoga Marketing **Confidence** Immortality Biographies Poetry **Psychology** Witchcraft Electronics Chemistry History **Law** Accounting **Philosophy** Anthropology Alchemy Drama Quantum Mechanics Atheism Sexual Health **Ancient History** **Entrepreneurship** Languages Sport Paleontology Needlework Islam **Metaphysics** Investment Archaeology Parenting Statistics Criminology **Motivational**

TREASURY OF THOUGHT.

FORMING

An Encyclopædia of Quotations

FROM

ANCIENT AND MODERN AUTHORS.

BY

MATURIN M. BALLOU.

I love to lose myself in other men's minds. — LAMB.

They have been at a great feast of languages, and stolen the scraps. — SHAKESPEARE.

Short sentences drawn from a long experience. — CERVANTES.

SEVENTH EDITION.

BOSTON:
HOUGHTON, MIFFLIN AND COMPANY.
The Riverside Press, Cambridge.
1881.

QUOTATION, SIR, IS A GOOD THING; THERE IS A COMMUNITY OF MIND IN IT; CLASSICAL QUOTATION IS THE PAROLE OF LITERARY MEN ALL OVER THE WORLD. —

Samuel Johnson.

HOW MANY OF US HAVE BEEN ATTRACTED TO REASON; FIRST LEARNED TO THINK, TO DRAW CONCLUSIONS, TO EXTRACT A MORAL FROM THE FOLLIES OF LIFE, BY SOME DAZZLING APHORISM! — *Bulwer Lytton.*

I HERE PRESENT THEE WITH A HIVE OF BEES, LADEN SOME WITH WAX AND SOME WITH HONEY. FEAR NOT TO APPROACH! THERE ARE NO HORNETS HERE. IF SOME WANTON BEE SHOULD CHANCE TO BUZZ ABOUT THINE EARS, STAND THY GROUND, AND HOLD THINE HANDS; THERE'IS NONE WILL STING THEE IF THOU STRIKE NOT FIRST. IF ANY DO, SHE HATH HONEY IN HER BAG WILL CURE THEE TOO. — *Francis Quarles.*

THUS HAVE I, AS WELL AS I COULD, GATHERED A POSEY OF OBSERVATIONS AS THEY GREW; AND IF SOME RUE AND WORMWOOD BE FOUND AMONG THE SWEET HERBS, THEIR WHOLESOMENESS WILL MAKE AMENDS FOR THEIR BITTERNESS. — *Lord Lyttelton.*

PREFACE.

LET EVERY BOOK-WORM, WHEN IN ANY FRAGRANT SCARCE OLD TOME HE DISCOVERS A SEN-
TENCE, A STORY, AN ILLUSTRATION, THAT DOES HIS HEART GOOD, HASTEN TO GIVE IT.—

Coleridge.

THE work herewith presented is the offspring of a desultory course of reading, extending through a period of more than twenty years. When, in the pleasant paths of study, an apothegm or vivid saying has been met with, bearing the impress of mind and mature thought, illustrating in a concise and significant manner a great truth, or exhibiting some marked phase of philosophy or peculiar aspect of life, with brief but happy expressions of familiar things, such gems have been transferred from their original setting for record and classification.

The incipient steps in this direction were the natural ones of a thoughtful reader, such as turned-down leaves and marginal notes, until a curiosity to compare the refined thought of one favorite author or classic authority with that of another upon the same theme led to a series of pencilled extracts upon various cardinal subjects. Mental research was thus gradually stimulated to collect from the shores of literature such golden sands as, from their brilliancy and suggestiveness, dazzled both the sense and the imagination.

For years this constantly growing collection was solely pursued as a matter of personal interest, and with no idea of future publication, until its volume had so increased, and its variety become so comprehensive, as to attract the attention of others who were casually aware of its existence. In a literary point of view, the undersigned claims no merit, save that of an industrious compiler, whose labor has been its own great reward, in the pleasurable memories it has aroused of those authors, ancient and modern, with whom so many delightful hours have been passed.

M. M. B.

TO

My Wife,

THE PATIENT AND CHEERFUL ASSOCIATE OF MY STUDIES, AFTER MORE THAN

THIRTY YEARS OF HAPPY COMPANIONSHIP,

THIS VOLUME

IS AFFECTIONATELY DEDICATED.

BY

THE COMPILER.

INDEX OF SUBJECTS.

xii

ENCYCLOPÆDIA OF QUOTATIONS.

A.

ABILITY.

The art of being able to make a good use of moderate abilities wins esteem, and often confers more reputation than real merit.—*Rochefoucauld.*

Men are often capable of greater things than they perform. They are sent into the world with bills of credit, and seldom draw to their full extent.—*Walpole.*

The force of his own merit makes his way, a gift that Heaven gives for him.—*Shakespeare.*

The abilities of a man must fall short on one side or other, like too scanty a blanket when you are abed : if you pull it upon your shoulders, you leave your feet bare; if you thrust it down upon your feet, your shoulders are uncovered.—*Sir W. Temple.*

The height of ability consists in a thorough knowledge of the real value of things, and of the genius of the age we live in.—*Rochefoucauld.*

An able man shows his spirit by gentle words and resolute actions ; he is neither hot nor timid.—*Chesterfield.*

No man's abilities are so remarkably shining, as to stand in need of a proper opportunity, a patron, and even the praises of a friend, to recommend them to the notice of the world.—*Pliny.*

Some persons of weak understanding are so sensible of that weakness, as to be able to make a good use of it.—*Rochefoucauld.*

ABSENCE.

'T is ever common, that men are merriest when they are from home.—*Shakespeare.*

Distance of time and place do generally cure what they seem to aggravate ; and taking leave of our friends resembles taking leave of the world, concerning which it hath been often said that it is not death, but dying, which is terrible.—*Fielding.*

The joy of meeting pays the pangs of absence ; else who could bear it ?—*Rowe.*

All flowers will droop in absence of the sun that waked their sweets.—*Dryden.*

What vigor absence adds to love !—*Flatman.*

I am not sure if the ladies understand the full value of the influence of absence, nor do I think it wise to teach it them, lest, like the Clelias and Mandanes of yore, they should resume the humor of sending their lovers into banishment. Distance, in truth, produces in idea the same effect as in real perspective. Objects are softened, and rounded, and rendered doubly graceful ; the harsher and more ordinary points of character are mellowed down, and those by which it is remembered are the more striking outlines that mark sublimity, grace, or beauty.—*Walter Scott.*

Absent in body, but present in spirit.—*Bible.*

Absence diminishes moderate passions and augments great ones, as the wind extinguishes candles and kindles the fire.—*Rochefoucauld.*

The absent are never without fault, nor the present without excuse.—*Franklin.*

Absence, like death, sets a seal on the image of those we have loved ; we cannot realize the intervening changes which time may have effected.—*Goldsmith.*

Our souls much farther than our eyes can see.—*Michael Drayton.*

I find the attraction of love is in an inverse proportion to the attraction of the Newtonian philosophy. Every mile-stone that marked my progress from Clarinda awakened a keener pang of attachment.—*Burns.*

Love reckons hours for months, and days for years ; and every little absence is an age.—*Dryden.*

Distance sometimes endears friendship, and absence sweeteneth it.—*Howell.*

Give me to drink mandragora, that I might sleep out this great gap of time my Antony is away.—*Shakespeare.*

1

What! keep a week away? Seven days and nights? eightscore eight hours? and lovers' absent hours, more tedious than the dial eightscore times? O weary reckoning!—*Shakespeare.*

The presence of those whom we love is as a double life; absence, in its anxious longing and sense of vacancy, is as a foretaste of death.—
Mrs. Jameson.

ABSTINENCE.

Ah, how much suffering might be spared sometimes by a single abstinence, by a single no answered in a firm tone to the voice of seduction!—*Lavater.*

To set the mind above the appetites is the end of abstinence, which one of the fathers observes to be, not a virtue, but the groundwork of a virtue. By forbearing to do what may innocently be done, we may add hourly new vigor to resolution, and secure the power of resistance when pleasure or interest shall lend their charms to guilt.—*Johnson.*

He who wishes to travel far is careful of his steed; drink, eat, sleep, and let us light a fire which shall continue to burn.—*Racine.*

The more a man denies himself, the more he shall obtain from God.—*Horace.*

The whole duty of man is embraced in the two principles of abstinence and patience: temperance in prosperity, and courage in adversity.
Seneca.

Always rise from table with an appetite, and you will never sit down without one.—
William Penn.

Endeavor to have as little to do with thy affections and passions as thou canst: and labor to thy power to make thy body content to go of thy soul's errands.—*Jeremy Taylor.*

His life is paralleled even with the stroke and line of his great justice; he doth with holy abstinence subdue that in himself which he spurs on his power to qualify in others.—
Shakespeare.

The stomach listens to no precepts. It begs and clamors. And yet it is not an obdurate creditor. It is dismissed with a small payment, if only you give it what you owe, and not as much as you can.—*Seneca.*

The temperate are the most truly luxurious. By abstaining from most things, it is surprising how many things we enjoy.—*Simms.*

Let not thy table exceed the fourth part of thy revenue: let thy provision be solid, and not far fetched, fuller of substance than art: be wisely frugal in thy preparation, and freely cheerful in thy entertainment: if thy guests be right, it is enough; if not, it is too much: too much is a vanity; enough is a feast.—*Quarles.*

A rich man cannot enjoy a sound mind nor a sound body, without exercise and abstinence; and yet these are truly the worst ingredients of poverty.—*Henry Home.*

Moderation is the silken string running through the pearl-chain of all virtues.—*Fuller.*

Temperance and labor are the two best physicians of man; labor sharpens the appetite, and temperance prevents him from indulging to excess.—*Rousseau.*

After all, it is continued temperance which sustains the body for the longest period of time, and which most surely preserves it free from sickness.—*Wilhelm von Humboldt.*

The miser's cheese is wholesomest.
Franklin.

When you have learned to nourish your body frugally, do not pique yourself upon it, nor, if you drink water, be saying upon every occasion, "I drink water." But first consider how much more frugal are the poor than we, and how much more patient of hardship.—
Epictetus.

The defensive virtue abstinence.—*Herrick.*

If thou desire to make the best advantage of the muses, either by reading, to benefit thyself, or by writing, others, keep a peaceful soul in a temperate body: a full belly makes a dull brain; and a turbulent spirit, a distracted judgment: the muses starve in a cook's shop and a lawyer's study.—*Quarles.*

ABUSE.

Abuse is often of service. There is nothing so dangerous to an author as silence. His name, like a shuttlecock, must be beat backward and forward, or it falls to the ground.—
Johnson.

It is the wit, the policy of sin, to hate those men we have abused.—*Sir W. Davenant.*

There are more people abusive to others than lie open to abuse themselves; but the humor goes round, and he that laughs at me to-day will have somebody to laugh at him to-morrow.—*Seneca.*

I never yet heard man or woman much abused, that I was not inclined to think the better of them; and to transfer any suspicion or dislike to the person who appeared to take delight in pointing out the defects of a fellow-creature.—*Jane Porter.*

Remember that it is not he who gives abuse or blows who affronts, but the view we take of these things as insulting. When, therefore, any one provokes you, be assured that it is your own opinion which provokes you.—
Epictetus

There is a time when men will not suffer bad things because their ancestors have suffered worse. There is a time when the hoary head of inveterate abuse will neither draw reverence nor obtain protection.—*Burke.*

When certain persons abuse us, let us ask ourselves what description of characters it is that they admire; we shall often find this a very consolatory question.—*Colton.*

ACCIDENT.

No accidents are so unlucky but that the prudent may draw some advantage from them; nor are there any so lucky but that the imprudent may turn to their prejudice.—
Rochefoucauld.

As the unthought-on accident is guilty of what we wildly do, so we profess ourselves to be the slaves of chance, and flies of every wind that blows.—*Shakespeare.*

ACQUIREMENTS.

That good sense which nature affords us is preferable to most of the knowledge that we can acquire.—*Comines.*

That which we acquire with the most difficulty we retain the longest; as those who have earned a fortune are usually more careful of it than those who have inherited one.—*Colton.*

ACTION.

There is no action of man in this life which is not the beginning of so long a chain of consequences, as that no human providence is high enough to give us a prospect to the end.—
Thomas of Malmesbury.

Man is an animal that cannot long be left in safety without occupation; the growth of his fallow nature is apt to run into weeds.—*Hillard.*

Wouldst thou know the lawfulness of the action which thou desirest to undertake, let thy devotion recommend it to Divine blessing: if it be lawful, thou shalt perceive thy heart encouraged by thy prayer; if unlawful, thou shalt find thy prayer discouraged by thy heart. That action is not warrantable which either blushes to beg a blessing, or, having succeeded, dares not present a thanksgiving.—*Quarles.*

Action hangs, as it were, "dissolved" in speech, in thoughts whereof speech is the shadow; and precipitates itself therefrom. The kind of speech in a man betokens the kind of action you will get from him.—*Carlyle.*

Speak out in acts; the time for words has passed, and deeds alone suffice.—*Whittier.*

To do an evil action is base; to do a good action, without incurring danger, is common enough; but it is the part of a good man to do great and noble deeds, though he risks everything.—*Plutarch.*

A contemplative life has more the appearance of a life of piety than any other; but it is the Divine plan to bring faith into activity and exercise.—*Cecil.*

All our actions take their lines from the complexion of the heart; as landscapes their variety from light.—*W. T. Bacon.*

Not alone to know, but to act according to thy knowledge, is thy destination,—proclaims the voice of my inmost soul. Not for indolent contemplation and study of thyself, nor for brooding over emotions of piety,—no, for action was existence given thee; thy actions, and thy actions alone, determine thy worth.—
Fichte.

The only true method of action in this world is to be in it, but not of it.—*Madame Swetchine.*

Man, being essentially active, must find in activity his joy, as well as his beauty and glory; and labor, like everything else that is good, is its own reward.—*Whipple.*

The only things in which we can be said to have any property are our actions. Our thoughts may be bad, yet produce no poison; they may be good, yet produce no fruit. Our riches may be taken away by misfortune, our reputation by malice, our spirits by calamity, our health by disease, our friends by death. But our actions must follow us beyond the grave; with respect to them alone, we cannot say that we shall carry nothing with us when we die, neither that we shall go naked out of the world.—
Colton.

Idlers cannot even find time to be idle, or the industrious to be at leisure. We must be always doing or suffering.—*Zimmermann.*

Unselfish and noble acts are the most radiant epochs in the biography of souls. When wrought in earliest youth, they lie in the memory of age like the coral islands, green and sunny, amidst the melancholy waste of ocean.—
Rev. Dr. Thomas.

Life is a short day; but it is a working-day. Activity may lead to evil; but inactivity cannot be led to good.—*Hannah More.*

Allowing the performance of an honorable action to be attended with labor, the labor is soon over, but the honor is immortal; whereas, should even pleasure wait on the commission of what is dishonorable, the pleasure is soon gone, but the dishonor is eternal.—*John Stewart.*

Our actions are like the terminations of verses, which we rhyme as we please.—
Rochefoucauld.

I have lived to know that the secret of happiness is never to allow your energies to stagnate.—*Adam Clarke.*

Be not too tame neither, but let your own discretion be your tutor; suit the action to the word, the word to the action; with this special observance, that you o'erstep not the modesty of nature.—*Shakespeare.*

All power appears only in transition. Permanent power is stuff.—*Novalis.*

Act! the wise are known by their actions; fame and immortality are ever their attendants. Mark with deeds the vanishing traces of swift-rolling time. Let us make happy the circle around us,—be useful as much as we may. For that fills up with soft rapture, that dissolves the dark clouds of the day!—*Salis.*

Be great in act, as you have been in thought.
Shakespeare.

Indolence is a delightful but distressing state; we must be doing something to be happy. Action is no less necessary than thought to the instinctive tendencies of the human frame.—*Hazlitt.*

It behooves the high for their own sake to do things worthily.—*Ben Jonson.*

It is hard to personate and act a part long; for where Truth is not at the bottom, Nature will always be endeavoring to return, and will peep out and betray herself one time or other.—*Tillotson.*

Strong reasons make strong actions.—
Shakespeare.

The Lord is a God of knowledge, and by him actions are weighed.—*Bible.*

Man is born for action; he ought to do something. Work, at each step, awakens a sleeping force and roots out error. Who does nothing, knows nothing. Rise! to work! If thy knowledge is real, employ it; wrestle with nature; test the strength of thy theories; see if they will support the trial; act!—*Aloysius.*

Our actions are our own; their consequences belong to Heaven.—*P. Francis.*

"There is nothing so terrible as activity without insight," says Goethe. "I would open every one of Argus's hundred eyes before I used one of Briareus's hundred hands," says Lord Bacon. "Look before you leap," says John Smith, all over the world.—*Whipple.*

Our acts make or mar us,—we are the children of our own deeds.—*Victor Hugo.*

Remember that in all miseries lamenting becomes fools, and action, wise folk.—
Sir P. Sidney.

A stirring dwarf we do allowance give before a sleeping giant.—*Shakespeare.*

Action is the highest perfection and drawing forth of the utmost power, vigor, and activity of man's nature.—*South.*

Better that we should err in action than wholly refuse to perform. The storm is so much better than the calm, as it declares the presence of a living principle. Stagnation is something worse than death. It is corruption also.—*Simms.*

The flighty purpose never is o'ertook unless the deed go with it.—*Shakespeare.*

Let us, if we must have great actions, make our own so. All action is of infinite elasticity, and the least admits of being inflated with celestial air, until it eclipses the sun and moon.—
Emerson.

Activity is the presence of function,—character is the record of function.—*Greenough.*

No man should be so much taken up in the search of truth, as thereby to neglect the more necessary duties of active life; for after all is done, it is action only that gives a true value and commendation to virtue.—*Cicero.*

Active natures are rarely melancholy. Activity and melancholy are incompatible.—*Bovee.*

Do not be afraid because the community teems with excitement. Silence and death are dreadful. The rush of life, the vigor of earnest men, the conflict of realities, invigorate, cleanse, and establish the truth.—*Beecher.*

Action is eloquence, and the eyes of the ignorant more learned than their ears.—
Shakespeare.

The activity of the young is like that of rail cars in motion,—they tear along with noise and turmoil, and leave peace behind them. The quietest nooks, invaded by them, lose their quietude as they pass, and recover it only on their departure. Time's best gift to us is serenity.—
Bovee.

Celerity is never more admired than by the negligent.—*Shakespeare.*

It is good policy to strike while the iron is hot; it is still better to adopt Cromwell's procedure, and make the iron hot by striking. The master-spirit who can rule the storm is great, but he is much greater who can both raise and rule it.—*E. L. Magoon.*

How slow the time to the warm soul, that, in the very instant it forms, would execute a great design!—*Thomson.*

Let's take the instant by the forward top; for we are old, and on our quickest decrees the inaudible and noiseless foot of time steals, ere we can effect them.—*Shakespeare.*

Hast thou not Greek enough to understand thus much: the end of man is an action and not a thought, though it were of the noblest.—*Carlyle.*

Deliberate with caution, but act with decision; and yield with graciousness, or oppose with firmness.—*Colton.*

The keen spirit seizes the prompt occasion; makes the thought start into instant action, and at once plans and performs, resolves and executes!—*Hannah More.*

The firefly only shines when on the wing; so is it with the mind; when once we rest, we darken.—*Bailey.*

Words are good, but there is something better. The best is not to be explained by words. The spirit in which we act is the chief matter. Action can only be understood and represented by the spirit. No one knows what he is doing while he is acting rightly, but of what is wrong we are always conscious.—*Goethe.*

It is vain to expect any advantage from our profession of the truth, if we be not sincerely just and honest in our actions.—*Archbishop Sharpe.*

Men's actions to futurity appear but as the events to which they are conjoined do give them consequence.—*Joanna Baillie.*

Thought and theory must precede all action that moves to salutary purposes. Yet action is nobler in itself than either thought or theory.—*Wordsworth.*

Every event that a man would master must be mounted on the run, and no man ever caught the reins of a thought except as it galloped by him.—*Holmes.*

Toil, feel, think, hope. A man is sure to dream enough before he dies without making arrangements for the purpose.—*Sterling.*

There is no word or action but may be taken with two hands,—either with the right hand of charitable construction, or the sinister interpretation of malice and suspicion; and all things do succeed as they are taken. To construe an evil action well is but a pleasing and profitable deceit to myself; but to misconstrue a good thing is a treble wrong,—to myself, the action, and the author.—*Bishop Hall.*

What a man knows should find its expression in what he does. The value of superior knowledge is chiefly in that it leads to a performing manhood.—*Bovee.*

Actions rare and sudden do commonly proceed from fierce necessity, or else from some oblique design, which is ashamed to show itself in the public road.—*Sir W. Davenant.*

The least movement is of importance to all nature. The entire ocean is affected by a pebble.—*Pascal.*

Act well at the moment, and you have performed a good action to all eternity.—*Lavater.*

Just in proportion as a man becomes good, divine, Christlike, he passes out of the region of theorizing, of system-building, and hireling service, into the region of beneficent activities. It is well to think well. It is divine to act well.—*Horace Mann.*

Life is an outward occupation, an actual work, in all ranks, and all situations.—*Wilhelm von Humboldt.*

ACTORS.

Notwithstanding all that Rousseau has advanced so very ingeniously upon plays and players, their profession is, like that of a painter, one of the imitative arts, whose means are pleasure, and whose end is virtue.—*Shenstone.*

Comedians are not actors; they are only imitators of actors.—*Zimmermann.*

They are the only honest hypocrites. Their life is a voluntary dream, a studied madness. The height of their ambition is to be beside themselves. To-day kings, to-morrow beggars, it is only when they are themselves that they are nothing. Made up of mimic laughter and tears, passing from the extremes of joy or woe at the prompter's call, they wear the livery of other men's fortunes; their very thoughts are not their own.—*Hazlitt.*

There is one way by which a strolling player may be ever secure of success; that is, in our theatrical way of expressing it, to make a great deal of the character. To speak and act as in common life is not playing, nor is it what people come to see; natural speaking, like sweet wine, runs glibly over the palate, and scarcely leaves any taste behind it; but being high in a part resembles vinegar, which grates upon the taste, and one feels it while he is drinking.—*Goldsmith.*

It is with some violence to the imagination that we conceive of an actor belonging to the relations of private life, so closely do we identify these persons in our mind with the characters which they assume upon the stage.—*Lamb.*

Where they do agree on the stage, their unanimity is wonderful.—*Sheridan.*

The actor is in the capacity of a steward to every living muse, and of an executor to every departed one: the poet digs up the ore; he sifts it from the dross, refines and purifies it for the mint; the actor sets the stamp upon it, and makes it current in the world.—*Cumberland.*

They are the abstract, and brief chronicles of the time.—*Shakespeare.*

All the world's a stage, and all the men and women merely players; they have their exits and their entrances, and one man in his time plays many parts.—*Shakespeare.*

The stage is a supplement to the pulpit, where virtue, according to Plato's sublime idea, moves our love and affection when made visible to the eye.—*Disraeli.*

God is the author, men are only the players. These grand pieces which are played upon earth have been composed in heaven.—*Balzac.*

Let those that play your clowns speak no more than is set down for them.—*Shakespeare.*

The most difficult character in comedy is that of the fool, and he must be no simpleton that plays that part.—*Cervantes.*

We that live to please must please to live.—*Johnson.*

In acting, barely to perform the part is not commendable; but to be the least out is contemptible.—*Steele.*

On the stage he was natural, simple, affecting; it was only when he was off that he was acting.—*Goldsmith.*

ADAPTATION.
To wade in marshes and sea margins is the destiny of certain birds, and they are so accurately made for this that they are imprisoned in those places. Each animal out of its habitat would starve. To the physician, each man, each woman, is an amplification of one organ. A soldier, a locksmith, a bank-clerk, and a dancer could not exchange functions. And thus we are victims of adaptation.—*Emerson.*

ADDRESS.
Brahmâ once asked of Force, "Who is stronger than thou?" She replied, "Address." *Victor Hugo.*

A man who knows the world will not only make the most of everything he does know, but of many things he does not know, and will gain more credit by his adroit mode of hiding his ignorance than the pedant by his awkward attempt to exhibit his erudition.—*Colton.*

Give a boy address and accomplishments, and you give him the mastery of palaces and fortunes where he goes. He has not the trouble of earning or owning them; they solicit him to enter and possess.—*Emerson.*

There is a certain artificial polish, a commonplace vivacity acquired by perpetually mingling in the *beau monde*, which, in the commerce of the world, supplies the place of natural suavity and good-humor, but is purchased at the expense of all original and sterling traits of character.—*Washington Irving.*

Address makes opportunities; the want of it gives them.—*Bovee.*

ADMIRATION.
It may be laid down as a general rule, that no woman who hath any great pretensions to admiration is ever well pleased in a company where she perceives herself to fill only the second place.—*Fielding.*

Admiration is a very short-lived passion, that immediately decays upon growing familiar with its object, unless it be still fed with fresh discoveries, and kept alive by a new perpetual succession of miracles rising up to its view.—*Addison.*

Those who are formed to win general admiration are seldom calculated to bestow individual happiness.—*Lady Blessington.*

Admiration is the daughter of ignorance.—*Franklin.*

Admiration and moderate contemplation have a great power to prolong life; for these detain the spirits upon pleasing subjects, without suffering them to tumultuate and act disorderly. But subtle, acute, and severe inquiries cut short life; for they fatigue and wear out the spirits.—*Byron.*

We always love those who admire us, but we do not always love those whom we admire.—*Rochefoucauld.*

There is a wide difference between admiration and love. The sublime, which is the cause of the former, always dwells on great objects and terrible; the latter on small ones and pleasing; we submit to what we admire, but we love what submits to us: in one case we are forced, in the other we are flattered, into compliance.—*Burke.*

Amid the most mercenary ages it is but a secondary sort of admiration that is bestowed upon magnificence.—*Shenstone.*

To cultivate sympathy you must be among living creatures, and thinking about them; and to cultivate admiration, you must be among beautiful things and looking at them.—*Ruskin.*

There is a long and wearisome step between admiration and imitation.—*Richter.*

The love of admiration leads to fraud, much more than the love of commendation; but, on the other hand, the latter is much more likely to spoil our good actions by the substitution of an inferior motive.—*Bishop Whately.*

Admiration must be continued by that novelty which first produces it; and how much soever is given, there must always be reason to imagine that more remains.—*Johnson.*

ADVERSITY.

Adversity has ever been considered as the state in which a man most easily becomes acquainted with himself, particularly being free from flatterers.—*Johnson.*

Prosperity is too apt to prevent us from examining our conduct, but as adversity leads us to think properly of our state, it is most beneficial to us.—*Johnson.*

Sweet are the uses of adversity, which, like the toad, though ugly and venomous, wears yet a precious jewel in his head.—*Shakespeare.*

The truly great and good, in affliction, bear a countenance more princely than they are wont; for it is the temper of the highest hearts, like the palm-tree, to strive most upwards when it is most burdened.—*Sir P. Sidney.*

Half the ills we hoard within our hearts are ills because we hoard them.—*Barry Cornwall.*

It is often better to have a great deal of harm happen to one than a little; a great deal may rouse you to remove what a little will only accustom you to endure.—*Greville.*

How full of briers is this working-day world!
Shakespeare.

Prosperity is the blessing of the Old Testament, adversity is the blessing of the New, which carrieth the greater benediction, and the clearer revelation of God's favor.—*Bacon.*

Prosperity is no just scale; adversity is the only balance to weigh friends.—*Plutarch.*

The willow which bends to the tempest often escapes better than the oak, which resists it; and so, in great calamities, it sometimes happens that light and frivolous spirits recover their elasticity and presence of mind sooner than those of a loftier character.—*Walter Scott.*

Adversity is the trial of principle. Without it, a man hardly knows whether he is honest or not.—*Fielding.*

Men think God is destroying them because he is tuning them. The violinist screws up the key till the tense cord sounds the concert pitch; but it is not to break it, but to use it tunefully, that he stretches the string upon the musical rack.—*Beecher.*

Adversity is the first path to truth.—*Byron.*

Our dependence upon God ought to be so entire and absolute that we should never think it necessary, in any kind of distress, to have recourse to human consolations.—
Thomas à Kempis.

Adversity borrows its sharpest sting from our impatience.—*Bishop Horne.*

He that can heroically endure adversity will bear prosperity with equal greatness of soul; for the mind that cannot be dejected by the former is not likely to be transported with the latter.—*Fielding.*

Heaven oft in mercy smites, even when the blow severest is.—*Joanna Baillie.*

The brightest crowns that are worn in heaven have been tried, and smelted, and polished, and glorified through the furnace of tribulation.—*Chapin.*

Clouds are the veil behind which the face of day coquettishly hides itself, to enhance its beauty.—*Richter.*

By adversity are wrought the greatest works of admiration, and all the fair examples of renown, out of distress and misery are grown.—
Daniel.

One month in the school of affliction will teach thee more than the great precepts of Aristotle in seven years; for thou canst never judge rightly of human affairs, unless thou hast first felt the blows, and found out the deceits of fortune.—*Fuller.*

Adversity has the effect of eliciting talents which in prosperous circumstances would have lain dormant.—*Horace.*

The gods in bounty work up storms about us, that give mankind occasion to exert their hidden strength, and throw out into practice virtues that shun the day, and lie concealed in the smooth seasons and the calms of life.—
Addison.

Affliction is the good man's shining scene; prosperity conceals his brightest rays; as night to stars, woe lustre gives to man.—*Young.*

For whom the Lord loveth he chasteneth.—
Bible.

In adversity be spirited and firm, and with equal prudence lessen your sail when filled with a too fortunate gale of prosperity.—*Horace.*

There is strength deep-bedded in our hearts, of which we reck but little till the shafts of heaven have pierced its fragile dwelling. Must not earth be rent before her gems are found?—
Mrs. Hemans.

Through danger safety comes — through trouble rest.—*John Marston.*

Affliction is the wholesome soil of virtue, where patience, honor, sweet humanity, calm fortitude, take root and strongly flourish.—
Mallet.

Much dearer be the things which come through hard distress.—*Spenser.*

*P*rosperity is a great teacher; adversity is a greater. Possession pampers the mind; privation trains and strengthens it.—*Hazlitt.*

He that has no cross deserves no crown.—
Quarles.

Genuine morality is preserved only in the school of adversity, and a state of continuous prosperity may easily prove a quicksand to virtue.—*Schiller.*

In the wounds our sufferings plough immortal love sows sovereign seed.—*Massey.*

The winter's frost must rend the burr of the nut before the fruit is seen. So adversity tempers the human heart, to discover its real worth.
Balzac.

Know how sublime a thing it is to suffer and be strong.—*Longfellow.*

Mr. Bettenham said that virtuous men were like some herbs and spices, that give not out their sweet smell till they be broken or crushed.
Bacon.

Those who have suffered much are like those who know many languages; they have learned to understand and be understood by all.—
Madame Swetchine.

A noble heart, like the sun, showeth its greatest countenance in its lowest estate.—
Sir P. Sidney.

There are minerals called hydrophanous, which are not transparent till they are immersed in water, when they become so; as the hydrophane, a variety of opal. So it is with many a Christian. Till the floods of adversity have been poured over him, his character appears marred and clouded by selfishness and worldly influences. But trials clear away the obscurity, and give distinctness and beauty to his piety.—*Professor Hitchcock.*

Let me embrace these sour adversities, for wise men say it is the wisest course.—
Shakespeare.

The most affluent may be stripped of all, and find his worldly comforts, like so many withered leaves, dropping from him.—*Sterne.*

He that has never known adversity is but half acquainted with others, or with himself.—
Colton.

ADVICE.

How is it possible to expect that mankind will take advice when they will not so much as take warning?—*Swift.*

Counsel and conversation is a good second education, that improves all the virtue and corrects all the vice of the former, and of nature itself.—*Clarendon.*

He that gives good advice builds with one hand; he that gives good counsel and example builds with the other; but he that gives good admonition and bad example builds with one hand and pulls down with the other.—*Bacon.*

He who can advise is sometimes superior to him who can give it.—*Von Knebel.*

Advice, as it always gives a temporary appearance of superiority, can never be very grateful, even when it is most necessary or most judicious; but, for the same reason, every one is eager to instruct his neighbors.—*Johnson.*

The worst men often give the best advice.—
Bailey.

If to do were as easy as to know what were good to do, chapels had been churches, and poor men's cottages, princes' palaces. It is a good divine that follows his own instructions: I can easier teach twenty what were good to be done, than be one of the twenty to follow mine own teaching.—*Shakespeare.*

Good counsels observed are chains to grace.
Fuller.

There is nothing of which men are more liberal than their good advice, be their stock of it ever so small; because it seems to carry in it an intimation of their own influence, importance, or worth.—*Young.*

Wait for the season when to cast good counsels upon subsiding passion.—*Shakespeare.*

Nothing is less sincere than our manner of asking and of giving advice. He who asks advice would seem to have a respectful deference for the opinion of his friend, whilst yet he only aims at getting his own approved of, and his friend responsible for his conduct. On the other hand, he who gives it repays the confidence supposed to be placed in him by a seemingly disinterested zeal, whilst he seldom means anything by the advice he gives but his own interest or reputation.—*Rochefoucauld.*

Let no man value at a little price a virtuous woman's counsel.—*George Chapman.*

No one was ever the better for advice: in general, what we called giving advice was properly taking an occasion to show our own wisdom at another's expense; and to receive advice was little better than tamely to afford another the occasion of raising himself a character from our defects.—*Lord Shaftesbury.*

Mishaps are mastered by advice discreet, and counsel mitigates the greatest smart.—*Spenser.*

When we feel a strong desire to thrust our advice upon others, it is usually because we suspect their weakness; but we ought rather to suspect our own.—*Colton.*

Advice is offensive, not because it lays us open to unexpected regret, or convicts us of any fault which has escaped our notice, but because it shows us that we are known to others as well as ourselves; and the officious monitor is persecuted with hatred, not because his accusation is false, but because he assumes the superiority which we are not willing to grant him, and has dared to detect what we desire to conceal.—*Johnson.*

How is it that even castaways can give such good advice ?—*Ninon de l'Enclos.*

A man takes contradiction and advice much more easily than people think, only he will not bear it when violently given, even though it be well founded. Hearts are flowers; they remain open to the softly falling dew, but shut up in the violent downpour of rain.—*Richter.*

Let no man presume to give advice to others that has not first given good counsel to himself.—*Seneca.*

There is as much difference between the counsel that a friend giveth and that a man giveth himself, as there is between the counsel of a friend and of a flatterer; for there is no such flatterer as a man's self, and there is no such remedy against flattery of a man's self as the liberty of a friend.—*Bacon.*

It has been well observed that few are better qualified to give others advice than those who have taken the least of it themselves.—*Goldsmith.*

It was the maxim, I think, of Alphonsus of Aragon, that dead counsellors are safest. The grave puts an end to flattery and artifice, and the information we receive from books is pure from interest, fear, and ambition. Dead counsellors are likewise most instructive, because they are heard with patience and with reverence.—*Johnson.*

Admonish your friends privately, but praise them openly.—*Publius Syrus.*

The greatest trust between man and man is the trust of giving counsel.—*Bacon.*

I lay very little stress either upon asking or giving advice. Generally speaking, they who ask advice know what they wish to do, and remain firm to their intentions. A man may allow himself to be enlightened on various points, even upon matters of expediency and duty; but, after all, he must determine his course of action for himself.—*Wilhelm von Humboldt.*

Remember this : they that will not be counselled cannot be helped. If you do not hear Reason, she will rap your knuckles.—*Franklin.*

There is nearly as much ability requisite to know how to profit by good advice as to know how to act for one's self.—*Rochefoucauld.*

Do not give to thy friends the most agreeable counsels, but the most advantageous.—*Tuckerman.*

We ask advice, but we mean approbation.—*Colton.*

No man is so foolish but he may give another good counsel sometimes, and no man so wise but he may easily err, if he takes no other counsel than his own. He that was taught only by himself had a fool for a master.
Ben Jonson.

Men give away nothing so liberally as their advice.—*Rochefoucauld.*

I forget whether advice be among the lost things which Ariosto says are to be found in the moon : that and time ought to have been there.—*Swift.*

Advice is seldom welcome. Those who need it most like it least.—*Johnson.*

He who calls in the aid of an equal understanding doubles his own ; and he who profits by a superior understanding raises his powers to a level with the height of the superior understanding he unites with.—*Burke.*

Harsh counsels have no effect ; they are like hammers which are always repulsed by the anvil.—*Helvetius.*

In order to convince it is necessary to speak with spirit and wit ; to advise, it must come from the heart.—*D'Aguesseau.*

Every man, however wise, requires the advice of some sagacious friend in the affairs of life.—*Plautus.*

It would truly be a fine thing if men suffered themselves to be guided by reason, that they should acquiesce in the true remonstrances addressed to them by the writings of the learned and the advice of friends. But the greater part are so disposed that the words which enter by one ear do incontinently go out of the other, and begin again by following the custom. The best teacher one can have is necessity.—
Francois la None.

Even the ablest pilots are willing to receive advice from passengers in tempestuous weather.
Cicero.

We give advice by the bucket, but take it by the grain.—*W. R. Alger.*

AFFECTATION.

Among the numerous stratagems by which pride endeavors to recommend folly to regard, there is scarcely one that meets with less success than affectation, or a perpetual disguise of the real character by fictitious appearances.—
Johnson.

Great vices are the proper objects of our detestation, smaller faults of our pity, but affectation appears to be the only true source of the ridiculous.—*Fielding.*

We are never made so ridiculous by the qualities we have, as by those we affect to have.—*Rochefoucauld.*

Affectation is certain deformity; by forming themselves on fantastic models, the young begin with being ridiculous, and often end in being vicious.—*Blair.*

In all the professions every one affects a particular look and exterior, in order to appear what he wishes to be thought; so that it may be said the world is made up of appearances.—*Rochefoucauld.*

Affectation is a greater enemy to the face than the small-pox.—*St. Evremond.*

Paltry affectation, strained allusions, and disgusting finery are easily attained by those who choose to wear them; they are but too frequently the badges of ignorance or of stupidity, whenever it would endeavor to please.—*Goldsmith.*

Affectation hides three times as many virtues as Charity does sins.—*Horace Mann.*

Affectation is to be always distinguished from hypocrisy, as being the art of counterfeiting those qualities, which we might with innocence and safety, be known to want. Hypocrisy is the necessary burden of villany; affectation part of the chosen trappings of folly.—*Johnson.*

Die of a rose in aromatic pain.—*Pope.*

Affectation proceeds from one of these two causes, — vanity or hypocrisy; for as vanity puts us on affecting false characters, in order to purchase applause; so hypocrisy sets us on an endeavor to avoid censure, by concealing our vices under an appearance of their opposite virtues.—*Fielding.*

Affectation in any part of our carriage is lighting up a candle to see our defects, and never fails to make us taken notice of, either as wanting sense or sincerity.—*Locke.*

All affectation is the vain and ridiculous attempt of poverty to appear rich.—*Lavater.*

When Cicero consulted the oracle at Delphos, concerning what course of studies he should pursue, the answer was, " Follow Nature." If every one would do this, affectation would be almost unknown.—*J. Beaumont.*

Avoid all affectation and singularity. What is according to nature is best, and what is contrary to it is always distasteful. Nothing is graceful that is not our own.—*Jeremy Collier.*

Hearts may be attracted by assumed qualities, but the affections are only to be fixed by those that are real.—*De Moy.*

I will not call vanity and affectation twins, because, more properly, vanity is the mother, and affectation is the darling daughter. Vanity is the sin, and affectation is the punishment; the first may be called the root of self-love, the other the fruit. Vanity is never at its full growth till it spreadeth into affectation, and then it is complete.—*Sir H. Saville.*

There is a pleasure in affecting affectation.—*Lamb.*

Affectation naturally counterfeits those excellences which are placed at the greatest distance from possibility of attainment, because, knowing our own defects, we eagerly endeavor to supply them with artificial excellence.—*Johnson.*

Affectation is as necessary to the mind as dress is to the body.—*Hazlitt.*

It is remarkable that great affectation and great absence of it (unconsciousness) are at first sight very similar; they are both apt to produce singularity.—*Bishop Whately.*

Affectation discovers sooner what one is than it makes known what one would fain appear to be.—*Stanislaus.*

AFFECTION.

There is so little to redeem the dry mass of follies and errors from which the materials of this life are composed, that anything to love or to reverence becomes, as it were, the Sabbath for the mind.—*Bulwer Lytton.*

Loving souls are like paupers. They live on what is given them.—*Madame Swetchine*

How often a new affection makes a new man! The sordid, cowering soul turns heroic. The frivolous girl becomes the steadfast martyr of patience and ministration, transfigured by deathless love. The career of bounding impulses turns into an anthem of sacred deeds.—*Chapin.*

It is sweet to feel by what fine-spun threads our affections are drawn together.—*Sterne.*

There are few mortals so insensible that their affections cannot be gained by mildness, their confidence by sincerity, their hatred by scorn or neglect.—*Zimmermann.*

The poor wren, the most diminutive of birds, will fight, her young ones in her nest, against the owl.—*Shakespeare.*

The affection of young ladies is of as rapid growth as Jack's beanstalk, and reaches up to the sky in a night.—*Thackeray.*

Alas! our young affections run to waste, or water but the desert.—*Byron.*

Universal love is a glove without fingers, which fits all hands alike, and none closely; but true affection is like a glove with fingers, which fits one hand only, and sits close to that one.— *Richter.*

No decking sets forth anything so much as affection.—*Sir P. Sidney.*

How sacred, how beautiful, is the feeling of affection in pure and guileless bosoms! The proud may sneer at it, the fashionable may call it fable, the selfish and dissipated may affect to despise it; but the holy passion is surely of heaven, and is made evil by the corruptions of those whom it was sent to bless and to preserve.—*Mordaunt.*

There are moments of mingled sorrow and tenderness, which hallow the caresses of affection.—*Washington Irving.*

One touch of nature makes the whole world kin.—*Shakespeare.*

Why doth Fate, that often bestows thousands of souls on a conqueror or tyrant, to be the sport of his passions, so often deny to the tenderest and most feeling hearts one kindred one on which to lavish their affections? Why is it that Love must so often sigh in vain for an object, and Hate never?—*Richter.*

Of all earthly music, that which reaches the farthest into heaven is the beating of a loving heart.—*Beecher.*

Affections injured by tyranny, or rigor of compulsion, like tempest-threatened trees, unfirmly rooted, never spring to timely growth.— *John Ford.*

There comes a time when the souls of human beings, women more even than men, begin to faint for the atmosphere of the affections they are made to breathe.—*Holmes.*

How cling we to a thing our hearts have nursed!—*Mrs. C. H. W. Esling*

If the deepest and best affections which God has given us sometimes brood over the heart like doves of peace, — they sometimes suck out our life-blood like vampires.—*Mrs. Jameson.*

I have given suck, and know how tender it is to love the babe that milks me.—*Shakespeare.*

Let the foundation of thy affection be virtue, then make the building as rich and as glorious as thou canst; if the foundation be beauty or wealth, and the building virtue, the foundation is too weak for the building, and it will fall: happy is he, the palace of whose affection is founded upon virtue, walled with riches, glazed with beauty, and roofed with honor.—*Quarles.*

Our happiness in this world depends on the affections we are enabled to inspire.— *Duchesse de Praslin.*

If there is anything that keeps the mind open to angel visits, and repels the ministry of ill, it is human love!—*Willis.*

The heart will commonly govern the head; and it is certain that any strong passion, set the wrong way, will soon infatuate even the wisest of men; therefore the first part of wisdom is to watch the affections.—*Dr. Waterland.*

The affections are immortal! they are the sympathies which unite the ceaseless generations.—*Bulwer Lytton.*

Our sweetest experiences of affection are meant to be suggestions of that realm which is the home of the heart.—*Beecher.*

AFFLICTION.

Affliction is a school of virtue: it corrects levity, and interrupts the confidence of sinning.— *Atterbury.*

The truth is, when we are under any affliction, we are generally troubled with a malicious kind of melancholy; we only dwell and pore upon the sad and dark occurrences of Providence, but never take notice of the more benign and bright ones. Our way in this world is like a walk under a row of trees, checkered with light and shade; and because we cannot all along walk in the sunshine, we therefore perversely fix only upon the darker passages, and so lose all the comfort of our comforts. We are like froward children who, if you take one of their playthings from them, throw away all the rest in spite.—*Bishop Hopkins.*

As threshing separates the wheat from the chaff, so does affliction purify virtue.—*Burton.*

God washes the eyes by tears until they can behold the invisible land where tears shall come no more. O love! O affliction! ye are the guides that show us the way through the great airy space where our loved ones walked; and, as hounds easily follow the scent before the dew be risen, so God teaches us, while yet our sorrow is wet, to follow on and find our dear ones in heaven.—*Beecher.*

It is from the remembrance of joys we have lost that the arrows of affliction are pointed.— *Mackenzie.*

It is a great thing, when our Gethsemane hours come, when the cup of bitterness is pressed to our lips, and when we pray that it may pass away, to feel that it is not fate, that it is not necessity, but divine love for good ends working upon us.—*Chapin.*

If you would not have affliction visit you twice, listen at once to what it teaches.—*Burgh.*

The cloud which appeared to the prophet Ezekiel carried with it winds and storms, but it was environed with a golden circle, to teach us that the storms of affliction, which happen to God's children, are eucompassed with brightness and smiling felicity.—*N. Caussin.*

When sorrows come, they come not single spies, but in battalions.—*Shakespeare.*

In thy silent wishing, thy voiceless, unuttered prayer, let the desire be not cherished that afflictions may not visit thee; for well has it been said, "Such prayers never seem to have wings. I am willing to be purified through sorrow, and to accept it meekly as a blessing. I see that all the clouds are angels' faces, and their voices speak harmoniously of the everlasting chime."—*Mrs. L. M. Child.*

Amid my list of blessings infinite stands this the foremost, "That my heart has bled."—*Young.*

Tears and sorrows and losses are a part of what must be experienced in this present state of life: some for our manifest good, and all, therefore, it is trusted, for our good concealed;—for our final and greatest good.—*Leigh Hunt.*

Afflictions clarify the soul.—*Quarles.*

There is an elasticity in the human mind, capable of bearing much, but which will not show itself until a certain weight of affliction be put upon it; its powers may be compared to those vehicles whose springs are so contrived that they get on smoothly enough when loaded, but jolt confoundedly when they have nothing to bear.—*Colton.*

Calamity is man's true touchstone.—*Fletcher.*

In a great affliction there is no light either in the stars or in the sun; for when the inward light is fed with fragrant oil, there can be no darkness though the sun should go out. But when, like a sacred lamp in the temple, the inward light is quenched, there is no light outwardly, though a thousand suns should preside in the heavens.—*Beecher.*

Afflictions sent by Providence melt the constancy of the noble-minded, but confirm the obduracy of the vile. The same furnace that hardens clay liquefies gold; and in the strong manifestations of divine power Pharaoh found his punishment, but David his pardon.—*Colton.*

With every anguish of our earthly part the spirit's sight grows clearer; this was meant when Jesus touched the blind man's lids with clay.—*Lowell.*

God afflicts with the mind of a father, and kills for no other purpose but that he may raise again.—*South.*

Man is born to trouble, as the sparks fly upward.—*Bible.*

The very afflictions of our earthly pilgrimage are presages of our future glory, as shadows indicate the sun.—*Richter.*

As the most generous vine, if it is not pruned, runs out into many superfluous stems, and grows at last weak and fruitless; so doth the best man, if he be not cut short of his desires and pruned with afflictions. If it be painful to bleed, it is worse to wither. Let me be pruned, that I may grow, rather than be cut up to burn.—*Bishop Hall.*

Corn is cleaned with wind, and the soul with chastening.—*George Herbert.*

No chastening for the present seemeth to be joyous, but grievous; nevertheless afterward it yieldeth the peaceable fruit of righteousness unto them which are exercised thereby.—*Bible.*

Fairer and more fruitful in spring the vine becomes from the skilful pruning of the husbandman; less pure had been the gums which the odorous balsam gives if it had not been cut by the knife of the Arabian shepherd.—*Metastasio.*

The good are better made by ill, as odors crushed are sweeter still!—*Rogers.*

No man ever stated his griefs as lightly as he might. For it is only the finite that has wrought and suffered; the infinite lies stretched in smiling repose.—*Emerson.*

The loss of a beloved connection awakens an interest in heaven before unfelt.—*Bovee.*

The great, in affliction, bear a countenance more princely than they are wont; for it is the temper of the highest heart, like the palm-tree, to strive most upward when it is most burdened.—*Sir P. Sidney.*

What seem to us but dim funereal tapers may be heaven's distant lamps.—*Longfellow.*

Extraordinary afflictions are not always the punishment of extraordinary sins, but sometimes the trial of extraordinary graces.—*Matthew Henry.*

The eternal stars shine out as soon as it is dark enough.—*Carlyle.*

As they lay copper in aquafortis before they begin to engrave it, so the Lord usually prepares us by the searching, softening discipline of affliction for making a deep, lasting impression of himself upon our hearts.—*J. T. Nottidge.*

With the wind of tribulation God separates, in the floor of the soul, the chaff from the corn.—*Molinos.*

Sanctified afflictions are spiritual promotions.
Matthew Henry.

God is now spoiling us of what would otherwise have spoiled us. When God makes the world too hot for his people to hold, they will let it go.—*T. Powell.*

How blunt are all the arrows of thy quiver in comparison with those of guilt!—*Blair.*

Afflictions are the medicine of the mind. If they are not toothsome, let it suffice that they are wholesome. It is not required in physic that it should please, but heal.—*Bishop Henshaw.*

'T is a physic that is bitter to sweet end.—
Shakespeare.

There will be no Christian but what will have a Gethsemane, but every praying Christian will find that there is no Gethsemane without its angel!—*Rev. T. Binney.*

AGE.

There are three classes into which all the women past seventy years of age, that ever I knew, were to be divided: 1. That dear old soul; 2. That old woman; 3. That old witch.—
Coleridge.

When a noble life has prepared old age, it is not the decline that it reveals, but the first days of immortality.—*Madame de Staël.*

The evening of life brings with it its lamps.—
Joubert.

Can man be so age-stricken that no faintest sunshine of his youth may revisit him once a year? It is impossible. The moss on our time-worn mansion brightens into beauty; the good old pastor, who once dwelt here, renewed his prime and regained his boyhood in the genial breezes of his ninetieth spring. Alas for the worn and heavy soul, if, whether in youth or age, it has outlived its privilege of springtime sprightliness!—*Hawthorne.*

Age makes us not childish, as some say; it finds us still true children.—*Goethe.*

Most long lives resemble those threads of gossamer, the nearest approach to nothing unmeaningly prolonged, scarce visible pathways of some worm from his cradle to his grave.—*Lowell.*

O sir, you are old; nature in you stands on the very verge of her confine; you should be ruled and led by some discretion, that discerns your state better than you yourself.—*Shakespeare.*

Age is rarely despised but when it is contemptible.—*Johnson.*

That which is usually called dotage is not the weak point of all old men, but only of such as are distinguished by their levity.—*Cicero.*

There is a quiet repose and steadiness about the happiness of age, if the life has been well spent. Its feebleness is not painful. The nervous system has lost its acuteness. Even in mature years we feel that a burn, a scald, a cut, is more tolerable than it was in the sensitive period of youth.—*Hazlitt.*

Old age is a tyrant, which forbids the pleasures of youth on pain of death.—*Rochefoucauld.*

Life grows darker as we go on, till only one pure light is left shining on it; and that is faith. Old age, like solitude and sorrow, has its revelations.—*Madame Swetchine.*

Old age likes to dwell in the recollections of the past, and, mistaking the speedy march of years, often is inclined to take the prudence of the winter time for a fit wisdom of midsummer days. Manhood is bent to the passing cares of the passing moment, and holds so closely to his eyes the sheet of "to-day," that it screens the "to-morrow" from his sight.—*Kossuth.*

To be happy, we must be true to nature, and carry our age along with us.—*Hazlitt.*

Winter, which strips the leaves from around us, makes us see the distant regions they formerly concealed; so does old age rob us of our enjoyments, only to enlarge the prospect of eternity before us.—*Richter.*

They say women and music should never be dated.—*Goldsmith.*

Old age is a lease nature only signs as a particular favor, and it may be, to one only in the space of two or three ages; and then with a pass to boot, to carry him through all the traverses and difficulties she has strewed in the way of his long career.—*Montaigne.*

Crabbed age and youth cannot live together.
Shakespeare.

If the memory is more flexible in childhood, it is more tenacious in mature age; if childhood has sometimes the memory of words, old age has that of things, which impress themselves according to the clearness of the conception of the thought which we wish to retain.—
De Bonstetten.

Old age has deformities enough of its own; do not add to it the deformity of vice.—*Cato.*

We should provide for our age, in order that our age may have no urgent wants of this world to absorb it from the meditation of the next. It is awful to see the lean hands of dotage making a coffer of the grave!—*Bulwer Lytton.*

There cannot live a more unhappy creature than an ill-natured old man, who is neither capable of receiving pleasures nor sensible of doing them to others.—*Sir W. Temple.*

A comfortable old age is the reward of a well-spent youth ; therefore instead of its introducing dismal and melancholy prospects of decay, it should give us hopes of eternal youth in a better world.—*Palmer.*

For my own part, I had rather be old only a short time than be old before I really am so.—*Cicero.*

He who would pass the declining years of his life with honor and comfort, should when young, consider that he may one day become old, and remember, when he is old, that he has once been young.—*Addison.*

Age, that lessens the enjoyment of life, increases our desire of living.—*Goldsmith.*

The damps of autumn sink into the leaves and prepare them for the necessity of their fall ; and thus insensibly are we, as years close round us, detached from our tenacity of life by the gentle pressure of recorded sorrows.—*Landor.*

The defects of the mind, like those of the face, grow worse as we grow old.—*Rochefoucauld.*

Old age is never honored among us, but only indulged, as childhood is ; and old men lose one of the most precious rights of man, — that of being judged by their peers.—*Goethe.*

Though I look old, yet I am strong and lusty ; for in my youth I never did apply hot and rebellious liquors in my blood ; nor did not with unbashful forehead woo the means of weakness and debility ; therefore my age is as a lusty winter, frosty, but kindly.—*Shakespeare.*

We do not count a man's years until he has nothing else to count.—*Emerson.*

I think that to have known one good old man — one man, who, through the chances and mischances of a long life, has carried his heart in his hand, like a palm-branch, waving all discords into peace — helps our faith in God, in ourselves, and in each other more than many sermons.—*G. W. Curtis.*

A healthy old fellow, who is not a fool, is the happiest creature living.—*Steele.*

Our life much resembles wine : when there is only a little remaining, it becomes vinegar ; for all the ills of human nature crowd to old age as if it were a workshop.—*Antiphanes.*

Age imprints more wrinkles in the mind, than it does in the face, and souls are never, or very rarely seen, that in growing old do not smell sour and musty. Man moves all together, both towards his perfection and decay.
Montaigne.

As we grow old we become more foolish and more wise.—*Rochefoucauld.*

The silver livery of advised age.—*Shakespeare.*

It is noticeable how intuitively in age we go back with strange fondness to all that is fresh in the earliest dawn of youth. If we never cared for little children before, we delight to see them roll in the grass over which we hobble on crutches. The grandsire turns wearily from his middle-aged, care-worn son, to listen with infant laugh to the prattle of an infant grandchild. It is the old who plant young trees ; it is the old who are most saddened by the autumn, and feel most delight in the returning spring.—
Bulwer Lytton.

A youthful age is desirable, but aged youth is troublesome and grievous.—*Chilo.*

True wisdom, indeed, springs from the wide brain which is fed from the deep heart ; and it is only when age warms its withering conceptions at the memory of its youthful fire, when it makes experience serve aspiration, and knowledge illumine the difficult paths through which thoughts thread their way into facts, — it is only then that age becomes broadly and nobly wise.—*Whipple.*

No wise man ever wished to be younger.—
Swift.

The mental powers acquire their full robustness when the cheek loses its ruddy hue, and the limbs their elastic step ; and pale thought sits on manly brows, and the watchman, as he walks his rounds, sees the student's lamp burning far into the silent night.—*Dr. Guthrie.*

Childhood itself is scarcely more lovely than a cheerful, kindly, sunshiny old age.—
Mrs. L. M. Child.

Last scene of all, that ends this strange, eventful history, is second childishness, and mere oblivion ; sans teeth, sans eyes, sans taste, sans everything.—*Shakespeare.*

The enthusiasm of old men is singularly like that of infancy.—*Gerard de Nerval.*

The tendency of old age, say the physiologists, is to form bone. It is as rare as it is pleasant, to meet with an old man whose opinions are not ossified.—*J. F. Boyse.*

It is difficult to grow old gracefully.—
Madame de Staël.

The heart never grows better by age ; I fear rather worse ; always harder. A young liar will be an old one ; and a young knave will only be a greater knave as he grows older —
Chesterfield.

Though sinking in decrepit age, he prematurely falls whose memory records no benefit conferred on him by man. They only have lived long who have lived virtuously. —*Sheridan.*

Men, like peaches and pears, grow sweet a little while before they begin to decay.—*Holmes.*

Time has laid his hand upon my heart gently, not smiting it; but as a harper lays his open palm upon his harp, to deaden its vibrations.—*Longfellow.*

Years do not make sages; they only make old men.—*Madame Swetchine.*

Men of age object too much, consult too long, adventure too little, repent too soon, and seldom drive business home to the full period, but content themselves with a mediocrity of success.—*Bacon.*

When men grow virtuous in their old age, they are merely making a sacrifice to God of the Devil's leavings.—*Swift.*

Time's chariot-wheels make their carriage-road in the fairest face.—*Rochefoucauld.*

I feel I am growing old for want of somebody to tell me that I am looking as young as ever. Charming falsehood! There is a vast deal of vital air in loving words.—*Landor.*

Years steal fire from the mind as vigor from the limb.—*Byron.*

Like a morning dream, life becomes more and more bright the longer we live, and the reason of everything appears more clear. What has puzzled us before seems less mysterious, and the crooked paths look straighter as we approach the end.—*Richter.*

What folly can be ranker? Like our shadows, our wishes lengthen as our sun declines.—*Young.*

Every man desires to live long; but no man would be old.—*Swift.*

Age and sufferings had already marked out the first incisions for death, so that he required but little effort to cut her down; for it is with men as with trees, they are notched long before felling, that their life-sap may flow out.—*Richter.*

We see time's furrows on another's brow; how few themselves, in that just mirror, see!—*Young.*

There is nothing more disgraceful than that an old man should have nothing to produce as a proof that he has lived long except his years.—*Seneca.*

Old men's lives are lengthened shadows; their evening sun falls coldly on the earth, but the shadows all point to the morning.—*Richter.*

How many persons fancy they have experience simply because they have grown old!—*Stanislaus.*

I venerate old age; and I love not the man who can look without emotion upon the sunset of life, when the dusk of evening begins to gather over the watery eye, and the shadows of twilight grow broader and deeper upon the understanding.—*Longfellow.*

The surest sign of age is loneliness. While one finds company in himself and his pursuits, he cannot be old, whatever his years may be.—*Alcott.*

As sailing into port is a happier thing than the voyage, so is age happier than youth; that is, when the voyage from youth is made with Christ at the helm.—*Rev. J. Pulsford.*

It is only necessary to grow old to become more indulgent. I see no fault committed that I have not committed myself.—*Goethe.*

Vanity in an old man is charming. It is a proof of an open nature. Eighty winters have not frozen him up, or taught him concealments. In a young person it is simply allowable; we do not expect him to be above it.—*Bovee.*

The smile upon the old man's lip, like the last rays of the setting sun, pierces the heart with a sweet and sad emotion. There is still a ray, there is still a smile; but they may be the last.—*Madame Swetchine.*

An aged Christian, with the snow of time on his head, may remind us that those points of earth are whitest which are nearest heaven.—*Chapin.*

Tell me what you find better or more honorable than age. Is not wisdom entailed upon it? Take the pre-eminence of it in everything; in an old friend, in old wine, in an old pedigree.—*Shakerly Marmion.*

The clock of his age had struck fifty-eight.—*Cellini.*

Natures that have much heat, and great and violent desires and perturbations, are not ripe for action till they have passed the meridian of their years.—*Bacon.*

A time there is when like a thrice-told tale long-rifled life of sweets can yield no more.—*Young.*

Mellowed by the stealing hours of time.—*Shakespeare.*

Age and youth look upon life from the opposite ends of the telescope; it is exceedingly long, — it is exceedingly short.—*Beecher.*

Nature is full of freaks, and now puts an old head on young shoulders, and then a young heart beating under fourscore winters.—*Emerson.*

As we advance in life the circle of our pains enlarges, while that of our pleasures contracts.—
Madame Swetchine.

Nature, as it grows again toward earth, is fashioned for the journey, dull and heavy.—
Shakespeare.

Old age was naturally more honored in times when people could not know much more than what they had seen.—*Joubert.*

Few people know how to be old.—
Rochefoucauld.

Old age is not one of the beauties of creation, but it is one of its harmonies. The law of contrasts is one of the laws of beauty. Under the conditions of our climate, shadow gives light its worth; sternness enhances mildness; solemnity, splendor. Varying proportions of size support and subserve one another.—
Madame Swetchine.

When men once reach their autumn, sickly joys fall off apace, as yellow leaves from trees.—
Young.

Gray hairs seem to my fancy like the light of a soft moon, silvering over the evening of life.—*Richter.*

We grizzle every day. I see no need of it. Whilst we converse with what is above us, we do not grow old, but grow young.—*Emerson.*

One's age should be tranquil, as one's childhood should be playful; hard work, at either extremity of human existence, seems to me out of place; the morning and the evening should be alike cool and peaceful; at midday the sun may burn, and men may labor under it.—
Dr. Arnold.

At twenty years of age, the will reigns; at thirty, the wit; and at forty, the judgment.—
Grattan.

Depend upon it, a man never experiences such pleasure or grief after fourteen years as he does before, unless in some cases, in his first love-making, when the sensation is new to him.—
Charles Kingsley.

We hope to grow old, yet we fear old age; that is, we are willing to live, and afraid to die.—
Bruyère.

Some one has said of a fine and honorable old age, that it was the childhood of immortality.—*Pindar.*

Cautious age suspects the flattering form, and only credits what experience tells.—*Johnson.*

Each departed friend is a magnet that attracts us to the next world, and the old man lives among graves.—*Richter.*

AGREEABLE.

The character in conversation which commonly passes for agreeable is made up of civility and falsehood.—*Swift.*

The art of being agreeable frequently miscarries through the ambition which accompanies it. Wit, learning, wisdom, — what can more effectually conduce to the profit and delight of society? Yet I am sensible that a man may be too invariably wise, learned, or witty to be agreeable; and I take the reason of this to be, that pleasure cannot be bestowed by the simple and unmixed exertion of any one faculty or accomplishment.—*Cumberland.*

If you wish to appear agreeable in society you must consent to be taught many things which you know already.—*Lavater.*

We may say of agreeableness, as distinct from beauty, that it consists in a symmetry of which we know not the rules, and a secret conformity of the features to each other, and to the air and complexion of the person.—
Rochefoucauld.

Most arts require long study and application; but the most useful art of all, that of pleasing, requires only the desire.—*Chesterfield.*

Nature has left every man a capacity of being agreeable, though not of shining in company; and there are a hundred men sufficiently qualified for both who, by a very few faults, that they might correct in half an hour, are not so much as tolerable.—*Swift.*

AGRICULTURE.

Agriculture is the most certain source of strength, wealth, and independence. Commerce flourishes by circumstances precarious, contingent, transitory, almost as liable to change as the winds and waves that waft it to our shores. She may well be termed the younger sister, for, in all emergencies, she looks to agriculture, both for defence and for supply.—*Colton.*

The first three men in the world were a gardener, a ploughman, and a grazier; and if any man object that the second of these was a murderer, I desire he would consider that as soon as he was so, he quitted our profession and turned builder.—*Cowley.*

In ancient times, the sacred plough employed the kings, and awful fathers of mankind.—
Thomson.

In the age of acorns, antecedent to Ceres and the royal ploughman Triptolemus, a single barley-corn had been of more value to mankind than all the diamonds that glowed in the mines of India.—*H. Brooke.*

He who would look with contempt upon the farmer's pursuit is not worthy the name of a man.—*Beecher.*

Trade increases the wealth and glory of a country; but its real strength and stamina are to be looked for among the cultivators of the land.—*Lord Chatham.*

He that sows his grain upon marble will have many a hungry belly before his harvest.— *Arbuthnot.*

In a moral point of view, the life of the agriculturist is the most pure and holy of any class of men; pure, because it is the most healthful, and vice can hardly find time to contaminate it; and holy, because it brings the Deity perpetually before his view, giving him thereby the most exalted notions of supreme power, and the most fascinating and endearing view of moral benignity.— *Lord John Russell.*

The farmers are the founders of civilization. *Daniel Webster.*

And he gave it for his opinion, that whoever could make two ears of corn, or two blades of grass, to grow upon a spot of ground where only one grew before, would deserve better of mankind, and do more essential service to his country, than the whole race of politicians put together.—*Swift.*

Command large fields, but cultivate small ones.—*Virgil.*

The frost is God's p   , which he drives through every inch of lgugland in the world, opening each clod, and pulverizing the whole.— *Fuller.*

"Agriculture, for an honorable and high-minded man," says Xenophon, "is the best of all occupations and arts by which men procure the means of living."—*Alcott.*

ALCHEMY.

Alchemy may be compared to the man who told his sons he had left them gold buried somewhere in his vineyard; where they by digging found no gold, but by turning up the mould, about the roots of their vines, procured a plentiful vintage. So the search and endeavors to make gold have brought many useful inventions and instructive experiments to light.— *Bacon.*

I have always looked upon alchemy in natural philosophy to be like enthusiasm in divinity, and to have troubled the world much to the same purpose.—*Sir W. Temple.*

ALLEGORY.

Allegories, when well chosen, are like so many tracks of light in a discourse, that make everything about them clear and beautiful.— *Addison.*

Allegory dwells in a transparent palace.— *Le Mierre.*

A man conversing in earnest, if he watch his intellectual processes, will find that a material image, more or less luminous, arises in his mind, contemporaneous with every thought, which furnishes the vestment of the thought. Hence, good writing and brilliant discourse are perpetual allegories.—*Emerson.*

AMBASSADOR.

An ambassador is an honest man sent to lie abroad for the commonwealth.—*Sir H. Wotton.*

AMBITION.

You have greatly ventured, but all must do so who would greatly win.—*Byron.*

To be ambitious of true honor, of the true glory and perfection of our natures, is the very principle and incentive of virtue; but to be ambitious of titles, of place, of ceremonial respects and civil pageantry, is as vain and little as the things are which we court.—*Sir P. Sidney*

Who soars too near the sun, with golden wings, melts them.—*Shakespeare.*

It is a true observation of ancient writers, that as men are apt to be cast down by adversity, so they are easily satiated with prosperity, and that joy and grief produce the same effects. For whenever men are not obliged by necessity to fight they fight from ambition, which is so powerful a passion in the human breast that however high we reach we are never satisfied.— *Machiavelli.*

Ambition becomes displeasing when it is once satiated; there is a reaction; and as our spirit, till our last sigh, is always aiming toward some object, it falls back on itself, having nothing else on which to rest; and having reached the summit, it longs to descend.—*Corneille.*

Nothing is too high for the daring of mortals: we storm heaven itself in our folly.—*Horace.*

If not for that of conscience, yet at least for ambition's sake, let us reject ambition, let us disdain that thirst of honor and renown, so low and mendicant, that it makes us beg it of all sorts of people.—*Montaigne.*

The towering hope of eagle-eyed ambition. *Smollett.*

The modesty of certain ambitious persons consists in becoming great without making too much noise; it may be said that they advance in the world on tiptoe.—*Voltaire.*

When ambitious men find an open passage, they are rather busy than dangerous; and if well watched in their proceedings, they will catch themselves in their own snare, and prepare a way for their own destruction.—*Quarles.*

He who surpasses or subdues mankind must look down on the hate of those below.—*Byron.*

2

Fling away ambition; by that sin fell the angels: how can man then, the image of his Maker, hope to win by it?—*Shakespeare.*

Ambition often puts men upon doing the meanest offices; so climbing is performed in the same posture with creeping.—*Swift.*

It is the nature of ambition to make men liars and cheats, and hide the truth in their breasts, and show, like jugglers, another thing in their mouths; to cut all friendships and enmities to the measure of their interest, and to make a good countenance without the help of a good will.—*Sallust.*

It is by attempting to reach the top at a single leap that so much misery is produced in the world.—*Cobbett.*

Ambition is a lust that is never quenched, grows more inflamed and madder by enjoyment.—*Otway.*

Every one has before his eyes an end which he pursues till death; but for many that end is a feather which they blow before them in the air.—*Nicoll.*

Vaulting ambition, which overleaps itself.—
Shakespeare.

Say what we will, you may be sure that ambition is an error; its wear and tear of heart are never recompensed, — it steals away the freshness of life, — it deadens its vivid and social enjoyments, — it shuts our souls to our own youth, — and we are old ere we remember that we have made a fever and a labor of our raciest years.—*Bulwer Lytton.*

Ambition thinks no face so beautiful as that which looks from under a crown.
Sir P. Sidney.

Like dogs in a wheel, birds in a cage, or squirrels in a chain, ambitious men still climb and climb, with great labor, and incessant anxiety, but never reach the top.—*Burton.*

Ambition hath but two steps: the lowest, blood; the highest, envy.—*Lilly.*

There is a native baseness in the ambition which seeks beyond its desert, that never shows more conspicuously than when, no matter how, it temporarily gains its object.—*Simms.*

Ambition is the mind's immodesty.—
Sir W. Davenant.

A slave has but one master; the ambitious man has as many masters as there are persons whose aid may contribute to the advancement of his fortune.—*Bruyère.*

Ambition is the germ from which all growth of nobleness proceeds.—*T. D. English.*

How dost thou wear, and weary out thy day, restless ambition, never at an end!—*Daniel.*

Ambition is frequently the only refuge which life has left to the denied or mortified affections. We chide at the grasping eye, the daring wing, the soul that seems to thirst for sovereignty only, and know not that the flight of this ambitious bird has been from a bosom or a home that is filled with ashes.—*Simms.*

The path of glory leads but to the grave.—
Gray.

Wisdom is corrupted by ambition, even when the quality of the ambition is intellectual. For ambition, even of this quality, is but a form of self-love.—*Henry Taylor.*

What is ambition? It is a glorious cheat! Angels of light walk not so dazzlingly the sapphire walls of heaven.— *Willis.*

Remarkable places are like the summits of rocks; eagles and reptiles only can get there.
Madame Necker.

Hard, withering toil only can achieve a name; and long days and months and years must be passed in the chase of that bubble, reputation, which, when once grasped, breaks in your eager clutch into a hundred lesser bubbles, that soar above you still.—*Mitchell.*

We frequently pass from love to ambition, but one seldom returns from ambition to love.—
Rochefoucauld.

Ambition makes the same mistake concerning power that avarice makes concerning wealth. She begins by accumulating power as a mean to happiness, and she finishes by continuing to accumulate it as an end.— *Colton.*

Ambition, like a torrent, never looks back.—
Ben Jonson.

Ambition, that high and glorious passion, which makes such havoc among the sons of men, arises from a proud desire of honor and distinction; and when the splendid trappings in which it is usually caparisoned are removed, will be found to consist of the mean materials of envy, pride, and covetousness.—*Burton.*

Ambition is an idol, on whose wings great minds are carried only to extreme, — to be sublimely great, or to be nothing.—*Southern.*

Moderation cannot have the credit of combating and subduing ambition, — they are never found together. Moderation is the languor and indolence of the soul, as ambition is its activity and ardor.—*Rochefoucauld.*

The cheat ambition, eager to espouse dominion, courts it with a lying show, and shines in borrowed pomp to serve a turn.—*Jeffrey.*

Dreams, indeed, are ambition ; for the very substance of the ambitious is merely the shadow of a dream. And I hold ambition of so airy and light a quality, that it is but a shadow's shadow.—*Shakespeare.*

Ambition is not a vice of little people.— *Montaigne.*

Ambition is a gilded misery, a secret poison, a hidden plague, the engineer of deceit, the mother of hypocrisy, the parent of envy, the original of vices, the moth of holiness, the blinder of hearts, turning medicines into maladies, and remedies into diseases. High seats are never but uneasy, and crowns are always stuffed with thorns.—*Rev. T. Brooks.*

Take away ambition and vanity, and where will be your heroes and patriots ?—*Seneca.*

I begin where most people end, with a full conviction of the emptiness of all sorts of ambition, and the unsatisfactory nature of all human pleasures.—*Pope.*

Ambition is to the mind what the cap is to the falcon ; it blinds us first, and then compels us to tower, by reason of our blindness. But alas ! when we are at the summit of a vain ambition, we are also at the depth of misery.— *Colton.*

It is the constant fault and inseparable ill quality of ambition never to look behind it.— *Seneca.*

The shadow, wheresoever it passes, leaves no track behind it ; and of the greatest personages of the world, when they are once dead, then there remains no more than if they had never lived. How many preceding emperors of the Assyrian monarchy were lords of the world as well as Alexander ! and now we remain not only ignorant of their monuments, but know not so much as their names. And of the same great Alexander, what have we at this day except the vain noise of his fame ?— *Jeremy Taylor.*

We should be careful to deserve a good reputation by doing well ; and when that care is once taken, not to be over anxious about the success.—*Rochester.*

Ambition sufficiently plagues her proselytes, by keeping themselves always in show, like the statue of a public place.—*Montaigne.*

Blood only serves to wash Ambition's hands.—*Byron.*

Ambition is torment enough for an enemy ; for it affords as much discontentment in enjoying as in want, making men like poisoned rats, which, when they have tasted of their bane, cannot rest till they drink, and then can much less rest till they die.—*Bishop Hall.*

Neither love nor ambition, as it has often been shown, can brook a division of its empire in the heart.—*Bovee.*

Ambition is a rebel both to the soul and reason, and enforces all laws, all conscience ; treads upon religion, and offers violence to nature's self.—*Ben Jonson.*

Alas ! ambition makes my little less.—*Young.*

Ambition is but avarice on stilts, and masked. God sometimes sends a famine, sometimes a pestilence, and sometimes a hero, for the chastisement of mankind ; none of them surely for our admiration.—*Landor.*

The ambitious deceive themselves when they propose an end to their ambition ; for that end, when attained, becomes a means.— *Rochefoucauld.*

There is a kind of grandeur and respect which the meanest and most insignificant part of mankind endeavor to procure in the little circle of their friends and acquaintance. The poorest mechanic, nay, the man who lives upon common alms, gets him his set of admirers, and delights in that superiority which he enjoys over those who are in some respects beneath him. This ambition, which is natural to the soul of man, might, methinks, receive a very happy turn ; and, if it were rightly directed, contribute as much to a person's advantage, as it generally does to his uneasiness and disquiet.—*Addison.*

Ambition is like choler, which is a humor that maketh men active, earnest, full of alacrity, and stirring, if it be not stopped ; but if it be stopped, and cannot have its way, it becometh fiery, and thereby malign and venomous.— *Bacon.*

Ambition, like love, can abide no lingering ; and ever urgeth on his own successes, hating nothing but what may stop them.— *Sir P. Sidney.*

We must distinguish between felicity and prosperity ; for prosperity leads often to ambition, and ambition to disappointment ; the course is then over, the wheel turns round but once, while the reaction of goodness and happiness is perpetual.—*Landor.*

One may easily enough guard against ambition till five-and-twenty. It is not ambition's day.—*Shenstone.*

We should reflect that whatever tempts the pride and vanity of ambitious persons is not so big as the smallest star which we see scattered in disorder and unregarded on the pavement of heaven.—*Jeremy Taylor.*

The tallest trees are most in the power of the winds, and ambitious men of the blasts of fortune.—*William Penn.*

A noble man compares and estimates himself by an idea which is higher than himself, and a mean man by one which is lower than himself. The one produces aspiration; the other, ambition. Ambition is the way in which a vulgar man aspires.—*Beecher.*

Ambition! deadly tyrant! inexorable master! what alarms, what anxious hours, what agonies of heart, are the sure portion of thy gaudy slaves?—*Mallet*

Don Quixote thought he could have made beautiful bird-cages and tooth-picks if his brain had not been so full of ideas of chivalry. Most people would succeed in small things if they were not troubled with great ambitions.—
Longfellow.

Ambition is like love, impatient both of delays and rivals.—*Denham.*

Ambition is, of all other, the most contrary humor to solitude; and glory and repose are so inconsistent that they cannot possibly inhabit one and the same place; and for so much as I understand, those have only their arms and legs disengaged from the crowd, their mind and intention remain engaged behind more than ever.—*Montaigne.*

Nothing can be more destructive to ambition, and the passion for conquest, than the true system of astronomy. What a poor thing is even the whole globe in comparison of the infinite extent of nature!—*Fontenelle.*

If love and ambition should be in equal balance, and come to jostle with equal force, I make no doubt but that the last would win the prize.—*Montaigne.*

Most natures are insolvent; cannot satisfy their own wants, have an ambition out of all proportion to their practical force, and so do lean and beg day and night continually.—
Emerson.

It is not for man to rest in absolute contentment. He is born to hopes and aspirations, as the sparks fly upwards, unless he has brutified his nature, and quenched the spirit of immortality, which is his portion.—*Southey.*

Where ambition can be so happy as to cover its enterprises even to the person himself, under the appearance of principle, it is the most incurable and inflexible of all human passions.—
Hume.

AMERICA.
The home of the homeless all over the earth.
Street.

America, — half-brother of the world !—
Bailey.

America is a fortunate country. She grows by the follies of our European nations.—*Napoleon.*

AMIABILITY.

The amiable is a duty most certainly, but must not be exercised at the expense of any of the virtues. He who seeks to do the amiable always, can only be successful at the frequent expense of his manhood.—*Simms.*

How easy it is to be amiable in the midst of happiness and success !—*Madame Swetchine.*

Amiable people, while they are more liable to imposition in casual contact with the world, yet radiate so much of mental sunshine that they are reflected in all appreciative hearts.—
Madame Deluzy.

That constant desire of pleasing, which is the peculiar quality of some, may be called the happiest of all desires in this, that it scarcely ever fails of attaining its ends, when not disgraced by affectation.—*Fielding.*

AMNESTY.

Amnesty, that noble word, the genuine dictate of wisdom.—*Æschines.*

AMUSEMENTS.

They are to religion like breezes of air to the flame, — gentle ones will fan it, but strong ones will put it out.—*Rev. Dr. Thomas.*

If those who are the enemies of innocent amusements had the direction of the world, they would take away the spring, and youth, the former from the year, the latter from human life.—*Balzac.*

The mind ought sometimes to be amused, that it may the better return to thought, and to itself.—*Phædrus.*

It is exceedingly deleterious to withdraw the sanction of religion from amusement. If we feel that it is all injurious we should strip the earth of its flowers and blot out its pleasant sunshine.—*Chapin.*

There is no such sport as sport by sport o'erthrown.—*Shakespeare.*

Let the world have their May-games, wakes, whetsunales, their dancings and concerts; their puppet-shows, hobby horses, tabors, bagpipes, balls, barley-breaks, and whatever sports and recreations please them best, provided they be followed with discretion.—*Burton.*

Amusement allures and deceives us, and leads us down imperceptibly in thoughtlessness to the grave.—*Pascal.*

The habit of dissipating every serious thought by a succession of agreeable sensations is as fatal to happiness as to virtue; for when amusement is uniformly substituted for objects of moral and mental interest, we lose all that elevates our enjoyments above the scale of childish pleasures.—*Anna Maria Porter.*

To find recreation in amusements is not happiness; for this joy springs from alien and extrinsic sources, and is therefore dependent upon and subject to interruption by a thousand accidents, which may minister inevitable affliction.—*Pascal.*

ANALOGY.

The instincts of the ant are very unimportant, considered as the ant's; but the moment a ray of relation is seen to extend from it to man, and the little drudge is seen to be a monitor, a little body with a mighty heart, then all its habits, even that said to be recently observed, that it never sleeps, become sublime.—*Emerson.*

ANCESTRY.

Some decent, regulated pre-eminence, some preference (not exclusive appropriation) given to birth, is neither unnatural nor unjust nor impolitic.—*Burke.*

He who boasts of his lineage boasts of that which does not properly belong to him.—*Seneca.*

It is, indeed, a blessing, when the virtues of noble races are hereditary; and do derive themselves from the imitation of virtuous ancestors.
Nabb.

Some men by ancestry are only the shadow of a mighty name.—*Lucan.*

It is only shallow-minded pretenders who either make distinguished origin a matter of personal merit, or obscure origin a matter of personal reproach. Taunt and scoffing at the humble condition of early life affect nobody in America but those who are foolish enough to indulge in them, and they are generally sufficiently punished by the published rebuke. A man who is not ashamed of himself need not be ashamed of his early condition.—*Daniel Webster.*

It is of no consequence of what parents any man is born, so that he be a man of merit.—
Horace.

The nobility of the Spencers has been illustrated and enriched by the trophies of Marlborough; but I exhort them to consider the "Faerie Queene," as the most priceless jewel of their coronet.—*Gibbon.*

Pride, in boasting of family antiquity, makes duration stand for merit.—*Zimmermann.*

He that boasts of his ancestors confesses that he has no virtue of his own. No person ever lived for our honor; nor ought that to be reputed ours, which was long before we had a being; for what advantage can it be to a blind man to know that his parents had good eyes? Does he see one whit the better?—*Charron.*

Philosophy does not regard pedigree; she did not receive *Plato* as a noble, but she made him so.—*Seneca.*

There may be, and there often is, indeed, a regard for ancestry which nourishes only a weak pride; as there is also a care for posterity, which only disguises an habitual avarice, or hides the workings of a low and grovelling vanity. But there is also a moral and philosophical respect for our ancestors, which elevates the character and improves the heart.—*Daniel Webster.*

If it is fortunate to be of noble ancestry, it is not less so to be such as that people do not care to be informed whether you are noble or ignoble.—*Bruyère.*

We sometimes see a change of expression in our companion, and say, his father or his mother comes to the windows of his eyes, and sometimes a remote relative. In different hours, a man represents each of several of his ancestors, as if there were seven or eight of us rolled up in each man's skin, — seven or eight ancestors at least, — and they constitute the variety of notes for that new piece of music which his life is.—*Emerson.*

It is a shame for a man to desire honor because of his noble progenitors, and not to deserve it by his own virtue.—*St. Chrysostom.*

Of all vanities of fopperies, the vanity of high birth is the greatest. True nobility is derived from virtue, not from birth. Titles, indeed, may be purchased, but virtue is the only coin that makes the bargain valid.—*Burton.*

The pride of ancestry is a superstructure of the most imposing height, but resting on the most flimsy foundation. It is ridiculous enough to observe the *hauteur* with which the old nobility look down on the new. The reason of this puzzled me a little, until I began to reflect that most titles are respectable only because they are old; if new, they would be despised, because all those who now admire the grandeur of the stream would see nothing but the impurity of the source.—*Colton.*

What can they see in the longest kingly line in Europe, save that it runs back to a successful soldier?—*Walter Scott.*

Title and ancestry render a good man more illustrious, but an ill one more contemptible. Vice is infamous, though in a prince, and virtue honorable, though in a peasant.—*Addison.*

Being well satisfied that, for a man who thinks himself to be somebody, there is nothing more disgraceful than to hold himself up as honored, not on his own account, but for the sake of his forefathers. Yet hereditary honors are a noble and splendid treasure to descendants.—*Plato.*

Pride of origin, whether high or low, springs from the same principle in human nature; one is but the positive, the other the negative, pole of a single weakness.—*Lowell.*

Take the title of nobility which thou hast received by birth, but endeavor to add to it another, that both may form a true nobility. There is between the nobility of thy father and thine own the same difference which exists between the nourishment of the evening and of the morrow. The food of yesterday will not serve thee for to-day, and will not give thee strength for the next.—*Jamakchari.*

I am no herald to inquire of men's pedigrees; it sufficeth me if I know their virtues.
　　　　　　　　　　　　　　Sir P. Sidney.

It was the saying of a great man, that if we could trace our descents, we should find all slaves to come from princes, and all princes from slaves; and fortune has turned all things topsy-turvy in a long series of revolutions: beside, for a man to spend his life in pursuit of a title, that serves only when he dies to furnish out an epitaph, is below a wise man's business.—*Seneca.*

When real nobleness accompanies that imaginary one of birth, the imaginary seems to mix with real, and becomes real too.—
　　　　　　　　　　　　　　Lord Greville.

Though you be sprung in direct line from Hercules, if you show a low-born meanness, that long succession of ancestors whom you disgrace are so many witnesses against you; and this grand display of their tarnished glory but serves to make your ignominy more evident.—*Boileau.*

I am one who finds within me a nobility that spurns the idle pratings of the great, and their mean boasts of what their fathers were, while they themselves are fools effeminate.—
　　　　　　　　　　　　　　Percival.

The character of the reputed ancestors of some men has made it possible for their descendants to be vicious in the extreme, without being degenerate; and there are some hereditary strokes of character by which a family may be as clearly distinguished as by the blackest features of the human face.—*Junius.*

It is better to be the builder of our own name than to be indebted by descent for the proudest gifts known to the books of heraldry.
　　　　　　　　　　　　　　Hosea Ballou.

Let him speak of his own deeds, and not of those of his forefathers. High birth is mere accident, and not virtue; for if reason had controlled birth, and given empire only to the worthy, perhaps Arbaces would have been Xerxes, and Xerxes Arbaces.—*Metastasio.*

The generality of princes, if they were stripped of their purple and cast naked on the world, would immediately sink to the lowest rank of society, without a hope of emerging from their obscurity.—*Gibbon.*

No man is nobler born than another, unless he is born with better abilities and a more amiable disposition. They who make such a parade with their family pictures and pedigrees, are, properly speaking, rather to be called notted or notorious than noble persons. I thought it right to say this much, in order to repel the insolence of men who depend entirely upon chance and accidental circumstances for distinction, and not at all on public services and personal merit.—*Seneca.*

A soldier, such as I am, may very well pretend to govern the state when he has known to defend it. The first who was king was a fortunate soldier. Whoever serves his country well has no need of ancestors.—*Voltaire.*

It has long seemed to me that it would be more honorable to our ancestors to praise them in words less, but in deeds to imitate them more.—*Horace Mann.*

By blood a king, in heart a clown.—
　　　　　　　　　　　　　　Tennyson.

Those who have nothing else to recommend them to the respect of others but only their blood, cry it up at a great rate, and have their mouths perpetually full of it. They swell and vapor, and you are sure to hear of their families and relations every third word.—*Charron.*

Those who depend on the merits of their ancestors may be said to search in the roots of the tree for those fruits which the branches ought to produce.—*Barrow.*

In the founders of great families, titles or attributes of honor are generally correspondent with the virtues of the person to whom they are applied; but in their descendants they are too often the marks rather of grandeur than of merit. The stamp and denomination still continue, but the intrinsic value is frequently lost.
　　　　　　　　　　　　　　Addison.

It is with antiquity as with ancestry, nations are proud of the one, and individuals of the other; but if they are nothing in themselves, that which is their pride ought to be their humiliation.—*Colton.*

The man who has nothing to boast of but his illustrious ancestry is like a potato, — the only good belonging to him is underground.—
　　　　　　　　　　　　　　Sir Thomas Overbury.

Nobility of birth is like a cipher; it has no power in itself, like wealth or talent; but it tells with all the power of a cipher when added to either of the other two.—*J. F. Boyes.*

We are very fond of some families because they can be traced beyond the Conquest, whereas indeed the farther back, the worse, as being the nearer allied to a race of robbers and thieves.—
　　　　　　　　　　　　　　De Foe.

ANGELS.

Millions of spiritual creatures walk the earth unseen, both when we sleep and when we wake.—*Milton.*

The guardian angel of life sometimes flies so high that man cannot see it; but he always is looking down upon us, and will soon hover nearer to us.—*Richter.*

They boast ethereal vigor, and are formed from seeds of heavenly birth.—*Virgil.*

Compare a Solomon, an Aristotle, or an Archimedes, to a child that newly begins to speak, and they do not more transcend such a one than the angelical understanding exceeds theirs, even in its most sublime improvements and acquisitions.—*South.*

Angels are bright still, though the brightest fell.—*Shakespeare.*

The angels may have wider spheres of action, may have nobler forms of duty, but right with them and with us is one and the same thing.—*Chapin.*

We are never like angels till our passion dies.—*Thomas Decker.*

Angels and ministers of grace defend us!—
Shakespeare.

ANGER.

Men often make up in wrath what they want in reason.—*W. R. Alger.*

Anger is an affected madness, compounded of pride and folly, and an intention to do commonly more mischief than it can bring to pass; and, without doubt, of all passions which actually disturb the mind of man, it is most in our power to extinguish, at least, to suppress and correct, our anger.—*Clarendon.*

Anger is like a full-hot horse, who being allowed his way, self-mettle tires him.—
Shakespeare.

Anger is like the waves of a troubled sea; when it is corrected with a soft reply, as with a little strand, it retires, and leaves nothing behind but froth and shells, — no permanent mischief.—*Jeremy Taylor.*

Anger causes us often to condemn in one what we approve of in another.—
Pasquier Quesnel.

Anger is the most impotent passion that accompanies the mind of man. It effects nothing it goes about; and hurts the man who is possessed by it more than any other against whom it is directed.—*Clarendon.*

He submits himself to be seen through a microscope, who suffers himself to be caught in a fit of passion.—*Lavater.*

He that would be angry and sin not must not be angry with anything but sin.—*Secker.*

To be angry about trifles is mean and childish; to rage and be furious is brutish; and to maintain perpetual wrath is akin to the practice and temper of devils.—*Dr. Watts.*

To be in anger is impiety, but who is man that is not angry?—*Shakespeare.*

Are you angry? Look at the child who has erred, he suspects no trouble, he dreams of no harm; you will borrow something of that innocence, you will feel appeased.—*Chateaubriand.*

To rule one's anger is well; to prevent it is better.—*Edwards.*

When anger rushes unrestrained to action, like a hot steed, it stumbles on its way. The man of thought strikes deepest and strikes safely.—*Savage.*

To be angry is to revenge the fault of others upon ourselves.—*Pope.*

He does anger too much honor, who calls it madness, which, being a distemper of the brain, and a total absence of all reason, is innocent of all the ill effects it may produce.—*Clarendon.*

Let not the sun go down upon your wrath.—
Bible.

The elephant is never won by anger; nor must that man who would reclaim a lion take him by the teeth.—*Dryden.*

An angry man who suppresses his passions thinks worse than he speaks; and an angry man that will chide speaks worse than he thinks.—*Bacon.*

To abandon yourself to rage is often to bring upon yourself the fault of another.—*Agapet.*

Had I a careful and pleasant companion that should show me my angry face in a glass, I should not at all take it ill; to behold man's self so unnaturally disguised and dishonored will conduce not a little to the impeachment of anger.—*Plutarch.*

He that will be angry for anything will be angry for nothing.—*Sallust.*

If anger proceeds from a great cause, it turns to fury; if from a small cause, it is peevishness; and so is always either terrible or ridiculous.—*Jeremy Taylor.*

Anger is blood, poured and perplexed into a froth; but malice is the wisdom of our wrath.—
Sir W. Davenant.

An angry man opens his mouth and shuts up his eyes.—*Cato.*

Anger is a noble infirmity, the generous failing of the just, the one degree that riseth above zeal, asserting the prerogative of virtue.—*Tupper.*

Never anger made good guard for itself.— *Shakespeare.*

The intoxication of anger, like that of the grape, shows us to others, but hides us from ourselves, and we injure our own cause, in the opinion of the world, when we too passionately and eagerly defend it.—*Colton.*

Lamentation is the only musician that always, like a screech-owl, alights and sits on the roof of an angry man.—*Plutarch.*

Anger is a transient hatred, or at least very like it.—*South.*

Anger manages everything badly.—*Stadius.*

Anger and the thirst of revenge are a kind of fever; fighting and lawsuits, bleeding, — at least, an evacuation. The latter occasions a dissipation of money; the former, of those fiery spirits which cause a preternatural fermentation.—*Shenstone.*

When a man is wrong and won't admit it, he always gets angry.—*Haliburton.*

Angry and choleric men are as ungrateful and unsociable as thunder and lightning, being in themselves all storm and tempest; but quiet and easy natures are like fair weather, welcome to all.—*Clarendon.*

When angry, count ten before you speak; if very angry, a hundred.—*Jefferson.*

The sun should not set upon our anger, neither should he rise upon our confidence. We should forgive freely, but forget rarely. I will not be revenged, and this I owe to my enemy; but I will remember, and this I owe to myself.—*Colton.*

Must I give way and room to your rash choler? Shall I be frighted when a madman stares?—*Shakespeare.*

Those passionate persons who carry their heart in their mouth are rather to be pitied than feared; their threatenings serving no other purpose than to forearm him that is threatened.— *Fuller.*

He that is slow to anger is better than the mighty; and he that ruleth his spirit, than he that taketh a city.—*Bible.*

As a conquered rebellion strengthens a government, or as health is more perfectly established by recovery from some diseases; so anger, when removed, often gives new life to affection.—*Fielding.*

Be ye angry, and sin not, therefore all anger is not sinful; I suppose because some degree of it, and upon some occasions, is inevitable. It becomes sinful, or contradicts, however, the rule of Scripture, when it is conceived upon slight and inadequate provocation, and when it continues long.—*Paley.*

Violence in the voice is often only the death-rattle of reason in the throat.—*J. F. Boyes.*

Never forget what a man has said to you when he was angry. If he has charged you with anything, you had better look it up. Anger is a bow that will shoot sometimes where another feeling will not.—*Beecher.*

An angry man is again angry with himself when he returns to reason.—*Publius Syrus.*

If anger is not restrained, it is frequently more hurtful to us than the injury that provokes it.—*Seneca.*

There is no passion that so much transports men from their right judgments as anger. No one would demur upon punishing a judge with death who should condemn a criminal upon the account of his own choler; why then should fathers and pedants be any more allowed to whip and chastise children in their anger? It is then no longer correction but revenge. Chastisement is instead of physic to children; and should we suffer a physician who should be animated against and enraged at his patient?—*Montaigne.*

Anger has some claim to indulgence, and railing is usually a relief to the mind.—*Junius.*

Consider how much more you often suffer from your anger and grief than from those very things for which you are angry and grieved.—*Marcus Antoninus.*

He best keeps from anger who remembers that God is always looking upon him.—*Plato.*

When I myself had twice or thrice made a resolute resistance unto anger, the like befell me that did the Thebans; who, having once foiled the Lacedæmonians (who before that time had held themselves invincible), never after lost so much as one battle which they fought against them.—*Plutarch.*

Anger begins with folly, and ends with repentance.—*Pythagoras.*

The round of a passionate man's life is in contracting debts in his passion, which his virtue obliges him to pay. He spends his time in outrage and acknowledgment, injury and reparation.—*Johnson.*

Anger is uneasiness or discomposure of the mind upon the receipt of any injury, with a present purpose of revenge.—*Locke.*

A lamb, that carries anger as the flint bears fire; who, much enforced, shows a hasty spark, and straight is cold again.—*Shakespeare.*

He injures the absent who contends with an angry man.—*Publius Syrus.*

Think when you are enraged at any one, what would probably become your sentiments should he die during the dispute.—*Shenstone.*

Wise anger is like fire from the flint; there is a great ado to bring it out; and when it does come, it is out again immediately.—
Matthew Henry.

Beware of him that is slow to anger; anger, when it is long in coming, is the stronger when it comes, and the longer kept. Abused patience turns to fury.—*Quarles.*

ANGLING.
We may say of angling as Dr. Boteler said of strawberries, "Doubtless God could have made a better berry, but doubtless God never did"; and so, if I might be judge, God never did make a more calm, quiet, innocent recreation than angling.—*Izaak Walton.*

The pleasantest angling is to see the fish cut with her golden oars the silver stream, and greedily devour the treacherous bait.—
Shakespeare.

Though no participator in the joys of more vehement sport, I have a pleasure that I cannot reconcile to my abstract notions of the tenderness due to dumb creatures, in the tranquil cruelty of angling. I can only palliate the wanton destructiveness of my amusement by trying to assure myself that my pleasure does not spring from the success of the treachery I practise toward a poor little fish, but rather from that innocent revelry in the luxuriance of summer life which only anglers enjoy to the utmost.—
Bulwer Lytton.

Angling is somewhat like poetry; men are to be born so.—*Izaak Walton.*

ANTICIPATION.
The events we most desire do not happen; or, if they do, it is neither in the time nor in the circumstances when they would have given us extreme pleasure.—*Bruyère.*

He who foresees calamities suffers them twice over.—*Porteus.*

All earthly delights are sweeter in expectation than enjoyment; but all spiritual pleasures more in fruition than expectation.—*Feltham.*

Suffering itself does less afflict the senses than the apprehension of suffering.—*Quintilian.*

All things that are, are with more spirit chased than enjoyed.—*Shakespeare.*

We can but ill endure, among so many sad realities, to rob anticipation of its pleasant visions.—*Henry Giles.*

Men spend their lives in anticipations, in determining to be vastly happy at some period or other, when they have time. But the present time has one advantage over every other, it is our own.—*Colton.*

Oft expectation fails, and most oft there where most it promises.—*Shakespeare.*

With every one, the expectation of a misfortune constitutes a dreadful punishment. Suffering then assumes the proportions of the unknown, which is the soul's infinite.—*Balzac.*

Things won are done, joy's soul lies in the doing.—*Shakespeare.*

In all worldly things that a man pursues with the greatest eagerness and intention of mind imaginable, he finds not half the pleasure in the actual possession of them, as he proposed to himself in the expectation.—*South.*

Nothing is so great an adversary to those who make it their business to please as expectation.—*Cicero.*

The pilot who is always dreading a rock or a tempest must not complain if he remain a poor fisherman. We must at times trust something to fortune, for fortune has often some share in what happens.—*Metastasio.*

I know that we often tremble at an empty terror; yet the false fancy brings a real misery.—
Schiller.

There would be few enterprises of great labor or hazard undertaken, if we had not the power of magnifying the advantages which we persuade ourselves to expect from them.—
Johnson.

Thou tremblest before anticipated ills, and still bemoanest what thou never losest.—*Goethe.*

To despond is to be ungrateful beforehand. Be not looking for evil. Often thou drainest the gall of fear while evil is passing by thy dwelling.—*Tupper.*

We expect everything, and are prepared for nothing.—*Madame Swetchine.*

Whatever advantage we snatch beyond a certain portion allotted us by nature, is like money spent before it is due, which, at the time of regular payment, will be missed and regretted.—
Johnson.

We part more easily with what we possess, than with our expectations of what we wish for; because expectation always goes beyond enjoyment.—*Henry Home.*

A man's desires always disappoint him; for though he meets with something that gives him satisfaction, yet it never thoroughly answers his expectation.—*Rochefoucauld.*

There is nothing so wretched or foolish as to anticipate misfortunes. What madness is it in your expecting evil before it arrives?—*Seneca.*

What need a man forestall his date of grief, and run to meet what he would most avoid?—*Milton.*

It is expectation makes a blessing dear; heaven were not heaven if we knew what it were.—*John Suckling.*

It is worse to apprehend than to suffer.—*Bruyère.*

Things temporal are sweeter in the expectation, things eternal are sweeter in the fruition; the first shames thy hope, the second crowns it; it is a vain journey, whose end affords less pleasure than the way.—*Quarles.*

ANTIQUITY.

Consider, for example, and you will find that almost all the transactions in the time of Vespasian differed little from those of the present day. You there find marrying and giving in marriage, educating children, sickness, death, war, joyous holidays, traffic, agriculture, flatterers, insolent pride, suspicions, laying of plots, longing for the death of others, newsmongers, lovers, misers, men canvassing for the consulship and for the kingdom; yet all these passed away, and are nowhere.—*Marcus Antoninus.*

Those we call the ancients were really new in everything.—*Pascal.*

All those things that are now held to be of the greatest antiquity were at one time new; what we to-day hold up by example will rank hereafter as precedent.—*Tacitus.*

Antiquity is a species of aristocracy with which it is not easy to be on visiting terms.—*Madame Swetchine.*

When ancient opinions and rules of life are taken away, the loss cannot possibly be estimated. From that moment we have no compass to govern us, nor can we know distinctly to what port to steer.—*Burke.*

Time's gradual touch has mouldered into beauty many a tower, which when it frowned with all its battlements was only terrible.—*Mason.*

I do by no means advise you to throw away your time in ransacking, like a dull antiquarian, the minute and unimportant parts of remote and fabulous times. Let blockheads read what blockheads wrote.—*Chesterfield.*

It is with antiquity as with ancestry, nations are proud of the one, and individuals of the other, but if they are nothing within themselves, that which is their pride ought to be their humiliation.—*Cotton.*

It is one proof of a good education, and of true refinement of feeling, to respect antiquity.—*Mrs. Sigourney.*

Antiquity! thou wondrous charm, what art thou? that, being nothing, art everything! When thou wert, thou wert not antiquity,— then thou wert nothing, but hadst a remoter antiquity, as thou calledst it, to look back to with blind veneration; thou thyself being to thyself flat, jejune, modern! What mystery lurks in this retroversion? or what half Januses are we, that cannot look forward with the same idolatry with which we forever revert! The mighty future is as nothing, being everything! The past is everything, being nothing! *Lamb.*

The pyramids, doting with age, have forgotten the names of their founders.—*Fuller.*

A thorough-paced antiquary not only remembers what all other people have thought proper to forget, but he also forgets what all other people think is proper to remember.—*Colton.*

Antiquity! I like its ruins better than its reconstructions.—*Joubert.*

Those were good old times, it may be thought, when baron and peasant feasted together. But the one could not read, and made his mark with a sword-pommel, and the other was held as dear as a favorite dog. Pure and simple times were those of our grandfathers, it may be. Possibly not so pure as we may think, however, and with a simplicity ingrained with some bigotry and a good deal of conceit.—*Chapin.*

Time consecrates; and what is gray with age becomes religion.—*Schiller.*

What subsists to-day by violence continues to-morrow by acquiescence, and is perpetuated by tradition; till at last the hoary abuse shakes the gray hairs of antiquity at us, and gives itself out as the wisdom of ages.—*Edward Everett.*

He who professes adherence to the national religion of England, on the ground that "it is the religion of his fathers," forgets, as do the hearers who applauded the sentiment, that, on this principle, the worship of Thor and Woden would claim precedence.—*Bishop Whately.*

Those old ages are like the landscape that shows best in purple distance, all verdant and smooth, and bathed in mellow light.—*Chapin.*

ANXIETY.

Generally we obtain very surely and very speedily what we are not too anxious to obtain.
Rousseau.

Anxiety is the poison of human life. It is the parent of many sins, and of more miseries. In a world where everything is doubtful, where you may be disappointed, and be blessed in disappointment, what means this restless stir and commotion of mind? Can your solicitude alter the cause or unravel the intricacy of human events?—*Blair.*

Better to be despised for too anxious apprehensions than ruined by too confident a security.—*Burke.*

APOLOGY.

No sensible person ever made an apology.—
Emerson.

A very desperate habit; one that is rarely cured. Apology is only egotism wrong side out. Nine times out of ten, the first thing a man's companion knows of his short-comings is from his apology.—*Holmes.*

Apologies only account for the evil which they cannot alter.—*Disraeli.*

APOTHEGMS.

A maxim is the exact and noble expression of an important and indisputable truth. Sound maxims are the germs of good; strongly imprinted in the memory, they nourish the will.—
Joubert.

Apothegms are the most infallible mirror to represent a man truly what he is.—*Plutarch.*

We content ourselves to present to thinking minds the original seeds from whence spring vast fields of new thought, that may be further cultivated, beautified, and enlarged.—
Chevalier Ramsay.

The genius, wit, and spirit of a nation are discovered by their proverbs.—*Bacon.*

An epigram often flashes light into regions where reason shines but dimly. Holmes disposed of a bigot at once, when he compared his mind to the pupil of the eye, — the more light you let into it the more it contracts.— *Whipple.*

Apothegms are, in history, the same as the pearls in the sand, or the gold in the mine.—
Erasmus.

Few of the many wise apothegms which have been uttered, from the time of the seven sages of Greece to that of poor Richard, have prevented a single foolish action.—*Macaulay.*

A man of maxims only is like a Cyclops with one eye, and that eye placed in the back of his head.—*Coleridge.*

The excellence of aphorisms consists not so much in the expression of some rare or abstruse sentiment, as in the comprehension of some useful truth in few words.—*Johnson.*

Aphorisms are portable wisdom, the quintessential extracts of thought and feeling.—
W. R. Alger.

A few words worthy to be remembered suffice to give an idea of a great mind. There are single thoughts that contain the essence of a whole volume, single sentences that have the beauties of a large work, a simplicity so finished and so perfect that it equals in merit and in excellence a large and glorious composition.—
Joubert.

The little and short sayings of nice and excellent men are of great value, like the dust of gold, or the least sparks of diamonds.—
Tillotson.

He may justly be numbered among the benefactors of mankind who contracts the great rules of life into short sentences, that may be easily impressed on the memory, and taught by frequent recollection to recur habitually to the mind.—*Johnson.*

Thoughts take up no room. When they are right, they afford a portable pleasure, which one may travel with, without any trouble or encumbrance.—*Jeremy Collier.*

He that lays down precepts for the governing of our lives, and moderating our passions, obliges humanity not only in the present, but in all future generations.—*Seneca.*

Under the veil of these curious sentences are hid those germs of morals which the masters of philosophy have afterwards developed into so many volumes.—*Plutarch.*

The wise men of old have sent most of their morality down to the stream of time in the light skiff of apothegm or epigram; and the proverbs of nations, which embody the common sense of nations, have the brisk concussion of the most sparkling wit.— *Whipple.*

I am of opinion that there are no proverbial sayings which are not true, because they are all sentences drawn from experience itself, who is the mother of all sciences.—*Cervantes.*

Abstracts, abridgments, summaries, etc, have the same use with burning-glasses, — to collect the diffused rays of wit and learning in authors, and make them point with warmth and quickness upon the reader's imagination.—
Swift.

Ethical maxims are bandied about as a sort of current coin of discourse, and, being never melted down for use, those that are of base metal are never detected.—*Bishop Whately.*

APPEARANCES.

A man may smile, and smile, and be a villain.—*Shakespeare.*

There are no greater wretches in the world than many of those whom people in general take to be happy.—*Seneca.*

By a kind of fashionable discipline, the eye is taught to brighten, the lip to smile, and the whole countenance to emanate with the semblance of friendly welcome, while the bosom is unwarmed by a single spark of genuine kindness and good-will.—*Washington Irving.*

With gloomy state, and agonizing pomp.—
Johnson.

There is no vice so simple, but assumes some mark of virtue on its outward parts.—
Shakespeare.

Surely you will not calculate any essential difference from mere appearances; for the light laughter that bubbles on the lip often mantles over brackish depths of sadness, and the serious look may be the sober veil that covers a divine peace. You know that the bosom can ache beneath diamond brooches; and how many blithe hearts dance under coarse wool!—*Chapin.*

How little do they see what is, who frame their hasty judgments upon that which seems!—
Southey.

O place! O form! how often dost thou with thy case, thy habit, wrench awe from fools, and tie the wiser souls to thy false seeming!—
Shakespeare.

A man of the world must seem to be that he wishes to be.—*Bruyère.*

In the condition of men, it frequently happens that grief and anxiety lie hid under the golden robes of prosperity; and the gloom of calamity is cheered by secret radiations of hope and comfort; as in the works of nature, the bog is sometimes covered with flowers, and the mine concealed in the barren crags.—*Johnson.*

I have always observed that to succeed in the world we must be foolish in appearance, but in reality wise.—*Montesquieu.*

Gilded tombs do worms enfold.—*Shakespeare.*

A miser grows rich by seeming poor; an extravagant man grows poor by seeming rich.—
Shenstone.

In civilized society external advantages make us more respected. A man with a good coat upon his back meets with a better reception than he who has a bad one. You may analyze this and say, What is there in it? But that will avail you nothing, for it is a part of a general system.—*Johnson.*

Beware, so long as you live, of judging men by their outward appearance.—*La Fontaine.*

APPETITE.

Reason should direct and appetite obey.—
Cicero.

Our appetites, of one or another kind, are excellent spurs to our reason, which might otherwise but feebly set about the great ends of preserving and continuing the species.—*Lamb.*

Good cheer is no hindrance to a good life.—
Aristippus.

There are so few invalids who are invariably and conscientiously untemptable by those deadly domestic enemies, sweetmeats, pastry, and gravies, that the usual civilities at a meal are very like being politely assisted to the grave.—
Willis.

Fat paunches have lean pates.—*Shakespeare.*

These appetites are very humiliating weaknesses. That our grace depends so largely upon animal condition is not quite flattering to those who are hyper-spiritual.—*Beecher.*

Choose rather to punish your appetites than to be punished by them.—*Tyrius Maximus.*

Hunger is a cloud out of which falls a rain of eloquence and knowledge; when the belly is empty, the body becomes spirit; when it is full, the spirit becomes body.—*Saadi.*

Animals feed, man eats; the man of intellect alone knows how to eat.—*Brillat Savarin.*

The youth who follows his appetites too soon seizes the cup, before it has received its best ingredients, and by anticipating his pleasures, robs the remaining parts of life of their share, so that his eagerness only produces a manhood of imbecility and an age of pain.—*Goldsmith.*

Doth not the appetite alter? A man loves the meat in his youth that he cannot endure in his age.—*Shakespeare.*

No man's body is as strong as his appetites, but Heaven has corrected the boundlessness of his voluptuous desires by stinting his strength and contracting his capacities.—*Tillotson.*

It is difficult to speak to the belly because it has no ears.—*Plutarch.*

Seest thou how pale the sated guest rises from supper, where the appetite is puzzled with varieties? The body, too, burdened with yesterday's excess, weighs down the soul, and fixes to the earth this particle of the divine essence.—*Horace.*

Hunger makes everything sweet except itself, for want is the teacher of habits.—*Antiphanes.*

Now good digestion wait on appetite, and health on both!—*Shakespeare.*

The lower your senses are kept, the better you may govern them. Appetite and reason are commonly like two buckets, — when one is at the top, the other is at the bottom. Now of the two, I had rather the reason-bucket be uppermost.—*Jeremy Collier.*

A well-governed appetite is a great part of liberty.—*Seneca.*

Appetite is the will's solicitor, the will is appetite's controller. No desire is properly called will, unless where reason and understanding prescribe the thing desired.—*Hooker.*

In grief I have always found eating a wondrous relief.—*Moore.*

Some men are born to feast, and not to fight ; whose sluggish minds, even in fair honor's field, still on their dinner turn.—*Joanna Baillie.*

The difference between a rich man and a poor man is this, — the former eats when he pleases, and the latter when he can get it.— *Sir Walter Raleigh.*

For the sake of health, medicines are taken by weight and measure ; so ought food to be, or by some similar rule.—*Skelton.*

APPLAUSE.

A universal applause is seldom less than two thirds of a scandal.—*L'Estrange.*

Such a noise arose as the shrouds make at sea in a stiff tempest, as loud and to as many tunes, — hats, cloaks, doublets, I think, flew up ; and had their faces been loose, this day they had been lost.—*Shakespeare.*

Applause is the spur of noble minds, the end and aim of weak ones.—*Colton.*

Flattery of the verbal kind is gross. In short, applause is of too coarse a nature to be swallowed in the gross, though the extract or tincture be ever so agreeable.—*Shenstone.*

The applause of a single human being is of great consequence.—*Johnson.*

Neither human applause nor human censure is to be taken as the test of truth ; but either should set us upon testing ourselves.— *Bishop Whately.*

When the million applaud you, seriously ask yourself what harm you have done ; when they censure you, what good !—*Colton.*

Applause waits on success : the fickle multitude, like the light straw that floats along the stream, glide with the current still, and follow fortune.—*Franklin.*

A slowness to applaud betrays a cold temper or an envious spirit.—*Hannah More.*

O popular applause ! what heart of man is proof against thy sweet, seducing charms ?— *Cowper.*

I would applaud thee to the very echo, that should applaud again.—*Shakespeare.*

Praise from the common people is generally false, and rather follows vain persons than virtuous ones.—*Bacon.*

APPRECIATION.

To love one that is great is almost to be great one's self.—*Madame Necker*

Praise is a debt we owe unto the virtues of others, and due unto our own from all whom malice hath not made mutes or envy struck dumb.—*Sir Thomas Browne.*

Were she perfect, one would admire her more, but love her less.—*Grattan.*

It is very singular how the fact of a man's death often seems to give people a truer idea of his character, whether for good or evil, than they have ever possessed while he was living and acting among them.—*Hawthorne.*

It is common, to esteem most what is most unknown.—*Tacitus.*

Nature and books belong to the eyes that see them. It depends on the mood of the man, whether he shall see the sunset or the fine poem. There are always sunsets, and there is always genius ; but only a few hours so serene that we can relish nature or criticism. The more or less depends on structure or temperament. Temperament is the iron wire on which the beads are strung. Of what use is fortune or talent to a cold and defective nature ?—*Emerson*

Men should allow others' excellences, to preserve a modest opinion of their own.—*Barrow.*

To guard the mind against the temptation of thinking that there are no good people, say to them : " Be such as you would like to see others, and you will find those who resemble you."—*Bossuet.*

To love her (Lady Elizabeth Hastings) was a liberal education.—*Steele.*

We must never undervalue any person. The workman loves not that his work should be despised in his presence. Now God is present everywhere, and every person is his work.— *De Sales.*

In this world there is one godlike thing, the essence of all that ever was or ever will be of godlike in this world, — the veneration done to human worth by the hearts of men.—*Carlyle.*

You think much too well of me as a man. No author can be as moral as his works, as no preacher is as pious as his sermons.—*Richter.*

Men prize the thing ungained more than it is.—*Shakespeare.*

Despise not any man, and do not spurn anything. For there is no man that hath not his hour, nor is there anything that hath not its place.—*Rabbi Ben Azai.*

To appreciate the noble is a gain which can never be torn from us.—*Goethe.*

No good writer was ever long neglected; no great man overlooked by men equally great. Impatience is a proof of inferior strength, and a destroyer of what little there may be.—*Landor.*

Sometimes a common scene in nature — one of the common relations of life — will open itself to us with a brightness and pregnancy of meaning unknown before. Sometimes a thought of this kind forms an era in life. It changes the whole future course. It is a new creation.
Channing.

You may fail to shine, in the opinion of others, both in your conversation and actions, from being superior, as well as inferior to them.
Greville.

We commend a horse for his strength, and sureness of foot, and not for his rich caparisons; a greyhound for his share of heels, not for his fine collar; a hawk for her wing, not for her jesses and bells. Why, in like manner, do we not value a man for what is properly his own? He has a great train, a beautiful palace, so much credit, so many thousand pounds a year, and all these are about him, but not in him.—*Montaigne.*

There is no surer mark of the absence of the highest moral and intellectual qualities than a cold reception of excellence.—*S. Bailey.*

People do not always understand the motives of sublime conduct, and when they are astonished they are very apt to think they ought to be alarmed. The truth is, none are fit judges of greatness but those who are capable of it.—
Jane Porter.

Next to excellence is the appreciation of it.—
Thackeray.

Every man stamps his value on himself. The price we challenge for ourselves is given us. There does not live on earth the man, be his station what it may, that I despise myself compared with him. Man is made great or little by his own will.—*Schiller.*

A man does but faintly relish that felicity which costs him nothing; happy they whom pain leads to pleasure.—*Henry Home.*

It is with certain good qualities as with the senses; those who are entirely deprived of them can neither appreciate nor comprehend them.—
Rochefoucauld.

Our companions please us less from the charms we find in their conversation than from those they find in ours.—*Greville.*

In an audience of rough people a generous sentiment always brings down the house. In the tumult of war both sides applaud an heroic deed.—*T. W. Higginson.*

To feel, to feel exquisitely, is the lot of very many; it is the charm that lends a superstitious joy to fear. But to appreciate belongs to the few; to one or two alone, here and there, the blended passion and understanding that constitute in its essence worship.—*Charles Auchester.*

We never know a greater character until something congenial to it has grown up within ourselves.—*Channing.*

In proportion as our own mind is enlarged, we discover a greater number of men of originality. Commonplace people see no difference between one man and another.—*Pascal.*

Contemporaries appreciate the man rather than the merit; posterity will regard the merit rather than the man.—*Buxton.*

The charming landscape which I saw this morning is indubitably made up of some twenty or thirty farms. Miller owns this field, Locke that, and Manning the woodland beyond. But none of them owns the landscape. There is a property in the horizon which no man has but he whose eye can integrate all the parts, that is, the poet. This is the best part of these men's farms, yet to this their warranty-deeds give no title.—*Emerson.*

He is incapable of a truly good action who knows not the pleasure in contemplating the good actions of others.—*Lavater.*

Whatever the benefits of fortune are, they yet require a palate fit to relish and taste them; it is fruition, and not possession, that renders us happy.—*Montaigne.*

Those who, from the desire of our perfection, have the keenest eye for our faults generally compensate for it by taking a higher view of our merits than we deserve.—*J. F. Boyes.*

I pity the man who can travel from Dan to Beersheba, and cry, "'T is all barren!" And so it is, and so is all the world to him who will not cultivate the fruits it offers.—*Sterne.*

The more enlarged is our own mind, the greater number we discover of men of originality. Your commonplace people see no difference between one man and another.—*Pascal.*

Do not justify all your actions. Do not appreciate the things as they touch you the nearest, and have not your eyes always fixed upon yourself.—*Richter.*

We are very much what others think of us. The reception our observations meet with gives us courage to proceed or damps our efforts.—
Hazlitt.

ARCHITECTURE.

The Gothic cathedral is a blossoming in stone, subdued by the insatiable demand of harmony in man. The mountain of granite blooms into an eternal flower, with the lightness and delicate finish as well as the aerial proportions and perspective of vegetable beauty.—*Emerson.*

A Gothic church is a petrified religion.—
Coleridge.

Architecture is the printing-press of all ages, and gives a history of the state of the society in which it was erected, from the cromlech of the Druids to those toy-shops of royal bad taste, — Carlton House and the Brighton Pavilion. The Tower and Westminster Abbey are glorious pages in the history of time, and tell the story of an iron despotism, and the cowardice of unlimited power.—*Lady Morgan.*

The architect must not only understand drawing, but music.—*Vitruvius.*

Architecture exhibits the greatest extent of the difference from nature which may exist in works of art. It involves all the powers of design, and is sculpture and painting inclusively. It shows the greatness of man, and should at the same time teach him humility.— *Coleridge.*

Architecture is frozen music !—
Madame de Staël.

In designing a house and gardens, it is happy when there is an opportunity of maintaining a subordination of parts; the house so luckily placed as to exhibit a view of the whole design. I have sometimes thought that there was room for it to resemble an epic or dramatic poem.—*Shenstone.*

Houses are built to live in, more than to look on ; therefore let use be preferred before uniformity except where both may be had.—
Bacon.

An instinctive taste teaches men to build their churches in flat countries with spire-steeples, which, as they cannot be referred to any other object, point as with silent finger to the sky and stars.— *Coleridge.*

Möller, in his Essay on Architecture, taught that the building which was fitted accurately to answer its end would turn out to be beautiful, though beauty had not been intended. I find the like unity in human structures rather virulent and pervasive.—*Emerson.*

Greek architecture is the flowering of geometry.—*Emerson.*

If cities were built by the sound of music, then some edifices would appear to be constructed by grave, solemn tones, — others to have danced forth to light fantastic airs.—*Hawthorne.*

ARGUMENT.

In argument similes are like songs in love : they much describe ; they nothing prove.—
Prior.

Some men at the approach of a dispute neigh like horses. Unless there be an argument, they think nothing is doing. Some talkers excel in the precision with which they formulate their thoughts, so that you get from them somewhat to remember ; others lay criticism asleep by a charm. Especially women use words that are not words, — as steps in a dance are not steps, — but reproduce the genius of that they speak of ; as the sound of some bells makes us think of the bell merely, whilst the church-chimes in the distance bring the church and its serious memories before us.—*Emerson.*

He that is not open to conviction is not qualified for discussion.—*Bishop Whately.*

An academical education, sir, bids me tell you, that it is necessary to establish the truth of your first proposition before you presume to draw inferences from it.—*Junius.*

Arguments, like children, should be like the subject that begets them.—*Thomas Decker.*

Reply with wit to gravity, and with gravity to wit ; make a full concession to your adversary, and give him every credit for those arguments you know you can answer, and slur over those you feel you cannot ; but above all, if he have the privilege of making his reply take especial care that the strongest thing you have to urge be the last.—*Colton.*

Arguments out of a pretty mouth are unanswerable.—*Addison.*

I never love those salamanders that are never well but when they are in the fire of contentions. I will rather suffer a thousand wrongs than offer one. I have always found that to strive with a superior is injurious ; with an equal, doubtful ; with an inferior, sordid and base ; with any, full of unquietness.—
Bishop Hall.

Be calm in arguing ; for fierceness makes error a fault, and truth discourtesy.—*Herbert.*

Argument, as usually managed, is the worst sort of conversation ; as it is generally in books the worst sort of reading.—*Swift.*

Wise men argue causes, and fools decide them.—*Anacharsis.*

If thou continuest to take delight in idle argumentation thou mayest be qualified to combat with the sophists, but will never know how to live with men.—*Socrates.*

He who establishes his argument by noise and command shows that reason is weak.—
Montaigne.

When we would show any one that he is mistaken, our best course is to observe on what side he considers the subject,—for his view of it is generally right on this side,—and admit to him that he is right so far. He will be satisfied with this acknowledgment, that he was not wrong in his judgment, but only inadvertent in not looking at the whole case.—*Pascal.*

As the scale of the balance must give way to the weight that presses it down, so the mind must of necessity yield to demonstration.—
Cicero.

Testimony is like an arrow shot from a long bow, the force of it depends on the strength of the hand that draws it. Argument is like an arrow from a cross-bow, which has equal force though drawn by a child.—*Boyle.*

Gratuitous violence in argument betrays a conscious weakness of the cause, and is usually a signal of despair.—*Junius.*

It is an excellent rule to be observed in all disputes, that men should give soft words and hard arguments; that they should not so much strive to vex as to convince each other.—
Wilkins.

Nothing is more certain than that much of the force, as well as grace, of arguments or instructions depends on their conciseness.—*Pope.*

In a debate, rather pull to pieces the argument of thy antagonist than offer him any of thy own; for thus thou wilt fight him in his own country.—*Fielding.*

ARISTOCRACY.

Amongst the masses—even in revolutions—aristocracy must ever exist; destroy it in nobility, and it becomes centred in the rich and powerful Houses of the Commons. Pull them down, and it still survives in the master and foreman of the workshop.—*Guizot.*

Aristocracy has three successive ages,—the age of superiorities, the age of privileges, and the age of vanities; having passed out of the first, it degenerates in the second, and dies away in the third.—*Chateaubriand.*

ARMY.

For the army is a school in which the niggardly become generous, and the generous prodigal; and if there are some soldiers misers, they are a kind of monsters, but very rarely seen.—*Cervantes.*

The army is a good book to open to study human life. One learns there to put his hand to everything, to the lowest and highest things. The most delicate and rich are forced to see living nearly everywhere poverty, and to live with it, and to measure his morsel of bread and draught of water.—*Alfred de Vigny.*

ARROGANCE.

What is so hateful to a poor man as the purse-proud arrogance of a rich one? Let fortune shift the scene, and make the poor man rich, he runs at once into the vice that he declaimed against so feelingly; these are strange contradictions in the human character.—
Cumberland.

When men are most sure and arrogant, they are commonly the most mistaken, and have then given views to passion, without that proper deliberation and suspense which can alone secure them from the grossest absurdities.—
Hume.

When Diogenes came to Olympia and perceived some Rhodian youths dressed with great splendor and magnificence, he said with a smile of contempt, " This is all arrogance." Afterwards some Lacedemónians came in his way, as mean and as sordid in their attire as the dress of the others was rich, " This," said he, ' is also arrogance."—*Ælian.*

Arrogance is the obstruction of wisdom —
Bion.

A man that loves to be peevish and paramount, and to play the sovereign at every turn, does but blast the blessings of life, and swagger away his own enjoyments; and not to enlarge upon the folly, not to mention the injustice of such a behavior, it is always the sign of a little, unbenevolent temper. It is disease and discredit all over, and there is no more greatness in it, than in the swelling of a dropsy.—
Jeremy Collier.

ART.

That which exists in nature is a something purely individual and particular. Art, on the contrary, is essentially destined to manifest the general.—*Schlegel.*

In sculpture, did ever anybody call the Apollo a fancy piece? Or say of the Laocoön how it might be made different? A masterpiece of art has in the mind a fixed place in the chain of being, as much as a plant or a crystal.—
Emerson.

It is not so much in buying pictures, as in being pictures, that you can encourage a noble school. The best patronage of art is not that which seeks for the pleasures of sentiment in a vague ideality, nor for beauty of form in a marble image, but that which educates your children into living heroes, and binds down the flights and the fondnesses of the heart into practical duty and faithful devotion.—*Ruskin.*

There is no more potent antidote to low sensuality than the adoration of the beautiful. All the higher arts of design are essentially chaste without respect to the object. They purify the thoughts as tragedy purifies the passions. Their accidental effects are not worth consideration, — there are souls to whom even a vestal is not holy.—*Schlegel.*

What is art? Nature concentrated.—*Balzac.*

It is only with the best judges that the highest works of art would lose none of their honor by being seen in their rudiments.—
J. F. Boyes.

Every common dauber writes rascal and villain under his pictures, because the pictures themselves have neither character nor resemblance. But the works of a master require no index. His features and coloring are taken from nature. The impression they make is immediate and uniform; nor is it possible to mistake his characters.—*Junius.*

The perfection of art is to conceal art.—
Quintilian.

Winckelmann wished to live with a work of art as a friend. The saying is true of pen and pencil. Fresh lustre shoots from Lycidas in a twentieth perusal. The portraits of Clarendon are mellowed by every year of reflection.—
Willmott.

Art must anchor in nature, or it is the sport of every breath of folly.—*Hazlitt.*

The names of great painters are like passing bells; in the name of Velasquez, you hear sounded the fall of Spain; in the name of Titian, that of Venice; in the name of Leonardo, that of Milan; in the name of Raphael, that of Rome. And there is profound justice in this; for in proportion to the nobleness of the power is the guilt of its use for purposes vain or vile; and hitherto the greater the art, the more surely has it been used, and used solely, for the decoration of pride, or the provoking of sensuality.—*Ruskin.*

Art, as far as it has ability, follows nature, as a pupil imitates his master: thus your art must be, as it were, God's grandchild.—*Dante.*

Art is the effort of man to express the ideas which nature suggests to him of a power above nature, whether that power be within the recesses of his own being, or in the Great First Cause of which nature, like himself, is but the effect.—*Bulwer Lytton.*

The only kind of sublimity which a painter or sculptor should aim at is to express by certain proportions and positions of limbs and features that strength and dignity of mind, and vigor and activity of body, which enables men to conceive and execute great actions.—*Burke.*

Art employs method for the symmetrical formation of beauty, as science employs it for the logical exposition of truth; but the mechanical process is, in the last, ever kept visibly distinct, while in the first it escapes from sight amid the shows of color and the curves of grace.—
Bulwer Lytton.

He that sips of many arts drinks of none. —
Fuller.

No man can thoroughly master more than one art or science. The world has never seen a perfect painter. What would it have availed for Raphael to have aimed at Titian's coloring, or for Titian to have imitated Raphael's drawing, but to have diverted each from the true bent of his natural genius, and to have made each sensible of his own deficiencies, without any probability of supplying them.—*Hazlitt.*

Many persons feel art, some understand it; but few both feel and understand it.—*Hillard.*

Art, not less eloquently than literature, teaches her children to venerate the single eye. Remember Matsys. His representations of miser-life are breathing. A forfeited bond twinkles in the hard smile. But follow him to an altar-piece. His Apostle has caught a stray tint from his usurer. Features of exquisite beauty are seen and loved; but the old nature of avarice frets under the glow of devotion. Pathos staggers on the edge of farce.—*Willmott.*

We speak of profane arts, but there are none properly such; every art is holy in itself, it is the son of eternal light.—*Tegner.*

Art is a jealous mistress, and, if a man have a genius for painting, poetry, music, architecture, or philosophy, he makes a bad husband, and an ill provider, and should be wise in season, and not fetter himself with duties which will imbitter his days, and spoil him for his proper work.—*Emerson.*

The highest problem of any art is to cause by appearance the illusion of a higher reality.—
Goethe.

All the arts, which have a tendency to raise man in the scale of being, have a certain common bond of union, and are connected, if I may be allowed to say so, by blood-relationship with one another.—*Cicero.*

A work of art is said to be perfect in proportion as it does not remind the spectator of the process by which it was created.—*Tuckerman.*

Moral beauty is the basis of all true beauty. This foundation is somewhat covered and veiled in nature. Art brings it out, and gives it more transparent forms. It is here that art, when it knows well its power and resources, engages in a struggle with nature in which it may have the advantage.—*Victor Cousin.*

3

Those critics who, in modern times, have the most thoughtfully analyzed the laws of æsthetic beauty, concur in maintaining that the real truthfulness of all works of imagination — sculpture, painting, written fiction — is so purely in the imagination, that the artist never seeks to represent the positive truth, but the idealized image of a truth.—*Bulwer Lytton.*

The artist belongs to his work, not the work to the artist.—*Novalis.*

Art is the microscope of the mind, which sharpens the wit as the other does the sight; and converts every object into a little universe in itself. Art may be said to draw aside the veil from nature. To those who are perfectly unskilled in the practice, unimbued with the principles of art, most objects present only a confused mass.—*Hazlitt.*

I think sculpture and painting have an effect to teach us manners, and abolish hurry.— *Emerson.*

I once asked a distinguished artist what place he gave to labor in art. "Labor," he in effect said, "is the beginning, the middle, and the end of art." Turning then to another — "And you," I inquired, "what do you consider as the great force in art?" "Love," he replied. In their two answers I found but one truth.—*Bovee.*

Ah! would that we could at once paint with the eyes! In the long way, from the eye through the arm to the pencil, how much is lost!—*Lessing.*

Art is a severe business; most serious when employed in grand and sacred objects. The artist stands higher than art, higher than the object. He uses art for his purposes, and deals with the object after his own fashion.—*Goethe.*

The great artist is the slave of his ideal.— *Bovee.*

The refining influence is the study of art, which is the science of beauty; and I find that every man values every scrap of knowledge in art, every observation of his own in it, every hint he has caught from another. For the laws of beauty are the beauty of beauty, and give the mind the same or a higher joy than the sight of it gives the senses. The study of art is of high value to the growth of the intellect.— *Emerson.*

The learned understand the reason of the art, the unlearned feel the pleasure.—*Quintilian.*

Art does not imitate nature, but it founds itself on the study of nature, — takes from nature the selections which best accord with its own intention, and then bestows on them that which nature does not possess, viz. the mind and the soul of man.—*Bulwer Lytton.*

Art neither belongs to religion nor to ethics; but, like these, it brings us nearer to the Infinite, one of the forms of which it manifests to us. God is the source of all beauty, as of all truth, of all religion, of all morality. The most exalted object, therefore, of art is to reveal in its own manner the sentiment of the Infinite.— *Victor Cousin.*

It is the end of art to inoculate men with the love of nature.—*Beecher.*

The mother of useful arts is necessity; that of the fine arts is luxury. For father the former has intellect; the latter genius, which itself is a kind of luxury.—*Schopenhauer.*

The true work of art is but a shadow of the divine perfection.—*Michael Angelo.*

Since I have known God in a saving manner, painting, poetry, and music have had charms unknown to me before. I have received what I suppose is a taste for them, or religion has refined my mind and made it susceptible of impressions from the sublime and beautiful. O, how religion secures the heightened enjoyment of those pleasures which keep so many from God, by their becoming a source of pride!—*Henry Martyn.*

The first essential to success in the art you practise is respect for the art itself.— *Bulwer Lytton.*

What a conception of art must those theorists have who exclude portraits from the proper province of the fine arts! It is exactly as if we denied that to be poetry in which the poet celebrates the woman he really loves. Portraiture is the basis and the touchstone of historic painting.—*Schlegel.*

The flitting sunbeam has been grasped and made to do man's bidding in place of the painter's pencil. And although Franklin tamed the lightning, yet not until yesterday has its instantaneous flash been made the vehicle of language; thus in the transmission of thought annihilating space and time.—*Professor Robinson.*

Art is based on a strong sentiment of religion, — on a profound and mighty earnestness; hence it is so prone to co-operate with religion. *Goethe.*

Art, however innocent, looks like deceiving. *Aaron Hill.*

Remember always, in painting as in eloquence, the greater your strength, the quieter will be your manner, and the fewer your words; and in painting, as in all the arts and acts of life, the secret of high success will be found, not in a fretful and various excellence, but in a quiet singleness of justly chosen aim.—*Ruskin.*

An amateur may not be an artist, though an artist should be an amateur.—*Disraeli.*

All things are artificial; for nature is the art of God.—*Sir Thomas Browne.*

Excellence in art is to be attained only by active effort, and not by passive impressions; by the manly overcoming of difficulties, by patient struggle against adverse circumstance, by the thrifty use of moderate opportunities. The great artists were not rocked and dandled into eminence, but they attained to it by that course of labor and discipline which no man need go to Rome or Paris or London to enter upon.—*Hillard.*

Art needs solitude or misery or passion. Lukewarm zephyrs wilt it. It is a rock-flower flourishing by stormy blasts and in stony soil.—*Alex. Dumas.*

The inglorious arts of peace.—*Andrew Marvell.*

The misfortune in the state is, that nobody can enjoy life in peace, but that everybody must govern; and in art, that nobody will enjoy what has been produced, but that every one wants to reproduce on his own account.—*Goethe.*

An artist has more than two eyes.—*Haliburton.*

All men are in some degree impressed by the face of the world; some men even to delight. This love of beauty is taste. Others have the same love in such excess that, not content with admiring, they seek to embody it in new forms. The creation of beauty is art.—*Emerson.*

A true artist should put a generous deceit on the spectators, and effect the noblest designs by easy methods.—*Burke.*

The summit charms us, the steps to it do not; with the heights before our eyes, we like to linger in the plain. It is only a part of art that can be taught; but the artist needs the whole. He who is only half instructed speaks much and is always wrong; who knows it wholly is content with acting and speaks seldom or late.—*Goethe.*

The highest art is artlessness.—*F. A. Durivage.*

Whatever may be the means, or whatever the more immediate end of any kind of art, all of it that is good agrees in this, that it is the expression of one soul talking to another, and is precious according to the greatness of the soul that utters it.—*Ruskin.*

In art, to express the infinite one should suggest infinitely more than is expressed.—*Goethe.*

Artists will sometimes speak of Rome with disparagement or indifference while it is before them; but no artist ever lived in Rome and then left it, without sighing to return.—*Hillard.*

This is an art which does mend nature,—change it rather; but the art itself is nature.—*Shakespeare.*

Many young painters would never have taken their pencils in hand if they could have felt, known, and understood, early enough, what really produced a master like Raphael.—*Goethe.*

The object of art is to crystallize emotion into thought, and then to fix it in form.—*François Delsarte.*

The power, whether of painter or poet, to describe rightly what he calls an ideal thing depends upon its being to him not an ideal but a real thing. No man ever did or ever will work well, but either from actual sight or sight of faith.—*Ruskin.*

In the fine arts, as in many other things, we know well only what we have not learned.—*Chamfort.*

The ordinary true, or purely real, cannot be the object of the arts. Illusion on a ground of truth,—that is the secret of the fine arts.—*Joubert.*

In old times men used their powers of painting to show the objects of faith; in later times they used the objects of faith that they might show their powers of painting.—*Ruskin.*

The enemy of art is the enemy of nature; art is nothing but the highest sagacity and exertions of human nature; and what nature will he honor who honors not the human?—*Lavater.*

The highest art is always the most religious; and the greatest artist is always a devout man. A scoffing Raphael or Michael Angelo is not conceivable.—*Blackie.*

In the art of design, color is to form what verse is to prose,—a more harmonious and luminous vehicle of the thought.—*Mrs. Jameson.*

The painter is, as to the execution of his work, a mechanic; but as to his conception, his spirit, and design, he is hardly below even the poet in liberal art.—*Steele.*

ARTIFICE.

Artifice is allowed to deceive a rival; we may employ everything against our enemies.—*Richelieu.*

The ordinary employment of artifice is the mark of a petty mind; and it almost always happens that he who uses it to cover himself in one place uncovers himself in another.—*Rochefoucauld.*

To know to dissemble is the knowledge of kings.—*Richelieu.*

Nature is mighty. Art is mighty. Artifice is weak. For nature is the work of a mightier power than man. Art is the work of man under the guidance and inspiration of a mightier power. Artifice is the work of .mere man, in the imbecility of his mimic understanding.—*Hare.*

ASKING.

I am prejudiced in favor of him who can solicit boldly, without impudence, — he has faith in humanity, he has faith in himself. No one who is not accustomed to give grandly can ask nobly and with boldness.—*Lavater.*

ASPIRATION.

There is not a heart but has its moments of longing, — yearning for something better, nobler, holier than it knows now.—*Beecher.*

What we truly and earnestly aspire to be, that in some sense we are. The mere aspiration, by changing the frame of the mind, for the moment realizes itself.—*Mrs. Jameson.*

Man ought always to have something which he prefers to life; otherwise life itself will appear to him tiresome and void.—*Seume.*

Aspirations after the holy, — the only aspiration in which the human soul can be assured that it will never meet with disappointment.—*Maria M'Intosh.*

Too low they build who build beneath the stars.—*Young.*

O that I had wings like a dove!—*Bible.*

We learn to treasure what is above this earth; we long for revelation, which nowhere burns more purely and more beautifully than in the New Testament.—*Goethe.*

ASSERTION.

It is an impudent kind of sorcery, to attempt to blind us with the smoke, without convincing us that the fire has existed.—*Junius.*

Assertion, unsupported by fact, is nugatory; surmise and general abuse, in however elegant language, ought not to pass for proofs.—*Junius.*

ASSOCIATES.

It is expedient to have an acquaintance with those who have looked into the world; who know men, understand business, and can give you good intelligence and good advice when they are wanted.—*Bishop Horne.*

He that walketh with wise men shall be wise; but a companion of fools shall be destroyed.—*Bible.*

He who comes from the kitchen smells of its smoke; he who adheres to a sect has something of its cant; the college air pursues the student, and dry inhumanity him who herds with literary pedants.—*Lavater.*

If men wish to be held in esteem, they must associate with those only who are estimable.—*Bruyère.*

Might I give counsel to any young hearer, I would say to him, Try to frequent the company of. your betters. In books and life is the most wholesome society; learn to admire rightly; the great pleasure of life is that. Note what the great men admired, — they admired great things; narrow spirits admire basely, and worship meanly.—*Thackeray.*

You may depend upon it that he is a good man whose intimate friends are all good.—*Lavater.*

Associate with men of good judgment; for judgment is found in conversation. And we make another man's judgment ours by frequenting his company.—*Fuller.*

Choose the company of your superiors, whenever you can have it; that is the right and true pride.—*Chesterfield.*

Be not deceived: evil communications corrupt good manners.—*Bible.*

When we live habitually with the wicked, we become necessarily either their victim or their disciple; when we associate, on the contrary, with virtuous men, we form ourselves in imitation of their virtues, or, at least, lose every day something of our faults.—*Agapet.*

No man can be provident of his time, who is not prudent in the choice of his company.—*Jeremy Taylor.*

A frequent intercourse and intimate connection between two persons make them so like, that not only their dispositions are moulded like each other, but their very face and tone of voice contract a certain analogy.—*Lavater.*

No man can possibly improve in any company for which he has not respect enough to be under some degree of restraint.—*Chesterfield.*

Company, villanous company, hath been the spoil of me.—*Shakespeare.*

What is companionship where nothing that improves the intellect is communicated, and where the larger heart contracts itself to the model and dimension of the smaller?—*Landor.*

In all societies, it is advisable to associate if possible with the highest; not that the highest are always the best, but because, if disgusted there, we can at any time descend; but if we begin with the lowest, to ascend is impossible.—*Colton.*

It is meet that noble minds keep ever with their likes; for who so firm, that cannot be seduced?—*Shakespeare.*

No company is far preferable to bad, because we are more apt to catch the vices of others than their virtues, as disease is far more contagious than health.—*Colton.*

There are like to be short graces where the devil plays host.—*Lamb.*

Bad company is like a nail driven into a post, which, after the first and second blow, may be drawn out with little difficulty; but being once driven up to the head, the pincers cannot take hold to draw it out, but which can only be done by the destruction of the wood.—*St. Augustine.*

It is best to be with those in time that we hope to be with in eternity.—*Fuller.*

Nothing is more deeply punished than the neglect of the affinities by which alone society should be formed, and the insane levity of choosing associates by others' eyes.—*Emerson.*

A companion that feasts the company with wit and mirth, and leaves out the sin which is usually mixed with them, he is the man; and let me tell you, good company and good discourse are the very sinews of virtue.—
Izaak Walton.

Costly followers are not to be liked; lest while a man maketh his train longer, he make his wings shorter.—*Bacon.*

Constant companionship is not enjoyable, any more than constant eating. We sit too long at the table of friendship, when we outsit our appetites for each other's thoughts.—*Bovee.*

The company in which you will improve most will be least expensive to you.—
Washington.

We gain nothing by being with such as ourselves. We encourage one another in mediocrity. I am always longing to be with men more excellent than myself.—*Lamb.*

It is good discretion not to make too much of any man at the first; because one cannot hold out that proportion.—*Bacon.*

It is certain that either wise bearing or ignorant carriage is caught, as men take diseases, one of another; therefore let men take heed of their company.—*Shakespeare.*

ASSOCIATION.
Association is the delight of the heart, not less than of poetry. Alison observes that an autumn sunset, with its crimson clouds, glimmering trunks of trees, and wavering tints upon the grass, seems scarcely capable of embellishment. But if in this calm and beautiful glow the chime of a distant bell steal over the fields, the bosom heaves with the sensation that Dante so tenderly describes.—*Willmott.*

Even a high dome and the expansive interior of a cathedral have a sensible effect upon manners. I have heard that stiff people lose some of their awkwardness under high ceilings.
Emerson.

How we delight to build our recollections upon some basis of reality, — a place, a country, a local habitation! how the events of life, as we look back upon them, have grown into the well-remembered background of the places where they fell upon us! Here is some sunny garden or summer lane, beautified and canonized forever with the flood of a great joy ; and here are dim and silent places, — rooms always shadowed and dark to us, whatever they may be to others, — where distress or death came once, and since then dwells forevermore.—*Washington Irving.*

I have only to take up this, or this, to flood my brain with memories.—*Madame Deluzy.*

There is no man who has not some interesting associations with particular scenes, or airs, or books, and who does not feel their beauty or sublimity enhanced to him by such connections.
Sir A. Alison.

He whose heart is not excited upon the spot which a martyr has sanctified by his sufferings, or at the grave of one who has largely benefited mankind, must be more inferior to the multitude in his moral, than he can possibly be raised above them in his intellectual nature.—
Southey.

That man is little to be envied whose patriotism would not gain force upon the plain of Marathon, or whose piety would not grow warmer among the ruins of Iona.—*Johnson.*

ASSURANCE.
Immoderate assurance is perfect licentiousness.—*Shenstone.*

Assurance and intrepidity, under the white banner of seeming modesty, clear the way to merit that would otherwise be discouraged by difficulties.—*Chesterfield.*

Assurance never failed to get admission into the houses of the great.—*Moore.*

ASTRONOMY.
Astronomy is one of the sublimest fields of human investigation. The mind that grasps its facts and principles receives something of the enlargement and grandeur belonging to the science itself. It is a quickener of devotion.—
Horace Mann.

Astronomy is the science of the harmony of infinite expanse.—*Lord John Russell.*

The contemplation of celestial things will make a man both speak and think more sublimely and magnificently when he descends to human affairs.— *Cicero.*

The narrow sectarian cannot read astronomy with impunity. The creeds of his church shrivel like dried leaves at the door of the observatory.—*Emerson.*

An undevout astronomer is mad.—*Young.*

ATHEISM.

There is no being eloquent for atheism. In that exhausted receiver the mind cannot use its wings, — the clearest proof that it is out of its element.—*Hare.*

Settle it, therefore, in your minds, as a maxim never to be effaced or forgotten, that atheism is an inhuman, bloody, ferocious system, equally hostile to every useful restraint, and to every virtuous affection; that leaving nothing above us to excite awe, nor round us to awaken tenderness, it wages war with heaven and earth: its first object is to dethrone God, its next to destroy man.—*Robert Hall.*

No atheist, as such, can be a true friend, an affectionate relation, or a loyal subject.—
Bentley.

Whoever considers the study of anatomy, I believe, will never be an atheist; the frame of man's body, and coherence of his parts, being so strange and paradoxical, that I hold it to be the greatest miracle of nature.—*Lord Herbert.*

The great atheists are, indeed, the hypocrites, which are ever handling holy things, but without feeling; so as they must need be cauterized in the end.—*Bacon.*

The owlet atheism, sailing on obscene wings across the noon, drops his blue-fringed lids, and shuts them close, and, hooting at the glorious sun in heaven, cries out, " Where is it ? " —
Coleridge.

A little philosophy inclineth man's mind to atheism, but depth in philosophy bringeth men's minds about to religion.—*Bacon.*

I should like to see a man sober in his habits, moderate, chaste, just in his dealings, assert that there is no God; he would speak at least without interested motives; but such a man is not to be found.—*Bruyère.*

Atheism is rather in the life than in the heart of man.—*Bacon.*

One would fancy that the zealots in atheism would be exempt from the single fault which seems to grow out of the imprudent fervor of religion. But so it is, that irreligion is propagated with as much fierceness and contention, wrath and indignation, as if the safety of mankind depended upon it.—*Addison.*

The statements of atheists ought to be perfectly clear of doubt. Now it is not perfectly clear that the soul is material.—*Pascal.*

The three great apostles of practical atheism, that make converts without persecuting, and retain them without preaching, are wealth, health, and power.—*Colton.*

Thank Heaven, the female heart is untenantable by atheism.—*Horace Mann.*

Atheism is the result of ignorance and pride, of strong sense and feeble reasons, of good eating and ill-living. It is the plague of society, the corrupter of manners, and the underminer of property.—*Jeremy Collier.*

By night an atheist half believes a God.—
Young.

Atheism is a system which can communicate neither warmth nor illumination, except from those fagots which your mistaken zeal has lighted up for its destruction.—*Colton.*

An atheist's laugh is a poor exchange for Deity offended.—*Burns.*

Supposing all the great points of atheism were formed into a kind of creed, I would fain ask whether it would not require an infinite greater measure of faith than any set of articles which they so violently oppose.—*Addison.*

The fool hath said in his heart, There is no God. They are corrupt; they have done abominable works.—*Bible.*

The footprint of the savage traced in the sand is sufficient to attest the presence of man to the atheist who will not recognize God, whose hand is impressed upon the entire universe.—*Hugh Miller.*

There are few men so obstinate in their atheism whom a pressing danger will not reduce to an acknowledgment of the divine power.
Plato.

ATTENTION.

Attention makes the genius; all learning, fancy, and science depend upon it. Newton traced back his discoveries to its unwearied employment. It builds bridges, opens new worlds, and heals diseases; without it taste is useless, and the beauties of literature are unobserved.—*Willmott.*

AUSTERITY.

Manners more reserved and harsh, less complaisant and frank, only serve to give a false idea of piety to the people of the world, who are already but too much prejudiced against it, and who believe that we cannot serve God but by a melancholy and austere life. Let us go on our way in the simplicity of our hearts, with the peace and joy that are the fruits of the Holy Spirit.—*Fenelon.*

AUTHORITY.

Nothing is more gratifying to the mind of man than power or dominion.—*Addison.*

Though Authority be a stubborn bear, yet he is oft led by the nose with gold.—
Shakespeare.

Meek young men grow up in libraries, believing it their duty to accept the views which Cicero, which Locke, which Bacon, have given; forgetful that Cicero, Locke, and Bacon were only young men in libraries when they wrote these books.—*Emerson.*

Authority, though it err like others, hath yet a kind of medicine in itself, that skins the vice of the top.—*Shakespeare.*

There is nothing sooner overthrows a weak head than opinion of authority; like too strong a liquor for a frail glass.—*Sir P. Sidney.*

Man, proud man! dressed in a little brief authority; most ignorant of what he's most assured, his glassy essence, — like an angry ape plays such fantastic tricks before high heaven as make the angels weep.— *Shakespeare.*

AUTHORS.

People may be taken in once, who imagine that an author is greater in private life than other men.—*Johnson.*

Professed authors who overestimate their vocation are too full of themselves to be agreeable companions. The demands of their egotism are inveterate. They seem to be incapable of that *abandon* which is the requisite condition of social pleasure; and bent upon winning a tribute of admiration, or some hint which they can turn to the account of pen-craft, there is seldom in their company any of the delightful unconsciousness which harmonizes a circle.—
Tuckerman.

Nature's chief masterpiece is writing well.—
Sheffield, Duke of Buckingham.

There is no author so poor who cannot be of some service, if only for a witness of his time.—*Claude Fauchet.*

The success of many works is found in the relation between the mediocrity of the authors' ideas and that of the ideas of the public.—
Chamfort.

Authors are the vanguard in the march of mind, the intellectual backwoodsmen, reclaiming from the idle wilderness new territories for the thought and activity of their happier brethren.—*Carlyle.*

It is quite as much of a trade to make a book as to make a clock. It requires more than mere genius to be an author.—*Bruyère.*

Our writings are so many dishes, our readers guests, our books like beauty; that which one admires another rejects; so are we approved as men's fancies are inclined.—*Burton.*

One hates an author that is all author; fellows in foolscap uniform turned up with ink.—
Byron.

Whoever has set his whole heart upon book-making had better be sought in his works, for it is only the lees of his cup of life which he offers, in person, to the warm lips of his fellows.
Tuckerman.

The motives and purposes of authors are not always so pure and high as, in the enthusiasm of youth, we sometimes imagine.—*Longfellow.*

The wonderful fortune of some writers deludes and leads to misery a great number of young people. It cannot be too often repeated that it is dangerous to enter upon a career of letters without some other means of living. An illustrious author has said in these times, "Literature must not be leant on as upon a crutch; it is little more than a stick.—*J. Petit, Senn.*

The familiar writer is apt to be his own satirist. Out of his own mouth is he judged.—
Whipple.

The faults of a brilliant writer are never dangerous on the long run; a thousand people read his work who would read no other; inquiry is directed to each of his doctrines; it is soon discovered what is sound and what is false; the sound become maxims, and the false beacons.—*Bulwer Lytton.*

The two most engaging powers of an author are to make new things familiar, and familiar things new.—*Thackeray.*

Those authors into whose hands nature has placed a magic wand, with which they no sooner touch us than we forget the unhappiness in life, than the darkness leaves our soul, and we are reconciled to existence, should be placed among the benefactors of the human race.—
Diderot.

A man is, I suspect, but of a second-rate order whose genius is not immeasurably above his works.—*Bulwer Lytton.*

It is a doubt whether mankind are most indebted to those who, like Bacon and Butler, dig the gold from the mine of literature, or those, who, like Paley, purify it, stamp it, fix its real value, and give it currency and utility.—
Colton.

We write from aspiration and antagonism, as well as from experience. We paint those qualities which we do not possess.—*Emerson.*

None but an author knows an author's cares.—*Cowper.*

To have invented that character (Fielding's Amelia) is not only a triumph of art, but it is a good action.—*Thackeray.*

I believe that there is much less difference between the author and his works than is currently supposed; it is usually in the physical appearance of the writer, — his manners, his mien, his exterior, — that he falls short of the ideal a reasonable man forms of him — rarely in his mind.—*Bulwer Lytton.*

The authors who affect contempt for a name in the world put their names to the books which they invite the world to read.—*Cicero.*

Dr. Johnson has said that the chief glory of a country arises from its authors. But then that is only as they are oracles of wisdom; unless they teach virtue, they are more worthy of a halter than of the laurel.—*Jane Porter.*

Nothing is so beneficial to a young author as the advice of a man whose judgment stands constitutionally at the freezing-point.—
Douglas Jerrold.

That an author's work is the mirror of his mind is a position that has led to very false conclusions. If Satan himself were to write a book it would be in praise of virtue, because the good would purchase it for use, and the bad for ostentation.—*Colton.*

Authors, like coins, grow dear as they grow old.—*Pope.*

To write well is to think well, to feel well, and to render well; it is to possess at once intellect, soul, and taste.—*Buffon.*

We may observe in humorous authors that the faults they chiefly ridicule have often a likeness in themselves. Cervantes had much of the knight-errant in him; Sir George Etherege was unconsciously the Fopling Flutter of his own satire; Goldsmith was the same hero to chambermaids, and coward to ladies that he has immortalized in his charming comedy; and the antiquarian frivolities of Jonathan Oldbuck had their resemblance in Jonathan Oldbuck's creator.—*Bulwer Lytton.*

He who purposes to be an author should first be a student.—*Dryden.*

Never write on a subject without having first read yourself full on it; and never read on a subject till you have thought yourself hungry on it.—*Richter.*

A writer who attempts to live on the manufacture of his imagination is continually coquetting with starvation.—*Whipple.*

There are three difficulties in authorship, — to write anything worth the publishing, to find honest men to publish it, and to get sensible men to read it.—*Colton.*

Young authors give their brains much exercise and little food.—*Joubert.*

There is infinite pathos in unsuccessful authorship. The book that perishes unread is the deaf mute of literature.—*Holmes.* ·

It is in vain a daring author thinks of attaining to the heights of Parnassus if he does not feel the secret influence of heaven and if his natal star has not formed him to be a poet.—
Boileau.

Never write anything that does not give you great pleasure; emotion is easily propagated from the writer to the reader.—*Joubert*

Certain I am that every author who has written a book with earnest forethought and fondly cherished designs will bear testimony to the fact that much which he meant to convey has never been guessed at in any review of his work; and many a delicate beauty of thought, on which he principally valued himself, remains, like the statue of Isis, an image of truth from which no hand lifts the veil.—*Bulwer Lytton.*

Of all unfortunate men one of the unhappiest is a middling author endowed with too lively a sensibility for criticism.—*Disraeli.*

How kind the " Critical Notices " — where small authorship comes to pick up chips of praise, fragrant, sugary, and sappy — always are to them! Well, life would be nothing without paper credit and other fictions; so let them pass current.—*Holmes.*

Friend, howsoever thou earnest by this book, I will assure thee thou wert least in my thoughts when I writ it.—*Bunyan.*

This is the highest miracle of genius, that things which are not should be as though they were, that the imaginations of one mind should become the personal recollections of another.—
Macaulay.

Clear writers, like clear fountains, do not seem so deep as they are: the turbid look the most profound.—*Landor.*

O thou who art able to write a book, which once in the two centuries or oftener there is a man gifted to do, envy not him whom they name city-builder, and inexpressibly pity him whom they name conqueror or city-burner.—
Carlyle.

So idle are dull readers, and so industrious are dull authors, that puffed nonsense bids fair to blow unpuffed sense wholly out of the field.—
Colton.

The triumphs of the warrior are bounded by the narrow theatre of his own age; but those of a Scott or a Shakespeare will be renewed with greater and greater lustre in ages yet unborn, when the victorious chieftain shall be forgotten, or shall live only in the song of the minstrel and the page of the chronicler.—*Prescott.*

The little mind who loves itself, will write and think with the vulgar; but the great mind will be bravely eccentric, and scorn the beaten road, from universal benevolence.—*Goldsmith.*

There is nothing more dreadful to an author than neglect; compared with which, reproach, hatred, and opposition are names of happiness; yet this worst, this meanest fate, every one who dares to write has reason to fear.—*Johnson.*

Every fool describes in these bright days his wondrous journey to some foreign court, and spawns his quarto, and demands your praise.—*Byron.*

From the moment one sets up for an author, one must be treated as ceremoniously, that is as unfaithfully, " as a king's favorite or a king."—*Pope.*

I have observed that vulgar readers almost always lose their veneration for the writings of the genius with whom they have had personal intercourse.—*Sir Egerton Brydges.*

There is a natural disposition with us to judge an author's personal character by the character of his works. We find it difficult to understand the common antithesis of a good writer and a bad man.—*Whipple.*

Satire lies respecting literary men during their life, and eulogy does so after their death.—*Voltaire.*

Authorship is, according to the spirit in which it is pursued, an infamy, a pastime, a day-labor, a handicraft, an art, a science, a virtue.—*Schlegel.*

Peace be with the soul of that charitable and courteous author, who, for the common benefit of his fellow-authors, introduced the ingenious way of miscellaneous writing!—*Shaftesbury.*

The wickedness of a loose or profane author, in his writings, is more atrocious than that of the giddy libertine or drunken ravisher; not only because it extends its effects wider (as a pestilence that taints the air is more destructive than poison infused in a draught), but because it is committed with cool deliberation.—*Johnson.*

One writer excels at a plan or a title-page; another works away at the body of the book; and a third is a dab hand at an index.—*Goldsmith.*

Spero Speroni explains admirably how an author who writes very clearly for himself is often obscure to his readers. " It is," he says, " because the author proceeds from the thought to the expression, and the reader from the expression to the thought."—*Chamfort.*

This is the magnanimity of authorship, when a writer having a topic presented to him, fruitful of beauties for common minds, waives his privilege, and trusts to the judicious few for understanding the reason of his abstinence.—*Lamb.*

Would a writer know how to behave himself with relation to posterity? Let him consider in old books what he finds that he is glad to know, and what omissions he most laments.—*Swift.*

Be very careful how you tell an author he is droll. Ten to one he will hate you; and if he does, be sure he can do you a mischief, and very probably will. Say you cried over his romance or his verses, and he will love you and send you a copy. You can laugh over that as much as you like, — in private.—*Holmes.*

To expect an author to talk as he writes is ridiculous; or even if he did you would find fault with him as a pedant.—*Hazlitt.*

For popular purposes, at least, the aim of literary artists should be similar to that of Rubens in his landscapes, of which, without neglecting the minor traits or finishing, he was chiefly solicitous to present the leading effect, or what we may call the inspiration.—*W. B. Clulow.*

No fathers or mothers think their own children ugly; and this self-deceit is yet stronger with respect to the offspring of the mind.—*Cervantes.*

Every author, indeed, who really influences the mind, who plants in it thoughts and sentiments which take root and grow, communicates his character. Error and immorality, — two words for one thing, for error is the immorality of the intellect, and immorality the error of the heart, — these escape from him if they are in him, and pass into the recipient mind through subtle avenues invisible to consciousness.—*Whipple.*

The most original modern authors are not so because they advance what is new, but simply because they know how to put what they have to say as if it had never been said before.—*Goethe.*

A man of letters is often a man with two natures, — one a book nature, the other a human nature. These often clash sadly.—*Whipple.*

AUTUMN.

A moral character is attached to autumnal scenes; the leaves falling like our years, the flowers fading like our hours, the clouds fleeting like our illusions, the light diminishing like our intelligence, the sun growing colder like our affections, the rivers becoming frozen like our lives, — all bear secret relations to our destinies.—*Chateaubriand.*

All-cheering Plenty, with her flowing horn, led yellow Autumn, wreathed with nodding corn.—*Burns.*

As fall the light autumnal leaves, one still the other following, till the bough strews all its honors.—*Dante.*

Autumn nodding o'er the yellow plain.—
Thomson.

Who is there who, at this season, does not feel his mind impressed with a sentiment of melancholy? or who is able to resist that current of thought, which, from such appearances of decay, so naturally leads him to the solemn imagination of that inevitable fate which is to bring on alike the decay of life, of empire, and of nature itself?—*Sir A. Alison.*

Wild is the music of autumnal winds amongst the faded woods.—*Wordsworth.*

The year growing ancient, not yet on summer's death, nor on the birth of trembling winter.—*Shakespeare.*

However constant the visitations of sickness and bereavement, the fall of the year is most thickly strewn with the fall of human life. Everywhere the spirit of some sad power seems to direct the time: it hides from us the blue heavens, it makes the green wave turbid; it walks through the fields, and lays the damp ungathered harvest low; it cries out in the night wind and the shrill hail; it steals the summer bloom from the infant cheek; it makes old age shiver to the heart; it goes to the churchyard, and chooses many a grave.—
James Martineau.

The melancholy days are come, the saddest of the year.—*Bryant.*

The teeming autumn, big with rich increase, bearing the wanton burden of the prime.—
Shakespeare.

AVARICE.

The lust of avarice has so totally seized upon mankind that their wealth seems rather to possess them than they possess their wealth.—
Pliny.

We are at best but stewards of what we falsely call our own; yet avarice is so insatiable that it is not in the power of liberality to content it.—*Seneca.*

This avarice sticks deeper; grows with more pernicious root than summer-seeding lust.—
Shakespeare.

Objects close to the eye shut out much larger objects on the horizon; and splendors born only of the earth eclipse the stars. So a man sometimes covers up the entire disc of eternity with a dollar, and quenches transcendent glories with a little shining dust.—*Chapin.*

It is surely very narrow policy that supposes money to be the chief good.—*Johnson.*

Had covetous men, as the fable goes of Briareus, each of them one hundred hands, they would all of them be employed in grasping and gathering, and hardly one of them in giving or laying out, but all in receiving, and none in restoring; a thing in itself so monstrous, that nothing in nature besides is like it, except it be death and the grave,—the only things I know which are always carrying off the spoils of the world, and never making restitution. For otherwise all the parts of the universe, as they borrow of one another, so they still pay what they borrow, and that by so just and well-balanced an equality that their payments always keep pace with their receipts.—
Dryden.

Avarice is more opposite to economy than liberality.—*Rochefoucauld.*

Many have been ruined by their fortunes; many have escaped ruin by the want of fortune. To obtain it, the great have become little, and the little great.—*Zimmermann.*

How quickly nature falls into revolt when gold becomes her object!—*Shakespeare.*

There are two considerations which always imbitter the heart of an avaricious man,—the one is a perpetual thirst after more riches, the other the prospect of leaving what he has already acquired.—*Fielding.*

A captive fettered at the oar of gain.—
Falconer.

He who is always in a hurry to be wealthy and immersed in the study of augmenting his fortune, has lost the arms of reason and deserted the post of virtue.—*Horace.*

Avarice increases with the increasing pile of gold.—*Juvenal.*

Some men are called sagacious, merely on account of their avarice; whereas a child can clench its fist the moment it is born.—*Shenstone.*

Poverty is in want of much, but avarice of everything.—*Publius Syrus.*

Parsimony is enough to make the master of the golden mines as poor as he that has nothing; for a man may be brought to a morsel of bread by parsimony as well as profusion —
Henry Home.

Avarice is the miser's dream, as fame is the poet's.—*Hazlitt.*

Because men believe not Providence, therefore they do so greedily scrape and hoard. They do not believe any reward for charity, therefore they will part with nothing.—*Barrow.*

It may be remarked, for the comfort of honest poverty, that avarice reigns most in those who have but few good qualities to recommend them. This is a weed that will grow only in a barren soil.—*Hughes.*

Study rather to fill your mind than your coffers; knowing that gold and silver were originally mingled with dirt, until avarice or ambition parted them.—*Seneca.*

For the love of money is the root of all evil.
Bible.

When a miser contents himself with giving nothing, and saving what he has got, and is in other respects guilty of no injustice, he is, perhaps, of all bad men the least injurious to society; the evil he does is properly nothing more than the omission of the good he might do. If, of all the vices, avarice is the most generally detested, it is the effect of an avidity common to all men; it is because men hate those from whom they can expect nothing. The greedy misers rail at sordid misers.—
Helvetius.

To be thankful for what we grasp exceeding our proportion, is to add hypocrisy to injustice.
Lamb.

The objects of avarice and ambition differ only in their greatness. A miser is as furious about a halfpenny, as the man of ambition about the conquest of a kingdom.—*Adam Smith.*

O cursed hunger of pernicious gold!—*Dryden.*

Avarice, in old age, is foolish; for what can be more absurd than to increase our provisions for the road, the nearer we approach to our journey's end ?—*Cicero.*

Avarice is the most opposite of all characters to that of God Almighty, whose alone it is to give and not receive.—*Shenstone.*

The avarice of the miser may be termed the grand sepulchre of all his other passions, as they successively decay. But unlike other tombs, it is enlarged by repletion and strengthened by age.—*Colton.*

The avaricious man is like the barren, sandy ground of the desert, which sucks in all the rain and dews with greediness, but yields no fruitful herbs or plants for the benefit of others.—*Zeno.*

O cursed lust of gold! when for thy sake the fool throws up his interest in both worlds, — first starved in this, then damned in that to come.—*Blair.*

The character of covetousness is what a man generally acquires more through some niggardliness or ill grace in little and inconsiderable things, than in expenses of any consequence.—*Pope.*

A poor spirit is poorer than a poor purse. A very few pounds a year would case a man of the scandal of avarice.—*Swift.*

Extreme avarice almost always makes mistakes. There is no passion that oftener misses its aim; nor on which the present has so much influence, in prejudice of the future.—
Rochefoucauld.

To me avarice seems not so much a vice as a deplorable piece of madness.—
Sir Thomas Browne.

Avarice has ruined more men than prodigality, and the blindest thoughtlessness of expenditure has not destroyed so many fortunes as the calculating but insatiable lust of accumulation.—*Colton.*

Avarice is insatiable and is always pushing on for more.—*L'Estrange.*

Avarice begets more vices than Priam did children, and like Priam survives them all. It starves its keeper to surfeit those who wish him dead, and makes him submit to more mortifications to lose heaven than the martyr undergoes to gain it.—*Colton.*

In plain truth, it is not want, but rather abundance, that creates avarice.—*Montaigne.*

Avarice often produces opposite effects; there is an infinite number of people who sacrifice all their property to doubtful and distant expectations; others despise great future advantages to obtain present interests of a trifling nature.—
Rochefoucauld.

It is one of the worst effects of prosperity to make a man a vortex instead of a fountain; so that, instead of throwing out, he learns only to draw in.—*Beecher.*

Poverty wants some, luxury many, and avarice all things.—*Cowley.*

Avarice is a uniform and tractable vice; other intellectual distempers are different in different constitutions of mind. That which soothes the pride of one will offend the pride of another; but to the favor of the covetous bring money, and nothing is denied.—*Johnson.*

Avarice is to the intellect what sensuality is to the morals.—*Mrs. Jameson.*

All the good things of this world are no further good to us than as they are of use; and whatever we may heap up to give to others, we enjoy only as much as we can use, and no more.
De Foe.

AWKWARDNESS.

Awkwardness is a more real disadvantage than it is generally thought to be; it often occasions ridicule, it always lessens dignity.—
Chesterfield.

B.

BABE.

It is well for us that we are born babies in intellect. Could we understand half what mothers say and do to their infants, we should be filled with a conceit of our own importance, which would render us insupportable through life. Happy the boy whose mother is tired of talking nonsense to him before he is old enough to know the sense of it.—*Hare.*

A babe is a mother's anchor.—*Beecher.*

A babe in a house is a well-spring of pleasure, a messenger of peace and love, a resting-place for innocence on earth, a link between angels and men.—*Tupper.*

The coarsest father gains a new impulse to labor from the moment of his baby's birth; he scarcely sees it when awake, and yet it is with him all the time. Every stroke he strikes is for his child. New social aims, new moral motives, come vaguely up to him.—*T. W. Higginson.*

A sweet new blossom of humanity, fresh fallen from God's own home to flower on earth.— *Gerald Massey.*

Welcome to the parents the puny struggler, strong in his weakness, his little arms more irresistible than the soldier's, his lips touched with persuasion which Chatham and Pericles in manhood had not. His unaffected lamentations when he lifts up his voice on high, or, more beautiful, the sobbing child, — the face all liquid grief, as he tries to swallow his vexation, — soften all hearts to pity and to mirthful and clamorous compassion.—*Emerson.*

Fragile beginnings of a mighty end.— *Mrs. Norton.*

Those who have lost an infant are never, as it were, without an infant child. Their other children grow up to manhood and womanhood, and suffer all the changes of mortality; but this one alone is rendered an immortal child; for death has arrested it with his kindly harshness, and blessed it into an eternal image of youth and innocence.—*Leigh Hunt.*

Good Christian people, here lies for you an inestimable loan; — take all heed thereof, in all carefulness employ it; — with high recompense, or else with heavy penalty will it one day be required back.—*Carlyle.*

Of all the joys that brighten suffering earth, what joy is welcomed like a new-born child ?— *Mrs. Norton.*

BACHELOR.

I have no wife or children, good or bad, to provide for : a mere spectator of other men's fortunes and adventures, and how they play their parts; which, methinks, are diversely presented unto me, as from a common theatre or scene.—*Burton.*

A man unattached and without wife, if he have any genius at all, may raise himself above his original position, may mingle with the world of fashion, and hold himself on a level with the highest; this is less easy for him who is engaged; it seems as if marriage put the whole world in their proper rank.—*Bruyère.*

BALLADS.

Vocal portraits of the national mind. *Lamb.*

A well-composed song strikes the mind and softens the feelings, and produces a greater effect than a moral work, which convinces our reason, but does not warm our feelings, nor effect the slightest alteration in our habits.— *Napoleon.*

Give me the writing of the ballads, and you make the laws.—*Fletcher of Saltoun.*

Ballads are the gypsy children of song, born under green hedgerows, in the leafy lanes and by-paths of literature, in the genial summer-time.—*Longfellow.*

BARGAIN.

I will give thrice so much land to any well-deserving friend; but in the way of bargain, mark me, I will cavil on the ninth part of a hair.—*Shakespeare.*

BASENESS.

Every base occupation makes one sharp in its practice, and dull in every other.— *Sir P. Sidney.*

There is a law of neutralization of forces, which hinders bodies from sinking beyond a certain depth in the sea; but in the ocean of baseness, the deeper we get, the easier the sinking.—*Lowell.*

Some kinds of baseness are nobly undergone. *Shakespeare.*

BASHFULNESS.

Conceit not so high a notion of any as to be bashful and impotent in their presence.— *Fuller.*

As those that pull down private houses adjoining to the temples of the gods prop up such parts as are contiguous to them, so, in undermining bashfulness, due regard is to be had to adjacent modesty, good-nature, and humanity. *Plutarch.*

The bashful virgin's sidelong look of love.— *Goldsmith.*

Bashfulness is more frequently connected with good sense than we find assurance; and impudence, on the other hand, is often the mere effect of downright stupidity.—*Shenstone.*

There are two distinct sorts of what we call bashfulness : this, the awkwardness of a booby, which a few steps in the world will convert into the pertness of a coxcomb ; that, a consciousness which the most delicate feelings produce, and the most extensive knowledge cannot always remove.—*Mackenzie.*

Bashfulness is an ornament to youth, but a reproach to old age.—*Aristotle.*

Nor do we accept as genuine the person not characterized by this blushing bashfulness, this youthfulness of heart, this sensibility to the sentiment of suavity and self-respect. Modesty is bred of self-reverence. Fine manners are the mantle of fair minds. None are truly great without this ornament.—*Alcott.*

Mere bashfulness without merit is awkwardness.— *Addison.*

We must prune it with care, so as only to remove the redundant branches, and not injure the stem, which has its root in the generous sensitiveness to shame.—*Plutarch.*

BATTLE.

The next dreadful thing to a battle lost is a battle won.—*Duke of Wellington.*

The cannons have their bowels full of wrath ; and ready mounted are they to spit forth their iron indignation against your walls.—
Shakespeare.

As well the soldier dieth who standeth still, as he that gives the bravest onset.—
Sir P. Sidney.

The fame of a battle-field grows with its years ; Napoleon storming the Bridge of Lodi, and Wellington surveying the towers of Salamanca, affect us with fainter emotions than Brutus reading in his tent at Philippi, or Richard bearing down with the English chivalry upon the white armies of Saladin.— *Willmott.*

Troops of heroes undistinguished die.—
Addison.

It was a goodly sight to see the embattled pomp, as with the step of stateliness the barbed steeds came on, to see the pennons rolling their long waves before the gale, and banners, broad and bright, tossing their blazonry.—*Southey.*

When Greeks joined Greeks, then was the tug of war. The labored battle sweat and conquest bled.—*D. K. Lee.*

BEARD.

He that hath a beard is more than a youth ; and he that hath none is less than a man.—
Shakespeare.

Such a beard as youth gone out had left in ashes.—*Tennyson.*

A beard like an artichoke, with dry shrivelled jaws.—*Sheridan.*

It has no bush below ; marry a little wool, as much as an unripe peach doth wear ; just enough to speak him drawing towards a man.—
Suckling.

Beard was never the true standard of brains.
Fuller.

Ambiguous things that ape goats in their visage, women in their shape.—*Byron.*

BEAU.

A beau is everything of a woman but the sex, and nothing of a man beside it.—*Fielding.*

BEAUTY.

Like other beautiful things in this world, its end (that of a shaft) is to be beautiful ; and, in proportion to its beauty, it receives permission to be otherwise useless. We do not blame emeralds and rubies because we cannot make them into heads of hammers.—*Ruskin.*

How goodness heightens beauty !—
Hannah More.

There is scarcely a single joy or sorrow within the experience of our fellow-creatures which we have not tasted ; yet the belief in the good and beautiful has never forsaken us. It has been medicine to us in sickness, richness in poverty, and the best part of all that ever delighted us in health and success.—*Leigh Hunt.*

Beauty is worse than wine, it intoxicates both the holder and the beholder.—*Zimmermann.*

Beauty is a fairy ; sometimes she hides herself in a flower-cup, or under a leaf, or creeps into the old ivy, and plays hide-and-seek with the sunbeams, or haunts some ruined spot, or laughs out of a bright young face.—*G. A. Sala.*

Beauty is like an almanac ; if it last a year it is well.—*Rev. T. Adams.*

Gaze not on beauty too much, lest it blast thee ; nor too long, lest it blind thee ; nor too near, lest it burn thee. If thou like it, it deceives thee ; if thou love it, it disturbs thee ; if thou hunt after it, it destroys thee. If virtue accompany it, it is the heart's paradise ; if vice associate it, it is the soul's purgatory. It is the wise man's bonfire, and the fool's furnace.—
Quarles.

In days of yore nothing was holy but the beautiful.—*Schiller.*

Sometimes there are living beings in nature as beautiful as in romance. Reality surpasses imagination ; and we see breathing, brightening, and moving before our eyes sights dearer to our hearts than any we ever beheld in the land of sleep.—*Jane Austen.*

The rose is fair, but fairer we it deem for that sweet odor which doth in it live.—
Shakespeare.

Beauty in a modest woman is like fire at a distance, or like a sharp sword; neither doth the one burn, nor the other wound those that come not too near them.—*Cervantes.*

That is the best part of beauty which a picture cannot express.—*Bacon.*

Beauty has so many charms, one knows not how to speak against it; and when it happens that a graceful figure is the habitation of a virtuous soul, when the beauty of the face speaks out the modesty and humility of the mind, and the justness of the proportion raises our thoughts up to the heart and wisdom of the great Creator, something may be allowed it, — and something to the embellishments which set it off; and yet, when the whole apology is read, it will be found at last that beauty, like truth, never is so glorious as when it goes the plainest.—*Sterne.*

The fringe of the garment of the Lord.—
·*Bailey.*

There is no more potent antidote to low sensuality than the adoration of beauty. All the higher arts of design are essentially chaste, without respect of the object. They purify the thoughts, as tragedy, according to Aristotle, purifies the passions.—*Schlegel.*

The very beautiful rarely love at all. Those precious images are placed above the reach of the passions.—*Landor.*

Beauty is as summer fruits, which are easy to corrupt and cannot last; and for the most part it makes a dissolute youth, and an age a little out of countenance; but if it light well, it makes virtues shine and vice blush.—*Bacon.*

In the forming of female friendships beauty seldom recommends one woman to another.—
Fielding.

Every good picture is the best of sermons and lectures. The sense informs the soul. Whatever you have, have beauty.—
Sydney Smith.

The beauty seen is partly in him who sees it.
Bovee.

O, it is the saddest of all things that even one human soul should dimly perceive · the beauty that is ever around us, "a perpetual benediction!" Nature, that great missionary of the Most High, preaches to us forever in all tones of love, and writes truth in all colors, on manuscripts illuminated with stars and flowers.
Mrs. L. M. Child.

Beauty can afford to laugh at distinctions; it is itself the greatest distinction.—*Bovee.*

Beauty is no local deity, like the Greek and Roman gods, but omnipresent.—*Bartol.*

In the true mythology, Love is an immortal child, and Beauty leads him as a guide; nor can we express a deeper sense than when we say, Beauty is the pilot of the young soul.—
Emerson.

Lovely sweetness is the noblest power of woman, and is far fitter to prevail by parley than by battle.—*Sir P. Sidney.*

A flower that dies when first it begins to bud.
Shakespeare.

No man receives the true culture of a man in whom the sensibility to the beautiful is not cherished; and I know of no condition in life from which it should be excluded. Of all luxuries this is cheapest and the most at hand; and it seems to me to be the most important to those conditions where coarse labor tends to give a grossness to the mind.—*Channing.*

Might but the sense of moral evil be as strong in me as is my delight in external beauty!
` *Dr. Arnold.*

To cultivate the sense of the beautiful is but one, and the most effectual, of the ways of cultivating an appreciation of the Divine goodness.
Bovee.

Beauty is the purgation of superfluities.—
Michael Angelo.

As amber attracts a straw, so does beauty admiration, which only lasts while the warmth continues; but virtue, wisdom, goodness, and real worth, like the loadstone, never lose their power. These are the true graces, which, as Homer feigns, are linked and tied hand in hand, because it is by their influence that human hearts are so firmly united to each other.—
Burton.

Beauty can give an edge to the bluntest sword.—*Sir P. Sidney.*

The beautiful is a manifestation of secret laws of nature, which, but for this appearance, had been forever concealed from us.—*Goethe.*

Beauty is an all-pervading presence. It unfolds to the numberless flowers of the spring; it waves in the branches of the trees and the green blades of grass; it haunts the depths of the earth and the sea, and gleams out in the hues of the shell and the precious stone. And not only these minute objects, but the ocean, mountains, the clouds, the heavens, the stars, the rising and setting sun, all overflow with beauty.—*Channing.*

A beautiful woman is the hell of the soul, the purgatory of the purse, and the paradise of the eyes.—*Fontenelle.*

In life, as in art, the beautiful moves in curves.—*Bulwer Lytton.*

Beauty, like truth and justice, lives within us ; like virtue, and like moral law, it is a companion of the soul.—*Bancroft.*

Even virtue is more fair when it appears in a beautiful person.—*Virgil.*

The useful encourages itself; for the multitude produce it, and no one can dispense with it: the beautiful must be encouraged; for few can set it forth, and many need it.—*Goethe.*

There is nothing that makes its way more directly to the soul than beauty.—*Addison.*

The most natural beauty in the world is honesty and moral truth. For all beauty is truth. True features make the beauty of a face, and true proportions the beauty of architecture ; as true measures that of harmony and music.—*Shaftesbury.*

Beauty, — the fading rainbow's pride.—
Halleck.

Beauty is a witch, against whose charms faith melteth into blood.—*Shakespeare.*

The perception of the beautiful is gradual, and not a lightning revelation ; it requires not only time, but some study.—*Ruffini.*

The good is always beautiful, the beautiful is good!—*Whittier.*

It was a very proper answer to him who asked why any man should be delighted with beauty, that it was a question that none but a blind man could ask ; since any beautiful object doth so much attract the sight of all men, that it is in no man's power not to be pleased with it.
Clarendon.

Rare is the union of beauty and virtue.—
Juvenal.

That which is striking and beautiful is not always good, but that which is good is always beautiful.—*Ninon de l'Enclos.*

Beauty itself is but the sensible image of the Infinite.—*Bancroft.*

As Congreve says, there is in true beauty something which vulgar souls cannot admire ; so can no dirt or rags hide this something from those souls which are not of the vulgar stamp.—
Fielding.

Beauty too rich for use, for earth too dear.—
Shakespeare.

What place is so rugged and so homely that there is no beauty, if you only have a sensibility to beauty ?—*Beecher.*

Beauty is truth, truth beauty, — that is all ye know on earth, and all ye need to know.—*Keats.*

To make the cunning artless, tame the rude, subdue the haughty, shake the undaunted soul ; yea, put a bridle in the lion's mouth, and lead him forth as a domestic cur, these are the triumphs of all-powerful beauty.—*Joanna Baillie.*

The essence of the beautiful is unity in variety—*Mendelssohn.*

Beautiful as sweet ! and young as beautiful ! and soft as young ! and gay as soft ! and innocent as gay !—*Young.*

Beauty draws us with a single hair.—*Pope.*

Beauty is the true prerogative of women, and so peculiarly their own, that our sex, though naturally requiring another sort of feature, is never in its lustre but when puerile and heardless, confused and mixed with theirs.—
Montaigne.

Heat cannot be separated from fire, or beauty from the eternal.—*Dante.*

If the nose of Cleopatra had been a little shorter, it would have changed the history of the world.—*Pascal.*

Thus was beauty sent from Heaven, the lovely ministress of truth and good in this dark world.—*Akenside.*

The common foible of women who have been handsome is to forget that they are no longer so.—*Rochefoucauld.*

For beauty is the bait which with delight doth man allure, for to enlarge his kind.—
Spenser.

Beauty is the mark God sets on virtue. Every natural action is graceful. Every heroic act is also decent, and causes the place and the bystanders to shine.—*Emerson.*

To give pain is the tyranny, — to make happy, the true empire of beauty.—*Steele.*

How much wit, good-nature, indulgences, how many good offices and civilities, are required among friends to accomplish in some years what a lovely face or a fine hand does in a minute !—*Bruyère.*

Whatever beauty may be, it has for its basis order, and for its essence unity.—*Father André.*

Unity and simplicity are the two true sources of beauty. Supreme beauty resides in God.—
Winckelmann.

Beauty attracts us men, but if, like an armed magnet, it is pointed with gold or silver beside, it attracts with tenfold power.—*Richter.*

Affect not to despise beauty, no one is freed from its dominion ; but regard it not a pearl of price, it is fleeting as the bow in the clouds.—
Tupper.

Could beauty have better commerce than with honesty ?—*Shakespeare.*

Methinks a being that is beautiful becometh more so as it looks on beauty, the eternal beauty of undying things.—*Byron.*

All orators are dumb when beauty pleadeth.
Shakespeare.

Beauty is only truly irresistible when it shows us something less transitory than itself, when it makes us dream of that which charms life beyond the fugitive moment which seduces us ; it is necessary for the soul to feel it when the senses have perceived it. The soul never wearies ; the more it admires, the more it is exalted.—*Madame de Krudener.*

Trust not too much to an enchanting face.—
Virgil.

Every trait of beauty may be referred to some virtue, as to innocence, candor, generosity, modesty, and heroism.—*St. Pierre.*

Beauty is bought by judgment of the eye, not uttered by base sale of chapmen's tongues.
Shakespeare.

An Indian philosopher, being asked what were, according to his opinion, the two most beautiful things in the universe, answered : The starry heavens above our heads, and the feeling of duty in our hearts.—*Bossuet.*

Beauty's tears are lovelier than her smiles.—
Campbell.

Where the mouth is sweet and the eyes intelligent, there is always the look of beauty, with a right heart.—*Leigh Hunt.*

The soul, by an instinct stronger than reason, ever associates beauty with truth.—
Tuckerman.

The divine right of beauty is the only divine right a man can acknowledge, and a pretty woman the only tyrant he is not authorized to resist.—*Junius.*

Beauty ! thou pretty plaything ! dear deceit !
Blair.

The sense of beauty is intuitive, and beauty itself is all that inspires pleasure without, and aloof from, and even contrarily to interest.— .
Coleridge.

If thou marry beauty, thou bindest thyself all thy life for that which, perchance, will neither last nor please thee one year.—*Raleigh.*

Loveliness needs not the foreign aid of ornament; but is, when unadorned, adorned the most.—*Thomson.*

Beauty lives with kindness.—*Shakespeare.*

Beauty is a great gift of Heaven; not for the purpose of female vanity, but a great gift for one who loves, and wishes to be beloved.—
Miss Edgeworth.

Beauty is such a fleeting blossom, how can wisdom rely upon its momentary delight ?—
Seneca.

The first distinction among men, and the first consideration that gave one precedence over another, was doubtless the advantage of beauty.
Montaigne.

Exquisite beauty resides with God. Unity and simplicity, joined together in different organs, are the principal sources of beauty. It resides in the good, the honest, and in the useful to the highest physical and intellectual degree.—*Vinkelman.*

Love that has nothing but beauty to keep it in good health is short-lived, and apt to have ague fits.—*Erasmus.*

Beauty is a short-lived tyranny.—*Socrates.*

No woman can be handsome by the force of features alone, any more than she can be witty only by the help of speech.—*Hughes.*

Beauty provoketh thieves sooner than gold.
Shakespeare.

Beauty of form affects the mind, but then it must be understood that it is not the mere shell that we admire; we are attracted by the idea that this shell is only a beautiful case adjusted to the shape and value of a still more beautiful pearl within. The perfection of outward loveliness is the soul shining through its crystalline covering.—*Jane Porter.*

We call comeliness a mischance in the first respect, which belongs principally to the face.—
Montaigne.

A thing of beauty is a joy forever.—*Keats.*

A beautiful form is better than a beautiful face; it gives a higher pleasure than statues or pictures ; it is the finest of the fine arts.—
Emerson.

There is no excellent beauty without some strangeness in the proportion.—*Bacon.*

The criterion of true beauty is that it increases on examination ; if false, that it lessens. There is something, therefore, in true beauty that corresponds with right reason, and is not merely the creation of fancy.—*Lord Greville.*

Is beauty vain because it will fade ? Then are earth's green robe and heaven's light vain.
— *Pierpont.*

Few have borne unconsciously the spell of loveliness.— *Whittier.*

Every year of my life I grow more convinced that it is the wisest and best to fix our attention on the beautiful and the good, and dwell as little as possible on the evil and the false.— *Cecil.*

Oesser taught me that the ideal of beauty is simplicity and tranquillity.— *Goethe.*

Beauty is a transitory flower ; even while it lasts it palls on the roving sense when held too near, or dwelling there too long.— *Jeffrey.*

How intoxicating is the triumph of beauty, and how right it is to name it queen of the universe ! How many courtiers, how many slaves, have submitted to it ! But, alas ! why must it be that what flatters our senses almost always deceives our souls ?— *Madame de Surin.*

It is seldom the case that beautiful persons are otherwise of great virtue.— *Bacon.*

That is true beauty which has not only a substance, but a spirit ; a beauty that we must intimately know, justly to appreciate.— *Colton.*

The contemplation of beauty in nature, in art, in literature, in human character, diffuses through our being a soothing and subtle joy, by which the heart's anxious and aching cares are softly smiled away.— *Whipple.*

O human beauty, what a dream art thou, that we should cast our life and hopes away on thee !— *Barry Cornwall.*

Beauty is a dangerous property, tending to corrupt the mind of the wife, though it soon loses its influence over the husband. A figure agreeable and engaging, which inspires affection, without the ebriety of love, is a much safer choice.— *Henry Home.*

Beauty is a frail good.— *Ovid.*

By cultivating the beautiful, we scatter the seeds of heavenly flowers ; by doing good, we foster those already belonging to humanity.— *Howard.*

In all things that live there are certain irregularities and deficiencies which are not only signs of life, but sources of beauty. No human face is exactly the same in its lines on each side, no leaf perfect in its lobes, no branch in its symmetry.— *Ruskin.*

Something of the severe hath always been appertaining to order and to grace ; and the beauty that is not too liberal is sought the most ardently, and loved the longest.— *Landor.*

Naught under heaven so strongly doth allure the sense of man, and all his mind possess, as beauty's love-bait.— *Spenser.*

It is the eternal law, that first in beauty should be first in might.— *Keats.*

The human heart yearns for the beautiful in all ranks of life. The beautiful things that God makes are his gift to all alike. I know there are many of the poor who have fine feeling and a keen sense of the beautiful, which rusts out and dies because they are too hard pressed to procure it any gratification.— *Mrs. Stowe*

Around that neck what dross are gold and pearl !— *Young.*

He who cannot see the beautiful side is a bad painter, a bad friend, a bad lover ; he cannot lift his mind and his heart so high as goodness.— *Joubert.*

Beauty soon grows familiar to the lover, fades in his eye, and palls upon the sense.—
Addison.

Nothing is arbitrary, nothing is insulated in beauty. It depends forever on the necessary and the useful. The plumage of the bird, the mimic plumage of the insect, has a reason for its rich colors in the constitution of the animal. Fitness is so inseparable an accompaniment of beauty, that it has been taken for it.
Emerson.

The dower of great beauty has always been misfortune, since happiness and beauty do not agree together.— *Calderon.*

Beauty is an exquisite flower, and its perfume is virtue.— *Ruffini.*

An agreeable figure and winning manner, which inspire affection without love, are always new. Beauty loses its relish, the graces never ; after the longest acquaintance, they are no less agreeable than at first.— *Henry Home.*

Liking is not always the child of beauty ; but whatsoever is liked, to the liker is beautiful.
Sir P. Sidney.

There should be, methinks, as little merit in loving a woman for her beauty as in loving a man for his prosperity ; both being equally subject to change.— *Pope.*

O, how much more doth beauty beauteous seem, by that sweet ornament which truth doth give !— *Shakespeare.*

We cannot approach beauty. Its nature is like opaline dove's-neck lustres, hovering and evanescent. Herein it resembles the most excellent things, which all have this rainbow character, defying all attempts at appropriation and use.— *Emerson.*

4

It is only through the morning gate of the beautiful that you can penetrate into the realm of knowledge. That which we feel here as beauty, we shall one day know as truth.— *Schiller.*

Whatever is beautiful is also profitable.— *Willmott.*

There is a certain period of the soul-culture when it begins to interfere with some of the characters of typical beauty belonging to the bodily frame, the stirring of the intellect wearing down the flesh, and the moral enthusiasm burning its way out to heaven, through the emaciation of the earthen vessel; and there is, in this indication of subduing the mortal by the immortal part, an ideal glory of perhaps a purer and higher range than that of the more perfect material form. We conceive, I think, more nobly of the weak presence of Paul than of the fair and ruddy countenance of David.— *Ruskin.*

Beauty is a possession not our own.—*Bion.*

The beautiful are never desolate, but some one always loves them.—*Bailey.*

Beauty hath no lustre save when it gleameth through the crystal web that purity's fine fingers weave for it.—*Maturin.*

BEES.

So work the honey-bees, — creatures that, by a rule in nature, teach the art of order to a peopled kingdom.—*Shakespeare.*

The little alms-men of spring bowers.— *Keats.*

Many-colored, sunshine-loving, spring-betokening bee! Yellow bee, so mad for love of early-blooming flowers!—*Professor Wilson.*

BEGGARS.

When beggars die there are no comets seen. *Shakespeare.*

In every civilized society there is found a race of men who retain the instincts of the aboriginal cannibal, and live upon their fellow-men as a natural food. These interesting but formidable bipeds, having caught their victim, invariably select one part of his body on which to fasten their relentless grinders. The part thus selected is peculiarly susceptible, providence having made it alive to the least nibble; it is situated just above the hip-joint; it is protected by a tegument of exquisite fibre, vulgarly called the breeches pocket.— *Bulwer Lytton.*

Sturdy beggars can bear stout denials.— *Colton.*

The true beggar is the only king above all comparison.—*Lessing.*

When paupers evince any consciousness of neglect, they are instantly spurned; if they complain this time of a scanty dole, the next they will have none. Though our donations are made to please ourselves, we insist upon those who receive our alms being pleased with them.—*Zimmermann.*

BEHAVIOR.

Levity of behavior is the bane of all that is good and virtuous.—*Seneca.*

Oddities and singularities of behavior may attend genius; when they do, they are its misfortunes and its blemishes. The man of true genius will be ashamed of them; at least he will never affect to distinguish himself by whimsical peculiarities.—*Sir W. Temple.*

I have known men disagreeably forward from their shyness.—*Arnold.*

What is becoming is honorable, and what is honorable is becoming.—*Tully.*

Any man shall speak the better when he knows what others have said, and sometimes the consciousness of his inward knowledge gives a confidence to his outward behavior, which of all other is the best thing to grace a man in his carriage.—*Feltham.*

Behavior is a mirror in which every one shows his image.—*Goethe.*

BELIEF.

Men willingly believe what they wish to be true.— *Cæsar.*

I am not afraid of those tender and scrupulous consciences, who are ever cautious of professing and believing too much; if they are sincerely in the wrong, I forgive their errors, and respect their integrity. The men I am afraid of are the men who believe everything, subscribe to everything, and vote for everything. *Bishop Shipley.*

The want of belief is a defect which ought to be concealed where it cannot be overcome.— *Swift.*

There are three means of believing, — by inspiration, by reason, and by custom. Christianity, which is the only rational institution, does yet admit none for its sons who do not believe by inspiration.—*Pascal.*

You do not believe, you only believe that you believe.—*Coleridge.*

When, in your last hour (think of this), all faculty in the broken spirit shall fade away, and sink into inanity, — imagination, thought, effort, enjoyment, — then will the flower of belief, which blossoms even in the night, remain to refresh you with its fragrance in the last darkness.—*Richter.*

It is a singular fact that most men of action incline to the theory of fatalism, while the greater part of men of thought believe in providence.—*Balzac.*

BENEDICTION.

The best wishes that can be forged in your thoughts be servants to you!—*Shakespeare.*

The benediction of these covering heavens fall on your heads like dew!—*Shakespeare.*

BENEVOLENCE.

To feel much for others and little for ourselves; to restrain our selfish, and to indulge our benevolent affections, constitute the perfection of human nature.—*Adam Smith.*

Doing good is the only certainly happy action of a man's life.—*Sir P. Sidney.*

He that does good to another does good also to himself, not only in the consequence, but in the very act; for the consciousness of well-doing is in itself ample reward.—*Seneca.*

When my friends are one-eyed, I look at their profile.—*Joubert.*

A life of passionate gratification is not to be compared with a life of active benevolence. God has so constituted our nature that a man cannot be happy unless he is, or thinks he is, a means of good. Judging from our own experience, we cannot conceive of a picture of more unutterable wretchedness than is furnished by one who knows that he is wholly useless in the world.—*Rev. Erskine Mason.*

Good deeds in this life are coals raked up in embers, to make a fire next day.—
Sir T. Overbury.

The disposition to give a cup of cold water to a disciple is a far nobler property than the finest intellect Satan has a fine intellect, but not the image of God.—*Howell.*

Better to expose ourselves to ingratitude than fail in assisting the unfortunate.—
Du Cœur.

Thy love shall chant itself its own beatitudes, after its own life working. A child-kiss, set on thy sighing lips, shall make thee glad; a poor man, served by thee, shall make thee rich; a rich man, helped by thee, shall make thee strong; thou shalt be served thyself by every sense of service which thou renderest.—
E. B. Browning.

Liberality consists less in giving profusely than in giving judiciously.—*Bruyère.*

When thou seest thine enemy in trouble, curl not thy whiskers in contempt; for in every bone there is marrow, and within every jacket there is a man.—*Saadi.*

There is nothing that requires so strict an economy as our benevolence. We should husband our means as the agriculturist his manure, which, if he spread over too large a superficies, produces no crop, — if over too small a surface, exuberates in rankness and in weeds.—*Colton.*

Men resemble the gods in nothing so much as in doing good to their fellow-creatures.—
Cicero.

It is another's fault if he be ungrateful, but it is mine if I do not give. To find one thankful man I will oblige a great many that are not so.—*Seneca.*

Benevolence and feeling ennoble the most trifling actions.—*Thackeray.*

Rich people who are covetous are like the cypress-tree, — they may appear well, but are fruitless; so rich persons have the means to be generous, yet some are not so, but they should consider they are only trustees for what they possess, and should show their wealth to be more in doing good than merely in having it.—
Bishop Hall.

Our hands we open of our own free will, and the good flies, which we can never recall.—
Goethe.

Nothing is so wholesome, nothing does so much for people's looks, as a little interchange of the small coin of benevolence.—*Ruffini.*

Never did any soul do good but it came readier to do the same again, with more enjoyment. Never was love or gratitude or bounty practised but with increasing joy, which made the practiser still more in love with the fair act.
Shaftesbury.

For his bounty, there was no winter in it; an autumn it was, that grew the more by reaping.—*Shakespeare.*

The opportunity of making happy is more scarce than we imagine; the punishment of missing it is, never to meet with it again; and the use we make of it leaves us an eternal sentiment of satisfaction or repentance.—*Rousseau.*

There is no use of money equal to that of beneficence; here the enjoyment grows on reflection.—*Mackenzie.*

There do remain dispersed in the soil of human nature divers seeds of goodness, of benignity, of ingenuity, which, being cherished, excited, and quickened by good culture, do, by common experience, thrust out flowers very lovely, and yield fruits very pleasant of virtue and goodness.—*Barrow.*

Doubtless that is the best charity which, Nilus-like, hath the several streams thereof seen, but the fountain concealed.—*Rev. T. Gouge.*

There cannot be a more glorious object in creation than a human being replete with benevolence, meditating in what manner he might render himself most acceptable to his Creator by doing most good to his creatures.—*Fielding.*

The office of liberality consisteth in giving with judgment.—*Cicero.*

No sincere desire of doing good need make an enemy of a single human being; that philanthropy has surely a flaw in it which cannot sympathize with the oppressor equally as with the oppressed.—*Lowell.*

The lower a man descends in his love, the higher he lifts his life.—*W. R. Alger.*

He is good that does good to others. If he suffers for the good he does, he is better still; and if he suffers from them to whom he did good, he is arrived to that height of goodness that nothing but an increase of his sufferings can add to it; if it proves his death, his virtue is at its summit, — it is heroism complete.—*Bruyère.*

We should do good whenever we can, and do kindness at all times, for at all times we can.—*Joubert.*

Time is short, your obligations are infinite. Are your houses regulated, your children instructed, the afflicted relieved, the poor visited, the work of piety accomplished ?—*Massillon.*

You are so to put forth the power that God has given you; you are so to give, and sacrifice to give, as to earn the eulogium pronounced on the woman, " She hath done what she could." Do it now. It is not a safe thing to leave a generous feeling to the cooling influences of a cold world. If you intend to do a mean thing, wait till to-morrow; if you are to do a noble thing, do it now, — now !—*Rev. Dr. Guthrie.*

Rare benevolence, the minister of God.— *Carlyle.*

There is scarcely a man who is not conscious of the benefits which his own mind has received from the performance of single acts of benevolence. How strange that so few of us try a course of the same medicine !—*J. F. Boyes.*

The greatest pleasure I know is to do a good action by stealth, and to have it found out by accident.—*Lamb.*

My God, grant that my bounty may be a clear and transparent river, flowing from pure charity, and uncontaminated by self-love, ambition, or interest. Thanks are due not to me, but thee, from whom all I possess is derived. And what are the paltry gifts for which my neighbor forgets to thank me, compared with the immense blessings for which I have so often forgotten to be grateful to thee !—*Gotthold.*

A beneficent person is like a fountain watering the earth, and spreading fertility ; it is, therefore, more delightful and more honorable to give than receive.—*Epicurus.*

Good, the more communicated, more abundant grows.—*Milton.*

The difference of the degrees in which the individuals of a great community enjoy the good things of life has been a theme of declaration and discontent in all ages ; and it is doubtless our paramount duty, in every state of society, to alleviate the pressure of the purely evil part of this distribution, as much as possible, and, by all the means we can devise, secure the lower links in the chain of society from dragging in dishonor and wretchedness.— *Herschel.*

Benevolence is allied to few vices; selfishness to fewer virtues.—*Henry Home.*

The true source of cheerfulness is benevolence. The pursuits of mankind are commonly frigid and contemptible, and the mistake comes, at last, to be detected. But virtue is a charm that never fades. The soul that perpetually overflows with kindness and sympathy will always be cheerful.—*Parke Godwin.*

BEREAVEMENT.

There is this pleasure in being bereaved, — the thought that time, which sadly overcometh all things, can alone restore the separated, and bring the mutually beloved together. Time, which plants the furrow and sows the seed of death, stands, to the faithful spirit, a messenger of light at that mysterious wicket-gate from whence we step and enter upon the vast unknown.—*W. G. Clark.*

BIBLE.

Intense study of the Bible will keep any man from being vulgar in point of style.— *Coleridge.*

I will answer for it, the longer you read the Bible, the more you will like it; it will grow sweeter and sweeter ; and the more you get into the spirit of it, the more you will get into the spirit of Christ.—*Romaine.*

I am of the opinion that the Bible contains more true sublimity, more exquisite beauty, more pure morality, more important history, and finer strains of poetry and eloquence, than can be collected from all other books, in whatever age or language they may have been written.— *Sir William Jones.*

As the moon, though darkened with spots, gives us a much greater light than the stars that seem all luminous, so do the Scriptures afford more light than the brightest human authors. In them the ignorant may learn all requisite knowledge, and the most knowing may learn to discern their ignorance.—*Boyle.*

Men cannot be well educated without the *B*ible. It ought, therefore, to hold the chief place in every situation of learning throughout Christendom ; and I do not know of a higher service that could be rendered to this republic than the bringing about this desirable result.—*Dr. Nott.*

There never was found, in any age of the world, either religion or law that did so highly exalt the public good as the *B*ible.—*Bacon.*

How admirable and beautiful is the simplicity of the Evangelists! They never speak injuriously of the enemies of Jesus Christ, of his judges, nor of his executioners. They report the facts without a single reflection. They comment neither on their Master's mildness when he was smitten, nor on his constancy in the hour of his ignominious death, which they thus describe : " And they crucified Jesus."—*Racine.*

The *B*ible is a window in this prison of hole through which we look into eternity.—*Dwight.*

The *B*ible goes equally to the cottage of the plain man and the palace of the king. It is woven into literature, and it colors the talk of the street. The bark of the merchant cannot sail to sea withou. it. No ship of war goes to the conflict but the *B*ible is there. It enters men's closets ; mingling in all grief and cheerfulness of life.—*Theodore Parker.*

A *B*ible and a newspaper in every house, a good school in every district, — all studied and appreciated as they merit, — are the principal support of virtue, morality, and civil liberty.—*Franklin.*

So far as I ever observed God's dealings with my soul, the flights of preachers sometimes entertained me, but it was Scripture expressions which did penetrate my heart, and in a way peculiar to themselves.—*J. Brown of Haddington.*

Scholars may quote *P*lato in studies, but the hearts of millions shall quote the *B*ible at their daily toil, and draw strength from its inspiration, as the meadows draw it from the brook.—*Conway.*

What is the *B*ible in your house? It is not the Old Testament, it is not the New Testament, it is not the Gospel according to Matthew or Mark or John ; it is the Gospel according to William, it is the Gospel according to Mary, it is the Gospel according to Henry and James, it is the Gospel according to your name. You write your own *B*ible.—*Beecher.*

It is a belief in the *B*ible, the fruits of deep meditation, which has served me as the guide of my moral and literary life. I have found it a capital safely invested, and richly productive of interest.—*Goethe.*

In morality there are books enough written both by ancient and modern philosophers, but the morality of the Gospel doth so exceed them all, that to give a man a full knowledge of true morality, I shall send him to no other book than the New Testament.—*Locke.*

The *B*ible is a precious storehouse, and the Magna Charta of a Christian. There he reads of his Heavenly Father's love, and of his dying Saviour's legacies. There he sees a map of his travels through the wilderness, and a landscape, too, of Canaan.—*Berridge.*

The *B*ible is the most betrashed book in the world. Coming to it through commentaries is much like looking at a landscape through garret windows, over which generations of numolested spiders have spun their webs.—*Beecher.*

I use the Scriptures, not as an arsenal to be resorted to only for arms and weapons, but as a matchless temple, where I delight to contemplate the beauty, the symmetry, and the magnificence of the structure, and to increase my awe and excite my devotion to the Deity there preached and adored.—*Boyle.*

The Scriptures teach us the best way of living, the noblest way of suffering, and the most comfortable way of dying.—*Flavel.*

Many will say " I can find God without the help of the *B*ible, or church, or minister." Very well. Do so if you can. The Ferry Company would feel no jealousy of a man who should prefer to swim to New York. Let him do so if he is able, and we will talk about it on the other shore ; but probably trying to swim would be the thing that would bring him quickest to the boat. So God would have no jealousy of a man's going to heaven without the aid of the *B*ible, or church, or minister ; but let him try to do so, and it will be the surest way to bring him back to them for assistance.—*Beecher.*

As the profoundest philosophy of ancient Rome and Greece lighted her taper at Israel's altar, so the sweetest strains of the pagan muse were swept from harps attuned on Zion's hill.—*Bishop Thomson.*

There are no songs comparable to the songs of Zion, no orations equal to those of the Prophets, and no politics like those which the Scriptures teach.—*Milton.*

A man may read the figure on the dial, but he cannot tell how the day goes unless the sun shines on the dial ; we may read the *B*ible over, but we cannot learn to purpose till the Spirit of God shine into our hearts.—*Rev. T. Watson.*

The *B*ible begins gloriously with *P*aradise, the symbol of youth, and ends with the everlasting kingdom, with the holy city. The history of every man should be a *B*ible.—*Novalis.*

The pure and noble, the graceful and dignified, simplicity of language is nowhere in such perfection as in the Scriptures and Homer. The whole book of Job, with regard both to sublimity of thought and morality, exceeds, beyond all comparison, the most noble parts of Homer.—*Pope.*

Every leaf is a spacious plain; every line a flowing brook; every period a lofty mountain.—*Hervey.*

BIGOTRY.

Bigotry murders religion, to frighten fools with her ghost.—*Cotton.*

Show me the man who would go to heaven alone if he could, and in that man I will show you one who will never be admitted into heaven.—*Feltham.*

A man who stole the livery of the court of heaven to serve the devil in.—*Pollok.*

There is no tariff so injurious as that with which sectarian bigotry guards its commodities. It dwarfs the soul by shutting out truths from other continents of thought, and checks the circulation of its own.—*Chapin.*

BIOGRAPHY.

Biography is the home aspect of history.—*Willmott.*

As it often happens that the best men are but little known, and consequently cannot extend the usefulness of their examples a great way, the biographer is of great utility, as, by communicating such valuable patterns to the world, he may perhaps do a more extensive service to mankind than the person whose life originally afforded the pattern.—*Fielding.*

A life that is worth writing at all is worth writing minutely.—*Longfellow.*

Biography, especially the biography of the great and good, who have risen by their own exertions from poverty and obscurity to eminence and usefulness, is an inspiring and ennobling study. Its direct tendency is to reproduce the excellence it records.—*Horace Mann.*

In reading the life of any great man you will always, in the course of his history, chance upon some obscure individual who, on some particular occasions, was greater than he whose life you are reading.—*Colton.*

There is properly no history, only biography.—*Emerson.*

My advice is, to consult the lives of other men as we would a looking-glass, and from thence fetch examples for our own imitation.—*Terence.*

One anecdote of a man is worth a volume of biography.—*Channing.*

Biography admonishes pride, when it displays Salmasius, the champion of kings, shivering under the eye and scourge of his wife; or bids us stand at the door of Milton's academy, and hear the scream and the ferule up stairs. It steals on the poet and the premier in their undress, — Cowley in dressing-gown and slippers, and Cecil with his treasurer's robe on the chair.—*Willmott.*

Biography is the most universally pleasant, universally profitable, of all reading.—*Carlyle.*

Of all studies, the most delightful and the most useful is biography. The seeds of great events lie near the surface; historians delve too deep for them. No history was ever true. Lives I have read which, if they were not, had the appearance, the interest, and the utility of truth.—*Landor.*

BIRTH.

What is birth to a man if it shall be a stain to his dead ancestors to have left such an offspring?—*Sir P. Sidney.*

Verily, I swear, it is better to be lowly born, and range with humble livers in content, than to be perked up in a glistering grief, and wear a golden sorrow.—*Shakespeare.*

Every anniversary of a birthday is the dispelling of a dream.—*Zschokke.*

A noble birth and fortune, though they make not a bad man good, yet they are a real advantage to a worthy one, and place his virtues in the fairest light.—*Lillo.*

Our birth is nothing but our death begun, as tapers waste that instant they take fire.—*Young.*

Custom forms us all; our thoughts, our morals, our most fixed belief, are consequences of our place of birth.—*Aaron Hill.*

High birth is a gift of fortune which should never challenge esteem towards those who receive it, since it costs them neither study nor labor.—*Bruyère.*

The birth of a child is the imprisonment of a soul.—*Simms.*

Called to the throne by the voice of the people, my maxim has always been, A career open to talent without distinction of birth. It is this system of equality for which the European oligarchy detests me.—*Napoleon.*

Birth is a shadow. Courage, self-sustained, outlords succession's phlegm, and needs no ancestors.—*Aaron Hill.*

I was born so high, our aerie buildeth in the cedar's top, and dallies with the wind, and scorns the sun.—*Shakespeare.*

BIRTHPLACE.

Whatever strengthens our local attachments is favorable both to individual and national character. Our home, our birthplace, our native land, — think for a while what the virtues are which arise out of the feelings connected with these words, and if you have any intellectual eyes, you will then perceive the connection between topography and patriotism.—*Southey.*

Those who wish to forget painful thoughts do well to absent themselves for a while from the ties and objects that recall them; but we can be said only to fulfil our destiny in the place that gave us birth.—*Hazlitt.*

BLESSEDNESS.

True blessedness consisteth in a good life and a happy death.—*Solon.*

Nothing raises the price of a blessing like its removal; whereas it was its continuance which should have taught us its value. There are three requisitions to the proper enjoyment of earthly blessings,— a thankful reflection on the goodness of the Giver, a deep sense of our unworthiness, a recollection of the uncertainty of long possessing them. The first would make us grateful; the second, humble; and the third, moderate.—*Hannah More.*

Blessedness is a whole eternity older than damnation.—*Richter.*

Blessings we enjoy daily; and for most of them, because they be so common, most men forget to pay their praises; but let not us, because it is a sacrifice so pleasing to Him that made the sun and us, and still protects us, and gives us flowers and showers and meat and content.—*Izaak Walton.*

The wise man starts and trembles at the perils of a bliss.—*Young.*

The beloved of the Almighty are the rich who have the humility of the poor, and the poor who have the magnanimity of the rich.—*Saadi.*

And let me tell you that every misery I miss is a new blessing.—*Izaak Walton.*

It is too generally true that all that is required to make men unmindful what they owe to God for any blessing is that they should receive that blessing often enough, and regularly enough.—*Bishop Whately.*

He alone is blessed who never was born.—*Prior.*

BLOCKHEAD.

A blockhead cannot come in, nor go away, nor sit, nor rise, nor stand, like a man of sense.—*Bruyère.*

Heaven and earth fight in vain against a dunce!—*Schiller.*

There never was any party, faction, sect, or cabal whatsoever, in which the most ignorant were not the most violent; for a bee is not a busier animal than a blockhead.—*Pope.*

BLUNTNESS.

He speaks home; you may relish him more in the soldier than in the scholar.—*Shakespeare.*

BLUSH.

The heart's meteors tilting in the face.—*Shakespeare.*

They teach us to dance; O that they could teach us to blush, did it cost a guinea a glow!—*Madame Deluzy.*

The bold defiance of a woman is the certain sign of her shame, — when she has once ceased to blush, it is because she has too much to blush for.—*Talleyrand.*

The man that blushes is not quite a brute.—*Young.*

How beautiful your reproof has made your daughter! That crimson hue and silver tears become her better than any ornament of gold and pearls. These may hang on the neck of a wanton, but those are never seen disconnected with moral purity. A full-blown rose, besprinkled with the purest dew, is not so beautiful as this child blushing beneath her parent's displeasure, and shedding tears of sorrow for her fault. A blush is the sign which nature hangs out to show where chastity and honor dwell.—*Gotthold.*

Give me the eloquent cheek, where blushes burn and die.—*Mrs. Osgood.*

Bid the cheek be ready with a blush, modest as Morning when she coldly eyes the youthful Phœbus.—*Shakespeare.*

Men blush less for their crimes than for their weaknesses and vanity.—*Bruyère.*

O, call not to this aged cheek the little blood which should keep warm my heart!—*Dryden.*

Blushing is the livery of virtue, though it may sometimes proceed from guilt; so it holds true of poverty, that it is the attendant of virtue, though sometimes it may proceed from mismanagement and accident.—*Bacon.*

It is better for a young man to blush than to turn pale.—*Cato.*

From every blush that kindles in thy cheeks ten thousand little loves and graces spring to revel in the roses.—*Rowe.*

The hue given back by the clouds from the reflected rays of the sun or the purple morn, such was the countenance of Diana when she was discovered unclothed.—*Ovid.*

What means, alas! that blood which flushes guilty in your face?—*Dryden.*

The blush is nature's alarm at the approach of sin, and her testimony to the dignity of virtue.—*Fuller.*

Like the last beam of evening thrown on a white cloud, just seen and gone.—*Walter Scott.*

Though looks and words, by the strong mastery of his practised will, are overruled, the mounting blood betrays an impulse in its secret spring too deep for his control.—*Southey.*

Like the faint streaks of light broke loose from darkness, and dawning into blushes.—
Dryden.

Troubled blood through his pale face was seen to come and go, with tidings from his heart, as it a running messenger had been.—
Spenser.

The inconvenience or the beauty of the blush, which is the greater?—*Madame Necker.*

BLUSTERING.

A killing tongue, and a quiet sword.—
Shakespeare.

It is with narrow-souled people as with narrow-necked bottles; the less they have in them, the more noise they make in pouring it out.—
Pope.

The Devil may be bullied, but not the Deity.
W. R. Alger.

Those that are the loudest in their threats are the weakest in the execution of them. In springing a mine, that which has done the most extensive mischief makes the smallest report; and again, if we consider the effect of lightning, it is probable that he that is killed by it hears no noise; but the thunderclap which follows, and which most alarms the ignorant, is the surest proof of their safety.—*Colton.*

The empty vessel makes the greatest sound.
Shakespeare.

A brave man is sometimes a desperado; a bully is always a coward.—*Haliburton.*

BOASTING.

Where there is much pretension, much has been borrowed; nature never pretends.—
Lavater.

There is this benefit in brag, that the speaker is unconsciously expressing his own ideal. Humor him by all means, draw it all out, and hold him to it.—*Emerson.*

A gentleman that loves to hear himself talk, and will speak more in a minute than he will stand to in a month.—*Shakespeare.*

To such as boasting show their scars a mock is due.—*Shakespeare.*

Commonly they use their feet for defence, whose tongue is their weapon.—*Sir P. Sidney.*

Lord Bacon told Sir Edward Coke when he boasted, "The less you speak of your greatness, the more I shall think of it." Mirrors are the accompaniments of dandies, not heroes. The men of history were not perpetually looking in the glass to make sure of their own size. Absorbed in their work they did it, and did it so well that the wondering world saw them to be great, and labelled them accordingly.—
Rev. S. Coley.

Who knows himself a braggart, let him fear this; for it will come to pass that every braggart shall be found an ass.—*Shakespeare.*

The honor is overpaid when he that did the act is commentator.—*Shirley.*

What art thou? Have not I an arm as big as thine? a heart as big? Thy words, I grant, are bigger, for I wear not my dagger in my mouth.—*Shakespeare.*

Where boasting ends, there dignity begins.
Young.

One man affirms that he has rode post a hundred miles in six hours: probably it is a lie; but supposing it to be true, what then? Why, he is a very good post-boy; that is all. Another asserts, and probably not without oaths, that he has drunk six or eight bottles of wine at a sitting; out of charity I will believe him a liar; for, if I do not, I must think him a beast.—
Chesterfield.

We wound our modesty, and make foul the clearness of our deservings, when of ourselves we publish them.—*Shakespeare.*

Men of real merit, and whose noble and glorious deeds we are ready to acknowledge, are yet not to be endured when they vaunt their own actions.—*Æschines.*

Conceit, more rich in matter than in words, brags of his substance, not of ornament; they are but beggars that can count their worth.—
Shakespeare.

Boasting and bravado may exist in the breast even of the coward, if he is successful through a mere lucky hit; but a just contempt of an enemy can alone arise in those who feel that they are superior to their opponent by the prudence of their measures.—*Thucydides.*

BODY.

What! know ye not that your body is the temple of the Holy Ghost which is in you, which ye have of God; and ye are not your own?—*Bible.*

These limbs, whence had we them ? — this stormy force ; this life-blood, with its burning passion ?   They are dust and shadow, — a shadow-system gathered round our me ; wherein, through some moments or years, the divine essence is to be revealed in the flesh.—*Carlyle.*

Every physician knows, though metaphysicians know little about it, that the laws which govern the animal machine are as certain and invariable as those which guide the planetary system, and are as little within the control of the human being who is subject to them.—
Priestley.

Our body is a well-set clock, which keeps good time ; but if it be too much or indiscreetly tampered with, the alarum runs out before the hour.—*Bishop Hall.*

God made the human body, and it is by far the most exquisite and wonderful organization which has come to use from the Divine hand. It is a study for one's whole life.   If an undevout astronomer is mad, an undevout physiologist is still madder.—*Beecher.*

BOLDNESS.

Fools rush in where angels fear to tread.—
Pope.

It deserves to be considered that boldness is ever blind, for it sees not dangers and inconveniences.   Whence it is bad in council though good in execution.   The right use of bold persons, therefore, is that they never command in chief, but serve as seconds, under the direction of others.   For in council it is good to see dangers, and in execution not to see them unless they are very great.—*Bacon.*

Fortune befriends the bold.—*Dryden.*

Carried away by the irresistible influence which is always exercised over men's minds by a bold resolution in critical circumstances.—
Guizot.

We make way for the man who boldly pushes past us.—*Bovee.*

BONDAGE.

Bondage is hoarse, and may not speak aloud.
Shakespeare.

A bond is necessary to complete our being, only we must be careful that the bond does not become bondage.—*Mrs. Jameson*

BOOKS.

After the pleasure of possessing books there is hardly anything more pleasant than that of speaking of them, and of communicating to the public the innocent richness of thought which we have acquired by the culture of letters.—*Nodier.*

We are as liable to be corrupted by books as by companions.—*Fielding.*

If I were to pray for a taste which would stand by me under every variety of circumstances, and be a source of happiness and cheerfulness to me through life, and a shield against its ills, however things might go amiss, and the world frown upon me, it would be a taste for reading.—*Herschel.*

It is in books the chief of all perfections to be plain and brief.—*Butler.*

The books which help you most are those which make you think the most.   The hardest way of learning is by easy reading : but a great book that comes from a great thinker, — it is a ship of thought, deep freighted with truth and with beauty.—*Theodore Parker.*

Great books, like large skulls, have often the least brains.— *W. B. Clulow.*

When a book raises your spirit, and inspires you with noble and courageous feelings, seek for no other rule to judge the work by ; it is good, and made by a good workman.—*Bruyère.*

Next to acquiring good friends, the best acquisition is that of good books.—*Colton.*

Books, says Lord Bacon, can never teach us the use of books ; the student must learn by commerce with mankind to reduce his speculations to practice.   No man should think so highly of himself as to think he can receive but little light from books ; no one so meanly, as to believe he can discover nothing but what is to be learned from them.—*Johnson.*

Books, like friends, should be few, and well chosen.—*Joineriana.*

Many readers judge of the power of a book by the shock it gives their feelings, — as some savage tribes determine the power of their muskets by their recoil ; that being considered best which fairly prostrates the purchaser.—
Longfellow.

A book is the only immortality.—
Rufus Choate.

Many books belong to sunshine, and should be read out of doors.   Clover, violets, and hedge roses breathe from their leaves ; they are most lovable in cool lanes, along field paths, or upon stiles overhung by hawthorn, while the blackbird pipes, and the nightingale bathes its brown feathers in the twilight copse.— *Willmott.*

It is always easy to shut a book, but not quite so easy to get rid of a lettered coxcomb.—
Colton.

In looking around me seeking for miserable resources against the heaviness of time, I open a book, and I say to myself, as the cat to the fox : I have only one good turn. but I need no other.—*Madame Necker.*

A good book is the best of friends, — the same to-day and forever.—*Tupper.*

The silent power of books is a great power in the world ; and there is a joy in reading them which those alone can know who read them with desire and enthusiasm. Silent, passive, and noiseless though they be, they may yet set in action countless multitudes, and change the order of nations.—*Henry Giles.*

Learning hath gained most by those books by which printers have lost.—*Fuller.*

The diffusion of these silent teachers — books — through the whole community is to work greater effects than artillery, machinery, and legislation. Its peaceful agency is to supersede stormy revolutions. The culture which it is to spread, whilst an unspeakable good to the individual, is also to become the stability of nations.—*Channing.*

Books are embalmed minds.—*Bovee.*

Books are faithful repositories, which may be awhile neglected or forgotten, but when they are opened again, will again impart their instruction. Memory, once interrupted, is not to be recalled ; written learning is a fixed luminary, which, after the cloud that had hidden it has passed away, is again bright in its proper station. Tradition is but a meteor, which, if it once falls, cannot be rekindled.—*Johnson.*

Every great book is an action, and every great action is a book.—*Luther.*

A man ought to inquire and find out what he really and truly has an appetite for ; what suits his constitution ; and that, doctors tell him, is the very thing he ought to have in general. And so with books.—*Carlyle.*

Every man is a volume if you know how to read him.—*Channing.*

Books, of which the principles are diseased or deformed, must be kept on the shelf of the scholar, as the man of science preserves monsters in glasses. They belong to the study of the mind's morbid anatomy, and ought to be accurately labelled. Voltaire will still be a wit, notwithstanding he is a scoffer ; and we may admire the brilliant spots and eyes of the viper, if we acknowledge its venom and call it a reptile.—*Willmott.*

Come, my best friends, my books ! and lead me on.—*Cowley.*

Most books fail, not so much from a want of ability in their authors, as from an absence in their productions of a thorough development of their ability.—*Bovee.*

Books, — lighthouses erected in the great sea of time.—*Whipple.*

A book should be luminous, but not voluminous.—*Bovee.*

Let us consider how great a commodity of doctrine exists in books ; how easily, how secretly, how safely they expose the nakedness of human ignorance without putting it to shame. These are the masters who instruct us without rods and ferules, without hard words and anger, without clothes or money. If you approach them, they are not asleep ; if investigating you interrogate them, they conceal nothing ; if you mistake them, they never grumble ; if you are ignorant, they cannot laugh at you.— *Richard de Bury.*

Books are the immortal sons deifying their sires.—*Plato.*

To divert myself from a troublesome fancy, it is but to run to my books ; they presently fix me to them, and drive the other out of my thoughts, and do not mutiny to see that I have only recourse to them for want of other more real, natural, and lively conveniences ; they always receive me with the same kindness.— *Montaigne.*

One must be rich in thought and character to owe nothing to books, though preparation is necessary to profitable reading ; and the less reading is better than more ; — book-struck men are of all readers least wise, however knowing or learned.—*Alcott.*

God be thanked for books. They are the voices of the distant and the dead, and make us heirs of the spiritual life of past ages.— *Channing.*

The greatest pleasure in life is that of reading while we are young. I have had as much of this pleasure perhaps as any one.—*Hazlitt.*

Without books God is silent, justice dormant, natural science at a stand, philosophy lame, letters dumb, and all things involved in Cimmerian darkness.—*Bartholin.*

Books are the true metempsychosis, — they are the symbol and presage of immortality. The dead men are scattered, and none shall find them. Behold they are here ! they do but sleep.—*Beecher.*

Many books owe their success to the good memories of their authors and the bad memories of their readers.—*Colton.*

Mankind are creatures of books, as well as of other circumstances ; and such they eternally remain, — proofs, that the race is a noble and believing race, and capable of whatever books can stimulate.—*Leigh Hunt.*

How many books there are whose reputation is made that would not obtain it were it now to make !—*Joubert.*

In comparing men and books, one must always remember this important distinction,— that one can put the books down at any time. As Macaulay says, "Plato is never sullen, Cervantes is never petulant, Demosthenes never comes unseasonably, Dante never stays too long."— *Willis.*

Books are a languid pleasure.—*Montaigne.*

Plays and romances sell as well as books of devotion, but with this difference,— more people read the former than buy them, and more buy the latter than read them.— *T. Hughes.*

Some books are drenched sands, on which a great soul's wealth lies all in heaps, like a wrecked argosy.—*Alexander Smith.*

The worth of a book is a matter of expressed juices.—*Bovee.*

Books are a guide in youth, and an entertainment for age. They support us under solitude, and keep us from becoming a burden to ourselves. They help us to forget the crossness of men and things, compose our cares and our passions, and lay our disappointments asleep. When we are weary of the living, we may repair to the dead, who have nothing of peevishness, pride, or design in their conversation.— *Jeremy Collier.*

He hath never fed of the dainties that are bred in a book.—*Shakespeare.*

A book becomes a mirror, with the author's face shining over it. Talent only gives an imperfect image,— the broken glimmer of a countenance. But the features of genius remain unruffled. Time guards the shadow. Beauty, the spiritual Venus,— whose children are the Tassos, the Spensers, the Bacons,— breathes the magic of her love, and fixes the face forever.— *Willmott.*

Some books are to be tasted, others to be swallowed, and some few to be chewed and digested.—*Bacon.*

Good books are to the young mind what the warming sun and the refreshing rain of spring are to the seeds which have lain dormant in the frosts of winter. They are more, for they may save from that which is worse than death, as well as bless with that which is better than life.—*Horace Mann.*

Books are not seldom talismans and spells.— *Cowper.*

Books are not absolutely dead things, but do contain a potency of life in them to be as active as that soul was whose progeny they are; nay, they do preserve, as in a vial, the purest efficacy and extraction of that living intellect that bred them.—*Milton.*

He that will have no books but those that are scarce evinces about as correct a taste in literature as he would do in friendship who would have no friends but those whom all the rest of the world have sent to Coventry.— *Colton.*

The last thing that we discover in writing a book is to know what to put at the beginning.— *Pascal.*

Books, as Dryden has aptly termed them, are spectacles to read nature. Æschylus and Aristotle, Shakespeare and Bacon, are priests who preach and expound the mysteries of man and the universe. They teach us to understand and feel what we see, to decipher and syllable the hieroglyphics of the senses.—*Hare.*

Those faithful mirrors, which reflect to our mind the minds of sages and heroes.—*Gibbon.*

Books are the best of things, well used; abused, among the worst. What is the right use? What is the one end, which all means go to effect? They are for nothing but to inspire. I had better never see a book than to be warped by its attraction clean out of my own orbit, and made a satellite instead of a system.—*Emerson.*

Without grace no book can live, and with it the poorest may have its life prolonged.— *Horace Walpole.*

Knowledge of books is like that sort of lantern which hides him who carries it, and serves only to pass through secret and gloomy paths of his own; but in the possession of a man of business it is as a torch in the hand of one who is willing and able to show those who are bewildered the way which leads to their prosperity and welfare.—*Steele.*

There was a time when the world acted upon books. Now books act upon the world.— *Joubert.*

Of many large volumes the index is the best portion and the usefullest. A glance through the casement gives whatever knowledge of the interior is needful. An epitome is only a book shortened; and, as a general rule, the worth increases as the size lessens.— *Willmott.*

You shall see a beautiful quarto page, where a neat rivulet of text shall meander through a meadow of margin.—*Sheridan.*

Men love better books which please them than those which instruct. Since their *ennui* troubles them more than their ignorance, they prefer being amused to being informed.— *L'Abbé Dubois.*

Those who are conversant with books well know how often they mislead us when we have not a living monitor at hand to assist us in comparing practice with theory.—*Junius.*

Thou mayst as well expect to grow stronger by always eating as wiser by always reading. Too much overcharges nature, and turns more into disease than nourishment. It is thought and digestion which makes books serviceable, and gives health and vigor to the mind.— *Fuller.*

The quantity of books in a library is often a cloud of witnesses of the ignorance of the owner.—*Oxenstiern.*

Many a man lives a burden upon the earth; but a good book is the precious life-blood of a master spirit, embalmed and treasured up on purpose for a life beyond life.—*Milton.*

A book may be compared to the life of your neighbor. If it be good, it cannot last too long; if bad, you cannot get rid of it too early.— *H. Brooke.*

Some new books it is necessary to read, — part for the information they contain, and others in order to acquaint one's self with the state of literature in the age in which one lives; but I would rather read too few than too many. *Lord Dudley.*

Many books require no thought from those who read them, and for a simple reason, — they made no such demand upon those who wrote them.—*Colton.*

Books, to judicious compilers, are useful, — to particular arts and professions absolutely necessary, — to men of real science they are tools; but more are tools to them.—*Johnson.*

Worthy books are not companions, they are solitudes; we lose ourselves in them, and all our cares.—*Bailey.*

There are persons who flatter themselves that the size of their works will make them immortal. They pile up reluctant quarto upon solid folio, as if their labors, because they are gigantic, could contend with truth and heaven! *Junius.*

Books, like proverbs, receive their chief value from the stamp and esteem of ages through which they have passed.—*Sir W. Temple.*

Do not believe that a book is good, if in reading it thou dost not become more contented with thy existence, if it does not rouse up in thee most generous feelings.—*Lavater.*

He who loves not books before he comes to thirty years of age will hardly love them enough afterwards to understand them.— *Clarendon.*

Books are the true levellers. They give to all who faithfully use them the society, the spiritual presence, of the best and greatest of our race.—*Channing.*

We ought to reverence books, to look at them as useful and mighty things. If they are good and true, whether they are about religion or politics, farming, trade, or medicine, they are the message of Christ, the maker of all things, the teacher of all truth.—*Rev. C. Kingsley.*

A book may be as great a thing as a battle.— *Disraeli.*

It is with books as with women, where a certain plainness of manner and of dress is more engaging than that glare of paint and airs and apparel which may dazzle the eye, but reaches not the affections.—*Hume.*

There is no book so poor that it would not be a prodigy if wholly made by a single man.— *Johnson.*

The past but lives in words; a thousand ages were blank if books had not evoked their ghosts, and kept the pale, unbodied shades to warn us from fleshless lips.—*Bulwer Lytton.*

Books that you may carry to the fire, and hold readily in your hand, are the most useful after all.—*Johnson.*

Books are the legacies that genius leaves to mankind, to be delivered down from generation to generation, as presents to the posterity of those that are yet unborn.—*Addison.*

When self-interest inclines a man to print, he should consider that the purchaser expects a pennyworth for his penny, and has reason to asperse his honesty if he finds himself deceived.— *Shenstone.*

There is a kind of physiognomy in the titles of books no less than in the faces of men, by which a skilful observer will as well know what to expect from the one as the other.—*Butler.*

A first book has some of the sweetness of a first love. The music of the soul passes into it. The unspotted eye illuminates it. Defects are unobserved; sometimes they grow even pleasing from their connection with an object that is dear, like the oblique eye in the girl to whom the philosopher was attached. Later surprises will amuse, and deeper sympathies may cheer us, but the charm loses its freshness, and the tenderness some of the balm.— *Willmott.*

It is books that teach us to refine our pleasures when young, and which, having so taught us, enable us to recall them with satisfaction when old.—*Leigh Hunt.*

Our favorites are few; since only what rises from the heart reaches it, being caught and carried on the tongues of men wheresoever love and letters journey.—*Alcott.*

The colleges, whilst they provide us with libraries, furnish no professors of books; and I think no chair is so much wanted.—*Emerson.*

BORES.

There are some kinds of men who cannot pass their time alone; they are the flails of occupied people.—*M. de Bonald.*

The secret of making one's self tiresome is not to know when to stop.—*Voltaire.*

There are few wild beasts more to be dreaded than a communicative man having nothing to communicate.—*Bovee.*

O, he is as tedious as is a tired horse, a railing wife; worse than a smoky house! —
Shakespeare.

It is to be hoped that, with all the modern improvements, a mode will be discovered of getting rid of bores; for it is too bad that a poor wretch can be punished for stealing your pocket-handkerchief or gloves, and that no punishment can be inflicted on those who steal your time, and with it your temper and patience, as well as the bright thoughts that might have entered into your mind (like the Irishman who lost the fortune before he had got it), but were frightened away by the bore.—
Byron.

We are almost always wearied in the company of persons with whom we are not permitted to be weary.—*Rochefoucauld.*

He will steal himself into a man's favor, and for a week escape a great deal of discoveries; but when you find him out, you have him ever after.—*Shakespeare.*

A tedious person is one a man would leap a steeple from.—*Ben Jonson.*

BORROWING.

The borrower runs in his own debt.—
Emerson.

Neither a borrower nor a lender be; for loan oft loses both itself and friend, and borrowing dulls the edge of husbandry.—*Shakespeare.*

Getting into debt is getting into a tanglesome net.—*Franklin.*

Charles Lamb, tired of lending his books, threatened to chain Wordsworth's poems to his shelves, adding, " For of those who borrow, some read slow; some mean to read, but don't read; and some neither read nor mean to read, but borrow, to leave you an opinion of their sagacity. I must do my money-borrowing friends the justice to say, that there is nothing of this caprice or wantonness of alienation in them. When they borrow my money, they never fail to make use of it."—*Talfourd.*

The reason why borrowed books are so seldom returned to their owners is that it is much easier to retain the books than what is in them.—*Montaigne.*

He that would have a short Lent let him borrow money to be repaid at Easter.—*Franklin.*

No remedy against this consumption of the purse; borrowing only lingers and lingers it out, but the disease is incurable.—*Shakespeare.*

BOUNTY.

The superfluous blossoms on a fruit-tree are meant to symbolize the large way God loves to do pleasant things.—*Beecher.*

From bounty issues power.—*Akenside.*

BRAINS.

The brain is the palest of all the internal organs, and the heart the reddest. Whatever comes from the brain carries the hue of the place it came from, and whatever comes from the heart carries the heat and color of its birth-place.—*Holmes.*

When God endowed human beings with brains, he did not intend to guarantee them.—
Montesquieu.

There are brains so large that they unconsciously swamp all individualities which come in contact or too near, and brains so small that they cannot take in the conception of any other individuality as a whole, only in part or parts.—
Mrs. Jameson.

BRAVERY.

No man can be brave who considers pain to be the greatest evil of life; nor temperate, who considers pleasure to be the highest good.—
Cicero.

A true knight is fuller of gay bravery in the midst than in the beginning of danger.—
Sir P. Sidney.

At the bottom of a good deal of the bravery that appears in the world there lurks a miserable cowardice. Men will face powder and steel because they cannot face public opinion.—
Chapin.

The best hearts, Trim, are ever the bravest, replied my uncle Toby.—*Sterne.*

Cato the elder, when somebody was praising a man for his foolhardy bravery, said " that there was an essential difference between a really brave man and one who had merely a contempt for life."—*Plutarch.*

That is a valiant flea that dares eat his breakfast on the lip of a lion!—*Shakespeare.*

The brave man is not he who feels no fear, for that were stupid and irrational; but he whose noble soul its fear subdues, and bravely dares the danger which it shrinks from.—
Joanna Baillie.

Who bravely dares must sometimes risk a fall.—*Smollett.*

A brave man is clear in his discourse, and keeps close to truth.—*Aristotle.*

Nature often enshrines gallant and noble hearts in weak bosoms, — oftenest, God bless her! in female breasts.—*Dickens.*

None but the brave deserve the fair.—
Dryden.

The bravery founded upon the hope of recompense, upon the fear of punishment, upon the experience of success, upon rage, upon ignorance of dangers, is common bravery, and does not merit the name. True bravery proposes a just end, measures the dangers, and, if it is necessary, the affront, with coldness.—*Francis la None.*

BREVITY.
Genuine good taste consists in saying much in a few words, in choosing among our thoughts, in having some order and arrangement in what we relate, in speaking with composure.—*Fenelon.*

It is excellent discipline for an author to feel that he must say all he has to say in the fewest possible words, or his reader is sure to skip them; and in the plainest possible words, or his reader will certainly misunderstand them. Generally, also, a downright fact may be told in a plain way; and we want downright facts at present more than anything else.—*Ruskin.*

Brevity is the soul of wit, and tediousness the limbs and outward flourishes.—*Shakespeare.*

These are my thoughts;—I might have spun them out to a greater length, but I think a little plot of ground thick sown is better than a great field which for the most part of it lies fallow.—*Bishop Norris.*

When a man has no design but to speak plain truth, he may say a great deal in a very narrow compass.—*Steele.*

And there is one rare strange virtue in their speeches, the secret of their mastery, — they are short.—*Halleck.*

Brevity is the best recommendation of a speech, not only in the case of a senator, but in that, too, of an orator.—*Cicero.*

Brevity in writing is what charity is to all other virtues, — righteousness is nothing without the one, nor authorship without the other.—
Sydney Smith.

Talk to the point, and stop when you have reached it. The faculty some possess of making one idea cover a quire of paper is not good for much. Be comprehensive in all you say or write. To fill a volume upon nothing is a credit to nobody; though Lord Chesterfield wrote a very clever poem upon nothing.—
John Neal.

Brevity is the body and soul of wit. It is wit itself, for it alone isolates sufficiently for contrasts; because redundancy or diffuseness produces no distinctions.—*Richter.*

When you introduce a moral lesson, let it be brief.—*Horace.*

It is the work of fancy to enlarge, but of judgment to shorten and contract; and therejore this must be as far above the other as judgment is a greater and nobler faculty than fancy or imagination.—*South.*

The one prudence in life is concentration.—
Emerson.

Rather to excite your judgment briefly than to inform it tediously.—*Bacon.*

A parsimony of words prodigal of sense.—
Disraeli.

If you would be pungent, be brief; for it is with words as with sunbeams, — the more they are condensed, the deeper they burn.—*Southey.*

Brevity is a great praise of eloquence.—
Cicero.

It is not a great Xerxes army of words, but a compact Greek ten thousand that march safely down to posterity.—*Lowell.*

Aiming at brevity, I become obscure.—
Horace.

BRIBERY.
Judges and senates have been bought for gold.—*Pope.*

Petitions, not sweetened with gold, are but unsavory and oft refused; or, if received, are pocketed, not read.—*Massinger.*

And sell the mighty space of our large honors for so much trash as may be grasped thus?
Shakespeare.

The universe would not be rich enough to buy the vote of an honest man.—*St. Gregory.*

BROTHERHOOD.
Man, man, is thy brother, and thy father is God.—*Lamartine.*

The era of Christianity, — peace, brotherhood, the Golden Rule as applied to governmental matters — is yet to come, and when it comes, then, and then only, will the future of nations be sure.—*Kossuth.*

Infinite is the help man can yield to man.—
Carlyle.

We are members of one great body. Nature planted in us a mutual love, and fitted us for a social life. We must consider that we were born for the good of the whole.—*Seneca.*

We must love men, ere to us they will seem worthy of our love.—*Shakespeare.*

The race of mankind would perish, did they cease to aid each other. From the time that the mother binds the child's head till the moment that some kind assistant wipes the death-damp from the brow of the dying, we cannot exist without mutual help. All, therefore, that need aid have a right to ask it from their fellow-mortals; no one who holds the power of granting can refuse it without guilt.— *Walter Scott.*

Be kindly affectioned one to another with brotherly love; in honor preferring one another.—*Bible.*

Nature has inclined us to love men.— *Cicero.*

However wretched a fellow-mortal may be, he is still a member of our common species.— *Seneca.*

To live is not to live for one's self alone; let us help one another.—*Menander.*

If we love one another, nothing, in truth, can harm us, whatever mischances may happen.—*Longfellow.*

The universe is but one great city, full of beloved ones, divine and human, by nature endeared to each other.—*Epictetus.*

Give bread to a stranger, in the name of the universal brotherhood which binds together all men under the common father of nature.— *Quintilian.*

BRUTE.
A singular fact, that, when man is a brute, he is the most sensual and loathsome of all brutes.—*Hawthorne.*

Notwithstanding that natural love in brutes is much more violent and intense than in rational creatures, Providence has taken care that it should be no longer troublesome to the parent than it is useful to the young; for so soon as the wants of the latter cease, the mother withdraws her fondness, and leaves them to provide for themselves.—*Addison.*

BURLESQUE.
What caricature is in painting, burlesque is in writing; and in the same manner the comic writer and painter correlate to each other; as in the former, the painter seems to have the advantage, so it is in the latter infinitely on the side of the writer. For the monstrous is much easier to paint than describe, and the ridiculous to describe than paint.—*Fielding.*

BUSINESS.
Formerly, when great fortunes were only made in war, war was a business; but now, when great fortunes are only made by business, business is war.—*Bovee.*

Business in a certain sort of men is a mark of understanding, and they are honored for it. Their souls seek repose in agitation, as children do by being rocked in a cradle. They may pronounce themselves as serviceable to their friends as troublesome to themselves. No one distributes his money to others, but every one therein distributes his time and his life. There is nothing of which we are so prodigal as of those two things, of which to be thrifty would be both commendable and useful.—*Montaigne.*

A man who cannot mind his own business is not fit to be trusted with the king's.—*Saville.*

Success in business is seldom owing to uncommon talents or original power which is untractable and self-willed, but to the greatest degree of commonplace capacity.—*Hazlitt.*

To business that we love, we rise betime and go to it with delight.—*Shakespeare.*

Rare almost as great poets, rarer, perhaps, than veritable saints and martyrs, are consummate men of business. A man, to be excellent in this way, requires a great knowledge of character, with that exquisite tact which feels unerringly the right moment when to act. A discreet rapidity must pervade all the movements of his thought and action. He must be singularly free from vanity, and is generally found to be an enthusiast who has the art to conceal his enthusiasm.—*Helps.*

The Christian must not only mind Heaven, but attend to his daily calling. Like the pilot who, while his eye is fixed upon the star, keeps his hand upon the helm.—*Rev.* T. *Watson.*

Every man has business and desire, such as it is.—*Shakespeare.*

To men addicted to delights, business is an interruption; to such as are cold to delights, business is an entertainment. For which reason it was said to one who commended a dull man for his application, "No thanks to him; if he had no business he would have nothing to do."— *Steele.*

The old proverb about having too many irons in the fire is an abominable old lie. Have all in, shovel, tongs, and poker.— *Adam Clarke.*

It is very sad for a man to make himself servant to a thing, his manhood all taken out of him by the hydraulic pressure of excessive business. I should not like to be merely a great doctor, a great lawyer, a great minister, a great politician, — I should like to be also something of a man.— *Theodore Parker*

Men of great parts are often unfortunate in the management of public business because they are apt to go out of the common road by the quickness of their imagination.—*Swift.*

Call on a business man at business times only, and on business; transact your business and go about your business, in order to give him time to finish his business.—
Duke of Wellington.

Stick to your legitimate business. Do not go into outside operations. Few men have brains enough for more than one business. To dabble in stocks, to put a few thousand dollars into a mine, and a few more into a manufactory, and a few more into an invention, is enough to ruin any man. Be content with fair returns. Do not become greedy. Do not think that men are happy in proportion as they are rich, and therefore do not aim too high. Be content with moderate wealth. Make friends. A time will come when all the money in the world will not be worth to you so much as one good stanch friend.—*Beecher.*

I do not give, but lend myself to business.—
Seneca.

The great secret both of health and successful industry is the absolute yielding up of one's consciousness to the business and diversion of the hour, — never permitting the one to infringe in the least degree upon the other.—
Sismondi.

There are in business three things necessary, — knowledge, temper, and time.—*Feltham.*

BUSYBODY.
They learn to be idle, wandering about from house to house; and not only idle, but tattlers also, and busybodies, speaking things which they ought not.—*Bible.*

A person who is too nice an observer of the business of the crowd, like one who is too curious in observing the labor of the bees, will often be stung for his curiosity.—*Pope.*

In private life I never knew any one interfere with other people's disputes, but that he heartily repented of it.—*Lord Carlisle.*

Always occupied with others' duties, never with our own, alas!—*Joubert.*

He is a treacherous supplanter and underminer of the peace of all families and societies. This being a maxim of an unfailing truth, that nobody ever pries into another man's concerns but with a design to do, or to be able to do him a mischief.—*South.*

His tongue, like the tail of Samson's foxes, carries firebrands, and is enough to set the whole field of the world on a flame. Himself begins table-talk of his neighbor at another's board, to whom he bears the first news, and adjures him to conceal the reporter; whose choleric answer he returns to his first host, enlarged with a second edition; so as it used to be done in the fight of unwilling mastiffs, he claps each on the side apart, and provokes them to an eager conflict.—*Bishop Hall.*

Have you so much leisure from your own business that you can take care of other people's that does not at all belong to you?—
Terence.

A person who constantly meddles to no purpose means to do harm, and is not sorry to find he has succeeded.—*Hazlitt.*

C.

CALAMITIES.
Times of general calamity and confusion have ever been productive of the greatest minds. The purest ore is produced from the hottest furnace, and the brightest thunderbolt is elicited from the darkest storm.—*Colton.*

Know, he that foretells his own calamity, and makes events before they come, twice over doth endure the pains of evil destiny.—
Sir W. Davenant.

It is only from the belief of the goodness and wisdom of a Supreme Being that our calamities can be borne in that manner which becomes a man.—*Mackenzie.*

Calamity is man's true touchstone.—
Beaumont and Fletcher.

CALUMNY.
His calumny is not only the greatest benefit a rogue can confer on us, but the only service he will perform for nothing.—*Lavater.*

Be thou as chaste as ice, as pure as snow, thou shalt not escape calumny.—*Shakespeare.*

Like the tiger, that seldom desists from pursuing man after having once preyed upon human flesh, the reader who has once gratified his appetite with calumny makes ever after the most agreeable feast upon murdered reputation!
Goldsmith.

I never listen to calumnies, because if they are untrue I run the risk of being deceived, and if they be true, of hating persons not worth thinking about.—*Montesquieu.*

Calumniators are those who have neither good hearts nor good understandings. We ought not to think ill of any one till we have palpable proof; and even then we should not expose them to others.—*Colton.*

Calumny will sear virtue itself: these shrugs, these hums and ha's.—*Shakespeare.*

Who stabs my name would stab my person too, did not the hangman's axe lie in the way.—*Crown.*

Calumny is a monstrous vice; for, where parties indulge in it, there are always two that are actively engaged in doing wrong, and one who is subject to injury. The calumniator inflicts wrong by slandering the absent; he who gives credit to the calumny before he has investigated the truth is equally implicated. The person traduced is doubly injured, — first by him who propagates, and secondly by him who credits, the calumny.—*Herodotus.*

Back-wounding calumny the whitest virtue strikes.—*Shakespeare.*

Close thine ear against him that shall open his mouth secretly against another : if thou receive not his words, they fly back and wound the reporter ; if thou receive them, they flee forward and wound the receiver.—*Quarles.*

There are calumnies against which even innocence loses courage.—*Napoleon.*

It is like the Greek fire used in ancient warfare, which burnt unquenched beneath the water ; or like the weeds which, when you have extirpated them in one place, are sprouting forth vigorously in another spot, at the distance of many hundred yards ; or, to use the metaphor of St. James, it is like the wheel which catches fire as it goes, and burns with fiercer conflagration as its own speed increases.—*F. W. Robertson.*

Calumny is only the noise of madmen.—*Diogenes.*

Calumny is like the wasp which worries you, and which it is not best to try to get rid of unless you are sure of slaying it ; for otherwise it returns to the charge more furious than ever.—*Chamfort.*

I am beholden to Calumny, that she hath so endeavored and taken pains to belie me. It shall make me set a surer guard on myself, and keep a better watch upon my actions.—*Ben Jonson.*

The celebrated Boerhaave, who had many enemies, used to say that he never thought it necessary to repeat their calumnies. "They are sparks," said he, "which, if you do not blow them, will go out of themselves."—*Disraeli.*

Those who ought to be secure from calumny are generally those who avoid it least.—*Stanislaus.*

He that lends an easy and credulous ear to calumny is either a man of very ill morals or has no more sense and understanding than a child.—*Menander.*

To persevere in one's duty and to be silent is the best answer to calumny.—*Washington.*

The pure in heart are slow to credit calumnies, because they hardly comprehend what motives can be inducements to the alleged crimes.—*Jane Porter.*

Cutting honest throats by whispers.—*Walter Scott.*

CANDOR.

I can promise to be candid, but I cannot promise to be impartial.—*Goethe.*

Fine speeches are the instruments of knaves or fools that use them, when they want good sense ; but honesty needs no disguise nor ornament : be plain.—*Otway.*

Candor is the brightest gem of criticism.—*Disraeli.*

He who, when called upon to speak a disagreeable truth, tells it boldly and has done, is both bolder and milder than he who nibbles in a low voice, and never ceases nibbling.—*Lavater.*

It is great, it is manly, to disdain disguise ; it shows our spirit, or it proves our strength.—*Young.*

I hold it cowardice to rest mistrustful where a noble heart hath pawned an open hand in sign of love.—*Shakespeare.*

A man should never be ashamed to own he has been in the wrong, which is but saying, in other words, that he is wiser to-day than he was yesterday.—*Pope.*

Making my breast transparent as pure crystal, that the world, jealous of me, may see the foulest thought my heart doth hold.—*Buckingham.*

CANT.

Is not cant the *materia prima* of the Devil, from which all falsehoods, imbecilities, abominations, body themselves ; from which no true thing can come ? For cant is itself properly a double-distilled lie, the second power of a lie.—*Carlyle.*

Those people are often the least worldly on whom they who make the loudest boast of their unworldliness seek basely to affix that opprobrious epithet. For they walk the world with a heart pure as it is cheerful ; they are, by that unpretending purity, saved from infection ; as there are as many fair and healthy faces to be seen in the smoke and stir of cities as in the rural wilds, so also are there as many fair and healthy spirits.—*Professor Wilson.*

Cant is the voluntary overcharging or prolongation of a real sentiment; hypocrisy is the setting up a pretension to a feeling you never had and have no wish for.—*Hazlitt.*

CARE.

All cares appear as large again as they are, owing to their emptiness and darkness; it is so with the grave.—*Richter.*

Second-hand cares, like second-hand clothes, come easily off and on.—*Dickens.*

Men do not avail themselves of the riches of God's grace. They love to nurse their cares, and seem as uneasy without some fret as an old friar would be without his hair girdle. They are commanded to cast their cares upon the Lord; but even when they attempt it, they do not fail to catch them up again, and think it meritorious to walk burdened.—*Beecher.*

Care keeps his watch in every old man's eye.
Shakespeare.

Quick is the succession of human events; the cares of to-day are seldom the cares of to-morrow; and when we lie down at night we may safely say to most of our troubles, Ye have done your worst, and we shall meet no more.—*Cowper.*

Our cares are the mothers, not only of our charities and virtues, but of our best joys and most cheering and enduring pleasures.—*Simms.*

Care, admitted as guest, quickly turns to be master.—*Bovee.*

Care seeks out wrinkled brows and hollow eyes, and builds himself caves to abide in them.
Beaumont and Fletcher.

Care is no cure, but rather corrosive for things that are not to be remedied.—*Shakespeare.*

Cares are often more difficult to throw off than sorrows; the latter die with time, the former grow upon it.—*Richter.*

To carry care to bed is to sleep with a pack on your back.—*Haliburton.*

Providence has given us hope and sleep as a compensation for the many cares of life.—
Voltaire.

O polished perturbation! golden care that keepest the ports of slumber open wide to many a watchful night!—*Shakespeare.*

CARICATURE.

Nothing conveys a more inaccurate idea of a whole truth than a part of a truth so promiuently brought forth as to throw the other parts into shadow. This is the art of caricature; and by the happy use of that art you might caricature the Apollo Belvidere.—
Bulwer Lytton.

The only good copies are those which point out the ridicule of bad originals.—
Rochefoucauld.

The great moral satirist, Hogarth, was once drawing in a room where many of his friends were assembled, and among them my mother. She was then a very young woman. As she stood by Hogarth, she expressed a wish to learn to draw caricature. "Alas, young lady," said Hogarth, "it is not a faculty to be envied! Take my advice, and never draw caricature; by the long practice of it, I have lost the enjoyment of beauty. I never see a face but distorted; I never have the satisfaction to behold the human face divine." We may suppose that such language from Hogarth would come with great effect; his manner was very earnest, and the confession is well deserving of remembrance.
Bishop Sandford.

A farce is that in poetry which grotesque (caricature) is in painting. The persons and actions of a farce are all unnatural, and the manners false, that is, inconsistent with the characters of mankind; and grotesque painting is the just resemblance of this.—*Dryden.*

CASTLES IN THE AIR.

Charming Alnaschar visions! it is the happy privilege of youth to construct you.—
Thackeray.

If you have built castles in the air, your work need not be lost; that is where they should be. Now put the foundations under them.—*Thoreau.*

A sigh can shatter a castle in the air.—
W. R. Alger.

Happy season of virtuous youth, when shame is still an impassable barrier, and the sacred air-cities of hope have not shrunk into the mean clay hamlets of reality; and man, by his nature, is yet infinite and free.—*Carlyle.*

Leave glory to great folks. Ah, castles in the air cost a vast deal to keep up!—
Bulwer Lytton.

In all assemblies, though you wedge them ever so close, we may observe this peculiar property, that over their heads there is room enough; but how to reach it is the difficult point. To this end the philosopher's way in all ages has been by erecting certain edifices in the air.—
Swift.

No tribute is laid on castles in the air.—
Churchill.

Ever building, building to the clouds, still building higher, and never reflecting that the poor narrow basis cannot sustain the giddy tottering column.—*Schiller.*

Thus we build on the ice, thus we write on the waves of the sea; the waves roaring pass away, the ice melts, and away goes our palace, like our thoughts.—*Herder.*

CAUSE.

I would seek unto God, and unto God would I commit my cause.—*Bible.*

Small causes are sufficient to make a man uneasy, when great ones are not in the way; for want of a block, he will stumble at a straw.
—*Swift.*

God befriend us, as our cause is just! —
Shakespeare.

A noble cause doth ease much a grievous case.—*Sir P. Sidney.*

CAUTION.

Man's caution often into danger turns, and his guard falling crushes him to death.— Young.

Pitchers have ears.—*Shakespeare.*

The bird alighteth not on the spread net when it beholds another bird in the snare. Take warning by the misfortunes of others, that others may not take example from you.—
Saadi.

All is to be feared where all is to be lost.—
Byron.

When you have need of a needle, you move your fingers delicately, with a wise caution. Use the same precaution with the inevitable dulness of life; give attention; keep yourself from imprudent precipitation; and do not take it by the point.—*Rance.*

When clouds are seen, wise men put on their cloaks.—*Shakespeare.*

Open your mouth and purse cautiously, and your stock of wealth and reputation shall, at least in repute, be great.—*Zimmermann.*

It is a good thing to learn caution by the misfortunes of others.—*Publius Syrus.*

CELERITY.

There is a medium between velocity and torpidity; the Italians say it is not necessary to be a stag, but we ought not to be a tortoise.—
Disraeli.

There is no secrecy comparable to celerity, like the motion of a bullet in the air which flieth so swift, it outruns the eye.—*Bacon.*

CENSURE.

Censure is the tax a man pays to the public for being eminent.—*Swift.*

Horace appears in good-humor while he censures, and therefore his censure has the more weight, as supposed to proceed from judgment, not from passion.— Young.

The readiest and surest way to get rid of censure is to correct ourselves.—*Demosthenes.*

The censure of those that are opposite to us is the nicest commendation that can be given us.
St. Evremond.

To arrive at perfection, a man should have very sincere friends, or inveterate enemies; because he would be made sensible of his good or ill conduct either by the censures of the one or the admonitions of the others.—*Diogenes.*

The villain's censure is extorted praise.—
Pope.

There are but three ways for a man to revenge himself of the censure of the world, — to despise it, to imitate the like, or to endeavor to live so as to avoid it; the first of these is usually pretended, the last is almost impossible, the universal practice is for the second.—*Swift.*

The death of censure is the death of genius.
Simms.

It is a folly for an eminent man to think of escaping censure, and a weakness to be affected with it. All the illustrious persons of antiquity, and indeed of every age in the world, have passed through this fiery persecution. There is no defence against reproach but obscurity; it is a kind of concomitant to greatness, as satires and invectives were an essential part of a Roman triumph.—*Addison.*

Few persons have sufficient wisdom to prefer censure which is useful to them to praise which deceives them.—*Rochefoucauld.*

Plutarch tells us of an idle and effeminate Etrurian who found fault with the manner in which Themistocles had conducted a recent campaign. "What," said the hero in reply, "have you, too, something to say about war, who are like the fish that has a sword, but no heart?" He is always the severest censor on the merits of others who has the least worth of his own.—*E. L. Magoon.*

It is harder to avoid censure than to gain applause; for this may be done by one great or wise action in an age. But to escape censure, a man must pass his whole life without saying or doing one ill or foolish thing.—*Hume.*

Some men's censures are like the blasts of rams' horns before the walls of Jericho; all a man's fame they lay level at one stroke, when all they go upon is only conceit, without any certain basis.—*J. Beaumont.*

CEREMONY.

When love begins to sicken and decay it useth an enforced ceremony.—*Shakespeare.*

If we use no ceremony towards others, we shall be treated without any. People are soon tired of paying trifling attentions to those who receive them with coldness, and return them with neglect.—*Hazlitt.*

It is superstition to repose our confidence in forms and ceremonies; but not to submit to them is pride.—*Pascal.*

Mankind are fond of inventing certain solemn and sounding expressions which appear to convey much, and in reality mean little; words that are the proxies of absent thoughts, and, like other proxies, add nothing to argument, while they turn the scales of decision.—*Shelley.*

To dispense with ceremony is the most delicate mode of conferring a compliment.— *Bulwer Lytton.*

All ceremonies are in themselves very silly things, but yet a man of the world should know them. They are the outworks of manners and decency, which would be too often broken in upon if it were not for that defence which keeps the enemy at a proper distance.—*Chesterfield.*

Ceremonies are different in every country; but true politeness is everywhere the same.— *Goldsmith.*

Ceremony was but devised at first to set a gloss on faint deeds, — hollow welcomes, recanting goodness, sorry e'er it is shown; but where there is true friendship there needs none.— *Shakespeare.*

Of what use are forms, seeing that at times they are empty? Of the same use as barrels, which at times are empty too.—*Hare.*

Truth and ceremony are two things. *Marcus Antoninus.*

I do not love much ceremony; suits in love should not, like suits in law, be rocked from term to term.—*Shirley.*

O ceremony, show me but thy worth! art thou aught else but place, degree, and form, creating fear and awe in other men?— *Shakespeare.*

As ceremony is the invention of wise men to keep fools at a distance, so good breeding is an expedient to make fools and wise men equals.— *Steele.*

No ashes are lighter than those of incense, and few things burn out sooner.—*Landor.*

Everything that tends to emancipate us from external restraint without adding to our own power of self-government is mischievous.— *Goethe.*

Ceremony is necessary as the outwork and defence of manners. — *Chesterfield.*

Ceremony keeps up things; it is like a penny glass to a rich spirit, or some excellent water; without it the water were spilt, and the spirit lost.—*Selden.*

There are ceremonious bows that throw you to a greater distance than the wrong end of any telescope.—*Ruffini.*

CHANCE.

There is no doubt such a thing as chance, but I see no reason why Providence should not make use of it.—*Simms.*

Chance is a term we apply to events to denote that they happen without any necessary or foreknown cause. When we say a thing happens by chance, we mean no more than that its cause is unknown to us, and not, as some vainly imagine, that chance itself can be the cause of anything.—*C. Buck.*

There are chords in the human heart — strange varying strings — which are only struck by accident; which will remain mute and senseless to appeals the most passionate and earnest, and respond at last to the slightest casual touch. In the most insensible or childish minds there is some train of reflection which art can seldom lead or skill assist, but which will reveal itself, as great truths have done, by chance, and when the discoverer has the plainest and simplest end in view.—*Dickens.*

Chance is but the pseudonyme of God for those particular cases which he does not choose to subscribe openly with his own sign-manual.— *Coleridge.*

Surely no man can reflect, without wonder, upon the vicissitudes of human life arising from causes in the highest degree accidental and trifling. If you trace the necessary concatenation of human events a very little way back, you may perhaps discover that a person's very going in or out of a door has been the means of coloring with misery or happiness the remaining current of his life.—*Lord Greville.*

The mines of knowledge are oft laid bare through the forked hazel wand of chance.— *Tupper.*

Chance never writ a legible book; chance never built a fair house; chance never drew a neat picture; it never did any of these things, nor ever will; nor can it be without absurdity supposed able to do them; which yet are works very gross and rude, very easy and feasible, as it were, in comparison to the production of a flower or a tree.—*Barrow.*

Chance corrects us of many faults that reason would not know how to correct.— *Rochefoucauld.*

Chance is always powerful; let your hook always be cast. In a pool where you least expect it there will be a fish.—*Ovid.*

There is no such thing as chance; and what seems to us merest accident springs from the deepest source of destiny.—*Schiller.*

The generality of men have, like plants, latent properties, which chance brings to light.—*Rochefoucauld.*

Many shining actions owe their success to chance though the 'general or statesman runs away with the applause.—*Henry Home.*

Be not too presumptuously sure in any business; for things of this world depend upon such a train of unseen chances that if it were in man's hands to set the tables, yet is he not certain to win the game.—*George Herbert.*

How often events, by chance, and unexpectedly, come to pass, which you had not dared even to hope for! —*Terence.*

CHANGE.

The world is a scene of changes, and to be constant in nature were inconstancy.—*Cowley.*

We do not know either unalloyed happiness or unmitigated misfortune. Everything in this world is a tangled yarn; we taste nothing in its purity, we do not remain two moments in the same state. Our affections, as well as bodies, are in a perpetual flux.—*Rousseau.*

What I possess I would gladly retain; change amuses the mind, yet scarcely profits.—*Goethe.*

Naught may endure but mutability.—*Shelley.*

Perfection is immutable. But for things imperfect, change is the way to perfect them. It gets the name of wilfulness when it will not admit of a lawful change to the better. Therefore constancy without knowledge cannot be always good. In things ill it is not virtue, but an absolute vice.—*Feltham.*

In the same brook none ever bathed him twice; to the same life none ever twice awoke.
Young.

All things human change.—*Tennyson.*

CHARACTER.

To know a people's character, we must see it at its homes, and look chiefly to the 'humbler abodes, where that portion of the people dwells which makes the broad basis of the national prosperity.—*Kossuth.*

There are beauties of character which, like the night-blooming Cereus, are closed against the glare and turbulence of every-day life, and bloom only in shade and solitude, and beneath the quiet stars.—*Tuckerman.*

Should any man tell you that a mountain had changed its place, you are at liberty to doubt it if you think fit; but if any one tells you that a man has changed his character, do not believe it.—*Mahomet.*

The craft with which the world is made runs also into the mind and character of men. No man is quite sane; each has a vein of folly in his composition, a slight determination of blood to the head, to make sure of holding him hard to some one point which Nature has taken to heart.—*Emerson.*

Character is very much a matter of health.—*Bovee.*

Some characters are like some bodies in chemistry; very good, perhaps, in themselves, yet fly off and refuse the least conjunction with each other.—*Lord Greville.*

Actions, looks, words, steps, form the alphabet by which you may spell character.—*Lavater.*

Character is always known. Thefts never enrich; alms never impoverish; murder will speak out of stone walls. The least admixture of a lie — for example, the taint of vanity, any attempt to make a good impression, a favorable appearance — will instantly vitiate the effect. But speak the truth, and all nature and all spirits help you with unexpected furtherance.—*Emerson.*

Circumstances form the character; but, like petrifying matters, they harden while they form.—*Landor.*

Instead of saying that man is the creature of circumstance, it would be nearer the mark to say that man is the architect of circumstance. It is character which builds an existence out of circumstance. Our strength is measured by our plastic power. From the same materials one man builds palaces, another hovels; one warehouses, another villas; bricks and mortar are mortar and bricks, until the architect can make them something else.—*Carlyle.*

Character is a perfectly educated will.—*Novalis.*

People of gloomy, uncheerful imaginations, or of envious, malignant tempers, whatever kind of life they are engaged in, will discover their natural tincture of mind in all their thoughts, words, and actions. As the finest wines have often the taste of the soil, so even the most religious thoughts often draw something that is particular from the constitution of the mind in which they arise.—*Addison.*

All men are alike in their lower natures; it is in their higher characters that they differ.—*Bovee.*

Never get a reputation for a small perfection if you are trying for fame in a loftier area. The world can only judge by generals, and it sees that those who pay considerable attention to minutiæ seldom have their minds occupied with great things.—*Bulwer Lytton.*

The effect of character is always to command consideration. We sport and toy and laugh with men or women who have none, but we never confide in them.—*Simms.*

Some men, like pictures, are fitter for a corner than a full light.—*Seneca.*

Duke Chartres used to boast that no man could have less real value for character than himself, yet he would gladly give twenty thousand pounds for a good one, because he could immediately make double that sum by means of it.—*Colton.*

The great hope of society is individual character.—*Channing.*

Ordinary people regard a man of a certain force and inflexibility of character as they do a lion. They look at him with a sort of wonder, perhaps they admire him; but they will on no account house with him.—*Merkel.*

Weakness of character is the only defect which cannot be amended.—*Rochefoucauld.*

The two most precious things this side the grave are our reputation and our life. But it is to be lamented that the most contemptible whisper may deprive us of the one, and the weakest weapon of the other.—*Colton.*

Give me the character and I will forecast the event. Character, it has in substance been said, is " victory organized."—*Bovee.*

The only equitable manner, in my opinion, of judging the character of a man is to examine if there are personal calculations in his conduct; if there are not, we may blame his manner of judging, but we are not the less bound to esteem him.—*Madame de Staël.*

There are peculiar ways in men, which discover what they are through the most subtle feints and close disguises.—*Bruyère.*

A man is known to his dog by the smell, to his tailor by the coat, to his friend by the smile; each of these know him, but how little or how much depends on the dignity of the intelligence. That which is truly and indeed characteristic of the man is known only to God.
Ruskin.

It is a quick and soft touch of many strings, all shutting up in one musical close; it is wit's descant on any plain song.—*Sir T. Overbury.*

We are sometimes as different from ourselves as we are from others.—*Rochefoucauld.*

Each man forms his duty according to his predominant characteristic; the stern require an avenging judge; the gentle, a forgiving father. Just so the pygmies declared that Jove himself was a pygmy.—*Bulwer Lytton.*

Characters never change. Opinions alter, — characters are only developed.—*Disraeli.*

A good character is, in all cases, the fruit of personal exertion. It is not inherited from parents, it is not created by external advantages, it is no necessary appendage of birth, wealth, talents, or station; but it is the result of one's own endeavors.—*Hawes.*

Best men are moulded out of faults.—
Shakespeare.

Joy and grief decide character. What exalts prosperity? what imbitters grief? what leaves us indifferent? what interests us? As the interest of man, so his God, — as his God, so he.—*Lavater.*

This is that which we call character, — a reserved force which acts directly by presence, and without means.—*Emerson.*

We should not be too hasty in bestowing either our praise or censure on mankind, since we shall often find such a mixture of good and evil in the same character, that it may require a very accurate judgment and a very elaborate inquiry to determine on which side the balance turns.—*Fielding.*

What is the true test of character, unless it be its progressive development in the bustle and turmoil, in the action and reaction, of daily life?—*Goethe.*

We must have a weak spot or two in a character before we can love it much. People that do not laugh or cry, or take more of anything than is good for them, or use anything but dictionary words, are admirable subjects for biographies. But we don't always care most for those flat-pattern flowers that press best in the herbarium.
Holmes.

The most brilliant qualities become useless when they are not sustained by force of character.—*Ségur.*

Character is the spiritual body of the person, and represents the individualization of vital experience, the conversion of unconscious things into self-conscious men.—*Whipple.*

Every man has in himself a continent of undiscovered character. Happy is he who acts the Columbus to his own soul.—*Sir J. Stephens*

A man's character is the reality of himself; his reputation, the opinion others have formed about him; character resides in him, reputation in other people; that is the substance, this is the shadow.—*Beecher.*

Gross and obscene natures, however decorated, seem impure shambles; but character gives splendor to youth, and awe to wrinkled skin and gray hairs.—*Emerson.*

Fine natures are like fine poems; a glance at the first two lines suffices for a guess into the beauty that waits you if you read on.— *Bulwer Lytton.*

It is an error common to many to take the character of mankind from the worst and basest amongst them; whereas, as an excellent writer has observed, nothing should be esteemed as characteristical of a species but what is to be found amongst the best and the most perfect individuals of that species.—*Fielding.*

The most striking characters are sometimes the product of an infinity of little accidents.— *Danton.*

It is a common error, of which a wise man will beware, to measure the worth of our neighbor by his conduct towards ourselves. How many rich souls might we not rejoice in the knowledge of, were it not for our pride!— *Richter.*

Character is a wish for a perfect education.— *Novalis.*

The noblest contribution which any man can make for the benefit of posterity is that of a good character. The richest bequest which any man can leave to the youth of his native land is that of a shining, spotless example.— *Winthrop.*

Strong characters are brought out by change of situation, and gentle ones by permanence.— *Richter.*

Only what we have wrought into our character during life can we take away with us.— *Wilhelm von Humboldt.*

Most natures are insolvent; cannot satisfy their own wants, have an ambition out of all proportion to their practical force, and so do lean and beg day and night continually.— *Emerson.*

Character, like porcelain ware, must be printed before it is glazed. There can be no change after it is burned in.—*Beecher.*

Character is what nature has engraven in us; can we then efface it?—*Voltaire.*

Remedy your deficiencies, and your merits will take care of themselves. Every man has in him good and evil. His good is his valiant army, his evil is his corrupt commissariat; reform the commissariat, and the army will do its duty.—*Bulwer Lytton.*

Certain trifling flaws sit as disgracefully on a character of elegance as a ragged button on a court dress.—*Lavater.*

The fine tints and fluent curves which constitute beauty of character.—*Bulwer Lytton.*

It is amusing to detect character in the vocabulary of each person. The adjectives habitually used, like the inscriptions on a thermometer, indicate the temperament.—*Tuckerman.*

Say not you know another entirely till you have divided an inheritance with him.— *Lavater.*

It is not what a man gets, but what a man is, that he should think of. He should first think of his character, and then of his condition. He that has character need have no fears about his condition. Character will draw after it condition. Circumstances obey principles.— *Beecher.*

As your enemies and your friends, so are you.—*Lavater.*

Talents are nurtured best in solitude, but character on life's tempestuous sea.—*Goethe.*

The amiable and the severe, Mr. Burke's sublime and beautiful, by different proportions, are mixed in every character. Accordingly, as either is predominant, men imprint the passions of love or fear. The best punch depends on a proper mixture of sugar and lemons.— *Shenstone.*

Individual character is in the right that is in strict consistence with itself. Self-contradiction is the only wrong.—*Schiller.*

A man who shows no defect is a fool or a hypocrite, whom we should mistrust. There are defects so bound to fine qualities that they announce them, — defects which it is well not to correct.—*Joubert.*

The most accomplished persons have usually some defect, some weakness in their characters, which diminishes the lustre of their brighter qualifications.—*Junius.*

Your disposition will be suitable to that which you most frequently think on; for the soul is, as it were, tinged with the color and complexion of its own thoughts.— *Marcus Antoninus.*

A man's character is like his shadow, which sometimes follows and sometimes precedes him, and which is occasionally longer, occasionally shorter, than he is.— *Madame de la Rochejaquelein.*

Those who quit their proper character to assume what does not belong to them are, for the greater part, ignorant both of the character they leave and of the character they assume.— *Burke.*

A German writer observes : "The noblest characters only show themselves in their real light. All others act comedy with their fellowmen even unto the grave."—*Lady Blessington.*

CHARITY.

As every lord giveth a certain livery to his servants, charity is the very livery of Christ. Our Saviour, who is the Lord above all lords, would have his servants known by their badge, which is love.—*Latimer.*

How white are the fair robes of Charity, as she walketh amid the lowly habitations of the poor!—*Hosea Ballou.*

The Shepherds led the Pilgrims to Mount Charity, where they showed them a man that had a bundle of cloth lying before him, out of which he cut coats and garments for the poor that stood about him; yet his bundle or roll of cloth was never the less. Then said they, "What should this be?" "This is," said the Shepherds, "to show you, that he who has a heart to give of his labor to the poor shall never want wherewithal. 'He that watereth shall be watered himself.' And the cake that the widow gave to the prophet did not cause that she had the less in her barrel."—*Bunyan.*

The heart of a girl is like a convent, — the holier the cloister, the more charitable the door. *Bulwer Lytton.*

To complain that life has no joys while there is a single creature whom we can relieve by our bounty, assist by our counsels, or enliven by our presence, is to lament the loss of that which we possess, and is just as irrational as to die of thirst with the cup in our hands.— *Fitzosborne.*

Charity is an eternal debt, and without limit.—*Pasquier Quesnel.*

If there be a pleasure on earth which angels cannot enjoy, and which they might almost envy man the possession of, it is the power of relieving distress, — if there be a pain which devils might pity man for enduring, it is the death-bed reflection that we have possessed the power of doing good, but that we have abused and perverted it to purposes of ill.—*Colton.*

That comes too late that comes for the asking.—*Seneca.*

Nothing truly can be termed mine own but what I make mine own by using well. Those deeds of charity which we have done shall stay forever with us; and that wealth which we have so bestowed we only keep; the other is not ours.—*Middleton.*

It is good to be charitable; but to whom? That is the point. As to the ungrateful, there is not one who does not at last die miserable. —*La Fontaine.*

Heaven be their resource who have no other but the charity of the world, the stock of which, I fear, is no way sufficient for the many great claims which are hourly made upon it.—*Sterne.*

Charity, though enjoined by the Christian law, and the law of nature itself, is withal so pleasant that if any duty can be said to be its own reward, or to pay us while we are discharging it, it is this.—*Fielding.*

A woman who wants a charitable heart wants a pure mind.—*Haliburton.*

The spirit of the world encloses four kinds of spirits, diametrically opposed to charity, — the spirit of resentment, spirit of aversion, spirit of jealousy, and the spirit of indifference.— *Bossuet.*

But when thou doest alms, let not thy left hand know what thy right hand doeth.—*Bible.*

I have much more confidence in the charity which begins in the home and diverges into a large humanity, than in the world-wide philanthropy which begins at the outside of our horizon to converge into egotism.— *Mrs. Jameson.*

Charity is the scope of all God's commands. *St. Chrysostom.*

When I die, I should be ashamed to leave enough to build me a monument if there were a wanting friend above ground. I would enjoy the pleasure of what I give by giving it alive and seeing another enjoy it.—*Pope.*

It is fruition, and not possession, that renders us happy.—*Montaigne.*

Posthumous charities are the very essence of selfishness, when bequeathed by those who, when alive, would part with nothing.—*Colton.*

Though we may sometimes unintentionally bestow our beneficence on the unworthy, it does not take from the merit of the act. For charity doth not adopt the vices of its objects.— *Fielding.*

True charity is not methodical, and scarcely judicious, so to speak, but is liable to excesses and transports.—*Massillon.*

Be not frightened at the hard words "imposition," "imposture"; give, and ask no questions. Cast thy bread upon the waters. Some have, unawares, entertained angels.—*Lamb.*

True charity is spontaneous and finds its own occasion; it is never the offspring of importunity, nor of emulation.—*Hosea Ballou.*

I would have none of that rigid, circumspect charity which is never done without scrutiny, and which always mistrusts the truth of the necessities laid open to it.—*Massillon.*

Our possessions are wholly in our performances. He owes nothing to whom the world owes nothing.—*Simms.*

It is an old saying, that charity begins at home; but this is no reason it should not go abroad. A man should live with the world as a citizen of the world; he may have a preference for the particular quarter or square, or even alley, in which he lives, but he should have a generous feeling for the welfare of the whole.— *Cumberland.*

Charity, — gently to hear, kindly to judge. *Shakespeare.*

Beneficence is a duty. He who frequently practises it, and sees his benevolent intentions realized, at length comes really to love him to whom he has done good.—*Kant*

For charity shall cover the multitude of sins.—*Bible.*

Charity is that rational and constant affection which makes us sacrifice ourselves to the human race, as if we were united with it, so as to form one individual, partaking equally in its adversity and prosperity.—*Confucius.*

Large charity doth never soil, but only whitens soft white hands.—*Lowell.*

A man should fear when he enjoys only what good he does publicly. Is it not the publicity, rather than the charity, that he loves?— *Beecher.*

The charities of life are scattered everywhere, enamelling the vales of human beings as the flowers paint the meadows. They are not the fruit of study, nor the privilege of refinement, but a natural instinct.—*Bancroft.*

Charity resembleth fire, which inflameth all things it toucheth.—*Erasmus.*

There is no dearth of charity in the world in giving, but there is comparatively little exercised in thinking and speaking.— *Sir P. Sidney.*

Be charitable and indulgent to every one but yourself.—*Joubert.*

Proportion thy charity to the strength of thy estate, lest God proportion thy estate to the weakness of thy charity; let the lips of the poor be the trumpet of thy gift, lest in seeking applause, thou lose thy reward. Nothing is more pleasing to God than an open hand and a close mouth.—*Quarles.*

A rich man without charity is a rogue; and perhaps it would be no difficult matter to prove that he is also a fool.—*Fielding.*

I have no respect for that self-boasting charity which neglects all objects of commiseration near and around it, but goes to the end of the earth in search of misery, for the purpose of talking about it.—*George Mason.*

Our true acquisitions lie only in our charities. We gain only as we give. There is no beggar so destitute as he who can afford nothing to his neighbor.—*Simms.*

My poor are my best patients. God pays for them.—*Boerhaave.*

We should give as we would receive, cheerfully, quickly, and without hesitation; for there is no grace in a benefit that sticks to the fingers. *Seneca.*

That charity is bad which takes from independence its proper pride, from mendicity its salutary shame.—*Southey.*

Flatter not thyself in thy faith to God, if thou wantest charity for thy neighbor; and think not thou hast charity for thy neighbor, if thou wantest faith to God; where they are not both together, they are both wanting; they are both dead, if once divided.—*Quarles.*

The secret pleasure of a generous act is the great mind's great bribe.—*Dryden.*

I thank Heaven I have often had it in my power to give help and relief, and this is still my greatest pleasure. If I could choose my sphere of action now, it would be that of the most simple and direct efforts of this kind.— *Niebuhr.*

In giving of thy alms, inquire not so much into the person, as his necessity. God looks not so much upon the merits of him that requires, as into the manner of him that relieves; if the man deserve not, thou hast given it to humanity. *Quarles.*

You must have a genius for charity as well as for anything else. As for doing good, that is one of the professions which are full.— *Thoreau.*

In all other human gifts and passions, though they advance nature, yet they are subject to excess; but charity alone admits no excess. For so we see, by aspiring to be like God in power the angels transgressed and fell; by aspiring to be like God in knowledge man transgressed and fell; but by aspiring to be like God in goodness or love neither man nor angel ever did or shall transgress. For unto that imitation we are called.—*Bacon.*

And learn the luxury of doing good. *Goldsmith.*

He who has never denied himself for the sake of giving has but glanced at the joys of charity. We owe our superfluity, and to be happy in the performance of our duty we must exceed it.—*Madame Swetchine.*

Wherever the tree of beneficence takes root, it sends forth branches beyond the sky!—*Saadi.*

The last best fruit which comes to late perfection, even in the kindliest soul, is tenderness toward the hard, forbearance toward the unforbearing, warmth of heart toward the cold, philanthropy toward the misanthropic.—*Richter.*

Cast thy bread upon the waters; for thou shalt find it after many days.—*Bible.*

Charity suffereth long, and is kind; charity envieth not; charity vaunteth not itself, is not puffed up, doth not behave itself unseemly, seeketh not her own, is not easily provoked, thinketh no evil; rejoiceth not in iniquity, but rejoiceth in the truth; beareth all things, believeth all things, hopeth all things, endureth all things.—*Bible.*

Charity is that sweet-smelling savor of Jesus Christ which vanishes and is extinguished from the moment that it is exposed.—
Massillon.

Active beneficence is a virtue of easier practice than forbearance after having conferred, or than thankfulness after having received, a benefit. I know not, indeed, whether it be a greater and more difficult exercise of magnanimity, for the one party to act as if he had forgotten, or for the other as if he constantly remembered, the obligation.—*Canning*

There can be no Christianity where there is no charity.—*Colton.*

It is with charity as with money,—the more we stand in need of it, the less we have to give away.—*Bovee.*

Shut not thy purse-strings always against painted distress. Act a charity sometimes. When a poor creature (outwardly and visibly such) comes before thee, do not stay to inquire whether the "seven small children," in whose name he implores thy assistance, have a veritable existence. Rake not into the bowels of unwelcome truth to save a halfpenny. It is good to believe him.—*Lamb.*

And now abideth faith, hope, charity, these three; but the greatest of these is charity.—
Bible.

The charities that soothe and heal and bless are scattered at the feet of man like flowers.—*Wordsworth.*

I will chide no breather in the world but myself; against whom I know most faults.—
Shakespeare.

Charity ever finds in the act reward, and needs no trumpet in the receiver.—
Beaumont and Fletcher.

We are rich only through what we give, and poor only through what we refuse.—
Madame Swetchine.

CHASTITY.

Not the mountain ice, congealed to crystals, is so frosty chaste as thy victorious soul, which conquers man and man's proud tyrant-passion.—*Dryden.*

Nothing makes a woman more esteemed by the opposite sex than chastity; whether it be that we always prize those most who are hardest to come at, or that nothing besides chastity, with its collateral attendants, truth, fidelity, and constancy, gives the man a property in the person he loves, and consequently endears her to him above all things.—*Addison.*

Chastity, once lost, cannot be recalled; it goes only once.—*Ovid.*

A pure mind in a chaste body is the mother of wisdom and deliberation, sober counsels and ingenuous actions, open deportment and sweet carriage, sincere principles and unprejudicate understanding, love of God and self-denial, peace and confidence, holy prayers and spiritual comfort, and a pleasure of spirit infinitely greater than the sottish pleasure of unchastity.—
Jeremy Taylor.

He comes too near that comes to be denied.
Sir Thomas Overbury.

There needs not strength to be added to inviolate chastity; the excellency of the mind makes the body impregnable.—*Sir P. Sidney.*

Of chastity, the ornaments are chaste.
Shakespeare.

Chaste as the icicle that is curdled by the frost from purest snow, and hangs on Dian's temple.—*Shakespeare.*

The woman that deliberates is lost.—
Addison.

Chaster than crystal on the Scythian cliffs, the more the proud winds court it, still the purer.—*Beaumont.*

A man defines his standing at the court of chastity by his views of women. He cannot be any man's friend nor his own if not hers.—
Alcott.

CHEERFULNESS.

I had rather have a fool to make me merry than experience to make me sad.—*Shakespeare.*

If good people would but make their goodness agreeable, and smile instead of frowning in their virtue, how many would they win to the good cause!—*Archbishop Usher.*

The most manifest sign of wisdom is continued cheerfulness.—*Montaigne.*

If the soul be happily disposed, everything becomes capable of affording entertainment, and distress will almost want a name.—*Goldsmith.*

Mirth is like a flash of lightning that breaks through a gloom of clouds and glitters for a moment. Cheerfulness keeps up a daylight in the mind, filling it with a steady and perpetual serenity.—*Johnson.*

If there is a virtue in the world at which we should always aim, it is cheerfulness.—*Bulwer Lytton.*

The lightsome countenance of a friend giveth such an inward decking to the house where it lodgeth, as proudest palaces have cause to envy the gilding.—*Sir P. Sidney.*

The industrious bee does not stop to complain that there are so many poisonous flowers and thorny branches in his road, but buzzes on, selecting the honey where he can find it, and passing quietly by the places where it is not. There is enough in this world to complain about and find fault with, if men have the disposition. We often travel on a hard and uneven road; but with a cheerful spirit, and a heart to praise God for his mercies, we may walk therein with comfort, and come to the end of our journey in peace.—*Dewey.*

An ounce of cheerfulness is worth a pound of sadness to serve God with.—*Fuller.*

Cheerfulness is a friend to grace, it puts the heart in tune to praise God. Uncheerful Christians, like the spies, bring an evil report on the good land; others suspect there is something unpleasant in religion, that they who profess it hang their harps upon the willows and walk so dejectedly. Be serious, yet cheerful. Rejoice in the Lord always.—*Rev. T. Watson.*

I have always preferred cheerfulness to mirth. The latter I consider as an art, the former as a habit of mind. Mirth is short and transient, cheerfulness fixed and permanent.—*Addison.*

The burden becomes light which is cheerfully borne.—*Ovid.*

True joy is a serene and sober motion, and they are miserably out that take laughing for rejoicing; the seat of it is within, and there is no cheerfulness like the resolutions of a brave mind.—*Seneca.*

The cheerful live longest in life, and after it, in our regards. Cheerfulness is the offshoot of goodness.—*Bovee.*

Be thou of good cheer.—*Bible.*

The habit of looking on the best side of every event is worth more than a thousand pounds a year.—*Johnson.*

Youth will never live to age unless they keep themselves in breath with exercise, and in heart with joyfulness.—*Sir P. Sidney.*

Let me play the fool; with mirth and laughter let old wrinkles come; and let my liver rather heat with wine than my heart cool with mortifying groans. Why should a man whose blood is warm within sit like his grandsire cut in alabaster, sleep when he wakes, and creep into the jaundice by being peevish?—*Shakespeare.*

The mind that is cheerful in its present state will be averse to all solicitude as to the future, and will meet the bitter occurrences of life with a smile.—*Horace.*

Cheerful looks make every dish a feast, and it is that which crowns a welcome.—*Massinger.*

A cheerful-temper spreads like the dawn, and all vapors disperse before it. Even the tear dries on the cheek, and the sigh sinks away half-breathed when the eye of benignity beams upon the unhappy.—*Jane Porter.*

To be free-minded and cheerfully disposed at hours of meat and sleep and of exercise is one of the best precepts of long lasting.—*Bacon.*

A light heart lives long.—*Shakespeare.*

I live in a constant endeavor to fence against the infirmities of ill-health, and other evils of life, by mirth; being firmly persuaded that every time a man smiles, but much more when he laughs, it adds something to his fragment of life.—*Sterne.*

Cheerfulness is health; the opposite, melancholy, is disease.—*Haliburton.*

I have observed that in comedies the best actor plays the droll, while some scrub rogue is made the fine gentleman or hero. Thus it is in the farce of life. Wise men spend their time in mirth; it is only fools who are serious.—*Bolingbroke.*

A merry heart doeth good like a medicine; but a broken spirit drieth the bones.—*Bible.*

Cheerfulness is always to be kept up if a man is out of pain; but mirth, to a prudent man, should always be accidental. It should naturally arise out of the occasion, and the occasion seldom be laid for it.—*Steele.*

To be happy, the passions must be cheerful and gay, not gloomy and melancholy. A propensity to hope and joy is real riches; one to fear and sorrow, real poverty.—*Hume.*

You find yourself refreshed by the presence of cheerful people. Why not make earnest effort to confer that pleasure on others? You will find half the battle is gained if you never allow yourself to say anything gloomy.—*Mrs. L. M. Child.*

The creed of the true saint is to make the best of life, and make the most of it.—*Chapin.*

I cannot tell how much I esteem and admire your good and happy temperament. What folly not to take advantage of circumstances, and enjoy gratefully the consolations which God sends us after the afflictive dispensations which he sometimes sees proper to make us feel! It seems to me to be a proof of great wisdom to submit with resignation to the storm, and enjoy the calm when it pleases him to give it us again. — *Madame de Sévigné.*

God is glorified, not by our groans, but our thanksgivings; and all good thought and good action claim a natural alliance with good cheer. — *Whipple.*

Give us, O give us, the man who sings at his work! Be his occupation what it may, he is equal to any of those who follow the same pursuit in silent sullenness. He will do more in the same time, — he will do it better, — he will persevere longer. One is scarcely sensible of fatigue whilst he marches to music. The very stars are said to make harmony as they revolve in their spheres. Wondrous is the strength of cheerfulness, altogether past calculation its powers of endurance. Efforts, to be permanently useful, must be uniformly joyous, — a spirit all sunshine, — graceful from very gladness, — beautiful because bright. — *Carlyle.*

A cheerful, easy, open countenance will make fools think you a good-natured man, and make designing men think you an undesigning one. — *Chesterfield.*

Cheerfulness is the best promoter of health. Repinings and murmurings of the heart give imperceptible strokes to those delicate fibres of which the vital parts are composed, and wear out the machine. Cheerfulness is as friendly to the mind as to the body. — *Addison.*

There seem to be some persons, the favorites of fortune and darlings of nature, who are born cheerful. "A star danced" at their birth. It is no superficial visibility, but a bountiful and beneficent soul that sparkles in their eyes and smiles on their lips. Their inborn geniality amounts to genius, — the rare and difficult genius which creates sweet and wholesome character, and radiates cheer. — *Whipple.*

What can the Creator see with greater pleasure than a happy creature? — *Lessing.*

Cheerfulness is just as natural to the heart of a man in strong health as color to his cheek; and wherever there is habitual gloom, there must be either bad air, unwholesome food, improperly severe labor, or erring habits of life. — *Ruskin.*

Cheerfulness bears the same friendly regard to the mind as to the body; it banishes all anxious care and discontent, soothes and composes the passions and keeps them in a perpetual calm. — *Addison.*

I have told you of the Spaniard who always put on his spectacles when about to eat cherries, that they might look bigger and more tempting. In like manner I make the most of my enjoyments; and though I do not cast my eyes away from my troubles, I pack them in as little compass as I can for myself, and never let them annoy others. — *Southey.*

When Goethe says that in every human condition foes lie in wait for us, "invincible only by cheerfulness and equanimity," he does not mean that we can at all times be really cheerful, or at a moment's notice; but that the endeavor to look at the better side of things will produce the habit, and that this habit is the surest safeguard against the danger of sudden evils. — *Leigh Hunt.*

Every human soul has the germ of some flowers within; and they would open if they could only find sunshine and free air to expand in. I always told you that not having enough of sunshine was what ailed the world. Make people happy, and there will not be half the quarrelling or a tenth part of the wickedness there is. — *Mrs. L. M. Child.*

Cheerfulness ought to be the *viaticum vitæ* of their life to the old; age without cheerfulness is a Lapland winter without a sun. — *Colton.*

Nothing will supply the want of sunshine to peaches, and, to make knowledge valuable, you must have the cheerfulness of wisdom. Whenever you are sincerely pleased you are nourished. The joy of the spirit indicates its strength. All healthy things are sweet-tempered. Genius works in sport, and goodness smiles to the last. — *Emerson.*

A cheerful temper, joined with innocence, will make beauty attractive, knowledge delightful, and wit good-natured. It will lighten sickness, poverty, and affliction, convert ignorance into an amiable simplicity, and render deformity itself agreeable. — *Addison.*

CHILDREN.

No man can tell but he that loves his children how many delicious accents make a man's heart dance in the pretty conversation of those dear pledges. — *Jeremy Taylor.*

Children have more need of models than of critics. — *Joubert.*

An infallible way to make your child miserable is to satisfy all his demands. Passion swells by gratification; and the impossibility of satisfying every one of his demands will oblige you to stop short at last, after he has become a little headstrong. — *Henry Home.*

I love these little people; and it is not a slight thing when they, who are so fresh from God, love us. — *Dickens.*

Children generally hate to be idle; all the care then is that their busy humor should be constantly employed in something of use to them.—*Locke.*

The whining schoolboy, with his satchel and shining morning face, creeping like snail unwillingly to school.—*Shakespeare.*

Happy season of childhood ! Kind Nature, that art to all a bountiful mother ; that visitest the poor man's hut with auroral radiance ; and for thy nursling hast provided a soft swathing of love and infinite hope wherein he waxes and slumbers, danced round by sweetest dreams !— *Carlyle.*

Childhood is the sleep of reason.—*Rousseau.*

The child's grief throbs against the round of its little heart as heavily as the man's sorrow ; and the one finds as much delight in his kite or drum as the other in striking the springs of enterprise or soaring on the wings of fame.— *Chapin.*

Who is not attracted by bright and pleasant children, to prattle, to creep, and to play with them ?—*Epictetus.*

Beware of fatiguing them by ill-judged exactness. If virtue offer itself to a child under a melancholy and constrained aspect, if liberty and license present themselves under an agreeable form, all is lost, your labor is in vain.— *Fenelon.*

Children have neither past nor future ; and, what scarcely ever happens to us, they enjoy the present.—*Bruyère.*

The least and most imperceptible impressions received in our infancy, have consequences very important, and of a long duration. It is with these first impressions, as with a river whose waters we can easily turn, by different canals, in quite opposite courses, so that from the insensible direction the stream receives at its source, it takes different directions, and at last arrives at places far distant from each other ; and with the same facility we may, I think, turn the minds of children to what direction we please.—*Locke.*

Living jewels dropped unstained from heaven.—*Pollok.*

If I were to choose among all gifts and qualities that which, on the whole, makes life pleasantest, I should select the love of children. No circumstance can render this world wholly a solitude to one who has this possession.— *T. W. Higginson.*

Children sweeten labors, but they make misfortunes more bitter ; they increase the cares of of life, but they mitigate the remembrance of death.—*Bacon.*

A creature undefiled by the taint of the world, unvexed by its injustice, unwearied by its hollow pleasures ; a being fresh from the source of light, with something of its universal lustre in it. If childhood be this, how holy the duty to see that in its onward growth it shall be no other ! —*Douglas Jerrold.*

Your little child is your only true democrat. *Mrs. Stowe.*

Children are very nice observers, and they will often perceive your slightest defects. In general, those who govern children forgive nothing in them, but everything in themselves. *Fenelon.*

I know that a sweet child is the sweetest thing in nature, not even excepting the delicate creatures which bear them ; but the prettier the kind of a thing is, the more desirable it is that it should be pretty of its kind. One daisy differs not much from another in glory ; but a violet should look and smell the daintiest.— *Lamb.*

A torn jacket is soon mended ; but hard words bruise the heart of a child.—*Longfellow.*

It always grieves me to contemplate the initiation of children into the ways of life when they are scarcely more than infants. It checks their confidence and simplicity, two of the best qualities that Heaven gives them, and demands that they share our sorrows before they are capable of entering into our enjoyments.— *Dickens.*

I hardly know so melancholy a reflection as that parents are necessarily the sole directors of the management of children, whether they have or have not judgment, penetration, or taste to perform the task.—*Lord Greville.*

In bringing up a child, think of its old age. *Joubert.*

Bring together all the children of the universe, you will see nothing in them but innocence, gentleness, and fear ; were they born wicked, spiteful, and cruel, some signs of it would come from them ; as little snakes strive to bite, and little tigers to tear. But nature having been as sparing of offensive weapons to man as to pigeons and rabbits, it cannot have given them an instinct to mischief and destruction.—*Voltaire.*

Blessed be the hand that prepares a pleasure for a child, for there is no saying when and where it may bloom forth.—*Douglas Jerrold.*

If a boy is not trained to endure and to bear trouble, he will grow up a girl ; and a boy that is a girl has all a girl's weakness without any of her regal qualities. A woman made out of a woman is God's noblest work ; a woman made out of a man is his meanest.—*Beecher.*

Who feels injustice, who shrinks before a slight, who has a sense of wrong so acute, and so glowing a gratitude to flow from grief at one's own kindness, as a generous boy?—*Thackeray.*

A child is an angel dependent on man.—
Count de Maistre.

When a child can be brought to tears, not from fear of punishment, but from repentance for his offence, he needs no chastisement. When the tears begin to flow from grief at one's own conduct, be sure there is an angel nestling in the bosom.—*Horace Mann.*

Happy child! the cradle is still to thee a vast space; become a man, and the boundless world will be too small to thee.—*Schiller.*

A child's eyes, those clear wells of undefiled thought,—what on earth can be more beautiful? Full of hope, love, and curiosity, they meet your own. In prayer, how earnest; in joy, how sparkling; in sympathy, how tender! The man who never tried the companionship of a little child has carelessly passed by one of the great pleasures of life, as one passes a rare flower without plucking it or knowing its value.—
Mrs. Norton.

That season of childhood, when the soul, on the rainbow bridge of fancy, glides along, dry-shod, over the walls and ditches of this lower earth.—*Richter.*

Children are the to-morrow of society.—
Whately.

Be very vigilant over thy child in the April of his understanding, lest the frost of May nip his blossoms. While he is a tender twig, straighten him; whilst he is a new vessel, season him; such as thou makest him, such commouly shalt thou find him. Let his first lesson be obedience, and his second shall be what thou wilt.—*Quarles.*

Childhood, who like an April morn appears, sunshine and rain, hopes clouded o'er with fears.
Churchill.

Be ever gentle with the children God has given you; watch over them constantly; reprove them earnestly, but not in anger. In the forcible language of Scripture, "Be not bitter against them." "Yes, they are good boys," I once heard a kind father say. "I talk to them very much, but do not like to beat my children,—the world will beat them." It was a beautiful thought, though not elegantly expressed.—
Elihu Burritt.

Our children that die young are like those spring bulbs which have their flowers prepared beforehand, and leave nothing to do but to break ground, and blossom, and pass away. Thank God for spring flowers among men, as well as among the grasses of the field.—*Beecher.*

I do not like punishments. You will never torture a child into duty; but a sensible child will dread the frown of a judicious mother more than all the rods, dark rooms, and scolding schoolmistresses in the universe.—*H. K. White.*

A man looketh on his little one as a being of better hope; in himself ambition is dead, but it hath a resurrection in his son.—*Tupper.*

A rose with all its sweetest leaves yet folded.
Byron.

Above all things endeavor to breed them up in the love of virtue, and that holy plain way of it which we have lived in, that the world in no part of it get into my family. I had rather they were homely than finely bred as to outward behavior; yet I love sweetness mixed with gravity, and cheerfulness tempered with sobriety.—*William Penn.*

Childhood shows the man, as morning shows the day.—*Milton.*

Truly there is nothing in the world so blessed or so sweet as the heritage of children.
Mrs. Oliphant.

Children are the hands by which we take hold of heaven. By these tendrils we clasp it and climb thitherward. And why do we think that we are separated from them? We never half knew them, nor in this world could.—
Beecher.

Call not that man wretched who, whatever ills he suffers, has a child to love.—*Southey.*

In trying to teach children a great deal in a short time, they are treated not as though the race they were to run was for life, but simply a three-mile heat.—*Horace Mann.*

I have often thought what a melancholy world this would be without children, and what an inhuman world without the aged.—*Coleridge.*

God sends children for another purpose than merely to keep up the race,—to enlarge our hearts, to make us unselfish, and full of kindly sympathies and affections; to give our souls higher aims, and to call out all our faculties to extended enterprise and exertion; to bring round our fireside bright faces and happy smiles, and loving, tender hearts. My soul blesses the Great Father every day, that he has gladdened the earth with little children.—*Mary Howitt.*

Children will grow up substantially what they are by nature,—and only that.—
Mrs. Stowe.

The children of the poor are so apt to look as if the rich would have been over-blest with such! Alas for the angel capabilities, interrupted so soon with care, and with after life so sadly unfulfilled!—*Willis.*

A child is man in a small letter, yet the best copy of Adam before he tasted of Eve or the apple; and he is happy whose small practice in the world can only write his character. His soul is yet a white paper unscribbled with observations of the world, wherewith at length it becomes a blurred note-book. He is purely happy because he knows no evil, nor hath made means by sin to be acquainted with misery.— *Bishop Earle.*

In praising or loving a child, we love and praise not that which is, but that which we hope for.—*Goethe.*

Just as the twig is bent the tree is inclined. *Pope.*

While childhood, and while dreams, reducing childhood, shall be left, imagination shall not have spread her holy wings totally to fly the earth.—*Lamb.*

Call not that man wretched, who whatever else he suffers as to pain inflicted, or pleasure denied, has a child for whom he hopes and on whom he doats.—*Coleridge.*

The plays of natural lively children are the infancy of art. Children live in a world of imagination and feeling. They invest the most insignificant object with any form they please, and see in it whatever they wish to see.— *Oehlenschläger.*

"Beware," said Lavater, "of him who hates the laugh of a child." "I love God and little children," was the simple yet sublime sentiment of Richter.—*Mrs. Sigourney*

What gift has Providence bestowed on man that is so dear to him as his children ?—*Cicero.*

The child is father of the man.—*Wordsworth.*

Of all sights which can soften and humanize the heart of men, there is none that ought so surely to reach it as that of innocent children, enjoying the happiness which is their proper and natural portion.—*Southey*

Is the world all grown up ? Is childhood dead ? Or is there not in the bosom of the wisest and the best some of the child's heart left, to respond to its earliest enchantments ?—*Lamb.*

Many children, many cares; no children, no felicity.—*Bovee.*

A child's existence is a bright, soft element of joy, out of which, as in Prospero's Island, wonder after wonder bodies itself forth, to teach by charming.—*Rodney.*

We should amuse our evening hours of life in cultivating the tender plants, and bringing them to perfection, before they are transplanted to a happier clime.—*Washington.*

Every child walks into existence through the golden gate of love.—*Beecher.*

A man shall see, where there is a house full of children, one or two of the eldest restricted, and the youngest ruined by indulgence; but in the midst, some that are, as it were, forgotten, who many times, nevertheless, prove the best.— *Bacon.*

The training of children is a profession where we must know to lose time in order to gain it.—*Rousseau.*

Children, like dogs, have so sharp and fine a scent, that they detect and hunt out everything, — the bad before all the rest. They also know well enough how this or that friend stands with their parents; and as they practise no dissimulation whatever, they serve as excellent barometers by which to observe the degree of favor or disfavor at which we stand with their parents.—*Goethe.*

The starlight smile of children.— *Epes Sargent.*

I can endure a melancholy man, but not a melancholy child: the former, in whatever slough he may sink, can raise his eyes either to the kingdom of reason or of hope; but the little child is entirely absorbed and weighed down by one black poison-drop of the present.— *Mrs. Norton.*

The scenes of childhood are the memories of future years.—*J. O. Choules.*

Heaven lies about us in our infancy.—· *Wordsworth.*

We should treat children as God does us, who makes us happiest when he leaves us under the influence of innocent delusions.—*Goethe.*

CHIVALRY.

The age of chivalry has gone, and one of calculators and economists has succeeded.— *Burke.*

Collision is as necessary to produce virtue in men, as it is to elicit fire in inanimate matter; and chivalry is the essence of virtue.— *Lord John Russell.*

CHOICE.

The measure of choosing well is whether a man likes what he has chosen.—*Lamb.*

CHRIST.

The best of men that ever wore earth about him was a sufferer, a soft, meek, patient, humble, tranquil spirit; the first true gentleman that ever breathed.—*Decker.*

In his death he is a sacrifice, satisfying for our sins; in the resurrection, a conqueror; in the ascension, a king; in the intercession, a high priest.—*Luther.*

Men who neglect Christ, and try to win heaven through moralities, are like sailors at sea in a storm, who pull, some at the bowsprit and some at the mainmast, but never touch the helm.—*Beecher.*

At his birth a star, unseen before in heaven, proclaims him come.—*Milton.*

The nature of Christ's existence is mysterious, I admit; but this mystery meets the wants of man. Reject it, and the world is an inexplicable riddle; believe it, and the history of our race is satisfactorily explained.—*Napoleon*

In him dwelleth all the fulness of the Godhead bodily.—*Bible.*

Unlike all other founders of a religious faith, Christ had no selfishness, no desire of dominance; and his system, unlike all other systems of worship, was bloodless, boundlessly beneficent, inexpressibly pure, and — most marvellous of all — went to break all bonds of body and soul, and to cast down every temporal and every spiritual tyranny.— *William Howitt.*

All the glory and beauty of Christ are manifested within, and there he delights to dwell; his visits there are frequent, his condescension amazing, his conversation sweet, his comforts refreshing; and the peace that he brings passeth all understanding.—*Thomas à Kempis.*

Rejecting the miracles of Christ, we still have the miracle of Christ himself.—*Bovee.*

He walked in Judæa eighteen hundred years ago; his sphere melody, flowing in wild native tones, took captive the ravished souls of men, and, being of a truth sphere melody, still flows and sounds, though now with thousand-fold accompaniments and rich symphonies, through all our hearts, and modulates and divinely leads them.—*Carlyle.*

CHRISTIANITY.

I do not want the walls of separation between different orders of Christians to be destroyed, but only lowered, that we may shake hands a little easier over them.—*Rowland Hill.*

Every Christian is born great because he is born for heaven.—*Massillon.*

It is more to the honor of a Christian soldier by faith to overcome the world, than by a monastical vow to retreat from it; and more for the honor of Christ to serve him in a city than to serve him in a cell.—*Matthew Henry.*

The relations of Christians to each other are like the several flowers in a garden that have upon each the dew of heaven, which, being shaken by the wind, they let fall the dew at each other's roots, whereby they are jointly nourished, and become nourishers of one another.—*Bunyan.*

Now you say, alas! Christianity is hard; I grant it; but gainful and happy. I contemn the difficulty when I respect the advantage. The greatest labors that have answerable requitals are less than the least that have no regard. Believe me, when I look to the reward, I would not have the work easier. It is a good Master whom we serve, who not only pays, but gives; not after the proportion of our earnings, but of his own mercy.—*Bishop Hall.*

Christianity has no ceremonial. It has forms, for forms are essential to order; but it disdains the folly of attempting to reinforce the religion of the heart by the antics of the mind.—*Rev. Dr. Croly.*

Alas! how has the social spirit of Christianity been perverted by fools at one time, and by knaves and bigots at another; by the self-tormentors of the cell, and the all-tormentors of the conclave!—*Colton.*

Ordinarily rivers run small at the beginning, grow broader and broader as they proceed, and become widest and deepest at the point where they enter the sea. It is such rivers that the Christian's life is like. But the life of the mere worldly man is like those rivers in Southern Africa, which proceeding from mountain freshets, are broad and deep at the beginning, and grow narrower and more shallow as they advance. They waste themselves by soaking into the sands, and at last they die out entirely. The farther they run, the less there is of them.—*Beecher.*

Christianity, which is always true to the heart, knows no abstract virtues, but virtues resulting from our wants, and useful to all.— *Chateaubriand.*

The real security of Christianity is to be found in its benevolent morality, in its exquisite adaptation to the human heart, in the facility with which its scheme accommodates itself to the capacity of every human intellect, in the consolation which it bears to every house of mourning, in the light with which it brightens the great mystery of the grave.—*Macaulay.*

He that loves Christianity better than truth will soon love his own sect or party better than Christianity, and will end by loving himself better than all.—*Coleridge.*

As to the Christian religion, besides the strong evidence which we have for it, there is a balance in its favor from the number of great men who have been convinced of its truth after a serious consideration of the question. Grotius was an acute man, a lawyer, a man accustomed to examine evidence, and he was convinced. Grotius was not a recluse, but a man of the world, who certainly had no bias on the side of religion. Sir Isaac Newton set out an infidel, and came to be a very firm believer.— *Johnson.*

Though the living man can wear a mask and carry on deceit, the dying Christian cannot counterfeit.—*Cumberland.*

Christianity commands us to pass by injuries; policy, to let them pass by us.—*Franklin.*

A Christian in this world is but gold in the ore; at death the pure gold is melted out and separated, and the dross cast away and consumed.—*Flavel.*

Christian graces are like perfumes; the more they are pressed, the sweeter they smell; like stars that shine brightest in the dark; like trees that shine brightest in the dark; like trees, the more they are shaken, the deeper root they take, and the more fruit they bear.—*Rev. John Mason.*

He who is truly a good man is more than half way to being a Christian, by whatever name he is called.—*South.*

Great books are written for Christianity much oftener than great deeds are done for it. City libraries tell us of the reign of Jesus Christ, but city streets tell us of the reign of Satan.—*Horace Mann.*

The other world is as to this like the east to the west. We cannot approach the one without turning away from the other.—*Abd-el-Kader.*

If ever Christianity appears in its power, it is when it erects its trophies upon the tomb; when it takes up its votaries where the world leaves them; and fills the breach with immortal hope in dying moments.—*Robert Hall.*

In becoming Christians, though we love some persons more than we did, let us love none less.—*Gambold.*

Christianity is indeed peculiarly fitted to the more improved stages of society, to the more delicate sensibilities of refined minds, and especially to that dissatisfaction with the present state which always grows with the growth of our moral powers and affections.—*Channing.*

I would give nothing for the Christianity of a man whose very dog and cat were not the better for his religion.—*Rowland Hill.*

A Christianity which will not help those who are struggling from the bottom to the top of society needs another Christ to die for it.—*Beecher.*

A Christian is God Almighty's gentleman.—*Hare.*

Christ was *vitæ magister*, not *scholæ*; and he is the best Christian whose heart beats with the purest pulse towards heaven; not he whose head spinneth out the finest cobwebs.—*Cudworth*

Christianity has carried civilization along with it, whithersoever it has gone; and, as if to show that the latter does not depend on physical causes, some of the countries the most civilized in the days of Augustus are now in a state of hopeless barbarism.—*Hare.*

The Church limits her sacramental services to the faithful. Christ gave himself upon the cross, a ransom for all.—*Pascal.*

Ours is a religion jealous in its demands, but how infinitely prodigal in its gifts! It troubles you for an hour, it repays you by immortality.—*Bulwer Lytton.*

CHURCH.

Surely the church is a place where one day's truce ought to be allowed to the dissensions and animosities of mankind.—*Burke.*

As in Noah's ark there were the clean and the unclean, raven and dove, leopard and kid, the cruel lion with the gentle lamb; so in the Church of Christ on earth you will find the same diversities and differences of human character.—*Rev. Dr. Guthrie.*

The way to preserve the peace of the Church is to preserve the purity of it.—*Matthew Henry.*

The clearest window that ever was fashioned, if it is barred by spiders' webs, and hung over with carcasses of insects, so that the sunlight has forgotten to find its way through, of what use can it be? Now, the Church is God's window; and if it is so obscured by errors that its light is darkness, how great is that darkness!—*Beecher.*

The Church has a good stomach; she has swallowed down whole countries, and has never known a surfeit; the Church alone can digest such ill-gotten wealth.—*Goethe.*

There ought to be such an atmosphere in every Christian church that a man going there and sitting two hours should take the contagion of heaven, and carry home a fire to kindle the altar whence he came.—*Beecher.*

Men say their pinnacles point to heaven. Why, so does every tree that buds, and every bird that rises as it sings. Men say their aisles are good for worship. Why, so is every mountain glen and rough sea-shore. But this they have of distinct and indisputable glory,—that their mighty walls were never raised, and never shall be, but by men who love and aid each other in their weakness.—*Ruskin.*

An I have not forgotten what the inside of a church is made of, I am a peppercorn, a brewer's horse.—*Shakespeare.*

CHURLISHNESS.

My master is of churlish disposition, and little recks to find the way to heaven by doing deeds of hospitality —*Shakespeare.*

CIRCUMSTANCES.

He is happy whose circumstances suit his temper; but he is more excellent who can suit his temper to any circumstances.—*Hume.*

Men are the sport of circumstances, when the circumstances seem the sport of men.—*Byron.*

When the Gauls laid waste Rome, they found the senators clothed in their robes, and seated in stern tranquillity in their curule chairs; in this manner they suffered death without resistance or supplication. Such conduct was in them applauded as noble and magnanimous; in the hapless Indians it was reviled as both obstinate and sullen. How truly are we the dupes of show and circumstances! How different is virtue, clothed in purple and enthroned in state, from virtue, naked and destitute, and perishing obscurely in a wilderness.—*Washington Irving.*

Circumstances! I make circumstances.—*Napoleon.*

It is our relation to circumstances that determines their influence upon us. The same wind that carries one vessel into port may blow another off shore.—*Bovee.*

CITIES.

The union of men in large masses is indispensable to the development and rapid growth of the higher faculties of men. Cities have always been the fireplaces of civilization whence light and heat radiated out into the dark, cold world.—*Theodore Parker.*

If you suppress the exorbitant love of pleasure and money, idle curiosity, iniquitous pursuits and wanton mirth, what a stillness would there be in the greatest cities!—*Bruyère.*

The city an epitome of the social world. All the belts of civilization intersect along its avenues. It contains the products of every moral zone. It is cosmopolitan, not only in a national, but a spiritual sense.—*Chapin.*

Cities force growth, and make men talkative and entertaining, but they make them artificial.—*Emerson.*

The most delicate beauty in the mind of women is, and ever must be, an independence of artificial stimulants for content. It is not so with men. The links that bind men to capitals belong to the golden chain of civilization, — the chain which fastens all our destinies to the throne of Jove. And hence the larger proportion of men in whom genius is pre-eminent have preferred to live in cities, though some of them have bequeathed to us the loveliest pictures of the rural scenes in which they declined to dwell.—*Bulwer Lytton.*

If you would know and not be known, live in a city.—*Colton.*

The number of objects we see from living in a large city amuses the mind like a perpetual raree-show, without supplying it with any ideas.—*Hazlitt.*

There is such a difference between the pursuits of men in great cities that one part of the inhabitants lives to little other purpose than to wonder at the rest. Some have hopes and fears, wishes and aversions, which never enter into the thoughts of others; and inquiry is laboriously exerted to gain that which those who possess it are ready to throw away.—*Johnson.*

God the first garden made, and the first city Cain.—*Cowley.*

I have found by experience that they who have spent all their lives in cities contract not only an effeminacy of habit, but of thinking.—*Goldsmith.*

I bless God for cities. Cities have been as lamps of life along the pathway of humanity and religion. Within them science has given birth to her noblest discoveries. Behind their walls freedom has fought her noblest battles. They have stood on the surface of the earth like great breakwaters, rolling back or turning aside the swelling tide of oppression. Cities, indeed, have been the cradles of human liberty. They have been the active centres of almost all church and state reformation.—*Rev. Dr. Guthrie.*

Men, by associating in large masses, as in camps and in cities, improve their talents, but impair their virtues, and strengthen their minds, but weaken their morals.—*Colton.*

The conditions of city life may be made healthy, so far as the physical constitution is concerned; but there is connected with the business of the city so much competition, so much rivalry, so much necessity for industry, that I think it is a perpetual, chronic, wholesale violation of natural law. There are ten men that can succeed in the country, where there is one that can succeed in the city.—*Beecher.*

Great towns are but a large sort of prison to the soul, like cages to birds, or pounds to beasts.—*Charron.*

Our large trading cities bear to me very nearly the aspect of monastic establishments in which the roar of the mill-wheel and the crane takes the place of other devotional music, and in which the worship of Mammon and Moloch is conducted with a tender reverence and an exact propriety; the merchant rising to his Mammon matins with the self-denial of an anchorite, and expiating the frivolities into which he may be beguiled in the course of the day by late attendance at Mammon vespers.—*Ruskin.*

Like Melrose Abbey, large cities should especially be viewed by moonlight.—*Willis.*

There is no solitude more dreadful for a stranger, an isolated man, than a great city. So many thousands of men and not one friend. — *Boiste.*

CIVILIZATION.

The ultimate tendency of civilization is towards barbarism. — *Hare.*

Such is the diligence with which, in countries completely civilized, one part of mankind labor for another, that wants are supplied faster than they can be formed, and the idle and luxurions find life stagnate for want of some desire to keep it in motion. This species of distress furnishes a new set of occupations; and multitudes are busied from day to day in finding the rich and the fortunate something to do. — *Johnson.*

The most civilized people are as near to barbarism as the most polished steel is to rust. Nations, like metals, have only a superficial brilliancy. — *Rivarol.*

A semi-civilized state of society, equally removed from the extremes of barbarity and of refinement, seems to be that particular meridian under which all the reciprocities and gratuities of hospitality do most really flourish and abound. For it so happens that the ease, the luxury, and the abundance of the highest state of civilization are as productive of selfishness as the difficulties, the privations, and the sterilities of the lowest. — *Colton.*

Ever since there has been so great a demand for type, there has been much less lead to spare for cannon-balls. — *Bulwer Lytton.*

There is often no material difference between the enjoyment of the highest ranks and those of the rudest stages of society. If the life of many young English noblemen, and an Iriquois in the forest, or an Arab in the desert are compared, it will be found that their real sources of happiness are nearly the same. — *Sir A. Alison.*

CLEANLINESS.

Let thy mind's sweetness have its operation upon thy body, clothes, and habitation. — *George Herbert.*

So great is the effect of cleanliness upon man, that it extends even to his moral character. Virtue never dwelt long with filth; nor do I believe there ever was a person scrupulously attentive to cleanliness who was a consummate villain. — *Rumford.*

Even from the body's purity the mind receives a secret sympathetic aid. — *Thomson.*

Beauty commonly produces love, but cleanliness preserves it. Age itself is not unamiable while it is preserved clean and unsullied; like a piece of metal constantly kept smooth and bright, we look on it with more pleasure than on a new vessel cankered with rust. — *Addison.*

Certainly this is a duty, not a sin. "Cleanliness is indeed next to godliness." — *John Wesley.*

CLEMENCY.

Clemency, which we make a virtue of, proceeds sometimes from vanity, sometimes from indolence, often from fear, and almost always from a mixture of all three. — *Rochefoucauld.*

In general, indulgence for those we know is rarer than pity for those we know not. — *Rivarol.*

No attribute so well befits the exalted seat supreme, and power's disposing hand, as clemency. Each crime must from its quality be judged; and pity there should interpose, where malice is not the aggressor. — *Sir William Jones.*

CLOUDS.

Those playful fancies of the mighty sky. — *Albert Smith.*

That looked as though an angel in his upward flight had left his mantle floating in midair. — *Joanna Baillie.*

Was I deceived, or did a sable cloud turn forth her silver lining on the night? — *Milton.*

COLOR.

Color is, in brief terms, the type of love. Hence it is especially connected with the blossoming of the earth; and again, with its fruits; also, with the spring and fall of the leaf, and with the morning and evening of the day, in order to show the waiting of love about the birth and death of man. — *Ruskin.*

COMFORT.

Of all the created comforts, God is the lender; you are the borrower, not the owner. — *Rutherford.*

It is a little thing to speak a phrase of common comfort, which by daily use has almost lost its sense; yet on the ear of him who thought to die unmourned it will fall like choicest music. — *Talfourd.*

In the exhaustless catalogue of Heaven's mercies to mankind, the power we have of finding some germs of comfort in the hardest trials must ever occupy the foremost place; not only because it supports and upholds us when we most require to be sustained, but because in this source of consolation there is something, we have reason to believe, of the Divine Spirit; something of that goodness which detects, amidst our own evil doings, a redeeming quality; something which, even in our fallen nature, we possess in common with the angels; which had its being in the old time when they trod the earth, and linger on it yet, in pity. — *Dickens.*

A beam of comfort, like the moon through clouds, gilds the black horror, and directs my way. — *Dryden.*

The comforts we enjoy here below are not like the anchor in the bottom of the sea that holds fast in a storm, but like the flag upon the top of the mast that turns with every wind.
Rev. Christopher Love.

I want a sofa, as I want a friend, upon which I can repose familiarly. If you can't have intimate terms and freedom with one and the other, they are of no good.—*Thackeray.*

Giving comfort under affliction requires that penetration into the human mind, joined to that experience which knows how to soothe, how to reason, and how to ridicule; taking the utmost care never to apply those arts improperly.—*Fielding.*

COMMANDER.

It is better to have a lion at the head of an army of sheep than a sheep at the head of an army of lions.—*De Foe.*

A brave captain is as a root, out of which (as branches) the courage of his soldiers doth spring.—*Sir P. Sidney.*

COMMERCE.

Commerce has made all winds her mistress.
Sterling.

Commerce, however we may please ourselves with the contrary opinion, is one of the daughters of fortune, inconstant and deceitful as her mother. She chooses her residence where she is least expected, and shifts her abode when her continuance is, in appearance, most firmly settled.—*Johnson.*

A well-regulated commerce is not, like law, physic, or divinity, to be overstocked with hands; but, on the contrary, flourishes by multitudes, and gives employment to all its professors.—*Addison.*

The first inventions of commerce are, like those of all other arts, cunning and short-sighted.—*Curran.*

As soon as the commercial spirit acquires vigor, and begins to gain an ascendant in any society, we discern a new genius in its policy, its alliances, its wars, and its negotiations.—
Dr. W. Robertson.

It may almost be held that the hope of commercial gain has done nearly as much for the cause of truth as even the love of truth.—
Bovee.

Nature seems to have taken a particular care to disseminate her blessings among the different regions of the world, with an eye to their mutual intercourse and traffic among mankind, that the nations of the several parts of the globe might have a kind of dependence upon one another, and be united together by their common interest.—*Addison.*

The trident of Neptune is the sceptre of the world.—*Antoine Lemierre.*

COMMON-SENSE.

Common-sense has given to words their ordinary signification, and common-sense is the genius of mankind.—*Guizot.*

Fine sense and exalted sense are not half as useful as common-sense. There are forty men of wit for one man of sense. And he that will carry nothing about him but gold will be every day at a loss for readier change.—*Pope.*

Common-sense is the average sensibility and intelligence of men undisturbed by individual peculiarities.—*W. R. Alger.*

Common-sense, alas in spite of our educational institutions, is a rare commodity.—*Bovee.*

To act with common-sense, according to the moment, is the best wisdom I know; and the best philosophy, to do one's duties, take the world as it comes, submit respectfully to one's lot, bless the goodness that has given us so much happiness with it, whatever it is, and despise affectation.—*Horace Walpole.*

In most old communities there is a common-sense even in sensuality. Vice itself gets gradually digested into a system, is amenable to certain laws of conventional propriety and honor, has for its object simply the gratification of its appetites, and frowns with quite a conservative air on all new inventions, all untried experiments in iniquity.—*Whipple.*

Common-sense punishes all departures from her, by forcing those who rebel into a desperate war with all facts and experience, and into a still more terrible civil war with each other and with themselves.—*Colton.*

Common-sense is nature's gift, but reason is an art.—*Beattie.*

Sydney Smith playfully says that common-sense was invented by Socrates, that philosopher having been one of its most conspicuous exemplars in conducting the contest of practical sagacity against stupid prejudice and illusory beliefs.—*Whipple.*

Common-sense is only a modification of talent. Genius is an exaltation of it; the difference is, therefore, in the degree, not nature.—
Bulwer Lytton.

COMPARISON.

I love not mine own parallel.—
Barry Cornwall.

Yet why repine? I have seen mansions on the verge of Wales that convert my farm-house into a Hampton Court, and where they speak of a glazed window as a great piece of magnificence. All things figure by comparison.—
Shenstone.

The botanist looks upon the astronomer as a being unworthy of his regard; and he that is growing great and happy by electrifying a bottle wonders how the world can be engaged by trifling prattle about war and peace.— *Johnson.*

The proud are always most provoked by pride.— *Young.*

When the moon shone, we did not see the candle, so doth the greater glory dim the less; a substitute shines brightly as a king, until a king be by; and then his state empties itself, as doth an inland brook into the main of waters.— *Shakespeare.*

COMPASSION.

Compassion to an offender who has grossly violated the laws is, in effect, a cruelty to the peaceable subject who has observed them.— *Junius.*

Want of compassion (however inaccurate observers have reported to the contrary) is not to be numbered among the general faults of mankind. The black ingredient which fouls our disposition is envy. Hence our eyes, it is to be feared, are seldom turned up to those who are manifestly greater, better, wiser, or happier than ourselves, without some degree of malignity, while we commonly look downward on the mean and miserable with sufficient benevolence and pity.— *Fielding.*

It is the crown of justice, and the glory, where it may kill with right, to save with pity. *Beaumont and Fletcher.*

There never was any heart truly great and generous that was not also tender and compassionate.— *South.*

Compassion is an emotion of which we ought never to be ashamed. Graceful, particularly in youth, is the tear of sympathy, and the heart that melts at the tale of woe. We should not permit ease and indulgence to contract our affections, and wrap us up in a selfish enjoyment; but we should accustom ourselves to think of the distresses of human life, of the solitary cottage, the dying parent, and the weeping orphan. Nor ought we ever to sport with pain and distress in any of our amusements, or treat even the meanest insect with wanton cruelty.— *Blair.*

COMPENSATION.

If the poor man cannot always get meat, the rich man cannot always digest it.— *Henry Giles.*

Where there is much general deformity nature has often, perhaps generally, accorded some one bodily grace even in over-measure. So, no doubt, with the intellect and disposition, only it is frequently less apparent, and we give ourselves but little trouble to discover it.— *J. F. Boyes.*

There is a third silent party to all our bargains. The nature and soul of things takes on itself the guaranty of the fulfilment of every contract, so that honest service cannot come to loss.— *Emerson.*

Nothing is pure and entire of a piece. All advantages are attended with disadvantages. A universal compensation prevails in all conditions of being and existence.— *Hume.*

If I have lost anything it was incidental; and the less money, the less trouble; the less favor, the less envy, — nay, even in those cases which put us out of our wits, it is not the loss itself, but the estimate of the loss that troubles us.— *Seneca.*

Curses always recoil on the head of him who imprecates them. If you put a chain around the neck of a slave, the other end fastens itself around your own.— *Emerson.*

As there is no worldly gain without some loss, so there is no worldly loss without some gain. If thou hast lost thy wealth, thou hast lost some trouble with it; if thou art degraded from thy honor, thou art likewise freed from the stroke of envy; if sickness hath blurred thy beauty, it hath delivered thee from pride. Set the allowance against the loss, and thou shalt find no loss great; he loses little or nothing that reserves himself.— *Quarles.*

Whatever difference may appear in the fortunes of mankind, there is, nevertheless, a certain compensation of good and evil which makes them equal.— *Rochefoucauld.*

The rose does not bloom without thorns. True; but would that the thorns did not outlive the rose!— *Richter.*

If poverty makes man groan, he yawns in opulence. When fortune exempts us from labor, nature overwhelms us with time.— *Rivarol.*

No evil is without its compensation.— *Seneca.*

Since we are exposed to inevitable sorrows, wisdom is the art of finding compensation.— *Lévis.*

COMPLACENCY.

Complaisance, though in itself it be scarce reckoned in the number of moral virtues, is that which gives a lustre to every talent a man can be possessed of. It was Plato's advice to an unpolished writer that he should sacrifice to the graces. In the same manner I would advise every man of learning, who would not appear in the world a mere scholar or philosopher, to make himself master of the social virtue which I have here mentioned.— *Addison.*

Complaisance renders a superior amiable, an equal agreeable, and an inferior acceptable.— *Addison.*

Complacency is a coin by the aid of which all the world can, for want of essential means, pay his club-bill in society. It is necessary, finally, that it may lose nothing of its merits, to associate judgment and prudence with it.—
Voltaire.

COMPLAINING.

Complaint is the largest tribute heaven receives, and the sincerest part of our devotion.—
Swift.

I have always despised the whining yelp of complaint, and the cowardly feeble resolve.—
Burns.

The usual fortune of complaint is to excite contempt more than pity.—*Johnson.*

I will not be as those who spend the day in complaining of headache, and the night in drinking the wine that gives the headache.—
Goethe.

We lose the right of complaining sometimes by forbearing it; but we often treble the force.—
Sterne.

COMPLIMENTS.

When two people compliment each other with the choice of anything, each of them generally gets that which he likes least.—*Pope.*

Deference is the most complicate, the most indirect, and the most elegant of all compliments.—*Shenstone.*

Compliments of congratulation are always kindly taken, and cost one nothing but pen, ink, and paper. I consider them as drafts upon good breeding, where the exchange is always greatly in favor of the drawer.—*Chesterfield.*

Compliments are only lies in court clothes.—
Sterling.

Though all compliments are lies, yet because they are known to be such, nobody depends on them, so there is no hurt in them; you return them in the same manner you receive them; yet it is best to make as few as one can.—
Lady Gethin.

CONCEIT.

The miller imagines that the corn grows only to make his mill turn.—*Goethe.*

Every man deems that he has precisely the trials and temptations which are the hardest of all for him to bear; but they are so, because they are the very ones he needs.—*Richter.*

A man — poet, prophet, or whatever he may be — readily persuades himself of his right to all the worship that is voluntarily tendered.—
Hawthorne.

An eagerness and zeal for dispute on every subject, and with every one, shows great self-sufficiency, that never-failing sign of great self-ignorance.—*Lord Chatham.*

Men educate each other in reason by contact or collision, and keep each other sane by the very conflict of their separate hobbies. Society as a whole is the deadly enemy of the particular crotchet of each, and solitude is almost the only condition in which the acorn of conceit can grow to the oak of perfect self-delusion.—
Whipple.

Conceit is the most contemptible and one of the most odious qualities in the world. It is vanity driven from all other shifts, and forced to appeal to itself for admiration.—*Hazlitt.*

Conceit is to nature what paint is to beauty; it is not only needless, but impairs what it would improve.—*Pope.*

No wonder we are all more or less pleased with mediocrity, since it leaves us at rest, and gives the same comfortable feeling as when one associates with his equals.—*Goethe.*

Conceit in weakest bodies strongest works.—
Shakespeare.

They say it was Liston's firm belief, that he was a great and neglected tragic actor; they say that every one of us believes in his heart, or would like to have others believe, that he is something which he is not.—*Thackeray.*

Conceit is just as natural a thing to human minds as a centre is to a circle. But little-minded people's thoughts move in such small circles that five minutes' conversation gives you an arc long enough to determine their whole curve. An arc in the movement of a large intellect does not differ sensibly from a straight line.—*Holmes.*

Conceit and confidence are both of them cheats; the first always imposes on itself, the second frequently deceives others too.—
Zimmermann.

The certain way to be cheated is to fancy one's self more cunning than others.—*Charron.*

None are so seldom found alone, and are so soon tired of their own company, as those coxcombs who are on the best terms with themselves.—*Colton.*

Nature descends down to infinite smallness. Great men have their parasites; and, if you take a large buzzing blue-bottle fly, and look at it in a microscope, you may see twenty or thirty little ugly insects crawling about it, which, doubtless, think their fly to be the bluest, grandest, merriest, most important animal in the universe, and are convinced the world would be at an end if it ceased to buzz.—
Sydney Smith.

Strong conceit, like a new principle, carries all easily with it, when yet above common-sense.
. *Locke.*

There is more hope of a fool than of him that is wise in his own conceit.—*Bible.*

Conceited men often seem a harmless kind of men, who, by an overweening self-respect, relieve others from the duty of respecting them at all.—*Beecher.*

Be not wise in your own conceits.—*Bible.*

One whom the music of his own vain tongue doth ravish like enchanting harmony.—
Shakespeare.

We judge of others for the most part by their good opinion of themselves; yet nothing gives such offence, or creates so many enemies, as that extreme self-complacency or superciliousness of manner, which appears to set the opinion of every one else at defiance.—*Hazlitt.*

Men are found to be vainer on account of those qualities which they fondly believe they have than of those which they really have.—
Voiture.

No man was ever so much deceived by another as by himself.—*Lord Greville.*

Be not righteous overmuch.—*Bible.*

Man believes himself always greater than he is, and is esteemed less than he is worth.—
Goethe.

All affectation and display proceed from the supposition of possessing something better than the rest of the world possesses. Nobody is vain of possessing two legs and two arms; because that is the precise quantity of either sort of limb which everybody possesses.—
Sydney Smith.

Every man, however little, makes a figure in his own eyes.—*Henry Home.*

Talk about conceit as much as you like, it is to human character what salt is to the ocean; it keeps it sweet and renders it endurable. Say rather it is like the natural unguent of the sea-fowl's plumage, which enables him to shed the rain that falls on him and the wave in which he dips. When one has had all his conceit taken out of him, when he has lost all his illusions, his feathers will soon soak through, and he will fly no more.—*Holmes.*

It is the admirer of himself, and not the admirer of virtue, that thinks himself superior to others.—*Plutarch.*

Conceited people are never without a certain degree of harmless satisfaction wherewith to flavor the waters of life.—*Madame Deluzy.*

How wise are we in thought! how weak in practice! our very virtue, like our will, is — nothing.—*Shirley.*

Dangerous conceits are in their nature poisons, which at the first are scarce found to distaste, but with a little act upon the blood, burn like the mines of sulphur.—*Shakespeare.*

There is scarcely any man, how much soever he may despise the character of a flatterer, but will condescend in the meanest manner to flatter himself.—*Fielding.*

He who gives himself airs of importance exhibits the credentials of impotence.—*Lavater.*

The best of lessons, for a good many people, would be to listen at a key-hole. It is a pity for such that the practice is dishonorable.—
Madame Swetchine.

The more any one speaks of himself, the less he likes to hear another talked of.—*Lavater.*

But the conceit of one's self and the conceit of one's hobby are hardly more prolific of eccentricity than the conceit of one's money. Avarice, the most hateful and wolfish of all the hard, cool, callous dispositions of selfishness, has its own peculiar caprices and crotchets. The ingenuities of its meanness defy all the calculations of reason, and reach the miraculous in subtlety.—*Whipple.*

The weakest spot in every man is where he thinks himself to be the wisest.—*Emmons.*

CONDUCT.

The integrity of men is to be measured by their conduct, not by their professions.—*Junius.*

CONFESSION.

Why does no man confess his vices? Because he is yet in them; it is for a waking man to tell his dream.—*Seneca.*

If thou wouldst be justified, acknowledge thy injustice; he that confesses his sin begins his journey toward salvation; he that is sorry for it mends his pace; he that forsakes it is at his journey's end.—*Quarles.*

That conduct sometimes seems ridiculous, in the eyes of the world, the secret reasons for which, may, in reality, be wise and solid.—
Rochefoucauld.

CONFIDENCE.

Fields are won by those who believe in the winning.—*T. W. Higginson.*

All confidence which is not absolute and entire is dangerous; there are few occasions but where a man ought either to say all or conceal all; for how little soever you have revealed of your secret to a friend, you have already said too much if you think it not safe to make him privy to all particulars.—*J. Beaumont.*

He who has lost confidence can lose nothing more.—*Boiste.*

To confide, even though to be betrayed, is much better than to learn only to conceal. In the one case, your neighbor wrongs you ; but in the other you are perpetually doing injustice to yourself.—*Simms.*

If we are truly prudent, we shall cherish, despite occasional delusions, those noblest and happiest of our tendencies, — to love and to confide.—*Bulwer Lytton.*

Never put much confidence in such as put no confidence in others. A man prone to suspect evil is mostly looking in his neighbor for what he sees in himself. As to the pure all things are pure, even so to the impure all things are impure.—*Hare.*

We may have the confidence of another without possessing his heart. If his heart be ours, there is no need of revelation or of confidence, — all is open to us.—*Du Cœur.*

A noble heart, like the sun, showeth its greatest confidence in its lowest estate.— *Sir P. Sidney.*

Where there is any good disposition, confidence begets faithfulness ; but distrust, if it do not produce treachery, never fails to destroy every inclination to evince fidelity. Most people disdain to clear themselves from the accusations of mere suspicion.—*Jane Porter.*

Trust not him who hath once broken faith. *Shakespeare.*

There is something captivating in spirit and intrepidity, to which we often yield as to a resistless power ; nor can he reasonably expect the confidence of others who too apparently distrusts himself.—*Hazlitt.*

For they can conquer who believe they can. *Dryden.*

Trust him little who praises all, him less who censures all, and him least who is indifferent about all.—*Lavater.*

People have generally three epochs in their confidence in man. In the first they believe him to be everything that is good, and they are lavish with their friendship and confidence. In the next, they have had experience, which has smitten down their confidence, and they then have to be careful not to mistrust every one, and to put the worst construction upon everything. Later in life, they learn that the greater number of men have much more good in them than bad, and that, even when there is cause to blame, there is more reason to p than condemn ; and then a spirit of confidence again awakens within them.— *Fredrika Bremer.*

Confidence is a plant of slow growth in an aged bosom.—*Johnson.*

Let not the quietness of any man's temper, much less the confidence he has in thy honesty and goodness, tempt thee to contrive any mischief against him ; for the more securely he relies on thy virtue, and the less mistrust he has of any harm from thee, the greater wickedness will it be to entertain even the thought of doing him an injury.—*Bishop Patrick.*

Trust him with little who, without proofs, trusts you with everything, or, when he has proved you, with nothing.—*Lavater.*

It is unjust and absurd of persons advancing in years, to expect of the young that confidence should come all and only on their side ; the human heart, at whatever age, opens only to the heart that opens in return.— *Miss Edgeworth.*

Confidence in conversation has a greater share than wit.—*Rochefoucauld.*

Confidence in another man's virtue is no slight evidence of a man's own.—*Montaigne.*

To reveal imprudently the spot where we are most sensitive and vulnerable is to invite a blow. The demi-god Achilles admitted no one to his confidence.—*Madame Swetchine.*

CONSCIENCE.

O conscience ! conscience ! man's most faithful friend.— *Crabbe.*

What a strange thing an old dead sin laid away in a secret drawer of the soul is ? Must it some time or other be moistened with tears, until it comes to life again, and begins to stir in our consciousness, as the dry wheat-animalcule, looking like a grain of dust, becomes alive if it is wet with a drop of water ?—*Holmes.*

The conscience is more wise than science.— *Lavater.*

I feel within me a peace above all earthly dignities, a still and quiet conscience. *Shakespeare.*

The great chastisement of a knave is not to be known, but to know himself.—*J. Petit Senn.*

A palsy may as well shake an oak, or a fever dry up a fountain, as either of them shake, dry up, or impair the delight of conscience. For it lies within, it centres in the heart, it grows into the very substance of the soul, so that it accompanies a man to his grave ; he never outlives it.—*South.*

What other dungeon is so dark as one's own heart? What jailer so inexorable as one's self ? —*Hawthorne.*

He that hath a scrupulous conscience is like a horse that is not well weighed ; he starts at every bird that flies out of the hedge.—*Selden.*

The most reckless · sinner against his own conscience has always in the background the consolation that he will go on in this course only this time, or only so long, but that at such a time he will amend.—*Fichte.*

Be more careful of your conscience than of your estate. The latter can be bought and sold; the former never.—*Hosea Ballou.*

God's vicegerent in the soul.—*Buchan.*

Some persons follow the dictates of their conscience only in the same sense in which a coachman may be said to follow the horses he is driving.— *Whately.*

It is as bad to clip conscience as to clip coin; it is as bad to give a counterfeit statement as a counterfeit bill.—*Chapin.*

Every man, however good he may be, has a yet better man dwelling in him, which is properly himself, but to whom nevertheless he is often unfaithful. It is to this interior and less mutable being that we should attach ourselves, not to the changeable, every-day man.— *Wilhelm von Humboldt.*

Man's conscience is the oracle of God!— *Byron.*

Better be with the dead, whom we, to gain our place, have sent to peace, than on the torture of the mind to lie in restless ecstasy.— *Shakespeare.*

Conscience, what art thou? thou tremendous power! who dost inhabit us without our leave; and art within ourselves, another self.— *Young.*

Rules of society are nothing, one's conscience is the umpire.— *Madame Dudevant.*

God, in his wrath, has not left this world to the mercy of the subtlest dialectician; and all arguments are happily transitory in their effect when they contradict the primal intuitions of conscience and the inborn sentiments of the heart.— *Whipple.*

If thou wouldst be informed what God has written concerning thee in heaven, look into thine own bosom, and see what graces he hath there wrought in thee.—*Fuller.*

What exile from himself can flee? —*Byron.*

Conscience is, at once, the sweetest and most troublesome of guests. It is the voice which demanded Abel of his brother, or that celestial harmony which vibrated in the ears of the martyrs, and soothed their sufferings — *Madame Swetchine.*

The voice of conscience is so delicate that it is easy to stifle it; but it is also so clear that it is impossible to mistake it.—*Madame de Staël.*

It is a blushing, shame-faced spirit, that mutinies in a man's bosom; it fills one full of obstacles; it made me once restore a purse of gold that by chance I found; it beggars any man that keeps it; it is turned out of all towns and cities for a dangerous thing; and every man that means to live well endeavors to trust to himself, and live without it.—*Shakespeare.*

Conscience is merely our own judgment of the moral rectitude or turpitude of our own actions.—*Locke.*

Man's first care should be to avoid the reproaches of his own heart; his next, to escape the censures of the world. If the last interferes with the former, it ought to be entirely neglected; but otherwise there cannot be a greater satisfaction to an honest mind than to see those approbations which it gives itself seconded by the applauses of the public.—*Addison.*

A good conscience is a continual Christmas. *Franklin.*

A tender conscience is an inestimable blessing; that is, a conscience not only quick to discern what is evil, but instantly to shun it, as the eyelid closes itself against the mote.— *Rev. N. Adams.*

I believe that we cannot live better than in seeking to become better, nor more agreeably than having a clear conscience.—*Socrates.*

There is no college for the conscience.— *Theodore Parker.*

Unnatural deeds do breed unnatural troubles; infected minds to their deaf pillows will discharge their secrets.—*Shakespeare.*

The moral conscience is a truly primitive faculty; it is a particular manner of feeling which corresponds to the goodness of moral actions, as taste is a manner of feeling which corresponds to beauty. Love men, immolate error.—*St. Augustine.*

O conscience, into what abyss of fears and horrors hast thou driven me, out of which I find no way, from deep to deeper plunged.— *Milton.*

A guilty conscience is like a whirlpool, drawing in all to itself which would otherwise pass by.—*Fuller.*

A man's own conscience is his sole tribunal, and he should care no more for that phantom "opinion" than he should fear meeting a ghost if he crossed the churchyard at dark.— *Bulwer Lytton.*

Conscience is a great ledger book in which all our offences are written and registered, and which time reveals to the sense and feeling of the offender.—*Burton.*

Conscience does make cowards of us all.—
Shakespeare.

Preserve your conscience always soft and sensitive. If but one sin force its way into that tender part of the soul and dwell there, the road is paved for a thousand iniquities.—
Watts.

Let us be thankful for health and competence, and, above all, for a quiet conscience.—
Izaak Walton.

We never do evil so thoroughly and heartily as when led to it by an honest but dwell perverted, because mistaken conscience.—*T. Edwards.*

No man ever offended his own conscience but first or last it was revenged upon him for it.
South.

We are born to lose and to perish, to hope and to fear, to vex ourselves and others; and there is no antidote against a common calamity but virtue; for the foundation of true joy is in the conscience.—*Seneca.*

Conscience is the mirror of our souls, which represents the errors of our lives in their full shape.—*Bancroft.*

A quiet conscience makes one so serene.—
Byron.

Our faults afflict us more than our good deeds console. Pain is ever uppermost in the conscience as in the heart.—*Madame Swetchine.*

In the commission of evil, fear no man so much as thyself; another is but one witness against thee, thou art a thousand; another thou mayest avoid, thyself thou canst not. Wickedness is its own punishment.—*Quarles.*

What a fool is he who locks his door to keep out spirits, who has in his own bosom a spirit he dares not meet alone; whose voice, smothered far down, and piled over with mountains of earthliness, is yet like the forewarning trumpet of doom!—*Mrs. Stowe.*

Conscience is the chamber of justice.
Origen.

Even in the fiercest uproar of our stormy passions, conscience, though in her softest whispers, gives to the supremacy of rectitude the voice of an undying testimony.—*Chalmers.*

The pulse of reason.—*Coleridge.*

O the wound of conscience is no scar, and time cools it not with his wing, but merely keeps it open with his scythe.—*Richter.*

Conscience, that vicegerent of God in the human heart, whose "still small voice" the loudest revelry cannot drown.—*W. H. Harrison.*

Remorse of conscience is like an old wound; a man is in no condition to fight under such circumstances. The pain abates his vigor and takes up too much of his attention.—
Jeremy Collier.

The conscience is the inviolable asylum of the liberty of man.—*Napoleon.*

A good conscience fears no witnesses, but a guilty conscience is solicitous even in solitude. If we do nothing but what is honest, let all the world know it; but if otherwise, what does it signify to have nobody else know it so long as I know it myself? Miserable is he who slights that witness!—*Seneca.*

A man never outlives his conscience, and that, for this cause only, he cannot outlive himself.—*South.*

A good conscience is to the soul what health is to the body; it preserves a constant ease and serenity within us, and more than countervails all the calamities and afflictions which can possibly befall us.—*Addison.*

Conscience is the sentinel of virtue.—*Johnson.*

Conscience signifies that knowledge which a man hath of his own thoughts and actions; and because, if a man judgeth fairly of his actions by comparing them with the law of God, his mind will approve or condemn him; this knowledge or conscience may be both an accuser and a judge.—*Swift.*

Alas, that we should be so unwilling to listen to the still and holy yearnings of the heart! A god whispers quite softly in our breast, softly yet audibly; telling us what we ought to seek and what to shun.—*Goethe.*

Most men are afraid of a bad name, but few fear their consciences.—*Pliny.*

It is a man's own dishonesty, his crimes, his wickedness, and boldness, that takes away from him soundness of mind; these are the furies, these the flames and firebrands, of the wicked.—
Cicero.

Conscience is a judge in every man's breast, which none can cheat or corrupt, and perhaps the only incorrupt thing about him; yet, inflexible and honest as this judge is (however polluted the bench on which he sits), no man can, in my opinion, enjoy any applause which is not there adjudged to be his due.—*Fielding.*

The world will never be in any manner of order or tranquility until men are firmly convinced that conscience, honor, and credit are all in one interest.—*Steele.*

There is no future pang can deal that justice on the self-condemned he deals on his own soul.—*Byron.*

Labor to keep alive in your breast that little spark of celestial fire called conscience.—*Washington.*

A man, so to speak, who is not able to bow to his own conscience every morning is hardly in a condition to respectfully salute the world at any other time of the day.—*Douglas Jerrold.*

A wounded conscience is able to unparadise paradise itself.—*Fuller.*

There is one court whose "findings" are incontrovertible, and whose sessions are held in the chambers of our own breast.—*Hosea Ballou.*

The good or evil we confer on others very often, I believe, recoils on ourselves; for as men of a benign disposition enjoy their own acts of beneficence equally with those to whom they are done, so there are scarce any natures so entirely diabolical as to be capable of doing injuries without paying themselves some pangs for the ruin which they bring on their fellow-creatures.—*Fielding.*

What we call conscience, in many instances, is only a wholesome fear of the constable.—*Bovee.*

As the stag which the huntsman has hit flies through bush and brake, over stock and stone, thereby exhausting his strength but not expelling the deadly bullet from his body; so does experience show that they who have troubled consciences run from place to place, but carry with them wherever they go their dangerous wounds.—*Gotthold.*

Conscience is the living law, and honor is to this law what piety is to religion.—*Boufflers.*

In matters of conscience first thoughts are best; in matters of prudence last thoughts are best.—*Rev. Robert Hall.*

A good conscience is never lawless in the worst regulated state, and will provide those laws for itself which the neglect of legislators had forgotten to supply.—*Fielding.*

There is no class of men so difficult to be managed in a State, as those whose intentions are honest, but whose consciences are bewitched.—*Napoleon.*

Conscience has no more to do with gallantry than it has with politics.—*Sheridan.*

The impulse which directs to right conduct, and deters from crime, is not only older than the ages of nations and cities, but coeval with that Divine Being who sees and rules both heaven and earth.—*Cicero.*

If you should escape the censure of others, hope not to escape your own.—*Henry Home.*

Conscience is the voice of the soul, the passions are the voice of the body. Is it astonishing that often these two languages contradict each other, and then to which must we listen? Too often reason deceives us; we have only too much acquired the right of refusing to listen to it; but conscience never deceives us; it is the true guide of man; it is to man what instinct is to the body, which follows it, obeys nature, and never is afraid of going astray.—*Rousseau.*

No infallible oracle out of the breast.—*Rev. Dr. Hedge.*

Leave her to heaven, and to those thorns that in her bosom lodge, to prick and sting her.—*Shakespeare.*

No outward tyranny can reach the mind. If conscience plays the tyrant, it would be greatly for the benefit of the world that she were more arbitrary, and far less placable than some men find her.—*Junius.*

Conscience warns us as a friend before it punishes us as a judge.—*Stanislaus.*

We should have all our communications with men, as in the presence of God; and with God, as in the presence of men.—*Colton.*

Conscience and covetousness are never to be reconciled; like fire and water they always destroy each other, according to the predominancy of the element.—*Jeremy Collier.*

Conscience is God's deputy in the soul.—*Rev. T. Adams.*

Who has a heart so pure but some uncleanly apprehensions keep leets and law-days, and in session sit with meditations awful?—*Shakespeare.*

I am more afraid of my own heart than of the Pope and all his Cardinals. I have within me the great pope, self.—*Luther.*

Our conscience is a fire within us, and our sins as the fuel; instead of warming, it will scorch us, unless the fuel be removed, or the heat of it allayed by penitential tears.—*Dr. Mason.*

Man is naturally more desirous of a quiet and approving, than of a vigilant and tender conscience, — more desirous of security than of safety.—*Whately.*

Conscience is a thousand swords.—*Shakespeare.*

Be fearful only of thyself, and stand in awe of none more than of thine own conscience. There is a Cato in every man; a severe censor of his manners. And he that reverences this judge will seldom do anything he need repent of.—*Burton.*

Conscience is Justice's best minister; it threatens, promises, rewards, and punishes and keeps all under its control; the busy must attend to its remonstrances, the most powerful submit to its reproof, and the angry endure its upbraidings. While conscience is our friend, all is peace; but if once offended, farewell the tranquil mind.—*Mary Wortley Montagu.*

Conscience and wealth are not always neighbors.—*Massinger.*

Conscience, that boon companion who sets a man free under the strong breastplate of innocence, that bids him on and fear not.—*Dante.*

The great theatre for virtue is conscience.— *Cicero.*

In the wildest anarchy of man's insurgent appetites and sins there is still a reclaiming voice,—a voice which, even when in practice disregarded, it is impossible not to own; and to which, at the very moment that we refuse our obedience, we find that we cannot refuse the homage of what ourselves do feel and acknowledge to be the best, the highest principles of our nature.—*Chalmers.*

CONSERVATISM.

A conservative is a man who will not look at the new moon, out of respect for that "ancient institution," the old one.—*Douglas Jerrold.*

We are reformers in spring and summer; in autumn and winter we stand by the old; reformers in the morning, conservers at night. Reform is affirmative, conservatism negative; conservatism goes for comfort, reform for truth.— *Emerson.*

A conservative young man has wound up his life before it was unreeled. We expect old men to be conservative; but when a nation's young men are so, its funeral bell is already rung.—*Beecher.*

The conservative may clamor against reform, but he might as well clamor against the centrifugal force. He sighs for the "good old times,"—he might as well wish the oak back into the acorn.—*Chapin.*

· Conservatism is a very good thing; but how many conservatives announce principles which might have shocked Dick Turpin, or nonsensicalities flat enough to have raised contempt in Jerry Sneak!—*Whipple.*

CONSISTENCY.

With consistency a great soul has simply nothing to do. He may as well concern himself with his shadow on the wall.—*Emerson.*

As flowers always wear their own colors and give forth their own fragrance every day alike, so should Christians maintain their character at all times and under all circumstances.—*Beecher.*

CONSOLATION.

One should never be very forward in offering spiritual consolations to those in distress. These, to be of any service, must be self-evolved in the first instance.—*Coleridge.*

Queen Elizabeth, in her hard, wise way, writing to a mother who had lost her son, tells her that she will be comforted in time; and why should she not do for herself what the mere lapse of time will do for her? —*Bentley.*

If a man makes me keep my distance, the comfort is he keeps his own at the same time.— *Swift.*

Consolation, indiscreetly pressed upon us when we are suffering under affliction only serves to increase our pain and to render our grief more poignant.—*Rousseau.*

As the bosom of earth blooms again and again, having buried out of sight the dead leaves of autumn, and loosed the frosty bands of winter; so does the heart, in spite of all that melancholy poets write, feel many renewed springs and summers. It is a beautiful and a blessed world we live in, and whilst that life lasts, to lose the enjoyment of it is a sin.— *A. W. Chambers.*

In a healthy state of the organism all wounds have a tendency to heal.— *Madame Swetchine.*

Nothing does so establish the mind amidst the rollings and turbulence of present things, as a look above them and a look beyond them, —above them, to the steady and good hand by which they are ruled; and beyond them, to the sweet and beautiful end to which, by that hand, they will be brought.—*Jeremy Taylor.*

God has commanded time to console the unhappy.—*Joubert.*

Before an affliction is digested, consolation ever comes too soon; and after it is digested, it comes too late; but there is a mark between these two, as fine almost as a hair, for a comforter to take aim at.—*Sterne.*

For every bad there might be a worse; and when one breaks his leg, let him be thankful it was not his neck.—*Bishop Hall.*

Apt words have power to suage the tumors of a troubled mind.—*Milton.*

Whoever can turn his weeping eyes to heaven has lost nothing; for there above is everything he can wish for here below. He only is a loser who persists in looking down on the narrow plains of the present time.—*Richter.*

Consolation heals without contact; somewhat like the blessed air which we need but to breathe.—*Madame Swetchine.*

CONSPIRACY.

Combinations of wickedness would overwhelm the world by the advantage which licentious principles afford, did not those who have long practised perfidy grow faithless to each other.—*Johnson.*

Conspiracies no sooner should be formed than executed.—*Addison.*

Conspiracies, like thunder-clouds, should in a moment form and strike like lightning, ere the sound is heard.—*John Dow.*

CONSTANCY.

As the faithful soldier never leaves his camp without the leave or command of his captain, so the good man, placed in this world in such a position as God pleases, never seeks to stir or leave it without the permission of his chief.—
Amayot.

O Heaven! Were man but constant, he were perfect.—*Shakespeare.*

The business of constancy chiefly is bravely to stand to, and stoutly to suffer those inconveniences which are not otherwise possible to be avoided.—*Montaigne.*

Constancy is a saint without a worshipper.
Boufflers.

I must confess there is something in the changeableness and inconstancy of human nature that very often both dejects and terrifies me. Whatever I am at present, I tremble to think what I may be. While I find this principle in me, how can I assure myself that I shall be always true to my God, my friend, or myself. In short, without constancy there is neither love, friendship, nor virtue in the world.—
Addison.

The constancy of the wise is only the art of keeping disquietude to one's self.—*Rochefoucauld.*

I am constant as the northern star, of whose true-fixed and resting quality there is no fellow in the firmament.—*Shakespeare.*

CONTEMPLATION.

In order to improve the mind, we ought less to learn than to contemplate.—*Descartes.*

There is a sweet pleasure in contemplation; all others grow flat and insipid upon frequent use; and when a man hath run through a set of vanities, in the declension of his age he knows not what to do with himself if he cannot think.—*Sir T. P. Blount.*

CONTEMPT.

None but the contemptible are apprehensive of contempt.—*Rochefoucauld.*

Contempt is the only way to triumph over calumny.—*Madame de Maintenon.*

Contempt is not a thing to be despised. It may be borne with a calm and equal mind, but no man, by lifting his head high, can pretend that he does not perceive the scorns that are poured down upon him from above.—*Burke.*

Contempt is a kind of gangrene, which, if it seizes one part of a character, corrupts all the rest by degrees.—*Johnson.*

Speak with contempt of no man. Every one hath a tender sense of reputation. And every man hath a sting, which he may, if provoked too far, dart out at one time or other.—
Burton.

It is very often more necessary to conceal contempt than resentment, the former being never forgiven, but the latter sometimes forgot.
Chesterfield.

Contempt is frequently regulated by fashion.
Zimmermann.

I have unlearned contempt; it is a sin that is engendered earliest in the soul, and doth beset it like a poison worm feeding on all its beauty.
Willis.

Contempt naturally implies a man's esteeming of himself greater than the person whom he contemns; he therefore that slights, that contemns an affront is properly superior to it; and he conquers an injury who conquers his resentments of it. Socrates, being kicked by an ass, did not think it a revenge proper for Socrates to kick the ass again.—*South.*

Despise not any man, and do not spurn anything. For there is no man that hath not his hour, nor is there anything that hath not its place.—*Rabbi Ben Azai.*

Contempt of others is the truest symptom of a base and bad heart, — while it suggests itself to the mean and the vile, and tickles their little fancy on every occasion, it never enters the great and good mind but on the strongest motives; nor is it then a welcome guest, — affording only an uneasy sensation, and bringing always with it a mixture of concern and compassion.—
Fielding.

He who feels contempt for any living thing hath faculties that he hath never used, and thought with him is in its infancy.—*Wordsworth.*

Wrongs are often forgiven, but contempt never is. Our pride remembers it forever. It implies a discovery of weaknesses, which we are much more careful to conceal than crimes. Many a man will confess his crimes to a common friend, but I never knew a man who would tell his silly weaknesses to his most intimate one.—*Chesterfield.*

O, what a deal of scorn looks beautiful in the contempt and anger of his lip!—*Shakespeare.*

The basest and meanest of all human beings are generally the most forward to despise others. So that the most contemptible are generally the most contemptuous.—*Fielding.*

Christ saw much in this world to weep over, and much to pray over; but he saw nothing in it to look upon with contempt.—*Chapin.*

CONTENTMENT.

Contentment is natural wealth; luxury, artificial poverty.—*Socrates.*

The fountain of content must spring up in the mind; and he who has so little knowledge of human nature as to seek happiness by changing anything but his own disposition will waste his life in fruitless efforts, and multiply the griefs which he proposes to remove.—*Johnson.*

One who is contented with what he has done will never become famous for what he will do. He has lain down to die. The grass is already growing over him.—*Bovee.*

There is scarce any lot so low, but there is something in it to satisfy the man whom it has befallen; Providence having so ordered things that in every man's cup, how bitter soever, there are some cordial drops,— some good circumstances, which, if wisely extracted, are sufficient for the purpose he wants them, — that is, to make him contented, and, if not happy, at least resigned.—*Sterne.*

I earn that I eat, get that I wear; owe no man hate, envy no man's happiness; glad of other men's good, content with my harm.—*Shakespeare.*

I say to thee be thou satisfied. It is recorded of the hares that with a general consent they went to drown themselves out of a feeling of their misery; but when they saw a company of frogs more fearful than they were, they began to take courage and comfort again. Confer thine estate with others.—*Burton.*

None is poor but the mean in mind, the timorous, the weak, and unbelieving; none is wealthy but the affluent in soul, who is satisfied and floweth over.—*Tupper.*

My God, give me neither poverty nor riches; but whatsoever it may be thy will to give, give me with it a heart which knows humbly to acquiesce in what is thy will.—*Gotthold.*

If men knew what felicity dwells in the cottage of a godly man, how sound he sleeps, how quiet his rest, how composed his mind, how free from care, how easy his position, how moist his mouth, how joyful his heart, they would never admire the noises, the diseases, the throngs of passions, and the violence of unnatural appetites that fill the house of the luxurious and the heart of the ambitious.—*Jeremy Taylor.*

The chief secret of comfort lies in not suffering trifles to vex us, and in prudently cultivating our undergrowth of small pleasures, since very few great ones, alas! are let on long leases.—*Sharp.*

Without content, we shall find it almost as difficult to please others as ourselves.—*Lord Greville.*

There is some help for all the defects of fortune; for, if a man cannot attain to the length of his wishes, he may have his remedy by cutting of them shorter.—*Cowley.*

For no chance is evil to him who is content, and to a man nothing is miserable unless it is unreasonable. No man can make another man to be his slave unless he hath first enslaved himself to life and death. No pleasure or pain, to hope or fear; command these passions, and you are freer than the Parthian kings.—*Jeremy Taylor.*

The highest point outward things can bring unto, is the contentment of the mind; with which no estate can be poor without which all estates will be miserable.—*Sir P. Sidney.*

If two angels were sent down from heaven, one to conduct an empire, and the other to sweep a street, — they would feel no inclination to change employments.—*John Newton.*

Our content is our best having.—*Shakespeare.*

Learn to be pleased with everything, with wealth so far as it makes us beneficial to others; with poverty, for not having much to care for; and with obscurity, for being unenvied.—*Plutarch.*

It is right to be contented with what we have, but never with what we are.—*Sir James Mackintosh.*

True contentment depends not upon what we have; a tub was large enough for Diogenes, but a world was too little for Alexander.—*Colton.*

The point of aim for our vigilance to hold in view is to dwell upon the brightest parts in every prospect, to call off the thoughts when running upon disagreeable objects, and strive to be pleased with the present circumstances surrounding us.—*Rev. J. Tucker.*

Contentment produces, in some measure, all those effects which the alchemist usually ascribes to what he calls the philosopher's stone; and if it does not bring riches, it does the same thing by banishing the desire for them.—*Addison.*

I have often said that all the unhappiness of men comes from not knowing how to remain quiet in a chamber.—*Pascal.*

If we are at peace with God and our own conscience, what enemy among men need we fear ? —*Hosea Ballou.*

Enjoy your own life without comparing it with that of another.—*Condorcet.*

Poor and content is rich, and rich enough; but riches, fineless, is as poor as winter to him that ever fears he shall be poor.—*Shakespeare.*

That is true plenty, not to have, but not to want riches.—*St. Chrysostom.*

A contented mind is the greatest blessing a man can enjoy in this world; and if in the present life his happiness arises from the subduing of his desires, it will arise in the next from the gratification of them.—*Addison.*

Content is to the mind like moss to a tree; it bindeth it up so as to stop its growth.— *Halifax.*

" What you demand is here, or at Ulubræ." You traverse the world in search of happiness, which is within the reach of every man; a contented mind confers it on all.—*Horace.*

We can console ourselves for not having great talents as we console ourselves for not having great places. We can be above both in our hearts.—*Vauvenargues.*

May I always have a heart superior, with economy suitable, to my fortune —*Shenstone.*

Take the good with the evil, for ye all are the pensioners of God, and none may choose or refuse the cup his wisdom mixeth.—*Tupper.*

A sense of contentment makes us kindly and benevolent to others; we are not chafed and galled by cares which are tyrannical because original. We are fulfilling our proper destiny, and those around us feel the sunshine of our own hearts.—*Bulwer Lytton.*

Contentment consisteth not in adding more fuel, but in taking away some fire.—*Fuller.*

Every one is well or ill at ease, according as he finds himself; not he whom the world believes, but he who believes himself to be so, is content; and in him alone belief gives itself being and reality.—*Montaigne.*

Happy the heart to whom God has given enough strength and courage to suffer for him, to find happiness in simplicity and the happiness of others.—*Lavater.*

Naught is had, all is spent, where our desire is got without content.—*Shakespeare.*

What is the highest secret of victory and peace ? To will what God wills, and strike a league with destiny.—*W. R. Alger.*

He is richest who is content with the least; for content is the wealth of nature.—*Socrates.*

Alas ! if the principles of contentment are not within us, the height of station and worldly grandeur will as soon add a cubit to a man's stature as to his happiness.—*Sterne.*

If we will take the good we find, asking no questions, we shall have heaping measures. The great gifts are not got by analysis. Everything good is on the highway. The middle region of our being is the temperate zone.— *Emerson.*

Contentment is a pearl of great price, and whoever procures it at the expense of ten thousand desires makes a wise and a happy purchase.—*Balguy.*

Contentment gives a crown where fortune hath denied it.—*Ford.*

Contentment is not happiness. An oyster may be contented. Happiness is compounded of richer elements.—*Bovee.*

It conduces much to our content if we pass by those things which happen to our trouble, and consider that which is pleasing and prosperous; that by the representation of the better the worse may be blotted out.—*Jeremy Taylor.*

CONTRADICTION.

We must not contradict, but instruct him that contradicts us; for a madman is not cured by another running mad also.—*Antisthenes.*

CONTRAST.

A learned man is a tank; a wise man is a spring.— *W. R. Alger.*

As the rose-tree is composed of the sweetest flowers and the sharpest thorns, — as the heavens are sometimes overcast, alternately tempestuous and serene; so is the life of man intermingled with hopes and fears, with joy and sorrows, with pleasure and with pains.—*Burton.*

Do not speak of your happiness to a man less fortunate than yourself.— *Plutarch.*

By Heaven ! upon the same man, as upon a vine-planted mount, there grow more kinds of wine than one; on the south side something little worse than nectar, on the north side something little better than vinegar.—*Richter.*

The rose and the thorn, sorrow and gladness, are linked together.—*Saadi.*

Strange as it may seem, the most ludicrous lines I ever wrote have been written in the saddest mood.— *Cowper.*

The superiority of some men is merely local. They are great because their associates are little.—*Johnson.*

No man needs money so much as he who despises it.—*Richter.*

If there be light, then there is darkness; if cold, then heat; if height, depth also; if solid, then fluid; hardness and softness, roughness and smoothness, calm and tempest, prosperity and adversity, life and death.—*Pythagoras.*

The coldest bodies warm with opposition, the hardest sparkle in collision.—*Junius.*

All things are double, one against another. Good is set against evil, and life against death; so is the godly against the sinner, and the sinner against the godly. Look upon all the works of the Most High, and there are two and two, one against another.—*Ecclesiasticus.*

Nature hath meal and bran, contempt and grace.—*Shakespeare.*

Cruel men are the greatest lovers of mercy, avaricious men of generosity, and proud men of humility; that is to say, in others, not in themselves.—*Colton.*

Shadow owes its birth to light.—*Gay.*

Men and statues that are admired in an elevated situation have a very different effect upon us when we approach them; the first appear less than we imagined them, the last bigger.—*Lord Greville.*

The good often sigh more over little faults than the wicked over great. Hence an old proverb, that the stain appears greater according to the brilliancy of what it touches.—
Palmieri.

The presence of the wretched is a burden to to the happy; and alas! the happy still more so to the wretched.—*Goethe.*

Those that are good manners at the court are as ridiculous in the country as the behavior of the country is most mockable at the court.—
Shakespeare.

Joy and grief are never far apart. In the same street the shutters of one house are closed, while the curtains of the next are brushed by shadows of the dance. A wedding-party returns from church, and a funeral winds to its door. The smiles and the sadnesses of life are the tragicomedy of Shakespeare. Gladness and sighs brighten and dim the mirror he beholds.—
Willmott.

Some people with great merit are very disgusting; others with great faults are very pleasing.—*Rochefoucauld.*

Is the jay more precious than the lark because his feathers are more beautiful? Or is the adder better than the eel because his painted skin contents the eye?—*Shakespeare.*

Where there is much light the shadow is deep.—*Goethe.*

CONVERSATION.

There is no real life but cheerful life; therefore valetudinarians should be sworn, before they enter into company, not to say a word of themselves until the meeting breaks up.—*Addison.*

He who sedulously attends, pointedly asks, calmly speaks, coolly answers, and ceases when he has no more to say, is in possession of some of the best requisites of man.—*Lavater.*

To speak well supposes a habit of attention which shows itself in the thought; by language we learn to think, and above all to develop thought.—*Bonstetten.*

As it is the characteristic of great wits to say much in few words, so it is of small wits to talk much and say nothing.—*Rochefoucauld.*

One could take down a book from a shelf ten times more wise and witty than almost any man's conversation. Bacon is wiser, Swift more humorous, than any person one is likely to meet with; but they cannot chime in with the exact frame of thought in which we happen to take them down from our shelves. Therein lies the luxury of conversation; and when a living speaker does not yield us that luxury, he becomes only a book on two legs.—*Campbell.*

Not only to say the right thing in the right place, but, far more difficult still, to leave unsaid the wrong thing at the tempting moment.—
G. A. Sala.

The progress of a private conversation betwixt two persons of different sexes is often decisive of their fate, and gives it a turn very distinct perhaps from what they themselves anticipated. Gallantry becomes mingled with conversation, and affection and passion come gradually to mix with gallantry. Nobles, as well as shepherd swains, will, in such a trying moment, say more than they intended; and queens, like village maidens, will listen longer than they should.—*Walter Scott.*

It is a secret known but to a few, yet of no small use in the conduct of life, that when you fall into a man's conversation, the first thing you should consider is whether he has a greater inclination to hear you, or that you should hear him.—*Steele.*

There is a sort of knowledge beyond the power of learning to bestow, and this is to be had in conversation; so necessary is this to the understanding the characters of men, that none are more ignorant of them than those learned pedants whose lives have been entirely consumed in colleges and among books; for however exquisitely human nature may have been described by writers the true practical system can be learned only in the world.—*Fielding.*

In table talk I prefer the pleasant and witty before the learned and grave.—*Montaigne.*

The first ingredient in conversation is truth, the next good sense, the third good humor, and the fourth wit.—*Sir W. Temple.*

He that questioneth much shall learn much, and content much ; but especially if he apply his questions to the skill of the persons whom he asketh ; for he shall give them occasion to please themselves in speaking, and himself shall continually gather knowledge ; but let his questions not be troublesome, for that is fit for a poser ; and let him be sure to leave other men their turn to speak ; nay, if there be any that would reign and take up all the time, let him find means to take them off, and bring others on, — as musicians used to do with those that dance too long galliards. If you dissemble sometimes your knowledge of that you are thought to know, you shall be thought, another time, to know that you know not.—*Bacon.*

Reasonable men are the best dictionaries of conversation.—*Goethe.*

The secret of pleasing in conversation is not to explain too much everything ; to say them half and leave a little for divination is a mark of the good opinion we have of others, and nothing flatters their self-love more.—
Rochefoucauld.

Those who speak always and those who never speak are equally unfit for friendship. A good proportion of the talent of listening and speaking is the base of social virtues.—*Lavater.*

The secret of tiring is to say everything that can be said on the subject.—*Voltaire.*

One of the first observations to make in conversation is the state, or the character, and the education of the person to whom we speak.
Madame Necker.

If conversation be an art, like painting, sculpture, and literature, it owes its most powerful charm to nature ; and the least shade of formality or artifice destroys the effect of the best collection of words.—*Tuckerman.*

There is no arena in which vanity displays itself under such a variety of forms as in conversation.—*Pascal.*

Conversation opens our views, and gives our faculties a more vigorous play ; it puts us upon turning our notions on every side, and holds them up to a light that discovers those latent flaws which would probably have lain concealed in the gloom of unagitated abstraction.—
Melmoth.

In the sallies of badinage a polite fool shines ; but in gravity he is as awkward as an elephant disporting.—*Zimmermann.*

The extreme pleasure we take in talking of ourselves should make us fear that we give very little to those who listen to us.—*Rochefoucauld.*

When we are in the company of sensible men, we ought to be doubly cautious of talking too much, lest we lose two good things, — their good opinion, and our own improvement ; for what we have to say we know, but what they have to say we know not.—*Colton.*

Silence is one great art of conversation.—
Hazlitt.

Our companions please us less from the charms we find in their conversation than from those they find in ours.—*Lord Greville.*

Conversation enriches the understanding, but solitude is the school of genius.—*Gibbon.*

In conversation, humor is more than wit, easiness more than knowledge ; few desire to learn, or think they need it ; all desire to be pleased, or, at least, to be easy.—
Sir W. Temple.

Conversation is an art in which a man has all mankind for competitors.—*Emerson.*

One of the best rules in conversation is, never say a thing which any of the company can reasonably wish we had rather left unsaid. Let the sage reflections of these philosophic minds be cherished.—*Swift.*

The less men think, the more they talk.
Montesquieu.

The perfection of conversation is not to play a regular sonata, but, like the Æolian harp, to await the inspiration of the passing breeze.—
Burke.

Conversation never sits easier upon us than when we now and then discharge ourselves in a symphony of laughter, which may not improperly be called the chorus of conversation.—
Steele.

The tone of good conversation is brilliant and natural ; it is neither tedious nor frivolous ; it is instructive without pedantry, gay without tumultuousness, polished without affectation, gallant without insipidity, waggish without equivocation.—*Rousseau.*

All men, well interrogated, answer well.—
Plato.

Topics of conversation among the multitude are generally persons, sometimes things, scarcely ever principles.—*W. B. Clulow.*

Never hold any one by the button or the hand in order to be heard out ; for if people are unwilling to hear you, you had better hold your tongue than them.—*Chesterfield.*

Those persons who never speak till they can make a hit are insufferable. They oblige you to fill up the embroidery of which they will only do the flowers.—*Madame Necker.*

I would establish but one general rule to be observed in all conversation, which is this, that men should not talk to please themselves, but those that hear them.—*Steele.*

Repose is as necessary in conversation as in a picture.—*Hazlitt.*

A conversation ought no more to be like a written discourse, than the latter like a conversation. What is pretty singular is, those who fall into the former blemish seldom escape the other; because, being in the habit of speaking as they would write, they imagine they ought to write as they speak. It should be a rule that a man cannot be too much on his guard when he writes to the public, and never too easy towards those with whom he converses.—*D'Alembert.*

It is when you come close to a man in conversation that you discover what his real abilities are. To make a speech in a public assembly is a knack.—*Johnson.*

Conversation is a traffic; and if you enter into it without some stock of knowledge to balance the account perpetually betwixt you, the trade drops at once.—*Sterne.*

Take, rather than give, the tone of the company you are in. If you have parts, you will show them more or less upon every subject; and if you have not, you had better talk sillily upon a subject of other people's than of your own choosing.—*Chesterfield.*

CONVERSION.

As to the value of conversions, God alone can judge. God alone can know how wide are the steps which the soul has to take before it can approach to a community with him, to the dwelling of the perfect, or to the intercourse and friendship of higher natures.—*Goethe.*

In what way, or by what manner of working God changes a soul from evil to good, how he impregnates the barren rock,—the priceless gems and gold,—is to the human mind an impenetrable mystery, in all cases alike.—*Coleridge.*

I have known men who thought the object of conversion was to cleanse them as a garment is cleansed, and that when they are converted they were to be hung up in the Lord's wardrobe, the door of which was to be shut, so that no dust could get at them. A coat that is not used the moths eat; and a Christian who is hung up so that he shall not be tempted, the moths eat him; and they have poor food at that.—*Beecher.*

COQUETRY.

The adoration of his heart had been to her only as the perfume of a wild flower which she had carelessly crushed with her foot in passing.—*Longfellow.*

To boast that we never coquet is itself a sort of coquetry.—*Rochefoucauld.*

Heartlessness and fascination, in about equal quantities, constitute the receipt for forming the character of a court coquette.—*Madame Deluzy.*

An accomplished coquette excites the passions of others in proportion as she feels none herself.—*Hazlitt.*

The characteristic of a coquette is affectation governed by whim; for as beauty, wit, good-nature, politeness, and health are sometimes affected by this creature, so are ugliness, folly, nonsense, ill-nature, ill-breeding, and sickness likewise put on by it in their turn. Its life is one constant lie; and the only rule by which you can form any judgment of them is that they are never what they seem.—*Fielding.*

All women seem by nature to be coquettes, though all do not practise coquetry. Some are restrained by reason, some by fear; none are aware of the extent of their coquetry.—*Rochefoucauld.*

There are many women who have never intrigued, and many men who have never gamed; but those who have done either but once are very extraordinary animals, and more worthy of a glass case when they die than half the exotics in the British Museum.—*Colton.*

There is one antidote only for coquetry, and that is true love.—*Madame Deluzy.*

A coquette is one that is never to be persuaded out of the passion she has to please, nor out of a good opinion of her own beauty; time and years she regards as things that only wrinkle and decay other women; forgets that age is written in the face, and that the same dress which became her when she was young now only makes her look the older. Affectation cleaves to her even in sickness and pain; she dies in a high-head and colored ribbons.—*Bruyère.*

The coquette who sacrifices the ease and reputation of as many as she is able to an ill-natured vanity, is a more pernicious creature than the wretch whom fondness betrays to make her lover happy, at the expense of her own reputation.—*Fielding.*

A coquette is a young lady of more beauty than sense, more accomplishments than learning, more charms of person than graces of mind, more admirers than friends, more fools than wise men for attendants.—*Longfellow.*

Women find it far more difficult to overcome their inclination to coquetry than to overcome their love.—*Rochefoucauld.*

CORRUPTION.

O that estates, degrees, and offices were not derived corruptly ! and that clear honor were purchased by the merit of the wearer ! —
Shakespeare.

Examine well his milk-white hand, the palm is hardly clean, — but here and there an ugly smutch appears. Foh ! It was a bribe that left it. He has touched corruption.— *Cowper.*

My business in the state made me a looker-on here in Vienna, where I have seen corruption boil and bubble till it o'errun the stew.—
Shakespeare.

Corruption is a tree whose branches are of an unmeasurable length ; they spread everywhere ; and the dew that drops from thence hath infected some chairs and stools of authority.—*Beaumont and Fletcher.*

Loathsome canker lives in sweetest bud.—
Shakespeare.

COUNTRY.

Seldom shall we see in cities, courts, and rich families, where men live plentifully and eat and drink freely, that perfect health, that athletic soundness and vigor of constitution which is commonly seen in the country, in poor houses and cottages, where nature is their cook, and necessity their caterer, and where they have no other doctor but the sun and fresh air, and that such a one as never sends them to the apothecary.—*South.*

One gets sensitive about losing mornings after getting a little used to them with living in the country. Each one of these endlessly varied daybreaks is an opera but once performed.—
Willis.

Nor rural sights alone, but rural sounds, exhilarate the spirit and restore the tone of languid nature.— *Cowper.*

There is virtue in country houses, in gardens and orchards, in fields, streams, and groves, in rustic recreations and plain manners, that neither cities nor universities enjoy.—*Alcott.*

Sir, when you have seen one green field, you have seen all green fields. Let us walk down Cheapside.—*Johnson.*

Ask any school-boy up to the age of fifteen where he would spend his holidays. Not one in five hundred will say, " In the streets of London," if you give him the option of green fields and running waters. It is, then, a fair presumption that there must be something of the child still in the character of the men or the women whom the country charms in maturer as in dawning life.—*Bulwer Lytton.*

Men are taught virtue and a love of independence by living in the country.—*Menander.*

The city reveals the moral ends of being, and sets the awful problem of life. The country soothes us, refreshes us, lifts us up with religious suggestion.— *Chapin.*

If country life be healthful to the body, it is no less so to the mind.—*Ruffini.*

Sunny spots of greenery.— *Coleridge.*

In those vernal seasons of the year, when the air is calm and pleasant, it were an injury and sullenness against nature not to go out and see her riches, and partake in her rejoicing with heaven and earth.—*Milton.*

I consider it the best part of an education to have been born and brought up in the country.
Alcott.

COURAGE.

True courage is the result of reasoning. A brave mind is always impregnable. Resolution lies more in the head than in the veins, and a just sense of honor and of infamy, of duty and of religion, will carry us farther than all the force of mechanism.—*Jeremy Collier.*

God is the brave man's hope and not the coward's excuse.— *Plutarch.*

Let him not imagine who aims at greatness that all is lost by a single adverse cast of fortune ; for if fortune has at one time the better of courage, courage may afterwards recover the advantage. He who is prepossessed with the assurance of overcoming at least overcomes the fear of failure ; whereas he who is apprehensive of losing loses, in reality, all hopes of subduing. Boldness and power are such inseparable companions that they appear to be born together ; and when once divided, they both decay and die at the same time.—*Archbishop Venn.*

If we survive danger, it steels our courage more than anything else.—*Niebuhr.*

Physical courage, which despises all danger, will make a man brave in one way ; and moral courage, which despises all opinion, will make a man brave in another. The former would seem most necessary for the camp, the latter for council ; but to constitute a great man, both are necessary ! — *Colton.*

Much danger makes great hearts most resolute.—*Marston.*

Women and men of retiring timidity are cowardly only in dangers which affect themselves, but the first to rescue when others are endangered.—*Richter.*

It is not our criminal actions that require courage to confess, but those which are ridiculous and foolish.—*Rousseau.*

Courage without discipline is nearer beastliness than manhood.—*Sir P. Sidney.*

An intrepid courage is at best but a holiday kind of virtue, to be seldom exercised, and never but in cases of necessity; affability, mildness, tenderness, and a word which I would fain bring back to its original signification of virtue, I mean good-nature, are of daily use; they are the bread of mankind and staff of life.—*Dryden.*

Courage consists not in blindly overlooking danger, but in seeing it and conquering it.—*Richter.*

True courage is cool and calm. The bravest of men have the least of a brutal bullying insolence; and in the very time of danger are found the most serene and free. Rage, we know, can make a coward forget himself and fight. But what is done in fury or anger can never be placed to the account of courage.—*Shaftesbury.*

Who hath not courage to revenge will never find generosity to forgive.—*Henry Home.*

The truest courage is always mixed with circumspection; this being the quality which distinguishes the courage of the wise from the hardiness of the rash and foolish.—*Jones of Nayland.*

The first mark of valor is defence.—*Sir P. Sidney.*

Courage is like the diamond,—very brilliant; not changed by fire, capable of high polish, but except for the purpose of cutting hard bodies, useless.—*Colton.*

Let us not despair too soon, my friend. Men's words are ever bolder than their deeds, and many a one who now appears resolute to meet every extremity with eager zeal, will on a sudden find in their breast a heart which he wot not of.—*Schiller.*

Courage enlarges, cowardice diminishes resources. In desperate straits the fears of the timid aggravate the dangers that imperil the brave. For cowards the road of desertion should be left open. They will carry over to the enemy nothing but their fears. The poltroon, like the scabbard, is an encumbrance when once the sword is drawn.—*Bovee.*

Before putting yourself in peril, it is necessary to foresee and fear it; but when one is there, nothing remains but to despise it.—*Fenelon.*

Courage, so far as it is a sign of race, is peculiarly the mark of a gentleman or a lady; but it becomes vulgar if rude or insensitive, while timidity is not vulgar, if it be a characteristic of race or fineness of make. A fawn is not vulgar in being timid, nor a crocodile "gentle" because courageous.—*Ruskin.*

A brave man thinks no one his superior who does him an injury; for he has it then in his power to make himself superior to the other by forgiving it.—*Pope.*

There is no courage but in innocence; no constancy but in an honest cause.—*Southern.*

Courage is always greatest when blended with meekness; intellectual ability is most admirable when it sparkles in the setting of a modest self-distrust; and never does the human soul appear so strong as when it foregoes revenge and dares to forgive an injury.—*Chapin.*

There is no impossibility to him who stands prepared to conquer every hazard; the fearful are the failing.—*Mrs. S. J. Hale.*

Courage ought to be guided by skill, and skill armed by courage. Neither should hardiness darken wit, nor wit cool hardiness. Be valiant as men despising death, but confident as unwonted to be overcome.—*Sir P. Sidney.*

Courage consists not in hazarding without fear, but being resolutely minded in a just cause.—*Plutarch.*

Courage is poorly housed that dwells in numbers; the lion never counts the herd that are about him, nor weighs how many flocks he has to scatter.—*Aaron Hill.*

Courage makes a man more than himself; for he is then himself plus his valor.—*W. R. Alger.*

By how much unexpected, by so much we must awake endeavor for defence; for courage mounteth with occasion.—*Shakespeare.*

Courage and modesty are the most unequivocal of virtues, for they are of a kind that hypocrisy cannot imitate; they too have this quality in common, that they are expressed by the same color.—*Goethe.*

Courage is adversity's lamp.—*Vauvenargues.*

Remember now, when you meet your antagonist, do everything in a mild, agreeable manner. Let your courage be as keen, but, at the same time, as polished, as your sword.—*Sheridan.*

I dare do all that may become a man; who dares do more is none.—*Shakespeare.*

The brave man is not he who feels no fear, for that were stupid and irrational; but he whose noble soul its fear subdues, and bravely dares the danger nature shrinks from.—*Joanna Baillie.*

COURTESY.

When we are saluted with a salutation, salute the person with a better salutation, or at least return the same, for God taketh an account of all things.—*Koran.*

Nothing costs less nor is cheaper than compliments of civility.—*Cervantes.*

When Zachariah ·Fox, the great merchant of Liverpool, was asked by what means he contrived to realize so large a fortune as he possessed, his reply was: "Friend, by one article alone, and in which thou mayest deal too, if thou pleasest, — it is civility."—*Bentley.*

What fairer cloak than courtesy for fraud ? — *Earl of Stirling.*

Hail! ye small sweet courtesies of life, for smooth do ye make the road of it, like grace and beauty, which beget inclinations to love at first sight; it is ye who open the door and let the stranger in.—*Sterne.*

There is a courtesy of the heart; it is allied to love. From it springs the purest courtesy in the outward behavior.—*Goethe.*

The small courtesies sweeten life; the greater ennoble it.—*Bovee.*

Courtesy which oft is sooner found in lowly sheds, with smoky rafters, than in tapestry halls and courts of princes, where it first was named. *Milton.*

O dissembling courtesy! how fine this tyrant can tickle where she wounds! —*Shakespeare.*

As the sword of the best-tempered metal is most flexible, so the truly generous are most pliant and courteous in their behavior to their inferiors.—*Fuller.*

Approved valor is made precious by natural courtesy.—*Sir P. Sidney.*

We must be as courteous to a man as we are to a picture, which we are willing to give the advantage of a good light.—*Emerson.*

Courtesy is a science of the highest importance. It is, like grace and beauty in the body, which charm at first sight, and lead on to further intimacy and friendship, opening a door that we may derive instruction from the example of others, and at the same time enabling us to benefit them by our example, if there be anything in our character worthy of imitation.— *Montaigne.*

There is no outward sign of courtesy that does not rest on a deep moral foundation.— *Goethe.*

It is a kind of good deed to say well; and yet words are no deeds.—*Shakespeare.*

Comely courtesy that unto every person knew her part.—*Spenser.*

A churlish courtesy rarely comes but either for gain or falsehood.—*Sir P. Sidney.*

Whilst thou livest, keep a good tongue in thy head.—*Shakespeare.*

Nothing is a courtesy unless it be meant us, and that friendly and lovingly. We owe no thanks to rivers that they carry our boats, or winds that they be favoring and fill our sails, or meats that they be nourishing; for these are what they are necessarily. Horses carry us, trees shade us; but they know it not.— *Ben Jonson.*

Civility is a desire to receive civility, and to be accounted well-bred.—*Rochefoucauld.*

If ever I should affect injustice, it would be in this, that I might do courtesies and receive none.—*Feltham.*

The whole of heraldry and of chivalry is in courtesy. A man of fine manners shall pronounce your name with all the ornament that titles of nobility could ever add.—*Emerson.*

When my friends are blind of one eye, I look at them in profile.—*Joubert.*

Great talents, such as honor, virtue, learning, and parts, are above the generality of the world, who neither possess them themselves, nor judge of them rightly in others; but all people are judges of the lesser talents, such as civility, affability, and an obliging, agreeable address and manner, because they feel the good effects of them, as making society easy and pleasing.—*Chesterfield.*

A good word is an easy obligation; but not to speak ill requires only our silence, which costs us nothing.—*Tillotson.*

COURTIER.

The chief requisites for a courtier are a flexible conscience and an inflexible politeness. *Lady Blessington.*

Poor wretches that depend on greatness's favor dream as I have done; wake and find nothing.—*Shakespeare.*

The court does not render a man contented, but it prevents his being so elsewhere.—*Bruyère.*

A courtier's dependant is a beggar's dog.— *Shenstone.*

Not a courtier, although they wear their faces to the bent of the king's looks, hath a heart that is not glad at the thing they scowl at. *Shakespeare.*

A court is an assemblage of noble and distinguished beggars.—*Talleyrand.*

COURTSHIP.

Courtship consists in a number of quiet attentions, not so pointed as to alarm, nor so vague as not to be understood.—*Sterne.*

With women worth the being won the softest lover ever best succeeds.—*Aaron Hill.*

If you cannot inspire a woman with love of you, fill her above the brim with love of herself; all that runs over will be yours.—*Colton.*

She half consents who silently denies.—*Ovid.*

He that can keep handsomely within rules, and support the carriage of a companion to his mistress, is much more likely to prevail than he who lets her see the whole relish of his life depends upon her. If possible, therefore, divert your mistress rather than sigh for her.—*Steele.*

She is a woman, therefore may be wooed; she is a woman, therefore may be won.—
Shakespeare.

Men dream in courtship, but in wedlock wake!—*Pope.*

I knelt, and with the fervor of a lip unused to the cool breath of reason, told my love.—
Willis.

The pleasantest part of a man's life is generally that which passes in courtship, provided his passion be sincere, and the party beloved kind with discretion. Love, desire, hope, all the pleasing emotions of the soul, rise in the pursuit.—*Addison.*

Men are April when they woo, December when they wed.—*Shakespeare.*

A town, before it can be plundered and deserted, must first be taken; and in this particular Venus has borrowed a law from her consort Mars. A woman that wishes to retain her suitor must keep him in the trenches; for this is a siege which the besieger never raises for want of supplies, since a feast is more fatal to love than a fast, and a surfeit than a starvation. Inanition may cause it to die a slow death, but repletion always destroys it by a sudden one.—
Colton.

I profess not to know how women's hearts are wooed and won. To me they have always been matters of riddle and admiration.—
Washington Irving.

She most attracts who longest can refuse.—
Aaron Hill.

That man that has a tongue, I say, is no man if with his tongue he cannot win a woman.—
Shakespeare.

Courtship is a fine bowling-green turf, all galloping round and sweethearting, a sunshine holiday in summer time; but when once through matrimony's turnpike, the weather becomes wintry, and some husbands are seized with a cold, aguish fit, to which the faculty give the name of indifference.—*G. A. Stevens.*

See how the skilful lover spreads his toils.—
Stillingfleet.

Let a woman once give you a task, and you are hers, heart and soul; all your care and trouble lend new charms to her for whose sake they are taken. To rescue, to revenge, to instruct, or protect a woman is all the same as to love her.—*Richter.*

COVETOUSNESS.

Some men are so covetous, as if they were to live forever; and others so profuse, as if they were to die the next moment.—*Aristotle.*

Covetousness, which is idolatry.—*Bible.*

Where necessity ends, desire and curiosity begin; and no sooner are we supplied with everything nature can demand than we sit down to contrive artificial appetites.—*Johnson.*

He deservedly loses his own property who covets that of another.—*Phædrus.*

To think well of every other man's condition, and to dislike our own, is one of the misfortunes of human nature. "Pleased with each other's lot, our own we hate."—*Burton.*

When all sins are old in us, and go upon crutches, covetousness does but then lie in her cradle.—*Decker.*

A circle cannot fill a triangle, so neither can the whole world, if it were to be compassed, the heart of man; a man may as easily fill a chest with grace as the heart with gold. The air fills not the body, neither doth money the covetous mind of man.—*Spenser.*

The soul of man is infinite in what it covets.
Ben Jonson.

The covetous person lives as if the world were made altogether for him, and not he for the world; to take in everything, and part with nothing.—*South.*

If money be not thy servant, it will be thy master. The covetous man cannot so properly be said to possess wealth, as that may be said to possess him.—*Bacon.*

Covetousness swells the principal to no purpose, and lessens the use to all purposes.—
Jeremy Taylor.

Covetous men need money least, yet they most affect it; but prodigals, who need it most, have the least regard for it.—*Alexander Wilson.*

Covetous men are fools, miserable wretches, buzzards, madmen, who live by themselves, in perpetual slavery, fear, suspicion, sorrow, discontent, with more of gall than honey in their enjoyments; who are rather possessed by their money than possessors of it.—*Burton*

Covetousness, like a candle ill made, smothers the splendor of a happy fortune in its own grease.—*F. Osborn.*

Covetousness, like jealousy, when it has once taken root, never leaves a man but with his life.—*Thomas Hughes.*

It was with good reason that God commanded through Moses that the vineyard and harvest were not to be gleaned to the last grape or grain ; but something to be left for the poor. For covetousness is never to be satisfied ; the more it has, the more it wants. Such insatiable ones injure themselves, and transform God's blessings into evil.—*Luther.*

Why are we so blind ?   That which we improve, we have, that which we hoard is not for ourselves.—*Madame Deluzy.*

When workmen strive to do better than well, they do confound their skill in covetousness.—*Shakespeare.*

The covetous man heaps up riches, not to enjoy them, but to have them ; and starves himself in the midst of plenty, and most nunaturally cheats and robs himself of that which is his own ; and makes a hard shift to be as poor and miserable with a great estate as any man can be without it.—*Tillotson.*

Those who give not till they die show that they would not then if they could keep it any longer.—*Bishop Hall.*

Suppose a more complete assemblage of sublunary enjoyments, and a more perfect system of earthly felicity than ever the sun beheld, the mind of man would instantly devour it, and, as if it was still empty and unsatisfied, would require something more.—*Leighton.*

Poor in abundance, famished at a feast, man's grief is but his grandeur in disguise, and discontent is immortality.—*Young.*

He that visits the sick in hopes of a legacy, let him be never so friendly in all other cases, I look upon him in this to be no better than a raven that watches a weak sheep only to peck out its eyes.—*Seneca.*

Covetousness, by a greediness of getting more, deprives itself of the true end of getting ; it loses the enjoyment of what it has got.—*Sprat.*

Although the beauties, riches, honors, sciences, virtues, and perfections of all men living were in the present possession of one, yet somewhat above and beyond all this would still be sought and earnestly thirsted for.—*Hooker.*

Covetousness is a sort of mental gluttony, not confined to money, but craving honor, and feeding on selfishness.—*Chamfort.*

The covetous man pines in plenty, like Tantalus up to the chin in water, and yet thirsty.—*Rev. T. Adams.*

Covetousness teaches men to be cruel and crafty, industrious and evil, full of care and malice ; and after all this, it is for no good to itself, for it dares not spend those heaps of treasure which it has snatched.—*Jeremy Taylor.*

Of covetousness we may truly say that it makes both the Alpha and Omega in the devil's alphabet, and that it is the first vice in corrupt nature which moves, and the last which dies.— *South.*

COWARDICE.

Cowards falter, but danger is often overcome by those who nobly dare.—*Queen Elizabeth.*

All mankind is one of these two cowards, either to wish to die when he should live, or live when he should die.—*Sir Robert Howard.*

What masks are these uniforms to hide cowards ! —*Duke of Wellington.*

It is a law of nature that faint-hearted men should be the fruit of luxurious countries, for we never find that the same soil produces delicacies and heroes.—*Herodotus.*

The craven's fear is but selfishness, like his merriment.—*Whittier.*

My valor is certainly going ! it is sneaking off ! I feel it oozing out, as it were, at the palms of my hands.—*Sheridan.*

Plenty and peace breed cowards ; hardness ever of hardiness is mother.—*Shakespeare.*

Lie not, neither to thyself, nor man, nor God. Let mouth and heart be one ; heat and speak together, and make both felt in action. It is for cowards to lie.—*George Herbert.*

It is vain for the coward to fly ; death follows close behind ; it is by defying it that the brave escape.—*Voltaire.*

When the passengers gallop by as if fear made them speedy, the cur follows them with an open mouth ; let them walk by in confident neglect, and the dog will not stir at all ; it is a weakness that every creature takes advantage of.—*J. Beaumont.*

Cowards die many times before their death ; the valiant taste of death but once.— *Shakespeare.*

Commonly they use their feet for defence, whose tongue is their weapon.—*Sir P. Sidney.*

If cowardice were not so completely a coward as to be unable to look steadily upon the effects of courage, he would find that there is no refuge so sure as dauntless valor.—*Jane Porter.*

You are the hare of whom the proverb goes, whose valor plucks dead lions by the beard.—*Shakespeare.*

One of the chief misfortunes of honest people is that they are cowardly.—*Voltaire.*

Mankind are dastardly when they meet with opposition.—*Franklin.*

Fear is the virtue of slaves: but the heart that loveth is willing.—*Longfellow.*

It is the coward who fawns upon those above him. It is the coward that is insolent whenever he dares be so.—*Junius.*

Cowardice is not synonymous with prudence. It often happens that the better part of diseretion is valor.—*Hazlitt.*

A coward ; a most devout coward ; religious in it.—*Shakespeare.*

COXCOMB.

A coxcomb begins by determining that his own profession is the first; and he finishes by deciding that he is the first of his profession.—*Colton.*

A coxcomb is ugly all over with the affectation of the fine gentleman.—*Johnson.*

A vulgar man is captious and jealous ; eager and impetuous about trifles. He suspects himself to be slighted, and thinks everything that is said meant at him.—*Chesterfield.*

None are so seldom found alone, and are so soon tired of their own company, as those coxcombs who are on the best terms with themselves.—*Colton.*

Foppery is never cured ; it is the bad stamina of the mind, which, like those of the body, are never rectified ; once a coxcomb, and always a coxcomb.—*Johnson.*

CREDITOR.

Creditors have better memories than debtors, and creditors are a superstitious sect, great observers of set days and times.—*Franklin.*

There is nothing in this world so fiendish as the conduct of a mean man when he has the power to revenge himself upon a noble one in adversity. It takes a man to make a devil ; and the fittest man for such a purpose is a snarling, waspish, red-hot, fiery creditor.—*Beecher.*

The most trifling actions that affect a man's credit are to be regarded. The sound of your hammer at five in the morning or nine at night, heard by a creditor, makes him easy six months longer ; but if he sees you at a billiard-table, or hears your voice at a tavern, when you should be at work, he sends for his money the next day.—*Franklin.*

The creditor whose appearance gladdens the heart of a debtor may hold his head in sunbeams and his foot on storms.—*Lavater.*

Credit is like a looking-glasss, which, when only sullied by a breath, may be wiped clear again, but if once cracked, can never be repaired.—*Walter Scott.*

CREDULITY.

The only disadvantage of an honest heart is credulity.—*Sir P. Sidney.*

The more gross the fraud, the more glibly will it go down, and the more greedily will it be swallowed, since folly will always find faith wherever impostors will find impudence.—*Bovee.*

We all know that a lie needs no other grounds than the invention of the liar; and to take for granted as truth all that is alleged against the fame of others is a species of credulity that men would blush at on any other subject.—*Jane Porter.*

Fear, if it be not immoderate, puts a guard about us that does watch and defend us ; but credulity keeps us naked, and lays us open to all the sly assaults of ill-intending men : it was a virtue when man was in his innocence; but since his fall, it abuses those that own it.—*Feltham.*

In all places, and in all times, those religionists who have believed too much have been more inclined to violence and persecution than those who have believed too little.—*Colton.*

I cannot spare the luxury of believing that all things beautiful are what they seem.—*Halleck.*

Credulity is the common failing of inexperienced virtue, and he who is spontaneously suspicious may be justly charged with radical corruption.—*Johnson.*

You believe that easily which you hope for earnestly.—*Terence.*

The general goodness which is nourished in noble hearts makes every one think that strength of virtue to be in another whereof they find assured foundation in themselves.—*Sir P. Sidney.*

Credulity is perhaps a weakness almost inseparable from eminently truthful characters.—*Tuckerman.*

We believe at once in evil; we only believe in good upon reflection. Is not this sad ?—*Madame Deluzy.*

O credulity, thou hast as many ears as fame has tongues, open to every sound of truth as of falsehood.—*Havard.*

It is a curious paradox, that precisely in proportion to our own intellectual weakness will be our credulity as to those mysterious powers assumed by others.—*Colton.*

Generous souls are still most subject to credulity.—*Sir W. Davenant.*

Men are most apt to believe what they least understand; and through the lust of human wit obscure things are more easily credited.—*Pliny.*

Superstition is certainly not the characteristic of this age. Yet some men are bigoted in politics who are infidels in religion. Ridiculous credulity! —*Junius.*

Your noblest natures are most credulous.—*Chapman.*

CREED.

In politics, as in religion, it so happens that we have less charity for those who believe the half of our creed than for those that deny the whole of it.—*Colton.*

He that will believe only what he can fully comprehend must have a very long head or a very short creed.—*Colton.*

CRIME.

Crimes sometimes shock us too much; vices almost always too little.—*Hare.*

There are crimes which become innocent, and even glorious, through their splendor, number, and excess; hence it is that public theft is called address, and to seize unjustly on provinces is to make conquests.—*Rochefoucauld.*

One crime is everything; two nothing.—*Madame Deluzy.*

Of all the adult male criminals in London, not two in a hundred have entered upon a course of crime who have lived an honest life up to the age of twenty; almost all who enter upon a course of crime do so between the ages of eight and sixteen.—*Earl of Shaftesbury.*

Heaven will permit no man to secure happiness by crime.—*Alfieri.*

Small crimes always precede great crimes. Whoever has been able to transgress the limits set by law may afterwards violate the most sacred rights; crime, like virtue, has its degrees, and never have we seen timid innocence pass suddenly to extreme licentiousness.—*Racine.*

Fear follows crime, and is its punishment.—*Voltaire.*

The contagion of crime is like that of the plague. Criminals collected together corrupt each other; they are worse than ever when at the termination of their punishment they re-enter society.—*Napoleon.*

Those who are themselves incapable of great crimes are ever backward to suspect others.—*Rochefoucauld.*

It is supposable that, in the eyes of angels, a struggle down a dark lane and a battle of Leipsic differ in nothing but excess of wickedness.—*Willmott.*

There is no den in the wide world to hide a rogue. Commit a crime, and the earth is made of glass. Commit a crime, and it seems as if a coat of snow fell on the ground, such as reveals in the woods the track of every partridge and fox, and squirrel and mole.—*Emerson.*

Most people fancy themselves innocent of those crimes of which they cannot be convicted.—*Seneca.*

The perfection of a thing consists in its essence; there are perfect criminals, as there are men of perfect probity.—*La Roche.*

CRISIS.

There is a moment of difficulty and danger at which flattery and falsehood can no longer deceive, and simplicity itself can no longer be misled.—*Junius.*

CRITICISM.

Criticism is the child and handmaid of reflection. It works by censure, and censure implies a standard.—*Richard Grant White.*

There is a certain meddlesome spirit which, in the garb of learned research, goes prying about the traces of history, casting down its monuments, and marring and mutilating its fairest trophies. Care should be taken to vindicate great names from such pernicious erudition.—*Washington Irving.*

Ten censure wrong for one who writes amiss.—*Pope.*

Neither praise nor blame is the object of true criticism. Justly to discriminate, firmly to establish, wisely to prescribe, and honestly to award,—these are the true aims and duties of criticism.—*Simms.*

Criticism is like champagne, nothing more execrable if bad, nothing more excellent if good; if meagre, muddy, vapid, and sour, both are fit only to engender colic and wind; but if rich, generous, and sparkling, they communicate a genial glow to the spirits, improve the taste, and expand the heart.—*Colton.*

There is scarcely a good critic of books born in our age, and yet every fool thinks himself justified in criticising persons.—*Bulwer Lytton.*

The purity of the critical ermine, like that of the judicial, is often soiled by contact with politics.—*Whipple.*

Doubtless criticism was originally benignant, pointing out the beauties of a work rather than its defects. The passions of men have made it malignant, as the bad heart of Procrustes turned the bed, the symbol of repose, into an instrument of torture.—*Longfellow.*

The most noble criticism is that in which the critic is not the antagonist so much as the rival of the author.—*Disraeli.*

It is quite cruel that a poet cannot wander through his regions of enchantment without having a critic forever, like the Old Man of the Sea, upon his back.—*Moore.*

Get your enemies to read your works in order to mend them, for your friend is so much your second self that he will judge too like you.
Pope.

Criticism must never be sharpened into anatomy. The delicate veins of fancy may be traced, and the rich blood that gives bloom and health to the complexion of thought be resolved into its elements. Stop there. The life of the imagination, as of the body, disappears when we pursue it.—*Willmott.*

Critics are sentinels in the grand army of letters, stationed at the corners of newspapers and reviews, to challenge every new author.—
Longfellow.

The critic, as he is currently termed, who is discerning in nothing but faults, may care little to be told that this is the mark of unamiable dispositions or of bad passions; but he might not feel equally easy, were he convinced that he thus gives the most absolute proofs of ignorance and want of taste.—*Macculloch.*

Is it in destroying and pulling down that skill is displayed? The shallowest understanding, the rudest hand, is more than equal to that task.—*Burke.*

The malignant deity Criticism dwelt on the top of a snowy mountain in Nova Zembla; Momus found her extended in her den upon the spoils of numberless volumes half devoured. At her right hand sat Ignorance, her father and husband, blind with age; at her left, Pride, her mother, dressing her up in the scraps of paper herself had torn. There was Opinion, her sister, light of foot, hoodwinked, and headstrong, yet giddy and perpetually turning. About her played her children, Noise and Impudence, Dulness and Vanity, Positiveness, Pedantry, and Ill Manners.—*Swift.*

It is a maxim with me that no man was ever written out of reputation but by himself.—
Bentley.

It is ridiculous for any man to criticise on the works of another who has not distinguished himself by his own performances.—*Addison.*

There are some books and characters so pleasant, or rather which contain so much that is pleasant, that criticism is perplexed or silent. The hounds are perpetually at fault among the sweet-scented herbs and flowers that grow at the base of Etna.—*J. F. Boyes.*

Of all the cants in this canting world, deliver me from the cant of criticism.—*Sterne.*

He who would reproach an author for obscurity should look into his own mind to see whether it is quite clear there. In the dusk the plainest writing is illegible.—*Goethe.*

One interesting feature of criticism is seen in the ease with which it discovers what Addison called the specific quality of an author. In Livy, it will be the manner of telling the story; in Sallust, personal identification with the character; in Tacitus, the analysis of the deed into its motive. If the same test be applied to painters, it will find the prominent faculty of Correggio to be manifested in harmony of effect; of Poussin, in the sentiment of his landscapes; and of Raffaelle, in the general comprehension of his subject.—*Willmott.*

Critics must excuse me if I compare them to certain animals called asses, who, by gnawing vines, originally taught the great advantage of pruning them.—*Shenstone.*

It is necessary a writing critic should understand how to write. And though every writer is not bound to show himself in the capacity of critic, every writing critic is bound to show himself capable of being a writer; for if he be apparently impotent in this latter kind, he is to be denied all title or character in the other.—
Shaftesbury.

Criticism is as often a trade as a science; it requiring more health than wit, more labor than capacity, more practice than genius.—*Bruyère.*

A true critic, in the perusal of a book, is like a dog at a feast, whose thoughts and stomach are wholly set upon what the guests fling away, and consequently is apt to snarl most when there are the fewest bones.—*Swift.*

The fangs of a bear and the tusks of a wild boar do not bite worse, and make deeper gashes, than a goosequill sometimes; no, not even the badger himself, who is said to be so tenacious of his bite that he will not give over his hold till he feels his teeth meet, and the bones crack.—*Howell.*

The eyes of critics, whether in commending or carping, are both on one side, like a turbot's.
Landor.

We rarely meet with persons that have true judgment; which, to many, renders literature a very tiresome knowledge. Good judges are as rare as good authors.—*St. Evremond.*

Criticism often takes from the tree caterpillars and blossoms together.—*Richter.*

Some critics are like chimney-sweepers; they put out the fire below, and frighten the swallows from their nests above; they scrape a long time in the chimney, cover themselves with soot, and bring nothing away but a bag of cinders, and then sing from the top of the house as if they had built it.—*Longfellow.*

If a faultless poem could be produced, I am satisfied it would tire the critics themselves, and annoy the whole reading world with the spleen.
Walter Scott.

It behooves the minor critic who hunts for blemishes to be a little distrustful of his own sagacity.—*Junius.*

Of all mortals a critic is the silliest; for, inuring himself to examine all things whether they are of consequence or not, never looks upon anything but with a design of passing sentence upon it; by which means he is never a companion, but always a censor.—*Steele.*

He wreathed the rod of criticism with roses.
Disraeli.

The pleasure of criticism takes from us that of being deeply moved by very beautiful things.
Bruyère.

A poet that fails in writing becomes often a morose critic. The weak and insipid white-wine makes at length excellent vinegar.—
Shenstone.

It is easy to criticise an author, but it is difficult to appreciate him.—*Vauvenargues.*

If men of wit and genius would resolve never to complain in their works of critics and detractors, the next age would not know that they ever had any.—*Swift.*

CRITICS.

Critics are a kind of freebooters in the republic of letters, who, like deer, goats, and divers other graminivorous animals, gain subsistence by gorging upon buds and leaves of the young shrubs of the forest, thereby robbing them of their verdure and retarding their progress to maturity.—*Washington Irving.*

To be a mere verbal critic is what no man of genius would be if he could; but to be a critic of true taste and feeling is what no man without genius could be if he would.—*Colton.*

He whose first emotion on the view of an excellent production is to undervalue it will never have one of his own to show.—*Aikin.*

The severest critics are always those who have either never attempted, or who have failed in original composition.—*Hazlitt.*

Professional critics are incapable of distinguishing and appreciating either diamonds in the rough state or gold in bars. They are traders, and in literature know only the coins that are current. Their criticism has scales and weights, but neither crucible nor touchstone.—*Joubert.*

It is the heart that makes the critic, not the nose.—*Max Müller.*

The exercise of criticism always destroys for a time our sensibility to beauty by leading us to regard the work in relation to certain laws of construction. The eye turns from the charms of nature to fix itself upon the servile dexterity of art.—*Alison.*

It is not enough for a reader to be unprejudiced. He should remember that a book is to be studied, as a picture is hung. Not only must a bad light be avoided, but a good one obtained. This taste supplies. It puts a history, a tale, or a poem in a just point of view, and there examines the execution.—*Willmott.*

Hold their farthing candle to the sun.—
Young.

CRUELTY.

The man who prates about the cruelty of angling will be found invariably to beat his wife.—*Christopher North.*

The cruelty of the effeminate is more dreadful than that of the hardy.—*Lavater.*

I would not enter on my list of friends (though graced with polished manners and fine sense, yet wanting sensibility) the man who needlessly sets foot upon a worm.—*Cowper.*

Cruelty and fear shake hands together.—
Balzac.

When the cruel fall into the hands of the cruel, we read their fate with horror, not with pity. Sylla commanded the bones of Marius to be broken, his eyes to be pulled out, his hands to be cut off, and his body to be torn in pieces with pincers, and Catiline was the executioner. "A piece of cruelty," says Seneca, "only fit for Marius to suffer, Catiline to execute, and Sylla to command."—*Colton.*

All cruelty springs from weakness.—*Seneca.*

Cruelty is no more the cure of crimes than it is the cure of sufferings. Compassion, in the first instance, is good for both ; I have known it to bring compunction when nothing else would.
Landor.

Much more may a judge overweigh himself in cruelty than in clemency.—*Sir P. Sidney.*

Let me be cruel, not unnatural ; I will speak daggers to her, but use none; my tongue and soul in this be hypocrites.—*Shakespeare.*

Detested sport, that owes its pleasures to another's pain.—*Cowper.*

Nothing is so pregnant as cruelty; so multifarious, so rapid, so ever teeming a mother is unknown to the animal kingdom; each of her experiments provokes another and refines upon the last; though always progressive, yet always remote from the end.—*Lavater.*

CULTIVATION.

It is very rare to find ground which produces nothing; if it is not covered with flowers, with fruit-trees and grains, it produces briers and pines. It is the same with man; if he is not virtuous, he becomes vicious.—*Bruyère.*

Partial culture runs to the ornate; extreme culture to simplicity.—*Bovee.*

The earth flourishes, or is overrun with noxious weeds and brambles, as we apply or withhold the cultivating hand. So fares it with the intellectual system of man. If you are a parent, then, consider that the good or ill dispositions and principles you please to cultivate in the mind of your infant may hereafter preserve a nation in prosperity, or hang its fate on the point of the sword.—*Horace Mann.*

Reading makes a full man, conference a ready man, and writing an exact man.—*Bacon.*

There is no reason why the brown hand of labor should not hold Thomson as well as the sickle. Ornamental reading shelters and even strengthens the growth of what is merely useful. A cornfield never returns a poorer crop because a few wild-flowers bloom in the hedge. The refinement of the poor is the triumph of Christian civilization.—*Willmott.*

A well-cultivated mind is, so to speak, made up of all the minds of preceding ages; it is only one single mind which has been educated during all this time.—*Fontenelle.*

It matters little whether a man be mathematically or philologically or artistically cultivated, so he be but cultivated.—*Goethe.*

Whatever expands the affections, or enlarges the sphere of our sympathies,—whatever makes us feel our relation to the universe, and all that it inherits, in time and in eternity, to the great and beneficent Cause of all, must unquestionably refine our nature, and 'elevate us in the scale of being.—*Channing.*

Cultivation to the mind is as necessary as food is to the body.—*Cicero.*

Not that the moderns are born with more wit than their predecessors, but, finding the world better furnished at their coming into it, they have more leisure for new thoughts, more light to direct them, and more hints to work upon.—*Jeremy Collier.*

As the soil, however rich it may be, cannot be productive without culture, so the mind, without cultivation, can never produce good fruit.—*Seneca.*

A man's nature runs either to herbs or weeds; therefore let him seasonably water the one and destroy the other.—*Lady Gethin.*

I am very sure that any man of common understanding may, by culture, care, attention, and labor, make himself whatever he pleases, except a great poet.—*Chesterfield.*

CUNNING.

Cunning leads to knavery; it is but a step from one to the other, and that very slippery; lying only makes the difference; add to that cunning, and it is knavery.—*Bruyère.*

This is the fruit of craft; like him that shoots up high, looks for the shaft, and finds it in his forehead.—*Middleton.*

Cunning is the art of concealing our own defects, and discovering other people's weaknesses.—*Hazlitt.*

Whoever appears to have much cunning has in reality very little; being deficient in the essential article, which is, to hide cunning.—
Henry Home.

Cunning pays no regard to virtue, and is but the low mimic of wisdom.—*Bolingbroke.*

The common practice of cunning is the sign of a small genius; it almost always happens that those who use it to cover themselves in one place lay themselves open in another.—
Rochefoucauld.

Cunning is none of the best nor worst qualities; it floats between virtue and vice; there is scarce any exigence where it may not, and perhaps ought not to be supplied by prudence.—
Bruyère.

Knowledge without justice ought to be called cunning rather than wisdom.—*Plato.*

All my own experience of life teaches me the contempt of cunning, not the fear. The phrase " profound cunning " has always seemed to me a contradiction in terms. I never knew a cunning mind which was not either shallow or on some point diseased.—*Mrs. Jameson.*

We take cunning for a sinister or crooked wisdom; and certainly there is a great difference between a cunning man and a wise man, not only in point of honesty, but in point of ability.
Bacon.

It has been a sort of maxim that the greatest art is to conceal art; but I know not how, among some people we meet with, their greatest cunning is to appear cunning.—*Steele.*

The most sure method of subjecting yourself to be deceived is to consider yourself more cunning than others.—*Rochefoucauld.*

Cunning is only the mimic of discretion, and may pass upon mean men in the same manner as vivacity is often mistaken for wit, and gravity for wisdom.—*Addison.*

Cunning is the dwarf of wisdom.— *W. R. Alger.*

Cunning has only private selfish aims, and sticks at nothing which may make them succeed. Discretion has large and extended views, and, like a well-formed eye, commands a whole horizon ; cunning is a kind of short-sightedness, that discovers the minutest objects which are near at hand, but is not able to discern things at a distance.—*Addison.*

In a great business there is nothing so fatal as cunning management.—*Junius.*

Those who are overreached by our cunning are far from appearing to us as ridiculous as we appear to ourselves when the cunning of others has overreached us.—*Rochefoucauld.*

Cunning to wisdom is as an ape to man.— *William Penn.*

The whole power of cunning is privative ; to say nothing, and to do nothing, is the utmost of its reach. Yet men, thus narrow by nature and mean by art, are sometimes able to rise by the miscarriages of bravery and the openness of integrity, and, watching failures and snatching opportunities, obtain advantages which belong to higher characters.—*Johnson.*

A cunning man overreaches no one half as much as himself.—*Beecher.*

Hurry and cunning are the two apprentices of despatch and of skill ; but neither of them ever learn their masters' trade.—*Colton.*

The bounds of a man's knowledge are easily concealed if he has but prudence.—*Goldsmith.*

The very cunn'ng conceal their cunning ; the indifferently shrewd boast of it.—*Bovee.*

The greatest of all cunning is to seem blind to the snares which we know to be laid for us. Men are never so easily deceived as while they are endeavoring to deceive others.— *Rochefoucauld.*

CURIOSITY.

Men are more inclined to ask curious questions than to obtain necessary instruction.— *Pasquier Quesnel.*

Of all the faculties of the human mind, curiosity is that which is the most fruitful or the most barren in effective results, according as it is well or badly directed.—*Palmieri.*

No heart is empty of the humor of curiosity, the beggar being as attentive in his station to an improvement of knowledge as the prince.— *Osborn.*

Avoid him who from mere curiosity asks three questions running about a thing that cannot interest him.—*Lavater.*

The over-curious are not over wise.— *Massinger.*

Who forces himself on others is to himself a load. Impetuous curiosity is empty and inconstant. Prying intrusion may be suspected of whatever is little.—*Lavater.*

The first and simplest emotion which we discover in the human mind is curiosity.—*Burke.*

Curiosity is a kernel of the forbidden fruit, which still sticketh in the throat of a natural man, sometimes to the danger of his choking.— *Fuller.*

The curiosity of an honorable mind willingly rests there where the love of truth does not urge it further onward, and the love of its neighbor bids it stop ; in other words, it willingly stops at the point where the interests of truth do not beckon it onward, and charity cries Halt ! *Coleridge.*

Curiosity is as much the parent of attention as attention is of memory.—*Whately.*

There are different kinds of curiosity, — one of interest, which causes us to learn that which would be useful to us ; and the other of pride which springs from a desire to know that of which others are ignorant.—*Rochefoucauld.*

The curiosity of knowing things has been given to man for a scourge.—*Bible.*

I loathe that low vice curiosity.—*Byron.*

There is philosophy in the remark that every man has in his own life follies enough, in the performance of his duty deficiencies enough, in his own mind trouble enough, without being curious after the affairs of others. *Dibdin.*

O this itch of the ear, that breaks out at the tongue ! Were not curiosity so over-busy, detraction would soon be starved to death.— *Douglas Jerrold.*

Curiosity is the direct incontinency of the spirit. Knock therefore at the door before you enter upon your neighbor's privacy ; and remember that there is no difference between entering into his house and looking into it.— *Jeremy Taylor.*

He who would pry behind the scenes oft sees a counterfeit.—*Dryden.*

Curiosity is the most superficial of all the affections; it changes its object perpetually; it has an appetite which is very sharp, but very easily satisfied, and it has always an appearance of giddiness, restlessness, and anxiety.—*Burke.*

Inquisitive people are the funnels of conversation; they do not take in anything for their own use, but merely to pass it to another.
Steele.

Curiosity is one of the permanent and certain characteristics of a vigorous intellect. Every advance into knowledge opens new prospects, and produces new incitements to further progress.—*Johnson.*

CURSES.
Let this pernicious hour stand aye accursed in the calendar ! —*Shakespeare.*

A curse is like a cloud, — it passes.—*Bailey.*

We let our blessings get mouldy, and then call them curses.—*Beecher.*

Dinna curse him, sir; I have heard a good man say that a curse was like a stone flung up to the heavens, and maist like to return on his head that sent it.— *Walter Scott.*

Curses are like young chickens and still come home to roost.—*Bulwer Lytton.*

CUSTOM.
The influence of costume is incalculable ; dress a boy as a man and he will at once change his own conception of himself.—*Bayle St. John.*

Custom does often reason overrule.—
Rochester.

Custom is the great leveller. It corrects the inequality of fortune by lessening equally the pleasures of the prince and the pains of the peasant.—*Henry Home.*

The way of the world is to make laws, but follow customs.—*Montaigne.*

Choose always the way that seems the best, however rough it may be. Custom will render it easy and agreeable.—*Pythagoras.*

New customs, though they be never so ridiculous, nay, let them be unmanly, yet are followed.—*Shakespeare.*

Can there be any greater dotage in the world than for one to guide and direct his courses by the sound of a bell, and not by his own judgment and discretion ? —*Rabelais.*

Custom is the law of fools.— *Vanbrugh*

There are not unfrequently substantial reasons underneath for customs that appear to us absurd.— *Charlotte Bronté.*

The custom and fashion of to-day will be the awkwardness and outrage of to-morrow. So arbitrary are these transient laws.—*Dumas.*

Custom is the law of one description of fools, and fashion of another ; but the .two parties often clash, for precedent is the legislator of the first and novelty of the last.— *Colton.*

Be not so bigoted to any custom as to worship it at the expense of truth.—*Zimmermann.*

Be not too rash in the breaking of an inconvenient custom ; as it was gotten, so leave it by degrees. Danger attends upon too sudden alterations ; he that pulls down a bad building by the great may be ruined by the fall, but he that takes it down brick by brick may live to build a better.— *Quarles.*

A custom more honored in the breach than the observance.—*Shakespeare.*

Men commonly think according to their inclinations, speak according to their learning and imbibed opinions; but generally act according to custom.—*Bacon.*

Custom, though never so ancient, without truth, is but an old error.—*Cyprian.*

As the world leads we follow.—*Seneca.*

Custom is the tyranny of the lower human faculties over the higher.—*Madame Necker*

Parents fear the destruction of natural affection in their children. What is this natural principle so liable to decay ? Habit is a second nature, which destroys the first. Why is not custom nature ? I suspect that this nature itself is but a first custom, as custom is a second nature.—*Pascal.*

There is no tyrant like custom, and no freedom where its edicts are not resisted.—*Bovee.*

Custom is a violent and treacherous schoolmistress. She, by little and little, slyly and unperceived, slips in the foot of her authority ; but having by this gentle and humble beginning, with the benefit of time, fixed and established it, she then unmasks a furious and tyrannic countenance, against which we have no more the courage or the power so much as to lift up our eyes.—*Montaigne.*

Custom may lead a man into many errors ; but it justifies none.—*Fielding.*

The ancients tell us what is best; but we must learn of the moderns what is fittest.—
Franklin.

CYNICISM.
Trust him little who smilingly praises all alike, him less who sneeringly censures all alike, him least who is coldly indifferent to all alike.—*Lavater.*

The cynic is one who never sees a good quality in a man, and never fails to see a bad one. He is the human owl, vigilant in darkness and blind to light, mousing for vermin, and never seeing noble game. The cynic puts all human actions into two classes, — openly bad and secretly bad. All virtue and generosity and disinterestedness are merely the appearance of good, but selfish at the bottom. He holds that no man does a good thing except for profit. The effect of his conversation upon your feelings is to chill and sear them ; to send you away sour and morose. His criticisms and hints fall indiscriminately upon every lovely thing, like frost upon flowers.—*Beecher.*

Indifference to all the actions and passions of mankind was not supposed to be such a distinguished quality at that time, I think. I have known it very fashionable indeed. I have seen it displayed with such success that I have encountered some fine ladies and gentlemen who might as well have been born caterpillars.—*Dickens.*

Don't hang a dismal picture on the wall, and do not daub with sables and glooms in your conversation. Don't be a cynic and disconsolate preacher. Don't bewail and bemoan. Omit the negative propositions. Nerve us with incessant affirmatives. Don't waste yourself in rejection, nor bark against the bad, but chant the beauty of the good. When that is spoken which has a right to be spoken, the chatter and the criticism will stop. Set down nothing that will not help somebody.—*Emerson.*

Nil admirari is the motto which men of the world always affect. They think it vulgar to wonder, or be enthusiastic. They have so much corruption and so much charlatanism that they think the credit of all high qualities must be delusive.—*Sir Egerton Brydges.*

There is so much trouble in coming into the world, and so much more, as well as meanness, in going out of it, that it is hardly worth while to be here at all.—*Lord Bolingbroke.*

D.

DANCING.

Learn to dance, not so much for the sake of dancing, as for coming into a room, and presenting yourself genteelly and gracefully. Women, whom you ought to endeavor to please, cannot forgive a vulgar and awkward air and gestures.—*Chesterfield.*

In swimming dance on airs soft billows float.—*Milton.*

I have suffered more from my bad dancing than from all the misfortunes and miseries of my life put together.—*Landor.*

I love these rural dances, — from my heart I love them. This world, at best, is full of care and sorrow ; the life of a poor man is also stained with the sweat of his brow, there is so much toil and struggling and anguish and disappointment, here below, that I gaze with delight on a scene where all those are laid aside and forgotten, and the heart of the toil-worn peasant seems to throw off its load.—*Longfellow.*

Well was it said by a man of sagacity, that dancing was a sort of privileged and reputable folly, and that the best way to be convinced of this was to close the ears, and judge of it by the eyes alone.—*Gotthold.*

No amusement seems more to have a foundation in our nature. The animation of youth overflows spontaneously in harmonious movements. The true idea of dancing entitles it to favor. Its end is to realize perfect grace in motion ; and who does not know that a sense of the graceful is one of the higher faculties of our nature ? —*Channing.*

The gymnasium of running, walking on stilts, climbing, etc. steels and makes hardy single powers and muscles ; but dancing, like a corporeal poesy, embellishes, exercises, and equalizes all the muscles at once.—*Richter.*

Dance, dance, as long as ye can ; we must travel through life, but why make a dead march of it ? —*Eliza Cook.*

Flushed with the beautiful motion of the dance.— *Willis.*

DANGER.

Dangers are no more light if they once seem light, and more dangers have deceived men than forced them ; nay, it were better to meet some dangers half-way, though they come nothing near, than to keep too long a watch upon their approaches ; for if a man watch too long, it is odds he will fall fast asleep.—*Bacon.*

That danger which is despised arrives the soonest.—*Laberius.*

A timid person is frightened before a danger, a coward during the time, and a courageous person afterwards.—*Richter.*

A man's opinion of danger varies at different times, in consequence of an irregular tide of animal spirits ; and he is actuated by considerations which he dares not avow.—*Smollett.*

We should never so entirely avoid danger as to appear irresolute and cowardly ; but, at the same time, we should avoid unnecessarily exposing ourselves to danger, than which nothing can be more foolish.— *Cicero.*

We triumph without glory when we conquer without danger.—*Corneille.*

Let the fear of a danger be a spur to prevent it; he that fears otherwise gives advantage to the danger; it is less folly not to endeavor the prevention of the evil thou fearest than to fear the evil which thy endeavor cannot prevent.—
Quarles.

Thou dwarf dressed up in giant's clothes, that showest far off still greater than thou art.—
Suckling.

Danger levels man and brute, and all are fellows in their need.—*Byron.*

DAUGHTER.

A daughter is an embarrassing and ticklish possession.—*Menander.*

To a father waxing old nothing is dearer than a daughter; sons have spirits of higher pitch, but less inclined to sweet endearing fondness.—*Euripides.*

Still harping on my daughter.—
Shakespeare.

DEATH.

Deliverer! God hath anointed thee to free the oppressed, and crush the oppressor.—
Bryant.

Living is death; dying is life. We are not what we appear to be. On this side of the grave we are exiles, on that citizens; on this side orphans, on that children; on this side captives, on that freemen; on this side disguised, unknown, on that disclosed and proclaimed as the sons of God.—*Beecher.*

If some men died and others did not, death would indeed be a most mortifying evil.—
Bruyère.

We hold death, poverty, and grief for our principal enemies; but this death, which some repute the most dreadful of all dreadful things, who does not know that others call it the only secure harbor from the storms and tempests of life, the sovereign good of nature, the sole support of liberty, and the common and sudden remedy of all evils?—*Montaigne.*

We so converse every night with the image of death that every morning we find an argument of the resurrection. Sleep and death have but one mother, and they have one name in common.—*Jeremy Taylor.*

Death shuns the naked throat and proffered breast; he flies when called to be a welcome guest.—*Sir Charles Sedley.*

We look at death through the cheap-glazed windows of the flesh, and believe him the monster which the flawed and cracked glass represents him.—*Lowell.*

Birth into this life was the death of the embryo life that preceded, and the death of this will be birth into some new mode of being.—
Rev. Dr. Hedge.

Friend to the wretch whom every friend forsakes, I woo thee, Death! Life and its joys I leave to those that prize them. Hear me, o gracious God! At thy good time let Death approach; I reck not, let him but come in genuine form, not with thy vengeance armed, too much for man to bear.—*Bishop Porteus.*

Death is so genuine a fact that it excludes falsehoods, or betrays its emptiness; it is a touchstone that proves the gold, and dishonors the baser metal.—*Hawthorne.*

I have heard that death takes us away from ill things, not from good. I have heard that when we pronounce the name of man we pronounce the belief of immortality.—*Emerson.*

It is infamy to die, and not be missed.—
Carlos Wilcox.

Of all the evils of the world which are reproached with an evil character, death is the most innocent of its accusation.—
Jeremy Taylor.

All my possessions for a moment of time.
— Last words of —*Queen Elizabeth.*

The birds of the air die to sustain thee; the beasts of the field die to nourish thee; the fishes of the sea die to feed thee. Our stomachs are their common sepulchre. Good God! with how many deaths are our poor lives patched up! how full of death is the life of momentary man!
Quarles.

When a man dies they who survive him ask what property he has left behind. The angel who bends over the dying man asks what good deeds he has sent before him.—*Koran.*

I have often thought of death, and I find it the least of all evils.—*Jeremy Taylor.*

Where all life dies, death lives.—*Milton.*

All death in nature is birth, and at the moment of death appears visibly the rising of life. There is no dying principle in nature, for nature throughout is unmixed life, which, concealed behind the old, begins again and develops itself. Death as well as birth is simply in itself, in order to present itself ever more brightly and more like to itself.—*Fichte.*

Men must endure their going hence, even as their coming hither; ripeness is all.—
Shakespeare.

I look upon death to be as necessary to our constitution as sleep. We shall rise refreshed in the morning.—*Franklin.*

Could we but know one in a hundred of the close approachings of the skeleton, we should lead a life of perpetual shudder. Often and often do his bony fingers almost clutch our throat, or his foot is put out to give us a cross buttock. But a saving arm pulls him back ere we have seen so much as his shadow.—
Professor Wilson.

Is death the last sleep? No, it is the last final awakening.—*Walter Scott.*

The churchyard is the market-place where all things are rated at their true value, and those who are approaching it talk of the world and its vanities with a wisdom unknown before.
Baxter.

Death is the tyrant of the imagination. His reign is in solitude and darkness, in tombs and prisons, over weak hearts and seething brains. He lives, without shape or sound, a phantasm, inaccessible to sight or touch, — a ghastly and terrible apprehension.—*Barry Cornwall.*

It is not I who die, when I die, but my sin and misery.—*Gotthold.*

It is an exquisite and beautiful thing in our nature, that, when the heart is touched and softened by some tranquil happiness or affectionate feeling, the memory of the dead comes over it most powerfully and irresistibly. It would seem almost as though our better thoughts and sympathies were charms, in virtue of which the soul is enabled to hold some vague and mysterious intercourse with the spirits of those whom we loved in life. Alas! how often and how long may these patient angels hover around us, watching for the spell which is so soon forgotten!—*Dickens.*

Cullen whispered in his last moments: "I wish I had the power of writing or speaking, for then I would describe to you how pleasant a thing it is to die."—*Dr. Derby.*

Death, remembered, should be like a mirror, who tells us life is but a breath; to trust it, error.—*Shakespeare.*

The good die first; and they whose hearts are dry as summer dust burn to the socket.—
Wordsworth.

If one were to think continually of death, the business of life would stand still. I am no friend to making religion appear too hard. Many good people have done harm by giving too severe notions to it.—*Johnson.*

The fear of approaching death, which in youth we imagine must cause inquietude to the aged, is very seldom the source of much uneasiness.—*Hazlitt.*

Death hath no advantage but where it comes a stranger.—*Jeremy Taylor.*

To fear death is the way to live long; to be afraid of death is to be long a dying.—*Quarles.*

O Death, what art thou? nurse of dreamless slumbers freshening the fevered flesh to a wakefulness eternal.—*Tupper.*

I scarcely know how it is, but the deaths of children seem to me always less premature than those of older persons. Not that they are in fact so, but it is because they themselves have little or no relation to time or maturity.—
Barry Cornwall.

Death is the ultimate boundary of human matters.—*Horace.*

To mourn deeply for the death of another loosens from myself the petty desire for, and the animal adherence to life. We have gained the end of the philosopher, and view without shrinking the coffin and the pall.—*Bulwer Lytton.*

All that nature has prescribed must be good; and as death is natural to us, it is absurdity to fear it. Fear loses its purpose when we are sure it cannot preserve us, and we should draw a resolution to meet it from the impossibility to escape it.—*Steele.*

O mighty Cæsar! dost thou lie so low? are all thy conquests, glories, triumphs, spoils, shrunk to this little measure? —*Shakespeare.*

If I were a writer of books, I would compile a register, with the comment of the various deaths of men; and it could not but be useful, for who should teach men to die would at the same time teach them to live.—*Montaigne.*

Who is it that called time the avenger, yet failed to see that death was the consoler? What mortal afflictions are there to which death does not bring full remedy? What hurts of hope and body does it not repair? "This is a sharp medicine," said Raleigh, speaking of the axe, "but it cures all disorders."—*Simms.*

Death is a black camel, which kneels at the gates of all.—*Abd-el-Kader.*

To neglect at any time preparation for death is to sleep on our post at a siege; to omit it in old age is to sleep at an attack.—*Johnson.*

Death, thou art infinite; it is life is little.—
Bailey.

One may live as a conqueror, a king, or a magistrate; but he must die as a man —
Daniel Webster.

To how many is the death of the beloved the parent of faith! —*Bulwer Lytton.*

The darkness of death is like the evening twilight; it makes all objects appear more lovely to the dying.—*Richter.*

8

Death to a good man is but passing through a dark entry, out of one little dusky room of his Father's house into another that is fair and large, lightsome and glorious, and divinely entertaining.—*Adam Clarke.*

The Pope can give no bull to dispense with death.—*Molière.*

Men may live fools, but fools they cannot die.—*Young.*

Death is the liberator of him whom freedom cannot release, the physician of him whom medicine cannot cure, and the comforter of him whom time cannot console.—*Colton.*

It were well to die if there be gods, and sad to live if there be none.—*Marcus Antoninus.*

Death is the only monastery; the tomb is the only cell, and the grave that adjoins the convent is the bitterest mock of its futility.—
Bulwer Lytton.

There is a sweet anguish springing up in our bosoms when a child's face brightens under the shadow of the waiting angel. There is an autumnal fitness when age gives up the ghost; and when the saint dies there is a tearful victory.—
Chapin.

The happiest of pillows is not that which love first presses; it is that which death has frowned on and passed over.—*Landor.*

Men fear death, as children fear the dark; and as that natural fear in children is increased by frightful tales, so is the other. Groans, convulsions, weeping friends, and the like show death terrible; yet there is no passion so weak but conquers the fear of it, and therefore death is not such a terrible enemy. Revenge triumphs over death, love slights it, honor aspires to it, dread of shame prefers it, grief flies to it, and fear anticipates it.—*Bacon.*

No evil is honorable: but death is honorable; therefore death is not evil.—*Zeno.*

Among the poor, the approach of dissolution is usually regarded with a quiet and natural composure, which it is consolatory to contemplate, and which is as far removed from the dead palsy of unbelief as it is from the delirious raptures of fanaticism. Theirs is a true, unhesitating faith, and they are willing to lay down the burden of a weary life, in the sure and certain hope of a blessed immortality.—*Southey.*

Death is the quiet haven of us all.—
Wordsworth.

Let death and exile, and all other things which appear terrible, be daily before your eyes, but death chiefly; and you will never entertain any abject thought, nor too eagerly covet anything.—*Epictetus.*

To me few things appear so beautiful as a very young child in its shroud. The little innocent face looks so sublimely simple and confiding among the terrors of death. Crimeless and fearless, that little mortal passed under the shadow and explored the mystery of dissolution. There is death, in its sublimest and purest image; no hatred, no hypocrisy, no suspicion, no care for the morrow, ever darkened that little one's face; death has come lovingly upon it; there is nothing cruel or harsh in its victory.—*Leigh Hunt.*

To die, I own, is a dread passage,—terrible to nature, chiefly to those who have, like me, been happy.—*Thomson.*

Can we wonder that men perish and are forgotten, when their noblest and most enduring works decay? Death comes even to monumental structures, and oblivion rests on the most illustrious names.—*Marcus Antoninus.*

Death comes equally to us all, and makes us all equal when it comes. The ashes of an oak in a chimney are no epitaph of that, to tell me how high or how large that was; it tells me not what flocks it sheltered while it stood, nor what men it hurt when it fell. The dust of great persons' graves is speechless too; it says nothing, it distinguishes nothing.—*Donne.*

Death alone of the gods loves not gifts, nor do you need to offer incense or libations; he cares not for altar nor hymn; the goddess of Persuasion alone of the gods has no power over him.—*Horace.*

At the last, when we die, we have the dear angels for our escort on the way. They who can grasp the whole world in their hands can surely also guard our souls, that they make that last journey safely.—*Luther.*

Soon as man, expert from time, has found the key of life, it opes the gates of death.—
Young.

Death, whether it regards ourselves or others, appears less terrible in war than at home. The cries of women and children, friends in anguish, a dark room, dim tapers, priests and physicians, are what affect us the most on the death-bed. Behold us already more than half dead and buried.—*Henry Home.*

Death is a friend of ours; and he that is not ready to entertain him is not at home.—
Bacon.

Some men make a womanish complaint, that it is a great misfortune to die before our time. I would ask what time? Is it that of Nature? But she, indeed, has lent us life, as we do a sum of money, only no certain day is fixed for payment. What reason then to complain if she demands it at pleasure, since it was on this condition you received it?—*Cicero.*

Ephemera die all at sunset, and no insect of this class has ever sported in the beams of the morning sun. Happier are ye, little human ephemera! Ye played only in the ascending beams, and in the early dawn, and in the eastern light; ye drank only of the prelibations of life; hovered for a little space over a world of freshness and of blossoms; and fell asleep in innocence before yet the morning dew was exhaled!—*Richter.*

That we shall die we know; it is but the time, and drawing days out, that men stand upon.—*Shakespeare.*

Earth has one angel less, and heaven one more, since yesterday. Already, kneeling at the throne, she has received her welcome, and is resting on the bosom of her Saviour. If human love have power to penetrate the veil, (and hath it not?) then there are yet living here a few who have the blessedness of knowing that an angel loves them.—*Hawthorne.*

How could the hand that gave such charms blast them again?—*Moore.*

It matters not at what hour of the day the righteous fall asleep; death cannot come to him untimely who is fit to die; the less of this cold world, the more of heaven,—the briefer life, the earlier immortality.—*H. H. Milman.*

Life is the jailer, death the angel sent to draw the unwilling bolts and set us free.—*Lowell.*

O, if the deeds of human creatures could be traced to their source, how beautiful would even death appear; for how much charity, mercy, and purified affection would be seen to have their growth in dusty graves!—*Dickens.*

Death ready stands to interpose his dart.—*Milton.*

Many persons sigh for death when it seems far off, but the inclination vanishes when the boat upsets, or the locomotive runs off the track, or the measles set in.—*T. W. Higginson.*

No better armor against the darts of death than to be busied in God's service.—*Thomas Fuller.*

Pale death enters with impartial step the cottages of the poor and the palaces of the rich.—*Horace.*

The realm of death seems an enemy's country to most men, on whose shores they are loathly driven by stress of weather; to the wise man it is the desired port where he moors his bark gladly, as in some quiet haven of the Fortunate Isles; it is the golden west into which his sun sinks, and, sinking, casts back a glory upon the leaden cloud-tack which had darkly besieged his day.—*Lowell.*

Death reigns in all the portions of our time. The autumn with its fruits provides disorders for us, and the winter's cold turns them into sharp diseases, and the spring brings flowers to strew our hearse, and the summer gives green turf and brambles to bind upon our graves. Calentures and surfeit, cold and agues, are the four quarters of the year, and all minister to death; and you can go no whither but you tread upon a dead man's bones.—*Bishop Taylor.*

Death and the sun are not to be looked at steadily.—*Rochefoucauld.*

Against specious appearances we must set clear convictions, bright and ready for use. When death appears as an evil, we ought immediately to remember that evils are things to be avoided, but death is inevitable.—*Epictetus.*

Death gives us sleep, eternal youth, and immortality.—*Richter.*

The more we sink into the infirmities of age, the nearer we are to immortal youth. All people are young in the other world. That state is an eternal spring, ever fresh and flourishing. Now, to pass from midnight into noon on the sudden, to be decrepit one minute and all spirit and activity the next, must be a desirable change. To call this dying is an abuse of language.—*Jeremy Collier.*

Ah! surely nothing dies but something mourns.—*Byron*

When death strikes down the innocent and young, for every fragile form from which he lets the panting spirit free, a hundred virtues rise, in shapes of mercy, charity, and love, to walk the world and bless it. Of every tear that sorrowing mortals shed on such green graves, some good is born, some gentler nature comes.—*Dickens.*

Death is a commingling of eternity with time; in the death of a good man eternity is seen looking through time.—*Goethe.*

Death is a mighty mediator. There all the flames of rage are extinguished, hatred is appeased, and angelic pity, like a weeping sister, bends with gentle and close embrace over the funeral urn.—*Schiller.*

If life be a pleasure, yet, since death also is sent by the hand of the same Master, neither should that displease us.—*Michael Angelo.*

There are flowers which only yield their fragrance to the night; there are faces whose beauty only fully opens out in death. No more wrinkles; no drawn, distorted lineaments; an expression of extreme humility, blended with gladness of hope; a serene brightness, and an ideal straightening of the outline, as if the Divine finger, source of supreme beauty, had been laid there.—*Madame de Gasparin.*

If thou expect death as a friend, prepare to entertain him ; if thou expect death as an enemy, prepare to overcome him ; death has no advantage but when he comes a stranger.—
Quarles.

The last enemy that shall be destroyed is death.—*Bible.*

Death did not first strike Adam, the first sinful man, nor Cain, the first hypocrite, but Abel, the innocent and righteous. The first soul that met with death, overcame death ; the first soul that parted from earth went to heaven. Death argues not displeasure, because he whom God loved best dies first, and the murderer is punished with living.—*Bishop Hall.*

It is impossible that anything so natural, so necessary, and so universal as death should ever have been designed by Providence as an evil to mankind.—*Swift.*

He that always waits upon God is ready whensoever he calls. Neglect not to set your accounts even ; he is a happy man who so lives as that death at all times may find him at leisure to die.—*Feltham.*

What! is there no bribing death ? — Dying words of—*Cardinal Beaufort.*

Everything dies, and on this spring morning, if I lay my ear to the ground, I seem to hear from every point of the compass, the heavy step of men who carry a corpse to its burial.—
Madame de Gasparin.

There is no finite life except unto death ; no death except unto higher life.—*Bunsen.*

Death, of all estimated evils, is the only one whose presence never incommoded anybody, and which only causes concern during its absence.—
Arcesilaus.

That which is so universal as death must be a benefit.—*Schiller.*

Death opens the gate of fame, and shuts the gate of envy after it ; it unlooses the chain of the captive, and puts the bondsman's task into another man's hand.—*Sterne.*

Death is the dropping of the flower that the fruit may swell.—*Beecher.*

Let dissolution come when it will, it can do the Christian no harm, for it will be but a passage out of a prison into a palace ; out of a sea of troubles into a haven of rest ; out of a crowd of enemies to an innumerable company of true, loving, and faithful friends ; out of shame, reproach, and contempt, into exceeding great and eternal glory.—*Bunyan.*

Life is the triumph of our mouldering clay ; death, of the spirit infinite ! divine ! — *Young.*

We die every day ; every moment deprives us of a portion of life and advances us a step toward the grave ; our whole life is only a long and painful sickness.—*Massillon.*

He who fears death has already lost the life he covets.—*Cato.*

Death is the wish of some, the relief of many, and the end of all. It sets the slave at liberty, carries the banished man home, and places all mortals on the same level, insomuch that life itself were a punishment without it.—*Seneca.*

Death is an equal doom to good and bad, the common inn of rest.—*Spenser.*

Setting is preliminary to brighter rising ; decay is a process of advancement ; death is the condition of higher and more fruitful life.—
Chapin.

Death but supplies the oil for the inextinguishable lamp of life.—*Coleridge.*

The day of our decease will be that of our coming of age ; and with our last breath we shall become free of the universe. And in some region of infinity, and from among its splendors, this earth will be looked back on like a lowly home, and this life of ours be remembered like a short apprenticeship to duty.—*Mountford.*

How wonderful is Death, — Death and his brother, Sleep ! —*Shelley.*

Death possesses a good deal of real estate, namely, the graveyard in every town.—
Hawthorne.

It seems as though, at the approach of a certain dark hour, the light of heaven infills those who are leaving the light of earth.—
Victor Hugo.

A short death is the sovereign good hap of human life.—*Pliny.*

The sense of death is most in apprehension ; and the poor beetle, that we tread upon, in corporal sufferance finds a pang as great as when a giant dies.—*Shakespeare.*

Death ? Translated into the heavenly tongue, that word means life ! —*Beecher.*

We sometimes congratulate ourselves at the moment of waking from a troubled dream, — it may be so the moment after death.—*Hawthorne.*

Death is not an end, but a transition crisis. All the forms of decay are but masks of regeneration, — the secret alembics of vitaliy.—
Chapin.

It seems to be remarkable that death increases our veneration for the good, and extenuates our hatred for the bad.—*Johnson.*

The tongues of dying men enforce attention, like deep harmony.—*Shakespeare.*

The whole life of a philosopher is the meditation of his death.— *Cicero.*

But the grave is not deep; it is the shining trend of an angel that seeks us. When the unknown hand throws the fatal dart at the end of man, then boweth he his head, and the dart only lifts the crown of thorns from his wounds.—
Richter.

Passing through nature to eternity.—
Shakespeare.

Death openeth the gate to good fame, and extinguisheth envy.—*Bacon.*

Like other tyrants, death delights to smite what, smitten, most proclaims the pride of power and arbitrary nod.—*Young.*

It is uncertain at what place death awaits thee. Wait thou for it at every place.—*Seneca.*

Death is as near to the young as to the old; here is all the difference : death stands behind the young man's back, before the old man's face.—*Rev. T. Adams.*

Not where death hath power may love be blest.—*Mrs. Hemans.*

Death lies on her like an untimely frost upon the sweetest flower of all the field.—
Shakespeare.

To close the eyes, and give a seemly comfort to the apparel of the dead, is poverty's holiest touch of nature.—*Dickens.*

What can they suffer that do not fear to die ?
Plutarch.

O eloquent, just, and mighty death ! whom none could advise thou hast persuaded, what none hath dared thou hast done, and whom all the world hath flattered thou only hast cast out of the world and despised ; thou hast drawn together all the far-stretched greatness, all the pride, cruelty, and ambition of men, and covered it all over with these two narrow words, *Hic jacet !*—*Sir Walter Raleigh.*

O death ! thou gentle end of human sorrows.
Rowe.

Death and love are the two wings which bear man from earth to heaven.—*Michael Angelo.*

Early, bright, transient, chaste as morning dew, she sparkled, was exhaled, and went to heaven.— *Young.*

The sleeping and the dead are but as pictures ; it is the eye of childhood that fears a painted devil.—*Shakespeare.*

That evil can never be great which is the last.—*Cornelius Nepos.*

Nothing can we call our own but death, and that small model of the barren earth which serves as paste and cover to our bones.—
Shakespeare.

Dear beauteous death, the jewel of the just.
Henry Vaughan.

It is not strange that a bright memory should come to a dying old man, as the sunshine breaks across the hills at the close of a stormy day ; nor that in the light of that ray the very clouds that made the day dark should grow gloriously beautiful.—*Hawthorne.*

There is no death ! What seems so is transition.—*Longfellow.*

There is nothing of evil in life for him who rightly comprehends that death is no evil ; to know how to die delivers us from all subjection and constraint.—*Montaigne.*

Cruel as death and hungry as the grave.
Thomson.

The bed of death brings every human being to his pure individuality ; to the intense contemplation of that deepest and most solemn of all relations, the relation between the creature and his Creator.—*Daniel Webster.*

Death borders upon our birth, and our cradle stands in the grave.—*Bishop Hall.*

The weariest and most loathed worldly life that age, ache, penury, and imprisonment can lay on nature is a paradise to what we fear of death.—*Shakespeare.*

Good men but see death, the wicked taste it.
Ben Jonson.

He that dies in an earnest pursuit is like one that is wounded in hot blood, who, for the time, scarce feels the hurt ; and therefore a mind fixed and bent upon somewhat that is good doth avert the dolors of death ; but above all, believe it, the sweetest canticle is, "Lord, now lettest thou thy servant depart in peace."—
Bacon.

If Socrates died like a sage, Jesus died like a God.—*Rousseau.*

If I must die, I will encounter darkness as a bride, and hug it in mine arms.—*Shakespeare.*

Death makes a beautiful appeal to charity. When we look upon the dead form, so composed and still, the kindness and the love that are in us all come forth.— *Chapin.*

Death is as the foreshadowing of life. We die that we may die no more.—*Hooker.*

The gods conceal from men the happiness of death, that they may endure life.—*Lucan.*

Death, which hateth and destroyeth a man, is believed; God, which hath made him and loves him, is always deferred.—
Sir Walter Raleigh.

I must sleep now. — Dying words of—
Byron.

DEBT.

A man who owes a little can clear it off in a very little time, and, if he is a prudent man, will; whereas a man who, by long negligence, owes a great deal, despairs of ever being able to pay, and therefore never looks into his accounts at all.—*Chesterfield.*

Man hazards the condition and loses the virtues of freeman, in proportion as he accustoms his thoughts to view without anguish or shame his lapse into the bondage of debtor.—
Bulwer Lytton.

Lose not thy own for want of asking for it; it will get thee no thanks.—*Fuller.*

Small debts are like small shot, — they are rattling on every side, and can scarcely be escaped without a wound; great debts are like cannon, of loud noise but little danger.—
Johnson.

Many delight more in giving of presents than in paying their debts.—*Sir P. Sidney.*

Paying of debts is, next to the grace of God, the best means in the world to deliver you from a thousand temptations to sin and vanity.—
Delany.

Debt is the fatal disease of republics, the first thing and the mightiest to undermine government and corrupt the people.—
Wendell Phillips.

Debt, grinding debt, whose iron face the widow, the orphan, and the s ns of genius fear and hate; — debt, which consumes so much time, which so cripples and disheartens a great spirit with cares that seem so base, is a preceptor whose lessons cannot be .foregone, and is needed most by those who suffer from it most.—
Emerson.

Debt is to man what the serpent is to the bird; its eye fascinates, its breath poisons, its coil crushes sinew and bone, its jaw is the pitiless grave.—*Bulwer Lytton.*

·A slight debt produces a debtor; a heavy one an enemy.—*Publius Syrus.*

Never be argued out of your soul, never be argued out of your honor, and never be argued into believing that soul and honor do not run a terrible risk if you limp into life with the load of a debt on your shoulders.—*Bulwer Lytton.*

DECEIT.

It is in disputes as in armies, where the weaker side sets up false lights, and makes a great noise, to make the enemy believe them more numerous and strong than they really are.
Swift.

Of all the agonies in life, that which is most poignant and harrowing — that which for the time annihilates reason, and leaves our whole organization one lacerated, mangled heart — is the conviction that we have been deceived where we placed all the trust of love.—*Bulwer Lytton.*

It is a pity we so often succeed in our attempts to deceive each other, for our double-dealing generally comes down upon ourselves. To speak a lie or to act a lie is alike contemptible in the sight of God and man.—*Everton.*

All false practices and affections of knowledge are more odious to God, and deserve to be so to men, than any want or defect of knowledge can be.—*Sprat.*

It is great, it is manly, to disdain disguise; it shows our spirit, or it proves our strength.—
Young.

It is as easy to deceive one's self without perceiving it as it is difficult to deceive others without their finding it out.—*Rochefoucauld.*

If a misplaced admiration shows imbecility, an affected criticism shows vice of character. Expose thyself rather to appear a beast than false.—*Diderot.*

He was justly accounted a skilful poisoner who destroyed his victims by bouquets of lovely and fragrant flowers. The art has not been lost; nay, is practised every day, — by the world.—*Latimer.*

Trust not in him that seems a saint.—*Fuller.*

The surest way of making a dupe is to let your victim suppose you are his.—*Bulwer Lytton.*

O that deceit should dwell in such a gorgeous palace!—*Shakespeare.*

There are falsehoods which represent truth so well that it would be judging ill not to be deceived by them.—*Rochefoucauld.*

We never deceive for a good purpose; knavery adds malice to falsehood.—*Bruyère.*

Deceit and falsehood, whatever conveniences they may for a time promise or produce, are, in the sum of life, obstacles to happiness. Those who profit by the cheat distrust the deceiver; and the act by which kindness was sought puts an end to confidence.—*Johnson.*

No man was ever so much deceived by another as by himself.—*Lord Greville.*

Ah, that deceit should steal such gentle shapes, and with a virtuous visor hide deep vice!
Shakespeare.

Some frauds succeed from the apparent candor, the open confidence, and the full blaze of ingenuousness that is thrown around them. The slightest mystery would excite suspicion, and ruin all. Such stratagems may be compared to the stars, they are discoverable by darkness and hidden only by light.—*Colton.*

Deceit is the false road to happiness; and all the joys we travel through to vice, like fairy banquets, vanish when we touch them.—
Aaron Hill.

It many times falls out that we deem ourselves much deceived in others because we first deceived ourselves.—*Sir P. Sidney.*

We are so accustomed to masquerade ourselves before others that we end by deceiving ourselves.—*Rochefoucauld.*

Life is the art of being well deceived.—
Hazlitt.

All deception in the course of life is indeed nothing else but a he reduced to practice, and falsehood passing from words into things.—
South.

Men, like musical instruments, seem made to be played upon.—*Bovee.*

Man is nothing but insincerity, falsehood, and hypocrisy, both in regard to himself and in regard to others. He does not wish that he should be told the truth, he shuns saying it to others; and all these moods, so inconsistent with justice and reason, have their roots in his heart.—*Pascal.*

The first and worst of all frauds is to cheat one's self. All sin is easy after that.—*Bailey.*

He who attempts to make others believe in means which he himself despises is a puffer; he who makes use of more means than he knows to be necessary is a quack; and he who ascribes to those means a greater efficacy than his own experience warrants is an impostor.—
Lavater.

He was no civil ruffian; none of those who lie with twisted looks, betray with shrugs.—
Thomson.

Men are so simple, and yield so much to necessity, that he who will deceive will always find him who will lend himself to be deceived.—
Machiavelli.

The true motives of our actions, like the real pipes of an organ, are usually concealed; but the gilded and hollow pretext is pompously placed in the front for show.—*Colton.*

As that g llant can best affect a pretended passion for one woman who has no true love for another, so he that has no real esteem for any of the virtues can best assume the appearance of them all.—*Colton.*

We have few faults that are not more excusable in themselves than are the means which we use to conceal them.—*Rochefoucauld.*

Cheaters must get some credit before they can cozen, and all falsehood, if not founded in some truth, would not be fixed in any belief.—
Fuller.

It is too much proved, that, with devotion's visage and pious action, we do sugar over the Devil himself.—*Shakespeare.*

Wiles and deceit are female qualities.—
Æschylus.

O, what a tangled web we weave when first we practise to deceive! — *Walter Scott.*

Many an honest man practises upon himself an amount of deceit sufficient, if practised upon another, and in a little different way, to send him to the state prison.—*Bovee.*

Men are never so easily deceived as while they are endeavoring to deceive others.—
Rochefoucauld.

Mankind in the gross is a gaping monster, that loves to be deceived, and has seldom been disappointed.—*Mackenzie.*

False face must hide what the false heart doth know.—*Shakespeare.*

The life even of a just man is a round of petty frauds; that of a knave a series of greater. We degrade life by our follies and vices, and then complain that the unhappiness which is only their accompaniment is inherent in the constitution of things.—*Bovee.*

We are never deceived; we deceive ourselves.
Goethe.

DECENCY.

Decency is the least of all laws, but yet it is the law which is the most strictly observed.
Rochefoucauld.

DECISION.

There is nothing more to be esteemed than a manly firmness and decision of character. I like a person who knows his own mind and sticks to it; who sees at once what is to be done in given circumstances and does it.—*Hazlitt.*

The woman who is resolved to be respected can make herself to be so even amidst an army of soldiers.—*Cervantes.*

When desperate ills demand a speedy cure, distrust is cowardice and prudence folly.—
Johnson.

Whatever we think out, whatever we take in hand to do, should be perfectly and finally finished, that the word, if it must alter, will only have to spoil it; we have then nothing to do but unite the severed, to recollect and restore the dismembered.—*Goethe.*

I hate to see things done by halves. If it be right, do it boldly; if it be wrong, leave it undone.—*Gilpin.*

DEFEAT.

What is defeat? Nothing but education, nothing but the first step to something better.— *Wendell Phillips.*

Defeat is a school in which truth always grows strong.—*Beecher.*

No man is defeated without some resentment which will be continued with obstinacy while he believes himself in the right, and asserted with bitterness, if even to his own conscience he is detected in the wrong.—*Johnson.*

BEFERENCE.

Deference is the most complicate, the most indirect, and the most elegant of all compliments.—*Shenstone.*

Deference often shrinks and withers as much upon the approach of intimacy as the sensitive plant does upon the touch of one's finger.— *Shenstone.*

DEFORMITY.

Do you suppose we owe nothing to Pope's deformity? He said to himself, " If my person be crooked, my verses shall be straight."— *Hazlitt.*

Deformed, unfinished, sent before my time into this breathing world, scarce half made up, and that so lamely and unfashionably, that dogs bark at me as I halt by them.—*Shakespeare.*

Many a man has risen to eminence under the powerful reaction of his mind in fierce counter-agency to the scorn of the unworthy, daily evoked by his personal defects, who with a handsome person would have sunk into the luxury of a careless life under the tranquillizing smiles of continual admiration.—*De Quincey.*

Deformity is daring; it is its essence to overtake mankind by heart and soul, and make itself the equal, ay, the superior of the rest.— *Byron.*

From whence comes it that a cripple in body does not irritate us, and that a crippled mind enrages us? It is because a cripple sees that we go right, and a distorted mind says that it is we who go astray. But for that we should have more pity and less rage.—*Pascal.*

DELAY.

In delay we waste our lights in vain, like lamps by day.—*Shakespeare.*

The procrastinator is not only indolent and weak, but commonly false too; most of the weak are false.—*Lavater.*

Defer no time; delays have dangerous ends. *Shakespeare.*

Procrastination is the thief of time; year after year it steals, till all are fled, and to the mercies of a moment leaves the vast concerns of an eternal scene.—*Young.*

O, how many deeds of deathless virtue and immortal crime the world had wanted had the actor said, " I will do this to-morrow " ! *Lord John Russell.*

Every delay is hateful, but it gives wisdom.— *Publius Syrus.*

That we would do we should do when we would, for this would changes, and hath abatements and delays as many as there are tongues, are hands, are accidents; and then this should is like a spendthrift's sigh, that hurts by easing. *Shakespeare.*

He who prorogues the honesty of to-day till to-morrow will probably prorogue his to-morrows to eternity.—*Lavater.*

Dull not device by coldness and delay.— *Shakespeare.*

Delay has ever been injurious to those who are prepared.—*Lucan.*

Go, fool, and teach a cataract to creep! can thirst, empire, vengeance, beauty, wait? —*Young.*

Some one speaks admirably of " the well-ripened fruit of sage delay."—*Balzac.*

Lingering labors come to naught.— *Robert Southwell.*

He that gives time to resolve gives leisure to deny, and warning to prepare.—*Quarles.*

Fearful commenting is leaden servitor to dull delay; delay leads impotent and snail-paced beggary.—*Shakespeare.*

DELICACY.

There is a certain delicacy which in yielding conquers; and with a pitiful look, makes one find cause to crave help one's self.— *Sir P. Sidney.*

Delicacy is to the affections what grace is to the beauty.—*Degerando.*

Weak men often, from the very principle of their weakness, derive a certain susceptibility, delicacy, and taste, which render them, in those particulars, much superior to men of stronger and more consistent minds who laugh at them.—*Lord Greville.*

An appearance of delicacy, and even of fragility, is almost essential to beauty.—*Burke.*

Friendship, love, and piety ought to be handled with a sort of mysterious secrecy ; they ought to be spoken of only in the rare moments of perfect confidence, to be mutually understood in silence. Many things are too delicate to be thought ; many more, to be spoken.—
Novalis.

The hand of little employment hath the daintier sense.—*Shakespeare.*

True delicacy, that most beautiful heart-leaf of humanity, exhibits itself most significantly in little things.—*Mary Howitt.*

Delicacy is to the mind what fragrance is to the fruit.—*Achilles Poincelot.*

The finest qualities of our nature, like the bloom on fruits, can be preserved only by the most delicate handling.—*Thoreau.*

DELUSION.

Were we perfectly acquainted with the object, we should never passionately desire it.—
Rochefoucauld.

The worst deluded are the self-deluded.—
Bovee.

No man is happy without a delusion of some kind. Delusions are as necessary to our happiness as realities.—*Bovee.*

When our vices quit us, we flatter ourselves with the belief that it is we who quit them.—
Rochefoucauld.

We strive as hard to hide our hearts from ourselves as from others, and always with more success ; for in deciding upon our own case we are both judge, jury, and executioner, and where sophistry cannot overcome the first, or flattery the second, self-love is always ready to defeat the sentence by bribing the third.—
Colton.

You think a man to be your dupe ; if he pretends to be so, who is the greatest dupe, — he or you ?—*Bruyère.*

DEMOCRACY.

It is the most beautiful truth in morals that we have no such thing as a distinct or divided interest from our race. In their welfare is ours, and by choosing the broadest paths to effect their happiness we choose the surest and the shortest to our own.—*Bulwer Lytton.*

Lycurgus being asked why he, who in other respects appeared to be so zealous for the equal rights of men, did not make his government democratical rather than oligarchical, " Go you," replied the legislator, " and try a democracy in your own house."—*Plutarch.*

The idea of bringing all men on an equality with each other has always been a pleasant dream ; the law cannot equalize men in spite of nature.— *Vauvenargues.*

In every village there will arise a miscreant to establish the most grinding tyranny by calling himself the people.—*Sir Robert Peel.*

" It is a great blessing," says Pascal, " to be born a man of quality, since it brings one man as far forward at eighteen or twenty as another man would be at fifty, which is a clear gain of thirty years." These thirty years are commonly wanting to the ambitious characters of democracies. The principle of equality, which allows every man to arrive at everything, prevents all men from rapid advancement.—
De Tocqueville.

If there were a people consisting of gods, they would be governed democratically. So perfect a government is not suitable to men.—
Rousseau.

Democracy is always the work of kings. Ashes, which in themselves are sterile, fertilize the land they are cast upon.—*Landor.*

DEPENDENCE.

God has made no one absolute. The rich depend on the poor, as well as the poor on the rich. The world is but a mere magnificent building ; all the stones are gradually cemented together. There is no one subsists by himself alone.—*Feltham.*

In an arch each single stone, which, if severed from the rest, would be perhaps defenceless, is sufficiently secured by the solidity and entireness of the whole fabric of which it is a part.—*Boyle.*

No degree of knowledge attainable by man is able to set him above the want of hourly assistance.—*Johnson.*

That acknowledgment of weakness which we make in imploring to be relieved from hunger and from temptation is surely wisely put in our daily prayer. Think of it, you who are rich, and take heed how you turn a beggar away.—*Thackeray.*

Dependence is a perpetual call upon humanity, and a greater incitement to tenderness and pity than any other motive whatsoever.—
Addison.

When we consider how weak we are in ourselves, yea, the very strongest of us, and how assaulted, we may justly wonder that we can continue one day in the state of grace ; but when we look on the strength by which we are guarded, the power of God, then we see the reason of our stability to the end ; for omnipotency supports us, and the everlasting arms are under us.—*Leighton.*

The greatest man living may stand in need of the meanest, as much as the meanest does of him.—*Fuller.*

There is none made so great but he may both need the help and service, and stand in fear of the power and unkindness, even of the meanest of mortals.—*Seneca.*

How beautifully is it ordered, that as many thousands work for one, so must every individual bring his labor to make the whole! The highest is not to despise the lowest, nor the lowest to envy the highest; each must live in all and by all. Who will not work, neither shall he eat. So God has ordered that men, being in need of each other, should learn to love each other, and bear each other's burdens.
G. A. Sala.

Heaven's eternal wisdom has decreed that man of man should ever stand in need.—
Theocritus.

Dependence goes somewhat against the grain of a generous mind ; and it is no wonder that it should do so, considering the unreasonable advantage which is often taken of the inequality of fortune.—*Jeremy Collier.*

Thou shalt know by experience how salt the savor is of others' bread, and how sad a path it is to climb and descend another's stairs.—
Dante.

DESERTS.

Use every man after his desert, and who should escape whipping ? Use them after your own honor and dignity ; the less they deserve, the more merit is in your bounty.—*Shakespeare.*

DESIRE.

Some desire is necessary to keep life in motion, and he whose real wants are supplied must admit those of fancy.—*Johnson.*

All impediments in fancy's course are motives of more fancy.—*Shakespeare.*

We never desire ardently what we desire rationally.—*Rochefoucauld.*

By annihilating the desires, you annihilate the mind. Every man without passions has within him no principle of action, nor motive to act.—*Helvetius.*

The shadows of our own desires stand between us and our better angels, and thus their brightness is eclipsed.—*Dickens.*

What we wish for in youth comes in heaps on us in old age.—*Goethe.*

Every desire bears its death in its very gratification. Curiosity languishes under repeated stimulants, and novelties cease to excite surprise, until at length we cannot wonder even at a miracle.—*Washington Irving.*

It is better to desire than to enjoy, to love than to be loved.—*Hazlitt.*

Every desire is a viper in the bosom, who, while he was chill, was harmless ; but when warmth gave him strength, exerted it in poison.—*Johnson.*

We trifle when we assign limits to our desires, since nature has set none.—*Bovee.*

The passions and desires, like the two twists of a rope, mutually mix one with the other, and twine inextricably round the heart ; producing good if moderately indulged, but certain destruction if suffered to become inordinate.
Burton.

Happy the man who early learns the wide chasm that lies between his wishes and his powers !—*Goethe.*

Unlawful desires are punished after the effect of enjoying ; but impossible desires are punished in the desire itself.—*Sir P. Sidney.*

While we desire, we do not enjoy ; and with enjoyment desire ceases, which should lend its strongest zest to it. This, however, does not apply to the gratification of sense, but to the passions, in which distance and difficulty have a principal share.—*Hazlitt.*

Before we passionately desire anything which another enjoys, we should examine into the happiness of its possessor.—*Rochefoucauld.*

Keep you in the rear of your affection, out of the shot and danger of desire.—*Shakespeare.*

He who can wait for what he desires takes the course not to be exceedingly grieved if he fails of it ; he, on the contrary, who labors after a thing too impatiently thinks the success when it comes is not a recompense equal to all the pains he has been at about it.—*Bruyère.*

Our nature is inseparable from desires, and the very word " desire " (the craving for something not possessed) implies that our present felicity is not complete.—*Hobbes.*

Heart's-ease is a flower which blooms from the grave of desire.—*W. R. Alger.*

There is nothing capricious in nature. In nature the implanting of a desire indicates that the gratification of that desire is in the constitution of the creature that feels it.—*Emerson.*

Ere yet we yearn for what is out of our reach, we are still in the cradle. When wearied out with our yearnings, desire again falls asleep, we are on the death-bed.—*Bulwer Lytton.*

However rich or elevated, a nameless something is always wanting to our imperfect fortune.—*Horace.*

*P*erish the lore that deadens young desire.—
Beattie.

In moderating, not in satisfying desires, lies peace.—*Heber.*

DESPAIR.

Sick in the world's regard, wretched and low.—*Shakespeare.*

There are some vile and contemptible men who, allowing themselves to be conquered by misfortune, seek a refuge in death.—*Agathon.*

Despair is the greatest of our errors.—
Vauvenargues.

Despair is like forward children, who, when you take away one of their playthings, throw the rest into the fire for madness. It grows angry with itself, turns its own executioner, and revenges its misfortunes on its own head.—
Charron.

Beware of desperate steps. The darkest day, live till to-morrow, will have passed away.
Cowper.

Despair, thou hast the noblest issues of all ill, which frailty brings us to ; for to be worse we fear not, and who cannot lose is ever a frank gamester.—*Sir Robert Howard.*

For me — I hold no commerce with despair !
Dawes.

Despair makes a despicable figure, and descends from a mean original. It is the offspring of fear, of laziness, of impatience ; it argues a defect of spirit and resolution, and oftentimes of honesty too.—*Jeremy Collier.*

It is late before the brave despair.—
Thomson.

Of all faults the greatest is the excess of impious terror, dishonoring divine grace. He who despairs wants love, wants faith ; for faith, hope, and love are three torches which blend their light together, nor does the one shine without the other.—*Metastasio.*

Despair gives the shocking ease to the mind that a mortification gives to the body.—
Lord Greville.

As a general rule, those who are dissatisfied with themselves will seek to go out of themselves into an ideal world. Persons in strong health and spirits, who take plenty of air and exercise, who are " in favor with their stars," and have a thorough relish of the good things of this life, seldom devote themselves in despair to religion or the Muses. Sedentary, nervous, hypochondriacal people, on the contrary, are forced, for want of an appetite for the real and substantial, to look out for a more airy food and speculative comforts.—*Hazlitt.*

To despond is to be ungrateful beforehand. Be not looking for evil. Often thou drainest the gall of fear while evil is passing thy dwelling.—*Tupper.*

Despair makes victims sometimes victors.—
Bulwer Lytton.

I am one whom the vile blows and buffets of the world have so incensed that I am reckless what I do to spite the world.—
Shakespeare.

Despair, — the last dignity of the wretched.—
Henry Giles.

A broken heart is a distemper which kills many more than is generally imagined, and would have a fair title to a place in the bills of mortality, did it not differ in one instance from all other diseases, namely, that no physicians can cure it.—*Fielding.*

Rage is for little wrongs ; despair is dumb.
Hannah More.

Lachrymal counsellors, with one foot in the cave of despair, and the other invading the peace of their friends, are the paralyzers of action, the pests of society, and the subtlest homicides in the world ; they poison with a tear ; and convey a dagger to the heart, while they press you to their bosoms.—*Jane Porter.*

Despair, sir, is a dauntless hero.—*Holcroft.*

All hope is lost of my reception into grace ; what worse ? For where no hope is left, is left no fear.—*Milton.*

Despair doth strike as deep a furrow in the brain as mischief or remorse.—
Barry Cornwall.

He that despairs degrades the Deity, and seems to intimate that he is insufficient, or not just to his word ; and in vain hath read the Scriptures, the world, and man.—*Feltham.*

The mild despairing of a heart resigned.
Coleridge.

I would not despair unless I knew the irrevocable decree was passed ; saw my misfortune recorded in the book of fate, and signed and sealed by necessity.—*Jeremy Collier.*

Despair is the damp of hell ; rejoicing is the serenity of heaven.—*Donne.*

The passage of providence lies through many crooked ways ; a despairing heart is the true prophet of approaching evil ; his actions may weave the webs of fortune, but not break them.—*Quarles.*

Some noble spirits mistake despair for content.—*Willis.*

Even every ray of hope destroyed and not a wish to gild the gloom.—*Burns.*

To doubt is worse than to have lost; and to despair is but to antedate those miseries that must fall on us.—*Massinger.*

The fact that God has prohibited despair gives misfortune the right to hope all things, and leaves hope free to dare all things.—
Madame Swetchine.

Try what repentance can; what can it not? yet what can it, when one cannot repent? O wretched state! O bosom black as death! O limèd soul, that, struggling to be free, art more engaged!—*Shakespeare.*

Despair defies even despotism; there is that in my heart would make its way through hosts with levelled spears.—*Byron.*

O God! O God! How weary, stale, flat, and unprofitable seem to me all the uses of this world!—*Shakespeare.*

Religion converts despair, which destroys, into resignation, which submits.—
Lady Blessington.

My day is closed! the gloom of night is come! a hopeless darkness settles over my fate.—*Joanna Baillie.*

DESPATCH.

True despatch is a rich thing. For time is the measure of business, as money is of wares, and business is bought at a dear hand where there is small despatch.—*Bacon.*

To choose time is to save time; and an unseasonable motion is but beating the air. There be three parts of business, — the preparation, the debate or examination, and the perfection; whereof, if you look for despatch, let the middle only be the work of many, and the first and last the work of few.—*Bacon.*

DESPONDENCY.

Life is a warfare; and he who easily desponds deserts a double duty, — he betrays the noblest property of man, which is dauntless resolution; and he rejects the providence of that All-gracious Being who guides and rules the universe.—*Jane Porter.*

To believe a business impossible is the way to make it so. How many feasible projects have miscarried through despondency, and been strangled in their birth by a cowardly imagination!—*Jeremy Collier.*

Despondency is not a state of humility; on the contrary, it is the vexation and despair of a cowardly pride, — nothing is worse; whether we stumble or whether we fall, we must only think of rising again and going on in our course.—*Fenelon.*

Some persons depress their own minds, despond at the first difficulty; and conclude that making any progress in knowledge, farther than serves their ordinary business, is above their capacities.—*Locke.*

DESPOTISM.

Despotism can no more exist in a nation until the liberty of the press be destroyed than the night can happen before the sun is set.—
Colton.

I will believe in the right of one man to govern a nation despotically when I find a man born into the world with boots and spurs, and a nation born with saddles on their backs.—
Algernon Sidney.

Travellers describe a tree in the island of Java whose pestiferous exhalations blight every tiny blade of grass within the compass of its shade. So it is with despotism.—*Ruffini.*

It is odd to consider the connection between despotism and barbarity, and how the making one person more than man makes the rest less.
Addison.

Despots govern by terror. They know that he who fears God fears nothing else; and therefore they eradicate from the mind, through their Voltaire, their Helvetius, and the rest of that infamous gang, that only sort of fear which generates true courage.—*Burke.*

In times of anarchy one may seem a despot in order to be a saviour.—*Mirabeau.*

As virtue is necessary in a republic, and honor in a monarchy, fear is what is required in a despotism. As for virtue, it is not at all necessary, and honor would be dangerous there.
Montesquieu.

When the savages of Louisiana wish to have fruit, they cut the tree at the bottom and gather the fruit. That is exactly a despotic government.—*Montesquieu.*

DESTINY.

That which God writes on thy forehead thou wilt come to.—*Koran.*

If the course of human affairs be considered, it will be seen that many things arise against which Heaven does not allow us to guard.—
Machiavelli.

Our minds are as different as our faces; we are all travelling to one destination, — happiness; but few are going by the same road.—
Colton.

Philosophers never stood in need of Homer or the Pharisees, to be convinced that everything is done by immutable laws, that everything is settled, that everything is a necessary effect of some previous cause.—*Voltaire.*

Resist as much as thou wilt; heaven's ways are heaven's ways.—*Lessing.*

Nature seems to have prescribed to every man at his birth the bounds of his virtues and vices.—*Rochefoucauld.*

What unknown power governs men! On what feeble causes do their destinies hinge! —
Voltaire.

I know that nothing comes to pass but what God appoints; our fate is decreed, and things do not happen by chance, but every man's portion of joy and sorrow is predetermined.—
Seneca.

That which is not allotted the hand cannot reach, and what is allotted will find you wherever you may be.—*Saadi.*

Man supposes that he directs his life and governs his actions, when his existence is irretrievably under the control of destiny.—*Goethe.*

There are but two future verbs which man may appropriate confidently and without pride: " I shall suffer," and " I shall die." —
Madame Swetchine.

Stern is the on-look of necessity. Not without a shudder may the hand of man grasp the mysterious urn of destiny.—*Schiller.*

Vast, colossal destiny, which raises man to fame, though it may also grind him to powder!
Schiller.

Death and life have their determined appointments; riches and honor depend upon Heaven.—*Confucius*

DEVOTION.
The life of a devotee is a crusade of which the heart is the Holy Land.—*Alfred de Musset.*

I find no quality so easy for a man to counterfeit as devotion, though his life and manner are not conformable to it; the essence of it is abstruse and occult, but the appearances easy and showy.—*Montaigne.*

To worship rightly is to love each other, each smile a hymn, each kindly deed a prayer.—
Whittier.

He who receives a sacrament does not perform a good work; he receives a benefit. In the mass we give Christ nothing; we only receive from him.—*Luther.*

All is holy where devotion kneels.—*Holmes.*

Private devotions and secret offices of religion are like the refreshing of a garden with the distilling and petty drops of a water-pot; but addressed from the temple, are like rain from heaven.—*Jeremy Taylor.*

Those who make use of devotion as a means and end generally are hypocrites.—*Goethe.*

The inward sighs of humble penitence rise to the ear of heaven, when pealed hymns are scattered with the sounds of common air.—
Joanna Baillie.

The secret heart is fair devotion's temple; there the saint, even on that living altar, lights the flame of purest sacrifice, which burns unseen, not unaccepted.—*Hannah More.*

Devotion, when it does not lie under the check of reason, is apt to degenerate into enthusiasm.—*Addison.*

DEW.
Dew-drops are the gems of morning, but the tears of mournful eve!—*Coleridge.*

That same dew, which sometime on the buds was wont to swell, like round and orient pearls, stood now within the pretty flowerets' eyes, like tears that did their own disgrace bewail.—
Shakespeare.

Those tears of the sky for the loss of the sun.—*Chesterfield.*

None can give the dew but God. It comes from above; it is of a celestial original; the nativity thereof is from " the womb of the morning." None can give grace but God.
Bishop Reynolds.

The starlight dews all silently their tears of love instil.—*Byron.*

DIET.
The chief pleasure (in eating) does not consist in costly seasoning or exquisite flavor, but in yourself. Do you seek for sauce by sweating.
Horace.

If thou wouldst preserve a sound body, use fasting and walking; if a healthful soul, fasting and praying; walking exercises the body, praying exercises the soul, fasting cleanses both.
Quarles.

Simple diet is best; for many dishes bring many diseases, and rich sauces are worse than even heaping several meats upon each other.—
Pliny.

Food, improperly taken, not only produces original diseases, but affords those that are already engendered both matter and sustenance; so that, let the father of disease be what it may, Intemperance is certainly its mother.—*Burton.*

Your worm is your only emperor for diet; we fat all creatures else to fat us, and we fa ourselves for maggots.—*Shakespeare.*

One meal a day is enough for a lion, and it ought to suffice for a man.—*Dr. George Fordyce.*

A chine of honest bacon would please my appetite more than all the marrow-puddings, for I like them better plain, having a very vulgar stomach.—*Dryden.*

A fig for your bill of fare; show me your bill of company.—*Swift.*

DIFFICULTY.

Hath fortune dealt thee ill cards? let wisdom make thee a good gamester. In a fair gale, every fool may sail, but wise behavior in a storm commends the wisdom of a pilot; to bear adversity with an equal mind is both the sign and glory of a brave spirit.—*Quarles.*

Fortune is the best school of courage when she is fraught with anger, in the same way as winds and tempests are the school of the sailor-boy.—*Metastasio.*

Difficulty is a severe instructor, set over us by the supreme ordinance of a paternal guardian and legislator, who knows us better than we know ourselves, as he loves us better too. He that wrestles with us strengthens our nerves and sharpens our skill. Our antagonist is our helper.
Burke.

It is as hard to come, as for a camel to thread the postern of a needle's eye.—
Shakespeare.

It is difficulties which give birth to miracles. It is not every calamity that is a curse, and early adversity is often a blessing. Perhaps Madame de Maintenon would never have mounted a throne had not her cradle been rocked in a prison. Surmounted obstacles not only teach, but hearten us in our future struggles; for virtue must be learnt, though, unfortunately, some of the vices come as it were by inspiration.—*Rev. Dr. Sharpe.*

Out of difficulties grow miracles.—*Bruyère.*

Accustom yourself to master and overcome things of difficulty; for if you observe, the left hand for want of practice is insignificant, and not adapted to general business; yet it holds the bridle better than the right, from constant use.—*Pliny.*

The greatest difficulties lie where we are not looking for them.—*Goethe.*

What is difficulty? Only a word indicating the degree of strength requisite for accomplishing particular objects; a mere notice of the necessity for exertion; a bugbear to children and fools; only a mere stimulus to men.—
Samuel Warren.

Our energy is in proportion to the resistance it meets. We can attempt nothing great but from a sense of the difficulties we have to encounter; we can persevere in nothing great but from a pride in overcoming them.—*Hazlitt.*

The three things most difficult are — to keep a secret, to forget an injury, and to make good use of leisure.—*Chilo.*

The more powerful the obstacle, the more glory we have in overcoming it; and the difficulties with which we are met are the maids of honor which set off virtue.—*Molière.*

There is no merit where there is no trial; and, till experience stamps the mark of strength, cowards may pass for heroes, faith for falsehood.
Aaron Hill.

Difficulties strengthen the mind, as well as labor does the body.—*Seneca.*

Difficulties are things that show what men are. In case of any difficulty remember that God, like a gymnastic trainer, has pitted you against a rough antagonist. For what end? That you may be an Olympic conqueror, and this cannot be without toil.—*Epictetus.*

Wisdom is not found with those who dwell at their ease; rather nature, when she adds brain, adds difficulty.—*Emerson.*

Difficulties are God's errands; and when we are sent upon them we should esteem it a proof of God's confidence, — as a compliment from God.—*Beecher.*

Difficulties, by bracing the mind to overcome them, assist cheerfulness, as exercise assists digestion.—*Bovee.*

DIFFIDENCE.

Persons extremely reserved are like old enamelled watches, which had painted covers, that hindered your seeing what o'clock it was.
Walpole.

Diffidence may check resolution and obstruct performance, but compensates its embarrassments by more important advantages; it conciliates the proud, and softens the severe; averts envy from excellence, and censure from miscarriage.—*Johnson.*

We are as often duped by diffidence as by confidence.—*Chesterfield.*

DIGNITY.

Lord Chatham and Napoleon were as much actors as Garrick or Talma. Now, an imposing air should always be taken as evidence of imposition. Dignity is often a veil between us and the real truth of things.—*Whipple.*

True dignity is never gained by place, and never lost when honors are withdrawn.—
Massinger.

Dignity of position adds to dignity of character, as well as to dignity of carriage. Give us a proud position, and we are impelled to act up to it.—*Bovee.*

Dignity consists not in possessing honors, but in deserving them.—*Aristotle.*

Dignity and love do not blend well, nor do they continue long together.—*Ovid.*

DILIGENCE.

What we hope ever to do with ease we may learn first to do with diligence.—*Johnson.*

Who makes quick use of the moment is a genius of prudence.—*Lavater.*

The expectations of life depend upon diligence; and the mechanic that would perfect his work must first sharpen his tools.—
Confucius.

Prefer diligence before idleness, unless you esteem rust above brightness.—*Plato.*

DIRT.

Dirt is not dirt, but only something in the wrong place.—*Lord Palmerston.*

DISAPPOINTMENT.

Oft expectation fails, and most oft there where it most promises; and oft it hits where hope is coldest, and despair most sits.—
Shakespeare.

The darling schemes and fondest hopes of man are frequently frustrated by time. While sagacity contrives, patience matures, and labor industriously executes, disappointment laughs at the curious fabric, formed by so many efforts, and gay with so many brilliant colors, and, while the artists imagine the work arrived at the moment of completion, brushes away the beautiful web, and leaves nothing behind.—
Dwight.

How disappointment tracks the steps of hope! —*Miss Landon.*

He that will do no good offices after a disappointment must stand still, and do just nothing at all. The plough goes on after a barren year; and while the ashes are yet warm, we raise a new house upon the ruins of a former.—
Seneca.

Bearing a life-long hunger in his heart.—
Tennyson.

It is generally known that he who expects much will be often disappointed; yet disappointment seldom cures us of expectation, or has any other effect than that of producing a moral sentence or peevish exclamation.—*Johnson.*

Life is as tedious as a twice-told tale, vexing the dull ear of a drowsy man.—*Shakespeare.*

In the light of eternity we shall see that what we desired would have been fatal to us, and that what we would have avoided was essential to our well-being.—*Fenelon.*

When we meet with better fare than was expected, the disappointment is overlooked even by the scrupulous. When we meet with worse than was expected, philosophers alone know how to make it better.—*Zimmermann.*

Man must be disappointed with the lesser things of life before he can comprehend the full value of the greater.—*Bulwer Lytton.*

It is folly to pretend that one ever wholly recovers from a disappointed passion. Such wounds always leave a scar. There are faces I can never look upon without emotion, there are names I can never hear spoken without almost starting.—*Longfellow.*

Mean spirits under disappointment, like small beer in a thunder-storm, always turn sour.—*Randolph.*

An old man once said, " When I was young I was poor; when old I became rich; but in each condition I found disappointment. When the faculties of enjoyment were, I had not the means; when the means came, the faculties were gone."—*Madame de Gasparin.*

Thus ever fade my fairy dreams of bliss.—
Byron.

It is sometimes of God's mercy that men in the eager pursuit of worldly aggrandizement are baffled; for they are very like a train going down an inclined plane, — putting on the brake is not pleasant, but it keeps the car on the track.—*Beecher.*

It never yet happened to any man since the beginning of the world, nor ever will, to have all things according to his desire, or to whom fortune was never opposite and adverse.—
Burton.

We mount to heaven mostly on the ruins of our cherished schemes, finding our failures were successes.—*Alcott.*

DISCERNMENT.

To succeed in the world, it is much more necessary to possess the penetration to discern who is a fool than to discover who is a clever man.—*Talleyrand.*

After a spirit of discernment the next rarest things in the world are diamonds and pearls.—
Bruyère.

Simple creatures, whose thoughts are not taken up, like those of educated people, with the care of a great museum of dead phrases, are very quick to see the live facts which are going on about them.—*Holmes.*

The idiot, the Indian, the child, and unschooled farmer's boy stand nearer to the light by which nature is to be read, than the dissector or the antiquary.—*Emerson.*

There seems to be no part of knowledge in fewer hands than that of discerning when to have done.—*Swift.*

DISCIPLINE.

Has it never occurred to us, when surrounded by sorrows, that they may be sent to us only for our instruction, as we darken the cages of birds when we wish to teach them to sing ?—*Richter.*

No evil propensity of the human heart is so powerful that it may not be subdued by discipline.—*Seneca.*

The heart must be divorced from its idols. Age does a great deal in curing the man of his frenzy ; but if God has a special work for a man, he takes a shorter and sharper course with him. This grievous loss is only a further and more expensive education for the work of the ministry ; it is but saying more closely, " Will you pay the price ? "— *Cecil.*

No pain, no palm ; no thorns, no throne ; no gall, no glory ; no cross, no crown.— *William Penn.*

A dull axe never loves grindstones, but a keen workman does ; and he puts his tool on them in order that it may be sharp. And men do not like grinding ; but they are dull for the purposes which God designs to work out with them, and therefore he is grinding them.— *Beecher.*

A stern discipline pervades all nature, which is a little cruel that it may be very kind.— *Spenser.*

We have all to be laid upon an altar ; we have all, as it were, to be subjected to the action of fire.—*G. J. W. Melville.*

DISCONTENT.

That which makes people dissatisfied with their condition is the chimerical idea they form of the happiness of others.—*Thomson.*

What is more miserable than discontent ?— *Shakespeare.*

Discontents are sometimes the better part of our life. I know not well which is the most useful ; joy I may choose for pleasure, but adversities are the best for profit ; and sometimes those do so far help me, as I should, without them, want much of the joy I have.—*Feltham.*

DISCOVERY.

It is a mortifying truth, and ought to teach the wisest of us humility, that many of the most valuable discoveries have been the result of chance rather than of contemplation, and of accident rather than of design.—*Colton.*

A new principle is an inexhaustible source of new views.—*Vauvenargues.*

DISCRETION.

The greatest parts, without discretion, as observed by an elegant writer, may be fatal to their owner ; as Polyphemus, deprived of his eyes, was only the more exposed on account of his enormous strength and stature.—*Addison.*

The better part of valor is discretion.— *Shakespeare.*

Jest not openly at those that are simple, but remember how much thou art bound to God, who hath made thee wiser. Defame not any woman publicly, though thou know her to be evil ; for those that are faulty cannot endure to be taxed, but will seek to be avenged of thee ; and those that are not guilty cannot endure unjust reproach.—*Sir Walter Raleigh.*

All persons are not discreet enough to know how to take things by the right handle.— *Cervantes.*

Without discretion, people may be overlaid with unreasonable affection, and choked with too much nourishment.—*Jeremy Collier.*

Discretion in speech is more than eloquence. *Bacon.*

Discretion is the perfection of reason, and a guide to us in all the duties of life ; cunning is a kind of instinct, that only looks out after our immediate interests and welfare. Discretion is only found in men of strong sense and good understanding ; cunning is often to be met with in brutes themselves, and in persons who are but the fewest removes from them.— *Bruyère.*

Discretion is the salt, and fancy the sugar of life ; the one preserves, the other sweetens it.— *Bovee.*

There are many more shining qualities in the mind of man, but there are none so useful as discretion.—*Addison.*

In a state where discretion begins, law, liberty, and safety end.—*Junius.*

There is no talent so useful towards rising in the world, or which puts men more out of the power of fortune, than that quality generally possessed by the dullest sort of men, and in common speech called " discretion," — a species of lower prudence, by the assistance of which people of the meanest intellectuals pass through the world in great tranquillity, neither giving nor taking offence. For want of a reasonable infusion of this aldermanly discretion, everything fails. Had Windham possessed discretion in debate, or Sheridan in conduct, they might have ruled their age.—*Swift.*

If a cause be good, the most violent attack of its enemies will not injure it so much as an injudicious defence of it by its friends.—*Colton.*

If thou art a master, be sometimes blind ; if a servant, sometimes deaf.—*Fuller.*

Never join with your friend when he abuses his horse or his wife, unless the one is about to be sold, and the other to be buried.—*Colton.*

DISEASE.

Diseases, desperate grown, by desperate appliance are relieved, or not at all.—*Shakespeare.*

DISGUISE.

Men would not live long in society, were they not the mutual dupes of each other.—
Rochefoucauld.

Were we to take as much pains to be what we ought to be as we do to disguise what we really are, we might appear like ourselves without being at the trouble of any disguise at all.—*Rochefoucauld.*

DISHONESTY.

Dishonesty is a forsaking of permanent for temporary advantages.—*Bovee.*

I have known a vast quantity of nonsense talked about bad men not looking you in the face. Don't trust that conventional idea. Dishonesty will stare honesty out of countenance any day in the week, if there is anything to be got by it.—*Dickens.*

Dishonest men conceal their faults from themselves as well as others ; honest men know and confess them.—*Rochefoucauld.*

Who purposely cheats his friend would cheat his God.—*Lavater.*

That which is won ill will never wear well, for there is a curse attends it, which will waste it ; and the same corrupt dispositions which incline men to the sinful ways of getting will incline them to the like sinful ways of spending.—*Matthew Henry.*

Dishonor waits on perfidy. A man should blush to think a falsehood ; it is the crime of cowards.—*Johnson.*

If you attempt to beat a man down and to get his goods for less than a fair price, you are attempting to commit burglary, as much as though you broke into his shop to take the things without paying for them. There is cheating on both sides of the counter, and generally less behind it than before it.—*Beecher.*

It is hard to say which of the two we ought most to lament, — the unhappy man who sinks under the sense of his dishonor, or him who survives it.—*Junius.*

DISPLAY.

They that govern most make least noise.—
Selden.

The lowest people are generally the first to find fault with show or equipage ; especially that of a person lately emerged from his obscurity. They never once consider that he is breaking the ice for themselves.—*Shenstone.*

The horses which make the most show are, in general, those which advance the least. It is the same with men ; and we ought not to confound that perpetual agitation which exhausts itself in vain efforts, with the activity which goes right to the end.—*Baron de Stassart.*

DISPUTE.

The more discussion the better, if passion and personality be eschewed ; and discussion, even if stormy, often winnows truth from error, — a good never to be expected in an uninquiring age.—*Channing.*

There is no dispute managed without passion, and yet there is scarce a dispute worth a passion.—*Sherlock.*

The pain of dispute exceeds by much its utility. All disputation makes the mind deaf ; and when people are deaf I am dumb.—*Joubert.*

It is true there is nothing displays a genius, I mean a quickness of genius, more than a dispute ; as two diamonds, encountering, contribute to each other's lustre. But perhaps the odds is much against the man of taste in this particular.—*Shenstone.*

DISSIMULATION.

Dissimulation is but a faint kind of policy ; for it asketh a strong wit and a strong heart, to know when to tell the truth and to do it.—
Bacon.

Dissimulation in youth is the forerunner of perfidy in old age ; its first appearance is the fatal omen of growing depravity and future shame. It degrades parts and learning, obscures the lustre of every accomplishment, and sinks us into contempt. The path of falsehood is a perplexing maze. After the first departure from sincerity, it is not in our power to stop ; one artifice unavoidably leads on to another, till, as the intricacy of the labyrinth increases, we are left entangled in our snare.—
Blair.

He who knows not how to dissimulate knows not how to rule.—*Metellus of Macedon.*

The harlot's cheek, beautied with plastering art, is not more ugly to the thing that helps it than is my deed to my most painted word.—
Shakespeare.

DISTINCTION.

All our distinctions are accidental ; beauty and deformity, though personal qualities, are neither entitled to praise nor censure ; yet it so happens that they color our opinion of those qualities to which mankind have attached responsibility.—*Zimmermann.*

Distinction, with a broad and powerful fan, puffing at all, winnows the light away.—
Shakespeare.

All that causes one man to differ from another is a very slight thing. What is it that is the origin of beauty or ugliness, health or weakness, ability or stupidity ? A slight difference in the organs, a little more or a little less bile. Yet this more or less is of infinite importance to men ; and when they think otherwise they are mistaken.—*Vauvenargues.*

DISTRUST.
The best use one can make of his mind is to distrust it.—*Fenelon.*

Nothing is more certain of destroying any good feeling that may be cherished towards us than to show distrust. To be suspected as an enemy is often enough to make a man become so ; the whole matter is over, there is no farther use of guarding against it. On the contrary, confidence leads us naturally to act kindly, we are affected by the good opinion which others entertain of us, and we are not easily induced to lose it.—*Madame de Sévigné.*

In distrust are the nerves of the mind.—
Demosthenes.

Excessive distrust is not less hurtful than its opposite. Most men become useless to him who is unwilling to risk being deceived.—
Vauvenargues.

This feeling of distrust is always the last which a great mind acquires ; he is deceived for a long time.—*Racine.*

A certain amount of distrust is wholesome, but not so much of others as of ourselves ; neither vanity nor conceit can exist in the same atmosphere with it.—*Madame Necker.*

DOCTRINE.
Every one cleaves to the doctrine he has happened upon, as to a rock against which he has been thrown by tempest.—*Cicero.*

As those wines which flow from the first treading of the grape are sweeter and better than those forced out by the press, which gives them the roughness of the husk and the stone, so are those doctrines best and sweetest which flow from a gentle crush of the Scriptures, and are not wrung into controversies and common-places.—*Bacon.*

Doctrine is nothing but the skin of truth set up and stuffed.—*Beecher.*

The question is not whether a doctrine is beautiful, but whether it is true. When we want to go to a place, we don't ask whether the road leads through a pretty country, but whether it is the right road, the road pointed out by authority, the turnpike-road.—*Hare.*

DOGMATISM.
Nothing can be more unphilosophical than to be positive or dogmatical on any subject ; and even if excessive scepticism could be maintained, it would not be more destructive to all just reasoning and inquiry. When men are the most sure and arrogant, they are commonly the most mistaken, and have there given reins to passion, without that proper deliberation and suspense which can alone secure them from the grossest absurdities.—*Hume.*

A dogmatical spirit inclines a man to be censorious of his neighbors. Every one of his opinions appears to him written, as it were, with sunbeams, and he grows angry that his neighbors do not see it in the same light. He is tempted to disdain his correspondents as men of low and dark understandings because they do not believe what he does.—*Watts.*

DOMESTIC.
The domestic man, who loves no music so well as his kitchen clock, and the airs which the logs sing to him as they burn on the hearth, has solaces which others never dream of.
Emerson.

Domestic worth, — that shuns too strong a light.—*Lord Lyttelton.*

Domestic happiness is the end of almost all our pursuits, and the common reward of all our pains. When men find themselves forever barred from this delightful fruition, they are lost to all industry, and grow careless of all their worldly affairs. Thus they become bad subjects, bad relations, bad friends, and bad men.—
Fielding.

A prince wants only the pleasure of private life to complete his happiness.—*Bruyère.*

Our notion of the perfect society embraces the family as its centre and ornament. Nor is there a paradise planted till the children appear in the foreground to animate and complete the picture.—*Alcott.*

Domestic happiness, thou only bliss of paradise that has survived the fall ! — *Cowper.*

A house kept to the end of prudence is laborious without joy ; a house kept to the end of display is impossible to all but a few women, and their success is dearly bought.—*Emerson.*

No money is better spent than what is laid out for domestic satisfaction. A man is pleased that his wife is dressed as well as other people, and the wife is pleased that she is dressed.—*Johnson.*

DOUBT.
Man was not made to question, but adore.—
Young.

Human knowledge is the parent of doubt.—
Lord Greville.

Our doubts are traitors, and make us lose the good we oft might win, by fearing to attempt.—
Shakespeare.

Can that which is the greatest virtue in philosophy, doubt (called by Galileo the father of invention), be in religion what the priests term it, the greatest of sins ?—*Bovee.*

Doubt is the vestibule which all must pass, before they can enter into the temple of wisdom ; therefore, when we are in doubt and puzzle out the truth by our own exertions, we have gained a something that will stay by us, and which will serve us again. But, if to avoid the trouble of the search, we avail ourselves of the superior information of a friend, such knowledge will not remain with us ; we have not bought, but borrowed it.—*Colton.*

Servile doubt argues an impotence of mind, that says we fear because we dare not meet misfortunes.—*Aaron Hill.*

When you doubt, abstain.—*Zoroaster.*

In contemplation, if a man begin with certainties, he shall end in doubts ; but if he will be content to begin with doubts, he shall end in certainties.—*Bacon.*

We know accurately only when we know little ; with knowledge doubt increases.—
Goethe.

To- be once in doubt is once to be resolved.—
Shakespeare.

A bitter and perplexed " What shall I do ? " is worse to man than worse necessity.—
Coleridge.

The wound of peace is surety, surety secure ; but modest doubt is called the beacon of the wise ; the tent that searches to the bottom of the worst.—*Shakespeare.*

I love sometimes to doubt, as well as know.—
Dante.

There is no weariness like that which rises from doubting, from the perpetual jogging of unfixed reason. The torment of suspense is very great ; and as soon as the wavering, perplexed mind begins to determine, be the determination which way soever, it will find itself at ease.—*South.*

Misgive that you may not mistake.—
Whately.

Weary the path that does not challenge reason. Doubt is an incentive to truth, and patient inquiry leadeth the way.—*Hosea Ballou.*

Who never doubted never half believed ; where doubt there truth is, — it is her shadow.—
Bailey.

DRAMA.
It is remarkable how virtuous and generously disposed every one is at a play. We uniformly applaud what is right, and condemn what is wrong, when it costs us nothing but the sentiment.—*Hazlitt.*

The real object of the drama is the exhibition of the human character.—*Macaulay.*

The drama embraces and applies all the beauties and decorations of poetry. The sister arts attend and adorn it. Painting, architecture, and music are her handmaids. The costliest lights of a people's intellect burn at her show. All ages welcome her.—*Willmott.*

The seat of wit, when one speaks as a man of the town and the world, is the playhouse.—
Steele.

Every movement of the theatre by a skilful poet is communicated, as it were, by magic to the spectators ; who weep, tremble, resent, rejoice, and are inflamed with all the variety of passions which actuate the several personages of the drama.—*Hume.*

The drama is the book of the people.—
Willmott.

There is so much of the glare and grief of life connected with the stage, that it fills me with most solemn thoughts.—*Henry Giles.*

DREAMS.
When monarch reason sleeps, this mimic wakes.—*Dryden.*

As dreams are the fancies of those that sleep, so fancies are but the dreams of those awake.—*Sir T. P. Blount.*

Dreaming is an act of pure imagination, attesting in all men a creative power which, if it were available in waking, would make every man a Dante or a Shakespeare.—*F. H. Hedge.*

Let not our babbling dreams affright our souls.—*Shakespeare.*

Dreams in their development have breath and tears and tortures, and the touch of joy ; they leave a weight upon our waking thoughts, they take a weight from off our waking toils, they do divide our being ; they become a portion of ourselves as of our time, and look like heralds of eternity.—*Byron.*

We are near waking when we dream that we dream.—*Novalis.*

Dreams are the bright creatures of poem and legend, who sport on the earth in the night season, and melt away with the first beam of the sun, which lights grim care and stern reality on their daily pilgrimage through the world.—
Dickens.

Dreams full oft are found of real events the forms and shadows.—*Joanna Baillie.*

Dreams are the children of an idle brain, begot of nothing but vain fantasy; which is as thin of substance as the air, and more inconstant than the wind.—*Shakespeare.*

Regard not dreams, since they are but the images of our hopes and fears.—*Cato.*

Nothing so much convinces me of the boundlessness of the human mind as its operations in dreaming.—*W. B. Clulow.*

The dreamer is a madman quiescent, the madman is a dreamer in action.—*F. H. Hedge.*

If we can sleep without dreaming, it is well that painful dreams are avoided. If, while we sleep, we can have any pleasing dreams, it is, as the French say, *tant gagné,* so much added to the pleasure of life.—*Franklin.*

As a wild maiden, with love-drinking eyes, sees in sweet dreams a beaming youth of glory.
Alexander Smith.

Metaphysicians have been learning their lesson for the last four thousand years, and it is high time that they should now begin to teach us something. Can any of the tribe inform us why all the operations of the mind are carried on with undiminished strength and activity in dreams, except the judgment, which alone is suspended and dormant?—*Colton.*

Every one turns his dreams into realities as far as he can; man is cold as ice to the truth, hot as fire to falsehood.—*La Fontaine.*

Dreams are like portraits; and we find they please because they are confessed resemblances.
Crabbe.

What the tender and poetic youth dreams to-day, and conjures up with inarticulate speech, is to-morrow the vociferated result of public opinion, and the day after is the character of nations.—*Emerson.*

Dreams where thought, in fancy's maze, runs mad.—*Young.*

DRESS.

Nothing can embellish a beautiful face more than a narrow band that indicates a small wound drawn crosswise over the brow.—
Richter.

The only medicine which does women more good than harm is dress.—*Richter*

Those who think that in order to dress well it is necessary to dress extravagantly or grandly make a great mistake. Nothing so well becomes true feminine beauty as simplicity.—
George D. Prentice.

But to please thyself, but dress to please others.—*Franklin.*

In Athens the ladies were not gaudily but simply arrayed, and we doubt whether any ladies ever excited more admiration. So also the noble old Roman matrons, whose superb forms were gazed on delightedly by men worthy of them, were always very plainly dressed.—
George D. Prentice.

There can be no kernel in this light nut; the soul of this man is in his clothes.
Shakespeare.

Next to clothes being fine, they should be well made, and worn easily; for a man is only the less genteel for a fine coat, if, in wearing it, he shows a regard for it, and is not as easy in it as if it was a plain one.—*Chesterfield.*

In the matter of dress one should always keep below one's ability.—*Montesquieu.*

Costly thy habit as thy purse can buy, but not expressed in fancy; rich, not gaudy; for the apparel oft proclaims the man.—*Shakespeare.*

Next to dressing for a rout or ball, undressing is a woe.—*Byron.*

No man ever stood lower in my estimation for having a patch in his clothes; yet I am sure there is greater anxiety to have fashionable, or at least clean and unpatched clothes, than to have a sound conscience. I sometimes try my acquaintances by some such test as this,—who could wear a patch, or two extra seams only, over the knee.—*Thoreau.*

A saint in crape is twice a saint in lawn.—
Pope.

Dress has a moral effect upon the conduct of mankind. Let any gentleman find himself with dirty boots, old surtout, soiled neckcloth, and a general negligence of dress, and he will in all probability find a corresponding disposition by negligence of address.—*Sir Jonah Barrington.*

The plainer the dress, with greater lustre does beauty appear. Virtue is the greatest ornament, and good sense the best equipage.—
Lord Halifax.

Beauty gains little, and homeliness and deformity lose much, by gaudy attire. Lysander knew this was in part true, and refused the rich garments that the tyrant Dionysius proffered to his daughters, saying " that they were fit only to make unhappy faces more remarkable."—
Zimmermann.

Through tattered clothes small vices do appear; robes and furred gowns hide all. Plate sin with gold, and the strong lance of justice hurtless breaks; arm it in rags, a pygmy's straw doth pierce it.—*Shakespeare.*

We sacrifice to dress till household joys and comforts cease. Dress drains our cellar dry, and keeps our larder lean.—*Cowper.*

It is not every man that can afford to wear a shabby coat; and worldly wisdom dictates to her disciples the propriety of dressing somewhat beyond their means, but of living within them; for every one sees how we dress, but none see how we live, except we choose to let them.—
Colton.

A fine coat is but a livery when the person who wears it discovers no higher sense than that of a footman.—*Addison.*

A lady of genius will give a genteel air to her whole dress by a well-fancied suit of knots, as a judicious writer gives a spirit to a whole sentence by a single expression.—*Gay.*

Women always show more taste in adorning others than themselves; and the reason is, that their persons are like their hearts, — they read another's better than they can their own.—
Richter.

In clothes clean and fresh there is a kind of youth with which age should surround itself.—
Joubert.

As the index tells us the contents of stories, and directs to the particular chapter, even so does the outward habit and superficial order of garments (in man or woman) give us a taste of the spirit, and demonstratively point (as it were a manual note from the margin) all the internal quality of the soul; and there cannot be a more evident, palpable, gross manifestation of poor, degenerate, dunghilly blood and breeding than a rude, unpolished, disordered, and slovenly outside.—*Massinger.*

And why take ye thought for raiment? Consider the lilies of the field, how they grow; they toil not, neither do they spin.—*Bible.*

Processions, cavalcades, and all that fund of gay frippery, furnished out by tailors, barbers, and tire-women, mechanically influence the mind into veneration; an emperor in his nightcap would not meet with half the respect of an emperor with a crown.—*Goldsmith.*

As you treat your body, so your house, your domestics, your enemies, your friends. Dress is a table of your contents.—*Lavater.*

Those who are incapable of shining but by dress would do well to consider that the contrast betwixt them and their clothes turns out much to their disadvantage. It is on this account I have sometimes observed with pleasure some noblemen of immense fortune to dress exceeding plain.—*Shenstone.*

No man is esteemed for gay garments but by fools and women.—*Sir Walter Raleigh.*

Men of quality never appear more amiable than when their dress is plain. Their birth, rank, title, and its appendages are at best invidious; and as they do not need the assistance of dress, so, by their disclaiming the advantage of it, they make their superiority sit more easy.—
Shenstone.

The vanity of loving fine clothes and new fashions, and valuing ourselves by them, is one of the most childish pieces of folly that can be.—
Sir Matthew Hale.

I would rather have a young fellow too much than too little dressed; the excess on that side will wear off, with a little age and reflection; but if he is negligent at twenty, he will be a sloven at forty, and stink at fifty years old. Dress yourself fine where others are fine, and plain where others are plain; but take care always that your clothes are well made and fit you, for otherwise they will give you a very awkward air.—*Chesterfield.*

Out of clothes out of countenance, out of countenance out of wit.—*Ben Jonson.*

A simple garb is the proper costume of the vulgar; it is cut for them, and exactly suits their measure; but it is an ornament for those who have filled up their life with great deeds. I liken them to beauty in dishabille, but more bewitching on that account.—*Bruyère.*

Be neither too early in the fashion, nor too long out of it, nor too precisely in it; what custom hath civilized is become decent, till then ridiculous; where the eye is the jury, thy apparel is the evidence.—*Quarles.*

As long as there are cold and nakedness in the land around you, so long can there be no question at all but that splendor of dress is a crime. In due time, when we have nothing better to set people to work at, it may be right to let them make lace and cut jewels; but as long as there are any who have no blankets for their beds, and no rags for their bodies, so long it is blanket-making and tailoring we must set people to work at, not lace.—*Ruskin.*

Too great carelessness, equally with excess in dress, multiplies the wrinkles of old age, and makes its decay the more conspicuous.—*Bruyère.*

All costume off a man is pitiful or grotesque. It is only the serious eye peering from and the sincere life passed within it, which restrain laughter and consecrate the costume of any people. Let Harlequin be taken with a fit of the colic, and his trappings will have to serve that mood too. When the soldier is hit by a cannon-ball rags are as becoming as purple.—
Thoreau.

In the indications of female poverty there can be no disguise. No woman dresses below herself from caprice.—*Lamb.*

It is the saying of an old divine, " Two things in my apparel I will chiefly aim at, — commodiousness and decency; more than these is not commendable, yet I hate an effeminate spruceness as much as a fantastic disorder. A neglected comeliness is the best ornament." It is said of the celebrated Mr. Whitfield, that he always was very clean and neat, and often said pleasantly " that a minister of the gospel ought to be without a spot."—*J. Beaumont.*

Rich apparel has strange virtues; it makes him that hath it without means esteemed for an excellent wit; he that enjoys it with means puts the world in remembrance of his means.—
Ben Jonson.

The person whose clothes are extremely fine I am too apt to consider as not being possessed of any superiority of fortune, but resembling those Indians who are found to wear all the gold they have in the world in a bob at the nose.— *Goldsmith.*

A rich dress adds but little to the beauty of a person. It may possibly create a deference, but that is rather an enemy to love.—*Shenstone.*

I have always a sacred veneration for any one I observe to be a little out of repair in his person, as supposing him either a poet or a philosopher; because the richest minerals are ever found under the most ragged and withered surfaces of the earth.—*Swift.*

A gentleman's taste in dress is, upon principle, the avoidance of all things extravagant. It consists in the quiet simplicity of exquisite neatness; but, as the neatness must be a neatness in fashion, employ the best tailor; pay him ready money, and, on the whole, you will find him the cheapest.—*Bulwer Lytton.*

DRUNKENNESS.

All excess is ill, but drunkenness is of the worst sort. It spoils health, dismounts the mind, and unmans men. It reveals secrets, is quarrelsome, lascivious, impudent, dangerous, and mad. He that is drunk is not a man, because he is, for so long, void of reason that distinguishes a man from a beast.—
William Penn.

Drunkenness is nothing else but a voluntary madness.—*Seneca.*

Man has evil as well as good qualities peculiar to himself. Drunkenness places him as much below the level of the brutes as reason elevates him above them.—*Sir G. Sinclair.*

Beware of drunkenness, lest all good men beware of thee; where drunkenness reigns, there reason is an exile, virtue a stranger, God an enemy; blasphemy is wit, oaths are rhetorie, and secrets are proclamations. Noah discovered that in one hour, drunk, which, sober, he kept secret six hundred years.— *Quarles.*

A drunken man is like a drowned man, a fool, and a madman; one draught above heat makes him a fool, the second mads him, and a third drowns him.—*Shakespeare.*

Some of the domestic evils of drunkenness are houses without windows, gardens without fences, fields without tillage, barns without roofs, children without clothing, principles, morals, or manners.—*Franklin.*

In the bottle discontent seeks for comfort, cowardice for courage, and bashfulness for confidence.—*Johnson.*

Drunkenness is the vice of a good constitution or of a bad memory, — of a constitution so treacherously good that it never bends till it breaks; or of a memory that recollects the pleasures of getting intoxicated, but forgets the pains of getting sober.— *Colton*

Habitual intoxication is the epitome of every crime.—*Douglas Jerrold.*

Drunkenness is a flattering devil, a sweet poison, a pleasant sin, which whosoever hath hath not himself; which whosoever doth commit doth not commit sin, but he himself is wholly sin.—*St. Augustine.*

Troops of furies march in the drunkard's triumph.—*Zimmermann.*

The bliss of the drunkard is a visible picture of the expectation of the dying atheist, who hopes no more than to lie down in the grave with the " beasts that perish."—*Jane Porter.*

A vine bears three grapes, — the first of pleasure, the second of drunkenness, and the third of repentance.—*Anacharsis.*

People say, " Do not regard what he says now he is in liquor." Perhaps it is the only time he ought to be regarded: *Aperit præcordia liber.*—*Shenstone.*

Of all vices take heed of drunkenness; other vices are but fruits of disordered affections, — this disorders, nay, banishes reason; other vices but impair the soul, — this demolishes her two chief faculties, the understanding and the will; other vices make their own way, — this makes way for all vices; he that is a drunkard is qualified for all vice.—*Quarles.*

Thirst teaches all animals to drink, but drunkenness belongs only to man.—*Fielding.*

They were red-hot with drinking; so full of valor, that they smote the air for breathing in their faces, beat the ground for kissing of their feet.—*Shakespeare.*

There is scarcely a crime before me that is not, directly or indirectly, caused by strong drink.—*Judge Coleridge.*

Those men who destroy a healthful constitution of body by intemperance and an irregular life do as manifestly kill themselves as those who hang or poison or drown themselves.—*Sherlock.*

The sight of a drunkard is a better sermon against that vice than the best that was ever preached upon that subject.—*Saville.*

If the headache should come before drunkenness, we should have a care of drinking too much; but Pleasure, to deceive us, marches before, and conceals her train.—*Montaigne.*

DUELS.

If all seconds were as averse to duels as their principals, very little blood would be shed in that way.—*Colton.*

With respect to duels, indeed, I have my own ideas. Few things in this so surprising world strike me with more surprise. Two little visual spectra of men, hovering with insecure enough cohesion in the midst of the unfathomable, and to dissolve therein, at any rate, very soon, make pause at the distance of twelve paces asunder, whirl around, and simultaneously, by the cunningest mechanism, explode one another into dissolution; and, off-hand, become air, and non-extant, — the little spitfires !— *Carlyle.*

Since bodily strength is but a servant to the mind, it were very barbarous and preposterous that force should be made judge over reason.— *Sir P. Sidney.*

Duelling, though barbarous in civilized, is a highly civilized institution among barbarous people; and when compared to assassination, is a prodigious victory gained over human passions.—*Sydney Smith.*

DULNESS.

What a comfort a dull but kindly person is, to be sure, at times ! A ground-glass shade over a gas-lamp does not bring more solace to our dazzled eyes than such a one to our minds.— *Holmes.*

There are some heads which have no windows, and the day can never strike from above; nothing enters from heavenward.—*Joubert.*

A dull man is so near a dead man that he is hardly to be ranked in the list of the living; and as he is not to be buried whilst he is half alive, so he is as little to be employed whilst he is half dead.—*Saville.*

DUTY.

The true way to render ourselves happy is to love our duty and find in it our pleasure.— *Madame de Motteville.*

Let men laugh when you sacrifice desire to duty, if they will. You have time and eternity to rejoice in.—*Theodore Parker.*

Amid all our ignorance and weakness what we best know is our duty—*Whately.*

There is little pleasure in the world that is true and sincere besides the pleasure of doing our duty and doing good. I am sure no other is comparable to this.—*Tillotson.*

Every subject's duty is the king's; but every subject's soul is his own.—*Shakespeare.*

We are apt to mistake our vocation by looking out of the way for occasions to exercise great and rare virtues, and by stepping over the ordinary ones that lie directly in the road before us.—*Hannah More.*

It is one of the worst of errors to suppose that there is any other path of safety except that of duty.—*Nevins.*

Duty itself is supreme delight when love is the inducement and labor. By such a principle the ignorant are enlightened, the hard-hearted softened, the disobedient reformed, and the faithful encouraged.—*Hosea Ballou.*

Fear God and keep his commandments, for this is the whole duty of man.—*Bible.*

There is a sanctity in suffering when meekly born. Our duty, though set about by thorns, may still be made a staff, supporting even while it tortures. Cast it away, and, like the prophet's wand, it changes to a snake.— *Douglas Jerrold.*

Only when the voice of duty is silent, or when it has already spoken, may we allowably think of the consequences of a particular action. *Hare.*

Let him who gropes painfully in darkness or uncertain light, and prays vehemently that the dawn may ripen into day, lay this precept well to heart: "Do the duty which lies nearest thee," which thou knowest to be a duty ! Thy second duty will already have become clearer.— *Carlyle.*

Who so escapes a duty avoids a gain.— *Theodore Parker.*

There are not good things enough in life to indemnify us for the neglect of a single duty.— *Madame Swetchine.*

Man owes two solemn debts, — one to society, and one to nature. It is only when he pays the second that he covers the first.— *Douglas Jerrold.*

A few strong instincts, and a few plain rules.— *Wordsworth.*

Stern duties need not speak sternly. He who stood firm before the thunder worshipped the "still small voice."—*Sidney Dobell.*

It is an impressive truth that sometimes in the very lowest forms of duty, less than which would rank a man as a villain, there is, nevertheless, the sublimest ascent of self-sacrifice. To do less would class you as an object of eternal scorn, to do so much presumes the grandeur of heroism.—*De Quincey.*

Perish discretion when it interferes with duty.—*Hannah More.*

There is no mean work save that which is sordidly selfish; there is no irreligious work save that which is morally wrong; while in every sphere of life "the post of honor is the post of duty."—*Chapin.*

Stern daughter of the voice of God!— *Wordsworth.*

No man's spirits were ever hurt by doing his duty; on the contrary, one good action, one temptation resisted and overcome, one sacrifice of desire or interest, purely for conscience' sake, will prove a cordial for weak and low spirits, far beyond what either indulgence or diversion or company can do for them.— *Paley.*

Duties are ours; events are God's.—*Cecil.*

I believe that we are conforming to the divine order and the will of Providence when we are doing even indifferent things that belong to our condition.—*Fenelon.*

Whether your time calls you to live or die, do both like a prince.—*Sir P. Sidney.*

Do not diverted from your duty by any idle reflections the silly world may make upon you, for their censures are not in your power, and consequently should not be any part of your concern.—*Epictetus.*

There is no evil which we cannot face or fly from but the consciousness of duty disregarded. *Daniel Webster.*

The consideration that human happiness and moral duty are inseparably connected will always continue to prompt me to promote the progress of the former by inculcating the practice of the latter.—*Washington.*

Every one regards his duty as a troublesome master from whom he would like to be free.— *La Roche.*

Let us do our duty in our shop or our kitchen, the market, the street, the office, the school, the home, just as faithfully as if we stood in the front rank of some great battle, and we knew that victory for mankind depended on our bravery, strength, and skill. When we do that the humblest of us will be serving in that great army which achieves the welfare of the world.—*Theodore Parker.*

Reverence the highest, have patience with the lowest. Let this day's performance of the meanest duty be thy religion. Are the stars too distant, pick up the pebble that lies at thy feet and from it learn the all.—*Margaret Fuller.*

Knowledge of our duties is the most useful part of philosophy.—*Whately.*

E.

EARNESTNESS.

Do you wish to become rich? You may become rich, that is, if you desire it in no half way, but thoroughly. A miser sacrifices all to his single passion; hoards farthings and dies possessed of wealth. Do you wish to master any science or accomplishment? Give yourself to it and it lies beneath your feet. Time and pains will do anything. This world is given as the prize for the men in earnest; and that which is true of this world is truer still of the world to come.—*F. W. Robertson.*

The most precious wine is produced upon the sides of volcanoes. Now bold and inspiring ideas are only born of a clear head that stands over a glowing heart.—*Horace Mann.*

Patience is only one faculty; earnestness the devotion of all the faculties. Earnestness is the cause of patience; it gives endurance, overcomes pain, strengthens weakness, braves dangers, sustains hope, makes light of difficulties, and lessens the sense of weariness in overcoming them.—*Bovee.*

I look upon enthusiasm in all other points but that of religion to be a very necessary turn of mind; as, indeed, it is a vein which nature seems to have marked with more or less strength in the tempers of most men.—*Fitzosborne.*

There is no substitute for thorough-going, ardent, and sincere earnestness.—*Dickens.*

Earnestness alone makes life eternity.— *Carlyle.*

A man without earnestness is a mournful and perplexing spectacle. But it is a consolation to believe, as we must of such a one, that he is the most effectual and compulsive of all schools.—*Sterling.*

A man is relieved and gay when he has put his heart into his work and done his best; but what he has said or done otherwise shall give him no peace.—*Emerson.*

Earnestness is enthusiasm tempered by reason.—*Pascal.*

EARTH.

Once every atom of this ground lived, breathed, and felt like me ! —*James Montgomery.*

Where is the dust that has not been alive ? The spade, the plough, disturb our ancestors ; from human mould we reap our daily bread.—
Young.

The earth, that is nature's mother, is her tomb.—*Shakespeare.*

Lean not on earth ; it will pierce thee to the heart ; a broken reed at best ; but oft a spear, on its sharp point Peace bleeds and Hope expires.—*Young.*

The waters deluge man with rain, oppress him with hail, and drown him with inundations ; the air rushes in storms, prepares the tempest, or lights up the volcano ; but the earth, gentle and indulgent, ever subservient to the wants of man, spreads his walks with flowers and his table with plenty ; returns with interest every good committed to her care, and though she produces the poison, she still supplies the antidote ; though constantly teased more to furnish the luxuries of man than his necessities, yet, even to the last, she continues her kind indulgence, and when life is over, she piously covers his remains in her bosom.—*Pliny.*

The flowers are but earth vivified.—
Lamartine.

Friend, hast thou considered the "rugged, all-nourishing earth," as Sophocles well names her; how she feeds the sparrow on the housetop, much more her darling man ? —*Carlyle.*

I believe this earth on which we stand is but the vestibule to glorious mansions through which a moving crowd forever press.—
Joanna Baillie.

Speak no harsh words of earth ; she is our mother, and few of us her sons who have not added a wrinkle to her brow.—*Alexander Smith.*

ECCENTRICITY.

Even beauty cannot palliate eccentricity.—
Balzac.

Oddities and singularities of behavior may attend genius ; but when they do, they are its misfortunes and blemishes. The man of true genius will be ashamed of them, or at least will never affect to be distinguished by them.—
Sir W. Temple.

Often extraordinary excellence, not being rightly conceived, does rather offend than please.—*Sir P. Sidney.*

ECHO.

That tuneful nymph, the babbling Echo, who has not learnt to conceal what is told her, nor yet is able to speak till another speaks.—*Ovid.*

Where we find echoes, we generally find emptiness and hollowness ; it is the contrary with the echoes of the heart.—*J. F. Boyes.*

The babbling gossip of the air.—
Shakespeare.

ECONOMY.

If you know how to spend less than you get you have the philosopher's stone.—*Franklin.*

All to whom want is terrible, upon whatever principle, ought to think themselves obliged to learn the sage maxims of our parsimonious ancestors, and attain the salutary arts of contracting expense ; for without economy none can be rich, and with it few can be poor.—
Johnson.

To make three guineas do the work of five.
Burns.

Nature is avariciously frugal ; in matter it allows no atom to elude its grasp ; in mind, no thought or feeling to perish. It gathers up the fragments that nothing he lost.—
Rev. Dr. Thomas.

Economy is an excellent lure to betray people into expense.—*Zimmermann.*

It is no small commendation to manage a little well. He is a good wagoner who can turn in a little room. To live well in abundance is the praise of the estate not of the person. I will study more how to give a good account of my little than how to make it more.—*Bishop Hall.*

Economy is of itself a great revenue.—
Cicero.

He who is taught to live upon little owes more to his father's wisdom than he that has a great deal left him does to his father's care.—
William Penn.

There is no gain so certain as that which arises from sparing what you have.—
Publius Syrus.

He regarded nothing to be cheap that was superfluous, for what one does not need is dear at a penny ; and it was better to possess fields, where the plough goes and cattle feed, than fine gardens that require much watering and sweeping.—*Plutarch.*

Beware of little expenses ; a small leak will sink a great ship.—*Franklin.*

Qualities not regulated run into their opposites. Economy before competence is meanness after it. Therefore economy is for the poor ; the rich may dispense with it.—*Bovee.*

No man is rich whose expenditures exceed his means ; and no one is poor whose incomings exceed his outgoings.—*Haliburton.*

Frugality is founded on the principle that all riches have limits.—*Burke.*

Men talk in raptures of youth and beauty, wit and sprightliness; but after seven years of union not one of them is to be compared to good family management, which is seen at every meal, and felt every hour in the husband's purse.—*Witherspoon.*

With parsimony a little is sufficient; and without it nothing is sufficient; whereas frugality makes a poor man rich.—*Seneca.*

Gain may be temporary and uncertain; but ever while you live expense is constant and certain; and it is easier to build two chimneys than to keep one in fuel.—*Franklin.*

Take care to be an economist in prosperity; there is no fear of your being one in adversity.—*Zimmermann.*

Economy is the parent of integrity, of liberty, and of ease, and the beauteous sister of temperance, of cheerfulness and health.—*Johnson.*

Sound economy is a sound understanding brought into action; it is calculation realized; it is the doctrine of proportion reduced to practice; it is foreseeing contingencies, and providing against them.—*Hannah More.*

Not to be covetous is money, not to be a purchaser is a revenue.—*Cicero.*

Economy is integrity and profuseness is a cruel and crafty demon, that gradually involves her followers in dependence and debts; that is, fetters them with irons that enter into their souls.—*Hawkesworth.*

Let honesty and industry be thy constant companions and spend one penny less than thy clear gains; then shall thy hide-bound pocket soon begin to thrive and will never again cry with the empty belly-ache; neither will creditors insult thee, nor want oppress, nor hunger bite, nor nakedness freeze thee.—*Franklin.*

The regard one shows economy is like that we show an old aunt who is to leave us something at last.—*Shenstone.*

Proportion and propriety are among the best secrets of domestic wisdom; and there is no surer test of integrity than a well-proportioned expenditure.—*Hannah More.*

Where there is a question of economy, I prefer privation.—*Madame Swetchine.*

The man who will live above his present circumstances is in great danger of living in a little time much beneath them, or, as the Italian proverb says : " The man who lives by hope will die by despair."—*Addison.*

EDITOR.

A journalist is a grumbler, a censurer, a giver of advice, a regent of sovereigns, a tutor of nations. Four hostile newspapers are more to be feared than a thousand bayonets.—*Napoleon.*

EDUCATION.

Education is the apprenticeship of life.—*Willmott.*

Jails and state prisons are the complement of schools; so many less as you have of the latter, so many more you must have of the former.—*Horace Mann.*

Let the soldier be abroad if he will, he can do nothing in this age. There is another personage less imposing in the eyes of some, perhaps insignificant. The schoolmaster is abroad, and I trust to him, armed with his primer, against the soldier in full military array.—*Lord Brougham.*

He is to be educated because he is a man, and not because he is to make shoes, nails, and pins.—*Channing.*

Knowledge does not comprise all which is contained in the large term of education. The feelings are to be disciplined, the passions are to be restrained; true and worthy motives are to be inspired; a profound religious feeling is to be instilled, and pure morality inculcated under all circumstances. All this is comprised in education.—*Daniel Webster.*

Education commences at the mother's knee, and every word spoken within the hearing of little children tends towards the formation of character. Let parents bear this ever in mind.—*Hosea Ballou.*

The real object of education is to give children resources that will endure as long as life endures; habits that time will ameliorate, not destroy; occupation that will render sickness tolerable, solitude pleasant, age venerable, life more dignified and useful, and death less terrible.—*Sydney Smith.*

No woman is educated who is not equal to the successful management of a family.—*Burnap.*

Promote as an object of primary importance institutions for the general diffusion of knowledge. In proportion as the structure of a government gives force to public opinion, it should be enlightened.—*Washington.*

We speak of educating our children. Do we know that our children also educate us ?—*Mrs. Sigourney.*

The sacred books of the ancient Persians say, If you would be holy, instruct your children, because all the good acts they perform will be imputed to you.—*Montesquieu.*

Any who says (with Mandeville in his treatise against charity schools), "If a horse knew as much as a man, I should not like to be his rider," ought to add, "If a man knew as little as a horse, I should not like to trust him to ride."— *Whately.*

Could we know by what strange circumstances a man's genius became prepared for practical success, we should discover that the most serviceable items in his education were never entered in the bills which his father paid for.—*Bulwer Lytton.*

The world is only saved by the breath of the school children.—*Talmud.*

Begin the education of the heart, not with the cultivation of noble propensities, but with the cutting away of those that are evil. When once the noxious herbs are withered and rooted out, then the more noble plants, strong in themselves, will shoot upwards. The virtuous heart, like the body, becomes strong and healthy more by labor than nourishment.—*Richter.*

The best education in the world is that got by struggling to get a living.— *Wendell Phillips.*

The true order of learning should be first, what is necessary ; second, what is useful ; and third, what is ornamental. To reverse this arrangement is like beginning to build at the top of the edifice.—*Mrs. Sigourney.*

School-houses are the republican line of fortifications.—*Horace Mann.*

Education is a better safeguard of liberty than a standing army. If we retrench the wages of the schoolmaster, we must raise those of the recruiting sergeant.—*Edward Everett.*

There are many things which we can afford to forget which it is yet well to learn.—*Holmes.*

It depends on education (that holder of the keys which the Almighty hath put into our hands) to open the gates which lead to virtue or to vice, to happiness or misery.—*Jane Porter.*

I call, therefore, a complete and generous education, that which fits a man to perform justly, skilfully, and magnanimously all the offices, both private and public, of peace and war.
Milton.

When a king asked Euclid, the mathematician, whether he could not explain his art to him in a more compendious manner, he was answered, that there was no royal way to geometry. Other things may be seized by might, or purchased with money ; but knowledge is to be gained only by study, and study to be prosecuted only in retirement.—*Johnson.*

Every fresh acquirement is another remedy against affliction and time.— *Willmott.*

I consider that it is on instruction and education that the future security and direction of the destiny of every nation chiefly and fundamentally rests.—*Kossuth.*

The wisest man may always learn something from the humblest peasant.— *J. Petit, Senn.*

Education, briefly, is the leading human souls to what is best, and making what is best out of them ; and these two objects are always attainable together, and by the same means ; the training which makes men happiest in themselves also makes them most serviceable to others.—*Ruskin.*

Education begins the gentleman, but reading, good company, and education must finish him.—*Locke.*

We know that the gifts which men have do not come from the schools. If a man is a plain, literal, factual man, you can make a great deal more of him in his own line by education than without education, just as you can make a great deal more of a potato if you cultivate it than if you do not ; but no cultivation in this world will ever make an apple out of a potato.— *Beecher.*

Education is our only political safety. Outside of this ark all is deluge.—*Horace Mann.*

Were it not better for a man in a fair room to set up one great light, or branching candlestick of lights, than to go about with a rushlight into every dark corner ? —*Bacon.*

Education is either from nature, from man, or from things ; the developing of our faculties and organs is the education of nature ; that of man is the application we learn to make of this very developing ; and that of things is the experience we acquire in regard to the different objects by which we are affected. All that we have not at our birth, and that we stand in need of at the years of maturity, is the gift of education.—*Rousseau.*

The best and most important part of every man's education is that which he gives himself.— *Gibbon.*

A father inquires whether his boy can construe Homer, if he understands Horace, and can taste Virgil ; but how seldom does he ask, or examine, or think whether he can restrain his passions, — whether he is grateful, generous, humane, compassionate, just, and benevolent.— *Lady Hervey.*

The pains we take in books or arts which treat of things remote from the necessaries of life is a busy idleness.— *Fuller.*

Public instruction should be the first object of government. - *Napoleon.*

The education of the present race of females is not very favorable to domestic happiness. For my own part, I call education, not that which smothers a woman with accomplishments, but that which tends to consolidate a firm and regular system of character; that which tends to form a friend, a companion, and a wife.— *Hannah More.*

In exalting the faculties of the soul, we annihilate, in a great degree, the delusion of the senses.—*Aimé-Martin.*

Virtue and talents, though allowed their due consideration, yet are not enough to procure a man a welcome wherever he comes. Nobody contents himself with rough diamonds, or wears them so. When polished and set, then they give a lustre.—*Locke.*

Man must either make provision of sense to understand, or of a halter to hang himself.— *Antisthenes.*

I too acknowledge the all-but omnipotence of early culture and nurture; hereby we have either a doddered dwarf-bush, or a high-towering, wide-shadowing tree! either a sick yellow cabbage, or an edible luxuriant green one. Of a truth, it is the duty of all men, especially of all philosophers, to note down with accuracy the characteristic circumstances of their education, — what furthered, what ·hindered, what in any way modified it.—*Carlyle.*

I think I should know how to educate a boy, but not a girl; I should be in danger of making her too learned.—*Niebuhr.*

Minds that are stupid and incapable of science are in the order of nature to be regarded as monsters and other extraordinary phenomena; minds of this sort are rare. Hence I conclude that there are great resources to be found in children, which are suffered to vanish with their years. It is evident, therefore, that it is not of nature, but of our own negligence, we ought to complain.—*Quintilian.*

All who have meditated on the art of governing mankind have been convinced that the fate of empires depends on the education of youth.—*Aristotle.*

Do not ask if a man has been through college. Ask if a college has been through him; if he is a walking university.—*Chapin.*

An intelligent class can scarce ever be, as a class, vicious; never, as a class, indolent. The excited mental activity operates as a counterpoise to the stimulus of sense and appetite.— *Edward Everett.*

As an apple is not in any proper sense an apple until it is ripe, so a human being is not in any proper sense a human being until he is educated.—*Horace Mann.*

All that a university or final highest school can do for us is still but what the first school began doing, — teach us to read. We learn to read in various languages, in various sciences; we learn the alphabet and letters of all manner of books. But the place where we are to get knowledge, even theoretic knowledge, is the books themselves. It depends on what we read, after all manner of professors have done their best for us. The true university of these days is a collection of books.—*Carlyle.*

Education is the chief defence of nations.— *Burke.*

How can man be intelligent, happy, or useful, without the culture and discipline of education? It is this that unlocks the prison-house of his mind, and releases the captive.— *Rev. Dr. Humphrey.*

In this country every one gets a mouthful of education, but scarcely any one a full meal.— *Theodore Parker.*

The greatest defect of common education is, that we are in the habit of putting pleasure all on one side, and weariness on the other; all weariness in study, all pleasure in idleness.— *Fenelon.*

Thalwell thought it very unfair to influence a child's mind by inculcating any opinions before it had come to years of discretion to choose for itself. I showed him my garden, and told him it was a botanical garden. " How so ? said he; " it is covered with weeds." " O," I replied, " that is only because it has not yet come to its age of discretion and choice. The weeds, you see, have taken the liberty to grow, and thought it unfair in me to prejudice the soil towards roses and strawberries."— *Coleridge.*

The aim of education should be to teach us rather how to think than what to think, — rather to improve our minds, so as to enable us to think for ourselves, than to load the memory with the thoughts of other men.—*Beattie.*

To be thoroughly imbued with the liberal arts refines the manners, and makes men to be mild and gentle in their conduct.—*Ovid.*

Man is an animal, formidable both from his passions and his reason ; his passions often urging him to great evils, and his reason furnishing means to achieve them. To train this animal, and make him amenable to order; to inure him to a sense of justice and virtue; to withhold him from ill courses by fear, and encourage him in his duty by hopes ; in short, to fashion and model him for society, hath been the aim of civil and religious institutions ; and, in all times, the endeavor of good and wise men. The aptest method for attaining this end hath been always judged a proper education.— *Bishop Berkeley.*

That there should one man die ignorant who had capacity for knowledge, this I call a tragedy, were it to happen more than twenty times in a minute, as by some computations it does.—*Carlyle.*

Unless the people can be kept in total darkness, it is the wisest way for the advocates of truth to give them full light.—*Whately.*

What we do not call education is more precious than that which we call so. We form no guess, at the time of receiving a thought, of its comparative value. And education often waste its efforts in attempts to thwart and balk this natural magnetism, which is sure to select what belongs to it.—*Emerson.*

As the fertilest ground must be manured, so must the highest flying wit have a Dædalus to guide him.—*Sir P. Sidney.*

We shall one day learn to supersede politics by education. What we call our root-and-branch reforms of slavery, war, gambling, intemperance, is only medicating the symptoms. We must begin higher up, namely, in education.
Emerson.

Capacity without education is deplorable, and education without capacity is thrown away.
Saadi.

EGOTISM.

The more you speak of yourself, the more you are likely to lie.—*Zimmermann.*

The awkwardness and embarrassment which all feel on beginning to write, when they themselves are the theme, ought to serve as a hint to authors that self is a subject they ought very rarely to descant upon.—*Colton.*

I shall never apologize to you for egotism. I think very few men writing to their friends have enough of it.—*Sydney Smith.*

It is a false principle, that because we are entirely occupied with ourselves, we must equally occupy the thoughts of others. The contrary inference is the fair one.—*Hazlitt.*

When all is summed up, a man never speaks of himself without loss; his accusations of himself are always believed, his praises never.—
Montaigne.

We like so much to talk of ourselves that we are never weary of those private interviews with a lover during the course of whole years, and for the same reason the devout like to spend much time with their confessor; it is the pleasure of talking of themselves, even though it be to talk ill.—*Madame de Sévigné.*

To speak highly of one with whom we are intimate is a species of egotism. Our modesty as well as our jealousy teaches us caution on this subject.—*Hazlitt.*

What hypocrites we seem to be whenever we talk of ourselves! Our words sound so humble, while our hearts are so proud.—*Hare.*

Egotism is the tongue of vanity.—*Chamfort.*

Every real master of speaking or writing uses his personality as he would any other serviceable material; the very moment a speaker or writer begins to use it, not for his main purpose, but for vanity's sake, as all weak people are sure to do, hearers and readers feel the difference in a moment.—*Holmes.*

Here is the egotist's code: everything for himself, nothing for others.—*Sanial-Dubay.*

The reason why lovers are never weary of one another is this, — they are always talking of themselves.—*Rochefoucauld.*

Seldom do we talk of ourselves with success. If I condemn myself, more is believed than is expressed; if I praise myself, much less.—
Henry Home.

The pest of society is egotists. There are dull and bright, sacred and profane, coarse and fine egotists. It is a disease that, like influenza, falls on all constitutions. In the distemper known to physicians as *chorea*, the patient sometimes turns round, and continues to spin slowly on one spot. Is egotism a metaphysical varioloid of this malady?—*Emerson.*

Do you wish men to speak well of you? Then never speak well of yourself.—*Pascal.*

He who thinks he can find in himself the means of doing without others is much mistaken; but he who thinks that others cannot do without him is still more mistaken.—*Rochefoucauld.*

It is never permissible to say, I say.—
Madame Necker.

There is scarce any man who cannot persuade himself of his own merit. Has he common-sense, he prefers it to genius; has he some diminutive virtues, he prefers them to great talents.—*Sewall.*

Let the degree of egotism be the measure of confidence.—*Lavater.*

Christian piety annihilates the egotism of the heart; worldly politeness veils and represses it.—*Pascal.*

Egotism is more like an offence than a crime; though it is allowable to speak of yourself, provided nothing is advanced in favor; but I cannot help suspecting that those who abuse themselves are, in reality, angling for approbation.—*Zimmermann.*

The personal pronoun "I" should be the coat of arms of some individuals.—*Rivarol*

ELEGANCE.

Elegance is something more than ease; it is more than a freedom from awkwardness or restraint. It implies, I conceive, a precision, a polish, a sparkling, spirited yet delicate.—
Hazlitt.

When the mind loses its feeling for elegance, it grows corrupt and grovelling, and seeks in the crowd what ought to be found at home.—
Landor.

Taste and elegance, though they are reckoned only among the smaller and secondary morals, yet are of no mean importance in the regulations of life. A moral taste is not of force to turn vice into virtue; but it recommends virtue with something like the blandishments of pleasure, and it infinitely abates the evils of vice.—*Burke.*

ELOQUENCE.

Eloquence is to the sublime what the whole is to its part.—*Bruyère.*

No man ever did or ever will become truly eloquent without being a constant reader of the Bible, and an admirer of the purity and sublimity of its language.—*Fisher Ames.*

In eloquence, the great triumphs of the art are when the orator is lifted above himself; when consciously he makes himself the mere tongue of the occasion and the hour, and says what cannot but be said. Hence the term "abandonment," to describe the self-surrender of the orator. Not his will, but the principle on which he is horsed, the great connection and crisis of events, thunder in the ear of the crowd.
Emerson.

As the grace of man is in the mind, so the beauty of the mind is eloquence.—*Cicero.*

Great is the power of eloquence; but never is it so great as when it pleads along with nature, and the culprit is a child strayed from his duty, and returned to it again with tears.—
Sterne.

Eloquence is relative. One can no more pronounce on the eloquence of any composition than the wholesomeness of a medicine without knowing for whom it is intended.—*Whately.*

Gentlemen, do you know what is the finest speech that I ever in my life heard or read? It is the address of Garibaldi to his Roman soldiers, when he told them: "Soldiers, what I have to offer you is fatigue, danger, struggle, and death; the chill of the cold night in the free air, and heat under the burning sun; no lodgings, no munitions, no provisions, but forced marches, dangerous watchposts, and the continual struggle with the bayonet against batteries;—those who love freedom and their country may follow me." That is the most glorious speech I ever heard in my life.—*Kossuth.*

It is of eloquence as of a flame; it requires matter to feed it, motion to excite it, and it brightens as it burns.—*Tacitus.*

Eloquence is in the assembly, not in the speaker.—*William Pitt.*

The receipt to make a speaker, and an applauded one too, is short and easy. Take common-sense *quantum sufficit:* add a little application to the rules and orders of the House [of Commons], throw obvious thoughts in a new light, and make up the whole with a large quantity of purity, correctness, and elegancy of style. Take it for granted that by far the greatest part of mankind neither analyze nor search to the bottom; they are incapable of penetrating deeper than the surface.—
Chesterfield.

His tongue dropped manna, and could make the worse appear the better reason, to perplex and dash maturest counsels.—*Milton.*

A just and reasonable modesty does not only recommend eloquence, but sets off every great talent which a man can be possessed of. It heightens all the virtues which it accompanies; like the shades of paintings, it raises and rounds every figure, and makes the colors more beautiful, though not so glowing as they would be without it.—*Addison.*

O Eloquence! thou violated fair, how thou art wooed and won to either bed of right or wrong!—*Havard.*

A cold-blooded learned man might, for anything I know, compose in his closet an eloquent book; but in public discourse, arising out of sudden occasions, he could by no possibility be eloquent.—*Erskine.*

Those who would make us feel must feel themselves.—*Churchill.*

There should be in eloquence that which is pleasing and that which is real; but that which is pleasing should itself be real.—*Pascal.*

The manner of your speaking is full as important as the matter, as more people have ears to be tickled than understandings to judge.—
Chesterfield.

In true eloquence I wish that the things be surmounted and that the discourse fill the imagination of him who hears, that he has no remembrance of words. An orator of past times said that his calling was to make little things appear and be grand.—*Montaigne.*

Eloquence, to produce her full effect, should start from the head of the orator, as Pallas from the brain of Jove, completely armed and equipped. Diffidence, therefore, which is so able a mentor to the writer, would prove a dangerous counsellor to the orator.—*Colton.*

Were we as eloquent as angels, we should please some more by listening than by talking. *Colton.*

True eloquence consists in saying all that is proper, and nothing more.—*Rochefoucauld.*

The pleasure of eloquence is in greatest part owing often to the stimulus of the occasion which produces it, — to the magic of sympathy, which exalts the feeling of each by radiating on him the feeling of all.—*Emerson.*

Brevity is a great praise of eloquence.— *Cicero.*

Power above powers! O heavenly eloquence! that, with the strong rein of commanding words, dost manage, guide, and master the high eminence of men's affections! —*Daniel.*

Thoughts that breathe and words that burn. *Gray.*

Eloquence, when at its highest pitch, leaves little room for reason or reflection, but addresses itself entirely to the fancy or the affections, captivates the willing hearers, and subdues their understanding. Happily, this pitch it seldom attains.—*Hume.*

Your words are like the notes of dying swans, too sweet to last! —*Dryden.*

There is as much eloquence in the tone of voice, in the eyes, and in the air of a speaker as in his choice of words.—*Rochefoucauld.*

The glorious burst of winged words! — *Tupper.*

True eloquence does not consist in speech. It cannot be brought from far. Labor and learning may toil in vain. Words and phrases may be marshalled in every way, but they cannot compass it. It must exist in the. man, in the subject, and in the occasion.— *Daniel Webster.*

When he spoke, what tender words he used! so softly that, like flakes of feathered snow, they melted as they fell.—*Dryden.*

Silence that spoke, and eloquence of eyes.— *Pope.*

Many are ambitious of saying grand things, that is, of being grandiloquent. Eloquence is speaking out, — a quality few esteem and fewer aim at.—*Hare.*

Eloquence the soul, song charms the senses. *Milton.*

Eloquence is a pictural representation of thought; and hence those who, after having painted it, make additions to it, give us a fancy picture, but not a portrait.—*Pascal.*

He has oratory who ravishes his hearers while he forgets himself.—*Lavater.*

In oratory affectation must be avoided; it being better for a man by a native and clear eloquence to express himself than by those words which may smell either of the lamp or inkhorn. *Lord Herbert.*

False eloquence is exaggeration, true eloquence is emphasis.— *W. R. Alger.*

Eloquence is the language of nature, and cannot be learned in the schools; the passions are powerful pleaders, and their very silence, like that of Garrick, goes directly to the soul; but rhetoric is the creature of art, which he who feels least will most excel in; it is the quackery of eloquence, and deals in nostrums, not in cures.— *Colton.*

EMPIRE.

Extended empire, like expanded gold, exchanges solid strength for feeble splendor.— *Johnson.*

EMPLOYMENT.

The Devil never tempted a man whom he found judiciously employed.—*Spurgeon.*

Employment is nature's physician, and is essential to human happiness.—*Galen.*

Employment and ennui are simply incompatible.—*Madame Deluzy.*

Be always employed about some rational thing, that the Devil find thee not idle.— *St. Jerome.*

EMULATION.

Emulation admires and strives to imitate great actions; envy is only moved to malice.— *Balzac.*

Emulation looks out for merits, that she may exert herself by a victory; envy spies out blemishes, that she may have another by a defeat.— *Colton.*

My heart laments that virtue cannot live out of the teeth of emulation.—*Shakespeare.*

Emulation is a noble passion; it is enterprising, but it is just; it makes the conquest for glory fair and generous. True emulation consists in striving to excel in everything commendable; it raises itself, but not by depressing others.—*J. Beaumont.*

It is scarce possible at once to admire and excel an author, as water rises no higher than the reservoir it falls from.—*Bacon.*

Emulation is a handsome passion; it is enterprising, but just withal. It keeps a man within the terms of honor, and makes the contest for glory just and generous. He strives to excel, but it is by raising himself, not by depressing others.—*Jeremy Collier.*

Worldly ambition is founded on pride or envy, but emulation, or laudable ambition, is actually founded in humility; for it evidently implies that we have a low opinion of our present attainments, and think it necessary to be advanced.—*Bishop Hall.*

Emulation is grief arising from seeing one's self exceeded or excelled by his concurrent, together with hope to equal or exceed him in time to come, by his own ability But envy is the same grief joined with pleasure conceived in the imagination of some ill-fortune that may befall him.—*Thomas Hobbes.*

Where there is emulation, there will be vanity; where there is vanity, there will be folly.— *Johnson.*

Emulation, even in the brutes, is sensitively "nervous." See the tremor of the thoroughbred racer before he starts. The dray-horse does not tremble, but he does not emulate. It is not his work to run a race. Says Marcus Antoninus, "It is all one to a stone whether it be thrown upward or downward." Yet the emulation of a man of genius is seldom with his contemporaries, that is, inwardly in his mind, although outwardly in his act it would seem so The competitors with whom his secret ambition seems to vie are the dead.—*Bulwer Lytton.*

Emulation hath a thousand sons, that one by one pursue; if you give way, or edge aside from the direct forthright, like to an entered tide, they all rush by, and leave you hindmost. *Shakespeare.*

There is emulation even in vice.— *Eugene Sue.*

Give me the boy who rouses when he is praised, who profits when he is encouraged, and who cries when he is defeated. Such a boy will be fired by ambition; he will be stung by reproach, and animated by preference; never shall I apprehend any bad consequences from idleness in such a boy.—*Quintilian.*

God grant that we may contend with other churches, as the vine with the olive, which of us shall bear the best fruit; but not as the brier with the thistle, which of us will be most unprofitable.—*Bacon.*

Emulation has been termed a spur to virtue, and assumes to be a spur of gold. But it is a spur composed of baser materials, and if tried in the furnace, will be found to want that fixedness which is the characteristic of gold.— *Colton.*

ENCOURAGEMENT.

Faint not; the miles to heaven are but few and short.—*Rutherford.*

Correction does much, but encouragement does more. Encouragement after censure is as the sun after a shower.—*Goethe.*

More hearts pine away in secret anguish for the want of kindness from those who should be their comforters than for any other calamity in life.—*Young.*

It may be proper for all to remember that they ought not to raise expectations which it is not in their power to satisfy; and that it is more pleasing to see smoke brightening into flame than flame sinking into smoke.—*Johnson.*

ENDURANCE.

There was never yet philosopher that could endure the toothache patiently, however they have writ the style of gods, and make a pish at chance and sufferance.—*Shakespeare*

Prolonged endurance tames the bold.— *Byron.*

There is a sort of natural instinct of human dignity in the heart of man which steels his very nerves not to bend beneath the heavy blows of a great adversity. The palm-tree grows best beneath a ponderous weight, even so the character of man. There is no merit in it, it is a law of psychology. The petty pangs of small daily cares have often bent the character of men, but great misfortunes seldom. There is less danger in this than in great good luck.—*Kossuth.*

A true-devoted pilgrim is not weary to measure kingdoms with his feeble steps.— *Shakespeare.*

There is nothing in the world so much admired as a man who knows how to bear unhappiness with courage.—*Seneca.*

Wounds and hardships provoke our courage, and when our fortunes are at the lowest, our wits and minds are commonly at the best.— *Charron.*

Whenever evil befalls us, we ought to ask ourselves, after the first suffering, how we can turn it into good. So shall we take occasion, from one bitter root, to raise perhaps many flowers.—*Leigh Hunt.*

The greater the difficulty the more glory in surmounting it. Skilful pilots gain their reputation from storms and tempests.—*Epicurus.*

Not in the achievement, but in the endurance of the human soul, does it show its divine grandeur and its alliance with the infinite God.—*Chapin.*

Stillest streams oft water fairest meadows, and the bird that flutters least is longest on the wing.—*Cowper.*

Our strength often increases in proportion to the obstacles which are imposed upon it; it is thus that we enter upon the most perilous plans after having had the shame of failing in more simple ones.—*Rapin.*

As in labor, the more one doth exercise, the more one is enabled to do, strength growing upon work; so, with the use of suffering, men's minds get the habit of suffering, and all fears and terrors are to them but as a summons to battle, whereof they know beforehand they shall come off victorious.—*Sir P. Sidney*

ENEMIES.

There is no little enemy.—*Franklin.*

A Christian should not discover that he has enemies by any other way than by doing more good to them than to others. "If thine enemy hunger, feed him; if he thirst, give him drink."
Bishop Wilson.

Make no enemies; he is insignificant indeed that can do thee no harm.—*Colton.*

Some men are more beholden to their bitterest enemies than to friends who appear to be sweetness itself. The former frequently tell the truth, but the latter never.—*Cato.*

I am persuaded that he who is capable of being a bitter enemy can never possess the necessary virtues that constitute a true friend.—
Fitzosborne.

If we could read the secret history of our enemies, we should find in each man's life sorrow and suffering enough to disarm all hostility.—*Longfellow.*

Plutarch has written an essay on the benefits which a man may receive from his enemies; and, among the good fruits of enmity, mentions this in particular, that by the reproaches which it casts upon us, we see the worst side of ourselves.—*Addison.*

That is a most wretched fortune which is without an enemy.—*Publius Syrus.*

Let us carefully observe those good qualities wherein our enemies excel us; and endeavor to excel them, by avoiding what is faulty, and imitating what is excellent in them.—*Plutarch.*

Men of sense often learn from their enemies. Prudence is the best safeguard. This principle cannot be learned from a friend, but an enemy extorts it immediately. It is from their foes, not their friends, that cities learn the lesson of building high walls and ships of war. And this lesson saves their children, their homes, and their properties.—*Aristophanes.*

Did a person but know the value of an enemy, he would purchase him with pure gold.—
Abbé de Raunci.

Be assured those will be thy worst enemies, not to whom thou hast done evil, but who have done evil to thee. And those will be thy best friends, not to whom thou hast done good, but who have done good to thee.—*Lavater.*

10

Everybody has enemies. To have an enemy is quite another thing. One must be somebody in order to have an enemy. One must be a force before he can be resisted by another force.
Madame Swetchine.

Our enemies are our outward consciences.—
Shakespeare.

With stupidity and sound digestion man may front much. But what in these dull, unimaginative days are the terrors of conscience to the diseases of the liver!—*Carlyle.*

A malicious enemy is better than a clumsy friend.—*Madame Swetchine.*

ENERGY.

Energy, even like the biblical grain of mustard-seed, will remove mountains.—
Hosea Ballou.

True wisdom, in general, consists in energetic determination.—*Napoleon.*

Energy will do anything that can be done in this world; and no talents, no circumstances, no opportunities, will make a two-legged animal a man without it.—*Goethe.*

He alone has energy that cannot be deprived of it.—*Lavater.*

It is with many enterprises as with striking fire; we do not meet with success except by reiterated efforts, and often at the instant when we despaired of success.—
Madame de Maintenon.

To impress we must be in earnest; to amuse it is only necessary to be kindly and fanciful.—
Tuckerman.

ENJOYMENT.

He scatters enjoyment who can enjoy much.
Lavater.

' Temper your enjoyments with prudence, lest there be written upon your heart that fearful word "satiety."—*Quarles.*

Light as a gossamer is the circumstance which can bring enjoyment to a conscience which is not its own accuser.—*William Carleton.*

Ye men of gloom and austerity, who paint the face of Infinite Benevolence with an eternal frown, read in the everlasting book, wide open to your view, the lesson it would teach. Its pictures are not in black and sombre hues, but bright and glowing tints; its music — save when ye drown it — is not in sighs and groans, but songs and cheerful sounds. Listen to the million voices in the summer air, and find one dismal as your own.—*Dickens.*

The less you can enjoy, the poorer, the scantier yourself, — the more you can enjoy, the richer, the more vigorous.—*Lavater.*

All solitary enjoyments quickly pall, or become painful, so that, perhaps, no more insufferable misery can be conceived than that which must follow incommunicable privileges. Only imagine a human being condemned to perpetual youth while all around him decay and die. O, how sincerely would he call upon death for deliverance!—*Archbishop Sharp.*

"Gratitude is memory of the heart." Therefore forget not to say often, with Bettine, "I have all I have ever enjoyed."—
Mrs. L. M. Child.

Providence has fixed the limits of human enjoyment by immovable boundaries, and has set, different gratifications at such a distance from each other, that no art or power can bring them together. This great law it is the business of every rational being to understand, that life may not pass away in an attempt to make contradictions consistent, to combine opposite qualities, and to unite things which the nature of their being must always keep asunder.—*Johnson.*

ENNUI.

I do pity unlearned gentlemen on a rainy day.—*Lord Falkland.*

Ennui, perhaps, has made more gamblers than avarice, more drunkards than thirst, and perhaps as many suicides as despair.—*Colton.*

Ennui, wretchedness, melancholy, groans, and sighs are the offering which these unhappy Methodists make to a Deity, who has covered the earth with gay colors, and scented it with rich perfumes; and shown us, by the plan and order of his works, that he has given to man something better than a bare existence, and scattered over his creation a thousand superfluous joys, which are totally unnecessary to the mere support of life.—*Sydney Smith.*

I have also seen the world, and after long experience have discovered that ennui is our greatest enemy, and remunerative labor our most lasting friend.—*Justus Möser.*

Ennui was born one day of uniformity.—
Motte.

The victims of ennui paralyze all the grosser feelings by excess, and torpefy all the finer by disuse and inactivity. Disgusted with this world and indifferent about another, they at last lay violent hands upon themselves, and assume no small credit for the *sang froid* with which they meet death. But alas! such beings can scarcely be said to die, for they have never truly lived.—*Colton.*

A scholar has no ennui.—*Richter.*

Ambition itself is not so reckless of human life as ennui; clemency is a favorite attribute of the former; but ennui has the taste of a cannibal.—*Bancroft.*

Ennui is a growth of English root, though nameless in our language.—*Byron*

"Ennui" is a word which the French invented, though of all nations in Europe they know the least of it.—*Bancroft.*

There is nothing so insupportable to man as to be in entire repose, without passion, occupation, amusement, or application. Then it is that he feels his own nothingness, isolation, insignificance, dependent nature, powerlessness, emptiness. Immediately there issue from his soul ennui, sadness, chagrin, vexation, despair.
Pascal.

That which renders life burdensome to us generally arises from the abuse of it.—*Rousseau.*

As the gout seems privileged to attack the bodies of the wealthy, so ennui seems to exert a similar prerogative over their minds.—*Colton.*

Ennui, the parent of expensive and ruinous vices.—*Ninon de l'Enclos.*

Social life is filled with doubts and vain aspirings; solitude, when the imagination is dethroned, is turned to weariness and ennui.—
Miss L. E. Landon.

Ennui is the desire of activity without the fit means of gratifying the desire.—*Bancroft.*

This ennui, for which we Saxons had no name, — this word of France, has got a terrific significance. It shortens life, and bereaves the day of its light.—*Emerson.*

We are amused through the intellect, but it is the heart that saves us from ennui.—
Madame Swetchine.

ENTERPRISE.

What passes in the world for talent or dexterity or enterprise is often only a want of moral principle. We may succed where others fail, not from a greater share of invention, but from not being nice in the choice of expedients.—*Hazlitt.*

The method of the enterprising is to plan with audacity and execute with vigor; to sketch out a map of possibilities, and then to treat them as probabilities.—*Bovee.*

The fact is, that to do anything in this world worth doing, we must not stand back shivering and thinking of the cold and danger, but jump in and scramble through as well as we can.—*Sydney Smith.*

Providence has hidden a charm in difficult undertakings which is appreciated only by those who dare to grapple with them.—
Madame Swetchine.

On the neck of the young man sparkles no gem so gracious as enterprise.—*Hafiz.*

ENTHUSIASM.

The same reason makes a man a religious enthusiast that makes a man an enthusiast in any other way, an uncomfortable mind in an uncomfortable body.—*Hazlitt.*

Enthusiasm is a virtue rarely to be met with in seasons of calm and unruffled prosperity. Enthusiasm flourishes in adversity, kindles in the hour of danger, and awakens to deeds of renown. The terrors of persecution only serve to quicken the energy of its purposes. It swells in proud integrity, and, great in the purity of its cause, it can scatter defiance amidst hosts of enemies.—*Dr. Chalmers.*

The best thing which we derive from history is the enthusiasm that it raises in us.—*Goethe.*

Enlist the interests of stern morality and religious enthusiasm in the cause of political liberty, as in the time of the old Puritans, and it will be irresistible.—*Coleridge.*

Every great and commanding movement in the annals of the world is the triumph of enthusiasm.—*Emerson.*

A mother should give her children a superabundance of enthusiasm; that after they have lost all they are sure to lose on mixing with the world, enough may still remain to prompt and support them through great actions. A cloak should be of three-pile, to keep its gloss in wear.—*Hare.*

Enthusiasm is the leaping lightning, not to be measured by the horse-power of the understanding.—*Emerson.*

Enthusiasm is grave, inward, self-controlled; mere excitement, outward, fantastic, hysterical, and passing in a moment from tears to laughter.
Sterling.

Nothing is so contagious as enthusiasm; it is the real allegory of the tale of Orpheus; it moves stones, it charms brutes. Enthusiasm is the genius of sincerity, and truth accomplishes no victories without it.—*Bulwer Lytton.*

Without enthusiasm, the adventurer could never kindle that fire in his followers which is so necessary to consolidate their mutual interests; for no one can heartily deceive numbers who is not first of all deceived himself.—
Warburton.

Enthusiasm is always connected with the senses, whatever be the object that excites it. The true strength of virtue is serenity of mind, combined with a deliberate and steadfast determination to execute her laws. That is the healthful condition of the moral life; on the other hand, enthusiasm, even when excited by representations of goodness, is a brilliant but feverish glow which leaves only exhaustion and languor behind.—*Kant.*

All noble enthusiasms pass through a feverish stage and grow wiser and more serene.—
Channing.

Let us recognize the beauty and power of true enthusiasm; and whatever we may do to enlighten ourselves and others, guard against checking or chilling a single earnest sentiment.
Tuckerman.

Every production of genius must be the production of enthusiasm.—*Disraeli.*

ENVY.

Base envy withers at another's joy.—
Thomson

Envy, like the worm, never runs but to the fairest fruit; like a cunning bloodhound, it singles out the fattest deer in the flock. Abraham's riches were the Philistines' envy; and Jacob's blessing bred Esau's hatred.—
J. Beaumont.

We ought to be guarded against every appearance of envy, as a passion that always implies inferiority wherever it resides.—*Pliny.*

There is a time in every man's education when he arrives at the conviction that envy is ignorance.—*Emerson.*

Envy, like a cold prison, benumbs and stupefies; and, conscious of its own impotence, folds its arms in despair.—*Jeremy Collier.*

Envy may justly be called "the gall of bitterness and bond of iniquity"; it is the most acid fruit that grows on the stock of sin, a fluid so subtle that nothing but the fire of divine love can purge it from the soul.—*Hosea Ballou.*

How can we explain the perpetuity of envy, — a vice which yields no return?—*Balzac.*

In our road through life we may happen to meet with a man casting a stone reverentially to enlarge the cairn of another which stone he has carried in his bosom to sling against that very other's head.—*Landor.*

Envy is more irreconcilable than hatred.—
Rochefoucauld.

We had rather do anything than acknowledge the merit of another if we can help it. We cannot bear a superior or an equal. Hence ridicule is sure to prevail over truth, for the malice of mankind, thrown into the scale, gives the casting weight.—*Hazlitt.*

Those who raise envy will easily incur censure.—*Churchill.*

They say that love and tears are learned without any master; and I may say that there is no great need of studying at the court to learn envy and revenge.—*N. Caussin.*

Whoever feels pain in hearing a good char acter of his neighbor will feel a pleasure in the reverse; and those who despair to rise in distinction by their virtues are happy if others can be depressed to a level with themselves.— *Rev. John Barker.*

Envy is a passion so full of cowardice and shame, that nobody ever had the confidence to own it.—*Rochester.*

The man that makes a character makes foes.— *Young.*

We are often infinitely mistaken, and take the falsest measures, when we envy the happiness of rich and great men; we know not the inward canker that eats out all their joy and delight, and makes them really much more miserable than ourselves.—*Bishop Hall.*

The hate which we all bear with the most Christian patience is the hate of those who envy us.—*Colton.*

Other passions have objects to flatter them, and seem to content and satisfy them for a while; there is power in ambition, pleasure in luxury, and pelf in covetousness; but envy can gain nothing but vexation.—*Montaigne.*

How bitter a thing it is to look into happiness through another man's eyes!—*Shakespeare.*

There is but one man who can believe himself free from envy, and it is he who has never examined his own heart.—*William Duncan.*

Envy, like flame, soars upwards.—*Livy.*

We are often vain of even the most criminal of our passions; but envy is a timid and shameful passion that we never dare acknowledge.— *Rochefoucauld.*

A weak mind is ambitious of envy, a strong one of respect.—*E. Wigglesworth.*

Do not envy the violet the dew-drop or glitter of a sunbeam; do not envy the bee the plant from which he draws some sweets. Do not envy man the little goods he possesses; for the earth is for him the plant from which he obtains some sweets, and his mind is the dew-drop which the world colors for an instant.— *Leopold Schefer.*

The hen of our neighbor appears to us a goose, says the Oriental proverb.— *Madame Deluzy.*

Men that make envy and crooked malice nourishment do bite the best.—*Shakespeare.*

Envy, if surrounded on all sides by the brightness of another's prosperity, like the scorpion confined within a circle of fire, will sting itself to death.—*Colton.*

Envy pierces more in the resolution of praises than in the exaggeration of its criticisms. *Achilles Poincelot.*

Men of noble birth are noted to be envious towards new men when they rise; for the distance is altered, and it is like a deceit of the eye, that when others come on they think themselves going back.—*Bacon.*

Envy is like a fly that passes all a body's sounder parts, and dwells upon the sores.— *Chapman.*

Envy feeds upon the living; after death it ceases,—then every man's well-earned honors defend him against calumny.—*Ovid.*

If our credit be so well built, so firm, that it is not easy to be shaken by calumny or insinuation, envy then commends us, and extols us beyond reason to those upon whom we depend, till they grow jealous, and so blow us up when they cannot throw us down.—*Clarendon.*

The truest mark of being born with great qualities is being born without envy.— *Rochefoucauld.*

A man that hath no virtue in himself ever envieth virtue in others; for men's minds will either feed upon their own good or upon others' evil; and who wanteth the one will prey upon the other.—*Bacon.*

Who can speak broader than he that has no house to put his head in? Such may rail against great buildings.—*Shakespeare.*

Envy,—the rottenness of the bones.—*Bible.*

If we did but know how little some enjoy of the great things that they possess, there would not be much envy in the world.—*Young.*

If envy, like anger, did not burn itself in its own fire, and consume and destroy those persons it possesses, before it can destroy those it wishes worst to, it would set the whole world on fire, and leave the most excellent persons the most miserable.—*Clarendon.*

Envy the attendant of the empty mind.— *Pindar.*

Every other sin hath some pleasure annexed to it, or will admit of some excuse; but envy wants both; we should strive against it, for if indulged in, it will be to us as a foretaste of hell upon earth.—*Burton.*

Surely, if we considered detraction to be bred of envy, nested only in deficient minds, we should find that the applauding of virtue would win us far more honor than the seeking slyly to disparage it. That would show we loved what we commended, while this tells the world we grudge at what we want in ourselves.—*Feltham.*

The envious man is in pain upon all occasions which ought to give him pleasure. The relish of his life is inverted; and the objects which administer the highest satisfaction to those who are exempt from this passion give the quickest pangs to persons who are subject to it. All the perfections of their fellow-creatures are odious. Youth, beauty, valor, and wisdom are provocations of their displeasure. What a wretched and apostate state is this! to be offended with excellence, and to hate a man because we approve him!—*Steele.*

There is some good in public envy, whereas in private there is none; for public envy is as an ostracism that eclipseth men when they grow too great; and therefore it is a bridle also to great ones to keep within bounds.—*Bacon.*

As a moth gnaws a garment, so doth envy consume a man.—*St. Chrysostom.*

I don't believe that there is a human creature in his senses, arrived to maturity, that at some time or other has not been carried away by this passion (sc. envy) in good earnest; and yet I never met with any one who dared own he was guilty of it but in jest.—*Mandeville.*

Many men profess to hate another, but no man owns envy, as being an enmity or displeasure for no cause but goodness or felicity.
Jeremy Taylor.

Envy is of all others the most ungratifying and disconsolate passion. There is power for ambition, pleasure for luxury, and pelf even for covetousness; but envy gets no reward but vexation.—*Jeremy Collier.*

No crime is so great as daring to excel.—
Churchill.

Newton found that a star, examined through a glass tarnished by smoke, was diminished into a speck of light. But no smoke ever breathed so thick a mist as envy or detraction.—
Willmott.

Envy, among other ingredients, has a mixture of the love of justice in it. We are more angry at undeserved than at deserved good fortune.—*Hazlitt.*

Envy makes us see what will serve to accuse others, and not perceive what may justify them.
Bishop Wilson.

Envy is an ill-natured vice, and is made up of meanness and malice. It wishes the force of goodness to be strained, and the measure of happiness abated. It laments over prosperity, and sickens at the sight of health. It oftentimes wants spirit as well as good-nature.—
Jeremy Collier.

Base natures joy to see hard hap happen to them they deem happy.—*Sir P. Sidney.*

The praise of the envious is far less creditable than their censure; they praise only that which they can surpass, but that which surpasses them they censure.—*Colton.*

Envy is blind, and has no other quality but that of detracting from virtue.—*Livy.*

Envy ought in strict truth to have no place whatever allowed it in the heart of man; for the goods of this present world are so vile and low that they are beneath it, and those of the future world are so vast and exalted that they are above it.—*Colton.*

We often glory in the most criminal passion; but that of envy is so shameful that we dare not even own it.—*Rochefoucauld.*

To pooh-pooh what we are never likely to possess is wonderfully easy. The confirmed celibate is loudest in his denunciations of matrimony. In Æsop, it is the tailless fox that advocates the disuse of tails. It is the grapes we cannot reach that we call sour.—
Æneas Sage.

In short, virtue cannot live where envy reigns, nor liberality subsist with niggardliness.
Cervantes.

It is because we have but a small portion of enjoyment ourselves that we feel so little pleasure in the good fortune of others. Is it possible for the happy to be envious?—
W. B. Clulow.

Of all hostile feelings, envy is perhaps the hardest to be subdued, because hardly any one owns it even to himself, but looks out for one pretext after another to justify his hostility.—
Whately.

Envy sets the strongest seal on desert.—
Ben Jonson.

An envious man waxeth lean with the fatness of his neighbors. Envy is the daughter of pride, the author of murder and revenge, the beginner of secret sedition, and the perpetual tormentor of virtue. Envy is the filthy slime of the soul; a venom, a poison, or quicksilver which consumeth the flesh, and drieth up the marrow of the bones.—*Socrates.*

The envious will die, but envy never.—
Molière.

To be an object of hatred and aversion to their contemporaries has been the usual fate of all those whose merit has raised them above the common level. The man who submits to the shafts of envy for the sake of noble objects pursues a judicious course for his own lasting fame. Hatred dies with its object, while merit soon breaks forth in full splendor, and his glory is handed down to posterity in never-dying strains.—*Thucydides.*

Envy always outlives the felicity of its object.—*Rochefoucauld.*

EQUALITY.

There are some races more cultured and advanced and ennobled by education than others; but there are no races nobler than others. All are equally destined for freedom.—*Alexander von Humboldt.*

Consider man, weigh well thy frame; the king, the beggar, are the same; dust formed us all.—*Gay.*

Equality is the share of every one at their advent upon earth, and equality is also theirs when placed beneath it.—*Ninon de l'Enclos.*

Your fat king, and your lean beggar, is but variable service; two dishes, but to one table; that is the end.—*Shakespeare.*

Who can in reason then or right assume monarchy over such as live by right his equals, if in power or splendor less, in freedom equal?—*Milton.*

Come forward, some great marshal, and organize equality in society, and your rod shall swallow up all the juggling old court goldsticks.—*Thackeray.*

Thersites's body is as good as Ajax's, when neither are alive.—*Shakespeare.*

So far is it from being true that men are naturally equal, that no two people can be half an hour together but one shall acquire an evident superiority over the other.—*Johnson.*

Whatever difference there may appear to be in men's fortunes, there is still a certain compensation of good and ill in all, that makes them equal.—*Charron.*

Kings and their subjects, masters and slaves, find a common level in two places,—at the foot of the cross, and in the grave.—*Colton.*

Golden lads and girls all must, as chimney-sweepers, come to dust.—*Shakespeare.*

All men are by nature equal, made all of the same earth by one Workman; and however we deceive ourselves, as dear unto God is the poor peasant as the mighty prince.—*Plato.*

As soon the dust of a wretch whom thou wouldest not, as of a prince whom thou couldst not look upon, will trouble thine eyes if the wind blow it thither; and when a whirlwind hath blown the dust of the churchyard into the church, and the man sweeps out the dust of the church into the churchyard, who will, undertake to sift those dusts again, and to pronounce, " This is the patrician, this is the noble flower, and this the yeoman, this the plebeian bran"?—*Rev. Dr. Donne.*

All men are equal, It is not birth, but virtue alone, that makes the difference.—*Voltaire.*

Equality is one of the most consummate scoundrels that ever crept from the brain of a political juggler,—a fellow who thrusts his hand into the pocket of honest industry or enterprising talent, and squanders their hard-earned profits on profligate idleness or indolent stupidity.—*Paulding.*

So let them ease their hearts with prate of equal rights, which man never knew.—*Byron.*

The king is but a man, as I am; the violet smells to him as it doth to me; the element shows to him as it doth to me; all his senses have but human conditions; his ceremonies laid by, in his nakedness he appears but a man; and though his affections are higher mounted than ours, yet, when they stoop, they stoop with the like wing.—*Shakespeare.*

All things whatsoever ye would that men should do to you, do ye even so to them.—*Bible.*

It is untrue that equality is a law of nature. Nature has no equality. Its sovereign law is subordination and dependence.—*Vauvenargues.*

Equality is deemed by many a mere speculative chimera, which can never be reduced to practice. But if the abuse is inevitable, does it follow that we ought not to try at least to mitigate it? It is precisely because the force of things tends always to destroy equality, that the force of the legislature must always tend to maintain it.—*Rousseau.*

In the gates of eternity, the black hand and the white hold each other with an equal clasp.—*Mrs. Stowe.*

EQUANIMITY.

In this thing one man is superior to another, that he is better able to bear adversity and prosperity.—*Philemon.*

Equanimity is the gem in Virtue's chaplet and St. Sweetness the loveliest in her calendar.—*Alcott.*

EQUITY.

Equity is a roguish thing; for law we have a measure, we know what to trust to; equity is according to the conscience of him that is chancellor, and as that is larger or narrower, so is equity. It is all one as if they should make the standard for the measure we call a foot a chancellor's foot. What an uncertain measure would this be? One chancellor has a long foot, another a short foot, a third an indifferent foot; it is the same thing in the chancellor's conscience—*Selden.*

EQUIVOCATION.

A sudden lie may be sometimes only manslaughter upon truth; but by a carefully constructed equivocation truth always is with malice aforethought deliberately murdered.—*Morley.*

There is no possible excuse for a guarded lie. Enthusiastic and impulsive people will sometimes falsify thoughtlessly, but equivocation is malice prepense.—*Hosea Ballou.*

ERROR.

Errors to be dangerous must have a great deal of truth mingled with them; it is only from this alliance that they can ever obtain an extensive circulation; from pure extravagance, and genuine, unmingled falsehood, the world never has, and never can sustain any mischief.—*Sydney Smith.*

Error is ever talkative.—*Goldsmith.*

Our understandings are always liable to error; nature and certainty are very hard to come at, and infallibility is mere vanity and pretence.—*Marcus Antoninus.*

Error is but the shadow of the truth.—*Stillingfleet.*

Consciousness of error is, to a certain extent, a consciousness of understanding; and correction of error is the plainest proof of energy and mastery.—*Landor.*

In all science error precedes the truth, and it is better it should go first than last.—*Horace Walpole.*

O hateful error, Melancholy's child! why dost thou show to the apt thoughts of men the things that are not! O error soon conceived, thou never comest unto a happy birth, but killest the mother that engendered thee!—*Shakespeare.*

No tempting form of error is without some latent charm derived from truth.—*Keith.*

. Truth only is prolific. Error, sterile in itself, produces only by means of the portion of truth which it contains. It may have offspring, but the life which it gives, like that of the hybrid races, cannot be transmitted.—*Madame Swetchine.*

There are few, very few, that will own themselves in a mistake.—*Swift.*

Error is a hardy plant; it flourisheth in every soil; in the heart of the wise and good, alike with the wicked and foolish; for there is no error so crooked but it hath in it some lines of truth, nor is any poison so deadly that it serveth not some wholesome use.—*Tupper.*

Error, when she retraces her steps, has farther to go before she can arrive at truth, than ignorance.—*Colton.*

There are errors which no wise man will treat with rudeness while there is a probability that they may be the refraction of some great truth still below the horizon.—*Coleridge.*

Spurn not a seeming error, but dig below its surface for the truth.—*Tupper.*

It is much easier to meet with error than to find truth; error is on the surface, and can be more easily met with; truth is hid in great depths, the way to seek does not appear to all the world.—*Goethe.*

There will be mistakes in divinity while men preach, and errors in governments while men govern.—*Sir Dudley Carlton.*

My principal method for defeating error and heresy is by establishing the truth. One purposes to fill a bushel with tares, but if I can fill it first with wheat, I may defy his attempts.—*Newton.*

Error is worse than ignorance.—*Bailey.*

For the first time, the best may err, art may persuade, and novelty spread out its charms. The first fault is the child of simplicity; but every other the offspring of guilt.—*Goldsmith.*

Find earth where grows no weed, and you may find a heart wherein no error grows.—*Knowles.*

Error is always more busy than ignorance. Ignorance is a blank sheet on which we may write; but error is a scribbled one from which we must first erase.—*Colton.*

The little I have seen of the world teaches me to look upon the errors of others in sorrow, not in anger. When I take the history of one poor heart that has sinned and suffered, and represent to myself the struggles and temptations it has passed through, the brief pulsations of joy, the feverish inquietude of hope and fear, the pressure of want, the desertion of friends, I would fain leave the erring soul of my fellow-man with Him from whose hand it came.—*Longfellow.*

It is only an error of judgment to make a mistake, but it argues an infirmity of character to adhere to it when discovered. Or, as the Chinese better say, "The glory is not in never falling, but in rising every time you fall."—*Bovee.*

All errors spring up in the neighborhood of some truth; they grow round about it, and, for the most part, derive their strength from such contiguity.—*Rev. T. Binney.*

Error is sometimes so nearly allied to truth that it blends with it as imperceptibly as the colors of the rainbow fade into each other.—*W. B. Clulow.*

How happy he who can still hope to lift himself from this sea of error! What we know not, that we are anxious to possess, and cannot use what we know.—*Goethe.*

We can get out of certain errors only at the top; that is, by raising our minds above human things.—*Joubert.*

There are in certain heads a kind of established errors against which reason has no weapons. There are more of these mere assertions current than one would believe. Men are very fond of proving their steadfast adherence to nonsense.—*Von Knebel.*

The more confidently secure we feel against our liability to any error, to which in fact we are liable, the greater must be our danger of falling into it.—*Whately.*

ESTEEM.

Esteem cannot be where there is no confidence, and there can be no confidence where there is no respect.—*Henry Giles.*

The esteem of wise and good men is the greatest of all temporal encouragements to virtue; and it is a mark of an abandoned spirit to have no regard to it.—*Burke.*

We acquire the love of people who, being in our proximity, are presumed to know us; and we receive reputation, or celebrity, from such as are not personally acquainted with us. Merit secures to us the regard of our honest neighbors, and good fortune that of the public. Esteem is the harvest of a whole life spent in usefulness; but reputation is often bestowed upon a chance action, and depends most on success.—*G. A. Sala.*

To be loved, we should merit but little esteem; all superiority attracts awe and aversion.—*Helvetius.*

The chief ingredients in the composition of those qualities that gain esteem and praise are good nature, truth, good sense, and good breeding.—*Addison.*

We have so exalted a notion of the human soul, that we cannot bear to be despised by it, or even not to be esteemed by it. Man, in fact, places all his happiness in this esteem.—*Pascal.*

Local esteem is far more conducive to happiness than general reputation. The latter may be compared to the fixed stars which glimmer so remotely as to afford little light and no warmth. The former is like the sun, each day shedding his prolific and cheering beams.—*W. B. Clulow.*

It is common to esteem most what is most unknown.—*Tacitus.*

There is graciousness and a kind of urbanity in beginning with men by esteem and confidence. It proves, at least, that we have long lived in good company with others and with ourselves.—*Joubert.*

Esteem has more engaging charms than friendship, and even love. It captivates hearts better, and never makes ingrates.—*Rochefoucauld.*

ESTIMATION.

It is seldom that a man labors well in his minor department unless he overrates it. It is lucky for us that the bee does not look upon the honeycomb in the same light we do.—*Whately.*

ETERNITY.

Eternity, thou pleasing, dreadful thought!—*Addison.*

Eternity is the divine treasure-house, and hope is the window, by means of which mortals are permitted to see, as through a glass darkly, the things which God is preparing.—*Mountford.*

The thought of eternity consoles for the shortness of life.—*Malesherbes.*

"What is eternity?" was a question once asked at the Deaf and Dumb Institution at Paris, and the beautiful and striking answer was given by one of the pupils, "The lifetime of the Almighty."—*John Bate.*

And can eternity belong to me, poor pensioner on the bounties of an hour?—*Young.*

Our imagination so magnifies this present existence, by the power of continual reflection on it, and so attenuates eternity, by not thinking of it at all, that we reduce an eternity to nothingness, and expand a mere nothing to an eternity; and this habit is so inveterately rooted in us that all the force of reason cannot induce us to lay it aside.—*Pascal.*

There is, I know not how, in the minds of men, a certain presage, as it were, of a future existence; and this takes the deepest root, and is most discoverable, in the greatest geniuses and most exalted souls.—*Cicero.*

The disappointed man turns his thoughts toward a state of existence where his wiser desires may be fixed with the certainty of faith; the successful man feels that the objects which he has ardently pursued fail to satisfy the cravings of an immortal spirit; the wicked man turneth away from his wickedness, that he may save his soul alive.—*Southey.*

All great natures delight in stability; all great men find eternity affirmed in the very promise of their faculties.—*Emerson.*

When at eve, at the bounding of the landscape, the heavens appear to recline so slowly on the earth, imagination pictures beyond the horizon an asylum of hope,—a native land of love; and nature seems silently to repeat that man is immortal.—*Madame de Staël.*

Let me dream that love goes with us to the shore unknown.—*Mrs. Hemans.*

In the life to come, at the first ray of its light our true characters, purified but preserving their identity, will more fully expand, and the result of the infinite diversity will be a complete unity.—*Madame de Gasparin.*

Beyond is all abyss, eternity, whose end no eye can reach.—*Milton.*

He that will often put eternity and the world before him, and who will dare to look steadfastly at both of them, will find that the more often he contemplates them, the former will grow greater and the latter less.—*Colton.*

ETHICS.

Ethics is the doctrine of manners, or science of philosophy, which teaches men their duty and the springs and principles of human conduct.—*Maunder.*

Art itself is essentially ethical; because every true work of art must have a beauty or grandeur of some kind, and beauty and grandeur cannot be comprehended by the beholder except through the moral sentiment. The eye is only a witness; it is not a judge. The mind judges what the eye reports to it; therefore, whatever elevates the moral sentiment to the contemplation of beauty and grandeur is in itself ethical.—*Bulwer Lytton.*

EVASION.

Evasion is unworthy of us, and is always the intimate of equivocation.—*Balzac.*

Evasions are the common shelter of the hard-hearted, the false and impotent, when called upon to assist; the real great alone plan instantaneous help, even when their looks or words presage difficulties.—*Lavater.*

EVENING.

The evening came. The setting sun stretched his celestial rods of light across the level landscape, and, like the Hebrews in Egypt, smote the rivers, the brooks, and the ponds, and they became as blood.—*Longfellow.*

Sober Evening takes her wonted station in the middle air, a thousand shadows at her beck.
Thomson.

Evening is the delight of virtuous age; it seems an emblem of the tranquil close of busy life,—serene, placid, and mild, with the impress of its great Creator stamped upon it; it spreads its quiet wings over the grave, and seems to promise that all shall be peace beyond it.—*Bulwer Lytton.*

Now came still evening on, and twilight gray had in her sober livery all things clad.—
Milton.

A paler shadow strews its mantle over the mountains; parting day dies like the dolphin, whom each pang imbues with a new color as it gasps away.—*Byron.*

Meek-eyed Eve, her cheek yet warm with blushes, slow retires through the Hesperian gardens of the west, and shuts the gates of day.
Mrs. Barbauld.

Night steals on; and the day takes its farewell, like the words of a departing friend, or the last tone of hallowed music in a minster's aisles, heard when it floats along the shade of elms, in the still place of graves.—*Percival.*

Vast and deep the mountain shadows grew.
Rogers.

EVIL.

The lives of the best of us are spent in choosing between evils.—*Junius.*

All animals are more happy than man. Look, for instance, on yonder ass: all allow him to be miserable; his evils, however, are not brought on by himself and his own fault; he feels only those which nature has inflicted. We, on the contrary, besides our necessary ills, draw upon ourselves a multitude of others.—
Menander.

The doing an evil to avoid an evil cannot be good.—*Coleridge.*

Imaginary evils soon become real ones by indulging our reflections on them; as he who in a melancholy fancy sees something like a face on the wall or the wainscot can, by two or three touches with a lead pencil, make it look visible, and agreeing with what he fancied.
Swift.

To overcome evil with good is good, to resist evil by evil is evil.—*Mohammed.*

All evil, in fact the very existence of evil, is inexplicable until we refer to the paternity of God. It hangs a huge blot in the universe until the orb of divine love rises behind it. In that apposition we detect its meaning. It appears to us but a finite shadow as it passes across the disk of infinite light.—*Chapin.*

Nothing is to be esteemed evil which God and nature have fixed with eternal sanction.—
Jeremy Taylor.

We sometimes learn more from the sight of evil than from an example of good; and it is well to accustom ourselves to profit by the evil which is so common, while that which is good is so rare.—*Pascal.*

The dread of evil is a much more forcible principle of human actions than the prospect of good.—*Locke.*

There is nothing evil but what is within us; the rest is either natural or accidental.—
Sir P. Sidney.

There are only two bad things in this world, sin and bile.—*Hannah More.*

That which the French proverb hath of sick ness is true of all evils, that they come on horseback, and go away on foot; we have often seen a sudden fall or one meal's surfeit hath stuck by many to their graves; whereas pleasures come like oxen, slow and heavily, and go away like post-horses, upon the spur.—
Bishop Hall.

Where evil may be done, it is right to ponder; where only suffered, know the shortest pause is much too long.—*Hannah More.*

Never let man imagine that he can pursue a good end by evil means, without sinning against his own soul! Any other issue is doubtful; the evil effect on himself is certain.—*Southey.*

The truest definition of evil is that which represents it as something contrary to nature; evil is evil because it is unnatural; a vine which should bear olive-berries, an eye to which blue seems yellow, would be diseased; an unnatural mother, an unnatural son, an unnatural act, are the strongest terms of condemnation.—*F. W. Robertson.*

In the history of man it has been very generally the case that when evils have grown insufferable they have touched the point of cure.—
Chapin.

If you do what you should not, you must bear what you would not.—*Franklin.*

Evil is easily discovered, there is an infinite variety; good is almost unique. But some kinds of evil are almost as difficult to discover as that which we call good; and often particular evil of this class passes for good. It needs even a certain greatness of soul to attain to this, as to that which is good.—*Pascal.*

If evil is inevitable, how are the wicked accountable? Nay, why do we call men wicked at all? Evil is inevitable, but it is also remediable.—*Horace Mann.*

He who will fight the Devil with his own weapon must not wonder if he finds him an over-match.—*South.*

By the very constitution of our nature moral evil is its own curse.—*Chalmers.*

As surely as God is good, so surely there is no such thing as necessary evil. For by the religious mind, sickness and pain and death are not to be accounted evils. Moral evils are of your own making; and undoubtedly the greater part of them may be prevented. Deformities of mind, as of body, will sometimes occur.—
Southey.

It is a proof of our natural bias to evil, that gain is slower and harder than loss in all things good; but in all things bad, getting is quicker and easier than getting rid of.—*Hare.*

To great evils we submit, we resent little provocations. I have before now been disappointed of a hundred-pound job and lost half a crown at rackets on the same day, and been more mortified at the latter than the former.—
Hazlitt.

We are neither obstinately nor wilfully to oppose evils, nor truckle under them for want of courage, but that we are naturally to give way to them, according to their condition and our own, we ought to grant free passage to diseases; and I find they stay less with me who let them alone. And I have lost those which are reputed the most tenacious and obstinate of their own defervescence, without any help or art, and contrary to their rules. Let us a little permit Nature to take her own way; she better understands her own affairs than we.—*Montaigne*

Philosophy triumphs easily over past and future evils, but present evils triumph over philosophy.—*Rochefoucauld.*

Many have puzzled themselves about the origin of evil. I am content to observe that there is evil, and that there is a way to escape from it; and with this I begin and end.—*Newton.*

We cannot do evil to others without doing it to ourselves.—*Desmahis.*

Every evil to which we do not succumb is a benefactor. As the Sandwich Islander believes that the strength and valor of the enemy he kills passes into himself, so we gain the strength of the temptation we resist.—*Emerson.*

The evil that men do lives after them; the good is oft interred with their bones.—
Shakespeare.

Evils in the journey of life are like the hills which alarm travellers upon their road; they both appear great at a distance, but when we approach them we find that they are far less insurmountable than we had conceived.—*Colton.*

There are times when it would seem as if God fished with a line, and the Devil with a net.—*Madame Swetchine.*

Good is positive. Evil is merely privative, not absolute. It is like cold, which is the privation of heat. All evil is so much death or nonentity.—*Emerson.*

He who is in evil is also in the punishment of evil.—*Swedenborg.*

As there is much beast and some devil in man, so is there some angel and some God in him. The beast and the devil may be conquered, but in this life never destroyed.—*Coleridge.*

There is this of good in real evils, they deliver us while they last from the petty despotism of all that were imaginary.—*Colton.*

There is some soul of goodness in things evil, would men observingly distil it out.—
Shakespeare.

There are thousands hacking at the branches of evil to one who is striking at the root.—
Thoreau.

With every exertion, the best of men can do but a moderate amount of good ; but it seems in the power of the most contemptible individual to do incalculable mischief.—
Washington Irving.

EVIL-SPEAKING.

Ill deeds are doubled with an evil word.—
Shakespeare.

It is not good to speak evil of all whom we know bad ; it is worse to judge evil of any who may prove good. To speak ill upon knowledge shows a want of charity ; to speak ill upon suspicion shows a want of honesty. I will not speak so bad as I know of many ; I will not speak worse than I know of any. To know evil of others and not speak it, is sometimes discretion ; to speak evil of others and not know it, is always dishonesty. He may be evil himself who speaks good of others upon knowledge, but he can never be good himself who speaks evil of others upon suspicion.—*Arthur Warwick.*

A good word is an easy obligation ; but not to speak ill requires only our silence, which costs us nothing.—*Tillotson.*

One doth not know how much an ill word may empoison liking.—*Shakespeare.*

A man has no more right to say an uncivil thing than to act one ; no more right to say a rude thing to another than to knock him down.
Johnson.

A knavish speech sleeps in a foolish ear.—
Shakespeare.

It is safer to affront some people than to oblige them ; for the better a man deserves, the worse they will speak of him.—*Seneca.*

Evil report, like the Italian stiletto, is an assassin's weapon, worthy only of the bravo.—
Madame de Maintenon.

When will talkers refrain from evil speaking ? When listeners refrain from evil hearing. At present there are many so credulous of evil, they will receive suspicions and impressions against persons whom they don't know, from a person whom they do know,— an authority good for nothing.—*Hare.*

Wherever the speech is corrupted the mind is also.—*Seneca.*

EXAGGERATION.

Exaggeration is a blood relation to falsehood and nearly as blamable.—*Hosea Ballou.*

The habit of exaggeration, like dram drinking, becomes a slavish necessity, and they who practise it pass their lives in a kind of mental telescope, through whose magnifying medium they look upon themselves and everything around them.—*J. B. Owen.*

EXAMPLE.

Allured to brighter worlds, and led the way.
Goldsmith.

If thou desire to see thy child virtuous, let him not see his father's vices ; thou canst not rebuke that in children that they behold practised in thee ; till reason be ripe, examples direct more than precepts ; such as thy behavior is before thy children's faces, such commonly is theirs behind their parents' backs.—*Quarles.*

Man is an imitative creature, and whoever is foremost leads the herd.—*Schiller.*

So admirably hath God disposed of the ways of men, that even the sight of vice in others is like a warning arrow shot for us to take heed. We should correct our own faults by seeing how uncomely they appear in others ; who will not abhor a choleric passion, and a saucy pride in himself, that sees how ridiculous and contemptible they render those who are infested with them ?—*J. Beaumont.*

He hath a daily beauty in his life.—
Shakespeare.

Example has more followers than reason. We unconsciously imitate what pleases us, and insensibly approximate to the characters we most admire. In this way, a generous habit of thought and of action carries with it an incalculable influence.—*Bovee.*

There is a transcendent power in example. We reform others unconsciously when we walk uprightly. *Madame Swetchine*

Nothing enlarges the gulf of atheism more than the wide passage which lies between the faith and lives of men pretending to teach Christianity.—*Stillingfleet.*

Though " the words of the wise be as nails fastened by the masters of the assemblies," yet sure their examples are the hammer to drive them in to take the deeper hold. A father that whipped his son for swearing, and swore himself whilst he whipped him, did more harm by his example than good by his correction.—
Fuller.

I am satisfied that we are less convinced by what we hear than by what we see.—*Herodotus.*

Think not, Sultan, that in the sequestered vale alone dwells virtue, and her sweet companion, with attentive eye, mild, affable benevolence ? No, the first great gift we can bestow on others is a good example.—*Sir Charles Morell*

We can do more good by being good than in any other way.—*Rowland Hill.*

Men trust rather to their eyes than to their ears; the effect of precepts is therefore slow and tedious, whilst that of examples is summary and effectual.—*Seneca.*

It is a well-known psychological fact that the conscience of children is formed by the influences that surround them; and that their notions of good and evil are the result of the moral atmosphere they breathe.—*Richter.*

It is a world of mischief that may be done by a single example of avarice or luxury. One voluptuous palate makes many more.—*Seneca.*

There are bad examples which are worse than crimes; and more states have perished from the violation of morality than from the violation of law.—*Montesquieu.*

None preaches better than the ant, and she says nothing.—*Franklin.*

Examples would indeed be excellent things were not people so modest that none will set, and so vain that none will follow them.—*Hare.*

"Not the cry, but the flight of a wild duck," says a Chinese author, "leads the flock to fly and follow."—*Richter.*

Be more prudent for your children than perhaps you have been for yourself. When they too are parents, they will imitate you, and each of you will have prepared happy generations, who will transmit, together with your memory, the worship of your wisdom.—
La Beaume.

Examples of vicious courses practised in a domestic circle corrupt more readily and more deeply when we behold them in persons in authority.—*Juvenal.*

Example is a dangerous lure; where the wasp got through the gnat sticks fast.—
La Fontaine.

The pulpit only "teaches" to be honest; the market-place "trains" to overreaching and fraud; and teaching has not a tithe of the efficiency of training. Christ never wrote a tract, but he went about doing good.—*Horace Mann.*

The road by precepts is tedious, by example, short and efficacious.—*Seneca.*

The corruption of the positively wicked is often less sad and fatal to society than the irregularities of a virtuous man who yields and falls.—*Desmahis.*

· They asked Lucmau the fabulist, From whom did you learn manners? He answered, From the unmannerly.—*Saadi.*

Precept is instruction written in the sand, the tide flows over it and the record is gone. Example is graven on the rock, and the lesson is not soon lost.—*Channing.*

Every man is bound to tolerate the act of which he himself has set the example.—*Phædrus.*

Nothing is so contagious as example; never was there any considerable good or ill done that does not produce its like. We imitate good actions through emulation, and bad ones through a malignity in our nature, which shame conceals, and example sets at liberty.—
Rochefoucauld.

Other men are lenses through which we read our own minds.—*Emerson.*

Men judge things more fully by the eye than by the ear; consequently a minister's practice is as much regarded, if not more, than his sermons.—*Bridges.*

It is certain, that either wise bearing or ignorant carriage is caught, as men take disease, one of another; therefore let men take heed of their company.—*Shakespeare.*

Preaching is of much avail, but practice is far more effective. A godly life is the strongest argument that you can offer to the sceptic.—
Hosea Ballou.

There are follies which are caught like contagious diseases.— *Rochefoucauld.*

A wise and good man will turn examples of all sorts to his own advantage. The good he will make his patterns, and strive to equal or excel them. The bad he will by all means avoid.—*Thomas à Kempis.*

Example is more forcible than precept. People look at my six days in the week, to see what I mean on the seventh.—*Cecil.*

No reproof or denunciation is so potent as the silent influence of a good example.—
Hosea Ballou.

My advice is to consult the lives of other men, as we would a looking-glass, and from thence fetch examples for our own imitation.—
Terence.

Be a pattern to others, and then all will go well; for as a whole city is infected by the licentious passions and vices of great men, so it is likewise reformed by their moderation.—
Cicero.

Alexander received more bravery of mind by the pattern of Achilles than by hearing the definition of fortitude.—*Sir P. Sidney.*

No man is so insignificant as to be sure his example can do no hurt.—*Clarendon.*

The sight of lovers feedeth those in love.—
Shakespeare.

People seldom improve when they have no other model but themselves to copy after.—
Goldsmith.

EXCELLENCE.

Excellence is never granted to man but as the reward of labor. It argues, indeed, no small strength of mind to persevere in the habits of industry without the pleasure of perceiving those advantages which, like the hands of a clock, whilst they make hourly approaches to their point, yet proceed so slowly as to escape observation.—*Sir Joshua Reynolds.*

A man that is desirous to excel should endeavor it in those things that are in themselves most excellent.—*Epictetus.*

Human excellence, parted from God, is like a fabled flower, which, according to Rabbis, Eve plucked when passing out of paradise, — severed from its native root, it is only the touching memorial of a lost Eden; sad, while charming, — beautiful, but dead.—*C. Stanford.*

Those who attain any excellence commonly spend life in one common pursuit; for excellence is not often gained upon easier terms.—
Johnson.

There is a moral excellence attainable by all who have the will to strive after it; but there is an intellectual and physical superiority which is above the reach of our wishes, and is granted to a few only.—*Crabb.*

EXCELSIOR.

What we truly and earnestly aspire to be, that in some sense we are. The mere aspiration, by changing the frame of the mind, for the moment realizes itself.—*Mrs. Jameson.*

It is but a base, ignoble mind that mounts no higher than a bird can soar.—*Shakespeare.*

Bright and illustrious illusions! Who can blame, who laugh at the boy, who not admire and commend him, for that desire of a fame outlasting the Pyramids by which he insensibly learns to live in a life beyond the present, and nourish dreams of a good unattainable by the senses? —*Bulwer Lytton.*

The movement of the species is upward, irresistibly upward.—*Bancroft.*

Lift thyself up, look around, and see something higher and brighter than earth, earthworms, and earthly darkness.—*Richter.*

Darwin remarks that we are less dazzled by the light at waking, if we have been dreaming of visible objects. Happy are those who have here dreamt of a higher vision! They will the sooner be able to endure the glories of the world to come.—*Novalis.*

Our natures are like oil; compound us with anything, yet still we strive to swim upon the top.—*Beaumont and Fletcher.*

Whilst we converse with what is above us, we do not grow old, but grow young.—
Emerson.

The desire of excellence is the necessary attribute of those who excel. We work little for a thing unless we wish for it. But we cannot of ourselves estimate the degree of our success in what we strive for; that task is left to others. With the desire for excellence comes, therefore, the desire for approbation. And this distinguishes intellectual excellence from moral excellence; for the latter has no necessity of human tribunal; it is more inclined to shrink from the public than to invite the public to be its judge.—*Bulwer Lytton.*

O sacred hunger of ambitious minds!—
Spenser.

Who shoots at the midday sun, though he be sure he shall never hit the mark, yet as sure he is that he shall shoot higher than he who aims but at a bush.—*Sir P. Sidney.*

By steps we may ascend to God.—*Milton.*

Man can only learn to rise from the consideration of that which he cannot surmount.—
Richter.

The little done vanishes from the sight of man, who looks forward to what is still to do.—
Goethe.

It is not to taste sweet things, but to do noble and true things, and vindicate himself under God's heaven as a God-made man, that the poorest son of Adam dimly longs. Show him the way of doing that, the dullest daydrudge kindles into a hero. They wrong man greatly who say he is to be seduced by ease. Difficulty, abnegation, martyrdom, death, are the allurements that act on the heart of man. Kindle the inner genial life of him, you have a flame that burns up all lower considerations.—
♦ *Carlyle.*

Lifted up so high I disdained subjection, and thought one step higher would set me highest.
Milton.

Fearless minds climb soonest unto crowns.—
Shakespeare.

Besides the pleasure derived from acquired knowledge, there lurks in the mind of man, and tinged with a shade of sadness, an unsatisfactory longing for something beyond the present, a striving towards regions yet unknown and unopened.—*Wilhelm von Humboldt.*

Too low they build who build beneath the stars.—*Young.*

EXCEPTIONS.

The exceptions of the scrupulous put one in mind of some general pardons where everything is forgiven except crimes.—*Fielding.*

EXCESS.

Let us teach ourselves that honorable step, not to outdo discretion.—*Shakespeare.*

To regard the excesses of the passions as maladies has so salutary an effect that this idea renders all moral sermons useless.—*Boiste.*

The misfortune is, that when a man has found honey, he enters upon the feast with an appetite so voracious that he usually destroys his own delight by excess and satiety.—*Knox.*

Whatever has exceeded its due bounds is ever in a state of instability.—*Seneca.*

Pleasures bring effeminacy, and effeminacy foreruns ruin ; such conquests, without blood or sweat, sufficiently do revenge themselves upon their intemperate conquerors.—*Quarles.*

They are as sick that surfeit with too much, as they that starve with nothing.—*Shakespeare.*

There is no unmixed good in human affairs ; the best principles, if pushed to excess, degenerate into fatal vices. Generosity is nearly allied to extravagance ; charity itself may lead to ruin ; the sternness of justice is but one step removed from the severity of oppression. It is the same in the political world ; the tranquillity of despotism resembles the stagnation of the Dead Sea ; the fever of innovation the tempests of the ocean. It would seem as if, at particular periods, from causes inscrutable to human wisdom, a universal frenzy seizes mankind ; reason, experience, prudence, are alike blinded ; and the very classes who are to perish in the storm are the first to raise its fury.—*Sir A. Alison.*

If a man get a fever, or a pain in the head with overdrinking, we are subject to curse the wine, when we should rather impute it to ourselves for the excess.—*Erasmus.*

The excesses of our youth are draughts upon our old age, payable with interest, about thirty years after date.—*Colton.*

The desire of power in excess caused angels to fall ; the desire of knowledge in excess caused man to fall ; but in charity is no excess, neither can man nor angels come into danger by it.—*Bacon.*

The body oppressed by excesses bears down the mind, and depresses to the earth any portion of the Divine Spirit we had been endowed with.—*Horace.*

· Violent delights have violent ends, and in their triumph die ; like fire and powder, which as they kiss consume.—*Shakespeare.*

Every morsel to a satisfied hunger is only a new labor to a tired digestion.—*South.*

It is a common thing to screw up justice to the pitch of an injury. A man may be over-righteous, and why not over-grateful too ? There is a mischievous excess that borders so close upon ingratitude that it is no easy matter to distinguish the one from the other ; but, in regard that there is good-will in the bottom of it, however distempered ; for it is effectually but kindness out of the wits.—*Seneca.* ,

There can be no excess to love, none to knowledge, none to beauty, when these attributes are considered in the purest sense.—*Emerson.*

He who indulges his sense in any excesses renders himself obnoxious to his own reason ; and, to gratify the brute in him, displeases the man, and sets his two natures at variance.— *Walter Scott.*

Let pleasure be ever so innocent, the excess is always criminal.—*St. Evremond.*

To gild refined gold, to paint the lily, is wasteful and ridiculous excess.—*Shakespeare.*

In its primary signification, all vice, that is, all excess, brings on its own punishment, even here. By certain fixed, settled, and established laws of him who is the God of nature, excess of every kind destroys that constitution which temperance would preserve. The debauchee offers up his body a " living sacrifice " to sin.— *Colton.*

As surfeit is the father of much fast, so every scope by the immoderate use turns to restraint. *Shakespeare.*

EXCUSE.

An excuse is worse and more terrible than a lie ; for an excuse is a lie guarded.—*Pope.*

EXERCISE.

In those vernal seasons of the year when the air is soft and pleasant, it were an injury and sullenness against Nature not to go out and see her riches, and partake of her rejoicings with heaven and earth.—*Milton.*

There are many troubles which you cannot cure by the Bible and the hymn-book, but which you can cure by a good perspiration and a breath of fresh air.—*Beecher.*

Such is the constitution of man, that labor may be styled its own reward ; nor will any external incitements be requisite if it be considered how much happiness is gained, and how much misery escaped, by frequent and violent agitation of the body.—*Johnson.*

By looking into physical causes our minds are opened and enlarged ; and in this pursuit, whether we take or whether we lose the game, the chase is certainly of service.—*Burke.*

EXPECTATION.

How slow this old moon wanes ! she lingers
my desires, like to a step-dame or a dowager.
Long withering out a young man's revenue.—
Shakespeare.

Uncertainty and expectation are joys of life.
Security is an insipid thing ; and the overtak-
ing and possessing of a wish discovers the folly
of the chase.—*Congreve.*

You give me nothing during your life, but
you promise to provide for me at your death.
If you are not a fool, you know what I wish
for.—*Martial.*

The great source of pleasure is variety.
Uniformity must tire at last, though it be uni-
formity of excellence. We love to expect, and
when expectation is disappointed or gratified,
we want to be again expecting.—*Johnson.*

With what a heavy and retarding weight
does expectation load the wing of time.—
William Mason.

›EXPEDIENCY.

Expediency is the science of exigencies.—
Kossuth

EXPERIENCE.

I learn several great truths ; as that it is im-
possible to see into the ways of futurity, that
punishment always attends the villain, that
love is the fond soother of the human breast.—
Goldsmith.

Our ancestors have travelled the iron age ;
the golden is before us.—
Bernardin de St. Pierre.

There are many arts among men, the knowl
edge of which is acquired bit by bit by expe-
ricuce. For it is experience that causeth our
life to move forward by the skill we acquire,
while want of experience subjects us to the ef
fects of chance.—*Plato.*

Experience wounded is the school where
man learns piercing wisdom out of smart.—
Lord Brooke.

Everything is worth seeing once, and the
more one sees, the less one either wonders or
admires.—*Chesterfield.*

Experience does take dreadfully high school-
wages, but he teaches like no other.—*Carlyle.*

He hazardeth much who depends for his
learning on experience. An unhappy master,
he that is only made wise by many shipwrecks ;
a miserable merchant, that is neither rich nor
wise till he has been bankrupt. By experience
we find out a short way by a long wandering. —
Roger Ascham.

To most men experience is like the stern
lights of a ship, which illumine only the track
it has passed.—*Coleridge.*

It may serve as a comfort to us in all our
calamities and afflictions that he that loses any-
thing and gets wisdom by it is a gainer by the
loss.—*L'Estrange.*

Experience is the common school-house of
fools and ill men. Men of wit and honesty be
otherwise instructed.—*Erasmus.*

Taught by experience to know my own
blindness, shall I speak as if I could not err,
and as if others might not in some disputed
points be more enlightened than myself ? —
Channing.

Would they could sell us experience, though
at diamond prices, but then no one would use
the article second-hand ! —*Balzac.*

Each successive generation plunges into the
abyss of passion, without the slightest regard to
the fatal effects which such conduct has pro-
duced upon their predecessors ; and lament,
when too late, the rashness with which they
slighted the advice of experience, and stifled the
voice of reason.—*Steele.*

Theories are very thin and unsubstantial ;
experience only is tangible.—*Hosea Ballou.*

Ah ! the youngest heart has the same waves
within it as the oldest, but without the plum-
met which can measure their depths.—*Richter.*

Oft have I thought, — jabber as he will, how
learned soever, man knows nothing but what
he has learned from experience ! — *Wieland.*

Experience is by industry achieved, and
perfected by the swift course of time.—
Shakespeare.

I scarcely exceed the middle age of man ;
yet between infancy and maturity I have seen
ten revolutions ! —*Lamartine*

If I might venture to appeal to what is so
much out of fashion at Paris, I mean to experi-
ence, I should tell you that in my course I have
known, and, according to my measure, have co-
operated with great men ; and I have never yet
seen any plan which has not been mended by
the observations of those who were much infe-
rior in understanding to the person who took the
lead in the business.—*Burke.*

The highest conceptions of the sages, who
in order to arrive at them have had to live many
days, have become the milk for children.—
Ballanche.

We are often prophets to others only be-
cause we are our own historians.—
Madame Swetchine.

No man was ever so completely skilled in the
conduct of life as not to receive new informa-
tion from age and experience.—*Terence.*

All reasoning is retrospect; it consists in the application of facts and principles previously known. This will show the very great importance of knowledge, especially of that kind called experience.—*J. Foster.*

All is but lip wisdom which wants experience.—*Sir P. Sidney.*

Experience keeps a dear school, but fools will learn in no other, and scarce in that; for it is true we may give advice, but we cannot give conduct.—*Franklin.*

Nobody will use other people's experience, nor has any of his own till it is too late to use it.—*Hawthorne.*

In all instances where our experience of the past has been extensive and uniform, our judgment concerning the future amounts to moral certainty.—*Beattie.*

Experience is a jewel, and it had need be so, for it is often purchased at an infinite rate.—
Shakespeare.

To some purpose is that man wise who gains his wisdom at another's expense.—
Plautus.

Each succeeding day is the scholar of that which preceded.—*Publius Syrus.*

The bitter past, more welcome is the sweet.
Shakespeare.

Every man's experience of to-day is that he was a fool yesterday and the day before yesterday. To-morrow he will most likely be of exactly the same opinion.—*Charles Mackay.*

Experience, that chill touchstone whose sad proof reduces all things from their hue.—*Byron.*

EXTENUATION.
Oftentimes excusing of a fault doth make the fault the worse by the excuse; as patches, set upon a little breach, discredit more, in hiding of the fault than did the fault before it was so patched.—*Shakespeare.*

EXTRAVAGANCE.
The passion of acquiring riches in order to support a vain expense corrupts the purest souls.—*Fenelon.*

Expense of time is the most costly of all expenses.—*Theophrastus.*

Prodigality is indeed the vice of a weak nature, as avarice is of a strong one; it comes of a weak craving for those blandishments of the world which are easily to be had for money.
Henry Taylor.

There is hope in extravagance, there is none in routine.—*Emerson.*

That is suitable to a man in point of ornamental expense, not which he can afford to have, but which he can afford to lose.— *Whately.*

A large retinue upon a small income, like a large cascade upon a small stream, tends to discover its tenuity.—*Shenstone.*

EXTREMES.
We feel neither extreme heat nor extreme cold. Qualities that are in excess are so much at variance with our feelings that they are impalpable; we do not feel them, though we suffer from their effects. The mind is equally affected by too great youth and by excessive old age, by too much and too little learning. In short, extremes are for us as if they were not, and as if we were not, in regard to them; they escape from us, or we from them.—*Pascal.*

Our age knows nothing but reactions, and leaps from one extreme to another.—*Niebuhr.*

Cruel men are the greatest lovers of mercy, avaricious men of generosity, and proud men of humility; that is to say, in others, not in themselves.—*Colton.*

No violent extreme endures.—*Carlyle.*

We must remember how apt man is to extremes, — rushing from credulity and weakness to suspicion and distrust.—*Bulwer Lytton.*

Everything runs to excess; every good quality is noxious, if unmixed; and, to carry the danger to the edge of ruin, nature causes each man's peculiarity to superabound.—
Emerson.

Shun equally a sombre air and vivacious sallies.—*Marcus Antoninus.*

The man who can be nothing but serious, or nothing but merry, is but half a man.—
Leigh Hunt.

Both in individuals and in masses violent excitement is always followed by remission, and often by reaction. We are all inclined to depreciate whatever we have overpraised, and, on the other hand, to show undue indulgence where we have shown undue rigor.—*Macaulay.*

Neither great poverty nor great riches will hear reason.—*Fielding.*

So near are the boundaries of panegyric and invective, that a worn-out sinner is sometimes found to make the best declaimer against sin. The same high-seasoned descriptions which in his unregenerate state served to inflame his appetites, in his new province of a moralist will serve him (a little turned) to expose the enormity of those appetites in other men.—*Lamb.*

Women are ever in extremes; they are either better or worse than men.—*Bruyère.*

It is a hard but good law of fate, that, as every evil, so every excessive power wears itself out.—*Herder.*

Extreme old age is childhood; extreme wisdom is ignorance, for so ·it may be called, since the man whom the oracle pronounced the wisest of men professed that he knew nothing; yea, push a coward to the extreme and he will show courage; oppress a man to the last, and he will rise above oppression.—*J. Beaumont.*

The greatest flood has the soonest ebb; the sorest tempest the most sudden calm; the hottest love the coldest end; and from the deepest desire oftentimes ensues the deadliest hate.—
Socrates.

Though little fire grows great with little wind, yet extreme gusts will blow out fire and all.—*Shakespeare.*

There is a mean in all things. Even virtue itself hath its stated limits; which not being strictly observed, it ceases to be virtue.—*Horace.*

Too austere a philosophy makes few wise men; too rigorous politics, few good subjects; too hard a religion, few religious persons whose devotion is of long continuance.—*St. Evremond.*

Pleasure and pain, though directly opposite, are yet so contrived by nature as to be constant companions; and it is a fact that the same motions and muscles of the face are employed both in laughing and crying.—
Charron.

Our senses will not admit anything extreme. Too much noise confuses us, too much light dazzles us, too great distance or nearness prevents vision, too great prolixity or brevity weakens an argument, too much pleasure gives pain, too much accordance annoys.—*Pascal.*

The blast that blows loudest is soon overblown.—*Smollett.*

That extremes beget extremes is an apothegm built on the most profound observation of the human mind.—*Colton.*

As great enmities spring from great friendships, and mortal distempers from vigorous health, so do the most surprising and the wildest frenzies from the high and lively agitations of our souls.—*Montaigne.*

Extremes, though contrary, have the like effects; extreme heat mortifies, like extreme cold; extreme love breeds satiety as well as extreme hatred; and too violent rigor tempts chastity as much as too much license.—
Chapman.

All extremes are error. The reverse of error is not truth, but error still. Truth lies between these extremes.—*Cecil.*

Mistrust the man who finds everything good, the man who finds everything evil, and still more, the man who is indifferent to everything.—
Lavater.

Extremity is the trier of spirits.—
Shakespeare.

EYES.

Flaw-seeing eyes, like needle points.—*Lowell.*

People forget that it is the eye which makes the horizon, and the rounding mind's eye which makes this or that man a type or representative of humanity with the name of hero or saint.—
Emerson.

The vista that shines through the eye to the heart.—*Moore.*

The eye speaks with an eloquence and truthfulness surpassing speech. It is the window out of which the winged thoughts often fly unwittingly. It is the tiny magic mirror on whose crystal surface the moods of feeling fitfully play, like the sunlight and shadow on a still stream.—
Tuckerman.

Such fierce vivacity as fires the eye of genius fancy-crazed.—*Coleridge.*

Speech is a laggard and a sloth, but the eyes shoot out an electric fluid that condenses all the elements of sentiment and passion in one single emanation.—*Horace Smith.*

That deadly Indian hug in which men wrestle with their eyes.—*Holmes.*

Little eyes must be good-tempered, or they are ruined. They have no other resource. But this will beautify them enough. They are made for laughing, and should do their duty.—
Leigh Hunt.

We credit most our sight; one eye doth please our trust far more than ten ear-witnesses.
Herrick.

Gradual as the snow, at heaven's breath, melts off and shows the azure flowers beneath, her lids unclosed, and the bright eyes were seen.—
Moore.

Crows pick out the eyes of the dead when they are no longer of any use. But flatterers destroy the souls of the living by blinding their eyes.—*Maximus.*

I prize the soul that slumbers in a quiet eye.
Eliza Cook.

O, the eye's light is a noble gift of Heaven! All beings live from light; each fair created thing, the very plants, turn with a joyful transport to the light.—*Schiller.*

The eyes of other people are the eyes that ruin us.—*Franklin.*

11

Men are born with two eyes, but with one tongue, in order that they should see twice as much as they say.—*Colton.*

I dislike an eye that twinkles like a star. Those only are beautiful which, like the planets, have a steady, lambent light, — are luminous, not sparkling.—*Longfellow.*

Pure vestal thoughts in the translucent fane of her still spirit.—*Tennyson.*

Ahab cast a covetous eye at Naboth's vineyard, David a lustful eye at Bathsheba. The eye is the pulse of the soul; as physicians judge of the heart by the pulse, so we by the eye; a rolling eye, a roving heart. The good eye keeps minute time, and strikes when it should; the lustful, crotchet-time, and so puts all out of tune.
    Rev. T. *Adams.*

The eye strays not while under the guidance of reason.—*Publius Syrus.*

Alack! there lies more peril in thine eye than twenty of their swords; look thou but sweet, and I am proof against their enmity.—
    Shakespeare.

Who has a daring eye tells downright truths and downright lies.—*Lavater.*

A pair of bright eyes with a dozen glances suffice to subdue a man; to enslave him, and inflame; to make him even forget; they dazzle him so, that the past becomes straightway dim to him; and he so prizes them, that he would give all his life to possess them. What is the fond love of dearest friends compared to his treasure? Is memory as strong as expectancy, fruition as hunger, gratitude as desire?
    Thackeray.

The eye of the master will do more work than both his hands.—*Franklin.*

Lovers are angry, reconciled, entreat, thank, appoint, and finally speak all things, by their eyes.—*Montaigne.*

Hell trembles at a heaven-directed eye.—
    Bishop Ken.

The eye observes only what the mind, the heart, and the imagination are gifted to see; and sight must be reinforced by insight before souls can be discerned as well as manners, ideas as well as objects, realities and relations as well as appearances and accidental connections.—
    Whipple.

Wait upon him whom thou art to speak to with thine eye; for there be many cunning men that have secret heads and transparent countenances.—*Burton.*

A wanton eye is a messenger of an unchaste heart.—*St. Augustine.*

What stars do spangle heaven with such beauty as those two eyes become that heavenly face?—*Shakespeare.*

Ah! the soft starlight of virgin eyes.—*Balzac.*

That fine part of our constitution, the eye, seems as much the receptacle and seat of our passions, appetites, and inclinations, as the mind itself; and at least it is the outward portal to introduce them to the house within, or rather the common thoroughfare to let our affections pass in and out. Love, anger, pride, and avarice all visibly move in those little orbs.—
    Addison.

The eye sees what it brings the power to see.
    Carlyle.

What an eye she has! methinks it sounds a parley of provocation.—*Shakespeare.*

Somebody once observed, — and the observation did him credit, whoever he was — that the dearest things in the world were neighbors' eyes, for they cost everybody more than anything else contributing to housekeeping.—
    Albert Smith.

The eyes have a property in things and territories not named in any title-deeds, and are the owners of our choicest possessions.—*Alcott.*

Eyes that droop like summer flowers.—
    Miss L. E. *Landon.*

One of the most wonderful things in nature is a glance; it transcends speech; it is the bodily symbol of identity.—*Emerson.*

There is a lore simple and sure, that asks no discipline of weary years, — the language of the soul, told through the eye.—*Mrs Sigourney.*

Heart on her lip and soul within her eyes.—
    Byron.

The eye is the window of the soul, the mouth the door. The intellect, the will, are seen in the eye; the emotions, sensibilities, and affections, in the mouth. The animals look for man's intentions right into his eyes. Even a rat, when you hunt him and bring him to bay, looks you in the eye.—*Hiram Powers.*

Sometimes from her eyes I did receive fair speechless messages.—*Shakespeare.*

When there is love in the heart there are rainbows in the eyes, which cover every black cloud with gorgeous hues.—*Beecher.*

Eyes not down-dropped nor over-bright, but fed with the clear-pointed flame of chastity.—
    Tennyson.

Where is any author in the world teaches such beauty as a woman's eye?—*Shakespeare.*

And eyes disclosed what eyes alone could tell.—*Dwight.*

Satan turned Eve's eye to the apple, Achan's eye to the wedge of gold, Ahab's eye to Naboth's vineyard, and then what work did he make with them!—*Rev. J. Alleine.*

Faster than his tongue did make offence, his eye did heal it up.—*Shakespeare.*

The eyes are the amulets of the mind.— *W. R. Alger.*

None but those who have loved can be supposed to understand the oratory of the eye, the mute eloquence of a look, or the conversational powers of the face. Love's sweetest meanings are unspoken ; the full heart knows no rhetoric of words, and resorts to the pantomime of sighs and glances.—*Bovee.*

Our eyes when gazing on sinful objects are out of their calling and God's keeping.— *Fuller.*

The eyes of women are Promethean fires.— *Shakespeare.*

Eyes are bold as lions, roving, running, leaping, here and there, far and near. . They speak all languages. They wait for no introduction ; they are no Englishmen ; ask no leave of age or rank ; they respect neither poverty nor riches, neither learning nor power, nor virtue, nor sex, but intrude, and come again, and go through and through you in a moment of time. What inundation of life and thought is discharged from one soul into another through them !—*Emerson.*

Men of cold passions have quick eyes.— *Hawthorne.*

Eyes will not see when the heart wishes them to be blind. Desire conceals truth as darkness does the earth.—*Seneca.*

Like a star glancing out from the blue of the sky !—*Whittier.*

A beautiful eye makes silence eloquent, a kind eye makes contradiction an assent, an enraged eye makes beauty deformed. This little member gives life to every other part about us ; and I believe the story of Argus implies no more than that the eye is in every part ; that is to say, every other part would be mutilated were not its force represented more by the eye than even by itself.—*Addison.*

Disdain and scorn ride sparkling in her eye, despising what they look on.—*Shakespeare.*

Tell me, sweet eyes, from what divinest star did ye drink in your liquid melancholy ? — *Bulwer Lytton.*

Those laughing orbs, that borrow from azure skies the light they wear.— *Frances S. Osgood.*

A lover's eyes will gaze an eagle blind.— *Shakespeare.*

The eye is the inlet to the soul, and it is well to beware of him whose visual organs avoid your honest regard.—*Hosea Ballou.*

The balls of sight are so formed that one man's eyes are spectacles to another to read his heart with.—*Johnson.*

Such eyes as may have looked from heaven, but never were raised to it before !—*Moore.*

The intelligence of affection is carried on by the eye only ; good-breeding has made the tongue falsify the heart, and act a part of continued restraint, while Nature has preserved the eyes to herself, that she may not be disguised or misrepresented.—*Addison.*

The curious questioning eye, that plucks the heart of every mystery.—*Grenville Mellen.*

The eyes are the pioneers that first announce the soft tale of love.—*Propertius.*

An eye like Mars, to threaten and command. *Shakespeare.*

Some eyes threaten like a loaded and levelled pistol, and others are as insulting as hissing or kicking ; some have no more expression than blueberries, while others are as deep as a well which you can fall into.—*Emerson.*

Love looketh from the eye, and kindleth love by looking.—*Tupper.*

Drink to me only with thine eyes, and I will pledge with mine.—*Ben Jonson.*

Sweet, silent rhetoric of persuading eyes.— *Sir W. Davenant.*

The eye is continually influenced by what it cannot detect ; nay, it is not going too far to say that it is most influenced by what it detects least. Let the painter define, if he can, the variations of lines on which depend the changes of expression in the human countenance.— *Ruskin.*

Eyes raised toward heaven are always beautiful, whatever they be.—*Joubert.*

F.

FACE.

A good face is the best letter of recommendation.—*Queen Elizabeth.*

No human face is exactly the same in its lines on each side, no leaf perfect in its lobes, no branch in its symmetry. All admit irregularity as they imply change; and to banish imperfection is to destroy expression, to check exertion, to paralyze vitality. All things are literally better, lovelier, and more beloved for the imperfections which have been divinely appointed, that the law of human life may be effort, and the law of human judgment mercy.
Ruskin.

He had a face like a benediction.—*Cervantes.*

What clear arched brows! What sparkling eyes! the lilies contending with the roses in her cheeks, who shall most set them off. What ruby lips!—*Massinger.*

All men's faces are true, whatsoever their hands are.—*Shakespeare.*

Look in the face of the person to whom you are speaking, if you wish to know his real sentiments; for he can command his words more easily than his countenance.—*Chesterfield.*

The cheek is apter than the tongue to tell an errand.—*Shakespeare.*

There are faces so fluid with expression, so flushed and rippled by the play of thought, that we can hardly find what the mere features really are. When the delicious beauty of lineaments loses its power, it is because a more delicious beauty has appeared, that an interior and durable form has been disclosed.
Emerson.

There is in every human countenance either a history or a prophecy, which must sadden, or at least soften, every reflecting observer.—*Coleridge.*

We are all sculptors and painters, and our material is our own flesh and blood and bones. Any nobleness begins at once to refine a man's features, any meanness or sensuality to imbrute them.—*Thoreau.*

Expression alone can invest beauty with supreme and lasting command over the eye.—*Fuseli.*

Alas! how few of nature's faces there are to gladden us with their beauty! The cares and sorrows and hungerings of the world change them as they change hearts; and it is only when those passions sleep, and have lost their hold forever, that the troubled clouds pass off, and leave heaven's surface clear.—*Dickens.*

That chastened brightness only gathered by those who tread the path of sympathy and love.
Bulwer Lytton.

Beauty depends more upon the movement of the face than upon the form of the features when at rest. Thus a countenance habitually under the influence of amiable feelings acquires a beauty of the highest order, from the frequeney with which such feelings are the originating causes of the movement or expressions which stamp their character upon it.—
Mrs. S. C. Hall.

A cheerful face is nearly as good for an invalid as healthy weather.—*Franklin.*

There remains in the faces of women who are naturally serene and peaceful, and of those rendered so by religion, an after-spring, and, later, an after-summer, the reflex of their most beautiful bloom.—*Richter.*

Fire burns only when we are near it; but a beautiful face burns and inflames, though at a distance.—*Xenophon.*

Her face had a wonderful fascination in it. It was such a calm, quiet face, with the light of the rising soul shining so peacefully through it. At times, it wore an expression of seriousness, of sorrow even; and then seemed to make the very air bright with what the Italian poets so beautifully call the "lampeggiar dell' angelico riso," — the lightning of the angelic smile.—
Longfellow.

In thy face I see the map of honor, truth, and loyalty.—*Shakespeare.*

Nature has laid out all her art in beautifying the face; she has touched it with vermilion, planted in it a double row of ivory, made it the seat of smiles and blushes, lighted it up and enlivened it with the brightness of the eyes, hung it on each side with curious organs of sense, given it airs and graces that cannot be described, and surrounded it with such a flowing shade of hair as sets all its beauties in the most agreeable light.—*Addison.*

The furrows of long thought dried up in tears.—*Byron.*

The face of a woman, whatever be the force or extent of her mind, whatever be the importance of the objects she pursues, is always an obstacle or a reason in the story of her life.—
Madame de Staël.

Her face, O call it pure, not pale!—*Coleridge.*

The loveliest faces are to be seen by moonlight, when one sees half with the eye and half with the fancy.—*Bovee.*

Those faces which have charmed us the most escape us the soonest.— *Walter Scott.*

As the language of the face is universal, so is it very comprehensive. No laconism can reach it. It is the short-hand of the mind, and crowds a great deal in a little room. A man may look a sentence as soon as speak a word. The strokes are small, but so masterly drawn that you may easily collect the image and proportions of what they resemble.—
Jeremy Collier.

Truth makes the face of that person shine who speaks and owns it.—*South.*

Faces are as legible as books, only with these circumstances to recommend them to 'our perusal, that they are read in much less time, and are much less likely to deceive us.—*Lavater.*

. That same face of yours looks like the title-page to a whole volume of roguery.—
Colley Cibber.

Her closed lips were delicate as the tinted pencilling of veins upon a flower; and on her check the timid blood had faintly melted through, like something that was half afraid of light.— *Willis.*

Features, — the great soul's apparent seat.—
Bryant.

Not the entrance of a cathedral, not the sound of a passing bell, not the furs of a magistrate, nor the sables of a funeral, were fraught with half the solemnity of face !—*Shenstone.*

A face like nestling luxury of flowers.—
Massey.

FACT.
Facts are to the mind the same thing as food to the body. On the due digestion of facts depend the strength and wisdom of the one, just as vigor and health depend on the other. The wisest in council, the ablest in debate, and the most agreeable companion in the commerce of human life, is that man who has assimilated to his understanding the greatest number of facts.—*Burke.*

FAILURE.
He only is exempt from failures who makes no efforts.— *Whately.*

Every failure is a step to success; every detection of what is false directs us towards what is true; every trial exhausts some tempting form of error. Not only so; but scarcely any attempt is entirely a failure; scarcely any theory, the result of steady thought, is altogether false; no tempting form of error is without some latent charm derived from truth.—
Professor Whewell.

Only the astrologer and the empyric never fail.— *Willmott.*

There is not a fiercer hell than failure in a great object.—*Keats.*

A failure establishes only this, that our determination to succeed was not strong enough.—
Bovee.

In the lexicon of youth, which fate reserves for a bright manhood, there is no such word as "fail"!—*Bulwer Lytton.*

FAITH.
It is impossible to be a hero in anything unless one is first a hero in faith.—*Jacobi.*

All sects, as far as reason will help them, gladly use it; when it fails them, they cry out it is a matter of faith, and above reason.—*Locke.*

Faith is not reason's labor, but repose.—
Young.

Judge not man by his outward manifestation of faith; for some there are who tremblingly reach out shaking hands to the guidance of faith; others who stoutly venture in the dark their human confidence, their leader, which they mistake for faith; some whose hope totters upon crutches; others who stalk into futurity upon stilts. The difference is chiefly constitutional with them.—*Lamb.*

Faith always implies the disbelief of a lesser fact in favor of a greater.—*Holmes.*

Faith, in order to be genuine and of any real value, must be the offspring of that divine love which Jesus manifested when he prayed for his enemies on the cross.—*Hosea Ballou.*

True faith nor biddeth nor abideth form.—
Bailey.

Faith and works are necessary to our spiritual life as Christians, as soul and body are to our natural life as men; for faith is the soul of religion, and works the body.— *Colton.*

Faith loves to lean on time's destroying arm.
Holmes.

Faith is the key that unlocks the cabinet of God's treasures; the king's messenger from the celestial world, to bring all the supplies we need out of the fulness that there is in Christ.—
. *J. Stephens.*

Faith may rise into miracles of might, as some few wise men have shown; faith may sink into credulities of weakness, as the mass of fools have witnessed.—*Tupper.*

Faith is necessary to victory.—*Hazlitt.*

It is by faith that poetry, as well as devotion, soars above this dull earth; that imagination breaks through its clouds, breathes a purer air, and lives in a softer light.—*Henry Giles.*

Faith is a certain image of eternity. All things are present to it, — things past, and things to come.—*Jeremy Taylor.*

Faith is the subtle chain that binds us to the Infinite.—*Mrs. E. Oakes Smith.*

Faith builds a bridge across the gulf of death, to break the shock blind nature cannot shun, and lands thought smoothly on the further shore.—*Young.*

The light of genius is sometimes so resplendent as to make a man walk through life, amid glory and acclamation ; but it burns very dimly and low when carried into " the valley of the shadow of death." But faith is like the evening star, shining into our souls the more brightly, the deeper is the night of death in which they sink.—*Mountford.*

The power of faith will often shine forth the most when the character is naturally weak.— *Hare.*

If thy faith have no doubts, thou hast just cause to doubt thy faith ; and if thy doubts have no hope, thou hast just reason to fear despair ; when therefore thy doubts shall exercise thy faith, keep thy hopes firm to qualify thy doubts ; so shall thy faith be secured from doubts ; so shall thy doubts be preserved from despair.— *Quarles.*

For modes of faith let graceless zealots fight. *Pope.*

In our age faith and charity are found, but they are found apart. We tolerate everybody, because we doubt everything ; or else we tolerate nobody, because we believe something.— *Mrs. E. B. Browning.*

Man is not made to question, but adore.— *Young.*

In your intercourse with sects, the sublime and abstruse doctrines of Christian belief belong to the Church ; but the faith of the individual, centred in his heart, is, or may be, collateral to them. Faith is subjective.—*Coleridge.*

Some wish they did ; but no man disbelieves. *Young.*

Never yet did there exist a full faith in the Divine Word (by whom light as well as immortality was brought into the world) which did not expand the intellect, while it purified the heart, — which did not multiply the aims and objects of the understanding, while it fixed and simplified those of the desires and passions.— *Coleridge.*

There is one inevitable criterion of judgment touching religious faith in doctrinal matters. Can you reduce it to practice ? If not, have none of it.—*Hosea Ballou.*

As the flower is before the fruit, so is faith before good works.— *Whately.*

Lay not the plummet to the line ; religion hath no landmarks ; no human keenness can discern the subtle shades of faith.—*Tupper.*

Faith is the substance of things hoped for, the evidence of things not seen.—*Bible.*

Faith converses with the angels, and antedates the hymns of glory ; every man that hath this grace is as certain that there are glories for him, if he persevere in duty, as if he had heard and sung the thanksgiving song for the blessed sentence of doomsday.—*Jeremy Taylor.*

The inventory of my faith for this lower world is soon made out. I believe in Him who made it.—*Madame Swetchine.*

Faith is the flame that lifts the sacrifice to heaven.—*J. Montgomery.*

Faith without works is like a bird without wings ; though she may hop with her companions on earth, yet she will never fly with them to heaven ; but when both are joined together, then doth the soul mount up to her eternal rest. *J. Beaumont.*

Faith, amid the disorders of a sinful life, is like the lamp burning in an ancient tomb — *Madame Swetchine.*

Faith is the root of all good works. A root that produces nothing is dead.—*Bishop Wilson.*

I know a courier, swift and sure, who will carry us to the absent, — faith. He knows the road ! have no fear ; he will not stumble or stray. *Madame de Gasparin.*

The steps of faith fall on the seeming void, and find the rock beneath.—*Whittier.*

Let us fear the worst, but work with faith ; the best will always take care of itself.— *Victor Hugo.*

Faith is letting down our nets into the untransparent deeps, at the Divine command, not knowing what we shall take.—*Faber.*

Have you not observed that faith is generally strongest in those whose character may be called the weakest ?—*Madame de Staël.*

Faith affirms many things, respecting which the senses are silent, but nothing that they deny. It is superior, but never opposed to their testimony.—*Pascal.*

Faith is a homely, private capital ; as there are public savings-banks and poor funds, out of which in times of want we can relieve the necessities of individuals, so here the faithful take their coin in peace.—*Goethe.*

Love is a bodily shape ; and Christian works are no more than animate faith and love, as flowers are the animate spring-tide.—*Longfellow.*

Faith consists in believing things because they are impossible. Faith is nothing more than submissive or deferential incredulity.—*Voltaire.*

There was never found in any age of the world either philosopher or sect, or law or discipline, which did so highly exalt the public good as the Christian faith.—*Bacon.*

Faith is the pencil of the soul, that pictures heavenly things.—*Thomas Burbridge.*

Strike from mankind the principle of faith, and men would have no more history than a flock of sheep.—*Bulwer Lytton.*

FALSEHOOD.
Falsehood is susceptible of an infinity of combinations, but truth has only one mode of being.—*Rousseau.*

There is a set of harmless liars, frequently to be met with in company, who deal much in the marvellous. Their usual intention is to please and entertain ; but as men are most delighted with what they conceive to be the truth, these people mistake the means of pleasing, and incur universal blame.—*Hume.*

A few men are sufficient to broach falsehoods, which are afterwards innocently diffused by successive relaters.—*Johnson.*

Falsehood and death are synonymous.—
Bancroft.

The gain of lying is nothing else but not to be trusted of any, nor to be believed when we speak the truth.—*Sir Walter Raleigh.*

Past all shame, so past all truth.—
Shakespeare.

He who tells a lie is not sensible how great a task he undertakes ; for he must be forced to invent twenty more to maintain that one.—*Pope.*

Although the Devil be the father of lies, he seems, like other great inventors, to have lost much of his reputation by the continual improvements that have been made upon him.—
Swift.

Not the least misfortune in a prominent falsehood is the fact that tradition is apt to repeat it for truth.—*Hosea Ballou.*

O, what a goodly outside falsehood hath !—
Shakespeare.

Falsehood, like poison, will generally be rejected when administered alone ; but when blended with wholesome ingredients, may be swallowed unperceived.—*Whately.*

Falsehood, like the dry-rot, flourishes the more in proportion as air and light are excluded.
Whately.

To tell a falsehood is like the cut of a sabre ; for though the wound may heal, the scar of it will remain.—*Saadi.*

Falsehood avails itself of haste and uncertainty.—*Tacitus.*

Falsehood is never so successful as when she baits her hook with truth, and no opinions so fatally mislead us as those that are not wholly wrong, as no watches so effectually deceive the wearer as those that are sometimes right.—*Colton.*

Falsehood is cowardice, — truth is courage.
Hosea Ballou.

Falsehood is difficult to be maintained. When the materials of a building are solid blocks of stone, very rude architecture will suffice ; but a structure of rotten materials needs the most careful adjustment to make it stand at all.—*Whately.*

Cowards tell lies, and those that fear the rod.—*Herbert.*

If there were no falsehood in the world, there would be no doubt ; if there were no doubt, there would be no inquiry ; if no inquiry, no wisdom, no knowledge, no genius.—*Landor.*

Falsehood always endeavored to copy the mien and attitudes of truth.—*Johnson.*

A lie should be trampled on and extinguished wherever found. I am for fumigating the atmosphere when I suspect that falsehood, like pestilence, breathes around me.—*Carlyle.*

Falsehoods not only disagree with truths, but usually quarrel among themselves.—
Daniel Webster.

Every lie, great or small, is the brink of a precipice, the depth of which nothing but Omniscience can fathom.—*Rev. Dr. Reade.*

Woe to falsehood ! it affords no relief to the breast, like truth ; it gives us no comfort, pains him who forges it, and like an arrow directed by a god flies back and wounds the archer.—
Goethe.

False modesty is the most decent of all falsehoods.—*Chamfort.*

Falsehood is fire in stubble ; — it likewise turns all the light stuff around it into its own substance for a moment, one crackling, blazing moment, and then dies ; and all its contents are scattered in the wind, without place or evidence of their existence, as viewless as the wind which scatters them.—*Coleridge.*

FAME.

Fame is an undertaker that pays but little attention to the living, but bedizens the dead, furnishes out their funerals, and follows them to the grave.— *Colton.*

Celebrity is the chastisement of merit and the punishment of talent.—*Chamfort.*

It is the penalty of fame that a man must ever keep rising. "Get a reputation and then go to bed," is the absurdest of all maxims. "Keep up a reputation or go to bed," would be nearer the truth.— *Chapin.*

Better than fame is still the wish for fame, the constant training for a glorious strife.— *Bulwer Lytton.*

Fame often rests at first upon something accidental, and often, too, is swept away, or for a time removed; but neither genius nor glory is conferred at once, nor do they glimmer and fall, like drops in a grotto, at a shout.—*Landor.*

The breath of popular applause.—*Herrick.*

What is fame? The advantage of being known by people of whom you yourself know nothing, and for whom you care as little.— *Stanislaus.*

Unlike the sun, intellectual luminaries shine brightest after they set.— *Colton.*

Those who despise fame seldom deserve it. We are apt to undervalue the purchase we cannot reach, to conceal our poverty the better. It is a spark which kindles upon the best fuel, and burns brightest in the bravest breast.— *Jeremy Collier.*

It often happens that those of whom we speak least on earth are best known in heaven. *N. Caussin.*

Raised by fortune to a ridiculous visibility. *Grattan.*

To be read by bare inscriptions, like many in Grüter, — to hope for eternity by enigmatical epithets or first letters of our names, — to be studied by antiquarians who we were, and have new names given us like many of the mummies, are cold consolation unto the students of perpetuity, even by everlasting languages.— *T. Hughes.*

What a heavy burden is a name that has become too soon famous! — *Voltaire.*

In itself a shadow. Soon as caught, contemned; it shrinks to nothing in the grasp. Consult the ambitious, it is ambition's cure.— *Young.*

To have fame follow us is well, but it is not a desirable avant-courier.—*Balzac.*

The thirst after fame is greater than that after virtue; for who embraces virtue if you take away its rewards? —*Juvenal.*

Happy indeed the poet of whom, like Orpheus, nothing is known but an immortal name! Happy next, perhaps, the poet of whom, like Homer, nothing is known but the immortal works. The more the merely human part of the poet remains a mystery, the more willing is the reverence given to his divine mission.— *Bulwer Lytton.*

Fame is a good so wholly foreign to our natures that we have no faculty in the soul adapted to it, nor any organ in the body to relish it; an object of desire placed out of the possibility of fruition.—*Addison.*

Though fame is smoke, its fumes are frankincense to human thoughts.—*Byron.*

Fame is the inheritance, not of the dead, but of the living. It is we who look back with lofty pride to the great names of antiquity, who drink of that flood of glory as of a river, and refresh our wings in it for future flight.—*Hazlitt.*

He that will sell his fame will also sell the public interest.—*Solon.*

In fame's temple there is always a niche to be found for rich dunces, importunate scoundrels, or successful butchers of the human race.— *Zimmermann.*

What is fame? a fancied life in others' breath.—*Pope.*

If opinion hath lighted the lamp of thy name, endeavor to encourage it with thy own oil, lest it go out and stink; the chronical disease of popularity is shame; if thou be once up, beware; from fame to infamy is a beaten road. — *Quarles.*

Fame is the perfume of heroic deeds.— *Socrates.*

The fame which bids fair to live the longest resembles that which Horace attributes to Marcellus, whose progress he compares to the silent, imperceptible growth of a tree.— *W. B. Clulow.*

There is no less danger from great fame than from infamy.—*Tacitus.*

Fame is like a river, that beareth up things light and swollen, and drowns things weighty and solid; but if persons of quality and judgment concur, then it filleth all round about, and will not easily away; for the odors of ointments are more durable than those of flowers.— *Bacon.*

Men think highly of those who rise rapidly in the world; whereas nothing rises quicker than dust, straw, and feathers.—*Hare.*

Fame is the shame of immortality, and is itself a shadow.—*Young.*

Fame is not won on downy plumes nor under canopies ; the man who consumes his days without obtaining it leaves such mark of himself on earth as smoke in air or foam on water.—*Dante.*

I awoke one morning and found myself famous.—*Byron.*

It is a very indiscreet and troublesome ambitiou which cares so much about fame ; about what the world says of us ; to be always looking in the faces of others for approval ; to be always anxious about the effect of what we do or say ; to be always shouting, to hear the echoes of our own voices.—*Longfellow.*

Fame, — next grandest word to God ! — *Alexander Smith.*

I am not covetous for gold ; but if it be a sin to covet honor, I am the most offending soul alive.—*Shakespeare.*

If fame is only to come after death, I am in no hurry for it.—*Martial.*

Fame may be compared to a scold ; the best way to silence her is to let her alone, and·she will at last be out of breath in blowing her own trumpet.—*Fuller.*

Milton neither aspired to present fame, nor even expected it ; but (to use his own words) his high ambition was "to leave something so written to after ages, that they should not willingly let it die." And Cato finely observed, he would much rather that posterity should inquire why no statues were erected to him, than why they were.—*Colton.*

Fame, — a flower upon a dead man's heart.— *Motherwell.*

A few words upon a tombstone, and the truth of those not to be depended on.—*Bovee.*

The greatest can but blaze, and pass away.— *Pope.*

After upwards of two thousand years Epicurus has been exonerated from the reproach that the doctrines of his philosophy recommended the pleasures of sensuality and voluptuousness as the chief good. Calumny may rest on genius a considerable part of a world's duration ; what then is the value of fame ?— *W. B. Clulow.*

The way to fame is like the way to heaven, through much tribulation.—*Steele.*

As the pearl ripens in the obscurity of its shell, so ripens in the tomb all the fame that is truly precious.—*Landor.*

A man's heart must be very frivolous if the possession of fame rewards the labor to attain it. For the worst of reputation is that it is not palpable or present, — we do not feel or see or taste it. People praise us behind our backs, but we hear them not; few before our faces, and who is not suspicious of the truth of such praise ? —*Bulwer Lytton.*

He who would acquire fame must not show himself afraid of censure. The dread of censure is the death of genius.—*Simms.*

To be rich, to be famous ? do these profit a year hence, when other names sound louder than yours, when you lie hidden away under ground, along with the idle titles engraven on your coffin ? But only true love lives after you, follows your memory with secret blessings, or pervades you, and intercedes for you. *Non omnis moriar*, if, dying, I yet live in a tender heart or two ; nor am lost and hopeless, living, if a sainted departed soul still loves and prays for me.—*Thackeray.*

Never get a reputation for a small perfection if you are trying for fame in a loftier area.— *Bulwer Lytton.*

Men's fame is like their hair, which grows after they are dead, and with just as little use to them.—*George Villiers.*

He lives in fame that died in virtue's cause.— *Shakespeare.*

There is not in the world so toilsome a trade as fame ; life concludes before you have so much as sketched your work.—*Bruyère.*

Among the writers of all ages, some deserve fame, and have it ; others neither have nor deserve it ; some have it, not deserving ; others, though deserving, yet totally miss it, or have it not equal to their deserts.—*Milton.*

What is the end of fame ? it is but to fill a certain portion of uncertain paper.—*Byron.*

If a man do not erect in this age his own tomb ere he dies, he shall live no longer in monument than the bell rings and the widow weeps.—*Shakespeare.*

Who despises fame will soon renounce the virtues that deserve it.—*Mallet.*

Fame is a revenue payable only to our ghosts ; and to deny ourselves all present satisfaction, or to expose ourselves to so much hazard for this, were as great madness as to starve ourselves, or fight desperately for food, to be laid on our tombs after our death.—*Mackenzie.*

Fame is a shuttlecock. If it be struck only at one end of a room it will soon fall to the floor. To keep it up, it must be struck at both ends.—*Johnson.*

Death makes no conquest of this conqueror; for now he lives in fame though not in life.—
Shakespeare.

Common fame is the only liar that deserveth to have some respect still reserved to it; though she telleth many an untruth, she often hits right, and most especially when she speaketh ill of men.—*Saville.*

Fame is no plant that grows on mortal soil.—*Milton.*

Of present fame think little and of future less; the praises that we receive after we are buried, like the posies that are strewn over our grave, may be gratifying to the living, but they are nothing to the dead: the dead are gone either to a place where they hear them not, or where, if they do, they will despise them.—
Colton.

The aspiring youth that fired the Ephesian dome outlives in fame the pious fool that raised it.—*Colley Cibber.*

Fame, they tell you, is air; but without air there is no life for any; without fame there is none for the best.—*Landor.*

To some characters, fame is like an intoxicating cup placed to the lips, — they do well to turn away from it who fear it will turn their heads. But to others fame is " love disguised," the love that answers to love in its widest, most exalted sense.—*Mrs. Jameson.*

There is no employment in the world so laborious as that of making to one's self a great name; life ends before one has scarcely made the first rough draught of his work.—*Bruyère.*

To get a name can happen but to few. A name, even in the most commercial nation, is one of the few things which cannot be bought. It is the free gift of mankind, which must be deserved before it will be granted, and is at last unwillingly bestowed.—*Johnson.*

The only pleasure of fame is that it proves the way to pleasure; and the more intellectual our pleasure, the better for the pleasure and for us too.—*Byron.*

Time has a doomsday book, upon whose pages he is continually recording illustrious names. But as often as a new name is written there, an old one disappears. Only a few stand in illuminated characters never to be effaced.—
Longfellow.

I have learned to prize the quiet lightning deed, not the applauding thunder at its heels, which men call fame.—*Alexander Smith.*

Of all the possessions of this life fame is the noblest; when the body has sunk into the dust the great name still lives.—*Schiller.*

Your fame is as the grass, whose hue comes and goes, and His might withers it by whose power it sprang from the lap of the earth.—
Dante.

Men's evil manners live in brass; their virtues we write in water.—*Shakespeare.*

Only the actions of the just smell sweet and blossom in the dust.—*James Shirley.*

FAMILIARITY.
When a man becomes familiar with his goddess, she quickly sinks into a woman.—
Addison.

The confidant of my vices is my master, though he were my valet.—*Goethe.*

All objects lose by too familiar a view.—
Dryden.

The ways suited to confidence are familiar to me, but not those that are suited to familiarity.—*Joubert.*

Make not thy friends too cheap to thee, nor thyself to thy friend.—*Fuller.*

Be thou familiar, but by no means vulgar.—
Shakespeare.

Familiarities are the aphides that imperceptibly suck out the juices intended for the germ of love.—*Landor.*

Though familiarity may not breed contempt, it takes off the edge of admiration.—*Hazlitt.*

Familiarity is a suspension of almost all the laws of civility, which libertinism has introduced into society under the notion of ease.—
Rochefoucauld.

Be not too familiar with thy servants; at first it may beget love, but in the end it will breed contempt.—*Fuller.*

FANATICISM.
Fanaticism is the child of false zeal and of superstition, the father of intolerance and of persecution.—*Rev. J. Fletcher.*

If you see one cold and vehement at the same time, set him down for a fanatic.—*Lavater.*

The downright fanatic is nearer to the heart of things than the cool and slippery disputant.—
Chapin.

Fanaticism is such an overwhelming impression of the ideas relating to the future world as disqualifies for the duties of life.—*Robert Hall.*

Fanaticism is a fire, which heats the mind indeed, but heats without purifying. It stimulates and ferments all the passions; but it rectifies none of them.— *Warburton.*

Everybody knows that fanaticism is religion caricatured ; bears, indeed, about the same relation to it that a monkey bears to a man ; yet, with many, contempt of fanaticism is received as a sure sign of hostility to religion.— *Whipple.*

That can never be reasoned down which was not reasoned up.—*Fisher Ames.*

What is fanaticism to-day is the fashionable creed to-morrow, and trite as the multiplication-table a week after.— *Wendell Phillips.*

The blind fanaticism of one foolish honest man may cause more evil than the united efforts of twenty rogues.—*Baron de Grimm.*

FANCY.
Fancy is imagination in her youth and adolescence. Fancy is always excursive ; imagination, not seldom, is sedate.—*Landor.*

Fancy, when once brought into religion, knows not where to stop. It is like one of those fiends in old stories which any one could raise, but which, when raised, could never be kept within the magic circle.— *Whately.*

So full of shapes is fancy, that it alone is high-fantastical.—*Shakespeare.*

Most marvellous and enviable is that fecundity of fancy which can adorn whatever it touches, which can invest naked fact and dry reasoning with unlooked-for beauty, make flowerets bloom even on the brow of the precipice, and, when nothing better can be had, can turn the very substance of rock itself into moss and lichens. This faculty is incomparably the most important for the vivid and attractive exhibition of truth to the minds of men.—*Fuller.*

Fancy rules over two thirds of the universe, the past and the future, while reality is confined to the present.—*Richter.*

It is the fancy, not the reason of things, that makes us so uneasy. It is not the place, nor the condition, but the mind alone, that can make anybody happy or miserable.— *L'Estrange.*

Our fancies are more giddy and unfirm, more longing, wavering, sooner lost and won, than women's are.—*Shakespeare.*

That queen of error, whom we call fancy and opinion, is the more deceitful because she does not always deceive. She would be the infallible rule of truth if she were the infallible rule of falsehood ; but being only most frequently in error, she gives no evidence of her real quality, for she marks with the same character both that which is true and that which is false.
Pascal.

Fancy restrained may be compared to a fountain, which plays highest by diminishing the aperture.— *Goldsmith.*

Touching everything lightly with the charm of poetry. – *Lucretius.*

Nothing is so atrocious as fancy without taste.—*Goethe.*

All impediments in fancy's course are motives of mere fancy.—*Shakespeare.*

The mere reality of life would be inconceivably poor without the charm of fancy, which brings in its bosom, no doubt, as many vain fears as idle hopes, but lends much oftener to the illusions it calls up a gay flattering hue than one which inspires terror.—
Wilhelm von Humboldt.

Fancy runs most furiously when a guilty conscience drives it.—*Fuller.*

Fancy has an extensive influence in morals. Some of the most powerful and dangerous feelings in nature, as those of ambition and envy, derive their principal nourishment from a cause apparently so trivial. Its effect on the common affairs of life is greater than might be supposed. Naked reality would scarcely keep the world in motion.—*W. B. Clulow.*

Every fancy you consult, consult your purse.
Franklin.

Every fancy that we would substitute for a reality is, if we saw aright, and saw the whole, not only false, but every way less beautiful and excellent than that which we sacrifice to it.—
Sterling.

Fancy borrows much from memory, and so looks back to the past.—*Ruffini.*

When my way is too rough for my feet, or too steep for my strength, I get off it to some smooth velvet path which fancy has scattered over with rosebuds of delights ; and, having taken a few turns in it, come back strengthened and refreshed.—*Sterne.*

A fretful fancy is constantly flinging its possessor into gratuitous tophets.— *W. R. Alger.*

FAREWELL.
For in that word, that fatal word, however we promise, hope, believe, there breathes despair.—*Byron.*

Where thou art gone, adieus and farewells are a sound unknown.— *Cowper.*

The bitter word, which closed all earthly friendships, and finished every feast of love, — farewell.—*Pollok.*

FASHION.
Seest thou not, I say, what a deformed thief this fashion is, how giddily he turns about all the hot bloods between fourteen and five-and-thirty ? —*Shakespeare.*

Fashion is a tyrant from which nothing frees us. We must suit ourselves to its fantastic tastes. But being compelled to live under its foolish laws, the wise man is never the first to follow, nor the last to keep it.—*Pascal.*

The fashion doth wear out more apparel than the man.—*Shakespeare.*

Fashion is gentility running away from vulgarity, and afraid of being overtaken by it. It is a sign the two things are not far asunder.—*Hazlitt.*

The secret of fashion is to surprise and never to disappoint.—*Bulwer Lytton.*

Thus grows up fashion, an equivocal semblance, the most puissant, the most fantastic and frivolous, the most feared and followed, and which morals and violence assault in vain.—*Emerson.*

Fashion is only the attempt to realize art in living forms and social intercourse.—*Holmes.*

Without depth of thought or earnestness of feeling or strength of purpose, living an unreal life, sacrificing substance to show, substituting the fictitious for the natural, mistaking a crowd for society, finding its chief pleasure in ridicule, and exhausting its ingenuity in expedients for killing time, fashion is among the last influences under which a human being who respects himself, or who comprehends the great end of life, would desire to be placed.—*Channing.*

Fashion seldom interferes with nature without diminishing her grace and efficiency.—*Tuckerman.*

The mere leader of fashion has no genuine claim to supremacy; at least, no abiding assurance of it. He has embroidered his title upon his waistcoat, and carries his worth in his watch-chain; and if he is allowed any real precedence for this it is almost a moral swindle,—a way of obtaining goods under false pretences.—*Chapin.*

A fop of fashion is the mercer's friend, the tailor's fool, and his own foe.—*Lavater.*

Manners have been somewhat cynically defined to be a contrivance of wise men to keep fools at a distance. Fashion is shrewd to detect those who do not belong to her train, and seldom wastes her attentions. Society is very swift in its instincts, and if you do not belong to it, resists and sneers at you, or quietly drops you.—*Emerson.*

Change of fashions is the tax which industry imposes on the vanity of the rich.—*Chamfort.*

Fashion is a great restraint upon your persons of taste and fancy; who would otherwise in the most trifling instances be able to distinguish themselves from the vulgar.—*Shenstone.*

Fashion is the veriest goddess of semblance and of shade; to be happy is of far less consequence to her worshippers than to appear so; even pleasure itself they sacrifice to parade, and enjoyment to ostentation.—*Colton.*

Fashion is, for the most part, nothing but the ostentation of riches.—*Locke.*

Fashion being the art of those who must purchase notice at some cheaper rate than that of being beautiful, loves to do rash and extravagant things. She must be forever new, or she becomes insipid.—*Lowell.*

Women cherish fashion because it rejuvenates them, or at least renews them.—*Madame de Preizeux.*

Those who seem to lead the public taste are, in general, merely outrunning it in the direction which it is spontaneously pursuing.—*Macaulay.*

We ought always to conform to the manners of the greater number, and so behave as not to draw attention to ourselves. Excess either way shocks, and every man truly wise ought to attend to this in his dress as well as language, never to be affected in anything, and follow without being in too great haste the changes of fashion.—*Molière.*

Every generation laughs at the old fashions, but follows religiously the new.—*Thoreau.*

I have been told by persons of experience in matters of taste, that the fashions follow a law of gradation, and are never arbitrary. The new mode is always only a step onward in the same direction as the last mode; and a cultivated eye is prepared for and predicts the new fashion.—*Emerson.*

We are taught to clothe our minds, as we do our bodies, after the fashion in vogue; and it is accounted fantastical, or something worse, not to do so.—*Locke.*

Where doth the world thrust forth a vanity (so it be new, there is no respect how vile) that is not quickly buzzed into the ears?—*Shakespeare.*

It is the rule of rules, and the general law of all laws, that every person should observe those of the place where he is.—*Montaigne.*

He alone is a man who can resist the genius of the age, the tone of fashion with vigorous simplicity and modest courage.—*Lavater.*

Fashion is the science of appearances, and it inspires one with the desire to seem rather than to be.—*Chapin.*

There would not be so much harm in the giddy following the fashions, if somehow the wise could always set them.—*Bovee.*

Avoid singularity. There may often be less vanity in following the new modes than in adhering to the old ones. It is true that the foolish invent them, but the wise may conform to, instead of contradicting them.—*Joubert.*

FATE.

What fates impose, that men must needs abide ; it boots not to resist both wind and tide.
Shakespeare.

God overrules all mutinous accidents, brings them under his laws of fate, and makes them all serviceable to his purpose.—*Marcus Antoninus.*

Heaven from all creatures hides the book of fate.—*Pope.*

The world throws its life into a hero or a shepherd, and puts him where he is wanted. Dante and Columbus were Italians in their time ; they would be Russians or Americans to-day.—*Emerson.*

Fate whirls on the bark, and the rough gale sweeps from the rising tide the lazy calm of thought.—*Bulwer Lytton.*

All things are in fate, yet all things are not decreed by fate.—*Plato.*

" Whosoever quarrels with his fate, does not understand it," says *Bettine* ; and among all her inspired sayings, she spoke none wiser.—
Mrs. L. M. Child.

There is a divinity that shapes our ends, rough-hew them how we will.—*Shakespeare.*

What must be shall be ; and that which is a necessity to him that struggles is little more than choice to him that is willing.—*Seneca.*

It is the best use of fate to teach a fatal courage. Go face the fire at sea, or the cholera in your friend's house, or the burglar in your own, or what danger lies in the way of duty, knowing you are guarded by the cherubim of destiny. If you believe in fate to your harm, believe it, at least, for your good.—*Emerson.*

Fate hath no voice but the heart's impulses.
Schiller.

All things are by fate, but poor blind man sees but a part of the chain, the nearest link, his eyes not carrying to that equal beam that poises all above.—*Dryden.*

The crown of manhood is a winter joy ; an evergreen, that stands the northern blast, and blossoms in the rigor of our fate.—*Young.*

Whatever may happen to thee, it was prepared for thee from all eternity ; and the implication of causes was from eternity spinning the thread of thy being and of that which is incident·to it.—*Marcus Antoninus.*

But, O vain boast ! who can control his fate ?—*Shakespeare.*

A strict belief in fate is the worst of slavery ; imposing upon our necks an everlasting lord or tyrant, whom we are to stand in awe of night and day ; on the other hand, there is some comfort that God will be moved by our prayers ; but this imports an inexorable necessity.—
Epicurus.

Fate with impartial hand turns out the doom of high and low ; her capacious urn is constantly shaking the names of all mankind.—*Horace.*

Fate is the friend of the good, the guide of the wise, the tyrant of the foolish, the enemy of the bad.—*W. R. Alger.*

FAULTS.

We are often more agreeable through our faults than through our good qualities.—
Rochefoucauld.

If the best man's faults were written on his forehead, he would draw his hat over his eyes.
Gray.

He who exhibits no faults is a fool or a hypocrite, whom we should mistrust. There are faults so intimately connected with fine qualities that they indicate them, and we do well not to correct them.—*Joubert.*

It is in nature's plague to spy into abuses ; and oft his jealousy shapes faults that are not.
Shakespeare.

There are some faults which, when well managed, make a greater figure than virtue itself.—*Rochefoucauld.*

It is not so much the being exempt from faults as the having overcome them that is an advantage to us ; it being with the follies of the mind as with weeds of a field, which, if destroyed and consumed upon the place where they grow, enrich and improve it more than if none had ever sprung there.—*Swift.*

Only those faults which we encounter in ourselves are insufferable to us in others.—
Madame Swetchine.

Why do we discover faults so much more readily than perfections ? —*Madame de Sévigné.*

Had we not faults of our own we should take less pleasure in observing those of others.
Rochefoucauld.

If we were faultless, we should not be so much annoyed by the defects of those with whom we associate. If we were to acknowledge honestly that we have not virtue enough to bear patiently with our neighbor's weaknesses, we should show our own imperfection, and this alarms our vanity.—*Fenelon.*

Just as you are pleased at finding faults, you are displeased at finding perfections.—
Lavater.

Best men oft are moulded out of faults.—
Shakespeare.

He shall be immortal who liveth till he be stoned by one without fault.—*Fuller.*

FEAR.

Why, what should be the fear? I do not set my life at a pin's fee; and for my soul, what can it do to that, being a thing immortal?—
Shakespeare.

All the passions seek that which nourishes them; fear loves the idea of danger.—*Joubert.*

Man begins life helpless. The babe is in paroxysms of fear the moment its nurse leaves it alone, and it comes so slowly to any power of self-protection that mothers say the salvation of the life and health of a young child is a perpetual miracle.—*Emerson.*

A certain degree of fear produces the same effects as rashness.—*Cardinal de Retz.*

Fear hath the common fault of a justice of peace, and is apt to conclude hastily from every slight circumstance, without examining the evidence on both sides.—*Fielding.*

I rather tell thee what is to be feared than what I fear; for always I am Cæsar.—
Shakespeare.

Noiseless as fear in a wide wilderness.—
Keats.

Such as are in immediate fear of losing their estates, of banishment, or of slavery, live in perpetual anguish, and lose all appetite and repose; whereas such as are actually poor slaves and exiles oftentimes live as merrily as men in a better condition; and so many people who, impatient of the perpetual alarms of fear, have hanged and drowned themselves give us sufficiently to understand that it is more importunate and insupportable than death itself.—*Montaigne.*

Fear has many eyes.—*Cervantes.*

Fear nothing but what thy industry may prevent; be confident of nothing but what fortune cannot defeat; it is no less folly to fear what is impossible to be avoided than to be secure when there is a possibility to be deprived.—*Quarles.*

Of all base passions, fear is most accursed.—
Shakespeare.

We must be afraid of neither poverty nor exile nor imprisonment; of fear itself only should we be afraid.—*Epictetus.*

I feel my sinews slackened with the fright, and a cold sweat trills down all over my limbs, as if I were dissolving into water.—*Dryden.*

From the moment fear begins I have ceased to fear.—*Schiller.*

In morals what begins in fear usually ends in wickedness; in religion what begins in fear usually ends in fanaticism. Fear, either as a principle or a motive, is the beginning of all evil.—*Mrs. Jameson.*

In time we hate that which we often fear.—
Shakespeare.

Fear guides more to their duty than gratitude; for one man who is virtuous from the love of virtue, from the obligation which he thinks he lies under to the Giver of all, there are ten thousand who are good only from their apprehension of punishment.—*Goldsmith.*

Present fears are less than horrible imaginings.—*Shakespeare.*

Fear is implanted in us as a preservative from evil; but its duty, like that of other passions, is not to overbear reason, but to assist it; nor should it be suffered to tyrannize in the imagination, to raise phantoms of horror, or to beset life with supernumerary distresses.—
Johnson.

Nothing routs us but the villany of our fears.—*Shakespeare.*

The thing in the world I am most afraid of is fear; and with good reason, that passion alone, in the trouble of it, exceeding all other accidents.—*Montaigne.*

Fear always springs from ignorance.—
Emerson.

In every mind where there is a strong tendency to fear there is a strong capacity to hate. Those who dwell in fear dwell next door to hate; and I think it is the cowardice of women which makes them such intense haters.—
Mrs. Jameson.

We often pretend to fear what we really despise, and more often to despise what we really fear.—*Colton.*

God planted fear in the soul as truly as he planted hope or courage. Fear is a kind of bell, or gong, which rings the mind into quick life and avoidance upon the approach of danger. It is the soul's signal for rallying.—*Beecher.*

Nothing is to be feared but fear.—*Bacon.*

Nothing is so rash as fear; and the counsels of pusillanimity very rarely put off, whilst they are always sure to aggravate, the evils from which they would fly.—*Burke.*

Good men have the fewest fears. He has but one great fear who fears to do wrong; he has a thousand who has overcome it.—*Bovee.*

Fear is far more painful to cowardice than death to true courage.—*Sir P. Sidney.*

Fear never was a friend to the love of God or man, to duty or conscience, truth, probity, or honor. It therefore can never make a good subject, a good citizen, or a good soldier, and, least of all, a good Christian; except the devils, who believe and tremble, are to be accounted good Christians.—*Henry Brooke.*

There is great beauty in going through life fearlessly. Half our fears are baseless, the other half discreditable.—*Bovee.*

Fear is the mother of foresight.—
Henry Taylor.

In how large a proportion of creatures is existence composed of one ruling passion, the most agonizing of all sensations, — fear.—
Bulwer Lytton.

There is nothing so ingenious as fear; it is even more ingenious than hatred, especially when its concern is with the preservation of money.—*Bayle St. John.*

Early and provident fear is the mother of safety.—*Burke.*

Fear sometimes adds wings to the heels, and sometimes nails them to the ground, and fetters them from moving.—*Montaigne.*

There is no fear in love; but perfect love casteth out fear, because fear hath torment.—
Bible.

Fearfulness, contrary to all other vices, maketh a man think the better of another, the worse of himself.—*Sir P. Sidney.*

Fear is the white-lipped sire of subterfuge and treachery.—*Mrs. Sigourney.*

Shun fear, it is the ague of the soul! a passion man created for himself, — for sure that cramp of nature could not dwell in the warm realms of glory.—*Aaron Hill.*

FEELINGS.

Feelings are like chemicals, — the more you analyze them the worse they smell. So it is best not to stir them up very much, only enough to convince one's self that they are offensively wrong, and then look away as far as possible, out of one's self, for a purifying power; and that we know can only come from Him who holds our hearts in his hands, and can turn us whither he will.—*Charles Kingsley.*

The feelings, like flowers and butterflies, last longer the later they are delayed.—*Richter.*

A word, a look, which at one time would make no impression, at another time wounds the heart; and like a shaft flying with the wind, pierces deep, which, with its own natural force, would scarce have reached the object aimed at.—*Sterne.*

When the heart is still agitated by the remains of a passion, we are more ready to receive a new one than when we are entirely cured.—
Rochefoucauld.

Every human feeling is greater and larger than the exciting cause.—*Coleridge.*

Some feelings are quite untranslatable; no language has yet been found for them. They gleam upon us beautifully through the dim twilight of fancy, and yet when we bring them close to us, and hold them up to the light of reason, lose their beauty all at once, as glow-worms which gleam with such a spiritual light in the shadows of evening, when brought in where the candles are lighted, are found to be only worms like so many others.—*Longfellow.*

Feelings come and go like light troops following the victory of the present; but principles, like troops of the line, are undisturbed, and stand fast.—*Richter.*

Life is a comedy to him who thinks, and a tragedy to him who feels.—*Horace Walpole.*

Fine feelings, without vigor of reason, are in the situation of the extreme feathers of a peacock's tail, — dragging in the mud.—
John Foster.

Our feelings were given us to excite to action, and when they end in themselves, they are impressed to no one good purpose that I know of.—*Bishop Sandford.*

The heart that is soonest awake to the flowers is always the first to be touched by the thorns.—*Moore.*

FICKLENESS.

There are three things a wise man will not trust, — the wind, the sunshine of an April day, and woman's plighted faith.—*Southey.*

He wears his faith but as the fashion of his hat; it ever changes with the next block.
Shakespeare.

We are all of us, in this world, more or less like St. January, whom the inhabitants of Naples worship one day, and pelt with baked apples the next.—*Madame Swetchine.*

It is plain there is not in nature a point of stability to be found; everything either ascends or declines; when wars are ended abroad, sedition begins at home; and when men are freed from fighting for necessity, they quarrel through ambition.—*Sir Walter Raleigh.*

Fickleness has its rise in the experience of the fallaciousness of present pleasures, and in the ignorance of the vanity of absent pleasures.—*Pascal.*

The uncertain glory of an April day.—
Shakespeare.

O perilous mouths, that bear in them one and the self-same tongue, either of commendation or approof! bidding the law make courtesy to their will; hooking both right and wrong to the appetite, to follow as it draws!—
Shakespeare.

Unstable as water, thou shalt not excel.—
Bible.

Irresolution loosens all the joints of a state; like an ague, it shakes not this or that limb, but all the body is at once in a fit. The irresolute man is lifted from one place to another, and hath no place left to rest on. He flecks from one egg to another; so hatcheth nothing, but addles all his actions.—*Feltham.*

FICTION.
Man is a poetical animal, and delights in fiction.—*Hazlitt.*

Addison acknowledged that he would rather inform than divert his reader; but he recollected that a man must be familiar with wisdom before he willingly enters on Seneca and Epictetus. Fiction allures him to the severe task by a gayer preface. Embellished truths are the illuminated alphabet of larger children.— *Willmott.*

FIDELITY.
Fidelity is the sister of justice.—*Horace.*

I am constant as the Northern Star, of whose true-fixed and resting quality there is no fellow in the firmament.—*Shakespeare.*

There is a third silent party to all our bargains. The nature and soul of things takes on itself the guaranty of the fulfilment of every contract, so that honest service cannot come to loss. If you serve an ungrateful master, serve him the more. Put God in your debt. Every stroke shall be repaid. The longer the payment is withholden, the better for you; for compound interest on compound interest is the rate and usage of this exchequer.—*Emerson.*

It is more difficult for a man to be faithful to his mistress when he is favored than when he is ill treated by her.—*Rochefoucauld.*

Trust reposed in noble natures obliges them the more.—*Dryden.*

It goes a great way towards making a man faithful, to let him understand that you think him so, and he that does but so much as suspect that I will deceive him gives me a sort of right to cozen him.—*Seneca.*

Nothing is more noble, nothing more venerable than fidelity. Faithfulness and truth are the most sacred excellences and endowments of the human mind.—*Cicero.*

FIRMNESS.
Firmness, both in sufferance and exertion, is a character which I would wish to possess. I have always despised the whining yelp of complaint, and the cowardly feeble resolve.—
Burns.

When firmness is sufficient, rashness is unnecessary.—*Napoleon.*

It is only persons of firmness that can have real gentleness; those who appear gentle are in general only of a weak character, which easily changes into asperity.—*Rochefoucauld.*

Firmness of purpose is one of the most necessary sinews of character, and one of the best instruments of success. Without it, genius wastes its efforts in a maze of inconsistencies.—
Chesterfield.

Rely on principles; walk erect and free, not trusting to bulk of body, like a wrestler; for one should not be unconquerable in the sense that an ass is. Who then is unconquerable? He whom the inevitable cannot overcome.—
Epictetus.

I know no real worth but that tranquil firmness which seeks dangers by duty, and braves them without rashness.—*Stanislaus.*

FLATTERY.
Men find it more easy to flatter than to praise.—*Richter.*

Know thyself, thy evil as thy good, and flattery shall not harm thee; yea, her speech shall be a warning, a humbling, and a guide. For wherein thou lackest most, there chiefly will the sycophant commend thee.—*Tupper.*

O that men's ears should be to counsel deaf, but not to flattery!—*Shakespeare.*

Of all wild beasts, preserve me from a tyrant; and of all tame—a flatterer.—
Ben Jonson.

Flatterers are the worst kind of traitors, for they will strengthen thy imperfections, encourage thee in all evils, correct thee in nothing, but so shadow and paint thy follies and vices as thou shalt never, by their will, discover good from evil, or vice from virtue.—
Sir Walter Raleigh.

A man finds no sweeter voice in all the world than that which chants his praise.—
Fontenelle.

If any man flatters me, I'll flatter him again, though he were my best friend.—*Franklin.*

It is scarcely credible to what degree discernment may be dazzled by the mist of pride, and wisdom infatuated by the intoxication of flattery; or how low the genius may descend by successive gradations of servility, and how swiftly it may fall down the precipice of falsehood.—*Johnson.*

If we would not flatter ourselves, the flattery of others could not harm us.—*Rochefoucauld.*

Flattery, though a base coin, is the necessary pocket money at court; where, by custom and consent, it has obtained such a currency that it is no longer a fraudulent, but a legal payment.—*Chesterfield.*

Flattery is the bellows blows up sin; the thing the which is flattered, but a spark, to which the blast gives heat and stronger glowing.—*Shakespeare.*

One would scarce ever be pleased if he did not flatter himself.—*Rochefoucauld.*

Flattery corrupts both the receiver and the giver; and adulation is not of more service to the people than to kings.—*Burke.*

There is nothing which so poisons princes as flattery, nor anything whereby wicked men more easily obtain credit and favor with them.—*Montaigne.*

Let the passion of flattery be ever so inordinate, the supply can keep pace with the demand, and in the world's great market, in which wit and folly drive their bargains with each other, there are traders of all sorts.—*Cumberland.*

No man flatters the woman he truly loves.—*Tuckerman.*

Hold! No adulation; it is the death of virtue! Who flatters is of all mankind the lowest, save he who courts the flattery.—*Hannah More.*

A flatterer is the shadow of a fool.—*Sir Thomas Overbury.*

To be flattered is grateful, even when we know that our praises are not believed by those who pronounce them; for they prove at least our power, and show that our favor is valued, since it is purchased by the meanness of falsehood.—*Johnson.*

Flattery is no more than what raises in a man's mind an idea of a preference which he has not.—*Burke.*

Delicious essence! how refreshing art thou to nature! how strongly are all its powers and all its weaknesses on thy side! how sweetly dost thou mix with the blood, and help it through the most difficult and tortuous passages to the heart!—*Sterne.*

Nothing is so great an instance of ill-manners as flattery. If you flatter all the company, you please none; if you flatter only one or two, you affront the rest.—*Swift.*

Applause is of too coarse a nature to be swallowed in the gross, though the extract or tincture be ever so agreeable.—*Shenstone.*

Flattery is like a painted armor, designed for show and not for use.—*Socrates.*

Flatterers of every age resemble those African tribes of which the credulous Pliny speaks, who made men, animals, and even plants perish, while fascinating them with praises.—*Richter.*

We sometimes hate what we hate flattery, when we only hate the manner in which we have been flattered.—*Rochefoucauld.*

Imitation is the sincerest of flattery.—*Colton.*

It is better to fall among crows than flatterers; for those devour the dead only, these the living.—*Antisthenes.*

The flatterer easily insinuates himself into the closet, while honest merit stands shivering in the hall or antechamber.—*Jane Porter.*

We must define flattery and praise; they are distinct. Trajan was encouraged to virtue by the panegyric of Pliny; Tiberius became obstinate in vice from the flattery of the senators.—*Louis the Sixteenth.*

There is not one of us that would not be worse than kings, if so continually corrupted as they are with a sort of vermin called flatterers.—*Montaigne.*

Some indeed there are, who profess to despise all flattery, but even these are, nevertheless, to be flattered, by being told that they do despise it.—*Colton.*

No flattery, boy! an honest man cannot live by it; it is a little, sneaking art, which knaves use to cajole and soften fools withal.—*Otway.*

No visor does become black villany so well as soft and tender flattery.—*Shakespeare.*

Allow no man to be so free with you as to praise you to your face. Your vanity by this means will want its food. At the same time your passion for esteem will be more fully gratified; men will praise you in their actions; where you now receive one compliment, you will then receive twenty civilities.—*Steele.*

Flattery is like base coin; it impoverishes him who receives it.—*Madame Voillez.*

The rich man despises those who flatter him too much, and hates those who do not flatter him at all.—*Talleyrand.*

There is no detraction worse than to over-praise a man, for if his worth prove short of what report doth speak of him, his own actions are ever giving the lie to his honor.—*Feltham.*

When I tell him he hates flattery, he says he does, being then most flattered.—*Shakespeare.*

I must be tolerably sure, before I congratulate men upon a blessing, that they have really received one.—*Burke.*

If you had told Sycorax that her son Caliban was as handsome as Apollo, she would have been pleased, witch as she was.—
Thackeray.

Among all the diseases of the mind, there is not one more epidemical or more pernicious than the love of flattery.—*Steele.*

The lie that flatters I abhor the most.—
Cowper.

Praise not people to their faces, to the end that they may pay thee in the same coin. This is so thin a cobweb that it may with little difficulty be seen through; it is rarely strong enough to catch flies of any considerable magnitude.—
Fuller.

Flatterers are the bosom enemies of princes.
South.

A flatterer is said to be a beast that biteth smiling. But it is hard to know them from friends, they are so obsequious and full of pro-testations; for as a wolf resembles a dog, so doth a flatterer a friend.—*Sir Walter Raleigh.*

Flattery, which was formerly a vice, is now grown into a custom.—*Publius Syrus.*

Beware of flattery; it is a flowery weed which oft offends the very idol vice whose shrine it would perfume.—*Fenton.*

The most dangerous of all flattery is the inferiority of those about us.—
Madame Swetchine.

Adroit observers will find that some who affect to dislike flattery may yet be flattered indirectly by a well-seasoned abuse and ridicule of their rivals.—*Colton.*

The love of flattery in most men proceeds from the mean opinion they have of themselves; in women, from the contrary.—*Swift.*

There is no tongue that flatters like a lov-er's; and yet in the exaggeration of his feelings flattery seems to him commonplace. Strange and prodigal exuberance, which soon exhausts itself by overflowing.—*Bulwer Lytton.*

Men are like stone jugs,— you may lug them where you like by the ears.—*Johnson.*

There is no flattery so adroit or effectual as that of implicit assent.—*Hazlitt.*

Give me flattery, — flattery the food of courts, that I may rock him, and lull him in the down of his desires.—*Beaumont.*

Not kings alone, — the people, too, have their flatterers.—*Mirabeau.*

Flattery is often a traffic of mutual mean-ness where, although both parties intend decep-tion, neither are deceived; since words that cost little are exchanged for hopes that cost less. But we must be careful how we flatter fools too little, or wise men too much; for the flatterer must act the very reverse of the physician, and administer the strongest dose only to the weak-est patient.—*Colton.*

Flatterers are the worst kind of enemies.—
Tacitus.

It requires but little acquaintance with the heart to know that woman's first wish is to be handsome; and that, consequently, the readiest method of obtaining her kindness is to praise her beauty.—*Johnson.*

The most skilful flattery is to let a person talk on, and be a listener.—*Addison.*

Meddle not with him that flattereth with his lips.—*Bible.*

Flattery is an ensnaring quality, and leaves a very dangerous impression. It swells a man's imagination, entertains his vanity, and drives him to a doting upon his own person.—
Jeremy Collier.

A fool flatters himself, a wise man flatters the fool.—*Bulwer Lytton.*

The most subtle flattery that a woman can receive is that conveyed by actions, not by words.—*Madame Necker.*

Parent of wicked, bane of honest deeds.—
Prior.

Christian! thou knowest thou carriest gun-powder about thee. Desire them that carry fire to keep at a distance. It is a dangerous crisis, when a proud heart meets with flattering lips.—*Flavel.*

When flatterers meet the Devil goes to din-ner.—*De Foe.*

People generally despise where they flatter, and cringe to those they would gladly overtop; so that truth and ceremony are two things.—
Marcus Antoninus.

It hath been well said that the arch-flatterer, with whom all the petty flatterers have intelli-gence, is a man's self.—*Bacon.*

Flattery is never so agreeable as to our blind side. Commend a fool for his wit, or a knave for his honesty, and they will receive you into their bosoms.—*Fielding.*

FLOWERS.

Sweet flowers are slow, and weeds make haste.—*Shakespeare.*

How the universal heart of man blesses flowers! They are wreathed round the cradle, the marriage altar, and the tomb. The Persian in the far East delights in their perfume, and writes his love in nosegays ; while the Indian child of the far West claps his hands with glee as he gathers the abundant blossoms, — the illuminated scriptures of the prairies. The cupid of the ancient Hindoos tipped his arrows with flowers, and orange flowers are a bridal crown with us, a nation of yesterday.—
Mrs. L. M. Child.

The budding rose above the rose full blown.
Wordsworth.

The instinctive and universal taste of mankind selects flowers for the expression of its finest sympathies, their beauty and their fleetingness serving to make them the most fitting symbols of those delicate sentiments for which language itself seems almost too gross a medium.—
Hillard.

Flowers are love's truest language.—
Park Benjamin.

There is not the least flower but seems to hold up its head, and to look pleasantly, in the secret sense of the goodness of its Heavenly Maker.—*South.*

Floral apostles ! that in dewy splendor weep without woe, and blush without a crime.—
Horace Smith.

There is to the poetical sense a ravishing prophecy and winsome intimation in flowers that now and then, from the influence of mood or circumstance, reasserts itself like the reminiscence of childhood, or the spell of love.—
Tuckerman.

A snow of blossoms, and a wild of flowers.—
Tickell.

Flowers are the sweetest things that God ever made and forgot to put a soul into.—
Beecher.

The little flower which sprung up through the hard pavement of poor Picciola's prison was beautiful from contrast with the dreary sterility which surrounded it. So here, amid rough walls, are there fresh tokens of nature. And O the beautiful lessons which flowers teach to children, especially in the city! The child's mind can grasp with ease the delicate suggestions of flowers.—*Chapin.*

To analyze the charms of flowers is like dissecting music ; it is one of those things which it is far better to enjoy than to attempt to understand.—*Tuckerman.*

The plants look up to heaven, from whence they have their nourishment.—*Shakespeare.*

Flowers so strictly belong to youth that we adult men soon come to feel that their beautiful generations concern not us ; we have had our day ; now let the children have theirs.—
Emerson.

The moss-clad violet, fragrant and concealed like hidden charity.—*J. F. Hollings.*

Flowers and fruits are always fit presents, — flowers, because they are a proud assertion that a ray of beauty outvalues all the utilities of the world.—*Emerson.*

There is to me a daintiness about early flowers that touches me like poetry. They blow out with such a simple loveliness among the common herbs of pastures, and breathe their lives so unobtrusively, like hearts whose beatings are too gentle for the world.—*Willis.*

In Eastern lands they talk in flowers, and they tell in a garland their loves and cares.—
Percival.

" If flowers have souls," said Undine, " the bees, whose nurses they are, must seem to them darling children at the breast. I once fancied a paradise for the spirits of departed flowers." " They go," answered I, "not into paradise, but into a middle state ; the souls of lilies enter into maidens' foreheads, those of hyacinths and forget-me-nots dwell in their eyes, and those of roses in their lips."—*Richter.*

Sweet flower, thou tellest how hearts as pure and tender as thy leaf, as low and humble as thy stem, will surely know the joy that peace imparts.—*Percival.*

Lovely flowers are the smiles of God's goodness.— *Wilberforce.*

Flowers should deck the brow of the youthful bride, for they are in themselves a lovely type of marriage. They should twine round the tomb, for their perpetually renewed beauty is a symbol of the resurrection. They should festoon the altar, for their fragrance and their beauty ascend in perpetual worship before the Most High.—*Mrs. L. M. Child.*

To me the meanest flower that blows can give thoughts that do often lie too deep for tears.
Wordsworth.

The herb feeds upon the juice of a good soil, and drinks in the dew of heaven as eagerly, and thrives by it as effectually, as the stalled ox that tastes everything that he eats or drinks.—*South.*

Look how the blue-eyed violets glance love to one another!—*T. B. Read.*

If thou wouldest attain to thy highest, go look upon a flower; what that does willessly, that do thou willingly.—*Schiller.*

These stars of earth, these golden flowers.— *Longfellow.*

Doubtless botany has its value; but the flowers knew how to preach divinity before men knew how to dissect and botanize them; they are apt to stop preaching, though, so soon as we begin to dissect and botanize them.— *H. N. Hudson.*

Foster the beautiful, and every hour thou callest new flowers to birth.—*Schiller.*

For the Infinite has sowed his name in the heavens in burning stars, but on the earth he has sowed his name in tender flowers.—*Richter.*

Where flowers degenerate man cannot live. *Napoleon.*

Full many a flower is born to blush unseen, and waste its sweetness on the desert air.— *Gray.*

He must have an artist's eye for color and form who can arrange a hundred flowers as tastefully, in any other way, as by strolling through a garden, and picking here one and there one, and adding them to the bouquet in the accidental order in which they chance to come. Thus we see every summer day the fair lady coming in from the breezy side hill with gorgeous colors and most witching effects. If only she could be changed to alabaster, was ever a finer show of flowers in so fine a vase? But instead of allowing the flowers to remain as they were gathered, they are laid upon the table, divided, rearranged on some principle of taste, I know not what, but never again have that charming naturalness and grace which they first had.—*Beecher.*

It is with flowers as with moral qualities; the bright are sometimes poisonous; but, I believe, never the sweet.—*Hare.*

Flowers are like the pleasures of the world. *Shakespeare.*

Honey, by some sweet mystery of the dew, is born of air, in bosoms of the flowers, liquid, — serene.—*Giovanni Rucellai.*

. The breath of flowers is far sweeter in the air (where it comes and goes like the warbling of music) than in the hand.—*Bacon.*

Flowers never emit so sweet and strong a fragrance as before a storm. Beauteous soul! when a storm approaches thee, be as fragrant as a sweet-smelling flower.—*Richter.*

Your voiceless lips, O flowers, are living preachers, — each cup a pulpit, and each leaf a book.—*Horace Smith.*

Not a flower but shows some touch, in freckle, streak, or stain, of His unrivalled pencil. He inspires their balmy odors, and imparts their hues.—*Cowper.*

The flower of sweetest smell is shy and lowly.—*Wordsworth.*

Flowers are the bright remembrances of youth; they waft us back, with their bland odorous breath, the joyous hours that only young life knows, ere we have learnt that this fair earth hides graves. *Countess of Blessington.*

I regard them, as Charles the Emperor did Florence, that they are too pleasant to be looked upon except on holidays.—*Izaak Walton.*

Often a nosegay of wild-flowers, which was to us, as village children, a grove of pleasure, has in after years of manhood, and in the town, given us by its old perfume an indescribable transport back into godlike childhood; and how, like a flower-goddess, it has raised us into the first embracing Aurora-clouds of our first dim feelings!—*Richter.*

Emblems of our own great resurrection, emblems of the bright and better land.— *Longfellow.*

Every rose is an autograph from the hand of the Almighty God on this world about us. He has inscribed his thoughts in these marvellous hieroglyphics which sense and science have been these many thousand years seeking to understand.—*Theodore Parker.*

Happy are they who can create a rose-tree or erect a honeysuckle.—*Gray.*

Most gladly would I give the blood-stained laurel for the first violet which March brings us, the fragrant pledge of the new-fledged year.— *Schiller.*

How like they are to human things! — *Longfellow.*

A passion for flowers is, I really think, the only one which long sickness leaves untouched with its chilling influence.—*Mrs. Hemans.*

To cultivate a garden is to walk with God, to go hand in hand with Nature in some of her most beautiful processes, to learn something of her choicest secrets, and to have a more intelligent interest awakened in the beautiful order of her works elsewhere.—*Bovee.*

FOE.

He makes no friend who never made a foe.— *Tennyson.*

FOOLISHNESS.

There is a foolish corner even in the brain of the sage.—*Aristotle.*

Take my word for this, reader, and say a fool told it you, if you please, that he who hath not a dram of folly in his mixture hath pounds of much worse matter in his composition.—*Lamb.*

This peculiar ill property has folly, that it enlarges men's desires while it lessens their capacities.—*South.*

Folly loves the martyrdom of fame.—*Byron.*

There are follies as catching as contagious disorders.—*Rochefoucauld.*

Folly consists in the drawing of false conclusions from just principles, by which it is distinguished from madness, which draws just conclusions from false principles.—*Locke.*

In folly's cup still laughs the bubble joy.—*Pope.*

The wise man has his follies no less than the fool; but it has been said that herein lies the difference, — the follies of the fool are known to the world, but are hidden from himself; the follies of the wise are known to himself, but hidden from the world.—*Colton.*

He who lives without folly is not so wise as he imagines.—*Rochefoucauld.*

I find nonsense singularly refreshing.—*Talleyrand.*

Folly hath often the same results as wisdom; but wisdom would not engage in her school-room so expensive an assistant as calamity.—*Landor.*

He must be a thorough fool who can learn nothing from his own folly.—*Hare.*

To pardon those absurdities in ourselves which we cannot suffer in others is neither better nor worse than to be more willing to be fools ourselves than to have others so.—*Pope.*

Fortune makes folly her peculiar care.—*Churchill.*

When our follies afford equal delight to ourselves and those about us, what is there to be desired more? We cannot discover the vast advantage of "seeing ourselves as others see us." It is better to have a contempt for any one than for ourselves.—*Hazlitt.*

It is the folly of the world, constantly, which confounds its wisdom. Not only out of the mouths of babes and sucklings, but out of the mouths of fools and cheats, we may often get our truest lessons.—*Holmes.*

Letting down buckets into empty wells, and growing old with drawing nothing up.—*Cowper.*

Men of all ages have the same inclinations, over which reason exercises no control. Thus wherever men are found, there are follies, ay, and the same follies.—*Fontenelle.*

He who has been once very foolish will never be very wise.—*Montaigne.*

FOOLS.

People have no right to make fools of themselves, unless they have no relations to blush for them.—*Haliburton.*

A rogue is a roundabout fool.—*Coleridge.*

A fool is often as dangerous to deal with as a knave, and always more incorrigible.—*Colton.*

For not only is Fortune herself blind, but she generally causes those men to be blind whose interests she has more particularly embraced. Therefore they are often haughty and arrogant; nor is there anything more intolerable than a prosperous fool. And hence we often see that men who were at one time affable and agreeable are completely changed by prosperity, despising their old friends, and clinging to new.—*Cicero.*

A fool's bolt is soon shot.—*Shakespeare.*

Were I to be angry at men being fools, I could here find ample room for declamation; but, alas! I have been a fool myself; and why should I be angry with them for being something so natural to every child of humanity?—*Goldsmith.*

No creature smarts so little as a fool.—*Pope.*

There is in human nature generally more of the fool than of the wise; and therefore those faculties by which the foolish part of men's minds are taken are more potent.—*Bacon.*

The fool or knave that wears a title lies.—*Young.*

This world is full of fools, and he who would not wish to see one must not only shut himself up alone, but must also break his looking-glass.—*Boileau.*

The multitude of fools is a protection to the wise.—*St. Augustine.*

To succeed in the world, it is much more necessary to possess the penetration to discover who is a fool than to discover who is a clever man.—*Cato.*

Their heads sometimes so little, that there is no room for wit; sometimes so long, that there is no wit for so much room.—*Fuller.*

A fool always finds a greater fool to admire him.—*Boileau.*

A man of wit would often be much embarrassed without the company of fools.— *Rochefoucauld.*

As I do live by food, I met a fool, who laid him down, and basked him in the sun, who railed on lady fortune in good terms, in good set terms, — and yet a motley fool.— *Shakespeare.*

A fool at forty is a fool indeed! — *Young.*

Though thou shouldst bray a fool in a mortar among wheat with a pestle, yet will not his foolishness depart from him.—*Bible.*

All men are fools, and with every effort they differ only in the degree.—*Boileau.*

If men are to be fools, it were better that they were fools in little matters than in great; dulness, turned up with temerity, is a livery all the worse for the facings; and the most tremendous of all things is a magnanimous dunce. *Sydney Smith.*

None but a fool is always right.—*Hare.*

The fool doth think he is wise, but the wise man knows himself to be a fool.—*Shakespeare.*

There are certain people fated to be fools; they not only commit follies by choice, but are even constrained to do so by fortune.— *Rochefoucauld.*

A fool must now and then be right, by chance.—*Cowper.*

The greatest of fools is he who imposes on himself, and in his greatest concern thinks certainly he knows that which he has least studied, and of which he is most profoundly ignorant.— *Shaftesbury.*

Of all thieves fools are the worst; they rob you of time and temper.—*Goethe.*

Fools are very often united in the strictest intimacies, as the lighter kinds of woods are the most closely glued together.—*Shenstone.*

To the fool-king belongs the world.— *Schiller.*

Men are so completely fools by necessity that he is but a fool in a higher strain of folly who does not confess his foolishness.—*Pascal.*

Fools are not mad folks.—*Shakespeare.*

The imputation of being a fool is a thing which mankind, of all others, is the most impatient of, it being a blot upon the prime and specific perfection of human nature.—*South.*

There are more fools than wise men; and even in the wise men more folly than wisdom.— *Chamfort.*

A fool can neither eat nor drink, nor stand nor walk, nor, in short, laugh nor cry nor take snuff, like a man of sense. How obvious the distinction!—*Shenstone.*

Fools with bookish knowledge are children with edged weapons; they hurt themselves, and put others in pain.—*Zimmermann.*

I am always afraid of a fool. One cannot be sure that he is not a knave as well.—*Hazlitt.*

A fool who has a flash of wit creates astonishment and scandal, like hack-horses setting out to gallop.—*Chamfort.*

Always win fools first. They talk much; and what they have once uttered they will stick to; whereas there is always time, up to the last moment, to bring before a wise man arguments that may entirely change his opinion. *Helps.*

In sallies of badinage a polite fool shines; but in gravity he is as awkward as an elephant disporting.—*Zimmermann.*

FOOTSTEPS.

The flower she touched on dipped and rose. *Tennyson.*

The grass stoops not, she treads on it so light.—*Shakespeare.*

Footprints on the sands of time.— *Longfellow.*

Her treading would not bend a blade of grass, or shake the downy blow-ball from his stalk!—*Ben Jonson.*

FOPPERY.

Dandies, when first-rate, are generally very agreeable men.—*Bulwer Lytton.*

Nature has sometimes made a fool; but a coxcomb is always of a man's own making.— *Addison.*

The all-importance of clothes has sprung up in the intellect of the dandy, without effort, like an instinct of genius; he is inspired with cloth, a poet of cloth.—*Carlyle.*

FORBEARANCE.

It is a noble and great thing to cover the blemishes and to excuse the failings of a friend; to draw a curtain before his stains, and to display his perfections; to bury his weaknesses in silence, but to proclaim his virtues upon the house-top.—*South.*

Whosoever shall smite thee on thy right cheek, turn to him the other also.—*Bible.*

FORCE.

Who overcomes by force hath overcome but half his foe.—*Milton.*

Force rules the world, and not opinion; but opinion is that which makes use of force.— *Pascal.*

FORETHOUGHT.

To have too much forethought is the part of a wretch; to have too little is the part of a fool. *Cecil.*

As a man without forethought scarcely deserves the name of a man, so forethought without reflection is but a metaphorical phrase for the instinct of a beast.—*Coleridge.*

To fear the worst oft cures the worst.— *Shakespeare.*

It is only the surprise and newness of the thing which makes that misfortune terrible which by premeditation might be made easy to us. For that which some people make light by sufferance, others do by foresight.—*Seneca.*

FORGETFULNESS.

Men are men; the best sometimes forget.— *Shakespeare.*

The pyramids themselves, doting with age, have forgotten the names of their founders.— *Fuller.*

The world forgetting, by the world forgot! *Pope.*

Though the past haunt me as a spirit, yet I ask not to forget!—*Mrs. Hemans.*

Forget thyself to marble.—*Milton.*

It is far off; and rather like a dream than an assurance that my remembrance warrants.— *Shakespeare.*

It is sure the hardest science to forget!— *Pope.*

FORGIVENESS.

There is a manner of forgiveness so divine that you are ready to embrace the offender for having called it forth.—*Lavater.*

The rarer action is in virtue than in vengeance.—*Shakespeare.*

He that cannot forgive others breaks the bridge over which he must pass himself; for every man has need to be forgiven. *Lord Herbert.*

Often forgive others, but never thyself.— *Publius Syrus.*

A more glorious victory cannot be gained over another man than this, that when the injury began on his part, the kindness should begin on ours.—*Tillotson.*

The sun should not set upon our anger, neither should he rise upon our confidence. We should forgive freely, but forget rarely. I will not be revenged, and this I owe to my enemy; but I will remember, and this I owe to myself.—*Colton.*

To err is human; to forgive, divine.—*Pope.*

A brave man thinks no one his superior who does him an injury: for he has it then in his power to make himself his superior to the other by forgiveness.—*Drummond.*

It is easier for the generous to forgive than for offence to ask it.—*Thomson.*

It is necessary to repent for years in order to efface a fault in the eyes of men; a single tear suffices with God.—*Chateaubriand.*

The narrow soul knows not the godlike glory of forgiving.—*Rowe.*

The brave only know how to forgive; it is the most refined and generous pitch of virtue human nature can arrive at. Cowards have done good and kind actions, — cowards have even fought, nay, sometimes even conquered; but a coward never forgave. It is not in his nature; the power of doing it flows only from a strength and greatness of soul, conscious of its own force and security, and above the little temptations of resenting every fruitless attempt to interrupt its happiness.—*Sterne.*

We pardon as long as we love.— *Rochefoucauld.*

Of him that hopes to be forgiven, it is indispensably required that he forgive. It is, therefore, superfluous to urge any other motive. On this great duty eternity is suspended; and to him that refuses to practise it, the throne of mercy is inaccessible, and the Saviour of the world has been born in vain.—*Johnson.*

They who forgive most shall be most forgiven.—*Bailey.*

When thou forgivest, — the man who has pierced thy heart stands to thee in the relation of the sea-worm that perforates the shell of the muscle which straightway closes the wound with a pearl.—*Richter.*

If thou wouldst find much favor and peace with God and man, be very low in thine own eyes. Forgive thyself little, and others much. *Leighton.*

We forgive too little, forget too much.— *Madame Swetchine.*

It is in vain for you to expect, it is impudent for you to ask of God, forgiveness on your own behalf, if you refuse to exercise this forgiving temper with respect to others.—*Bishop Hoadly.*

God pardons like a mother, who kisses the offence into everlasting forgetfulness.—*Beecher.*

Humanity is never so beautiful as when praying for forgiveness, or else forgiving another.—*Richter.*

The truly great man is as apt to forgive as his power is able to revenge.—*Sir P. Sidney.*

If you bethink yourself of any crime, unreconciled as yet to heaven and grace, solicit for it straight.—*Shakespeare.*

There is an ugly kind of forgiveness in this world, — a kind of hedgehog forgiveness, shot out like quills. Men take one who has offended, and set him down before the blowpipe of their indignation, and scorch him, and burn his fault into him; and when they have kneaded him sufficiently with their fiery fists, then — they forgive him.—*Beecher.*

Young men soon give, and soon forget affronts; old age is slow in both.—*Addison.*

He who has not forgiven an enemy has never yet tasted one of the most sublime enjoyments of life.—*Lavater.*

Hath any wronged thee? be bravely revenged; slight it, and the work is begun; forgive it, and it is finished; he is below himself that is not above an injury.—*Quarles.*

Great souls forgive not injuries till time has put their enemies within their power, that they may show forgiveness is their own.—*Dryden.*

It is easier to forgive an enemy than a friend. *Madame Deluzy.*

" I can forgive, but I cannot forget," is only another way of saying " I will not forgive." A forgiveness ought to be like a cancelled note, torn in two and burned up, so that it never can be shown against the man.—*Beecher.*

That curse shall be — forgiveness! —*Byron.*

Forgiveness is commendable, but apply not ointment to the wound of an oppressor.—*Saadi.*

FORTITUDE.

Where true fortitude dwells, loyalty, bounty, friendship, and fidelity may be found.—*Gay.*

It is sufficient to have a simple heart in order to escape the harshness of the age, in order not to fly from the unfortunate; but it is to have some understanding of the imperishable law, to seek them in the forgetfulness against which they dare not complain, to prefer them in their ruin, to admire them in their struggles. *Sénancour.*

In struggling with misfortunes lies the true proof of virtue.—*Shakespeare.*

Fortitude has its extremes as well as the rest of the virtues, and, ought, like them, to be always attended by prudence.—*Voet.*

Learn to labor and to wait.—*Longfellow.*

The fortitude of a Christian consists in patience, not in enterprises which the poets call heroic, and which are commonly the effects of interest, pride, and worldly honor.—*Dryden.*

True fortitude I take to be the quiet possession of a man's self, and an undisturbed doing his duty, whatever evil besets or danger lies in his way.—*Locke*

The vulgar refuse or crouch beneath their load; the brave bear theirs without repining.—*Mallet.*

Fortitude implies a firmness and strength of mind, that enables us to do and suffer as we ought. It rises upon an opposition, and, like a river, swells the higher for having its course stopped.—*Jeremy Collier.*

True fortitude is seen in great exploits, that justice warrants and that wisdom guides.—*Addison.*

Fortitude is the guard and support of the other virtues; and without courage a man will scarce keep steady to his duty, and fill up the character of a truly worthy man.—*Locke*

Gird your hearts with silent fortitude, suffering yet hoping all things.—*Mrs. Hemans.*

Blessed are those whose blood and judgment are so well commingled that they are not a pipe for Fortune's finger to sound what stop she please.—*Shakespeare.*

Fortitude, itself an essential virtue, is a guard to every other virtue.—*Locke.*

Fortitude is not the appetite of formidable things, nor inconsult rashness; but virtue fighting for a truth, derived from knowledge of distinguishing good or bad causes.—*Nabb.*

Fortitude is the marshal of thought, the armor of the will, and the fort of reason.—*Bacon.*

Bid that welcome which comes to punish us, and we punish it, seeming to bear it lightly.—*Shakespeare.*

FORTUNE.

Will Fortune never come with both hands full and write her fair words still in foulest letters? She either gives a stomach, and no food, — such are the poor, in health; or else a feast, and takes away the stomach, — such are the rich, that have abundance and enjoy it not.—*Shakespeare.*

The less we deserve good fortune, the more we hope for it.—*Molière.*

What real good does an addition to a fortune already sufficient procure ? Not any. Could the great man, by having his fortune increased, increase also his appetites, then precedence might be attended with real amusement.—*Goldsmith.*

If fortune wishes to make a man estimable she gives him virtues; if she wishes to make him esteemed she gives him success.—*Joubert.*

Fortune does us neither good nor hurt; she only presents us the matter, and the seed, which our soul, more powerfully than she, turns and applies as she best pleases; being the sole cause and sovereign mistress of her own happy or unhappy condition.—*Montaigne*

Those who lament for fortune do not often lament for themselves.—*Voltaire.*

Fortune is said to be blind, but her favorites never are. Ambition has the eye of the eagle, prudence that of the lynx ; the first looks through the air, the last along the ground.—
Bulwer Lytton.

Fortune is brittle as glass, and when she is most refulgent, she is often most unexpectedly broken.—*Publius Syrus.*

The heavens do not send good haps in handfuls; but let us pick out our good by little, and with care, from out much bad, that still our little world may know its king.—*Sir P. Sidney.*

Fortune is like a market, where many times if you wait a little the price will fall.—*Bacon.*

This is most true, and all history bears testimony to it, that men may second Fortune, but they cannot thwart her, — they may weave her web, but they cannot break it.—*Machiavelli.*

A fortunate shepherd is nursed in a rude cradle in some wild forest, and, if fortune smile, has risen to empire. That other, swathed in purple by the throne, has at last, if fortune frown, gone to feed the herd.—*Metastasio.*

Fortune dreads the brave, and is only terrible to the coward.—*Seneca.*

It is a madness to make Fortune the mistress of events, because in herself she is nothing, but is ruled by Prudence.—*Dryden.*

Fortune, to show us her power in all things, and to abate our presumption, seeing she could not make fools wise, has made them fortunate.
Montaigne.

It has been remarked that almost every character which has excited either attention or pity has owed part of its success to merit, and part to a happy concurrence of circumstances in its favor. Had Cæsar or Cromwell exchanged countries, the one might have been a sergeant, and the other an exciseman.—*Goldsmith.*

Fortune, like a coy mistress, loves to yield her favors, though she makes us wrest them from her.—*Bovee.*

The bad fortune of the good turns their faces up to heaven ; and the good fortune of the bad bows their heads down to the earth.—*Saadi.*

O, how full of error is the judgment of mankind ! They wonder at results when they are ignorant of the reasons. They call it fortune when they know not the cause, and thus worship their own ignorance changed into a deity.—
Metastasio.

Many have been ruined by their fortunes ; many have escaped ruin by the want of fortune. To obtain it, the great have become little, and the little great.—*Zimmermann.*

Fortune does not change men; it only unmasks them.—*Madame Riccoboni.*

The good, we do it ; the evil, that is fortune ; man is always right, and destiny always wrong.
La Fontaine.

O Fortune, Fortune ! all men call thee fickle.
Shakespeare.

Fortune is ever seen accompanying industry, and is as often trundling in a wheelbarrow as lolling in a coach and six.—*Goldsmith.*

Fortune brings in some boats that are not steered.—*Shakespeare.*

It is with fortune as with fantastical mistresses, — she makes sport with those that are ready to die for her, and throws herself at the feet of others that despise her.—*J. Beaumont.*

That strumpet — Fortune.—*Shakespeare.*

The wheel of fortune turns incessantly round, and who can say within himself, I shall to-day be uppermost ? —*Confucius.*

What men usually say of misfortunes, that they never come alone, may with equal truth be said of good fortune; nay, of other circumstances which gather round us in a harmonious way, whether it arise from a kind of fatality, or that man has the power of attracting to himself things that are mutually related.—*Goethe.*

We do not commonly find men of superior sense amongst those of the highest fortune.—
Juvenal.

I have heard Cardinal Imperiali say : " There is no man whom Fortune does not visit once in his life ; but when she does not find him ready to receive her, she walks in at the door, and flies out at the window."—*Montesquieu.*

We do not know what is really good or bad fortune.—*Rousseau.*

The old Scythians painted blind Fortune's powerful hands with wings, to show her gifts come swift and suddenly, which, if her favorite be not swift to take, he loses them forever.—
Chapman.

Our probity is not less at the mercy of fortune than our property.—*Rochefoucauld.*

It cannot be denied but outward accidents conduce much to fortune's favor, — opportunity, death of others, occasion fitting virtue; but chiefly the mould of a man's fortune is in his own hands.—*Bacon.*

We rise to fortune by successive steps; we descend by only one.—*Stanislaus.*

A man is thirty years old before he has any settled thoughts of his fortune; it is not completed before fifty. He falls to building in his old age, and dies by the time his house is in a condition to be painted and glazed.—*Bruyère.*

Fortune! There is no fortune; all is trial, or punishment, or recompense, or foresight.—
Voltaire.

Men have made an all-powerful goddess of fortune, that they may attribute to her all their follies.—*Madame Necker.*

Fortune is the rod of the weak and the staff of the brave.—*Lowell.*

So quickly sometimes has the wheel turned round, that many a man has lived to enjoy the benefit of that charity which his own piety projected.—*Sterne.*

Though Fortune's malice overthrow my state, my mind exceeds the compass of her wheel.—*Shakespeare.*

There are some men who are Fortune's favorites, and who, like cats, light forever upon their legs.—*Colton.*

All our advantages are those of fortune; birth, wealth, health, beauty, are her accidents; and when we cry out against fate, it were well we should remember Fortune can take naught save what she gave.—*Byron.*

Every man is the architect of his own fortune.—*Sallust.*

In human life there is a constant change of fortune; and it is unreasonable to expect an exemption from the common fate. Life itself decays, and all things are daily changing.—
Plutarch.

There are some natures that will take hurt from any conditions of life; and the man that prosperity ripens into a spendthrift is precisely the man that poverty would have soured into a churl.—*Alexander Smith.*

The power of fortune is confessed only by the miserable, for the happy impute all their success to prudence or merit.—*Swift.*

It is we that are blind, not Fortune; because our eye is too dim to discern the mystery of her effects, we foolishly paint her blind, and hoodwink the providence of the Almighty.—
Sir Thomas Browne.

We treat Fortune like a mistress, — the more she yields, the more we demand.—
Madame Roland.

Fortune rules in all things, and advances and depresses things more out of her own will than right and justice.—*Sallust.*

Fortune, not wisdom, human life doth sway.
Cicero.

The way of fortune is like the milky way in the sky, which is a meeting or knot of a number of small stars, not seen asunder, but giving light together; so are there a number of little and scarce discerned virtues, or rather faculties and customs, that make men fortunate.—*Bacon.*

Dame Fortune, like most others of the female sex, is generally most indulgent to the nimble-mettled blockheads.—*Otway.*

Fortune has rarely condescended to be the companion of Genius; others find a hundred by-roads to her palace; there is but one open, and that a very indifferent one, for men of letters.—
Disraeli.

Good and bad fortune are found severally to visit those who have the most of the one or the other.—*Rochefoucauld.*

When Fortune means to men most good, she looks upon them with a threatening eye. —
Shakespeare.

They are generally better satisfied whom Fortune never favored, than those whom she has forsaken.—*Seneca.*

Fortune, like other females, prefers a lover to a master, and submits with impatience to control; but he that wooes her with opportunity and importunity will seldom court her in vain.
Colton.

Some are born great, some achieve greatness, and some have greatness thrust upon them.—*Shakespeare.*

We should manage our fortune like our constitution; enjoy it when good, have patience when bad, and never apply violent remedies but in cases of necessity.—*Rochefoucauld.*

The old saying is expressed with depth and significance: " On the pinnacle of fortune man does not long stand firm."—*Goethe.*

To be thrown upon one's own resources is to be cast in the very lap of fortune; for our faculties then undergo a development, and display an energy, of which they were previously unsusceptible.—*Franklin.*

Fortune gives too much to many, but to none enough.—*Martial.*

Lucky men are favorites of Heaven.—*Dryden.*

The moderation of fortunate people comes from the calm which good fortune gives to their tempers.—*Rochefoucauld.*

We are sure to get the better of Fortune if we do but grapple with her.—*Seneca.*

It requires greater virtues to support good than bad fortune.—*Rochefoucauld.*

FRAILTY.

Frailty, thy name is woman!—*Shakespeare.*

Though thou seest another openly offend, or even commit some enormous sin, yet thou must not from thence take occasion to value thyself for thy superior goodness; for thou canst not tell how long thou wilt be able to persevere in the narrow path of virtue. All men are frail, but thou shouldst reckon none so frail as thyself.—*Thomas à Kempis.*

Man with frailty is allied by birth.—
Bishop Lowth.

FRANCE.

The sun rises bright in France, and fair sets be.—*Allan Cunningham.*

Studious to please, and ready to submit; the supple Gaul was born a parasite.—*Johnson.*

A monarchy tempered by songs.—*Chamfort.*

France is a dog-hole, and it no more merits the tread of a man's foot.—*Shakespeare.*

Decayed in thy glory and sunk in thy worth.
Byron.

FRANKNESS.

He speaks home; you may relish him more in the soldier than in the scholar.—
Shakespeare.

It is wrong to believe that frank sentiments and the candor of the mind are the exclusive share of the young; they ornament oftentimes old age, upon which they seem to spread a chaste reflection of the modest graces of their younger days, where they shine with the same brightness as those flowers which are often seen peeping, fresh and laughing, from among ruins.—
Poincelot.

FRAUD.

All frauds, like the "wall daubed with untempered mortar," with which men think to buttress up an edifice, always tend to the decay of the system they are devised to support.—*Whately.*

Though fraud in all other actions be odious, yet in matters of war it is laudable and glorious, and he who overcomes his enemies by stratagem is as much to be praised as he who overcomes them by force.—*Machiavelli*

FREEDOM.

The man who stands upon his own soil, who feels, by the laws of the land in which he lives, — by the laws of civilized nations, — he is the rightful and exclusive owner of the land which he tills, is, by the constitution of our nature, under a wholesome influence, not easily imbibed from any other source.—
Edward Everett.

Void of freedom, what would virtue be?—
Lamartine.

The cause of freedom is identified with the destinies of humanity, and in whatever part of the world it gains ground by and by, it will be a common gain to all those who desire it.—
Kossuth.

There is no legitimacy upon earth but in a government which is the choice of the nation.—
Joseph Bonaparte.

The sea, as well as air, is a free and common thing to all; and a particular nation cannot pretend to have the right to the exclusion of all others, without violating the rights of nature and public usage.—*Queen Elizabeth*

We do not know of how much a man is capable if he has the will, and to what point he will raise himself if he feels free.—*J. von Müller.*

The man who seeks freedom for anything but freedom's self is made to be a slave.—
De Tocqueville.

The water-lily, in the midst of waters, opens its leaves and expands its petals, at the first pattering of the shower, and rejoices in the rain-drops with a quicker sympathy than the packed shrubs in the sandy desert.—*Coleridge*

None are more hopelessly enslaved than those who falsely believe they are free.—*Goethe.*

The greatest glory of a free-born people is to transmit that freedom to their children.—
Havard.

To have freedom is only to have that which is absolutely necessary to enable us to be what we ought to be, and to possess what we ought to possess.—*Rahel.*

Countries are well cultivated, not as they are fertile, but as they are free.—*Montesquieu.*

Whatever natural right men may have to freedom and independency, it is manifest that some men have a natural ascendency over others.—*Lord Greville.*

Freedom is the ferment of freedom. The moistened sponge drinks up water greedily; the dry one sheds it.—*Holmes.*

Progress, the growth of power, is the end and boon of liberty; and, without this, a people may have the name, but want the substance and spirit of freedom.—*Channing.*

Many politicians are in the habit of laying it down as a self-evident proposition, that no people ought to be free till they are fit to use their freedom. The maxim is worthy of the fool in the old story, who resolved not to go into the water till he had learned to swim!—
Macaulay.

Know ye not who would be free themselves must strike the blow? by their right arms the conquest must be wrought?—*Byron.*

FREE SPEECH.
There is tonic in the things that men do not love to hear; and there is damnation in the things that wicked men love to hear. Free speech is to a great people what winds are to oceans and malarial regions, which waft away the elements of disease, and bring new elements of health. And where free speech is stopped miasma is bred, and death comes fast.—*Beecher.*

FRIENDSHIP.
In your friendships and in your enmities let your confidence and your hostilities have certain bounds; make not the former dangerous, nor the latter irreconcilable. There are strange vicissitudes in business.—*Chesterfield.*

We call friendship the love of the Dark Ages.
Madame de Salm.

A wound in the friendship of young persons, as in the bark of young trees, may be so grown over as to leave no scar. The case is very different in regard to old persons and old timber. The reason of this may be accountable from the decline of the social passions, and the prevalence of spleen, suspicion, and rancor towards the latter part of life.—*Shenstone.*

Friendship! mysterious cement of the soul! sweetener of life! and solder of society!—*Blair.*

Friendship is more firmly secured by lenity towards failings than by attachment to excellences. The former is valued as a kindness which cannot be claimed; the latter is exacted as the payment of a debt to merit.—
W. B. Clulow.

Friendship is a vase, which, when it is flawed by heat or violence or accident, may as well be broken at once; it never can be trusted after. The more graceful and ornamental it was, the more clearly do we discern the hopelessness of restoring it to its former state. Coarse stones, if they are fractured, may be cemented again; precious ones never.—*Landor.*

The friendships of the world are oft confederacies in vice, or leagues of pleasure.—*Addison.*

Charity commands us, where we know no ill, to think well of all; but friendship that always goes a step higher, gives a man a peculiar right and claim to the good opinion of his friend.—
South.

We must love our friends as true amateurs love paintings; they have their eyes perpetually fixed on the fine parts, and see no others.—
Madame d'Épinay.

The light of friendship is like the light of phosphorus, — seen plainest when all around is dark.
Crowell.

We value the devotedness of friendship rather as an oblation to vanity than as a free interchange of hearts; an endearing contract of sympathy, mutual forbearance, and respect!—
Jane Porter.

False friends are like our shadow, keeping close to us while we walk in the sunshine, but leaving us the instant we cross into the shade.—
Bovee.

Friendship is infinitely better than kindness.
Cicero.

Whatever the number of a man's friends, there will be times in his life when he has one too few.—*Bulwer Lytton.*

To say, with La Rochefoucauld, that "in the adversity of our best friends there is something that does not displease us," and to say that in the prosperity of our best friends there is something that does not please us, seems to be the same thing; yet I believe the first is false, and the latter true.—*Lord Greville.*

My friends! There are no friends!—
Aristotle.

Friendship, like love, is self-forgetful. The only inequality it knows is one that exalts the object, and humbles self.—*Henry Giles.*

A friendship will be young after the lapse of a century. A passion is old at the end of three months.—*Nigu.*

Be on such terms with your friend as if you knew that he might one day become your enemy.—*Laberius.*

What is commonly called friendship is no more than a partnership; a reciprocal regard for one another's interests, and an exchange of good offices; in a word, a mere traffic, wherein self-love always proposes to be a gainer.—
Rochefoucauld.

Kindred weaknesses induce friendships as often as kindred virtues.—*Bovee.*

Our most intimate friend is not he to whom we show the worst, but the best of our nature.—*Hawthorne.*

Nothing is more dangerous than an imprudent friend; better is it to have to deal with a prudent enemy.—*La Fontaine.*

Life is to be fortified by many friendships. To love and to be loved is the greatest happiness of existence.—*Sydney Smith.*

Friendship is love without its flowers or veil.
Hare.

We love everything on our own account; we even follow our own taste and inclination when we prefer our friends to ourselves ; and yet it is this preference alone that constitutes true and perfect friendship.—*Rochefoucauld.*

He who has ceased to enjoy his friend's superiority has ceased to love him.—
Madame Swetchine.

Every friend is to the other a sun, and a sunflower also. He attracts and follows.—
Richter.

When danger threats, the friend comes forth resolved and shields his friend; in Fortune's golden smiles what need of friends ? her favoring power wants no auxiliary.—*Euripides.*

He that doth a base thing in zeal for his friend burns the golden thread that ties their hearts together.—*Jeremy Taylor.*

Wise were the kings who never chose a friend till with full cups they had unmasked his soul, and seen the bottom of his deepest thoughts.—*Horace.*

How were friendship possible? In mutual devotedness to the good and true ; otherwise impossible, except as armed neutrality or hollow commercial league. A man, be the heavens ever praised, is sufficient for himself; yet were ten men, united in love, capable of being and of doing what ten thousand singly would fail in. Infinite is the help man can yield to man.—
Carlyle.

A faithful friend is the true image of the Deity.—*Napoleon.*

As the shadow in early morning, is friendship with the wicked ; it dwindles hour by hour. But friendship with the good increases, like the evening shadows, till the sun of life sets.—
Herder.

The amity that wisdom knits not, folly may easily nutie.—*Shakespeare.*

Real friendship is a slow grower ; and never thrives unless engrafted upon a stock of known and reciprocal merit.—*Chesterfield.*

A friend loveth at all times ; and a brother is born for adversity.—*Bible.*

When the first time of love is over, there comes a something better still. Then comes that other love ; that faithful friendship which never changes, and which will accompany you with its calm light through the whole of life. It is only needful to place yourself so that it may come, and then it comes of itself. And then everything turns and changes itself to the best.
Fredrika Bremer.

That friendship will not continue to the end that is begun for an end.—*Quarles.*

With a clear sky, a bright sun, and a gentle breeze, you will have friends in plenty ; but let Fortune frown, and the firmament be overcast, and then your friends will prove like the strings of the lute, of which you will tighten ten before you find one that will bear the stretch and keep the pitch.—*Gotthold.*

If we would build on a sure foundation in friendship, we must love our friends for their sakes rather than for our own.—*Charlotte Brontë.*

True friends are the whole world to one another ; and he that is a friend to himself is also a friend to mankind. Even in my studies the greatest delight I take is of imparting it to others; for there is no relish to me in the possessing of anything without a partner.—*Seneca.*

We may have many acquaintances, but we can have but few friends ; this made Aristotle say that he that hath many friends hath none.
Johnson.

What an argument in favor of social connections is the observation that by communicating our grief we have less, and by communicating our pleasure we have more.—*Lord Greville.*

There have been fewer friends on earth than kings.—*Cowley.*

We say, in common discourse, that a man may be his own enemy ; and the frequency of the fact makes the expression intelligible. But that a man should be the bitterest enemy of his friends implies a contradiction of a peculiar nature. There is something in it which cannot be conceived without a confusion of ideas, nor expressed without a solecism in language ; yet a man is often injured by the assistance of his friend, whose impulse, however generous and sincere, combines neither prudence for its regulation nor skill for its successful adoption.—
Junius.

There is no man so friendless but that he can find a friend sincere enough to tell him disagreeable truths.—*Bulwer Lytton.*

Women bestow on friendship only what they borrow from love.—*Chamfort.*

He who disguises tyranny, protection, or even benefits under the air and name of friendship reminds me of the guilty priest who poisoned the sacramental bread.—*Chamfort.*

To what gods is sacrificed that rarest and sweetest thing upon earth, friendship? To vanity and to interest.—*Malesherbes.*

There are no rules for friendship. It must be left to itself; we cannot force it any more than love.—*Hazlitt.*

Old friends are the great blessings of one's latter years. Half a word conveys one's meaning. They have memory of the same events, and have the same mode of thinking. I have young relations that may grow upon me, for my nature is affectionate, but can they grow old friends? My age forbids that. Still less can they grow companions. Is it friendship to explain half one says? One must relate the history of one's memory and ideas ; and what is that to the young but old stories ? —
Horace Walpole.

A friendship that makes the least noise is very often the most useful; for which reason I should prefer a prudent friend to a zealous one.
Addison.

Take heed of a speedy professing friend; love is never lasting which flames before it burns.—*Feltham.*

These hearts which suck up friendship like water, and yield it again with the first touch, might as well expect to squeeze a sponge and find it hold its moisture, as to retain affections which they are forever dashing from them.—
Jane Porter.

We lose some friends for whom we regret more than we grieve; and others for whom we grieve, yet do not regret.—*Rochefoucauld.*

A principal fruit of friendship is the ease and discharge of the fulness and swellings of the heart, which passions of all kinds do cause and induce.—*Bacon.*

There is nothing that is meritorious but virtue and friendship, and, indeed, friendship itself is but a part of virtue.—*Pope.*

A friend should bear his friend's infirmities.
Shakespeare.

The most elevated and pure souls cannot bear, even from the lips of the most contemptible men, these words, "friendship," "sensibility," "virtue," without immediately attaching to them all the grandeur of which their heart is susceptible.—*Richter.*

Friendship consists properly in mutual offices, and a generous strife in alternate acts of kindness.—*South.*

Friendship is constant in all other things, save in the office and affairs of love.—
Shakespeare.

If thy friends be of better quality than thyself, thou mayest be sure of two things: the first, that they will be more careful to keep thy counsel, because they have more to lose than thou hast; the second, they will esteem thee for thyself, and not for that which thou dost possess.—*Sir Walter Raleigh.*

The greatest medicine is a true friend.—
Sir W. Temple.

I have never believed that friendship supposed the obligation of hating those whom your friends did not love, and I believe rather it obliges me to love those whom they love.—
Morellet.

Friendship is made fast by interwoven benefits.—*Sir P. Sidney.*

We learn our virtues from the bosom friends who love us; our faults from the enemy who hates us. We cannot easily discover our real form from a friend. He is a mirror on which the warmth of our breath impedes the clearness of the reflection.—*Richter.*

Friendship is the wine of life.—*Young.*

Perfect friendship puts us under the necessity of being virtuous. As it can only be preserved among estimable persons, it forces us to resemble them. You find in friendship the surety of good counsel, the emulation of good example, sympathy in our griefs, succor in our distress.—
Madame de Lambert.

He who reckons ten friends has not one.—
Malesherbes.

Friends are discovered rather than made; there are people who are in their own nature friends, only they don't know each other; but certain things, like poetry, music, and paintings are like the Freemason's sign, — they reveal the initiated to each other.—*Mrs. Stowe.*

Friendship requires deeds.—*Richter.*

Friendship is the only thing in the world concerning the usefulness of which all mankind are agreed.— *Cicero.*

Be careful to make friendship the child, and not the father of virtue ; for many strongly knit minds are rather good friends than good men ; so, as though they do not like the evil their friend does, yet they like him who does the evil ; and though no counsellors of the offence, they yet protect the offender.—*Sir P. Sidney.*

Old friends are best. King James used to call for his old shoes ; they were easiest for his feet.—*Selden.*

When men are friends there is no need of justice ; but when they are just, they still need friendship.—*Aristotle.*

The ideal of friendship is to feel as one while remaining two.—*Madame Swetchine.*

The noblest part of a friend is an honest boldness in the notifying of errors. He that tells me of a fault, aiming at my good, I must think him wise and faithful, — wise in spying that which I see not ; faithful in a plain admonishment, not tainted with flattery.— *Feltham.*

Friendships which are born in misfortune are more firm and lasting than those which are formed in happiness.—*D'Urfey.*

There are jilts in friendship as well as in love, and by the behavior of some men in both, one would almost imagine that they industriously sought to gain the affections of others with a view only of making the parties miserable.— *Fielding.*

Friends are as companions on a journey, who ought to aid each other to persevere in the road to a happier life.—*Pythagoras.*

Do not allow grass to grow on the road of friendship.—*Madame Geoffrin.*

Take heed how you place your good-will upon any other ground than proof of virtue. Neither length of acquaintance, mutual secrecies, nor height of benefits, can bind a vicious heart ; no man being good to others that is not good in himself.—*Sir P. Sidney.*

Friendship is a cadence of divine melody melting through the heart.—*Mildmay.*

False friendship, like the ivy, decays and ruins the walls it embraces ; but true friendship gives new life and animation to the object it supports.—*Burton.*

Rare as is true love, true friendship is rarer. *La Fontaine.*

If two men are united, the wants of neither are any greater, in some respects, than they would be were they alone, and their strength is superior to the strength of two separate men.— *Sénancour.*

Friendship is the medicine for all misfortune ; but ingratitude dries up the fountain of all goodness.—*Richelieu.*

Feast-won, fast-lost, one cloud of winter showers, these flies are couched.—*Shakespeare.*

If a man does not make new acquaintances as he advances through life, he will soon find himself left alone. A man should keep his friendships in constant repair—*Johnson.*

We have social strengths. Our affection towards others creates a sort of vantage or purchase which nothing will supply. I can do that by another which I cannot do alone. I can say to you what I cannot first say to myself. Other men are lenses through which we read our own minds.—*Emerson.*

The youth of friendship is better than its old age.—*Hazlitt.*

Love and esteem are the first principles of friendship, which always is imperfect where either of these two is wanting.—*Budgell.*

Friendship is like those ancient altars where the unhappy, and even the guilty, found a sure asylum.—*Madame Swetchine.*

He who has not the weakness of friendship has not the strength.—*Joubert.*

Friendship, gift of heaven, delight of great souls ; friendship which kings, so distinguished for ingratitude, are unhappy enough not to know.—*Voltaire.*

Friendship is stronger than kindred.— *Publius Syrus.*

People young, and raw, and soft-natured, think it an easy thing to gain love, and reckon their own friendship a sure price of any man's ; but when experience shall have shown them the hardness of most hearts, the hollowness of others, and the baseness and ingratitude of almost all, they will then find that a true friend is the gift of God, and that He only who made hearts can unite them.—*South.*

Purchase no friends by gifts ; when thou ceasest to give such will cease to love.—*Fuller.*

Friendship is full of dregs.—*Shakespeare.*

The friendship of high and sanctified spirits loses nothing by death but its alloy ; failings disappear, and the virtues of those whose " faces we shall behold no more " appear greater and more sacred when beheld through the shades of the sepulchre.—*Robert Hall.*

The difficulty is not so great to die for a friend as to find a friend worth dying for.— *Henry Home.*

The generality of friends puts us out of conceit with friendship ; just as the generality of religious people puts us out of conceit with religion.—*Rochefoucauld.*

To be influenced by a passion for the same pursuits, and to have similar dislikes, is the rational ground-work of lasting friendship.— *Cicero.*

The corpse of friendship is not worth embalming.—*Hazlitt.*

Those who want friends to open themselves unto are cannibals of their own hearts.—*Bacon.*

The qualities of your friends will be those of your enemies,—cold friends, cold enemies; half friends, half enemies; fervid enemies, warm friends.—*Lavater.*

I love a friendship that flatters itself in the sharpness and vigor of its communications.—*Montaigne.*

True friends visit us in prosperity only when invited, but in adversity they come without invitation.—*Theophrastus.*

Friendship is given us by nature, not to favor vice, but to aid virtue.—*Cicero.*

I would give more for the private esteem and love of one than for the public praise of ten thousand.—*W. R. Alger.*

Let friendship creep gently to a height; if it rush to it, it may soon run itself out of breath.
Fuller.

A man that is fit to make a friend of must have conduct to manage the engagement, and resolution to maintain it. He must use freedom without roughness, and oblige without design. Cowardice will betray friendship, and covetousness will starve it. Folly will be nauseous, passion is apt to ruffle, and pride will fly out into contumely and neglect.—*Jeremy Collier.*

Something like home, that is not home, is to be desired; it is to be found in the house of a friend.—*Sir William Temple.*

Dread more the blunderer's friendship than the calumniator's enmity.—*Lavater.*

True friendship is a plant of slow growth, and must undergo and withstand the shocks of adversity before it is entitled to the appellation.
Washington.

Friendship improves happiness and abates misery, by the doubling of our joy and the dividing of our grief.—*Cicero.*

True friendship cannot be among many. For since our faculties are of a finite energy, it is impossible our love can be very intense when divided among many. No, the rays must be contracted to make them burn.—*John Norris.*

He who cannot feel friendship is alike incapable of love. Let a woman beware of the man who owns that he loves no one but herself.—*Talleyrand.*

There is a power in love to divine another's destiny better than that other can, and by heroic encouragements, hold him to his task. What has friendship so signal as its sublime attraction to whatever virtue is in us?—*Emerson.*

Friendship hath the skill and observation of the best physician, the diligence and vigilance of the best nurse, and the tenderness and patience of the best mother.—*Clarendon.*

Friendship is the shadow of the evening, which strengthens with the setting sun of life.—*La Fontaine.*

Be slow to fall into friendship; but when thou art in continue firm and constant.—*Socrates.*

Nature loves nothing solitary, and always reaches out to something, as a support, which ever in the sincerest friend is most delightful.—*Cicero.*

No better relation than a prudent and faithful friend.—*Franklin.*

In friendship, we see only the faults which may injure our friends. In love, we see only the faults by which we ourselves suffer.—*Du Cœur.*

The friends thou hast, and their adoption tried, grapple them to thy soul with hooks of steel.—*Shakespeare.*

One of the surest evidences of friendship that one individual can display to another is telling him gently of a fault. If any other can excel it, it is listening to such a disclosure with gratitude, and amending the error.—*Bulwer Lytton.*

Friends should be weighed, not told; who boasts to have won a multitude of friends has never had one.—*Coleridge.*

The loss of a friend is like that of a limb. Time may heal the anguish of the wound, but the loss cannot be repaired.—*Southey.*

He will find himself in a great mistake that either seeks for a friend in a palace or tries him at a feast.—*Seneca.*

Friendship throws a greater lustre on prosperity, while it lightens adversity by sharing in its griefs and anxieties.—*Cicero.*

Summer friends vanish when the cask is drained to the dregs, their necks refusing to halve the yoke that sorrow draws.—*Horace.*

I have too deeply read mankind to be amused with friendship; it is a name invented merely to betray credulity; it is intercourse of interest, not of souls.—*Havard.*

We should remember that it is quite as much a part of friendship to be delicate in its demands as to be ample in its performances.—*J. F. Boyes.*

Friendship is too pure a pleasure for a mind cankered with ambition, or the lust of power and grandeur.—*Junius.*

It is a common saying, and because founded in truth, has become a proverb, that friendships ought to be immortal, but enmities mortal.—
Livy.

Convey thy love to thy friend as an arrow to the mark, to stick there ; not as a ball against the wall, to rebound back to thee.—*Quarles.*

There is nothing so great that I·fear to do for my friend ; nor nothing so small that I will disdain to do for him.—*Sir P. Sidney.*

FRUGALITY.
Frugality is founded on the principle that all riches have limits.—*Burke.*

Frugality may be termed the daughter of prudence, the sister of temperance, and the parent of liberty. He that is extravagant will quickly become poor, and poverty will enforce dependence and invite corruption.—*Johnson.*

The world has not yet learned the riches of frugality.—*Cicero.*

He that spareth in everything is an inexcusable niggard. He that spareth in nothing is an inexcusable madman. The mean is to spare in what is least necessary, and to lay out more liberally in what is most required in our several circumstances.—*Lord Halifax.*

By sowing frugality we reap liberty? a golden harvest.—*Agesilaus.*

Frugality is good if liberality be joined with it. The first is leaving off superfluous expenses ; the last is bestowing them to the benefit of others that need. The first without the last begets covetousness ; the last without the first begets prodigality.—*William Penn.*

He seldom lives frugally who lives by chance. Hope is always liberal, and they that trust her promises make little scruple of revelling to-day on the profits of to-morrow.
Johnson.

FUN.
Fun has no limits. It is like the human race and face ; there is a family likeness among all the species, but they all differ.—*Haliburton.*

FUTURITY.
It ever is the marked propensity of restless and aspiring minds to look into the stretch of dark futurity.—*Joanna Baillie.*

While a man is stringing a harp, he tries the strings, not for music, but for construction. When it is finished it shall be played for melodies. God is fashioning the human heart for future joy. He only sounds a string here and there to see how far his work has progressed.—
Beecher.

If there was no future life, our souls would not thirst for it.—*Richter.*

13

Everything that looks to the future elevates human nature ; for never is life so low or so little as when occupied with the present.—
Landor.

The future is always fairy-land to the young. Life is like a beautiful and winding lane, on either side bright flowers, and beautiful butterflies and tempting fruits, which we scarcely pause to admire and to taste, so eager are we to hasten to an opening which we imagine will be more beautiful still. But by degrees, as we advance, the trees grow bleak ; the flowers and butterflies fail, the fruits disappear, and we find we have arrived — to reach a desert waste.—
G. A. Sala.

Age and sorrow have the gift of reading the future by the sad past.—*Rev. J. Farrar.*

Boast not thyself of to-morrow ; for thou knowest not what a day may bring forth.—
Bible.

One might as well attempt to calculate mathematically the contingent forms of the tinkling bits of glass in a kaleidoscope as to look through the tube of the future and foretell its pattern.—*Beecher.*

Coming events cast their shadows before.—
Campbell.

It has been well observed that we should treat futurity as an aged friend, from whom we expect a rich legacy. Let us do nothing to forfeit his esteem, and treat him with respect, not with servility. But let us not be too prodigal when we are young, nor too parsimonious when we are old, otherwise we shall fall into the common error of those who, when they had the power to enjoy, had not the prudence to acquire ; and when they had the prudence to acquire, had no longer the power to enjoy.—*Colton.*

O Heaven ! that one might read the book of fate, and see the revolution of the times.—
Shakespeare.

Futurity is impregnable to mortal ken : no prayer pierces through heaven's adamantine walls. Whether the birds fly right or left, whatever be the aspect of the stars, the book of nature is a maze, dreams are a lie, and every sign a falsehood.—*Schiller.*

When all else is lost, the future still remains.—*Bovee.*

There is, I know not how, in the minds of men, a certain presage, as it were, of a future existence, and this takes the deepest root, and is most discoverable in the greatest geniuses and most exalted souls.—*Cicero.*

The future does not come from before to meet us, but comes streaming up from behind over our heads.—*Rahel.*

The veil which covers the face of futurity is woven by the hand of mercy.—*Bulwer Lytton*.

Why will any man be so impertinently officious as to tell me all prospect of a future state is only fancy and delusion? Is there any merit in being the messenger of ill news? If it is a dream, let me enjoy it, since it makes me both the happier and better man.—*Addison*.

We are always looking into the future, but we see only the past.—*Madame Swetchine*.

Sure there is none but fears a future state; and when the most obdurate swear, do not their trembling hearts belie their boasting tongues.—*Dryden*.

We are born for a higher destiny than that of earth; there is a realm where the rainbow never fades, where the stars will be spread before us like islands that slumber on the ocean, — and where the beings that pass before us like shadows will stay in our presence forever.— *Bulwer Lytton*.

How narrow our souls become when absorbed in any present good or ill! it is only the thought of the future that makes them great.— *Richter*.

The golden age is not in the past, but in the future; not in the origin of human experience, but in its consummate flower; not opening in Eden, but out from Gethsemane.— *Chapin*.

O, if this were seen, the happiest youth — viewing his progress through, what perils past, what crosses to ensue — would shut the book and sit him down and die.—*Shakespeare*.

Since we stay not here, being people but of a day's abode, and our age is like that of a fly, and contemporary with that of a gourd, we must look somewhere else for an abiding city, a place in another country, to fix our house in, whose walls and foundation is God, where we must rest, or else be restless forever.— *Jeremy Taylor*.

We may believe that we shall know each other's forms hereafter; and in the bright fields of the better land call the lost dead to us.— *Willis*.

If that marvellous microcosm, man, with all the costly cargo of his faculties and powers, were indeed a rich argosy, fitted out and freighted only for shipwreck and destruction, who amongst us that tolerate the present only from the hope of the future, who that have any aspirings of a high and intellectual nature about them, could be brought to submit to the disgusting mortifications of the voyage? —*Colton*.

It is vain to be always looking towards the future and never acting towards it.— *J. F. Boyes*.

The dead carry our thoughts to another and a nobler existence. They teach us, and especially by all the strange and seemingly untoward circumstances of their departure from this life, that they and we shall live in a future state forever.—*Orville Dewey*.

It is easy to see, hard to foresee.—*Franklin*.

We bewail our friends as if there were no better futurity yonder, and bewail ourselves as if there were no better futurity here; for all our passions are born atheists and infidels.— *Richter*.

It is one of God's blessings that we cannot foreknow the hour of our death; for a time fixed, even beyond the possibility of living, would trouble us more than doth this uncertainty.—*James the Sixth*.

Divine wisdom, intending to detain us some time on earth, has done well to cover with a veil the prospect of life to come; for if our sight could clearly distinguish the opposite bank, who would remain on this tempestuous coast? — *Madame de Staël*.

It is heaven itself that points out an hereafter, and intimates eternity to man.—*Addison*.

My mind can take no hold on the present world, nor rest in it a moment, but my whole nature rushes onward with irresistible force towards a future and better state of being.—*Fichte*.

The grand difficulty is to feel the reality of both worlds, so as to give each its due place in our thoughts and feelings, to keep our mind's eye and our heart's eye ever fixed on the land of promise, without looking away from the road along which we are to travel toward it.—*Hare*.

To me there is something thrilling and exalting in the thought that we are drifting forward into a splendid mystery, — into something that no mortal eye has yet seen, no intelligence has yet declared.—*Chapin*.

Look not mournfully into the past, — it comes not back again; wisely improve the present, — it is thine; go forth to meet the shadowy future without fear, and with a manly heart.— *Longfellow*.

God will not suffer man to have the knowledge of things to come; for if he had prescience of his prosperity, he would be careless; and, understanding of his adversity, he would be senseless.—*St. Augustine*.

G.

GALLANTRY.

Gallantry thrives most in the atmosphere of the court.—*Madame Necker.*

A gallant man is above ill words.—*Selden.*

Love is the smallest part of gallantry.—*Rochefoucauld.*

Gallantry, though a fashionable crime, is a very detestable one ; and the wretch who pilfers from us in the hour of distress is an innocent character compared to the plunderer who wantouly robs us of happiness and reputation.—*Rev. H. Kelley.*

The gallantry of the mind consists in agreeable flattery.—*Rochefoucauld.*

GAMBLING.

Gaming is the destruction of all decorum ; the prince forgets at it his dignity, and the lady her modesty.—*Marchioness d'Alembert.*

Keep flax from fire, youth from gaming.—*Franklin.*

Gambling houses are temples where the most sordid and turbulent passions contend ; there no spectator can be indifferent. A card or a small quare of ivory interests more than the loss of an empire, or the ruin of an unoffending group of infants, and their nearest relatives.—*Zimmermann.*

Who gets by play proves loser in the end.—*Heath.*

I look upon every man as a suicide from the moment he takes the dice-box desperately in his hand ; and all that follows in his fatal career from that time is only sharpening the dagger before he strikes it to his heart.—*Cumberland.*

It is possible that a wise and good man may be prevailed on to game ; but it is impossible that a professed gamester should be a wise and good man.—*Lavater.*

Gaming is a vice the more dangerous as it is deceitful ; and, contrary to every other species of luxury, flatters its votaries with the hopes of increasing their wealth ; so that avarice itself is so far from securing us against its temptations that it often betrays the more thoughtless and giddy part of mankind into them.—*Fielding.* ·

The gamester, if he die a martyr to his profession, is doubly ruined. He adds his soul to every other loss, and by the act of suicide, renounces earth to forfeit heaven.—*Colton.*

Play not for gain, but sport ; who plays for more than he can lose with pleasure stakes his heart.—*George Herbert.*

An assembly of the states, a court of justice, shows nothing so serious and grave as a table of gamesters playing very high ; a melancholy solicitude clouds their looks : envy and rancor agitate their minds while the meeting lasts, without regard to friendship, alliances, birth, or distinctions.—*Bruyère.*

It is lost at dice, what ancient honor won.—*Shakespeare.*

If thy desire to raise thy fortunes encourage thy delights to the casts of fortune, be wise betimes, lest thou repent too late ; what thou gettest, thou gainest by abused providence ; what thou losest, thou losest by abused patience ; what thou winnest is prodigally spent ; what thou losest is prodigally lost ; it is an evil trade that prodigality drives ; and a bad voyage where the pilot is blind.—*Quarles.*

Games of chance are traps to catch schoolboy novices and gaping country squires, who begin with a guinea and end with a mortgage.—*Cumberland.*

The exercises I wholly condemn are dieing and carding, especially if you play for any great sum of money, or spend any time in them, or use to come to meetings in dicing-houses, where cheaters meet and cozen young gentlemen out of all their money.—*Lord Herbert.*

Gaming is the child of avarice, but the parent of prodigality.—*Colton.*

Sports and gaming, whether pursued from a desire of gain or love of pleasure, are as ruinous to the temper and disposition of the party addicted to them, as they are to his fame and fortune.—*Burton.*

Gaming finds a man a cully, and leaves him a knave.—*T. Hughes.*

The coldness of a losing gamester lessens the pleasure of the winner. I would no more play with a man that slighted his ill fortune than I would make love to a woman who undervalued the loss of her reputation.—*Congreve.*

All gaming, since it implies a desire to profit at the expense of another, involves a breach of the tenth commandment.—*Whately.*

It is well for gamesters that they are so numerous as to make a society of themselves ; for it would be a strange abuse of terms to rank those among society at large, whose profession it is to prey upon all who compose it.—*Cumberland.*

By gaming we lose both our time and treasure, — two things most precious to the life of man.—*Feltham.*

The passion of gaming is almost never un accompanied ; and, to those of our sex especially, is always the source or the occasion of all the others.—*Massillon.*

Be assured that, although men of eminent genius have been guilty of all other vices, none worthy of more than a secondary name has ever been a gamester. Either an excess of avarice, or a deficiency of what, in physics, is called excitability, is the cause of it; neither of which can exist in the same bosom with genius, with patriotism, or with virtue.—*Landor.*

Lookers-on many times see more than gamesters.—*Bacon.*

There is nothing that wears out a fine face like the vigils of a card-table, and those cutting passions which naturally attend them. Haggard looks and pale complexions are the natural indications of a female gamester.—*Addison.*

It is the child of avarice, the brother of iniquity, and the father of mischief.—*Washington.*

That reproach of modern times, that gulf of time and fortune, the passion for gaming, which is so often the refuge of the idle sons of pleasure and often, alas! the last resource of the ruined.—*Blair.*

Gaming has been resorted to by the affluent as a refuge from ennui; it is a mental dram, and may succeed for a moment, but, like all other stimuli, it produces indirect debility; and those who have recourse to it will find that the sources of their ennui are far more inexhaustible than those of their purse.—*Colton.*

GAYETY.

Gayety pleases more when we are assured that it does not cover carelessness.—*Madame de Staël.*

Gayety is to good-humor as animal perfumes to vegetable fragrance. The one overpowers weak spirits, the other recreates and revives them. Gayety seldom fails to give some pain; good-humor boasts no faculties which every one does not believe in his own power, and pleases principally by not offending.—*Johnson.*

Some people are commended for a giddy kind of good-humor, which is as much a virtue as drunkenness.—*Pope.*

Is there anything in life so lovely and poetical as the laugh and merriment of a young girl, who, still in harmony with all her powers, sports with you in luxuriant freedom, and in her mirthfulness neither despises nor dislikes? Her gravity is seldom as innocent as her playfulness; still less that haughty discontent which converts the youthful Psyche into a dull, thick, buzzing, wing-drooping night-moth.—*Richter.*

Gayety is the soul's health; sadness is its poison.—*Stanislaus.*

Leaves seem light and useless, and idle and wavering, and changeable,—they even dance; yet God has made them part of the oak. In so doing, he has given us a lesson, not to deny the stout-heartedness within because we see the lightsomeness without.—*Leigh Hunt.*

Gayety is often the reckless ripple over depths of despair.—*Chapin.*

GENEROSITY.

Any one may do a casual act of good-nature; but a continuation of them shows it a part of the temperament.—*Sterne.*

Some are unwisely liberal; and more delight to give presents than to pay debts.—*Sir P. Sidney.*

A giving hand, though foul, shall have fair praise.—*Shakespeare.*

There is a story of some mountains of salt in Cumana, which never diminished, though carried away in much abundance by merchants; but when once they were monopolized to the benefit of a private purse, then the salt decreased, till afterwards all were allowed to take of it, when it had a new access and increase. The truth of this story may be uncertain, but the application is true; he that envies others the use of his gifts decays then, but he thrives most that is most diffusive.—*Spencer.*

Generosity, wrong placed, becometh a vice; a princely mind will undo a private family.—*Fuller.*

True generosity is a duty as indispensably necessary as those imposed upon us by the law. It is a rule imposed upon us by reason, which should be the sovereign law of a rational being.—*Goldsmith.*

The generous who is always just, and the just who is always generous, may, unannounced, approach the throne of Heaven.—*Lavater.*

When you give, take to yourself no credit for generosity, unless you deny yourself something in order that you may give.—*Henry Taylor.*

Bounty, being free itself, thinks all others so.—*Shakespeare.*

Men of the noblest dispositions think themselves happiest when others share their happiness with them.—*Duncan.*

There is greatness in being generous, and there is only simple justice in satisfying creditors. Generosity is the part of the soul raised above the vulgar.—*Goldsmith.*

The secret pleasure of a generous act is the great mind's great bribe.—*Dryden.*

All my experience of the world teaches me that in ninety-nine cases out of a hundred the safe side and the just side of a question is the generous side and the merciful side.—
Mrs. Jameson.

In this world, it is not what we take up, but what we give up, that makes us rich.—*Beecher.*

O the world is but a word ; were it all yours to give it in a breath, how quickly were it gone ! —*Shakespeare.*

There is no grace in a benefit that sticks to the fingers.—*Seneca.*

Wherever I find a great deal of gratitude in a poor man, I take it for granted there would be as much generosity if he were a rich man.—
Pope.

What seems to be generosity is often no more than disguised ambition ; which overlooks a small interest, in order to gratify a great one.—
Rochefoucauld.

Generosity during life is a very different thing from generosity in the hour of death ; one proceeds from genuine liberality and benevolence, the other from pride or fear.—
Horace Mann.

Almost always the most indigent are the most generous.—*Stanislaus.*

The reputation of generosity is to be purchased pretty cheap ; it does not depend so much upon a man's general expense, as it does upon his giving handsomely where it is proper to give at all. A man, for instance, who should give a servant four shillings would pass for covetous, while he who gave him a crown would be reckoned generous ; so that the difference of those two opposite characters turns upon one shilling.—*Chesterfield.*

How much easier it is to be generous than just ! Men are sometimes bountiful who are not honest.—*Junius.*

He that gives all, though but little, gives much ; because God looks not to the quantity of the gift, but to the quality of the givers : he that desires to give more than he can hath equalled his gift to his desire, and hath given more than he hath.—*Quarles.*

If there be any truer measure of a man than by what he does, it must be by what he gives.—
South.

One great reason why men practise generosity so little in the world is their finding so little there. Generosity is catching ; and if so many escape it, it is in a small degree for the same reason that countrymen escape the small-pox, — because they meet with no one to give it to them.—*Lord Greville.*

It is not enough to help the feeble up, but to support him after.—*Shakespeare.*

He who gives what he would as readily throw away gives without generosity ; for the essence of generosity is in self-sacrifice.—
Henry Taylor.

They that do an act that does deserve requital pay first themselves the stock of such content.—*Sir Robert Howard.*

GENIUS.

The effusions of genius are entitled to admiration rather than applause, as they are chiefly the effect of natural endowment, and sometimes appear to be almost involuntary.—*W. B. Clulow.*

Genius may at times want the spur, but it stands as often in need of the curb.—*Longinus.*

Nature seems to delight in disappointing the assiduities of art, with which it would rear dulness to maturity, and to glory in the vigor and luxuriance of her chance productions. She scatters the seeds of genius to the winds, and though some may perish among the stony places of the world, and some may be choked by the thorns and brambles of early adversity, yet others will now and then strike root even in the clefts of the rock, struggle bravely up into sunshine, and spread over their sterile birthplace all the beauties of vegetation.—
Washington Irving.

Genius is the instinct of enterprise. A boy came to Mozart, wishing to compose something, and inquiring the way to begin. Mozart told him to wait. " You composed much earlier." " But asked nothing about it," replied the musician.—*Willmott.*

Genius unexerted is no more genius than a bushel of acorns is a forest of oaks.—*Beecher.*

Obey thy genius, for a minister it is unto the throne of fate. Draw to thy soul, and centralize the rays which are around of the Divinity.—*Bailey.*

The whole difference between a man of genius and other men, it has been said a thousand times, and most truly, is that the first remains in great part a child, seeing with the large eyes of children, in perpetual wonder, not conscious of much knowledge, — conscious, rather, of infinite ignorance, and yet infinite power ; a fountain of eternal admiration, delight, and creative force within him meeting the ocean of visible and governable things around him.—*Ruskin.*

The first and last thing which is required of genius is the love of truth.—*Goethe.*

Men of genius do not excel in any profession because they labor in it, but they labor in it because they excel.—*Hazlitt.*

Was genius ever ungrateful? Mere talents are dry leaves, tossed up and down by gusts of passion, and scattered and swept away; but Genius lies on the bosom of Memory, and Gratitude at her feet.—*Landor.*

It is possible, by measuring and administering quantities of color, to paint a room wall so that it shall not hurt the eye; but there are no laws by observing which we can become Titians. It is possible so to measure and administer syllables as to construct harmonious verse; but there are no laws by which we can write Iliads.—*Ruskin.*

Genius, the Pythian of the beautiful, leaves its large truths a riddle to the dull.—
Bulwer Lytton.

There is nothing so remote from vanity as true genius. It is almost as natural for those who are endowed with the highest powers of the human mind to produce the miracles of art, as for other men to breathe or move. Correggio, who is said to have produced some of his divinest works almost without having seen a picture, probably did not know that he had done anything extraordinary.—*Hazlitt.*

The merit of great men is not understood, but by those who are formed to be such themselves; genius speaks only to genius.
Stanislaus.

The richest genius, like the most fertile soil, when uncultivated, shoots up into the rankest weeds; and instead of vines and olives for the pleasure and use of man, produces to its slothful owner the most abundant crop of poisons.—
Hume.

Genius grafted on womanhood is like to overgrow it and break its stem, as you may see a grafted fruit-tree spreading over the stock which cannot keep pace with its evolutions.—
Holmes.

The light of genius never sets, but sheds itself upon other faces, in different hues of splendor. Homer glows in the softened beauty of Virgil, and Spenser revives in the decorated learning of Gray.—*Willmott.*

Genius always gives its best at first, prudence at last.—*Lavater.*

As well might a lovely woman look daily in her mirror, yet not be aware of her beauty, as a great soul be unconscious of the powers with which Heaven has gifted him; not so much for himself, as to enlighten others, — a messenger from God himself, with a high and glorious mission to perform. Woe unto him who abuses that mission!—*Chambers.*

Every man who observes vigilantly and resolves steadfastly grows unconsciously into genius.—*Bulwer Lytton.*

Talent is often to be envied, and genius very commonly to be pitied. It stands twice the chance of the other of dying in a hospital, in jail, in debt, in bad repute. It is a perpetual insult to mediocrity; its every word is a trespass against somebody's vested ideas.—*Holmes.*

Ill-directed genius torments and harasses a community; it again and again perils the position of the possessor. Well if it do not eventually wreck his fortunes and blast his name.—*Follett.*

Men of genius are often dull and inert in society; as the blazing meteor, when it descends to earth, is only a stone.—*Longfellow.*

It is the habit of party in England to ask the alliance of a man of genius, but to follow the guidance of a man of character.—
Lord John Russell.

Of what use is genius, if the organ is too convex or too concave, and cannot find a focal distance within the actual horizon of human life?
Emerson.

This is the method of genius, to ripen fruit for the crowd by those rays of whose heat they complain.—*Margaret Fuller.*

How often we see the greatest genius buried in obscurity!—*Plautus.*

If one listens to the faintest but constant suggestions of his genius, which are certainly true, he sees not to what extremes, or even insanity, it may lead him; and yet that way, as he grows more resolute and faithful, his road lies.—*Thoreau.*

I know no such thing as genius, — genius is nothing but labor and diligence.—*Hogarth.*

What we call genius may, perhaps, with more strict propriety, be described as the spirit of discovery. Genius is the very eye of intellect and the wing of thought. It is always in advance of its time. It is the pioneer for the generation which it precedes. For this reason it is called a seer, — and hence its songs have been prophecies.—*Simms.*

Genius, — the free and harmonious play of all the faculties of a human being.—*Alcott.*

Genius is supposed to be a power of producing excellences which are out of the reach of the rules of art, — a power which no precepts can teach, and which no industry can acquire.—
Sir Joshua Reynolds.

A person of genius should marry a person of character. Genius does not herd with genius. The musk-deer and the civet-cat are never found in company. They don't care for strange scents, — they like plain animals better than perfumed ones.—*Holmes.*

Genius is subject to the same laws which regulate the production of cotton and molasses.
Macaulay.

To carry on the feelings of childhood into the powers of manhood, to combine the child's sense of wonder and novelty with the appearances which every day for perhaps forty years has rendered familiar, — this is the character and privilege of genius, and one of the marks which distinguish genius from talent.—*Coleridge.*

There is no great genius free from some tincture of madness.—*Seneca.*

When a true genius appears in the world, you may know him by this sign, that the dunces are all in confederacy against him.—*Swift.*

Genius is the gold in the mine, talent is the miner who works and brings it out.—
Lady Blessington.

As what we call genius arises out of the disproportionate power and size of a certain faculty, so the great difficulty lies in harmonizing with it the rest of the character.—
Mrs. Jameson.

Heaven and earth, advantages and obstacles, conspire to educate genius.—*Fuseli.*

The effusions of genius, or rather the manifestations of what is called talent, are often the effects of distempered nerves and complexional spleen, as pearls are morbid secretions.—
Robert Walsh.

Genius finds its own road and carries its own lamp.—*Willmott.*

There never appear more than five or six men of genius in an age, but if they were united the world could not stand before them.—*Swift.*

Genius may be almost defined as the faculty of acquiring poverty.—*Whipple.*

Genius does not seem to derive any great support from syllogisms. Its carriage is free ; its manner has a touch of inspiration. We see it come, but we never see it walk.—
Count de Maistre.

Genius is allied to a warm and inflammable constitution, delicacy of taste to calmness and sedateness. Hence it is common to find genius in one who is a prey to every passion ; but seldom delicacy of taste. Upon a man possessed of this blessing, the moral duties, no less than the fine arts, make a deep impression, and counterbalance every irregular desire ; at the same time, a temper calm and sedate is not easily moved, even by a strong temptation.—
Henry Home.

Genius does what it must, and talent does what it can.—*Owen Meredith.*

The only difference between a genius and one of common capacity is that the former anticipates and explores what the latter accidentally hits upon. But even the man of genius himself more frequently employs the advantages that chance presents to him. It is the lapidary that gives value to the diamond, which the peasant has dug up without knowing its worth.
Abbé Raynal.

A genius is never to be acquired by art, but is the gift of nature.—*Gay.*

Genius is only great patience.—*Buffon.*

Genius is not a single power, but a combination of great powers. It reasons, but it is not reasoning ; it judges, but it is not judgment ; it imagines, but it is not imagination ; it feels deeply and fiercely, but it is not passion. It is neither, because it is all.—*Whipple.*

Genius is the power of carrying the feelings of childhood into the powers of manhood.—
Coleridge.

Genius is independent of situation.—
Churchill.

The drafts which true genius draws upon posterity, although they may not always be honored so soon as they are due, are sure to be paid with compound interest in the end.—*Colton.*

Genius must be born, and never can be taught.—*Dryden.*

The highest genius never flowers in satire, but culminates in sympathy with that which is best in human nature, and appeals to it.—
Chapin.

Genius is to other gifts what the carbuncle is to the precious stones. It sends forth its own light, whereas other stones only reflect borrowed light.—*A. Schopenhauer.*

With the offspring of genius, the law of parturition is reversed ; the throes are in the conception, the pleasure in the birth.—*Colton.*

One genius has made many clever artists.—
Martial.

All the means of action, the shapeless masses, — the materials, — lie everywhere about us. What we need is the celestial fire to change the flint into transparent crystal, bright and clear. That fire is genius !—*Longfellow.*

Genius makes its observations in short-hand ; talent writes them out at length.—*Bovee.*

The three indispensables of genius are understanding, feeling, and perseverance. The three things that enrich genius are contentment of mind, the cherishing of good thoughts, and the exercise of memory.—*Southey.*

A man's genius is always, in the beginning of life, as much unknown to himself as to others; and it is only after frequent trials, attended with success, that he dares think himself equal to those undertakings in which those who have succeeded have fixed the admiration of mankind.—*Hume.*

Talent, lying in the understanding, is often inherited; genius, being the action of reason and imagination, rarely or never.—*Coleridge.*

Men do not make their homes unhappy because they have genius, but because they have not enough genius. A mind and sentiments of a higher order would render them capable of seeing and feeling all the beauty of domestic ties.—*Wordsworth.*

Genius, without religion, is only a lamp on the outer gate of a palace. It may serve to cast a gleam of light on those that are without while the inhabitant sits in darkness.—
Hannah More.

The faculty of growth.—*Coleridge.*

Genius ever stands with nature in solemn union, and what the one foretells the other shall fulfil.—*Schiller.*

The proportion of genius to the vulgar is like one to a million; but genius without tyranny, without pretension, that judges the weak with equity, the superior with humanity, and equals with justice, is like one to ten millions.—
Lavater.

GENTILITY.

There cannot be a surer proof of low origin, or of an innate meanness of disposition, than to be always talking and thinking of being genteel.
Hazlitt.

How weak a thing is gentility if it wants virtue!—*Fuller.*

I would have you not stand so much on your gentility, which is an airy and mere borrowed thing from dead men's dust and bones; and none of yours except you make and hold it.
Ben Jonson.

GENTLEMAN.

God knows that all sorts of gentlemen knock at the door; but whenever used in strictness and with any emphasis, the name will be found to point at original energy.—*Emerson.*

Men of courage, men of sense, and men of letters are frequent; but a true gentleman is what one seldom sees.—*Steele.*

The taste of beauty and the relish of what is decent, just, and amiable perfects the character of the gentleman and the philosopher.—
Shaftesbury.

To make a fine gentleman, several trades are required, but chiefly a barber.—*Goldsmith.*

He that can enjoy the intimacy of the great, and on no occasion disgust them by familiarity, or disgrace himself by servility, proves that he is as perfect a gentleman by nature as his companions are by rank.—*Colton.*

The real gentleman should be gentle in everything, at least in everything that depends on himself, — in carriage, temper, constructions, aims, desires.—*Hare.*

Education begins the gentleman, but reading, good company, and reflection must finish him.—*Locke.*

That man will never be a perfect gentleman who lives only with gentlemen. To be a man of the world we must view that world in every grade and in every perspective.—*Bulwer Lytton.*

Repose and cheerfulness are the badge of the gentleman, — repose in energy.—*Emerson.*

A gentleman is a rarer thing than some of us think for. Which of us can point out many such in his circle, — men whose aims are generous, whose truth is constant and elevated; who can look the world honestly in the face, with an equal manly sympathy for the great and the small? We all know a hundred whose coats are well made, and a score who have excellent manners; but of gentlemen how many? Let us take a little scrap of paper and each make out his list.—*Thackeray.*

It is difficult to believe that a true gentleman will ever become a gamester, a libertine, or a sot.
Chapin.

The true gentleman is extracted from ancient and worshipful parentage. When a pepin is planted on a pepin-stock, the fruit growing thence is called a renate, a most delicious apple, as both by sire and dame well descended. Thus his blood must needs be well purified who is gentilely born on both sides.—*Fuller.*

We sometimes meet an original gentleman, who, if manners had not existed, would have invented them.—*Emerson.*

The character of a gentleman is a relative term, which can hardly subsist where there is no marked distinction of persons. The diffusion of knowledge, of artificial and intellectual equality, tends to level this distinction, and to confound that nice perception and high sense of honor which arises from conspicuousness of sitnation, and a perpetual attention to personal propriety and the claims of personal respect.—
Hazlitt.

You may depend upon it, religion is, in its essence, the most gentlemanly thing in the world. It will alone gentilize, if unmixed with cant; and I know nothing else that will, alone. Certainly not the army, which is thought to be the grand embellisher of manners.—*Coleridge.*

Custom is not at once overthrown ; and he is even now deemed a gentleman who has arms recorded in the Herald's office, and at the same time follows none, except a liberal employment.
Shenstone.

Gentleman is a term which does not apply to any station, but to the mind and the feelings in every station.—*Talfourd.*

The grand old name of gentleman, defamed by every charlatan, and soiled with all ignoble use.—*Tennyson.*

We may daily discover crowds acquire sufficient wealth to buy gentility, but very few that possess the virtues which ennoble human nature, and (in the best sense of the word) constitute a gentleman.—*Shenstone.*

Perhaps propriety is as near a word as any to denote the manners of the gentleman ; elegance is necessary to the fine gentleman ; dignity is proper to noblemen ; and majesty to kings ! *Hazlitt.*

He is the best gentleman that is the son of his own deserts, and not the degenerated heir of another's virtue.—*Victor Hugo.*

GENTLENESS.

True gentleness is founded on a sense of what we owe to Him who made us, and to the common nature which we all share. It arises from reflection on our own failings and wants, and from just views of the condition and the duty of man. It is native feeling heightened and improved by principle.—*Blair.*

Soft is the music that would charm forever.
Wordsworth.

Gentleness corrects whatever is offensive in our manners.—*Blair.*

With regard to manner, be careful to speak in a soft, tender, kind, and loving way. Even when you have occasion to rebuke, be careful to do it with manifest kindness. The effect will be incalculably better.—*Hosea Ballou*

Let gentleness thy strong enforcement be.—
Shakespeare.

Experience has caused it to be remarked that in the country where the laws are gentle, the minds of the citizens are struck by it, as it is elsewhere by the most severe.—
Catherine the Second.

Gentleness ! more powerful than Hercules.
Ninon de l'Enclos.

Good words do more than hard speeches ; as the sunbeams without any noise will make the traveller cast off his cloak, which all the blustering winds could not do, but only make him bind it closer to him.—*Leighton.*

What thou wilt, thou rather shalt enforce it with thy smile, than hew to it with thy sword.—*Shakespeare.*

Better make penitents by gentleness than hypocrites by severity.—*St. Francis de Sales.*

The power of gentleness is irresistible.—
H. Martyn.

GIBBET.

The gibbet is a species of flattery to the human race. Three or four persons are hung from time to time for the sake of making the rest believe that they are virtuous.—
Sanial-Dubay.

GIFTS.

It is a cold, lifeless business when you go to the shops to buy something, which does not represent your life and talent, but a goldsmith's.
Emerson.

He who loves with purity considers not the gift of the lover, but the love of the giver.—
Thomas à Kempis.

It passes in the world for greatness of mind, to be perpetually giving and loading people with bounties ; but it is one thing to know how to give, and another thing not to know how to keep. Give me a heart that is easy and open, but I will have no holes in it ; let it be bountiful with judgment, but I will have nothing run out of it I know not how.—*Seneca.*

Gifts are like fish-hooks ; for who is not aware that the greedy char is deceived by the fly which he swallows ? —*Martial.*

Posthumous charities are the very essence of selfishness, when bequeathed by those who, when alive, would part with nothing.—*Colton.*

People do not care to give alms without some security for their money ; and a wooden leg or a withered arm is a sort of draft upon heaven for those who choose to have their money placed to account there.—*Mackenzie.*

For the will and not the gift makes the giver.
Lessing.

Those Spaniards in Mexico who were chased of the Indians tell us what to do with our goods in our extremity. They being to pass over a river in their flight, as many as cast away their gold swam over safe ; but some, more covetous, keeping their gold, were either drowned with it, or overtaken and slain by the savages : you have received, now learn to give.—*Bacon.*

A gift — its kind, value, and appearance ; the silence or the pomp that attends it ; the style in which it reaches you — may decide the dignity or vulgarity of the giver.—*Lavater.*

He was one of those men, moreover, who possess almost every gift except the gift of the power to use them.—*Charles Kingsley.*

If we will take the good we find, asking no questions, we shall have heaping measures. The great gifts are not got by analysis. Everything good is on the highway.—*Emerson.*

It is a proof of boorishness to confer a favor with a bad grace; it is the act of giving that is hard and painful. How little does a smile cost?
Bruyère.

When thou makest presents, let them be of such things as will last long; to the end they may be in some sort immortal, and may frequently refresh the memory of the receiver.—
Fuller.

We are as answerable for what we give as for what we receive; nay, the misplacing of a benefit is worse than the not receiving of it; for the one is another person's fault, but the other is mine.—*Seneca.*

Give freely to him that deserveth well and asketh nothing; and that is a way of giving to thyself.—*Fuller.*

Gifts are the greatest usury, because a two-fold retribution is an urged effect that a noble mind prompts us to; and it is said we pay the most for what is given us.—*J. Beaumont.*

When you give, give with joy and smiling.
Joubert.

The secret of giving affectionately is great and rare; it requires address to do it well; otherwise we lose instead of deriving benefit from it. This man gives lavishly in a way that obliges no one; the manner of giving is worth more than the gift. Another loses intentionally at a game, thus disguising his present; another forgets a jewel, which would have been refused as a gift. A generous booby seems to be giving alms to his mistress when he is making a present.—*Corneille.*

Every gift which is given, even though it be small is in reality great, if it be given with affection.—*Pindar.*

Liberty is of more value than any gifts; and to receive gifts is to lose it. Be assured that men most commonly seek to oblige thee only that they may engage thee to serve them.—
Saadi.

Some men give so that you are angry every time you ask them to contribute. They give so that their gold and silver shoot you like a bullet. Other persons give with such beauty that you remember it as long as you live; and you say, "It is a pleasure to go to such men." There is some men that give as springs do: whether you go to them or not, they are always full; and your part is merely to put your dish under the ever-flowing stream. Others give just as a pump does where the well is dry, and the pump leaks.—*Beecher.*

Rich gifts wax poor when givers prove unkind.—*Shakespeare.*

God's love gives in such a way that it flows from a Father's heart, the wellspring of all good. The heart of the giver makes the gift dear and precious; as among ourselves we say of even a trifling gift, "It comes from a hand we love," and look not so much at the gift as at the heart.—*Luther.*

The making presents to a lady one addresses is like throwing armor into an enemy's camp, with a resolution to recover it.—*Shenstone.*

Gifts are as gold that adorns the temple; grace is like the temple that sanctifies the gold.
Burkitt.

God hands gifts to some, whispers them to others.—*W. R. Alger.*

No man esteems anything that comes to him by chance; but when it is governed by reason, it brings credit both to the giver and receiver; whereas those favors are in some sort scandalous that make a man ashamed of his patron.—*Seneca.*

Who gives a trifle meanly is meaner than the trifle.—*Lavater.*

He gives not best that gives most; but he gives most who gives best. If then I cannot give bountifully, yet I will give freely; and what I want in my hand, supply by my heart. He gives well that gives willingly.—
Arthur Warwick.

Gifts, they weigh like mountains on a sensitive heart. To me they are oftener punishments than pleasures.—*Madame Fee.*

That which is given with pride and ostentation is rather an ambition than a bounty.—
Seneca.

GLADNESS.
For from the crushed flowers of gladness on the road of life a sweet perfume is wafted over to the present hour, as marching armies often send out from heaths the fragrance of trampled plants.—*Richter.*

True gladness doth not always speak; joy, bred and born but in the tongue, is weak.—
Ben Jonson.

Nations and men are only the best when they are the gladdest, and deserve heaven when they enjoy it.—*Richter.*

GLOOM.
Gloom and sadness are poison to us, and the origin of hysterics. You are right in thinking that this disease is in the imagination : you have defined it perfectly; it is vexation which causes it to spring up, and fear that supports it.—
Madame de Sévigné.

He who is only just is stern ; he who is only wise lives in gloom.— *Voltaire.*

GLORY.

Glory is a poison, good to be taken in small doses.—*Balzac.*

He that first likened glory to a shadow did better than he was aware of. They are both of them things excellently vain. Glory also, like a shadow, goes sometimes before the body, and sometimes in length infinitely exceeds it.—
Montaigne.

The love of glory can only create a great hero ; the contempt of it creates a great man.—
Talleyrand.

Wood burns because it has the proper stuff for that purpose in it ; and a man becomes renowned because he has the necessary stuff in him. Renown is not to be sought, and all pursuit of it is vain. A person may, indeed, by skilful conduct and various artificial means, make a sort of name for himself ; but if the inner jewel is wanting, all is vanity, and will not last a day.—*Goethe.*

The paths of glory lead but to the grave.—
Gray.

Glory is like a circle in the water, which never ceaseth to enlarge itself, till, by broad spreading, it disperse to naught.—*Shakespeare.*

Is death more cruel from a private dagger than in the field from murdering swords of thousands ? Or does the number slain make slaughter glorious ? —*Cibber.*

What is glory ?—in the socket see how dying tapers flare !—*Wordsworth.*

Glory is safe when it is deserved ; it is not so with popularity ; one lasts like a mosaic, the other is effaced like a crayon drawing.—
Boufflers.

Glory grows guilty of detested crimes.—
Shakespeare.

There are two things which ought to teach us to think but meanly of human glory ; the very best have had their calumniators, the very worst their panegyrists.—*Colton.*

Our greatest glory consists not in never falling, but in rising every time we fall.—
Goldsmith.

True glory consists in doing what deserves to be written, in writing what deserves to be read, and in so living as to make the world happier and better for our living in it.—*Pliny.*

Glory is so enchanting that we love whatever we associate with it, even though it be death.—*Pascal.*

Glory darts her soul-pervading ray on thrones and cottages, regardless still of all the artificial nice distinctions vain human customs make.—
Hannah More.

Glory is the fair child of peril.—*Smollett.*

Those great actions whose lustre dazzles us are represented by politicians as the effects of deep design ; whereas they are commonly the effects of caprice and passion.—*Rochefoucauld.*

Let us not disdain glory too much, — nothing is finer, except virtue. The height of happiness would be to unite both in this life.—
Chateaubriand.

True glory is a flame lighted at the skies.—
Horace Mann.

Rising glory occasions the greatest envy, as kindling fires the greatest smoke. Envy is the reverse of charity ; and as that is the supreme source of pleasure, so this is of pain. Envy has under its banner, hatred, calumny, treachery, with the meagreness of famine, the venom of pestilence, and the rage of war.—*Spenser.*

True glory takes root, and even spreads ; all false pretences, like flowers, fall to the ground ; nor can any counterfeit last long.—*Cicero.*

Glory, the casual gift of thoughtless crowds ! Glory, the bribe of avaricious virtue !—*Johnson*

Real glory springs from the silent conquest of ourselves ; and without that the conqueror is naught but the first slave.—*Thomson.*

The road to glory would cease to be arduous if it were trite and trodden ; and great minds must be ready not only to take opportunities, but to make them.—*Colton.*

Glory fills the world with virtue, and, like a beneficent sun, covers the whole earth with flowers and with fruits.—*Vauvenargues.*

No flowery road leads to glory !—
La Fontaine.

The shortest way to arrive at glory should be to do that for conscience which we do for glory. And the virtue of Alexander appears to me with much less vigor in his theatre, than that of Socrates in his mean and obscure employment. I can easily conceive Socrates in the place of Alexander, but Alexander in that of Socrates I cannot.—*Montaigne.*

The glory of a people and of an age is always the work of a small number of great men, and disappears with them.—
Baron de Grimm.

Men are guided less by conscience than by glory ; and yet the shortest way to glory is to be guided by conscience.—*Henry Home.*

Who is it that does not voluntarily exchange his health, his repose, and his very life for reputation and glory? The most useless, frivolous, and false coin that passes current amongst us.—*Montaigne.*

Glory relaxes often and debilitates the mind; censure stimulates and contracts, — both to an extreme. Simple fame is, perhaps, the proper medium.—*Shenstone.*

GLUTTONY.

Old friendships are sometimes destroyed by toasted cheese, and hard salted meat has led to suicide. I have come to the conclusion that mankind consume twice too much food. —
Sydney Smith.

The turnpike road to people's hearts, I find, lies through their mouths.—*Dr. John Wolcott.*

But for the cravings of the belly, not a bird would have fallen into the snare; nay, nay, the fowler would not have spread his net. The belly is chains to the hands and fetters to the feet. He who is a slave to his belly seldom worships God.—*Saadi.*

I am a great eater of beef, and I believe that does harm to my wit.—*Shakespeare.*

Gluttony is the source of all our infirmities, and the fountain of all our diseases. As a lamp is choked by a superabundance of oil, a fire extinguished by excess of fuel, so is the natural health of the body destroyed by intemperate diet.—*Burton.*

Born merely for the purpose of digestion.—
Bruyère.

Swinish gluttony never looks to heaven amidst its gorgeous feast; but with besotted, base ingratitude, cravens and blasphemes his feeder.—*Milton.*

Gluttony and drunkenness have two evils attendant on them; they make the carcass smart, as well as the pocket.—*Marcus Antoninus.*

He was a kind and thankful toad, whose heart dilated in proportion as his skin was filled with good cheer; and whose spirits rose with eating, as some men's do with drink.—
Washington Irving.

Let me have men about me that are fat; sleek-headed men, and such as sleep o' nights; yonder Cassius has a lean and hungry look; he thinks too much; such men are dangerous.—
Shakespeare.

As houses well stored with provisions are likely to be full of mice, so the bodies of those that eat much are full of diseases.—*Diogenes.*

He is a very valiant trencher-man; he hath an excellent stomach.—*Shakespeare.*

When I behold a fashionable table set out in all its magnificence, I fancy that I see gouts and dropsies, fevers and lethargies, with other innumerable distempers lying in ambuscade among the dishes. Nature delights in the most plain and simple diet. Every animal, but man, keeps to one dish. Herbs are the food of this species, fish of that, and flesh of a third. Man falls upon everything that comes in his way; not the smallest fruit or excrescence of the earth, scarce a berry or a mushroom can escape him.—
Addison.

He that prolongs his meals, and sacrifices his time as well as his other conveniences, to his luxury, how quickly does he outset his pleasure!—*South.*

Such, whose sole bliss is eating, who can give but that one brutal reason why they live.—
Juvenal.

Why, at this rate, a fellow that has but a groat in his pocket may have a stomach capable of a ten-shilling ordinary.—*Congreve.*

Some men find happiness in gluttony and in drunkenness, but no delicate viands can touch their taste with the thrill of pleasure, and what generosity there is in wine steadily refuses to impart its glow to their shrivelled hearts.—
Whipple.

The pleasures of the palate deal with us like Egyptian thieves, who strangle those whom they embrace.—*Seneca.*

GOD.

He who bridles the fury of the billows knows also to put a stop to the secret plans of the wicked. Submitting with respect to his holy will, I fear God, and have no other fear.—
Racine.

How did the atheist get his idea of that God whom he denies? —*Coleridge.*

To God belongeth the east and the west; therefore, whithersoever ye turn yourselves to pray, there is the word of God; for God is omnipresent and omniscient.—*Koran.*

Born of God, attach thyself to him, as a plant to its root, that ye may not be withered.—
Demophilus.

Space is the statue of God.—*Joubert.*

Nothing is more ancient than God, for he was never created; nothing more beautiful than the world, it is the work of that same God; nothing more active than thought, for it flies over the whole universe; nothing stronger than necessity, for all must submit to it.—*Thales.*

God governs the world, and we have only to do our duty wisely, and leave the issue to him.—*John Jay.*

It is one of my favorite thoughts, that God maflifests himself to men in all the wise, good, humble, generous, great, and magnanimous men.—*Lavater.*

O, there is naught on earth worth being known but God and our own souls!—*Bailey.*

They that deny a God destroy man's nobility; for certainly man is like the beasts in his body; and if he is not like God in his spirit, he is an ignoble creature.—*Bacon.*

A foe to God was never true friend to man.— *Young.*

Many people have their own God; and he is much what the French may mean when they talk of *Le bon Dieu,* — very indulgent, rather weak, near at hand when we want anything, but far away, out of sight, when we have a mind to do wrong. Such a God is as much an idol as if he were an image of stone.—*Hare.*

There is no God but God, the living, the self-subsisting.—*Koran.*

There is something very sublime, though very fanciful, in Plato's description of the Supreme Being, that "truth is his body and light his shadow."—*Addison.*

I know by myself how incomprehensible God is, seeing I cannot comprehend the parts of my own being.—*St. Bernard.*

Happy the man who sees a God employed in all the good and ill that checker life! — *Cowper.*

When we would think of God, how many things we find which turn us away from him, and tempt us to think otherwise. All this is evil, yet it is innate.—*Pascal.*

If God were not a necessary Being of himself, he might almost seem to be made for the use and benefit of men.—*Tillotson.*

God is all love; it is he who made everything, and he loves everything that he has made.— , *Henry Brooke.*

How calmly may we commit ourselves to the hands of Him who bears up the world, — of him who has created, and who provides for the joys even of insects, as carefully as if he were their father!—*Richter.*

We cannot think too oft there is a never, never sleeping Eye, which reads the heart, and registers our thoughts.—*Bacon.*

Think not thy love to God merits God's love to thee; his acceptance of thy duty crowns his own gifts in thee; man's love to God is nothing but a faint reflection of God's love to man.—*Quarles.*

It is the nature of every artificer to tender and esteem his own work; and if God should not love his creature, it would reflect some disparagement upon his workmanship, that he should make anything that he could not own. God's power never produces what his goodness cannot embrace. God oftentimes, in the same man, distinguishes between the sinner and the creature; as a creature he can love him, while as a sinner he does afflict him.— *South.*

If God did not exist, it would be necessary to invent one.—*Voltaire.*

God is the light which, never seen itself, makes all things visible, and clothes itself in colors. Thine eye feels not its ray, but thine heart feels its warmth.—*Richter.*

We always believe that God is like ourselves: the indulgent affirm him indulgent; the stern, terrible.—*Joubert.*

With God is terrible majesty. Touching the Almighty, we cannot find him out; he is excellent in power, and in judgment, and in plenty of justice; he will not afflict.—*Bible.*

At whose sight all the stars hide their diminished heads.—*Milton.*

I cannot but take notice of the wonderful love of God to mankind, who, in order to encourage obedience to his laws, has annexed a present as well as a future reward to a good life; and has so interwoven our duty and happiness together, that, while we are discharging our obligations to the one, we are, at the same time, making the best provision for the other.— *Melmoth.*

I fear God, and next to God, I chiefly fear him who fears him not.—*Saadi.*

So long as the word "God" endures in a language will it direct the eyes of men upwards. It is with the Eternal as with the sun, which, if but its smallest part can shine uneclipsed, prolongs the day, and gives its rounded image in the dark chamber.—*Richter.*

God is goodness itself; and whatsoever is good is of him.—*Sir P. Sidney.*

In all thy actions think God sees thee; and in all his actions labor to see him; that will make thee fear him; this will move thee to love him; the fear of God is the beginning of knowledge, and the knowledge of God is the perfection of love.—*Quarles.*

We know God easily, provided we do not constrain ourselves to define him.—*Joubert.*

I ask no truer image of my Heavenly Father than I find reflected in my own heart, — all loving, all forgiving.—*Hosea Ballou.*

Of what consequence is it that anything should be concealed from man? Nothing is hidden from God; he is present in our minds and comes into the midst of our thoughts. Comes, do I say? — as if he were ever absent! — *Seneca.*

When we have broken our god of tradition, and ceased from our god of rhetoric, then may God fire the heart with his presence.— *Emerson.*

If we look closely at this earth, where God seems so utterly forgotten, we shall find that it is he, after all, who commands the most fidelity and the most love.—*Madame Swetchine.*

O Thou above all gods supreme! who broughtest the world out of darkness, and gavest man a heart to feel! By whatsoever name thou art addressed, — God, Father, or Jehovah; the God of Romulus or of Abraham, — not the God of one man but the Father and Judge of all! —*Klopstock.*

The God of merely traditional believers is the great Absentee of the universe.— *W. R. Alger.*

God should be the object of all our desires, the end of all our actions, the principle of all our affections, and the governing power of our whole souls.—*Massillon.*

As a countenance is made beautiful by the soul's shining through it, so the world is beautiful by the shining through it of a God.— *Jacobi.*

If you wish to behold God, you may see him in every object around; search in your breast, and you will find him there. And if you do not yet perceive where he dwells, confute me, if you can, and say where he is not.— *Metastasio.*

Yet forget not that "the whole world is a phylactery, and everything we see an item of the wisdom, power, or goodness of God."— *Sir Thomas Browne.*

Amid so much war and contest and variety of opinion, you will find one consenting conviction in every land, that there is one God, the King and Father of all.—*Maximus Tyrius.*

The very impossibility in which I find myself to prove that God is not discovers to me his existence.—*Bruyère.*

The slender capacity of man's heart cannot comprehend, much less utter, that unsearchable depth and burning zeal of God's love towards us.—*Luther.*

God has been pleased to prescribe limits to his own power, and to work his ends within these limits.—*Paley.*

It takes something of a poet to apprehend and get into the depth, the lusciousness, the spiritual life of a great poem. And so we must be in some way like God in order that we may see God as he is.—*Chapin.*

GOD-LIKE.

Were not the eye made to receive the rays of the sun it could not behold the sun; if the peculiar power of God lay not in us, how could the godlike charm us? —*Goethe.*

GOLD.

Though authority be a stubborn bear, yet he is oft led by the nose with gold.—*Shakespeare.*

Gold is a wonderful clearer of the understanding; it dissipates every doubt and scruple in an instant; accommodates itself to the meanest capacities; silences the loud and clamorous, and brings over the most obstinate and inflexible.—*Addison.*

It is much better to have your gold in the hand than in the heart.—*Fuller.*

It is gold which buys admittance; and it is gold which makes the true man killed, and saves the thief; nay, sometime hangs both thief and true man; what can it not do and undo?— *Shakespeare.*

How few, like Daniel, have God and gold together! — *George Villiers.*

Those who worship gold in a world so corrupt as this we live in have at least one thing to plead in defence of their idolatry, — the power of their idol. It is true that, like other idols, it can neither move, see, hear, feel, nor understand; but, unlike other idols, it has often communicated all these powers to those who had them not, and annihilated them in those who had. This idol can boast of two peculiarities; it is worshipped in all climates, without a single temple, and by all classes, without a single hypocrite.—*Colton.*

Gold glitters most where virtue shines no more, as stars from absent suns have leave to shine.—*Young.*

Gold, — worse poison to men's souls, doing more murders in this loathsome world, than these poor compounds that thou mayst not sell.—*Shakespeare.*

If all were rich, gold would be penniless.— *Bailey.*

Gold is Cæsar's treasure, man is God's; thy gold hath Cæsar's image, and thou hast God's; give therefore those things unto Cæsar which are Cæsar's, and unto God which are God's.—*Quarles.*

How quickly nature falls to revolt when gold becomes her object! —*Shakespeare.*

And mammon wins his way where seraphs might despair.—*Byron.*

Commerce has set the mark of selfishness, the signet of its all-enslaving power, upon a shining ore and called it gold.—*Shelley.*

Give him gold enough, and marry him to a puppet, or an aglet-baby; or an old trot with never a tooth in her head, though she have as many diseases as two and fifty horses; why, nothing comes amiss, so money comes withal.— *Shakespeare.*

Gold is the fool's curtain, which hides all his defects from the world.—*Feltham.*

It is observed of gold, by an old epigrammatist, "that to have it is to be in fear, and to want it, to be in sorrow."—*Johnson.*

Saint-seducing gold.—*Shakespeare.*

Midas longed for gold, and insulted the Olympians. He got gold, so that whatever he touched became gold, and he, with his long ears, was little the better for it. Midas had insulted Apollo and the gods; the gods gave him his wish, and a pair of long ears, which also were a good appendage to it. What a truth in these old fables!—*Carlyle.*

Spurned by the young, but hugged by the old!—*Hood.*

I know not whether there exists such a thing as a coin stamped with a pair of pinions; but I wish this were the device which monarchs put upon their dollars and ducats, to show that riches make to themselves wings, and fly away. *Gotthold.*

As the touchstone tries gold, so gold tries men.—*Chilo.*

O what a world of vile ill-favored faults looks handsome in three hundred pounds a year!—*Shakespeare.*

Gold, — the picklock that never fails.— *Massinger.*

Thou valiant Mars! thou ever young, fresh, loved, and delicate wooer, whose blush doth thaw the consecrated snow that lies on Dian's lap! thou visible god, that solderest close impossibilities, and makest them kiss! that speak-est with every tongue, to every purpose! O thou touch of hearts!—*Shakespeare.*

Gold, like the sun, which melts wax and hardens clay, expands great souls and contracts bad hearts.—*Rivarol.*

GOOD-BREEDING.

Good-breeding is as necessary a quality in conversation, to accomplish all the rest, as grace in motion and dancing.—*Sir W. Temple.*

One principal point of good-breeding is to suit our behavior to the three several degrees of men, — our superiors, our equals, and those below us.—*Swift.*

Good-breeding is surface Christianity.— *Holmes.*

A man endowed with great perfections, without good-breeding, is like one who has his pockets full of gold, but always wants change for his ordinary occasions.—*Steele.*

Good qualities are the substantial riches of the mind; but it is good-breeding that sets them off to advantage.—*Locke.*

Good-breeding is the art of showing men, by external signs, the internal regard we have for them. It arises from good sense, improved by conversing with good company.—*Cato.*

A man's own good-breeding is the best security against other people's ill-manners.— *Chesterfield.*

Some young people do not sufficiently understand the advantages of natural charms, and how much they would gain by trusting to them entirely. They weaken these gifts of Heaven, so rare and fragile, by affected manners and an awkward imitation. Their tones and their gait are borrowed; they study their attitudes before the glass until they have lost all trace of natural manner, and, with all their pains, they please but little.—*Bruyère.*

Good-breeding is the result of much good sense, some good-nature, and a little self-denial for the sake of others, and with a view to obtain the same indulgence from them.—*Chesterfield.*

One may know a man that never conversed in the world, by his excess of good-breeding.— *Addison.*

Perhaps the summary of good-breeding may be reduced to this rule. "Behave unto all men as you would they should behave unto you." This will most certainly oblige us to treat all mankind with the utmost civility and respect, there being nothing that we desire more than to be treated so by them.—*Fielding.*

The highest point of good-breeding, if any one can hit it, is to show a very nice regard to your own dignity, and with that in your heart, to express your value for the man above you.— *Steele.*

There are few defects in our nature so glaring as not to be veiled from observation by politeness and good-breeding.—*Stanislaus.*

Good-breeding carries along with it a dignity that is respected by the most petulant. Ill-breeding invites and authorizes the familiarity of the most timid.—*Chesterfield.*

As ceremony is the invention of wise men to keep fools at a distance, so good-breeding is an expedient to make fools and wise men equals.— *Steele.*

There is no society or conversation to be kept up in the world without good-nature, or something which must bear its appearance, and supply its place. For this reason mankind have been forced to invent a kind of artificial humanity, which is what we express by the word " good-breeding." For, if we examine thoroughly the idea of what we call so, we shall find it to be nothing else but an imitation and mimicry of good-nature, or, in other terms, affability, complaisance, and easiness of temper reduced into an art.—*Addison.*

The scholar without good-breeding is a pedant; the philosopher, a cynic; the soldier, a brute; and every man disagreeable.— *Chesterfield.*

It is not wit merely, but temper, which must form the well-bred man. In the same manner, it is not a head merely, but a heart and resolution, which must complete the real philosopher. *Shaftesbury.*

We see a world of pains taken, and the best years of life spent, in collecting a set of thoughts in a college for the conduct of life; and, after all, the man so qualified shall hesitate in his speech to a good suit of clothes, and want common sense before an agreeable woman. Hence it is that wisdom, valor, justice, and learning cannot keep a man in countenance that is possessed with these excellences, if he wants that inferior art of life and behavior called good-breeding.—*Steele.*

Good breeding shows itself most where to an ordinary eye it appears the least.—*Addison.*

Good manners is the art of making those people easy with whom we converse. Whoever makes the fewest persons uneasy is the best bred in the company.—*Swift.*

GOOD-NATURE.
Good-nature is the very air of a good mind, the sign of a large and generous soul, and the peculiar soil in which virtue prospers.— *Goodman.*

Good-nature is more agreeable in conversation than wit, and gives a certain air to the countenance which is more amiable than beauty. It shows virtue in the fairest light; takes off in some measure from the deformity of vice; and makes even folly and impertinence supportable. *Addison.*

Good sense and good-nature are never separated, though the ignorant world has thought otherwise. Good-nature, by which I mean beneficence and candor, is the product of right reason.—*Dryden.*

Good-humor will sometimes conquer ill-humor, but ill-humor will conquer it oftener; and for this plain reason good-humor must operate on generosity, ill-humor on meanness.— *Lord Greville.*

Nothing can constitute good-breeding that has not good-nature for its foundation.— *Bulwer Lytton.*

Good nature is that benevolent and amiable temper of mind which disposes us to feel the misfortunes and enjoy the happiness of others, and, consequently, pushes us on to promote the latter and prevent the former; and that without any abstract contemplation on the beauty of virtue, and without the allurements or terrors of religion.—*Fielding.*

All other knowledge is hurtful to him who has not the science of honesty and good-nature. *Montaigne.*

That inexhaustible good-nature which is the most precious gift of Heaven, spreading itself like oil over the troubled sea of thought, and keeping the mind smooth and equable in the roughest weather.— *Washington Irving.*

Good-nature is stronger than tomahawks.— *Emerson.*

Good humor, gay spirits, are the liberators, the sure cure for spleen and melancholy. Deeper than tears, these irradiate the tophets with their glad heavens. Go laugh, vent the pits, transmuting imps into angels by the alchemy of smiles. The satans flee at the sight of these redeemers.—*Alcott.*

There are persons of that general philanthropy and easy tempers, which the world in contempt generally calls good-natured, who seem to be sent into the world with the same design with which men put little fish into a pond, in order only to be devoured by the voracious water-hero.—*Fielding.*

Honest good-humor is the oil and wine of a merry meeting, and there is no jovial companionship equal to that where the jokes are rather small and the laughter abundant.— *Washington Irving.*

Good-nature is the beauty of the mind, and, like personal beauty, wins almost without anything else, — sometimes, indeed, in spite of positive deficiencies.—*Hanway.*

GOODNESS.
Goodness is generous and diffusive; it is largeness of mind, and sweetness of temper, balsam in the blood, and justice sublimated to a richer spirit.—*Jeremy Collier.*

Experience has convinced me that there is a thousand times more goodness, wisdom, and love in the world than men imagine.— *Gehler.*

Your goodness must have some edge to it, else it is none.—*Emerson.*

One of the almost numberless advantages of goodness is, that it blinds its possessor to many of those faults in others which could not fail to be detected by the morally defective. A consciousness of unworthiness renders people extremely quick-sighted in discerning the vices of their neighbors; as persons can easily discover in others the symptoms of those diseases beneath which they themselves have suffered.—*Godfrey.*

Goodness is beauty in its best estate.—
Marlowe.

It is only great souls that know how much glory there is in being good.—*Sophocles.*

The life of a truly good man consists in the perpetual enjoyment of an intercourse with the good, in the seeking for good, and in the contemplation.—*Lavater.*

Let no man think lightly of good, saying in his heart, It will not benefit me. Even by the falling of water-drops a water-pot is filled; the wise man becomes full of good, even if he gather it little by little.—*Buddha.*

We may be as good as we please, if we please to be good.—*Barrow.*

He that is a good man is three quarters of his way towards the being a good Christian, wheresoever he lives, or whatsoever he is called. *South.*

God's livery is a very plain one; but its wearers have good reason to be content. If it have not so much gold-lace about it as Satan's, it keeps out foul weather better, and is besides a great deal cheaper.—*Lowell.*

How far that little candle throws his beams! so shines a good deed in a naughty world.—
Shakespeare.

The soul is strong that trusts in goodness.—
Massinger.

In the heraldry of Heaven goodness precedes greatness; so on earth it is more powerful. The lowly and the lovely may frequently do more in their own limited sphere than the gifted:—
Bishop Horne.

A good man enlarges the term of his own existence.—*Martial.*

Our whole life is startlingly moral. There is never an instant's truce between virtue and vice. Goodness is the only investment that never fails.—*Thoreau.*

Few persons have courage enough to seem as good as they really are.—*Hare.*

None deserve the character of being good who have not spirit enough to be bad; goodness, for the most part, is either indolence or impotence.—*Rochefoucauld.*

A charmed life old goodness hath; the tares may perish, but the grain is not for death.—
Whittier.

O, if the good deeds of human creatures could be traced to their source, how beautiful would even death appear; for how much charity, mercy, and purified affection would be seen to have growth in dusty graves!—*Dickens.*

You are not very good if you are not better than your best friends imagine you to be.—
Lavater.

A good deed is never lost; he who sows courtesy reaps friendship, and he who plants kindness gathers love; pleasure bestowed upon a grateful mind was never sterile, but generally gratitude begets reward.—*Basil.*

Goodness consists not in the outward things we do, but in the inward thing we are. To be is the great thing.—*Chapin.*

True goodness is like the glow-worm in this, that it shines most when no eyes, except those of Heaven, are upon it.—*Hare.*

Little men build up great ones, but the snow colossus soon melts; the good stand under the eye of God, and therefore stand.—
Landor.

It is pleasant to be virtuous and good, because that is to excel many others; it is pleasant to grow better, because that is to excel ourselves; it is pleasant to mortify and subdue our lusts, because that is victory; it is pleasant to command our appetites and passions, and to keep them in due order within the bounds of reason and religion, because this is empire.—
Tillotson.

How indestructibly the good grows, and propagates itself, even among the weedy entanglements of evil!—*Carlyle.*

A good man doubles the length of his existence; to have lived so as to look back with pleasure on our past existence is to live twice.—
Martial.

Goodness does not more certainly make men happy, than happiness makes them good. We must distinguish between felicity and prosperity; for prosperity leads often to ambition, and ambition to disappointment; the course is then over, the wheel turns round but once; while the reaction of goodness and happiness is perpetual.—*Landor.*

Every day should be distinguished by at least one particular act of love.—*Lavater.*

If for anything he loved greatness, it was because therein he might exercise his goodness.— *Sir P. Sidney.*

Live for something. Do good, and leave behind you a monument of virtue that the storm of time can never destroy. Write your name, in kindness, love, and mercy, on the hearts of thousands you come in contact with year by year; you will never be forgotten. No, your name, your deeds, will be as legible on the hearts you leave behind as the stars on the brow of evening. Good deeds will shine as the stars of heaven.— *Chalmers.*

Goodness admits of no excess, but error.— *Bacon.*

There is no odor so bad as that which arises from goodness tainted. It is human, it is divine carrion.— *Thoreau.*

To love the public, to study universal good, and to promote the interest of the whole world, as far as lies within our power, is the height of goodness, and makes that temper which we call divine.—*Shaftesbury.*

His daily prayer, far better understood in acts than words, was simply doing good.— *Whittier.*

Nothing good bursts forth all at once. The lightning may dart out of a black cloud; but the day sends his bright heralds before him, to prepare the world for his coming.—*Hare.*

GOOD-TASTE.

Good taste is the modesty of the mind; that is why it cannot be either imitated or acquired. *Madame de Girardin.*

GOSPEL.

God writes the gospel, not in the Bible alone, but on trees and flowers and clouds and stars.—*Luther.*

The gospel comes to the sinner at once, with nothing short of complete forgiveness as the starting-point of all his efforts to be holy. It does not say, " Go and sin no more, and I will not condemn thee " ; it says at once, " Neither do I condemn thee ; go and sin no more."— *Rev. Dr. Bonar.*

I am not ashamed of the gospel of Christ; for it is the power of God unto salvation to every one that believeth ; to the Jew first, and also to the Greek.—*Bible.*

GOSSIP.

I will not say it is not Christian to make beads of others' faults, and tell them over every day ; I say it is infernal. If you want to know how the Devil feels, you do know, if you are such an one.—*Beecher.*

Love and scandal are the best sweeteners of tea.—*Fielding.*

Truth is not exciting enough to those who depend on the characters and lives of their neighbors for all their amusement.—*Bancroft.*

We are disgusted by gossip ; yet it is of importance to keep the angels in their proprieties. *Emerson.*

Such as are still observing upon others are like those who are always abroad at other men's houses, reforming everything there while their own runs to ruin.—*Pope.*

I take it as a matter not to be disputed, that if all knew what each said of the other, there would not be four friends in the world. This seems proved by the quarrels and disputes caused by the disclosures which are occasionally made.—*Pascal.*

A knavish speech sleeps in a foolish ear.— *Shakespeare.*

Let the greatest part of the news thou hearest be the least part of what thou believest, lest the greatest part of what thou believest be the least part of what is true. Where lies are easily admitted, the father of lies will not easily be excluded.—*Quarles.*

GOVERNMENT.

The principal foundation of all states are good laws and good arms.—*Machiavelli.*

The wonder is not that the world is so easily governed, but that so small a number of persons will suffice for the purpose. There are dead weights in political and legislative bodies as in clocks, and hundreds answer as pulleys who would never do for politicians.—*Simms.*

Wish you to know if a soul is of free being and temper, put to the proof his respect for the magistrates.—*Riouffe.*

Let them obey who know how to rule.— *Shakespeare.*

Government is only a necessary evil, like other go-carts and crutches. Our need of it shows exactly how far we are still children. All governing overmuch kills the self-help and energy of the governed.— *Wendell Phillips.*

We are often governed by people not only weaker than ourselves, but even by those whom we think so.—*Lord Greville.*

A man must first govern himself, ere he be fit to govern a family ; and his family, ere he be fit to bear the government of the commonwealth.—*Sir Walter Raleigh.*

They that govern most make least noise. You see when they row in a barge, they that do drudgery work, slash, and puff, and sweat; but he that governs sits quietly at the stern, and scarce is seen to stir.—*Selden.*

Monarch, thou wishest to cover thyself with glory; be the first to submit to the laws of thy empire.—*Bias.*

There be three sorts of government, — monarchical, aristocratical, democratical; and they are apt to fall three several ways into ruin, — the first, by tyranny; the second, by ambition; the last, by tumults. A commonwealth grounded upon any one of these is not of long continuance; but, wisely mingled, each guards the other and makes that government exact.—*Quarles.*

Society is well governed when the people obey the magistrates, and the magistrates the laws.—*Solon.*

The very idea of the power and the right of the people to establish government presupposes the duty of every individual to obey the established government.— *Washington.*

Which is the best government? That which teaches self-government.—*Goethe.*

The science of government is merely a science of combinations, of applications and of exceptions, according to time, place, and circumstances.—*Rousseau.*

All governments are, to a certain extent, a treaty with the Devil.—*Jacobi.*

With common men, there needs too oft the show of war to keep the substance of sweet peace; and for a king, it is sometimes better to be feared than loved.—*Shakespeare.*

All government, all exercise of power, no matter in what form, which is not based in love and directed by knowledge, is a tyranny.—*Mrs. Jameson.*

.One of the most important, but one of the most difficult things to a powerful mind is to be its own master; a pond may lay quiet in a plain, but a lake wants mountains to compass and hold it in.—*Addison.*

Power exercised with violence has seldom been of long duration, but temper and moderation generally produce permanence in all things.—*Seneca.*

When Tarquin the Proud was asked what was the best mode of governing a conquered city, he replied only by beating down with his staff all the tallest poppies in his garden.—*Livy.*

The power is detested, and miserable is the life of him who wishes rather to be feared than loved.—*Cornelius Nepos.*

In all governments there must of necessity be both the law and the sword; laws without arms would give us not liberty but licentiousness, and arms without laws would produce not subjection but slavery.—*Colton.*

Though a soldier, in time of peace, is like a chimney in summer, yet what wise man would pluck down his chimney because his almanac tells him it is the middle of June?—*T. Hughes.*

Refined policy ever has been the parent of confusion, and ever will be so as long as the world endures. Plain good intention, which is as easily discovered at the first view as fraud is surely detected at last, is of no mean force in the government of mankind.—*Burke.*

A statesman, we are told, should follow public opinion. Doubtless, as a coachman follows his horses; having firm hold on the reins and guiding them.—*Hare.*

The surest way to prevent seditions (if the times do bear it) is to take away the matter of them; for if there be fuel prepared it is hard to tell whence the spark shall come that shall set it on fire.—*Bacon.*

The aggregate happiness of society, which is best promoted by the practice of a virtuous policy, is or ought to be the end of all government.— *Washington.*

Of all the difficulties in a state, the temper of a true government most felicifies and perpetnates it; too sudden alterations distemper it. Had Nero tuned his kingdom as he did his harp, his harmony had been more honorable, and his reign more prosperous.—*Quarles.*

All men would be masters of others, and no man is lord of himself.—*Goethe.*

There is no slight danger from general ignorance; and the only choice which Providence has graciously left to a vicious government is either to fall by the people, if they are suffered to become enlightened, or with them, if they are kept enslaved and ignorant.—*Coleridge.*

A mercantile democracy may govern long and widely; a mercantile aristocracy cannot stand.—*Landor.*

An established government has an infinite advantage by that very circumstance of its being established, — the bulk of mankind being governed by authority, not reason, and never attributing authority to anything that has not the recommendation of antiquity.—*Hume.*

The worst governments are always the most chargeable, and cost the people dearest; as all men in courts of judicature pay more for the wrongs that are done them than for the right.—*Butler.*

Government began in tyranny and force, began in the feudalism of the soldier and bigotry of the priest; and the ideas of justice and humanity have been fighting their way, like a thunder-storm, against the organized selfishness of human nature.— *Wendell Phillips.*

The administration of government, like a guardianship, ought to be directed to the good of those who confer, and not of those who receive the trust.—*Cicero.*

When any one person or body of men seize into their hands the power in the last resort, there is properly no longer a government, but what Aristotle and his followers call the abuse and corruption of one.—*Swift.*

The surest way of governing, both in a private family and a kingdom, is for a husband and a prince sometimes to drop their prerogative.—*Bishop Hughes.*

It is among the evils, and perhaps not the smallest, of democratical governments, that the people must feel before they will see. When this happens, they are roused to action. Hence it is that those kinds of government are so slow.— *Washington.*

GRACE.

Grace has been defined, the outward expression of the inward harmony of the soul.—*Hazlitt.*

Grace is to the body what good sense is to the mind.—*Rochefoucauld.*

Grace is in a great measure a natural gift; elegance implies cultivation, or something of more artificial character. A rustic, uneducated girl may be graceful, but an elegant woman must be accomplished and well trained. It is the same with things as with persons; we talk of a graceful tree, but of an elegant house or other building. Animals may be graceful, but they cannot be elegant. The movements of a kitten or a young fawn are full of grace; but to call them "elegant" animals would be absurd.— *Whately.*

Every natural action is graceful.—*Emerson.*

To some kind of men their graces serve them but as enemies.—*Shakespeare.*

Let grace and goodness be the principal loadstone of thy affections. For love, which hath ends, will have an end; whereas that which is founded on true virtue will always continue.—*Dryden.*

God appoints our graces to be nurses to other men's weaknesses.—*Beecher.*

It is graceful in a man to think and to speak with propriety, to act with deliberation, and in every occurrence of life to find out and persevere in the truth. On the other hand, to be imposed upon, to mistake, to falter, and to be deceived, is as ungraceful as to rave or to be insane.—*Cicero.*

Beauty, devoid of grace, is a mere hook without the bait.—*Talleyrand.*

There is a language in her eye, her cheeks, her lip, nay, her foot speaks.—*Shakespeare.*

Grace is a quality different from beauty, though nearly allied to it, which is never observed without affecting us with emotions of peculiar delight, and which it is, perhaps, the first object of the arts of sculpture and painting to study and to present.—*Sir A. Alison.*

Grace was in all her steps, heaven in her eye, in every gesture dignity and love.—*Milton.*

She was the pride of her familiar sphere, — the daily joy of all who on her gracefulness might gaze, and in the light and music of her way have a companion's portion.— *Willis.*

The mother grace of all the graces is Christian good-will.—*Beecher.*

Grace is in garments, in movements, in manners; beauty in the nude, and in forms. This is true of bodies; but when we speak of feelings, beauty is in their spirituality, and grace in their moderation.—*Joubert.*

Whatever is graceful is virtuous, and whatever is virtuous is graceful.—*Cicero.*

Natural graces, that extinguish art.—*Shakespeare.*

Grace in women has more effect than beauty. We sometimes see a certain fine self-possession, an habitual voluptuousness of character, which reposes on its own sensations, and derives pleasure from all around it, that is more irresistible than any other attraction. There is an air of languid enjoyment in such persons, "in their eyes, in their arms, and their hands, and their face," which robs us of ourselves, and draws us by a secret sympathy towards them.—*Hazlitt.*

A pleasing figure is a perpetual letter of recommendation.—*Bacon.*

Gracefulness cannot subsist without ease; delicacy is not debility; nor must a woman be sick in order to please. Infirmity and sickness may excite our pity, but desire and pleasure require the bloom and vigor of health.—*Rousseau.*

Grace is the beauty of form under the influence of freedom.—*Schiller.*

The Hand that hath made you fair hath made you good; the goodness that is cheap in beauty makes beauty brief in goodness; but grace, being the soul of your complexion, should keep the body of it ever fair.—*Shakespeare.*

Snatch a grace beyond the reach of art.—*Pope.*

Grace imitates modesty, as politeness imitates kindness.—*Joubert.*

Virtue, without the graces, is like a rich diamond unpolished, — it hardly looks better than a common pebble; but when the hand of the master rubs off the roughness, and forms the sides into a thousand brilliant surfaces, it is then that we acknowledge its worth, admire its beauty, and long to wear it in our bosoms.— *Jane Porter.*

That word " grace " in an ungracious mouth is but profane.—*Shakespeare.*

All actions and attitudes of children are graceful because they are the luxuriant and immediate offspring of the moment, — divested of affectation, and free from all pretence.— *Fuseli.*

GRAMMAR.
Grammar, which knows how to lord it over kings, and with high hand makes them obey its laws.—*Molière.*

GRANDEUR.
Grandeur and beauty are so very opposite that you often diminish the one as you increase the other. Vanity is most akin to the latter, simplicity to the former.—*Shenstone.*

GRATITUDE.
To the generous mind the heaviest debt is that of gratitude, when it is not in our power to repay it.—*Franklin.*

If gratitude is due from children to their earthly parents, how much more is the gratitude of the great family of man due to our Father in heaven ! —*Hosea Ballou.*

Now it was well said, whoever said it, " That he who hath the loan of money has not repaid it, and he who has repaid has not the loan; but he who has acknowledged a kindness has it still, and he who has a feeling of it has requited it."—*Cicero.*

He that preaches gratitude pleads the cause both of God and men ; for without it we can neither be sociable nor religious.—*Seneca.*

I thank my Heavenly Father for every manifestation of human love, I thank him for all experiences, be they sweet or bitter, which help me to forgive all things, and to enfold the whole world with a blessing.—*Mrs. L. M. Child.*

We seldom find people ungrateful so long as we are in a condition to render them service. *Rochefoucauld.*

Cicero calls gratitude the mother of virtues ; reckons it is the most capital of all duties ; and uses the words " grateful " and "good " as synonymous terms, inseparably united in the same character.—*John Bate.*

He who remembers the benefits of his parents is too much occupied with his recollections to remember their faults.—*Béranger.*

The law of the pleasure in having done anything for another is, that the one almost immediately forgets having given, and the other remembers eternally having received.—*Seneca.*

He who receives a good turn should never forget it ; he who does one should never remember it.—*Charron.*

There are minds so impatient of inferiority that their gratitude is a species of revenge ; and they return benefits, not because recompense is a pleasure, but because obligation is a pain.— *Johnson.*

The feeling of gratitude has all the ardor of a passion in noble hearts.—*Achilles Poincelot.*

It is another's fault if he be ungrateful, but it is mine if I do not give. To find one thankful man I will oblige a great many that are not so.—*Seneca.*

It is not best to refine gratitude ; it evaporates in the process of subtilization.— *Nicole.*

Epicurus says " gratitude is a virtue that has commonly profit annexed to it." And where is the virtue, say I, that has not ? But still the virtue is to be valued for itself, and not for the profit that attends it.—*Seneca.*

Gratitude is a duty which ought to be paid, but which none have a right to expect. *Rousseau.*

He that has nature in him must be grateful ; it is the *C*reator's primary great law, that links the chain of beings to each other.— *Madden.*

He enjoys much who is thankful for little. A grateful mind is a great mind.—*Secker.*

Gratitude is the fairest blossom which springs from the soul ; and the heart of man knoweth none more fragrant. While its opponent, ingratitude, is a deadly weed ; not only poisonous in itself, but impregnating the very atmosphere in which it grows, with fetid vapors. *Hosea Ballou.*

Gratitude is a duty none can be excused from, because it is always at our own disposal.— *Charron.*

Gratitude in the generality of men is only a strong and secret wish to receive still greater benefits.—*Rochefoucauld.*

It is a dangerous experiment to call in gratitude as an ally to love. Love is a debt which inclination always pays, obligation never.— *Pascal.*

There is as much greatness of mind in the owning of a good turn as in the doing of it ; and we must no more force a requital out of season than be wanting in it.—*Seneca.*

The gratitude of place-expectants is a lively sense of future favors.—*Sir Robert Walpole.*

So long as we stand in need of a benefit, there is nothing dearer to us; nor anything cheaper when we have received it.—*L'Estrange.*

Small service is true service while it lasts.— *Wordsworth.*

O call not to my mind what you have done! It sets a debt of that account before me, which shows me poor and bankrupt even in hopes! — *Congreve.*

It is a species of agreeable servitude, to be under an obligation to those we esteem.— *Queen Christina.*

It is a very high mind to which gratitude is not a painful sensation. If you wish to please, you will find it wiser to receive, solicit even, favors, than accord them; for the vanity of the obligor is always flattered, that of the obligee rarely.—*Bulwer Lytton.*

Those who make us happy are always thankful to us for being so. Their gratitude is the reward of their own benefits.— *Madame Swetchine.*

The reason for misreckoning in expected returns of gratitude is that the pride of the giver and receiver can never agree about the value of the obligation.—*Rochefoucauld.*

From David learn to give thanks in everything. Every furrow in the book of Psalms is sown with seeds of thanksgiving.— *Jeremy Taylor.*

He that precipitates a return does as good as say, I am weary of being in this man's debt; not but that the hastening of a requital, as a good office, is a commendable disposition, but it is another thing to do it as a discharge; for it looks like casting off a heavy and troublesome burden.—*Seneca.*

A single grateful thought towards heaven is the most perfect prayer.—*Lessing.*

There is a selfishness even in gratitude, when it is too profuse; to be over-thankful for one favor is in effect to lay out for another.— *Cumberland.*

As flowers carry dew-drops, trembling on the edges of the petals, and ready to fall at the first waft of wind or brush of bird, so the heart should carry its beaded words of thanksgiving; and at the first breath of heavenly flavor, let down the shower, perfumed with the heart's gratitude.—*Beecher.*

People follow their interest; one man is grateful for his convenience, and another man is ungrateful for the same reason.—*Seneca.*

If I only have will to be grateful, I am so.— *Seneca.*

Almost every one takes pleasure in repaying trifling obligations, very many feel gratitude for those that are moderate; but there is scarcely any one who is not ungrateful for those that are weighty.—*Rochefoucauld.*

O Lord, that lends me life, lend me a heart replete with thankfulness.—*Shakespeare.*

Gratitude is like the good faith of traders, — it maintains commerce; and we often pay, not because it is just to discharge our debts, but that we may more readily find people to trust us.—*Rochefoucauld.*

Thankfulness is the tune of angels.— *Spenser.*

As gratitude is a necessary, and a glorious, so also is it an obvious, a cheap, and an easy virtue; so obvious that wherever there is life there is place for it, so cheap that the covetous man may be gratified without expense, and so easy that the sluggard may be so likewise without labor.—*Seneca.*

Beggar that I am, I am even poor in thanks, but I thank you.—*Shakespeare.*

GRAVE.
The world's sweet inn from pain and wearisome turmoil.—*Spenser.*

The Stoics, who thought the souls of wise men had their habitations about the moon, might make slight account of subterranean depositions, whereas the Pythagoreans and transcorporating philosophers, who were to be after buried, held great care of their interment, and the Platonic rejected not a due care of the grave.—*Sir T. Browne.*

The grave is a common treasury, to which we must all be taken.—*Burke.*

However bright the comedy before, the last act is always stained with blood. The earth is laid upon our head, and there it lies forever.— *Pascal.*

Earth's highest station ends in — Here he lies.—*Young.*

The grave — dread thing! — men shiver when thou art named; Nature, appalled, shakes off her wonted firmness.—*Blair.*

The disciples found angels at the grave of Him they loved; and we should always find them too, but that our eyes are too full of tears for seeing.—*Beecher.*

The reconciling grave swallows distinction first, that made us foes; there all lie down in peace together.—*Southern.*

It buries every error, covers every defect, extinguishes every resentment. From its peaceful bosom spring none but fond regrets and tender recollections. Who can look down upon the grave of an enemy, and not feel a compunctious throb that he should have warred with the poor handful of dust that lies mouldering before him? —*Washington Irving.*

How peaceful and how powerful is the grave! —*Byron.*

There the wicked cease from troubling ; and there the weary be at rest. There the prisoners rest together ; they hear not the voice of the oppressor. The small and great are there ; and the servant is free from his master.—*Bible.*

How populous, how vital is the grave! — *Young.*

As a tract of country narrowed in the distance expands itself when we approach, thus the way to our near grave appears to us as long as it did formerly when we were far off.—*Richter.*

A grave, wherever found, preaches a short, pithy sermon to the soul.—*Hawthorne.*

Dark lattice ! letting in eternal day ! — *Young.*

When the dusk of evening had come on, and not a sound disturbed the sacred stillness of the place, — when the bright moon poured in her light on tomb and monument, on pillar, wall, and arch, and most of all (it seemed to them) upon her quiet grave, — in that calm time, when all outward things and inward thoughts teem with assurances of immortality, and worldly hopes and fears are humbled in the dust before them, — then, with tranquil and submissive hearts they turned away, and left the child with God.—*Dickens.*

My heart is its own grave ! — *Miss L. E. Landon.*

Without settled principle and practical virtue, life is a desert; without Christian piety, the contemplation of the grave is terrible.— *Sir William Knighton.*

An angel's arm can't snatch me from the grave, — legions of angels can't confine me there ! — *Young.*

The grave is, I suspect, the sole commonwealth which attains that dead flat of social equality that life in its every principle so heartily abhors.—*Bulwer Lytton.*

The grave is a sacred workshop of nature ! a chamber for the figure of the body ; death and life dwell here together as man and wife. They are one body, they are in union ; God has joined them together, and what God hath joined together let no man put asunder.—*Hippel.*

The earth opens impartially her bosom to receive the beggar and the prince.—*Horace.*

Always the idea of unbroken quiet broods around the grave. It is a port where the storms of life never beat, and the forms that have been tossed on its chafing waves lie quiet forevermore. There the child nestles as peacefully as ever it lay in its mother's arms, and the workman's hands lie still by his side, and the thinker's brain is pillowed in silent mystery, and the poor girl's broken heart is steeped in a balm that extracts its secret woe, and is in the keeping of a charity that covers all blame.—*Chapin.*

That temple of silence and reconciliation.— *Macaulay.*

We go to the grave of a friend, saying " A man is dead " ; but angels throng about him, saying " A man is born."—*Beecher.*

Some showers (tears) sprinkled upon my grave would do well and comely.— *Jeremy Taylor.*

We adorn graves with flowers and redolent plants, just emblems of the life of man, which has been compared in the Holy Scriptures to those fading beauties whose roots, being buried in dishonor, rise again in glory.—*Evelyn.*

If thou hast no inferiors, have patience awhile, and thou shalt have no superiors. The grave requires no marshal.—*Quarles.*

That unfathomed, boundless sea, the silent grave ! —*Longfellow.*

GRAVITY.

Gravity is a mysterious carriage of the body invented to cover the defects of the mind.— *Rochefoucauld.*

Gravity is of the very essence of imposture ; it does not only mistake other things, but is apt perpetually almost to mistake itself.— *Shaftesbury.*

Too much gravity argues a shallow mind. *Lavater.*

There is a gravity which is not austere nor captious, which belongs not to melancholy nor dwells in contraction of heart ; but arises from tenderness and hangs upon reflection.—*Landor.*

What doth gravity out of his bed at midnight ? —*Shakespeare.*

As in a man's life, so in his studies, I think it is the most beautiful and humane thing in the world, so to mingle gravity with pleasure that the one may not sink into melancholy nor the other rise up into wantonness.—*Pliny.*

Gravity is only the bark of wisdom, but it preserves it.—*Confucius.*

Gravity is twin brother to stupidity. *Bovee.*

There is a false gravity that is a very ill symptom; and it may be said that as rivers which run very slowly have always the most mud at the bottom, so a stolid stiffness in the constant course of a man's life is a sign of a thick bed of mud at the bottom of his brain.—
Saville.

Gravity is the ballast of the soul.—*Fuller.*

A grave aspect to a grave character is of much more consequence than the world is generally aware of; a barber may make you laugh, but a surgeon ought rather to make you cry.—
Fielding.

The body's wisdom to conceal the mind.—
Young.

Yorick sometimes, in his wild way of talking, would say that gravity was an arrant scoundrel, and, he would add, of the most dangerous kind too, because a sly one; and that he verily believed more honest well-meaning people were bubbled out of their goods and money by it in one twelvemonth than by pocket-picking and shop-lifting in seven.—*Sterne.*

Piety enjoins no man to be dull.—*South.*

That gloomy outside, like a rusty chest, contains the shining treasures of a soul resolved and brave.—*Dryden.*

Gravity is the best cloak for sin in all countries.—*Fielding.*

GREATNESS.
It is to be lamented that great characters are seldom without a blot.—*Washington.*

Few footprints of the great remain in the sand before the ever-flowing tide. Long ago it washed out Homer's. Curiosity follows him in vain; Greece and Asia perplex us with a rival Stratford-upon-Avon. The rank of Aristophanes is only conjectured from his gift to two poor players in Athens. The age made no sign when Shakespeare, its noblest son, passed away.—*Willmott.*

Greatness, once fallen out with fortune, must fall out with men too.—*Shakespeare.*

There is something on earth greater than arbitrary power. The thunder, the lightning, and the earthquake are terrific, but the judgment of the people is more.—*Daniel Webster.*

There never was a great man unless through divine inspiration.—*Cicero.*

All grandeur that has not something corresponding to it in personal merit and heroic acts, is a deliberate burlesque, and an insult on common sense and human nature.—*Hazlitt.*

Distinction is an eminence that is attained but too frequently at the expense of a fireside.
Simms.

Great men, said Themistocles, are like the oaks, under the branches of which men are happy in finding a refuge in the time of storm and rain. But when they have to pass a sunny day under them, they take pleasure in cutting the bark and breaking the branches.—*Goethe.*

It is always a sign of poverty of mind when men are ever aiming to appear great; for they who are really great never seem to know it.—*Cecil.*

The truly great consider, first, how they may gain the approbation of God, and, secondly, that of their own consciences; having done this, they would then willingly conciliate the good opinion of their fellow-men.—*Colton.*

In order to do great things, it is necessary to live as if one was never to die.
Vauvenargues.

Such is the destiny of great men that their superior genius always exposes them to be the butt of the envenomed darts of calumny and envy.—*Voltaire.*

The world cannot do without great men, but great men are very troublesome to the world.—*Goethe.*

None think the great unhappy but the great.
Young.

Subtract from a great man all that he owes to opportunity and all that he owes to chance, all that he has gained by the wisdom of his friends and by the folly of his enemies, and the giant will often be left a pygmy.—*Barlow.*

The world knows nothing of its greatest men.—*Jeremy Taylor.*

In life we shall find many men that are great, and some men that are good, but very few men that are both great and good.—*Colton.*

Great men lose somewhat of their greatness by being near us; ordinary men gain much.—
Landor.

What millions died that Cæsar might be great!—*Campbell.*

The reason why great men meet with so little pity or attachment in adversity would seem to be this: the friends of a great man were made by his fortunes, his enemies by himself; and revenge is a much more punctual paymaster than gratitude.—*Colton.*

The superiority of some men is merely local. They are great because their associates are little.—*Johnson.*

Greatness stands upon a precipice; and if prosperity carry a man never so little beyond his poise, it overbears and dashes him to pieces.—*Colton.*

It is with glory as with beauty; for as a single fine lineament cannot make a handsome face, neither can a single good quality render a man accomplished; but a concurrence of many fine features and good qualities makes true beauty and true honor.—*Bruyère.*

Like the air-invested heron, great persons should conduct themselves; and the higher they be, the less they should show.—*Sir P. Sidney.*

It is not in the nature of true greatness to be exclusive and arrogant.—*Beecher.*

A contemplation of God's works, a generous concern for the good of mankind, and the unfeigned exercise of humility only, denominate men great and glorious.—*Addison.*

Great warriors, like great earthquakes, are principally remembered for the mischief they have done.—*Bovee.*

That man lives greatly, whatever his fate or fame, who greatly dies.—*Young.*

The greatness of action includes immoral as well as moral greatness, — Cortes and Napoleon, as well as Luther and Washington.—*Whipple.*

The highest and most lofty trees have the most reason to dread the thunder.—*Rollin.*

They that stand high have many blasts to shake them; and if they fall, they dash themselves to pieces.—*Shakespeare.*

We observe with confidence that the truly strong mind, view it as intellect or morality, or under any other aspect, is nowise the mind acquainted with its strength; that here the sign of health is unconsciousness.—*Carlyle.*

Great souls are not those which have less passion and more virtue than common souls, but only those which have greater designs.—*Rochefoucauld.*

Speaking generally, no man appears great to his contemporaries, for the same reason that no man is great to his servants, — both know too much of him.—*Colton.*

Nothing can make a man truly great but being truly good, and partaking of God's holiness.—*Matthew Henry.*

He only is great who has the habits of greatness; who, after performing what none in ten thousand could accomplish, passes on like Samson, and "tells neither father nor mother of it."—*Lavater.*

The great would not think themselves demigods if the little did not worship them.—*Boiste.*

The truly strong and sound mind is the mind that can embrace equally great things and small. I would have a man great in great things, and elegant in little things.—*Johnson.*

However brilliant an action may be, it ought not to pass for great when it is not the result of a great design.—*Rochefoucauld.*

The great are only great because we are on our knees; let us rise up.—*Prudhomme.*

Great men undertake great things because they are great; and fools, because they think them easy.—*Vauvenargues.*

The greatest man is he who chooses right with the most invincible resolution; who resists the sorest temptation from within and without; who bears the heaviest burdens cheerfully; who is calmest in storms, and most fearless under menaces and frowns; whose reliance on truth, on virtue, and on God is most unfaltering.—*Seneca.*

A great soul is above insult, injustice, grief, and mockery.—*Bruyère.*

Rightly to be great is not to stir without great argument, but greatly to find quarrel in a straw when honor is at the stake.—*Shakespeare.*

The just temper of human mind in this matter may, nevertheless, be told shortly. Greatness can only be rightly estimated when minuteness is justly reverenced. Greatness is the aggregation of minuteness; nor can its sublimity be felt truthfully by any mind unaccustomed to the affectionate watching of what is least.—*Ruskin.*

It is, alas! the poor prerogative of greatness, to be wretched and unpitied.—*Congreve.*

There is no man so great as not to have some littleness more predominant than all his greatness. Our virtues are the dupes, and often only the plaything of our follies.—*Bulwer Lytton.*

Copiousness and simplicity, variety and unity, constitute real greatness of character.—*Lavater.*

It appears to be among the laws of nature, that the mighty of intellect should be pursued and carped by the little, as the solitary flight of one great bird is followed by the twittering petulance of many smaller.—*Landor.*

Great souls attract sorrows as mountains do storms. But the thunder-clouds break upon them, and they thus form a shelter for the plains around.—*Richter.*

There is something of oddity in the very idea of greatness, for we are seldom astonished at a thing very much resembling ourselves.— *Goldsmith.*

The great make us feel, first of all, the indifference of circumstances. They call into activity the higher perceptions, and subdue the low habits of comfort and luxury; but the higher perceptions find their objects everywhere; only the low habits need palaces and banquets. *Emerson.*

Everything great is not always good, but all good things are great.—*Demosthenes.*

He that makes himself famous by his eloquence, justice, or arms illustrates his extraction, let it be never so mean; and gives inestimable reputation to his parents. We should never have heard of Sophroniscus, but for his son, Socrates; nor of Ariosto and Gryllus, if it had not been for Xenophon and Plato.— *Seneca.*

As the swollen columns of ascending smoke, so solid swells thy grandeur, pygmy man!— *Young.*

There never was a great truth but it was reverenced; never a great institution, nor a great man, that did not, sooner or later, receive the reverence of mankind.—*Theodore Parker.*

Greatness appeals to the future.—*Emerson.*

I will not go so far as to say, with a living poet, that the world knows nothing of its greatest men; but there are forms of greatness, or at least of excellence, where "die and make no sign"; there are martyrs that miss the palm, but not the stake; heroes without the laurel, and conquerors without the triumph.—*G. A. Sala.*

In the truly great, virtue governs with the sceptre of knowledge.—*Sir P. Sidney.*

The great men of earth are the shadowy men, who, having lived and died, now live again and forever through their undying thoughts. Thus living, though their footfalls are heard no more, their voices are louder than the thunder, and unceasing as the flow of tides or air.—*Beecher.*

What your heart thinks great is great. The soul's emphasis is always right.—*Emerson.*

For as much as to understand and to be mighty are great qualities, the higher that they be, they are so much the less to be esteemed if goodness also abound not in the possessor.— *Sir P. Sidney.*

Be substantially great in thyself, and more than thou appearest unto others; and let the world be deceived in thee, as they are in the lights of heaven.—*Sir Thomas Browne.*

The greatest men have not always the best heads; many indiscretions may be pardoned to a brilliant and ardent imagination. The prudence and discretion of a cold heart are not worth half so much as the follies of an ardent mind.—*Baron de Grimm.*

O, be sick, great greatness, and bid thy ceremony give thee cure! Thinkest thou the fiery fever will go out with titles blown from adulation?—*Shakespeare.*

If wrecks and ruins and desolation of kingdoms are marks of greatness, why do we not worship a tempest, and erect a statue to the plague? A panegyric upon an earthquake is every jot as reasonable as upon such conquests as these.—*Jeremy Collier.*

To be great is to be misunderstood.— *Emerson.*

Greatness is like a laced coat from Monmouth Street, which fortune lends us for a day to wear; to-morrow puts it on another's back.—*Fielding.*

Great men stand like solitary towers in the city of God, and secret passages, running deep beneath external nature, give their thoughts intercourse with higher intelligences, which strengthens and consoles them, and of which the laborers on the surface do not even dream.— *Longfellow.*

Great is not great to the greater.— *Sir P. Sidney.*

Greatness lies not in being strong, but in the right using of strength; and strength is not used rightly when it only serves to carry a man above his fellows for his own solitary glory. He is greatest whose strength carries up the most hearts by the attraction of his own. *Beecher.*

Without great men, great crowds of people in a nation are disgusting; like moving cheese, like hills of ants or of fleas, — the more, the worse.—*Emerson.*

GREETING.

As ships meet at sea a moment together, when words of greeting must be spoken, and then away upon the deep; so men meet in this world; and I think we should cross no man's path without hailing him, and if he needs giving him supplies.—*Beecher.*

GRIEF.

O, grief hath changed me since you saw me last; and careful hours, with Time's deformed hand, have written strange defeatures in my face!—*Shakespeare.*

The truth is, we pamper little griefs into great ones, and bear great ones as well as we can.— *Hazlitt.*

The grief that does not speak whispers the overfraught heart and bids it break.—
Shakespeare.

I grieve that grief can teach me nothing, nor carry me one step into real nature.—
Emerson.

The person who grieves suffers his passion to grow upon him ; he indulges it, he loves it ; but this never happens in the case of actual pain, which no man ever willingly endured for any considerable time.—*Burke.*

The sickness of the heart is most easily got rid of by complaining and soothing confidence.
Goethe.

Great grief makes sacred those upon whom its hand is laid. Joy may elevate, ambition glorify, but sorrow alone can consecrate.—
Horace Greeley.

Grief boundeth where it falls, not with an empty hollowness, but weight.—*Shakespeare.*

They truly mourn that mourn without a witness.—*Byron.*

What is grief ? It is an obscure labyrinth into which God leads man, that he may be experienced in life, that he may remember his faults and abjure them, that he may appreciate the calm which virtue gives.—*Leopold Scheffer.*

Woman's grief is like a summer storm, short as it is violent.—*Joanna Baillie.*

Some grief shows much of love ; but much of grief shows still some want of wit.—
Shakespeare.

Grief knits two hearts in closer bonds than happiness ever can ; and common sufferings are far stronger links than common joys.
Lamartine.

Grief is a stone that bears one down, but two bear it lightly.—*W. Hauff.*

Grief or misfortune seems to be indispensable to the development of intelligence, energy, and virtue. The proofs to which the people are submitted, as with individuals, are necessary then to draw them from their lethargy, to disclose their character.—*Fearon.*

Nothing speaks our grief so well as to speak nothing.—*Crashaw.*

Each substance of a grief hath twenty shadows, which show like grief itself, but are not so ; for sorrow's eye, glazed with blinding tears, divides one thing entire to many objects.
Shakespeare.

Light griefs are plaintive, but great ones are dumb.—*Seneca.*

How beautiful is sorrow when it is dressed by virgin innocence ! it makes felicity in others seem deformed.—*Sir W. Davenant.*

A heavier task could not have been imposed than I to speak my griefs unspeakable.—
Shakespeare.

Grief still treads upon the heels of pleasure.
Congreve.

Grief is a flower as delicate and prompt to fade as happiness. Still, it does not wholly die. Like the magic rose, dried and unrecognizable, a warm air breathed on it will suffice to renew its bloom.—*Madame de Gasparin.*

Every one can master a grief, but he that has it.—*Shakespeare.*

In youth, grief comes with a rush and overflow, but it dries up, too, like the torrent. In the winter of life it remains a miserable pool, resisting all evaporation.—*Madame Swetchine.*

Grief is the culture of the soul, it is the true fertilizer.—*Madame de Girardin.*

O the things unseen untold, undreamt of, which like shadows pass hourly over that mysterious world, a mind to ruin struck by grief ! —
Mrs. Hemans.

No grief is so acute but time ameliorates it.
Cicero.

Of permanent griefs there are none, for they are but clouds. The swifter they move through the sky, the more follow after them ; and even the immovable ones are absorbed by the other, and become smaller till they vanish.—*Richter.*

A plague of sighing and grief, it blows a man up like a bladder ! —*Shakespeare.*

As a fresh wound shrinks from the hand of the surgeon, then gradually submits to and even calls for it ; so a mind under the first impression of a misfortune shuns and rejects all comfort, but at length, if touched with tenderness, calmly and willingly resigns itself.—*Pliny the Younger.*

He conquers grief who can take a firm resolution.—*Goethe.*

Excess of grief for the deceased is madness ; for it is an injury to the living, and the dead know it not.—*Xenophon.*

My grief lies all within, and these external manners of laments are merely shadows to the unseen grief, that swells with silence to the tortured soul.—*Shakespeare.*

If the internal griefs of every man could be read, written on his forehead, how many who now excite envy would appear to be the objects of pity ? —*Metastasio.*

Trembling lips, tuned to such grief that they say bright words sadly.—*Sydney Dobell.*

Grief is only the memory of widowed affection. The more intense the delight in the presence of the object, the more poignant must be the impression of the absence.—
James Martineau.

Grief alone can teach us what is man.—
Bulwer Lytton.

I am not prone to weeping as our sex commonly are; the want of which vain dew perchance shall dry your pities; but I have that honorable grief lodged here which burns worse than tears drown.—*Shakespeare.*

That eating canker grief, with wasteful spite, preys on the rosy bloom of youth and beauty.—
Rowe.

As warmth makes even glaciers trickle, and opens streams in the ribs of frozen mountains, so the heart knows the full flow and life of its grief only when it begins to melt and pass away.—*Beecher.*

Great griefs medicine the less.—*Shakespeare.*

That grief is the most durable which flows inward, and buries its streams with its fountain, in the depths of the heart.—*Jane Porter.*

Grief, like a tree, has tears for its fruit.—
Philemon.

He wrote poems and relieved himself very much. When a man's grief or passion is at this point, it may be loud, but it is not very severe. When a gentleman is cudgelling his brain to find any rhyme for sorrow besides " borrow " or " to-morrow," his woes are nearer at an end than he thinks.—*Thackeray.*

Well has it been said, that there is no grief like the grief which does not speak.—*Longfellow.*

Those great and stormy passions do so spend the whole stock of grief that they presently admit a comfort and contrary affection; while a sorrow that is even and temperate goes on to its period with expectation and the distance of a just time.—*Jeremy Taylor.*

Griefs assured are felt before they come.—
Dryden.

There are moods in which we court suffering, in the hope that here, at least, we shall find reality, sharp peaks and edges of truth. But it turns out to be scene-painting and counterfeit. The only thing grief has taught me is to know how shallow it is.—*Emerson.*

GRUMBLING.

I pity the man who can travel from Dan to Beersheba, and cry, it is all barren.—*Sterne.*

Those who complain most are most to be complained of.—*Matthew Henry.*

The very large, very respectable, and very knowing class of misanthropes who rejoice in the name of grumblers, — persons who are so sure that the world is going to ruin, that they resent every attempt to comfort them as an insult to their sagacity, and accordingly seek their chief consolation in being inconsolable, their chief pleasure in being displeased.—
Whipple.

GUILE.

O, what authority and show of truth can cunning sin cover itself withal!—*Shakespeare.*

GUILT.

Beside one deed of guilt, how blest is guiltless woe!—*Bulwer Lytton.*

He who is conscious of secret and dark designs, which, if known, would blast him, is perpetually shrinking and dodging from public observation, and is afraid of all around him, and much more of all above him.—*Wirt.*

The guilty mind debases the great image that it wears, and levels us with brutes.—
Havard.

There is no man so good, that so squares all his thoughts and actions to the laws, that he is not faulty enough to deserve hanging ten times in his life. Nay, and such a one too, as it were great pity to make away, and very unjust to punish. And such a one there may be, as has no way offended the laws, who nevertheless would not deserve the character of a virtuous man, and that philosophy would justly condemn to be whipped ; so unequal and perplexed is this relation.—*Montaigne.*

God hath yoked to guilt her pale tormentor, — misery.—*Bryant.*

Think not that guilt requires the burning torches of the Furies to agitate and torment it. Their own frauds, their crimes, their remembrances of the past, their terrors of the future, — these are the domestic furies that are ever present to the mind of the impious.—*Robert Hall.*

Guilt is a spiritual Rubicon.—*Jane Porter.*

It is easy to defend the innocent ; but who is eloquent enough to defend the guilty ? —
Publius Syrus.

Let no man trust the first false step of guilt ; it hangs upon a precipice, whose steep descent in last perdition ends.—*Young.*

Guilt, though it may attain temporal splendor, can never confer real happiness. The evident consequences of our crimes long survive their commission, and, like the ghosts of the murdered, forever haunt the steps of the malefactor.—*Walter Scott.*

It is base to filch a purse, daring to embezzle a million, but it is great beyond measure to steal a crown. The sin lessens as the guilt increases.—*Schiller.*

The mind of guilt is full of scorpions.—
Shakespeare.

From the body of one guilty deed a thousand ghostly fears and haunting thoughts proceed.— *Wordsworth.*

Guilt is a poor, helpless, dependent being. Without the alliance of able, diligent, and let me add, fortunate fraud, it is inevitably undone. If the guilty culprit be obstinately silent, it forms a deadly presumption against him ; if he speaks, talking tends only to his discovery, and his very defence often furnishes the materials for his conviction.—*Junius.*

Be sure your sin will find you out.—*Bible.*

They whose guilt within their bosoms lie imagine every eye beholds their blame.—
Shakespeare.

They who once engage in iniquitous designs miserably deceive themselves when they think that they will go so far and no farther ; one fault begets another, one crime renders another necessary ; and thus they are impelled continually downward into a depth of guilt, which at the commencement of their career they would have died rather than have incurred.—*Southey.*

Life is not the supreme good ; but of all earthly ills the chief is guilt.—*Schiller.*

Our sins, like to our shadows, when our day was in its glory, scarce appeared ; toward our evening, how great and monstrous ! —*Suckling.*

Those whom guilt stains it equals.—*Lucan.*

When guilt is in its blush of infancy, it trembles in a tenderness of shame ; and the first eye that pierces through the veil that hides the secret brings it to the face.—*Southern.*

Let the galled jade wince.—*Shakespeare.*

Let wickedness escape as it may at the bar, it never fails of doing justice upon itself; for every guilty person is his own hangman.—
Seneca.

GUNPOWDER.

Such I hold to be the genuine use of gunpowder ; that it makes all men alike tall. Nay, if thou be cooler, cleverer than I, — if thou have more mind though all but no body whatever, then canst thou kill me first, and art the taller. Hereby at last is the Goliath powerless and the David resistless ; savage animalism is nothing, inventive spiritualism is all.—*Carlyle.*

Gunpowder is the emblem of politic revenge, for it biteth first, and barketh afterwards ; the bullet being at the mark before the report is heard, so that it maketh a noise, not by way of warning, but of triumph.—*Fuller.*

H.

HABIT.

A single bad habit will mar an otherwise faultless character, as an ink-drop soileth the pure white page.—*Hosea Ballou.*

Habit is ten times nature.— *Wellington.*

Like flakes of snow that fall unperceived upon the earth, the seemingly unimportant events of life succeed one another. As the snow gathers together, so are our habits formed. No single flake that is added to the pile produces a sensible change ; no single action creates, however it may exhibit, a man's character.—
Jeremy Taylor.

If an idiot were to tell you the same story every day for a year, you would end by believing him.—*Burke.*

Habit hath so vast a prevalence over the human mind that there is scarce anything too strange or too strong to be asserted of it. The story of the miser who, from long accustoming to cheat others, came at last to cheat himself, and with great delight and triumph picked his own pocket of a guinea to convey to his hoard, is not impossible or improbable.—*Fielding.*

Habit, if not resisted, soon becomes necessity.—*St. Augustine.*

Habit in most cases hardens and encrusts by taking away the keener edge of our sensations : but does it not in others quicken and refine, by giving a mechanical facility and by engrafting an acquired sense ? —*Hazlitt.*

Every base occupation makes one sharp in its practice and dull in every other.—
Sir P. Sidney.

For the honest people, relations increase with the years. For the vicious, inconveniences increase. Inconstancy is the defect of vice ; the influence of habit is one of the qualities of virtue.—*Madame Necker.*

How use doth breed a habit in a man ! —
Shakespeare.

I trust everything, under God, to habit, upon which, in all ages, the lawgiver, as well as the schoolmaster, has mainly placed his reliance, — habit, which makes everything easy, and casts all difficulties upon the deviation from the wonted course.—*Lord Brougham.*

Habits, though in their commencement like the filmy line of the spider, trembling at every breeze, may in the end prove as links of tempered steel, binding a deathless being to eternal felicity or woe.—*Mrs. Sigourney.*

All habits gather by unseen degrees.—
Dryden.

It must be conceded that, after affection, habit has its peculiar value. It is a little stream which flows softly, but freshens everything along its course.—*Madame Swetchine.*

It is almost as difficult to make a man unlearn his errors as his knowledge.—*Colton.*

A young man ought to cross his own rules, to awake his vigor, and to keep it from growing faint and rusty. And there is no course of life so weak and sottish as that which is carried on by rule and discipline.—*Montaigne.*

A new cask will long preserve the tincture of the liquor with which it is impregnated.—
Horace.

I will govern my life and my thoughts as if the whole world were to see the one and to read the other; for what does it signify to make anything a secret to my neighbor, when to God (who is the Searcher of our hearts) all our privacies are open ? —*Seneca.*

Habit is a cable. We weave a thread of it every day, and at last we cannot break it.—
Horace Mann.

The habit of virtue cannot be formed in a closet. Habits are formed by acts of reason in a persevering struggle through temptation.—
Bernard Gilpin.

Habit is our primal fundamental law; habit and imitation,— there is nothing more perennial in us than these two. They are the source of all working and all apprenticeship, of all practice and all learning, in this world.—
Carlyle.

In the great majority of things habit is a greater plague than ever afflicted Egypt; in religious character it is a grand felicity.—
John Foster.

Those who are in the power of evil habits must conquer them as they can, — and conquered they must be, or neither wisdom nor happiness can be attained; but those who are yet subject to their influence may, by timely caution, preserve their freedom; they may effectually resolve to escape the tyrant, whom they will very vainly resolve to conquer.—*Johnson.*

Habits work more constantly and with greater facility than reason; which, when we have most need of it, is seldom fairly consulted, and more rarely obeyed.—*Locke.*

I have often found a small stream at its fountain-head, that, when followed up, carried away the camel with his load.—*Saadi.*

Vicious habits are so great a stain to human nature, and so odious in themselves, that every person actuated by right reason would avoid them, though he were sure they would be always concealed both from God and man, and had no future punishment entailed upon them.
Cicero.

Habit is the deepest law of human nature.—
Carlyle.

And it is a singular truth that, though a man may shake off national habits, accent, manner of thinking, style of dress, — though he may become perfectly identified with another nation, and speak its language well, perhaps better than his own, — yet never can he succeed in changing his handwriting to a foreign style.—
Disraeli.

Lord Tenterden, the celebrated judge, expired with these words on his lips, " Gentlemen of the jury, you will now consider your verdict."
Lord Campbell.

The chains of habit are generally too small to be felt till they are too strong to be broken.
Johnson.

We are so wonderfully formed that, whilst we are creatures vehemently desirous of novelty, we are as strongly attached to habit and custom. But it is the nature of things which hold us by custom to affect us very little whilst we are in possession of them, but strongly when they are absent.—*Burke.*

Habit, with its iron sinews, clasps and leads us day by day.—*Lamartine.*

A man who has passed his life on shipboard will pace the length of his quarter-deck on the terrace before his house, were it a mile in length.—*Cumberland.*

As the stream gradually wears the channel deeper in which it runs, and thus becomes more surely bound to its accustomed course ; so the current of the mind and heart grows more and more restricted to the course in which habit has taught them to flow. These intellectual and moral habits form many peculiarities of character, and chiefly distinguish one individual from another. They, are, therefore of the utmost importance.—*S. G. Goodrich.*

Habit is too arbitrary a master for my liking.—*Lavater.*

This law is the magistrate of a man's life. It is not the pilot directing the vessel ; it is the vessel abandoned to the force of the current, the influence of the tides, and the control of the winds.—*Joseph Johnson.*

Habit, to which all of us are more or less slaves.—*La Fontaine.*

A tendency to resume the same mode of action at stated times is peculiarly the characteristic of the nervous system; and on this account regularity is of great consequence in exercising the moral and intellectual power. All nervous diseases have a marked tendency to observe regular periods; and the natural inclination to sleep at the approach of night is another instance of the same fact.—*Dr. Combe.*

I will be slave to no habit; therefore farewell tobacco.—*Hosea Ballou.*

HAIR.

There seems a life in hair, though it be dead.—*Leigh Hunt.*

By common consent gray hairs are a crown of glory; the only object of respect that can never excite envy.—*Bancroft.*

Now Jove, in his next commodity of hair, send thee a beard!—*Shakespeare.*

Fair tresses man's imperial race ensnare.—
Pope.

Hair is the most delicate and lasting of our materials, and survives us, like love. It is so light, so gentle, so escaping from the idea of death, that, with a lock of hair belonging to a child or friend, we may almost look up to heaven and compare notes with the angelic nature,—may almost say, "I have a piece of thee here not unworthy of thy being now."—
Leigh Hunt.

Her luxuriant hair,—it was like the sweep of a swift wing in visions!—*Willis.*

Her hair was not more sunny than her heart, though like a natural golden coronet it circled her dear head with careless art.—*Lowell.*

Soft hair, on which light drops a diadem.—
Massey.

How ill white hairs become a fool and jester!—*Shakespeare.*

A silver line, that from the brow to the crown, and in the middle, parts the braided hair, just serves to show how delicate a soil the golden harvest grows in.—*Wordsworth.*

The hoary head is a crown of glory if it bè found in the way of righteousness.—*Bible.*

HAND.

I love a hand that meets mine own with grasp that causes some sensation.—
Mrs. F. S. Osgood.

His noble hand did win what he did spend.—
Shakespeare.

The hand is the mind's only perfect vassal, and when, through age or illness, the connection between them is interrupted, there are few more affecting tokens of human decay.—
Tuckerman.

Venerable to me is the hard hand,—crooked, coarse,—wherein, notwithstanding, lies a cunning virtue, indispensably royal as of the seeptre of the planet.—*Carlyle.*

A dazzling white hand, veined cerulean.—
Massey.

Her hand, in whose comparison all whites are ink writing their own reproach, to whose soft seizure the cygnet's down is harsh, and spirit of sense hard as the palm of ploughman!
Shakespeare.

Neither the naked hand nor the understanding, left to itself, can do much; the work is accomplished by instruments and helps, of which the need is not less for the understanding than the hand.—*Bacon.*

HANDSOME.

Handsomeness is the more animal excellence, beauty the more imaginative. A handsome Madonna I cannot conceive, and never saw a handsome Venus; but I have seen many a handsome country girl, and a few very handsome ladies.—*Hare.*

HAPPINESS.

Happiness is only evident to us in this life by deliverance from evil; we have not real and positive good. "Happy he who sees the day!" said a blind man; but a man who sees clearly does not say so. "Happy he who is healthy!" said an invalid; when he is well he does not feel the happiness of health.—*Nicole.*

The sunshine of life is made up of very little beams, that are bright all the time.—*Aikin.*

We take greater pains to persuade others that we are happy than in endeavoring to think so ourselves.—*Confucius.*

All rational happiness consists in a proper and just exercise of those abilities and graces which our Heavenly Father has mercifully bestowed upon us. The higher we rise, and the broader we extend in the knowledge of moral holiness, righteousness, and truth, the more happy we are capable of being.—*Hosea Ballou.*

The most happy man is he who knows how to bring into relation the end and beginning of his life.—*Goethe.*

The happiness of life is made up of minute fractions,—the little, soon-forgotten charities of a kiss, a smile, a kind look, a heartfelt compliment in the disguise of a playful raillery, and the countless other infinitesimals of pleasant thought and feeling.—*Coleridge.*

If we cannot live so as to be happy, let us at least live so as to deserve happiness.—*Fichte.*

Happiness is unrepented pleasure.—*Socrates.*

No mockery in this world ever sounds to me so hollow as that of being told to cultivate happiness. Happiness is not a potato, to be planted in a mould and tilled with manure. Happiness is a glory shining far down upon us from heaven. She is a divine dew, which the soul feels dropping upon it from the amaranth bloom and golden fruitage of paradise.—*Charlotte Brontë.*

Happiness is like the statue of Isis, whose veil no mortal ever raised.—*Landor.*

We take our ideas from sounds which folly has invented, — fashion, bon-ton, and virtue are the names of certain idols to which we sacrifice the genuine pleasures of the soul. In this world of resemblance we are content with personating happiness, — to feel it is an art beyond us.—*Mackenzie.*

There must be some mixture of happiness in everything but sin.—*Mrs. Sigourney.*

All external accessions receive taste and color from the internal constitution, as clothes warm us not with their heat but our own, which they are adapted to cover and keep in.—*Montaigne.*

No person is either so happy or so unhappy as he imagines.—*Rochefoucauld.*

The happiness of life consists, like the day, not in single flashes (of light), but in one continuous mild serenity. The most beautiful period of the heart's existence is in this calm, equable light, even although it be only moonshine or twilight. Now the mind alone can obtain for us this heavenly cheerfulness and peace.—*Richter.*

The rays of happiness, like those of light, are colorless when unbroken.—*Longfellow.*

What is earthly happiness? that phantom of which we hear so much and see so little; whose promises are constantly given and constantly broken, but as constantly believed; that cheats us with the sound instead of the substance, and with the blossom instead of the fruit.—*Colton.*

The bitter past more welcome is the sweet.—*Shakespeare.*

Happiness in this world, when it comes, comes incidentally. Make it the object of pursuit, and it leads us a wild-goose chase, and is never attained.—*Hawthorne.*

Happiness is a ball after which we run wherever it rolls, and we push it with our feet when it stops.—*Goethe.*

Happiness is much more equally divided than some of us imagine. One man shall possess most of the materials, but little of the thing; another may possess much of the thing, but very few of the materials. In this particular view of it, happiness has been beautifully compared to the manna in the desert, — he that gathered much had nothing over, and he that gathered little had no lack.—*Colton.*

Happiness and virtue reach upon each other, — the best are not only the happiest, but the happiest are usually the best.—*Bulwer Lytton.*

Happiness consists in the multiplicity of agreeable consciousness.—*Johnson.*

Indolence of body and mind, when we aim at no more, is very frequently enjoyed; but the very inquiry after happiness has something restless in it, which a man who lives in a series of temperate meals, friendly conversations, and easy slumbers gives himself no trouble about. While men of refinement are talking of tranquillity, he possesses it.—*Steele.*

It is a kind of happiness to know to what extent we may be unhappy.—*Rochefoucauld.*

There is this difference between happiness and wisdom, that he that thinks himself the happiest man really is so; but he that thinks himself the wisest is generally the greatest fool.—*Colton.*

Our happiness in this world depends on the affections we are enabled to inspire.—*Duchess de Praslin.*

False happiness renders men stern and proud, and that happiness is never communicated. True happiness renders them kind and sensible, and that happiness is always shared.—*Montesquieu.*

Men of the noblest dispositions think themselves happiest when others share their happiness with them.—*Jeremy Taylor.*

O, how bitter a thing it is to look into happiness through another man's eyes!—*Shakespeare.*

To diminish envy, let us consider not what others possess, but what they enjoy; mere riches may be the gift of lucky accident or blind chance, but happiness must be the result of prudent preference and rational design.—*Colton.*

Noiseless falls the foot of time that only treads on flowers.—*Spencer.*

False happiness is like false money, — it passes for a time as well as the true, and serves some ordinary occasions; but when it is brought to the touch we find the lightness and alloy, and feel the loss.—*Pope.*

Happiness can be built on virtue alone, and must of necessity have truth for its foundation.—*Coleridge.*

No one can be said to be happy until he is dead.—*Solon.*

Happiness is a roadside flower growing on the highways of usefulness; plucked, it shall wither in thy hand; passed by, it is fragrance to thy spirit. Trample the thyme beneath thy feet; be useful, be happy.—*Tupper.*

Happiness is a rare cosmetic.—*G. J. W. Melville.*

There are two ways of being happy,—we may either diminish our wants or augment our means,—either will do, the result is the same; and it is for each man to decide for himself, and do that which happens to be the easiest. If you are idle or sick or poor, however hard it may be to diminish your wants, it will be harder to augment your means. If you are active and prosperous, or young, or in good health, it may be easier for you to augment your means than to diminish your wants. But if you are wise, you will do both at the same time, young or old, rich or poor, sick or well; and if you are very wise, you will do both in such a way as to augment the general happiness of society.—*Franklin.*

There is in man a higher aim than love of happiness; he can do without happiness, and instead thereof find blessedness.—*Carlyle.*

Happiness depends on the prudent constitution of the habits; and it is the business of religion, not so much to extinguish our desires, as to regulate and direct them to valuable, well-chosen objects.—*Paley.*

Even felicity, unless it moderate itself, oppresseth.—*Seneca.*

Happiness is in taste and not in things; and it is by having what we love that we are happy, not by having what others find agreeable.—*Rochefoucauld.*

Into the composition of every happiness enters the thought of having deserved it.—*Joubert.*

False happiness loves to be in a crowd, and to draw the eyes of the world upon her. She does not receive any satisfaction from the applauses which she gives herself, but from the admiration which she raises in others.—*Addison.*

Silence is the perfectest herald of joy; I were but little happy if I could say how much.—*Shakespeare.*

There is one way of attaining what we may term, if not utter, at least mortal happiness; it is this,—a sincere and unrelaxing activity for the happiness of others.—*Bulwer Lytton.*

The body is like a piano, and happiness is like music. It is needful to have the instrument in good order.—*Beecher.*

Hume's doctrine was that the circumstances vary, the amount of happiness does not; that the beggar cracking fleas in the sunshine under a hedge, and the duke rolling by in his chariot, the girl equipped for her first ball, and the orator returning triumphant from the debate, had different means, but the same quantity of pleasant excitement.—*Emerson.*

No man is ap who does not think himself so.—*Marcus Aptoninus.*

"Is not life useful when it is happy?" asks the egotist. "Is it not sufficiently happy when it is useful?" asks the good man.—*Madame Swetchine.*

Happiness is that single and glorious thing, which is the very light and sun of the whole animated universe; and where she is not, it were better that nothing should be. Without her wisdom is but a shadow, and virtue a name; she is their sovereign mistress.—*Colton.*

Beware what earth calls happiness; beware all joys but joys that never can expire.—*Young.*

Human happiness, according to the most received notions, seems to consist in three ingredients,—action, pleasure, and indolence. And though these ingredients ought to be mixed in different proportions, according to the particular disposition of the person, yet no one ingredient can be entirely wanting without destroying in some measure the relish of the whole composition.—*Hume.*

Happiness is no other than soundness and perfection of mind.—*Marcus Antoninus.*

In vain do they talk of happiness who never subdued an impulse in obedience to a principle. He who never sacrificed a present to a future good, or a personal to a general one, can speak of happiness only as the blind do of colors.—*Horace Mann.*

There is even a happiness that makes the heart afraid.—*Hood.*

True happiness is of a retired nature, and an enemy to pomp and noise. It arises, in the first place, from the enjoyment of one's self, and in the next, from the friendship and conversation of a few select companions.—*Addison.*

Happiness is neither within us nor without us; it is in the union of ourselves with God.—*Pascal.*

It is one main point of happiness that he that is happy doth know and judge himself to be so. The knowledge and consideration of it are the fruition of it.—*Coleridge.*

The common course of things is in favor of happiness; happiness is the rule, misery the exception. Were the order reversed, our attention would be called to examples of health and competency, instead of disease and want.—
Paley.

The soul's calm sunshine and the heartfelt joy.—*Pope.*

That wherein God himself is happy, and the holy angels happy, and in the defect of which the devils are unhappy, — that dare I call happiness. Whatsoever conduceth unto this may with an easy metaphor deserve that name ; whatsoever else the world terms happiness is to me a story out of *P*liny, — an apparition, or real delusion, wherein there is no more of happiness than the name.—
Sir Thomas Browne.

Happy in that we are not over-happy, on fortune's cap we are not the very button.—
Shakespeare.

It is one species of despair to have no room to hope for any addition to one's happiness. His following wish must then be to wish he had some fresh object for his wishes, — a strong argument that our minds and bodies were both meant to be forever active.—*Shenstone.*

The best advice on the art of being happy is about as easy to follow as advice to be well when one is sick.—*Madame Swetchine.*

Perfect happiness, I believe, was never intended by the Deity to be the lot of one of his creatures in this world; but that he has very much put in our power the nearness of our approaches to it is what I have steadfastly believed.—*Jefferson.*

If it were now to die, it were now to be most happy ; for I fear my soul hath her content so absolute, that not another comfort like to this succeeds in unknown fate.—*Shakespeare.*

Surely happiness is reflective, like the light of heaven ; and every countenance bright with smiles, and glowing with innocent enjoyment, is a mirror transmitting to others the rays of a supreme and ever-shining benevolence.—
Washington Irving.

Happiness lies beyond either pain or pleasure, — is as sublime a thing as virtue itself, indivisible from it ; and under this point of view it seems a perilous mistake to separate them.—
Mrs. Jameson.

This near miss of happiness is a great misery.
Leighton.

The happiness of man depends on no creed and no book ; it depends on the dominion of truth, which is the Redeemer and Saviour, the Messiah and the King of Glory.—*Rabbi Wise.*

There is a gentle element, and man may breathe it with a calm, unruffled soul, and drink its living waters, till his heart is pure; and this is human happiness.— *Willis.*

The happy man is he who distinguishes the boundary between desire and delight, and stands firmly on the higher ground, — he who knows that pleasure is not only not possession, but is often to be lost, and always to be endangered by it.—*Landor.*

Real happiness is cheap enough, yet how dearly we pay for its counterfeit ! —*Hosea Ballou.*

Happiness is the fine and gentle rain which penetrates the soul, but which afterwards gushes forth in springs of tears.—*Maurice de Guérin.*

God loves to see his creatures happy; our lawful delight is his ; they know not God that think to please him with making themselves miserable. The idolaters thought it a fit service for Baal to cut and lance themselves ; never any holy man looked for thanks from the true God by wronging himself.—*Bishop Hall.*

Oft when blind mortals think themselves secure, in height of bliss, they touch the brink of ruin.—*Thomson.*

The great blessings of mankind are within us and within our reach ; but we shut our eyes, and, like people in the dark, we fall foul upon the very thing we search for, without finding it.
Seneca.

To be happy is not the purpose of our being, but to deserve happiness.—*Fichte.*

Youth is too tumultuous for felicity ; old age too insecure for happiness. The period most favorable to enjoyment, in a vigorous, fortunate, and generous life, is that between forty and sixty. Life culminates at sixty.—
Bovee.

Wouldst thou ever roam abroad ? See, what is good lies by thy side. Only learn to catch happiness, for happiness is ever by you.—
Goethe.

Every one speaks of it, few know it.—
Madame Roland.

Happiness is a sunbeam which may pass through a thousand bosoms without losing a particle of its original ray ; nay, when it strikes on a kindred heart, like the converged light on a mirror, it reflects itself with redoubled brightness. Happiness is not perfected till it is shared.
Jane Porter.

The haunts of happiness are varied and rather unaccountable, but I have more often seen her among little children, and home firesides, and in country houses, than anywhere else, — at least, I think so.—*Sydney Smith.*

Happiness and vice are mutually exclusive; happiness and repentance mutually prejudicial. Happiness and virtue clasp hands and walk together —*Madame Swetchine.*

How sad a sight is human happiness to those whose thoughts can pierce beyond an hour ! — *Young.*

Were a man of pleasure to arrive at the full extent of his several wishes, he must immediately feel himself miserable.—*Shenstone.*

It is ever thus with happiness ; it is the gay to-morrow of the mind that never comes.—
Barry Cornwall.

Whatever be the cause of happiness may be made likewise the cause of misery. The medicine which, rightly applied, has power to cure, has, when rashness or ignorance prescribes it, the same power to destroy.—*Johnson.*

He who has no wish to be happier is the happiest of men.— *W. R. Alger.*

If one only wished to be happy, this could be readily accomplished ; but we wish to be happier than other people ; and this is almost always difficult, for we believe others to be happier than they are.—*Montesquieu.*

To enjoy true happiness, we must travel into a very far country, and even out of ourselves ; for the pearl we seek for is not to be found in the Indian, but in the empyrean ocean.
Sir Thomas Browne.

So scanty is our present allowance of happiness, that in many situations life could scarcely be supported if hope were not allowed to relieve the present hour by pleasures borrowed from the future.—*Johnson.*

Felicity, pure and unalloyed felicity, is not a plant of earthly growth ; her gardens are the skies.—*Burton.*

Happiness is the perpetual possession of being well deceived ; for it is manifest what mighty advantages fiction has over truth ; and the reason is at our elbow, because imagination can build nobler scenes and produce more wonderful revolutions than fortune or nature will be at the expense to furnish.—*Swift.*

That state of life is most happy where superfluities are not required and necessaries are not wanting.—*Plutarch.*

We never enjoy perfect happiness ; our most fortunate successes are mingled with sadness ; some anxieties always perplex the reality of our satisfaction.— *Corneille.*

Happiness is a matter of opinion, of fancy, in fact, but it must amount to conviction, else it is nothing.—*Chamfort.*

HARMONY.

Harmonious words render ordinary ideas acceptable ; less ordinary, pleasant ; novel and ingenious ones, delightful. As pictures and statues, and living beauty, too, show better by music-light, so is poetry irradiated, vivified, glorified, and raised into immortal life by harmony.—*Landor.*

HARVEST.

Nature's bank-dividends.—*Haliburton.*

The plump swain at evening bringing home four months' sunshine bound in sheaves.—
Lowell.

HASTE.

Haste and rashness are storms and tempests, breaking and wrecking business, but nimbleness is a full, fair wind, blowing it with speed to the haven.—*Fuller.*

Haste is of the Devil.—*Koran.*

Though I am always in haste, I am never in a hurry.—*John Wesley.*

It is of no use running ; to set out betimes is the main point.—*La Fontaine.*

Whoever is in a hurry shows that the thing he is about is too big for him. Haste and hurry are very different things.—
Chesterfield.

Haste is needful in a desperate case.—
Shakespeare.

Manners require time, as nothing is more vulgar than haste.—*Emerson.*

Haste trips up its own heels, fetters and stops itself.—*Seneca.*

Hasten slowly, and without losing heart put your work twenty times upon the anvil.—
Boileau.

Stay awhile to make an end the sooner.—
Sir Amyas Paulet.

Fraud and deceit are ever in a hurry. Take time for all things. Great haste makes great waste.—*Franklin.*

Wisely, and slow ; they stumble that run fast.—*Shakespeare.*

Unreasonable haste is the direct road to error.—*Molière.*

Haste turns usually upon a matter of ten minutes too late, and may be avoided by a habit like that of Lord Nelson, to which he ascribed his success in life, of being ten minutes too early.—*Bovee.*

Modest wisdom plucks me from over-credulous haste.—*Shakespeare.*

HATRED.

Men love in haste, but they detest at leisure.
Byron.

Hannah More said to Horace Walpole: "If I wanted to punish an enemy, it should be by fastening on him the trouble of constantly hating somebody."—*John Bate.*

Heaven has no rage like love to hatred turned.—*Congreve.*

Better is a dinner of herbs where love is than a stalled ox and hatred therewith.—*Bible.*

Hate no one, — hate their vices, not themselves.—*Brainard.*

Hatred is active, and envy passive disgust; there is but one step from envy to hate.
Goethe.

Dislike what deserves it, but never hate; for that is of the nature of malice, which is applied to persons, not things.—*William Penn.*

It is the nature of the human disposition to hate him whom you have injured.—*Tacitus.*

Hatred is the vice of narrow souls; they feed it with all their littlenesses, and make it the pretext of base tyrannies.—*Balzac.*

The hatred of those who are the most nearly connected is the most inveterate.—*Tacitus.*

Hatred is keener than friendship, less keen than love.—*Vauvenargues.*

All men naturally hate one another. I hold it a fact, that if men knew exactly what one says of the other, there would not be four friends in the world.—*Pascal.*

Plutarch says very finely, that a man should not allow himself to hate even his enemies.—*Addison.*

When our hatred is too keen, it places us beneath those we hate.—*Rochefoucauld.*

There is this difference between hatred and pity; pity is a thing often avowed, seldom felt; hatred is a thing often felt, seldom avowed.
Colton.

Hatred is self-punishment.—*Hosea Ballou.*

If you hate your enemies, you will contract such a vicious habit of mind as by degrees will break out upon those who are your friends, or those who are indifferent to you.—*Plutarch.*

The madness of the heart.—*Byron.*

Hatred is nearly always honest, — rarely if ever assumed. So much cannot be said for love.—*Ninon de l'Enclos.*

Cruelty is commonplace; and hatred, like the eagle, that carries up its prey to dash it down to a more certain death, seems to elevate the object it is about to destroy.—*Grattan.*

The greatest hatred, like the greatest virtue and the worst dogs, is quiet.—*Richter.*

Hatred is blind as well as love.—*Plutarch.*

With a hard and horrible aspect, like a new and extraordinary beast of prey behind the grating, does a real though unarmed hatred present itself for the first time before a good heart.—*Richter.*

Thousands are hated, whilst none are loved without a real cause.—*Lavater.*

To be deprived of the person we love is a happiness in comparison of living with one we hate.—*Bruyère.*

I like a good hater!—*Johnson.*

The passion of hatred is so durable and so inveterate that the surest prognostic of death in a sick man is a wish for reconciliation.—
Bruyère.

Let them hate, provided they fear.—*Cicero.*

Hate is of all things the mightiest divider, nay, is division itself. To couple hatred, therefore, though wedlock try all her golden links, and borrow to her aid all the iron manacles and fetters of law, it does but seek to twist a rope of sand.—*Milton.*

We are almost always guilty of the hate we encounter.—*Vauvenargues.*

I am misanthropos, and hate mankind; for thy part, I do wish thou wert a dog, that I might love thee something.—*Shakespeare.*

Hatred does not cease by hatred, hatred ceases by love; this is the eternal rule.—
Buddha.

HEAD.

After all, the head only reproduces what the heart creates; and so we give the mocking-bird credit when he imitates the loving murmurs of the dove.—*G. J. W. Melville.*

The head has the most beautiful appearance, as well as the highest station, in a human figure.—*Addison.*

The head truly enlightened will presently have a wonderful influence in purifying the heart; and the heart really affected with goodness will much conduce to the directing of the head.—*Sprat.*

A woman's head is always influenced by her heart; but a man's heart is always influenced by his head.—*Lady Blessington.*

Some people carry their hearts in their heads very many carry their heads in their hearts. The difficulty is to keep them apart, yet both actively working together.—*Hare*

HEALTH.

Anguish of mind has driven thousands to suicide; anguish of body, none. This proves that the health of the mind is of far more consequence to our happiness than the health of the body, although both are deserving of much more attention than either of them receives.— *Colton.*

Preserving the health by too strict a regimen is a wearisome malady.—*Rochefoucauld.*

He that loses his conscience has nothing left that is worth keeping. Therefore be sure you look to that. And in the next place look to your health; and if you have it, praise God, and value it next to a good conscience; for health is the second blessing that we mortals are capable of, a blessing that money cannot buy, therefore value it, and be thankful for it.— *Izaak Walton.*

A sound mind in a sound body, if the former be the glory of the latter, the latter is indispensable to the former.—*Edwards.*

Life is not to live, but to be well.— *Martial.*

In these days half our diseases come from the neglect of the body in the overwork of the brain. In this railway age the wear and tear of labor and intellect go on without pause or self-pity. We live longer than our forefathers; but we suffer more from a thousand artificial anxieties and cares. They fatigued only the muscles; we exhaust the finer strength of the nerves.—*Bulwer Lytton.*

Physic, for the most part, is nothing else but the substitute of exercise and temperance.— *Addison.*

There is this difference between those two temporal blessings, health and money, — money is the most envied, but the least enjoyed; health is the most enjoyed, but the least envied; and this superiority of the latter is still more obvious when we reflect that the poorest man would not part with health for money, but that the richest would gladly part with all their money for health.—*Colton.*

The only way for a rich man to be healthy is, by exercise and abstinence, to live as if he was poor.—*Sir W. Temple.*

The first wealth is health. Sickness is poor-spirited, and cannot serve any one; it must husband its resources to live. But health or fulness answers its own ends, and has to spare, runs over, and inundates the neighborhoods and creeks of other men's necessities.—*Emerson.*

Health, beauty, vigor, riches, and all the other things called goods, operate equally as evils to the vicious and unjust, as they do as benefits to the just.—*Plato.*

Health is the greatest of all possessions, and it is a maxim with me, that a hale cobbler is a better man than a sick king.—*Bickerstaff.*

O blessed health! thou art above all gold and treasure; it is thou who enlargest the soul, and openest all its powers to receive instruction, and to relish virtue. He that has thee has little more to wish for! and he that is so wretched as to want thee wants everything with thee.—*Sterne.*

What a searching preacher of self-command is the varying phenomenon of health! — *Emerson.*

The morbid states of health, the irritableness of disposition arising from unstrung nerves, the impatience, the crossness, the fault-finding of men, who, full of morbid influences, are unhappy themselves, and throw the cloud of their troubles like a dark shadow upon others, teach us what eminent duty there is in health.— *Beecher.*

People who are always taking care of their health are like misers, who are hoarding up a treasure which they have never spirit enough to enjoy.—*Sterne.*

HEART.

To try to conceal our own heart is a bad means to read that of others.—*Rousseau.*

The human heart is like a millstone in a mill; when you put wheat under it, it turns, and grinds, and bruises the wheat into flour; if you put no wheat in, it still grinds on; but then it is itself it grinds and slowly wears away.—*Luther.*

He who has most of heart knows most of sorrow.—*Bailey.*

Many flowers open to the sun, but only one follows him constantly. Heart, be thou the sunflower, not only open to receive God's blessing, but constant in looking to him.—*Richter.*

The human heart is like heaven; the more angels the more room.—*Fredrika Bremer.*

Never believe to be right those who, having but a piece of metal in their chests, would persuade you that to be cold is to be wise. Warmth is the vivifying influence of the universe, and the heart is the source of noble deeds.—*Kossuth.*

A good heart is worth gold.—*Shakespeare.*

As the heart is, so is love to the heart. It partakes of its strength or weakness, its health or disease.—*Longfellow.*

What Is the human mind, however enriched with acquisition or strengthened by exercise, unaccompanied by an ardent and sensitive heart? Its light may illumine, but it cannot inspire. It may shed a cold and moonlight radiance upon the path of life, but it warms no flower into bloom; it sets free no ice-bound fountain.— *Tuckerman.*

Be persuaded that your only treasures are those which you carry in your heart.
Demophilus.

The heart never grows better by age, I fear rather worse; always harder. A young liar will be an old one; and a young knave will only be a greater knave as he grows older.— *Chesterfield.*

The heart ought to give charity, when the hand cannot.—*Pasquier Quesnel.*

There are many people the brilliancy of whose minds only depends upon the heart. When they open that, it is hardly possible for it not to throw out some fire.—*Desmahis.*

Out of the abundance of the heart the mouth speaketh.—*Bible.*

How mighty is the human heart, with all its complicated energies; this living source of all that moves the world! this temple of liberty, this kingdom of heaven, this altar of God, this throne of goodness, so beautiful in holiness, so generous in love!—*Henry Giles.*

All who know their own minds know not their own hearts.—*Rochefoucauld.*

How easy it is for one benevolent being to diffuse pleasure around him; and how truly is a kind heart a fountain of gladness, making everything in its vicinity to freshen into smiles!
Washington Irving.

The wrinkles of the heart are more indelible than those of the brow.—*Madame Deluzy.*

The heart of a man is a short word, — a small substance, scarce enough to give a kite a meal; yet great in capacity, yea, so indefinite in desire that the round globe of the world cannot fill the three corners of it. When it desires more, and cries " Give — give! " I will set it over to .the infinite good,' where the more it hath, it may desire more, and see more to be desired.—*Bishop Hall.*

Every man must, in a measure, be alone in the world. No heart was ever cast in the same mould as that which we bear within us.—
Berne.

A good heart is the sun and moon, or, rather, the sun, and not the moon; for it shines bright and never changes, but keeps its course truly.—*Shakespeare.*

If wrong our hearts, our heads are right in vain.—*Young.*

A human heart can never grow old if it takes a lively interest in the pairing of birds, the reproduction of flowers, and the changing tints of autumn leaves.—*Mrs. L. M. Child.*

Memory, wit, fancy, acuteness, cannot grow young again in old age; but the heart can.—
Richter.

What sad faces one always sees in the asylums for orphans! It is more fatal to neglect the heart than the head.—*Theodore Parker.*

A human heart is a skein of such imperceptibly and subtly interwoven threads, that even the owner of it is often himself at a loss how to unravel it.—*Ruffini.*

What the heart has once owned and had, it shall never lose.—*Beecher.*

When the heart is still agitated by the remains of a passion, we are more ready to receive a new one than when we are entirely cured.—*Rochefoucauld.*

Alas! there is no instinct like the heart!—
Byron.

Nothing is less in our power than the heart, and, far from commanding it, we are forced to obey it.—*Rousseau.*

How idly of the human heart we speak, giving it gods of clay! —*Willis.*

All our actions take their hues from the complexion of the heart, as landscapes their variety from light.—*Bacon.*

A good heart will, at all times, betray the best head in the world.—*Fielding.*

When the heart of man is serene and tranquil, he wants to enjoy nothing but himself; every movement, even corporeal movement, shakes the brimming nectar cup too rudely.—
Richter.

The heart will break, yet brokenly live on.
Byron.

If my heart were as poor as my understanding, I should be happy; for I am thoroughly persuaded that such poverty is a means of salvation.—*Pascal.*

The hardest trial of the heart is, whether it can bear a rival's failure without triumph.—
Aikin.

Smooth your way to the head through the heart. The way of reason is a good one; but it is commonly something longer, and perhaps not so sure.—*Chesterfield.*

The heart is deceitful above all things, and desperately wicked; who can know it?—*Bible.*

The heart, when broken, is like sweet gums and spices, when beaten; for as such cast their fragrant scent into the nostrils of men, so the heart, when broken, casts its sweet smell into the nostrils of God. The incense, which was a type of prayer of old, was to be beaten or bruised, and so to be burned in the censer. The heart must be beaten or bruised, and then the sweet scent will come out.—*Bunyan.*

The heart must glow before the tongue can gild.—*W. R. Alger.*

The heart must be at rest before the mind, like a quiet lake under an unclouded summer evening, can reflect the solemn starlight and the splendid mysteries of heaven.—*Macdonald Clarke.*

The dreariest poverty is that of the heart. Banish this, and we shall all be rich.—*Bovee.*

If you should take the human heart and listen to it, it would be like listening to a sea-shell; you would hear in it the hollow murmur of the infinite ocean to which it belongs, from which it draws its profoundest inspiration, and for which it yearns.—*Chapin.*

Keep thy heart with all diligence, for out of it are the issues of life.—*Bible.*

To judge human character rightly, a man may sometimes have very small experience provided he has a very large heart.—*Bulwer Lytton.*

The heart is the best logician.—*Wendell Phillips.*

We should not trust the heart too much. The heart speaks to us very gladly, as our mouth expresses itself. If the mouth were as much inclined to speak the feelings of the heart, it would have been the fashion long ago to put a padlock on the mouth.—*Lessing.*

Those there are whose hearts have a look southward, and are open to the whole noon of nature; be thou of such.—*Bailey.*

If a good face is a letter of recommendation, a good heart is a letter of credit.—*Bulwer Lytton.*

Where the heart goes before, like a lamp, and illumines the pathway, many things are made clear that else lie hidden in darkness.—*Longfellow.*

The thoughts we have had, the pictures we have seen, can be again called back before the mind's eye and before the imagination; but the heart is not so obliging; it does not reproduce its pleasing emotions.—*Goethe.*

Never morning wore to evening but some heart did break.—*Tennyson.*

Wealth and want equally harden the human heart, as frost and fire are both alien to the human flesh. Famine and gluttony alike drive nature away from the heart of man.—*Theodore Parker.*

Mind is the partial side of men; the heart is everything.—*Rivarol.*

The nice, calm, cold thought, which in women shapes itself so rapidly that they hardly know it as thought, should always travel to the lips via the heart. It does so in those women whom all love and admire.—*Holmes.*

A temple of the Holy Ghost, and yet oft lodging fiends.—*Pollok.*

The human heart has a sigh lonelier than the cry of the bittern.—*W. R. Alger.*

The heart has often been compared to the needle for its constancy; has it ever been so for its variations? Yet were any man to keep minutes of his feelings from youth to age, what a table of variations would they present! how numerous, how diverse, and how strange!—*Hare.*

The heart of a wise man should resemble a mirror, which reflects every object without being sullied by any.—*Confucius.*

What a proof of the Divine tenderness is there in the human heart itself, which is the organ and receptacle of so many sympathies! When we consider how exquisite are those conditions by which it is even made capable of so much suffering,—the capabilities of a child's heart, of a mother's heart,—what must be the nature of Him who fashioned its depths, and strung its chords?—*Chapin.*

The heart is like a musical instrument of many strings, all the chords of which require putting in harmony.—*Saadi.*

Heaven's Sovereign saves all beings but himself that hideous sight,—a naked human heart.—*Young.*

Each heart is a world. You find all within yourself, that you find without. The world that surrounds you is the magic glass of the world within you. To know yourself you have only to set down a true statement of those that ever loved or hated you.—*Lavater.*

My heart resembles the ocean; has storm, and ebb and flow; and many a beautiful pearl lies hid in its depths below.—*Heinrich Heine.*

When the heart speaks, glory itself is an illusion.—*Napoleon.*

HEARTLESSNESS.

A man, whose blood is very snow-broth.—
Shakespeare.

HEAVEN.

It is heaven upon earth to have a man's
mind move in charity, rich in Providence, stern
upon the poles of truth.—*Bacon.*

What, after all, is heaven, but a transition
from dim guesses and blind struggling with a
mysterious and adverse fate to the fulness of all
wisdom, — from ignorance, in a word, to knowl-
edge, but knowledge of what order ? —
Bulwer Lytton.

In a better world we will find our young
years and our old friends.—*J. Petit, Senn.*

One should go to sleep at night as homesick
passengers do, saying, " Perhaps in the morning
we shall see the shore." To us who are Chris-
tians is it not a solemn but a delightful thought
that perhaps nothing but the opaque bodily eye
prevents us from beholding the gate which is
open just before us, and nothing but the dull
ear prevents us from hearing the ringing of
those bells of joy which welcome us to the heav-
enly land ?—*Beecher.*

Heaven's gates are not so highly arched as
princes' palaces; they that enter there must
go upon their knees.—*Daniel Webster.*

· Heaven is the day of which grace is the
dawn ; the rich, ripe fruit of which grace is the
lovely flower; the inner shrine of that most
glorious temple to which grace forms the ap-
proach and outer court.—*Rev. Dr. Guthrie.*

Heaven, — it is God's throne. The earth, —
it is his footstool.—*Bible.*

The joys of heaven are without example,
above experience, and beyond imagination,— for
which the whole creation wants a comparison ;
we, an apprehension ; and even the Word of
God, a revelation.—*Bishop Norris.*

No fountain so small but that heaven may
be imaged in its bosom.—*Hawthorne.*

. The poets fabulously fancied that the giants
scaled heaven by heaping mountain upon moun-
tain. What was their fancy is the gospel truth.
If you would get to heaven you must climb
thither by putting Mount Sion upon Mount
Sinai.—*Bishop Hopkins.*

There is but one way to heaven for the
learned and the unlearned.—*Jeremy Taylor.*

Heaven hath many tongues to talk of
it, more eyes to behold it, but few hearts that
rightly affect it.—*Bishop Hall.*

Ah, what without a heaven would be even
love ! — a perpetual terror of the separation that
must one day come.—*Bulwer Lytton.*

Nothing is farther than earth from heaven ;
nothing is nearer than heaven to earth.—*Hare.*

Some people think black is the color of
heaven, and that the more they can make their
faces look like midnight, the more evidence
they have of grace. But God, who made the
sun and the flowers, never sent me to proclaim
to you such a lie as that.—*Beecher.*

Heaven, the treasury of everlasting joy !
Shakespeare.

If I am allowed to give a metaphorical allu-
sion to the future state of the blessed, I should
imagine it by the orange-grove in that sheltered
glen on which the sun is now beginning to shine,
and of which the trees are, at the same time,
loaded with sweet golden fruit and balmy silver
flowers. Such objects may well portray a state
in which hope and fruition become one eternal
feeling.—*Sir H. Davy.*

They have destroyed the beaten track to
heaven ; we are now compelled to make for our-
selves ladders.—*Joubert.*

. Perfect purity, fulness of joy, everlasting
freedom, perfect rest, health and fruition,
complete security, substantial and eternal
good.—*Hannah More.*

If the way of heaven be narrow, it is not
long ; and if the gate be strait, it opens into
endless life.—*Bishop Beveridge.*

Perhaps God does with his heavenly garden
as we do with our own. He may chiefly stock
it from nurseries, and select for transplanting
what is yet in its young and tender age, —
flowers before they have bloomed, and trees ere
they begin to bear.—*Rev. Dr. Guthrie.*

He who seldom thinks of heaven is not like-
ly to get thither ; as the only way to hit the
mark is to keep the eye fixed upon it.—
Bishop Horne.

Heaven will be inherited by every man who
has heaven in his soul. " The kingdom of God
is within you."—*Beecher.* ·

By heaven, we understand a state of happi-
ness infinite in degree, and endless in duration.
Franklin.

HEIRS.

He who sees his heir in his own child, car-
ries his eye over hopes and possessions lying
far beyond his gravestone, viewing his life, even
here, as a period but closed with a comma. He
who sees his heir in another man's child, sees
the full stop at the end of the sentence.—
Bulwer Lytton.

What madness is it for a man to starve
himself to enrich his heir, and so turn a friend
into an enemy ! For his joy at your death will
be proportioned to what you leave him.—*Seneca.*

An heiress, remaining unmarried, is a prey to all manner of extortion and imposition, and with the best intentions, becomes — through a bounty — a corruption to her neighborhood and a curse to the poor; or, if experience shall put her on her guard, she will lead a life of suspicion and resistance, to the injury of her own mind and nature.—*Jeremy Taylor.*

HERALDRY.

A court of heraldry sprung up to supply the place of crusade exploits, to grant imaginary shields and trophies to families that never wore real armor, and it is but of late that it has been discovered to have no real jurisdiction.—
Shenstone.

We may talk what we please of lilies, and lions rampant, and spread eagles, in fields of *d'or* or *d'argent*, but if heraldry were guided by reason, a plough in a field arable would be the most noble and ancient arms.—*Cowley.*

HEREAFTER.

If our Creator has so bountifully provided for our existence here, which is but momentary, and for our temporal wants, which will soon be forgotten, how much more must he have done for our enjoyment in the everlasting world!—
Hosea Ballou.

The light here is not the true; I await a better.—*Ducis.*

When I read the several dates on the tombs of some that died yesterday and some six hundred years ago, I consider that Great Day when we shall all of us be contemporaries, and make our appearance together.—*Addison.*

When a noble life has prepared old age, it is not the decline that it recalls, but the first days of immortality.—*Madame de Staël.*

HERO.

Nobody, they say, is a hero to his valet. Of course; for a man must be a hero to understand a hero. The valet, I dare say, has great respect for some person of his own stamp.—*Goethe.*

Of two heroes, he who esteems his rivals the most is the greatest.—*Beaumelle.*

Heroes in history seem to us poetic because they are there. But if we should tell the simple truth of some of our neighbors, it would sound like poetry.—*G. W. Curtis.*

There are heroes in evil as well as in good.—
Rochefoucauld.

The prudent sees only the difficulties, the bold only the advantages, of a great enterprise; the hero sees both, diminishes those, makes these preponderate, and conquers.—*Lavater.*

Worship your heroes from afar; contact withers them.—*Madame Necker.*

A hero is — as though one should say — a man of high achievement, who performs famous exploits, — who does things that are heroical, and in all his actions and demeanor is a hero indeed.—*H. Brooke.*

Heroes are not known by the loftiness of their carriage, as the greatest braggarts are generally the merest cowards.—*Rousseau.*

It were well if there were fewer heroes; for I scarcely ever heard of any, excepting Hercules, but did more mischief than good. These overgrown mortals commonly use their will with their right hand, and their reason with their left.—*Jeremy Collier.*

The heroes of literary history have been no less remarkable for what they have suffered than for what they have achieved.—*Johnson.*

The heroic soul does not sell its justice and its nobleness. It does not ask to dine nicely and to sleep warm. The essence of greatness is the perception that virtue is enough. Poverty is its ornament. It does not need plenty, and can very well abide its loss.—*Emerson.*

The gentle breath of peace would leave him on the surface neglected and unmoved. It is only the tempest that lifts him from his place.—
Junius.

However great the advantages which Nature bestows on us, it is not she alone, but Fortune in conjunction with her, which makes heroes.—
Rochefoucauld.

In analyzing the character of heroes, it is hardly possible to separate altogether the share of fortune from their own.—*Hallam.*

HEROISM.

The grandest of heroic deeds are those which are performed within four walls and in domestic privacy.—*Richter.*

Heroism is no extempore work of transient impulse, — a rocket rushing fretfully up to disturb the darkness by which, after a moment's insulting radiance, it is ruthlessly swallowed up, — but a steady fire, which darts forth tongues of flame. It is no sparkling epigram of action, but a luminous epic of character.—*Whipple.*

Self-trust is the essence of heroism.
Emerson.

Heroism, — the divine relation which, in all times, unites a great man to other men.—
Carlyle.

The greatest obstacle to being heroic is the doubt whether one may not be going to prove one's self a fool; the truest heroism is to resist the doubt; and the profoundest wisdom to know when it ought to be resisted, and when to be obeyed.—*Hawthorne.*

Every heroic act measures itself by its contempt of some external good. But it finds its own success at last, and then the prudent also extol.—*Emerson.*

There is an army of memorable sufferers who suffer inwardly and not outwardly. The world's battle-fields have been in the heart chiefly. More heroism has there been displayed in the household and in the closet, I think, than on the most memorable military battle-fields of history.—*Beecher.*

I believe in great men, but not in demigods.—*Bovee.*

Take away ambition and vanity, and where will be your heroes or patriots?—*Seneca.*

HISTORY.

Historians rarely descend to those details from which alone the real state of a community can be collected. Hence posterity is too often deceived by the vague hyperboles of poets and rhetoricians, who mistake the splendor of a court for the happiness of a people.—*Macaulay.*

That which history can give us best is the enthusiasm which it raises in our hearts.—
Goethe.

History presents the pleasantest features of poetry and fiction, — the majesty of the epic, the moving accidents of the drama, the surprises and moral of the romance. Wallace is a ruder Hector ; Robinson Crusoe is not stranger than Crœsus ; the Knights of Ashby never burnish the page of Scott with richer lights of lance and armor, than the Carthaginians, winding down the Alps, cast upon Livy.—*Willmott.*

History is only time furnished with dates and rich with events.—*Rivarol.*

The more we know of history, the less shall we esteem the subjects of it ; and to despise our species is the price we must too often pay for our knowledge of it.—*Colton.*

All history is a lie!—*Sir Robert Walpole.*

Providence conceals itself in the details of human affairs, but becomes unveiled in the generalities of history.—*Lamartine.*

What is public history but a register of the successes and disappointments, the vices, the follies, and the quarrels, of those who engage in contention for power ?—*Paley.*

All history is but a romance, unless it is studied as an example.—*Rev. Dr. Croly.*

History is the great looking-glass through which we may behold with ancestral eyes, not only the various deeds of past ages and the odd accidents that attend time, but also discern the different humors of men.—*Howell.*

History is a perspective glass, carrying the mind to a vast distance, and taking in the remotest objects of antiquity.—*Dryden.*

History maketh a young man to be old, without either wrinkles or gray hairs, privileging him with the experience of age, without either the infirmities or inconveniences thereof.—*Fuller.*

What is history but a fable agreed upon ?—
Napoleon.

It is when the hour of conflict is over, that history comes to a right understanding of the strife, and is ready to exclaim : " Lo! God is here, and we knew it not."—*Bancroft.*

A cultivated reader of history is domesticated in all families ; he dines with Pericles, and sups with Titian.—*Willmott.*

They who have employed the study of it as they ought for their instruction, for the regulation of their private manners, and the management of public affairs, must agree with me that it is the most pleasant school of wisdom.—
Dryden.

Her ample page rich with the spoils of time.
Gray.

Not to know what has been transacted in former times is to continue always a child. If no use is made of the labors of past ages, the world must remain always in the infancy of knowledge.—*Cicero.*

There is no history worthy of attention but that of a free people ; the history of a people subjected to despotism is only a collection of anecdotes.—*Chamfort.*

I have read somewhere or other in Dionysius of Halicarnassus, I think, that history is philosophy teaching by examples.—*Bolingbroke.*

Even the lowest book of Chronicles partakes of the spirit of the age in which it was written. The fourteenth century records a comet with greater parade and awe than the nineteenth ; and an account of an important event changes its aspect within four-and-twenty hours.—*Goethe.*

History is a sacred kind of writing, because truth is essential to it, and where truth is, there God himself is, so far as truth is concerned.—
Cervantes.

The present state of things is the consequence of the past ; and it is natural to inquire as to the sources of the good we enjoy, or the evils we suffer. If we act only for ourselves, to neglect the study of history is not prudent ; if intrusted with the care of others, it is not just.—
Johnson.

Truth is very liable to be left-handed in history.—*Alex. Dumas.*

To study history is to study literature. The biography of a nation embraces all its works. No trifle is to be neglected. A mouldering medal is a letter of twenty centuries. Antiquities which have been beautifully called history defaced, compose its fullest commentary. In these wrecks of many storms, which time washes to the shore, the scholar looks patiently for treasure.—*Willmott.*

History is the revelation of Providence.—*Kossuth.*

Truth comes to us from the past, as gold is washed down from the mountains of Sierra Nevada, in minute but precious particles, and intermixed with infinite alloy, the *débris* of the centuries.—*Bovee.*

For historians ought to be precise, truthful, and quite unprejudiced, and neither interest nor fear, hatred nor affection, should cause them to swerve from the path of truth, whose mother is history, the rival of time, the depository of great actions, the witness of what is past, the example and instruction to the present, and monitor to the future.—*Cervantes.*

History is neither more nor less than biography on a large scale.—*Lamartine.*

Geologists complain that when they want specimens of the common rocks of a country, they receive curious spars; just so, historians give us the extraordinary events and omit just what we want,—the every-day life of each particular time and country.—*Whately.*

Every great writer is a writer of history, let him treat on almost what subject he may. He carries with him, for thousands of years, a portion of his times; and indeed, if only his own effigy were there, it would be greatly more than a fragment of his country.—*Landor.*

Histories used often to be stories. The fashion now is to leave out the story. Our histories are stall-fed; the facts are absorbed by the reflections, as the meat sometimes is by the fat.—*Hare.*

The reign of Antoninus is marked by the rare advantage of furnishing very few materials for history, which is indeed little more than the register of the crimes, follies, and misfortunes of mankind.—*Gibbon.*

We find but few historians of all ages, who have been diligent enough in their search for truth. It is their common method to take on trust what they distribute to the public; by which means a falsehood, once received from a famed writer, becomes traditional to posterity.—*Dryden.*

A history will live, though written ever so indifferently; and is generally less suspected than the rhetoric of the muses.—*Shenstone.*

Oratory and poetry are of little value unless they reach the highest perfection; but history, in whatever way it may be executed, is a source of pleasure.—*Pliny the Younger.*

History is a great painter, with the world for canvas, and life for a figure. It exhibits man in his pride, and nature in her magnificence,—Jerusalem bleeding under the Roman, or Lisbon vanishing in flame and earthquake. History must be splendid. Bacon called it the pomp of business. Its march is in high places, and along the pinnacles and points of great affairs.—*Willmott.*

Most historians take pleasure in putting into the mouths of princes what they have neither said nor ought to have said.—*Voltaire.*

Great men are the inspired (speaking and acting) texts of that divine book of revelations, whereof a chapter is completed from epoch to epoch, and by some named history.—*Carlyle.*

History makes haste to record great deeds, but often neglects good ones.—*Hosea Ballou.*

The student is to read history actively and not passively; to esteem his own life the text, and books the commentary. Thus compelled, the muse of history will utter oracles as never to those who do not respect themselves.—*Emerson.*

HOBBY.

Hobbies should be wives, not mistresses. It will not do to have more than one at a time. One hobby leads you out of extravagance; a team of hobbies you cannot drive till you are rich enough to find corn for them all. Few men are rich enough for that.—*Bulwer Lytton.*

HOLIDAY.

If all the year were playing holidays, to sport would be as tedious as to work; but when they seldom come, they wished for come.—*Shakespeare.*

HOLINESS.

If it be the characteristic of a worldly man that he desecrates what is holy, it should be of the Christian to consecrate what is secular, and to recognize a present and presiding divinity in all things.—*Chalmers.*

Blessed is the memory of those who have kept themselves unspotted from the world! yet more blessed and more dear the memory of those who have kept themselves unspotted in the world!—*Mrs. Jameson.*

The symmetry of the soul.—*Philip Henry.*

Everything holy is before what is unholy; guilt presupposes innocence, not the reverse; angels, but not fallen ones, were created. Hence man does not properly rise to the highest, but first sinks gradually down from it, and then afterwards rises again; a child can never be considered too innocent and good.—*Richter.*

HOME.

The first indication of domestic happiness is the love of one's home.—*M. de Montlosier.*

The strength of a nation, especially of a republican nation, is in the intelligent and well-ordered homes of the people.—*Mrs. Sigourney.*

There is a magic in that little word,—it is a mystic circle that surrounds comforts and virtues never known beyond its hallowed limits.
Southey.

The first sure symptom of a mind in health is rest of heart, and pleasure felt at home.—*Young.*

It is indeed at home that every man must be known by those who would make a just estimate either of his virtue or felicity; for smiles and embroidery are alike occasional, and the mind is often dressed for show in painted honor and fictitious benevolence.—*Johnson.*

Home should be the centre of joy, equatorial and tropical.—*Beecher.*

If ever household affections and loves are graceful things, they are graceful in the poor. The ties that bind the wealthy and the proud to home may be forged on earth, but those which link the poor man to his humble hearth are of the true metal and bear the stamp of heaven.—*Dickens.*

The paternal hearth, that rallying-place of the affections.—*Washington Irving.*

Are you not surprised to find how independent of money peace of conscience is, and how much happiness can be condensed in the humblest home? A cottage will not hold the bulky furniture and sumptuous accommodations of a mansion; but if God be there, a cottage will hold as much happiness as might stock a palace.—*Dr. James Hamilton.*

To Adam Paradise was home. To the good among his descendants home is paradise.—*Hare.*

It was the policy of the good old gentleman to make his children feel that home was the happiest place in the world; and I value this delicious home-feeling as one of the choicest gifts a parent can bestow.—*Washington Irving.*

He is happiest, be he king or peasant, who finds peace in his home.—*Goethe.*

A house is never perfectly furnished for enjoyment unless there is a child in it rising three years old, and a kitten rising six weeks.—*Southey.*

There is no happiness in life, there is no misery, like that growing out of the dispositions which consecrate or desecrate a home.—*Chapin.*

The domestic relations precede, and, in our present existence, are worth more than all our other social ties. They give the first throb to the heart, and unseal the deep fountains of its love. Home is the chief school of human virtue. Its responsibilities, joys, sorrows, smiles, tears, hopes, and solicitudes form the chief interest of human life.—*Channing.*

Home-keeping youth have ever homely wits.
Shakespeare.

HOMELINESS.

Homeliness has this advantage over its enemy, beauty. It is that it is as difficult for an ugly woman to be calumniated as for a pretty woman not to be.—*Stahl.*

HONESTY.

The world is so corrupt that a reputation for honesty is acquired by not doing wrong.—*De Lévis.*

The man who is so conscious of the rectitude of his intentions as to be willing to open his bosom to the inspection of the world is in possession of one of the strongest pillars of a decided character. The course of such a man will be firm and steady, because he has nothing to fear from the world, and is sure of the approbation and support of Heaven.—*Wirt.*

Rich honesty dwells like a miser, in a poor house, as your pearl in your foul oyster.—*Shakespeare.*

It would be an unspeakable advantage, both to the public and private, if men would consider that great truth, that no man is wise or safe but he that is honest.—*Sir Walter Raleigh.*

An honest man's the noblest work of God.
Pope.

It should seem that indolence itself would incline a person to be honest, as it requires infinitely greater pains and contrivance to be a knave.—*Shenstone.*

An honest man is able to speak for himself when a knave is not.—*Shakespeare.*

Socrates, being asked the way to honest fame, said, "Study to be what you wish to seem."—*John Bate.*

A straight line is the shortest in morals as well as in geometry.—*Rahel.*

Nothing more completely baffles one who is full of trick and duplicity himself than straightforward and simple integrity in another. A knave would rather quarrel with a brother-knave than with a fool, but he would rather avoid a quarrel with one honest man than with both.—*Colton.*

The more honesty a man has, the less he affects the air of a saint.—*Lavater.*

God only looks to pure, and not to full hands.—*Laberius.*

There is no man but for his own interest hath an obligation to be honest. There may be sometimes temptations to be otherwise ; but, all cards cast up, he shall find it the greatest ease, the highest profit, the best pleasure, the most safety, and the noblest fame, to hold the horns of this altar, which, in all assays, can in himself protect him.—*Feltham.*

It is much easier to ruin a man of principle than a man of none, for he may be ruined through his scruples. Knavery is supple and can bend ; but honesty is firm and upright, and yields not.—*Colton.*

Honesty needs no disguise nor ornament; be plain.—*Otway.*

Put it out of the power of truth to give you an ill character; and if anybody reports you not to be an honest man, let your practice give him the lie; and to make all sure, you should resolve to live no longer than you can live honestly ; for it is better to be nothing than a knave.—*Marcus Antoninus.*

To be honest as this world goes is to be one man picked out of ten thousand.—*Shakespeare.*

Honesty is not only the deepest policy, but the highest wisdom ; since, however difficult it may be for integrity to get on, it is a thousand times more difficult for knavery to get off ; and no error is more fatal than that of those who think that Virtue has no other reward because they have heard that she is her own.—*Colton.*

The man who pauses in his honesty wants little of a villain.—*H. Martyn.*

A right mind and generous affection hath more beauty and charms than all other symmetries in the world besides ; and a grain of honesty and native worth is of more value than all the adventitious ornaments, estates, or preferments ; for the sake of which some of the better sort so oft turn knaves.—*Shaftesbury.*

I like people to be saints ; but I want them to be first and superlatively honest men.—*Madame Swetchine.*

The best kind of glory is that which is reflected from honesty, such as was the glory of Cato and Aristides ; but it was harmful to them both, and is seldom beneficial to any man while he lives.—*Cowley.*

Honest men are the gentlemen of nature.—*Bulwer Lytton.*

Irritated one day at the bad faith of Madame Jay, Mirabeau said to her, "Madame Jay, if probity did not exist, we ought to invent it as the best means of getting rich."—*Dumont.*

Prefer loss before unjust gain ; for that brings grief but once, this forever.—*Chilo.*

There is no terror in your threats ; for I am armed so strong in honesty that they pass by me as the idle wind which I respect not.—*Shakespeare.*

It is with honesty in one particular as with wealth, — those that have the thing care less about the credit of it than those who have it not. No poor man can well afford to be thought so, and the less of honesty a finished rogue possesses the less he can afford to be supposed to want it.—*Colton.*

Honesty coupled to beauty is to have honey a sauce to sugar.—*Shakespeare.*

The first step towards greatness is to be honest, says the proverb ; but the proverb fails to state the case strong enough. Honesty is not only "the first step towards greatness," — it is greatness itself.—*Bovee.*

It is necessary in this life, — at first honesty ; then usefulness, which follows nearly always, for they cannot be separated.—*Palmieri.*

What is becoming is honest, and whatever is honest must always be becoming.—*Cicero.*

No legacy is so rich as honesty.—*Shakespeare.*

Honest and courageous people have very little to say about either their courage or their honesty. The sun has no need to boast of his brightness, nor the moon of her effulgence.—*Hosea Ballou.*

He who freely praises what he means to purchase, and he who enumerates the faults of what he means to sell, may set up a partnership with honesty.—*Lavater.*

The most natural beauty in the world is honesty and moral truth. For all beauty is truth. True features make the beauty of a face, and true proportions the beauty of architecture ; as true measure that of harmony and music. In poetry which is all fable, truth is still the perfection.—*Shaftesbury.*

Probity is as rarely in accord with interest as reason is with passion.—*Sanial-Dubay.*

An entirely honest man, in the severe sense of the word, exists no more than an entirely dishonest knave ; the best and the worst are only approximations to those qualities. Who are those that never contradict themselves? yet honesty never contradicts itself. Who are they that always contradict themselves? yet knavery is mere self-contradiction. Thus the knowledge of man determines not the things themselves, but their proportions, the quantum of congruities and incongruities.—*Lavater.*

"Honesty is the best policy"; but he who acts on that principle is not an honest man.— *Whately.*

HONOR.

Be not ashamed of thy virtues; honor is a good brooch to wear in a man's hat at all times.—*Ben Jonson.*

Purity is the feminine, truth the masculine of honor.—*Hare.*

The Athenians erected a large statue of Æsop, and placed him, though a slave, on a lasting pedestal, to show that the way to honor lies open indifferently to all.—*Phædrus.*

Honor's train is longer than his foreskirt.— *Shakespeare.*

The knot that binds me by the law of courtesy pinches me more than that of legal constraint, and I am much more at ease when bound by a scrivener than by myself. Is it not reason that my conscience should be much more engaged when men simply rely upon it? In a bond my faith owes nothing, because it has nothing lent it. Let them trust to the security they have taken without me; I had much rather break the walls of a prison, and the laws themselves, than my own word.—*Montaigne.*

Let honor be to us as strong an obligation, as necessity is to others.—*Pliny.*

Where the meekness of self-knowledge veileth the front of self-respect, there look thou for the man whose name none can know but they will honor.—*Tupper.*

Act well your part; there all the honor lies. *Pope.*

Clear and round dealing is the honor of man's nature, and mixture of falsehood is like alloy in coin of gold and silver, which may make the metal work the better, but it embaseth it; for these windings and crooked courses are the goings of the serpent, which goeth basely upon the belly and not on the feet.— *Bacon.*

Honor is a fine imaginary notion, that draws in raw and unexperienced men to real mischiefs, while they hunt a shadow.—*Addison.*

The journey of high honor lies not in smooth ways.—*Sir P. Sidney.*

Honor is the most capricious in her rewards. She feeds us with air, and often pulls down our house, to build our monument.—*Colton.*

If well-respected honor bid me on, I hold as little counsel with weak fear as you.— *Shakespeare.*

No one ever lost his honor, except he who had it not.—*Publius Syrus.*

Honors soften fatigue. It is easier riding in a gilded and embossed saddle. Atlas, while he sustains the world upon his shoulders, is himself sustained by the admiration his feat excites.—*Bovee.*

Honor is unstable, and seldom the same; for she feeds upon opinion, and is as fickle as her food. She builds a lofty structure on the sandy foundation of the esteem of those who are of all beings the most subject to change.— *Colton.*

That chastity of honor which felt a stain like a wound.—*Burke.*

Honor hath three things in it, — the vantage-ground to do good, the approach to kings and principal persons, and the raising of a man's own fortunes.—*Bacon.*

See that you come not to woo honor, but to wed it.—*Shakespeare.*

To be ambitious of true honor, of the true glory and perfection of our natures, is the very principle and incentive of virtue; but to be ambitions of titles, of place, of ceremonial respects and civil pageantry, is as vain and little as the things are which we court.—*Sherlock.*

Discretion and hardy valor are the twins of honor, and, nursed together, make a conqueror; divided, but a talker.—*Beaumont and Fletcher.*

Honor with some is a sort of paper credit, with which men are obliged to trade who are deficient in the sterling cash of morality and religion.—*Zimmermann.*

Woman's honor is nice as ermine, —will not bear a soil.—*Dryden.*

Let none presume to wear an undeserved dignity. O that estates, degrees, and offices were not derived corruptly! and that clear honor were purchased by the merit of the wearer!—*Shakespeare.*

Our own heart, and not other men's opinions, forms our true honor.—*Coleridge.*

Your honors here may serve you for a time, as it were for an hour, but they will be of no use to you beyond this world. Nobody will have heard a word of your honors in the other life. Your glory, your shame, your ambitions, and all the treasures for which you push hard and sacrifice much will be like wreaths of smoke. For these things, which you mostly seek, and for which you spend your life, only tarry with you while you are on this side of the flood.—*Beecher.*

Honor is like the eye, which cannot suffer the least impurity without damage; it is a precious stone, the price of which is lessened by the least flaw.—*Bossuet.*

Unblemished honor is the flower of virtue! the vivifying soul! and he who slights it will leave the other dull and lifeless dross.— *Thomson.*

Too much honor, — O, it is a burden, it is a burden too heavy for a man that hopes for heaven.—*Shakespeare.*

Honor is like an island, rugged and without a landing-place; we can nevermore re-enter when we are once outside of it.—*Boileau.*

Honor pricks me on. Yea, but how if honor prick me off, when I come on? how then? Can honor set a leg? No. Or an arm? No. Or take away the grief of a wound? No. Honor hath no skill in surgery, then? No. What is honor? A word. What is that word honor? Air. A trim reckoning! Who hath it? He that died o' Wednesday. Doth he feel it? No. Doth he hear it? No. Is it insensible, then? Yea, to the dead. But will it not live with the living? No. Why? Detraction will not suffer it, — therefore, I 'll none of it! Honor is a mere scutcheon; and so ends my catechism.—*Shakespeare.*

Honor, the moral conscience of the great! — *Sir W. Davenant.*

High honor is not only gotten and born by pain and danger, but must be nursed by the like, else it vanisheth as soon as it appears to the world.—*Sir P. Sidney.*

The giving riches and honors to a wicked man is like giving strong wine to him that hath a fever.—*Plutarch.*

Honor is not love of innocence, but praise; the fear of censure, not the scorn of sin.— *Aaron Hill.*

Honor is but the reflection of a man's own actions shining bright in the face of all about him, and from thence rebounding upon himself.—*South.*

HOPE.
We never shed so many tears as at the age of hope; but when we have lost hope, we look on everything with dry eyes, and tranquillity springs from incapacity.—*Rivarol.*

Hope deferred maketh the heart sick; but when the desire cometh, it is as a tree of life.— *Bible.*

There are hopes, the bloom of whose beauty would be spoiled by the trammels of description; too lovely, too delicate, too sacred for words, they should be only known through the sympathy of hearts.—*Dickens.*

Hope is the only good which is common to all men; those who have nothing more possess hope still.—*Thales.*

Hope is the last thing that dies in man, and though it be exceedingly deceitful, yet it is of this good use to us, that while we are travelling through life it conducts us in an easier and more pleasant way to our journey's end.— *Rochefoucauld.*

The shadow of human life is traced upon a golden ground of immortal hope.—*Hillard.*

Hope is a lover's staff.—*Shakespeare.*

Hope is a prodigal young heir, and experience is his banker, but his drafts are seldom honored, since there is often a heavy balance against him, because he draws largely on a small capital, is not yet in possession, and if he were, would die.—*Colton.*

Hope! fortune's cheating lottery; when for one prize an hundred blanks there be! — *Cowley.*

Hope animates the wise, and lures the presumptuous and indolent who repose inconsiderately on her promises.— *Vauvenargues.*

The miserable have no other medicine, but only hope.—*Shakespeare.*

For present grief there is always a remedy. However much thou sufferest, hope. The greatest happiness of man is hope.— *Leopold Schefer.*

Hope is a willing slave; despair is free.— *Dawes.*

Used with due abstinence, hope acts as a healthful tonic; intemperately indulged, as an enervating opiate. The visions of future triumph, which at first animate exertion, if dwelt upon too intently, will usurp the place of the stern reality; and noble objects will be contemplated, not for their own inherent worth, but on account of the day-dreams they engender. Thus hope, aided by imagination, makes one man a hero, another a somnambulist, and a third a lunatic; while it renders them all enthusiasts. *Sir J. Stephen.*

Hope springs eternal in the human breast.— *Pope.*

Hope is a flatterer, but the most upright of all parasites; for she frequents the poor man's hut, as well as the palace of his superior.— *Shenstone.*

From the lowest depth, there is a path to the loftiest height.— *Carlyle.*

In the treatment of nervous cases, he is the best physician who is the most ingenious inspirer of hope.— *Coleridge.*

Hope itself is a pain, while it is overmatched by fear.—*Sir P. Sidney.*

A loving heart encloses within itself an unfading and eternal Eden. Hope is like a bad clock, forever striking the hour of happiness, whether it has come or not.—*Richter.*

Hope, deceitful as she is, serves at least to conduct us through life by an agreeable path.—*Rochefoucauld.*

No hope so bright but is the beginning of its own fulfilment.—*Emerson.*

Hope is the ruddy morning ray of joy, recollection is its golden tinge; but the latter is wont to sink amid the dews and dusky shades of twilight; and the bright blue day which the former promises breaks indeed, but in another world, and with another sun.—*Richter.*

Hope is a leaf-joy which may be beaten out to a great extension, like gold.—*Bacon.*

Hope is like the wing of an angel, soaring up to heaven, and bearing our prayers to the throne of God.—*Jeremy Taylor.*

Hope travels through, nor quits us when we die.—*Pope.*

Hope is the chief blessing of man; and that hope only is rational of which we are sensible that it cannot deceive us.—*Johnson.*

Hope never spread her golden wings but in unfathomable seas.—*Emerson.*

"Hast thou hope?" they asked of John Knox, when he lay a-dying. He spoke nothing, but raised his finger and pointed upwards, and so died.—*Carlyle.*

For hope is but the dream of those that wake.—*Matthew Prior.*

The setting of a great hope is like the setting of the sun. The brightness of our life is gone, shadows of the evening fall around us, and the world seems but a dim reflection itself, — a broader shadow. We look forward into the coming lonely night; the soul withdraws itself. Then stars arise, and the night is holy.—*Longfellow.*

A propensity to hope and joy is real riches; one to fear and sorrow, real poverty.—*Hume.*

Thales, being asked what was the most universal possession, answered, "Hope"; for they have it who have nothing else.—*Epictetus.*

Hope, alas! is our waking dream.—*Madame de Girardin.*

It is when our budding hopes are nipped beyond recovery by some rough wind, that we are the most disposed to picture to ourselves what flowers they might have borne if they had flourished.—*Dickens.*

True hope is swift, and flies with swallow's wings.—*Shakespeare.*

Hope is a vigorous principle; it is furnished with light and heat to advise and execute; it sets the head and heart to work, and animates a man to do his utmost. And thus, by perpetually pushing and assurance, it puts a difficulty out of countenance, and makes a seeming impossibility give way.—*Jeremy Collier.*

Folly ends where genuine hope begins.—*Cowper.*

It is best to hope only for things possible and probable; he that hopes too much shall deceive himself at last, especially if his industry does not go along with his hopes; for hope without action is a barren undoer.—*Feltham.*

Hope is such a bait, it covers any book.—*Ben Jonson.*

This comforts me, that the most weatherbeaten vessel cannot properly be seized on for a wreck which hath any quick cattle remaining therein. My spirits are not as yet forfeited to despair, having one lively spark of hope in my heart because God is even where he was before.—*Fuller.*

Hope is brightest when it dawns from fears.—*Walter Scott.*

The good man's hope is laid far, far beyond the sway of tempests, or the furious sweep of mortal desolation.—*H. K. White.*

Where no hope is left, is left no fear.—*Milton.*

Hope is a pleasant acquaintance, but an unsafe friend. Hope is not the man for your banker, though he may do for a travelling companion.—*Haliburton.*

The night is past, — joy cometh with the morrow.—*Bulwer Lytton.*

All which happens in the whole world happens through hope. No husbandman would sow a grain of corn, if he did not hope it would spring up and bring forth the ear. How much more are we helped on by hope in the way to eternal life!—*Luther.*

His worth shines forth the brightest who in hope always confides; the abject soul despairs.—*Euripides.*

While there is hope left, let not the weakness of sorrow make the strength of resolution languish.—*Sir P. Sidney.*

Hope is the best part of our riches. What sufficeth it that we have the wealth of the Indies in our pockets, if we have not the hope of heaven in our souls?—*Bovee.*

Where there is no hope there can be no endeavor.—*Johnson.*

Hope is to a man as a bladder to a learning swimmer, — it keeps him from sinking in the bosom of the waves, and by that help he may attain the exercise ; but yet it many times makes him venture beyond his height, and then if that breaks, or a storm rises, he drowns without recovery. How many would die, did not hope sustain them ! How many have died by hoping too much ! This wonder we find in Hope, that she is both a flatterer and a true friend.—*Feltham.*

The sickening pang of hope deferred.—
Walter Scott.

O what a valiant faculty is hope, that in a mortal subject, and in a moment makes nothing of usurping infinity and immensity, and of supplying her master's indigence at her pleasure with all things he can imagine or desire ! Nature has given us this passion for a pretty toy to play withal.—*Montaigne.*

There are many that measure not the end of their hopes by the possession of them, but by their precedent labor, which they overvalue.—
Jeremy Taylor.

The fortunate have many parasites ; hope is the only one that vouchsafes attendance upon the wretched and the beggar.—*Shenstone.*

Hope is a light diet, but very stimulating.—
Balzac.

The reasonableness of a project ought to be its foundation ; and hope, the ladder only which conducts the architect to the heights of the building.—*Jane Porter.*

The flights of the human mind are not from enjoyment to enjoyment, but from hope to hope.—*Johnson.*

Hope of ill gain is the beginning of loss.—
Democritus.

Hope calculates its schemes for a long and durable life, presses forward to imaginary points of bliss, and grasps at impossibilities ; and consequently very often ensnares men into beggary, ruin, and dishonor.—*Addison.*

Hope is like the sun, which, as we journey towards it, casts the shadow of our burden behind us.—*Samuel Smiles.*

Hope is love's happiness, but not its life.—
Miss L. E. Landon.

Hope is the best possession. None are completely wretched but those who are without hope ; and few are reduced so low as that.—*Hazlitt.*

Hope is a working-man's dream.—*Pliny.*

16

Man is, properly speaking, based upon hope , he has no other possession but hope ; this world of his is emphatically the place of hope.—
Carlyle.

I will despair, and be at enmity with cozening Hope ; he is a flatterer.—*Shakespeare.*

Hope is like the cork to the net, which keeps the soul from sinking in despair ; and fear is like the lead to the net, which keeps it from floating in presumption.—*Bishop Watson.*

HORSEMANSHIP.

And witch the world with noble horsemanship.—*Shakespeare.*

A good rider on a good horse is as much above himself and others as the world can make him.—*Lord Herbert.*

I will not change my horse with any that treads but on four pasterns. When I bestride him I soar, I am a hawk ; he trots the air ; the earth sings when he touches it.—*Shakespeare.*

HOSPITALITY.

Let not the emphasis of hospitality lie in bed and board ; but let truth and love and honor and courtesy flow in all thy deeds.—
Emerson.

Like many other virtues, hospitality is practised in its perfection by the poor. If the rich did their share, how would the woes of this world be lightened !—*Mrs. Kirkland.*

Provision is the foundation of hospitality, and thrift the fuel of magnificence.—
Sir P. Sidney.

It is an excellent circumstance that hospitality grows best where it is most needed. In the thick of men it dwindles and disappears, like fruit in the thick of a wood ; but where men are planted sparely it blossoms and matures, like apples on a standard or an espalier. It flourishes where the inn and lodging-house cannot exist.—*Hugh Miller.*

Breaking through the chills of ceremony and selfishness, and thawing every heart into a flow.
Washington Irving.

If a man be gracious to strangers, it shows that he is a citizen of the world and his heart is no island, cut off from other islands, but a continent that joins them.—*Bacon.*

Be not forgetful to entertain strangers ; for thereby some have entertained angels unawares.
Bible.

The pleasantest hospitality waiteth not for curious costliness, when it can give cleanly sufficieney. More cometh of pride and greater friendliness to your own ostentation, than to the comfort of the guest.—*Sir P. Sidney.*

There is an emanation from the heart in genuine hospitality which cannot be described but is immediately felt and puts the stranger at once at his ease.— *Washington Irving.*

Small cheer and great welcome make a merry feast.—*Shakespeare.*

For people to make invitations to their house and table, or offers of their fortune and services, is nothing. To be as good as their word is all the expense and difficulty.—*Bruyère.*

As you receive the stranger so you receive your God.—*Lavater.*

The magnanimous know very well that they who give time or money or shelter to the stranger, — so it be done for love and not for ostentation, — do, as it were, put God under obligation to them, so perfect are the compensations of the universe.—*Emerson.*

It is not the quantity of the meat, but the cheerfulness of the guests, which makes the feast.— *Clarendon.*

HUMANITY.

You lie nearest to the river of life when you bend to it. You cannot drink but as you stoop.
J. H. Evans.

Humanity is the peculiar characteristic of great minds; little vicious minds abound with anger and revenge, and are incapable of feeling the exact pleasure of forgiving their enemies.— *Chesterfield.*

There is nothing on earth divine beside humanity.—*Melanchthon.*

There is but one temple in the world, and that is the body of man. Nothing is holier than this high form. Bending before men is a reverence done to this revelation in the flesh. We touch heaven when we lay our hand on a human body.—*Novalis.*

Humanity is the Son of God.—
Theodore Parker.

What a vile and abject thing is man if he do not raise himself above humanity.—*Seneca.*

True humanity consists not in a squeamish ear; it consists not in starting or shrinking at tales of misery, but in a disposition of heart to relieve it. True humanity appertains rather to the mind than to the nerves, and prompts men to use real and active endeavors to execute the actions which it suggests. – *Charles James Fox.*

Our humanity were a poor thing but for the Divinity that stirs within us.—*Bacon.*

I did not give to the man (being reproached for giving to an unworthy one), I gave to humanity.—*Aristotle.*

I am a man; I count nothing human foreign to me.—*Terence.*

The sentiment of humanity, indeed, or a hypocritical affectation of it, has become infused into almost all literature and speech, from the sermons of Dr. Channing to the *feuilletons* of Eugene Sue. It is exceedingly difficult for a man to be as narrow as he could have been had he lived a century ago.— *Whipple.*

The greatest wits I have conversed with are men eminent for their humanity.—*Addison.*

No piled-up wealth, no social station, no throne, reaches as high as that spiritual plane upon which every human being stands by virtue of his humanity.—*Chapin.*

Humanity is the equity of the heart.—
Confucius.

The most eloquent speaker, the most ingenious writer, and the most accomplished statesman cannot effect so much as the mere presence of the man who tempers his wisdom and his vigor with humanity.—*Lavater.*

I never knew a young man remarkable for heroic bravery whose very aspect was not lighted up by gentleness and humanity.—*Lord Erskine.*

HUMAN NATURE.

Human nature is so weak that the honest men who have no religion make me fret with their perilous virtue, as rope-dancers with their dangerous equilibrium.—*De Lévis.*

There do remain dispersed in the soil of human nature divers seeds of goodness, of benignity, of ingenuity, which being cherished, excited, and quickened by good culture, do by common experience thrust out flowers very lovely, and yield fruits very pleasant of virtue and goodness.—*Mrs. L. M. Child.*

As there is much beast and some devil in man, so is there some angel and some God in him. The beast and the devil may be conquered, but in this life never wholly destroyed.
Coleridge.

A man's nature is best perceived in privateness, for there is no affectation; in passion, for that putteth a man out of his precepts; and in a new case or experiment, for there custom leaveth him.—*Bacon.*

The scrutiny of human nature on a small scale is one of the most dangerous of employments; the study of it on a large scale is one of the safest and truest.—*Isaac Taylor.*

HUMILITY.

Much misconstruction and bitterness are spared to him who thinks naturally upon what he owes to others, rather than what he ought to expect from them.—*Madame Guizot.*

Humility, — that low, sweet root from which al! heavenly virtues shoot.—*Moore.*

There is many a wounded heart without a contrite spirit. The ice may be broken into a th usand pieces; it is ice still; but expose it to the beams of the *Sun* of Righteousness, and then it will melt.—*Middleton.*

Humility, like darkness, reveals the heavenly lights.—*Thoreau.*

Humility is the softened shadow before the stature of Excellence, and lieth lowly on the ground, beloved and lovely as the violet; it is the fair handmaid that calleth Worth her brother, the gentle, silent nurse that fostereth infant virtues.—*Tupper.*

Search others for their virtues, and thyself for thy vices.—*Fuller.*

Some one called *Sir* Richard Steele the "vilest of mankind," and he retorted with proud humility, "It would be a glorious world if I were."—*Bovee.*

The street is full of humiliations to the proud.—*Emerson.*

Antigones, being near death, said to his daughter: "O my well-beloved child! work at turning the spindle, it is a sufficient heritage for the poor; and if one day thou art united to a husband, preserve the manners and virtues of the Grecian mothers. That is the richest dower for a woman."—*Antipater.*

Humble yourself, says the proud priest.— *Bovee.*

There will come a time when three words, uttered with charity and meekness, shall receive a far more blessed reward than three thousand volumes written with disdainful sharpness of wit.—*Hooker.*

I do not aspire to send my javelin beyond the sun.—*Pindar.*

Cleobulus, being asked why he sought not to be advanced to honor and preferment, made this reply: "O friend, as long as I study and practise humility, I know where I am; but when I shall hunt after dignities and promotion, I am afraid I shall lose myself!" *John Bate.*

Humanity is progress, or it is nothing.— *Simms.*

Nature hath so distributed her gifts among her children as to promote a mutual helpfulness, and what, perhaps, is still more precious, a mutual humility among men.—*Chalmers.*

We cannot think too highly of our nature, nor too humbly of ourselves.—*Colton.*

To put up with the world humbly is better than to control it. This is the very acme of virtue. Religion leads to it in a day; philosophy only conducts to it by a lengthened life, misery, or death.—*Lamartine.*

Sense shines with a double lustre when it is set in humility. An able and yet humble man is a jewel worth a kingdom.— *William Penn.*

There is nothing so clear-sighted and sensible as a noble mind in a low estate.— *Jane Porter.*

When I look upon the tombs of the great, every emotion of envy dies within me; when I read the epitaphs of the beautiful, every inordinate desire goes out.—*Addison.*

After crosses and losses, men grow humbler and wiser.—*Franklin.*

It is easy to look down on others; to look down on ourselves is the difficulty.— *Lord Peterborough.*

Humanity cannot be degraded by humiliation. It is its very character to submit to such things. There is a consanguinity between benevolence and humility. They are virtues of the same stock.—*Burke.*

It must be very grateful to the man who humbly estimates his own claims that the world always heartily approves his judgment.— *Simms.*

Among all the other virtues, humility, the lowest, is pre-eminent. It is the safest, because it is always at anchor; and that man may be truly said to live the most content in his calling that strives to live within the compass of it. *Richter.*

Humility is the Christian's greatest honor; and the higher men climb, the farther they are from heaven.—*Burder.*

The sufficiency of my merit is to know that my merit is not sufficient.—*St. Augustine.*

May exalting and humanizing thoughts forever accompany me, making me confident without pride, and modest without servility.— *Leigh Hunt.*

Meekness and courtesy will always recommend the first address, but soon pall and nauseate unless they are associated with more sprightly qualities.—*Johnson.*

Only a great pride, that is, a great and reverential repose in one's own being, renders possible a noble humility.—*D. A. Wasson.*

Everything may be mimicked by hypocrisy but humility and love united. The more rare, the more radiant when they meet.—*Lavater.*

If opinion hath cried thy name up, let thy modesty cry thy heart down, lest thou deceive it, or it thee; there is no less danger in a great name than a bad, and no less honor in deserving of praise than in the enduring it.—
Quarles.

Modest humility is beauty's crown, for the beautiful is a hidden thing and shrinks from its own power.—*Schiller.*

Humility is a cuirass which turns aside the blows dealt by the enmity of man; but that cuirass is defective at the heart.—
Madame Swetchine.

Humility is the solid foundation of all the virtues.—*Confucius.*

If thou desire the love of God and man, be humble; for the proud heart, as it loves none but itself, so it is beloved of none but by itself; the voice of humility is God's music, and the silence of humility is God's rhetoric. Humility enforces where neither virtue nor strength can prevail nor reason.—*Quarles.*

Be wise; soar not too high to fall, but stoop to rise.—*Massinger.*

True dignity abides with him alone who, in the silent hour of inward thought, can still suspect and still revere himself, in lowliness of heart.—*Wordsworth.*

The beloved of the Almighty are the rich who have the humility of the poor, and the poor who have the magnanimity of the rich.—
Saadi.

Humility is the first lesson we learn from reflection; and self-distrust, the first proof we give of having obtained a knowledge of ourselves.—
Zimmermann.

To be humble to superiors is duty; to equals, is courtesy; to inferiors, is nobleness; and to all, safety; it being a virtue that, for all her lowliness, commandeth those souls it stoops to.—*Moore.*

It is in vain to gather virtues without humility; for the Spirit of God delighteth to dwell in the hearts of the humble.—*Erasmus.*

Whatever obscurities may involve religious tenets, humility and love constitute the essence of true religion; the humble is formed to adore, the loving to associate with eternal love.—
Lavater.

Humbleness is always grace, always dignity.—
Lowell.

Shall we speak of the inspiration of a poet or a priest, and not of the heart impelled by love and self-devotion to the lowliest work in the lowliest way of life?—*Dickens.*

By humility and the fear of the Lord are riches, honor, and life.—*Bible.*

It is a fair and fragrant flower; in its appearance modest, in its situation low and hidden; it doth not flaunt its beauties to every vulgar eye, or throw its odors upon every passing gale; it is unknown to the earthly botanist, it discovers itself only to the spiritual searcher; neither does he find it among those gay and gaudy tribes of flowers with which the generality are so easily captivated, but in some obscure and unfrequented spot, where the prints of human footsteps are rarely seen.—*Caspipini.*

Blessed are the meek, for they shall inherit the earth.—*Bible.*

All the world, all that we are, and all that we have, our bodies and our souls, our actions and our sufferings, our conditions at home, our accidents abroad, our many sins, and our seldom virtues, are as so many arguments to make our souls dwell low in the deep valley of humility.—*Jeremy Taylor.*

Humility is the first of the virtues—for other people.—*Holmes.*

Humility is the hall-mark of wisdom. Socrates, whom the oracle, that is, the united opinion of the world in which he moved, pronounced to be the wisest man, was content with the title of a lover, rather than a professor, of wisdom.
Jeremy Collier.

It is easy to be humble where humility is a condescension; easy to concede where we know ourselves wronged; easy to forgive where vengeance is in our power.—*Mrs. Jameson.*

Lowliness is the base of every virtue; and he who goes the lowest builds the safest. My God keeps all his pity for the proud.—*Bailey.*

The loveliest, sweetest flower that bloomed in paradise, and the first that died, has rarely blossomed since on mortal soil. It is so frail, so delicate, a thing it is gone if it but look upon itself; and she who ventures to esteem it hers proves by that single thought she has it not.—
Mrs. E. Fry.

The bird of wisdom flies low, and seeks her food under hedges; the eagle himself would be starved if he always soared aloft and against the sun.—*Landor.*

Humility is not a weak and timid quality. It must be carefully distinguished from a grovelling spirit. There is such a thing as an honest pride and self-respect. We should think something of our humanity, and not cast it under men's feet. Though we may be servants of all, we should be servile to none.—*Chapin.*

The more sinful man feels himself, the more Christian he is.—*Novalis.*

I am afraid humility to genius is as an extinguisher to a candle.—*Shenstone.*

Humility is a virtue all preach, none practise, and yet everybody is content to bear. The master thinks it good doctrine for his servant, the laity for the clergy, and the clergy for the laity.—*Selden.*

If man makes himself a worm he must not complain when he is trodden on.—*Kant.*

We are sent to the pismire for industry, to the lion for valor, to the dove for innocence, to the serpent for wisdom; but for humility unto God himself, as an attribute more peculiar to his excellence.—*Feltham.*

Who seems proud wants at least the look of humility, — light without splendor, fire without heat, humility without meekness, what are they? *Lavater.*

Humility mainly becometh the converse of man with his Maker, but oftentimes it seemeth out of place of man with man; render unto all men their due, but remember thou also art a man, and cheat not thyself of the reverence which is owing to thy reasonable being.— *Tupper.*

The fullest and best ears of corn hang lowest towards the ground.—*Bishop Reynolds.*

HUMOR.
Wit may be a thing of pure imagination, but humor involves sentiment and character. Humor is of a genial quality, and is closely allied to pity.—*Henry Giles.*

Humor, which is the pensiveness of wit, enjoys a longer and a wider life. After one brilliant explosion, the repartee is worthless. The shrunken firework offends the eye; but the quiet suggestiveness of Mr. Shandy is interesting as ever; and the details of the great army in Flanders will last as long as the passage of Hannibal.—*Willmott.*

Men of humor are, in some degree, men of genius; wits are rarely so, although a man of genius may, amongst other gifts, possess wit, — as Shakespeare.—*Coleridge.*

Humor is wit and love.—*Thackeray.*

Humor is one of the elements of genius; but if it predominates, it becomes a make-shift. Humor accompanies the decline of art, which it destroys and annihilates.—*Goethe.*

Whenever you find Humor, you find Pathos close by its side.—*Whipple.*

Humor is a quality which dwells in the same character with pathos, and which is always mingled with sensibility, being the offspring of a sympathizing fancy.—*Henry Giles.*

It is not in the power of every one to taste humor, however he may wish it; it is the gift of God! and a true feeler always brings half the entertainment along with him.—*Sterne.*

Humor is the harmony of the heart.— *Douglas Jerrold.*

HYPOCRISY.
O cunning enemy, that to catch a saint, with saints dost bait thy hook! Most dangerous is that temptation that doth goad us on to sin in loving virtue.—*Shakespeare.*

Hypocrisy is the necessary burden of villany. *Johnson.*

Lord love you! when we see what some people do all the week, — people who are stanch at church, remember, — I can't help thinking there are a good many poor souls who are only Christians at morning and afternoon service.—*Dickens.*

An thou canst not smile as the wind sits, thou wilt catch cold shortly.—*Shakespeare.*

Hypocrisy, of course, delights in the most sublime speculations; for, never intending to go beyond speculation, it costs nothing to have it magnificent.—*Burke.*

If Satan ever laughs, it must be at hypocrites; they are the greatest dupes he has. *Colton.*

Hypocrisy itself does great honor, or rather justice, to religion, and tacitly acknowledges it to be an ornament to human nature. The hypocrite would not be at so much pains to put on the appearance of virtue, if he did not know it was the most proper and effectual means to gain the love and esteem of mankind. *Addison.*

Hypocrisy is the homage that vice pays to virtue.—*Rochefoucauld.*

An atheist is but a mad, ridiculous derider of piety; but a hypocrite makes a sober jest of God and religion; he finds it easier to be upon his knees than to rise to a good action.—*Pope.*

The world is all title-page; there is no contents; the world is all face; the man who shows his heart is hooted for his nudities, and scorned.—*Young.*

If hypocrites go to hell by the road to heaven, we may carry on the metaphor, and add that as all the virtues demand their respective tolls, the hypocrite has a by-way to avoid them, and to get into the main road again. And all would be well if he could escape the last turnpike in the journey of life, where all must pay, where there is no by-path, and where the toll is death.—*Colton.*

Trust not him that seems a saint.—*Fuller.*

Who by kindness and smooth attention can insinuate a hearty welcome to an unwelcome guest is a hypocrite superior to a thousand plain dealers.—*Lavater.*

Though I do hate him as I do hell pains, yet for necessity of present lift, I must show out a flag and sign of love, which is indeed but sign.
Shakespeare.

To beguile the time, look like the time; bear welcome in your eyes, your hand, your tongue; look like the innocent flower, but be the serpent under it.—*Shakespeare.*

While every vice is hid by hypocrisy, every virtue is suspected to be hypocrisy. This excuses the bad from imitating virtue, the ungenerous from rewarding it; and the suspicion is looked upon as wisdom, as if it was not as necessary a part of wisdom to know what to believe as what to reject.—
Mary Wortley Montagu.

The only vice that cannot be forgiven is hypocrisy. The repentance of a hypocrite is itself hypocrisy.—*Hazlitt.*

Hypocrisy has been styled " the homage which vice renders to virtue"; but if Virtue herself could be consulted, she would probably think the courteous custom " better honored in the breach than the observance." No man who loves truth himself can value another's professing truth which is not truth to him.—
Whately.

Hypocrites do the Devil's drudgery in Christ's livery.—*Matthew Henry.*

For all those with whom we live are like actors on a stage; they assume whatever dress and appearance may suit their present purpose, and they speak and act in strict keeping with this character. In this way we find it difficult to get at their real sentiments, or to bring into clear day the truth, which they have hid in a cloud of darkness.—*Polybius.*

Some that smile have in their heart, I fear, millions of mischief.—*Shakespeare.*

For it is more disgraceful for men in high office to improve their private fortune by specious fraud than by open violence. Might makes right in the one case; while in the other man throws over his proceedings the cloak of despicable cunning.—*Thucydides.*

The hypocrite had left his mask, and stood in naked ugliness.—*Pollok.*

It is not that the hypocrite despises a good character that he is not one himself, but because he thinks he can purchase it at a cheaper rate than the practice of it, and thus obtain all the applause of a good man, merely by pretending to be so.—*Fielding.*

Satan was the first that practised falsehood under saintly show, deep malice to conceal, couched with revenge.—*Milton.*

For every man's nature is concealed with many folds of disguise, and covered as it were with various veils. His brows, his eyes, and very often his countenance, are deceitful, and his speech is most commonly a lie.—*Cicero.*

The hypocrite and the Pharisee, like some beasts, are only valuable for their skin and their fine colors.—*Cudworth.*

Surely the mischief of hypocrisy can never be enough inveighed against. When religion is in request, it is the chief malady of the Church, and numbers die of it; though because it is a subtle and inward evil, be little perceived. It is to be feared there are many sick of it, that look well and comely in God's outward worship, and they may pass well in good weather, in times of peace; but days of adversity are days of trial.—*Bishop Hall.*

Hypocrisy is folly. It is much easier, safer, and pleasanter to be the thing which a man aims to appear, than to keep up the appearance of being what he is not.—*Cecil.*

False face must hide what the false heart doth know.—*Shakespeare.*

A hypocrite in society lives in the same apprehension with a thief, who lies concealed in the midst of the family he is to rob; for this fancies himself perceived when he is least so; every motion alarms him; he fears he is discovered, and is suspicious that every one who enters the room knows where he is hid, and is coming to seize him. And thus, as nothing hates more violently than fear, many an innocent person, who suspects no evil intended him, is detested by him who intends it.—*Fielding.*

The hypocrite shows the excellency of virtue by the necessity he thinks himself under of seeming to be virtuous.—*Johnson.*

Hypocrites place religion chiefly in externals, in the outward practices of devotion, objectless, like machines, and performed as the service of thralls to God; among other things, they have the characteristic sign of being more alive to the religious life of others than to their own.—
Fichte.

There is some virtue in almost every vice except hypocrisy; and even that, while it is a mockery of virtue, is at the same time a compliment to it.—*Hazlitt.*

He hath put forth his hands against such as be at peace with him; he hath broken his covenant; the words of his mouth were smoother than butter, but war was in his heart; his words were softer than oil, yet were they drawn swords.—*Bible.*

I.

IDEAL.

We build statues of snow, and weep to see them melt.— *Walter Scott.*

All men need something to poetize and idealize their life a little, — something which they value for more than its use, and which is a symbol of their emancipation from the mere materialism and drudgery of daily life.— *Theodore Parker.*

Every life has its actual blanks, which the ideal must fill up, or which else remain bare and profitless forever.—*Julia Ward Howe.*

Achievement is only the eminence whence we survey something better to be achieved. Ideality is only the *avant-courier* of the mind, and where that, in a healthy and normal state, goes, I hold it to be a prophecy that realization can follow.—*Horace Mann.*

The ideal itself is but truth clothed in the forms of art.—*Octave Feuillet.*

Every man has at times in his mind the ideal of what he should be, but is not. This ideal may be high and complete, or it may be quite low and insufficient; yet, in all men that really seek to improve, it is better than the actual character. Perhaps no one is so satisfied with himself that he never wishes to be wiser, better, and more holy.—*Theodore Parker.*

What we need most is not so much to realize the ideal as to idealize the real.— *F. H. Hedge.*

Alas! we know that ideals can never be completely embodied in practice. Ideals must ever lie a great way off, — and we will thankfully content ourselves with any not intolerable approximation thereto! Let no man, as Schiller says, too querulously " measure by a scale of perfection the meagre product of reality " in this poor world of ours.—*Carlyle.*

Ideal beauty is a fugitive which is never located.—*Madame Sévigné.*

A large portion of human beings live not so much in themselves as in what they desire to be. They create what is called an ideal character, in an ideal form, whose perfections compensate in some degree for the imperfections of their own.— *Whipple.*

Freedom is only in the land of dreams, and the beautiful only blooms in song.—*Schiller.*

IDEAS.

By what strange law of mind is it that an idea long overlooked, and trodden underfoot as a useless stone, suddenly sparkles out in new light, as a discovered diamond? —*Mrs. Stowe.*

Our land is not more the recipient of the men of all countries than of their ideas.—*Bancroft.*

Common speakers have only one set of ideas, and one set of words to clothe them in; and these are always ready at the mouth; so people come faster out of a church when it is almost empty than when a crowd is at the door.—*Swift.*

Our ideas, like pictures, are made up of lights and shadows.—*Joubert.*

The ideas, as well as children of our youth, often die before us; and our minds represent to us those tombs to which we are approaching, where, though the brass and marble remain, yet the inscriptions are effaced by time and the imagery moulders away. The pictures drawn in our minds are laid on in fading colors, and if not sometimes refreshed, vanish and disappear.—*Locke.*

It is a proof of mediocrity of intellect to be addicted to relating stories.—*Bruyère.*

An idea, like a ghost (according to the common notion of ghosts), must be spoken to a little before it will explain itself.—*Dickens.*

To have ideas is to gather flowers. To think is to weave them into garlands.— *Madame Swetchine.*

A sublime idea remains the same, from whatever brain or in whatever region it had its birth.— *W. Menzel.*

Events are only the shells of ideas; and often it is the fluent thought of ages that is crystallized in a moment by the stroke of a pen or the point of a bayonet.—*Chapin.*

Ideas are pitiless.—*Lamartine.*

Bred to think, as well as to speak by rote, we furnish our minds as we furnish our houses, — with the fancies of others, and according to the mode and age of our country; we pick up our ideas and notions in common conversation, as in schools.—*Bolingbroke.*

The dilution of ideas which I love is intolerable to me. I like sugar, and hate syrup.— *Madame Swetchine.*

Ideas are, like matter, infinitely divisible. It is not given to us to get down, so to speak, to their final atoms, but to their molecular groupings the way is never ending, and the progress infinitely delightful and profitable.— *Bovee.*

Ideas are ofttimes shy of the close furniture of words.—*Tupper.*

IDLENESS.

I can wonder at nothing more than how a man can be idle, — but of all others, a scholar, — in so many improvements of reason, in such sweetness of knowledge, in such variety of studies, in such importunity of thoughts. To find wit in poetry; in philosophy, profoundness; in history, wonder of events; in oratory, sweet eloquence; in divinity, supernatural light and holy devotion, — as so many rich metals in their proper mines, — whom would it not ravish with delight? —*Bishop Hall.*

Disciplined inaction.—*Mackintosh.*

Idleness is an inlet to disorder, and makes way for licentiousness. People that have nothing to do are quickly tired of their own company.—*Jeremy Collier.*

Enjoyment stops where indolence begins.—
Pollok.

Idleness is the badge of gentry, the bane of body and mind, the nurse of naughtiness, the step-mother of discipline, the chief author of all mischief, one of the seven deadly sins, the cushion upon which the Devil chiefly reposes, and a great cause not only of melancholy, but of many other diseases; for the mind is naturally active, and if it be not occupied about some honest business, it rushes into mischief or sinks into melancholy.—*Burton.*

The bees can abide no drones amongst them; but as soon as they begin to be idle, they kill them.—*Plato.*

I look upon indolence as a sort of suicide; for the man is efficiently destroyed, though the appetite of the brute may survive.—*Chesterfield.*

An idler is a watch that wants both hands.—
Cowper.

Employment, which Galen calls "nature's physician," is so essential to human happiness that indolence is justly considered as the mother of misery.—*Burton.*

Much bending breaks the bow; much unbending, the mind.—*Bacon.*

Laziness grows on people; it begins in cobwebs, and ends in iron chains. The more business a man has to do, the more he is able to accomplish; for he learns to economize his time.
Judge Hale.

The idle walk slowly, as the poor never lag to await them.—*Hunter.*

Rather do what is nothing to the purpose than be idle; that the Devil may find thee doing. The bird that sits is easily shot, when fliers scape the fowler. Idleness is the Dead Sea that swallows all the virtues, and the self-made sepulchre of a living man.—*Quarles.*

Sure He that made us with such large discourse, looking before and after, gave us not that capability and godlike reason to rust in us unused.—*Shakespeare.*

Watch, for the idleness of the soul approaches death.—*Demophilus.*

Perhaps every man may date the predominance of those desires that disturb his life, and contaminate his conscience, from some unhappy hour when too much leisure exposed him to their incursions; for he has lived with little observation, either on himself or others, who does not know that to be idle is to be vicious.—
Johnson.

A poor idle man cannot be an honest man.—
Achilles Poincelot.

In such a world as ours the idle man is not so much a biped as a bivalve; and the wealth which breeds idleness, of which the English peerage is an example, and of which we are beginning to abound in specimens in this country, is only a sort of human oyster bed, where heirs and heiresses are planted, to spend a contemptible life of slothfulness in growing plump and succulent for the grave-worms' banquet.—
Horace Mann.

Idleness is emptiness; the tree in which the sap is stagnant, remains fruitless.—
Hosea Ballou.

If you ask me which is the real hereditary sin of human nature, do you imagine I shall answer pride or luxury or ambition or egotism? No; I shall say indolence. Who conquers indolence will conquer all the rest. Indeed, all good principles must stagnate without mental activity.—*Zimmermann.*

A thousand evils do afflict that man which hath to himself an idle and unprofitable carcass.
Sallust.

Indolence, indeed, is never at a loss for a smooth lie or delicious sophism to justify inaction, and, in our day, has rationalized it into a philosophy of the mind, and idealized it into a school of poetry, and organized it into a "hospital of incapables." It promises you the still ecstasy of a divine repose, while it lures you surely down into the vacant dulness of inglorious sloth. It provides a primrose path to stagnant pools, to an Arcadia of thistles, and a Paradise of mud.—*Whipple.*

The man who lives in vain lives worse than in vain. He who lives to no purpose lives to a bad purpose.—*Nevins.*

He that embarks in the voyage of life will always wish to advance, rather by the impulse of the wind, than the strokes of the oar; and many founder in their passage while they lie waiting for the gale.—*Johnson.*

The idle always have a mind to do something.—*Vauvenargues.*

Indolent people, whatever taste they may have for society, seek eagerly for pleasure, and find nothing. They have an empty head and seared hearts.—*Zimmermann.*

Idleness is the stupidity of the body, and stupidity the idleness of the mind.—*Seume.*

It is deceiving one's self to believe that it is only violent passions, like those of love and ambition, which are able to triumph over others. Slothfulness, as languishing as it is, permits none to be its mistress; it usurps all the designs and all the actions of life; it destroys and consumes insensibly the passions and the virtues.—*Rochefoucauld.*

Troubles spring from idleness, and grievous toils from needless ease.—*Franklin.*

Idleness often takes the name of repose, and thinks to shield itself from the just blame that it merits.—*Oxenstiern.*

Too much idleness, I have observed, fills up a man's time much more completely, and leaves him less his own master, than any sort of employment whatsoever.—*Burke.*

Stagnation is something worse than death, it is corruption also.—*Simms.*

The idle man is the Devil's cushion, on which he taketh his free ease, who as he is incapable of any good, so he is fitly disposed for all evil motions. The standing water soon stinketh; whereas the current ever keeps clear and cleanly, conveying down all noisome matter that might infect it by the force of his stream.—*Bishop Hall.*

A moral in the style of Seneca: It is better to do the idlest thing in the world than to sit idle for half an hour.—*Sterne.*

Drones suck not eagles' blood, but rob bee-hives.—*Shakespeare.*

To be idle and to be poor have always been reproaches; and therefore every man endeavors with his utmost care to hide his poverty from others, and his idleness from himself.—*Johnson.*

The frivolous work of polished idleness.—*Mackintosh.*

Avoid idleness, and fill up all the spaces of thy time with severe and useful employment; for lust easily creeps in at those emptinesses where the soul is unemployed and the body is at ease; for no easy, healthful idle person was ever chaste if he could be tempted; but of all employments, bodily labor is the most useful, and of the greatest benefit for driving away the Devil.—*Jeremy Taylor.*

Idleness is a constant sin, and labor is a duty. Idleness is the Devil's home for temptation, and for unprofitable, distracting musings; while labor profiteth others and ourselves.—*Baxter.*

How sweet and sacred idleness is!—*Landor.*

The Turks have a proverb, which says that the Devil tempts all other men, but that idle men tempt the Devil.—*Colton.*

Idleness belongs more to the mind than to the body.—*Rochefoucauld.*

They that do nothing are in the readiest way to do that which is worse than nothing.—*Zimmermann.*

A mind quite vacant is a mind distressed.—*Cowper.*

How long shall we sit in our porticos praising idle and musty virtues, which any work would make impertinent? As if one, were to begin the day with long-suffering, and hire a man to hoe his potatoes.—*Thoreau.*

Idleness is many gathered miseries in one name.—*Richter.*

Idleness is the grand Pacific Ocean of life, and in that stagnant abyss the most salutary things produce no good, the most noxious, no evil. Vice, indeed, abstractedly considered, may be, and often is engendered in idleness; but the moment it becomes efficiently vice, it must quit its cradle and cease to be idle.—*Colton.*

He is not only idle who does nothing, but he is idle who might be better employed.—*Socrates.*

That which some would call idleness I will call the sweetest part of my life, and that is my thinking.—*Feltham.*

Idleness is a disease that must be combated; but I would not advise a rigid adherence to a particular plan of study. I myself have never persisted in any plan for two days together. A man ought to read just as inclination leads him; for what he reads as a task will do him little good.—*Johnson.*

Do not allow Idleness to deceive you; for, while you give him to-day, he steals to-morrow from you.—*Crowquill.*

The idle, who are neither wise for this world nor the next, are emphatically fools at large.—*Tillotson.*

Sloth makes all things difficult, but industry all easy; and he that riseth late must trot all day, and shall scarce overtake his business at night; while laziness travels so slowly that poverty soon overtakes him.—*Franklin.*

Idleness is as fatiguing as repose is sweet.—
De Lévis.

It is no more possible for an idle man to keep together a certain stock of knowledge than it is possible to keep together a stock of ice exposed to the meridian sun. Every day destroys a fact, a relation, or an influence; and the only method of preserving the bulk and value of the pile is by constantly adding to it.—
Sydney Smith.

As pride is sometimes hid under humility, idleness is often covered by turbulence and hurry.—*Johnson.*

Indolence is, methinks, an intermediate state between pleasure and pain, and very much unbecoming any part of our life after we are out of the nurse's arms.—*Steele.*

IGNORANCE.

Ignorance is the curse of God; knowledge, the wing wherewith we fly to heaven.—
Shakespeare.

The ignorance that knows itself, judges and condemns itself, is not an absolute ignorance; which to be, it must be ignorant of itself.—
Montaigne.

Better to be unborn, than untaught; for ignorance is the root of misfortune.—*Plato.*

So long as thou art ignorant, be not ashamed to learn. Ignorance is the greatest of all infirmities; and when justified, the chiefest of all follies—*Izaak Walton.*

Ignorance gives a sort of eternity to prejudice, and perpetuity to error.—*Robert Hall.*

There is a sort of ignorance strong and generous, that yields nothing in honor and courage to knowledge; and ignorance, which to conceive requires no less knowledge than knowledge itself.—*Montaigne.*

Ignorant men differ from beasts only in their figure.—*Cleanthes.*

He hath not eat paper, as it were; hath not drunk ink: his intellect is not replenished; he is only an animal, only sensible in the duller parts.—*Shakespeare.*

If thou art wise, thou knowest thy own ignorance; and thou art ignorant if thou knowest not thyself.—*Luther.*

Thy ignorance in unrevealed mysteries is the mother of a saving faith, and thy understanding in revealed truths is the mother of a sacred knowledge; understand not therefore that thou mayest believe, but believe that thou mayest understand; understanding is the wages of a lively faith, and faith is the reward of an humble ignorance.—*Quarles.*

Be not sorry that men do not know you, but be sorry that you are ignorant of men.—*Confucius.*

As if anything were so common as ignorance. The multitude of fools is a protection to the wise.—*Cicero.*

O thou monster, Ignorance, how deformed dost thou look!—*Shakespeare.*

The wisdom of the ignorant somewhat resembles the instinct of animals; it is diffused but in a very narrow sphere, but within the circle it acts with vigor, uniformity, and success.
Goldsmith.

Ignorance is the night of the mind, but a night without moon or star.—*Confucius.*

Talk to a blind man,—he knows he wants the sense of sight, and willingly makes the proper allowances. But there are certain internal senses which a man may want, and yet be wholly ignorant that he wants them. It is most unpleasant to converse with such persons on subjects of taste, philosophy, or religion. Of course there is no reasoning with them, for they do not possess the facts on which the reasoning must be grounded.—*Coleridge.*

A wise man in the company of those who are ignorant has been compared by the sages to a beautiful girl in the company of blind men.
Saadi.

I would as lief be a brute beast as an ignorant rich man.—*Bishop Hall.*

There is one peculiar imperfection connected with our want of correct information, which we should particularly guard against,—I mean that of being positive in proportion to our ignorance!—*Hosea Ballou.*

There is no darkness but ignorance.—
Shakespeare.

We think there is shame in doubt and ignorance, and we like better to decide at hazard, than to be conscious that we are not informed enough of things to give judgment. We are full of ignorance and errors; and nevertheless we are at the greatest trouble in the world to draw from the lips of men this confession, so just and so conformable to their natural condition: "I am mistaken, and I know nothing."
Nicole.

They most assume who know the least.—
Gay.

Nothing is so good for an ignorant man as silence; and if he was sensible of this he would not be ignorant.—*Saadi.*

He that is not aware of his ignorance will be only misled by his knowledge.—*Whately.*

The man who feels himself ignorant should, at least, be modest.—*Johnson.*

It is impossible to make people understand their ignorance, for it requires knowledge /to perceive it; and therefore he that can perceive it hath it not.—*Jeremy Taylor.*

Nothing is more terrible than active ignorance.—*Goethe.*

Ignorance, when voluntary, is criminal, and a man may be properly charged with that evil which he neglected or refused to learn how to prevent.—*Johnson.*

There are times when ignorance is bliss indeed.—*Dickens.*

There are two sorts of ignorance: we philosophize to escape ignorance; we start from the one, we repose in the other; they are the goals from which and to which we tend; and the pursuit of knowledge is but a course between two ignorances, as human life is only a travelling from grave to grave.—*Sir William Hamilton.*

Scholars are frequently to be met with who are ignorant of nothing — saving their own ignorance.—*Zimmermann.*

It is not wisdom, but ignorance, which teaches men presumption. Genius may be sometimes arrogant, but nothing is so diffident as knowledge.—*Bulwer Lytton.*

Ignorance is a prolonged infancy only deprived of its charm.—*De Boufflers.*

It is thus that we walk through the world like the blind, not knowing whither we are going, regarding as bad what is good, regarding as good what is bad, and ever in entire ignorance.—*Madame de Sévigné.*

Nothing so haughty and assuming as ignorance, where self-conceit bids it set up for infallible.—*South.*

Ignorance is the mother of fear, as well as of admiration. A man intimately acquainted with the nature of things has seldom occasion to be astonished.—*Henry Home.*

Man is arrogant in proportion to his ignorance. Man's natural tendency is to egotism. Man, in his infancy of knowledge, thinks that all creation was formed for him.—*Bulwer Lytton.*

O Ignorance! thou art fallen man's best friend!—*H. K. White.*

A man is never astonished or ashamed that he don't know what another does, but he is surprised at the gross ignorance of the other in not knowing what he does.—*Haliburton.*

The true instrument of man's degradation is his ignorance.—*Lady Morgan.*

It is with nations as with individuals, those who know the least of others think the highest of themselves; for the whole family of pride and ignorance are incestuous, and mutually beget each other.—*Colton.*

From ignorance our comfort flows. The only wretched are the wise.—*Matthew Prior.*

Ignorance lies at the bottom of all human knowledge, and the deeper we penetrate, the nearer we arrive unto it. For what do we truly know, or what can we clearly affirm, of any one of those important things upon which all our reasonings must of necessity be built, — time and space, life and death, matter and mind?—*Colton.*

Ignorance is but a dull remedy for evils.—*Seneca.*

Ignorance breeds monsters to fill up all the vacancies of the soul that are unoccupied by the verities of knowledge. He who dethrones the idea of law bids chaos welcome in its stead.—*Horace Mann.*

There is nothing more frightful than a bustling ignorance.—*Goethe.*

He that had never seen a river imagined the first he met with to be the sea, and the greatest things that have fallen within our knowledge we conclude the extremes that nature makes of the kind.—*Montaigne.*

There is nothing more daring than ignorance.—*Menander.*

Too much attention cannot be bestowed on that important, yet much neglected branch of learning, — the knowledge of man's ignorance.—*Whately.*

ILL-NATURE.
The world is so full of ill-nature that I have lampoons sent me by people who cannot spell, and satires composed by those who scarce know how to write.—*Addison.*

It is impossible that an ill-natured man can have a public spirit; for how should he love ten thousand men who never loved one?—*Pope.*

Though I carry always some ill-nature about me, yet it is, I hope, no more than is in this world necessary for a preservative.—*Marvell.*

Ill-humor is nothing more than an inward feeling of our own want of merit, a dissatisfaction with ourselves which is always united with an envy that foolish vanity excites.—*Goethe.*

If thou be a severe, sour-complexioned man, then here I disallow thee to be a competent judge.—*Izaak Walton.*

ILLS.

Philosophy easily triumphs over past and future ills; but present ills triumph over philosophy.—*Rochefoucauld.*

All ills spring from some vice, either in ourselves or others; and even many of our diseases proceed from the same origin. Remove the vices, and the ills follow. You must only take care to remove all the vices. If you remove part, you may render the matter worse. By banishing vicious luxury, without curing sloth and an indifference to others, you only diminish industry in the state, and add nothing to men's charity or their generosity.—*Hume.*

Think of the ills from which you are exempt.—*Joubert.*

We satisfied ourselves the other day that there was no real ill in life except severe bodily pain; everything else is the child of the imagination, and depends on our thoughts; all other ills find a remedy, either from time or moderation, or strength of mind.—*Madame de Sévigné.*

To the greater part of mankind it is less dangerous to do an injury than much service.·
Rochefoucauld.

O, yet we trust that somehow good will be the final goal of ill!—*Tennyson.*

ILLUSION.

When the boys come into my yard for leave to gather horse-chestnuts, I own I enter into nature's game, and affect to grant the permission reluctantly, fearing that any moment they will find out the imposture of that showy chaff. But this tenderness is quite unnecessary; the enchantments are laid on very thick. Their young life is thatched with them. Bare and grim to tears is the lot of the children in the hovel I saw yesterday; yet not the less they hang it round with frippery romance, like the children of the happiest fortune.—*Emerson.*

There is no such thing as real happiness in life. The justest definition that was ever given of it was " a tranquil acquiescence under an agreeable delusion."—I forget where.—*Sterne.*

ILL-WILL.

It is a true word of Gerson, that in a pennyworth of strife there is not a halfpennyworth of love; and we say truly, ill-will never said well.
Bishop Hall.

Such is the charity of some, that they never owe any man any ill-will, making present payment thereof.—*Fuller.*

IMAGINATION.

The imagination magnifies small objects, so as to fill the mind with a fantastic estimate; and with haughty insolence contracts the great to its own dwarfish measure, — as, for instance, in speaking of God.—*Pascal.*

The soul without imagination is what an observatory would be without a telescope.—
Beecher.

The world of reality has its limits; the world of imagination is boundless. Not being able to enlarge the one, let us contract the other; for it is from their difference alone that all the evils arise which render us really unhappy.—*Rousseau.*

Imagination rules the world.—*Napoleon.*

It is the divine attribute of the imagination, that it is irrepressible, unconfinable; that when the real world is shut out, it can create a world for itself, and with a necromantic power can conjure up glorious shapes and forms, and brilliant visions to make solitude populous, and irradiate the gloom of a dungeon.—
Washington Irving.

I did wed myself to things of light from infancy.—*Keats.*

Imagination is that faculty which arouses the passions by the impression of exterior objects; it is influenced by these objects, and consequently it is in affinity with them; it is contagious; its fear or courage flies from imagination to imagination; the same in love, hate, joy, or grief: hence I conclude it to be a most subtle atmosphere.—*Lord John Russell.*

Whatever makes the past or the future predominate over the present exalts us in the scale of thinking beings.—*Johnson.*

Imagination, in a poet, is a faculty so wild and lawless that, like a high-ranging spaniel, it must have clogs to it, lest it outrun the judgment.—*Dryden.*

There is nothing more fearful than imagination without taste.— *Goethe.*

The faculty of imagination is the great spring of human activity, and the principal source of human improvement. As it delights in presenting to the mind scenes and characters more perfect than those which we are acquainted with, it prevents us from ever being completely satisfied with our present condition, and engages us continually in the pursuit of some untried enjoyment, or of some ideal excellence. Hence the ardor of the selfish to better their fortunes, and to add to their personal accomplishments; and hence the zeal of the patriot and the philosopher to advance the virtue and the happiness of the human race. Destroy this faculty, and the condition of man will become as stationary as that of the brutes.—*Dugald Stewart.*

Imagination is a mettled horse, that will break the rider's neck, when a donkey would have carried him to the end of his journey slow but sure.—*Southey.*

The imagination, give it the least license, dives deeper and soars higher than nature goes.—*Thoreau.*

What I can fancy, but can never express.—*Juvenal.*

Imagination is the ruler of our dreams,—a circumstance that may account for the peculiar vividness of the impressions they produce. Let reason be the ruler of our waking thoughts.—*W. B. Clulow.*

Such is the power of imagination, that even a chimerical pleasure in expectation affects us more than a solid pleasure in possession.— *Henry Home.*

But what is the imagination? Only an arm or weapon of the interior energy; only the precursor of the reason.—*Emerson.*

Imagination, excited in those who are novices as to its effects, and who have felt it so little that they have never learnt to control it, is like wine, as Waller has described it.— *J. F. Boyes.*

Imagination disposes of everything; it creates beauty, justice, and happiness, which is everything in this world.—*Pascal.*

Imagination is the organ through which the soul within us recognizes a soul without us; the spiritual eye by which the mind perceives and converses with the spiritualities of nature under her material forms; which tends to exalt even the senses into soul by discerning a soul in the objects of sense.—*H. N. Hudson.*

Imagination is the eye of the soul.—*Joubert.*

If we except the blessings of strength, health, and the testimony of a good conscience, all the other conveniences and pleasures of life depend on opinion. Except pain of body and remorse of conscience, all our evils are imaginary.— *Rousseau.*

Imagination is not thought, neither is fancy reflection; thought paceth like a hoary sage, but imagination hath wings as an eagle.— *Tupper.*

The imagination often magnifies the veriest trifle, by a false and romantic preference, till it fills the whole soul; or, in its heedless presumption, brings down the most elevated subjects to our own low standard.—*Pascal.*

An uncommon degree of imagination constitutes poetical genius.—*Dugald Stewart.*

Plenty and indigence depend upon the opinion every one has of them; and riches, no more than glory or health, have no more beauty or pleasure than their possessor is pleased to lend them.—*Montaigne.*

The imagination acquires by custom a certain involuntary, unconscious power of observation and comparison, correcting its own mistakes, and arriving at precision of judgment, just as the outward eye is disciplined to compare, adjust, estimate, measure, the objects reflected on the back of its retina. The imagination is but the faculty of glassing images; and it is with exceeding difficulty, and by the imperative will of the reasoning faculty resolved to mislead it, that it glasses images which have no prototype in truth and nature.— *Bulwer Lytton.*

The imagination is of so delicate a texture that even words wound it.—*Hazlitt.*

Our griefs, as well as our joys, owe their strongest colors to our imaginations. There is nothing so grievous to be borne that pondering upon will not make heavier; and there is no pleasure so vivid that the animation of fancy cannot enliven.—*Jane Porter.*

The lunatic, the lover, and the poet are of imagination all compact.—*Shakespeare.*

Mere thought convinces; feeling always persuades. If imagination furnishes the fact with wings, feeling is the great, stout muscle which plies them, and lifts him from the ground. Thought sees beauty, emotion feels it.— *Theodore Parker.*

Delighting in the most sublime speculations, —for, never intending to go beyond speculation, it costs nothing to have it magnificent.—*Burke*

Thanks be to our sick minds that abate our joys, and put them out of taste with them, as with themselves. They entertain both themselves and all they receive,—one while better, and another worse,—according to their insatiable, vagabond, and versatile essence.— *Montaigne.*

Pure imagination, of which the loveliest of winged creatures is the fitting emblem, seems always to gain in vigor and grace by the tempests it encounters, and in contrary winds to show the brightest plumage.—*Willmott.*

IMITATION.

I hardly know so true a mark of a little mind as the servile imitation of others.— *Lord Greville.*

The secret of some men's attractions might be safely told to all the world, for under any other management but that of the possessor, they would cease to attract. Those who attempted to imitate them would find that they had got the fiddle, but not the fiddlestick.— *Colton.*

It is a poor wit who lives by borrowing the words, decisions, mien, inventions, and actions of others.—*Lavater.*

A good imitation is the most perfect originality.— *Voltaire.*

It is certain that either wise bearing or ignorant carriage is caught as men take diseases, one of another.—*Shakespeare.*

To be as good as our fathers, we must be better. Imitation is not discipleship. When some one sent a cracked plate to China to have a set made, every piece in the new set had a crack in it.— *Wendell Phillips.*

He who imitates what is evil always goes beyond the example that is set; on the contrary, he who imitates what is good always falls short.
Guicciardini.

For imitation is natural to man from his infancy. Man differs from other animals particularly in this, that he is imitative, and acquires his rudiments of knowledge in this way; besides, the delight in it is universal.—*Aristotle.*

O imitators, a servile race, how often have your attacks roused my bile and often my laughter ! —*Horace.*

It is by imitation, far more than by precept, that we learn everything ; and what we learn thus, we acquire not only more effectually, but more pleasantly. This forms our manners, our opinions, our lives.—*Burke.*

It is very true that precepts are useful ; but practice and imitation go far beyond them ; hence the importance of watching early habits, that they may be free from what is objectionable.
Sir William Knighton.

Man is an imitative creature, and whoever is foremost leads the herd.—*Schiller.*

Some imitation is involuntary and unconscious. Genius is nourished from within and without. Its food is self-grown and gathered. Like a rich-bearing tree, it absorbs the juices of the soil and the balm of the air, but draws from its own blood the life that swells out the trunk, and gives color and flavor to the fruit.—*Willmott.*

Even a man's exact imitation of the song of the nightingale displeases us when we discover that it is a mimicry, and not the nightingale.—*Kant.*

You may imitate, but never counterfeit.—*Balzac.*

No single character is ever so great that a nation can afford to form itself upon it. Imitation belittles. This appears in the instance of the Chinese. The Chinese are so many Confucii, in miniature. And so with the Jews. Moses, the lawgiver, is poorly represented by Moses, the old clothesman; or even by *Dives,* the banker.—*Bovee.*

The only good copies are those which enable us to see the laughableness of bad originals.—
Rochefoucauld.

We only imitate what we believe.— *Willmott.*

IMMODESTY.

Immodest words admit of no defence.—
Pope.

The chariest maid is prodigal enough, if she unmask her beauty to the moon.—*Shakespeare.*

IMMORTALITY.

We are much better believers in immortality than we can give grounds for. The real evidence is too subtle, or is higher than we can write down in propositions.—*Emerson.*

For does this soul within me, this spirit of thought and love and infinite desire, dissolve as well as the body? Has Nature, who quenches our bodily thirst, who rests our weariness, and perpetually encourages us to endeavor onwards, prepared no food for this appetite of immortality?—*Leigh Hunt.*

Without a belief in personal immortality religion surely is like an arch resting on one pillar, like a bridge ending in an abyss.—
Max Müller.

How gloomy would be the mansions of the dead to him who did not know that he should never die; that what now acts shall continue its agency, and what now thinks shall think on forever ! —*Johnson.*

There may be beings, thinking beings, near or surrounding us, which we do not perceive, which we cannot imagine. We know very little; but, in my opinion, we know enough to hope for the immortality, the individual immortality, of the better part of man.—
Sir H. Davy.

It is only our mortal duration that we measure by visible and measurable objects; and there is nothing mournful in the contemplation for one who knows that the Creator made him to be the image of his own eternity, and who feels that in the desire for immortality he has sure proof of his capacity for it.—*Southey.*

We do not believe immortality because we have proved it, but we forever try to prove it because we believe it.—*James Martineau.*

When the stiffened body goes down to the tomb, sad, silent, remorseless,— I feel there is no death for the man. That clod which yonder dust shall cover is not my brother. The dust goes to its place, man to his own. It is then I feel my immortality. I look through the grave into heaven. I ask no miracle, no proof, no reasoning for me. I ask no risen dust to teach me immortality. I am conscious of eternal life.—*Theodore Parker.*

Still seems it strange that thou shouldst live forever? Is it less strange that thou shouldst live at all? This is a miracle; and that no more.—*Young.*

Bonaparte was visiting the picture-gallery of Soult with Dénon, and was struck with one of Raffaelle's pictures, which Dénon complimented with the term "immortal." "How long may it last?" asked Bonaparte. "Well, some four or five hundred years longer," said Dénou. "*Belle immortalité!*" said Bonaparte, disdainfully.—*Lady Morgan.*

A man really and practically looking onwards to an immortal life, on whatever grounds, exhibits to us the human soul in an ennobled attitude.—*Whewell.*

We are born for a higher destiny than that of earth; there is a realm where the rainbow never fades, where the stars will be spread before us like islands that slumber on the ocean, and where the beings that pass before us like shadows will stay in our presence forever.— *Bulwer Lytton.*

I feel my immortality oversweep all pains, all tears, all time, all fears, — and peal, like the eternal thunders of the deep, into my ears this truth, — thou livest forever!—*Byron.*

It is well known that the belief of a future state is a troublesome check on the human passions, and that it will never succeed in making tranquil and resolute libertines without having first made unbelievers.—*Massillon.*

Faith in the hereafter is as necessary for the intellectual as the moral character; and to the man of letters, as well as to the Christian, the present forms but the slightest portion of his existence.—*Southey.*

Every natural longing has its natural satisfaction. If we thirst, God has created liquids to gratify thirst. If we are susceptible of attachment, there are beings to gratify that love. If we thirst for life and love eternal, it is likely that there are an eternal life and an eternal love to satisfy that craving.—*F. W. Robertson.*

What is human is immortal!— *Bulwer Lytton.*

O, what a fate is that of man! As often as I hear of some undeserved wretchedness, my thoughts rest on that world where all will be made straight, and where the labors of the sorrowful will end in joy. O that we could call up in the hearts of the afflicted such thoughts!— *Fichte.*

Men do not believe in the next world as they do in London or Boston: they do not launch upon the *ignotum mare* with a shadow of that prophetic belief which girded up the heart of Columbus.—*Lowell.*

Our dissatisfaction with any other solution is the blazing evidence of immortality.— *Emerson.*

The soul aspires to immortality.— *Lope de Vega.*

IMPATIENCE.

Impatience dries the blood sooner than age or sorrow.—*Chapin.*

Impatience is a quality sudden, eager, and insatiable, which grasps at all, and admits of no delay; scorning to wait God's leisure, and attend humbly and dutifully upon the issues of his wise and just Providence.—*South.*

Impatience waiteth on true sorrow.— *Shakespeare.*

The schoolboy counts the time till the return of the holidays; the minor longs to be of age; the lover is impatient till he is married.— *Addison.*

We would willingly, and without remorse, sacrifice not only the present moment, but all the interval (no matter how long) that separates us from any favorite object.—*Hazlitt.*

Impatience is the principal cause of most of our irregularities and extravagances. I would sometimes have paid a guinea to be at some particular ball or assembly, and something has prevented my going there. After it was over, I would not give a shilling to have been there. I would pay a crown at any time for a venison ordinary. But after having dined on beef or mutton, I would not give a penny to have had it venison.—*Sterne.*

You are convinced by experience that very few things are brought to a successful issue by impetuous desire, but most by calm and prudent forethought.—*Thucydides.*

Such is our impatience, such our hatred of procrastination, in everything but the amendment of our practices'and the adornment of our nature, one would imagine we were dragging Time along by force, and not he us.—*Landor.*

Nothing is more unreasonable than to entangle our spirits in wildness and amazement, like a partridge fluttering in a net, which she breaks not, though she breaks her wings.— *Jeremy Taylor.*

The beautiful laws of time and space, once dislocated by our inaptitude, are holes and dens. If the hive be disturbed by rash and stupid hands, instead of honey, it will yield us bees.— *Emerson.*

I have not so great a struggle with my vices, great and numerous as they are, as I have with my impatience. My efforts are not absolutely useless; yet I have never been able to conquer this ferocious wild beast.—*Calvin.*

Whosoever is out of patience is out of possession of his soul. Men must not turn bees, and kill themselves in stinging others.—*Bacon.*

In all evils which admit a remedy, impatience should be avoided, because it wastes that time and attention in complaints which, if properly applied, might remove the cause.—*Johnson.*

IMPERFECTION.

What an absurd thing it is to pass over all the valuable parts of a man, and fix our attention on his infirmities! —*Addison.*

It is only imperfection that complains of what is imperfect. The more perfect we are, the more gentle and quiet we become towards the defects of others.—*Fenelon.*

Imperfection is in some sort essential to all that we know of life. It is the sign of life in a mortal body, that is to say, of a state of progress and change. Nothing that lives is, or can be rigidly perfect; part of it is decaying, part nascent. The foxglove blossom — a third part bud, a third part past. a third part in full bloom — is a type of the life of this world.—*Ruskin.*

IMPOSITION.

There are cases in which a man would have been ashamed not to have been imposed on. There is a confidence necessary to human intercourse, and without which, men are more injured by their suspicions than they could be by the perfidy of others.—*Burke.*

I could hardly feel much confidence in a man who had never been imposed upon.—*Hare.*

To the generality of men you cannot give a stronger hint for them to impose upon you than by imposing upon yourself.—*Fielding.*

IMPOSSIBILITY.

Never let me hear that foolish word again.—*Mirabeau.*

My Lord Anson, at the Admiralty, sends word to Chatham, then confined to his chamber by one of his most violent attacks of the gout, that it is impossible for him to fit out a naval expedition within the period to which he is limited. "Impossible!" cried Chatham, glaring at the messenger; "who talks to me of impossibilities?" Then starting to his feet, and forcing out great drops of agony on his brow with the excruciating torment of the effort, he exclaimed, "Tell Lord Anson that he serves under a minister who treads on impossibilities!" — *Whipple.*

Impossible! — it is not good French.—*Napoleon.*

Nothing is impossible; there are ways which lead to everything; and if we had sufficient will we should always have sufficient means.—*Rochefoucauld.*

IMPRISONMENT.

Let them fear bondage who are slaves to fear; the sweetest freedom is an honest heart.—*John Ford.*

IMPROVEMENT.

To hear always, to think always, to learn always, it is thus that we live truly. He who aspires to nothing, who learns nothing, is not worthy of living.—*Helps.*

It is necessary to try to surpass one's self always; this occupation ought to last as long as life.—*Queen Christiana.*

Judge of thine improvement, not by what thou speakest or writest, but by the firmness of thy mind, and the government of thy passions and affections.—*Fuller.*

Infinite toil would not enable you to sweep away a mist; but by ascending a little, you may often look over it altogether. So it is with our moral improvement; we wrestle fiercely with a vicious habit, which could have no hold upon us if we ascended into a higher moral atmosphere.—*Helps.*

IMPROVIDENCE.

It has always been more difficult for a man to keep than to get; for, in the one case, fortune aids, which often assists injustice; but in the other case, sense is required. Therefore, we often see a person deficient in cleverness rise to wealth; and then, from want of sense, roll head over heels to the bottom.—*Count Basil.*

There are men born under that constellation which maketh them, I know not how, as unapt to enrich themselves as they are ready to impoverish others.—*Hooker.*

IMPUDENCE.

The way to avoid the imputation of impudence is, not to be ashamed of what we do, but never to do what we ought to be ashamed of.—*Tully.*

Receive no satisfaction for premeditated impertinence; forget it, forgive it, — but keep him inexorably at a distance who offered it.—*Lavater.*

A true and genuine impudence is ever the effect of ignorance, without the least sense of it.—*Steele.*

A man has no more right to say an uncivil thing than to act one; no more right to say a rude thing to another than to knock him down.—*Johnson.*

The man who cannot blush, and who has no feelings of fear, has reached the acme of impudence.—*Menander.*

What was said by the Latin poet of labor — that it conquers all things — is much more true when applied to impudence.—*Fielding.*

Impudence is no virtue, yet able to beggar them all; being for the most part in good plight, when the rest starve, and capable of carrying her followers up to the highest preferments; as useful in a court as armor in a camp.
Sir Thomas Osborne.

There is no better provision for life than impudence and a brazen face.—*Menander.*

IMPULSE.
Since the generality of persons act from impulse much more than from principle, men are neither so good nor so bad as we are apt to think them.—*Hare.*

All our first movements are good, generous, heroical; reflection weakens and kills them.—
Aimé-Martin.

A true history of human events would show that a far larger proportion of our acts are the results of sudden impulses and accidents than of that reason of which we so much boast.—
Cooper.

Act upon your impulses, but pray that they may be directed by God.—*Emerson Tennent.*

The Indian who fells the tree that he may gather the fruit, and the Arab who plunders the caravans of commerce, are actuated by the same impulse of savage nature, and relinquish for momentary rapine the long and secure possession of the most important blessings.—*Gibbon.*

What persons are by starts, they are by nature. You see them, at such times, off their guard. Habit may restrain vice, and virtue may be obscured by passion, but intervals best discover the man.—*Sterne.*

INCONSISTENCY.
I have known several persons of great fame for wisdom in public affairs and councils governed by foolish servants. I have known great ministers, distinguished for wit and learning, who preferred none but dunces. I have known men of valor cowards to their wives. I have known men of cunning perpetually cheated. I knew three ministers who would exactly compute and settle the accounts of a kingdom, wholly ignorant of their own economy.—
Horace Walpole.

How often in this world the actions that we condemn are the result of sentiments that we love and opinions that we admire!—
Mrs. Jameson.

We all complain of the shortness of time, and yet have much more than we know what to do with. Our lives are spent either in doing nothing at all, or in doing nothing to the purpose, or in doing nothing that we ought to do; we are always complaining our days are few, and acting as though there would be no end of them.—*Seneca.*

INCONSTANCY.
Infidelity, like death, admits of no degrees.—
Madame de Girardin.

Such an act, that blurs the grace and blush of modesty; calls virtue hypocrite; takes off the rose from the fair forehead of an innocent love, and sets a blister there.—*Shakespeare.*

Clocks will go as they are set; but man, irregular man, is never constant, never certain.—
Otway.

We pardon infidelities, but we do not forget them.—*Madame de Lafayette.*

Nothing that is not a real crime makes a man appear so contemptible and little in the eyes of the world as inconstancy, especially when it regards religion or party.—*Addison.*

Inconstancy falls off ere it begins.—
Shakespeare.

INCREDULITY.
The incredulous are the most credulous. They believe the miracles of Vespasian, in order not to believe those of Moses.—*Pascal.*

Incredulity robs us of many pleasures, and gives us nothing in return.—*Lowell.*

Of all the signs of a corrupt heart and a feeble head, the tendency of incredulity is the surest. Real philosophy seeks rather to solve than to deny.—*Bulwer Lytton.*

There lives more faith in honest doubt, believe me, than in half the creeds.—*Tennyson.*

Incredulity is not wisdom, but the worst kind of folly. It is folly, because it causes ignorance and mistake, with all the consequents of these; and it is very bad, as being accompanied with disingenuity, obstinacy, rudeness, uncharitableness, and the like bad dispositions; from which credulity itself, the other extreme sort of folly, is exempt.—*Barrow.*

Nothing is so contemptible as that affectation of wisdom, which some display, by universal incredulity.—*Goldsmith.*

The amplest knowledge has the largest faith. Ignorance is always incredulous. Tell an English cottager that the belfries of Swedish churches are crimson, and his own white steeple furnishes him with a contradiction.—*Willmott.*

Some men will believe nothing but what they can comprehend; and there are but few things that such are able to comprehend.—
St. Evremond.

INDECISION.
There is nothing more pitiable in the world than an irresolute man, oscillating between two feelings, who would willingly unite the two, and who does not perceive that nothing can unite them.—*Goethe.*

17

When a man has not a good reason for doing a thing, he has one good reason for letting it alone.—*Rev. Thomas Scott.*

The wavering mind is a base property.— *Euripides.*

In matters of great concern, and which must be done, there is no surer argument of a weak mind than irresolution; to be undetermined where the case is so plain, and the necessity so urgent. To be always intending to live a new life, but never to find time to set about it; this is as if a man should put off eating, and drinking, and sleeping, from one day and night to another, till he is starved and destroyed.— *Tillotson.*

INDEPENDENCE.

It is not the greatness of a man's means that makes him independent, so much as the smallness of his wants.—*Cobbett.*

The word "independence" is united to the accessory ideas of dignity and virtue. The word "dependence" is united to the ideas of inferiority and corruption.—*Bentham.*

Independence, like honor, is a rocky island, without a beach.—*Napoleon.*

Independency may be found in comparative, as well as absolute abundance; I mean where a person contracts his desires within the limits of his fortune.—*Shenstone.*

The greatest of all human benefits, that at least without which no other benefit can be truly enjoyed, is independence.—*Parke Godwin.*

Let Fortune do her worst, whatever she makes us lose, as long as she never makes us lose our honesty and our independence.—*Pope.*

It is easy in the world to live after the world's opinion; it is easy in solitude to live after your own; but the great man is he who, in the midst of the crowd, keeps with perfect sweetness the independence of solitude.— *Emerson.*

The man is best served who has no occasion to put the hands of others at the end of his own arms.—*Rousseau.*

Nothing is at last sacred but the integrity of your own mind. Absolve you to yourself, and you shall have the suffrage of the world.— *Emerson.*

Happy the man to whom Heaven has given a morsel of bread without laying him under the obligation of thanking any other for it than Heaven itself.—*Cervantes.*

These two things, contradictory as they may seem, must go together, — manly dependence and manly independence, manly reliance and manly self-reliance.—*Wordsworth.*

INDIFFERENCE.

What is a woman's surest guardian angel ? Indifference.—*Madame Deluzy.*

A lady of fashion will sooner excuse a freedom, flowing from admiration, than a slight resulting from indifference. The first offence has the pleasing apology of her attractions; the last is bold and without an alleviation. But the mode in which she disposes of the two only shows that her love of admiration is stronger than her sense of propriety.—*Colton.*

INDISCRETION.

We waste our best years in distilling the sweetest flowers of life into potions which, after all, do not immortalize, but only intoxicate.— *Longfellow.*

We may outrun by violent swiftness that which we run at, and lose by overrunning.— *Shakespeare.*

Young men soon give and soon forget affronts.—*Addison.*

There is a ripe season for everything; and if you slip or anticipate it, you dim the grace of the matter, be it ever so good.—*Hackett.*

Wicked is not much worse than indiscreet. *Donne.*

An indiscreet man is more hurtful than an ill-natured one; for, as the latter will only attack his enemies, and those he wishes ill to, the other injures indifferently both friends and foes. *Addison.*

Fools take ingenious abuse for kindness and often make one in the laugh that is carrying on at their own expense.—*Zimmermann.*

Three things too much and three too little are pernicious to man : to speak much and know little; to spend much and have little; to presume much and be worth little.—*Cervantes.*

Indiscretion and wickedness, be it known, are first cousins.—*Ninon de l'Enclos.*

We, ignorant of ourselves, beg often our own harms, which the wise powers deny us for our good ; so find we profit by losing our prayers.—*Shakespeare.*

The generality of men expend the early part of their lives in contributing to render the latter part miserable.—*Bruyère.*

A man should be careful never to tell tales of himself to his own disadvantage ; people may be amused, and laugh at the time, but they will be remembered, and brought up against him upon some subsequent occasion.—*Johnson.*

A prodigal course is like the sun's; but not, like his, recoverable.—*Shakespeare.*

Indiscretion, rashness, falsehood, levity, and malice produce each other.—*Lavater.*

Imprudence, silly talk, foolish vanity, and vain curiosity, are closely allied ; they are children of one family.—*La Fontaine*

INDIVIDUALITY.

Every great man is a unique. The Scipionism of Scipio is precisely that part he could not borrow.—*Emerson.*

The stupidest fellow, if he would but reveal with childlike honesty how he feels and he thinks, when the stars wink at him, when he sees the ocean for the first time, when music comes over the waters, or when he and his beloved look into each other's eyes, — would he but reveal this, the world would hail him as a genius in his way.—*Mrs. L. M. Child.*

Thou art in the end what thou art. Put on wigs with millions of curls, set thy foot upon ell-high rocks. Thou abidest ever, — what thou art.—*Goethe.*

In the particularities of everybody's mind and fortune, there are particular advantages, by which they are to be held.—*Sir P. Sidney.*

Human faculties are common, but that which converges these faculties into my identity separates me from every other man. That other man cannot think my thoughts, he cannot speak my words, he cannot do my works. He cannot have my sins, I cannot have his virtues.
Henry Giles.

Individuality is everywhere to be spared and respected as the root of everything good.—
Richter.

Experience serves to prove that the worth and strength of a state depend far less upon the form of its institutions than upon the character of its men ; for the nation is only the aggregate of individual conditions, and civilization itself is but a question of personal improvement.—
Samuel Smiles.

There is in every man a certain feeling, that he has been what he is from all eternity, and by no means became such in time.—
Schelling.

The worth of a state, in the long run, is the worth of the individuals composing it.—
J. S. Mill.

Every individual nature has its own beauty. One is struck in every company, at every fireside, with the riches of nature, when he hears so many tones, all musical, sees in each person original manners, which have a proper and peculiar charm, and reads new expressions of face. He perceives that nature has laid for each the foundations of a divine building, if the soul will build thereon.—*Emerson.*

Most painters have painted themselves. So have most poets ; not so palpably indeed and confessedly, but still more assiduously. Some have done nothing else.—*Hare.*

We move too much in platoons ; we march by sections ; we do not live in our vital individuality enough ; we are slaves to fashion, in mind and in heart, if not to our passions and appetites.—*Chapin.*

He who would not be frustrate of his hope to write well hereafter in laudable things ought himself to be a true poem.—*Milton.*

Each mind has its own method ! A true man never acquires after college rules. What you have aggregated in a natural manner surprises and delights when it is produced. For we cannot oversee each other's secret.—
Emerson.

Not nations, not armies, have advanced the race ; but here and there, in the course of ages, an individual has stood up and cast his shadow over the world.—*Chapin*

INDOLENCE.

The paralysis of the soul.—*Lavater.*

What is often called indolence, is in fact the unconscious consciousness of incapacity.
H. C. Robinson.

Indolence is a kind of centripetal force.—
Shenstone.

If you ask me which is the real hereditary sin of human nature, do you imagine I shall answer pride, or luxury, or ambition, or egotism ? No ; I shall say indolence. Who conquers indolence will conquer all the rest. Indeed all good principles must stagnate without mental activity.—*Zimmermann.*

Go to the ant, thou sluggard ; consider her ways, and be wise.—*Bible.*

Of all our faults, that which we most readily admit is indolence. We persuade ourselves that it cherishes all the peaceful virtues ; and that, without entirely destroying the others, it merely suspends their functions.—
Rochefoucauld.

Indolence is the sleep of the mind.—
Vauvenargues.

It should seem that indolence itself would incline a person to be honest ; as it requires infinitely greater pains and contrivance to be a knave.—*Shenstone.*

Indolence and stupidity are first cousins.—
Rivarol.

We have more indolence in the mind than in the body.—*Rochefoucauld.*

Better not to know what we should practise than not to practise what we know; and less danger dwells in unaffected ignorance than unactive knowledge.—*Quarles.*

INDUSTRY.

"To be employed," said the poet Gray, "is to be happy." "It is better to wear out than rust out," said Bishop Cumberland. "Have we not all eternity to rest in?" exclaimed Arnauld.—*Samuel Smiles.*

Diligence is the mother of good luck.—*Franklin.*

Many are discontented with the name of idler, who are nevertheless content to do worse than nothing.—*Zimmermann.*

Why, man of idleness, labor has rocked you in the cradle, and nourished your pampered life; without it, the woven silk and wool upon your back would be in the shepherd's fold. For the meanest thing that ministers to human want, save the air of heaven, man is indebted to toil; and even the air, in God's wise ordination, is breathed with labor.—*Chapin.*

One loses all the time which he can employ better.—*Rousseau.*

At the working-man's house hunger looks in, but dares not enter; nor will the bailiff or the constable enter; for industry pays debts as despair increaseth them.—*Franklin*

The end of labor is to gain leisure. It is a great saying.—*Aristotle.*

I have observed that as long as one lives and bestirs himself, he can always find food and raiment, though it may not be of the choicest description.—*Goethe.*

In this theatre of man's life, it is reserved only for God and angels to be lookers-on.—*Pythagoras.*

What a solemn and striking admonition to youth is that inscribed on the dial at All Souls, Oxford — *periunt et imputantur,* — the hours perish, and are laid to our charge; for time, like life, can never be recalled. Melancthon noted down the time lost by him, that he might thereby reanimate his industry, and not lose an hour.—*Samuel Smiles.*

The laborer is worthy of his hire.—*Bible.*

God has so made the mind of man that a peculiar deliciousness resides in the fruits of personal industry.—*Wilberforce.*

If you have great talents, industry will improve them; if moderate abilities, industry will supply their deficiencies. Nothing is denied to well-directed labor; nothing is ever to be attained without it.—*Sir J. Reynolds.*

Well for the drones of the social hive that there are bees of an industrious turn, willing, for an infinitesimal share of the honey, to undertake the labor of its fabrication.—*Hood.*

There is always hope in a man that actually and earnestly works. In idleness alone is there perpetual despair.—*Carlyle.*

The celebrated Galen said employment was nature's physician. It is indeed so important to happiness, that indolence. is justly considered the parent of misery.—*Colton.*

There is no art or science that is too difficult for industry to attain to; it is the gift of tongues, and makes a man understood and valued in all countries, and by all nations. It is the philosopher's stone, that turns all metals, and even stones, into gold, and suffers no want to break into its dwelling. It is the northwest passage, that brings the merchant's ships as soon to him as he can desire. In a word, it conquers all enemies, and makes fortune itself pay contribution.—*Clarendon.*

According to Swift, even angels are not to be passive. The royal arms of Lilliput, he says, are "an angel lifting a lame beggar from the earth."—*Samuel Smiles.*

The more we do, the more we can do; the more busy we are, the more leisure we have.—*Hazlitt.*

Industry is not only the instrument of improvement, but the foundation of pleasure. He who is a stranger to it may possess, but cannot enjoy; for it is labor only which gives relish to pleasure. It is the appointed vehicle of every good to man. It is the indispensable condition of possessing a sound mind in a sound body.—*Blair.*

The way to wealth is as plain as the way to market. It depends chiefly on two words, industry and frugality; that is, waste neither time nor money, but make the best use of both.—*Franklin.*

Seest thou a man diligent in his business? he shall stand before kings.—*Bible.*

I would not waste my spring of youth in idle dalliance; I would plant rich seeds to blossom in my manhood, and bear fruit when I am old.—*Hillhouse.*

No man is born into the world whose work is not born with him; there is always work, and tools to work withal, for those who will; and blessed are the horny hands of toil!—*Lowell.*

A man should inure himself to voluntary labor; and not give up to indulgence and pleasure; as they beget no good constitution of body, nor knowledge of the mind.—*Socrates.*

Time is incalculably long, and every day is a vessel into which very much may be poured, if one will really fill it up.—*Goethe.*

Industry need not wish.—*Franklin.*

A divine benediction is always invisibly breathed on painful and lawful diligence. Thus, the servant employed in making and blowing of the fire (though sent away thence as soon as it burneth clear) ofttimes getteth by his pains a more kindly and continuing heat than the master himself, who sitteth down by the same; and thus persons, industriously occupying themselves, thrive better on a little of their own honest getting, than lazy heirs on the large revenues left unto them.—*Fuller.*

Hell itself must yield to industry.—
Ben Jonson.

Everything is sold to skill and labor; and where nature furnishes the materials, they are still rude and unfinished, till industry, ever active and intelligent, refines them from their brute state, and fits them for human use and convenience.—*Hume.*

That man is but of the lower part of the world that is not brought up to business and affairs.—
Feltham.

There is none so innocent as not to be evil spoken of; none so wicked as to want all commendation. There are too many who condemn the just, and not a few who justify the wicked. I often hear both envy and flattery speaking falsehoods, of myself to myself; and may not the like tongues perform the like tasks of others to others? I will know others by what they do themselves; but not learn myself by what I hear of others. I will be careful of mine own actions, not credulous of others' relations.—
Arthur Warwick.

Means are always in our power; ends are very seldom so.—*Fielding.*

Excellence is never granted to man, but as the reward of labor. It argues, indeed, no small strength of mind to persevere in the habits of industry, without the pleasure of perceiving those advantages, which, like the hand of a clock, whilst they make hourly approaches to their point, yet proceed so slowly as to escape observation.—*Sir J. Reynolds.*

INFAMY.
Infamy is where it is received. If thou art a mud wall, it will stick; if marble, it will rebound; if thou storm at it, it is thine; if thou contemn it, it is his.—*Quarles.*

INFIDELITY.
There is one single fact, which one may oppose to all the wit and argument of infidelity, namely, that no man ever repented of being a Christian on his death-bed.—*Hannah More.*

Charles II., hearing the celebrated Vossius, a freethinker, repeating some incredible stories of the Chinese, turned to those about him and said, "This learned divine is a very strange man,—he believes everything but the Bible."
Samuel Smiles.

General infidelity is the hardest soil which the propagators of a new religion can have to work upon.—*Paley.*

A sceptical young man one day conversing with the celebrated Dr. Parr, observed that he would believe nothing which he could not understand. "Then, young man, your creed will be the shortest of any man's I know.—*Helps.*

To destroy the ideas of immortality of the soul, is to add death to death.—
Madame de Souza.

What can be more foolish than to think that all this rare fabric of heaven and earth could come by chance, when all the skill of art is not able to make an oyster?—*Jeremy Taylor.*

Infidelity and Faith look both through the same perspective-glass, but at contrary ends. Infidelity looks through the wrong end of the glass; and, therefore, sees those objects near which are afar off, and makes great things little,—diminishing the greatest spiritual blessings, and removing far from us threatened evils; Faith looks at the right end, and brings the blessings that are far off in time close to our eye, and multiplies God's mercies, which, in the distance, lost their greatness.—*Bishop Hall.*

They that deny a God, destroy a man's nobility; for certainly man is of kin to the beasts by his body; and if he is not kin to God by his spirit, he is a base and ignoble creature.—
Bacon.

No men deserve the title of infidels so little as those to whom it has been usually applied; let any of those who renounce Christianity, write fairly down in a book all the absurdities that they believe instead of it, and they will find that it requires more faith to reject Christianity than to embrace it.—*Colton.*

When once infidelity can persuade men that they shall die like beasts, they will soon be brought to live like beasts also.—*South.*

Infidelity is one of those coinages,—a mass of base money that won't pass current with any heart that loves truly, or any head that thinks correctly. And infidels are poor sad creatures; they carry about them a load of dejection and desolation, not the less heavy that it is invisible. It is the fearful blindness of the soul.—
Chalmers.

INFINITE.
It is only the finite that has wrought and suffered; the infinite lies stretched in smiling repose.—*Emerson.*

The infinite is more sure than any other fact. The infinite of terror, of hope, of pity; did it not at any moment disclose itself to thee, indubitable, unnamable? Came it never, like the gleam of preternatural eternal oceans, like the voice of old eternities, far-sounding through thy heart of hearts?—*Carlyle.*

INFLUENCE.

Planets govern not the soul nor guide the destinies of men, but trifles, lighter than straws, are levers in the building up of character.—*Tupper.*

Virtue will catch as well as vice by contact; and the public stock of honest manly principle will daily accumulate.—*Burke.*

Giant, in the fable, acquired new strength every time he touched the earth; so some brave minds gain fresh energy from that which depresses and crushes others.—*Murphy.*

When we are at peace with ourselves and the world, it is as though we gazed upon outward things through a golden-tinted glass, and saw a glory resting upon them all. We know that it cannot be long thus; sin and sorrow, and blinding tears, will dim the mirror of our inmost thoughts; but we must pray and look again, and by and by the cloud will pass away.—*G. A. Sala.*

Not one false man but does uncountable mischief.—*Carlyle.*

It is an old saying, and one of fearful and fathomless import, that we are forming characters for eternity. Forming characters! Whose? our own or others? Both,—and in that momentous fact lies the peril and responsibility of our existence. Who is sufficient for the thought?—*Elihu Burritt.*

The colder the country, the coarser the appetites; the more heat in the atmosphere, the more fire in the blood; the highest virtue of the tropics is therefore chastity; of colder regions, temperance.—*Bovee.*

It is noticed that the consideration of the great periods and spaces of astronomy induces a dignity of mind, and an indifference to death. The influence of fine scenery, the presence of mountains, appeases our irritations and elevates our friendships. Even a high dome, and the expansive interior of a cathedral, have a sensible effect on manners.—*Emerson.*

The words that a father speaks to his children in the privacy of home are not heard by the world, but, as in whispering-galleries, they are clearly heard at the end, and by posterity.—*Richter.*

If you would be well with a great mind, leave him with a favorable impression of you; if with a little mind, leave him with a favorable opinion of himself.—*Coleridge.*

Good words do more than hard speeches, as the sunbeams without any noise will make the traveller cast off his cloak, which all the blustering winds could not do, but only make him bind it closer to him.—*Leighton.*

Let a man overcome anger by love, let him overcome evil by good; let him overcome the greedy by liberality, the liar by truth.—*Buddha.*

Looking where others look, and conversing with the same things, we catch the charm which lured them. Napoleon said, "You must not fight too often with one enemy, or you will teach him all your art of war." Talk much with any man of vigorous mind, and we acquire very fast the habit of looking at things in the same light, and on each occurrence we anticipate his thought.—*Emerson.*

There is no action of man in this life which is not the beginning of so long a chain of consequences as that no human providence is high enough to give us a prospect to the end.—*Thomas of Malmesbury.*

How gladly would I lead mankind from the vain prospects of life, to prospects of innocence and ease, where every breeze breathes health, and every sound is but the echo of tranquillity.—*Goldsmith.*

INGRATITUDE.

You may rest upon this as an unfailing truth, that there neither is, nor ever was, any person remarkably ungrateful, who was not also insufferably proud; nor any one proud who was not equally ungrateful.—*South.*

How sharper than a serpent's tooth it is to have a thankless child!—*Shakespeare.*

He who does a kindness to an ungrateful person sets his seal to a flint, and sows his seed upon the sand; upon the former he makes no impression, and from the latter finds no production.—*South.*

If there be a crime of deeper dye than all the guilty train of human vices, it is ingratitude.—*H. Brooke.*

It is a great happiness to get off, without injury and heart-burning, from one who has had the ill-luck to be served by you. It is a very onerous business, this of being served, and the debtor naturally wishes to give you a slap.—*Emerson.*

He that calls a man ungrateful sums up all the evil that a man can be guilty of.—*Swift.*

I hate ingratitude more in a man than lying, vainness, babbling, drunkenness, or any taint of vice, whose strong corruption inhabits our frail blood.—*Shakespeare.*

Men may be ungrateful, but the human race is not so.—*De Boufflers.*

To be ungrateful is to be unnatural. The head may be thus guilty, not the heart.—*Rivarol.*

Not to return one good office for another is inhuman; but to return evil for good is diabolical. There are too many even of this sort, who, the more they owe, the more they hate. There is nothing more dangerous than to oblige those people; for when they are conscious of not paying the debt, they wish the creditor out of the way.—*Seneca.*

Ingratitude! thou marble-hearted fiend, more hideous, when thou showest thee in a child, than the sea-monster!—*Shakespeare.*

He that is ungrateful has no guilt but one; all other crimes may pass for virtues in him.—*Young.*

Ingratitude takes away less pleasure from the benefactor than from the ingrate.—*Lingrée.*

Ingratitude is monstrous; and for the multitude to be ungrateful were to make a monster of the multitude; of the which, we being members, should bring ourselves to be monstrous members.—*Shakespeare.*

Brutes leave ingratitude to man.—*Colton.*

An extraordinary haste to discharge an obligation is a sort of ingratitude.—*Rochefoucauld.*

Flints may be melted,—we see it daily,—but an ungrateful heart cannot; no, not by the strongest and the noblest flame.—*South.*

Ingratitude is treason to mankind.—*Thomson.*

We do not marvel at the sunrise of a joy, only at its sunset! Then, on the other hand, we are amazed at the commencement of a sorrow-storm, but that it should go off in gentle showers we think quite natural.—*Richter.*

Filial ingratitude! Is it not as this mouth should tear this hand for lifting food to it.—*Shakespeare.*

Ingratitude is a nail which, driven into the tree of courtesy, causes it to wither; it is a broken channel, by which the foundations of the affections are undermined; and a lump of soot, which, falling into the dish of friendship, destroys its scent and flavor.—*Basil.*

We fancy we suffer from ingratitude, while in reality we suffer from self-love.—*Landor.*

Ingratitude never so thoroughly pierces the human breast as when it proceeds from those in whose behalf we have been guilty of transgressions.—*Fielding.*

Ingratitude is of all crimes what in ourselves we account the most venial, in others the most unpardonable.—*Henry Home.*

As the deepest hate may spring from the most violent love, so the greatest ingratitude may arise from the largest benefits. It is said that Cicero was slain by one whom his oratory had defended when he was accused of his father's murder.—*J. Beaumont.*

I am rapt, and cannot cover the monstrous bulk of this ingratitude with any size of words! *Shakespeare.*

Ingratitude is too base to return a kindness, and too proud to regard it; much like the tops of mountains, barren, indeed, but yet lofty; they produce nothing, they feed nobody, they clothe nobody, yet are high and stately, and look down upon all the world about them.—*South.*

Ingratitude calls forth reproaches, as gratitude brings fresh kindnesses.—*Madame de Sévigné.*

I hate that ambition which inforceth ingratitude; which, being the basest of vices, cannot but soil and disgrace a man graced with such honors. I am not preferred with honor if debased with ingratitude.—*Arthur Warwick.*

Ingratitude is always a kind of weakness. I have never seen that clever men have been ungrateful.—*Goethe.*

There be three usual causes of ingratitude, upon a benefit received,—envy, pride, covetousness; envy, looking more at others' benefits than our own; pride, looking more at ourselves, than the benefit; covetousness, looking more at what we would have than what we have.—*Bishop Hall.*

He that forgets his friend is ungrateful to him; but he that forgets his Saviour is unmerciful to himself.—*Bunyan.*

To pass now to the matter of gratitude and ingratitude; there never was any man yet so wicked as not to approve the one, and detest the other; as the two things in the whole world, the one to be the most abominated, the other the most esteemed. The very story of an ungrateful action puts us out of all patience and gives us a loathing for the author of it.—*Seneca.*

Ingratitude is the abridgment of all baseness,—a fault never found unattended with other viciousness.—*Fuller.*

The worst of ingratitude lies not in the ossified heart of him who commits it, but we find it in the effect it produces on him against whom it was committed.—*Landor.*

Man is, beyond dispute, the most excellent of created beings, and the vilest animal is a dog; but the sages agree that a grateful dog is better than an ungrateful man.—*Saadi.*

The ungrateful person is a monster,.which is all throat and belly; a kind of thoroughfare or common sewer, for the good things of the world to pass into; and of whom, in respect of all kindnesses conferred on him, may be verified that observation of the lion's den, before which appeared the footsteps of many that had gone in thither, but no prints of any that ever came out thence.—*South.*

INHERITANCE.

They who provide much wealth for their children, but neglect to improve them in virtue, do like those who feed their horses high, but never train them to the *ménage.*—*Socrates.*

Say not you know another, until you have divided an inheritance with him.—*Lavater.*

Enjoy what thou hast inherited from thy sires if thou wouldst possess it; what we employ not is an oppressive burden; what the moment brings forth, that only can it profit by.—*Goethe.*

INJURY.

An injury unanswered in time grows weary of itself; and dies away in an involuntary remorse. In bad dispositions, capable of no restraint but fear, it has a different effect, — the silent digestion of one wrong provokes a second.
Sterne.

No man is hurt but by himself.—*Diogenes.*

To wilful men, the injuries that they themselves procure must be their schoolmasters.—
Shakespeare.

It is equally difficult to stifle in the beginning the sentiment of injury, and to preserve it after a certain number of years.—*Bruyère.*

Christianity commands us to pass by injuries; policy, to let them pass by us.—*Franklin.*

Men are not only prone to lose the remembrance of benefits and of injuries; they even hate those who have obliged them, and cease to hate those who have grievously injured them.—
Rochefoucauld.

Slight small injuries, and they will become none at all.—*Fuller.*

Nothing can work me damage except myself; the harm that I carry about with me, and never am a real sufferer but by my own fault.—*St. Bernard.*

There is no ghost so difficult to lay as the ghost of an injury.—*Alexander Smith.*

If men wound you with injuries, meet them with patience; hasty words rankle the wound, soft language dresses it, forgiveness cures it, and oblivion takes away the scar. It is more noble by silence to avoid an injury than by argument to overcome it.—*J. Beaumont.*

He who has injured thee was either stronger or weaker; if weaker, spare him; if stronger, spare thyself.—*Seneca.*

No man ever did a designed injury to another, without doing a greater to himself.—
Henry Home.

Recompense injury with justice, and recompense kindness with kindness.—*Confucius.*

As a Christian should do no injuries to others, so he should forgive the injuries that others do to him. It is to be like God, who is a good-giving God, and a sin-forgiving God.—
R. Venning.

Lay silently the injuries you receive upon the altar of oblivion.—*Hosea Ballou.*

INJUSTICE.

Surely they who devour the possessions of orphans unjustly shall swallow down nothing but fire into their bellies, and shall broil in raging flames.—*Koran.*

If thou sustain injustice, console thyself; the true unhappiness is in doing it.—*Democritus.*

There is no greater evil among men than a testament framed with injustice; where caprice hath guided the boon, or dishonesty refused what was due.—*Tupper.*

Fraud is the ready minister of injustice.—
Burke.

He whose first emotion, on the view of an excellent work, is to undervalue it, will never have one of his own to show.—*Aikin.*

The wronged side is always the safest.—
Rev. Dr. Sibbes.

An unjust acquisition is like a barbed arrow, which must be drawn backward with horrible anguish, or else will be your destruction.—
Jeremy Taylor.

The greatest of all injustice is that which goes under the name of law; and of all sorts of tyranny the forcing the letter of the law against the equity is the most insupportable.—
L'Estrange.

He who commits injustice is ever made more wretched than he who suffers it.—*Plato.*

Injustice arises either from precipitation or indolence, or from a mixture of both. The rapid and the slow are seldom just; the unjust wait either not at all or wait too long.—
Lavater.

Did the mass of men know the actual selfishness and injustice of their rulers, not a government would stand a year. The world would foment with revolution.—*Theodore Parker.*

No one will dare maintain that it is better to do injustice than to bear it.—*Aristotle.*

It is not possible to found a lasting power upon injustice, perjury, and treachery. These may, perhaps, succeed for once, and borrow for awhile, from hope, a gay and flourishing appearance. But time betrays their weakness, and they fall into ruin of themselves. For, as in structures of every kind, the lower parts should have the greatest firmness, — so the grounds and principles of actions should be just and true.—*Demosthenes.*

One man receives crucifixion as the reward of his villany; another a regal crown.—*Juvenal.*

What renders man unjust? Are not errors and prejudices the causes of the abuses of power? If you really wish to prevent the commission of injustice, you must first remove error and prejudice. Any one intrusted with power will abuse it, if not also animated with the love of truth and virtue, no matter whether he be a prince or one of the people.—*La Fontaine.*

INNOCENCE.

There is no courage but in innocence; no constancy but in an honest cause.—*Southern.*

I do not believe in virtue, but I do believe in innocence. They are very different. Innocence is ignorance.—*Madame de Girardin.*

It is not quality, but innocence, which exempts men from reproof.—*Addison.*

Of all sights which can soften and humanize the heart of man, there is none that ought so surely to reach it as that of innocent children enjoying the happiness which is their proper and natural portion.—*Southey.*

The innocent seldom find an uneasy pillow.—*Cowper.*

The innocence that feels no risk and is taught no caution is more vulnerable than guilt, and oftener assailed.—*Willis.*

Alas! innocence is but a poor substitute for experience.—*Bulwer Lytton.*

What a power there is in innocence! whose very helplessness is its safeguard; in whose presence even Passion himself stands abashed, and stands worshipper at the very altar he came to despoil.—*Moore.*

Unto the pure all things are pure.—*Bible.*

Innocence is a flower which withers when touched, but blooms not again, though watered with tears.—*Hooper.*

There is a heroic innocence, as well as a heroic courage.—*St. Evremond.*

We have not the innocence of Eden; but by God's help and Christ's example we may have the victory of Gethsemane.—*Chapin.*

Innocence and ignorance are sisters. But there are noble and vulgar sisters. Vulgar innocence and ignorance are mortal, they have pretty faces, but wholly without expression, and of a transient beauty; the noble sisters are immortal, their lofty forms are unchangeable, and their countenances are still radiant with the light of Paradise.—*Novalis.*

To be innocent is to be not guilty; but to be virtuous is to overcome our evil inclinations.—*William Penn.*

How the innocent, as in a gentle slumber, pass away!—*Massinger.*

There are some reasoners who frequently confound innocence with the mere incapacity of guilt; but he that never saw, or heard, or thought of strong liquors, cannot be proposed as a pattern of sobriety.—*Johnson.*

Innocence finds not near so much protection as guilt.—*Rochefoucauld.*

Unstained thoughts do seldom dream on evil; birds never limed no secret bushes fear.—*Shakespeare.*

Let our lives be pure as snow-fields, where our footsteps leave a mark, but not a stain.—*Madame Swetchine.*

Innocence is always unsuspicious.—*Haliburton*

Coerced innocence is like an imprisoned lark, — open the door, and it is off forever. The bird that roams through the sky and the groves unrestrained knows how to dodge the hawk and protect itself; but the caged one, the moment it leaves its bars and bolts behind, is pounced upon by the fowler or the vulture.—*Haliburton.*

Innocence and mystery never dwell long together.—*Madame Necker.*

Innocence is like p   armor, it adorns and it defends.—*South.*olished

How many bitter thoughts does the innocent man avoid! Serenity and cheerfulness are his portion. Hope is continually pouring its balm into his soul. His heart is at rest, whilst others are goaded and tortured by the stings of a wounded conscience, the remonstrances and risings up of principles which they cannot forget; perpetually teased by returning temptations, perpetually lamenting defeated resolutions.—*Paley.*

The silence often of pure innocence persuades when speaking fails.—*Shakespeare.*

He is armed without that is innocent within; be this thy screen, and this thy wall of brass.— *Horace.*

What stronger breastplate than a heart untainted ? —*Shakespeare.*

INNOVATION.

A spirit of innovation is generally the result of a selfish temper and confined views. People will not look forward to posterity who never look backward to their ancestors.—*Burke.*

INQUISITIVENESS.

In ancient days the most celebrated precept was, " Know thyself"; in modern times it has been supplanted by the more fashionable maxim, "Know thy neighbor, and everything about him."—*Johnson.*

Inquisitive people are the funnels of conversation; they do not take in anything for their own use, but merely to pass it to another.— *Steele.*

Inquisitiveness or curiosity is a kernel of the forbidden fruit, which still sticketh in the throat of a natural man, and sometimes to the danger of his choking.—*Fuller.*

Inquisitiveness is an uncomely guest.— *Sir P. Sidney.*

The man who is inquisitive into the secrets of your affairs with which he has no concern, should be an object of your caution. Men no more desire another's secrets to conceal them, than they would another's purse, for the pleasure only of carrying it.—*Fielding.*

An inquisitive man is a creature naturally very vacant of thought itself, and therefore forced to apply itself to foreign assistance.— *Steele.*

Few men are raised in our estimation by being too closely examined.—*Balzac.*

Shun the inquisitive, for thou wilt be sure to find him leaky; open ears do not keep conscientiously what has been intrusted to them, and a word once spoken flies never to be recalled.—*Horace.*

INSENSIBILITY.

A thorough and mature insensibility is rarely to be acquired, but by a steady perseverance in infamy.—*Junius.*

INSPIRATION.

There is a God within us, who breathes that divine fire, by which we are animated.— *Ovid.*

INSTINCT.

The active part of man consists of powerful instincts. Some are gentle and continuous, others violent and short; some baser, some nobler, all necessary.—*F. W. Newman.*

There is not, in my opinion, anything more mysterious in nature than this instinct in animals, which thus rise above reason and fall infinitely short of it.—*Addison.*

We are too good for pure instinct.—*Goethe.*

Human sagacity, stimulated by human wants, seizes first on the nearest natural assistant. The power of his own arm is an early lesson among the studies of primitive man. This is animal strength; and from this he rises to the conception of employing, for his own use, the strength of other animals.—*Daniel Webster.*

Our instinct inspires us, — warns us, our intelligence scents out what our reason does not discover, for instinct is the nose of the mind.— *Madame de Girardin.*

How often we feel and know, either pleasurably or painfully, that another is looking on us, before we have ascertained the fact with our own eyes ! How often we prophesy truly to ourselves the approach of friend or enemy just before either has really appeared ! How strangely and abruptly we become convinced, at a first introduction, that we shall secretly love this person and loathe that, before experience has guided us with a single fact in relation to their characters ! — *Wilkie Collins.*

A goose flies by a chart which the Royal Geographical Society could not mend.—*Holmes.*

Beasts, birds, and insects, even to the minutest and meanest of their kind, act with the unerring providence of instinct; man, the while, who possesses a higher faculty, abuses it, and therefore goes blundering on. They, by their unconscious and unhesitating obedience to the laws of nature, fulfil the end of their existence ; he, in wilful neglect of the laws of God, loses sight of the end of his.—*Southey.*

We only listen to those instincts which are our own, and only give credit to the evil when it has befallen us.—*La Fontaine.*

Who taught the parrot his " Welcome"? Who taught the raven in a drought to throw pebbles into a hollow tree where she espied water, that the water might rise so as she might come to it ? Who taught the bee to sail through such a vast sea of air, and to find the way from a flower in a field to her hive ? Who taught the ant to bite every grain of corn that she burieth in her hill, lest it should take root and grow ? —*Bacon.*

INSTRUCTION.

The wise are instructed by reason, ordinary minds by experience ; the stupid by necessity; and brutes by instinct.— *Cicero.*

The heavens and the earth, the woods and the wayside, teem with instruction and knowledge to the curious and thoughtful.—*Hosea Ballou.*

Let us consider how great a commodity of doctrine exists in books; how easily, how secretly, how safely they expose the nakedness of human ignorance without putting it to shame. These are the masters who instruct us without rods and ferules, without hard words and anger, without clothes or money. If you approach them they are not asleep; if investigating you interrogate them, they conceal nothing; if you mistake them they never grumble; if you are ignorant, they cannot laugh at you.—
Richard de Bury.

INSULT.

The slight that can be conveyed in a glance, in a gracious smile, in a wave of the hand, is often the *ne plus ultra* of art. What insult is so keen, or so keenly felt, as the polite insult, which it is impossible to resent?—*Julia Kavanagh.*

Whatever be the motive of insult, it is always best to overlook it; for folly scarcely can deserve resentment, and malice is punished by neglect.—*Johnson.*

As it is the nature of a kite to devour little birds, so it is the nature of some minds to insult and tyrannize over little people; this being the means which they use to recompense themselves for their extreme servility and condescension to their superiors; for nothing can be more reasonable than that slaves and flatterers should exact the same taxes on all below them which they themselves pay to all above them.—
Fielding.

Injuries accompanied with insults are never forgiven: all men, on these occasions, are good haters, and lay out their revenge at compound interest.—*Colton.*

Receive no satisfaction for premeditated impertinence; forget it, forgive it, but keep him inexorably at a distance who offered it.—
Lavater.

Thus the greater proportion of mankind are more sensitive to contemptuous language than unjust acts; for they can less easily bear insult than wrong.—*Plutarch.*

The way to procure insults is to submit to them. A man meets with no more respect than he exacts.—*Hazlitt.*

There is an insolence which none but those who deserve some contempt themselves can bestow, and those only who deserve no contempt can bear.—*Fielding.*

Injuries may be atoned for, and forgiven; but insults admit of no compensation. They degrade the mind in its own esteem, and force it to recover its level by revenge.—*Junius.*

INTELLECT.

Intellect lies behind genius, which is intellect constructive. Intellect is the simple power anterior to all action or construction.—*Emerson.*

It is only the intellect that can be thoroughly and hideously wicked. It can forget everything in the attainment of its ends. The heart recoils; in its retired places some drops of childhood's dew still linger, defying manhood's fiery noon.—*Lowell.*

The starlight of the brain.—*Willis.*

The growth of the intellect is spontaneous in every expansion. The mind that grows could not predict the time, the means, the mode of that spontaneity. God enters by a private door into every individual.—*Emerson.*

Intellect, — brain force.—*Schiller.*

The march of intellect is proceeding at quick time; and if its progress be not accompanied by a corresponding improvement in morals and religion, the faster it proceeds, with the more violence will you be hurried down the road to ruin.—*Southey.*

The march of intellect, which licks all the world into shape, has even reached the devil.—
Goethe.

Man gains wider dominion by his intellect than by his right arm. The mustard-seed of thought is a pregnant treasury of vast results. Like the germ in the Egyptian tombs, its vitality never perishes; and its fruit will spring up after it has been buried for long ages.—*Chapin.*

A man of intellect is lost unless he unites energy of character to intellect. When we have the lantern of Diogenes we must have his staff.
Chamfort.

The intellect has only one failing, which, to be sure, is a very considerable one; it has no conscience. Napoleon is the readiest instance of this. If his heart had borne any proportion to his brain, he had been one of the greatest men in all history.—*Lowell.*

God has placed no limits to the exercise of the intellect he has given us, on this side of the grave.—*Bacon.*

The nearer anything comes to mental joy, the purer and choicer it is. It is the observation not only of Aristotle, but of every one almost, " Some things delight merely because of their novelty "; and that surely upon this account, because the mind, which is the spring of joy, is more fixed and intense upon such things. The rosebud thus pleases more than the blown rose.—*Lamb.*

In these beings so minute, and as it were such nonentities, what wisdom is displayed, what power, what unfathomable perfection.—
Pliny.

The intellect of the wise is like glass; it admits the light of heaven and reflects it.—*Hare.*

Intellect and industry are never incompatible. There is more wisdom, and will be more benefit, in combining them than scholars like to believe, or than the common world imagine; life has time enough for both, and its happiness will be increased by the union.— *Sir E. Turner.*

While the world lasts, the sun will gild the mountain-tops before it shines upon the plain.— *Bulwer Lytton.*

There never was a man all intellect; but just in proportion as men become so they become like lofty mountains, all ice and snow the higher they rise above the warm heart of the earth.— *Chapin.*

INTELLIGENCE.
That alone can be called true refinement which elevates the soul of man, purifying the manners by improving the intellect.— *Hosea Ballou.*

They who have read about everything are thought to understand everything, too, but it is not always so; reading furnishes the mind only with materials of knowledge; it is thinking that makes what we read ours. We are of the ruminating kind, and it is not enough to cram ourselves with a great load of collections,—we must chew them over again.— *Channing.*

If a man empties his purse into his head, no one can take it from him.— *Franklin.*

The superior man is he who develops, in harmonious proportions, his moral, intellectual and physical nature. This should be the end at which men of all classes should aim, and it is this only which constitutes real greatness.— *Douglas Jerrold.*

Wise men are instructed by reason; less intelligent men by experience; the most ignorant by necessity, and animals by instinct.— *Cicero.*

Prejudices, it is well known, are most difficult to eradicate from the heart whose soil has never been loosened or fertilized by education; they grow there, firm as weeds among rocks.— *Charlotte Bronté.*

It is the mind that makes the body rich;— and as the sun breaks through the darkest clouds so honor peereth in the meanest habit.— *Shakespeare.*

God having capacitated men for the reception of instruction, for a growth in wisdom, knowledge, and understanding, has made it the nature of intellect to strive and improve in intellectual power.— *Hosea Ballou.*

We must despise no sort of talents, they all have their separate duties and uses; all the happiness of man for their object; they all improve, exalt and gladden life.— *Sydney Smith.*

Alexander the Great valued learning so highly, that he used to say he was more indebted to Aristotle for giving him knowledge than to his father Philip for life.— *Samuel Smiles.*

A man cannot leave a better legacy to the world than a well-educated family.— *Rev. Thomas Scott.*

God multiplies intelligence, which communicates itself, like fire, *ad infinitum.* Light a thousand torches at one touch, the flame remains always the same.— *Joubert.*

The intellectual powers of man are not given merely for self; they are not intended to aid his own cunning, and craft, and intrigues, and conspiracies, and enrichment. They will do nothing for these base purposes. The instinct of a tiger, a vulture, or a fox will do better. Genius and abilities are given as lamps to the world, not to self.— *Sir Egerton Brydges.*

It is no proof of a man's understanding to be able to confirm whatever he pleases; but to be able to discern that what is true is true, and that what is false is false, this is the mark and character of intelligence.— *Swedenborg.*

INTEMPERANCE.
I never drink. I cannot do it, on equal terms with others. It costs them only one day; but me three,— the first in sinning, the second in suffering, and the third in repenting.— *Sterne.*

Every inordinate cup is unblessed and the ingredient is a devil.— *Shakespeare.*

Who hath woe? who hath sorrow? who hath contentions? who hath babbling? who hath wounds without cause? who hath redness of eyes? They that tarry long at the wine; they that go to seek mixed wine. Look not thou upon the wine when it is red, when it giveth his color in the cup, when it moveth itself aright; at the last it biteth like a serpent, and stingeth like an adder.— *Bible.*

O, that men should put an enemy in their mouths to steal away their brains!— *Shakespeare.*

While you are in the habit of intemperance, you often drink up the value of an acre of land in a night.— *Father Mathew.*

When the cup of any sensual pleasure is drained to the bottom, there is always poison in the dregs. Anacreon himself declares, that "the flowers swim at the top of the bowl!"— *Jane Porter.*

Wise men mingle mirth with their cares, as a help either to forget or overcome them; but to resort to intoxication for the ease of one's mind is to cure melancholy by madness.— *Charron,*

In our world, death deputes intemperance to do the work of age.— *Young.*

No man oppresses thee, O free and independent franchiser! but does not this stupid porter-pot oppress thee? No son of Adam can bid thee come or go ; but this absurd pot of heavy wet, this can and does! Thou art the thrall, not of Cedric the Saxon, but of thy own brutal appetites, and this scoured dish of liquor. And thou pratest of thy " liberty," thou entire block-head! — *Carlyle.*

He that tempts me to drink beyond my measure, civilly invites me to a fever.— *Jeremy Taylor.*

The habit of using ardent spirits, by men in office, has occasioned more injury to the public, and more trouble to me, than all other causes. And were I to commence my administration again, the first question I would ask, respecting a candidate for office would be, " Does he use ardent spirits ? "—*Jefferson.*

In what pagan nation was Moloch ever propitiated by such an unbroken and swift-moving procession of victims as are offered to this Moloch of Christendom, Intemperance ? — *Horace Mann.*

As surfeit is the father of much fast, so every scope, by the immoderate use, turns to restraint.—*Shakespeare.*

Intemperance is a dangerous companion. It throws people off their guard ; betrays them to a great many indecencies, to ruinous passions, to disadvantages in fortune ; makes them discover secrets, drive foolish bargains, engage in play, and often to stagger from the tavern to the stews.—*Jeremy Collier.*

It is not fitting that the evil produced by men should be imputed to things ; let those bear the blame who make an ill use of things in themselves good.—*Isocrates.*

Every apartment devoted to the circulation of the glass, may be regarded as a temple set apart for the performance of human sacrifices. And they ought to be fitted up like the ancient temples in Egypt, in a manner to show the real atrocity of the superstition that is carried on within their walls.—*Beddoes.*

Greatness of any kind has no greater foe than a habit of drinking.— *Walter Scott.*

INTENTIONS.

Hell is full of good meanings and wishes.— *George Herbert.*

To be always intending to lead a new life, but never to find time to set about it, this is as if a man should put off eating, and drinking, and sleeping, from one day and night to another, till he is starved and destroyed.—*Tillotson.*

Purposes, like eggs, unless they be hatched into action, will run into rottenness.— *Samuel Smiles.*

Hell is paved with good intentions.— *Johnson.*

If religion might be judged of, according to men's intentions, there would scarcely be any idolatry in the world.—*Bishop Hall.*

Many good purposes lie in the churchyard. *Philip Henry.*

INTEREST.

Interest speaks all languages, and acts all parts, even that of disinterestedness itself.— *Rochefoucauld.*

Interest has the security, though not the virtue of a principle. As the world goes, it is the surest side ; for men daily leave both relations and religion to follow it.— *William Penn.*

Interest is the spur of the people, but glory that of great souls.—*Rousseau.*

How difficult a thing it is to persuade a man to reason against his own interest, though he is convinced that equity is against him. *Dr. John Trusler.*

Interest blinds some people, and enlightens others.—*Rochefoucauld.*

It is more than possible, that those who have neither character nor honor may be wounded in a very tender part, — their interest. *Junius.*

When interest is at variance with conscience, any distinction to make them friends will serve the hollow-hearted.—*Henry Home.*

Interest makes some people blind and others quick-sighted. We promise according to our hopes, and perform according to our fears. Virtues are lost in interest, as rivers are swallowed up in the sea.—*J. Beaumont.*

The virtues and vices are all put in motion by interest.—*Rochefoucauld.*

INTERFERENCE.

He that passeth by, and meddleth with strife belonging not to him, is like one that taketh a dog by the ears.—*Bible.*

That is the briefest and sagest of maxims which bids us to " meddle not."—*Colton.*

INTOLERANCE.

As no roads are so rough as those that have just been mended, so no sinners are so intolerant as those that have just turned saints.—*Colton.*

The Devil loves nothing better than the intolerance of reformers, and dreads nothing so much as their charity and patience.—*Lowell.*

Those who, having magnified into serious evils by injudicious opposition heresies in themselves insignificant, yet appeal to the magnitude of those evils to prove that their opposition was called for, act like unskilful physicians, who, when by violent remedies they have aggravated a trifling disease into a dangerous one, urge the violence of the symptoms which they themselves have produced in justification of their practice.—*Whately.*

The intolerant man is the real pedant.—*Richter.*

Some men will not shave on Sunday, and yet they spend all the week in shaving their fellow-men; and many folks think it very wicked to black their boots on Sunday morning, yet they do not hesitate to black their neighbor's reputation on week-days.—*Beecher.*

It were better to be of no church, than to be bitter for any.—*William Penn.*

It appears an extraordinary thing to me, that since there is such a diabolical spirit in the depravity of human nature, as persecution for difference of opinion in religious tenets, there never happened to be any inquisition, any *auto da fé*, any crusade, among the Pagans.—*Sterne.*

INTRIGUE.

There are many women who never have had one intrigue; but there are few who have had only one.—*Rochefoucauld.*

Intrigue is a court distemper.
Madame Deluzy.

INTUITION.

Intuition is the clear conception of the whole at once. It seldom belongs to man to say without presumption " I came, I saw, I conquered."
Lavater.

This, therefore, is a law not found in books, but written on the fleshly tablets of the heart, which we have not learned from man, received, or read, but which we have caught up from Nature herself, sucked in and imbibed; the knowledge of which we were not taught, but for which we were made; we received it not by education, but by intuition.—*Cicero.*

INVENTION.

Man hath found out inventions, to cheat him of the weariness of life, to help him to forget realities and hide the misery of guilt.—*Tupper.*

Invention, strictly speaking, is little more than a new combination of those images which have been previously gathered and deposited in the memory. Nothing can be made of nothing; he who has laid up no material can produce no combinations.—*Sir J. Reynolds.*

Founders and senators of states and cities, lawgivers, extirpers of tyrants, fathers of the people, and other eminent persons in civil government, were honored but with titles of worthies or demigods; whereas such as were inventors and authors of new arts, endowments, and commodities towards man's life, were ever consecrated among the gods themselves.—*Bacon.*

Invention is activity of mind, as fire is air in motion; a sharpening of the spiritual sight, to discern hidden aptitudes.—*Tupper.*

The great inventor is one who has walked forth upon the industrial world, not from universities, but from hovels; not as clad in silks and decked with honors, but as clad in fustian and grimed with soot and oil.—*Isaac Taylor.*

Where we cannot invent, we may at least improve; we may give somewhat of novelty to that which was old, condensation to that which was diffuse, perspicuity to that which was obscure, and currency to that which was recondite.
Colton.

Invention is the talent of youth, and judgment of age.—*Swift.*

It is frivolous to fix pedantically the date of particular inventions. They have all been invented over and over fifty times. Man is the arch machine, of which all these shifts drawn from himself are toy models. He helps himself on each emergency by copying or duplicating his own structure, just so far as the need is.—*Emerson.*

A fine invention is nothing more than a fine deviation from, or enlargement on a fine model. Imitation, if noble and general, insures the best hope of originality.—*Bulwer Lytton.*

IRONY.

Clap an extinguisher upon your irony, if you are unhappily blessed with a vein of it.—*Lamb.*

Irony is an insult conveyed in the form of a compliment; insinuating the most galling satire under the phraseology of panegyric; placing its victim naked on a bed of briers and thistles, thinly covered with rose-leaves; adorning his brow with a crown of gold, which burns into his brain; teasing and fretting, and riddling him through and through, with incessant discharges of hot shot from a masked battery; laying bare the most sensitive and shrinking nerves of his mind, and then blandly touching them with ice, or smilingly pricking them with needles.—*Whipple.*

ISOLATION.

Eagles fly alone; they are but sheep which always herd together.—*Sir P. Sidney.*

J.

JEALOUSY.

It is with jealousy as with the gout. When such distempers are in the blood, there is never any security against their breaking out, and that often on the slightest occasions, and when least suspected.—*Fielding.*

Jealousy lives upon doubts,—it becomes madness, or ceases entirely, as soon as we pass from doubt to certainty.—*Rochefoucauld.*

Jealousy—it is a green-eyed monster, which doth mock the meat it feeds on.—*Shakespeare.*

Jealousy may often explain blindness. When Le Brun heard of the death of Le Sueur, he said that he felt as if a thorn had just been taken out of his foot. Bellino warns Titian that he will never succeed in painting; and Titian, crowned with fame, scowls upon the dawning honors of Tintoretto.—*Willmott.*

O, the pain of pains is when the fair one, whom our soul is fond of, gives transport, and receives it from another.—*Young.*

There is not so much danger in a known foe as a suspected friend.—*Nabb.*

O Jealousy! thou most unnatural offspring of a too tender parent! that in excess of fondness feeds thee, like the pelican, but with her purest blood; and in return thou tearest the bosom whence thy nurture flows.—*Frowde.*

We may kill those of whom we are jealous, but we do not hate them.—*Fielding.*

Jealousy is like a polished glass held to the lips when life is in doubt; if there be breath, it will catch the damp and show it.—*Dryden.*

O, what damned minutes tells he o'er, who dotes, yet doubts; suspects, yet strongly loves!
Shakespeare.

All the other passions condescend at times to accept the inexorable logic of facts; but jealousy looks facts straight in the face, ignores them utterly, and says that she knows a great deal better than they can tell her.—*Helps.*

Trifles light as air are to the jealous confirmations strong as proofs of holy writ.—
Shakespeare.

No passion more base, nor one which seeks to hide itself more than jealousy. It is ashamed of itself; if it appears, it carries its stain and disgrace on the forehead. We do not wish to acknowledge it to ourselves, it is so ignominious; but hidden and ashamed in the character, we would be confused and disconcerted if it appeared, by which we are convinced of our bad minds and debased courage.—*Bossuet.*

Where love reigns, disturbing jealousy doth call himself affection's sentinel.—*Shakespeare.*

Of all the passions, jealousy is that which exacts the hardest service, and pays the bitterest wages. Its service is to watch the success of our enemy; its wages, to be sure of it.—
Colton.

A jealous man sleeps dog sleep.—
Sir Thomas Overbury.

It is very puzzling, sometimes, to distinguish between jealousy and envy, for they often run into one another, and are blended together. The most valid distinction seems to be this, that jealousy is always personal. The envious man desires some good which another possesses; the jealous man would often be content to be without the good so that that other did not possess it.—*Helps.*

Thou grand counterpoise for all the transports beauty can inspire.—*Young*

Love may exist without jealousy, although this is rare; but jealousy may exist without love, and this is common; for jealousy can feed on that which is bitter, no less than on that which is sweet, and is sustained by pride, as often as by affection.—*Colton.*

There is in jealousy more of self-love than of love.—*Rochefoucauld.*

People who are jealous, or particularly careful of their own rights and dignity, always find enough of those who do not care for either to keep them continually uncomfortable.—
Barnes.

Love often reillumes his extinguished flame at the torch of jealousy.—*Lady Blessington.*

We are more jealous of frivolous accomplishments with brilliant success, than of the most estimable qualities without. Dr. Johnson envied Garrick whom he despised, and ridiculed Goldsmith, whom he loved.—*Hazlitt.*

Jealousy is an awkward homage which inferiority renders to merit.—*Madame de Puisieux.*

It is said that jealousy is love, but I deny it; for though jealousy be procured by love, as ashes are by fire, yet jealousy extinguishes love as ashes smother the flame.—
Margaret of Navarre.

O Jealousy, each other passion's calm to thee, thou conflagration of the soul!—*Young.*

The jealous man's disease is of so malignant a nature that it converts all it takes into its own nourishment.—*Addison.*

Jealousy is a painful passion; yet without some share of it, the agreeable affection of love has difficulty to subsist in its full force and violence.—*Hume.*

Jealousy dislikes the world to know it.—
Byron.

Jealousy is, in some sort, rational and just; it aims at the preservation of a good which belongs, or which we think belongs, to us; whereas envy is a frenzy that cannot endure, even in idea, the good of others.—*Rochefoucauld.*

Jealousy is the fear or apprehension of superiority; envy our uneasiness under it.—
Shenstone.

O Jealousy! thou merciless destroyer, more cruel than the grave! what ravages does thy wild war make in the noblest bosoms!—
Mallet.

The jealous is possessed by a "fine mad devil" and a dull spirit at once.—*Lavater.*

Foul Jealousy! that turnest love divine to joyless dread, and makest the loving heart with hateful thoughts to languish and to pine.—
Spenser.

Jealousy is always born with love, but does not always die with it.—*Rochefoucauld.*

All jealousy must still be strangled in its birth, or time will soon conspire to make it strong enough to overcome the truth.—
Sir W. Davenant.

Jealousy is cruel as the grave; the coals thereof are coals of fire, which hath a most vehement flame.—*Bible.*

Where jealousy is the jailer, many break the prison, it opening more ways to wickedness than it stoppeth; so that where it findeth one, it maketh ten dishonest.—*Fuller.*

The cancer of jealousy on the breast can never wholly be cut out, if I am to believe great masters of the healing art.—*Richter.*

O jealousy, thou ugliest fiend of hell! thy deadly venom preys on my vitals, turns the healthful hue of my fresh cheek to haggard sallowness, and drinks my spirit up.—
Hannah More.

To doubt is an injury; to suspect a friend is breach of friendship; jealousy is a seed sown but in vicious minds; prone to distrust, because apt to deceive.—*Lord Lansdowne.*

JEERING.

Scoff not at the natural defects of any which are not in their power to amend. O, it is cruel to beat a cripple with his own crutches!—
Fuller.

Jeer not others upon any occasion. If they be foolish, God hath denied them understanding; if they be vicious, you ought to pity, not revile them; if deformed, God framed their bodies, and will you scorn his workmanship? Are you wiser than your Creator? If poor, poverty was designed for a motive to charity, not to contempt; you cannot see what riches they have within.—*South.*

JESTING.

Take heed of jesting; many have been ruined by it. It is hard to jest, and not sometimes jeer too; which oftentimes sinks deeper than we intended, or expected.—*Fuller.*

The jest which is expected is already destroyed.—*Johnson.*

When jesting is so handsomely and innocently used, as not to defile or discompose the mind of the speaker, not to wrong or harm the hearer, not to derogate from any worthy subject of discourse, not to infringe decency, to disturb peace, to violate any of the grand duties incumbent on us, it cannot be condemned.—
Barrow.

A jest is a very serious thing.—*Churchill.*

Raillery is sometimes more insupportable than wrong; because we have a right to resent injuries, but it is ridiculous to be angry at a jest.—*Rochefoucauld.*

Wanton jests make fools laugh, and wise men frown.—*Fuller.*

Never risk a joke, even the least offensive in its nature and the most common, with a person who is not well-bred, and possessed of sense to comprehend it.—*Bruyère.*

Wit loses its respect with the good when seen in company with malice; and to smile at the jest which plants a thorn in another's breast is to become a principal in the mischief.—
Sheridan.

A joker is near akin to a buffoon; and neither of them is the least related to wit.—
Chesterfield.

Laughter should dimple the cheek, not furrow the brow. A jest should be such, that all shall be able to join in the laugh which it occasions; but if it bears hard upon one of the company, like the crack of a string, it makes a stop in the music.—*Feltham.*

A jest's prosperity lies in the ear of him that hears it, never in the tongue of him that makes it.—*Shakespeare.*

Beware of biting jests; the more truth they carry with them, the greater wounds they give, the greater smarts they cause, and the greater scars they leave behind them.—*Lavater.*

He that will lose his friend for a jest deserves to die a beggar by the bargain. Such let thy jests be, that they may not grind the credit of thy friend ; and make not jests so long till thou becomest one.—*Fuller.*

It is dangerous to jest with God, death, or the Devil ; for the first neither can nor will be mocked ; the second mocks all men at one time or another ; and the third puts an eternal sarcasm on those that are too familiar with him.— *J. Beaumont.*

Be not affronted at a jest. If one throw never so much salt at thee, thou wilt receive no harm, unless thou art raw and ulcerous.— *Junius.*

He who never relaxes into sportiveness is a wearisome companion ; but beware of him who jests at everything ! such men disparage, by some ludicrous association, all objects which are presented to their thoughts, and thereby render themselves incapable of any emotion which can either elevate or soften them ; they bring upon their moral being an influence more withering than the blasts of the desert.— *Southey.*

If a habit of jesting lowers a man, it is to the level of humanity. Wit nourishes vanity ; reason has a much stronger tincture of pride in it.—*Hazlitt.*

JEWELS.
Dumb jewels often, in their silent kind, more than quick words, do move a woman's mind.—*Shakespeare.*

JOY.
Profound joy has more of severity than gayety in it.—*Montaigne.*

True joy is a serene and sober motion ; and they are miserably out, that take laughing for rejoicing ; the seat of it is within, and there is no cheerfulness like the resolutions of a brave mind, that has fortune under its feet.—*Seneca.*

He who can conceal his joys is greater than he who can hide his griefs.—*Lavater.*

Real joy seems dissonant from the human character in its present condition ; and if it be felt, it must come from a higher region, for the world is shadowed by sorrow ; thorns array the ground ; the very clouds, while they weep fertility on our mountains, seem also to shed a tear on man's grave who departs, unlike the beauties of summer, to return no more ; who fades unlike the sons of the forest, which another summer beholds new clothed, when he is unclothed and forgotten.—*Rev. Dr. Andrews.*

By the degree of thy joy in seeing the joy of thy fellow-creature, and that of thy pain in his suffering, thou canst be able to judge of the degree of thy goodness.—*Lavater.*

How beat our hearts big with tumultuous joy ! —*Somerville.*

Joy wholly from without, is false, precarious, and short. From without it may be gathered ; but, like gathered flowers, though fair, and sweet for a season, it must soon wither, and become offensive. Joy from within is like smelling the rose on the tree ; it is more sweet and fair, it is lasting ; and, I must add, immortal.—*Young.*

Whole years of joy glide unperceived away, while sorrow counts the minutes as they pass.— *Havard.*

A man would have no pleasure in discovering all the beauties of the universe, even in heaven itself, unless he had a partner to whom he might communicate his joys.—*Cicero.*

What is joy ? A sunbeam between two clouds.—*Madame Deluzy.*

Joys are our wings, sorrows are our spurs.— *Richter.*

Joy is the happiness of love. It is love exulting. It is love aware of its own felicity, and resting in riches, which it has no fear of exhausting. It is love taking a view of its treasures, and surrendering itself to bliss without foreboding.—*Rev. J. Hamilton.*

It is a joy to think the best we can of human kind.— *Wordsworth.*

Little joys refresh us constantly, like housebread, and never bring disgust ; and great ones, like sugar-bread, briefly, and then satiety.— *Richter.*

Tranquil pleasures last the longest. We are not fitted to bear long the burden of great joys.—*Bovee.*

Mortal joy is ever on the wing and hard to bind ; it can only be kept in a closed box ; with silence we best guard the fickle good, and swift it vanishes if a flippant tongue haste to raise the lid.—*Schiller.*

Joy ? — a moon by fits reflected in a swamp or watery bog.— *Wordsworth.*

There are joys which long to be ours. God sends ten thousand truths, which come about us like birds seeking inlet ; but we are shut up to them, and so they bring us nothing, but sit and sing awhile upon the roof, and then fly away.— *Beecher.*

True joy is only hope put out of fear.— *Lord Brooke*

Joy descends gently upon us like the evening dew, and does not patter down like a hailstorm.—*Richter.*

18

Who partakes in another's joys is a more humane character than he who partakes in his griefs.—*Lavater.*

Joy never feasts so high, as when the first course is of misery.—*Suckling.*

Great joy, especially after a sudden change and revolution of circumstances, is apt to be silent, and dwells rather in the heart than on the tongue.—*Fielding.*

Far beneath a soul immortal is a mortal joy.
　　　　　　　　　　　Young.

In this world, full often our joys are only the tender shadows which our sorrows cast.—
　　　　　　　　　　　Beecher.

Here below is not the land of happiness; I know it now; it is only the land of toil, and every joy which comes to us is only to strengthen us for some greater labor that is to succeed.—
　　　　　　　　　　　Fichte.

Joy kneels, at morning's rosy prime, in worship to the rising sun.—*J. G. Brooks.*

Trouble is a thing that will come without our call; but true joy will not spring up without ourselves.—*Bishop Patrick.*

There is not a joy the world can give like that it takes away.—*Byron.*

Joy is the mainspring in the whole round of everlasting nature; joy moves the wheels of the great timepiece of the world; she it is that loosens flowers from their buds, suns from their firmaments, rolling spheres in distant space seen not by the glass of the astronomer.—
　　　　　　　　　　　Schiller.

Of joys departed, not to return, how painful the remembrance!—*Blair.*

Remember the wheel is always in motion, and the spoke which is uppermost will soon be under; therefore mix trembling with all your joy.—*Philip Henry.*

The greatest felicity that felicity hath is to spread.—*Hooker.*

The very society of joy redoubles it; so that, whilst it lights upon my friend it rebounds upon myself, and the brighter his candle burns the more easily will it light mine.—*South.*

The joy resulting from the diffusion of blessings to all around us is the purest and sublimest that can ever enter the human mind, and can be conceived only by those who have experienced it. Next to the consolations of divine grace, it is the most sovereign balm to the miseries of life, both in him who is the object of it, and in him who exercises it.—
　　　　　　　　　　Bishop Porteus.

Joy is an exchange; joy flies monopolies! it calls for two; rich fruit! Heaven-planted! never plucked by one.—*Young.*

The beams of joy are made hotter by reflection.—*Fuller.*

Extreme joy is not without a certain delightful pain: by extending the heart beyond its limits; and by so forcibly a holding of all the senses to any object, it confounds their mutual working (but not without a charming kind of ravishment), from the free use of their functions.
　　　　　　　　　　Sir P. Sidney.

Every nation may traffic in charity, and commute for pleasure.—*Jeremy Taylor.*

JUDGMENT.

As the touchstone which tries gold, but is not itself tried by the gold; such is he, who has the standard of judgment.—*Epictetus.*

Outward judgment often fails, inward justice never.—*Theodore Parker.*

It behooves us always to bear in mind, that while actions are always to be judged by the immutable standard of right and wrong, the judgments which we pass upon men must be qualified by considerations of age, country, station, and other accidental circumstances; and it will then be found that he who is most charitable in his judgment is generally the least unjust.
　　　　　　　　　　Southey.

Hear one side, and you will be in the dark; hear both sides, and all will be clear.—
　　　　　　　　　　Haliburton.

Men are not to be judged by their looks, habits, and appearances; but by the character of their lives and conversations, and by their works.—*L'Estrange.*

In forming a judgment, lay your hearts void of fore-taken opinions; else, whatsoever is done or said, will be measured by a wrong rule; like them who have the jaundice, to whom everything appeareth yellow.—*Sir P. Sidney.*

Men's judgments sway on that side fortune leans.—*George Chapman.*

For we must all appear before the judgment-seat of Christ, that every one may receive the things done in his body, according to that he hath done, whether it be good or bad.—*Bible.*

A man has generally the good or ill qualities which he attributes to mankind.—
　　　　　　　　　　Shenstone.

The judgment is like a pair of scales, and evidences like the weights; but the will holds the balances in its hand; and even a slight jerk will be sufficient, in many cases, to make the lighter scale appear the heavier.—*Whately.*

Everything, even piety, is dangerous in a man without judgment.—*Stanislaus.*

The most necessary talent in a man of conversation is a good judgment. He that has this in perfection is master of his companion, without letting him see it; and has the same advantage over men of any other qualifications whatsoever, as one that can see would have over a blind man of ten times his strength.—*Steele.*

It is with our judgments as our watches, none go just alike, yet each believes his own.—*Pope.*

Without the proper and sober estimate of men, we have neither prudence in the affairs of life, nor toleration for contrary opinions, — we tempt the cheater and then condemn him — we believe so strongly in one faith, that we would sentence dissentients as heretics. It is experience alone that teaches us that he who is discreet is seldom betrayed, and that out of the opinions we condemn, spring often the actions we admire.—*Bulwer Lytton.*

The instinctive feeling of a great people is often wiser than the wisest men.—*Kossuth.*

It is a maxim received in life, that in general, we can determine more wisely for others than for ourselves. The reason of it is so clear in argument, that it hardly wants the confirmation of experience.—*Junius.*

Judge thyself with a judgment of sincerity, and thou wilt judge others with a judgment of charity.—*Mason.*

Judges ought to be more learned than witty, more reverent than plausible, and more advised than confident. Above all things, integrity is their portion and proper virtue.—*Bacon.*

Wise judges are we of each other!—*Richelieu.*

It is very questionable, in my mind, how far we have the right to judge one of another, since there is born within every man the germs of both virtue and vice. The development of one or the other is contingent upon circumstances.—*Hosea Ballou.*

Forbear to judge, for we are sinners all.—*Shakespeare.*

There is but one indivisible point from which we should look at a picture; all others are too near, too distant, too high or too low. Perspective fixes this point precisely in the art of painting; but who shall fix it in regard to truth and morals?— *Pascal.*

Many judge rashly, only for the pleasure they take to discourse, and make conjectures of other men's manners and humors by way of exercising their wits.—*De Sales.*

The world is undone by looking at things at a distance.—*Sir Thomas More.*

In equality of conjectures, we are not to take hold of the worse; but rather to be glad we find any hope, that mankind is not grown monstrous; it being, undoubtedly, less evil a guilty man should escape than a guiltless perish.—*Sir P. Sidney.*

Every one complains of the badness of his memory, but nobody of his judgment.—*Rochefoucauld.*

How would you be if He, which is the top of judgment, should but judge you as you are? *Shakespeare.*

The wise will determine from the gravity of the case; the irritable, from sensibility to oppression; the high-minded, from disdain and indignation at abusive power in unworthy hands.—*Burke.*

Lynx-eyed towards our neighbors, and moles to ourselves.—*La Fontaine.*

Surely extraordinary events have not the best title to our studious attention. To study nature or man, we ought to know things that are in the ordinary course, not the unaccountable things that happen out of it.—*Fisher Ames.*

The world is an excellent judge in general, but a very bad one in particular.—*Lord Greville.*

O, how full of error is the judgment of mankind. They wonder at results when they are ignorant of the reasons. They call it Fortune when they know not the cause, and thus worship their own ignorance changed into a deity. — *Metastasio.*

There is so much of good among the worst, so much of evil in the best, such seeming partialities in providence, so many things to lessen and expand, yea, and with all man's boast, so little real freedom of his will, that to look a little lower than the surface, garb, or dialect, or fashion, thou shalt feebly pronounce for a saint, and faintly condemn for a sinner.—*Tupper.*

The seat of knowledge is in the head; of wisdom, in the heart. We are sure to judge wrong if we do not feel right.—*Hazlitt.*

A surface judgment is a daring one indeed if it presumes to be other than a pleasant one.—*Miss Mulock.*

The vulgar mind fancies that judgment is implied chiefly in the capacity to censure; and yet there is no judgment so exquisite as that which knows properly how to approve.—*Simms.*

We do not judge men by what they are in themselves, but by what they are relatively to us.—*Madame Swetchine.*

Fools measure actions after they are done by the event; wise men beforehand, by the rules of reason and right. The former look to the end to judge of the act. Let me look to the act, and leave the end to God.—*Bishop Hale.*

Think wrongly, if you please, but in all cases think for yourself.—*Lessing.*

Judgment is not a swift-growing plant; it requires time and culture to mature it, while fancy often springs up and blossoms in a single hour. The fragrance of the first, however, is lasting, while that of the latter is as transient as its stem is fragile.—*Hosea Ballou.*

I see men's judgments are a parcel of their fortunes; and things outward do draw the inward quality after them.—*Shakespeare.*

While I am ready to adopt any well-grounded opinion, my inmost heart revolts against receiving the judgments of others respecting persons, and whenever I have done so, I have bitterly repented of it.—*Niebuhr.*

I will chide no heathen in the world, but myself, against whom I know most faults.— *Shakespeare.*

There are some minds like either convex or concave mirrors, who represent objects such as they receive them, but they never receive them as they are.—*Joubert.*

If judges would make their decisions just, they should behold neither plaintiff, defendant, nor pleader, but only the cause itself.— *Livingston.*

We rarely meet with persons that have true judgment; which to many renders literature a very tiresome knowledge. Good judges are as rare as good authors.—*St. Evremond.*

Despise not any man, and do not spurn anything; for there is no man that has not his hour, nor is there anything that has not its place.—*Rabbi Ben Azai.*

Human nature is so constituted, that all see, and judge better in the affairs of other men, than in their own.—*Terence.*

That was excellently observed, say I, when I read a passage in an author, where his opinion agrees with mine. When we differ, there I pronounce him to be mistaken.—*Swift.*

A man may see how this world goes with no eyes. Look with thine ears. See how yon justice rails upon yon simple thief. Hark, in thine ear; change places; and handy-dandy, which is the justice, which is the thief?— *Shakespeare.*

One man's word is no man's word; we should quietly hear both sides.—*Goethe.*

Rashly, nor ofttimes truly, doth man pass judgment on his brother; for he seeth not the springs of the heart, nor heareth the reasons of the mind.—*Tupper.*

The judgment of the world stands upon matter of fortune.—*Sir P. Sidney.*

God does not weigh criminality in our scales. We have one absolute, with the seal of authority upon it; and with us an ounce is an ounce, and a pound a pound. God's measure is the heart of the offender, — a balance which varies with every one of us, a balance so delicate that a tear cast in the other side may make the weight of error kick the beam.—*Lowell.*

If thou be a severe, sour-complexioned man, then I here disallow thee to be a competent judge.—*Izaak Walton.*

No man can judge another, because no man knows himself, for we censure others but as they disagree from that humor which we fancy laudable in ourselves, and commend others but for that wherein they seem to quadrate and consent with us.—*Sir Thomas Browne.*

This is the tax a man must pay to his virtues, — they hold up a torch to his vices, and render those frailties notorious in him which would have passed without observation in another.—*Colton.*

Invention is the talent of youth, and judgment of age; so that our judgment grows harder to please, when we have fewer things to offer it; this goes through the whole commerce of life.—*Swift.*

And how his audit stands, who knows, save Heaven?—*Shakespeare.*

In our judgment of human transactions, the law of optics is reversed; we see the most indistinctly the objects which are close around us.— *Whately.*

The judgment may be compared to a clock or watch, where the most ordinary machine is sufficient to tell the hours; but the most elaborate alone can point out the minutes and seconds, and distinguish the smallest differences of time.—*Fontenelle.*

To judge by the event, is an error all abuse and all commit; for in every instance, courage, if crowned with success, is heroism; if clouded by defeat, temerity.—*Colton.*

JUSTICE.

Justice is the freedom of those who are equal. Injustice is the freedom of those who are unequal.—*Jacobi.*

To be perfectly just is an attribute of the divine nature; to be so to the utmost of our abilities, is the glory of man.—*Addison.*

What is justice? — To give every man his own.—*Aristotle.*

Justice without power is inefficient; power without justice is tyranny. Justice without power is opposed, because there are always wicked men. Power without justice is soon questioned. Justice and power must therefore be brought together, so that whatever is just may be powerful, and whatever is powerful may be just.—*Pascal.*

Let us be sacrificers, but no butchers.—
Shakespeare.

Antiquity always begets the opinion of right; and whatever disadvantageous sentiments we may entertain of mankind, they are always found to be prodigal both of blood and treasure in the maintenance of public justice.—
Hume.

The virtue of justice consists in moderation, as regulated by wisdom.—*Aristotle.*

Justice always whirls in equal measure.
Shakespeare.

We ought always to deal justly, not only with those who are just to us, but likewise with those who endeavor to injure us; and this, too, for fear lest by rendering them evil for evil, we should fall into the same vice.—*Hierocles.*

All religion and all ethics are summed up in justice.— *Conway.*

Even Joe Miller in his jests has an eye to poetical justice; generally gives the victory or turns the laugh on the side of merit. No small compliment to mankind!—*Shenstone.*

Justice without strength, and strength without justice; fearful misfortunes!—*Joubert.*

Justice, as defined in the Institutes of Justitian, nearly two thousand years ago, and as it is felt and understood by all who understand human relations and human rights, is: "Constans to perpetua voluntas, jus suum cuique tribuere," — "a constant and perpetual will to render to every one that which is his own."—
J. Q. Adams.

Good my liege, for justice all place a temple, and all season, summer! Do you deny me justice? —*Bulwer Lytton.*

Man is unjust, but God is just; and finally justice triumphs.—*Longfellow.*

Justice is never so slender to us as when we first practise it. It grows in the imagination. It is enlarged by experience. It includes more elements, it touches things with a finer stroke, and it demands more exquisite duties, every single day and year that a man lives, who lives at all right.—*Beecher.*

He who is only just is cruel. Who upon the earth could live, were all judged justly? —*Byron.*

If thou desire rest unto thy soul, be just; he that doth no injury fears not to suffer injury; the unjust mind is always in labor; it either practises the evil it hath projected, or projects to avoid the evil it hath deserved.—*Quarles.*

Justice is the key-note of the world, and all else is ever out of tune.—*Theodore Parker.*

Justice and truth are two points of such exquisite delicacy, that our coarse and blunted instruments will not touch them accurately. If they do find out the point, so as to rest upon it, they bruise and injure it, and lean at last more on the error that surrounds it than on the truth itself.—*Pascal.*

God gives manhood but one clew to success, — utter and exact justice; that he guarantees shall be always expediency.—*Wendell Phillips.*

How can a people be free that has not learned to be just? —*Abbé Sieyès.*

Justice is in general only a lively apprehension of being deprived of what belongs to us; hence arise our great consideration and respect for all the interests of our neighbor, and our scrupulous care to avoid doing him an injury.—
Rochefoucauld.

I do not see why we should not be as just to an ant as to a human being.—*Charles Kingsley.*

It must always be remembered that the actions of public men will be the subject of thought at a future period; when interest is stifled, and passion is silent; when fear has ceased to agitate, and discord is at rest; but when conscience has resumed its sway over the human heart. Nothing but what is just, therefore, can finally be expedient, because nothing else can secure the permanent concurrence of mankind.—*Sir A. Alison.*

The injustice of men subserves the justice of God, and often his mercy.—
Madame Swetchine.

Robes and fur gowns hide all. Plate sins with gold, and the strong lance of justice hurtless breaks; arm it in rags, a pygmy's straw doth pierce it.—*Shakespeare.*

Heaven is above all yet; there sits a judge that no king can corrupt.—*Shakespeare.*

Things should not be done by halves; if it be right, do it boldly; if it be wrong, leave it undone. Every day is a little life, and our whole life is but a day repeated.—*Bishop Hall.*

All are not just because they do no wrong; but he who will not wrong me when he may, he is the truly just.— *Cumberland.*

No obligation to justice does force a man to be cruel, or to use the sharpest sentence. A just man does justice to every man and to everything; and then, if he be also wise, he knows there is a debt of mercy and compassion due to the infirmities of man's nature; and that is to be paid; and he that is cruel and ungentle to a sinning person, and does the worst to him, dies in his debt and is unjust.—
Jeremy Taylor.

Justice consists in doing no injury to men; decency, in giving them no offence.—*Cicero.*

Justice, is the insurance which we have on our lives and property; to which may be added, and obedience is the premium which we pay for it.—*William Penn.*

He who goes no further than bare justice stops at the beginning of virtue.—*Blair.*

I am told thou callest thyself a king; know, if thou art one, that the poor have rights; and power, in all its pride, is less than justice.—
Aaron Hill.

How many sentences have I seen more criminal than the crimes themselves? All which makes me remember the ancient opinions, "That there is a necessity a man must do wrong by retail, who will do right in gross; and injustice in little things, that will come to do justice in great; that human justice is formed after the model of physic," according to which, all that is utile is also just and honest; "That nature of herself proceeds contrary to justice in most of her works"; and of what is received by the Cyrenaicks, "That there is nothing just of itself, but that customs and laws make justice."—
Montaigne.

The sentiment of justice is so natural, so universally acquired by all mankind, that it seems to me independent of all law, all party, all religion.—*Voltaire.*

The failings of good men are commonly more published in the world than their good deeds; and one fault of a well-deserving man shall meet with more reproaches than all his virtues praise, — such is the force of ill-will and ill-nature.—*Willis.*

Justice is the bread of the nation; it is always hungry for it.—*Chateaubriand.*

The integrity of the heart, when it is strengthened by reason, is the principal source of justice and wit; an honest man thinks nearly always justly.—*Rousseau.*

Use every man after his desert, and who should escape whipping?—*Shakespeare.*

If strict justice be not the rudder of all our other virtues, the faster we sail, the farther we shall find ourselves from that haven where we would be.—*Colton.*

Sophistry may perplex truth, ingenuity may warp the decrees of justice, and ridicule may raise an undeserved laugh; but where free inquiry prevails, errors will be corrected, justice will be revered, and ridicule will be retorted on those who have abused its influence.—*Ennius.*

The only way to make the mass of mankind see the beauty of justice, is by showing them in pretty plain terms the consequence of injustice.
Sydney Smith.

It is necessary, in order to do well, to join strength to justice; but with this difference; that strength obeys justice as feudal dame and mistress, and does nothing in the spite of her authority, wish, or command.—
Michel l'Hospital.

Justice is the great, but simple principle, and the whole secret of success in all government: as absolutely essential to the training of an infant, as to the control of a mighty nation.
Simms.

Justice is the first virtue of those who command, and stops the complaints of those who obey.—*Diderot.*

Justice is as strictly due between neighbor nations, as between neighbor citizens. A highwayman is as much a robber when he plunders in a gang, as when single; and a nation that makes an unjust war is only a great gang of robbers.—*Franklin.*

Justice is the idea of God, the ideal of man, the rule of conduct writ in the nature of mankind.—*Theodore Parker.*

Justice is that which is by law established; and hence, all our established laws are to be necessarily accounted just, because they are established.—*Pascal.*

Justice is itself the great standing policy of civil society; and any eminent departure from it, under any circumstance, lies under the suspicion of being no policy at all.—*Burke.*

This even-handed justice commends the ingredients of our poisoned chalice to our own lips.—*Shakespeare.*

K.

KINDNESS.

Ask thyself daily to how many ill-minded persons thou hast shown a kind disposition.—
Marcus Antoninus.

Ministers who threaten death and destruction employ weapons of weakness. Argument and kindness are alone effectual, flavored by the principles of Divine love.—*Hosea Ballou.*

The great duty of life is not to give pain; and the most acute reasoner cannot find an excuse for one who voluntarily wounds the heart of a fellow-creature. Even for their own sakes people should show kindness and regard to their dependants. They are often better served in trifles, in proportion as they are rather feared than loved; but how small is this gain compared with the loss sustained in all the weightier affairs of life ? Then the faithful servant shows himself at once as a friend, while one who serves from fear shows himself as an enemy.—
Fredrika Bremer.

Well has Ennius said, "Kindnesses misplaced are nothing but a curse and disservice."—
Cicero.

Life is made up, not of great sacrifices or duties, but of little things, in which smiles and kindness, and small obligations, given habitually, are what win and preserve the heart, and secure comfort.—*Sir H. Davy.*

Kindness in women, not their beauteous looks, shall win my love.—*Shakespeare.*

One man has kindness deep within him; and when the occasion comes, the rind or shell is cracked, and the kernel is found. Such a man's heart, too long clouded, like a sun in a storm-muffled day, shoots through some opening rift, and glows for a period in glory. But there are other natures that are always cloudless. With them, a cloud is the exception, shining is the rule.—*Beecher.*

There are few occasions when ceremony may not be easily dispensed with, but kindness, never.—*Hosea Ballou.*

Heaven in sunshine will require the kind.—
Byron.

Kind words prevent a good deal of that perverseness, which rough and imperious usage often produces in generous minds.—*Locke.*

Clemency alone makes us equal with the gods.—*Claudianus.*

A more glorious victory cannot be gained over another man than this, that when the injury began on his part, the kindness should begin on ours.—*Tillotson.*

Kindness in ourselves is the honey that blunts the sting of unkindness in another.—
Landor.

Kindness nobler ever than revenge.—
Shakespeare.

Always say a kind word if you can, if only that it may come in, perhaps, with singular opportuneness, entering some mournful man's darkened room, like a beautiful firefly, whose happy circumvolutions he cannot but watch, forgetting his many troubles.—*Helps.*

Kindness is the golden chain by which society is bound together.—*Goethe.*

Gentle feelings produce profoundly beneficial effects upon stern natures. It is the spring rain which melts the ice-covering of the earth, and causes it to open to the beams of heaven.—
Fredrika Bremer.

A language which the dumb can speak, and the deaf can understand.—*Bovee.*

We have a great deal more kindness than is ever spoken. Maugre all the selfishness that chills like east-winds the world, the whole human family is bathed with an element of love like a fine ether.—*Emerson.*

Kindness gives birth to kindness.—
Sophocles.

Good and friendly conduct may meet with an unworthy, with an ungrateful, return; but the absence of gratitude on the part of the receiver cannot destroy the self-approbation which recompenses the giver : and we may scatter the seeds of courtesy and kindness around us at so little expense. Some of them will inevitably fall on good ground, and grow up into benevolence in the minds of others; and all of them will bear fruit of happiness in the bosom whence they spring. Once blest are all the virtues ; twice blest sometimes.—*Bentham.*

Kindness is virtue itself.—*Lamartine.*

That best portion of a good man's life, his little, nameless, unremembered acts of kindness and of love.— *Wordsworth.*

A willing heart adds feather to the heel, and makes the clown a winged Mercury.—
Joanna Baillie.

I had rather never receive a kindness than never bestow one. Not to return a benefit is the greater sin, but not to confer it is the earlier.—*Seneca.*

An effort made for the happiness of others lifts us above ourselves.—*Mrs. L. M. Child.*

A tender-hearted and compassionate dispo-sition which inclines men to pity and feel the misfortunes of others, and which is, even for its own sake, incapable of involving any man in ruin and misery, is of all tempers of mind the most amiable; and though it seldom receives much honor, is worthy of the highest.— .
Fielding.

I have sped by land and sea, and mingled with much people, but never yet could find a spot unsunned by human kindness.—*Tupper.*

The last, best fruit which comes to late per-fection, even in the kindliest soul, is tenderness toward the hard, forbearance toward the unfor-bearing, warmth of heart toward the cold, phi-lanthropy toward the misanthropic.—*Richter.*

It is more beautiful to overcome injury by the power of kindness than to oppose to it the obstinacy of hatred.—*Valerius Maximus.*

Let your best love draw to that point which seeks best to preserve it.—*Shakespeare.*

The happiness of life may be greatly in-creased by small courtesies in which there is no parade, whose voice is too still to tease, and which manifest themselves by tender and affec-tionate looks, and little kind acts of attention.—
Sterne.

Who will not give some portion of his ease, his blood, his wealth, for others' good, is a poor frozen churl.—*Joanna Baillie.*

Kind hearts are more than coronets, and simple faith than Norman blood.—*Tennyson.*

Kindnesses do not always produce what we expect; from a hand which we hate they are regarded as offences; the more we lavish on one who may hate us, the more arms we give to him who wishes to betray us.—*Corneille.*

You may ride us with one soft kiss a thou-sand furlongs, ere with spur we heat an acre.—
Shakespeare.

In the intercourse of social life, it is by little acts of watchful kindness recurring daily and hourly, — and opportunities of doing kindnesses if sought for are forever starting up, — it is by words, by tones, by gestures, by looks, that affec-tion is won and preserved. He who neglects these trifles, yet boasts that, whenever a great sacrifice is called for, he shall be ready to make it, will rarely be loved. The likelihood is, he will not make it; and if he does, it will be much rather for his own sake than for his neighbor's.
G. A. Sala.

The cheapest of all things is kindness, its ex-ercise requiring the least possible trouble and self-sacrifice. "Win hearts," said Burleigh to Queen Elizabeth, "and you have all men's hearts and purses."—*Samuel Smiles.*

Violence and harshness make men disgusted and close up their hearts. Where there is long opposition, a kind word easily finds entrance.—
Herder.

He who confers a favor should at once for-get it, if he is not to show a sordid ungenerous spirit. To remind a man of a kindness con-ferred on him, and to talk of it, is little different from reproach.—*Demosthenes.*

KINGS.

It is the misfortune of kings that they scarcely ever do that good that they have a mind to do; and through surprise, and the insinuations of flatterers, they often do that mischief they never intended.—*Fenelon.*

Uneasy lies the head that wears a crown.—
Shakespeare.

A king that would not feel his crown too heavy for him must wear it every day; but if he think it too light, he knoweth not of what metal it is made.—*Bacon.*

The king that faithfully judgeth the poor, his throne shall be established forever.—*Bible.*

A king ruleth as he ought, a tyrant as he lists; a king to the profit of all, a tyrant only to please a few.—*Aristotle.*

What have kings that privates have not too, save ceremony?—*Shakespeare*

O, unhappy state of kings! it is well the robe of majesty is gay, or who would put it on?
Hannah More.

Wise kings have generally wise councillors, as — he must be a wise man himself who is capable of distinguishing one.—*Diogenes.*

Kings ought to be kings in all things.—
Adrian.

The people are fashioned according to the example of their king; and edicts are of less power than the model which his life exhibits.—
Claudian.

Royalty consists not in vain pomp, but in great virtues.—*Agesilaus.*

The king is but a man, as I am: the violet smells to him as it doth to me; the element shows to him as it doth to me; all his senses have but human conditions; his ceremonies laid by, in his nakedness he appears but a man; and though his affections are higher mounted than ours, yet, when they stoop, they stoop with the like wing.—*Shakespeare.*

What has surprised me most in history, is to read of so few kings who have abdicated their thrones, — not above a dozen or two at the most!—*Sterne.*

He who reflects attentively upon the duties of a king trembles at the sight of a crown.— *De Lévis.*

It is manifest that the power of kings and magistrates is nothing else but what is only derivative, transferred, and committed to them in trust from the people to the common good of them all, in whom the power yet remains fundamentally, and cannot be taken from them without a violation of their natural birthright. *Milton.*

Kings, chiefly in this, should imitate God; their mercy should be above all their works.— *William Penn.*

He was a king blessed of the King of kings. *Shakespeare.*

KISSES.
The kiss, snatched hasty from the sidelong maid.—*Thomson.*

Kisses are like grains of gold or silver found upon the ground, of no value themselves, but precious as showing that a mine is near.— *George Villiers.*

A kiss from my mother made me a painter. *Benjamin West.*

One kiss — so ends all record of my crime! it is the seal upon the tomb of Hope, by which like some lost, sorrowing angel, sits sad memory evermore.—*Bulwer Lytton.*

It is time to fear when tyrants seem to kiss. *Shakespeare.*

There is the kiss of welcome and of parting; the long, lingering, loving, present one; the stolen, or the mutual one; the kiss of love, of joy, and of sorrow; the seal of promise, and the receipt of fulfilment. Is it strange, therefore, that a woman is invincible, whose armory consists of kisses, smiles, sighs, and tears? — *Haliburton.*

God pardons like a mother, who kisses the offence into everlasting forgetfulness.—*Beecher.*

It is the passion that is in a kiss that gives to it its sweetness; it is the affection in a kiss that sanctifies it.—*Bovee.*

Upon thy cheek lay I this zealous kiss, as seal to the indenture of my love.—*Shakespeare.*

The fragrant infancy of opening flowers, flowed to my senses in that meeting kiss.— *Southern.*

The gentle wind, a sweet and passionate wooer kisses the blushing leaf.—*Longfellow.*

Now by the jealous queen of Heaven, that kiss I carried from thee, dear; my true lip hath virgined it ever since.—*Shakespeare.*

Then kissed me hard, as if he plucked up kisses by the roots, that grew upon my lips.— *Shakespeare.*

A long, long kiss, a kiss of youth and love. *Byron.*

And with a velvet lip print on his brow such language as the tongue hath never spoken.— *Mrs. Sigourney.*

Mercy and truth are met together: righteousness and peace have kissed each other.— *Bible.*

Teach not thy lip such scorn; for it was made for kissing, lady, not for such contempt. *Shakespeare.*

I clasp thy waist, I feel thy bosom's beat — O, kiss me into faintness sweet and dim.— *Alexander Smith.*

It is delightful to kiss the eyelashes of the beloved — is it not? But never so delightful as when fresh tears are on them.—*Landor.*

Let me drink often of this living spring, to nourish new invention.—*Massinger.*

And steal immortal kisses from her lips; which even in pure and vestal modesty still blush as thinking their own kisses sin. *Shakespeare.*

O Love, O fire! once he drew with one long kiss my whole soul through my lips, as sunlight drinketh dew.—*Tennyson.*

For lovers, lacking (God warn us!) matter, the cleanliest shift is to kiss. -*Shakespeare.*

KNAVERY.
The worst of all knaves are those who can mimic their former honesty.—*Lavater.*

Every base occupation makes one sharp in its practice, and dull in every other.— *Sir P. Sidney.*

His tongue and his heart are always at variance, and fall out like rogues in the street, to pick somebody's pocket. They never agree but like Herod and Pilate, to do mischief. His conscience never stands in his light, when the devil holds a candle to him; for he has stretched it so thin that it is transparent.—*Butler.*

Knavery's plain face is never seen till used. *Shakespeare.*

Craftiness is a quality in the mind, and a vice in the character.—*Sanial-Dubay.*

Cunning leads to knavery; it is but a step from one to the other, and that very slippery; lying only makes the difference; add that to cunning, and it is knavery.—*Bruyère.*

Men, who are knaves individually, are in the mass very honorable people.—*Montesquieu.*

A thorough-paced knave will rarely quarrel with one whom he can cheat. His revenge is plunder ; therefore he is usually the most forgiving of beings, upon the principle that if he come to an open rupture, he must defend himself, and this does not suit a man whose vocation it is to keep his hands in the pockets of another.—*Colton.*

The craftiest wiles are too short and ragged a cloak to cover a bad heart.—*Lavater.*

Many a would-be great knave is, from intellectual deficiency, only a small knave.—
Whately.

Knaves will thrive when honest plainness knows not how to live.—*Shirley.*

His knowledge of human nature must be limited indeed, and he must have mixed, but little with the world — who is not aware, that a very honest man, with a very good understanding may be deceived by a knave.—*Junius.*

Every knave is a thorough knave, and a thorough knave is a knave throughout.—
Bishop Berkeley.

Knaves easily believe that others are like to themselves : they can hardly be deceived, and they do not deceive others for any length of time.—*Bruyère.*

Knavery is supple, and can bend, but honesty is firm and upright and yields not.—*Colton.*

KNOWLEDGE.

. The more we have read, the more we have learned, the more we have meditated, the better conditioned we are to affirm that we know nothing.—*Voltaire.*

All that is known is comprehended, not according to its own force, but according rather to the faculty of those knowing.—*Boethius.*

Knowledge and good parts, managed by grace, are like the rod in Moses' hand, wonder-workers ; but turn to serpents when they are cast upon the ground, and employed in promoting wicked designs.—*Arrowsmith.*

If you have knowledge, let others light their candles at it.—*Fuller.*

The more we know, the greater our thirst for knowledge. The water-lily, in the midst of waters, opens its leaves and expands its petals at the first pattering of showers, and rejoices in the raindrops with a quicker sympathy than the parched shrub in the sandy desert.—*Coleridge.*

Knowledge is the treasure, but judgment the treasurer, of a wise man.—*William Penn.*

Virtue is an angel ; but she is a blind one, and must ask of Knowledge to show her the pathway that leads to her goal. Mere knowledge, on the other hand, like a Swiss mercenary, is ready to combat either in the ranks of sin or under the banners of righteousness ; ready to forge cannon-balls, or to print New Testaments ; to navigate a corsair's vessel or a missionary ship.—*Horace Mann.*

Half our knowledge we must snatch, not take.—*Pope.*

Manners must adorn knowledge, and smooth its way through the world. Like a great rough diamond, it may do very well in a closet by way of curiosity and also for its intrinsic value.—*Chesterfield.*

Every person has two educations, one which he receives from others, and one, more important, which he gives to himself.—*Gibbon.*

Knowledge conquered by labor becomes a possession,—a property entirely our own. A greater vividness and permanency of impression is secured, and facts thus acquired become registered in the mind in a way that mere imparted information can never produce.—*Samuel Smiles.*

Many of the supposed increasers of knowledge have only given a new name, and often a worse, to what was well known before.—*Hare.*

Nothing in this life, after health and virtue, is more estimable than knowledge,— nor is there anything so easily attained, or so cheaply purchased, — the labor only sitting still, and the expense but time, which, if we do not spend, we cannot save.—*Sterne.*

Knowledge is leagued with the universe, and findeth a friend in all things ; but ignorance is everywhere a stranger, unwelcome ; ill at ease and out of place.—*Tupper.*

It is of great importance to the honor of learning that men of business should know erudition is not like a lark, which flies high, and delights in nothing but singing ; but that it is rather like a hawk, which soars aloft indeed, but can stoop when she finds it convenient, and seize her prey.—*Bacon.*

It is knowledge that destroys enthusiasm and dispels all those prejudices of admiration which people simpler minds with so many idols of enchantment. Philosophy, which has led to the exact investigation of causes, has robbed the world of much of its sublimity, and by preventing us from believing much, and from wondering at anything, has taken away half our enthusiasm, and more than half our admiration.—
Jeffrey.

In many instances we clearly perceive that more or less knowledge dispensed to man would have proved detrimental to his state.—*Blair.*

For one effect of knowledge is to deaden the force of the imagination and the original energy of the whole man; under the weight of his knowledge he cannot move so lightly as in the days of his simplicity. The pack-horse is furnished for the journey, the war-horse is armed for war; but the freedom of the field and the lightness of the limb are lost for both.—*Ruskin.*

Your learning, like the lunar beam, affords light, but not heat; it leaves you undevout, frozen at heart, while speculation shines.—
Young.

Every man of sound brain whom you meet knows something worth knowing better than yourself. A man, on the whole, is a better preceptor than a book. But what scholar does not allow that the dullest book can suggest to him a new and a sound idea?—*Bulwer Lytton.*

Knowledge is power.—*Bacon.*

Knowledge is a comfortable and necessary retreat and shelter for us in an advanced age; and if we do not plant it while young, it will give us no shade when we grow old.—
Chesterfield.

Knowledge comes, but wisdom lingers.—
Tennyson.

Those who come last seem to enter with advantage. They are born to the wealth of antiquity. The materials for judging are prepared, and the foundations of knowledge are laid to their hands. Besides, if the point was tried by antiquity, antiquity would lose it; for the present age is really the oldest and has the largest experience to plead.—*Jeremy Collier.*

Knowledge is not happiness, and science but an exchange of ignorance for that which is another kind of ignorance.—*Byron.*

He that enlarges his curiosity after the works of nature demonstrably multiplies the inlets to happiness; therefore we should cherish ardor in the pursuit of useful knowledge, and remember that a blighted spring makes a barren year, and that the vernal flowers, however beautiful and gay, are only intended by nature as preparatives to autumnal fruits.—*Johnson.*

It is odd how folks will force disagreeable knowledge upon us,—crab-apples, that we must eat and defy the stomach-ache.—
Douglas Jerrold.

Knowledge and timber should not be much used until they are seasoned.—*Holmes.*

The highest knowledge can be nothing more than the shortest and clearest road to truth; all the rest is pretension, not performance, mere verbiage and grandiloquence, from which we can learn nothing, but that it is the external sign of an internal deficiency.—*Colton.*

That learning which thou gettest by thy own observation and experience, is far beyond that which thou gettest by precept; as the knowledge of a traveller exceeds that which is got by reading.—*Thomas à Kempis.*

Knowledge and wisdom, far from being one, have ofttimes no connection. Knowledge dwells in heads replete with thoughts of other men; wisdom in minds attentive to their own.—
Cowper.

The wisest man that ever was, being asked what he knew, made answer, "He knew this, that he knew nothing." By which, he verified what has been said, that the greatest part of what we know is the least of what we do not; that is to say, that even what we think we know, is but a piece, and a very little one, of our ignorance.—*Montaigne.*

Knowledge is our ultimate good.—*Socrates.*

He who calls in the aid of an equal understanding, doubles his own; and he who profits of a superior understanding raises his powers to a level with the height of the superior understanding he unites with.—*Burke.*

Knowledge may not be as a courtesan for pleasure and vanity only; or as a bondwoman, to acquire and gain for her master's use; but as a spouse, for generation, fruit, and comfort.—
Bacon.

A little knowledge leads the mind from God. Unripe thinkers use their learning to authenticate their doubts; while unbelief has its own dogma, more peremptory than the inquisitor's. Patient meditation brings the scholar back to humbleness. He learns that the grandest truths appear slowly.—*Willmott.*

He that does not know those things which are of use and necessity for him to know is but an ignorant man, whatever he may know besides.—*Tillotson.*

Knowledge hath a bewildering tongue, and she will stoop and lead you to the stars, and witch you with her mysteries,—till gold is a forgotten dross, and power and fame toys of an hour, and woman's careless love light as the breath that breaks it.—*Willis.*

The essence of knowledge is, having it, to apply it; not having it, to confess your ignorance.—*Confucius.*

It is the property of all true knowledge, especially spiritual, to enlarge the soul by filling it; to enlarge it without swelling it; to make it more capable, and more earnest to know, the more it knows.—*Sprat.*

It is always safe to learn, even from our enemies; seldom safe to venture to instruct even our friends.—*Colton.*

A man may do very well with a very little knowledge, and scarce be found out, in mixed company; everybody is so much more ready to produce his own than to call for a display of your acquisitions.—*Lamb.*

Diffused knowledge immortalizes itself.—
Mackintosh.

Knowledge always desires increase; it is like fire, which must first be kindled by some external agent, but which will afterwards propagate itself.—*Johnson.*

Human knowledge is the parent of doubt.—
Lord Greville.

It doth invest us with grand and glorious privileges, and grant to us a largess of beatitude. We enter our studies and enjoy a society which we alone can bring together. We raise no jealousy by conversing with one in preference to another; we give no offence to the most illustrious by questioning him as long as he will, and leaving him abruptly.—*Landor.*

Knowledge, unemployed, will preserve us from vice, for vice is but another name for ignorance; but knowledge employed is virtue.—
Bulwer Lytton.

Ignorance is the curse of God, knowledge the wing wherewith we fly to heaven.—
Shakespeare.

When we rise in knowledge, as the prospect widens, the objects of our regard become more obscure; and the unlettered peasant, whose views are only directed to the narrow sphere around him, beholds nature with a finer relish, and tastes her blessings with a keener appetite, than the philosopher whose mind attempts to grasp a universal system.—*Goldsmith.*

To know things well, we should know them in detail; but this being in a manner infinite, our knowledge must needs be superficial and imperfect.—*Rochefoucauld.*

The first step to knowledge is to know that we are ignorant.—*Cecil.*

What fulness of granary and storehouse, what freights for ship and car, come from agricultural knowledge,—that is, from mind,—where once the barrenness of earth and the barrenness of ignorance spread a common solitude!—*Horace Mann.*

He that would make a real progress in knowledge must dedicate his age as well as youth,—the latter-growth as well as the first-fruits—at the altar of truth.—*Bishop Berkeley.*

Every generation enjoys the use of a vast hoard bequeathed to it by antiquity, and transmits that hoard, augmented by fresh acquisitions, to future ages.—*Macaulay.*

The desire of knowledge, like the thirst of riches, increases ever with the acquisition of it.
Sterne.

There is nothing so charming as the knowledge of literature; of that branch of literature, I mean, which enables us to discover the infinity of things, the immensity of Nature, the heavens, the earth, and the seas; this is that branch which has taught us religion, moderation, magnanimity, and that has rescued the soul from obscurity; to make her see all things above and below, first and last, and between both; it is this that furnishes us wherewith to live well and happily, and guides us to pass our lives without displeasure and without offence.—*Cicero.*

It is no wonder if a great deal of knowledge, which is not capable of making a man wise, has a natural tendency to make him vain and arrogant.—*Addison.*

Seldom ever was any knowledge given to keep, but to impart; the grace of this rich jewel is lost in concealment.—*Bishop Hall.*

The tree of knowledge is grafted upon the tree of life; and that fruit which brought the fear of death into the world, budding on an immortal stock, becomes the fruit of the promise of immortality.—*Sir H. Davy.*

It is not the number of facts he knows, but how much of a fact he is himself, that proves the man.—*Bovee.*

Man often acquires just so much knowledge as to discover his ignorance, and attains so much experience as to regret his follies, and then dies.—*W. B. Clulow.*

The dangers of knowledge are not to be compared with the dangers of ignorance. Man is more likely to miss his way in darkness than in twilight; in twilight than in full sun.—
Whately.

As in geometry, the oblique must be known, as well as the right; and in arithmetic, the odd as well as the even; so in actions of life, who seeth not the filthiness of evil, wanteth a great foil to perceive the beauty of virtue.—
Sir P. Sidney.

The itch of impertinent and unprofitable knowledge hath been the hereditary disease of the sons of Adam and Eve. How many have perished to know that which hath procured their perishing!—*Bishop Hall.*

One part of knowledge consists in being ignorant of such things as are not worthy to be known.—*Crates.*

Imparting knowledge, is only lighting other men's candle at our lamp, without depriving ourselves of any flame.—*Jane Porter.*

Knowledge is the consequence of time, and multitude of days are fittest to teach wisdom.—
Jeremy Collier.

Man, if he compare himself with all that he can see, is at the zenith of power; but if he compare himself with all that he can conceive, he is at the nadir of weakness.—*Colton.*

Knowledge without education is but armed injustice.—*Horace.*

That learning which makes us acquainted with ourselves, with the powers and faculties of the human mind, with divine truth, which is plainly revealed, with its power on the mind and heart, with the concatenations of cause and effect and to understand our every-day duty, which grows out of our wants and the wants of those about us, is learning of a better quality than that which only enables us to call things by different names, without giving us a knowledge of their qualities either for good or evil.—
Hosea Ballou.

Of knowledge there is no satiety — but satisfaction and appetite are perpetually interchangeable.—*Bacon.*

The study of literature nourishes youth, entertains old age, adorns prosperity, solaces adversity, is delightful at home, and unobtrusive abroad.—*Cicero.*

Knowledge is boundless, — human capacity, limited.—*Chamfort.*

Knowledge perverted, is knowledge no longer. .Vinegar which exposed to the sun, breeds small serpents, or at best slimy eels, not comestible, once was wine.—*Bulwer Lytton.*

Knowledge hath clipped the lightning's wings, and mewed it up for a purpose.—
Tupper.

The knowledge which we have acquired ought not to resemble a great shop without order, and without an inventory; we ought to know what we possess, and be able to make it serve us in need.—*Leibnitz.*

Charles V. has said that a man who knew four languages was worth four men.—
M. de Montlosier.

Every increase of knowledge may possibly render depravity more depraved, as well as it may increase the strength of virtue. It is in itself only power; and its value depends on its application.—*Sydney Smith.*

Knowledge is not a shop for profit or sale, but a rich storehouse for the glory of the Creator, and the relief of men's estate.—*Bacon.*

Knowledge has its penalties and pains, as well as its prizes.—*Bulwer Lytton.*

People disparage knowing and the intellectual life, and urge doing. I am very content with knowing, if only I could know. That is an august entertainment and would suffice me a great while. To know a little would be worth the expense of this world.—*Emerson.*

Much which passes in the world for knowledge is but a slight and trivial thing.—*South.*

An honest and educated man can do many good and useful things, which an honest ignorant man would not dare do; the first knows that he will act as becomes him; the second knows not, hesitates, and abstains. It is thus with a child who fears to walk in darkness; a man walks without fear, he knows that there is no danger.—*Bruyère.*

What we know here is very little, but what we are ignorant of is immense.—*La Place.*

As soon as a true thought has entered our mind, it gives a light which makes us see a crowd of other objects which we have never perceived before.—*Chateaubriand.*

I envy no man that knows more than myself, but pity them that know less.—
Sir Thomas Browne.

If a man empties his purse into his head, no man can take it away from him. An investment in knowledge always pays the best interest.—*Franklin.*

Knowledge of the world is dearly bought at the price of moral purity.—*E. Wigglesworth.*

Knowledge will not be acquired without pains and application. It is troublesome and deep digging for pure waters; but when once you come to the spring, they rise up and meet you.—*Felton.*

Those only who know little, can be said to know anything. The greater the knowledge the greater the doubt.—*Goethe.*

There are in knowledge these two excellences; first, that it offers to every man the most selfish and the most exalted, his peculiar inducement to good. It says to the former, "Serve mankind, and you serve yourself"; to the latter, "In choosing the best means to secure your own happiness, you will have the sublime inducement of promoting the happiness of mankind." The second excellence of knowledge is that even the selfish man, when he has once begun to love virtue from little motives, loses the motives as he increases the love, and at last worships the deity, where before he only coveted the gold upon its altar.—*Bulwer Lytton.*

It is in knowledge as it is in plants. If you mean to use the plant, it is no matter for the roots; if you mean it to grow, it is safer to rest upon roots than slips.—*Bacon.*

Knowledge that terminates in curiosity and speculation is inferior to that which is useful; and of all useful knowledge that is the most so which consists in a due care and just notion of ourselves.—*St. Bernard.*

The best part of our knowledge is that which teaches us where knowledge leaves off and ignorance begins.—*Holmes.*

That is indeed a twofold knowledge, which profits alike by the folly of the foolish, and the wisdom of the wise. It is both a shield and a sword; it borrows its security from the darkness, and its confidence from the light.—*Colton.*

Knowledge has been deemed long enough an argand-lamp to illuminate a drawing-room; it is time it should be known as a sun, whose beams, resting upon the mountain-tops, penetrate into profoundest valleys.—*Melton.*

All wish to possess knowledge, but few, comparatively speaking, are willing to pay the price.—*Juvenal*

Knowledge has its boundary line, where it abuts on ignorance; on the outside of that boundary line are ignorance and miracles; on the inside of it are science and no miracles.— *Horace Mann.*

Pleasure is a shadow, wealth is vanity, and power a pageant; but knowledge is ecstatic in enjoyment, perennial in fame, unlimited in space, and infinite in duration. In the performance of its sacred offices, it fears no danger, spares no expense, looks in the volcano, dives into the ocean, perforates the earth, wings its flight into the skies, explores sea and land, contemplates the distant, examines the minute, comprehends the great, ascends to the sublime — no place too remote for its grasp, no height too exalted for its reach.—*De Witt Clinton.*

Falling in love with the utility of knowledge as a means, men sometimes cease to pursue it as an end; and while turning aside to pick up the golden apples of pleasure or profit, or applause, miss the more excellent prize at the end of the course.—*H. N. Hudson.*

L.

LABOR.

The gods sell everything good for labor.— *Epicharmus.*

Labor is one of the great elements of society, the great substantial interest on which we all stand.—*Daniel Webster.*

Next to faith in God is faith in labor.— *Bovee.*

God has laid upon us many severe trials in this world; but he has created labor for us, and all is compensated. Thanks to labor, the bitterest tears are dried; a serious consoler, it always promises less than it bestows; a pleasure unparalleled, it is still the salt of other pleasures. Everything abandons you, — gayety, wit, love, — labor alone is always present, and the profound enjoyment it produces. Have I said enough? No; for to these privileges of labor, we must add a greater yet; that it is like the sun, — God has made it for the whole world.— *E. Legouvé.*

The lottery of honest labor, drawn by Time, is the only one whose prizes are worth taking up and carrying home.—*Theodore Parker.*

Labor rids us of three great evils, — irksomeness, vice, and poverty.—*Voltaire.*

It is the primal curse, but softened into mercy, made the pledge of cheerful days, and nights without a groan.—*Cowper.*

Hard workers are usually honest. Industry lifts them above temptation.—*Bovee.*

There is a perennial nobleness and even sacredness in work. Were he ever so benighted, forgetful of his high calling, there is always hope in a man that actually and earnestly works. *Carlyle.*

Labor is the Lethe of the Past and of the Present.—*Richter.*

It is not work that kills men, it is worry. Work is healthy, you can hardly put more upon a man than he can bear. Worry is rust upon the blade. It is not the revolution that destroys the machinery, but the friction. Fear secretes acids, but love and trust are sweet juices.— *Beecher.*

From labor health, from health contentment springs.—*Beattie.*

It is only by labor that thought can be made healthy, and only by thought that labor can be made happy; and the two cannot be separated with impunity.—*Ruskin.*

As we are born to work, so others are born to watch over us while we are working.— *Goldsmith.*

It is to labor, and to labor only, that man owes everything possessed of exchangeable value. Labor is the talisman that has raised him from the condition of the savage; that has changed the desert and the forest into cultivated fields; that has covered the earth with cities, and the ocean with ships; that has given us plenty, comfort, and elegance, instead of want, misery, and barbarism.—*M'Culloch.*

Hard labor is not whenever you are very actively employed, but when you must be.— *Whately.*

Venerable to me is the hard hand,—crooked, coarse,—wherein, notwithstanding, lies a cunning virtue, indefeasibly royal, as of the sceptre of this planet. Venerable, too, is the rugged face, all weather-tanned, besoiled with its rude intelligence; for it is the face of a man living manlike.—*Carlyle.*

The fruit derived from labor is the sweetest of all pleasures.—*Vauvenargues.*

The labor of the body relieves us from the fatigues of the mind; and this it is which forms the happiness of the poor.—*Rochefoucauld.*

Clay and rock are given us; not brick and squared stone. God gives us no raiment; he gives us flax and sheep. If we would have coats on our backs, we must take them off our flocks, and spin them and weave them. If we would have anything of benefit, we must earn it, and, earning it, must become shrewd, inventive, ingenious, active, enterprising.—*Beecher.*

Genius easily hews out its figure from the block; but the sleepless chisel gives it life.— *Willmott.*

Observe, without labor nothing prospers.— *Sophocles.*

This labor and sweat of our brows is so far from being a curse, that without it our very bread would not be so great a blessing. Is it not labor that makes the garlic and the pulse, the sycamore and the cresses, the cheese of the goats, and the butter of the sheep, to be savory and pleasant as the flesh of the roebuck, or the milk of the kine, the marrow of oxen, or the thighs of birds? If it were not for labor, men neither could eat so much, nor relish so pleasantly, nor sleep so soundly, nor be so healthful, nor so useful, so strong nor so patient, so noble nor so untempted.— *Jeremy Taylor.*

I find that successful exertion is a powerful means of exhilaration, which discharges itself in good-humor upon others.—*Chalmers.*

Shun no toil, to make yourself remarkable by some talent or other. Yet do not devote yourself to one branch exclusively. Strive to get clear notions about all. Give up no science entirely, for science is but one.—*Seneca.*

Toil and pleasure, in their natures opposite, are yet linked together in a kind of necessary connection.—*Livy.*

Labor is the ornament of the citizen; the reward of toil is when you confer blessings on others; his high dignity confers honor on the king; be ours the glory of our hands.—*Schiller.*

What is there that is illustrious that is not also attended by labor?—*Cicero.*

All true work is sacred; in all true work, were it but true hand-labor, there is something of divineness. Labor, wide as the earth, has its summit in heaven. Sweat of the brow; and up from that to sweat of the brain; sweat of the heart, which includes all Kepler calculations, Newton meditations, all sciences, all spoken epics, all acted heroisms.—*Carlyle.*

Love labor; for if thou dost not want it for food, thou mayst for physic.—*William Penn.*

Sulky labor and the labor of sorrow are little worth. Whatever a man does with a guilty feeling he is apt to do wrong; and whatever he does with a melancholy feeling he is likely to do by halves. If you could only shed tranquillity over the conscience and infuse joy into the soul, you would do more to make the man a thorough worker than if you could lend him the force of Hercules, or the hundred arms of Briareus.—*Wilberforce.*

The labor we delight in physics pain.— *Shakespeare.*

Thou wilt never be better pleased than when thou hast much to do of such things as thou knowest thyself able to go through with; for business by its motion addeth heat, and a delightful vigor to the spirits; while the unemployed, like standing waters, corrupt with their own idleness.—*Fuller.*

Learning is pleasurable, but doing is the height of enjoyment.—*Novalis.*

There is no doubt of the essential nobility of that man who pours into life the honest vigor of his toil, over those who compose the feathery foam of fashion that sweeps along Broadway; who consider the insignia of honor to consist in wealth and indolence; and who, ignoring the family history, paint coats of arms to cover up the leather aprons of their grandfathers.— *Chapin.*

LANDSCAPE.

However, I think a plain space near the eye gives it a kind of liberty it loves; and then the picture, whether you choose the grand or beautiful, should be held up at its proper distance. Variety is the principal ingredient in beauty; and simplicity is essential to grandeur.— *Shenstone.*

A moss-rose is beautiful because it is bordered; it is a landscape seen through trees. So a view through half-raised window-curtains and distant scenery through a long suite of rooms; so are lights on foregrounds, and shadows on backgrounds, in all pictures.— *Sylvester Judd.*

LANGUAGE.

In the commerce of speech use only coin of gold and silver.—*Joubert.*

Language is the armory of the human mind, and at once contains the trophies of its past, and the weapons of its future conquests.—*Coleridge.*

Language is the dress of thought.—*Johnson.*

Language is the amber in which a thousand precious and subtle thoughts have been safely embedded and preserved. It has arrested ten thousand lightning flashes of genius, which unless fixed and arrested might have been as bright, but would have also been as quickly passing and perishing as the lightning.—*Trench.*

Language is not only the vehicle of thought, it is a great and efficient instrument in thinking.—*Sir H. Davy.*

Decorum of language is the natural expression of honest manners. The decorum of language should be a law of taste, as well as a moral law ; and it is for this reason that decorum should be the most respected among a nation where corruption of manners is carried to the least excess.—*Rœderer.*

Even as a hawk flieth not high with one wing, even so a man reacheth not to excellence with one tongue.—*Roger Ascham.*

Felicity, not fluency, of language is a merit.
Whipple.

It is curious that some learned dunces, because they can write nonsense in languages that are dead, should despise those that talk sense in languages that are living. "To acquire a few tongues," says a French writer, " is the task of a few years, but to be eloquent in one, is the labor of a life."—*Colton.*

The language denotes the man. A coarse or refined character finds its expression naturally in a coarse or refined phraseology.—*Bovee.*

As we go back in history, language becomes more picturesque, until its infancy, when it is all poetry ; or all spiritual facts are represented by natural symbols. The same symbols are found to make the original elements of all languages. It has moreover been observed, that the idioms of all languages approach each other in passages of the greatest eloquence and power.—*Emerson.*

A man who is ignorant of foreign languages is also ignorant of his own language.—*Goethe.*

Language is properly the servant of thought, but not unfrequently becomes its master. The conceptions of a feeble writer are greatly modified by his style ; a man of vigorous powers makes his style bend to his conceptions ; a fact compatible enough with the acknowledgment of Dryden, that a rhyme had often helped him to an idea.—*W. B. Clulow.*

Every man is more able to explain the subject of an art than its professors ; a farmer will tell you in two words that he has broken his leg, but a surgeon, after a long discourse, will leave you as ignorant as you were before.—*Swift.*

LAUGHTER.

A laugh is worth a hundred groans in any market.—*Lamb.*

What was talked of as the golden chain of Jove was nothing but a succession of laughs, a chromatic scale of merriment, reaching from earth to Olympus.—*Douglas Jerrold.*

They laugh that win.—*Shakespeare.*

Laughter is one of the very privileges of reason, being confined to the human species.—
Leigh Hunt.

It is a good thing to laugh, at any rate ; and if a straw can tickle a man, it is an instrument of happiness. Beasts can weep when they suffer, but they cannot laugh.—*Dryden.*

With mirth and laughter let old wrinkles come.—*Shakespeare.*

No man who has once heartily and wholly laughed can be altogether irreclaimably depraved.—*Carlyle.*

Those who laugh at serious propensities love serious trifles.—*Vauvenargues.*

I dare say there has been more by us in some one play laughed into wit and virtue than has been by twenty tedious lectures drawn from sin.—*Randolph.*

Man is the only creature endowed with the power of laughter ; is he not also the only one that deserves to be laughed at ? —*Lord Greville.*

The ludicrous has its place in the universe ; it is not a human invention, but one of the divine ideas, illustrated in the practical jokes of kittens and monkeys long before Aristophanes or Shakespeare.—*Holmes.*

No one is more profoundly sad than he who laughs too much.—*Richter.*

O, glorious laughter ! thou man-loving spirit, that for a time doth take the burden from the weary back, that doth lay salve to the weary feet, bruised and cut by flints and shards.—
Douglas Jerrold.

Laughter is, indeed, akin to weeping ; and true humor is as closely allied to pity as it is abhorrent to derision.—*Henry Giles.*

In a natural state, tears and laughter go hand in hand ; for they are twin-born. Like two children sleeping in one cradle, when one wakes and stirs, the other wakes also.—*Beecher.*

The loud laugh that spoke the vacant mind.
Goldsmith.

It may be remarked in general, that the laugh of men of wit is for the most part but a faint, constrained kind of half-laugh, as such persons are never without some diffidence about them; but that of fools is the most honest, natural, open laugh in the world.—*Steele.*

Men show their character in nothing more clearly than by what they think laughable.
Goethe.

The man who cannot laugh is only fit for treasons, stratagems, and spoils; but his own whole life is already a treason and a stratagem.
Carlyle.

That laughter costs too much which is purchased by the sacrifice of decency.—*Quintilian.*

"He who laughs," said the mother of Goethe, "can commit no deadly sin." The Emperor Titus thought he had lost a day if he had passed it without laughing. Sterne contends that every laugh lengthens the term of our lives. Wisdom, which represents the marriage of truth and virtue, is by no means synonymous with gravity. She is L'Allegro as well as Il Penseroso, and jests as well as preaches.—*Whipple.*

He who always prefaces his tale with laughter is poised between impertinence and folly.
Lavater.

Though laughter is looked upon by the philosophers as the property of reason, the excess of it has been always considered as the mark of folly.—*Addison.*

Laugh if you are wise.—*Martial.*

Genuine and innocent wit is surely the flavor of the mind. Man could not direct his way by plain reason, and support his life by tasteless food; but God has given us wit, and flavor, and brightness, and laughter, and perfumes, to enliven the days of man's pilgrimage, and to charm his pained steps over the burning marl.—*Sydney Smith.*

I am persuaded that every time a man smiles — but much more so when he laughs — it adds something to this fragment of life.—*Sterne.*

If we consider the frequent reliefs we receive from laughter, and how often it breaks the gloom which is apt to depress the mind, one would take care not to grow too wise for so great a pleasure of life.—*Addison.*

Laughing cheerfulness throws the light of day on all the paths of life; the evil fog of gloom hovers in every distance; sorrow is more confusing and distracting than so-called giddiness.—*Richter.*

A laugh to be joyous must flow from a joyous heart, for without kindness there can be no true joy.— *Carlyle.*

Wrinkle not thy face with too much laughter, lest thou become ridiculous; neither wanton thy heart with too much mirth, lest thou become vain: the suburbs of folly is vain mirth, and profuseness of laughter is the city of fools.—
Quarles.

The riotous tumult of a laugh, I take it, is the mob-law of the features, and propriety the magistrate who reads the riot-act.—*Holmes.*

Laughter is a very good counterpoise to the spleen; and it seems but reasonable that we should be capable of receiving joy from what is no real good to us, since we can receive grief from what is no real evil.—*Addison.*

Let materialists blaspheme as gingerly and acutely as they will; they must find confusion in laughter.—*Douglas Jerrold.*

LAW.

Laws are essential emanations from the self-poised character of God; they radiate from the sun to the circling edge of creation. Verily, the mighty Lawgiver hath subjected himself unto laws.—*Tupper.*

A countryman between two lawyers, is like a fish between two cats.—*Franklin.*

These written laws are just like spiders' webs; the small and feeble may be caught and entangled in them, but the rich and mighty force through and despise them.—*Anacharsis.*

A fish hangs in the net, like a poor man's right in the law, it will hardly come out.—
Shakespeare.

So great is the force of laws, and of particular forms of government, and so little dependence have they on the humors and tempers of men, that consequences almost as general and certain may sometimes be deduced from them, as any which the mathematical sciences afford us.—*Hume.*

The English laws punish vice; the Chinese laws do more, they reward virtue.—*Goldsmith.*

In all governments, there must of necessity be both the law and the sword; laws without arms would give us not liberty, but licentiousness; and arms without laws, would produce not subjection, but slavery. The law, therefore, should be unto the sword what the handle is to the hatchet; it should direct the stroke, and temper the force.— *Colton.*

The plaintiff and defendant in an action at law are like two men ducking their heads in a bucket, and daring each other to remain longest under water.—*Johnson.*

19

To seek the redress of grievances by going to law, is like sheep running for shelter to a bramble bush.—*Dilwyn.*

Alas! how many causes that can plead well for themselves in the courts of Westminster, and yet in the general court of the universe, and free soul of man, have no word to utter!— *Carlyle.*

The people's safety is the law of God.— *James Otis.*

The law is the standard and guardian of our liberty; it circumscribes and defends it; but to imagine liberty without a law, is to imagine every man with his sword in his hand to destroy him who is weaker than himself; and that would be no pleasant prospect to those who cry out most for liberty.—*Clarendon.*

Law and equity are two things which God hath joined, but which man hath put asunder.— *Colton.*

As the laws are above magistrates, so are the magistrates above the people; and it may truly be said, that the magistrate is a speaking law, and the law a silent magistrate.—*Cicero.*

A prince who falleth out with laws breaketh with his best friends.—*Saville.*

Laws are generally found to be nets of such a texture, as the little creep through, the great break through, and the middle size are alone entangled in.—*Shenstone.*

Law that shocks equity is reason's murderer.—*Aaron Hill.*

The science of legislation is like that of medicine in one respect,—that it is far more easy to point out what will do harm than what will do good.—*Colton.*

Laws are silent in the midst of arms.— *John Bate.*

Equity judgeth with lenity, laws with extremity. In all moral cases, the reason of the law is the law.—*Walter Scott.*

The laws keep up their credit, not because they are all just, but because they are laws. This is the mystical foundation of their authority, and they have no other.—*Montaigne.*

We are all slaves of the laws, to live free of power at last.—*Cicero.*

Whoever goes to law, goes into a glass house, where he understands little or nothing of what he is doing; where he sees a whole matter blown up into fifty times the size of its intrinsic contents, and through which, if he can perceive any other objects, he perceives them all discolored and distorted.—*Skelton.*

Law is a bottomless pit, it is a cormorant, a harpy that devours everything.—*Arbuthnot.*

The greatest of all injustice is that which goes under the name of law; and of all sorts of tyranny, the forcing the letter of the law against the equity is the most insupportable.— *L'Estrange.*

The law is a pretty bird, and has charming wings. It would be quite a bird of paradise if it did not carry such a terrible bill.— *Douglas Jerrold.*

Laws are not made like lime-twigs or nets, to catch everything that toucheth them; but rather like sea-marks, to guide from shipwreck the ignorant passenger.—*Sir P. Sidney.*

Laws grind the poor, and rich men rule the law.—*Goldsmith.*

The universal and absolute law is that natural justice which cannot be written down, but which appeals to the hearts of all. Written laws are formulas in which we endeavor to express the least imperfectly possible that which, under such or such determined circumstances, natural justice demands.— *Victor Cousin.*

Let us consider the reason of the case. For nothing is law that is not reason.— *Sir John Powell.*

In civil jurisprudence it too often happens that there is so much law, there is no room for justice, and that the claimant expires of wrong, in the midst of right, as mariners die of thirst in the midst of water.—*Colton.*

The character that needs law to mend it, is hardly worth the tinkering.—*Douglas Jerrold.*

Bad laws are the worst sort of tyranny. In such a country as this, they are of all bad things the worst, worse by far than anything else; and they derive a particular malignity even from the wisdom and soundness of the rest of our institutions.—*Burke.*

To make an empire durable, the magistrates must obey the laws, and the people the magistrates.—*Solon.*

A law overcharged with severity, like a blunderbuss overloaded with powder, will each of them grow rusty by disuse, and neither will be resorted to, from the shock and the recoil that must inevitably follow their explosion.— *Colton.*

Let but the public mind once become thoroughly corrupt, and all attempts to secure property, liberty, or life, by mere force of laws written on parchment, will be as vain as to put up printed notices in an orchard to keep off canker-worms.—*Horace Mann.*

When the state is most corrupt, then the laws are most multiplied.—*Tacitus.*

To embarrass justice by multiplicity of laws, or to hazard it by confidence in judges, seems to be the opposite rocks on which all civil institutions have been wrecked, and between which legislative wisdom has never yet found an open passage.—*Johnson.*

The plainest case in many words entangling.—*Joanna Baillie.*

Every instance of a man's suffering the penalty of the law, is an instance of the failure of that penalty in effecting its purpose, which is, to deter.—*Whately.*

Law, man's sole guardian ever since the time when the old Brazen Age, in sadness saw love fly the world!—*Schiller.*

Laws are the sovereigns of sovereigns.— *Louis the Fourteenth.*

We see insurmountable multitudes obeying, in opposition to their strongest passions, the restraints of a power which they scarcely perceive, and the crimes of a single individual marked and punished at the distance of half the earth.—*Sir Thomas Browne.*

Litigious terms, fat contentions, and flowing fees.—*Milton.*

Ignorance of the law excuses no man; not that all men know the law, but because it is an excuse every man will plead, and no man can tell how to confute him.—*Selden.*

Law should be like death, which spares no one.—*Montesquieu.*

To go to law, is for two persons to kindle a fire at their own cost to warm others and singe themselves to cinders; and because they cannot agree as to what is truth and equity, they will both agree to unplume themselves, that others may be decorated with their feathers.—*Feltham.*

Law when kept is nothing else but law; whereas law broken is both law and executioner.—*Menander.*

The law is what we must do; the gospel what God will give.—*Luther.*

Laws, written, if not on stone tables, yet on the azure of infinitude, in the inner heart of God's creation, certain as life, certain as death! I say, the laws are there, and thou shalt not disobey them. It were better for thee not. Better a hundred deaths than yes! Terrible "penalties" withal, if thou still need penalties, are there for disobeying!—*Carlyle.*

We should never create by law what can be accomplished by morality.—*Montesquieu.*

As the law dissolves all contracts without a valuable consideration,—a valuable consideration often dissolves the law.—*Fielding.*

As to lawyers,—their profession is supported by the indiscriminate defence of right and wrong.—*Junius.*

We must not make a scarecrow of the law, setting it up to fear the birds of prey, and let it keep one shape, till custom make it their perch, and not their terror.—*Shakespeare.*

Strict laws are like steel bodice, good for growing limbs; but when the joints are knit they are not helps but burdens.— *Sir Francis Fane.*

Laws are the silent assessors of God.— *W. R. Alger.*

Use law and physic only for necessity; they that use them otherwise abuse themselves into weak bodies, and light purses; they are good remedies, bad businesses, and worse recreations.—*Quarles.*

A multitude of laws in a country is like a great number of physicians, a sign of weakness and malady.—*Voltaire.*

The law is a sort of hocus-pocus science, that smiles in your face while it picks your pocket; and the glorious uncertainty of it is of more use to the professors than the justice of it.—*Charles Macklin.*

They are the best laws, by which the king hath the greatest prerogative, and the people the best liberty.—*Bacon.*

Of law there can be no less acknowledged than that her seat is the bosom of God, her voice the harmony of the world. All things in heaven and earth do her homage; the very least, as feeling her care, and the greatest, as not exempt from her power; both angels and men, and creatures of what condition soever, though each in different sort and manner, yet all with uniform consent admiring her as the mother of peace and joy.—*Hooker.*

As diseases must necessarily be known before their remedies, so passions come into being before the laws which prescribe limits to them.— *Livy.*

Reason is the life of the law; nay, the common law itself is nothing else but reason.— *Coke.*

Where nothing is certain but the expense.— *Samuel Butler.*

It is impossible for men so much as to murder each other without statutes and maxims, and an idea of justice and honor. War has its laws as well as peace.—*Hume.*

No man knows any one except himself, whom he judges fit to be set free from the coercion of laws, and to be abandoned entirely to his own choice. By this consideration have all civilized nations been induced to the enaction of penal laws; laws by which every man's danger becomes every man's safety, and by which, though all are restrained, yet all are benefited.

Johnson.

The law is past depth to those that, without heed, do plunge into it.—*Shakespeare.*

LEARNING.

Learning is not to be tacked to the mind, but we must fuse and blend them together, not merely giving the mind a slight tincture, but a thorough and perfect dye. And if we perceive no evident change and improvement, it would be better to leave it alone; learning is a dangerous weapon, and apt to wound its master if it be wielded by a feeble hand, and by one not well acquainted with its use.—*Montaigne.*

Learning passes for wisdom among those who want both.—*Sir W. Temple.*

Learning, like money, may be of so base a coin, as to be utterly void of use; or, if sterling, may require good management, to make it serve the purpose of sense or happiness.—
Shenstone.

Learning is like mercury, one of the most powerful and excellent things in the world in skilful hands; in unskilful, the most mischievous.—*Pope.*

The end of learning is to know God, and out of that knowledge to love him, and to imitate him, as we may the nearest, by possessing our souls of true virtue.—*Milton.*

Learning once made popular is no longer learning; it has the appearance of something which we have bestowed upon ourselves, as the dew appears to rise from the field which it refreshes.—*Johnson.*

And it is without all controversy, that learning doth make the mind of men gentle, generous, amiable, and pliant to government; whereas ignorance makes them churlish, thwarting, and mutinous; and the evidence of time doth clear this assertion, considering that the most barbarous, rude, and unlearned times have been most subject to tumults, seditions, and changes.
Bacon.

He who learns and makes no use of his learning, is a beast of burden, with a load of books. Comprehendeth the ass whether he carries on his back a library or a bundle of fagots?
Saadi.

The learning and knowledge that we have is at the most but little compared with that of which we are ignorant.—*Plato.*

The most learned are often the most narrow minded men.—*Hazlitt.*

No man is the wiser for his learning: it may administer matter to work in, or objects to work upon; but wit and wisdom are born with a man.—*Selden.*

He that wants good sense is unhappy in having learning, for he has thereby only more ways of exposing himself; and he that has sense knows that learning is not knowledge, but rather the art of using it.—*Steele.*

Learning puffeth men up: words are but wind and learning is nothing but words; *ergo,* learning is nothing but wind.—*Swift.*

Your learning, like the lunar beam, affords light, but not heat; it leaves you undevout, frozen at heart, while speculation shines.—
Young.

Many persons after once they become learned, cease to be good: all other knowledge is hurtful to him who has not the science of honesty and good-nature.—*Montaigne.*

Learning teaches how to carry things in suspense without prejudice till you resolve.—
Bacon.

He that knoweth not that which he ought to know is a brute beast among men; he that knoweth no more than he hath need of is a man amongst brute beasts; and he that knoweth all that may be known is as a god amongst men.—*Pythagoras.*

The Chinese, whom it might be well to disparage less and imitate more, seem almost the only people among whom learning and merit have the ascendency, and wealth is not the standard of estimation.—*W. B. Clulow.*

Wear your learning, like your watch, in a private pocket; and do not pull it out and strike it, merely to show that you have one. If you are asked what o'clock it is, tell it, but do not proclaim it hourly and unasked, like the watchman.—*Chesterfield.*

"A little learning is a dangerous thing," and yet it is what all must attain before they can arrive at great learning; it is the utmost acquisition of those who know the most, in comparison of what they do not know. The field of science may be compared to an American forest in which the more trees a man cuts down, the greater is the expanse of wood he sees around him.—*Whately.*

The sweetest and most inoffensive path of life leads through the avenues of science and learning; and whoever can either remove any obstruction in this way, or open up any new prospect, ought so far, to be esteemed a benefactor to mankind.—*Hume.*

There is in some tempers such a natural barrenness, that, like the sands of Arabia, they are never to be cultivated and improved. And some will never learn anything because they understand everything too soon.—*Sir T. P. Blount.*

The great art to learn much is to undertake a little at a time.—*Locke.*

Learning gives us a fuller conviction of the imperfections of our nature; which one would think, might dispose us to modesty: for the more a man knows, the more he discovers his ignorance.—*Jeremy Collier.*

Till a man can judge whether they be truths or no, his understanding is but little improved; and thus men of much reading are greatly learned, but may be little knowing.—*Locke.*

Learning hath its infancy, when it is almost childish; then its youth, when luxurious and juvenile; then its strength of years, when solid; and lastly its old age, when dry and exhaust.—*Bacon.*

Mere learning is only a compiler, and manages the pen as the compositor picks out the type—each sets up a book with the hand. Stone-masons collected the dome of St. Paul's, but Wren hung it in air.— *Willmott.*

Learning, ye wise fathers, and good bringingup, and not blind and dangerous experience, is the readiest way that must lead your children, first to wisdom, and then to worthiness, if ever ye propose they shall come there.— *Roger Ascham.*

We should ask not who is the most learned, but who is the best learned.—*Montaigne.*

LEISURE.
Leisure is time for doing something useful; this leisure the diligent man will obtain, but the lazy man never; so that, as poor Richard says, a life of leisure and a life of laziness are two things.—*Franklin.*

There is room enough in human life to crowd almost every art and science in it. If we pass "no day without a line,"— visit no place without the company of a book, — we may with ease fill libraries, or empty them of their contents.—*Hazlitt.*

Leisure is pain; takes off our chariot wheels; how heavily we drag the load of life.— *Young.*

Leisure and solitude are the best effect of riches, because the mother of thought. Both are avoided by most rich men, who seek company and business, which are signs of being weary of themselves.—*Sir W. Temple.*

Remove but the temptations of leisure, and the bow of Cupid will lose its effect.—*Ovid.*

Leisure, the highest happiness upon earth, is seldom enjoyed with perfect satisfaction, except in solitude. Indolence and indifference do not always afford leisure; for true leisure is frequently found in that interval of relaxation which divides a painful duty from an agreeable recreation; a toilsome business from the more agreeable occupations of literature and philosophy.—*Zimmermann.*

I pant beyond expression for two days of absolute and unbroken leisure. If it were not for my love of beautiful nature and poetry, my heart would have died within me long ago.— *Lord Jeffrey.*

LENDING.
And whatever you lend, let it be your money, and not your name. Money you may get again, and, if not, you may contrive to do without it; name once lost you cannot get again, and, if you can contrive to do without it, you had better never have been born.— *Bulwer Lytton.*

Loan oft loses both itself and friend.— *Shakespeare.*

Lend not beyond thy ability, nor refuse to lend out of thy ability; especially when it will help others more than it can hurt thee. If thy debtor be honest and capable, thou hast thy money again, if not with increase, with praise. If he prove insolvent, do not ruin him to get that which it will not ruin thee to lose; for thou art but a steward, and another is thy owner, master, and judge.— *William Penn.*

LENITY.
Lenity is a part of justice; but she must not speak too loud for fear of waking justice.— *Joubert.*

Lenity will operate with greater force, in some instances, than rigor. It is, therefore, my first wish to have my whole conduct distinguished by it.— *Washington.*

Lenity has almost always wisdom and justice on its side.—*Hosea Ballou.*

LETTERS.
The best time to frame an answer to the letters of a friend is the moment you receive them. Then the warmth of friendship, and the intelligence received most forcibly co-operate.— *Shenstone.*

Letters which are warmly sealed are often but coldly opened.—*Richter.*

A profusion of fancies and quotations is out of place in a love-letter. True feeling is always direct, and never deviates into by-ways to cull flowers of rhetoric.—*Bovee.*

In a heavy oppressive atmosphere, when the spirits sink too low, the best cordial is to read over all the letters of one's friends.—*Shenstone.*

Let your letter be written as accurately as you are able, — I mean with regard to language, grammar, and stops; for as to the matter of it the less trouble you give yourself the better it will be. Letters should be easy and natural, and convey to the persons to whom we send them just what we should say to the persons if we were with them.—*Chesterfield.*

The true character of epistolary style is playfulness and urbanity.—*Joubert.*

Perhaps there is no greater test of a man's regularity and easiness of conscience than his readiness to face the postman. Blessed is he who is made happy by the sound of a rat-tat! The good are eager for it; but the naughty tremble at the sound thereof.—*Thackeray.*

To write a good love-letter, you ought to begin without knowing what you mean to say, and to finish without knowing what you have written.—*Rousseau.*

Here are a few of the unpleasantest words that ever blotted paper! —*Shakespeare.*

LEVITY.

In infants, levity is a prettiness; in men a shameful defect; but in old age, a monstrous folly.—*Rochefoucauld.*

The lively and mercurial are as open books, with the leaves turned down at the notable passages. Their souls sit at the windows of their eyes, seeing and to be seen.—*Bovee.*

There is always some levity even in excellent minds; they have wings to rise, and also to stray.—*Joubert.*

Levity of behavior is the bane of all that is good and virtuous.—*Seneca.*

LIBERALITY.

· He that defers his charity until he is dead is, if a man weighs it rightly, rather liberal of another man's goods than his own.—*Bacon.*

Liberality consists less in giving much than in giving with discretion.—*Du Cœur.*

Frugality is good, if liberality be joined with it. The first is leaving off superfluous expenses; the last bestowing them to the benefit of others that need. The first without the last begins covetousness; the last without the first begins prodigality. Both together make an excellent temper. Happy the place where that is found.—*William Penn.*

What we call liberality is seldom more than the vanity of giving; we are fonder of the vanity than the generosity of the action.—
Rochefoucauld.

Be rather bountiful, than expensive.—
William Penn.

Liberality consists rather in giving seasonably than much.—*Bruyère.*

Liberality is the best way to gain affection; for we are assured of their friendship to whom we are obliged.—*St. Evremond.*

No communications can exhaust genius, no gifts impoverish charity.—*Lavater.*

There is no brilliancy in silver when hidden in the earth, Crispus Sallustius, thou foe to money, if it does not throw lustre around by moderate use.—*Horace.*

Gold that is put to use more gold begets.—
Shakespeare.

There is that scattereth, and yet increaseth; and there is that withholdeth more than is meet, but it tendeth to poverty. The liberal soul shall be made fat, and he that watereth shall be watered also himself. He that hath pity on the poor, lendeth to the Lord; and that which he hath given will he pay him again.—*Bible.*

Liberality should be tempered with judgment, not with profuseness.—*Hosea Ballou.*

In defiance of all the torture, of all the might, of all the malice of the world, the liberal man will ever be rich; for God's providence is his estate, God's wisdom and power are his defence, God's love and favor are his reward, and God's word is his security.—
Barrow.

The liberality of some men is but indifference clad in the garb of candor.— *Whately.*

LIBERTY.

Give me the centralism of liberty; give me the imperialism of equal rights.—
Charles Sumner.

Liberty is to the collective body, what health is to every individual body. Without health no pleasure can be tasted by man; without liberty, no happiness can be enjoyed by society.—
Bolingbroke.

If liberty with law is fire on the hearth, liberty without law is fire on the floor.—*Hillard.*

The only rational liberty is that which is born of subjection, reared in fear of God and love of man, and made courageous in the defence of a trust, and the prosecution of a duty.—
Simms.

O Liberty! Liberty! how many crimes are committed in thy name.—*Madame Roland.*

Reason and virtue alone can bestow liberty.—
Shaftesbury.

Liberty is a principle; its community is its security, — exclusiveness is its doom.—*Kossuth.*

The only liberty that is valuable is a liberty connected with order; that not only exists along with order and virtue, but which cannot exist at all without them. It inheres in good and steady government, as in its substance and vital principle.—*Burke.*

As liberty is not a fruit of all climates, it is not within the reach of all people.—*Rousseau.*

The spirit of liberty is not merely, as multitudes imagine, a jealousy of our own particular rights, but a respect for the rights of others, and an unwillingness that any man, whether high or low, should be wronged and trampled under foot.—*Channing.*

The human race is in the best condition, when it has the greatest degree of liberty.—*Dante.*

Liberty, that best gift, dealt out by the impartial hand of nature, even to the brute creation.—*Tacitus.*

Is life so dear, or peace so sweet, as to be purchased at the price of chains and slavery? Forbid it, Almighty God! I know not what course others may take; but, as for me, give me liberty, or give me death!—*Patrick Henry.*

Personal liberty is the paramount essential to human dignity and human happiness.—*Bulwer Lytton.*

What is life? it is not to stalk about and draw fresh air, or gaze upon the sun. It is to be free.—*Addison.*

We hold these truths to be self-evident: that all men are created equal; that they are endowed by their Creator with inalienable rights: that among these are life, liberty, and the pursuit of happiness.—*Thomas Jefferson.*

Diogenes has well said, that the only way to preserve his liberty was being always ready to die without pain.—*Goethe.*

Liberty knows nothing but victories. Soldiers call Bunker Hill a defeat; but liberty dates from it though Warren lay dead on the field.—*Wendell Phillips.*

Liberty consists in the power of doing that which is permitted by the law.—*Cicero.*

Liberty will not descend to a people, a people must raise themselves to liberty; it is a blessing that must be earned before it can be enjoyed. That nation cannot be free, where reform is a common hack, that is dismissed with a kick the moment it has brought the rider to his place.—*Colton.*

Give me the liberty to know, to think, to believe, and to utter freely, according to conscience, above all other liberties.—*Milton.*

The most culpable of the excesses of liberty is the harm she does herself.—*Madame Swetchine.*

Liberty is an old fact. It has had its heroes and its martyrs in almost every age. As I look back through the vista of centuries, I can see no end of the ranks of those who have toiled and suffered in its cause, and who wear upon their breasts its stars of the legion of honor.—*Chapin.*

O, give me liberty! for even were paradise my prison, still I should long to leap the crystal walls.—*Dryden.*

The tree of liberty only grows when watered by the blood of tyrants.—*Bertrand Barère.*

Liberty is one of the most precious gifts which heaven has bestowed on man; with it we cannot compare the treasures which the earth contains or the sea conceals; for liberty, as for honor, we can and ought to risk our lives; and, on the other hand, captivity is the greatest evil that can befall man.—*Cervantes.*

Liberty has no actual rights which are not grafted upon justice. Her principal duty is to defend it.—*Madame Swetchine.*

What is so beneficial to the people as liberty, which we see not only to be greedily sought after by men, but also by beasts, and to be preferred to all things.—*Cicero.*

A bird in a cage is not half a bird.—*Beecher.*

True liberty consists in the privilege of enjoying our own rights, not in the destruction of the rights of others.—*Pinckard.*

Liberty must be a mighty thing; for by it God punishes and rewards nations.—*Madame Swetchine.*

Liberty is not idleness, it is an unconstrained use of time; it is the choice of work and of exercise. To be free, in a word, is not to be doing nothing, it is to be one's own master as to what one ought to do or not to do. What a blessing in this sense is liberty!—*Bruyère.*

The fruition of liberty is not so pleasing, as a conceit of the want of it is irksome.—*Howell.*

Easier were it to hurl the rooted mountain from its base than force the yoke of slavery upon men determined to be free.—*Southey.*

All men love Liberty and seem bent on destroying her.—*Voltaire.*

Free people, remember this maxim: We may acquire liberty, but it is never recovered if it is once lost.—*Rousseau.*

Liberty and Union, now and forever, one and inseparable.—*Daniel Webster.*

The liberty of a people consists in being governed by laws which they have made themselves, under whatsoever form it be of government; the liberty of a private man, in being master of his own time and actions, as far as may consist with the laws of God, and of his country.—
Cowley.

Liberty, when it begins to take root, is a plant of rapid growth.—*Washington.*

LIBRARY.

Libraries are the wardrobes of literature, whence men, properly informed, might bring forth something for ornament, much for curiosity, and more for use.—*James Dyer.*

Consider what you have in the smallest chosen library. A company of the wisest and wittiest men that could be picked out of all civil countries, in a thousand years, have set in best order the results of their learning and wisdom. The men themselves were hid and inaccessible, solitary, impatient of interruption, fenced by etiquette; but the thought which they did not uncover to their bosom friend is here written out in transparent words to us, the strangers of another age.—*Emerson.*

A library is but the soul's burial-ground. It is the land of shadows.—*Beecher.*

What laborious days, what watchings by the midnight lamp, what rackings of the brain, what hopes and fears, what long lives of laborious study, are here sublimized into print, and condensed into the narrow compass of these surrounding shelves!—*Horace Smith.*

Great collections of books are subject to certain accidents besides the damp, the worms, and the rats; one not less common is that of the borrowers, not to say a word of the purloiners!
Disraeli.

My library was dukedom large enough.—
Shakespeare.

The gloomy recess of an ecclesiastical library is like a harbor, into which a far-travelling curiosity has sailed with its freight, and cast anchor. The ponderous tomes are bales of the mind's merchandise. Odors of distant countries and times steal from the red leaves, the swelling ridges of vellum, and the titles in tarnished gold.—*Willmott.*

Libraries are as the shrines where all the relics of saints full of true virtue, and that without delusion or imposture, are preserved and reposed.—*Bacon*

LICENSE.

A popular license, is indeed the many-headed tyrant.—*Sir P. Sidney.*

For there is no air that men so greedily draw in, that diffuses itself so soon, and that penetrates so deep as that of license.—
Montaigne.

LICENTIOUSNESS.

The freedom of some is the freedom of the herd of swine that ran violently down a steep place into the sea and were drowned.—
Rev. W. Jay.

Headstrong liberty is lashed with woe.—
Shakespeare.

Human brutes, like other beasts, find snares and poison in the provisions of life, and are allured by their appetites to their destruction.—
Swift.

LIFE.

Each thing lives according to its kind; the heart by love, the intellect by truth, the higher nature of man by intimate communion with God.—*Chapin.*

He is but the counterfeit of a man, who hath not the life of a man.—*Shakespeare.*

Life in itself is neither good nor evil, it is the scene of good or evil, as you make it; and, if you have lived a day, you have seen all; one day is equal, and like to all other days; there is no other light, no other shade, this very sun, this moon, these very stars, this very order and revolution of things, is the same your ancestors enjoyed, and that shall also entertain your posterity.—*Montaigne.*

We always live prospectively, never retrospectively, and there is no abiding moment.—
Jacobi.

It is impossible to live pleasurably without living prudently, and honorably, and justly; or to live prudently, and honorably, and justly without living pleasurably.—*Epicurus.*

And he that lives to live forever never fears dying.—*William Penn.*

Was there ever a long, happy day, I wonder, even though it fell at midsummer? Did not the sun hurry on his way, and set at noon, just as the tide of our happiness was rising highest? Are not twelve hours of bliss distilled into minutes? and when the moment of parting comes, does it not seem as if we had but that instant clasped hands in joyous greeting?—
F. G. Trafford.

It matters not how a man dies, but how he lives.—*Johnson.*

Oft in my way have I stood still, though but a casual passenger, so much I felt the awfulness of life.—*Wordsworth.*

Life is a malady in which sleep soothes us every sixteen hours; it is a palliation; death is the remedy.—*Chamfort.*

We live in deeds, not years; in thoughts, not breaths; in feelings, not in figures on a dial. We should count time by heart-throbs. He most lives who thinks most, feels the noblest, acts the best.—*Bailey.*

The life of man is summed in birthdays and in sepulchres.—*H. K. White.*

Let us make haste to live, since every day to a wise man is a new life; for he has done his business the day before, and so prepared himself for the next, that if it be not his last, he knows yet that it might have been so. No man enjoys the true taste of life, but he who is willing and ready to quit it.—*Seneca.*

Life is the art of being well deceived.—*Hazlitt.*

There appears to exist a greater desire to live long than to live well! Measure by man's desires, he cannot live long enough; measure by his good deeds, and he has not lived long enough; measure by his evil deeds, and he has lived too long.—*Zimmermann.*

The great error is, placing such an estimate on this life, as if our being depended on it, and we were nothing after death.—*Rousseau*

He that embarks in the voyage of life will always wish to advance, rather by the impulse of the wind than the strokes of the oar; and many founder in their passage, while they lie waiting for the gale.—*Johnson.*

O God! how lovely still is life!—*Schiller.*

Our brains are seventy-year clocks. The angel of life winds them up at once for all, then closes the cases, and gives the key into the hand of the angel of resurrection. " Tic-tac, tic-tac ! " go the wheels of thought; our will cannot stop them; madness only makes them go faster. Death alone can break into the case, and, seizing the ever-swinging pendulum which we call the heart, silence at last the clicking of the terrible escapement we have carried so long beneath our aching foreheads.—*Holmes.*

That man lives twice that lives the first life well.—*Herrick.*

This world is not a platform where you will hear Thalberg-piano-playing. It is a piano manufactory, where are dust and shavings and boards, and saws and files and rasps and sandpapers. The perfect instrument and the music will be hereafter.—*Beecher.*

Life, however short, is made still shorter by waste of time.—*Johnson.*

Life, as we call it, is nothing but the edge of the boundless ocean of existence where it comes upon soundings.—*Holmes.*

Life, whether in this world or any other, is the sum of our attainment, our experience, our character. The conditions are secondary. In what other world shall we *be* more surely than we are here ? —*Chapin.*

We live mortal lives for immortal good. And really this world is so mysterious, that there is not one of its commonest ways but is perhaps sublimer to walk on than we at all think.—*Mountford.*

What is our life but an endless flight of winged facts or events ? —*Emerson.*

Life everywhere! The air is crowded with birds, — beautiful, tender, intelligent birds, to whom life is a song and a thrilling anxiety, the anxiety of love. The air is swarming with insects — those little animated miracles. The waters are peopled with innumerable forms, from the animalcule, so that one hundred and fifty millions of them would not weigh a grain, to the whale, so large that it seems an island as it sleeps upon the waves.—*G. A. Sala.*

If we begin to die when we live, and long life be but a prolongation of death, our life is a sad composition ; we live with death, and die not in a moment.—*Sir Thomas Browne.*

The line of life is a ragged diagonal between duty and desire.—*W. R. Alger.*

That life is long which answers life's great end ; the time that bears no fruit deserves no name; the man of wisdom is the man of years. *Young.*

Life, like a dome of many-colored glass, stains the white radiance of eternity.—*Shelley.*

Life is sweet as nitrous oxide; and the fisherman dripping all day over a cold pond, the switchman at the railway intersection, the farmer in the field, the negro in the rice-swamp, the fop in the street, the hunter in the woods, the barrister with the jury, the belle at the ball, all ascribe a certain pleasure to their employment, which they themselves give it.—*Emerson.*

Life is a dream and death an awakening.—*Beaumelle.*

Life is a crucible. We are thrown into it, and tried. The actual weight and value of a man are expressed in the spiritual substance of the man. All else is dross.—*Chapin.*

Live virtuously, my lord, and you cannot die too soon, nor live too long.—*Lady Rachel Russell.*

The fraction of life can be increased in value not so much by increasing your numerator as by lessening your denominator. Nay, unless my Algebra deceives me, unity itself divided by zero will give infinity.—*Carlyle.*

A minute analysis of life at once destroys that splendor which dazzles the imagination. Whatsoever grandeur can display, or luxury enjoy, is procured by offices of which the mind shrinks from the contemplation. All the delicacies of the table may be traced back to the shambles and the dunghill ; all magnificence of building was hewn from the quarry, and all the pomp of ornament dug from among the damps and darkness of the mine.—*Johnson.*

Life is a shuttle.—*Shakespeare.*

In my opinion, he only may be truly said to live, and enjoy his being, who is engaged in some laudable pursuit, and acquires a name by some illustrious action or useful art.—*Sallust.*

Life, when hospitably taken, is a simple affair. Very little suffices to enrich us. Being, a fountain and fireside, a web of cloth, a garden, a few friends, and good books, a chosen task, health and peace of mind, — these are a competent estate, embracing all we need.—*Alcott.*

Life has been compared to a race ; but the allusion still improves by observing that the most swift are ever the most apt to stray from the course.—*Goldsmith.*

Man's life is an appendix to his heart.— *South.*

To live is not merely to breathe, it is to act ; it is to make use of our organs, senses, faculties, of all those parts of ourselves which give us the feeling of existence. The man who has lived longest is not the man who has counted most years, but he who has enjoyed life most. Such a one was buried a hundred years old, but he was dead from his birth. He would have gained by dying young ; at least he would have lived till that time.—*Rousseau.*

To live long, it is necessary to live slowly.— *Cicero.*

For we are but of yesterday, and know nothing, because our days upon earth are a shadow.—*Bible.*

They who are most weary of life, and yet are most unwilling to die, are such who have lived to no purpose, — who have rather breathed than lived.—*Clarendon.*

Life itself is a bubble and a scepticism, and a sleep within a sleep.—*Emerson.*

As it is the chief concern of wise men to retrench the evils of life by the reasonings of philosophy, it is the employment of fools to multiply them by the sentiments of superstition. *Addison.*

A wide, rich heaven hangs above you, but it hangs high. A wide, rough world is around you, and it lies very low.—*D. G. Mitchell.*

The woof of life is dark, but it is shot with a warp of gold.—*F. W. Robertson.*

What is this life but a circulation of little mean actions ? We lie down and rise again, dress and undress, feed and grow hungry, work or play, and are weary ; and then we lie down again and the circle returns.—*Bishop Burnet.*

Life went a-maying with nature, hope, and poesy, when I was young.—*Coleridge.*

Life consists not of a series of illustrious actions or elegant enjoyments. The greater part of our time passes in compliance with necessities, in the performance of daily duties, in the removal of small inconveniences, in the procurement of petty pleasures ; and we are well or ill at ease, as the main stream of life glides on smoothly, or is ruffled by small obstacles and frequent interruption.—*Johnson.*

Life is real, life is earnest.—*Longfellow.*

Life at the greatest and best is but a forward child, that must be humored and coaxed a little till it falls asleep, and then all the care is over. *Goldsmith.*

Life is as the current spark on the miner's wheel of flints ; while it spinneth there is light; stop it, all is darkness.—*Tupper.*

The laugh of mirth that vibrates through the heart ; the tears that freshen the dry wastes within ; the music that brings childhood back ; the prayer that calls the future near ; the doubt which makes us meditate ; the death which startles us with mystery ; the hardship which forces us to struggle ; the anxiety that ends in trust ; are the true nourishment of our natural being.—*James Martineau.*

To make good use of life, one should have in youth the experience of advanced years, and in old age the vigor of youth.—*Stanislaus.*

With most men life is like backgammon, half skill and half luck.—*Holmes.*

The nearest approximation to an understanding of life is to feel it — to realize it to the full — to be a profound and inscrutable mystery.—*Bovee.*

Such is the condition of life, that something is always wanting to happiness. In youth we have warm hopes, which are soon blasted by rashness and negligence ; and great designs, which are defeated by inexperience. In age, we have knowledge and prudence, without spirit to exert, or motives to prompt them.—*Johnson.*

A man is thirty years old before he has any settled thoughts of his fortune ; it is not completed before fifty, he falls a building in his old age, and dies by the time his house is in a condition to be painted and glazed.—*Bruyère.*

They only have lived long who have lived virtuously.—*Sheridan.*

Beneath me flows the Rhine, and, like the stream of time, it flows amid the ruins of the past. I see myself therein, and know that I am old. Thou, too, shalt be old. Be wise in season. Like the stream of thy life runs the stream beneath us. Down from the distant Alps, out into the wide world, it bursts away, like a youth from the house of his fathers. Broad-breasted and strong, and with earnest endeavors, like manhood, it makes itself a way through these difficult mountain-passes. And at length in old age, it falters, and its steps are weary and slow, and it sinks into the sand, and through its grave passes into the great ocean, which is its eternity.—*Longfellow.*

Life is not intellectual or critical, but sturdy. Its chief good is for well-mixed people who can enjoy what they find without question.— *Emerson.*

Life is a comedy to him who thinks and a tragedy to him who feels.—*Horace Walpole.*

If this life is unhappy, it is a burden to us, which it is difficult to bear; if it is in every respect happy, it is dreadful to be deprived of it; so that in either case the result is the same, for we must exist in anxiety and apprehension.—*Bruyère.*

How sour sweet music is, when time is broke, and no proportion kept! So is it in the music of men's lives.—*Shakespeare.*

The truest end of life is to know the life that never ends.— *William Penn.*

Life is too much for most. So much of age, so little of youth; living for the most part in the moment, and dating existence by the memory of its burdens.—*Alcott.*

Human life is everywhere a state in which much is to be endured, and little enjoyed.— *Johnson.*

There is no fooling with life, when it is once turned beyond forty; the seeking of a fortune then is but a desperate after-game; it is a hundred to one if a man fling two sixes, and recover all; especially if his hand be no luckier than mine.—*Cowley.*

Life, like the water of the seas, freshens only when it ascends towards heaven.—*Richter.*

O, that I less could fear to lose this being, which like a snowball in my coward hand, the more it is grasped, the faster melts away!— *Dryden.*

Life is rather a state of embryo, a preparation for life; a man is not completely born till he has passed through death.—*Franklin.*

Life is short — while we speak it flies; enjoy, then, the present, and forget the future; such is the moral of ancient poetry, a graceful and a wise moral, — indulged beneath a southern sky, and all deserving the phrase applied to it, — " the philosophy of the garden."—*Bulwer Lytton.*

As sad dreams betoken a glad future, so may it be with the so often tormenting dream of life when it is over.—*Richter.*

We should live as though our life would be both long and short.—*Bias.*

It is not perhaps much thought of, but it is certainly a very important lesson, to learn how to enjoy ordinary life, and to be able to relish your being without the transport of some passion, or gratification of some appetite.—*Steele.*

Live as long as you may, the first twenty years are the longest half of your life.—*Southey.*

Art is long, life short, judgment difficult, opportunity fleeting. To act is easy, to think is difficult; to act according to our thoughts is troublesome. Every beginning is agreeable; the threshold is the place of expectation. The boy is astonished, his impressions guide him, he learns as he plays, earnestness comes on him by surprise. Imitation is born with us, but what we ought to imitate is not easily discovered. The excellent is seldom found, more seldom prized.—*Goethe.*

This span of life was lent for lofty duties, not for selfishness; not to be wiled away for aimless dreams, but to improve ourselves, and serve mankind.—*Sir Aubrey de Vere.*

Making their lives a prayer.—*Whittier.*

So much are men enamored of their miserable lives, that there is no condition so wretched to which they are not willing to submit, provided they may live.—*Montaigne.*

Life is as tedious as a twicetold tale, vexing the dull ear of a drowsy man.—*Shakespeare.*

What is life? A gulf of troubled waters, where the soul, like a vexed bark, is tossed upon the waves of pain and pleasure by the wavering breath of passions.—*Miss L. E. Landon.*

I am convinced the world will get tired, at least, I hope so, of this eternal guffaw about all things. After all, life has something serious in it. It cannot be all comic history of humanity. *Douglas Jerrold.*

No man takes care to live well, but long, when yet it is in everybody's power to do the former, and in no man's to do the latter. We consume our lives in providing the very instruments of life and govern ourselves still with a regard to the future, so that we do not properly live, but are about to live.—*Seneca.*

We talk of human life as a journey, but how variously is that journey performed! There are those who come forth girt, and shod, and mantled, to walk on velvet lawns and smooth terraces, where every gale is arrested and every beam is tempered. There are others who walk on the Alpine paths of life, against driving misery, and through stormy sorrows, over sharp afflictions; walk with bare feet and naked breast, jaded, mangled, and chilled.—
Sydney Smith.

We are such stuff as dreams are made of, and our little life is rounded with a sleep.—
Shakespeare.

The end of life is to be like unto God; and the soul following God, will be like unto him; He being the beginning, middle, and end of all things.—*Socrates.*

Life's harvest reap like the wheat's fruitful ear.—*Mrs. Jameson.*

Plunge boldly into the thick of life! each lives it, not to many is it known; and seize it where you will, it is interesting.—*Goethe.*

The secret of prolonging life is not to abridge it.—*Henry Giles.*

No man can promise himself even fifty years of life, but any man may, if he please, live in the proportion of fifty years in forty,—let him rise early, that he may have the day before him, and let him make the most of the day, by determining to expend it on two sorts of acquaintance only,—those by whom something may be got, and those from whom something may be learned.—*Colton.*

There is nothing of which men are so fond and withal so careless as life.—*Bruyère.*

Think of "living"! Thy life, wert thou the "pitifullest of all the sons of earth," is no idle dream, but a solemn reality. It is thy own; it is all thou hast to front eternity with. Work, then, even as he has done, and does, "like a star, unhasting, yet unresting."—*Carlyle.*

Yet through all, we know this tangled skein is in the hands of One who sees the end from the beginning; he shall yet unravel all.—
Alexander Smith.

Life, like some cities, is full of blind alleys, leading nowhere; the great art is to keep out of them.—*Bovee.*

O, how full of briers is this working-day world!—*Shakespeare.*

He lives long that lives well; and time misspent, is not lived, but lost. Besides, God is better than his promise if he takes from him a long lease, and gives him a freehold of a better value.—*Fuller.*

So much of our time is preparation, so much is routine, and so much retrospect, that the pith of each man's genius contracts itself to a very few hours.—*Emerson.*

Though we seem grieved at the shortness of life in general, we are wishing every period of it at an end. The minor longs to be at age, then to be a man of business, then to make up an estate, then to arrive at honors, then to retire.—*Addison.*

While we are reasoning concerning life, life is gone.—*Hume.*

The web of our life is of a mingled yarn, good and ill together; our virtues would be proud, if our faults whipped them not; and our crimes would despair, if they were not cherished by our virtues.—*Shakespeare.*

We hold not to the prosperity of the wicked and the misfortunes of the just; for life is a book where the *errata* are at the end.—
J. Petit, Senn.

Life is short, if it merits that name only when it is agreeable; since, if we reckoned together all our happy years, we should with difficulty make a life of some months out of a great number of years.—*Diderot.*

All die who have lived; all have not lived who die!—*Zimmermann.*

How mysterious is this human life, with all its diversities of contrast and compensation; this web of checkered destinies; this sphere of manifold allotment, where man lives in his greatness and grossness, a little lower than the angels, a little higher than the brutes.—
Henry Giles.

Man spends his life in reasoning on the past, complaining of the present, and trembling for the future.—*Rivarol.*

Life is but a walking shadow; a poor player, that struts and frets his hour upon the stage, and then is heard no more; it is a tale told by an idiot, full of sound and fury, signifying nothing.—*Shakespeare.*

Life is like wine; he who would drink it pure must not drain it to the dregs.—
Sir W. Temple.

The true harvest of my daily life is somewhat as intangible and indescribable as the tints of morning or evening. It is a little star-dust caught, a segment of the rainbow which I have clutched.—*Thoreau.*

Life is made up, not of great sacrifices or duties, but of little things, in which smiles and kindness, and small obligations given habitually, are what win and preserve the heart and secure comfort.—*Sir H. Davy.*

If life, like the olive, is a bitter fruit, then grasp both with the press and they will afford the sweetest oil.—*Richter.*

We paint our lives in fresco. The soft and fusile plaster of the moment hardens under every stroke of the brush into eternal rock.— *Sterling.*

On what strange grounds we build our hopes and fears! Man's life is all a mist, and in the dark our fortunes meet us.—*Dryden.*

The great art of life is to play for much, and stake little.—*Johnson.*

The date of human life is too short to recompense the cares which attend the most private condition; therefore it is, that our souls are made, as it were, too big for it; and extend themselves in the prospect of a longer existence. *Steele.*

Life is the jailer of the soul in this filthy prison, and its only deliverer is death; what we call life is a journey to death, and what we call death is a passport to life.—*Colton.*

In the species with which we are best acquainted, namely, our own, I am far, even as an observer of human life, from thinking that youth is its happiest season, much less the only happy one.—*Paley.*

The color of our whole life is generally such as the three or four first years in which we are our own masters make it.—*Cowper.*

We sleep, but the loom of life never stops; and the pattern which was weaving when the sun went down is weaving when it comes up to-morrow.—*Beecher.*

Man carries under his hat a private theatre, wherein a greater drama is acted than is ever performed on the mimic stage, beginning and ending in eternity.—*Carlyle.*

Life is a casket not precious in itself, but valuable in proportion to what fortune, or industry, or virtue has placed within it.—*Landor.*

LIGHT.
When the new light we beg for shines in upon us, there be those who envy and oppose, if it come not first in at their casements.— *Milton.*

Light is no less favorable to merit than unfavorable to imposture.—*Henry Home.*

The first creation of God in the works of the days was the light of the sense; the last was the light of the reason: and his Sabbath-work ever since is the illumination of the spirit.—*Bacon.*

Is not light grander than fire? It is the same element in a state of purity.—*Carlyle.*

Our moments of light are moments of happiness; in the mind, when it is clear weather it is fine weather.—*Joubert.*

Where there is much light, the shade is deepest.—*Goethe.*

Children always turn toward the light. O that grown-up people in this would become like little children!—*Hare.*

Thy nimble pencil paints the landscape as thou goest.—*Cowley.*

And as the eye is the best composer, so light is the first of painters. There is no object so foul that intense light will not make beautiful. And the stimulus it affords to the sense, and a sort of infinitude which it hath like space and time, make all matter gay.—*Emerson.*

Light is, as it were, a divine humidity.— *Joubert.*

The light in the world comes principally from two sources, — the sun, and the student's lamp.—*Bovee.*

Light ethereal, first of things, quintessence pure.—*Milton.*

O the eye's light is a noble gift of Heaven. All beings live from light, each fair created thing, — the very plants turn with a joyful transport to the light.—*Schiller.*

Light is the symbol of truth.—*Lowell.*

A drop of light is better to give or to receive than an ocean of obscurities.—*Joubert.*

LITERATURE.
When a learned man, intoxicated with his reading, takes a first step in the world, it is very often a false step; if he takes counsel only of his books, he runs the risk of never succeeding in his projects.—*St. Evremond.*

I never knew a man of letters ashamed of his profession.—*Thackeray.*

Let literature be an honorable augmentation to your arms, not constitute the coat or fill the escutcheon.—*Coleridge.*

Literature is so common a luxury, that the age has grown fastidious. The moralist is expected to allure men to virtue by his beautiful rhetoric. Philosophy must be illustrated by charming metaphors or captivating fiction; and history, casting aside the tedious garb of formal narrative, is required to assume a scenic costume, and teem with the connected interest of a fascinating tale.—*Tuckerman.*

The decline of literature indicates the decline of the nation. The two keep pace in their downward tendency.—*Goethe.*

It is the glorious doom of literature that the evil perishes and the good remains.—
Bulwer Lytton.

Literature has now become a game; in which the booksellers are the kings; the critics, the knaves; the public, the pack; and the poor author, the mere table, or thing played upon.—
Colton.

Literature, as a field for glory, is an arena where a tomb may be more easily found than laurels; as a means of support, it is the very chance of chances.—*Henry Giles.*

Literature is the immortality of speech.—
Willmott.

A beautiful literature springs from the depth and fulness of intellectual and moral life, from an energy of thought and feeling, so which nothing, as we believe, ministers so largely as enlightened religion.—*Channing.*

Let your literary compositions be kept from the public eye for nine years at least.—*Horace.*

Literature has her quacks no less than medicine, and they are divided into two classes; those who have erudition without genius, and those who have volubility without depth; we shall get second-hand sense from the one, and original nonsense from the other.—*Colton.*

In science, read, by preference, the newest works; in literature, the oldest. The classic literature is always modern.—*Bulwer Lytton.*

I have never tasted pleasures so true as those I have found in the study of books, in writing, or in music. The days that succeed brilliant entertainments are always melancholy, but those which follow days of study are delicions; we have gained something; we have acquired some new knowledge, and we recall the past day not only without disgust and without regret, but with consummate satisfaction.—
Madame de Genlis.

There is such a thing as literary fashion, and prose and verse have been regulated by the same caprice that cuts our coats and cocks our hats.—*Disraeli.*

Experience enables me to depose to the comfort and blessing that literature can prove in seasons of sickness and sorrow, — how powerfully intellectual pursuits can help in keeping the head from crazing, and the heart from breaking.—*Hood.*

Literature is a great staff, but a sorry crutch.
Walter Scott.

Nothing lives in literature but that which has in it the vitality of creative art; and it would be safe advice to the young to read nothing but what is old.—*Whipple.*

The selection of a subject is to the author what choice of position is to the general, — once skilfully determined, the battle is already half won. Of a few writers it may be said, that they are popular in despite of their subjects — but of a great many more it may be observed that they are popular because of them.
Bovee.

To literary composition we may apply the saying of an ancient philosopher: "A little thing gives perfection, although perfection is not a little thing."—*Disraeli.*

In literary concerns, few things are done well that do not emanate spontaneously from the writer's fancy. To act on the advice or views of others, is almost a certain presage of failure. Where there is not genius or inclination to devise, there is seldom ability or patience to execute.—*W. B. Clulow.*

In literary performances, as in Gothic architecture, the taste of the age is largely in favor of the pointed styles. Our churches and our books must bristle all over with points.—*Bovee.*

The great standard of literature, as to purity and exactness of style, is the Bible.—*Blair.*

Other relaxations are peculiar to certain times, places, and stages of life, but the study of letters is the nourishment of our youth, and the joy of our old age. They throw an additional splendor on prosperity, and are the resource and consolation of adversity; they delight at home, and are no embarrassment abroad; in short, they are company to us at night, our fellow-travellers on a journey, and attendants in our rural recesses.—*Cicero.*

Literature is the thought of thinking souls.
Carlyle.

There never was a literary age whose dominant taste was not sickly. The success of excellent authors consists in making wholesome works agreeable to morbid tastes.—*Joubert.*

No man's life is free from struggles and mortification, not even the happiest; but every one may build up his own happiness by seeking mental pleasures, and thus making himself independent of outward fortune.—*Humboldt.*

Literature is a fragment of a fragment. Of all that ever happened, or has been said, but a fraction has been written; and of this but little is extant.—*Goethe.*

A country which has no national literature, or a literature too insignificant to force its way abroad, must always be, to its neighbors at least, in every important spiritual respect, an unknown and unestimated country.—*Carlyle.*

In literature, to-day, there are plenty of good masons but few good architects.—*Joubert.*

LOGIC.

Ethics makes a man's soul mannerly and wise; but logic is the armory of reason, furnished with all offensive and defensive weapons.
Fuller.

Logic works; metaphysic contemplates.—
Joubert.

Logic is the essence of truth, and truth is the most powerful tyrant; but tyrants hate the truth.—*Kozlay.*

LOQUACITY.

Nature has given us two ears, two eyes, and but one tongue; to the end, we should hear and see more than we speak.—*Socrates.*

Thou mayst esteem a man of many words and many lies much alike.—*Fuller.*

There are braying men in the world as well as braying asses; for what is loud and senseless talking and swearing any other than braying?—*L'Estrange.*

Every absurdity has a champion to defend it; for error is always talkative.—*Goldsmith.*

Words must be fitted to a man's mouth: it was well said of the fellow that was to make a speech for my lord Mayor, when he desired to take measure of his lordship's mouth.—*Selden.*

No fool can be silent at a feast.—*Solon.*

· Those who have few affairs to attend to are great speakers. The less men think, the more they talk.—*Montesquieu.*

The tongue of a fool is the key of his counsel, which, in a wise man, wisdom hath in keeping.
Socrates.

A talkative fellow may be compared to an unbraced drum, which beats a wise man out of his wits.—*Feltham.*

Speaking much is a sign of vanity; for he that is lavish in words is a niggard in deed.—
Sir Walter Raleigh.

Gratiano speaks an infinite deal of nothing, more than any man in all Venice: his reasons are as two grains of wheat hid in two bushels of chaff; you shall seek all day ere you find them; and, when you have them, they are not worth the search.—*Shakespeare.*

As a vessel is known by the sound, whether it be cracked or not, so men are proved by their speeches, whether they be wise or foolish.—
Demosthenes.

Be always less willing to speak than to hear; what thou hearest, thou receivest; what thou speakest, thou givest. It is more glorious to give, more profitable to receive.—*Quarles.*

Many a man's tongue shakes out his master's undoing.—*Shakespeare.*

Surely in much talk there cannot choose but be much vanity. Loquacity is the fistula of the mind, — ever running and almost incurable, let every man, therefore, be a Phocion or Pythagorean, to speak briefly to the point or not at all; let him labor like them of Crete, to show more wit in his discourse than words, and not to pour out of his mouth a flood of the one, when he can hardly wring out of his brains a drop of the other.—*Spencer.*

They only babble who practise not reflection. I shall think, — and thought is silence.—
Sheridan.

He draweth out the thread of his verbosity finer than the staple of his argument.—
Shakespeare.

LOSSES.

Losses are comparative, imagination only makes them of any moment.—*Pascal.*

What is taken from the fortune, also, may haply be so much lifted from the soul. The greatness of a loss, as the proverb suggests, is determinable, not so much by what we have lost, as by what we have left.—*Bovee.*

LOVE.

There is music in the beauty, and the silent note which Cupid strikes, far sweeter than the sound of an instrument.—*Sir Thomas Browne.*

The maid that loves goes out to sea upon a shattered plank, and puts her trust in miracles for safety.—*Young.*

When God formed the rose, he said, " Thou shalt flourish and spread thy perfume." When he commanded the sun to emerge from chaos, he added, " Thou shalt enlighten and warm the world." When he gave life to the lark, he enjoined upon it to soar and sing in the air. Finally, he created man and told him to love. And seeing the sun shine, perceiving the rose scattering its odors, hearing the lark warble in the air, how can man help loving? —*Grün.*

The greatest pleasure of life is love.—
Sir W. Temple.

Love is like a hunter, who cares not for the game when once caught, which he may have pursued with the most intense and breathless eagerness. Love is strongest in pursuit; friendship in possession.—*Emerson.*

To love in order to be loved in return, is man; but to love for the pure sake of loving, is almost the characteristic of an angel.—
Lamartine.

Base men, being in love, have then a nobility in their natures more than is native to them.
Shakespeare.

LOVE. 304 LOVE.

If fun is good, truth is still better, and love best of all — *Thackeray.*

O, let us prize the first-blown bud of love, let us love now in this fairest youth, when love can find a full and fond return.—*Percival.*

Love is a local anguish — I am fifty miles distant, and am not half so miserable.— *Coleridge.*

A murderous guilt shows not itself more soon than love that would seem hid; love's night is noon.—*Shakespeare.*

Mutual love, the crown of all our bliss.— *Milton.*

I say to you truly, the heart of him who loves is a paradise on earth; he has God in himself, for God is love.—*Lamennais.*

It is better to have loved and lost, than never to have loved at all.—*Tennyson.*

Nothing but real love — (how rare it is; has one human heart in a million ever known it?) — nothing but real love can repay us for the loss of freedom — the cares and fears of poverty — the cold pity of the world that we both despise and respect.—*Bulwer Lytton.*

All true love is grounded on esteem.— *Buckingham.*

They are the true disciples of Christ, not who know most, but who love most.— *Spanheim.*

Love is a superstition that doth fear the idol which itself has made.—*Sir Thomas Overbury.*

There is nothing in this world so sweet as love, and next to love, the sweetest thing is hate.—*Longfellow.*

To reveal its complacence by gifts is one of the native dialects of love.—*Mrs. Sigourney.*

Love covers a multitude of sins. When a scar cannot be taken away, the next kind office is to hide it. Love is never so blind as when it is to spy faults.—*South.*

Love reckons hours for months, and days for years; and every little absence is an age.— *Dryden.*

The cure for all the ills and wrongs, the cares, the sorrows, and the crimes of humanity, all lie in that one word "love." It is the divine vitality that everywhere produces and restores life. To each and every one of us, it gives the power of working miracles if we will.— *Mrs. L. M. Child.*

Where love has once obtained influence, any seasoning, I believe, will please.—*Plautus.*

To give, that is, to love; to receive, that is, to learn and love; in delicate souls, that is to love already and much. The happiness of giving and receiving is the secret and life of the moral world.—*Degerando.*

To love, is to be useful to yourself; to cause love, is to be useful to others.—*Béranger.*

That is the true season of love, when we believe that we alone can love, that no one could ever have loved so before us, and that no one will love in the same way after us.—*Goethe.*

It is astonishing how little one feels poverty when one loves.—*Bulwer Lytton.*

No cord or cable can draw so forcibly, or bind so fast, as love can do with only a single thread.—*Burton.*

That you may be beloved be amiable. *Ovid.*

Where there exists the most ardent and true love, it is often better to be united in death than separated in life.—*Valerius Maximus.*

A man of sense may love like a madman, but not like a fool.—*Rochefoucauld.*

Ridicule, perhaps, is a better expedient against love, than sober advice; and I am of opinion, that Hudibras and Don Quixote may be as effectual to cure the extravagance of this passion, as any one of the old philosophers.—*Addison.*

The law of heaven is love.—*Hosea Ballou.*

It makes us proud when our love of a mistress is returned; it ought to make us prouder still when we can love her for herself alone, without the aid of any such selfish reflection. This is the religion of love.—*Hazlitt.*

Let him who does not choose to be considered a lazy fellow fall in love.—*Ovid.*

True love can no more be diminished by showers of evil than flowers are marred by timely rain.—*Sir P. Sidney.*

Love lessens woman's delicacy and increases man's.—*Richter.*

There is an English song beginning, "Love knocks at the door." He knocks less often than he finds it open.—*Madame Swetchine.*

Loving goes by haps; some Cupid kills with arrows, some with traps.—*Shakespeare.*

The accepted and betrothed lover has lost the wildest charms of his maiden in her acceptance of him. She was heaven whilst he pursued her as a star, — she cannot be heaven if she stoops to such a one as he.—*Emerson.*

It is sweet to feel by what fine-spun threads our affections are drawn together.—*Sterne.*

The comparison of love to fire holds good in one respect, that the fiercer it burns the sooner it is extinguished.—*Henry Home.*

Love me little, love me long.—*Marlowe.*

The plainest man that can convince a woman that he is really in love with her, has done more to make her in love with him than the handsomest man, if he can produce no such conviction. For the love of woman is a shoot, not a seed, and flourishes most vigorously only when ingrafted on that love which is rooted in the breast of another.—*Colton.*

Love seldom haunts the breast where learning lies.—*Pope.*

Fear is a bad guardian of a thing that requires to last, while, on the other hand, affection is faithful to the end.—*Cicero.*

Hate makes us vehement partisans, but love still more so.—*Goethe.*

There is a gloom in deep love, as in deep water; there is a silence in it that suspends the foot; and the folded arms and the dejected head are the images it reflects.—*Landor.*

Love is but another name for that inscrutable presence by which the soul is connected with humanity.—*Simms.*

The beings who appear cold, but are only timid, adore where they dare to love.—
Madame Swetchine.

We can receive anything from love, for that is a way of receiving it from ourselves ; but not from any one who assumes to bestow.—
Emerson.

Man, while he loves, is never quite depraved.—*Lamb.*

It is possible that a man can be so changed by love that one could not recognize him to be the same person.—*Terence.*

Solid love, whose root is virtue, can no more die, than virtue itself.—*Erasmus.*

Love and friendship exclude each other. Love begins by love, and the strongest friendship could only give birth to a feeble love.—
Du Cœur.

Love never reasons, but profusely gives ; gives, like a thoughtless prodigal, its all, and trembles then lest it has done too little.—
Hannah More.

Man's lóvc is of man's life a thing, a part, — it is woman's whole existence.—*Byron.*
20

It is more common to see an extreme love than a perfect friendship.—*Du Cœur.*

Love is the weapon which Omnipotence reserved to conquer rebel man when all the rest had failed. Reason he parries ; fear he answers blow for blow ; future interest he meets with present pleasure ; but love, that sun against whose melting beams the winter cannot stand — that soft subliming slumber which wrestles down the giant, there is not one human being in a million, nor a thousand men in all earth's huge quintillion, whose clay heart is hardened against love.—*Tupper.*

Love gives itself, but is not bought.—
Longfellow.

Let us not love those things much which we are not sure to live long to love, nor to have long if we should.—*Fuller.*

There is, in human nature, an essential, though somewhat mysterious, connection of love with fear.—*Henry Taylor.*

Love sacrifices all things to bless the thing it loves.—*Bulwer Lytton.*

True love were very unlovely, if it were half so deadly as lovers term it.—*Sir P. Sidney*

Love one human being with warmth and purity, and thou wilt love the world. The heart, in that celestial sphere of love, is like the sun in its course. From the drop in the rose, to the ocean, all is for him a mirror, which he fills and brightens.—*Richter.*

There is but one kind of love, but there are a thousand different copies of it.—
Rochefoucauld.

If thou neglectest thy love to thy neighbor, in vain thou professest thy love to God ; for by thy love to God, the love to thy neighbor is begotten, and by the love to thy neighbor, thy love to God is nourished.—*Quarles.*

It is weakness to love ; often it is another weakness to cease to love.—*Du Cœur.*

Love, when founded in the heart, will show itself in a thousand unpremeditated sallies of fondness ; but every cool, deliberate exhibition of the passion only argues little understanding, or great insincerity.—*Goldsmith.*

What concentrated joy, or woe, in blessed or blighted love.—*Tupper.*

The most lovable heart is that which loves the most readily ; but that which easily loves also easily forgets.—*Goethe.*

We can sometimes love what we do not understand, but it is impossible completely to understand what we do not love.—*Mrs. Jameson*

There are few people who are not ashamed of their amours when the fit is over.—*Rochefoucauld.*

In love we are all fools alike.—*Gay.*

The love which grows slowly and by degrees resembles friendship too much to be a violent passion.—*Du Cœur.*

The more you love your mistress, the readier you are to hate her.—*Rochefoucauld.*

The reason why all men honor love is because it looks up, and not down; aspires and not despairs.—*Emerson.*

It is better to desire than to enjoy, to love than to be loved.—*Hazlitt.*

Ripening love is the stillest; the shady flowers in this spring, as in the other, shun sunlight.—*Richter.*

Love dies by satiety, and forgetfulness inters it.—*Du Cœur.*

The heart needs not for its heaven much space, nor many stars therein, if only the star of love has arisen.—*Richter.*

Love, which is only an episode in the life of man, is the entire history of woman's life.— *Madame de Staël.*

Love is a science, rather than a sentiment. It is taught and learned. One is never master of it at the first step.—*Madame Deluzy.*

Love, one time, layeth burdens; another time, giveth wings.—*Sir P. Sidney.*

There are people who would never have been in love if they had never heard love spoken of. *Rochefoucauld.*

Whatever, below God, is the object of our love, will, at some time or other, be the matter of our sorrow.—*Cecil.*

There are several remedies which will cure love, but there are no infallible ones.— *Rochefoucauld.*

We, that are true lovers, run into strange capers; but as all is mortal in nature, so is all nature in love mortal in folly.—*Shakespeare.*

Friendship often ends in love; but love in friendship—never.—*Colton.*

To say the least to the disadvantage of this passion, it is putting your peace in the power of another, which is rarely safe even in your own.—*Young.*

In her first passion, woman loves her lover; in all the others, all she loves is love.—*Byron.*

Beauty may be the object of liking—great qualities of admiration—good ones of esteem—but love only is the object of love.—*Fielding.*

We love those who admire us, but not those whom we admire.—*Rochefoucauld.*

O love, when thou gettest dominion over us, we may bid good by to prudence.— *La Fontaine.*

We are cured of love as we are consoled in sorrow; the heart has not the power always to mourn, or always to love.—*Du Cœur.*

Love can hope, where reason would despair. *Lyttelton.*

Love is an alchemist that can transmute poison into food,—and a spaniel, that prefers even punishment from one hand, to caresses from another. But it is in love, as in war, we are often more indebted for our success to the weakness of the defence, than to the energy of the attack; for mere idleness has ruined more women than passion; vanity more than idleness, and credulity more than either.—*Colton.*

But love is blind, and lovers cannot see the pretty follies that themselves commit.— *Shakespeare.*

Love sees what no eye sees; love hears what no ear hears; and what never rose in the heart of man love prepares for its object.—*Lavater.*

To love deeply in one direction makes us more loving in all others.—*Madame Swetchine.*

Love is of the nature of a burning glass, which kept still in one place, fireth; changed often, it doth nothing.—*Suckling.*

Love mocks all sorrows but its own, and damps each joy he does not yield.—*Lady Dacre.*

Novelty is to love like bloom to fruit; it gives a lustre, which is easily effaced, but never returns.—*Rochefoucauld.*

Love is represented as the fulfilling of the law,—a creature's perfection. All other graces, all divine dispensations, contribute to this, and are lost in it as in a heaven. It expels the dross of our nature; it overcomes sorrow; it is the full joy of our Lord.—*Hooker.*

Humble love, and not proud science, keeps the door of heaven.—*Young.*

Days are like years in the love of the young, when no bar, no obstacle, is between their hearts,—when the sun shines, and the course runs smooth,—when their love is prosperous and confessed.—*Bulwer Lytton.*

Love with men is not a sentiment, but an idea.—*Madame de Girardin.*

Love, like fire, cannot subsist without continual motion, and ceases to exist as soon as it ceases to hope or fear.—*Rochefoucauld.*

Our very wretchedness grows dear to us when suffering for one we love.—*Bulwer Lytton.*

Love, it has been said, flows downward. The love of parents for their children has always been far more powerful than that of children for their parents; and who among the sons of men ever loved God with a thousandth part of the love which God has manifested to us?—*Hare.*

No disguise can long conceal love where it is, nor feign it where it is not.—*Rochefoucauld.*

Love is merely a madness; and, I tell you, deserves as well a dark house and a whip as madmen do: and the reason why they are not so punished and cured is, that the lunacy is so ordinary that the whippers are in love too.—
Shakespeare.

O love, the beautiful and brief!—*Schiller.*

Love not only occupies the higher lobes of the brain, but crowds out the lower to make room for its expansion.—*Horace Mann.*

If a man loves a woman for her beauty, does he love her? No; for the small-pox, which destroys her beauty without killing her, causes his love to cease. And if any one loves me for my judgment or my memory, does he really love me? No; for I can lose these qualities without ceasing to be.—*Pascal.*

In love, the deceit generally outstrips the distrust.—*Rochefoucauld.*

All brave men love; for he only is brave who has affections to fight for, whether in the daily battle of life or in physical contests.—
· *Hawthorne.*

A youth's love is the more passionate: virgin love is the more idolatrous.—*Hare.*

Must love be ever treated with profaneness as a mere illusion? or with coarseness as a mere impulse? or with fear as a mere disease? or with shame as a mere weakness? or with levity as a mere accident? whereas it is a great mystery and a great necessity, lying at the foundation of human existence, morality, and happiness, — mysterious, universal, inevitable as death.—*Harriet Martineau.*

The truth of truths is love.—*Bailey.*

Of the uses of adversity which are sweet, none are sweeter than those which grow out of disappointed love.—*Henry Taylor.*

Alas for love, if thou art all, and naught beyond, O Earth!—*Mrs. Hemans.*

A man loved by a beautiful and virtuous woman, carries a talisman that renders him invulnerable; every one feels that such a one's life has a higher value than that of others.—
Madame Dudevant.

Heaven's harmony is universal love.—
Cowper.

There are no little events with the heart. It magnifies everything; it places in the same scales the fall of an empire of fourteen years and the dropping of a woman's glove, and almost always the glove weighs more than the empire.—*Balzac.*

As love without esteem is volatile and capricious, esteem without love is languid and cold.
Johnson.

There is in the heart of woman such a deep well of love that no age can freeze it.—
Bulwer Lytton.

The consciousness of being loved softens the keenest pang even at the moment of parting; yea, even the eternal farewell is robbed of half of its bitterness when uttered in accents that breathe love to the last sigh.—*Addison.*

A smile that glowed celestial rosy red, love's proper hue.—*Milton.*

Love makes itself understood by the simplest beings; it bears with it a charm which moves the indifferent, and the eyes of two young lovers have a language whose sweetness penetrates even those who have never loved.—
Madame Desbordes-Valmore.

Love is the virtue of woman.—
Madame Dudevant.

The young girl who begins to experience the necessity of loving seeks to hide it; but the desire of pleasing betrays the secret of her heart and sometimes reveals her hopes.—*Beauchêne.*

Prosperity is the very bond of love.—
Shakespeare.

There is nothing half so sweet in life as love's young dream.—*Moore.*

In matters of love and appetite beware of surfeits. Nothing contributes so much to the duration of either as moderation in their gratification.—*Bovee.*

O love! what is it in this world of ours which makes it fatal to be loved?—*Byron.*

Love is heaven, and heaven is love.—
Walter Scott.

We never love truly but once. It is the first time. Succeeding passions are less involuntary.—*Du'Cœur.*

Though love use reason for its precision, he admits him not for his councillor.—
Shakespeare.

There is a sweet and holy blindness in Christian love, even as there is a blindness of life; yea, and of genius, too, in the moment of productive energy.—*Sir Thomas Browne.*

I have heard that whoever loves is in no condition old.—*Emerson.*

When there is love in the heart, there are rainbows in the eyes, which cover every black cloud with gorgeous hues.—*Beecher.*

Successful love takes a load off our hearts, and puts it upon our shoulders.—*Bovee.*

Beneath the odorous shade of the boundless forests of Chili the native youth repeats the story of love as sincerely as it was ever chanted in the valley of Vaucluse. The affections of family are not the growth of civilization.—
Bancroft.

The worst effect of gold — love, alas! is bought and sold.—*Anacreon.*

Love sought, is good, — but given unsought, is better.—*Shakespeare.*

All love is sweet, given or returned. Common as light is love, and its familiar voice wearies not ever.—*Shelley.*

Love is the piety of the affections.—
Theodore Parker.

The greatest happiness of life is the conviction that we are loved, loved for ourselves — say rather, loved in spite of ourselves.—
Victor Hugo.

Love at two-and-twenty is a terribly intoxicating draught.—*Ruffini.*

At love's perjuries they say Jove laughs.—
Shakespeare.

Love is of such superlative worth that it is more honorable to be its victim than its conqueror.—*Bovee.*

What a miserable world! — trouble if we love, and trouble if we do not love.—
Count de Maistre.

Equality is no rule in love's grammar.—
Beaumont and Fletcher.

Love seizes on us suddenly, without giving warning, and our disposition or our weakness favors the surprise; one look, one glance, from the fair fixes and determines us.—*Bruyère.*

Suits in love should not, like suits in law, be racked from term to term.—*Shirley.*

A man's want of beauty is of small account if he be not deficient in other amiable qualities, for there is no conquest without the affections, and what mole can be so blind as a woman in love.—*Ninon de l'Enclos.*

Excessive love in loathing ever ends.—*Ovid.*

Love, be it true love, is ever simple, and thinks itself unseen of the world, because it is itself so blind.—*Madame de Puisieux.*

O heart, love is thy bane and thy antidote.—
Madame Dudevant.

How wayward is this foolish love, that, like a testy babe, will scratch the nurse, and presently, all humbled, kiss the rod.—*Shakespeare.*

Love makes obedience lighter than liberty.—
W. R. Alger.

Where love and wisdom drink out of the same cup, in this everyday world, it is the exception.—*Madame Necker.*

The worst thing an old man can be is a lover.—*Otway.*

Why is it so difficult to love wisely, so easy to love too well?—*Miss M. E. Braddon.*

Love is an affair of credulity.—*Ovid.*

The poets, the moralists, the painters, in all their descriptions, allegories, and pictures, have represented love as a soft torment, a bitter sweet, a pleasing pain, or an agreeable distress.—
Addison.

The greatest miracle of love is the reformation of a coquette.—*Rochefoucauld.*

He loves but lightly who his love can tell.—
Petrarch.

It is the show and seal of nature's truth, where love's strong passion is impressed in youth.—*Shakespeare.*

Who love too much, hate in the like extreme.—*Pope.*

Providence has so ordained it, that only two women have a true interest in the happiness of a man, — his own mother, and the mother of his children. Besides these two legitimate kinds of love, there is nothing between the two creatures except vain excitement, painful and vain delusion.—*Octave Feuillet.*

Love is a reality which is born in the fairy region of romance.—*Talleyrand.*

Love has its instinct. It knows how to find the way to the heart, as the feeblest insect moves to its flower with an irresistible will which nothing daunts.—*Balzac.*

LOVE. 309 LOVE.

It is ever the invisible that is the object of our profoundest worship. With the lover it is not the seen but the unseen that he muses upon.
Bovee.

To love is everything ; love is God.—
Léon Gozlan.

There is no permanent love but that which has duty for its eldest brother ; so that if one sleeps the other watches, and honor is safe.—
Stahl.

They love least, that let men know their love.—*Shakespeare.*

Love makes its record in deeper colors as we grow out of childhood into manhood ; as the emperors signed their names in green ink when under age, but when of age, in purple.—
Longfellow.

Paradise is always where love dwells.—
Richter.

Love is God's loaf; and this is that feeding for which we are taught to pray, " Give us this day our daily bread."—*Beecher.*

Man loves little and often, woman much and rarely.—*Basta.*

There can be no barrenness in full summer. The very sand will yield something. Rocks will have mosses, and every rift will have its wind-flower, and every crevice a leaf; while from the fertile soil will be reared a gorgeous troop of growths, that will carry their life in ten thousand forms, but all with praise to God. And so it is when the soul knows its summer. Love redeems its weakness, clothes its barrenness, enriches its poverty, and makes its very desert to bud and blossom as the rose.—
Beecher.

A woman often thinks she is regretting the lover, when she is only regetting the love.—
Madame d'Arconville.

However dull a woman may be, she will understand all there is in love ; however intelligent a man may be, he will never know but half of it.—*Madame Fée.*

Love is precisely to the moral nature what the sun is to the earth.—*Balzac.*

Love is, I believe, an entirely personal poem. There is nothing which is not at once true and false in all that authors have written of it.—
Balzac.

It is not decided that women love more than men, but it is indisputable that they love better.
Sanial-Dubay.

O, how this spring of love resembleth the uncertain glory of an April day ! —*Shakespeare.*

It is the beautiful necessity of our nature to love something.—*Douglas Jerrold.*

Love is a flame which burns in heaven and whose soft reflections radiate to us. Two worlds are opened, two lives given to it. It is by love that we double our being ; it is by love that we approach God.—*Aimé-Martin.*

Honest men love women ; those who deceive them adore them.—*Beaumarchais.*

True love is eternal, infinite, and always like itself. It is equal and pure, without violent demonstrations : it is seen with white hairs and is always young in the heart.—*Balzac.*

Love is incompatible with fear.—
Publius Syrus.

Love is like what is called the Milky Way in heaven, a brilliant mass formed by thousands of little stars, of which each perhaps is nebulous.—
Henri Beyle.

Of all the agonies in life, that which is most poignant and harrowing ; that which for the time annihilates reason, and leaves our whole organization one lacerated, mangled heart, is the conviction that we have been deceived where we placed all the trust of love.—
Bulwer Lytton.

Love is wholly in him who loves; the beloved is only a pretext.—*Alphonse Karr.*

A woman cannot love a man she feels to be her inferior; love without veneration and enthusiasm is only friendship.—
Madame Dudevant.

One half, the finest half, of life is hidden from the man who does not love with passion.—
Henri Beyle.

As the nature of love is divine, that is to say immortal, when we think we have destroyed it, we have only buried it in our hearts.—
Madame Dudevant.

If a man fancies he loves his mistress for her own sake, he is much mistaken.—*Rochefoucauld.*

A man may be a miser of his wealth ; he may tie up his talent in a napkin ; he may hug himself in his reputation ; but he is always generous in his love. Love cannot stay at home ; a man cannot keep it to himself. Like light it is constantly travelling. A man must spend it, must give it away.—*Rev. Dr. Macleod.*

Love is a smoke raised with the fume of sighs.—*Shakespeare.*

Love is like a charming romance which is read with avidity, and often with such impatience that many pages are skipped to reach the dénouement sooner.—*Sylvain Maréchal.*

Nothing more excites to everything noble and generous, than virtuous love.—*Henry Home.*

Let grace and goodness be the principal loadstone of thy affections. For love which hath ends will have an end; whereas that which is founded on true virtue will always continue.—*Dryden.*

Prudence and love are inconsistent; in proportion, as the last increases, the other decreases.—*Rochefoucauld.*

He who has fostered the sweet poison of love by fondling it finds it too late to refuse the yoke which he has of his own accord assumed.—*Seneca.*

The heart of a young woman in love is a golden sanctuary which often enshrines an idol of clay.—*Paulin Limayrac.*

The heart that has once been bathed in love's pure fountain retains the pulse of youth forever. Death can only take away the sorrowful from our affections; the flower expands; the colorless film that enveloped it falls off and perishes.—*Landor.*

If love live on hope, it dies with it; it is a fire which goes out from want of fuel.—*Corneille.*

Poetry has no echo more sonorous and more prolonged than the heart of youth in which love is first born.—*Lamartine.*

Fears accomplish much in love. The husband of the Middle Ages was loved by his wife for his very severity. The bride of William the Conqueror, having been beaten by him, recognized him by this token for her lord and husband.—*Michelet.*

The life of a woman may be divided into three epochs; in the first she dreams of love, in the second she makes love, in the third she regrets it.—*St. Prosper.*

It is in the heart that God has placed the genius of women, because the works of this genius are all works of love.—*Lamartine.*

It is an observation founded on much experience, that all persons are doomed to be in love once in their lives.—*Fielding.*

Celestial love, with the affections of good and truth, and the perceptions thence derived and at the same time with the delights of these affections and the thoughts thence derived, may be compared to a tree with beautiful branches, leaves, and fruits; the life's love is that tree; the branches, with the leaves, are the affections of good and truth, with their perceptions; and the fruits are the delights of the affections with their thoughts.—*Swedenborg.*

Love is an image of God, and not a lifeless image, nor one painted on paper, but the living essence of the Divine Nature which beams full of all goodness.—*Martin Luther.*

In the old age of love, as in that of life, we still live for its evils, but no longer for its pleasures.—*Rochefoucauld.*

An oyster may be crossed in love.—*Sheridan.*

Better to love amiss than nothing to have loved.—*Crabbe.*

If there exists a love pure and exempt from the mixture of our other passions, it is that which lies hidden at the bottom of the heart, and of which we are ignorant ourselves.—*Rochefoucauld.*

What is man's love! his vows are broke, even while his parting kiss is warm.—*Halleck.*

As nice as we are in love, we forgive more faults in that than in friendship. Expostulations betwixt friends end generally ill, but well betwixt lovers.—*Henry Home.*

O artless love, where the soul moves the tongue, and only nature speaks what nature thinks.—*Dryden.*

I will not be sworn but love may transform me to an oyster; but I'll take my oath on it, till he have made an oyster of me he shall never make me such a fool.—*Shakespeare*

Love is such an affection, as cannot so properly be said to be in the soul as the soul to be in that.—*South.*

Love reigns a very tyrant in my heart, attended on his throne by all his guards of furious wishes, fears, and nice suspicions.—*Otway.*

Oh! must the cup that holds the sweetest vintage of the vine of life taste bitter at the dregs? Is there no story, no legend, no love passage, which shall end even as the bow that God hath bent in heaven, o'er the sad waste of mortal histories, promising respite to the rain of tears?—*Matthew Arnold.*

When we love we live.—*Congreve.*

The motto of chivalry is also the motto of wisdom; to serve all and love but one.—*Balzac.*

Life is a sleep, love is a dream; and you have lived if you have loved.—*Alfred de Musset.*

A lover is the very fool of nature, made sick by his own wantonness of thought, his fevered fancy.—*Thomson.*

The greatest tyranny is to love where we are not loved again.—*Balzac.*

Love as if you should hereafter hate; and hate as if you should hereafter love.—*Chilo.*

The true one of youth's love, proving a faithful helpmate in those years when the dream of life is over, and we live in its realities.
Southey.

Let me but bear your love, I'll bear your cares.—*Shakespeare.*

Who ever passed the tomb of Abelard and Heloise in the ground of Père la Chaise without a heart-swell? There is no deep love which has not in it an element of solemnity. It moves through the soul as if it were an inspiration of God, and carries with it something of the awe and shadow of eternity.—*Beecher.*

Words of love are works of love.—
W. R. Alger.

A heat full of coldness, a sweet full of bitterness, a pain full of pleasantness, which maketh thoughts have eyes, and hearts, and ears; bred by desire, nursed by delight, weaned by jealousy, killed by dissembling, buried by ingratitude; and this is love.—*Lyly.*

Love requires not so much proofs, as expressions, of love. Love demands little else than the power to feel and to requite love.—*Richter.*

A love, that makes breath poor, and speech unable.—*Shakespeare.*

Those know little of real love or grief who do not know how much we deceive ourselves when we pretend to aim at the cure of either; it is with those, as with some distempers of the body, nothing is in the least agreeable to us, but what serves to heighten the disease.—
Fielding.

I have enjoyed the happiness of this world, I have lived and have loved.—*Schiller.*

Love is an alliance of friendship and animalism; if the former predominate, it is a passion exalted and refined; but if the latter, gross and sensual.—*Colton.*

Cupid makes it his sport to pull the warrior's plumes.—*Sir P. Sidney.*

See how she leans her cheek upon her hand! O that I were a glove upon that hand, that I might touch that cheek!—*Shakespeare.*

We say, Love is blind, and the figure of Cupid is drawn with a bandage round his eyes. Blind;—yes, because he does not see what he docs not like; but the sharpest-sighted hunter in the universe is Love, for finding what he seeks and only that.—*Emerson.*

The love which arises suddenly is the most difficult to cure.—*Du Cœur.*

Were I to fall in love again (which is a great passion, and therefore I hope I have done with it), it would be, I think, with prettiness, rather than with majestical beauty.—*Cowley.*

It is a miserable thing to love where one hates; and yet it is not inconsistent.—
Shenstone.

Love is a secondary passion in those who love most, a primary in those who love least. He who is inspired by it in a high degree is inspired by honor in a higher; it never reaches its plenitude of growth and perfection but in the most exalted minds.—*Landor.*

Life outweighs all things, if love lies within it.—*Goethe.*

What is specially true of love is, that it is a state of extreme impressionability; the lover has more senses and finer senses than others; his eye and ear are telegraphs; he reads omens on the flower and cloud and face and form and gesture, and reads them aright.—*Emerson.*

The punishment of those who have loved women too much is to love them always.—
Joubert.

Love teaches cunning even to innocence; and, when he gets possession, his first work is to dig deep within a heart, and there lie hid, and, like a miser in the dark, to feast alone.—
Dryden.

In love, anger is always false.—
Publius Syrus.

Affection can withstand very severe storms of rigor, but not a long polar frost of downright indifference. Love will subsist on wonderfully little hope, but not altogether without it.—
Walter Scott.

The only victory over love is flight.—
Napoleon.

We love a girl for very different things than understanding. We love her for her beauty, her youth, her mirth, her confidingness, her character, with its faults, caprices, and God knows what other inexpressible charms; but we do not love her understanding. Her mind we esteem (if it is brilliant), and it may greatly elevate her in our opinion; nay, more, it may enchain us when we already love. But her understanding is not that which awakens and inflames our passions.—*Goethe.*

The beginning and end of love are marked by the embarrassment felt when the parties are left to themselves.—*Bruyère.*

So great a happiness do I esteem it to be loved that I really fancy every blessing both from gods and men ready to descend spontaneously upon him who is loved.—*Xenophon.*

Find me a reasonable lover against his weight in gold.—*Plautus.*

Love is not a fire which can be confined within the breast; everything betrays us, — the voice, silence, the eyes; and its fires imperfectly covered only burst forth the more.—*Racine.*

How delightful it would be to love, if one loved always; but alas! there are no eternal loves.—*Madame Scudéri.*

A happiness that is quite undisturbed becomes tiresome; we must have ups and downs; the difficulties which are mingled with love awaken passion and increase pleasure.—
Molière.

True love, like the eye, can bear no flaw.—
Lavater.

Whoever may desire fully to understand the folly of mankind has only to consider the causes and the effects of love. The cause of it is, " I know not what " (Corneille), and the effects from it are positively frightful. This " I know not what," this little thing which we can scarcely understand, moves the whole earth, princes, armies, the entire world.—*Pascal.*

To be loved we should merit but little esteem; all superiority attracts awe and aversion.
Helvetius.

Love may be likened to a disease in this respect, that when it is denied a vent in one part, it will certainly break out in another; hence what a woman's lips often conceal, her eyes, her blushes, and many little involuntary actions betray.—*Fielding.*

Our first and last love is — self-love.—
Bovee.

Genuine love, however rated as the chief passion of the human heart, is but a poor dependant, a retainer upon other passions, — admiration, gratitude, respect, esteem, pride in the object. Divest the boasted sensation of these, and it is no more than the impression of a twelvemonth, by courtesy or vulgar error termed love.—*Mrs. Inchbald.*

Love has made its best interpreter a sigh.—
Byron.

This is the monstrosity in love, — that the will is infinite, and the execution confined; that the desire is boundless, and the act a slave to limit.—*Shakespeare.*

Love, like men, dies oftener of excess than of hunger; it lives on love, but it resembles those Alpine flowers which feed themselves by suction from the wet clouds and die if you besprinkle them.—*Richter.*

Love is the fulfilling of the law.—*Bible.*

It is vain to try to conceal one's self; the most discreet love allows its secret to escape by some slight token.—*Racine.*

For faults are beauties in a lover's eyes.—
Theocritus.

Ah, with how little attention one listens to reason when the heart is touched by so charming a poison! and when the patient loves his disease, how unwilling he is to allow a remedy to be applied! —*Corneille.*

Quench, O quench not that flame! it is the breath of your being.—*Longfellow.*

As few germs, comparatively, live to be flowers; so few of our early loves ripen into " the bright consummate flower " of affection founded on appreciation.—*Bovee.*

All love may be expelled by other love, as poisons are by poisons.—*Dryden.*

How sweet is the prayer of the virgin heart to its love! Thy virtues won me. With virtue preserve me! Dost thou love me? Keep me, then, still worthy to be loved! —*Sir P. Sidney.*

The soul of woman lives in love.—
Mrs. Sigourney.

In love all is risk. In the grove or before the altar, in an embrace or a golden ring, by the chirping of a cricket or at the sound of trumpets and kettle-drums, it is all only a risk; chance does it all.—*Goethe.*

Alas, that love, so gentle in his view, should be so tyrannous and rough in proof!—
Shakespeare.

The love of a delicate female is always shy and silent. Even when fortunate, she scarcely breathes it to herself; but when otherwise, she buries it in the recesses of her bosom, and there lets it cower and brood among the ruins of her peace.— *Washington Irving.*

Love's feeling is more soft and sensible than are the tender horns of cockled snails; love's tongue proves dainty Bacchus gross in taste.—
Shakespeare.

Love has power to give in a moment what toil can scarcely reach in an age.—*Goethe.*

Nothing makes love sweeter and tenderer than a little previous scolding and freezing, just as the grape-clusters acquire by a frost before vintage thinner skins and better flavor.
Richter.

Love is strong as death. Many waters cannot quench love, neither can the floods drown it; if a man would give all the substance of his house for love it would utterly be contemned.—*Bible.*

It is the privilege of human nature above brutes, to love those that disoblige us.—
Marcus Antoninus.

The bitterest satires and noblest eulogies on married life have come from poets. Love, indeed, has ever been the inspiration of poetry. From Theocritus all the way down to the young gentleman that drizzled in yesterday's newspaper, it has provoked millions on millions of good and bad verses, most of which have been kindly gathered by Oblivion under her dusky wing.—*Whipple.*

Love is old, old as eternity, but not outworn; with each new being born or to be born.
Byron.

The judicial character is not captivating in females. A woman fascinates a man quite as often by what she overlooks as by what she sees. Love prefers twilight to daylight.—*Holmes.*

Gather the rose of love while yet is time.—
Spenser.

A lover's hope resembles the bean in the nursery tale; let it once take root, and it will grow so rapidly, that, in the course of a few hours, the giant Imagination builds a castle on the top, and by and by comes Disappointment with the curtal axe, and hews down both the plant and the superstructure.—*Walter Scott.*

Love has no age, as it is always renewing itself.—*Pascal.*

If ever (as that ever may be near) you meet in some fresh cheek the power of fancy, then shall you know the wounds invisible that love's keen arrows make.—*Shakespeare.*

Without belief in its perpetuity, love would be nothing; constancy magnifies it.—*Balzac.*

Love is not altogether a delirium, yet it has many points in common therewith. I call it rather a discerning of the infinite in the finite, — of the idea made real.—*Carlyle.*

When love is well timed, it is not a fault to love: the strong, the brave, the virtuous, and the wise sink in the soft captivity together.—
Addison.

Love is omnipresent in nature as motive and reward. Love is our highest word, and the synonyme of God.—*Emerson.*

Woman is rather made to be loved than to love, like the flowers which feel nothing of their perfume, but yield it to be felt by others. Women are the true flowers of love.—
Alphonse Esquiros.

Love is ever busy with his shuttle, is ever weaving into life's dull warp bright gorgeous flowers and scenes Arcadian.—*Longfellow.*

As the rays come from the sun, and yet are not the sun, even so our love and pity, though they are not God, but merely a poor, weak image and reflection of him, yet from him alone they come. If there is mercy in our hearts, it comes from the fountain of mercy. If there is the light of love in us, it is a ray from the full sun of his love.—*Charles Kingsley.*

Woman's love, like lichens upon a rock, will still grow where even charity can find no soil to nurture itself.—*Bovee.*

It is not love that steals the heart from love; it is the hard world and its perplexing cares, its petrifying selfishness, its pride, its low ambition, and its paltry aims.—*Charlotte Bowles.*

Gold does not satisfy love, it must be paid in its own coin.—*Madame Deluzy.*

Love is the greatest thing that God can give us, for himself is love; and it is the greatest thing we can give to God, for it will also give ourselves, and carry with it all that is ours. The apostle calls it the bond of perfection; it is the old, and it is the new, and it is the great commandment, and it is all the commandments, for it is the fulfilling of the law. It does the work of all the other graces without any instrument but its own immediate virtue.—
Jeremy Taylor.

Never yet was known the power could vanished love recall.—*Dickens.*

The platform or the altar of love may be analyzed and explained; it is constructed of virtue, beauty, and affection. Such is the pyre, such is the offering; but the ethereal spark must come from heaven, that lights the sacrifice.—*Jane Porter.*

Great spirits and great business do keep out this weak passion.—*Bacon.*

In love we never think of moral qualities, and scarcely of intellectual ones. Temperament and manner alone, with beauty, excite love. —
Hazlitt.

The oath of a lover is no stronger than the word of a tapster; they are both the confirmers of false reckoning.—*Shakespeare.*

The martyr of its fond fidelity.—
Miss L. E. Landon.

If we can still love those who have made us suffer, we love them all the more. It is as if the principle that conflict is a necessary law of progress were applicable even to love.—
Mrs. Jameson.

Love delights in paradoxes. Saddest when it has most reason to be gay, sighs are the signs of its deepest joy, and silence is the expression of its yearning tenderness.—*Bovee.*

This weak impress of love is as a figure trenched in ice; which, with an hour's heat, dissolves to water, and doth lose its form.— *Shakespeare.*

Her eyes, her lips, her cheeks, her shape, her features, seem to be drawn by love's own hand ; by love himself in love.—*Dryden.*

O, love can take what shape he pleases, and when once begun his fiery inroad in the soul, how vain the after-knowledge which his presence gives ! We weep or rave, but still he lives, and lives master and lord, amidst pride and tears and pain.—*Barry Cornwall.*

Love is never lasting which flames before it burns.—*Feltham.*

Love is exactly like war in this ; that a soldier, though he has escaped three weeks compiete o' Saturday night, may nevertheless be shot through his heart on Sunday morning.— *Sterne.*

Love is a fire self-fed, and does not need hope to preserve the flame.—*Shiel.*

O love ! thy essence is thy purity ! Breathe one unhallowed breath upon thy flame, and it is gone forever, and but leaves a sullied vase, its pure light lost in shame ! — *Miss L. E. Landon.*

It is an old story, yet remains ever new.— *Heinrich Heine.*

Love is like the spirit in Ezekiel's wheels, that made them move so swiftly ; so that dulness, sluggishness, and wearisomeness is quickly dispelled by heavenly love, as the ice is presently dissolved by the sunbeams.— *Anthony Burgess.*

The great lever by which to raise and save the world is the unbounded love and mercy of God.—*Beecher.*

Love has this in common with scruples, that it is exasperated by the reflections used to free us from them. If it were practicable, the only way to extinguish our passion is never to think of it.—*Bruyère.*

It is far happier to be deceived than unde-ceived by those we love.—*Rochefoucauld.*

Do anything but love ; or if thou lovest and art a woman, hide thy love from him whom thou dost worship ; never let him know how dear he is ; flit like a bird before him ; lead him from tree to tree, from flower to flower ; but be not won, or thou wilt, like that bird, when caught and caged, be left to pine neglected and perish in forgetfulness.—*Miss L. E. Landon.*

These are the charming agonies of love, whose misery delights.—*Thomson.*

Love ! love ! when thou gettest hold of us we may safely say, adieu, prudence ! — *La Fontaine.*

No man, or woman, was ever cured of love by discovering the falseness of his or her lover. The living together for three long, rainy days in the country has done more to dispel love than all the perfidies in love that have ever been committed.—*Helps.*

The breath of divine knowledge is the bellows of divine love, and the flame of divine love is the perfection of divine knowledge. – *Quarles.*

Soon or late Love is his own avenger.— *Byron.*

Certainly, the lover is no lover, or but a very small-hearted one, who does not see much beauty in the faults of the mistress of his affections.—*Helps.*

The most likely method we can take to hasten the removal of what we love is, to value it too much — to think on it with endless anxiety — to live on its favor with solicitude. It shall soon either become a thorn in our side, or be taken away.—*Cecil.*

Adieu, valor ! rust, rapier ! be still, drum ! for your manager is in love ; yea, he loveth.— *Shakespeare.*

This is the great instrument and engine of nature, the bond and cement of society, the spring and spirit of the universe. Love is such an affection as cannot so properly be said to be in the soul, as the soul to be in that. It is the whole man wrapt up into one desire, all the powers, vigor, and faculties of the soul abridged into one inclination.—*South.*

Love is a familiar ; love is a devil ; there is no evil angel but love. Yet Samson was so tempted ; and he had an excellent strength ; yet was Solomon so seduced ; and he had a very good wit.—*Shakespeare.*

My love is so true that I can neither hide it where it is, nor show it where it is not.— *Dryden.*

Love, like the opening of the heavens to the saints, shows for a moment, even to the dullest man, the possibilities of the human race. He has faith, hope, and charity for another being, perhaps but a creation of his imagination ; still, it is a great advance for a man to be profoundly loving even in his imaginations.— *Helps.*

Love is indeed heaven upon earth ; since heaven above would not be heaven without it ; for where there is not love is fear ; but, "Perfect love casteth out fear." And yet we naturally fear most to offend what we most love.— *William Penn.*

As long as love prevails in the house, space of the breadth of a sword is satisfactory; as soon as it disappears, sixty hand-breadths are not sufficient.—*Talmud.*

They that love beyond the world cannot be separated by it.—*William Penn.*

Love is the crowning grace of humanity, the holiest right of the soul, the golden link which binds us to duty and truth, the redeeming principle that chiefly reconciles the heart to life, and is prophetic of eternal good.—*Petrarch.*

Love is more pleasing than marriage, because romances are more amusing than history.
Chamfort.

Love's heralds should be thoughts, which ten times faster glide than the sun's beams, driving back shadows over lowering hills.—
Shakespeare.

Love's voice doth sing as sweetly in a beggar as·a king.—*Decker.*

Love is full of unbefitting strains; all wanton as a child, skipping, and vain; formed by the eye, and therefore, like the eye, full of strange shapes, of habits, and of forms.—*Shakespeare.*

Sweet is true love, though given in vain.—
Tennyson.

Methinks all poets should be gentle, fair, and ever young, and ever beautiful; I would have all poets to be like to this, — gold-haired and rosy-lipped, to sing of love.—
Alexander Smith.

If thou hast not broke from company abruptly, as my passion now makes me, thou hast not loved.—*Shakespeare.*

O, let the ,steps of youth be cautious how they advance into a dangerous world, our duty only can conduct us safe, our passions are seducers; but of all the strongest love.—
Southey.

But to see her was to love her, love but her, and love forever.—*Burns.*

It is both a misery and a shame for a man to be a bankrupt in love; which he may easily pay, and be never the more impoverished. I will be in no man's debt for good-will; but will at least return every man his own measure, if not with usury.—*Bishop Hall.*

Love is the hardest lesson in Christianity; but, for that reason, it should be most our care to learn it.—*William Penn.*

God gives us love. Something to love he lends us; but when love is grown to ripeness, that on which it throve falls off, and love is left alone.—*Tennyson.*

Was not this love, indeed! We men may say more, swear more; but, indeed, our shows are more than will; for still we prove much in our vows, but little in our love.—*Shakespeare.*

If he loves me, the merit is not mine, the fault will be if he ceases.—*Landor.*

Love informs us as the sun doth colors: and as the sun, reflecting his warm beams against the earth, begets all fruits and flowers, so love, fair shining in the inward man, brings forth in him the honorable fruits of valor, wit, virtue, and haughty thoughts, brave resolutions, and divine discourse.—*Chapman.*

Love is a kind of warfare.—*Ovid.*

To me, it is a delightful thought that, during the familiarity of constant proximity, the heart gathers up in silence the nutriment of love, as the diamond, even beneath water, imbibes the light it emits.—*Richter.*

Love will not be spurred to what it loathes.
Shakespeare.

She that is loved is safe.—*Jeremy Taylor.*

Stimulate the heart to love and the mind to be early accurate, and all other virtues will rise of their own accord, and all vices will be thrown out.—*Coleridge.*

Love is the master-key that opens every ward of the heart of man.—*J. H. Evans.*

Fair soul, in your fine frame hatn love no quality? If the quick fire of youth light not your mind, you are no maiden, but a monument.—*Shakespeare.*

Love has the tendency of pressing together all the lights — all the rays emitted from the beloved object by the burning-glass of fantasy, — into one focus, and making of them one radiant sun without any spots.—*Goethe.*

Of all the paths leading to a woman's love, pity is the straightest.—*Beaumont and Fletcher.*

The truth of lovers is likened to the Arabian Phœnix; but where no one can tell. If thou knowest where it dies, and rises again from its ashes, point out to me the spot, and I promise to preserve a steadfast love to thee.—*Metastasio.*

For now my love is thawed; which, like a waxen image against a fire, bears no impression of the thing it was.—*Shakespeare.*

Love swells like the Solway, but ebbs like its tide.—*Walter Scott.*

Love is a thing most nice, and must be fed to such a height; but never surfeited; what is beyond the mean is ever ill.—*Herrick.*

Greater love hath no man than this, that a man lay down his life for his friend.—*Bible.*

They that cannot be induced to fear for love will never be inforced to love for fear; love opens the heart, fear shuts it, that encourages, this compels; and victory meets encouragement, but flees compulsion.—*Quarles.*

I could not love thee, dear, so much, loved I not honor more.—*Lovelace.*

Nothing can sweeten felicity itself but love.— *Jeremy Taylor.*

As in the sweetest bud the eating canker dwells, so eating love inhabits in the finest wits of all.—*Shakespeare.*

A Briton, even in love, should be a subject, not a slave! — *Wordsworth.*

We never can say why we love, but only that we love. The heart is ready enough at feigning excuses for all that it does or imagines of wrong: but ask it to give a reason for any of its beautiful and divine motions, and it can only look upwards and be dumb.—*Lowell.*

Love is an egotism of two.— *Antoine de la Salle.*

If thou hast not sat as I do now, wearying thy hearer in thy mistress' praise, thou hast not loved.—*Shakespeare.*

A woman is more considerate in affairs of love than a man; because love is more the study and business of her life.— *Washington Irving.*

The true measure of loving God is to love him without measure.—*St. Bernard.*

Divine love is a sacred flower, which in its early bud is happiness, and in its full bloom is heaven.—*Hervey.*

Love needs new leaves every summer of life, as much as your elm-tree, and new branches to grow broader and wider, and new flowers to cover the ground.—*Mrs. Stowe.*

How shall I do to love? Believe. How shall I do to believe? Love.—*Leighton.*

Those who have loved have little relish for friendship. The devotee of strong drink finds wine insipid.—*Alex. Dumas.*

There lives within the very flame of love a kind of wick, or snuff, that will abate it; and nothing is at a like goodness still; for goodness, growing to a pleurisy, dies in his own too much. *Shakespeare.*

Love's sweetest meanings are unspoken; the full heart knows no rhetoric of words.—*Bovee.*

Perish the lover whose imperfect flame forgets one feature of the nymph he loved.— *Shenstone.*

The first sigh of love is the last of wisdom.— *Antoine Bret.*

The height of heights is love. The philosopher dries into a skeleton like that he investigates, unless love teaches him.— *T. W. Higginson.*

To be wise and love exceeds man's might.— *Shakespeare.*

I have heard that love is the loadstone of love; how true it is!—*Ninon de l'Enclos.*

The doubts of love are never to be wholly overcome; they grow with its various anxieties, timidities, and tendernesses; and are the very fruits of the reverence in which the admired object is beheld.—*Jane Porter.*

Sweet love is food for fortune's tooth.— *Shakespeare.*

Is not every true lover a martyr?—*Hare.*

We endow those whom we love, in our fond, passionate blindness, with power upon our souls too absolute to be a mortal's trust.— *Mrs. Hemans.*

Love is the occupation of the idle man, the amusement of a busy one, and the shipwreck of a sovereign.—*Napoleon.*

Love never contracts its circles: they widen by as fixed and sure a law as those around a pebble cast into still water.—*Lowell.*

Stony limits cannot hold love out.— *Shakespeare.*

It is not the earliest blossoms which are most permanent, those which bloom in mid-season last the longest. So of that blossom of the heart, — love.—*Ninon de l'Enclos.*

He that loveth maketh his own the grandeur he loves.—*Emerson.*

Love is the fountain of pleasure; the passion which gives everything we do or enjoy its relish and agreeableness.—*Atterbury.*

Love is the only possession which we can carry with us beyond the grave.— *Madame Necker.*

Take away love, and not physical nature only, but the heart of the moral world, would be palsied.—*Southey.*

The poet's heart is an unlighted torch, which gives no help to his footsteps till love has touched it with flame.—*Lowell.*

O powerful love! that, in some respects, makes a beast a man; in some other, a man a beast.—*Shakespeare.*

What a man pays for bread and butter is worth its market value, and no more. What he pays for love's sake is gold indeed, which has a lure for angel's eyes, and rings well upon God's touchstone.—*Lowell.*

Two sentiments alone suffice for man, were he to live the age of the rocks, — love, and the contemplation of the Deity.— *Watts.*

I do much wonder that one man, seeing how much another man is a fool when he dedicates his behavior to love, will, after he hath laughed at such shallow follies in others, become the argument of his own scorn, by falling in love.
Shakespeare.

Ah! the spendthrift, love; it gives all and everything with the first sigh! —
Madame de Genlis.

Love, and you shall be loved. All love is mathematically just, as much as the two sides of an algebraic equation.—*Emerson.*

Wish chastely, and love dearly.—
Shakespeare.

Pure love and suspicion cannot dwell together: at the door where the latter enters, the former makes its exit.—*Alex. Dumas.*

Scorn, at first, makes after-love the more.—
Shakespeare.

There is a vein of inconsistency in every woman's heart, within whose portals love hath entered.—*Madame Deluzy.*

LOWLINESS.
Lowliness is young ambition's ladder, whereto the climber upward turns his face; but when he once attains the upmost round, he then unto the ladder turns his back, looks in the clouds, scorning the base degrees by which he did ascend.—*Shakespeare.*

LUCK.
I never knew an early-rising, hard-working, prudent man, careful of his earnings, and strictly honest, who complained of bad luck. A good character, good habits, and iron industry are impregnable to the assaults of all the ill-luck that fools ever dreamed of.—*Addison.*

Luck is ever waiting for something to turn up. Labor, with keen eyes and strong will, will turn up something. Luck lies in bed, and wishes the postman would bring him the news of a legacy. Labor turns out at six o'clock, and with busy pen or ringing hammer lays the foundation of a competence. Luck whines. Labor whistles. Luck relies on chance. Labor on character.—*Cobden.*

Never have anything to do with an unlucky place, or an unlucky man. I have seen many clever men, very clever men, who had not shoes to their feet. I never act with them. Their advice sounds very well, but they cannot get on themselves; and if they cannot do good to themselves, how can they do good to me? —
Rothschild.

Pitch a lucky man into the Nile, says the Arabian proverb, and he will come up with a fish in his mouth! — *Willis.*

Shallow men believe in luck, believe in circumstances: It was somebody's name, or he happened to be there at the time, or it was so then, and another day it would have been otherwise. Strong men believe in cause and effect. The man was born to do it, and his father was born to be the father of him and of this deed, and, by looking narrowly, you shall see there was no luck in the matter, but it was all a problem in arithmetic, or an experiment in chemistry.—*Emerson.*

There are no chances so unlucky from which clever people are not able to reap some advantage, and none so lucky that the foolish are not able to turn to their own disadvantage.—
Rochefoucauld.

Virtue without success is a fair picture shown by an ill light; but lucky men are favorites of heaven; all own the chief, when fortune owns the cause.—*Dryden.*

LUST.
It is the difference betwixt lust and love, that this is fixed, that volatile. Love grows, lust wastes, by enjoyment: and the reason is, that one springs from an union of souls, and the other springs from an union of sense.—
William Penn.

The blood of youth burns not with such excess as gravity's revolt to wantonness.—
Shakespeare.

Lust is a vice sooner condemned than banished; easily spoke against, but yet it will fawn as smoothly on our flesh as Circe on the Græcian travellers, when she detained them in the shape of beasts.— *W. Mason.*

Nature is content with little; grace with less; but lust with nothing.—*Matthew Henry.*

It is the grand battle of life, to teach lust the limits of Divine law, to break it into the taste of the bread of heaven, and make it understand that man doth not live by bread alone, but by every word that cometh out of the mouth of God.—*Rev. J. B. Brown.*

Capricious, wanton, bold, and brutal lust is meanly selfish; when resisted, cruel; and, like the blast of pestilential winds, taints the sweet bloom of nature's fairest forms.—*Milton.*

When vile lust, as virtue never will be moved, though lewdness court it in a shape of heaven, so lust, though to a radiant angel joined, will sate itself in a celestial bed, and prey on garbage.—*Shakespeare.*

So long as lust (whether of the world or flesh) smells sweet in our nostrils, so long we are loathesome to God.—*Colton.*

Lust is, of all the frailities of our nature, what most we ought to fear; the headstrong beast rushes along, impatient of the course; nor hears the rider's call, nor feels the rein.—*Rowe.*

Lust—hard by hate.—*Milton.*

Lust is an enemy to the purse, a foe to the person, a canker to the mind, a corrosive to the conscience, a weakness of the wit, a besotter of the senses, and finally, a mortal bane to all the body.—*Pliny.*

Lust is a captivity of the reason and an enraging of the passions. It hinders business and distracts counsel. It sins against the body and weakens the soul.—*Jeremy Taylor.*

Any enemy to whom you show kindness becomes your friend, excepting lust, the indulgence of which increases its enmity.—*Saadi.*

Light and lust are deadly enemies.—
Shakespeare.

As pills that are outwardly fair, gilt, and rolled in sugar, but within are full of bitterness: even so lustful pleasure is no sooner hatched but repentance is at hand, ready to supplant her.—*Daniel Cawdrey*

I know the very difference that lies 'twixt hallowed love and base unholy lust; I know the one is as a golden spur, urging the spirit to all noble aims; the other but a foul and miry pit, o'erthrowing it in midst of its career.—
Fanny Kemble Butler.

LUXURY.

Such luxuriants have but false appetites; like those gluttons, that by sauce force them, where they have no stomach, and sacrifice to their palate, not their health: which cannot be without great vanity, nor that without some sin.
William Penn.

There be that make it their glory to feed high, and fare deliciously every day, and to maintain their bodies elementary, search the elements, the earth, the sea, and air, to maintain the fire of their appetites. They that thus make their bellies their gods do make their glory their shame.—*Arthur Warwick.*

They that deliver themselves up to luxury are still either tormented with too little, or oppressed with too much; and are equally miserable by being either deserted or overwhelmed.—*Seneca.*

Luxury makes a man so soft, that it is hard to please him, and easy to trouble him; so that his pleasures at last become his burden. Luxury is a nice master, hard to be pleased.—
Sir G. Mackenzie.

The wealthy and the noble, when they expend large sums in decorating their houses with the rare and costly efforts of genius, with busts from the chisel of a Canova, and with cartoons from the pencil of a Raphael, are to be commended if they do not stand still here, but go on to bestow some pains and cost, that the master himself be not inferior to the mansion, and that the owner be not the only thing that is little amidst everything else that is great.—
Colton.

Sedition is bred in the lap of luxury, and its chosen emissaries are the beggared spendthrift and the impoverished libertine.—*Bancroft.*

All luxury corrupts either the morals or the taste.—*Joubert.*

Let us consider what we call vicious luxury. No gratification, however sensual, can of itself be esteemed vicious. A gratification is only vicious when it engrosses all a man's expense, and leaves no ability for such acts of duty and generosity as are required by his situation and fortune. The same care and toil that raise a dish of peas at Christmas would give bread to a whole family during six months.—*Hume.*

Falsely luxurious, will not man awake?—
Thomson.

It was a shrewd saying, whoever said it, "that the man who first brought ruin on the Roman people was he who pampered them by largesses and amusements."—*Plutarch.*

On the soft bed of luxury, most kingdoms have expired.—*Young.*

You cannot spend money in luxury without doing good to the poor. Nay, you do more good to them by spending it in luxury,— you make them exert industry, whereas by giving it, you keep them idle.—*Johnson.*

Fell luxury! more perilous to youth than storms or quicksands, poverty or chains.—
Hannah More.

I know it is more agreeable to walk upon carpets than to lie upon dungeon floors, I know it is pleasant to have all the comforts and luxuries of civilization; but he who cares only for these things is worth no more than a butterfly, contented and thoughtless, upon a morning flower; and who ever thought of rearing a tombstone to a last-summer's butterfly?—
Beecher.

Avarice and luxury, those pests which have ever been the ruin of every great state.—*Livy.*

'Garrick showed Dr. Johnson his fine house, gardens, statues, pictures, etc. at Hampton Court. "Ah! David, David," said the doctor, "these are the things which make a death-bed terrible!"—*John Bate.*

We read on the forehead of those who are surrounded by a foolish luxury, that Fortune sells what she is thought to give!—*La Fontaine.*

Luxury among the great is probably rather a moral than a political evil. But vices, no more than diseases, will stop with them; for bad habits are as infectious by example, as the plague itself is by contact.—*Fielding.*

Luxury possibly may contribute to give bread to the poor; but if there were no luxury, there would be no poor.—*Henry Home.*

The more various our artificial necessities, the wider is our circle of pleasure; for all pleasure consists in obviating necessities as they rise; luxury, therefore, as it increases our wants, increases our capacity for happiness.—
Goldsmith.

Luxury, that alluring pest with fair forehead, which, yielding always to the will of the body, throws a deadening influence over the senses, and weakens the limbs more than the drugs of Circe's cup.—*Claudian.*

LYING.
Although the Devil be the father of lies, he seems, like other great inventors, to have lost much of his reputation by the continual improvements that have been made upon him.—
Swift.

All lies disgrace a gentleman, white or black, although I grant there is a difference. To say the least of it, it is a dangerous habit, for white lies are but the gentlemen ushers to black ones. I know of but one point on which a lie is excusable, and that is, when you wish to deceive the enemy. Then, your duty to your country warrants your lying till you are black in the face; and, for the very reason that it goes against your grain, it becomes, as it were, a sort of virtue.—*Marryat.*

The most intangible, and therefore the worst, kind of a lie is a half truth. This is the peculiar device of a " conscientious " detractor.—
Washington Allston.

A lie always needs a truth for a handle to it, else the hand would cut itself which sought to drive it home upon another. The worst lies, therefore, are those whose blade is false, but whose handle is true.—*Beecher.*

No lie you can speak or act, but it will come, after longer or shorter circulation, like a bill drawn on Nature's reality, and be presented there for payment,—with the answer: No effects.—*Carlyle.*

They begin with making falsehood appear like truth, and end with making truth itself appear like falsehood.—*Shenstone.*

Habitual liars invent falsehoods not to gain any end or even to deceive their hearers, but to amuse themselves: It is partly practice and partly habit. It requires an effort in them to speak the truth.—*Hazlitt.*

Sin has many tools, but a lie is the handle which fits them all.—*Holmes.*

Lying is a disgraceful vice, and one that Plutarch paints in most disgraceful colors, when he says that it is " affording testimony that one first despises God, and then fears men." It is not possible more happily to describe its horrible, disgusting, and abandoned nature; for can we imagine anything more vile than to be cowards with regard to men, and brave with regard to God?—*Montaigne.*

A lie has no legs, and cannot stand; but it has wings, and can fly far and wide.—
Warburton.

Though people may have no interest in what they say, we must not, therefore, conclude absolutely that they are not telling a lie; for there are people who lie simply for the sake of lying.—*Pascal.*

The gain of lying is nothing else but not to be trusted of any, nor to be believed when we say the truth.—*Sir Walter Raleigh.*

After a tongue has once got the knack of lying, it is not to be imagined how impossible almost it is to reclaim it. Whence it comes to pass, that we see some men, who are otherwise very honest, so subject to this vice.—*Montaigne.*

Liars are the cause of all the sins and crimes in the world.—*Epictetus.*

When thou art obliged to speak, be sure to speak the truth; for equivocation is half-way to lying, and lying is the whole way to hell.—
William Penn.

It is more from carelessness about truth, than from intentional lying, that there is so much falsehood in the world.—*Johnson.*

He who has not a good memory should never take upon him the trade of lying.—
Montaigne.

Lord, Lord, how this world is given to lying!
Shakespeare.

He who tells a lie is not sensible how great a task he undertakes; for he must be forced to invent twenty more to maintain one.—*Pope.*

And, after all, what is a lie? It is but the truth in masquerade.—*Byron.*

How much less sociable is false speaking than silence? *Monialyne.*

———

Truth is always consistent with itself, and needs nothing to help it out; it is always near at hand, sits upon our lips, and is ready to drop out before we are aware; a lie is troublesome, and sets a man's invention upon the rack, and one trick needs a great many more to make it good. It is like building upon a false foundation, which continually stands in need of props to shore it up, and proves at last more chargeable than to have raised a substantial building at first upon a true and solid foundation.—*Addison.*

———

A great lie is like a great fish on dry land; it may fret and fling, and make a frightful bother, but it cannot hurt you. You have only to keep still and it will die of itself.—
Crabbe.

———

Nothing is rarer than a solitary lie; for lies breed like Surinam toads; you cannot tell one but out it comes with a hundred young ones on its back.— *Washington Allston*

———

When the world has once got hold of a lie, it is astonishing how hard it is to get it out of the world. You beat it about the head, till it seems to have given up the ghost, and lo! the next day it is as healthy as ever.—
Bulwer Lytton.

———

Though I never scruple a lie to serve a friend, it hurts one's conscience to be found out! —*Sheridan.*

———

As universal a practice as lying is, and as easy a one as it seems, I do not remember to have heard three good lies in all my conversation.—*Swift.*

———

A lie, though it be killed and dead, can sting sometimes, — like a dead wasp.—
Mrs. Jameson.

———

One lie must be thatched with another, or it will soon rain through.—*Dr. Owen.*

———

Half the vices in the world rise out of cowardice, and one who is afraid of lying is usually afraid of nothing else.—*James Anthony Froude.*

M.

MACHINERY.
There is this immense benefit in machinery, that it carries on those operations which debase the mind and injure the faculties. A man, by constantly performing the same operations, becomes unfit for any other. Machinery requires attention, intellectual exertion, and bodily labor of various kinds.—*Sir H. Davy.*

MAIDENHOOD.
Pale primroses, that die unmarried ere they can behold bright Phœbus in his strength, — a malady most incident to maids.—*Shakespeare.*

———

The blushing beauties of a modest maid.—
Dryden.

———

Let the words of a virgin, though in a good cause, and to as good purpose, be neither violent, many, nor first, nor last; it is less shame for a virgin to be lost in a blushing silence than to be found in a bold eloquence.—*Quarles.*

———

A maiden hath no tongue, but thought.—
Shakespeare.

———

Nature has thrown a veil of modest beauty over maidenhood and moss-roses.— *Willis.*

———

A maiden never bold; of spirit so still and quiet, that her motion blushed at herself.—
Shakespeare.

———

She had grown, in her unstained seclusion, bright and pure as a first opening lilac, when it spreads its clear leaves to the sweetest dawn of May.—*Percival.*

Her form was fresher than the morning rose when the dew wets its leaves; unstained and pure as the lily, or the mountain snow.—
Thomson.

———

The honor of a maid is her name; and no legacy is so rich as honesty.—*Shakespeare.*

———

A loving maiden grows unconsciously more bold.—*Richter.*

MADNESS.
Ecstasy! my pulse, as yours, doth temperately keep time, and make as healthful music. It is not madness that I have uttered: bring me to the test, and I the matter will re-word; which madness would gambol from.—*Shakespeare.*

———

Insanity is often the logic of an accurate mind overtasked.—*Holmes.*

———

O this poor brain! ten thousand shapes of fury are whirling there, and reason is no more.
Fielding.

———

There is a pleasure, sure, in being mad, which none but mad men know.—*Dryden.*

———

Madness is consistent; which is more than can be said for poor reason. Whatever may be the ruling passion at the time continues equally so throughout the whole delirium, though it should last for life. Madmen are always constant in love; which no man in his senses ever was. Our passions and principles are steady in frenzy; but begin to shift and waver, as we return to reason.—*Sterne.*

O, that way madness lies ; let me shun that.
Shakespeare.

Montesquieu wittily observes, that, by building professed madhouses, men tacitly insinuate that all who are out of their senses are to be found only in those places.— *Warton.*

Without one glimpse of reason or of heaven.
Moore.

Now see that noble and most sovereign reason, like sweet bells jangled, out of time, and harsh.— *Shakespeare.*

MAGNANIMITY.

Magnanimity is sufficiently defined by its name ; yet we may say of magnanimity, that it is the good sense of pride, and the noblest way of acquiring applause.— *Rochefoucauld.*

Magnanimity is above circumstance ; and any virtue which depends on that is more of constitution than of principle.— *Jane Porter.*

A great mind will neither give an affront nor bear it.— *Henry Home.*

If you desire to be magnanimous, undertake nothing rashly, and fear nothing thou undertakest ; fear nothing but infamy ; dare anything but injury ; the measure of magnanimity is neither to be rash nor timorous.— *Quarles.*

Of all virtues, magnanimity is the rarest. There are a hundred persons of merit for one who willingly acknowledges it in another.—
Hazlitt.

MAJORITY.

It never troubles the wolf how many the sheep be.— *Virgil.*

We go by the major vote, and if the majority are insane, the same must go to the hospital. As Satan said, " Evil, be thou my good," so they say, " Darkness, be thou my light."— *Horace Mann.*

One and God make a majority.—
Frederick Douglass.

A better principle than this, that " the majority shall rule," is this other, that justice shall rule. " Justice," says the Code of Justinian, " is the constant and perpetual desire to render every man his due."— *Bovee.*

The voice of the majority is no proof of justice.— *Schiller.*

A man in the right, with God on his side, is in the majority, though he be alone, for God is multitudinous above all populations of the earth.— *Beecher.*

MALICE.

Malice sucks up the greatest part of her own venom, and poisons herself.— *Montaigne.*

Those that have nothing else to say must tell stories ; fools over Burgundy, and ladies over tea, must have something that is sharp to relish their liquor ; malice is the piquant sauce of such conversation, and without it their entertainment would prove mighty insipid.—
Farquhar.

Malice, scorned, puts out itself ; but, argued, gives a kind of credit to a false accusation.—
Massinger.

But for that blindness which is inseparable from malice, what terrible powers of evil would it possess ! Fortunately for the world, its venom, like that of the rattlesnake, when most poisonous, clouds the eye of the reptile, and defeats its aim.— *Simms.*

Speak of me as I am ; nothing extenuate, nor set down aught in malice.— *Shakespeare.*

Malice, in its false witness, promotes its tale with so cunning a confusion ; so mingles truths with falsehoods, surmises with certainties, causes of no moment with matters capital, that the accused can absolutely neither grant nor deny, plead innocence nor confess guilt.—
Sir P. Sidney.

There is an alchemy of quiet malice by which women can concoct a subtle poison from ordinary trifles.— *Hawthorne.*

There is no small degree of malicious craft in fixing upon a season to give a mark of enmity and ill-will ; a word, a look, which at one time would make no impression, at another time wounds the heart, and, like a shaft flying with the wind, pierces deep, which, with its own natural force, would scarce have reached the object aimed at.— *Sterne.*

When malice is joined to envy, there is given forth poisonous and feculent matter, as ink from the cuttle-fish.— *Plutarch.*

Wit loses its respect with the good, when seen in company with malice ; and to smile at the jest which plants a thorn in another's breast is to become a principal in the mischief.
Sheridan.

As the malicious disposition of mankind is too well known, and the cruel pleasure which they take in destroying the reputation of others, the use we are to make of this knowledge is, to afford no handle for reproach ; for bad as the world is, it seldom falls on any one who hath not given some slight cause for censure.—
Fielding.

When malice has reason on its side, it looks forth bravely, and displays that reason in all its lustre. When austerity and self-denial have not realized true happiness, and the soul returns to the dictates of nature, the reaction is fearfully extravagant.— *Pascal.*

21

Even in the midst of compassion we feel within I know not what tart-sweet titillation of malicious pleasure in seeing others suffer; children have the same feeling.—*Montaigne.*

Friendship closes its eyes rather than see the moon eclipsed; while malice denies that it is ever at the full.—*Hare.*

Malice is the Devil's picture. Lust makes men brutish, and malice makes them devilish. Malice is mental murder; you may kill a man and never touch him; "Whosoever hateth his brother is a murderer."—*T. Watson.*

MAMMON.

Mammon has enriched his thousands, and has damned his ten thousands.—*South.*

MAN.

As there is much beast and some devil in man, so is there some angel and some God in him. The beast and the devil may be conquered, but, in this life, never wholly destroyed.— *Coleridge.*

Man is more than constitutions.—*Whittier.*

The record of life runs thus: Man creeps into childhood,— bounds into youth,— sobers into manhood,— softens into age,— totters into second childhood, and slumbers into the cradle prepared for him,— thence to be watched and cared for.—*Henry Giles.*

Do you know what a man is? Are not birth, beauty, good shape, discourse, manhood, learning, gentleness, virtue, youth, liberality, and such like, the spice and salt that season a man?—*Shakespeare.*

Poor pensioner on the bounty of an hour.— *Young.*

A man in old age is like a sword in a shop window. Men that look upon the perfect blade do not imagine the process by which it was completed. Man is a sword, daily life is the workshop, and God is the artificer; and those cares which beat upon the anvil, and file the edge, and eat in, acid-like, the inscription upon his hilt,— these are the very things that fashion the man.—*Beecher.*

Whenever I contemplate man in the actual world or the ideal, I am lost amidst the infinite multiformity of his life, but always end in wonder at the essential unity of his nature.— *Henry Giles.*

Man was sent into the world to be a growing and exhaustless force. The world was spread out around him to be seized and conquered. Realms of infinite truth burst open above him, inviting him to tread those shining coasts along which Newton dropped his plummet, and Herschel sailed,— a Columbus of the skies.—*Chapin.*

There are but three classes of men, the retrogade, the stationary, and the progressive.— *Lavater.*

It is an error to suppose that a man belongs to himself. No man does. He belongs to his wife, or his children, or his relations, or his creditors, or to society in some form or other. It is for their especial good and behalf that he lives and works, and they kindly allow him to retain a certain percentage of his gains to administer to his own pleasures or wants. He has his body, and that is all, and even for that he is answerable to society. In short, society is the master and man is the servant; and it is entirely according as society proves a good or bad master, whether he turns out a bad or a good servant.—*G. A. Sala.*

So weak is man, so ignorant and blind, that did not God sometimes withhold in mercy what we ask, we should be ruined at our own request. *Hannah More.*

Man — living, feeling man — is the easy sport of the overmastering present.—*Schiller.*

Now the basest thought possible concerning man is, that he has no spiritual nature; and the foolishest misunderstanding of him possible is, that he has, or should have, no animal nature. For his nature is nobly animal, nobly spiritual, — coherently and irrevocably so; neither part of it may, but at its peril, expel, despise, or defy the other.—*Ruskin.*

Man is the metre of all things, the hand is the instrument of instruments, and the mind is the form of forms.—*Aristotle.*

Omit a few of the most abstruse sciences, and mankind's study of man occupies nearly the whole field of literature. The burden of history is what man has been; of law, what he does; of physiology, what he is; of ethics, what he ought to be; of revelation, what he shall be.—*George Finlayson.*

Men, in general, are but great children.— *Napoleon.*

For man is a plant, not fixed in the earth, nor immovable, but heavenly, whose head, rising as it were from a root upwards, is turned towards heaven.—*Plutarch.*

Man is forever the same; the same under every form, in all situations and relations that admit of free and unrestrained exertion. The same regard which you have for yourself you have for others, for nature, for the invisible *Numen,* which you call God. Who has witnessed one free and unconstrained act of yours has witnessed all.—*Lavater.*

Man is an animal that makes bargains; no other animal does this,— one dog does not change a bone with another.—*Adam Smith.*

Man is a noble animal, splendid in ashes, pompous in the grave.—*Sir Thomas Browne.*

What a chimera is man! What a singular phenomenon! what a chaos! what a scene of contrariety! A judge of all things, yet a feeble worm; the shrine of truth, yet a mass of doubt and uncertainty; at once the glory and the scorn of the universe. If he boasts, I lower him; if he lowers himself, I raise him; either way I contradict him, till he learns that he is a monstrous, incomprehensible mystery.—*Pascal.*

No man is so great as mankind.
Theodore Parker.

Man is greater than a world, than systems of worlds; there is more mystery in the union of soul with the physical than in the creation of a universe.—*Henry Giles.*

Man is an animal that cooks his victuals.—
Burke.

Man is the highest product of his own history. The discoverer finds nothing so grand or tall as himself, nothing so valuable to him. The greatest star is that at the little end of the telescope, — the star that is looking, not looked after, nor looked at.—*Theodore Parker.*

If there are men in whom the ridiculous has never appeared, it is because they have not been well searched.—*Rochefoucauld.*

Of all the animals which fly in the air, walk on the ground, or swim in the sea, from Paris to Peru, from Japan to Rome, the most foolish animal in my opinion is man.—*Boileau.*

Men are but children of a larger growth; our appetites are apt to change as theirs, and full as craving too, and full as vain.—*Dryden.*

O rich and various man! thou palace of sight and sound, carrying in thy senses the morning and the night, and the unfathomable galaxy; in thy brain, the geometry of the city of God; in thy heart, the power of love and the realms of right and wrong. An individual man is a fruit which it cost all the foregoing ages to form and ripen. He is strong, not to do, but to live; not in his arms, but in his heart; not as an agent, but as a fact.—*Emerson.*

Man is the end towards which all the animal creation has tended from the first appearance of the first Palæozoic fishes.—*Agassiz.*

A man ought to carry himself in the world as an orange-tree would if it could walk up and down in the garden, — swinging perfume from every little censer it holds up to the air.—
Beecher.

He is a man who knows how to die for his God and his country; his heart, his lips, his arms, are faithful unto death.—*Ernest Arndt.*

Man is the image and glory of God, but the woman is the glory of the man.—*Bible.*

Man perfected by society is the best of all animals; he is the most terrible of all when he lives without law and without justice. If he finds himself an individual who cannot live in society, or who pretends he has need of only his own resources, do not consider him as a member of humanity; he is a savage beast or a god.—*Aristotle.*

Man is the jewel of God, who has created this material world to keep his treasure in.—
Theodore Parker.

Man is a central creature between the animals, that is to say, the most perfect form, which unites the traits of all in the most complete epitome.—*Herder.*

Man is an individual animal with narrow faculties, but infinite desires, which he is anxious to concentrate in some one object within the grasp of his imagination, and where, if he cannot be all that he wishes himself, he may at least contemplate his own pride, vanity, and passions, displayed in their most extravagant dimensions in a being no bigger and no better than himself.—*Hazlitt.*

Lord, we know what we are, but know not what we may be.—*Shakespeare.*

Man is too near all kinds of beasts, — a fawning dog, a roaring lion, a thieving fox, a robbing wolf, a dissembling crocodile, a treacherous decoy, and a rapacious vulture.—*Cowley.*

How poor, how rich, how abject, how august, how complicate, how wonderful, is man!—*Young.*

A man is like a bit of Labrador spar, which has no lustre as you turn it in your hand, until you come to a particular angle; then it shows deep and beautiful colors.—*Emerson.*

To despise our own species is the price we must too often pay for a knowledge of it.—
Colton.

What a piece of work is a man! How noble in reason! How infinite in faculties! In form and moving, how express and admirable! In action, how like an angel! In apprehension, how like a God.—*Shakespeare.*

Look what a little vain dust we are! —
Addison.

Men are, in the state, what musical instruments are in an orchestra; they render the sounds more or less agreeable according as they are well or badly touched.—*Beaumelle.*

God made him, and therefore let him pass for a man.—*Shakespeare.*

Man is improvable. Some people think he is only a machine, and that the only difference between a man and a mill is, that one is carried by blood and the other by water.—*Horace Mann.*

Every man is exceptional.—*Emerson.*

God hath given to mankind a common library, his creatures; and to every man a proper book, himself, being an abridgment of all the others: if thou read with understanding, it will make thee a great master of philosophy, and a true servant to the divine Author; if thou but barely read, it will make thee thy own wise man, and the Author's fool.—*Quarles.*

Man should be ever better than he seems; and shape his acts, and discipline his mind, to walk adorning earth, with hope of heaven.—
Sir Aubrey de Vere.

Man is but a little thing in the midst of the objects of nature, yet, by the moral quality radiating from his countenance, he may abolish all considerations of magnitude, and, in his manners, equal the majesty of the world.—
Emerson.

Bounded in his nature, infinite in his desires, man is a fallen god who has a recollection of heaven.—*Lamartine.*

Born to be ploughed with years, and sown with cares, and reaped by Death, lord of the human soil.—*Byron.*

" We touch heaven when we lay our hand on a human body!" This sounds much like a mere flourish of rhetoric; but it is not so. If well meditated, it will turn out to be a scientific fact; the expression, in such words as can be had, of the actual truth of the thing. We are the miracle of miracles,—the great inscrutable mystery of God. We cannot understand it, we know not how to speak of it; but we may feel and know, if we like, that it is verily so.—*Carlyle.*

The proper study of mankind is man.—
Pope.

Man is physically as well as metaphysically a thing of shreds and patches, borrowed unequally from good and bad ancestors, and a misfit from the start.—*Emerson.*

Man! thou pendulum betwixt a smile and tear.—*Byron.*

It has always struck me that there is a far greater distinction between man and man than between many men and most other animals.—
Basil Hall.

Man, if he compare himself with all that he can see, is at the zenith of power; but if he compare himself with all that he can conceive, he is at the nadir of weakness.—*Colton.*

This is the state of man: to-day he puts forth the tender leaves of hope; to-morrow blossoms and bears his blushing honors thick upon him; the third day comes a frost, a killing frost; and when he thinks, good easy man, full surely his greatness is a ripening, nips his root, and then he falls.—*Shakespeare.*

Mankind at large always resemble frivolous children; they are impatient of thought, and wish to be amused.—*Emerson.*

Half dust, half deity, alike unfit to sink or soar.—*Byron.*

Man is by nature weak; he is born in and to a state of dependence; he therefore naturally seeks and looks about for help, and where he observes the greatest power, it is there that he applies and prays for protection.—*H. Brooke.*

MANAGEMENT.

As in the greater world for man, so in the little world of man,—as in the outward riches of the one, so in the inner treasures of the other, many possess much, and enjoy but little; many have much, and use but little; others use much, and but little well. I shall not so much endeavor to have much wherewithal to do as to do much with that little I have. It shall not so much grieve me that I am a poor treasurer, as joy me if I had been a good steward. I could wish I had more to use well, but more wish well to use that I have. If he were so blamed that employed not one talent well, what would become of me if I had ten and abused them?—
Arthur Warwick.

MANNERS.

There is certainly something of exquisite kindness and thoughtful benevolence in that rarest of gifts,—fine breeding.—*Bulwer Lytton.*

It is meat and drink to me to see a clown.—
Shakespeare.

I could better eat with one who did not respect the truth or the laws than with a sloven and unpresentable person. Moral qualities rule the world, but at short distances the senses are despotic.—*Emerson.*

A mien austere oft veils a vicious heart.—
Martial.

There is a policy in manner. I have heard one, not inexperienced in the pursuit of fame, give it his earnest support, as being the surest passport to absolute and brilliant success.—
Tuckerman.

Unbecoming forwardness oftener proceeds from ignorance than impudence.—*Lord Greville.*

Prepare yourself for the world, as the athletæ used to do for their exercises; oil your mind and your manners, to give them the necessary suppleness and flexibility; strength alone will not do.—*Chesterfield.*

Good-breeding shows itself most where to an ordinary eye it appears the least.—*Addison.*

There is not any benefit so glorious in itself but it may be exceedingly sweetened and improved by the manner of conferring it. The virtue, I know, rests in the intent, but the beauty and ornament of an obligation lies in the manner of it.—*Seneca.*

There are some people who give with the air of refusal.—*Queen Christiana.*

How often have I seen the most solid merit and knowledge neglected, unwelcome, and even rejected; while flimsy parts, little knowledge, and less merit, introduced by the Graces, have been received, cherished, and admired! — *Chesterfield.*

Virtue itself offends when coupled with forbidding manners.—*Bishop Middleton.*

Society loves Creole natures, and sleepy, languishing manners, so that they cover sense, grace, and good-will, — the air of drowsy strength which disarms criticism.—*Emerson.*

The immoral man, who invades another's property, is justly punished for it; and the ill-bred man, who by his ill manners invades and disturbs the quiet and comforts of private life, is by common consent as justly banished society. For my own part, I really think, next to the consciousness of doing a good action, that of doing a civil one is the most pleasing; and the epithet which I should covet the most, next to that of Aristides, would be that of well-bred.—*Chesterfield.*

It is the manner which is better than all.— *Sir P. Sidney.*

Manners must adorn knowledge, and smooth its way through the world. Like a great rough diamond, it may do very well in a closet by way of curiosity, and also for its intrinsic value.— *Chesterfield.*

To be good and disagreeable is high treason against the royalty of virtue.—*Hannah More.*

A man whose great qualities want the ornament of exterior attractions is like a naked mountain with mines of gold, which will be frequented only till the treasure is exhausted.— *Johnson.*

It is not enough to have reason ; it is spoilt, it is dishonored, by sustaining a brusk and haughty manner.—*Fenelon.*

Manners are the shadows of virtues, the momentary display of those qualities which our fellow-creatures love and respect. If we strive to become, then, what we strive to appear, manners may often be rendered useful guides to the performance of our duties.—*Sydney Smith.*

The more generally persons are pleasing, the less profoundly do they please.—*H. Beyle.*

There is no policy like politeness ; and a good manner is the best thing in the world, either to get a good name, or to supply the want of it.—*Bulwer Lytton.*

Many young persons believe themselves natural when they are only impolite and coarse.— *Rochefoucauld.*

What better school for manners than the company of virtuous women ; where the mutual endeavor to please must insensibly polish the mind, where the example of the female softness and modesty must communicate itself to their admirers, and where the delicacy of the sex puts every one on his guard lest he give offence ? —*Hume.*

Manner is everything with some people, and something with everybody.— *Bishop Middleton.*

Parents are commonly more careful to bestow wit on their children than the art of speaking well than doing well ;. but their manners ought to be the great concern.—*Fuller.*

I can forgive a crime, — it may have some grand motive, — but never an awkwardness.— *Madame Recamier.*

What a rare gift, by the by, is that of manners ! how difficult to define, how much more difficult to impart ! Better for a man to possess them than wealth, beauty, or talent; they will more than supply all.—*Bulwer Lytton.*

I don't believe in the goodness of disagreeable people.—*Orville Dewey.*

There is a certain artificial polish, a commonplace vivacity, acquired by perpetually mingling in the *beau monde*, which, in the commerce of the world, supplies the place of natural suavity and good-humor ; but it is purchased at the expense of all original and sterling traits of character.— *Washington Irving.*

A well-bred man is always sociable and complaisant.—*Montaigne.*

Manners are of more importance than laws. Upon them, in a great measure, the laws depend. The law can touch us here and there, now and then. Manners are what vex or soothe, corrupt or purify, exalt or debase, barbarize or refine, by a constant, steady, uniform, insensible operation, like that of the air we breathe in. They give their whole form and colors to our lives. According to their quality they aid morals, they supply them, or they totally destroy them.—*Burke.*

Grace is to the body what good sense is to the mind.—*Rochefoucauld.*

One of the most important rules of the science of manners is an almost absolute silence in regard to yourself.—*Balzac.*

The distinguishing trait of people accustomed to good society is a calm, imperturbable quiet which pervades all their actions and habits, from the greatest to the least. They eat in quiet, move in quiet, live in quiet, and lose their wife, or even their money, in quiet; while low persons cannot take up either a spoon or an affront without making such an amazing noise about it.—*Bulwer Lytton.*

Striking manners are bad manners.—
Robert Hall.

In conversation use some, but not too much ceremony; it teaches others to be courteous too. Demeanors are commonly paid back in their own coin.—*Fuller.*

Men's evil manners live in brass; their virtues we write in water.—*Shakespeare.*

There is a probity of manners, as well as of conscience, and a true Christian will regard in a degree the conventionalities of society.—
De Boufflers.

The true art of being agreeable is to appear well pleased with all the company, and rather to seem well entertained with them than to bring entertainment to them. A man thus disposed may have not much learning, nor any wit; but if he has common sense, and something friendly in his behavior, it conciliates men's minds more than the brightest parts without this disposition.—*Addison.*

Good manners are the settled medium of social, as specie is of commercial, life; returns are equally expected for both; and people will no more advance their civility to a bear, than their money to a bankrupt.—*Chesterfield.*

There are some people that even mind and the usage of the world will not teach; and without wanting the most perfect politeness they often wound the heart.—*Madame de Staël.*

Manners are the ornament of action.
Samuel Smiles.

Pride, ill-nature, and want of sense, are the three great sources of ill manners; without some one of these defects, no man will behave himself ill for want of experience, or what, in the language of fools, is called knowing the world.—*Swift.*

Civility costs nothing, and buys everything.
Mary Wortley Montagu.

A man's fortune is frequently decided by his first address. If pleasing, others at once conclude he has merit; but if ungraceful, they decide against him.—*Chesterfield.*

Wisdom, valor, justice, and learning cannot keep a man in countenance that is possessed with these excellences, if he wants that inferior art of life and behavior called good-breeding.—*Steele.*

There is a nobility in the world of manners.
Schiller.

Your manners are always under examination, and by committees little suspected, — a police in citizen's clothes, — but who are awarding or denying you very high prizes when you least think of it.—*Emerson.*

A company attitude is rarely anybody's best.
Miss Sedgwick.

It is easier to polish the manners than to reform the heart, to disguise a fault than to conquer it. He who can venture to appear as he is must be what he ought to be, — a difficult and arduous task, which often requires the sacrifice of many a darling inclination and the exertion of many a painful effort.—*Bowdler.*

An imposing air should always be taken as an evidence of imposition. Dignity is often a veil between us and the real truth of things.—
Whipple.

It is certain that either wise bearing or ignorant carriage is caught, as men take diseases, one of another; therefore let men take heed of their company.—*Shakespeare.*

Manners easily and rapidly mature into morals.—*Horace Mann.*

Morals and manners, which give color to life, are of greater importance than laws, which are but one of their manifestations. The law touches us here and there, but manners are about us everywhere, pervading society like the air we breathe. Good manners, as we call them, are neither more nor less than good behavior, consisting of courtesy and kindness.—
Samuel Smiles.

All good conversation, manners, and action come from a spontaneity which forgets usages and makes the moment great.—*Emerson.*

With virtue, capacity, and good conduct, one still can be insupportable. The manners, which are neglected as small things, are often those which decide men for or against you. A slight attention to them would have prevented their ill judgments.—*Bruyère.*

Fine manners are the mantle of fair minds.—
Alcott.

Genius invents fine manners, which the baron and the baroness copy very fast, and, by the advantage of a palace, better the instruction. They stereotype the lesson they have learned into a mode.—*Emerson.*

I take it for a rule, that the natural, and not the acquired, man is the companion. Learning, wit, gallantry, and good-breeding are all but subordinate qualities in society, and are of no value, but as they are subservient to benevolence, and tend to a certain manner of being or appearing equal to the rest of the company.—*Steele.*

There are some persons on whom their faults sit well, and others who are made ungraceful by their good qualities.—*Rochefoucauld.*

Manners are the happy ways of doing things; each one a stroke of genius or of love, now repeated and hardened into usage, they form at last a rich varnish, with which the routine of life is washed, and its details adorned. If they are superficial, so are the dew-drops which give such a depth to the morning meadows.—*Emerson.*

They asked Lucman, the fabulist, From whom did you learn manners? He answered: From the unmannerly.—*Saadi.*

Nothing, except what flows from the heart, can render even external manners truly pleasing.—*Blair.*

In society, good temper and animal spirits are nearly everything. They are of more importance than sallies of wit or refinements of understanding. They give a general tone of cheerfulness •and satisfaction to the company. The French have the advantage over us in external manners. They breathe a lighter air, and have a brisker circulation of the blood.—*Hazlitt.*

Adorn yourself with all those graces and accomplishments which without solidity are frivolous; but without which, solidity is to a great degree useless.—*Chesterfield.*

In manners, tranquillity is the supreme power.—*Madame de Maintenon.*

Impure manners prepare the heart for unclean spirits, and give them the opportunity they desire. We have heard of certain arts to call up the Devil, but a man need only live like a swine, and he will be sure to have his company.—*Jones of Nayland.*

Nothing so much prevents our being natural, as the desire of appearing so.—*Rochefoucauld.*

I never judge from manners, for I once had my pocket picked by the civilest gentleman I ever met with, and one of the mildest persons I ever saw was Ali Pacha.—*Byron.*

Frugality of manners is the nourishment and strength of bodies politic; it is that by which they grow and subsist, until they are corrupted by luxury,—the natural cause of their decay and ruin.—*Bishop Berkeley.*

Good manners are a part of good morals.—*Whately.*

Truth, justice, and reason lose all their force, and all their lustre, when they are not accompanied with agreeable manners.—*Thomson.*

Manners are the root, laws only the trunk and branches. Manners are the archetypes of laws. Manners are laws in their infancy; laws are manners fully grown,—or, manners are children, which, when they grow up, become laws.—*Horace Mann.*

Marriage, indeed, may qualify the fury of his passion; but it very rarely mends a man's manners.—*Congreve.*

As a man's salutation, so is the total of his character; in nothing do we lay ourselves so open as in our manner of meeting and salutation.—*Lavater.*

The manner of saying or of doing anything goes a great way in the value of the thing itself. It was well said of him that called a good office that was done harshly, and with an ill-will, a stony piece of bread; it is necessary for him that is hungry to receive it, but it almost chokes a man in the going down.—*Seneca.*

Manners are stronger than laws.—*Alexander Carlile.*

Manners are the shadows of virtues; the momentary display of those qualities which our fellow-creatures love and respect. If we strive to become, then, what we strive to appear, manners may often be rendered useful guides to the performance of our duties.—*Sydney Smith.*

You will, I believe, in general, ingratiate yourself with others, still less by paying them too much court than too little.—*Lord Greville.*

There is not, perhaps, a more whimsical figure in nature than a man of real modesty who assumes an air of impudence; who, while his heart beats with anxiety, studies ease and affects good-humor.—*Goldsmith.*

There is a deportment which suits the figure and talents of each person; it is always lost when we quit it to assume that of another.—*Rousseau.*

The manner of a vulgar man has freedom without ease, and the manner of a gentleman has ease without freedom.—*Chesterfield.*

Bad manners are a species of bad morals. A conscientious man will not grossly offend in that way.—*Bovee.*

To be always thinking about your manners is not the way to make them good; because the very perfection of manners is not to think about yourself.—*Whately.*

MARTYRS.

The martyrs to vice far exceed the martyrs to virtue, both in endurance and in number. So blinded are we by our passions, that we suffer more to be damned than to be saved.—*Colton.*

Christianity has made martyrdom sublime, and sorrow triumphant.—*Chapin.*

No language can fitly express the meanness, the baseness, the brutality, with which the world has ever treated its victims of one age and boasts of the next. Dante is worshipped at that grave to which he was hurried by persecution. Milton, in his own day, was "Mr. Milton, the blind adder, that spit his venom on the king's person"; and soon after, "the mighty orb of song." These absurd transitions from hatred to apotheosis, this recognition just at the moment when it becomes a mockery, saddens all intellectual history.—*Whipple.*

It is the cause, and not the death, that makes the martyr.—*Napoleon.*

Two things are necessary to a modern martyr,—some to pity, and some to persecute, some to regret, and some to roast him. If martyrdom is now on the decline, it is not because martyrs are less zealous, but because martyr-mongers are more wise.—*Colton.*

When we read, we fancy we could be martyrs; when we come to act, we cannot bear a provoking word.—*Hannah More*

It is said all martyrdoms looked mean when they were suffered.—*Emerson.*

To die for truth is not to die for one's country, but to die for the world. Truth, like the Venus de Medici, will pass down in thirty fragments to posterity; but posterity will collect and recompose them into a goddess. Then, also, thy temple, O eternal Truth! that now stands half below the earth, made hollow by the sepulchres of its witnesses, will raise itself in the total majesty of its proportions, and will stand in monumental granite; and every pillar on which it rests will be fixed in the grave of a martyr.—*Richter.*

It is more difficult, and calls for higher energies of soul, to live a martyr than to die one.—*Horace Mann.*

He that dies a martyr proves that he was not a knave, but by no means that he was not a fool; since the most absurd doctrines are not without such evidence as martyrdom can produce. A martyr, therefore, by the mere act of suffering, can prove nothing but his own faith.—*Colton.*

Those who completely sacrifice themselves are praised and admired; that is the sort of character men like to find in others.—*Rahel.*

O, how much those men are to be valued who, in the spirit with which the widow gave up her two mites, have given up themselves! How their names sparkle! How rich their very ashes are! How they will count up in heaven!—*Chapin.*

And they stoned Stephen, calling upon God, and saying, Lord Jesus, receive my spirit. And he kneeled down, and cried with a loud voice, Lord, lay not this sin to their charge. And when he had said this, he fell asleep.—*Bible.*

For some not to be martyred is a martyrdom.—*Donne.*

The torments of martyrdom are probably most keenly felt by the bystanders. The torments are illusory. The first suffering is the last suffering, the latter hurts being lost on insensibility. Our affections and wishes for the external welfare of the hero tumultuously rush to expression in tears and outcries; but we, like him, subside into indifferency and defiance, when we perceive how short is the longest arm of malice, how serene is the sufferer.—*Emerson.*

MASTER.

I follow him to serve my turn upon him; we cannot all be masters, nor all masters cannot be truly followed.—*Shakespeare.*

It is not only paying wages, and giving commands, that constitutes a master of a family; but prudence, equal behavior, with a readiness to protect and cherish them, is what entitles a man to that character in their very hearts and sentiments.—*Steele.*

The many still must labor for the one! It is nature's doom.—*Byron.*

It is proper for every one to consider, in the case of all men, that he who has not been a servant cannot become a praiseworthy master; and it is meet that we should plume ourselves rather on acting the part of a servant properly than that of the master, first, towards the laws, (for in this way we are servants of the gods), and next, towards our elders.—*Plato.*

If thou art a master, be sometimes blind; if a servant, sometimes deaf.—*Fuller.*

We must truly serve those whom we appear to command; we must bear with their imperfections, correct them with gentleness and patience, and lead them in the way to heaven.—*Fenelon.*

The measure of a master is his success in bringing all men round to his opinion twenty years later.—*Emerson.*

It is a common law of nature, which no time will ever change, that superiors shall rule their inferiors.—*Dionysius.*

There is nothing so good to make a horse fat, as the eye of his master.—*Diogenes.*

MATRIMONY.

I chose my wife, as she did her wedding gown, for qualities that would wear well.—*Goldsmith.*

Have ever more care that thou be beloved of thy wife, rather than thyself besotted on her; and thou shalt judge of her love by these two observations: first, if thou perceive she have a care of thy estate, and exercise herself therein; the other, if she study to please thee, and be sweet unto thee in conversation, without thy instruction; for love needs no teaching nor precept.—*Sir Walter Raleigh.*

He that takes a wife takes care.—*Franklin.*

The reason why so few marriages are happy is because young ladies spend their time in making nets, not in making cages.—*Swift.*

Up to twenty-one, I hold a father to have power over his children as to marriage; after that age, authority and influence only. Show me one couple unhappy merely on account of their limited circumstances, and I will show you ten who are wretched from other causes.—*Coleridge.*

No man can either live piously or die righteous without a wife.—*Richter.*

Two persons who have chosen each other out of all the species with a design to be each other's mutual comfort and entertainment have, in that action, bound themselves to be good-humored, affable, discreet, forgiving, patient, and joyful, with respect to each other's frailties and perfections, to the end of their lives.—*Addison.*

To be man's tender mate was woman born, and in obeying nature she best serves the purposes of heaven.—*Schiller.*

Marriage has in it less of beauty, but more of safety, than the single life; it hath not more ease, but less danger; it is more merry and more sad; it is fuller of sorrows and fuller of joys; it lies under more burdens, but is supported by all the strengths of love and charity; and those burdens are delightful. Marriage is the mother of the world, and preserves kingdoms, and fills cities and churches and heaven itself.—*Jeremy Taylor.*

Strong are the instincts with which God has guarded the sacredness of marriage.—*Maria M'Intosh.*

He that hath wife and children hath given hostages to fortune; for they are impediments to great enterprises, either of virtue or mischief. Certainly wife and children are a kind of discipline of humanity.—*Bacon.*

Never marry but for love; but see that thou lovest what is lovely.—*William Penn.*

The good husband keeps his wife in the wholesome ignorance of unnecessary secrets. They will not be starved with the ignorance, who perchance may surfeit with the knowledge of weighty counsels, too heavy for the weaker sex to bear. He knows little who will tell his wife all he knows.—*Steele.*

Should all despair that have revolted wives, the tenth of mankind would hang themselves.—*Shakespeare.*

It is the most momentous question a woman is ever called upon to decide, whether the faults of the man she loves are beyond remedy and will drag her down, or whether she is competent to be his earthly redeemer and lift him to her own level.—*Holmes.*

Humble wedlock is far better than proud virginity.—*St. Augustine.*

A married man falling into misfortune is more apt to retrieve his situation in the world than a single one, chiefly because his spirits are soothed and retrieved by domestic endearments, and his self-respect kept alive by finding that although all abroad be darkness and humiliation, yet there is a little world of love at home over which he is a monarch.—*Jeremy Taylor.*

First get an absolute conquest over thyself, and then thou wilt easily govern thy wife.—*Fuller.*

In the opinion of the world, marriage ends all; as it does in a comedy. The truth is precisely the reverse. It begins all. So they say of death, "It is the end of all things." Yes, just as much as marriage.—*Madame Swetchine.*

What, therefore, God hath joined together let not man put asunder.—*Bible.*

If idleness be the root of all evil, then matrimony is good for something, for it sets many a poor woman to work.—*Vanbrugh.*

Men are April when they woo, December when they wed.—*Shakespeare.*

Marriage is a desperate thing; the frogs in Æsop were extremely wise; they had a great mind to some water, but they would not leap into the well, because they could not get out again.—*Selden.*

A world-without-end bargain.—*Shakespeare.*

It is a mistake to consider marriage merely as a scheme of happiness. It is also a bond of service. It is the most ancient form of that social ministration which God has ordained for all human beings, and which is symbolized by all the relations of nature.—*Chapin.*

Go down the ladder when thou marriest a wife; go up when thou choosest a friend.—
Rabbi Ben Azai.

We are not very much to blame for our bad marriages. We live amid hallucinations, and this especial trap is laid to trip up our feet with, and all are tripped up first or last. But the mighty mother, who had been so sly with us, as if she felt she owed us some indemnity, insinnates into the Pandora box of marriage some deep and serious benefits, and some great joys.
Emerson.

Men are generally more careful of the breed of their horses and dogs than of their children.
William Penn.

When it shall please God to bring thee to man's estate, use great providence and circumspection in choosing thy wife. For from thence will spring all thy future good or evil; and it is an action of life, like unto a stratagem of war; wherein a man can err but once!—
Sir P. Sidney.

As the husband is, the wife is; if mated with a clown.—*Tennyson.*

The man at the head of the house can mar the pleasure of the household; but he cannot make it. That must rest with the woman, and it is her greatest privilege.—*Helps.*

It is in vain for a man to be born fortunate, if he be unfortunate in his marriage.—*Dacier.*

Save the love we pay to Heaven, there is none purer, holier, than that a virtuous woman feels for him she would cleave through life to. Sisters part from sisters, brothers from brothers, children from their parents, but such woman from the husband of her choice never!—
Sheridan Knowles.

To be a man in a true sense is, in the first place, and above all things, to have a wife.—
Michelet.

A man may be cheerful and contented in celibacy, but I do not think he can ever be happy; it is an unnatural state, and the best feelings of his nature are never called into action.
Southey.

The amity that wisdom knits not, folly may easily nutie.—*Shakespeare.*

Not whom you marry, but how much you marry, is the real question among the Hon. Tom Shuffletons of every age.—*Whipple.*

Marriages are best of dissimilar material.—
Theodore Parker.

To love early and marry late is to hear a lark singing at dawn, and at night to eat it roasted for supper.—*Richter.*

Mistress, know yourself; down on your knees, and thank Heaven, fasting, for a good man's love. For I must tell you friendly in your ear, — sell when you can; you are not for all markets.—
Shakespeare.

God has set the type of marriage everywhere throughout the creation. Each creature seeks its perfection in another. The very heavens and earth picture it to us.— *Luther.*

O love of loves! to thy white hand is given of earthly happiness the golden key!—
Rev. Dr. Croly.

For parents to restrain the inclinations of their children in marriage is an usurped power. For how can Nature give another the power to direct those affections which she has not enabled even ourselves to govern! —*Fielding.*

Marriage is the nursery of heaven! —
Jeremy Taylor.

As a great part of the uneasiness of matrimony arises from mere trifles, it would be wise in every young married man to enter into an agreement with his wife, that in all disputes of this kind the party who was most convinced they were right should always surrender the victory. By which means both would be more forward to give up the cause.—*Fielding.*

Two consorts in heaven are not two, but one angel.—*Swedenborg.*

It is a delightful thought, that, during the familiarity of constant proximity, the heart gathers up in silence the nutriment of love, as the diamond, even beneath water, imbibes the light it emits. Time, which deadens hatred, secretly strengthens love.—*Richter.*

Man is the circled oak; woman the ivy.—
Aaron Hill.

Deceive not thyself by over-expecting happiness in the marriage state. Look not therein for contentment greater than God will give, or a creature in this world can receive, namely, to be free from all inconveniences. Marriage is not, like the hill of Olympus, wholly clear without clouds.—*Fuller.*

Maids are May when they are maids, but the sky changes when they are wives.
Shakespeare.

An idol may be undeified by many accidental causes. Marriage, in particular, is a kind of counter-apotheosis, or a deification inverted. When a man becomes familiar with his goddess, she quickly sinks into a woman.—
Addison.

Marriage to maids is like a war to men; the battle causes fear, but the sweet hopes of winning at the last still draws them in.—*Lee.*

A latent discontent is the secret spur of most of our enterprises. Marriage, by making us more contented, causes us often to be less enterprising.—*Bovee.*

Hail, wedded love, mysterious law, true source of human offspring!—*Milton.*

Her gentle spirit commits itself to yours to be directed, as from her lord, her governor, her king.—*Shakespeare.*

She that hath a wise husband must entice him to an eternal dearness by the veil of modesty and the grave robes of chastity, the ornament of meekness and the jewels of faith and charity. She must have no painting but blushings; her brightness must be purity, and she must shine round about with sweetness and friendship; and she shall be pleasant while she lives, and desired when she dies.— *Jeremy Taylor.*

Only so far as a man is happily married to himself is he fit for married life and family life generally.—*Novalis.*

Take the daughter of a good mother.— *Fuller.*

Marriage is the best state for man in general; and every man is a worse man in proportion as he is unfit for the married state.—*Johnson.*

Marriage is a feast where the grace is sometimes better than the dinner.—*Colton.*

All the molestations of marriage are abundantly recompensed with other comforts which God bestoweth on them who make a wise choice of a wife.—*Fuller.*

Husbands and wives talk of the cares of matrimony, and bachelors and spinsters bear them. *Wilkie Collins.*

If you wish to marry suitably, marry your equal.—*Ovid.*

In the career of female fame, there are few prizes to be obtained which can vie with the obscure state of a beloved wife or a happy mother.—*Jane Porter.*

There are good marriages, but there are no delightful ones.—*Rochefoucauld.*

The land of marriage has this peculiarity, that strangers are desirous of inhabiting it, while its natural inhabitants would willingly be banished from thence.—*Montaigne.*

It is not good that man should be alone.— *Bible.*

Let still the woman take an elder than herself; so wears she to him, so sways she level in her husband's heart.—*Shakespeare.*

Such a large sweet fruit is a complete marriage, that it needs a very long summer to ripen in and then a long winter to mellow and season it.—*Theodore Parker.*

A man finds himself seven years older the day after his marriage.—*Bacon.*

The bloom or blight of all men's happiness! *Byron.*

Of all the actions of a man's life, his marriage does least concern other people; yet, of all actions of our life, it is most meddled with by other people.—*Selden.*

He that would have fine guests, let him have a fine wife.—*Johnson.*

From my experience, not one in twenty marries the first love; we build statues of snow and weep to see them melt.—*Walter Scott.*

The instances, that second marriage move, are base respects of thrift, but none of love.— *Shakespeare.*

As a looking-glass, if it is a true one, faithfully represents the face of him that looks in it, so a wife ought to fashion herself to the affection of her husband; not to be cheerful when he is sad, nor sad when he is cheerful.—*Erasmus.*

Men should keep their eyes wide open before marriage, and half shut afterwards.— *Madame Scudéri.*

It is to be feared that they who marry where they do not love will love where they do not marry.— *Fuller.*

But earthlier happy is the rose distilled than that which, withering on the virgin thorn, grows, lives, and dies in single blessedness.— *Shakespeare.*

MEANNESS.

I have so great a contempt and detestation for meanness, that I could sooner make a friend of one who had committed murder, than of a person who could be capable, in any instance, of the former vice. Under meanness, I comprehend dishonesty; under dishonesty, ingratitude; under ingratitude, irreligion; and under this latter, every species of vice and immorality in human nature.—*Sterne.*

Superior men, and yet not always virtuous, there have been, alas! But there never has been a mean man, and at the same time virtuous.—*Confucius.*

I have great hope of a wicked man, slender hope of a mean one. A wicked man may be converted and become a prominent saint. A mean man ought to be converted six or seven times, one right after the other, to give him a fair start and put him on an equality with a bold, wicked man.—*Beecher.*

MEDICINE.

The disease and its medicine are like two factions in a besieged town; they tear one another to pieces, but both unite against their common enemy, Nature.—*Jeffrey.*

By medicine life may be prolonged, yet death will seize the doctor too.—*Shakespeare.*

The bitterness of the portion, and the abhorrence of the patient are necessary circumstances to the operation. The nature that would eat rhubarb like buttered turnips would frustrate the use and nature of it. It must be something to trouble and disturb the stomach that must purge and cure it.—*Montaigne.*

The poets did well to conjoin music and medicine, because the office of medicine is but to tune the curious harp of man's body.—*Bacon.*

MEDIOCRITY.

Mediocrity can talk; but it is for genius to observe.—*Disraeli.*

The highest order of mind is accused of folly, as well as the lowest. Nothing is thoroughly approved but mediocrity. The majority has established this, and it fixes its fangs on whatever gets beyond it either way.—*Pascal.*

Nothing in the world is more haughty than a man of moderate capacity when once raised to power.—*Baron Wessenberg.*

Mediocrity is not allowed to poets, either by the gods or men.—*Horace.*

We meet with few utterly dull and stupid souls; the sublime and transcendent are still fewer; the generality of mankind stand between these two extremes; the interval is filled with multitudes of ordinary geniuses, but all very useful, and the ornaments and supports of the commonwealth.—*Bruyère.*

Minds of moderate calibre ordinarily condemn everything which is beyond their range.—*Rochefoucauld.*

Persevering mediocrity is much more respectable, and unspeakably more useful, than talented inconstancy.—*Dr. James Hamilton.*

The virtue of the soul does not consist in flying high, but walking orderly; its grandeur does not exercise itself in grandeur, but in mediocrity.—*Montaigne.*

Mediocrity is beneath a brave soul.—*Lady Blessington.*

The art of putting well into play mediocre qualities often begets more reputation than true merit achieves.—*Rochefoucauld.*

Mediocrity only of enjoyment is allowed to man.—*Blair.*

There are certain things in which mediocrity is not to be endured, such as poetry, music, painting, public speaking.—*Bruyère.*

MEDITATION.

Meditation is the soul's perspective glass, whereby, in her long removes, she discerneth God, as if he were nearer at hand.—*Feltham.*

Meditation is a busy search in the storehouse of phantasy for some ideas of matters, to be cast in the moulds of resolution into some forms of words or actions; in which search, when I have used my greatest diligence, I find this is the best conclusion, that to meditate on the best is the best of meditations; and a resolution to make a good end is a good end of my resolutions.—*Arthur Warwick.*

The man of meditation is happy, not for an hour or a day, but quite round the circle of his years.—*Isaac Taylor.*

Meditation is the tongue of the soul and the language of our spirit; and our wandering thoughts in prayer are but the neglects of meditation and recessions from that duty; and according as we neglect meditation, so are our prayers imperfect, — meditation being the soul of prayer and the intention of our spirit.—*Jeremy Taylor.*

Chewing the food of sweet and bitter fancy.—*Shakespeare.*

There is a sweet pleasure in contemplation. All others grow flat and insipid on frequent use; and when a man hath run through a set of vanities, in the declension of his age he knows not what to do with himself, if he cannot think.—*Sir T. P. Blount.*

Meditation is the life of the soul; action is the soul of meditation; honor is the reward 'of action: so meditate, that thou mayst do; so do, that thou mayst purchase honor: for which purchase, give God the glory.—*Quarles.*

MEETING.

Sir, you are very welcome to our house; it must appear in other ways than words, therefore I scant this breathing courtesy.—*Shakespeare.*

Absence, with all its pains, is by this charming moment wiped away.—*Thomson.*

Ah me! the world is full of meetings such as this, — a thrill, a voiceless challenge and reply, and sudden partings after! —*Willis.*

The joys of meeting pay the pangs of absence; else who could bear it?—*Rowe.*

MELANCHOLY.

Melancholy spreads itself betwixt heaven and earth, like envy between man and man, and is an everlasting mist.—*Byron.*

Make not a bosom friend of a melancholy, sad soul. He will be sure to aggravate thy adversity, and lessen thy prosperity. He goes always heavy loaded; and thou must bear half. — *Fenelon.*

Melancholy is the convalescence of grief.— *Madame Dufrénoy.*

Whatever is highest and holiest is tinged with melancholy. The eye of genius has always a plaintive expression, and its natural language is pathos. A prophet is sadder than other men; and He who was greater than all prophets was " a man of sorrow and acquainted with grief."—*Mrs. L. M. Child.*

O melancholy, who ever yet could sound thy bottom? —*Shakespeare.*

Melancholy advanceth men's conceits more than any humor whatever.—*Burton.*

There is a shadow on my heart I cannot fling aside.—*Alice Cary.*

O, it is your only fine humor, sir; your true melancholy breeds your perfect fine wit, sir; I am melancholy myself divers times, sir, and then do I no more, but take a pen and paper presently, and overflow you half a score or a dozen of sonnets at a sitting.—*Ben Jonson.*

Nothing is so dainty sweet as lovely melancholy.—*Samuel Fletcher.*

I once gave a lady two-and-twenty receipts against melancholy: one was a bright fire; another, to remember all the pleasant things said to her; another, to keep a box of sugar-plums in the chimney-piece and a kettle simmering on the hob. I thought this mere trifling at the moment, but have in after life discovered how true it is that these little pleasures often banish melancholy better than higher and more exalted objects; and that no means ought to be thought too trifling which can oppose it either in ourselves or in others.— *Sydney Smith.*

Great men are always of a nature originally melancholy.—*Aristotle.*

If you are melancholy for the first time, you will find, upon a little inquiry, that others have been melancholy many times, and yet are cheerful now.—*Leigh Hunt.*

How weary, stale, flat, and unprofitable seem to me all the uses of this world!— *Shakespeare.*

There is not a string attuned to mirth but has its chord of melancholy.—*Hood.*

Melancholy is a kind of demon that haunts our island, and often conveys herself to us in an easterly wind.—*Addison.*

Melancholy attends on the best joys of a merely ideal life.—*Margaret Fuller.*

There are some people who think that they should be always mourning, that they should put a continual constraint upon themselves, and feel a disgust for those amusements to which they are obliged to submit. For my own part, I confess that I know not how to conform myself to these rigid notions. I prefer something more simple, which I also think would be more pleasing to God.—*Fenelon.*

It is impious in a good man to be sad.— *Shakespeare.*

Melancholy sees the worst of things, — things as they may be, and not as they are. It looks upon a beautiful face, and sees but a grinning skull.—*Bovee.*

MEMORY.

Memory is not wisdom; idiots can rote volumes; yet what is wisdom without memory? A babe that is strangled in its birth.—*Tupper.*

The two offices of memory are collection and distribution.—*Johnson.*

Memory is the friend of wit, but the treacherous ally of invention; there are many books that owe their success to two things, — the good memory of those who write them, and the bad memory of those who read them.—*Colton.*

Memory always obeys the commands of the heart.—*Rivarol.*

How can such deeply imprinted images sleep in us at times, till a word, a sound, awake them! —*Lessing.*

Memory, bosom-spring of joy.—*Coleridge.*

It is an old saying, that we forget nothing, as people in fever begin suddenly to talk the language of their infancy; we are stricken by memory sometimes, and old affections rush back on us as vivid as in the time when they were our eyes, when their accents thrilled in our ears, — when, with passionate tears and grief, we flung ourselves upon their hopeless corpses. Parting is death, — at least, as far as life is concerned. A passion comes to an end; it is carried off in a coffin, or, weeping in a post-chaise, it drops out of life one way or the other, and the earth-clods close over it, and we see it no more. But it has been part of our souls, and it is eternal.—*Thackeray.*

O memory, thou bitter sweet, — both a joy and a scourge! —*Madame de Staël.*

Memory can glean, but can never renew. It brings us joys faint as is the perfume of the flowers, faded and dried, of the summer that is gone.—*Beecher.*

Memory is the primary and fundamental power, without which there could be no other intellectual operation.—*Johnson.*

Memory, like books which remain a long time shut up in the dust, needs to be opened from time to time; it is necessary, so to speak, to open its leaves, that it may be ready in time of need.—*Seneca.*

Memory, the warder of the brain.—
Shakespeare.

We consider ourselves as defective in memory, either because we remember less than we desire, or less than we suppose others to remember.—*Johnson.*

Memory, the daughter of attention, is the teeming mother of wisdom.—*Tupper.*

Memory, a source of pleasure and instruction, rather than that dreadful engine of colloquial oppression, into which it is sometimes erected.—*Sydney Smith.*

Great memories, which retain all indifferently, are the mistresses of an inn, and not the mistresses of a house.—*Madame Necker.*

It is the treasure-house of the mind, wherein the monuments thereof are kept and preserved.
Fuller.

There is a voice from the tomb sweeter than song; there is a remembrance of the dead, to which we turn even from the charms of the living. These we would not exchange for the song of pleasure or the bursts of revelry.—
Washington Irving.

The memory is the receptacle and sheath of all science.—*Cicero.*

To know by heart is not to know; it is to hold that which one has given his memory to keep.—*Montaigne.*

The memory is a treasurer to whom we must give funds, if we would draw the assistance we need.—*Rawe.*

The memory of past favors is like a rainbow, bright, vivid, and beautiful; but it soon fades away. The memory of injuries is engraved on the heart, and remains forever.—
Haliburton.

Memory seldom fails when its office is to show us the tombs of our buried hopes.—
Lady Blessington.

It haunts me still, though many a year has fled, like some wild melody.—*Rogers.*

Memory is the cabinet of imagination, the treasury of reason, the registry of conscience, and the council-chamber of thought.—*Basile.*

A memory without blot or contamination must be an exquisite treasure, an inexhaustible source of pure refreshment.—
Charlotte Bronté.

Memory is ever active, ever true. Alas, if it were only as easy to forget!—
Ninon de l'Enclos.

There is nothing steadfast in life but our memories. We are sure of keeping intact only that which we have lost.—*Madame Swetchine.*

Experience teaches that a strong memory is generally joined to a weak judgment.
Montaigne.

It is usually the case that those who have sharp and ready wits possess weak memories, while that which is acquired with labor and perseverance is always retained longest; for every hard-gained acquisition of knowledge is a sort of annealing upon the mind.—
Plutarch.

In the man whose childhood has known caresses, there is always a fibre of memory which can be touched to gentle issues.—
Marian Evans.

Aristotle calls it the scribe of the soul; and Bernard calls the memory the stomach of the soul, because it hath a retentive faculty, and turns heavenly food into blood and sph'its.—
T. Watson.

But O for the touch of a vanished hand, and the sound of a voice that is still!—
Tennyson.

Every man complains of his memory, but no man complains of his judgment.—
Rochefoucauld.

Joy's recollection is no longer joy, while sorrow's memory is a sorrow still.—*Byron.*

The course of none has been along so beaten a road that they remember not fondly some resting-places in their journeys, some turns of their path in which lovely prospects broke in upon them, some soft plats of green refreshing to their weary feet. Confiding love, generous friendship, disinterested humanity, require no recondite learning, no high imagination, to enable an honest heart to appreciate and feel them.—*Talfourd.*

Memory tempers prosperity, mitigates adversity, controls youth, and delights old age.—
Lactantius.

Through the shadowy past, like a tomb-searcher, memory ran, lifting each shroud that time had cast o'er buried hopes.—*Moore.*

Memory, like a purse, if it be over full that it cannot shut, all will drop out.—*Fuller.*

A scent, a note of music, a voice long unheard, the stirring of the summer breeze, may startle us with the sudden revival of long-forgotten feelings and thoughts.—*Talfourd.*

Along the pebbled shore of memory.—*Keats.*

The ghost of one bright hour comes from its grave and stands before me.—
Alexander Smith.

Memory is the golden thread linking all the mental gifts and excellences together.—
E. P. Hood.

Beasts and babies remember, that is, recognize; man alone recollects. This distinction was made by Aristotle.—*Coleridge.*

Time but the impression deeper makes, as streams their channels deeper wear.—*Burns.*

MENDICANTS.

Mendicants have great comforts; they require a good address, though they can dispense with a good dress; this dispensation is exclusively theirs; they have little to care for, and their expectations are great; of them nothing is required; and what forms their calamity forms likewise a fund for its own emergencies.—
Zimmermann.

MERCY.

Mercy abandons the arena of battle.—*Abbott.*

There is no better rule to try a doctrine by, than the question, Is it merciful, or is it unmerciful? If its character is that of mercy, it has the image of Jesus, who is the way, the truth and the life.—*Hosea Ballou.*

Sweet mercy is nobility's true badge.—
Shakespeare.

The sun is the eye of the world; and he is indifferent to the negro or the cold Russian; to them that dwell under the line, and them that stand near the tropics, — the scalded Indian, or the poor boy that shakes at the foot of the Riphean hills; so is the mercy of God.—
Jeremy Taylor.

Mercy turns her back to the unmerciful.—
Quarles.

No ceremony that to great ones belongs, — not the king's crown nor the deputed sword, the marshal's truncheon nor the judge's robe, become them with one half so good a grace as mercy does.—*Shakespeare.*

The greatest attribute of Heaven is mercy.—
Beaumont and Fletcher.

We may imitate the Deity in all his attributes; but mercy is the only one in which we can pretend to equal him. We cannot, indeed, give like God; but surely we may forgive like him.—*Sterne.*

Great minds erect their never-failing trophies on the firm base of mercy.—*Massinger.*

We believe that God's power is without limit; why should we not believe the same of his mercy? —*Bovee.*

As the sun's rays will irradiate even the murky pool, and make its stagnant waters to shine like silver, so doth God's goodness and tender mercy, towards the greatest sinner, and the blackest heart, make his own image visible there! —*Hosea Ballou.*

If thou hast fear of those who command thee, spare those who obey thee.—
Rabbi Ben Azai.

The quality of mercy is not strained; it droppeth, as the gentle rain from heaven, upon the place beneath; it is twice blessed; it blesseth him that gives, and him that takes; it is an attribute to God himself; and earthly power doth then show likest God's when mercy seasons justice.—*Shakespeare.*

Hate shuts her soul when dove-eyed Mercy pleads.—*Charles Sprague.*

Merciful heaven! thou rather, with thy sharp and sulphurous bolt, splittest the unwedgeable and gnarled oak, than the soft myrtle.—
Shakespeare.

Mercy to him that shows it is the rule.—
Cowper.

As freely as the firmament embraces the world, so mercy must encircle friend and foe. The sun pours forth impartially his beams through all the regions of infinity; heaven bestows the dew equally on every thirsty plant. Whatever is good and comes from on high is universal and without reserve; but in the heart's recesses darkness dwells.—*Schiller.*

A God all mercy is a God unjust.—*Young.*

If the end of one mercy were not the beginning of another, we were undone.—
Philip Henry.

How would you be if He, which is the top of judgment, should but judge you as you are? O, think on that, and mercy then will breathe within your lips like man new made.—
Shakespeare.

Blessed are the merciful, for they shall obtain mercy.—*Bible.*

The most perfect would be the most exacting and severe; but, fortunately, mercy is one of the attributes of perfection.—*J. F. Boyes.*

We do pray for mercy; and that same prayer doth teach us all to render the deeds of mercy.—*Shakespeare.*

MERIT.

The sufficiency of my merit is to know that my merit is not sufficient.—*St. Augustine.*

Contemporaries appreciate the man rather than his merit; posterity will regard the merit rather than the man.—*Colton.*

True merit, like a river, the deeper it is, the less noise it makes.—*Lord Halifax.*

Real merit of any kind cannot long be concealed; it will be discovered, and nothing can depreciate it, but a man's exhibiting it himself. It may not always be rewarded as it ought; but it will always be known.—*Chesterfield.*

Nature makes merit, and fortune puts it to work.—*Rochefoucauld.*

Charms strike the sight, but merit wins the soul.—*Pope.*

Merit has rarely risen of itself, but a pebble or a twig is often quite sufficient for it to spring from to the highest ascent. There is usually some baseness before there is any elevation.—
Landor.

Merit is born with men; happy those with whom it dies!—*Queen Christina.*

Merit is never so conspicuous as when coupled with an obscure origin, just as the moon never appears so lustrous as when it emerges from a cloud.—*Bovee.*

The world more frequently recompenses the appearance of merit, than merit itself.—
Rochefoucauld.

I know not why we should delay our tokens of respect to those who deserve them, until the heart that our sympathy could have gladdened has ceased to beat. As men cannot read the epitaphs inscribed upon the marble that covers them, so the tombs that we erect to virtue often only prove our repentance that we neglected it when with us.—*Bulwer Lytton.*

There is a proud modesty in merit.—
Dryden.

It is the witness still of excellency, to put a strange face on his own perfection.—
Shakespeare.

I am told so many ill things of a man, and I see so few in him, that I begin to suspect he has a real but troublesome merit, as being likely to eclipse that of others.—*Bruyère.*

There is merit without elevation, but there is no elevation without some merit.—
Rochefoucauld.

They are but beggars that can count their worth.—*Shakespeare.*

Merit in appearance is oftener rewarded than merit itself.—*Rochefoucauld.*

It never occurs to fools that merit and good fortune are closely united.—*Goethe.*

If you wish particularly to gain the good graces and affection of certain people, men or women, try to discover their most striking merit, if they have one, and their dominant weakness, for every one has his own, then do justice to the one, and a little more than justice to the other.—*Chesterfield.*

The best evidence of merit is a cordial recognition of it whenever and wherever it may be found.—*Bovee.*

Know you not, master, to some kind of men their graces serve them but as enemies? O, what a world is this, when what is comely envenoms him that wears it!—*Shakespeare.*

Merit, like fruit, has its season.—
Rochefoucauld.

A person may not merit favor, as that is only the claim of man, but can never demerit charity, for that is the command of God.—
Sterne.

Real merit requires as much labor, to be placed in a true light, as humbug to be elevated to an unworthy eminence; only the success of the false is temporary, that of the true, immortal.—*F. A. Durivage.*

Elevation is to merit what dress is to a handsome person.—*Rochefoucauld.*

I will not be concerned at men's not knowing me; I will be concerned at my own want of ability.—*Confucius.*

Who shall go about to cozen fortune and be honorable without the stamp of merit! Let none presume to wear an undeserved dignity.—
Shakespeare.

METAPHOR.

An epithet or metaphor drawn from nature ennobles art; an epithet or metaphor drawn from art degrades nature.—*Johnson.*

METAPHYSICS.

Metaphysics are the anatomy of the soul.—
De Boufflers.

When he (the metaphysician) has, after long pursued and baffled endeavors, rolled aside some huge difficulty which lay in his path, he will find beneath it a passage to the bright subtleties of his nature, through which he may range at will, and gather immortal fruits, like Aladdin in the subterranean gardens.—
Talfourd.

Algebra is the metaphysics of arithmetic.—
Sterne.

When he to whom we speak and he who speaks does not understand, that is metaphysics.
Voltaire.

METHOD.

Method is essential, and enables a larger amount of work to be got through with satisfaction. "Method," said Cecil (afterward Lord Burleigh), " is like packing things in a box ; a good packer will get in half as much again as a bad one." Cecil's despatch of business was extraordinary ; his maxim being, " The shortest way to do many things is to do only one thing at once."—*Samuel Smiles.*

Method is the hinge of business, and there is no method without order and punctuality.—
Hannah More.

Though every one who possesses merit is not necessarily a great man, yet every great man must possess it in a very superior degree, whether he be a poet, a philosopher, a statesman, a general ; for every great man exhibits the talent of organization or construction, whether it be in a poem, a philosophical system, a policy, or a strategy. And without method there is no organization nor construction.—*Bulwer Lytton.*

Make the most of time, it flies away so fast ; yet method will teach you to win time.—*Goethe.*

Method is simply an adaptation to the fact. The sculptor discovers what form of tool will hollow a knee-joint, and he saves time for the face. Philosophers and theologians grow stiff in that joint because they refuse to walk in Nature's way.—*John Weiss.*

To live is not to learn, but to apply.
E. Legouvé.

Method means primarily a way or path of transit. From this we are to understand that the first idea of method is a progressive transition from one step to another in any course. If in the right course, it will be the true method ; if in the wrong, we cannot hope to progress.—
Coleridge.

Methods are the masters of masters.—
Talleyrand.

You must elect your work ; you shall take what your brains can, and drop all the rest. Only so can that amount of vital force accumulate which can make the step from knowing to doing. No matter how much faculty of idle seeing a man has, the step from knowing to doing is rarely taken. It is a step out of a chalk circle of imbecility into fruitfulness.—
Emerson.

Irregularity and want of method are only supportable in men of great learning or genius, who are often too full to be exact, and therefore choose to throw down their pearls in heaps before the reader rather than be at the pains of stringing them.—*Addison.*
22

The right mental method keeps every man cool and safe in the dark, like the healthy child who goes up the dim winding staircase to its slumber, having gone up so often in the noontime that the night shineth like the day.—*John Weiss.*

MIDNIGHT.

This dead of midnight is the noon of thought, and wisdom mounts her zenith with the stars.—*Mrs. Barbauld.*

The stifled hum of midnight, when traffic has lain down to rest, and the chariot wheels of Vanity, still rolling here and there through distant streets, are bearing her to halls roofed in and lighted to the due pitch for her ; and only vice and misery, to prowl or to moan like night birds, are abroad.—*Carlyle.*

That hour, of night's black arch the keystone.—*Burns.*

The midnight bell did, with his iron tongue and brazen mouth, sound one unto the drowsy race of night.—*Shakespeare.*

Midnight brought on the dusky hour friendliest to sleep and silence.—*Milton.*

The night, proceeding on with silent pace, stood in her noon, and viewed with equal face her sleepy rise and her declining race.—*Dryden.*

In the dead vast and middle of the night.—
Shakespeare.

Midnight, — strange mystic hour, — when the veil between the frail present and the eternal future grows thin.—*Mrs. Stowe.*

About the noon of night.—*Ben Jonson.*

Now had night measured, with her shadowy cone, half-way up hill this vast sublunar vault.
Milton.

It is now the very witching time of night ; when churchyards yawn, and hell itself breathes out contagion to this world : now could I drink hot blood, and do such business as the bitter day would quake to look on.—*Shakespeare.*

MIND.

Men have marble, women waxen, minds.—
Shakespeare.

The human mind cannot create anything It produces nothing until, after having been fertilized by experience and meditation, its acquisitions are the germs of its productions.—
Buffon.

The mind grows narrow in proportion as the soul grows corrupt.—*Rousseau.*

Attention to the mind is the natural prayer that we make to interior truth, that we may discover it.—*Malebranche.*

That which causes us to think is dear to us, as everything which gives an even imperceptible impulse to our faculties is agreeable.— *Lavater.*

The commonest and coarsest clocks mark the hours; it is only those which are made with the greatest art which mark the minutes. So ordinary minds feel the difference between a simple probability and an entire certainty; but it is only the delicate minds which feel the greater or less certainty or probability, and who mark, that is to say, the minutes by their feelings.—*Fontenelle.*

By the measure of a spirited mind, we find there are many original men; the common people do not discover the difference between men.— *Pascal.*

There are those who prefer the language of the mind to that of the soul. They are very like those who are indifferent to the sight of a starry night, and who run to an exhibition of fireworks.—*Richter.*

The more accurately we search into the human mind, the stronger traces we everywhere find of His wisdom who made it.—*Burke.*

There are some minds which have only surface without depth; there are some which have depth without surface; there are others, finally, which have both advantages. The first deceive the world and even themselves. The world deceives itself in the second, by not taking them for what they really are; but they do not deceive themselves. It is only the last who deceive neither the world nor themselves.—*Nicole.*

There are some minds of which we can say, they make light; and for others only, they are warm.—*Joubert.*

There is nothing so elastic as the human mind. Like imprisoned steam, the more it is pressed the more it rises to resist the pressure. The more we are obliged to do, the more we are able to accomplish.—*T. Edwards.*

We find means to cure folly, but none to reclaim a distorted mind.—*Rochefoucauld.*

The mind of the greatest man in the world is not so independent but that he may be subject to being troubled by the least jumble which is made around him, — it need not be the noise of a cannon to disturb his thoughts; it need only be the noise of a weather-cock or pulley.— *Pascal.*

We disjoint the mind like the body. *Joubert.*

The mind is but a barren soil; a soil which is soon exhausted, and will produce no crop, or only one, unless it be continually fertilized and enriched with foreign matter.—*Sir J. Reynolds.*

For it is the mind that makes the body rich, and as the sun breaks through the darkest cloud, so honor appeareth in the meanest habit. *Shakespeare.*

Mental courage, infinitely rarer than valor, supposes the most eminent qualities.—*Diderot.*

A mind too vigorous and active serves only to consume the body to which it is joined, as the richest jewels are soonest found to wear their settings.—*Goldsmith.*

We measure minds by their stature; it would be better to esteem them by their beauty. *Joubert.*

The sovereign good of man is a mind that subjects all things to itself, and is itself subject to nothing; such a man's pleasures are modest and reserved, and it may be a question whether he goes to heaven, or heaven comes to him; for a good man is influenced by God himself, and has a kind of divinity within him.—*Seneca.*

The mind is its own place, and in itself can make a heaven of hell, a hell of heaven.—*Milton.*

The best way to prove the clearness of our mind is by showing its faults; as when a stream discovers the dirt at the bottom, it convinces us of the transparency and purity of the water.—*Pope.*

There are some cloudy days for the mind as well as for the world; and the man who has the most genius is twenty times a day in the clouds.—*Beaumelle.*

Great minds lower, instead of elevate, those who do not know how to support them.— *Rochefoucauld.*

Our minds are like our stomachs; they are whetted by the change of their food, and variety supplies both with fresh appetite.—*Quintilian.*

The mind is chameleon-like in one respect, it receives hues from without; but it is unlike it in another respect, for it retains them. *, Bayle St. John.*

Mind unemployed is mind unenjoyed.— *Bovee.*

Mind is not as merchandise which decreaseth in the using, but like to the passions of men, which rejoice and expand in exertion.— *Tupper.*

The common mind is the true Parian marble, fit to be wrought into likeness to a God.— *Bancroft.*

Whatever that be which thinks, which understands, which wills, which acts, it is something celestial and divine; and, upon that account, must necessarily be eternal.—*Cicero.*

Minds which never rest are subject to many digressions.—*Joubert.*

The mind is nourished at a cheap rate; neither cold nor heat, nor age itself, can interrupt this exercise ; give, therefore, all your care to a possession which ameliorates even in its old age.—*Seneca.*

The mind does not know what diet it can feed on until it has been brought to the starvation point.—*Holmes.*

The mind, like all other things, will become impaired, the sciences are its food, — they nourish, but at the same time they consume it.—*Bruyère.*

Minds of moderate calibre ordinarily condemn everything which is beyond their range.—*Rochefoucauld.*

We may doubt of the existence of matter, if we please, and, like Berkeley, deny it, without subjecting ourselves to the shame of a very conclusive confutation ; but there is this remarkable difference between matter and mind : he that doubts the existence of mind, by doubting, proves it.—*Colton.*

The mind wears the colors of the soul, as a valet those of his master.—*Madame Swetchine.*

Different minds incline to different objects ; one pursues the vast alone, the wonderful, the wild ; another sighs for harmony and grace, and gentlest beauty.—*Akenside.*

The very might of the human intellect reveals its limits.—*Madame Swetchine.*

For as the strength of the mind surpasses that of the body, in the same way the sufferings of the mind are more severe than the pains of the body.—*Cicero.*

Frivolous curiosity about trifles, and laborious attention to little objects, which neither require nor deserve a moment's thought, lower a man, who from thence is thought (and not unjustly) incapable of greater matters. Cardinal de Retz very sagaciously marked out Cardinal Chigi for a little mind, from the moment he told him that he had wrote three years with the same pen, and that it was an excellent good one still.—*Chesterfield.*

Strength of mind is exercise, not rest.—*Pope.*

The march of the human mind is slow.—*Burke.*

The mind has a certain vegetative power, which cannot be wholly idle. If it is not laid out and cultivated into a beautiful garden, it will of itself shoot up in weeds or flowers of a wild growth.—*Steele.*

As sight is in the eye, so is the mind in the soul l—*Sophocles.*

A weak mind sinks under prosperity, as well as under adversity. A strong mind has two highest tides, — when the moon is at the full, and when there is no moon.—*Hare.*

The mind doth shape itself to its own wants, and can bear all things.—*Joanna Baillie.*

For in the mind, as in a field, though some things may be sown and carefully brought up, yet what springs naturally is most pleasing.—*Tacitus.*

A well-cultivated mind is, so to speak, made up of all the minds of preceding ages ; it is only one single mind which has been educated during all this time.—*Fontenelle.*

The mind has its arrangement ; it proceeds from principles to demonstrations. The heart has a different mode of proceeding.—*Pascal.*

Nothing can be so quick and sudden as the operations of the mind, especially when hope, or fear, or jealousy, to which the other two are but journeymen, set it to work.—*Fielding.*

A weak mind is like a microscope, which magnifies trifling things, but cannot receive great ones.— *Chesterfield.*

The great business of a man is to improve his mind and govern his manners ; all other projects and pursuits, whether in our power to compass or not, are only amusements.—*Pliny.*

He who cannot contract the sight of his mind as well as dilate it wants a great talent in life.—*Bacon.*

Thought alone, and its quick elements, — will, passion, reason, imagination, — cannot die. What has thought to do with time or place or circumstance ? —*Shelley.*

It is ordained in the eternal constitution of things, that men of intemperate minds cannot be free ; their passions forge their fetters.—*Burke.*

It is the mind that makes us rich and happy, in what condition soever we are, and money signifies no more to it than it does to the gods.—*Seneca.*

The failure of the mind in old age is often less the result of natural decay than of disuse. Ambition has ceased to operate ; contentment brings indolence ; indolence, decay of mental power, *ennui*, and sometimes death. Men have been known to die, literally speaking, of disease induced by intellectual vacancy.—*Sir Benjamin Brodie.*

Few minds wear out ; more rust out.—*Bovee.*

Old minds are like old horses, you must exercise them if you wish to keep them in working order.—*John Adams.*

It often happens that subjects are presented instinctively to our mind in a more finished state than they could be by the most consummate human art.—*Rochefoucauld.*

How excellently composed is that mind which shows a piercing wit, quite void of ostentation; high erected thoughts, seated in a heart of courtesy; and eloquence, as sweet in the uttering, as slow to come to the uttering; and a behavior so noble, as gives beauty to pomp, and majesty to adversity.—*Sir P. Sidney.*

Mind is the brightness of the body, — lights it, when strength, its proper but less subtle fire, begins to fail.—*J. S. Knowles.*

Sublime is the dominion of the mind over the body, that for a time can make flesh and nerve impregnable, and string the sinews like steel, so that the weak become so mighty.—
Mrs. Stowe.

The mind itself must, like other things, sometimes be unbent; or else it will be either weakened or broken.—*Sir P. Sidney.*

Anguish of mind has driven thousands to suicide; anguish of body, none. This proves that the health of the mind is of far more consequence to our happiness than the health of the body, although both are deserving of much more attention than either of them receives.—
Colton.

As the mind must govern the hands, so in every society the man of intelligence must direct the man of labor.—*Johnson.*

The mind forges from knowledge an archangel's spear, and, with the spirits that compel the world, conflicts for empire.—*Willis.*

MINORITY.

Votes should be weighed, not counted! —
Schiller.

This minority is great and formidable. I do not know whether, if I aimed at the total overthrow of a kingdom, I should wish to be encumbered with a large body of partisans.—
Burke.

MIRACLE.

Miracles are ceased; and therefore we must needs admit the means, how things are perfected.—*Shakespeare.*

Miracle is the pet child of faith.—*Goethe.*

MIRTH.

Harmless mirth is the best cordial against the consumption of the spirit; wherefore jesting is not unlawful, if it trespasseth not in quantity, quality, or season.—*Fuller.*

Mirth is God's medicine. Everybody ought to bathe in it. Grim care, moroseness, anxiety, — all this rust of life, ought to be scoured off by the oil of mirth. It is better than emery. Every man ought to rub himself with it. A man without mirth is like a wagon without springs, in which one is caused disagreeably to jolt by every pebble over which it runs.—
Beecher.

Man is the merriest species of the creation; all above or below him are serious.—*Addison.*

There is nothing like fun, is there? I have n't any myself, but I do like it in others. O, we need it! We need all the counterweights we can muster to balance the sad relations of life. God has made sunny spots in the heart; why should we exclude the light from them? —
Haliburton.

Most of the appearing mirth in the world is not mirth, but art. The wounded spirit is not seen, but walks under a disguise.—*South.*

I love such mirth as does not make friends ashamed to look upon one another next morning; or men, that cannot well bear it, to repent of the money they spend when they be warmed with drink; and take this for a rule, you may pick out such times and such companies, that you may make yourself merrier for a little than a great deal of money; for "it is the company and not the charge that makes the feast."—
Izaak Walton.

Who cannot make one in the circle of harmless merriment without a secret cause of grief or seriousness may be suspected of pride, hypocrisy, or formality.—*Lavater.*

From the crown of his head to the sole of his foot he is all mirth; he hath twice or thrice cut Cupid's bowstring, and the little hangman dare not shoot at him; he hath a heart as sound as a bell; and his tongue is the clapper; for what his heart thinks, his tongue speaks.—
Shakespea. e.

I have observed, that in comedy, the best actor plays the part of the droll, while some scrub rogue is made the hero, or fine gentleman. So, in this farce of life, wise men pass their time in mirth, whilst fools only are serious.—
Bolingbroke.

Frame thy mind to mirth and merriment, which bars a thousand harms, and lengthens life.—*Shakespeare.*

Mirthfulness is in the mind, and you cannot get it out. It is the blessed spirit that God has set in the mind to dust it, to enliven its dark places, and to drive asceticism, like a foul fiend, out the back-door. It is just as good, in its place, as conscience or veneration. Praying can no more be made a substitute for smiling than smiling can for praying.—*Beecher.*

A single burst of mirth is worth a whole season full of cries, with melancholy.—*Hood.*

Gayety and a light heart, in all virtue and decorum, are the best medicine for the young, or rather for all. Solitude and melancholy are poison. They are deadly to all, but, above all, to the young.—*Talfourd.*

Plato allowed mirth and wine to old men, but forbade them both to young ones. To be merry and wise, might have been a proverb deduced from this law. But Plato's reason was truly philosophic, that, while our natural cheerfulness and spirits remain, we should never use incitements. To spur a free horse soon makes a jade of him.—*Sterne.*

A merrier man within the limit of becoming mirth, I never spent an hour's talk withal; his eye begets occasion for his wit.—*Shakespeare.*

Let not mirth be thy profession, lest thou become a make-sport. He that hath but gained the title of a jester, let him assure himself the fool is not far off.—*Quarles.*

The highest gratification we receive here from company is mirth, which at the best is but a fluttering, unquiet motion.—*Pope*

MISANTHROPY.

Man delights not me,—nor woman neither.
Shakespeare.

Sombre thoughts and fancies often require little real soil or substance to flourish in; they are the dark pine-trees which take root in, and frown over the rifts of the scathed and petrified heart, and are chiefly nourished by the rain of unavailing tears, and the vapors of fancy.—
J. F. Boyes.

Let the misanthrope shun men and abjure; the most are rather lovable than hateful.—
Tupper.

Melancholy is the nurse of frenzy.—
Shakespeare.

We readily excuse paralytics from labor; and shall we be angry with a hypochondriac for not being cheerful in company? Must we stigmatize such an unfortunate person as peevish, positive, and unfit for society? His disorder may no more suffer him to be merry, than the gout will suffer another to dance. The advising a melancholic to be cheerful is like bidding a coward be courageous, or a dwarf be taller.—
Wollaston.

That dye is on me that makes my whitest part black.—*Shakespeare.*

There cannot live a more unhappy creature than an ill-natured old man, who is neither capable of receiving pleasures nor sensible of doing them to others.—*Sir W. Temple.*

Men possessing minds which are morose, solemn, and inflexible, enjoy, in general, a greater share of dignity than of happiness.—
Bacon.

Out of the ashes of misanthropy benevolence rises again; we find many virtues where we had imagined all was vice, many acts of disinterested friendship where we had fancied all was calculation and fraud,—and so gradually from the two extremes we pass to the proper medium; and, feeling that no human being is wholly good or wholly base, we learn that true knowledge of mankind which induces us to expect little and forgive much. The world cures alike the optimist and the misanthrope.—
Bulwer Lytton.

The opinions of the misanthropical rest upon this very partial basis, that they adopt the bad faith of a few as evidence of the worthlessness of all.—*Bovee.*

MISCHIEF.
In life it is difficult to say who do you the most mischief,—enemies with the worst intentions, or friends with the best.—*Bulwer Lytton.*

O mischief! thou art swift to enter in the thoughts of desperate men!—*Shakespeare.*

The sower of the seed is assuredly the author of the whole harvest of mischief.—
Demosthenes.

Now let it work. Mischief, thou art afoot, take thou what course thou wilt.—*Shakespeare.*

Few men are so clever as to know all the mischief they do.—*Rochefoucauld.*

It shocks me to think how much mischief almost every man may do, who will but resolve to do all he can.—*Sterne.*

MISER.
How vilely he has lost himself, that becomes a slave to his servant, and exalts him to the dignity of his Maker! Gold is the God, the wife, the friend, of the money-monger of the world.—*William Penn.*

The prodigal robs his heir, the miser robs himself.—*Bruyère.*

To cure us of our immoderate love of gain, we should seriously consider how many goods there are that money will not purchase, and these the best; and how many evils there are that money will not remedy, and these the worst.—*Colton.*

Money never can be well managed if sought solely through the greed of money for its own sake. In all meanness there is a defect of intellect as well as of heart. And even the cleverness of avarice is but the cunning of imbecility.—*Bulwer Lytton.*

History tells us of illustrious villains, but there never was an illustrious miser.—
St. Evremond.

I can compare our rich misers to nothing so fitly as a whale; he plays and tumbles, driving the poor fry before him, and at last devours them all at a mouthful.—*Shakespeare.*

The miser is as much in want of that which he has as of that which he has not.—
Publius Syrus.

A thorough miser must possess considerable strength of character, to bear the self-denial imposed by his penuriousness. Equal sacrifices, endured voluntarily in a better cause, would make a saint or a martyr.
W. B. Clulow.

Groan under gold, yet weep for want of bread.—*Young.*

Misers, as death approaches, are heaping up a chest of reasons to stand in more awe of him.
Shenstone.

A miser is sometimes a grand personification of fear. He has a fine horror of poverty; and he is not content to keep want from the door, or at arm's length, but he places it, by heaping wealth upon wealth, at a sublime distance!—
Lamb.

The miser is the pauper *par excellence;* he is the man who is surest of not being loved for himself.—*Rivarol.*

The miser, starving his brother's body, starves also his own soul, and at death shall creep out of his great estate of injustice, poor and naked and miserable.—*Theodore Parker.*

The life of a miser is a play of which we applaud only the closing scene.—*Sanial-Dubay.*

But is it not some reproach on the economy of Providence that such a one, who is a mean, dirty fellow, should have amassed wealth enough to buy half a nation? Not in the least. He made himself a mean, dirty fellow for that very end. He has paid his health, his conscience, his liberty for it; and will you envy him his bargain?—*Mrs. Barbauld.*

Misers mistake gold for their good; whereas it is only the means of obtaining it.—
Rochefoucauld.

Of all the vices, avarice is the most generally detested; it is the effect of an avidity common to all men; it is because men hate those from whom they can expect nothing. The greedy misers rail at sordid misers.—
Helvetius.

He heapeth up riches, and knoweth not who shall gather them.—*Bible.*

MISERY.
We become innocent when we become miscrable.—*La Fontaine.*

Misery is caused, for the most part, not by a heavy crush of disaster, but by the corrosion of less visible evils, which canker enjoyment, and undermine security. The visit of an invader is necessarily rare, but domestic animosities allow no cessation.—*Johnson.*

Misery acquaints a man with strange bed-fellows.—*Shakespeare.*

Man is so great that his greatness appears even in the consciousness of his misery. A tree does not know itself to be miserable. It is true that it is misery indeed to know one's self to be miserable; but then it is greatness also. In this way, all man's miseries go to prove his greatness. They are the miseries of a mighty potentate, of a dethroned monarch.—
Pascal.

No scene of mortal life but teems with mortal woe.—*Walter Scott.*

The misery of human life is made up of large masses, each separated from the other by certain intervals. One year the death of a child; years after, a failure in trade; after another longer or shorter interval, a daughter may have married unhappily: in all but the singularly unfortunate, the integral parts that compose the sum-total of the unhappiness of a man's life are easily counted and distinctly remembered.—*Coleridge.*

Miserable men commiserate not themselves; bowelless unto others, and merciless unto their own bowels.—*Sir Thomas Browne.*

Small miseries, like small debts, hit us in so many places, and meet us at so many turns and corners, that what they want in weight they make up in number, and render it less hazardous to stand the fire of one cannon-ball, than a volley composed of such a shower of bullets.—*Colton.*

Sick in the world's regard, wretched and low.—*Shakespeare.*

Misery and ignorance are always the cause of great evils. Misery is easily excited to anger, and ignorance soon yields to perfidious counsels.—*Addison.*

The miserable are sacred.—*Seneca.*

If misery be the effect of virtue, it ought to be reverenced; if of ill-fortune, to be pitied; and if of vice, not to be insulted; because it is, perhaps, itself a punishment adequate to the crime by which it was produced; and the humanity of that man can deserve no panegyric who is capable of reproaching a criminal in the hands of the executioner.—*Johnson.*

We should pass on from crime to crime, heedless and remorseless, if misery did not stand in our way, and our own pains admonish us of our folly.—*Johnson.*

And twins, even from the birth, are misery and man!—*Homer.*

Notwithstanding the sight of all those miseries which wring us, and threaten our destruction, we have still an instinct that we cannot repress, which elevates us above our sorrows.—*Pascal.*

Man is only miserable so far as he thinks himself so.—*Sannazaro.*

What a situation is that of the great! They only live in the future, and are only happy in hope. There is no peace in ambition; it is always gloomy, and often unreasonably so. The kindness of the king, the regards of the courtiers, the attachment of my domestics, and the fidelity of a large number of friends, make me happy no longer.—*Madame de Pompadour.*

A misery is not to be measured from the nature of the evil, but from the temper of the sufferer.—*Addison.*

MISFORTUNE.
I believe, indeed, that it is more laudable to suffer great misfortunes than to do great things.—*Stanislaus.*

There is a Russian proverb which says that misfortune is next door to stupidity; and it will generally be found that men who are constantly lamenting their ill luck are only reaping the consequences of their own neglect, mismanagement, improvidence, or want of application.—*Samuel Smiles.*

After all, our worst misfortunes never happen, and most miseries lie in anticipation.—*Balzac.*

I may grieve with the smart of an evil as soon as I feel it, but I will not smart with the grief of an evil as soon as I hear of it. My evil, when it cometh, may make my grief too great; why, then, should my grief, before it comes, make my evil greater?—*Arthur Warwick.*

A noble nature may catch a wrench.—*Shakespeare.*

Seneca has attempted not only to pacify us in misfortune, but almost to allure us to it by representing it as necessary to the pleasures of the mind. He invites his pupil to calamity as the Sirens allured the passengers to their coasts, by promising that they shall return with increase of knowledge.—*Johnson.*

Rats and conquerors must expect no mercy in misfortunes.—*Colton.*

Then was I as a tree whose boughs did bend with fruit; but in one night, a storm or robbery, call it what you will, shook down my mellow hangings, nay, my leaves, and left me bare to weather.—*Shakespeare.*

The greatest misfortune of all is not to be able to bear misfortune.—*Bias.*

Misfortune sprinkles ashes on the head of the man, but falls like dew on the head of the woman, and brings forth germs of strength of which she herself had no conscious possession.—*Anna Cora Mowatt.*

Misfortune does not always wait on vice, nor is success the constant guest of virtue.—*Havard.*

It is often better to have a great deal of harm happen to one; a great deal may arouse you to remove what a little will only accustom you to endure.—*Lord Greville.*

Who hath not known ill fortune never knew himself, or his own virtue.—*Mallet.*

We should learn, by reflecting on the misfortunes which have attended others, that there is nothing singular in those which befall ourselves.—*Melmoth.*

Misfortune is, like the honest man, as good as her word.—*Madame Swetchine.*

The injuries of life, if rightly improved, will be to us as the strokes of the statuary on his marble, forming us to a more beautiful shape, and making us fitter to adorn the heavenly temple.—*Mather.*

Most of our misfortunes are more supportable than the comments of our friends upon them.—*Colton.*

Nothing is a misery, unless our weakness apprehend it so; we cannot be more faithful to ourselves in anything that is manly, than to make ill fortune as contemptible to us as it makes us to others.—*Beaumont and Fletcher.*

O, give me thy hand, one writ with me in sour misfortune's book!—*Shakespeare.*

When misfortunes happen to such as dissent from us in matters of religion, we call them judgments; when to those of our own sect, we call them trials; when to persons neither way distinguished, we are content to attribute them to the settled course of things.—*Shenstone.*

When any calamity has been suffered, the first thing to be remembered is, how much has been escaped.—*Johnson.*

The less we parade our misfortunes the more sympathy we command.—*Orville Dewey.*

Ovid finely compares a man of broken fortune to a falling column ; the lower it sinks, the greater weight it is obliged to sustain.—
Goldsmith.

Misfortune makes of certain souls a vast desert through which rings the voice of God.—
Balzac.

It is seldom that God sends such calamities upon man as men bring upon themselves and suffer willingly.—*Jeremy Taylor.*

Cicero has said of men : " They are like wines ; age sours the bad and betters the good." We can say that misfortune has the same effect upon them.—*Ricker.*

The quivering flesh, though torture-torn, may live, but souls, once deeply wounded, heal no more.—*Ebenezer Elliott.*

Misfortune has in it at least this good, that it corrects all those little passions which agitate the idle and corrupted.—
Mademoiselle de l'Espinasse.

Heaven sends us misfortunes as a moral tonic !—*Lady Blessington.*

In misfortune we often mistake dejection for constancy ; we bear it without daring to look on it ; like cowards, who suffer themselves to be murdered without resistance.—*Rochefoucauld.*

Woes cluster ; rare are solitary woes ; they love a train, they tread each other's heel.—
Young.

If all men would bring their misfortunes together in one place, most would be glad to take his own home again, rather than to take a proportion out of the common stock.—*Solon.*

Little minds are tamed and subdued by misfortune ; but great minds rise above it.—
Washington Irving.

When I was happy I thought I knew men, but it was fated that I should know them in misfortune only.—*Napoleon.*

Misfortune is never mournful to the soul that accepts it ; for such do always see that every cloud is an angel's face. Every man deems that he has precisely the trials and temptations which are the hardest of all others for him to bear ; but they are so, simply because they are the very ones he most needs.—
Mrs. L. M. Child.

Men do not go out to meet misfortune as we do. They learn it ; and we — we divine it.—
Madame Swetchine.

We exaggerate misfortune and happiness alike. We are never either so wretched or so happy as we say we are.—*Balzac.*

We all bear the misfortunes of other people with an heroic constancy.—*Rochefoucauld.*

I am convinced that we have a degree of delight, and that no small one, in the real misfortunes and pains of others.—*Burke.*

You were used to say, extremity was the trier of spirits ; that common chances common men could bear ; that when the sea was calm, all boats alike showed mastership in floating.—
Shakespeare.

There is a certain sort of man whose doom in the world is disappointment, who excels in it, and whose luckless triumphs in his meek career of life, I have often thought, must be regarded by the kind eyes above with as much favor as the splendid successes and achievements of coarser and more prosperous men.—
Thackeray.

The effect of supreme and irrevocable misfortune is to elevate those souls which it does not deprive of all virtue.—*Guizot.*

MISTAKE.

Being a mortal, you have stumbled ; in this mortal life it is a wonder when a man has been happy throughout his life.—*Bato*

To step aside is human.—*Burns.*

Any man may commit a mistake, but none but a fool will continue in it.—*Cicero.*

We learn wisdom from failure much more than from success ; we often discover what will do by finding out what will not do ; and probably he who never made a mistake never made a discovery. Horne Tooke used to say of his studies in intellectual philosophy, that he had become all the better acquainted with the country through having had the good luck sometimes to lose his way.—*Samuel Smiles.*

All flesh doth frailty breed !—*Spenser.*

MISTRUST.

The world is an old woman, that mistakes any gilt farthing for a gold coin ; whereby, being often cheated, she will henceforth trust nothing but the common copper.—*Carlyle.*

MOB.

The scum that rises upmost, when the nation boils.—*Dryden.*

As a goose is not alarmed by hissing, nor a sheep by bleating ; so neither be you terrified by the voice of a senseless multitude.—
Maximus.

The mob is a sort of bear ; while your ring is through its nose, it will even dance under your cudgel ; but should the ring slip, and you lose your hold, the brute will turn and rend you.—*Jane Porter.*

The blind monster with uncounted heads, the still discordant, wavering multitude.— *Shakespeare.*

A mob is usually a creature of very mysterious existence, particularly in a large city. Where it comes from, or whither it goes, few men can tell. Assembling and dispersing with equal suddenness, it is as difficult to follow to its various sources as the sea itself; nor does the parallel stop here, for the ocean is not more fickle and uncertain, more terrible when roused, more unreasonable or more cruel.—*Dickens.*

The multitude is always in the wrong.— *Roscommon.*

The mob is a monster, with the hands of *B*riareus, but the head of Polyphemus, — strong to execute, but blind to perceive.—*Colton.*

The multitude unawed is insolent; once seized with fear, contemptible and vain.— *Mallet.*

There is nothing so little to be expected or hoped for from this many-headed monster, when so incensed, as humanity and good-nature; it is much more capable of reverence and fear.— *Montaigne.*

The many-headed multitude, whom inconstancy only doth by accident guide to well-doing! Who can set confidence there, where company takes away shame, and each may lay the fault upon his fellow?—*Sir P. Sidney.*

Things are neither good nor bad, as they appear to the judgment of the mob.—*Tacitus.*

I will not choose what many men desire, because I will not jump with common spirits, and rank me with the barbarous multitude.— *Shakespeare.*

It has been very truly said that the mob has many heads, but no brains.—*Rivarol.*

Let there be an entire abstinence from intoxicating drinks throughout this country during the period of a single generation, and a mob would be as impossible as combustion without oxygen.—*Horace Mann.*

You have many enemies, that know not why they are so, but, like the village curs, bark when their fellows do.—*Shakespeare.*

I am always ill at ease when tumults arise among the mob, — people who have nothing to lose. They use as a pretext that to which we also must appeal, and bring misery on the land. *Goethe.*

The blind, unwieldy monster, which at first rattles its heavy bones, threatening to swallow high and low, the near and distant, with gaping jaws, at last stumbles over a thread.—*Schiller.*

More are made insurgents by firing on them than by feeding them; and men are more dangerous in the field than in the kitchen.—*Landor.*

License they mean when they cry liberty.— *Milton.*

A mob is a society of bodies voluntarily bereaving themselves of reason, and traversing its work. The mob is man voluntarily descending to the nature of the beast. Its fit hour of activity is night. Its actions are insane, like its whole constitution.—*Emerson.*

The dregs may stir themselves as they please; they fall back to the bottom by their own coarseness.—*Joubert.*

When roused to rage the maddening populace storms, their fury, like a rolling flame, bursts forth unquenchable; but give its violence ways, it spends itself, and as its force abates, learns to obey and yields it to your will.— *Euripides.*

Every numerous assembly is a mob; consequently everything there depends upon instantaneous turns.—*Cardinal de Retz.*

It is an easy and vulgar thing to please the mob, and not a very arduous task to astonish them; but essentially to benefit and to improve them is a work fraught with difficulty, and teeming with danger.—*Colton.*

Human affairs are not so happily arranged that the best things please the most men. It is the proof of a bad cause when it is applauded by the mob.—*Seneca.*

MODERATION.

The pursuit even of the best of things ought to be calm and tranquil.—*Cicero.*

Remember to comport thyself in life as at a banquet. If a plate is offered thee, extend thy hand and take it moderately; if it be withdrawn, do not detain it. If it come not to thy side, make not thy desire loudly known, but wait patiently till it be offered thee. Use the same moderation towards thy wife and thy children, towards honors and riches.—*Epictetus.*

Moderation is the inseparable companion of wisdom, but with it genius has not even a nodding acquaintance.—*Colton.*

Moderation cannot have the credit of combating and subduing ambition, — they are never found together. Moderation is the languor and indolence of the soul, as ambition is its activity and ardor.—*Rochefoucauld.*

It is certainly a very important lesson to learn how to enjoy ordinary things, and to be able to relish your being, without the transport of some passion, or gratification of some appetite.—*Steele.*

MODERATION.　346　MODESTY.

Life's enchanted cup but sparkles near the brim.—*Byron.*

Moderation, which consists in an indifference about little things, and in a prudent and well-proportioned zeal about things of importance, can proceed from nothing but true knowledge, which has its foundation in self-acquaintance.—*Lord Chatham.*

Such moderation with thy bounty join, that thou mayest nothing give that is not thine.—*Denham.*

There are times when moderation must be hypocrisy.—*Bayle St. John.*

It is no mean happiness to be seated in the mean; superfluity comes sooner by white hairs, but competency lives longer.—*Shakespeare.*

Moderation consists in being moved as angels are moved.—*Joubert.*

To go beyond the bounds of moderation is to outrage humanity. The greatness of the human soul is shown by knowing how to keep within proper bounds. So far from greatness consisting in going beyond its limits, it really consists in keeping within it.—*Pascal.*

There is a German proverb which says that Take-it-Easy and Live-Long are brothers.—*Bovee.*

There is a great purpose served in society by that law of nature in virtue of which it is that great bodies move slowly.—*Chalmers.*

To live long, it is necessary to live slowly.—*Cicero.*

Howsoever varied the courses of our life, whatsoever the phases of pleasure and ambition through which it has swept along, still, when in memory we would revive the times that were comparatively the happiest, those times will be found to have been the calmest.—*Bulwer Lytton.*

It is best to rise from life as from a banquet, neither thirsty nor drunken.—*Aristotle.*

There is a mean in all things. Even virtue itself hath its stated limits; which not being strictly observed, it ceases to be virtue.—*Horace.*

I knew a wise man that had for a by-word, when he saw men hasten to a conclusion, "Stay a little, that we may end the sooner."—*Bacon.*

Tranquil pleasures last the longest. We are not fitted to bear long the burden of great joys.—*Bovee.*

Moderation resembles temperance. We are not so unwilling to eat more, as afraid of doing ourselves harm by it.—*Rochefoucauld.*

Everything that exceeds the bounds of moderation has an unstable foundation.—*Seneca.*

As if we had an infectious touch, we by our manner of handling corrupt things, that in themselves are laudable and good, — we may grasp virtue so hard, till it become vicious, if we embrace it too straight, and with too violent a desire. Those who say, there is never any excess in virtue, for as much as it is no virtue, when it once becomes excess, only play upon words.—*Montaigne.*

The flowers swim at the top of the bowl.—*Anacreon.*

The boundary of man is moderation. When once we pass that pale our guardian angel quits his charge of us.—*Feltham.*

Assume in adversity the countenance of prosperity, and in prosperity moderate the temper.—*Livy.*

Only actions give life strength; only moderation gives it a charm.—*Richter.*

Fortify yourself with moderation; for this is an impregnable fortress.—*Epictetus.*

MODESTY.

Let us be careful to distinguish modesty, which is ever amiable, from reserve, which is only prudent. A man is hated sometimes for pride, when it was an excess of humility gave the occasion.—*Shenstone.*

True modesty is a discerning grace.—*Cowper.*

"God will punish," say the Orientals, "him who sees and him who is seen." Beautiful and terrible recommendation of modesty!—*Joubert.*

It is often found that modesty and humility not only do no good, but are positively hurtful, when they are shown to the arrogant who have taken up a prejudice against you, either from envy or from any other cause.—*Machiavelli.*

Full many a flower is born to blush unseen, and waste its sweetness on the desert air.—*Gray.*

It is remarked that the modest deportment of real wise men, when contrasted to the assuming air of the young and ignorant, may be compared to the differences of wheat, which while its ear is empty holds up its head proudly, but as soon as it is filled with grain bends modestly down, and withdraws from observation.—*J. Beaumont.*

That chastity of look which seems to hang, a veil of purest light, over all her beauties, and by forbidding most inflames desires.—*Young.*

Modesty seldom resides in a breast that is not enriched with nobler virtues.—*Goldsmith.*

The gravest events dawn with no more noise than the morning star makes in rising. All great developments complete themselves in the world, and modestly wait in silence, praising themselves never, and announcing themselves not at all. We must be sensitive, and sensible, if we would see the beginnings and endings of great things. That is our part.—*Beecher.*

Modesty is policy, no less than virtue.—
Simms.

Those actions have much more grace and lustre that slip from the hand of him that does them negligently, and without noise; and that some honest man after chooses out, and raises from the shade, to produce it to the light, upon its own account.—*Montaigne.*

· Modesty is of the color of virtue.—*Diogenes.*

I think that few people are aware how early it is right to respect the modesty of an infant.—*Harriet Martineau.*

The modest man has everything to gain, and the arrogant man everything to lose; for modesty has always to deal with generosity, and arrogance with envy —*Rivarol.*

The woman and the soldier who do not defend the first pass will never defend the last.
Fielding.

Bashfulness is not so much the effect of an ill education, as the proper gift and provision of wise nature. Every stage of life has its own set of manners, that is suited to it, and best becomes it. Each is beautiful in its season; and you might as well quarrel with the child's rattle, and advance him directly to the boy's top and span-farthing, as expect from diffident youth the manly confidence of riper age.—
Bishop Hurd.

Modesty is not only an ornament, but also a guard to virtue.—*Addison.*

In the modesty of fearful duty I read as much as from the rattling tongue of saucy and audacious eloquence.—*Shakespeare.*

Modesty makes large amends for the pain it gives the persons who labor under it, by the prejudice it affords every worthy person in their favor.—*Shenstone.*

Modesty is a sweet song-bird no open cage-door can tempt to flight.—*Hafiz.*

Wrap thyself in the decent veil that the arts or the graces weave for thee, O human nature! It is only the statue of marble whose nakedness the eye can behold without shame and offence!—*Bulwer Lytton.*

Modesty winneth good report, but scorn cometh close upon servility.—*Tupper.*

God intended for women two preventatives against sin, modesty and remorse; in confession to a mortal priest the former is removed by his absolution, the latter is taken away.—
Miranda of Piedmont

Modesty is the citadel of beauty and virtue.
Demades.

Be simple and modest in your deportment, and treat with indifference whatever lies between virtue and vice. Love the human race; obey God.—*Marcus Antoninus.*

Modesty once extinguished knows not how to return.—*Seneca.*

A just and reasonable modesty does not only recommend eloquence, but sets off every great talent which a man can be possessed of; it heightens all the virtues which it accompanies.—*Addison.*

Women and men of retiring timidity are cowardly only in dangers which affect themselves, but the first to rescue when others are endangered.—*Richter.*

No padlocks, bolts, or bars can secure a maiden so well as her own reserve.—*Cervantes.*

No age, sex, or condition is above or below the absolute necessity of modesty; but without it one is vastly beneath the rank of man.—
Barton.

Modesty is to merit as shades to figures in a picture; giving it strength and beauty.—
Bruyère.

Nothing can atone for the want of modesty, without which beauty is ungraceful and wit detestable.—*Steele.*

I know not what the world may think of my labors, but to myself it seems that I have been but a child playing on the sea-shore; now finding some pebble rather more polished, and now some shell rather more agreeably variegated than another, while the immense ocean of truth extended itself unexplored before me.—
Sir Isaac Newton.

A modest person seldom fails to gain the good-will of those he converses with, because nobody envies a man who does not appear to be pleased with himself.—*Steele.*

Modesty in a man is never to be allowed as a good quality, but a weakness, if it suppresses his virtue, and hides it from the world, when he has at the same time a mind to exert himself.—*Johnson.*

The greatest ornament of an illustrious life is modesty and humility, which go a great way in the character even of the most exalted princes.—*Napoleon.*

Modesty, that becomes all men, is especially becoming in one who has great merit, in that he has everything to excuse pride.—*Bovee.*

The mark of the man of the world is absence of pretension. He does not make a speech; he takes a low business-tone, avoids all brag, is nobody, dresses plainly, promises not at all, performs much, speaks in monosyllables, hugs his fact. He calls his employment by its lowest name, and so takes from evil tongues their sharpest weapon.—*Emerson.*

Modest expression is a beautiful setting to the diamond of talent and genius.—*Chapin.*

There are numbers in the world who do not want sense to make a figure, so much as an opinion of their own abilities, to put them upon recording their observations, and allowing them the same importance which they do to those which others print.—*Shenstone.*

Mere bashfulness without merit is awkward; and merit without modesty insolent. But modest merit has a double claim to acceptance.—*T. Hughes.*

Modesty was designed by *P*rovidence as a guard to virtue, and that it might be always at hand it is wrought into the mechanism of the body. It is likewise proportioned to the occasions of life, and strongest in youth when passion is so too.—*Jeremy Collier.*

Modesty is the appendage of sobriety, and is to chastity, to temperance, and to humility as the fringes are to a garment.—*Jeremy Taylor.*

Modesty never rages, never murmurs, never pouts when it is ill-treated; it pines, it beseeches, it languishes.—*Steele.*

True modesty avoids everything that is criminal; false modesty everything that is unfashionable.—*Addison.*

MONEY.
Money is a handmaiden, if thou knowest to use it; a mistress, if thou knowest not.—*Horace.*

When money represents many things, not to love it would be to love nearly nothing. To forget true needs can be only a feeble moderation; but to know the value of money and to sacrifice it always, maybe to duty, maybe even to delicacy,—that is real virtue.—*De Senancour.*

If money go before, all ways do lie open.—*Shakespeare.*

O money, money, how blindly thou hast been worshipped, and how stupidly abused! Thou art health and liberty and strength, and he that has thee may rattle his pockets at the foul fiend!—*Lamb.*

The value of a dollar is to buy just things; a dollar goes on increasing in value with all the genius and all the virtue of the world. A dollar in a university is worth more than a dollar in a jail; in a temperate, schooled, law-abiding community than in some sink of crime, where dice, knives, and arsenic are in constant play.—*Emerson.*

Money is a bottomless sea, in which honor, conscience, and truth may be drowned.—*Kozlay.*

Misery assails riches as lightning does the highest towers; or as a tree that is heavy laden with fruit breaks its own boughs, so do riches destroy the virtue of their possessor.—*Burton.*

Many people take no care of their money till they have come nearly to the end of it, and others do just the same with their time.—*Goethe.*

Money is a good servant, but a dangerous master.—*Bouhours.*

Whoever has sixpence is sovereign over all men,—to the extent of the sixpence; commands cooks to feed him, philosophers to teach him, kings to mount guard over him,—to the extent of sixpence.—*Carlyle.*

He that wants money, means, and content is without three good friends.—*Shakespeare.*

Certainly man's wicked angel is in money. I often catch myself with something bold as a lion bouncing from my heart, when the shilling rattles, and the lion as small as any weasel slinks back again.—*Douglas Jerrold.*

A wise man should have money in his head, but not in his heart.—*Swift.*

What a dignity it gives an old lady, that balance at the bankers! How tenderly we look at her faults if she is a relative; what a kind, good-natured old creature we find her!—*Thackeray.*

Money is not required to buy one necessity of the soul.—*Thoreau.*

Money never made a man happy yet, nor will it. There is nothing in its nature to produce happiness. The more a man has, the more he wants. Instead of its filling a vacuum, it makes one. If it satisfies one want, it doubles and trebles that want another way. That was a true proverb of the wise man, rely upon it: "*Better* is little with the fear of the Lord, than great treasure, and trouble therewith."—*Franklin.*

The picklock that never fails.—*Massinger.*

Money is a terrible blab; she will betray the secrets of her owner whatever he do to gag her. His virtues will creep out in her whisper, his vices she will cry aloud at the top of her tongue.—*Bulwer Lytton.*

Put not your trust in money, but put your money in trust.—*Holmes.*

Money is only thus far a standard of value; that which it can measure is perishable; that which it cannot is immortal.—*Bovee.*

Money often costs too much, and power and pleasure are not cheap.—*Emerson.*

Alexander being asked why he did not gather money and lay it up in a public treasury, "For fear," said he, " lest, being keeper thereof, I should be infected and corrupted." A good caution for them who love to bear the bag.—*Venning.*

If you make money your god, it will plague you like the devil.—*Fielding.*

By doing good with his money, a man as it were stamps the image of God upon it, and makes it pass current for the merchandise of heaven.—*Rutledge.*

Money is like manure, of very little use except it be spread.—*Bacon.*

Covetous men need money least, yet most affect it; and prodigals, who need it most, do least regard it.—*Theodore Parker.*

The philosophy which affects to teach us a contempt of money does not run very deep.— *Henry Taylor.*

If Heaven allotted to each man seven guardian angels, five of them, at least, would be found night and day hovering over his pocket. *Bulwer Lytton.*

All love has something of blindness in it, but the love of money especially.—*South.*

Money is both the generation and corruption of purchased honor; honor is both the child and slave of potent money: the credit which honor hath lost, money hath found. When honor grew mercenary, money grew honorable. The way to be truly noble is to contemn both. *Quarles.*

Money is life to us wretched mortals.— *Hesiodus.*

It happens a little unluckily, that the persons who have the most intimate contempt of money are the same that have the strongest appetites for the pleasures it procures.— *Shenstone.*

Great mammon!—greatest god below the sky.—*Spenser.*

Money and time are the heaviest burdens of life, and the unhappiest of all mortals are those who have more of either than they know how to use.—*Johnson.*

To cure us of our immoderate love of gain, we should seriously consider how many goods there are that money will not purchase, and these the best; and how many evils there are that money will not remedy, and these the worst.— *Colton.*

Men are seldom more innocently employed than when they are making money.—*Johnson.*

The Romans worshipped their standard; and the Roman standard happened to be an eagle. Our standard is only one tenth of an eagle,—a dollar,—but we make all even by adoring it with tenfold devotion.—*E. A. Poe.*

Money is oftentimes the only patent of nobility, beside lofty pretensions.—*Zimmermann.*

Money does all things for reward; some are pious and honest as long as they thrive upon it, but if the devil himself gives better wages, they soon change their party.—*Seneca.*

Why, nothing comes amiss, so money comes withal.—*Shakespeare.*

MONOMANIA.

The man with but one idea in his head is sure to exaggerate that to top-heaviness, and thus he loses his equilibrium.—*Aaron Hill.*

The greatest part of mankind labor under one delirium or another; and Don Quixote differed from the rest, not in madness, but the species of it. The covetous, the prodigal, the superstitious, the libertine, and the coffee-house politician, are all Quixotes in their several way. *Fielding.*

Adhesion to one idea is monomania; to a few, slavery.—*Bovee.*

MONUMENTS.

Monuments are the grappling-irons that bind one generation to another.—*Joubert.*

The monument of the greatest man should be only a bust and a name. If the name alone is insufficient to illustrate the bust, let them both perish.—*Landor.*

No man who needs a monument ever ought to have one.—*Hawthorne.*

Those only deserve a monument who do not need one, that is, who have raised themselves a monument in the minds and memories of men. *Hazlitt.*

Monuments themselves memorials need.— *Crabbe.*

While we feel that the mightiest must yield to the stern law of necessity, we know that the very monuments which record the decay of their outward frame are so many proofs and symbols that they shall never really expire.—*Talfourd.*

Monuments, like men, submit to fate.—*Pope.*

If I have done any deed worthy of remembrance, that deed will be my monument. If not, no monument can preserve my memory.—
Agesilaus.

MOON.

The moon, the governess of floods, pale in her anger, washes all the air, that rheumatic diseases do abound; and, through this distemperature, we see the seasons alter.—
Shakespeare.

See the fair rising moon, ere day's remaining twilight scarce is spent, hangs up her ready lamp, and with mild lustre drives back the hovering shade.—*T. Hughes.*

The cold chaste moon, the queen of heaven's bright isles.—*Shelley.*

I know not that there is anything in nature more soothing to the mind than the contemplation of the moon, sailing, like some planetary bark, amidst a sea of bright azure. The subject is certainly hackneyed; the moon has been sung by poet and poetaster. Is there any marvel that it should be so?—*Simms.*

The queen of night shines fair with all her virgin stars about her.—*Otway.*

How sweet the moonlight sleeps upon this bank! Here will we sit, and let the sounds of music creep in our ears; soft stillness, and the night, become the touches of sweet harmony.—
Shakespeare.

O moon! old boughs lisp forth a holier din, the while they feel thine airy fellowship: thou dost bless everywhere with silver lip, kissing dead things to life.—*Keats.*

MOONLIGHT.

When *Phœbe* doth behold her silver visage in the watery glass, decking with liquid pearl the bladed grass.—*Shakespeare.*

Soft moonlight and tender love harmonize together wonderfully.—*Ninon de l'Enclos.*

MORALITY.

The morality of some people is in remnants, — never enough to make a coat.—*Joubert.*

The morality of an action depends upon the motive from which we act. If I fling half a crown to a beggar with intention to break his head, and he picks it up and buys victuals with it, the physical effect is good; but with respect to me, the action is very wrong.—*Johnson.*

Morality is a curb, not a spur.—*Joubert.*

The moral of the steed is in the spur of his rider; of the slave, in the eye of his master; of the woman, in the sense of her weakness and dependence.—*Simms.*

The health of a community is an almost unfailing index of its morals.—
James Martineau.

Morality without religion, is only a kind of dead reckoning, — an endeavor to find our place on a cloudy sea by measuring the distance we have to run, but without any observation of the heavenly bodies.—*Longfellow.*

All sects are different, because they come from men; morality is everywhere the same, because it comes from God.—*Voltaire.*

Nothing seems important to me but so far as it is connected with morals. If the mind cannot feel and treat mathematics and music and everything else as a trifle, it has been seduced and enslaved.—*Cecil.*

I think I restrict myself within bounds in saying, that, so far as I have observed in this life, ten men have failed from defect in morals where one has failed from defect in intellect.—
Horace Mann.

Let us with caution indulge the supposition that morality can be maintained without religion. Reason and experience both forbid us to expect that national morality can prevail in exclusion of religious principle.—*Washington.*

Morality is but the vestibule of religion.—
Chapin.

We are come too late, by several thousand years, to say anything new in morality. The finest and most beautiful thoughts concerning manners have been carried away before our times, and nothing is left for us but to glean after the ancients, and the most ingenious of the moderns.—*Bruyère.*

To give a man a full knowledge of true morality, I would send him to no other book than the New Testament.—*Locke*

Infinite toil would not enable you to sweep away a mist, but, by ascending a little, you may often overlook it altogether. So it is with our moral improvement, we wrestle fiercely with a vicious habit, which could have no hold upon us if we ascended into a higher moral atmosphere.—*Helps.*

Morality has need, that it may be well received, of the mask of fable and the charm of poetry; truth pleases less when it is naked, and is the only virgin in this vast universe whom one likes to see a little clothed.—
De Boufflers.

If we are told a man is religious we still ask what are his morals? But if we hear at first that he has honest morals, and is a man of natural justice and good temper, we seldom think of the other question, whether he be religious and devout. —*Shaftesbury.*

MORNING.

Spill not the morning (the quintessence of the day) in recreation, for sleep itself is a recreation. Add not, therefore, sauce to sauces.—*Fuller.*

Merry larks are ploughmen's clocks.—*Shakespeare.*

Let the day have a blessed baptism by giving your first waking thoughts into the bosom of God. The first hour of the morning is the rudder of the day.—*Beecher.*

Under the opening eyelids of the morn.—*Milton.*

Nor is a day lived if the dawn is left out of it, with the prospects it opens. Who speaks charmingly of nature or of mankind, like him who comes bibulous of sunrise and the fountains of waters ? —*Alcott.*

The silent hours steal on, and flaky darkness breaks within the east.—*Shakespeare.*

The meek-eyed Morn appears, mother of dews.—*Thomson.*

Let your sleep be necessary and healthful, not idle and expensive of time, beyond the needs and conveniences of nature ; and sometimes be curious to see the preparation which the sun makes when he is coming forth from his chambers of the east.—*Jeremy Taylor.*

See how the morning opes her golden gates, and takes her farewell of the glorious sun.—*Shakespeare.*

The morning hour has gold in its mouth.—*Franklin.*

I see the spectacle of morning from the hill-top over against my house, from daybreak to sunrise, with emotions which an angel might share. The long slender bars of cloud float like fishes in the sea of crimson light. From the earth, as a shore, I look out into that silent sea. I seem to partake its rapid transformations ; the active enchantment reaches my dust, and I dilate and conspire with the morning wind.—*Emerson.*

The breezy call of incense-breathing morn.—*Gray.*

Light is in her wane ; day's early flush glows like a hectic on her fading cheek, wasting its beauty.—*Longfellow.*

Sweet is the breath of morn, her rising sweet with charm of earliest birds.—*Milton.*

Look, love, what envious streaks do lace the severing clouds in yonder east ! night's candles are burnt out, and jocund day stands tiptoe on the misty mountain-tops.—*Shakespeare.*

Morn, in the white wake of the morning star, came furrowing all the orient into gold.—*Tennyson.*

The morning steals upon the night, melting the darkness.—*Shakespeare.*

See ! the dapple gray coursers of the morn beat up the light with their bright silver hoofs, and chase it through the sky.—*J. Marston.*

The morn is up again, the dewy morn, with breath all incense, and with cheek all bloom.—*Byron.*

There was a small clear lake, from whence the morning, like a beauty, came fresh from her bath.—*Miss L. E. Landon.*

Modest as Morning when she coldly eyes the youthful Phœbus.—*Shakespeare.*

MOROSENESS.

Moroseness is the evening of turbulence.—*Landor.*

There is no mockery like the mockery of that spirit that looks around in the world and believes that all is emptiness.—*Chapin.*

MORTALITY.

To smell a fresh turf of earth is wholesome for the body ; no less are thoughts of mortality cordial to the soul. "Dust thou art, and unto dust thou shalt return."—*Fuller.*

Short is the life of those who possess great accomplishments, and seldom do they reach a good old age. Whatever thou lovest, pray that thou mayest not set too high a value on it.—*Martial.*

When we see our enemies and friends gliding away before us, let us not forget that we are subject to the general law of mortality, and shall soon be where our doom will be fixed forever.—*Johnson.*

MOSSES.

Meek creatures ! the first mercy of the earth, veiling with hushed softness its dintless rocks ; creatures full of pity, covering with strange and tender honor the scarred disgrace of ruin, — laying quiet finger on the trembling stones, to teach them rest. No words, that I know of, will say what these mosses are. None are delicate enough, none perfect enough, none rich enough.—*Ruskin.*

They will not be gathered, like the flowers, for chaplet or love-token ; but of these the wild bird will make its nest, and the wearied child his pillow.—*Ruskin.*

MOTHER.

What are Raphael's Madonnas but the shadow of a mother's love, fixed in permanent outline forever ?—*T. W. Higginson.*

" What is wanting," said Napoleon one day to Madame Campan, " in order that the youth of France be well educated ? " " Good mothers," was the reply. The Emperor was most forcibly struck with this answer. " Here," said he, " is a system in one word."—*Abbott.*

I think it must somewhere be written, that the virtues of mothers shall, occasionally, be visited on their children, as well as the sins of fathers.—*Dickens.*

At first babes feed on the mother's bosom, but always on her heart.—*Beecher.*

A father may turn his back on his child, brothers and sisters may become inveterate enemies, husbands may desert their wives, wives their husbands. But a mother's love endures through all; in good repute, in bad repute, in the face of the world's condemnation, a mother still loves on, and still hopes that her child may turn from his evil ways, and repent; still she remembers the infant smiles that once filled her bosom with rapture, the merry laugh, the joyful shout of his childhood, the opening promise of his youth; and she can never be brought to think him all unworthy.—*Washington Irving.*

If there be aught surpassing human deed or word or thought, it is a mother's love ! —*Marchioness de Spadara.*

Observe how soon, and to what a degree, this influence begins to operate ! Her first ministration for her infant is to enter, as it were, the valley of the shadow of death, and win its life at the peril of her own ! How different must an affection thus founded be from all others ! —*Mrs. Sigourney.*

The future destiny of the child is always the work of the mother.—*Napoleon.*

The instruction received at the mother's knee, and the paternal lessons, together with the pious and sweet souvenirs of the fireside, are never effaced entirely from the soul.—*Lamennais.*

I would desire for a friend the son who never resisted the tears of his mother.—*Lacretelle.*

Unhappy is the man for whom his own mother has not made all other mothers venerable.—*Richter.*

Men are what their mothers made them. You may as well ask a loom which weaves huckaback, why it does not make cashmere, as expect poetry from this engineer, or a chemical discovery from that jobber.—*Emerson.*

Youth fades; love droops; the leaves of friendship fall; a mother's secret hope outlives them all ! —*Holmes.*

Stories first heard at a mother's knee are never wholly forgotten, — a little spring that never quite dries up in our journey through scorching years.—*Ruffini.*

"An ounce of mother," says the Spanish proverb, " is worth a pound of clergy."—*T. W. Higginson.*

Even He that died for us upon the cross, in the last hour, in the unutterable agony of death, was mindful of his mother, as if to teach us that this holy love should be our last worldly thought, — the last point of earth from which the soul should take its flight for heaven.—*Longfellow.*

It is generally admitted, and very frequently proved, that virtue and genius, and all the natural good qualities which men possess, are derived from their mothers.—*Hook.*

The mother's heart is the child's schoolroom.—*Beecher.*

There is in all this cold and hollow world no fount of deep, strong, deathless love, save that within a mother's heart.—*Mrs. Hemans.*

A mother's love is indeed the golden link that binds youth to age; and he is still but a child, however time may have furrowed his cheek, or silvered his brow, who can yet recall, with a softened heart, the fond devotion, or the gentle chidings, of the best friend that God ever gives us.—*Bovee.*

Maternal love ! thou word that sums all bliss.—*Pollok.*

No language can express the power and beauty and heroism and majesty of a mother's love. It shrinks not where man cowers, and grows stronger where man faints, and over the wastes of worldly fortune sends the radiance of its quenchless fidelity like a star in heaven.—*Chapin.*

If the whole world were put into one scale, and my mother into the other, the world would kick the beam.—*Lord Langdale.*

Happy he with such a mother ! faith in womankind beats with his blood, and trust in all things high comes easy to him, and though he trip and fall, he shall not blind his soul with clay.—*Tennyson.*

MOTIVE.

We should often have reason to be ashamed of our most brilliant actions if the world could see the motives from which they spring.—*Rochefoucauld.*

Motives are better than actions. Men drift into crime. Of evil they do more than they contemplate, and of good they contemplate more than they do.—*Bovee.*

Many actions, like the Rhone, have two sources, — one pure, the other impure.—*Hare.*

To bring motives under faithful examination is a high state of religious character. With regard to the depravity of the heart we live daily in the disbelief of our own creed. We indulge thoughts and feelings which are founded upon the presumption that all around us are imperfect and corrupted, but that we are exempted.— *Cecil.*

Distinction is the consequence, never the object, of a great mind.— *Washington Allston.*

The difference there is betwixt honor and honesty seems to be chiefly the motive; the mere honest man does that from duty which the man of honor does for the sake of character.
Shenstone.

He that does good for good's sake seeks neither praise nor reward, though sure of both at last.— *William Penn.*

Socrates, in the Phædon, makes a great difference between virtue and habit, with regard to the allotments hereafter. He says that a person who behaves well from a moral principle shall be entitled to an infinitely higher reward than one who fills up the same measure of duty merely from use or exercise. This is a fine reflection in a Pagan. The Christian divines carry their distinction much farther, by giving the same advantage to religion over morals that Socrates does to morals over habit.
Sterne.

Prudent men lock up their motives, letting familiars have a key to their hearts, as to their garden.—*Shenstone.*

Motives are symptoms of weakness, and supplements for the deficient energy of the living principle, the law within us. Let them then be reserved for those momentous acts and duties in which the strongest and best-balanced natures must feel themselves deficient, and where humility no less than prudence prescribes deliberation.— *Coleridge.*

It is not virtue, but a deceptive copy and imitation of virtue, when we are led to the performance of duty by pleasure as its recompense.
Cicero.

Great actions, the lustre of which dazzles us, are represented by politicians as the effects of deep design; whereas they are commonly the effects of caprice and passion. Thus the war between Augustus and Antony, supposed to be owing to their ambition to give a master to the world, arose probably from jealousy.—
Rochefoucauld.

If a man speaks or acts with a pure thought, happiness follows him like a shadow that never leaves him.—*Buddha.*

The motives of the best actions will not bear too strict an inquiry. It is allowed that the cause of most actions, good or bad, may be resolved into the love of ourselves; but the self-love of some men inclines them to please others, and the self-love of others is wholly employed in pleasing themselves. This makes the great distinction between virtue and vice.—*Swift.*

In the eye of that Supreme Being to whom our whole internal frame is uncovered, dispositions hold the place of actions.—*Blair.*

The attendant on William Rufus, who discharged at a deer an arrow, which glanced against a tree and killed the king, was no murderer, because he had no such design. And, on the other hand, a man who should lie in wait to assassinate another, and pull the trigger of a gun with that intent, would be morally a murderer, not the less though the gun should chance to miss fire.— *Whately.*

The two great movers of the human mind are the desire of good, and the fear of evil.—
Johnson.

He who does evil that good may come pays a toll to the Devil to let him into heaven.—*Hare.*

God made man to go by motives, and he will not go without them, any more than a boat without steam, or a balloon without gas.—
Beecher.

It is motive alone that gives real value to the actions of men, and disinterestedness puts the cap to it.—*Bruyère.*

What if a man save my life with a draught that was prepared to poison me ? The providence of the issue does not at all discharge the obliquity of the intent. And the same reason holds good even in religion itself. It is not the incense, or the offering that is acceptable to God, but the purity and devotion of the worshipper.—*Seneca.*

MUNIFICENCE.
Munificence is not quantity, but quality.—
Pascal.

The proofs of true munificence must be drawn from the uses to which a man of wealth applies his fortune.—*Junius.*

MURDER.
Nor cell, nor chain, nor dungeon speaks to the murderer like the voice of solitude.
Maturin.

The great King of kings hath in the table of his law commanded that thou shalt do no murder; wilt thou then spurn at his edict, and fulfil a man's ? —*Shakespeare.*

Blood, though it sleep a time, yet never dies.— *Chapman.*

23

From the earliest dawning of policy to this day, the invention of men has been sharpening and improving the mystery of murder, from the first rude essay of clubs and stones to the present perfection of gunnery, cannoneering, bombarding, mining.—*Burke.*

One murder made a villain ; millions a hero. Numbers sanctified the crime! —*Porteus.*

It is an hard case, that the laws should not have made any manner of difference between murdering an honest man and only executing a scoundrel. I really think that these things should always be rated *ad valorem.*—*Sterne.*

Murder, though it have no tongue, will speak with most miraculous organ.—*Shakespeare.*

MUSIC.
Music, once admitted to the soul, becomes a sort of spirit, and never dies. It wanders perturbedly through the halls and galleries of the memory, and is often heard again, distinct and living as when it first displaced the wavelets of the air.—*Bulwer Lytton.*

Some of the fathers went so far as to esteem the love of music a sign of predestination ; as a thing divine, and reserved for the felicities of heaven itself.—*Sir W. Temple.*

Some scrap of a childish song hath often been a truer alms than all the benevolent societies could give. This is the best missionary, knowing when she may knock at the door of the most curmudgeonly hearts, without being turned away unheard. For poesy is love's chosen apostle, and the very almoner of God. She is the home of the outcast, and the wealth of the needy.—*Lowell.*

The soul of art best loved when love is by.
Rev. J. B. Brown.

How sour sweet music is, when time is broke, and no proportion kept! —*Shakespeare.*

Music is the only sensual gratification which mankind may indulge · in to excess without injury to their moral or religious feelings.—
Addison.

I am constitutionally susceptible of noises. A carpenter's hammer, in a warm summer noon, will fret me into more than midsummer madness. But those unconnected, unset sounds are nothing to the measured malice of music.—
Lamb.

Music is the fourth great material want of our natures, — first food, then raiment, then shelter, then music.—*Bovee.*

Music is the art of the prophets, the only art that can calm the agitations of the soul ; it is one of the most magnificent and delightful presents God has given us.—*Luther.*

Let me die to the sounds of the delicious music.—Last words of—*Mirabeau.*

I think sometimes, could I only have music on my own terms ; could I live in a great city, and know where I could go whenever I wished the ablution and inundation of musical waves, that were a bath and a medicine.—*Emerson.*

Sweetest melodies are those that are by distance made more sweet.— *Wordsworth.*

It calls in my spirits, composes my thoughts, delights my ear, recreates my mind, and so not only fits me for after business, but fills my heart, at the present, with pure and useful thoughts ; so that when the music sounds the sweetliest in my ears, truth commonly flows the clearest into my mind. And hence it is that I find my soul is become more harmonious, by being accustomed so much to harmony, and so averse to all manners of discord, that the least jarring sounds, either in notes or words, seem very harsh and unpleasant to me.—
Bishop Beveridge.

Before which of us has not childhood been a thousand times called up by Music ? and to which of us has she not spoken, and asked, " Are the rosebuds which I gave thee not yet blown ? " Alas! blown indeed they are, — but they were pale, white roses.—*Richter.*

I was all ear, and took in strains that might create a soul under the ribs of death.—*Milton.*

The meaning of song goes deep. Who is there that, in logical words, can express the effect music has on us ? A kind of inarticulate, unfathomable speech, which leads us to the edge of the infinite, and lets us for moments gaze into that.—*Carlyle.*

The musician and the orator fall short of the full power of their science, if the hearer is left in possession of himself.—*Cecil.*

If you love music, hear it ; go to operas, concerts, and pay fiddlers to play to you ; but I insist upon your neither piping nor fiddling yourself. It puts a gentleman in a very frivolous, contemptible light ; brings him into a great deal of bad company ; and takes up a great deal of time, which might be much better employed.—*Chesterfield.*

Music is the medicine of an afflicted mind, a sweet sad measure is the balm of a wounded spirit ; and joy is heightened by exultant strains.—*Henry Giles.*

Music is nothing else but wild sounds civilized into time and tune. Such the extensiveness thereof, that it stoopeth so low as brute beasts, yet mounteth as high as angels. For horses will do more for a whistle than for a whip, and by hearing their bells jingle away their weariness.—*Fuller.* ·

Music, of all the liberal arts, has the greatest influence over the passions, and is that to which the legislator ought to give the greatest encouragement.—*Napoleon.*

Music is a discipline, and a mistress of order and good manners; she makes the people milder and gentler, more moral and more reasonable.—*Luther.*

There is something in the shape of harps as though they had been made by music.—*Bailey.*

In part of Lord Kames's Elements of Criticism, he says that "music improves the relish of a banquet." That I deny,—any more than painting might do. They may both be additional pleasures, as well as conversation is, but are perfectly distinct notices; and cannot, with the least propriety, be said to mix or blend with the repast, as none of them serve to raise the flavor of the wine, the sauce, the meat, or help to quicken appetite. But music and painting both add a spirit to devotion, and elevate the ardor.—*Sterne.*

Music is a prophecy of what life is to be, the rainbow of promise translated out of seeing into hearing.—*Mrs. L. M. Child.*

Even the miner, while clanking his chains, sings as he lightens his labor with untaught music; he too sings, who bending low on the oozy sand, drags the slow barge against the stream.—*Ovid.*

Away! away! thou speakest to me of things which in all my endless life I have not found, and shall not find.—*Richter.*

The lines of poetry, the periods of prose, and even the texts of Scripture most frequently recollected and quoted, are those which are felt to be pre-eminently musical.—*Shenstone.*

The man that hath no music in himself, nor is not moved with concord of sweet sounds, is fit for treasons, stratagems, and spoils.— *Shakespeare.*

Music is one of the fairest and most glorious gifts of God, to which Satan is a bitter enemy; for it removes from the heart the weight of sorrow, and the fascination of evil thoughts.— *Luther.*

I ever held this sentence of the poet as a canon of my creed, "that whom God loveth not, they love not music."—*T. Morley.*

The direct relation of music is not to ideas, but emotions. Music, in the works of its greatest masters, is more marvellous, more mysterious, than poetry.—*Henry Giles.*

If music be the food of love, play on, give me excess of it; that, surfeiting, the appetite may sicken, and so die.—*Shakespeare.*

Those who love music are gentle and honest in their tempers. I always loved music, and would not, for a great matter, be without the little skill which I possess in the art.—*Luther.*

The stormy music of the drum.—*Campbell.*

Curran's favorite mode of meditation was with his violin in his hand; for hours together would he forget himself, running voluntaries over the strings, while his imagination, collecting its tones, was opening all his faculties for the coming emergency at the bar.—*Disraeli.*

Almost all my tragedies were sketched in my mind, either in the act of hearing music or a few hours after.—*Alfieri.*

A good ear for music, and a good taste for music are two very different things which are often confounded; and so is comprehending and enjoying every object of sense and sentiment.—*Lord Greville.*

All of heaven we have below.—*Addison.*

I remember once strolling along the margin of a stream, in one of those low, sheltered valleys on Salisbury Plain, where the monks of former ages planted chapels and built hermits' cells. There was a little parish church near, but tall elms and quivering alders hid it from the sight, when, all on a sudden, I was startled by the sound of the full organ pealing on the ear, accompanied by rustic voices, and the willing choir of village maids and children. It rose, indeed, "like an exhalation of rich distilled perfumes."—*Hazlitt.*

Let me have music dying, and I seek no more delight.—*Keats.*

In the germ, when the first trace of life begins to stir, music is the nurse of the soul; it murmurs in the ear, and the child sleeps; the tones are companions of his dreams,—they are the world in which he lives.—*Bettina.*

There is music in all things, if men had ears.—*Byron.*

Lord Bacon had music often played in the room adjoining his study. Milton listened to his organ for his solemn inspirations; and music was ever necessary to Warburton. The symphonies which awoke in the poet sublime emotions might have composed the inventive mind of the great critic in the visions of his theoretical mysteries.—*Disraeli.*

Music!—O, how faint, how weak, language fades before thy spell!—*Moore.*

Without the definiteness of sculpture and painting, music is, for that very reason, far more suggestive. Like Milton's Eve, an outline, an impulse, is furnished, and the imagination does the rest.—*Tuckerman.*

Music, sphere - descended maid, friend of pleasure, wisdom's aid!—*Collins.*

It is a bird-flight of the soul, when the heart declares itself in song. The affections that clothe themselves with wings are passions that have been subdued to virtues.—*Simms.*

Music washes away from the soul the dust of every-day life.—*Auerbach.*

It is the medicine of the breaking heart.—
Sir A. Hunt.

Lord, what music hast thou provided for thy saints in heaven, when thou affordest bad men such music on earth!—*Izaak Walton.*

Under the influence of music we are all deluded in some way. We imagine that the performers must dwell in the regions to which they lift their hearers. We are reluctant to admit that a man may blow the most soul-animating strains from his trumpet and yet be a coward; or melt an audience to tears with his violin, and yet be a heartless profligate.—
Hillard.

Music has charms to soothe the savage breast, to soften rocks, and bend the knotted oak.—
Congreve.

Music is the mediator between the spiritual and the sensual life. Although the spirit be not master of that which it creates through music, yet it is blessed in this creation, which, like every creation of art, is mightier than the artist.—*Beethoven.*

Music,—we love it for the buried hopes, the garnered memories, the tender feelings it can summon at a touch.—*Miss L. E. Landon.*

I am never merry when I hear sweet music.
Shakespeare.

Had I children, my utmost endeavors would be to make them musicians. Considering I have no ear, nor even thought of music, the preference seems odd, and yet it is embraced on frequent reflection.—*Horace Walpole.*

Like the faint, exquisite music of a dream.
Moore.

The effect of good music is not caused by its novelty. On the contrary, it strikes us more the more familiar we are with it.—*Goethe.*

Music moves us, and we know not why; we feel the tears, but cannot trace their source. Is it the language of some other state, born of its memory? For what can wake the soul's strong instinct of another world, like music?—
Miss L. E. Landon.

Music is the child of prayer, the companion of religion.—*Chateaubriand.*

Next to theology I give to music the highest place and honor. And we see how David and all the saints have wrought their godly thoughts into verse, rhyme, and song.—
Luther.

It is in learning music that many youthful hearts learn love.—*Ricard.*

Such is the sociableness of music, it conforms itself to all companies, both in mirth and mourning; complying to improve that passion with which it finds the auditors most affected.—
Fuller.

Music is the only one of the fine arts in which not only man, but all other animals, have a common property, — mice and elephants, spiders and birds.—*Richter.*

O, it came over my ear like the sweet south, that breathes upon a bank of violets, stealing and giving odor!—*Shakespeare*

Amongst the instrumentalities of love and peace, surely there can be no sweeter, softer, more effective voice than that of gentle, peace-breathing music.—*Elihu Burritt.*

MUTABILITY.

Be not too anxious for the few things that life requires; youth is flying rapidly past and beauty is vanishing, while withered age puts to flight amorous play and gentle sleep. The flowers of spring do not retain their bloom, nor does the ruddy moon always shine with the same lustre; why then, O man, dost thou disquiet thyself forever with schemes that are far beyond the power of man?—*Horace.*

Look at the fate of summer flowers, which blow at daybreak, droop ere even-song.—
Wordsworth.

When Anaxagoras was told of the death of his son, he only said, "I knew he was mortal." So we in all casualties of life should say, "I knew my riches were uncertain, that my friend was but a man." Such considerations would soon pacify us, because all our troubles proceed from their being unexpected.—*Plutarch.*

The mutable rank-scented many.—
Shakespeare.

It may serve as a comfort to us, in all our calamities and afflictions, that he that loses anything and gets wisdom by it is a gainer by the loss.—*L'Estrange.*

All our life goeth like Penelope's web,— what one hour effects the next destroys.—
St. Augustine.

At last some curious traveller from Lima will visit England, and give a description of the ruins of St. Paul's, like the editions of Balbec and Palmyra.—*Horace Walpole.*

Can we wonder that men perish and are forgotten, when their noblest and most enduring works decay? Death comes even to monumental structures, and oblivion rests on the most illustrious names.—*Ausonius.*

Nothing maintains its bloom forever; age succeeds to age.—*Cicero.*

Mutability is the badge of infirmity. It is seldom that a man continues to wish and design the same thing two days alike. Now he is for marrying; and now a mistress is preferred to a wife. Now he is ambitious and aspiring; presently the meanest servant is not more humble than he. This hour he squanders his money away; the next he turns miser. Sometimes he is frugal and serious; at other times profuse, airy, and gay.—*Charron.*

The uncertainty of events disturbs the purest enjoyments.—*De Lévis.*

The worthy gentleman who has been snatched from us at the moment of the election, and in the middle of the contest, whilst his desires were as warm and his hopes as eager as ours, has feelingly told us what shadows we are, and what shadows we pursue.—*Burke.*

Ye gods, ready to grant the highest prosperity, and slow to preserve it! —*Lucan.*

In human life there is a constant change of fortune; and it is unreasonable to expect an exemption from the common fate. Life itself decays, and all things are daily changing.— *Plutarch.*

Clocks will go as they are set; but man, irregular man, is never constant, never certain. *Otway.*

We see scarcely anything, just or unjust, that does not change its quality with its climate. Three degrees of latitude upset all the principles of jurisprudence; a meridian determines what is truth, or a few years of settled authority. Fundamental laws may vary. Right has its epochs. Droll justice, indeed, that a river or a mountain limits! Truth on one side of the Pyrenees is error on the other.—*Pascal.*

Man must be prepared for every event of life, for there is nothing that is durable.— *Menander.*

Time, whose millioned accidents creep in betwixt vows, and change decrees of kings, tan sacred beauty, blunt the sharpest intents, divert strong minds to the course of altering things.—*Shakespeare.*

The blessings of health and fortune, as they have a beginning, so they must also have an end. Everything rises but to fall, and increases but to decay.—*Sallust.*

Like madness is the glory of this life, as this pomp shows to a little oil, and root. We make ourselves fools, to disport ourselves; and spend our flatteries, to drink those men, upon whose age we void it up again with poisonous spite and envy.—*Shakespeare.*

MYSTERY.

As defect of strength in us makes some weights to be unmovable, so likewise defect of understanding makes some truths to be mysterious.—*Bishop Sherlock.*

Mystery magnifies danger, as a fog the sun; the hand that warned Belshazzar derived its horrifying influence from the want of a body.— *Colton.*

It is the dim haze of mystery that adds enchantment to pursuit.—*Rivarol.*

Most men take least notice of what is plain, as if that was of no use; but puzzle their thoughts to be themselves in those vast depths and abysses which no human understanding can fathom.—*Bishop Sherlock.*

There are more things in heaven and earth than are dreamt of in your philosophy.— *Shakespeare.*

To make anything very terrible, obscurity seems, in general, to be necessary. When we know the full extent of any danger, when we can accustom our eye to it, a great deal of the apprehension vanishes.—*Burke.*

A proper secrecy is the only mystery of able men; mystery is the only secrecy of weak and cunning ones.—*Chesterfield.*

Mystery and innocence are not akin.— *Hosea Ballou.*

We injure mysteries, which are matters of faith, by any attempt at explanation in order to make them matters of reason. Could they be explained, they would cease to be mysteries; and it has been well said that a thing is not necessarily against reason because it happens to be above it.—*Colton.*

Where there is mystery, it is generally supposed that there must also be evil.—*Byron.*

MYTHOLOGY.

Mythology is not religion. It may rather be regarded as the ancient substitute, the poetical counterpart, for dogmatic theology.— *Hare.*

The heathen mythology not only was not true, but was not even supported as true; it not only deserved no faith, but it demanded none. The very pretension to truth, the very demand of faith, were characteristic distinctions of Christianity.—*Whately.*

N.

NAME.

"A person with a bad name is already half hanged," saith the old proverb.—*Whipple.*

With the vulgar and the learned, names have great weight; the wise use a writ of inquiry into their legitimacy when they are advanced as authority.—*Zimmermann.*

Good name in man and woman is the immediate jewel of their souls.—*Shakespeare.*

In honest truth, a name given to a man is no better than a skin given to him; what is not natively his own falls off and comes to nothing.
Landor.

Ravished with the whistling of a name.—
Pope.

Favor or disappointment has been often conceded as the name of the claimant has affected us; and the accidental affinity or coincidence of a name, connected with ridicule or hatred, with pleasure or disgust, has operated like magic.—*Disraeli.*

Some to the fascination of a name surrender judgment hoodwinked.—*Cowper.*

Some men do as much begrudge others a good name, as they want one themselves; and perhaps that is the reason of it.—*William Penn.*

What is in a name? That which we call a rose by any other name would smell as sweet.—
Shakespeare.

Who hath not owned, with rapture-smitten frame, the power of grace, the magic of a name?—*Cowper.*

It was a charming fancy of the Pythagoreans to exchange names when they met, that so they might partake of the virtues each admired in the other. And, knowing the power of names, they used only such as were musical and pleasing.—*Alcott.*

I do beseech you (chiefly, that I may set it in my prayers), what is your name?—
Shakespeare.

Steine humorously exhorts all godfathers not to Nicodemus a man into nothing.—
Disraeli.

NATIONALITY.

A nation's character is the sum of its splendid deeds; they constitute one common patrimony, the nation's inheritance. They awe foreign powers, they arouse and animate our own people.—*Henry Clay.*

Nationality is the aggregated individuality of the greatest men of the nation.—*Kossuth.*

National progress is the sum of individual industry, energy, and uprightness, as national decay is of individual idleness, selfishness, and vice.—*Samuel Smiles.*

NATIVE LAND.

A man's love for his native land lies deeper than any logical expression, among those pulses of the heart which vibrate to the sanctities of home, and to the thoughts which leap up from his fathers' graves.—*Chapin.*

NATURE.

Nature does not capriciously scatter her secrets as golden gifts to lazy pets and luxurions darlings, but imposes tasks when she presents opportunities, and uplifts him whom she would inform. The apple that she drops at the feet of Newton is but a coy invitation to follow her to the stars.—*Whipple.*

Nature is man's religious book, with lessons for every day.—*Theodore Parker.*

All things are engaged in writing their history. The planet, the pebble, goes attended by its shadow. The rolling rock leaves its scratches on the mountain; the river, its channel in the soil; the animal, its bones in the stratum; the fern and leaf, their modest epitaph in the coal. The falling drop makes its sculpture in the sand or the stone. Not a foot steps into the snow or along the ground, but prints, in characters more or less lasting, a map of its march. Every act of the man inscribes itself in the memories of its fellows, and in his own manners and face. The air is full of sounds, the sky of tokens, the ground is all memoranda and signatures, and every object covered over with hints which speak to the intelligent.—
Emerson.

How hard it is to hide the sparks of nature!
Shakespeare.

Nature never deserts the wise and pure; no plot so narrow, be but nature there, no waste so vacant, but may well employ each faculty of sense, and keep the heart awake to love and beauty!—*Coleridge.*

Art may err, but nature cannot miss.—
Dryden.

Let not a man trust his victory over his nature too far; for nature will lie buried a great time, and yet revive upon the occasion of temptation,—like as it was with Æsop's damsel, turned from a cat to a woman, who sat very demurely at the board's end till a mouse ran before her.—*Bacon.*

I have been reasoning all my life, and find that all argument will vanish before one touch of nature.—*Colman.*

Sympathy with nature is a part of the good man's religion.—*F. H. Hedge.*

Take a thorn-bush and sprinkle it for a whole year with water,—it will yield nothing but thorns. Take a date-tree, leave it without culture, and it will always produce dates. Nobility is the date-tree, and the Arab populace is a bush of thorns.—*Abd-el-Kader.*

Nature, the vicar of the Almighty Lord.— *Chaucer.*

Nature always springs to the surface and manages to show what she is. It is vain to stop or try to drive her back. She breaks through every obstacle, pushes forward, and at last makes for herself a way.—*Boileau.*

Nature cannot be surprised in undress. Beauty breaks in everywhere.—*Emerson.*

Everything made by man may be destroyed by man; there are no ineffaceable characters except those engraved by nature; and nature makes neither princes, nor rich men, nor great lords.—*Rousseau.*

Nature ever provides for her own exigencies. *Seneca.*

There are forces in all bodies, some of which cause them to unite, and others to separate. We call these attraction, affinity, adhesion, repulsion, reaction, resistance; but when applied to sentient beings, we vary the names, and denote the same qualities by the words love, friendship, sympathy, hatred, enmity, and antipathy; and we say in common language that the former belong to physical, and the latter to moral beings.—*Drummond.*

Nature, through all her kingdoms, insures herself.—*Emerson.*

Lavish thousands of dollars on your baby-clothes, and after all the child is prettiest when every garment is laid aside. That becoming nakedness, at least, may adorn the chubby darling of the poorest home.—*T. W. Higginson.*

Nature is frugal, and her wants are few.— *Young.*

Nature wears not the pale livery which inspires meditation or solemn joy; her face seems wreathed in a perpetual smile. The landscape breathes, indeed, of intoxicating delight; it invites to present joy; but it leads to no tender reminiscences of the past, nor gives solemn indications of the future.—*Talfourd.*

Looks through nature up to nature's God.— *Pope.*

Nature has perfections, in order to show that she is the image of God; and defects, in order to show that she is only his image.—*Pascal.*

The more a man follows Nature, and is obedient to her laws, the longer he will live; the farther he deviates from these, the shorter will be his existence.—*C. W. Hufeland.*

In nature things move violently to their place, and calmly in their place.—*Bacon.*

Nature is a frugal mother, and never gives without measure. When she has work to do, she qualifies men for that and sends them equipped.—*Emerson.*

Nature is commanded by obeying her.— *Bacon.*

There is no trifling with nature; it is always true, grave, and severe; it is always in the right, and the faults and errors fall to our share. It defies incompetency, but reveals its secrets to the competent, the truthful, and the pure.—*Goethe.*

A man's own manner and character is what best becomes him.—*Cicero.*

Hill and valley, seas and constellations, are but stereotypes of divine ideas appealing to and answered by the living soul of man.—*Chapin.*

The works of nature and the works of revelation display religion to mankind in characters so large and visible, that those who are not quite blind may in them see and read the first principles and most necessary parts of it, and from thence penetrate into those infinite depths filled with the treasures of wisdom and knowledge.— *Locke.*

Nature is God's Old Testament.— *Theodore Parker.*

Read nature; nature is a friend to truth; nature is Christian, preaches to mankind, and bids dead matter aid us in our creed.—*Young.*

It were happy if we studied nature more in natural things; and acted according to nature, whose rules are few, plain, and most reasonable. Let us begin where she begins, go her pace, and close always where she ends, and we cannot miss of being good naturalists.— *William Penn.*

Nature and wisdom always say the same.— *Juvenal.*

I follow nature as the surest guide, and resign myself with implicit obedience to her sacred ordinances.—*Cicero.*

Nature is the chart of God, mapping out all his attributes.—*Tupper.*

All the gestures of children are graceful; the reign of distortion and unnatural attitude commences with the introduction of the dancing-master.—*Sir Joshua Reynolds.*

Knowing that nature never did betray the heart that loved her.—*Wordsworth.*

Nature was his nurse and playfellow. For him she would let slip between the leaves golden shafts of sunlight that fell just within his grasp; she would send wandering breezes to visit him with the balm of bay and resinous gums; to him the tall red-woods nodded familiarly and sleepily, the bumble-bees buzzed, and the rooks cawed a slumberous accompaniment.—
Bret Harte.

Nature alone is permanent.—*Longfellow.*

Nature stretches out her arms to embrace man, only let his thoughts be of equal greatness. Willingly does she follow his footstep with the violet and the rose, and bend her lines of grandeur and grace to the decoration of her darling child.—*Emerson.*

The poetry of earth is never dead.—*Keats.*

He that follows nature is never out of his way. Nature is sometimes subdued, but seldom extinguished.—*Bacon.*

God has placed nature by the side of man as a friend who remains always near to guide and console him in life; as a protecting genius who conducts him, as well as all species, to a harmonious unity with himself. The earth is the maternal bosom which bears all the races; nature arouses man from the sleep in which he would remain without thought of himself, inspires him, and preserves thus in humanity activity and life.—*Ritter.*

Nature, like a kind and smiling mother, lends herself to our dreams and cherishes our fancies.—*Victor Hugo.*

O Lord, how manifold are thy works! in wisdom hast thou made them all; the earth is full of thy riches.—*Bible.*

Nature is no spendthrift, but takes the shortest way to her ends. As the general says to his soldiers, "If you want a fort, build a fort," so nature makes every creature do its own work and get its living, be it planet, animal, or tree.—*Emerson.*

One touch of nature makes the whole world kin.—*Shakespeare.*

The laws of nature are just, but terrible. There is no weak mercy in them. Cause and consequence are inseparable and inevitable. The elements have no forbearance. The fire burns, the water drowns, the air consumes, the earth buries. And perhaps it would be well for our race if the punishment of crimes against the laws of man were as inevitable as the punishment of crimes against the laws of nature,— were man as unerring in his judgments as nature.—*Longfellow.*

Nature is but a name for an effect, whose cause is God.—*Cowper.*

Nature is sanitive, refining, elevating. How cunningly she hides every wrinkle of her inconceivable antiquity under roses and violets and morning dew! Every inch of the mountains is scarred by unimaginable convulsions, yet the new day is purple with the bloom of youth and love.—*Emerson.*

The living, visible garment of God.—*Goethe.*

There is a signature of wisdom and power impressed upon the works of God, which evidently distinguishes them from the feeble imitations of men. Not only the splendor of the sun, but the glimmering light of the glowworm, proclaims his glory.—*Rev. John Newton.*

All nature's difference keeps all nature's peace.—*Pope.*

Natural objects themselves, even when they make no claim to beauty, excite the feelings, and occupy the imagination. Nature pleases, attracts, delights, merely because it is nature. We recognize in it an Infinite Power.
Wilhelm von Humboldt.

The time-vesture of God, that reveals him to the wise, and hides him from the foolish.—
Carlyle.

When storms lower, and wintry winds oppress thee, Nature, dear goddess, is beautiful, always beautiful! Every little flake of snow is such a perfect crystal, and they fall together so gracefully, as if fairies of the air caught waterdrops and made them into artificial flowers to garland the wings of the wind!—
Mrs. L. M. Child.

There is but one book for genius, — nature.
Madame Deluzy.

What profusion is there in His work! When trees blossom there is not a single breastpin, but a whole bosom-full of gems; and of leaves they have so many suits that they can throw them away to the winds all summer long. What unnumbered cathedrals has He reared in the forest shades, vast and grand, full of curious carvings, and haunted evermore by tremulous music; and in the heavens above, how do stars seem to have flown óut of His hand faster than sparks out of a mighty forge! —*Beecher.*

Nature is an Æolian harp, a musical instrument, whose tones are the re-echo of higher strings within us.—*Novalis.*

Give nature a place to stand upon, and she cannot be entirely subdued by art. An orange-tree in a box is still a tree, and even a yew cut into the shape of St. George and the dragon is more of a growth than a manufacture.—
Hillard.

Nature! my mother Nature! as the infant in the harsh slavery of schools pines for home. I yearn within the dark walls of cities, and amid the hum of unfamiliar men, for thy sweet embrace, and thy bosom whereon to lay my head, and weep wild tears at my will!—
Bulwer Lytton.

If we did not take great pains, and were not at great expense to corrupt our nature, our nature would never corrupt us.—*Clarendon.*

Nature gives to every time and season some beauties of its own; and from morning to night, as from the cradle to the grave, is but a succession of changes so gentle and easy that we can scarcely mark their progress.—*Dickens.*

Thou fool! Nature alone is antique, and the oldest art a mushroom; that idle crag thou sittest on is six thousand years of age.—*Carlyle.*

Perhaps, if we could penetrate nature's secrets, we should find that what we call weeds are more essential to the well being of the world than the most precious fruit or grain.—*Hawthorne.*

Shakespeare paints so very closely to nature, and with such marking touches, that he gives the very look an actor ought to wear when he is on his scene.—*Cumberland.*

In nature, all is managed for the best with perfect frugality and just reserve, profuse to none, but bountiful to all; never employing on one thing more than enough, but with exact economy retrenching the superfluous, and adding force to what is principal in everything.—
Shaftesbury.

Surely there is something in the unruffled calm of nature that overawes our little anxieties and doubts; the sight of the deep-blue sky and the clustering stars above seems to impart a quiet to the mind.—*T. Edwards.*

Nature is the most thrifty thing in the world; she never wastes anything; she undergoes change, but there is no annihilation,—the essence remains, matter is eternal.—
Rev. T. Binney.

Nature never says that which reason will contradict.—*Juvenal.*

Nature without learning is like a blind man; learning without nature is like the maimed; practice without both these is incomplete. As in agriculture a good soil is first sought for, then a skilful husbandman, and then good seed; in the same way nature corresponds to the soil, the teacher to the husbandman, precepts and instruction to the seed.—
Plutarch.

Laboring art can never ransom nature from her inaidable estate.—*Shakespeare.*

Search out the wisdom of Nature, there is depth in all her doings; she seemeth prodigal of power, yet her rules are the maxims of frugality.—*Tupper.*

NEATNESS.

We must avoid fastidiousness; neatness, when it is moderate, is a virtue; but when it is carried to an extreme, it narrows the mind.—
Fenelon.

NECESSITY.

Necessity is the argument of tyrants, it is the creed of slaves.—*William Pitt.*

A people never fairly begins to prosper till necessity is treading on its heels. The growing want of room is one of the sources of civilization. Population is power, but it must be a population that, in growing, is made daily apprehensive of the morrow.—*Simms.*

Necessity does everything well.—*Emerson.*

Necessity is a bad recommendation to favors of any kind, which as seldom fall to those who really want them, as to those who really deserve them.—*Fielding.*

There is no virtue like necessity.—
Shakespeare.

There is no contending with necessity, and we should be very tender how we censure those that submit to it. It is one thing to be at liberty to do what we will, and another thing to be tied up to do what we must.—*L'Estrange.*

The necessities that exist are in general created by the superfluities that are enjoyed.—
Zimmermann.

We ought to be thankful to nature for having made those things which are necessary easy to be discovered; while other things that are difficult to be known are not necessary.—
Epicurus.

What fate imposes, men must needs abide; it boots not to resist both wind and tide.—
Shakespeare.

We are ruined, not by what we really want, but by what we think we do; therefore, never go abroad in search of your wants; if they be real wants, they will come home in search of you; for he that buys what he does not want will soon want what he cannot buy.—*Colton.*

Necessity is stronger than human nature.—
Dionysius.

No picture of life can have any veracity that does not admit the odious facts. A man's power is hooped in by a necessity, which, by many experiments, he touches on every side, until he learns its arc.—*Emerson.*

Need teacheth unlawful things.—*Seneca.*

Necessity, that great refuge and excuse for human frailty, breaks through all law; and he is not to be accounted in fault whose crime is not the effect of choice, but force.—*Pascal.*

Necessity is stronger far than art.—*Æschylus.*

Though fancy may be the patient's complaint, necessity is often the doctor's.—*Zimmermann.*

Necessity is cruel, but it is the only test of inward strength. Every fool may live according to his own likings.—*Goethe.*

Even God is said to be unable to use force against necessity.—*Plato.*

Fear is the underminer of all determinations; and necessity, the victorious rebel of all laws.—*Sir P. Sidney.*

Necessity is always the first stimulus to industry, and those who conduct it with prudence, perseverance, and energy will rarely fail. Viewed in this light, the necessity of labor is not a chastisement, but a blessing, — the very root and spring of all that we call progress in individuals and civilization in nations.—*Samuel Smiles.*

We cannot conquer fate and necessity, yet we can yield to them in such a manner as to be greater than if we could.—*Landor.*

Necessity may be the mother of lucrative, but is the death of poetical invention.—*Shenstone.*

Necessity, like electricity, is in ourselves and all things, and no more without us than within us.—*Bailey.*

Necessity, — thou best of peacemakers, as well as surest prompter of invention.—*Scott.*

The word "necessary" is miserably applied. It disordereth families, and overturneth government, by being so abused. Remember that children and fools want everything; and therefore there is no stronger evidence of a crazy understanding than the making too large a catalogue of things necessary.—*Lord Halifax.*

Necessity makes dastards valiant men.—*Herrick.*

What need the bridge much broader than the flood? The fairest grant is the necessity; look, what will serve is fit.—*Shakespeare.*

Nothing is intolerable that is necessary.—*Jeremy Taylor.*

Not mine this saying, but the sentence of the sage, — nothing is stronger than necessity.—*Euripides.*

The iron hand of necessity commands, and her stern decree is supreme law, to which the gods even must submit. In deep silence rules the uncounselled sister of eternal fate. Whatever she lays upon thee, endure; perform whatever she commands.—*Goethe.*

Necessity never made a good bargain.—*Franklin.*

When God will educate a man, he compels him to learn bitter lessons. He sends him to school to the Necessities rather than to the Graces, that by knowing all suffering he may know also the eternal consolations.—*Celia Burleigh.*

Necessity of action takes away the fear of the act, and makes bold resolution the favorite of fortune.—*Quarles.*

NEGLECT.

Every man has something to do which he neglects, every man has faults to conquer which he delays to combat.—*Johnson.*

A wise and salutary neglect.—*Burke.*

A little neglect may breed great mischief; for want of a nail the shoe was lost; for want of a shoe the horse was lost; and for want of a horse the rider was lost; being overtaken and slain by an enemy, all for want of care about a horse-shoe nail.—*Franklin.*

Negligence is the rust of the soul, that corrodes through all her best resolves.—*Feltham.*

The best ground, untilled, soonest runs out into rank weeds. A man of knowledge that is either negligent' or uncorrected cannot but grow wild and godless.—*Bishop Hall.*

In persons grafted in a serious trust, negligence is a crime.—*Shakespeare.*

NEGRO.

The negro is an exotic of the most gorgeous and superb countries of the world, and he has deep in his heart a passion for all that is splendid, rich, and fanciful; a passion which, rudely indulged by an untrained taste, draws on him the ridicule of the colder and more correct white race.—*Mrs. Stowe.*

The image of God cut in ebony.—*Fuller.*

In the negro countenance you will often meet with strong traits of benignity. I have felt yearnings of tenderness towards some of these faces, or rather masks, that have looked out kindly upon one in casual encounters in the streets and highways.—*Lamb.*

NEUTRALITY.

A wise neuter joins with neither, but uses both, as his honest interest leads him.—*William Penn.*

Neutrality is no favorite with Providence, for we are so formed that it is scarcely possible for us to stand neuter in our hearts, although we may deem it prudent to appear so in our actions.—*Colton.*

The cold neutrality of an impartial judge.—*Burke.*

There is in some men a dispassionate neutrality of mind, which, though it generally passes for good temper, can neither gratify nor warm us: it must indeed be granted that these men can only negatively offend; but then it should also be remembered that they cannot positively please.—*Lord Greville.*

Neutral men are the Devil's allies.—*Chapin.*

Neutrality in things good or evil is both odious and prejudicial; but in matters of an indifferent nature is safe and commendable. Herein taking of parts maketh sides, and breaketh unity. In an unjust cause of separation, he that favoreth both parts may perhaps have least love of either side, but hath most charity in himself.—*Bishop Hall.*

Neutrality, as a lasting principle, is an evidence of weakness.—*Kossuth.*

As for the ass's behavior in such nice circumstances, whether he would starve sooner than violate his neutrality to the two bundles of hay, I shall not presume to determine.—*Addison.*

NEWS.

Ill news is winged with fate, and flies apace.—*Dryden.*

The first bringer of unwelcome news hath but a losing office.—*Shakespeare.*

When ill news comes too late to be serviceable to your neighbor, keep it to yourself.—*Zimmermann.*

Ill news are swallow-winged, but what is good walks on crutches.—*Massinger.*

. Evil news rides post, while good news bates.—*Milton.*

Though it be honest, it is never good to bring bad news. Give to a gracious message an host of tongues; but let ill tidings tell themselves, when they be felt.—*Shakespeare*

News as wholesome as the morning air.—*Chapman.*

NICKNAME.

A good name will wear out; a bad one may be turned; a nickname lasts forever.—*Zimmermann.*

There is also an evil report; light, indeed, and easy to raise, but difficult to carry, and still more difficult to get rid of.—*Hesiodus.*

Names alone mock destruction; they survive the doom of all creation.—*H. Trevanion.*

Nicknames stick to people, and the most ridiculous are the most adhesive.—*Haliburton.*

NIGHT.

The night shows stars and women in a better light.—*Byron.*

The contemplation of night should lead to elevating rather than to depressing ideas. Who can fix his mind on transitory and earthly things, in presence of those glittering myriads of worlds; and who can dread death or solitude in the midst of this brilliant, animated universe, composed of countless suns and worlds, all full of light and life and motion?—*Richter.*

Come, civil night, thou sober-suited matron, all in black.—*Shakespeare.*

As his wife has been given to man as his best half, so night is the half of life, and by far the better part of life.—*Goethe.*

Night,—when good men rest and infants sleep.—*Joanna Baillie.*

The night is made for tenderness,—so still that the low whisper, scarcely audible, is heard like music,—and so deeply pure that the fond thought is chastened as it springs and on the lip made holy.—*Willis.*

Night! that great shadow and profile of the day.—*Richter.*

How absolute and omnipotent is the silence of night! And yet the stillness seems almost audible! From all the measureless depths of air around us comes a half-sound, a half-whisper, as if we could hear the crumbling and falling away of earth and all created things, in the great miracle of nature, decay and reproduction, ever beginning, never ending,—the gradual lapse and running of the sand in the great hour-glass of Time.—*Longfellow.*

Even lust and envy sleep.—*Dryden.*

In her starry shade of dim and solitary loveliness, I learn the language of another world.—*Byron.*

Mind and night will meet, though in silence, like forbidden lovers.—*Bailey.*

Few are the faults we flatter when alone; vice sinks in her allurements, is ungilt, and looks, like other objects, black by night.—*Young.*

Night is a lively masquerade of day.—*J. Montgomery.*

The crickets sing, and man's over-labored sense repairs itself by rest.—*Shakespeare.*

The worm of conscience is the companion of the owl: the light is shunned by sinners and evil spirits only.—*Schiller.*

O majestic night! nature's great ancestor!
Young.

The cripple, tardy-gaited night, who, like a foul and ugly witch, doth limp so tediously away.—*Shakespeare.*

NOBILITY.

The original of all men is the same; and virtue is the only nobility.—*Seneca.*

Nature's noblemen are everywhere,—in town and out of town, gloved and rough-handed, rich and poor. Prejudice against a lord, because he is a lord, is losing the chance of finding a good fellow, as much as prejudice against a ploughman because he is a ploughman.
Willis.

Nobility, without virtue, is a fine setting without a gem.—*Jane Porter.*

Fishwomen cry noble oysters. They certainly are full as noble as any family blazoned out in Collins's peerage. If not of as ancient an house, of as old a bed at least. And to show their richness too, pearls and they are congenial.—*Sterne.*

He who is lord of himself, and exists upon his own resources, is a noble but a rare being.—
Sir E. Brydges.

Talent and worth are the only eternal grounds of distinction. To these the Almighty has affixed his everlasting patent of nobility. Knowledge and goodness,—these make degrees in heaven, and they must be the g   i scale of a true democracy.—*Miss Sedgmidwat ng*

All nobility in its beginnings was somebody's natural superiority.—*Emerson.*

We must have kings, we must have nobles; nature is always providing such in every society, only let us have the real instead of the titular. In every society, some are born to rule, and some to advise. The chief is the chief all the world over, only not his cap and plume. It is only this dislike of the pretender which makes men sometimes unjust to the true and finished man.—*Emerson.*

Nobility should be elective, not hereditary.—
Zimmermann.

Nobility is a graceful ornament to the civil order. It is the Corinthian capital of polished society. It is indeed one sign of a liberal and benevolent mind to incline to it with some sort of partial propensity.—*Burke.*

If a man be endued with a generous mind, this is the best kind of nobility.—*Plato.*

The rank is but the guinea's stamp, the man 's the gowd for a' that.—*Burns.*

Nobility is a river that sets with a constant and undeviating current directly into the great Pacific Ocean of time; but, unlike all other rivers, it is more grand at its source than at its termination.—*Colton.*

NOISE.

Many an irksome noise, go a long way off, is heard as music,—a proud, sweet satire on the meanness of our lives.—*Thoreau.*

It is with narrow-souled people as with narrow-necked bottles,—the less they have in them, the more noise they make in pouring it out.—*Pope.*

NONSENSE.

Hudibras has defined nonsense, as Cowley does wit, by negatives. Nonsense, says he, is that which is neither true nor false. These two great properties of nonsense, which are always essential to it, give it such a peculiar advantage over all other writings, that it is incapable of being either answered or contradicted.—
Addison.

To write or talk concerning any subject, without having previously taken the pains to understand it, is a breach of the duty which we owe to ourselves, though it may be no offence against the laws of the land. The privilege of talking and even publishing nonsense is necessary in a free state; but the more sparingly we make use of it the better.—*Coleridge.*

There are greater depths and obscurities, greater intricacies and perplexities, in an elaborate and well-written piece of nonsense, than in the most abstruse and profound tract of school divinity.—*Addison.*

NOTHING.

Nothing! thou elder brother even to shade.
Rochester.

Gratiano speaks an infinite deal of nothing.
Shakespeare.

NOTORIETY.

As for being much known by sight, and pointed out, I cannot comprehend the honor that lies withal; whatsoever it be, every mountebank has it more than the best doctor.—*Cowley.*

A proverb and a by-word among all people.
Bible.

Even the greatest actions of a celebrated person labor under this disadvantage, that however surprising and extraordinary they may be, they are no more than what are expected from him.—*Addison.*

NOVELS.

The habitual indulgence in such reading is a silent, mining mischief.—*Hannah More.*

Lessons of wisdom have never such power over us as when they are wrought into the heart through the groundwork of a story which engages the passions ; is it that we are like iron, and must first be heated before we can be wrought upon ? or is the heart so in love with deceit, that where a true report will not reach it, we must cheat it with a fable in order to come at the truth ? —*Sterne.*

Fiction is a potent agent for good, — in the hands of the good.—*Madame Necker.*

Writers of novels and romances in general bring a double loss on their readers, — they rob them both of their time and money ; representing men, manners, and things, that never have been, nor are likely to be ; either confounding or perverting history and truth, inflating the mind, or committing violence upon the understanding.—*Mary Wortley Montagu.*

Novels may teach us as wholesome a moral as the pulpit. There are " sermons in stones," in healthy books, and " good in everything."— *Colton.*

Legitimately produced, and truly inspired, fiction interprets humanity, informs the understanding, and quickens the affections. It reflects ourselves, warns us against prevailing social follies, adds rich specimens to our cabinets of character, dramatizes life for the unimaginative, daguerreotypes it for the unobservant, multiplies experience for the isolated or inactive, and cheers age, retirement, and invalidism with an available and harmless solace.— *Tuckerman.*

Romance is the poetry of literature.— *Madame Necker.*

I suppose as long as novels last, and authors aim at interesting their public, there must always be in the story a virtuous and gallant hero ; a wicked monster, his opposite ; and a pretty girl, who finds a champion. Bravery and virtue conquer beauty ; and vice, after seeming to triumph through a certain number of pages, is sure to be discomfited in the last volume, when justice overtakes him, and honest folks come by their own.—*Thackeray.*

Novels do not force their fair readers to sin, they only instruct them how to sin ; the consequences of which are fully detailed, and not in a way calculated to seduce any but weak minds ; few of their heroines are happily disposed of.— *Zimmermann.*

They are tales of adventures which did not occur in God's creation, but only in the waste chambers (to be let unfurnished) of certain human heads, and which are part and parcel only of the sum of nothings ; which, nevertheless, obtain some temporary remembrance, and lodge extensively at this epoch of the world in similar, still more unfurnished chambers.—*Carlyle.*

' The importance of the romantic element does not rest upon conjecture. Pleasing testimonies abound. Hannah More traced her earliest impressions of virtue to works of fiction ; and Adam Clarke gives a list of tales that won his boyish admiration. Books of entertainment led him to believe in a spiritual world ; and he felt sure of having been a coward, but for romances. He declared that he had learned more of his duty to God, his neighbor, and himself from Robinson Crusoe than from all the books, except the Bible, that were known to his youth.— *Willmott.*

We gild our medicines with sweets ; why not clothe truth and morals in pleasant garments as well ? —*Chamfort.*

A fiction which is designed to inculcate an object wholly alien to the imagination 'sins against the first law of art ; and if a writer of fiction narrow his scope to particulars so positive as polemical controversy in matters ecclesiastical, political, or moral, his work may or may not be an able treatise, but it must be a very poor novel.—*Bulwer Lytton.*

NOVELTY.
Novelty is only in request ; and it is as dangerous to be aged in any kind of course as it is virtuous to be constant in any undertaking.—*Shakespeare.*

Novelty has charms that our minds can hardly withstand. The most valuable things, if they have for a long while appeared among us, do not make any impression as they are good, but give us a distaste as they are old. But when the influence of this fantastical humor is over, the same men or things will come to be admired again, by a happy return of our good taste.—*Thackeray.*

All wonder is the effect of novelty upon ignorance.—*Johnson.*

All, with one consent, praise new-born gauds, though they are made and moulded of things past.—*Shakespeare.*

Natural objects please, in proportion as they are uncommon, by fixing the attention more steadily on their beauties or differences. The same principle of the effect of novelty in exciting the attention may account perhaps for the extraordinary discoveries and lies told by travellers, who, opening their eyes for the first time in foreign parts, are startled at every object they meet.—*Hazlitt.*

The earth was made so various, that the mind of desultory man, studious of change and pleased with novelty, might be indulged.— *Cowper.*

It is not only old and early impressions that deceive us ; the charms of novelty have the same power.—*Pascal.*

O.

OATHS.

It is a great sin to swear unto a sin, but greater sin to keep a sinful oath.— *Shakespeare.*

Oaths are the counterfeit money with which we pay the sacrifice of love.— *Ninon de l'Enclos.*

The gods are deaf to hot and peevish vows; they are polluted offerings, more abhorred than spotted livers in the sacrifice.—*Shakespeare.*

The accusing spirit, which flew up to Heaven's chancery with the oath, blushed as he gave it in; and the recording angel, as he wrote it down, dropped a tear upon the word and blotted it out forever.—*Sterne.*

Rash oaths, whether kept or broken, frequently produce guilt.—*Johnson.*

Come, swear it, damn thyself, lest, being like one of heaven, the devils themselves should fear to seize thee; therefore be double-damned, swear, — thou art honest.—*Shakespeare.*

Oaths are but words, and words but wind.— *Butler.*

It is not the many oaths that make the truth, but the plain single vow, that is vowed true.—*Shakespeare.*

Whoever considers the number of absurd and ridiculous oaths necessary to be taken at present in most countries, on being admitted into any society or profession whatever, will be less surprised to find prevarication still prevailing, where perjury has led the way.— *Abbé Raynal.*

Oaths are straws, men's faiths are wafer-cakes, and hold-fast is the only dog.— *Shakespeare.*

Of all men, a philosopher should be no swearer; for an oath, which is the end of controversies in law, cannot determine any here, where reason only must induce.— *Sir Thomas Browne.*

Recognized probity is the surest of all oaths. *Madame Necker.*

For it comes to pass oft, that a terrible oath, with a swaggering accent sharply twanged off, gives manhood more approbation than ever proof itself would have earned him.— *Shakespeare.*

An oath ! why, it is the traffic of the soul, it is law within a man; the seal of faith, the bond of every conscience; unto whom we set our thoughts like hands.—*Decker.*

OBEDIENCE.

No principle is more noble as there is none more holy, than that of a true obedience.— *Henry Giles.*

To say a blind custom of obedience should be a surer obligation than duty taught and understood is to say a blind man may tread surer with a guide than a seeing man with a light.—*Bacon.*

Let them obey that know how to rule.— *Shakespeare.*

Following the most ancient law of nature, which makes the weak obey the strong, beginning from God and ending with the irrational part of creation. For these are taught by nature to use the advantages which their strength gives them over the weak.—*Plutarch.*

We will obey the voice of the Lord our God, that it may be well with us.—*Bible.*

The first law that ever God gave to man was a law of pure obedience: it was a commandment naked and simple, wherein man had nothing to inquire after, or to dispute, forasmuch as to obey is the proper office of a rational soul, acknowledging a heavenly superior and benefactor. From obedience and submission spring all other virtues, as all sin does from self-opinion.—*Montaigne.*

Remember, rather, obedience is the mother of success, wedded to safety; so the wise assure us.—*Æschylus.*

It is foolish to strive with what we cannot avoid; we are born subjects, and to obey God is perfect liberty: he that does this shall be free, safe, and quiet; all his actions shall succeed to his wishes.—*Seneca.*

The virtue of Paganism was strength; the virtue of Christianity is obedience.—*Hare.*

Let the ground of all thy religious actions be obedience: examine not why it is commanded, but observe it because it is commanded. True obedience neither procrastinates nor questions.—*Quarles.*

Obedience is not truly performed by the body of him whose heart is dissatisfied. The shell without a kernel is not fit for store.— *Saadi.*

Obedience is our universal duty and destiny; wherein whoso will not bend must break; too early and too thoroughly we cannot be trained to know that "would," in this world of ours, is a mere zero to "should," and for most part as the smallest of fractions even to "shall."—*Carlyle.*

One very common error misleads the opinion of mankind, that, universally, authority is pleasant, submission painful. In the general course of human affairs, the very reverse of this is nearer to the truth. Command is anxiety; obedience, ease.—*Paley.*

He praiseth God best that serveth and obeyeth him most; the life of thankfulness consists in the thankfulness of the life.—*Burkitt.*

Obedience, as it regards the social relations, the laws of society, and the laws of nature and of nature's God, should commence at the cradle and end only at the tomb.—*Hosea Ballou.*

OBESITY.

Falstaff sweats to death, and lards the lean earth as he walks along.—*Shakespeare.*

There is something cordial in a fat man, everybody likes him, and he likes everybody. Food does a fat man good; it clings to him; it fructifies upon him; he swells nobly out, and fills a generous space in life.—*Henry Giles.*

Let me have men about me that are fat; sleek-headed men, and such as sleep o' nights: yonder *C*assius has a lean and hungry look; methinks too much: such men are dangerous.— *Shakespeare.*

As many suffer from too much as too little. A fat body makes a lean mind.—*Bovee.*

OBLIGATION.

To feel oppressed by obligation is only to prove that we are incapable of a proper sentiment of gratitude. To receive favors from the unworthy is simply to admit that our selfishness is superior to our pride. Most men remember obligations, but not often to be grateful for them. The proud are made sour by the remembrance and the vain silent.—*Simms.*

We are solemnly obliged to the children of those who have loved us.—*Achilles Poincelot.*

What do I owe to my times, to my country, to my neighbors, to my friends? Such are the questions which a virtuous man ought to ask himself often.—*Lavater.*

Obligation is thraldom, and thraldom is hateful.—*Hobbes.*

It is a secret, well known to all great men, that by conferring an obligation they do not always procure a friend, but are certain of creating many enemies.—*Fielding.*

There is one thing diviner than duty, namely, the bond of obligation transmuted into liberty.—*W. R. Alger.*

We are always much better pleased to see those whom we have obliged than those who have obliged us.—*Rochefoucauld.*

It is no great misfortune to oblige ungrateful people, but an unsupportable one to be forced to be under an obligation to a scoundrel. *Bailey.*

Trifling favors are readily acknowledged, though cheaply esteemed; but important ones are most rarely remembered.—*Ruffini.*

To owe an obligation to a worthy friend is a happiness, and can be no disparagement.— *Charron.*

An extraordinary haste to discharge an obligation is a sort of ingratitude.— *Rochefoucauld.*

Base natures ever judge a thing above them, and hate a power they are too much obliged to. *Otway.*

Some pretend want of power to make a competent return; and you shall find in others a kind of graceless modesty, that makes a man ashamed of requiting an obligation, because it is a confession that he has received one.— *Seneca.*

OBLIVION.

Oblivion is a second death, which great minds dread more than the first.—*De Boufflers.*

Fame is a vapor; popularity an accident; riches take wings; the only certainty is oblivion *Horace Greeley*

Oblivion is the rule, and fame the exception, of humanity.—*Rivarol.*

OBSCURITY.

There is no defence against reproach but obscurity; it is a kind of concomitant to greatness, as satires and invectives were an essential part of a Roman triumph.—*Addison.*

The obscurity of a writer is generally in proportion to his incapacity.—*Quintilian.*

How many people make themselves abstract to appear profound! The greatest part of abstract terms are shadows that hide a vacuum.— *Joubert.*

Obscurity and Innocence, twin sisters, escape temptations which would pierce their gossamer armor, in contact with the world.—*Chamfort.*

Lost in the dreary shades of dull obscurity.— *Shenstone.*

To be nameless in worthy deeds exceeds an infamous history. The *C*anaanitish woman lives more happily without a name than Herodias with one; and who would not rather have been the penitent thief than Pilate?— *Sir Thomas Browne.*

Objects imperfectly discerned take forms from the hope or fear of the beholder.—*Johnson.*

OBSERVATION.

He only is an acute observer who can observe minutely without being observed.
Lavater.

An old man's memory.—*Swift.*

To behold is not necessarily to observe, and the power of comparing and combining is only to be obtained by education. It is much to be regretted that habits of exact observation are not cultivated in our schools; to this deficiency may be traced much of the fallacious reasoning, the false philosophy, which prevails.—
Wilhelm von Humboldt.

For he is but a bastard to the time that doth not smack of observation.—*Shakespeare.*

Observation may trip now and then without throwing you, for her gait is a walk; but inference always gallops, and if she stumbles you are gone.—*Holmes.*

The hearing ear and the seeing eye.—*Bible.*

OBSTINACY.

Obstinacy and heat in argument are surest proofs of folly. Is there anything so stubborn, obstinate, disdainful, contemplative, grave, or serious, as an ass?—*Montaigne.*

Obstinacy, sir, is certainly a great vice; and in the changeful state of political affairs it is frequently the cause of great mischief. It happens, however, very unfortunately, that almost the whole line of other and masculine virtues — constancy, gravity, magnanimity, fortitude, fidelity, and firmness — are closely allied to this disagreeable quality, of which you have so just an abhorrence; and in their excess all these virtues very easily fall into it.—*Burke.*

Obstinacy is ever most positive when it is most in the wrong.—*Madame Necker.*

Obstinacy is the strength of the weak. Firmness founded upon principle, upon the truth and right, order and law, duty and generosity, is the obstinacy of sages.—*Lavater.*

Obstinacy and vehemency in opinion are the surest proofs of stupidity.—*Barton.*

There is something in obstinacy which differs from every other passion. Whenever it fails, it never recovers, but either breaks like iron, or crumbles sulkily away, like a fractured arch. Most other passions have their periods of fatigue and rest, their sufferings and their cure; but obstinacy has no resource, and the first wound is mortal.—*Johnson.*

I believe that obstinacy, or the dread of control and discipline, arises not so much from self-willedness as from a conscious defect of voluntary power; as foolhardiness is not seldom the disguise of conscious timidity.—*Coleridge.*

There are few, very few, that will own themselves in a mistake.—*Swift.*

Obstinacy and contention are common qualities, most appearing in, and best becoming, a mean and illiterate soul.—*Montaigne.*

An obstinate man does not hold opinions, but they hold him.—*Pope.*

OBTUSENESS.

There are few things more singular than the blindness which, in matters of the highest importance to ourselves, often hides the truth that is plain as noon to all other eyes.—
Rev. Dr. Croly.

Obtuseness is sometimes a virtue.—*Rivarol.*

Instead of watching the bird as it flies above our heads, we chase his shadow along the ground; and, finding we cannot grasp it, we conclude it to be nothing.—*Hare.*

Other men's sins are before our eyes; our own, behind our back.—*Seneca.*

OCCUPATION.

Indolence is a delightful but distressing state; we must be doing something to be happy. Action is no less necessary than thought to the instinctive tendencies of the human frame.—
Hazlitt.

Occupation is the necessary basis of all enjoyment.—*Leigh Hunt.*

The great happiness of life, I find, after all, to consist in the regular discharge of some mechanical duty.—*Schiller.*

No thoroughly occupied man was ever yet very miserable.—*Landor.*

You cannot give an instance of any man who is permitted to lay out his own time contriving not to have tedious hours.—*Johnson.*

Employment, which Galen calls "nature's physician," is so essential to human happiness that indolence is justly considered as the mother of misery.—*Burton.*

Occupation is the scythe of time.—*Napoleon.*

You see men of the most delicate frames engaged in active and professional pursuits who really have no time for illness. Let them become idle, — let them take care of themselves, let them think of their health, — and they die! The rust rots the steel which use preserves.—
Bulwer Lytton.

We protract the career of time by employment, we lengthen the duration of our lives by wise thoughts and useful actions. Life to him who wishes not to have lived in vain is thought and action.—*Zimmermann.*

One man, perhaps, proves miserable in the study of the law, who might have flourished in that of physic or divinity: another runs his head against the pulpit, who might have been serviceable to his country at the plough; and a third proves a very dull and heavy philosopher, who possibly would have made a good mechanic, and have done well enough at the useful philosophy of the spade or anvil.—*South.*

The price of excellence is labor, and time that of immortality.—*Fuseli.*

Cheerfulness is the daughter of employment; and I have known a man come home in high spirits from a funeral, merely because he has had the management of it.—*Dr. Horne.*

I take it to be a principal rule of life, not to be too much addicted to any one thing.—
Terence.

Let a man choose what condition he will, and let him accumulate around him all the goods and all the gratifications seemingly calculated to make him happy in it; if that man is left at any time without occupation or amusement, and reflects on what he is, the meagre, languid felicity of his present lot will not bear him up. He will turn necessarily to gloomy anticipations of the future; and except, therefore, his occupation calls him out of himself, he is inevitably wretched.—*Pascal.*

Any engagement which is innocent is better than none; as the writing of a book, the building of a house, the laying out of a garden, the digging of a fish-pond,— even the raising of a cucumber or a tulip.—*Paley.*

A good man and a wise man may at times be angry with the world, at times grieved for it; but be sure no man was ever discontented with the world if he did his duty in it. If a man of education, who has health, eyes, hands, and leisure, wants an object, it is only because God Almighty has bestowed all those blessings upon a man who does not deserve them.—*Southey.*

If every man works at that for which nature fitted him, the cows will be well tended.—
La Fontaine.

It is observed at sea that men are never so much disposed to grumble and mutiny as when least employed. Hence an old captain, when there was nothing else to do, would issue the order to " scour the anchor."—*Samuel Smiles.*

OFFENCE.
Where the offence is, let the great axe fall.—
Shakespeare.

We are so desirous of vengeance that people often offend us by not giving offence.—
Madame Deluzy.

The offender never pardons.—*George Herbert.*
24

In such a time as this it is not meet that every nice offence should bear its comment.—
Shakespeare.

It is pride which fills the world with so much harshness and severity. We are rigorous to offences as if we had never offended.—*Blair.*

All is not offence that indiscretion finds, and dotage terms, so.—*Shakespeare.*

If a man offend a harmless, pure, and innocent person, the evil falls back upon that fool, like light dust thrown up against the wind.—
Buddha.

When any one has offended me, I try to raise my soul so high that the offence cannot reach it.—*Descartes.*

OFFICE.
When a king creates an office, Providence creates immediately a fool to buy it.—*Colbert.*

All see, and most admire, the glare which hovers round the external happiness of elevated office.— *Washington.*

When impious men bear sway, the post of honor is a private station.—*Shakespeare*

If a due participation of office is a matter of right, how are vacancies to be obtained? Those by death are few; by resignation, none.—
Jefferson.

Five things are requisite to a good officer,— ability, clean hands, despatch, patience, and impartiality.— *William Penn.*

It is the curse of service; preferment goes by letter and affection, not by the old gradation where each second stood heir to the first.—
Shakespeare.

If ever this free people, if this government itself, is ever utterly demoralized, it will come from this human wriggle and struggle for office, — that is, a way to live without work.—
Abraham Lincoln.

High office is like a pyramid; only two kinds of animals reach the summit, — reptiles and eagles.—*D'Alembert.*

OMNIPOTENCE.
The same Being that fashioned the insect, whose existence is only discerned by a microscope, and gave that invisible speck a system of ducts and other organs to perform its vital functions, created the enormous mass of the planet thirteen hundred times larger than our earth, and launched it in its course round the sun, and the comet, wheeling with a velocity that would carry it round our globe in less than two minutes of time, and yet revolving through so prodigious a space that it takes near six centuries to encircle the sun!—*Lord Brougham.*

OPINION.

All power, even the most despotic, rests ultimately on opinion.—*Hume.*

The greater part of men have no opinion, still fewer an opinion of their own, well reflected and founded upon reason.—*Seume.*

Stiff in opinion, always in the wrong.—
Dryden.

Do not think of knocking out another person's brains because he differs in opinion from you. It would be as rational to knock yourself on the head because you differ from yourself ten years ago.—*Horace Mann.*

The masses procure their opinions ready made in open market.—*Colton.*

The world is governed much more by opinion than by laws. It is not the judgment of courts, but the moral judgment of individuals and masses of men, which is the chief wall of defence around property and life. With the progress of society, this power of opinion is taking the place of arms.—*Channing.*

He who has no opinion of his own, but depends upon the opinion and taste of others, is a slave.—*Klopstock.*

A plague of opinion! a man may wear it on both sides, like a leather jerkin.—*Shakespeare.*

That was excellently observed, say I, when I read a passage in an author where his opinion agrees with mine. When we differ, there I pronounce him to be mistaken.—*Swift.*

Opinion is, as it were, the queen of world, but force is its tyrant.—*Pascal.*

Social opinion is like a sharp knife. There are foolish people who regard it only with terror, and dare not touch or meddle with it; there are more foolish people who, in rashness or defiance, seize it by the blade, and get cut and mangled for their pains; and there are wise people, who grasp it discreetly and boldly by the handle, and use it to carve out their own purposes.—*Mrs. Jameson.*

Everything is mere opinion.—
Marcus Antoninus.

Opinions, like showers, are generated in high places, but they invariably descend into lower ones, and ultimately flow down to the people, as rain unto the sea.—*Colton.*

In many matters of opinion, our first and last coincide, though on different grounds; it is the middle stage which is farthest from the truth. Childhood often holds a truth with its feeble fingers, which the grasp of manhood cannot retain, and which it is the pride of utmost age to recover.—*Ruskin.*

Modest doubt is called the beacon of the wise.—*Shakespeare.*

Common opinions often conflict with common sense; for reason in most minds is no match for prejudices, a hydra whose heads grow faster than they can be cut off.—
E. Wigglesworth.

No liberal man would impute a charge of unsteadiness to another for having changed his opinion.—*Cicero.*

Opinion is the main thing which does good or harm in the world. It is our false opinions of things which ruin us.—*Marcus Antoninus.*

Predominant opinions are generally the opinions of the generation that is vanishing.—
Disraeli.

An ambitious desire of being distinguished from the crowd leads men sometimes to combat, in theory, received opinions; while a timorous self-love, that dreads all new and dangerous attempts, through the apprehension of miscarrying obliges them to follow those very opinions in practice.—*D'Alembert.*

Public opinion is a second conscience.—
W. R. Alger.

Public opinion is a weak tyrant compared with our own private opinion. What a man thinks of himself, that it is which determines, or rather indicates, his fate.—*Thoreau.*

The mind revolts against certain opinions, as the stomach rejects certain foods.—*Hazlitt.*

Who confers reputation? who gives respect and veneration to persons, to books, to great men? Who but Opinion? How utterly insufficient are all the riches of the world without her approbation!—*Pascal.*

Opinion crowns with an imperial voice.—
Shakespeare.

If your physician does not think it good for you to sleep, to drink wine, or to eat such and such meals, never trouble yourself. I will soon find you another who shall not be of his opinion.—*Montaigne.*

Race and temperament go for much in influencing opinion.—*Lady Morgan.*

Popular opinion is the old fable of the lion's great supper. The delicacies of the forest were spread before the guests; but the swine asked, "Have you no grains?"—*Willmott.*

A confident expectation that no argument will be adduced that will change our opinions is very different from a resolution that none ever shall. We may print but not stereotype our opinions.—*Whately.*

The only sin which we never forgive in each other is difference of opinion.—*Emerson.*

That queen of error, whom we call Fancy and Opinion, is the more deceitful because she does not deceive always. She would be the infallible rule of truth if she were the infallible rule of falsehood; but being only most frequently in error, she gives no evidence of her real quality, for she marks with the same character both that which is true and that which is false.—*Pascal.*

O, even holy justice cannot escape the voice of censure! Opinion is ever on the side of the unfortunate; envy always will pursue the laurelled conqueror.—*Schiller.*

Opinion is a medium between knowledge and ignorance.—*Plato.*

To maintain an opinion because it is thine, and not because it is true, is to prefer thyself above the truth.—*Venning.*

We must always think our opinions are right, but not think our opinions right always.
Whately.

He is a strong man who can hold down his opinion. A man cannot utter two or three sentences without disclosing to intelligent ears precisely where he stands in life and thought, namely, whether in the kingdom of the senses and the understanding, or in that of ideas and imagination, in the realm of intuitions and duty.—*Emerson.*

Correct opinions, well established on any subject, are the best preservative against the seductions of error.—*Bishop Mant.*

Weed your better judgments of all opinion that grows rank in them.—*Shakespeare.*

When we know that the opinions of even the greatest multitudes are the standard of rectitude, I shall think myself obliged to make those opinions the masters of my conscience. But if it may be doubted whether Omnipotence itself is competent to alter the essential constitution of right and wrong, sure I am, that such things as they and I are possessed of no such power.—*Burke.*

He who is master of all opinions can never be the bigot of any.—*W. R. Alger.*

I could never divide myself from any man upon the difference of an opinion, or be angry with his judgment for not agreeing in that from which within a few days I might dissent myself.—*Sir Thomas Browne.*

It is on opinion only that government is founded; and this maxim extends to the most despotic and most military governments, as well as to the most free and most popular.—*Hume.*

We are too much inclined to underrate the power of moral influence, and the influence of public opinion, and the influence of the principles to which great men — the lights of the world and of the present age — have given their sanction.—*Daniel Webster.*

In all things reason should prevail; it is quite another thing to be stiff, than steady in an opinion.—*William Penn.*

An originator of an opinion precedes the time; you cannot both precede and reflect it. What ten years ago was philosophy is now opinion.—*Bulwer Lytton.*

Opinions are accidental in people, — have a poverty-stricken air. A man valuing himself as the organ of this or that dogma is a dull companion enough; but opinion native to the speaker is sweet and refreshing, and inseparable from his image.—*Emerson.*

We think very few people sensible except those who are of our opinion.—*Rochefoucauld.*

Among the best men are diversities of opinions; which are no more, in true reason, to breed hatred, than one that loves black should be angry with him that is clothed in white; for thoughts are the very apparel of the mind.—
Sir P. Sidney.

Private opinion is weak, but public opinion is almost omnipotent.—*Beecher.*

When men first take up an opinion, and then afterwards seek for reasons for it, they must be contented with such as the absurdity of it will afford.—*South.*

Statutes are mere milestones, telling how far yesterday's thought had travelled; and the talk of the sidewalk to-day is the law of the land. With us law is nothing unless close behind it stands a warm, living public opinion.
Wendell Phillips.

If I for my opinion bleed, opinion shall be surgeon to my hurt, and keep me on the side where still I am.—*Shakespeare.*

It is opinion, that tormentor of the wise and the ignorant, that has exalted the appearance of virtue above virtue itself. Hence the esteem of men becomes not only useful, but necessary, to every one, to prevent him sinking below the common level. The ambitious man grasps at it, as being necessary to his designs; the vain man sues for it, as a testimony of his merit; the honest man demands it, as his due; and most men consider it as necessary to their existence.—*Beccaria.*

We should always keep a corner of our heads open and free, that we may make room for the opinions of our friends. Let us have heart and head hospitality.—*Joubert.*

We are not, indeed, satisfied with our own opinions, whatever we may pretend, till they are ratified and confirmed by suffrage of the rest of mankind. We dispute and wrangle forever; we endeavor to get men to come to us when we do not go to them.—
Sir Joshua Reynolds.

It is not only arrogant, but it is profligate, for a man to disregard the world's opinion of himself.—*Cicero.*

Men will die for an opinion as soon as for anything else. Whatever excites the spirit of contradiction is capable of producing the last effects of heroism, which is only the highest pitch of obstinacy in a good or a bad cause, in wisdom or folly.—*Hazlitt.*

A right opinion is that which connects distant truths by the shortest train of intermediate propositions.—*Johnson.*

That the voice of the common people is the voice of God is as full of falsehood as commonness. For who sees not that those black-mouthed hounds, upon the mere scent of opinion, as freely spend their mouths in hunting counter, or, like Actæon's dogs, in chasing an innocent man to death, as if they followed the chase of truth itself, in a fresh scent.—
Arthur Warwick.

Opinion is a sovereign mistress of effects.—
Shakespeare.

Provided that we look to our consciences, no matter for opinion. Let me deserve well, though I hear ill. The common people take stomach and audacity for the marks of magnanimity and honor; and if a man be soft and modest, they look upon him as an easy fop.—
Seneca.

Opinion, the blind goddess of fools, foe to the virtuous, and only friend to undeserving persons.—*George Chapman.*

As for the differences of opinion upon speculative questions, if we wait until they are reconciled, the action of human affairs must be suspended forever. But neither are we to look for perfection in any one man nor for agreement among many.—*Junius.*

Opinion is a light, vain, crude, and imperfect thing, settled in the imagination, but never arriving at the understanding, there to obtain the tincture of reason.—*Ben Jonson.*

Opinion is a bold bastard gotten between a strong fancy and a weak judgment; it is less dishonorable to be ingenuously doubtful than rashly opinionate.—*Quarles.*

Those are opinions which come from the heart, and whoever has no fixed opinions has no constant feelings.—*Joubert.*

While I am ready to adopt any well-grounded opinion, my inmost soul revolts against receiving the judgment of others respecting persons; and whenever I have done so I have bitterly repented of it.—*Niebuhr.*

It is always considered as a piece of impertinence in England, if a man of less than two or three thousand a year has any opinions at all upon important subjects.—*Sydney Smith.*

OPPORTUNITY.

Take all the swift advantage of the hours.—
Shakespeare.

It is common to overlook what is near by keeping the eye fixed on something remote. In the same manner present opportunities are neglected and attainable good is slighted by minds busied in extensive ranges, and intent upon future advantages. Life, however short, is made shorter by waste of time; and its progress towards happiness, though naturally slow, is made still slower by unnecessary labor.—
. *Johnson.*

Opportunity is rare, and a wise man will never let it go by him.—*Bayard Taylor.*

Many do with opportunities as children do at the seashore; they fill their little hands with sand, and then let the grains fall through, one by one, till all are gone.—*Rev. T. Jones.*

How oft the sight of means to do ill deeds makes deeds ill done!—*Shakespeare.*

No man possesses a genius so commanding that he can attain eminence, unless a subject suited to his talents should present itself, and an opportunity occurs for this development.—
Pliny.

Opportunity is the great bawd.—*Franklin.*

Miss not the occasion; by the forelock take that subtle power, the never-halting time.—
Wordsworth.

If we do not watch, we lose our opportunities; if we do not make haste, we are left behind; 'our best hours escape us, the worst are come. The purest part of our life runs first, and leaves only the dregs at the bottom; and that time which is good for nothing else we dedicate to virtue; and only propound to begin to live at an age that very few people arrive at.—
Seneca.

Little opportunities should be improved.—
Fenelon.

To be a great man it is necessary to turn to account all opportunities.—*Rochefoucauld.*

I will listen to any one's convictions, but pray keep your doubts to yourself. I have plenty of my own.—*Goethe.*

The sure way to miss success is to miss the opportunity.—*Philarète Chasles.*

There is a tide in the affairs of men, which, taken at the flood, leads on to fortune; omitted, all the voyage of their life is bound in shallows and in miseries.—*Shakespeare.*

We must not only strike the iron while it is hot, but strike it till it is made hot.—*Sharp.*

A genius and great abilities are often wanting, sometimes only opportunities. Some deserve praise for what they have done, and others for what they would have done.—*Bruyère.*

Alas! for the treachery of opportunity!—
Ninon de l'Enclos.

Do not wait for extraordinary circumstances to do good actions; try to use ordinary situations.—*Richter.*

The race is not to the swift, nor the battle to the strong, neither yet bread to the wise, nor yet riches to men of understanding, nor yet favor to men of skill; but time and chance happeneth to them all.—*Bible.*

The public man needs but one patron, namely, the lucky moment.—*Bulwer Lytton.*

There sometimes wants only a stroke of fortune to discover numberless latent good or bad qualities, which would otherwise have been eternally concealed; as words written with a certain liquor appear only when applied to the fire.—*Lord Greville.*

A word spoken in season, at the right moment, is the mother of ages.—*Carlyle.*

The best men are not those who have waited for chances, but who have taken them,—besieged the chance, conquered the chance, and made the chance their servitor.—*Chapin.*

A little fire is quickly trodden out; which, being suffered, rivers cannot quench.—
Shakespeare.

A wise man will make more opportunities than he finds.—*Bacon.*

For Opportunity has all her hair on her forehead; but when she has passed, you cannot call her back. She has no tuft whereby you can lay hold on her, for she is bald on the back part of her head, and never returns.—*Rabelais.*

We must take the current when it serves, or lose our ventures.—*Shakespeare.*

When Heaven half opens its arms, he who is faint-hearted deserves not anything; it is this want of faith that often keeps Heaven from bestowing its blessings; and even when they descend, it is apt to send them away.—*Corneille.*

Thou strong seducer, opportunity.—*Dryden.*

Do well while thou mayst, lest thou do evil when thou would not: he that takes not advantage of a good power shall lose the benefit of a good will.—*Quarles.*

Who makes quick use of the moment is a genius of prudence.—*Lavater.*

Opportunity, to statesmen, is as the just degree of heat to chemists; it perfects all the work.—*Suckling.*

There is never but one opportunity of a kind.—*Thoreau.*

I undertake to show you that you have means and powers to exhibit greatness of soul and a manly spirit; but what occasion you have to find fault and complain, do you show me, if you can.—*Epictetus.*

The May of life only blooms once.—*Schiller.*

The opportunity to do mischief is found a hundred times a day, and that of doing good once a year.—*Voltaire.*

O Opportunity! thy guilt is great!—
Shakespeare.

OPPOSITION.

A certain amount of opposition is a great help to a man. Kites rise against and not with the wind. Even a head wind is better than none. No man ever worked his passage anywhere in a dead calm. Let no man wax pale, therefore, because of opposition.—*John Neal.*

He that wrestles with us strengthens our nerves, and sharpens our skill. Our antagonist is our helper. – *Burke.*

If any man will oppose or contradict the most evident truths, it will not be easy to find arguments wherewith to convince him. And yet this, notwithstanding, ought neither to be imputed to any inability in the teacher, nor to any strength of wit in the denier, but only to a certain dead insensibility in him.—*Epictetus.*

Opposition always inflames the enthusiast, never converts him.—*Schiller.*

As the arrival of enemies makes a town to fortify itself, so that ever after it remains stronger; and hence a man may say, that enemies were no small cause to the town's strength; so, to a mind once fixed in a well-pleasing determination, who hopes by annoyance to overthrow it, doth but teach it to knit together all its best grounds; and so, perchance, of a chanceable purpose, make an unchangeable resolution.—*Sir P. Sidney.*

A strenuous soul hates cheap success. It is the ardor of the assailant that makes the vigor of the defendant.—*Emerson.*

We are told by naturalists that birds-of-paradise fly best against the wind; it drifts behind them the gorgeous train of feathers, which only entangles their flight with the gale.—*Willmott.*

All impediments in fancy's course are motives of more fancy.—*Shakespeare.*

The more powerful the obstacle, the more glory we have in overcoming it; and the difficulties with which we are met are the maids of honor which set off virtue.—*Molière.*

It is not the victory that makes the joy of noble hearts, but the combat.—*Montalembert.*

It is not ease, but effort,— not facility, but difficulty, that makes men. There is, perhaps, no station in life in which difficulties have not to be encountered and overcome before any decided measure of success can be achieved.—*Samuel Smiles.*

Such is the nature of the human mind, that it always lays hold on every mind that approaches it: and as it is wonderfully fortified by an unanimity of sentiments, so is it shocked and disturbed by any contrariety. Hence the eagerness, which most people discover in a dispute, and hence their impatience of opposition, even in the most speculative and indifferent opinions.—*Hume.*

OPPRESSION.

The camomile, the more it is trodden on, the faster it grows.—*Shakespeare.*

There is no happiness for him who oppresses and persecutes; no, there can be no repose for him. For the sighs of the unfortunate cry for vengeance to Heaven.—*Pestalozzi.*

The smallest worm will turn, being trodden on.—*Shakespeare.*

A desire to resist oppression is implanted in the nature of man.—*Tacitus.*

I never could believe that Providence had sent a few men into the world, ready booted and spurred to ride, and millions ready saddled and bridled to be ridden.—*Richard Rumbold.*

An extreme rigor is sure to arm everything against it.—*Burke.*

Oppression is more easily borne than insult.—*Junius.*

Fishes live in the sea, as men do a-land; the great ones eat up the little ones.—*Shakespeare.*

ORATORY.

He is the eloquent man who can treat subjects of an humble nature with delicacy, lofty things impressively, and moderate things temperately.—*Cicero.*

Those orators who give us much noise and many words, but little argument and less wit, and who are the loudest when least lucid, should take a lesson from the great volume of Nature; she often gives us the lightning without the thunder, but never the thunder without the lightning.—*Burritt.*

What orators want in depth, they give you in length.—*Montesquieu*

There is no power like that of oratory. Cæsar controlled men by exciting their fears; Cicero, by captivating their affections and swaying their passions. The influence of the one perished with its author; that of the other continues to this day.—*Henry Clay.*

Eloquence is the companion of peace, the associate of a life of leisure.—*Cicero.*

The passions are the only orators that always succeed. They are, as it were, nature's art of eloquence, fraught with infallible rules. Simplicity, with the aid of the passions, persuades more than the utmost eloquence without it.—*Rochefoucauld.*

Suit the action to the word, the word to the action; with this special observance, that you overstep not the modesty of nature.—*Shakespeare.*

The language of the heart — the language which "comes from the heart" and "goes to the heart" — is always simple, always graceful, and always full of power, but no art of rhetoric can teach it. It is at once the easiest and most difficult language, — difficult, since it needs a heart to speak it; easy, because its periods though rounded and full of harmony, are still unstudied.—*Bovee.*

Eloquence is vehement simplicity.—*Cecil.*

As thought supplies materials for discourse, so discourse gives precision to thought, as well as often assists its evolution. The best orators owe half their inspiration to the music of their own voice. Yet profundity of ideas is commonly an impediment to fluency of words — *W. B. Clulow*

Brilliant thoughts are, I consider, as it were the eyes of eloquence; but I would not that the body were all eyes, lest the other members should lose their proper functions.—*Vauvenargues*

Extemporaneous speaking is, indeed, the groundwork of the orator's art: preparation is the last finish, and the most difficult of all his accomplishments. To learn by heart as a school boy, or to prepare as an orator, are two things, not only essentially different, but essentially antagonistic to each other, for the work most opposed to an effective oration is an elegant essay.—*Bulwer Lytton.*

The elegancy of the style, and the turn of the periods make the chief impression upon the hearers. Give them but one or two round and harmonious periods in a speech, which they will retain and repeat; and they will go home as well satisfied, as people do from an opera, humming all the way one or two favorite tunes that have struck their ears and were easily caught. Most people have ears, but few have judgment; tickle those ears, and, depend upon it, you will catch their judgments, such as they are.—*Chesterfield.*

Every man should study conciseness in speaking; it is a sign of ignorance not to know that long speeches, though they may please the speaker, are the torture of the hearer.—*Feltham.*

Nothing appears to me to be nobler than to keep assemblies of men entranced by the charms of eloquence, wielding their minds at will, impelling them at one time, and at another dissuading them from their previous intentions.—*Cicero.*

It is the first rule in oratory that a man must appear such as he would persuade others to be; and that can be accomplished only by the force of his life.—*Swift.*

Oratory, like the drama, abhors lengthiness; like the drama, it must keep doing. It avoids, as frigid, prolonged metaphysical soliloquy. Beauties themselves, if they delay or distract the effect which should be produced on the audience, become blemishes.—*Bulwer Lytton.*

Oratory is the huffing and blustering spoiled child of a semi-barbarous age. The press is the foe of rhetoric, but the friend of reason; and the art of declamation has been sinking in value from the moment that speakers were foolish enough to publish, and readers wise enough to read.—*Colton.*

ORDER.

Order in a house ought to be like the machines in an opera, whose effect produces a great pleasure, but whose ends must be hid.—*Madame Necker.*

Order is heaven's first law.—*Pope.*

The order of the Eternal manifests itself in the sun which rises and the heavens which fall.—*Jens Baggesen.*

Order gave each thing view.—*Shakespeare.*

Order is the sanity of the mind, the health of the body, the peace of the city, the security of the state. As the beams to a house, as the bones to the microcosm of man, so is order to all things.—*Southey.*

So work the honey-bees, creatures that by a rule in nature teach the act of order to a peopled kingdom.—*Shakespeare.*

Let all things be done decently and in order.—*Bible.*

Order is a lovely nymph, the child of Beauty and Wisdom; her attendants are Comfort, Neatness, and Activity; her abode is the valley of happiness: she is always to be found when sought for, and never appears so lovely as when contrasted with her opponent, Disorder.—*Johnson.*

All are born to observe good order, but few are born to establish it.—*Joubert.*

There are persons who are never easy unless they are putting your books and papers in order,—that is, according to their notions of the matter,—and hide things, lest they should be lost, where neither the owner nor anybody else can find them. This is a sort of magpie faculty. If anything is left where you want it, it is called litter. There is a pedantry in housewifery, as well as in the gravest concerns.—*Hazlitt.*

Every blade of grass in the field is measured; the green cups and the colored crowns of every flower are curiously counted; the stars of the firmament wheel in cunningly calculated orbits; even the storms have their laws.—*Blakie.*

He who has no taste for order will be often wrong in his judgment, and seldom considerate or conscientious in his actions.—*Lavater.*

Creation is the production of order. What a simple, but, at the same time, comprehensive and pregnant principle is here! Plato could tell his disciples no ultimate truth of more pervading significance. Order is the law of all intelligible existence.—*Blakie.*

Order, thou eye of action.—*Aaron Hill.*

ORIGINALITY.

Originality is simply a fresh pair of eyes. "If you want to astonish the whole world," said Rahel, "tell the simple truth."—*T. W. Higginson.*

Originality provokes originality.—*Goethe.*

Every human being is intended to have a character of his own, to be what no other is, to do what no other can do.—*Channing.*

He who thinks for himself, and imitates rarely, is a free man.—*Klopstock.*

It is a special trick of low cunning to squeeze out knowledge from a modest man, who is eminent in any science; and then to use it as legally acquired, and pass the source in total silence.—*Horace Walpole.*

It is better to create than to be learned. Creating is the true essence of life.—*Niebuhr.*

Those writers who lie on the watch for novelty can have little hope of greatness; for great things cannot have escaped former observation.—*Johnson.*

Originality!· what do they mean by it? The action of the world upon us commences with the hour of our birth, and ends only with our death. It is here and there and everywhere. There is nothing we can claim as our own but energy, strength, and volition. Very little of me would be left, if I could but say what I owe to my great predecessors and contemporaries.—*Goethe.*

All effort at originality must end either in the quaint or the monstrous, for no man knows himself as an original.—*Washington Allston.*

I would rather be the author of one original thought than conqueror of a hundred battles. Yet moral excellence is so much superior to intellectual, that I ought to esteem one virtue more valuable than a hundred original thoughts.—*W. B. Clulow.*

Every man is an original and solitary character. None can either understand or feel the book of his own life like himself.—*Cecil.*

The little mind who loves itself will write and think with the vulgar; but the great mind will be bravely eccentric, and scorn the beaten road, from universal benevolence.—*Goldsmith.*

When will poets learn that a grass-blade of their own raising is worth a barrow-load of flowers from their neighbor's garden?—*Lowell.*

All we can possibly say of the most original authors nowadays is not, that they say anything new, but only that they are capable of saying such and such things themselves, "if they had never been said before them."—*Sterne.*

If you would create something, you must be something.—*Goethe.*

Those who are ambitious of originality, and aim at it, are necessarily led by others, since they seek to be different from them.—*Whately.*

ORNAMENT.

Plutarch has a fine expression, with regard to some woman of learning, humility, and virtue; — that her ornaments were such as might be purchased without money, and would render any woman's life both glorious and happy.—*Sterne.*

The world is still deceived with ornament.—*Shakespeare.*

Flowers of rhetoric in sermons and serious discourses are like the blue and red flowers in corn, pleasing to those who come only for amusement, but prejudicial to him who would reap profit from it.—*Pope.*

Modern education too often covers the fingers with rings, and at the same time cuts the sinews at the wrists.—*Sterling.*

Dumb jewels often, in their silent kind, more than quick words, do move a woman's mind.—*Shakespeare.*

We all originally came from the woods; it is hard to eradicate from any of us the old taste for the tattoo and the war-paint; and the moment that money gets into our pockets, it somehow or another breaks out in ornaments on our person, without always giving refinement to our manners.—*Whipple.*

Ornaments were invented by modesty.—*Joubert.*

When I behold the passion for ornamentation, and the corresponding power, I feel as if women had so far shown what they are bad for, rather than what they are good for.—*Julia Ward Howe.*

All finery is a sign of littleness.—*Lavater.*

Ornament is but the guiled shore to a most dangerous sea: the beauteous scarf veiling an Indian beauty; in a word, the seeming truth which cunning times put on to entrap the wisest.—*Shakespeare.*

The true ornament of matrons is virtue, not apparel.—*Justin.*

Orators and stage-coachmen, when the one wants argument and the other a coat of arms, adorn their cause and their coaches with rhetoric and flower-pots.—*Shenstone.*

OSTENTATION.

I have seldom seen much ostentation and much learning met together. The sun, rising and declining, makes long shadows; at midday, when he is highest, none at all.—*Bishop Hall.*

That book in many's eyes doth share the glory that in gold clasps locks in the golden story.—*Shakespeare.*

Show is not substance; realities govern wise men.—*William Penn.*

Education, indeed, has made the fondness for fine things next to natural; the corals and bells teach infants on the breasts to be delighted with sound and glitter.—*H. Brooke.*

Where there is much pretension, much has been borrowed; nature never pretends.—*Lavater.*

An ostentatious man will rather relate a blunder or an absurdity he has committed, than be debarred from talking of his own dear person.—*Addison.*

Do what good thou canst unknown ; and be not vain of what ought rather to be felt than seen.— *William Penn.*

It appears to be an axiom founded on truth, that whoever shows you that he is either in himself or his equipage as gaudy as he can, convinces you that he is more so than he can afford. Whenever a man's expense exceeds his income, he is indifferent in the degree.—*Fielding.*

Surely half the world must be blind ; they can see nothing unless it glitters.—*Hare.*

Excess in apparel is another costly folly. The very trimming of the vain world would clothe all the naked ones.— *William Penn.*

As you see in a pair of bellows, there is a forced breath without life, so in those that are puffed up with the wind of ostentation, there may be charitable words without works.—
Bishop Hall.

Ostentation is the signal-flag of hypocrisy. The charlatan is verbose and assumptive ; the Pharisee is ostentatious, because he is a hypocrite. Pride is the master sin of the Devil ; and the Devil is the father of lies.—*Chapin.*

Heaven must scorn the humility which we telegraph thither by genuflection ; it must prefer the manliness that stands by all created gifts, and looks itself in the face without pretence of worship.—*John Weiss.*

P.

PAIN.

Often pains too long retained increase even to the breaking of the heart. If they could be exhaled, we should see that they do not merit the bitterness which they have caused.—*Fenelon.*

Pain addeth zest unto pleasure, and teacheth the luxury of health.—*Tupper.*

Nature has placed mankind under the government of two sovereign masters, pain and pleasure. It is for them alone to point out what we ought to do, as well as to determine what we shall do. On the one hand, the standard of right and wrong ; on the other, the chain of causes and effects, are fastened to their throne.—*Bentham.*

Pain may be said to follow pleasure as its shadow.—*Colton.*

The alleviating of pain is a certain symptom of the development of that liberty dear to the people.—*Montesquieu.*

Long pains, with use of bearing, are half eased.—*Dryden.*

As an enemy is made more fierce by our flight, so Pain grows proud to see us truckle under it. She will surrender upon much better terms to those who make head against her.—
Montaigne.

Pain is less subject than pleasure to caprices of expression.—*Johnson.*

Pain is the deepest thing we have in our nature, and union through pain has always seemed more real and holy than any other.—
Hallam.

The most painful part of our bodily pain is that which is bodiless, or immaterial, namely, our impatience, and the delusion that it will last forever.—*Richter.*

Pain itself is not without its alleviations. It may be violent and frequent, but it is seldom both violent and long-continued ; and its pauses and intermissions become positive pleasures. It has the power of shedding a satisfaction over intervals of ease, which, I believe, few enjoyments exceed.—*Paley.*

Pain pays the income of each precious thing.—*Shakespeare.*

PAINTING.

Painting is silent poetry, and poetry is a speaking picture.—*Simonides.*

Stothard learned the art of combining colors by closely studying butterflies' wings ; he would often say that no one knew what he owed to these tiny insects. A burnt stick and a barn-door served Wilkie in lieu of pencil and canvas.—*Samuel Smiles.*

The best portraits are those in which there is a slight mixture of caricature.—*Macaulay.*

The painter who is content with the praise of the world in respect to what does not satisfy himself is not an artist, but an artisan ; for though his reward be only praise, his pay is that of a mechanic.— *Washington Allston.*

A picture is a poem without words.—
Horace.

There are pictures by Titian so steeped in golden splendors, that they look as if they would light up a dark room like a solar lamp.—
Hillard.

The love of gain never made a painter ; but it has marred many.— *Washington Allston.*

Softness of manner seems to be in painting what smoothness of syllables is in language, affecting the sense of sight or hearing, previous to any correspondent passion.—*Shenstone.*

Portrait - painting may be to the painter what the practical knowledge of the world is to the poet, provided he considers it as a school by which he is to acquire the means of perfection in his art, and not as the object of that perfection.—*Burke.*

A room hung with pictures is a room hung with thoughts.—*Sir Joshua Reynolds.*

Painting, when we have allowed for the pleasure of imitation, can only affect simply by the images it presents; and even in painting, a judicious obscurity in some things contributes to the effect of the picture.—*Burke.*

What a vanity is painting, which attracts admiration by the resemblance of things, that in the original we do not admire!—*Pascal.*

A painter that would draw a rose, though he may flourish some likeness of it in figure and color, yet he can never paint the scent and fragrancy; or if he would draw a flame, he cannot put a constant heat into his colors. All the skill of cunning artisans and mechanics cannot put a principle or life into a statue of their own making. Neither are we able to enclose in words and letters the life, soul, and essence of any spiritual truths.—*Cudworth.*

Blest be the art that can immortalize, — the art that baffles time's tyrannic claim to quench it.—*Cowper.*

The first merit of pictures is the effect which they can produce upon the mind; and the first step of a sensible man should be to receive involuntary effects from them. Pleasure and inspiration first, analysis afterward.—*Beecher.*

A picture is an intermediate something between a thought and a thing.—*Coleridge.*

The first degree of proficiency is, in painting, what grammar is in literature, — a general preparation for whatever species of the art the student may afterwards choose for his more particular application. The power of drawing, modelling, and using colors is very properly called the language of the art.—*Sir Joshua Reynolds.*

Ah! would that we could at once paint with the eyes! In the long way, from the eye through the arm to the pencil, how much is lost!—*Lessing.*

The masters painted for joy, and knew not that virtue had gone out of them. They could not paint the like in cold blood. The masters of English lyric wrote their songs so. It was a fine efflorescence of fine powers.—*Emerson.*

PANIC.
A panic is a sudden desertion of us, and a going over to the enemy, of our imagination.—*Bovee.*

The stampede of our self-possession.—*Rivarol.*

PARADISE.
Remembrance is the only paradise out of which we cannot be driven away. Indeed, our first parents were not to be deprived of it.—*Richter.*

Every man has a paradise around him till he sins, and the angel of an accusing conscience drives him from his Eden. And even then there are holy hours, when this angel sleeps, and man comes back, and with the innocent eyes of a child looks into his lost paradise again, — into the broad gates and rural solitudes of nature —*Longfellow.*

PARDON.
Virtue pardons the wicked, as the sandal-tree perfumes the axe which strikes it.—*Saadi.*

To pardon those absurdities in ourselves which we cannot suffer in others, is neither better nor worse than to be more willing to be fools ourselves than to have others so.—*Pope.*

Amnesty, that noble word, the genuine dictate of wisdom.—*Æschines*

Mercy is not itself, that oft looks so pardon is still the nurse of second woe.—*Shakespeare.*

To err is human ; to forgive, divine !—*Pope.*

They who forgive most shall be most forgiven.—*Bailey.*

The man who pardons easily courts injury.—*Corneille.*

Nothing in this low and ruined world bears the meek impress of the Son of God so surely as forgiveness.—*Alice Cary.*

Pardon others often, thyself never —*Publius Syrus*

God pardon them that are the cause thereof! A virtuous and a Christian-like conclusion, to pray for them that have done scath to us.—*Shakespeare.*

Thou art a God ready to pardon, gracious and merciful, slow to anger, and of great kindness.—*Bible.*

PARENT.
The voice of parents is the voice of gods, for to their children they are heaven's lieutenants.—*Shakespeare.*

A suspicious parent makes an artful child.—*Haliburton.*

In a father's love, like a well-drawn picture, he eyes all his children alike (if there be a parity of deserts), never parching one to drown another.—*Fuller.*

When thou art contemplating some base deed, forget not thy child's tender years, but let the presence of thy infant son act as a check on thy headlong course to sin.—*Juvenal.*

Next to God, thy parents; next them, the magistrate.—*William Penn.*

Certain it is that there is no kind of affection so purely angelic as that of a father to a daughter. He beholds her both with and without regard to her sex. In love to our wives there is desire; to our sons there is ambition; but in that to our daughters there is something which there are no words to express.—*Addison.*

PARTING.

Adieu! I have too grieved a heart to take a tedious leave.—*Shakespeare.*

Let our parting be full as charitable as our meeting was; that the pale envious world, glad of the food of others' miseries, civil dissensions, and nuptial strifes, may not feed fat with ours.
Middleton.

The air is full of farewells to the dying, and mournings for the dead.—*Longfellow.*

What! gone without a word? ay, so true love should do; it cannot speak, for truth hath better deeds, than words, to grace it.—*Shakespeare.*

How blessings brighten as they take their flight!—*Young.*

Parting and forgetting? What faithful heart can do these? Our great thoughts, our great affections, the truths of our life, never leave us. Surely they cannot separate from our consciousness; shall follow it whithersoever that shall go; and are of their nature divine and immortal.—*Thackeray.*

To die and part is a less evil; but to part and live, there, there is the torment.—
Lord Lansdowne.

Farewell! God knows when we shall meet again. I have a faint cold fear thrills through my veins, that almost freezes up the heat of life.
Shakespeare.

I have no parting sigh to give, so take my parting smile.—*Miss L. E. Landon.*

Time, which deadens hatred, secretly strengthens love; and in the hour of threatened separation its growth is manifested at once in radiant brightness.—*Richter.*

Abruptness is an eloquence in parting, when spinning out the time is but the weaving of new sorrow.—*Suckling.*

Let us not unman each other,—part at once; all farewells should be sudden, when forever.—*Byron.*

We cannot part with our friends. We cannot let our angels go. We do not see that they only go out that archangels may come in. We are idolators of the old. We do not believe in the richness of the soul, in its proper eternity and omnipresence.—*Emerson.*

Every parting is a form of death, as every reunion is a type of heaven.—*T. Edwards.*

A chord, stronger or weaker, is snapped asunder in every parting, and Time's busy fingers are not practised in re-splicing broken ties. Meet again you may; will it be in the same way? with the same sympathies? with the same sentiments? Will the souls, hurrying on in diverse paths, unite once more, as if the interval had been a dream? Rarely, rarely.—
Bulwer Lytton.

Parting is worse than death; it is death of love!—*Dryden.*

At length this joy, these dreams, this parting, dissolved themselves into that nameless melancholy in which the overflowing of happiness covers the borders of pain, because our breasts are ever more easily overflowed than filled.—*Richter.*

There is such sweet pain in parting, that I could hang forever on thine arms, and look away my life into thine eyes.—*Otway.*

Eyes, look your last; arms, take your last embrace!—*Shakespeare.*

PARTY.

Party standards are shadows in which patriotism is buried.—*Bernardin de St. Pierre.*

Nothing can be proposed so wild or so absurd as not to find a party, and often a very large party to espouse it.—*Cecil.*

Party is the madness of many for the gain of a few.—*Pope.*

The tendency of party-spirit has ever been to disguise and propagate and support error.—
Whately.

PASSION.

The way to conquer men is by their passions; catch but the ruling foible of their hearts, and all their boasted virtues shrink before you.
Tolson.

Passion is the drunkenness of the mind.—
South.

Passionate persons are like men who stand upon their heads; they see all things the wrong way.—*Plato.*

Nothing doth so fool a man as extreme passion. This doth make them fools which otherwise are not, and show them to be fools which are so.—*Bishop Hall.*

The worst of slaves is he whom passion rules.—*H. Brooke.*

Alas! in strong natures, if resistance to temptation is of granite, so the passions that they admit are of fire.—*Bulwer Lytton.*

In all disputes, so much as there is of passion, so much there is of nothing to the purpose; for then reason, like a bad hound, spends upon a false scent, and forsakes the question first started.—*Sir Thomas Browne.*

The brain may devise laws for the blood; but a hot temper leaps over a cold decree.—
Shakespeare.

Mirabeau said: " There are none but men of strong passions capable of going to greatness; none but such capable of meriting the public gratitude." Passion, though a bad regulator, is a powerful spring.—*Emerson.*

The only praiseworthy indifference is an acquired one; we must feel as well as control our passions.—*Richter.*

The passions are at once tempters and chastisers. As tempters, they come with garlands of flowers on brows of youth; as chastisers, they appear with wreaths of snakes on the forehead of deformity. They are angels of light in their delusion; they are fiends of torment in their inflictions.—*Henry Giles.*

If we resist our passions, it is more through their weakness than from our strength.—
Rochefoucauld.

Great passions are incurable diseases. The very remedies make them worse.—*Goethe.*

People have a custom of excusing the enormities of their conduct by talking of their passions, as if they were under the control of a blind necessity, and sinned because they could not help it.—*Cumberland.*

All the passions seek that which nourishes them; fear loves the idea of danger.—*Joubert.*

Almost all men are born with every passion to some extent, but there is hardly a man who has not a dominant passion to which the others are subordinate. Discover this governing passion in every individual; search into the recesses of his heart, and observe the different effects of the same passion in different people. And when you have found the master passion of a man, remember never to trust to him where that passion is concerned.—*Chesterfield.*

A great passion has no partner.—*Lavater.*

It is the strong passions which, rescuing us from sloth, can alone impart to us that continuous and earnest attention necessary to great intellectual effort.—*Helvétius.*

The pleasure of being master of one's self and of one's passion should be balanced with that of contenting them; it will rise above, if we know what is liberty.—*Bossuet.*

We condemn generally the passions of others by other passions either like or unlike.—
Pasquier Quesnel.

Men spend their lives in the service of their passions, instead of employing their passions in the service of their lives.—*Steele.*

Strong passions are the life of manly virtues. But they need not necessarily be evil because they are passions and because they are strong. The passions may be likened to blood horses, that need training and the curb only, to enable them whom they carry to achieve the most glorious triumphs.—*Simms.*

He submits to be seen through a microscope, who suffers himself to be caught in a fit of passion.—*Lavater.*

Our passions are like convulsion fits, which, though they make us stronger for the time, leave us the weaker ever after.—*Pope.*

Passion is universal humanity. Without it religion, history, romance, and art would be useless.—*Balzac.*

Passion makes the will lord of the reason.—
Shakespeare.

The blossoms of passion, gay and luxuriant flowers, are brighter and fuller of fragrance, but they beguile us and lead us astray, and their odor is deadly.—*Longfellow.*

O you much partial gods! why gave ye men affections, and not power to govern them? What I by fate should shun I most affect.—
Lodovick Barrey.

The passions are like those demons with which Afrasahiab sailed down the Orus. Our only safety consists in keeping them asleep. If they wake, we are lost.—*Goethe.*

Moreover, brain is always to be bought, but passion never comes to market.—*Lowell.*

I don't mean to say that principle is not a finer thing than passion; but passions existed before principles, they came into the world with us; principles are superinduced.—
Mrs. Jameson.

He only employs his passion who can make no use of his reason.—*Cicero.*

Men are not blindly betrayed into corruption, but abandon themselves to their passions with their eyes open; and lose the direction of truth, because they do not attend to her voice, not because they do not understand it.—*Johnson.*

Passion often makes a fool of the most ingenious man, and often makes the greatest blockheads ingenious.—*Thomson.*

Even virtue itself, all perfect as it is, requires to be inspirited by passion; for duties are but coldly performed, which are but philosophically fulfilled.—*Mrs. Jameson.*

Let the sap of reason quench the fire of passion.—*Shakespeare.*

The passions of mankind are partly protective, partly beneficent, like the chaff and grain of the corn; but none without their use, none without nobleness when seen in balanced unity with the rest of the spirit which they are charged to defend.—*Ruskin.*

The passions of the men of society differ as much from the passions of the natural man as the fruits of a grafted tree from those of a wild one.—*De Boufflers.*

Passion lives above all analysis and estimate, and arrives at its conclusions by intuition. D. G. *Mitchell.*

It is much more easy to inspire a passion than a faith. Were beauty but as solicitous of the one as of the other object, she need never fear that her myrtles will change to willows.— *Simms.*

Passion looks not beyond the moment of its existence. Better, it says, the kisses of love to-day, than the felicities of heaven afar off.— *Bovee.*

Passion, in its first violence, controls interest, as the eddy for a while runs against the stream.—*Johnson.*

All passions are good or bad, according to their objects: where the object is absolutely good, there the greatest passion is too little, where absolutely evil, there the least passion is too much; where indifferent, there a little is enough.—*Quarles.*

Give me that man that is not passion's slave, and I will wear him in my heart's core, aye, in my heart of hearts.—*Shakespeare.*

The passions may be humored till they become our master, as a horse may be pampered till he gets the better of his rider; but early discipline will prevent mutiny, and keep the helm in the hands of reason.—*Cumberland.*

The passions are like fire, useful in a thousand ways and dangerous only in one, through their excess.—*Bovee.*

In the heart of man there is a perpetual succession of the passions; so that the destruction of one is almost always the production of another.—*Rochefoucauld.*

Steel assassinates; the passions kill. Where is the difference?—*Madame Deluzy.*

The way to avoid evil is not by maiming our passions, but by compelling them to yield their vigor to our moral nature. Thus they become, as in the ancient fable, the harnessed steeds which bear the chariot of the sun.— *Beecher.*

Passion makes the best observations and the most wretched conclusions. It is a telescope whose field is so much the brighter as it is narrower.—*Richter.*

The passions should be purged; all may become innocent if they are well directed and moderated. Even hatred may be a commendable feeling when it is caused by a lively love of good. Whatever makes the passions purer makes them stronger, more durable, and more enjoyable.—*Joubert.*

A genuine passion is like a mountain stream: it admits of no impediment; it cannot go backwards; it must go forward.—*Bovee.*

It is the passions which do and undo everything. If reason ruled, nothing would get on. It is said that pilots fear beyond everything those halcyon seas where the vessel obeys not the helm, and that they prefer wind at the risk of storms. The passions in men are the winds necessary to put everything in motion, though they often cause storms.—*Fontenelle.*

Passion costs me too much to bestow it upon every trifle.—*Rev. Thomas Adam.*

The passions often engender their contraries; avarice sometimes produces prodigality, and prodigality avarice; we are often resolute from weakness, and daring from timidity.— *Rochefoucauld.*

Passions, new-born, at first are in our power; but, when their tide runs strong, they sweep resolves—*Aaron Hill.*

If you can once engage people's pride, love, pity, ambition (or whichever is their prevailing passion) on your side, you need not fear what their reason can do against you.—*Chesterfield.*

Violent passions are formed in solitude. In the bustle of the world no object has time to make a deep impression.—*Henry Home.*

Pleasure and revenge have ears more deaf than adders to the voice of any true decision.— *Shakespeare.*

The passions are the only orators who never fail to persuade. They are, if we may so speak, nature's art of eloquence, the rules of which never fail; and the simplest man, moved by passion, is more persuasive than the most eloquent who has none.—*Rochefoucauld*

As rivers, when they overflow, drown those grounds, and ruin those husbandmen, which, whilst they flowed calmly betwixt their banks, they fertilized and enriched; so our passions, when they grow exorbitant and unruly, destroy those virtues, to which they may be very serviceable whilst they keep within their bounds.— *Boyle.*

Our headstrong passions shut the door of our souls against God.— *Confucius.*

As our bodies are compounded of different elements, so are our minds of various passions. And as the blending of the former creates the union of body, so is all virtue produced by the balancing or commixing of the several affections and propensities of the soul. As our bodies are formed of clay, so are even our virtues made up of meanness or vice. Add vain-glory to avarice and it rises to ambition. Lust inspires the lover, and selfish wants the friend. Prudence arises from fear, and courage arises from madness or from pride.—*Sterne.*

We use up in the passions the stuff that was given us for happiness.—*Joubert.*

Nothing so apt to inflame passion as hopes and fears: a young woman of a calm temper and modest deportment is less apt to attract lovers, than one who is changeable and coquettish; a man of sense and gravity is less apt to succeed with a fine woman than the·gay, the giddy, the fluttering coxcomb.—*Henry Home.*

All passions exaggerate; and they are passions only because they do exaggerate.— *Chamfort.*

What a mistake to suppose that the passions are strongest in youth! The passions are not stronger, but the control over them is weaker! They are more easily excited, they are more violent and apparent; but they have less energy, less durability, less intense and concentrated power than in maturer life.— *Bulwer Lytton.*

We may always accomplish much more than we conceive, provided passion fans the flame which the imagination has lighted; for life is insupportable when unanimated by the soft affections of the heart.—*Zimmermann.*

Passion may not unfitly be termed the mob of the man, that commits a riot upon his reason. *William Penn.*

Happy is he who is engaged in controversy with his own passions, and comes off superior; who makes it his endeavor that his follies and weaknesses may die before himself, and who daily meditates on mortality and immortality.— *Jortin.*

Passions are as easily evaded as impossible to moderate.—*Montaigne.*

Men will always act according to their passions. Therefore the best government is that which inspires the nobler passions and destroys the meaner.—*Jacobi.*

To be without passion is worse than a beast; to be without reason is to be less than a man. Since I can be without neither, I am blessed in that I have both. For if it be not against reason to be passionate, I will not be passionate against reason. I will both grieve and joy if I have reason for it, but no joy nor grief above reason. I will so joy at my good as not to take evil by my joy, so grieve at any evil as not to increase my evil by my grief. For it is not a folly to have passion, but to want reason. I would be neither senseless nor beastly.— *Arthur Warwick.*

Passion is the great mover and spring of the soul. When men's passions are strongest, they may have great and noble effects; but they are then also apt to fall into the greatest miscarriages.—*Sprat.*

Passion, as it has been well said, when in a state of solemn and omnipotent vehemence, always appears to be calmness to him whom it domineers; not unfrequently to others also, as the tide at its highest flood looks tranquil, and neither way inclines.—*Mrs. Jameson.*

Our passions never wholly die, but, in the last cantos of life's romantic epos, they rise up again, and do battle, like some of Ariosto's heroes, who have already been quietly interred, and ought to be turned to dust.—*Longfellow.*

Many persons in reasoning on the passions, make a continual appeal to common-sense. But passion is without common-sense, and we must frequently discard the one in speaking of the other.—*Hazlitt.*

Words may be counterfeit, false coined, and current only from the tongue, without the mind; but passion is in the soul, and always speaks the heart.—*Southern.*

The most commonplace people become highly imaginative when they are in a passion. Whole dramas of insult, injury, and wrong pass before their minds, — efforts of creative genius, for there is sometimes not a fact to go upon.—*Helps.*

PAST.

Tell us not that the past, examined by cold philosophy, was no better and no loftier than the present; it is not thus seen by pure and generous eyes. Let the past perish, when it ceases to reflect on the magic mirror the beautiful romance which is its noblest reality, though perchance but the shadow of delusion.— *Bulwer Lytton.*

No hand can make the clock strike for me the hours that are passed.—*Byron.*

Earth has scarcely an acre that does not remind us of actions that have long preceded our own, and its clustering tombstones loom up like reefs of the eternal shore, to show us where so many human barks have struck and gone down.—*Chapin.*

Our reverence for the past is just in proportion to our ignorance of it.—*Theodore Parker.*

It is necessary to look forward as well as backward, as some think it always necessary to regulate their conduct by things that have been done of old times; but that past which is so presumptuously brought forward as a precedent for the present, was itself founded on an alteration of some past that went before it.—
Madame de Staël.

Some are so very studious of learning what was done by the ancients that they know not how to live with the moderns.—*William Penn.*

But there have been human hearts, constituted just like ours, for six thousand years. The same stars rise and set upon this globe that rose upon the plains of Shinar or along the Egyptian Nile; and the same sorrows rise and set in every age.—*Beecher.*

Things without remedy should be without regard; what is done is done.—*Shakespeare.*

Many classes are always praising the by-gone time, for it is natural that the old should extol the days of their youth; the weak, the area of their strength; the sick, the season of their vigor; and the disappointed, the spring-tide of their hopes!—*C. Bingham*

The past is the sepulchre of our dead emotions,—*Bovee.*

Every brave life appears to us out of the past not so brave as it really was, for the forms of terror with which it fought are overthrown. Against the many-armed future threatening from its clouds, only the great soul has courage; every one can be courageous towards the spent-out, disclothed past.—*Richter.*

Well does Agathon say, " Of this alone is even God deprived, the power of making that which is past never to have been."—*Aristotle.*

There have been many men who left behind them that which hundreds of years have not worn out. The earth has Socrates and Plato to this day. The world is richer yet by Moses and the old prophets than by the wisest statesmen. We are indebted to the past. We stand in the greatness of ages that are gone rather than in that of our own. But of how many of us shall it be said that, being dead, we yet speak?—
Beecher.

Gone, glimmering through the dream of things that were.—*Byron.*

The admiration bestowed on former times is the bias of all times; the golden age never was the present age.—*Henry Home.*

To him who has thought, or done, or suffered much, the level days of his childhood seem at an immeasurable distance, far off as the age of chivalry, or as the line of Sesostris.—
Talfourd.

I have, besides, a great love for the past. Only what refers to it is eternal and unchangeable like death, and at the same time warm and gladsome like life.—*Wilhelm von Humboldt.*

Things past may be repented, but not re-called.—*Livy.*

It is delightful to transport one's self into the spirit of the past, to see how a wise man has thought before us, and to what a glorious height we have at last reached.—*Goethe.*

So sad, so fresh, the days that are no more.
Tennyson.

There is nothing like the dead cold hand of the past to take down our tumid egotism, and lead us into the solemn flow of the life of our race.—*Holmes.*

Study the past if you would divine the future.—*Confucius.*

It is the past only which we really enjoy as soon as we become sensible of duration. Each bygone instant of delight becomes rapidly present to us, and " bears a glass which shows us many more."—*Talfourd.*

Let us not burden our remembrances with a heaviness that is gone.—*Shakespeare.*

PATIENCE.

Patience is the panacea; but where does it grow, or who can swallow it?—*Shenstone.*

Patience is the key of content.—*Mahomet.*

Patience is the ballast of the soul, that will keep it from rolling and tumbling in the greatest storms; and he that will venture out without this to make him sail even and steady will certainly make shipwreck and drown himself, first in the cares and sorrows of this world, and then in perdition.—*Bishop Hopkins.*

To know how to wait is the great secret of success.—*De Maistre.*

We increase our losses ourselves, and club with fortune to undo us, when with them we lose our patience, too; as infants that, being robbed of some of their baubles, throw away the rest in childish anger.—*Wycherley.*

Upon the heat and flame of thy distemper, sprinkle cool patience.—*Shakespeare.*

It the wicked flourish, and thou suffer, be not discouraged. They are fatted for destruction; thou art dieted for health.—*Fuller.*

Patience and gentleness are power.—
Leigh Hunt.

He who can wait for what he desires, takes the course not to be exceedingly grieved if he fails of it. He, on the contrary, who labors after a thing too impatiently, thinks the success, when it comes, is not a recompense equal to all the pains he has been at about it.—*Bruyère.*

Patience, when it is a divine thing, is active, not passive.—*Lowell.*

That which in mean men we entitle patience is pale, cold cowardice in noble breasts.—
Shakespeare.

Arm the obdured breast with stubborn patience as with triple steel.—*Milton.*

To bear, is to conquer our fate.—*Campbell.*

Accustom yourself to that which you bear ill, and you will bear it well.—*Seneca.*

Beware the fury of a patient man.—*Dryden.*

If thou intendest to vanquish the greatest, the most abominable, and wickedest enemy, who is able to do thee mischief both in body and soul, and against whom thou preparest all sorts of weapons, but cannot overcome, then know that there is a sweet and loving physical herb to serve thee, named *Patientia.*—*Luther.*

Though patience be a tired mare, yet she will plod.—*Shakespeare.*

Man without patience is the lamp without oil, and pride in a rage is a bad counsellor.—
Musset.

Our real blessings often appear to us in the shape of pains, losses, and disappointments; but let us have patience, and we soon shall see them in their proper figures.—*Addison.*

How poor are they who have not patience! What wound did ever heal but by degrees?—
Shakespeare.

If we could have a little patience, we should escape much mortification; time takes away as much as it gives.—*Madame de Sévigné.*

They also serve who only stand and wait.—
Milton.

The conflict of patience is such that the vanquished is better than the vanquisher.—
Euripides.

Patience! Hence,—the word was made for brutes of burden, not for birds of prey.—*Byron.*

But patience is the virtue of an ass, that trots beneath his burden and is quiet.—
Lord Lansdowne.

Patience is bitter, but its fruit is sweet.—
Rousseau.

It is all men's office to speak patience to those that wring under the load of sorrow; but no man's virtue, nor sufficiency, to be so moral, when he shall endure the like himself.—
Shakespeare.

Patience is so like Fortitude, that she seems either her sister or her daughter.—*Aristotle.*

He that can have patience can have what he will.—*Franklin.*

Endurance is the crowning quality, and patience all the passion of great hearts.—*Lowell.*

There is no such thing as preaching patience into people unless the sermon is so long that they have to practise it while they hear. No man can learn patience except by going out into the burly-burly world, and taking life just as it blows. Patience is but lying to and riding out the gale.—*Beecher.*

Day follows the murkiest night, and when the time comes, the latest fruits also ripen!—
Schiller.

A patient and humble temper gathers blessings that are marred by the peevish and overlooked by the aspiring.—*Chapin.*

Fortify courage with the true rampart of patience.—*Sir P. Sidney.*

Nothing does so much honor to a woman as her patience, and nothing does her so little as the patience of her husband.—*Joubert.*

Patience is the art of hoping.—*Vauvenargues.*

Patience! why, it is the soul of peace; of all the virtues, it is nearest kin to heaven; it makes men look like gods. The best of men that ever wore earth about him was a Sufferer,—a soft, meek, patient, humble, tranquil spirit; the first true gentleman that ever breathed.—
Decker.

Patience and time do more than strength or passion.—*La Fontaine.*

All that I have accomplished, or expect or hope to accomplish, has been and will be by that plodding, patient, persevering process of accretion which builds the ant-heap, particle by particle, thought by thought, fact by fact.—
Elihu Burritt.

Never think that God's delays are God's denials. Hold on; hold fast; hold out. Patience is genius.—*Buffon.*

Patience is the support of weakness; impatience is the ruin of strength.—*Colton.*

There is no road too long to the man who advances deliberately and without undue haste; there are no honors too distant to the man who prepares himself for them with patience.— *Bruyère.*

Talk of patience when you have borne him who has none without repining.—*Lavater.*

Patience is even more rarely manifested in the intellect than it is in the temper.—*Helps.*

PATRIOTISM.

He who loathes war, and will do everything in his power to avert it, but who will, in the last extremity, encounter its perils, from love of country and of home, — who is willing to sacrifice himself and all that is dear to him in life, to promote the well-being of his fellow-man, will ever receive a worthy homage.—*Abbott.*

The noblest motive is the public good.— *Virgil.*

My idea is that there are duties toward our native land common to every citizen, and even public institutions and education must have such a direction as to enable every citizen to fulfil his duty toward his fatherland.—*Kossuth.*

I have learned by much observation that nothing will satisfy a patriot but a place! — *Junius.*

The love of country produces good manners, and good manners also love of country. The less we satisfy our particular passions, the more we leave to our general.—*Montesquieu.*

The proper means of increasing the love we bear our native country is to reside some time in a 'foreign one.—*Shenstone.*

This is a maxim which I have received by hereditary tradition, not only from my father, but also from my grandfather and his ancestors, that after what I owe to God, nothing should be more dear or more sacred than the love and respect I owe to my country.—*De Thou.*

National enthusiasm is the great nursery of genius.—*Tuckerman.*

It matters not with what principle the new-born patriot is animated, if the measures he supports are beneficial to the community. The nation is interested in his conduct. His motives are his own. The properties of a patriot are perishable in the individual; but there is a quick succession of subjects, and the breed is worth preserving.—*Junius.*

Be just, and fear not : let all the ends thou aimest at be thy country's, thy God's, and truth's.—*Shakespeare.*

Had I a dozen sons, — each in my love alike, —I had rather have eleven die nobly for their country, than one voluptuously surfeit out of action.—*Shakespeare.*

PATRONAGE.

The parson knows enough, who knows a duke!—*Cowper.*

Is not a patron, my lord, one who looks with unconcern on a man struggling for life in the water, and when he has reached ground encumbers him with help ? —*Johnson.*

PAYMENT.

Pay not before thy work be done; if thou dost, it will never be well done; and thou wilt have but a pennyworth for twopence.— *Franklin.*

PEACE.

There is nothing so likely to produce peace as to be well prepared to meet the enemy.— *Washington.*

Peace is rarely denied to the peaceful.— *Schiller.*

Like the rainbow, peace rests upon the earth, but its arch is lost in heaven. Heaven bathes it in hues of light, — it springs up amid tears and clouds, — it is a reflection of the eternal sun, — it is an assurance of calm, — it is the sign of a great covenant between God and man, — it is an emanation from the distant orb of immortal light.—*Colton.*

Peace hath her victories no less renowned than war.—*Milton.*

We love peace, as we abhor pusillanimity; but not peace at any price. There is a peace more destructive of the manhood of living man than war is destructive of his material body. Chains are worse than bayonets.— *Douglas Jerrold.*

All things that speak of heaven speak of peace.—*Bailey.*

Peace shows itself more in patience than in judgment; so it is better to be unjustly accused than to accuse others, even with justice.— *St. Martin.*

Peace is the evening star of the soul, as virtue is its sun, and the two are never far apart.— *Colton.*

Peace is lovely ! a beauteous boy, he lies couched by the tranquil brook, where the skipping lambkins feed joyfully around him in the sunny meadow ! His flute discourses sweet music, waking up the echoes of the hills, or else the murmurs of the streamlet lull him to sleep in the sunset's ruddy sheen.—*Schiller.*

Peace is the happy, natural state of man ; war his corruption, his disgrace.—*Thomson.*

25

I am a man of peace. God knows how I love peace. But I hope I shall never be such a coward as to mistake oppression for peace.—
Kossuth.

A peace is of the nature of a conquest; for then both parties nobly are subdued, and neither party loser.—*Shakespeare.*

They shall beat their swords into ploughshares, and their spears into pruning-hooks; nation shall not lift up sword against nation, neither shall they learn war any more.—*Bible.*

Speak, move, act in peace, as if you were in prayer. In truth, this is prayer.—*Fenelon.*

No peace was ever won from fate by subterfuge or agreement; no peace is ever in store for any of us, but that which we shall win by victory over shame or sin, — victory over the sin that oppresses, as well as over that which corrupts.—*Ruskin.*

Blessed are the peacemakers, for they shall be called the children of God.—*Bible.*

There are interests by the sacrifice of which peace is too dearly purchased. One should never be at peace to the shame of his own soul, — to the violation of his integrity or of his allegiance to God.—*Chapin.*

In peace, there is nothing so becomes a man as modest stillness and humility.—*Shakespeare.*

Peace does not dwell in outward things, but within the soul. We may preserve it in the midst of the bitterest pain, if our will remain firm and submissive. Peace in this life springs from acquiescence even in disagreeable things, not in an exemption from suffering.—*Fenelon.*

Peace is the masterpiece of reason.—
Johann Müller.

PEDANT.

Bristling with horrid Greek, and puffed with pride!—*Boileau.*

A well-read fool is the most pestilent of blockheads; his learning is a flail which he knows not how to handle, and with which he breaks his neighbor's shins as well as his own. Keep a fellow of this description at arm's length, as you value the integrity of your bones.—*Stanislaus.*

The vacant skull of a pedant generally furnishes out a throne and temple for vanity.—
Shenstone.

Deep versed in books, and shallow in himself.—*Milton.*

PEDANTRY.

Pedantry crams our heads with learned lumber, and takes out our brains to make room for it.—*Colton.*

Pedantry prides herself on being wrong by rules; while common-sense is contented to be right, without them. The former would rather stumble in following the dead, than walk upright by the profane assistance of the living.—
Colton.

A pedant holds more to instruct us with what he knows, than of what we are ignorant.
J. Petit Senn.

Pedantry is properly the overrating any kind of knowledge we pretend to; and if that kind of knowledge be a trifle in itself, the pedantry is the greater.—*Swift.*

Pedantry and taste are as inconsistent as gayety and melancholy.—*Lavater.*

Pedantry and bigotry are millstones, able to sink the best book which carries the least part of their dead weight. The temper of the pedagogue suits not with the age; and the world, however it may be taught, will not be tutored.
Shaftesbury.

A man who has been brought up among books, and is able to talk of nothing else, is a very indifferent companion, and what we call a pedant. But we should enlarge the title, and give it to every one that does not know how to think out of his profession and particular way of life.—*Addison.*

A pedant is a precocious old man.—
De Boufflers.

Pedantry, in the common acceptation of the word, means an absurd ostentation of learning and stiffness of phraseology, proceeding from a misguided knowledge of books, and a total ignorance of men.—*Mackenzie.*

PEN.

The strokes of the pen need deliberation as much as those of the sword need swiftness.—
Julia Ward Howe.

Beneath the rule of men entirely great, pen is mightier than the sword. Behold the arch enchanter's wand! itself a nothing, but taking sorcery from the master hand to paralyze the Cæsars, and to strike the broad earth breathless!—*Bulwer Lytton.*

O nature's noblest gift, — my gray goose-quill!—*Byron.*

Scholars are men of peace; they bear no arms, but their tongues are sharper than Actius's sword, their pens carry further and give a louder report than thunder. I had rather stand in the shock of a basilisk than in the fury of a merciless pen.—
Sir Thomas Browne.

Take away the sword; states can be saved without it; bring the pen!—*Bulwer Lytton.*

PENETRATION.

Penetration has an air of divination ; it pleases our vanity more than any other quality of the mind.—*Rochefoucauld.*

PERCEPTION.

The more sand has escaped from the hourglass of our life, the clearer we should see through it.—*Richter.*

Make a point never so clear, it is great odds that a man whose habits and the bent of whose mind lie a contrary way, shall be unable to comprehend it. So weak a thing is reason in competition with inclination.—*Bishop Berkeley.*

Penetration seems a kind of inspiration ; it gives one an idea of prophecy.—*Lord Greville.*

All papas and mammas have exactly that sort of sight which distinguishes objects at a distance clearly, while they need spectacles to see those under their very noses.—*Ruffini.*

PERFECTION.

Among the other excellences of man, this is one, that he can form an idea of perfection much beyond what he has experience of in himself ; and is not limited in his conception of wisdom and virtue.—*Hume.*

Aim at perfection in everything, though in most things it is unattainable ; however, they who aim at it, and persevere, will come much nearer to it than those whose laziness and despondency make them give it up as unattainable.—*Chesterfield.*

Perfection is attained by slow degrees ; she requires the hand of time.—*Voltaire.*

To arrive at perfection, a man should have very sincere friends or inveterate enemies ; because he would be made sensible of his good or ill conduct, either by the censures of the one or the admonitions of the other.—*Diogenes.*

God never made his work for man to mend.
Dryden.

Every true specimen of perfection, or even excellence, of whatever kind it may be, from the moral down to the physical, elevates every instance of an inferior degree of excellence that we meet with, and sheds over it a portion of its own perfection.—*Francis Lieber.*

PERSECUTION.

Persecution often does in this life, what the last day will do completely, — separate the wheat from the tares.—*Milner.*

Persecution is not wrong because it is cruel ; but it is cruel because it is wrong.—*Whately.*

Wherever you see persecution, there is more than a probability that truth lies on the persecuted side.—*Bishop Latimer.*

The way of this world is, to praise dead saints, and persecute living ones.—
Rev. N. Howe.

The history of persecution is a history of endeavors to cheat nature, to make water run up hill, to twist a rope of sand. It makes no difference whether the actors be many or one, a tyrant or a mob.—*Emerson.*

Blessed are they which are persecuted for righteousness' sake, for theirs is the kingdom of heaven.—*Bible.*

As long as the waters of persecution are upon the earth, so long we dwell in the ark ; but where the land is dry, the dove itself will be tempted to a wandering course of life, and never to return to the house of her safety.—
Jeremy Taylor.

Persecution to persons in a high rank stands them in the stead of eminent virtue.—
Cardinal de Retz.

PERSEVERANCE.

Yet I argue not against Heaven's hand or will, nor bate a jot of heart or hope, but still bear up and steer right onward.—*Milton.*

Perseverance and audacity generally win.—
Madame Deluzy.

Great works are performed, not by strength, but by perseverance. Yonder palace was raised by single stones, yet you see its height and spaciousness. He that shall walk with vigor three hours a day will pass in seven years a space equal to the circumference of the globe.—
Johnson.

To climb steep hills requires slow pace at first.—*Shakespeare.*

It is all very well to tell me that a young man has distinguished himself by a brilliant first speech. He may go on, or he may be satisfied with his first triumph ; but show me a young man who has not succeeded at first, and nevertheless has gone on, and I will back that young man to do better than most of those who have succeeded at the first trial.—
Charles James Fox.

Few things are impossible to diligence and skill.—*Johnson.*

The virtue lies in the struggle, not the prize.
R. M. Milnes.

There are two ways of attaining an important end, — force and perseverance. Force falls to the lot only of the privileged few, but austere and sustained perseverance can be practised by the most insignificant. Its silent power grows irresistible with time.—*Madame Swetchine.*

Nothing is so hard but search will find it out.—*Herrick.*

That policy that can strike only while the iron is hot will be overcome by that perseverance which, like Cromwell's, can make the iron hot by striking; and he that can only rule the storm must yield to him who can both raise and rule it.—*Colton.*

The nerve that never relaxes, the eye that never blenches, the thought that never wanders, — these are the masters of victory.—*Burke.*

Every noble work is at first impossible.— *Carlyle.*

Perseverance merits neither blame nor praise; it is only the duration of our inclinations and sentiments, which we can neither create nor extinguish.—*Rochefoucauld.*

To the persevering mortal, the blessed Immortals are swift.—*Zoroaster.*

I hold a doctrine, to which I owe not much, indeed, but all the little I ever had, namely, that with ordinary talent and extraordinary perseverance, all things are attainable.— *Sir T. F. Buxton.*

When I take the humor of a thing once, I am like your tailor's needle, — I go through.— *Ben Jonson.*

The conditions of conquest are always easy. We have but to toil awhile, endure awhile, believe always, and never turn back.—*Simms.*

If there be one thing on earth which is truly admirable, it is to see God's wisdom blessing an inferiority of natural powers, where they have been honestly, truly, and zealously cultivated. *Dr. Arnold.*

Perseverance is a Roman virtue, that wins each godlike act, and plucks success even from the spear-proof crest of rugged danger.— *Havard.*

A falling drop at last will cave a stone.— *Lucretius.*

All the performances of human art, at which we look with praise or wonder, are instances of the resistless force of perseverance; it is by this that the quarry becomes a pyramid, and that distant countries are united with canals. If a man was to compare the effect of a single stroke of a pickaxe, or of one impression of the spade, with the general design and last result, he would be overwhelmed by the sense of their disproportion; yet those petty operations, incessantly continued, in time surmount the greatest difficulties, and mountains are levelled, and oceans bounded, by the slender force of human beings.—*Johnson.*

The block of granite, which was an obstacle in the pathway of the weak, becomes a stepping-stone in the pathway of the strong.—*Carlyle.*

Few things are impracticable in themselves; and it is for want of application, rather than of means, that men fail of success.—*Rochefoucauld.*

Victory belongs to the most persevering.— *Napoleon.*

Perseverance, dear my lord, keeps honor bright. To have none is to hang quite out of fashion, like a rusty nail in monumental mockery.—*Shakespeare.*

It gives power to weakness, and opens to poverty the world's wealth. It spreads fertility over the barren landscape, and bids the choicest fruits and flowers spring up and flourish in the desert abode of thorns and briers.— *S. G. Goodrich.*

Whoever perseveres will be crowned.— *Herder.*

Even in social life, it is persistency which attracts confidence, more than talents and accomplishments.—*Whipple.*

No rock so hard but that a little wave may beat admission in a thousand years.—*Tennyson.*

For some men, like unskilful jockeys, give up their designs when they have almost reached the goal; while others, on the contrary, obtain a victory over their opponents, by exerting, at the last moment, more vigorous efforts than before.—*Polybius.*

Hard pounding, gentlemen; but we will see who can pound the longest.— *Wellington at Waterloo.*

PERSUASION.

Few are open to conviction, but the majority of men are open to persuasion.—*Goethe.*

It is only for those to employ force who possess strength without judgment; but the well advised will have recourse to other means. Besides, he who pretends to carry his point by force hath need of many associates; but the man who can persuade knows that he is himself sufficient for the purpose: neither can such a one be supposed forward to shed blood; for, who is there would choose to destroy a fellow-citizen, rather than make a friend of him by mildness and persuasion? — *Xenophon.*

PERVERSENESS.

Some men, like spaniels, will only fawn the more when repulsed, but will pay little heed to a friendly caress.—*Abd-el-Kader.*

Perseverance is one of the primitive impulses of the human heart; one of the indivisible primary faculties or sentiments which give direction to the character of man.—*Edgar A. Poe.*

When once a man is determined to believe, the very absurdity of the doctrine confirms him in his faith.—*Junius.*

For so remarkably perverse is the nature of man, that he despises whoever courts him, and admires whoever will not bend before him.—*Thucydides.*

PHILANTHROPY.

What word sums up the highest Christian virtue if not philanthropy ?—*T. W. Higginson.*

This is true philanthropy, that buries not its gold in ostentatious charity, but builds its hospital in the human heart.—*Harley.*

Philanthropy, like charity, must begin at home. From this centre our sympathies may extend in an ever-widening circle.—*Lamb.*

PHILOSOPHY.

True philosophy is that which renders us to ourselves, and all others who surround us, better, and at the same time more content, more patient, more calm, and more ready for all decent and pure enjoyment.—*Lavater.*

Adversity's sweet milk, philosophy.—*Shakespeare.*

Philosophy has given us several plausible rules for attaining peace and tranquillity of mind, but they fall very much short of bringing men to it.—*Tillotson.*

If we take in hand any volume of divinity, or school metaphysics, for instance, let us ask, does it contain any abstract reasoning concerning quantity or number ? No. Does it contain any experimental reasoning concerning matter of fact and existence ? No. Commit it then to the flames ; for it can contain nothing but sophistry and illusion.—*Hume.*

This same philosophy is a good horse in a stable, but an arrant jade on a journey.—*Goldsmith.*

" Wonder," says Aristotle, " is the first cause of philosophy." This is quite as true in the progress of the individual as in that of the concrete mind ; and the constant aim of philosophy is to destroy its parent.—*Bulwer Lytton.*

Philosophy is as far separated from impiety as religion is from fanaticism.—*Diderot.*

Philosophy can merely resolve what is given to her : giving is not the act of analysis, but of genius, which carries on its combinations according to objective laws, under the dim but sure guidance of the pure reason.—*Schiller.*

All philosophy lies in two words, " sustain " and " abstain."—*Epictetus.*

Philosophy is a bully that talks very loud when the danger is at a distance ; but the moment she is hard pressed by the enemy she is not to be found at her post, but leaves the brunt of the battle to be borne by her humbler but steadier comrade, Religion.—*Colton.*

Philosophy is reason with the eyes of the soul.—*Simms.*

A philosopher has a system ; he views things according to his theory ; he is unavoidably partial ; and, like Lucian's painter, he paints his one-eyed princes in profile.—*Bulwer Lytton.*

The philosopher is he to whom the highest has descended, and the lowest has mounted up ; who is the equal and kindly brother of all.—*Carlyle.*

Be a philosopher ; but amidst all your philosophy, be still a man.—*Hume.*

The condition and characteristic of a vulgar person is, that he never looks for either help or harm from himself, but only from externals. The condition and characteristic of a philosopher is that he looks to himself for all help or harm.—*Epictetus.*

To study philosophy is nothing but to prepare one's self to die.—*Cicero.*

When Philosophy has gone as far as she is able, she arrives at almightiness, and in that labyrinth is lost ; where, not knowing the way, she goes on by guess and cannot tell whether she is right or wrong ; and like a petty river, is swallowed up in the boundless ocean of Omnipotency.—*Feltham.*

Philosophy, while it soothes the reason, damps the ambition.—*Bulwer Lytton.*

Hncheson, in his philosophic treatise on beauty, harmony, and order, plus's and minus's you to heaven or hell by algebraic equations, so that none but an expert mathematician can ever be able to settle his accounts with St. Peter, and perhaps St. Matthew, who had been an officer in the customs, must be called in to audit them.—*Sterne.*

What is philosophy ? It is something that lightens up, that makes bright.—*Victor Cousin.*

Philosophy is to poetry what old age is to youth ; and the stern truths of philosophy are as fatal to the fictions of the one, as the chilling testimonies of experience are to the hopes of the other.—*Colton.*

Philosophy abounds more than philosophers, and learning more than learned men.—*W. B. Clulow.*

Philosophy is a proud, sullen detector of the poverty and misery of man. It may turn him from the world with a proud, sturdy contempt ; but it cannot come forward and say, here are rest, grace, pardon, peace, strength, and consolation.—*Cecil.*

The business of philosophy is to circumnavigate human nature.—*Hare.*

Make philosophy thy journey, theology thy journey's end: philosophy is a pleasant way, but dangerous to him that either tires or retires; in this journey it is safe neither to loiter nor to rest, till thou hast attained thy journey's end; he that sits down a philosopher rises up an atheist.—*Quarles.*

Philosophy will clip an angel's wings.—
Keats.

Philosophy is the art and law of life, and it teaches us what to do in all cases, and, like good marksmen to hit the white at any distance.—*Seneca.*

The first business of the philosopher is to part with self-conceit.—*Epictetus.*

To be a husbandman is but a retreat from the city; to be a philosopher, from the world; or rather a retreat from the world, as it is man's, into the world, as it is God's.—*Cowley.*

Is it not in philosophy as in love? The more we have of it, and the less we talk about it, the better.—*Landor.*

Tooth-drawers are practical philosophers that go upon a very rational hypothesis, — not to cure, but to take away the part affected.—
Steele.

Queen of arts and daughter of heaven.—
Burke.

Philosophy, the formatrix of judgment and manners, has the privilege of having a hand in everything.—*Montaigne.*

The great source of calamity lies in regret or anticipation; he, therefore, is most wise, who thinks of the present alone, regardless of the past or future. This is impossible to a man of pleasure; it is difficult to the man of business; and is, in some degree, attainable by the philosopher. Happy were we all born philosophers, all born with a talent of thus dissipating our own cares by spreading them upon all mankind.
Goldsmith.

Philosophy is a goddess, whose head indeed is in heaven, but whose feet are upon earth; she attempts more than she accomplishes, and promises more than she performs.—*Colton.*

All that philosophy can teach is to be stubborn or sullen under misfortunes.—*Goldsmith.*

In wonder all philosophy began; in wonder it ends; and admiration fills up the interspace. But the first is the wonder offspring of ignorance; the last is the parent of adoration.—
Coleridge.

How charming is divine philosophy! not harsh nor crabbed, as dull fools suppose, but musical as is Apollo's lute! —*Milton.*

Philosophy is, to tell the truth, a homesickness, an effort to return home.—*Novalis.*

Philosophical studies are beset by one peril, a person easily brings himself to think that he thinks; and a smattering of science encourages conceit. He is above his companions. A hieroglyphic is a spell. The gnostic dogma is cuneiform writing to the million. Moreover, the vain man is generally a doubter. It is Newton who sees himself in a child on the seashore, and his discoveries in the colored shells.
Willmott.

It is the bounty of nature that we live, but of philosophy, that we live well; which is, in truth, a greater benefit than life itself.—*Seneca.*

Sublime philosophy! thou art the patriarch's ladder, reaching heaven, and bright with beckoning angels; but, alas! we see thee, like the patriarch, but in dreams, by the first step, dull slumbering on the earth.—*Bulwer Lytton.*

There are more things in heaven and earth, Horatio, than are dreamt of in your philosophy.—*Shakespeare.*

There is a philosophy full of flowers, of amenity, and of sportiveness, as sprightly as it is sublime.—*Joubert.*

Philosophy is a modest profession, it is all reality and plain dealing; I hate solemnity and pretence, with nothing but pride at the bottom.
Pliny.

Philosophy, when superficially studied, excites doubt; when thoroughly explored, it dispels it.—*Bacon.*

Do not all charms fly at the mere touch of cold philosophy? —*Keats.*

Philosophy does not look into pedigrees. She did not find Plato noble, but she made him so.—*Seneca.*

He who philosophizes for himself meets, at every step, with difficulties, of which he who philosophizes for a school experiences nothing.
Jacobi.

Admiration is the foundation of all philosophy, inquisition the progress, and ignorance the end.—*Montaigne.*

A little philosophy inclineth men's minds to atheism; but depth in philosophy bringeth men's minds to religion.—*Bacon.*

All philosophy is only forcing the trade of happiness, when nature seems to deny the means.—*Goldsmith.*

Philosophy alone makes the mind invincible and places us out of the reach of fortune, so that all her arrows fall short of us.—*Seneca.*

Comte's philosophy in practice might be compendiously described as Catholicism minus Christianity.—*Professor Huxley.*

Philosophy, if rightly defined, is naught but the love of wisdom.—*Cicero.*

It is easy for men to write and talk like philosophers, but to act with wisdom, there is the rub ! —*Rivarol.*

The discovery of what is true, and the practice of that which is good, are the two most important objects of philosophy.—*Voltaire.*

PHYSIC — PHYSICIAN.

Physic, for the most part, is nothing else but the substitute of exercise or temperance.—
Addison.

Throw physic to the dogs, I 'll none of it.—
Shakespeare.

Physic is of little use to a temperate person, for a man's own observation on what he finds does him good, and what hurts him, is the best physic to preserve health.—*Bacon.*

Take physic, pomp; expose thyself to feel what wretches feel.—*Shakespeare.*

The rich patient cures the poor physician much more often than the poor physician the rich patient; and it is rather paradoxical, that the rapid recovery of the one usually depends upon the procrastinated disorder of the other.—
Colton.

We have not only multiplied diseases, but we have made them more fatal.—*Rush.*

In the actual condition of medical science, the physician mostly plays but the part of simple spectator of the sad episodes which his profession furnishes him.—*Magendie.*

A murder-loving devil has taken possession of the medical chairs; for none but a devil would recommend to physicians blood-letting as a necessary means.— *Van Helmont.*

Physician, heal thyself.—*Bible.*

Some persons will tell you, with an air of the miraculous, that they recovered although they were given over ; whereas they might with more reason have said, they recovered because they were given over.— *Colton.*

Time is generally the best doctor.—*Ovid.*

Experience is properly upon its own dunghill in the subject of physic, where reason wholly gives it place. Tiberius said that " whoever had lived twenty years ought to be responsible to himself for all things that were hurtful or wholesome to him, and know how to order himself without physic."—*Montaigne.*

Though fancy may be the patient's complaint, necessity is often the doctor's.—
Zimmermann.

I think you might dispense with half your doctors, if you would only consult Doctor Sun more, and be more under the treatment of these great hydropathic doctors, the clouds ! —
Beecher.

A man who pours drugs of which he knows little into a body of which he knows less.—
Voltaire.

Apollo was held the god of physic and sender of diseases ; both were originally the same trade, and still continue so ! —*Swift.*

Guy Patin recommends to a patient to have no doctor but a horse, and no apothecary but an ass ! —*Chesterfield.*

PHYSIOGNOMY.

There is nothing truer than physiognomy, taken in connection with manner.—*Dickens.*

Spite of Lavater, faces are oftentimes great lies. They are the paper money of society, for which, on demand, there frequently proves to be no gold in the human coffer.—
F. G. Trafford.

There is no art whereby to find the mind's construction in the face.—*Shakespeare.*

It is believed that physiognomy is only a simple development of the features already marked out by nature. It is my opinion, however, that in addition to this development, the features come insensibly to be formed and assume their shape from the frequent and habitual expression of certain affections of the soul. These affections are marked on the countenance ; nothing is more certain than this; and when they turn into habits, they must leave on it durable impressions.—*Rousseau.*

Pickpockets and beggars are the best practical physiognomists, without having read a line of Lavater, who, it is notorious, mistook a philosopher for a highwayman.— *Colton.*

He who observes the speaker more than the sound of words will seldom meet with disappointments.—*Lavater.*

The scope of an intellect is not to be measured with a tape-string, or a character deciphered from the shape or length of a nose.—
Bovee.

PIETY.

Piety is the only proper and adequate relief of decaying man. He that grows old without religious hopes, as he declines into imbecility, and feels pains and sorrows incessantly crowding upon him, falls into a gulf of bottomless misery, in which every reflection must plunge him deeper and deeper.—*Johnson.*

Let us learn upon earth those things which can call us to heaven.—*St. Jerome.*

I do not doubt but that genuine piety is the spring of peace of mind ; it enables us to bear the sorrows of life, and lessens the pangs of death : the same cannot be said of hypocrisy.—*Bruyère.*

True piety hath in it nothing weak, nothing sad, nothing constrained. It enlarges the heart ; it is simple, free, and attractive.—*Fenelon.*

Piety is a kind of modesty. It makes us cast down our thoughts, just as modesty makes us cast down our eyes in presence of whatever is forbidden.—*Joubert.*

We are surrounded by motives to piety and devotion, if we would but mind them. The poor are designed to excite our liberality ; the miserable, our pity ; the sick, our assistance ; the ignorant, our instruction ; those that are fallen, our helping hand. In those who are vain, we see the vanity of the world ; in those who are wicked, our own frailty. When we see good men rewarded, it confirms our hope ; and when evil men are punished, it excites our fear.—*Bishop Wilson.*

Let us carry only in this life that perfection which we have given to our soul.—*Orfila.*

Let it not be imagined that the life of a good Christian must necessarily be a life of melancholy and gloominess ; for he only resigns some pleasures, to enjoy others infinitely greater.—*Pascal.*

The root of sanctity is sanity. A man must be healthy before he can be holy. We bathe first, and then perfume.—*Madame Swetchine.*

Our piety must be weak and imperfect if it do not conquer our fear of death.—*Fenelon.*

Piety is indifferent whether she enters at the eye or the ear. There is none of the senses at which she does not knock one day or other. The Puritans forgot this, and thrust Beauty out of the meeting-house and slammed the door in her face.—*Lowell.*

A beauty of holiness, which effloresces on the countenance, the manner, and the outward path.—*Dr. Chalmers.*

We must labor unceasingly to render our piety reasonable, and our reason pious.—*Madame Swetchine.*

A good man regards the root ; he fixes the root, and all else flows out of it. The root is filial piety ; the fruit brotherly love.—*Confucius.*

PITY.

Man may dismiss compassion from his heart, but God will never.—*Cowper.*

We pity in others only those evils which we have ourselves experienced.—*Rousseau.*

Nature has cast me in so soft a mould, that but to hear a story feigned for pleasure, of some sad lover's death, moistens my eyes, and robs me of my manhood.—*Dryden.*

Pity best taught by fellowship of woe.—*Coleridge.*

Pity those whom nature abuses, but never those who abuse nature.—*J. Vanbrugh.*

Pity is to many of the unhappy a source of comfort in hopeless distresses, as it contributes to recommend them to themselves, by proving that they have not lost the regard of others ; and Heaven seems to indicate the duty even of barren compassion, by inclining us to weep for evils which we cannot remedy.—*Johnson.*

Pity is the virtue of the law, and none but tyrants use it cruelly.—*Shakespeare.*

Pity and forbearance, and long-sufferance and fair interpretation, and excusing our brother, and taking in the best sense, and passing the gentlest sentence, are as certainly our duty, and owing to every person that does offend and can repent, as calling to account can be owing to the law, and are first to be paid ; and he that does not so is an unjust person.—*Jeremy Taylor.*

Pity swells the tide of love.—*Young.*

How sometimes nature will betray its folly, its tenderness ! and make itself a pastime to harder bosoms.—*Shakespeare.*

Pity, the tenderest part of love.—*Yalden.*

Let us pity the wicked man ; for it is very sad to seek happiness where it does not exist. Let our compassion express itself in efforts to bring him gently back to sacred principle, and if he persist, let us pity him the more for a blindness so fatal to himself.—*De Charnage.*

Pity is akin to love.—*Southern.*

How different is the ready hand, tearful eye, and soothing voice, from the ostentatious appearance which is called pity !—*Jane Porter.*

Soft pity enters at an iron gate.—*Shakespeare.*

Pity and friendship are passions incompatible with each other ; and it is impossible that both can reside in any breast, for the smallest space, without impairing each other.—*Goldsmith.*

Of all the paths that lead to a woman's love, pity is the straightest.—*Beaumont and Fletcher.*

Friends should be very delicate and careful in administering pity as medicine, when enemies use the same article as poison.—
J. F. Boyes.

It is easy to condemn; it is better to pity.—
Abbott.

He hath a tear for pity, and a hand open as day for melting charity.—*Shakespeare*

Pity is a sense of our own misfortunes in those of another man; it is a sort of foresight of the disasters which may befall ourselves. We assist others, in order that they may assist us on like occasions; so that the services we offer to the unfortunate are in reality so many anticipated kindnesses to ourselves.—*Rochefoucauld.*

Pity is love when grown into excess.—
Sir H. Howard.

PLAGIARISM.
Borrowed garments never keep one warm. A curse goes with them, as with Harry Gill's blankets. Nor can one get smuggled goods safely into kingdom-come. How lank and pitiful does one of these gentry look, after posterity's customs-officers have had the plucking of him!—*Lowell.*

They lard their lean books with the fat of other's works.—*Burton.*

There is a very pretty Eastern tale, of which the fate of plagiarists often reminds us. The slave of a magician saw his master wave his wand, and heard him give orders to the spirits who arose at the summons. The slave stole the wand, and waved it himself in the air; but he had not observed that his master used the left hand for that purpose. The spirits thus irregularly summoned, tore the thief to pieces instead of obeying his orders.—*Macaulay.*

Plagiarists are always suspicious of being stolen from.—*Coleridge.*

Most plagiarists, like the drone, have neither taste to select, industry to acquire, nor skill to improve, but impudently pilfer the honey ready prepared, from the hive.—*Colton.*

As monarchs have a right to call in the specie of a state, and raise its value, by their own impression; so are there certain prerogative geniuses, who are above plagiaries, who cannot be said to steal, but, from their improvement of a thought, rather to borrow it, and repay the commonwealth of letters with interest again; and may more properly be said to adopt, than to kidnap a sentiment, by leaving it heir to their own fame.—*Sterne.*

Horace or Boileau have said such a thing before you. I take your word for it, but I said it as my own, and may not I have the same just thoughts after them, as others may have after me?—*Bruyère.*

No earnest thinker is a plagiarist pure and simple. He will never borrow from others that which he has not already, more or less, thought out for himself.—*Charles Kingsley.*

Borrowed thoughts, like borrowed money, only show the poverty of the borrower.—
Lady Blessington.

If we steal thoughts from the moderns, it will be cried down as plagiarism; if from the ancients, it will be cried up as erudition. But in this respect every author is a Spartan, being more ashamed of the discovery than of the depredation.—*Colton.*

Away, ye imitators, servile herd!—*Horace.*

Honest thinkers are always stealing from each other. Our minds are full of waifs and estrays which we think are our own. Innocent plagiarism turns up everywhere.—*Holmes.*

Touching plagiarism in general, it is to be remembered that all men who have sense and feeling are being continually helped; they are taught by every person whom they meet and enriched by everything that falls in their way. The greatest is he who has been oftenest aided; and, if the attainments of all human minds could be traced to their real sources, it would be found that the world had been laid most under contribution by the men of most original power, and that every day of their existence deepened their debt to their race, while it enlarged their gifts to it.—*Ruskin.*

Plagiarists, at least, have the merit of preservation.—*Disraeli.*

Steal! to be sure they may, and, egad, serve your best thoughts as gypsies do stolen children,—disfigure them to make them pass for their own.—*Sheridan.*

It is a special trick of low cunning to squeeze out knowledge from a modest man, who is eminent in any science; and then to use it as legally acquired, and pass the source in total silence.—*Horace Walpole.*

Literature is full of coincidences, which some love to believe plagiarisms. There are thoughts always abroad in the air, which it takes more wit to avoid than to hit upon.—
Holmes.

PLEASURE.
Pleasure never comes sincere to man; but lent by heaven upon hard usury—*Dryden.*

Our pleasures travel by express; our pains by parliamentary. Through the loveliest scenes the joy-train of our lives rushes swiftly. At the pretty wayside stations we are able but to touch hands with cherished friends, and behold! we are off again; but if we have grief for our engine-driver, care for the stoker, how we creep along the lines!—*F. G. Trafford.*

Pleasure itself is painful at the bottom.—
Montaigne.

Pleasure is one of those commodities which are sold at a thousand shops, and bought by a thousand customers, but of which nobody ever fairly finds possession. Either they know not well how to use, or the commodity will not keep, for no one has ever yet appeared to be satisfied with his bargain. It is too subtle for transition, though sufficiently solid for sale.—
Simms.

Pleasure can be supported by illusion, but happiness rests upon truth.—*Chamfort*

There are only three pleasures in life pure and lasting, and all derived from inanimate things,—books, pictures, and the face of nature. What is the world but a heap of ruined friendships, but the grave of love ? —*Hazlitt.*

All worldly pleasure is correspondent to a like measure of anxiety.—*F. Osborn.*

If you suppress the exorbitant love of pleasure and money, idle curiosity, iniquitous pursuits and wanton mirth, what a stillness would there be in the great cities ! The necessaries of life do not occasion at most a third part of the hurry.—*Bruyère.*

The pleasure of all things increases by the same danger that should deter it.—*Seneca.*

There is no just and lawful pleasure, wherein intemperance and excess is not to be condemned ; but, to speak the truth, is not man a most miserable creature the while? It is scarce, by his natural condition, in his power to taste one pleasure pure and entire ; and yet must he be contriving doctrines and precepts to curtail that little he has : he is not yet wretched enough unless, by art and study, he augment his own misery.—*Montaigne.*

Mistake not. Those pleasures are not pleasures that trouble the quiet and tranquillity of thy life.—*Jeremy Taylor.*

The amiable is the voluptuous in expression or manner. The sense of pleasure in ourselves is that which excites it in others ; or, the art of pleasing is to seem pleased.—*Hazlitt.*

Pleasure of every kind quickly satisfies.—
Burke.

If I give way to pleasure, I must also yield to grief, to poverty, to labor, ambition, anger, until I am torn to pieces by my misfortunes and my lust.—*Seneca.*

We smile at the ignorance of the savage who cuts down the tree in order to reach its fruits ; but the fact is that a blunder of this description is made by every person who is over eager and impatient in the pursuit of pleasure.—*Channing.*

The sweetest pleasures are those which do not exhaust hope.—*De Lévis.*

The cheapest pleasures are the best, and nothing is more costly than sin, yet we mortgage futurity, counting it but little loss.—
Tupper.

Pleasure's couch is virtue's grave.—*Duganne.*

People should be guarded against temptation to unlawful pleasures by furnishing them the means of innocent ones. In every community there must be pleasures, relaxations, and means of agreeable excitement ; and if innocent are not furnished, resort will be had to criminal. Man was made to enjoy as well as labor, and the state of society should be adapted to this principle of human nature.—*Channing.*

Choose such pleasures as recreate much, and cost little.—*Fuller.*

Relaxation is a physical and moral necessity. Animals, even to the simplest and dullest, have their games, their sports, their diversions. The toil-worn artisan, stooping and straining over his daily task, which taxes eye and brain and limb, ought to have opportunity and means for an hour or two of relaxation after that task is concluded.—*Horace Greeley.*

But grant to life some perquisites of joy ; a time there is, when, like a thrice-told tale, long-rifled life of sweets can yield no more.—*Young.*

The roses of pleasure seldom last long enough to adorn the brow of him who plucks them, and they are the only roses which do not retain their sweetness after they have lost their beauty.—*Blair.*

He that is violent in the pursuit of pleasure won't mind to turn villain for the purchase.—
Marcus Antoninus.

Would you judge of the lawfulness or unlawfulness of pleasures, take this rule : whatever weakens your reason impairs the tenderness of your conscience, obscures your sense of God, or takes off the relish of spiritual things ; in short, whatever increases the strength and authority of your body over your mind, that thing is sin to you, however innocent it may be in itself.—
Southey.

Put this restriction on your pleasures ; be cautious that they injure no being which has life.—*Zimmermann.*

Pleasure when it is a man's chief purpose disappoints itself ; and the constant application to it palls the faculty of enjoying it, though it leaves the sense of our inability for that we wish, with a disrelish of everything else. Thus the intermediate seasons of the man of pleasure are more heavy than one would impose upon the vilest criminal.—*Steele.*

None has more frequent conversations with disagreeable self than the man of pleasure ; his enthusiasms are but few and transient; his appetites, like angry creditors, continually making fruitless demands for what he is unable to pay ; and the greater his former pleasures, the more strong his regret, the more impatient his expectations.—*Goldsmith.*

In diving to the bottom of pleasures we bring up more gravel than pearls.—*Balzac.*

There is a limit to enjoyment, though the sources of wealth be boundless ; and the choicest pleasures of life lie within the ring of moderation.—*Tupper.*

All pleasure must be bought at the price of pain. The difference between false pleasure and true pleasure is put thus : for the true, the price is paid before you enjoy it; for the false, after you enjoy it.—*John Foster.*

These natural pleasures, indeed, are really without price, both because they are below all price in their attainment, and above it in their enjoyment.—*Hume.*

Pleasure is the reflex of unimpeded energy.
Sir William Hamilton.

Pleasures are not of such a solid nature that we can dive into them ; we must merely skim over them ; they resemble those boggy lands over which we must run lightly, without stopping to put down our feet.—*Fontenelle.*

The seeds of repentance are sown in youth by pleasure, but the harvest is reaped in age and pain.—*Colton.*

The slave of pleasure soon sinks into a kind of voluptuous dotage; intoxicated with present delights, and careless of everything else, his days and his nights glide away in luxury or vice, and he has no care but to keep thought away ; for thought is troublesome to him who lives without his own approbation.—*Johnson.*

Pleasure may be called the short cut to the tomb, as it shortens time, which is the way.—
Douglas Jerrold.

Pleasure is a necessary reciprocal ; no one feels, who does not at the same time give it. To be pleased, one must please. What pleases you in others will in general please them in you.—*Chesterfield.*

The pungency of pleasure is as transient as the foam that mantles round its brimming cup.
Henry Giles.

The pleasures of the world are deceitful; they promise more than they give. They trouble us in seeking them, they do not satisfy us when possessing them, and they make us despair in losing them.—*Madame de Lambert.*

Pleasure blinds, so to say, the eyes of the mind, and has no fellowship with virtue.—
Cicero.

Centries, or wooden frames, are put under the arches of a bridge, to remain no longer than till the latter are consolidated. Even so pleasures are the Devil's scaffolding to build a habit upon ; that formed and steady, the pleasures are sent for fire-wood, and the hell begins in this life.—*Coleridge.*

There is no sterner moralist than pleasure.
Byron.

There are, indeed, some spirits so ardent, that change of employment to them is rest, and their only fatigue a cessation from activity. But even these, if they make pleasure a business, will be equally subject to *ennui*, with more phlegmatic minds ; for mere pleasure, although it may refresh the weary, wearies the refreshed.
Colton.

The sweetest pleasure is in imparting it.—
Bovee.

No enjoyment, however inconsiderable, is confined to the present moment. A man is the happier for life from having made once an agreeable tour, or lived for any length of time with pleasant people, or enjoyed any considerable interval of innocent pleasure.—*Sydney Smith.*

I look upon it as an equal injustice to loath natural pleasures as to be too much in love with them.—*Montaigne.*

There is'not a little generalship and stratagem required in the managing and marshalling of our pleasures, so that each shall not mutually encroach to the destruction of all. For pleasures are very voracious, too apt to worry one another, and each, like Aaron's serpent, is prone to swallow up the rest. Thus, drinking will soon destroy the power, gaming the means, and sensuality the taste, for other pleasures less seductive, but far more salubrious and permanent, as they are pure.—*Colton.*

Pleasure soon exhausts us and itself also ; but endeavor never does.—*Richter.*

But no enjoyment is transitory ; the impression which it leaves is lasting, and what is done with diligence and toil imparts to the spectator a secret force, of which one cannot say how far the effect may reach.—*Goethe.*

He who can at all times sacrifice pleasure to duty approaches sublimity.—*Lavater.*

Pleasures, riches, honor, and joy are sure to have care, disgrace, adversity, and affliction in their train. There is no pleasure without pain, no joy without sorrow. O the folly of expecting lasting felicity in a vale of tears, or a paradise in a ruined world ! —*Gotthold.*

Give me health and a day, and I will make ridiculous the pomp of emperors.—*Emerson.*

It is my firm conviction that man has only himself to blame, if his life appears to him at any time void of interest and of pleasure. Man may make life what he pleases, and give it as much worth, both for himself and others, as he has energy for. Over his moral and intellectual being his sway is complete.—
Wilhelm von Humboldt.

Mental pleasures never cloy; unlike those of the body, they are increased by repetition, approved of by reflection, and strengthened by enjoyment.—*Cotton.*

I never could tread a single pleasure under foot.—*Robert Browning.*

The art of pleasing consists in being pleased. To be amiable is to be satisfied with one's self and others. Good-humor is essential to pleasautry.—*Hazlitt.*

Venture not to the utmost bounds of even lawful pleasures; the limits of good and evil join.—*Fuller.*

Amid the roses fierce Repentance rears her snaky crest.—*Thomson.*

It is owned that the most noble and excellent gift of Heaven to man is reason; and it is as sure, that of all the enemies reason has to engage with, pleasure is the most capital.—
Cicero.

It is but just that we should purchase our pleasures, but the moment when we pay is a hard one.—*Madame Swetchine.*

Even in the moments of intensest enjoyment our pleasures are multiplied by the quick-revolving images of thought; we feel the past and future in each fragment of the instant, even as the flavor of every drop of some delicious liquid is heightened and prolonged on the lips.—
Talfourd.

Shenstone, an artist in landscape gardening, said he knew the turn in his life which led to unhappiness, — it was when he made pleasure his aim.—*G. S. Bowes.*

The shadow of our pleasures is the pain that seems so surely to follow them.—
Madame Dudevant.

Pleasure is a word of dubious import; pleasure is in general dangerous, and pernicious to virtue; to be able, therefore, to furnish pleasure that is harmless, pleasure pure and unalloyed, is as great a power as man can possess.
Johnson.

It is the rarest pleasures which especially delight us.—*Tyrius Maximus.*

Often and often to me, and instinctively, has an innocent pleasure felt like a foretaste of infinite delight, an antepast of heaven. Nor can I believe otherwise than that pure happiness is of a purifying effect; like Jewish bread from heaven, no doubt it is meant to invigorate as well as to gratify.—*Mountford.*

The end of pleasure is to support the offices of life, to relieve the fatigues of business, to reward a regular action, and to encourage the continuance.—*Jeremy Collier.*

Pleasures waste the spirits more than pains; therefore the latter can be endured longer, and in greater degree, than the former.—
Zimmermann.

When the idea of any pleasure strikes your imagination, make a just computation between the duration of the pleasure and that of the repentance that is likely to follow it.—*Epictetus.*

No state can be more destitute than that of a person, who, when the delights of sense forsake him, has no pleasures of the mind.—*Burgh.*

Pleasures do but weaken our minds, and send us for our support to fortune, who gives us money only as the wages of slavery.—*Seneca.*

There are pleasures for keeping as enjoying, — for using delicately, the zest lasting long, the more affluent when tasted with moderation and seldom.—*Alcott.*

The man of pleasure little knows the perfect joy he loses for the disappointing gratifications which he pursues.—*Addison.*

Pleasure and sorrow are twins.—
Daniel Cowdrey.

Writers of every age have endeavored to show that pleasure is in us, and not in the object offered for our amusement. If the soul be happily disposed, everything becomes capable of affording entertainment, and distress will almost want a name.—*Goldsmith.*

Pleasures are like poppies spread; you seize the flower, its bloom is shed!—*Burns.*

Pleasure and pain, which are two sentiments so different in themselves, differ not so much in their cause. From the instance of tickling, it appears, that the movement of pleasure, pushed a little too far, becomes pain; and the movement of pain a little moderated becomes pleasure.—*Fontenelle.*

The loss of pain is generally thought to be purchased too dear by the loss of pleasure.—
Sir W. Temple.

The size of a man's sense and improvement is discovered by his pleasures as much as by anything else.—*Jeremy Collier.*

Most pleasures, like flowers when gathered, die.—*Young.*

Pleasures of high flavor, like pine-apples, have the misfortune, that, like pine-apples, they make the gums bleed.—*Richter.*

All earthly delights are sweeter in expectation than enjoyment; but all spiritual pleasures more in fruition than expectation.—*Feltham.*

Pleasure and pain spring not so much from the nature of things as from our manner of considering them. Pleasure, especially, is never an invariable effect of particular circumstances. Largely that is pleasure which is thought to be so.—*Bovee.*

Pleasure is like a building; the more high the narrower it grows; cedars die soonest at the top.—*Shakespeare.*

It is sad to think how few our pleasures really are; and for the which we risk eternal good.—*Bailey.*

On a thin coating of ice winter conducts their steps, a deep pool is beneath. Such is the slight surface of your pleasures. Glide on, mortals, do not halt.—*Pierre-Charles Roy.*

Cultivate not only the cornfields of your mind, but the pleasure-grounds also.—*Whately.*

Let a man keep the law, any law, and his way will be strewn with satisfactions. There is more difference in the quality of our pleasures than in the amount.—*Emerson.*

POETRY.

In the hands of genius, the driest stick becomes an Aaron's rod, and buds and blossoms out in poetry. Is he a Burns? the sight of a mountain daisy unseals the fountains of his nature, and he embalms the " bonny gem " in the beauty of his spirit. Is he a Wordsworth? at his touch all nature is instinct with feeling; the spirit of beauty springs up in the footsteps of his going, and the darkest, nakedest grave becomes a sunlit bank empurpled with blossoms of life.—*H. N. Hudson.*

He tames grief that fetters it in verse.
Rev. Dr. Donne.

Poets are never young in one sense. Their delicate ear hears the far-off whispers of eternity, which coarser souls must travel towards for scores of years before their dull sense is touched by them.—*Holmes.*

Superstition is the poesy of life, so that it does not injure the poet to be superstitious.—
Goethe.

Poetry is in itself strength and joy, whether it be crowned by all mankind, or left alone in its own magic hermitage.—*Sterling.*

Try a good poem as you would sound a pipkin; and if it rings well upon the knuckle, be sure there is no flaw in it. Verse without rhyme is a body without a soul (for " the chief lie consisteth in the rhyme ") or a bell without a clapper; which, in strictness, is no bell, as being neither of use nor delight.—*Swift*

A poet must needs be before his own age, to be even with posterity.—*Lowell.*

As the falcon launched trustingly heavenward is lost to view, the course of the higher poetry often soars beyond the ken of the multitude; and, as the humble birds carol blithely round our dwellings, so the meeker lays of the muse linger tunefully about the heart.—
Tuckerman.

Sad is his lot who, once at least in his life, has not been a poet.—*Lamartine.*

Over all life broods Poesy, like the calm blue sky with its motherly, rebuking face. She is the great reformer, and where the love of her is strong and healthy, wickedness and wrong cannot long prevail.—*Lowell.*

None ever was a great poet that applied himself much to anything else.—
Sir W. Temple.

We have more poets than judges and interpreters of poetry. It is easier to write an indifferent poem than to understand a good one. There is, indeed, a certain low and moderate sort of poetry, that a man may well enough judge by certain rules of art; but the true, supreme, and divine poesy is equally above all rules and reason. And whoever discerns the beauty of it with the most assured and most steady sight sees no more than the quick reflection of a flash of lightning.—*Montaigne.*

As nightingales do upon glow-worms feed, so poets live upon the living light of nature and of beauty.—*Bailey.*

Genius in the poet, like the nomad of Arabia, ever a wanderer, still ever makes a home where the well or the palm-tree invites it to pitch the tent. Perpetually passing out of himself and his own positive circumstantial condition of being into other hearts and into other conditions, the poet obtains his knowledge of human life by transporting his own life into the lives of others.—*Bulwer Lytton.*

Poetry is right royal. It puts the individual for the species, the one above the infinite many.
Hazlitt.

A poet ought not to pick nature's pocket. Let him borrow, and so borrow as to repay by the very act of borrowing. Examine nature accurately, but write from recollection, and trust more to the imagination than the memory.—*Coleridge.*

In poetry, which is all fable, truth still is the perfection.—*Shaftesbury.*

Poetry reveals to us the loveliness of nature, brings back the freshness of youthful feeling, revives the relish of simple pleasures, keeps unquenched the enthusiasm which warmed the spring-time of our being, refines youthful love, strengthens our interest in human nature, by vivid delineations of its tenderest and softest feelings, and, through the brightness of its prophetic visions, helps faith to lay hold on the future life.—*Channing.*

Poets utter great and wise things which they do not themselves understand.—*Plato.*

Poetry is music in words, and music is poetry in sound; both excellent sauce, but they have lived and died poor, that made them their meat.—*Fuller.*

Those feel it (poetry) most, and write it best, who forget that it is a work of art.— *Macaulay.*

Poetry deserves the honor it obtains as the eldest offspring of literature, and the fairest. It is the fruitfulness of many plants growing into one flower, and sowing itself over the world in shapes of beauty and color, which differ with the soil that receives and the sun that ripens the seed. In Persia, it comes up the rose of Hafiz; in England, the many-blossomed tree of Shakespeare.—*Willmott.*

Poetry is the morning dream of great minds. *Lamartine.*

Poets should turn philosophers in age, as Pope did. We are apt to grow chilly, when we sit out our fire.—*Sterne.*

Poetry is only born after painful journeys into the vast regions of thought.—*Balzac.*

What I object to is, not the poetry of sadness, but the sadness of poetry. Many of the poets make out the fountain of poetry to be only a fountain of tears.—*Bovee.*

You arrive at truth through poetry, and I arrive at poetry through truth.—*Joubert.*

Poetry should be an alterative; modern playwrights have converted it into a sedative, which they administer in such unseasonable quantities that, like an over-dose of opium, it makes one sick.—*Hare.*

A poet is the translator of the silent language of nature to the world.—*R. W. Griswold.*

It is not metres, but a metre-making agreement, that makes a poem, — a thought so passionate and alive, that, like the spirit of a plant or an animal, it has an architecture of its own, and adorns nature with a new thing.—*Emerson.*

Poetry is the art of substituting shadows, and of lending existence to nothing.—*Burke.*

Poetical taste is the only magician whose wand is not broken. No hand, except its own, can dissolve the fabric of beauty in which it dwells. Genii, unknown to Arabian fable, wait at the portal. Whatever is most precious from the loom or the mine of fancy is poured at its feet. Love, purified by contemplation, visits and cheers it; unseen musicians are heard in the dark; it is Psyche in the palace of Cupid.— *Willmott.*

Poesy is of so subtle a spirit, that in the pouring out of one language into another it will evaporate.—*Denham.*

Thoughts that breathe, and words that burn. *Gray.*

All poets pretend to write for immortality, but the whole tribe have no objection to present pay, and present praise. Lord Burleigh is not the only statesman who has thought one hundred pounds too much for a song, though sung by Spenser; although Oliver Goldsmith is the only poet who ever considered himself to have been overpaid.—*Colton.*

Poetry is the record of the best and happiest moments of the happiest and best minds.— *Shelley.*

Poetry is the attempt which man makes to render his existence harmonious.—*Carlyle.*

To a poet nothing can be useless. Whatever is beautiful, and whatever is dreadful, must be familiar to his imagination; he must be conversant with all that is awfully vast or elegantly little.—*Johnson.*

Poetry is truth dwelling in beauty.— *Gilfillan.*

Poetry has been to me its own exceeding great reward; it has given me the habit of wishing to discover the good and beautiful in all that meets and surrounds me.—*Coleridge.*

Sweet food of sweetly uttered knowledge.— *Sir P. Sidney.*

The poet in prose or verse — the creator — can only stamp his images forcibly on the page in proportion as he has forcibly felt, ardently nursed, and long brooded over them.— *Bulwer Lytton.*

There are so many tender and holy emotions flying about in our inward world, which, like angels, can never assume the body of an outward act; so many rich and lovely flowers spring up which bear no seed, that it is a happiness poetry was invented, which receives into its limbus all these incorporeal spirits, and the perfume of all these flowers.—*Richter.*

Poetry is the natural religion of literature.—
Willmott.

The truest poetry is the most feigning;
and lovers are given to poetry; and what they
swear in poetry, may be said, as lovers they do
feign.—*Shakespeare.*

Poetry and consumption are the most flat-
tering of diseases.—*Shenstone.*

. *Poetry* is born to be the companion of
youth. Those hours may be fleeting as they
are fair. The flower of the grass is not with-
ered sooner. Temptations and cares overleap
the garden. A blazing sword appears at the
gate. The hard paths of toil are to be trodden ;
the soil of life is to he tilled.— *Willmott.*

Poets are all who love, who feel great truths,
and tell them.—*Bailey.*

Now half or more of the beauties of poetry
depend on metaphor or allusion, neither of
which, by a mind uncultivated, can be applied
to their proper counterparts. Their beauty,
of consequence, is like a picture to a blind man.
Shenstone.

How often has poetry been inestimable as a
lonely protest against atheism in a bad age ! —
Emerson.

Language — the machine of the poet — is
best fitted for his purpose in its rudest state.
Nations, like individuals, first perceive, and
then abstract. They advance from particular
images to general terms. Hence the vocabu-
lary of an enlightened society is philosophical ;
that of a half-civilized people is poetical.—
Macaulay.

Poetry is the utterance of truth, — deep,
heartfelt truth. The true poet is very near the
oracle.— *Chapin.*

He who finds elevated and lofty pleasures in
the feeling of poetry is a true poet, though he
had never composed a line of verse in his entire
lifetime.—*Madame Dudevant.*

Poetry is the key to the hieroglyphics of
nature.—*Hare.*

A poet's mind should be clear and unsul-
lied ; and the muses being virgins, their per-
formances should agree with their condition.—
Jeremy Collier.

Poets are too frequently merely poets.—
Disraeli.

Poetry uses the rainbow tints for special
effects, but always keeps its essential object in
the purest white light of truth.—*Holmes.*

Poetry is the robe, the royal apparel, in
which truth asserts its divine origin.—*Beecher.*

The world is full of poetry. The air is
living with its spirit ; and the waves dance to
the music of its melodies, and sparkle in its
brightness.—*Percival.*

There is a pleasure in poetic pains which
only poets know.— *Cowper.*

Let the rules of art become a second nature
to the poet ; let him succeed in applying them
as moral laws are naturally applied by a well-
educated man, and then imagination will re-
cover all its power and all its freedom.—
Schiller.

Ye stars, that are the poetry of heaven ! —
Byron.

As Dante is said to have combined in his
immortal poem the fulness of the Middle Ages,
Burke combined in his own character the poe-
try of the British aristocracy.—*Bancroft.*

Modern poets put a great deal of water in
their ink.— *Goethe.*

Poetry is the breath and finer spirit of all
knowledge ; it is the impassioned expression
which is the countenance of all science.—
Wordsworth.

The intellect colored by the feelings.—
Professor Wilson.

Poetry is the offspring of rarest beauty, be-
got by imagination upon thought, and clad by
taste and fancy, in habiliments of grace.—
Simms.

You will find poetry nowhere unless you
bring some with you.—*Joubert.*

A drainless renown of light is poesy ; it is
the supreme of power ; the might half slumber-
ing on its own right arm ! —*Keats.*

A man may play the fool in everything else
but in poetry.—*Montaigne.*

Poetry is most just to its divine origin when
it administers the comforts and breathes the
thoughts of religion.— *Wordsworth.*

Poetry, the sister spirit of music.—
Madame le Vert.

Poetry and philosophy revolve around the
same centre, and differ, like comets and fixed
stars, only in the orbit they describe.— *Colton.*

I have met with most poetry on trunks ; so
that I am apt to consider the trunk-maker as
the sexton of authorship.—*Byron.*

Poetry is something to make us wiser and
better, by continually revealing those types of
beauty and truth which God has set in all
men's souls.—*Lowell.*

Poetry, with all its obscurity, has a more general as well as a more powerful dominion over the passions, than the art of painting.—
Burke.

Milton said, that no man could write epics who did not live epics.— *Whipple.*

That which moveth the heart most is the best poetry; it comes nearest unto God, the source of all power.—*Landor.*

I wish our clever young poets would remember my homely definitions of prose and poetry; that is, prose — words in their best order; poetry — the best words in the best order.—*Coleridge.*

Poetry comes nearer to vital truth than history.—*Plato.*

There is as much difference between good poetry and fine verses, as between the smell of a flower-garden and of a perfumer's shop.—
Hare.

Everything perishes except truth, and the worship of truth, and poetry, which is its enduring language.—*Jeremy Taylor.*

Of all kinds of ambition, that which pursues poetical fame is the wildest.—*Goldsmith.*

He who, in an enlightened and literary society, aspires to be a great poet, must first become a little child.—*Macaulay.*

A poet who shoots all his arrows at the stars may chance to hit us now and then, but it is only by good luck.—*Lowell.*

Sculpture and painting are moments of life; poetry is life itself, and everything around it and above it.—*Landor.*

POLICY.
Let go thy hold when a great wheel runs down the hill, lest it break thy neck with following it; but the great one that goes up the hill, let him draw thee after.—*Shakespeare.*

We are less thought of for what we are, than for what we have.—*J. Petit, Senn.*

I have heard some of the first judges of whist say, that it was not those who played best by the true laws of the game that would win most, but those who played best to the false play of others; and I am sure it is true of the great game of the world.—*Lord Greville.*

The Devil knew not what he did when he made man politic; he crossed himself by it.—
Shakespeare.

It is not juggling that is to be blamed, but much juggling; for the world cannot be governed without it.—*Selden.*

Were the king at noonday to say, "This day is night," it would behoove us to reply, "Lo! there are the moon and seven stars!"—
Saadi.

By a kind of fashionable discipline, the eye is taught to brighten, the lip to smile, and the whole countenance to emanate with the semblance of friendly welcome, while the bosom is unwarmed by a single spark of genuine kindness and good-will.— *Washington Irving.*

There are times when we are diverted out of errors, but could not be preached out of them.—
Stephen Montague.

A few drops of oil will set the political machine at work, when a ton of vinegar would only corrode the wheels and canker the movements.—*Colton.*

An thou canst not smile as the wind sits, thou wilt catch cold shortly.—*Shakespeare.*

Lay a bridge of silver for a flying enemy.—
Cervantes.

If thou be strong enough to encounter with the times, keep thy station; if not, shift a foot to gain advantage of the times. He that acts a beggar to prevent a thief is never the poorer; it is a great part of wisdom sometimes to seem a fool.—*Quarles.*

Men must learn now with pity to dispense, for policy sits above conscience.—*Shakespeare.*

POLITENESS.
Bowing, ceremonious, formal compliments, stiff civilities, will never be politeness; that must be easy, natural, unstudied; and what will give this but a mind benevolent and attentive to exert that amiable disposition in trifles to all you converse and live with? —*Chatham.*

The true effect of genuine politeness seems to be rather ease than pleasure.—*Johnson.*

The only true source of politeness is consideration, — that vigilant moral sense which never loses sight of the rights, the claims, and the sensibilities of others. This is the one quality, over all others, necessary to make a gentleman.—*Simms.*

Politeness is to goodness what words are to thoughts.—*Joubert.*

Not to perceive the little weaknesses and the idle but innocent affectations of the company may be allowable as a sort of polite duty. The company will be pleased with you if you do, and most probably will not be reformed by you if you do not.—*Chesterfield.*

In the great world, malevolence and disdain never appear in any other garb than that of cold and ceremonious politeness.—*Lathy.*

Politeness has been well defined as benevolence in small things.—*Macaulay.*

That politeness which we put on; in order to keep the assuming and the presumptuous at a proper distance, will generally succeed. But it sometimes happens, that these obtrusive characters are on such excellent terms with themselves, that they put down this very politeness to the score of their own great merits and high pretensions, meeting the coldness of our reserve with a ridiculous condescension of familiarity, in order to set us at ease with ourselves.—*Colton.*

Politeness has been defined to be artificial good-nature; but we may affirm, with much greater propriety, that good-nature is natural politeness.—*Stanislaus.*

I consider that the spirit of politeness is a certain desire to bring it about, that, by our words and manners, others may be pleased with us and with themselves.—*Montesquieu.*

"Politeness," says Witherspoon, "is real kindness kindly expressed"; an admirable definition, and so brief that all may easily remember it. This is the sum and substance of all true politeness. Put it in practice, and all will be charmed with your manners.— *Mrs. Sigourney.*

Good-breeding is benevolence in trifles, the preference of others to ourselves in the little daily occurrences of life.—*Lord Chatham.*

In all the affairs of human life, social as well as political, I have remarked that courtesies of a small and trivial character are the ones which strike deepest to the grateful and appreciating heart.—*Henry Clay.*

Wisdom and virtue are by no means sufficient, without the supplemental laws of good-breeding, to secure freedom from degenerating into rudeness, or self-esteem from swelling into insolence. A thousand incivilities may be committed, and a thousand offices neglected, without any remorse of conscience, or reproach from reason.—*Johnson.*

It is because gold is rare that gilding has been invented, which, without having its solidity, has all its brilliancy. Thus, to replace the kindness we lack, we have devised politeness which has all its appearance.—*De Lévis.*

Politeness is nothing more than an elegant and concealed species of flattery, tending to put the person to whom it is addressed in good-humor and respect with himself.—*Cumberland.*

Politeness does not always inspire goodness, equity, complaisance, and gratitude; it gives at least the appearance of these qualities, and makes man appear outwardly, as he should be within.—*Bruyère.*

26

Nothing is more dissimilar than natural and acquired politeness. The first consists in a willing abnegation of self; the second in a compelled recollection of others.—*Chesterfield.*

True politeness is consideration for the opinions of others. It has been said of dogmatism, that it is only puppyism come to its full growth; and certainly the worst form this quality can assume is that of opinionativeness and arrogance.—*Samuel Smiles.*

As charity covers a multitude of sins before God, so does politeness before men.— *Lord Greville.*

The polite of every country seem to have but one character. A gentleman of Sweden differs but little, except in trifles, from one of any other country. It is among the vulgar we are to find those distinctions which characterize a people.—*Goldsmith.*

It seems to me that the spirit of politeness is a certain attention in causing that, by our words and by our manners, others may be content with us and with themselves.—*Bruyère*

Politeness is not always a sign of wisdom; but the want of it always leaves room for a suspicion of folly, if folly and imprudence are the same.—*Landor.*

Good-breeding is not confined to externals, much less to any particular dress or attitude of the body; it is the art of pleasing, or contributing as much as possible to the ease and happiness of those with whom you converse.— *Fielding.*

When two goats met on a bridge which was too narrow to allow either to pass or return, the goat which lay down that the other might walk over it was a finer gentleman than Lord Chesterfield.—*Cecil.*

He is truly well-bred who knows when to value and when to despise those national peculiarities, which are regarded by some with so much observance; a traveller of taste at once perceives that the wise are polite all the world over, but that fools are polite only at home.— *Bacon.*

True politeness is perfect ease and freedom. It simply consists in treating others just as you love to be treated yourself.—*Chesterfield.*

All politeness is owing to liberty. We polish one another, and rub off our corners and rough sides by a sort of amicable collision. To restrain this, is inevitably to bring a rust upon men's understandings.—*Shaftesbury.*

There is no policy like politeness; and a good manner is the best thing in the world, either to get a good name, or supply the want of it.—*Bulwer Lytton.*

Politeness may be regarded as the zero of friendship's thermometer.—*De Boufflers.*

Among well-bred people a mutual deference is affected, contempt of others is disguised: authority concealed; attention given to each in his turn; and an easy stream of conversation maintained without vehemence, without interruption, without eagerness for victory, and without any airs of superiority.—*Hume.*

Politeness is to goodness what words are to thought. It tells not only on the manners, but on the mind and the heart; it renders the feelings, the opinions, the words, moderate and gentle.—*Joubert.*

Politeness is a mixture of discretion, civility, complaisance, and circumspection spread over all we do and say.—*St. Evremond.*

Do not press your young children into book learning; but teach them politeness, including the whole circle of charities which spring from the consciousness of what is due to their fellow-beings.—*Spurzheim.*

As for politeness, whoever keeps good company, and is not polite, must have formed a resolution, and taken some pains not to be so; otherwise he would naturally and insensibly acquire the air, the address, and the turn of those he converses with.—*Chesterfield.*

Politeness is a kind of anæsthetic which envelops the asperities of our character, so that other people be not wounded by them. We should never be without it, even when we contend with the rude.—*Joubert.*

POLITICS.
He knows very little of mankind who expects, by any facts or reasoning, to convince a determined party-man.—*Lavater.*

Party is the madness of many for the gain of a few.—*Pope.*

If we mean to support the liberty and independence which has cost us so much blood and treasure to establish, we must drive far away the demon of party spirit and local reproach.—*Washington.*

Politics is the science of exigencies.—*Theodore Parker.*

Some have said that it is not the business of private men to meddle with government,—a bold and dishonest saying, which is fit to come from no mouth but that of a tyrant or a slave. To say that private men have nothing to do with government is to say that private men have nothing to do with their own happiness or misery; that people ought not to concern themselves whether they be naked or clothed, fed or starved, deceived or instructed, protected or destroyed.—*Cato.*

Men naturally sympathize with the calamities of individuals; but they are inclined to look on a fallen party with contempt rather than with pity.—*Macaulay.*

The politics of courts are so mean that private people would be ashamed to act in the same way; all is trick and finesse, to which the common cause is sacrificed.—*Nelson.*

A statesman, we are told, should follow public opinion. Doubtless, as a coachman follows his horses; having firm hold on the reins, and guiding them.—*Hare.*

In politics, merit is rewarded by the possessor being raised, like a target, to a position to be fired at.—*Bovee.*

People who declare that they belong to no party certainly do not belong to ours.—*J. Petit, Senn.*

I hate all bungling as I do sin, but partienlarly bungling in politics, which leads to the misery and ruin of many thousands and millions of people.—*Goethe.*

He that aspires to be the head of a party will find it more difficult to please his friends than to perplex his foes. He must often act from false reasons which are weak, because he dares not avow the true reasons which are strong.—*Colton.*

Political men, like goats, usually thrive best among inequalities.—*Landor.*

There is scarcely anything more harmless than political or party malice. It is best to leave it to itself. Opposition and contradiction are the only means of giving it life or duration.—*Witherspoon.*

Measures, not men, have always been my mark.—*Goldsmith.*

Perhaps I do not know what I was made for; but one thing I certainly never was made for, and that is to put principles on and off at the dictation of a party, as a lackey changes his livery at his master's command.—*Horace Mann.*

Responsibility educates, and politics is but another name for God's way of teaching the masses ethics, under the responsibility of great present interests.—*Wendell Phillips.*

There is an infinity of political errors which, being once adopted, become princip s.—*Abbé Raynal.*

The amelioration of the condition of mankind, and the increase of human happiness ought to be the leading objects of every political institution, and the aim of every individual, according to the measure of his power, in the situation he occupies.—*Hamilton.*

Politics resemble religion; attempting to divest either of ceremony is the most certain mode of bringing either into contempt.—
Goldsmith.

Great political questions stir the deepest nature of one half the nation; but they pass far above and over the heads of the other half.
Wendell Phillips.

A politician weakly and amiably in the right is no match for a politician tenaciously and pugnaciously in the wrong. You cannot, by tying an opinion to a man's tongue, make him the representative of that opinion; and at the close of any battle for principles, his name will be found neither among the dead nor among the wounded, but among the missing.—
Whipple.

Such, for wise purposes it is presumed, is the turbulence of human passions in party disputes, when victory, more than truth, is the palm contended for, that "the post of honor is a private station."—*Washington.*

There is no Canaan in politics. As health lies in labor, and there is no royal road to it but through toil, so there is no republican road to safety but in constant distrust.—
Wendell Phillips.

The violation of party faith is of itself too common to excite surprise or indignation. Political friendships are so well understood that we can hardly pity the simplicity they deceive.
Junius.

Politicians think that by stopping up the chimney they can stop its smoking. They try the experiment, they drive the smoke back, and there is more smoke than ever; but they do not see that their want of common-sense has increased the evil they would have prevented.—
Borne.

The strife of politics tends to unsettle the calmest understanding, and ulcerate the most benevolent heart. There are no bigotries or absurdities too gross for parties to create or adopt under the stimulus of political passions.—
Whipple.

A politician thinks of the next election; a statesman of the next generation. A politician looks for the success of his party; a statesman, for that of the country. The statesman wishes to steer, while the politician is satisfied to drift.—*James Freeman Clarke.*

POPULACE.
The multitude which is not brought to act as unity is confusion. That unity which has not its origin in the multitude is tyranny.—
Pascal.

The public sense is in advance of private practice.—*Chapin.*

The pliant populace, those dupes of novelty.
Mallet.

Our slippery people, whose love is never linked to the deserver till his deserts are passed.—*Shakespeare.*

Nothing is so uncertain as the minds of the multitude.—*Leiz.*

The proverbial wisdom of the populace at gates, on roads, and in markets instructs the attentive ear of him who studies man more fully than a thousand rules ostentatiously arranged.—*Lavater.*

The multitude is always in the wrong.—
Earl of Roscommon.

There are occasions when the general belief of the people, even though it be groundless, works its effect as sure as truth itself.—*Schiller.*

The many-headed monster of the pit.—*Pope.*

This gives force to the strong,—that the multitude have no habit of self reliance or original action.—*Emerson.*

POPULARITY.
A generous nation is grateful even for the preservation of its rights, and willingly extends the respect due to the office of a good prince into an affection for his person.—*Junius*

A habitation giddy and unsure hath he that buildeth on the vulgar heart.—*Shakespeare.*

Could the departed, whoever he may be, return in a week after his decease, he would almost invariably find himself at a higher or a lower point than he had formerly ocenpied on the scale of public appreciation.—*Hawthorne.*

The rude reproaches of the rascal herd for the selfsame actions, if successful, would be as grossly lavish in their praise.—
Thomson.

Applause waits on success; the fickle multitude, like the light straw that floats along the stream, glide with the current still, and follow fortune.—*Franklin.*

The great secrets of being courted are, to shun others, and seem delighted with yourself.
Bulwer Lytton.

The most agreeable recompense which we can receive for things which we have done is to see them known, to have them applauded with praises which honor you.—*Molière.*

It is not so difficult a task to plant new truths as to root out old errors; for there is this paradox in men,—they run after that which is new, but are prejudiced in favor of that which is old.—*Colton.*

Our merit gains us the esteem of the virtuous; our star, that of the public.—
Rochefoucauld.

Seek not the favor of the multitude; it is seldom got by honest and lawful means. But seek the testimony of few; and number not voices, but weigh them.—*Kant.*

Popular opinion is the greatest lie in the world.—*Carlyle.*

The vulgar and common esteem is seldom happy in hitting right; and I am much mistaken, if, amongst the writings of my time, the worst are not those which have most gained the popular applause.—*Montaigne.*

Yet has the popular voice much potency.—
Æschylus.

The greatness of a popular character is less according to the ratio of his genius than the sympathy he shows with the prejudices and even the absurdities of his time. Fanatics do not select the cleverest, but the most fanatical leaders ; as was evidenced in the choice of Robespierre by the French Jacobins, and in that of Cromwell by the English Puritans.—
Lamartine.

There are people who, like new songs, are in vogue only for a time.—*Rochefoucauld.*

I put no account on him who esteems himself just as the popular breath may chance to raise him.—*Goethe.*

As inclination changes, thus ebbs and flows the unstable tide of public judgment.—*Schiller.*

The love of popularity seems little else than the love of being beloved ; and is only blamable when a person aims at the affections of a people by means in appearance honest, but in their end pernicious and destructive.—*Shenstone.*

Whatever is popular deserves attention.—
Mackintosh.

Be as far from desiring the popular love as fearful to deserve the popular hate ; ruin dwells in both : the one will hug thee to death; the other will crush thee to destruction : to escape the first, be not ambitious ; to avoid the second, be not seditious.—*Quarles.*

Woe unto you when all men speak well of you ! —*Bible.*

Those men who are commended by everybody must be very extraordinary men ; or, which is more probable, very inconsiderable men.—*Lord Greville.*

There is what is called the highway to posts and honors, and there is a cross and by way, which is much the shortest.—*Bruyère.*

Avoid popularity ; it has many snares, and no real benefit.—*William Penn.*

The common people are but ill judges of a man's merits; they are slaves to fame, and their eyes are dazzled with the pomp of titles and large retinue. No wonder, then, that they bestow their honors on those who least deserve them.—*Horace.*

POSITION.
The higher we rise, the more isolated we become ; and all elevations are cold.—
De Boufflers.

Lord Bacon has compared those who move in higher spheres to those heavenly bodies in the firmament, which have much admiration, but little rest. And it is not necessary to invest a wise man with power, to convince him that it is a garment bedizened with gold, which dazzles the beholder by its splendor, but oppresses the wearer by its weight.—*Colton.*

In general, it is not very difficult for little minds to attain splendid situations. It is much more difficult for great minds to attain the place to which their merit fully entitles them.—
Baron de Grimm.

A great many men, — some comparatively small men now, — if put in the right position, would be Luthers and Columbuses.—*Chapin.*

POSITIVENESS.
Positiveness is a most absurd foible. If you are in the right, it lessens your triumph ; if in the wrong, it adds shame to your defeat.—
Sterne.

The most positive men are the most credulous, since they most believe themselves, and advise most with their falsest flatterer and worst enemy, — their own self-love.—*Pope.*

Every one of his opinions appears to himself to be written with sunbeams.—*Watts.*

Positiveness is a good quality for preachers and orators, because whoever would obtrude his thoughts and reasons upon a multitude will convince others the more, as he appears convinced himself.—*Swift.*

POSTERITY.
It is pleasant to observe how free the present age is in laying taxes on the next. "Future ages shall talk of this ; they shall be famous to all posterity" ; whereas their time and thoughts will be taken up about present things, as ours are now.—*Swift.*

Of this our ancestors complained, we ourselves do so, and our posterity will equally lament, because goodness has vanished, evil habits prevail, while human affairs grow worse and worse, sinking into an abyss of wickedness.—*Seneca.*

Time will unveil all things to posterity; it is a chatterer, and speaks to those who do not question it.—*Euripides.*

We are too careless of posterity; not considering that as they are, so the next generation will be.—*William Penn.*

What does not wasting time change! The age of our parents, worse than that of our grandsires, has brought us forth more impious still, and we shall produce a more vicious progeny.—*Horace.*

If we would amend the world we should mend ourselves; and teach our children to be, not what we are, but what they should be.—*William Penn.*

POVERTY.

It is an ill thing to be ashamed of one's poverty; but much worse not to make use of lawful means to avoid it.—*Thucydides.*

It is the great privilege of poverty to be happy unenvied, to be healthy without physic, secure without a guard, and to obtain from the bounty of nature what the great and wealthy are compelled to procure by the help of art.—*Johnson.*

There is a noble manner of being poor, and who does not know it will never be rich.—*Seneca.*

Few things in this world trouble people more than poverty, or the fear of poverty; and indeed it is a sore affliction; but, like all other ills that flesh is heir to, it has its antidote, its reliable remedy. The judicious application of industry, prudence, and temperance is a certain cure.—*Hosea Ballou.*

Want of prudence is too frequently the want of virtue; nor is there on earth a more powerful advocate for vice than poverty.—*Goldsmith.*

Poverty has, in large cities, very different appearances. It is often concealed in splendor, and often in extravagance. It is the care of a very great part of mankind to conceal their indigence from the rest. They support themselves by temporary expedients, and every day is lost in contriving for to-morrow.—*Johnson.*

My poverty, but not my will, consents.—*Shakespeare.*

Seneca, with two millions out at usury, can afford to chant the praises of poverty; but for our own part, we prefer the fine extravagance of that philosopher who declared that "no man was as rich as all men ought to be."—*Whipple.*

We want fewer things to live in poverty with satisfaction, than to live magnificently with riches.—*St. Evremond.*

The real wants of nature are the measure of enjoyments, as the foot is the measure of the shoe. We can call only the want of what is necessary poverty.—*St. Clement.*

Lord God, I thank thee that thou hast been pleased to make me a poor and indigent man upon earth. I have neither house nor land nor money, to leave behind me. Thou hast given me wife and children, whom I now restore to thee. Lord, nourish, teach, and preserve them as thou hast me.—*Luther.*

He travels safe and not unpleasantly, who is guarded by poverty and guided by love.—*Sir P. Sidney.*

Chill penury weighs down the heart itself; and though it sometimes be endured with calmness, it is but the calmness of despair.—*Mrs. Jameson.*

The greatest hardship of poverty is that it tends to make men ridiculous.—*Juvenal.*

Rags, which are the reproach of poverty, are the beggar's robes, and graceful insignia of his profession, his tenure, his full dress, the suit in which he is expected to show himself in public.—*Lamb.*

What is even poverty itself, that a man should murmur under it? It is but as the pain of piercing a maiden's ear, and you hang precious jewels in the wound.—*Richter.*

Through tattered clothes small vices do appear; robes and furred gowns hide all.—*Shakespeare.*

Poverty is, except where there is an actual want of food and raiment, a thing much more imaginary than real. The shame of poverty, — the shame of being thought poor, — it is a great and fatal weakness, though arising in this country, from the fashion of the times themselves.—*Cobbett.*

In one important respect a man is fortunate in being poor. His responsibility to God is so much the less.—*Bovee.*

If rich, it is easy enough to conceal our wealth; but, if poor, it is not quite so easy to conceal our poverty. We shall find that it is less difficult to hide a thousand guineas than one hole in our coat.—*Colton.*

It is not poverty so much as pretence that harasses a ruined man, — the struggle between a proud mind and an empty purse, — the keeping up a hollow show that must soon come to an end. Have the courage to appear poor, and you disarm poverty of its sharpest sting.—*Mrs. Jameson.*

Poverty is the test of civility and the touchstone of friendship.—*Hazlitt.*

Poverty often deprives a man of all spirit and virtue. It is hard for an empty bag to stand upright.—*Franklin.*

Not to be able to bear poverty is a shameful thing, but not to know how to chase it away by work is a more shameful thing yet.—
Pericles.

To be poor, and to seem poor, is a certain method never to rise.—*Goldsmith.*

Poverty is only contemptible when it is felt to be so. Doubtless the best way to make our poverty respectable is to seem never to feel it as an evil.—*Bovee.*

Men praise poverty, as the African worships Mumbo Jumbo, — from terror of the malign power, and a desire to propitiate it.—
Alexander Smith.

It is only luxury and avarice that make poverty grievous to us; for it is a very small matter that does our business, and when we have provided against cold, hunger, and thirst, all the rest is but vanity and excess.—*Seneca.*

Poverty makes people satirical, soberly, sadly, bitterly satirical.—*Haines Friswell.*

That man is to be accounted poor, of whatever rank he be, and suffers the pains of poverty, whose expenses exceed his resources ; and no man is, properly speaking, poor, but he.—
Paley.

If poverty is the mother of crimes, want of sense is the father of them.—*Bruyère.*

Poverty must make a match, or make an assignation, or make some bargain scandalous to the man who drives it. More shillings conceded to the making of a shirt would double the religion of mankind.—*John Weiss.*

Poverty palls the most generous spirits ; it cows industry, and casts resolution itself into despair.—*Addison.*

There is nothing keeps longer than a middling fortune, and nothing melts away sooner than a great one. Poverty treads upon the heels of great and unexpected riches.—*Bruyère.*

Poverty snatches the reins out of the hand of piety.—*Saadi.*

It would be a considerable consolation to the poor and discontented, could they but see the means whereby the wealth they covet has been acquired, or the misery that it entails.—
Zimmermann.

It is impossible to diminish poverty by the multiplication of goods ; for, manage as we may, misery and suffering will always cleave to the border of superfluity.—*Jacobi.*

He had a prince's mind imprisoned in a poor man's purse.—*Fuller.*

O poverty! or what is called a reverse of fortune ! among the many bitter ingredients that thou hast in thy most bitter cup, thou hast not one so insupportably bitter as that which brings us in close and hourly contact with the earthenware and huckaback beings of the nether world. Even the vulgarity of inanimate things it requires time to get accustomed to ; but living, breathing, bustling, plotting, planning, human vulgarity is a species of moral ipecacuanha, enough to destroy any comfort.—*Carlyle.*

Poverty, labor, and calamity are not without their luxuries, which the rich, the indolent, and the fortunate in vain seek for.—*Hazlitt.*

The poor man is a kind of money that is not current ; the subject of every idle housewife's chat ; the offscum of the people ; the dust of the street, first trampled under foot and then thrown on the dunghill ; in conclusion, the poor man is the rich man's ass.—*Alfarache.*

We should not so much esteem our poverty as a misfortune, were it not that the world treats it so much as a crime.—*Bovee.*

There is not such a mighty difference as some men imagine between the poor and the rich ; in pomp, show, and opinion there is a great deal, but little as to the pleasures and satisfactions of life : they enjoy the same earth and air and heavens ; hunger and thirst make the poor man's meat and drink as pleasant and relishing as all the varieties which cover the rich man's table ; and the labor of a poor man is more healthful, and many times more pleasant, too, than the ease and softness of the rich.—
Sherlock.

Poverty possesses this disease; through want it teaches a man evil.—*Euripides.*

How like a railway-tunnel is the poor man's life, with the light of childhood at one end, the intermediate gloom, and only the glimmer of a future life at the other extremity ! —*Bovee.*

When we have only a little we should be satisfied ; for this reason, that those best enjoy abundance who are contented with the least, and so that the pains of poverty are removed, simple fare can give a relish equal to the most expensive luxuries.—*Epicurus.*

An avowal of poverty is a disgrace to no man ; to make no effort to escape from it is indeed disgraceful.—*Thucydides.*

That poverty which is not the daughter of the spirit is but the mother of shame and reproach ; it is a disreputation that drowns all the other good parts that are in man ; it is a disposition to all kind of evil ; it is man's greatest foe.—*Alfarache.*

For a generous and noble spirit cannot be expected to dwell in the breast of men who are struggling for their daily bread.—*Dionysius.*

Wealth and poverty are seen for what they are. It begins to be seen that the poor are only they who feel poor, and poverty consists in feeling poor. The rich, as we reckon them, and among them the very rich, in a true scale would be found very indigent and ragged.—*Emerson.*

It requires a great deal of poetry to gild the pill of poverty, and then it will pass current only in theory; the reality is a dead failure! — *Madame Deluzy.*

Poor and content is rich, and rich enough; but riches, fineless, is as poor as winter to him that ever fears he shall be poor.—*Shakespeare.*

The extent of poverty in the world is much exaggerated. Our sensitiveness makes half our poverty; our fears, — anxieties for ills that never happen, — a greater part of the other half.— *Bovee.*

Nature makes us poor only when we want necessaries, but custom gives the name of poverty to the want of superfluities.—*Johnson.*

No man is poor who does not think himself so. But if in a full fortune with impatience he desires more, he proclaims his wants and his beggarly condition.—*Jeremy Taylor.*

All I desire is, that my poverty may not be a burden to myself, or make me so to others; and that is the best state of fortune that is neither directly necessitous nor far from it. A mediocrity of fortune, with gentleness of mind, will preserve us from fear or envy; which is a desirable condition; for no man wants power to do mischief.—*Seneca.*

Poverty persuades a man to do and suffer everything that he may escape from it.—*Lucian.*

One solitary philosopher may be great, virtuous, and happy in the depth of poverty, but not a whole people.—*Isaak Iselin.*

POWER.

Arbitrary power is the natural object of temptation to a prince; as wine or women to a young fellow, or a bribe to a judge, or avarice to old age, or vanity to a woman.—*Swift.*

I know of nothing sublime which is not some modification of power.—*Burke.*

It is an observation no less just than common, that there is no stronger test of a man's real character than power and authority, exciting, as they do, every passion, and discovering every latent vice.—*Plutarch.*

All violence, all that is dreary and repels, is not power, but the absence of power.—*Emerson.*

I will tell you where there is power: where the dew lies upon the hills, and the rain has moistened the roots of the various plants; where the sunshine pours steadily; where the brook runs babbling along, there is a beneficent power.—*Chapin.*

Power is seldom innocent, and envy is the yokefellow of eminence.—*Tupper.*

Power is always the more immoderate and the more jealous when it rises out of usurpation; but those who contend for liberty of any kind should, in no instance, be its abettors.— *Landor.*

It is godlike to have power, but not to kill. *Beaumont and Fletcher.*

Nothing, indeed, but the possession of some power can with any certainty discover what at the bottom is the true character of any man. *Burke.*

We have more power than will; and it is often by way of excuse to ourselves that we fancy things are impossible.—*Rochefoucauld.*

Power is so characteristically calm that calmness in itself has the aspect of power. And forbearance implies strength.— *Bulwer Lytton.*

Power obeys reality, and not appearances; power is according to quality, and not quantity. *Emerson.*

Power and courtly influence form an intoxicating draught even when raised to the lips of an ascetic and a saint.—*Sir J. Stephen.*

Power is ever stealing from the many to the few. The manna of popular liberty must be gathered each day, or it is rotten.— *Wendell Phillips.*

Beware of dissipating your powers; strive constantly to concentrate them. Genius thinks it can do whatever it sees others doing, but it is sure to repent of every ill-judged outlay.— *Goethe.*

Power safely defied touches its downfall.— *Macaulay.*

Power, like the diamond, dazzles the beholder, and also the wearer; it dignifies meanness; it magnifies littleness; to what is contemptible, it gives authority; to what is low, exaltation.— *Colton.*

Even in war moral power is to physical as three parts out of four.—*Napoleon.*

The greater a man is in power above others, the more he ought to excel them in virtue. None ought to govern who is not better than the governed.—*Publius Syrus.*

Power and liberty are like heat and moisture; where they are well mixed, everything prospers; where they are single, they are destructive.—*Saville.*

Power will intoxicate the best hearts, as wine the strongest heads. No man is wise enough, nor good enough to be trusted with unlimited power.—*Colton.*

Power is according to quality and not quantity. How much more are men than nations!—*Emerson.*

Nothing really succeeds which is not based on reality; sham, in a large sense, is never successful; in the life of the individual, as in the more comprehensive life of the state, pretension is nothing and power is everything.—*Whipple.*

Where power is absent we may find the robe of genius, but we miss the throne.—*Landor.*

Experience constantly proves that every man who has power is impelled to abuse it; he goes on till he is pulled up by some limits. Who would say it! virtue even has need of limits.—*Montesquieu.*

As thou directest the power, harm or advantage will follow, and the torrent that swept the valley may be led to turn a mill.—*Tupper.*

There is always room for a man of force, and he makes room for many. Society is a troop of thinkers, and the best heads among them take the best places. A feeble man can see the farms that are fenced and tilled, the houses that are built. The strong man sees the possible houses and farms. His eye makes estates as fast as the sun breeds clouds.—*Emerson.*

Nothing destroys authority so much as the unequal and untimely interchange of power, pressed too far, and relaxed too much.—*Bacon.*

PRAISE.

Be not too great a niggard in the commendations of him that professes thy own quality: if he deserve thy praise, thou hast discovered thy judgment; if not, thy modesty: honor either returns or reflects to the giver.—*Quarles.*

It is always esteemed the greatest mischief a man can do to those whom he loves, to raise men's expectations of them too high by undue and impertinent commendations.—*Sprat.*

No ashes are lighter than those of incense, and few things burn out sooner.—*Landor.*

What a person praises is perhaps a surer standard, even, than what he condemns, of his character, information, and abilities. No wonder, then, that in this prudent country most people are so shy of praising anything.—*Hare.*

For the good, when praised, feel something of disgust, if to excess commended.—*Euripides.*

Among the smaller duties of life, I hardly know any one more important than that of not praising where praise is not due. Reputation is one of the prizes for which men contend : it is, as Mr. Burke calls it, "the cheap defence and ornament of nations." It produces more labor and more talent than twice the wealth of a country could ever rear up. It is the coin of genius, and it is the imperious duty of every man to bestow it with the most scrupulous justice and the wisest economy.—*Sydney Smith.*

Praise is so pleasing to the mind of man, that it is the original motive of almost all our actions.—*Johnson.*

We praise all good thoughts, all good words, all good deeds, which are and will be, and we likewise keep clean and pure all that is good.—*Zend Avesta.*

Praise, like gold and diamonds, owes its value only to its scarcity. It becomes cheap as it becomes vulgar, and will no longer raise expectation or animate enterprise.—*Johnson.*

It is not he who searches for praise who finds it.—*Rivarol.*

Praise follows Truth afar off, and only overtakes her at the grave; Plausibility clings to her skirts and holds her back till then.—*Lowell.*

Words of praise, indeed, are almost as necessary to warm a child into a genial life as acts of kindness and affection. Judicious praise is to children what the sun is to flowers.—*Bovee.*

It is a great happiness to be praised of them that are most praiseworthy.—*Sir P. Sidney.*

I should entertain a mean opinion of myself if all men or the most part praised and admired me ; it would prove me to be somewhat like them.—*Landor.*

Praise in the beginning is agreeable enough, and we receive it as a favor; but when it comes in great quantities, we regard it only as a debt, which nothing but our merit could extort.—*Goldsmith.*

Those who are greedy of praise prove that they are poor in merit.—*Plutarch.*

Praise was originally a pension paid by the world; but the moderns, finding the trouble and charge too great in collecting it, have lately bought out the fee-simple; since which time the right of presentation is wholly in ourselves.—*Swift.*

We are all excited by the love of praise, and it is the noblest spirits that feel it most.—*Cicero.*

To be forward to praise others implies either great eminence, that can afford to part with applause ; or great quickness of discernment, with confidence in our own judgments ; or great sincerity and love of truth, getting the better of our self-love.—*Hazlitt.*

Praise undeserved is satire in disguise.—
Pope.

Allow no man to be so familiar with you as to praise you to your face. Your vanity by this means will want its food ; at the same time your passion for esteem will be more fully gratified : men will praise you in their actions; where you now receive one compliment, you will then receive twenty civilities.—*Steele.*

Praise is the reflection of virtue ; but it is glass, or body, which giveth the reflection.—
Bacon.

I will not much commend others to themselves, I will not at all commend myself to others. So to praise any to their faces is a kind of flattery, but to praise myself to any is the height of folly. He that boasts his own praises speaks ill of himself, and much derogates from his true deserts. It is worthy of blame to affect commendation.—*Arthur Warwick.*

Praise never gives us much pleasure unless it concur with our own opinion, and extol us for those qualities in which we chiefly excel.—
Hume.

A little praise is good for a shy temper ; it teaches it to rely on the kindness of others.—
Landor.

There are reproaches which praise, and praises which slander.—*Rochefoucauld.*

Praise is the symbol which represents sympathy, and which the mind insensibly substitutes for its recollection and language.—
Mackintosh.

His praise is lost who waits till all commend.—*Pope.*

It is a fault against politeness to praise immoderately, in the presence of those who are singing or playing to you upon an instrument, some other person who has these same talents ; as before those who read you their verses, another poet.—*Bruyère.*

Praise is only praise when well addressed.—
Gay.

Whenever you commend, add your reasons for doing so ; it is this which distinguishes the approbation of a man of sense from the flattery of sycophants and admiration of fools.—*Steele.*

To praise anything well is an argument of much more wit than to abuse.—*Tillotson.*

Let another man praise thee, and not thine own mouth : a stranger, and not thine own lips.—*Bible.*

Solid pudding against empty praise.—
Pope.

We are not fond of praising, and never praise any one except from interested motives. Praise is a clever, concealed, and delicate flattery, which gratifies in different ways the giver and the receiver. The one takes it as a recompense of his merit, and the other bestows it to display his equity and discernment.—
Rochefoucauld.

I know no manner of speaking so offensive as that of giving praise and closing it with an exception.—*Steele.*

They are the most frivolous and superficial of mankind, who can be much delighted with that praise which they themselves know to be altogether unmerited.—*Adam Smith.*

Half-uttered praise is to the curious mind, as to the eye half-veiled beauty is, more precious than the whole.—*Joanna Baillie.*

Every one that has been long dead has a due proportion of praise allotted him, in which, while he lived, his friends were too profuse and his enemies too sparing.—*Addison.*

Cram us with praise, and make us as fat as tame things. One good deed, dying tongueless, slaughters a thousand waiting upon that ; our praises are our wages. You may ride us with one soft kiss a thousand furlongs, ere with spur we heat an acre.—*Shakespeare.*

We always make our friend appear awkward and ridiculous by giving him a laced suit of tawdry qualifications, which nature never intended him to wear.—*Junius.*

Praise no man too liberally before his face, nor censure him too lavishly behind his back : the one savors of flattery ; the other of malice ; and both are reprehensible : the true way to advance another's virtue is to follow it ; and the best means to cry down another's vice is to decline it.—*Quarles.*

Men are offended if we bestow on them praises which show that we quite understand the extent of their abilities ; few people are modest enough to endure without annoyance that their depth should be fathomed.—
Vauvenargues.

As the Greek said, " Many men know how to flatter, few men know how to praise."
Wendell Phillips.

Thou mayst be more prodigal of praise when thou writest a letter than when thou speakest in presence.—*Fuller.*

Praise has different effects, according to the mind it meets with; it makes a wise man modest, but a fool more arrogant, turning his weak brain giddy.—*Feltham.*

True praise is frequently the lot of the humble; false praise is always confined to the great.—*Henry Home.*

There is a species of ferocity in rejecting indiscriminately all kinds of praises; we should be accessible to those which are given to us by good people, who praise in us sincerely praiseworthy things.—*Bruyère.*

Sweet is the breath of praise when given by those whose own high merit claims the praise they give.—*Hannah More.*

The shame that arises from praise which we do not deserve often makes us do things we should never otherwise have attempted.—*Rochefoucauld.*

Praise is but virtue's shadow; who courts her doth more the handmaid than the dame admire.—*Heath.*

The praises of others may be of use in teaching us, not what we are, but what we ought to be.—*Hare.*

Commend a fool for his wit, or a knave for his honesty, and they will receive you into their bosom.—*Fielding.*

Praise is the daughter of present power.—*Swift.*

It is no flattery to give a friend a due character; for commendation is as much the duty of a friend as reprehension.—*Plutarch.*

We should not be too niggardly in our praise, for men will do more to support a character than to raise one.—*Colton.*

PRAYER.

I desire no other evidence of the truth of Christianity than the Lord's Prayer.—*Madame de Staël.*

The protection of God cannot, without sacrilege, be invoked but in behalf of justice and right.—*Kossuth.*

For the most part, we should pray rather in aspiration than petition, rather by hoping than requesting; in which spirit also we may breathe a devout wish for a blessing on others upon occasions when it might be presumptuous to beg it.—*Leigh Hunt.*

Faith builds in the dungeon and the lazar-house its sublimest shrines; and up, through roofs of stone, that shut out the eye of heaven, ascends the ladder where the angels glide to and fro, — prayer.—*Bulwer Lytton.*

Our prayer and God's mercy are like two buckets in a well; while the one ascends, the other descends.—*Bishop Hopkins.*

We should pray with as much earnestness as those who expect everything from God; we should act with as much energy as those who expect everything from themselves.—*Colton.*

A good man's prayers will from the deepest dungeon climb heaven's height, and bring a blessing down.—*Joanna Baillie.*

Each time thou wishest to decide upon performing some enterprise, raise the eyes to heaven, pray God to bless thy project; if thou canst make that prayer, accomplish thy work.—*Leopold Schefer.*

Leave not off praying to God; for either praying will make thee leave off sinning, or continuing in sin will make thee desist from praying.—*Fuller.*

Prayer is not eloquence, but earnestness; not the definition of helplessness, but the feeling of it; not figures of speech, but compunction of soul.—*Hannah More.*

Heaven is never deaf but when man's heart is dumb.—*Quarles.*

Prayer among men is supposed a means to change the person to whom we pray; but prayer to God doth not change him, but fits us to receive the things prayed for.—*Stillingfleet.*

Between the humble and contrite heart and the majesty of Heaven there are no barriers. The only password is prayer.—*Hosea Ballou.*

Good prayers never come creeping home. I am sure I shall receive either what I ask or what I should ask.—*Bishop Hall.*

More things are wrought by prayer than the world dreams of.—*Tennyson.*

"Prayer," says St. Jerome, "is a groan." Ah! our groans are prayers as well. The very cry of distress is an involuntary appeal to that invisible Power whose aid the soul invokes.—*Madame Swetchine.*

Prayer is the voice of faith.—*Horne.*

Thou, when thou prayest, enter into thy closet, and when thou hast shut thy door, pray to thy Father which is in secret; and thy Father, which seeth in secret, shall reward thee openly.—*Bible.*

The first petition that we are to make to Almighty God is. for a good conscience, the next for health of mind, and then of body.—*Seneca.*

The greatest prayer is patience.—*Buddha.*

Let prayer be the key of the morning and the bolt of the evening.—*Matthew Henry.*

Prayer has a right to the word "ineffable." It is an hour of outpourings which words cannot express, — of that interior speech which we do not articulate, even when we employ it.—*Madame Swetchine.*

We pray for trifles without so much as a thought of the greatest blessings; and we are not ashamed, many times, to ask God for that which we should blush to own to our neighbor.—*Seneca.*

Prayer is the slender nerve that moveth the muscles of Omnipotence.—*Tupper.*

No man can hinder our private addresses to God; every man can build a chapel in his breast, himself the priest, his heart the sacrifice, and the earth he treads on the altar.—*Jeremy Taylor.*

The simple heart that freely asks in love, obtains.—*Whittier.*

The best and sweetest flowers of Paradise God gives to his people when they are upon their knees. Prayer is the gate of heaven, or key to let us in to Paradise.—*Rev. T. Brooks.*

Is not prayer a study of truth, a sally of the soul into the unfound infinite? No man ever prayed heartily without learning something.—*Emerson.*

Prayer purifies: it is a self-preached sermon.—*Richter.*

When a pump is frequently used, the water pours out at the first stroke, because it is high; but, if the pump has not been used for a long time, the water gets low, and when you want it you must pump a long while; and the water comes only after great efforts. It is so with prayer. If we are instant in prayer, every little circumstance awakens the disposition to pray, and desire and words are always ready; but, if we neglect prayer, it is difficult for us to pray, for the water in the well gets low.—*Felix Neff.*

Prayer is to religion what thinking is to philosophy. To pray is to make religion.—*Novalis.*

O, when the heart is full, when bitter thoughts come crowding thickly up for utterance, and the poor common words of courtesy are such a very mockery, how much the bursting heart may pour itself in prayer!—*Willis.*

Prayers are but the body of the bird; desires are its angel's wings.—*Jeremy Taylor.*

Prayer is the wing wherewith the soul flies to heaven, and meditation the eye wherewith we see God.—*St. Ambrose.*

In prayer it is better to have a heart without words than words without a heart.—*Bunyan.*

Prayer is intended to increase the devotion of the individual, but if the individual himself prays he requires no formula; he pours himself forth much more naturally in self-chosen and connected thoughts before God, and scarcely requires words at all. Real inward devotion knows no prayer but that arising from the depths of its own feelings.—*Wilhelm von Humboldt.*

Embark in no enterprise which you cannot submit to the test of prayer.—*Hosea Ballou.*

The Ædiles among the Romans had their doors always standing open, that all who had petitions might have free access to them. The door of heaven is always open for the prayers of God's people.—*T. Watson.*

Prayer is a shield to the soul, a sacrifice to God, and a scourge for Satan.—*Bunyan.*

Perfect prayers without a spot or blemish, though not one word be spoken, and no phrases known to mankind be tampered with, always pluck the heart out of the earth and move it softly, like a censer, to and fro beneath the face of heaven.—*John Weiss.*

If He prayed who was without sin, how much more it becometh a sinner to pray!—*St. Cyprian.*

We, ignorant of ourselves, beg often our own harm, which the wise powers deny us for our good; so find we profit by losing of our prayers.—*Shakespeare.*

When we pray for any virtue, we should cultivate the virtue as well as pray for it; the form of your prayers should be the rule of your life; every petition to God is a precept to man. Look not, therefore, upon your prayers as a short method of duty and salvation only, but as a perpetual monition of duty, by what we require of God we see what he requires of us.—*Jeremy Taylor.*

A Christian will find his parenthesis for prayer, even through his busiest hours.—*Cecil.*

Premeditation of thought and brevity of expression are the great ingredients of that reverence that is required to a pious and acceptable prayer.—*South.*

PREACHING.

It requires as much reflection and wisdom to know what is not to be put into a sermon as what is.—*Cecil.*

Remember that God is as near to our mouth when we speak, as that man is who leans his ear to our whispers.—*Young.*

I love a serious preacher, who speaks for my sake and not for his own ; who seeks my salvation, and not his own vainglory. He best deserves to be heard who uses speech only to clothe his thoughts, and his thoughts only to promote truth and virtue. Nothing is more detestable than a professed declaimer, who retails his discourses as a quack does his medicine.—*Massillon.*

Some plague the people with too long sermons ; for the faculty of listening is a tender thing, and soon becomes weary and satiated.—*Luther.*

The meanness of the earthen vessel, which conveys to others the gospel treasure, takes nothing from the value of the treasure. A dying hand may sign a deed of gift of incalculable value. A shepherd's boy may point out the way to a philosopher. A beggar may be the bearer of an invaluable present.—*Cecil.*

Many a meandering discourse one hears, in which the preacher aims at nothing, and — hits it.—*Whately.*

The minister should preach as if he felt that although the congregation own the church, and have bought the pews, they have not bought him. His soul is worth no more than any other man's, but it is all he has, and he cannot be expected to sell it for a salary. The terms are by no means equal. If a parishioner does not like the preaching, he can go elsewhere and get another pew, but the preacher cannot get another soul.—*Chapin.*

Grant that I may never rack a Scripture simile beyond the true intent thereof, lest, instead of sucking milk, I squeeze blood out of it.—*Fuller.*

The Christian ministry is the worst of all trades, but the best of all professions.—*Newton.*

All things with which we deal preach to us. What is a farm but a mute gospel ? The chaff and the wheat, weeds and plants, blight, rain, insects, sun, — it is a sacred emblem from the first furrow of spring to the last stack which the snow of winter overtakes in the fields.—*Emerson.*

It was said of one who preached very well, and lived very ill, " that when he was out of the pulpit it was pity he should ever go into it ; and when he was in the pulpit, it was pity he should ever come out of it."—*Fuller.*

The defects of a preacher are soon spied. Let a preacher be endued with ten virtues, and have but one fault, that one fault will eclipse and darken all his virtues and gifts, so evil is the world in these times.—*Luther.*

The minister's brain is often the " poorbox " of the church.—*Whipple.*

Gospel ministers should not only be like dials on watches, or mile-stones upon the road, but like clocks and larums, to sound the alarm to sinners. Aaron wore bells as well as pomegranates, and the prophets were commanded to lift up their voice like a trumpet. A sleeping sentinel may be the loss of the city.—*Bishop Hall.*

It is a good divine that follows his own instructions.—*Shakespeare.*

The grand aim of a minister must be the exhibition of gospel truth. Statesmen may make the greatest blunders in the world, but that is. not his affair. Like a king's messenger, he must not stop to take care of a person fallen down : if he can render any kindness consistently with his duty, he will do it ; if not, he will prefer his office.—*Cecil.*

A preacher should have the skill to teach the unlearned simply, roundly, and plainly ; for teaching is of more importance than exhorting.—*Luther.*

Whatever is preached to us, and whatever we learn, we should still remember that it is man that gives, and man that receives ; it is a mortal hand that presents it to us, it is a mortal hand that accepts it.—*Montaigne.*

Pulpit discourses have insensibly dwindled from speaking to reading ; a practice of itself sufficient to stifle every germ of eloquence.—*Sydney Smith.*

Of all sorts of flattery, that which comes from a solemn character and stands before a sermon is the worst-complexioned. Such commendation is a satire upon the author, makes the text look mercenary, and disables the discourse from doing service.—*Jeremy Collier.*

A good discourse is that from which one can take nothing without taking the life.—*Fenelon.*

It is a glorious occupation, vivifying and self-sustaining in its nature, to struggle with ignorance, and discover to the inquiring minds of the masses the clear cerulean blue of heavenly truth.—*Hosea Ballou.*

He who the sword of heaven will bear should be as holy as severe.—*Shakespeare.*

The theatre has often been at variance with the pulpit ; they ought not to quarrel. How much is it to be wished that in both the celebration of nature and of God were intrusted to none but men of noble minds ! —*Goethe.*

In pulpit eloquence, the grand difficulty lies here ; to give the subject all the dignity it so fully deserves, without attaching any importance to ourselves. The Christian messenger cannot think too highly of his Prince, or too humbly of himself.—*Colton.*

· That is not the best sermon which makes the hearers go away talking to one another, and praising the speaker, but which makes them go away thoughtful and serious, and hastening to be alone.—*Burnet.*

The pulpit is a clergyman's parade; the parish is his field of active service.—*Southey.*

The object of preaching is constantly to remind mankind of what mankind are constantly forgetting; not to supply the defects of human intelligence, but to fortify the feebleness of human resolutions.—*Sydney Smith.*

This I quarrelled at, that he went far from his text to come close to me, and so was faulty himself in telling me of my faults.—*Fuller.*

When I compare the clamorous preaching and passionate declamation too common in the Christian world with the composed dignity, the deliberate wisdom, the freedom from all extravagance, which characterized Jesus, I can imagine no greater contrast; and I am sure that the fiery zealot is no representative of Christianity.—*Channing.*

O that our prelates would be as diligent to sow the corn of good doctrine, as Satan is to sow cockle and darnel! —*Latimer.*

I should not like to preach to a congregation who all believed as I believe. I would as lief preach to a basket of eggs in their smooth compactness and oval formality.—*Chapin*

Nothing is text but what is spoken of in the Bible and meant there for person and place; the rest is application; which a discreet man may do well; but it is his scripture, not the Holy Ghost's. First, in your sermons use your logic, and then your rhetoric; rhetoric without logic is like a tree with leaves and blossoms, but no root.—*Selden.*

· Sermons in stones, and good in everything.
Shakespeare.

When men come with nets in their ears, it is good for the preacher to have neither fish nor fowl in his tongue. But blessed be God, now we need not lie at so close a guard.—*Fuller.*

The life of a pious minister is visible rhetoric.—*Hooker.*

Formerly, it was the fashion to preach the natural; now it is the ideal. People too often forget that these things are profoundly compatible; that in a beautiful work of imagination the natural should be ideal, and the ideal natural.—*Schlegel.*

Men of God have always, from time to time, walked among men, and made their commission felt in the heart and soul of the commonest hearer.—*Emerson.*

Reasons are the pillars of the fabric of a sermon, but similitudes are the windows which give the best light. The faithful minister avoids such stories whose mention may suggest bad thoughts to the auditors, and will not use a light comparison to make thereof a grave application, for fear lest his poison go further than his antidote.—*Fuller.*

A minister, without boldness, is like a smooth file, a knife without an edge, a sentinel that is afraid to let off his gun. If men will be bold in sin, ministers must be bold to reprove.
Rev. W. Gurnall.

Some clergymen make a motto, instead of a theme, of their texts.—*Hosea Ballou.*

I would have every minister of the gospel address his audience with the zeal of a friend, with the generous energy of a father, and with the exuberant affection of a mother.—*Fenelon.*

Preaching, in the first sense of the word, ceased as soon as ever the gospel was written.—*Selden.*

Evil ministers of good things are as torches — a light to others, a waste to none but themselves only.—*Hooker.*

Sir, a woman's preaching is like a dog standing on his hinder legs. It is not done well, but you wonder to see it done at all.—*Johnson.*

The world looks at ministers out of the pulpit to know what they mean when in it.—*Cecil.*

The clergy are at present divided into three sections: an immense body who are ignorant; a small proportion who know and are silent; and a minute minority who know and speak according to their knowledge.—*Professor Huxley.*

PRECEDENT.

One precedent creates another. They soon accumulate, and constitute law. What yesterday was fact, to-day is doctrine. Examples are supposed to justify the most dangerous measures; and where they do not suit exactly, the defect is supplied by analogy.—*Junius.*

Precedents are the band and disgrace of legislature. They are not wanted to justify right measures, are absolutely insufficient to excuse wrong ones. They can only be useful to heralds, dancing-masters, and gentlemen ushers.—*Sterne.*

PRECEPT.

If to do were as easy as to know what were good to do, chapels had been churches, and poor men's cottages, princes' palaces. It is a good divine that follows his own instructions: I can easier teach twenty what were good to be done, than be one of the twenty to follow mine own teaching.—*Shakespeare.*

Precepts are like seeds ; they are little things which do much good ; if the mind which receives them has a disposition, it must not be doubted that his part contributes to the generation, and adds much to that which has been collected.—*Seneca.*

It was observed of the Jesuits, that they constantly inculcated a thorough contempt of worldly things in their doctrines, but eagerly grasped at them in their lives. They were wise in their generation ; for they cried down worldly things, because they wanted to obtain them, and cried up spiritual things, because they wanted to dispose of them.—*Colton.*

Precepts or maxims are of great weight ; and a few useful ones at hand do more toward a happy life than whole volumes that we know not where to find.—*Seneca.*

Most precepts that are given are so general that they cannot be applied, except by an exercise of just as much discretion as would be sufficient to frame them.—*Whately.* .

He that lays down precepts for the government of our lives and moderating our passions obliges human nature, not only in the present, but in all succeeding generations.—*Seneca.*

I thought that to forgive our enemies had been the highest effort of the heathen ethic ; but that the returning good for evil was an improvement of the Christian morality. But I had the mortification to meet with that interloper, Socrates, in Plato, enforcing the divine precept of loving our enemies. Perhaps for this reason, among others, he was styled by Erasmus "a Christian before Christianity."—*Sterne.*

Precepts are the rules by which we ought to square our lives. When they are contracted into sentences, they strike the affections ; whereas admonition is only blowing of the coal.—*Seneca.*

PREFERMENT.

It is the curse of service ; preferment goes by letter and affection, not by the old gradation, when each second stood heir to the first.—
Shakespeare.

PREJUDICE.

The prejudices of youth pass away with it. Those of old age last only because there is no other age to be hoped for.—*Stanislaus.*

Every one is forward to complain of the prejudices that mislead other men and parties, as if he were free, and had none of his own. This being objected on all sides, it is agreed that it is a fault and a hindrance to knowledge. What now is the cure ? No other but this, that every man should let alone others' prejudices and examine his own.—*Locke.*

Even when we fancy we have grown wiser, it is only. it may be, that new prejudices have displaced old ones.—*Bovee.*

Prejudice is a mist, which in our journey through the world often dims the brightest and obscures the best of all the good and glorious objects that meet us on our way.—*Shaftesbury.*

Instead of casting away all our old prejudices, we cherish them to a very considerable degree, and, to take more shame to ourselves, we cherish them because they are prejudices ; and the longer they have lasted and the more generally they have prevailed, the more we cherish them. We are afraid to put men to live and trade each on his own private stock of reason ; because we suspect that this stock in each man is small, and that the individuals would do better to avail themselves of the general bank and capital of nations and of ages.—
Burke.

Every period of life has its peculiar prejudices ; whoever saw old age, that did not applaud the past, and condemn the present times ?
Montaigne.

Some persons believe everything that their kindred, their parents, and their tutors believe. The veneration and the love which they have for their ancestors incline them to swallow down all their opinions at once, without examining what truth or falsehood there is in them. Men take their principles by inheritance, and defend them as they would their estates, because they are born heirs to them.—*Watts.*

There is nothing stronger than human prejudice. A crazy sentimentalism, like that of Peter the Hermit, hurled half of Europe upon Asia, and changed the destinies of kingdoms.—
Wendell Phillips.

Reasoning against a prejudice is like fighting against a shadow ; it exhausts the reasoner, without visibly affecting the prejudice. Argument cannot do the work of instruction any more than blows can take the place of sunlight.
Charles Mildmay.

Prejudice is the child of ignorance.—*Hazlitt.*

Because a total eclipse of the sun is above my own head, I will not therefore insist that there must be an eclipse in America also ; and because snowflakes fall before my own nose, I need not believe that the Gold Coast is snowed up also.—*Richter.*

Never suffer the prejudice of the eye to determine the heart.—*Zimmermann.*

No wise man can have a contempt for the prejudices of others ; and he should even stand in a certain awe of his own, as if they were aged parents and monitors. They may in the end prove wiser than he.—*Hazlitt.*

Prejudice and self-sufficiency naturally proceed from inexperience of the world and ignorance of mankind.—*Addison.*

The confirmed prejudices of a thoughtful life are as hard to change as the confirmed habits of an indolent life ; and as some must trifle away age because they trifled away youth, others must labor on in a maze of error because they have wandered there too long to find their way out.—*Bolingbroke.*

To lay aside all prejudice is to lay aside all principles. He who is destitute of principles is governed, theoretically and practically, by whims.—*Jacobi.*

They that are against superstition oftentimes run into it of the wrong side. If I wear all colors but black, then I am superstitious in not wearing black.—*Selden.*

Prejudices are what rule the vulgar crowd.— *Voltaire.*

Prejudice may be considered as a continual false medium of viewing things ; for prejudiced persons not only never speak well, but also never think well, of those whom they dislike, and the whole character and conduct is considered with an eye to that particular thing which offends them.—*Butler.*

Opinions founded on prejudice are always sustained with the greatest violence.—*Jeffrey.*

Prejudice is an equivocal term ; and may as well mean right opinions taken upon trust and deeply rooted in the mind, as false and absurd opinions so derived, and grown into it.—*Hurd.*

When we destroy an old prejudice, we have need of a new virtue.—*Madame de Staël.*

None are too wise to be mistaken, but few are so wisely just as to acknowledge and correct their mistakes, and especially the mistakes of prejudice.—*Barrow.*

National antipathy is the basest, because the most illiberal and illiterate of all prejudices.— *Jane Porter.*

Prejudice squints when it looks, and lies when it talks.—*Duchess d'Abrantes.*

The prejudices of ignorance are more easily removed than the prejudices of interest ; the first are all blindly adopted, the second wilfully preferred.—*Bancroft.*

Remember, when the judgment is weak the prejudice is strong.—*Kane O'Hara.*

When prejudices are caught up from bad passions, the worst of men feel intervals of remorse to soften and disperse them ; but when they arise from a generous though mistaken source, they are hugged closer to the bosom, and the kindest and most compassionate natures feel a pleasure in fostering a blind and unjust resentment.—*Lord Erskine.*

Moral prejudices are the stopgaps of virtue ; and, as is the case with other stopgaps, it is often more difficult to get either out or in through them than through any other part of the fence.—*Hare.*

Prejudice is never easy unless it can pass itself off for reason.—*Hazlitt.*

Removing prejudices is, alas ! too often removing the boundary of a delightful near prospect in order to let in a shockingly extensive one.—*Lord Greville.*

PRESENT.

This moment is a flower too fair and brief.— *Moore.*

Look upon every day, O youth, as the whole of life, not merely as a section, and enjoy the present without wishing through haste, to spring on to another.—*Richter.*

The present eye praises the present object.— *Shakespeare.*

Busy not yourself in looking forward to the events of to-morrow ; but whatever may be those of the days Providence may yet assign you neglect not to turn them to advantage.— *Horace.*

Devote each day to the object then in time, and every evening will find something done.— *Goethe.*

Enjoy the blessings of this day if God sends them ; and the evils bear patiently and sweetly. For this day only is ours ; we are dead to yesterday, and we are not born to to-morrow.— *Jeremy Taylor.*

Every man's life lies within the present ; for the past is spent and done with, and the future is uncertain.—*Marcus Antoninus.*

Men spend their lives in anticipations, in determining to be vastly happy at some period or other, when they have time. But the present time has one advantage over every other, — it is our own. Past opportunities are gone, future are not come. We may lay in a stock of pleasures, as we would lay in a stock of wine ; but if we defer the tasting of them too long, we shall find that both are soured by age. *Colton.*

Live this day as if the last.—*Bishop Kerr.*

Let any man examine his thoughts, and he will find them ever occupied with the past or the future. We scarcely think at all of the present ; or if we do, it is only to borrow the light which it gives, for regulating the future. The present is never our object ; the past and the present we use as means ; the future only is our end. Thus, we never live, we only hope to live.—*Pascal.*

One of our poets — which is it ? — speaks of an everlasting now.—*Southey*.

One of the illusions is that the present hour is not the critical, decisive hour. Write it on your heart that every day is the best day in the year. No man has learned anything rightly, until he knows that every day is Doomsday.— *Emerson*.

The present moment is a powerful deity.— *Goethe*.

Make use of time, if thou lovest eternity know, yesterday cannot be recalled, to-morrow cannot be assured: to-day is only thine; which if thou procrastinate, thou losest; which lost, is lost forever: one to-day is worth two to-morrows.—*Quarles*.

Duty and to-day are ours; results and futurity belong to God.—*Horace Greeley*.

We think very little of time present; we anticipate the future, as being too slow, and, with a view to hasten it onward, we recall the past to stay it as too swiftly gone. We are so thoughtless, that we thus wander through the hours which are not here, regardless only of the moment that is actually our own.—*Pascal*.

Every day is a gift I receive from Heaven; let us enjoy to-day that which it bestows on me. It belongs not more to the young than to me, and to-morrow belongs to no one.—*Mancroix*.

Shun to seek what is hid in the womb of the morrow, and set down as gain in life's ledger whatever time fate shall have granted thee.—*Horace*.

Each present joy or sorrow seems the chief. *Shakespeare*.

Shakespeare says, we are creatures that look before and after; the more surprising that we do not look round a little, and see what is passing under our very eyes.—*Carlyle*.

PRESS.
This country is not priest-ridden, but press-ridden.—*Longfellow*.

The liberty of the press is a blessing when we are inclined to write against others, and a calamity when we find ourselves overborne by the multitude of our assailants.—*Johnson*.

The press is the foe of rhetoric, but the friend of reason.—*Colton*.

The productions of the press, fast as steam can make and carry them, go abroad through all the land, silent as snowflakes, but potent as thunder. It is an additional tongue of steam and lightning, by which a man speaks his first thought, his instant argument or grievance, to millions in a day.—*Chapin*.

What gunpowder did for war, the printing-press has done for the mind; and the statesman is no longer clad in the steel of special education, but every reading man is his judge.— *Wendell Phillips*.

When the press is the echo of sages and reformers, it works well; when it is the echo of turbulent cynics, it merely feeds political excitement.—*Lamartine*.

The invention of printing added a new element of power to the race. From that hour, in a most especial sense, the brain and not the arm, the thinker and not the soldier, books and not kings, were to rule the world; and weapons, forged in the mind, keen-edged and brighter than the sunbeam, were to supplant the sword and the battle-axe.— *Whipple*.

The Reformation was cradled in the printing-press, and established by no other instrument.—*Agnes Strickland*.

Much has been accomplished; more than people are aware, — so gradual has been the advance. How noiseless is the growth of corn! Watch it night and day for a week, and you will never see it growing; but return after two months, and you will find it all whitening for the harvest. Such, and so imperceptible in the stages of their motion, are the victories of the press.—*De Quincey*.

A journalist is a grumbler, a censurer, a giver of advice, a regent of sovereigns, a tutor of nations. Four hostile newspapers are more to be feared than a thousand bayonets.— *Napoleon*.

Let it be impressed upon your minds, let it be instilled into your children, that the liberty of the press is the palladium of all the civil, political, and religious rights.—*Junius*.

A man possessed of intellectual talents would be more blamable in confining them to his own private use, than the mean-spirited miser that did the same by his money. The latter is indeed obliged to bid adieu to what he communicates! the former enjoys his treasures, even while he renders others the better for them.—*Shenstone*.

PRETENSION.
He who gives himself airs of importance exhibits the credentials of impotence.—*Lavater*.

It is the care of a very great part of mankind to conceal their indigence from the rest. They support themselves by temporary expedients, and every day is lost in contriving for to-morrow.—*Johnson*.

When you see a man with a great deal of religion displayed in his shop window, you may depend upon it he keeps a very small stock of it within.—*Spurgeon*.

The desire of appearing clever often prevents our becoming so.—*Rochefoucauld.*

Hearts may be attracted by assumed qualities, but the affections are not to be fixed but by those which are real.—*De Moy.*

The more honesty a man has, the less he affects the air of a saint.—*Lavater.*

Who makes the fairest show means most deceit.—*Shakespeare.*

The most accomplished way of using books at present is to serve them as some do lords, learn their titles, and then boast of their acquaintance.—*Swift.*

Pretension almost always overdoes the original, and hence exposes itself.—*Hosea Ballou.*

When half-gods go, the gods arrive.—*Emerson.*

True glory strikes root, and even extends itself; all false pretensions fall as do flowers, nor can anything feigned be lasting.—*Cicero.*

The higher the rank the less pretence, because there is less to pretend to.—*Bulwer Lytton.*

The greatest cosmopolites are generally the neediest beggars, and they who embrace the entire universe with love, for the most part, love nothing but their narrow self.—*Herder.*

We are only vulnerable and ridiculous through our pretensions.—*Madame de Girardin.*

It is no disgrace not to be able to do everything; but to undertake, or pretend to do what you are not made for, is not only shameful, but extremely troublesome and vexatious.—*Plutarch.*

For in religion as in friendship, they who profess most are ever the least sincere.—*Sheridan.*

PREVENTION.
Laws act after crimes have been committed; prevention goes before them both.—*Zimmermann.*

PRIDE.
Pride is handsome, economical; pride eradicates so many vices, letting none subsist but itself, that it seems as if it were a great gain to exchange vanity for pride.—*Emerson.*

Pride goeth before destruction, and an haughty spirit before a fall.—*Bible.*

It is pride which fills the world with so much harshness and severity. We are rigorous to offences as if we had never offended.—*Blair.*

The best manners are stained by the addition of pride.—*Claudian.*

It seems rather extraordinary that pride, which is constantly struggling, and often imposing on itself, to gain some little pre-eminence, should so seldom hint to us the only certain, as well as laudable way of setting ourselves above another man, and that is, by becoming his benefactor.—*Fielding.*

Pride would never owe, nor self-love ever pay.—*Rochefoucauld.*

Pride is a virtue,—let not the moralist be scandalized,—pride is also a vice. Pride, like ambition, is sometimes virtuous and sometimes vicious, according to the character in which it is found, and the object to which it is directed.—*Lord Greville.*

Pride always indemnifies itself, and takes care to be no loser, even when it renounces vanity.—*Rochefoucauld.*

Pride counterbalances all our miseries, for it either hides them, or, if it discloses them, boasts of that disclosure. Pride has such a thorough possession of us, even in the midst of our miseries and faults, that we are prepared to sacrifice life with joy, if it may but be talked of.—*Pascal.*

One thing pride has, which no other vice that I know of has; it is an enemy to itself, and a proud man cannot endure to see pride in another.—*Feltham.*

All pride is willing pride.—*Shakespeare.*

When a man's pride is subdued it is like the sides of Mount Ætna. It was terrible during the eruption, but when that is over and the lava is turned into soil, there are vineyards and olive-trees which grow up to the top.—*Beecher.*

How pomp is followed!—*Shakespeare.*

What a lesson, indeed, is all history and all life to the folly and fruitlessness of pride! The Egyptian kings had their embalmed bodies preserved in massive pyramids, to obtain an earthly immortality. In the seventeenth century they were sold as quack medicines, and now they are burnt for fuel! The Egyptian mummies, which Cambyses or time hath spared, avarice now consumeth. Mummy is become merchandise.—*Whipple.*

Pride and weakness are Siamese twins, knit together by indissoluble hyphen.—*Lowell.*

As to environments, the kingliest Being ever born in the flesh lay in a manger. What a miserable thing to see clay in brocade and velvet shrugging its shoulders at clay in coarse woollen and with black thumbs!—*Chapin.*

When a beautiful woman yields to temptation, let her consult her pride, though she forgets her virtue.—*Junius.*

There are so many things to lower a man's top-sails, — he is such a dependent creature, — he is to pay such court to his stomach, his food, his sleep, his exercise, — that, in truth, a hero is an idle word. Man seems formed to be a hero in suffering, not a hero in action. Men err in nothing more than in the estimate which they make of human labor.—*Cecil.*

Men of fine parts, they say, are often proud; I answer, dull people are seldom so, and both act upon an appearance of reason.—*Shenstone.*

I think half the troubles for which men go slouching in prayer to God are caused by their intolerable pride. Many of our cares are but a morbid way of looking at our privileges. We let our blessings get mouldy, and then call them curses.—*Beecher.*

The proud are ever most provoked by pride.
Cowper.

It seems that nature, which has so wisely disposed our bodily organs with a view to our happiness, has also bestowed on us pride, to spare us the pain of being aware of our imperfections.—*Rochefoucauld.*

Pride is not the heritage of man; humility should dwell with frailty, and atone for ignorance, error, and imperfection.—
Sydney Smith.

All that the wisdom of the proud can teach is to be stubborn or sullen under misfortune.—*Goldsmith.*

Pride is the common forerunner of a fall. It was the Devil's sin, and the Devil's ruin; and has been, ever since, the Devil's stratagem, who, like an expert wrestler, usually gives a man a lift before he gives him a throw.—*South.*

We rise in glory as we sink in pride.—
Young.

He who will be wiser than his Maker is but seeming wise. He who will deaden one half of his nature to invigorate the other half will become at best a distorted prodigy. Dark as are the pages, and mystic the character in which the truth is inscribed, he who can decipher the roll will read there, that self-adoring pride is the head-string of stoicism, whether heathen or Christian.—*Sir J. Stephen.*

Dignity and pride are of too near relationship for intermarriage.—*Madame Deluzy*

Men say, "By pride the angels fell from heaven." By pride they reached a place from which they fell !—*Joaquin Miller.*

If he could only see how small a vacancy his death would leave, the proud man would think less of the place he occupies in his lifetime.—*E. Legouvé.*

There are no friends more inseparable than pride and hardness of heart, humility and love, falsehood and impudence.—*Lavater.*

To acknowledge our faults when we are blamed is modesty; to discover them to one's friends, in ingenuousness, is confidence; but to preach them to all the world, if one does not take care, is pride.—*Confucius.*

Deep is the sea, and deep is hell, but pride mineth deeper; it is coiled as a poisonous worm about the foundations of the soul.—*Tupper.*

You who are ashamed of your poverty, and blush for your calling, are a snob; as are you who boast of your pedigree, or are proud of your wealth.—*Thackeray.*

O world, how apt the poor are to be proud !
Shakespeare.

Very few public men but look upon the public as their debtors and their prey; so much for their pride and honesty.—
Zimmermann.

This life will not admit of equality; but surely that man who thinks he derives consequence and respect from keeping others at a distance is as base-minded as the coward who shuns the enemy from the fear of an attack.—*Goethe.*

As the swollen columns of ascending smoke, so solid swells thy grandeur, pygmy man ! —
Young.

The sordid meal of the Cynics contributed neither to their tranquillity nor to their modesty. Pride went with Diogenes into his tub; and there he had the presumption to command Alexander the haughtiest of all men.—
Henry Home.

Haughty people seem to me to have, like the dwarfs, the stature of a child and the face of a man.—*Joubert.*

When pride and presumption walk before, shame and loss follow very closely.
Louis the Eleventh.

Pride may be allowed to this or that degree, else a man cannot keep up his dignity. In gluttons there must be eating, in drunkenness there must be drinking; it is not the eating, nor it is not the drinking, that is to be blamed, but the excess So in pride.—*Selden.*

Earthly pride is like the passing flower, that springs to fall, and blossoms but to die.—
H. K. White.

The disesteem and contempt of others is inseparable from pride. It is hardly possible to overvalue ourselves but by undervaluing our neighbors.—*Clarendon.*

There is this paradox in pride, — it makes some men ridiculous, but prevents others from becoming so.— *Colton.*

If it were ever allowable to forget what is due to superiority of rank, it would be when the privileged themselves remember it.— *Madame Swetchine.*

It is the nature of man to be proud, when man by nature hath nothing to be proud of. He more adorneth the creature than he adoreth the Creator ; and makes not only his belly his god, but his body. I am ashamed of their glory whose glory is their shame. If nature will needs have me to be proud of something, I will be proud only of this, that I am proud of nothing.—*Arthur Warwick.*

There is a certain noble pride through which merits shine brighter than through modesty.— *Richter.*

Is it not the wound our pride sustains by being deceived that makes us more averse to hypocrites than the most audacious and bare-faced villain ? —*Shenstone.*

The most ridiculous of all animals is a proud priest ; he cannot use his own tools without cutting his own fingers.— *Colton.*

In beginning the world, if you don't wish to get chafed at every turn, fold up your pride carefully, put it under lock and key, and only let it out to air upon grand occasions. Pride is a garment all stiff brocade outside, all grating sackcloth on the side next to the skin. Even kings don't wear the dalmaticum except at a coronation.—*Bulwer Lytton.*

There is none so homely but loves a looking-glass.—*South.*

Pride differs in many things from vanity, and by gradations that never blend, although they may be somewhat indistinguishable. Pride may perhaps be termed a too high opinion of ourselves founded on the overrating of certain qualities that we do actually possess ; whereas vanity is more easily satisfied, and can extract a feeling of self-complacency, from qualifications that are imaginary.— *Colton.*

Pride is observed to defeat its own end, by bringing the man who seeks esteem and reverence into contempt.—*Bolingbroke.*

A proud man never shows his pride so much as when he is civil.—*Lord Greville.*

As Plato entertained some friends in a room where there was a couch richly ornamented, Diogenes came in very dirty, as usual, and getting upon the couch, and trampling on it, said, "I trample upon the pride of Plato." Plato mildly answered, "But with greater pride, Diogenes ! "—*Erasmus.*

Pride is like the beautiful acacia, that lifts its head proudly above its neighbor plants, — forgetting that it too, like them, has its roots in the dirt.—*Bovee.*

There are proud men of so much delicacy that it almost conceals their pride, and perfectly excuses it.—*Landor.*

Pride, which inspires us with so much envy, serves also to moderate it.—*Rochefoucauld.*

Pride either finds a desert or makes one ; submission cannot tame its ferocity, nor satiety fill its voracity, and it requires very costly food — its keeper's happiness.— *Colton.*

The infinitely little have a pride infinitely great.— *Voltaire.*

John Bunyan had a great dread of spiritual pride ; and once, after he had preached a very fine sermon, and his friends crowded round to shake him by the hand, while they expressed the utmost admiration of his eloquence, he interrupted them, saying : "Ay ! you need not remind me of that, for the Devil told me of it before I was out of the pulpit ! "—*Southey.*

Pride is a vice, which pride itself inclines every man to find in others, and to overlook in himself.—*Johnson.*

The pride of the heart is the attribute of honest men ; pride of manners is that of fools ; the pride of birth and rank is often the pride of dupes.—*Duclos.*

Men are sometimes accused of pride, merely because their accusers would be proud themselves were they in their places.—*Shenstone.*

Fly pride, says the peacock ! —*Shakespeare.*

The seat of pride is in the heart, and only there ; and if it be not there, it is neither in the look nor in the clothes.—*Clarendon.*

It is with nations as with individuals, those who know the least of others think the highest of themselves ; for the whole family of pride and ignorance are incestuous, and mutually beget each other.— *Colton.*

If a man has a right to be proud of anything, it is of a good action done as it ought to be, without any base interest lurking at the bottom of it.—*Sterne.*

Pride hath no other glass to show itself but pride.—*Shakespeare.*

Pride is as loud a beggar as want, and a great deal more saucy. When you have bought one fine thing, you must buy ten more, that your appearance may be all of a piece ; but it is easier to suppress the first desire than to satisfy all that follow it.—*Franklin.*

Though Diogenes lived in a tub, there might be, for aught I know, as much pride under his rags, as in the fine-spun garments of the divine Plato.—*Swift.*

Infidelity, alas! is not always built upon doubt, for this is diffident; nor philosophy always upon wisdom, for this is meek; but pride is neither.—*Colton.*

To be proud and inaccessible is to be timid and weak.—*Massillon.*

He that is proud eats up himself; pride is his own glass, his own trumpet, his own chronicle; and whatever praises itself but in the deed devours the deed in the praise.—*Shakespeare.*

Pride is increased by ignorance; those assume the most who know the least.—*Gay.*

Pride, though it cannot prevent the holy affections of nature from being felt, may prevent them from being shown.—*Jeremy Taylor.*

Pride, like the magnet, constantly points to one object, self; but, unlike the magnet, it has no attractive pole, but at all points repels.—*Colton.*

Pride is the ape of charity, in show not much unlike, but somewhat fuller of action. In seeking the one, take heed thou light not upon the other. They are two parallels, never but asunder: charity feeds the poor, so does pride; charity builds an hospital, so does pride. In this they differ: charity gives her glory to God; pride takes her glory from man.—*Quarles.*

There are some who feel more pride in sealing a letter with the head of Homer, than even that blind old bard did in reciting his Iliad.—*Hazlitt.*

Pride, the never-failing vice of fools.—*Pope.*

Vanity is a confounded donkey, very apt to put his head between his legs, and chuck us over; but pride is a fine horse, that will carry us over the ground, and enable us to distance our fellow-travellers.—*Marryat.*

Of all the marvellous works of the Deity, perhaps there is nothing that angels behold with such supreme astonishment as a proud man.—*Colton.*

When flowers are full of heaven-descended dews, they always hang their heads; but men hold theirs the higher the more they receive, getting proud as they get full.—*Beecher*

PRINCIPLES.

I knew a man who was governed by no one principle in the world but fear. He had no manner of objection to going to church, but lest "the Devil might take it ill."—*Sterne.*

Men are not made truly religious by performing certain actions which are externally good; but men must have righteous principles in the first place, and then they will not fail to perform virtuous actions.—*Luther.*

He who knows right principles is not equal to him who loves them.—*Confucius.*

I have all reverence for principles which grow out of sentiments; but as to sentiments which grow out of principles, you shall scarcely build a house of cards thereon.—*Jacobi.*

PROCRASTINATION.

We pass our life in deliberation, and we die upon it.—*Pasquier Quesnel.*

Delays have dangerous ends.—*Shakespeare.*

Procrastination has been called a thief, — the thief of time. I wish it were no worse than a thief. It is a murderer; and that which it kills is not time merely, but the immortal soul.—*Nevins.*

Whatever things injure your eye you are anxious to remove; but things which affect your mind you defer.—*Horace.*

To-morrow, and to-morrow, and to-morrow creeps in this petty pace, from day to day, to the last syllable of recorded time; and all our yesterdays have lighted fools the way to dusty death.—*Shakespeare.*

Never leave that till to-morrow which you can do to-day.—*Franklin.*

Delays in business are dangerous. I must send for the smith next week, and in the mean time will take a minute of it.—*Addison.*

By the streets of "By and By" one arrives at the house of "Never."—*Cervantes.*

To be always intending to live a new life, but never to find time to set about it; this is as if a man should put off eating and drinking and sleeping from one day and night to another, till he is starved and destroyed.—*Tillotson.*

Faith in to-morrow, instead of Christ, is Satan's nurse for man's perdition.—*Rev. Dr. Cheever.*

PROFANITY.

Profane swearing has always seemed to be a most voluntary sin. Most erring people when they do wrong count upon some good to be derived from their conduct; but for profanity there is no excuse.—*Hosea Ballou.*

Immodest words admit of no defence.—*Pope.*

From a common custom of swearing men easily slide into perjury; therefore, if thou wouldst not be perjured, do not use thyself to swear.—*Hierocles.*

Of all the dark catalogue of sins there is not one more vile and execrable than profaneness. It commonly does, and loves to cluster with other sins; and he who can look up and insult his Maker to his face needs but little improvement in guilt to make him a finished devil.— *S. H. Cox.*

The foolish and wicked practice of profane cursing and swearing is a vice so mean and low that every person of sense and character detests and despises it.— *Washington.*

Ill deeds are doubled with an evil word.— *Shakespeare.*

Swearing is properly a superfluity of naughtiness, and can only be considered as a sort of pepper-corn rent, in acknowledgment of the Devil's right of superiority.—*Robert Hall.*

Blasphemous words betray the vain foolishness of the speaker.—*Sir P. Sidney.*

The sourest man is not wholly hopeless when he will not blaspheme before his son.— *Theodore Parker.*

There are braying men in the world as well as braying asses; for what is loud and senseless talking and swearing any other than braying? *L'Estrange.*

The Devil tempts men through their ambition, their cupidity, or their appetite, until he comes to the profane swearer, whom he catches without any reward.—*Horace Mann.*

Nothing is a greater sacrilege than to prostitute the great name of God to the petulancy of an idle tongue.—*Jeremy Taylor.*

Profaneness is a brutal vice. He who indulges in it is no gentleman. I care not what his stamp may be in society. I care not what clothes he wears, or what culture he boasts. Despite all his refinement, the light and habitual taking of God's name betrays a coarse nature and a brutal will.—*Chapin.*

PROFLIGATE.

It is pleasant to see a notorious profligate seized with a concern for religion, and converting his spleen into zeal.—*Addison.*

PROGRESS.

The books which once we valued more than the apple of the eye we have quite exhausted. What is that but saying that we have come up with the point of view which the universal mind took through the eyes of one scribe; we have been that man, and have passed on.— *Emerson.*

He only is advancing in life whose heart is getting softer, whose blood warmer, whose brain quicker, whose spirit is entering into living peace.—*Ruskin.*

What are the aims which are at the same time duties? They are the perfecting of ourselves, the happiness of others.—*Kant.*

It is wonderful how soon a piano gets into a log-hut on the frontier. You would think they found it under a pine-stump. With it comes a Latin grammar, and one of those tow-head boys has written a hymn on Sunday. Now let colleges, now let senates take heed! for here is one who, opening these fine tastes on the basis of the pioneer's iron constitution, will gather all their laurels in his strong hands. *Emerson.*

Indeed, the grandest of all laws is the law of progressive development. Under it, in the wide sweep of things, men grow wiser as they grow older; societies better.—*Bovee.*

All attempts to urge men forward, even in the right path, beyond the measure of their light, are impracticable; and unlawful, if they were practicable: augment their light, conciliate their affections, and they will follow of their own accord.—*Robert Hall.*

The individual and the race are always moving, and as we drift into new latitudes new lights open in the heaven more immediately over us.—*Chapin.*

" Can any good come out of Nazareth? " This is always the question of the wiseacres and the knowing ones. But the good, the new, comes from exactly that quarter whence it is not looked for, and is always something different from what is expected. Everything new is received with contempt, for it begins in obscurity. It becomes a power unobserved.— *Feuerbach.*

All our progress is an unfolding, like the vegetable bud. You have first an instinct, then an opinion, then a knowledge, as the plant has root, bud, and fruit. Trust the instinct to the end, though you can render no reason.— *Emerson.*

Every step of progress which the world has made has been from scaffold to scaffold, and from stake to stake.— *Wendell Phillips.*

If virtue promises happiness, prosperity, and peace, then progress in virtue is certainly progress in each of these. For to whatever point the perfection of anything brings us, progress is always an approach towards it.— *Epictetus.*

We are never present with, but always beyond ourselves. Fear, desire, and hope are still pushing us on towards the future.— *Montaigne.*

Some men so dislike the dust kicked up by the generation they belong to, that, being unable to pass, they lag behind it.—*Hare.*

Mankind never loses any good thing, physical, intellectual, or moral, till it finds a better, and then the loss is a gain. No steps backward is the rule of human history. What is gained by one man is invested in all men, and is a permanent investment for all time.—
Theodore Parker.

Some falls are means the happier to rise.—
Shakespeare.

However slow the progress of mankind may be, or however imperceptible the gain in a single generation, the advancement is evident enough in the long run. There was a time when the most part of the inhabitants of Britain would have been as much startled at questioning the truth of the doctrine of transubstantiation as they would in this age at the most sceptical doubts on the being of a God.—
Locke.

Now by St. Paul the work goes bravely on.
Colley Cibber.

The progress from infancy to boyhood is imperceptible. In that long dawn of the mind we take but little heed. The years pass by us, one by one, little distinguishable from each other. But when the intellectual sun of our life is risen, we take due note of joy and sorrow.
Barry Cornwall.

By a peculiar prerogative, not only each individual is making daily advances in the sciences, and may make advances in morality (which is the science, by way of eminence, of living well and being happy), but all mankind together are making a continual progress in proportion as the universe grows older; so that the whole human race, during the course of so many ages, may be considered as one man, who never ceases to live and learn.—*Pascal.*

There is a frightful interval between the seed and the timber.—*Johnson.*

Intellectually, as politically, the direction of all true progress is towards greater freedom, and along an endless succession of ideas.—
Bovee.

Society moves slowly towards civilization, but when we compare epochs half a century or even quarter of a century apart, we perceive many signs that progress is made.
Mrs. L. M. Child.

Westward the course of empire takes its way.—*Bishop Berkeley.*

A man's genius is always, in the beginning of life, as much unknown to himself as to others; and it is only after frequent trials, attended with success, that he dares think himself equal to the undertakings in which those who have succeeded have fixed the admiration of mankind.—*Hume.*

The greatest evils of society are goods that have refused to go on, but have sat down on the highway, saying to the world, "We stop here; do you stop also."—*Julia Ward Howe.*

Our course heavenward is something like the plan of the zealous pilgrims to Jerusalem of old, who for every three steps forward took one backward.—*Richter.*

The world owes all its onward impulses to men ill at ease. The happy man inevitably confines himself within ancient limits.—
Hawthorne.

The true law of the race is progress and development. Whenever civilization pauses in the march of conquest, it is overthrown by the barbarian.—*Simms.*

Nature knows no pause in progress and development, and attaches her curse on all inaction.—*Goethe.*

Works of true merit are seldom very popular in their own day; for knowledge is on the march, and men of genius are the *præstolatores* or *videttes*, that are far in advance of their comrades. They are not with them, but before them; not in the camp, but beyond it.—*Colton.*

If a man is not rising upward to be an angel, depend upon it, he is sinking downward to be a devil. He cannot stop at the beast.—
Coleridge.

Bacon said, time is the greatest of innovators; he might also have said the greatest of improvers. And I like Madame de Staël's observation on this subject quite as well as Lord Bacon's; it is this: "That past which is so presumptuously brought forward as a precedent for the present was itself founded on an alteration of some past that went before it."—*Colton.*

I am suffocated and lost when I have not the bright feeling of progression.—
Margaret Fuller.

It is always hard to go beyond your public. If they are satisfied with cheap performance, you will not easily arrive at better. If they know what is good, and require it, you will aspire and burn until you achieve it. But from time to time, in history, men are born a whole age too soon.—*Emerson.*

Progress is the law of life,—man is not man as yet.—*Robert Browning.*

The mind naturally makes progress, and the will naturally clings to objects; so that for want of right objects, it will attach itself to wrong ones.—*Pascal.*

Not because I raise myself above something, but because I raise myself to something, do I approve myself.—*Jacobi.*

Let us labor for that larger and larger comprehension of truth, that more and more thorough repudiation of error, which shall make the history of mankind a series of ascending developments.—*Horace Mann.*

Progress, — the stride of God ! —
Victor Hugo.

The first party of painted savages who raised a few huts upon the Thames did not dream of the London they were creating, or know that in lighting the fire on their hearth they were kindling one of the great foci of Time. . . . . All the grand agencies which the progress of mankind evolves are formed in the same unconscious way. . They are the aggregate result of countless single wills, each of which, thinking merely of its own end, and perhaps fully gaining it, is at the same time enlisted by Providence in the secret service of the world.—*James Martineau.*

PROMISE.

He who is the most slow in making a promise is the most faithful in the performance of it.
Rousseau.

In religion, not to do as thou sayest is to unsay thy religion in thy deeds, and to undo thyself by doing.—*R. Venning.*

I had rather do and not promise, than promise and not do.—*Arthur Warwick.*

Thou oughtest to be nice, even to superstition, in keeping thy promises; and therefore thou shouldst be equally cautious in making them.—*Fuller.*

An acre of performance is worth the whole world of promise.—*Howell.*

Liberal of cruelty are those who pamper with promises; promisers destroy while they deceive, and the hope they raise is dearly purchased by the dependence that is sequent to disappointment.—*Zimmermann.*

We promise according to our hopes, and perform according to our fears.—*Rochefoucauld.*

Promises, — the ready money that was first coined and made current by the law of nature, to support that society and commerce that was necessary for the comfort and security of mankind.—*Clarendon.*

A mind that is conscious of its integrity scorns to say more than it means to perform.—
Burns.

Every brave man is a man of his word; to such base vices he cannot stoop, and shuns more than death the shame of lying.—*Corneille.*

Magnificent promises are always to be suspected.—*Theodore Parker.*

The man who is wantonly profuse of his promises ought to sink his credit as much as a tradesman would by uttering a great number of promissory notes payable at a distant day. The truest conclusion in both cases is, that neither intend or will be able to pay. And as the latter most probably intends to cheat you of your money, so the former at least designs to cheat you of your thanks.—*Fielding.*

I do know when the blood burns, how prodigal the soul lends the tongue vows.—
Shakespeare.

A promise is a child of the understanding and the will; the understanding begets it, the will brings it forth. He that performs delivers the mother: he that breaks it murders the child. If he be begotten in the absence of the understanding it is a bastard, but the child must be kept. If thou mistrust thy understanding, promise not; if thou hast promised, break it not: it is better to maintain a bastard than to murder a child.—*Quarles.*

It is easy to promise, and alas! how easy to forget! —*Alfred de Musset.*

Promising is the very air of the time; it opens the eyes of expectation: performance is ever the duller for his act; and, but in the plainer and simpler kind of people, the deed of saying is quite out of use. To promise is most courtly and fashionable; performance is a kind of will, or testament, which argues a great sickness in his judgment that makes it.—
Shakespeare.

He who promiseth runs in debt.—*Talmud.*

A promise against law or duty is void in its own nature. If it be just, I promised it; if unjust, I only said it.—*Agesilaus.*

PROSPERITY.

Everything in the world may be endured, except only a succession of prosperous days.—
Goethe.

What Anacharsis said of the vine may aptly enough be said of prosperity. She bears the three grapes of drunkenness, pleasure, and sorrow; and happy is it if the last can cure the mischief which the former work. When afflictions fail to have their due effect, the case is desperate.—*Bolingbroke.*

Prosperity seems to be scarcely safe, unless it be mixed with a little adversity.
Hosea Ballou.

As riches and favor forsake a man, we discover him to be a fool; but nobody could find it out in his prosperity.—*Bruyère.*

Prosperity is not without many fears and distastes; and adversity is not without comforts and hopes.—*Bacon.*

A weak mind sinks under prosperity as well as under adversity. A strong and deep one has two highest tides, — when the moon is at the full, and when there is no moon.—*Hare.*

To rejoice in the prosperity of another is to partake of it.—*William Austin.*

Many are not able to suffer and endure prosperity; it is like the light of the sun to a weak eye, — glorious indeed in itself, but not proportioned to such an instrument.—
Jeremy Taylor.

O, how portentous is prosperity! How comet-like; it threatens while it shines! —
Young.

The increase of a great number of citizens in prosperity is a necessary element to the security, and even to the existence of a civilized people.—*Buret.*

There is a glare about worldly success which is very apt to dazzle men's eyes.—*Hare.*

It is one of the worst effects of prosperity to make a man a vortex, instead of a fountain; so that, instead of throwing out, he learns only to draw in.—*Beecher.*

To bring the best human qualities to anything like perfection, to fill them with the sweet juices of courtesy and charity, prosperity, or, at all events, a moderate amount of it, is required, —just as sunshine is needed for the ripening of peaches and apricots.—*Alexander Smith.*

Prosperity is often an equivocal word denoting merely affluence of possession.—*Blair.*

Prosperity is the touchstone of virtue; for it is less difficult to bear misfortunes than to remain uncorrupted by pleasure.—*Tacitus.*

Watch lest prosperity destroy generosity.—
Beecher.

Greatness stands upon a precipice, and if prosperity carries a man never so little beyond his poise, it overbears and dashes him to pieces.
Seneca.

He that swells in prosperity will be sure to shrink in adversity.—*Colton.*

So use prosperity, that adversity may not abuse thee: if in the one, security admits no fears, in the other, despair will afford no hopes; he that in prosperity can foretell a danger can in adversity foresee deliverance.
Quarles.

Prosperity too often has the same effect on a Christian that a calm at sea has on a Dutch mariner; who frequently, it is said, in those circumstances, ties up the rudder, gets drunk, and goes to sleep.—*Bishop Horne.*

It is the bright day that brings forth the adder, and that craves wary walking.—
Shakespeare.

During our prosperity, and while things flow agreeably to our desire, we ought with great care to avoid pride and arrogance; for, as it discovers weakness not to bear adversity with equanimity, so also with prosperity: equanimity, in every condition of life, is a noble attribute.—*Cicero.*

Prosperity, alas! is often but another name for pride.—*Mrs. Sigourney.*

They who lie soft and warm in a rich estate seldom come to heat themselves at the altar.—
South.

There is ever a certain languor attending the fulness of prosperity. When the heart has no more to wish, it yawns over its possessions, and the energy of the soul goes out, like a flame that has no more to devour.—*Young.*

PROVERBS.

The wisdom of nations lies in their proverbs, which are brief and pithy. Collect and learn them; they are notable measures and directions for human life; you have much in little; they save time in speaking; and upon occasion may be the fullest and safest answers.—
William Penn.

Proverbs were anterior to books, and formed the wisdom of the vulgar, and in the earliest ages were the unwritten laws of morality.—
Disraeli.

Proverbs may be said to be the abridgments of wisdom.—*Joubert.*

The pithy quaintness of old Howell has admirably described the ingredients of an exquisite proverb to be sense, shortness, and salt.—
Disraeli.

If you hear a wise sentence or an apt phrase, commit it to your memory.—*Sir Henry Sidney.*

Patch grief with proverbs.—*Shakespeare.*

We frequently fall into error and folly, not because the true principles of action are not known, but because for a time they are not remembered; he may, therefore, justly be numbered among the benefactors of mankind who contracts the great rules of life into short sentences that may early be impressed on the memory, and taught by frequent recollection to occur habitually to the mind.—*Johnson.*

For I am proverbed with a grandsire phrase.
Shakespeare.

Jewels five words long, that on the stretched forefinger of all Time sparkle forever.—
Tennyson.

The wit of one man, and the wisdom of many.—*Earl Russell.*

Proverbs are mental gems gathered in the diamond districts of the mind.—*W. R. Alger.*

Proverbs were bright shafts in the Greek and Latin quivers.—*Disraeli.*

The Scripture vouches Solomon for the wisest of men; and they are his proverbs that prove him so. The seven wise men of Greece, so famous for their wisdom all the world over, acquired all that fame each of them by a single sentence consisting of two or three words.—
South.

The genius, wit, and spirit of a nation are discovered by their proverbs.—*Bacon.*

Short sentences drawn from a long experience.—*Cervantes.*

PROVIDENCE.

To make our reliance upon Providence both pious and rational, we should, in every great enterprise we take in hand, prepare all things with that care, diligence, and activity, as if there were no such thing as Providence for us to depend upon; and again, when we have done all this, we should as wholly and humbly rely upon it, as if we had made no preparations at all.—
South.

We are not to lead events, but to follow them.—*Epictetus.*

Divine Providence tempers his blessings to secure their better effect. He keeps our joys and our fears on an even balance, that we may neither presume nor despair. By such compositions God is pleased to make both our crosses more tolerable and our enjoyments more wholesome and safe.—*W. Wogan.*

There's a divinity that shapes our ends, rough-hew them how we will.—*Shakespeare.*

It is remarkable that Providence has given us all things for our advantage near at hand; but iron, gold, and silver, being both the instruments of blood and slaughter and the price of it, nature has hidden in the bowels of the earth.
Seneca.

He that will watch Providence shall never want a Providence to watch.—*Flavel.*

The decrees of Providence are inscrutable; in spite of man's short-sighted endeavors to dispose of events according to his own wishes and his own purposes, there is an Intelligence beyond his reason, which holds the scales of justice and promotes his well-being, in spite of his puny efforts.—*J. Morier.*

God hangs the greatest weights upon the smallest wires.—*Bacon.*

If God but cares for our inward and eternal life, if by all the experiences of this life he is reducing it and preparing for its disclosure, nothing can befall us but prosperity. Every sorrow shall be but the setting of some luminous jewel of joy. Our very mourning shall be but the enamel around the diamond; our very hardships but the metallic rim that holds the opal, glancing with strange interior fires.—*Beecher.*

A cockle-fish may as soon crowd the ocean into its narrow shell, as vain man ever comprehend the decrees of God!—*Bishop Beveridge.*

There is a special providence in the fall of a sparrow. If it be now, it is not to come; if it be not to come, it will be now; if it be not now, yet it will come: the readiness is all. Since no man has aught of what he leaves, what is it to leave betimes?—*Shakespeare.*

Providence has a wild, rough, incalculable road to its end, and it is of no use to try to whitewash its huge, mixed instrumentalities, or to dress up that terrific benefactor in a clean shirt and white neckcloth of a student in divinity.—*Emerson.*

The heavens do not send good haps in handfuls, but let us pick out our good by little, and with care, from out much bad, that still our little world may know its king.—*Sir P. Sidney.*

Duties are ours; events are God's. This removes an infinite burden from the shoulders of a miserable, tempted, dying creature. On this consideration only can he securely lay down his head and close his eyes.—*Cecil.*

Gifts come from on high in their own peculiar forms.—*Goethe.*

I asked a hermit once in Italy how he could venture to live alone, in a single cottage, on the top of a mountain, a mile from any habitation? He replied that "Providence was his very next-door neighbor."—*Sterne.*

There is a sweet little cherub that sits up aloft, to keep watch for the life of poor Jack.—
Dibdin.

You may say, "I wish to send this ball so as to kill the lion crouching yonder, ready to spring upon me. My wishes are all right, and I hope Providence will direct the ball." Providence won't. You must do it; and if you do not, you are a dead man.—*Beecher.*

He who sends the storm steers the vessel.—
Rev. T. Adams.

There could not be a greater chance than that which brought to light the powder treason, when Providence (as it were) snatched a king and kingdom out of the very jaws of death only by the mistake of a word in the direction of a letter.—*South.*

A man's heart deviseth his way, but the Lord directeth his steps.—*Bible.*

Round about what is lies a whole mysterious world of what might be, — a psychological romance of possibilities and things that do not happen. By going out a few minutes sooner or later, by stopping to speak with a friend at a corner, by meeting this man or that, or by turning down this street instead of the other, we may let slip some great occasion of good, or avoid some impending evil, by which the whole current of our lives would have been changed. There is no possible solution to the dark enigma but the one word " Providence."—
Longfellow.

We must follow, not force Providence.—
Shakespeare.

Long may it remain in this mixed world a question not easy of decision, which is the more beautiful evidence of the Almighty's goodness, the soft white hand formed for the ministrations of sympathy and tenderness, or the rough hard hand which the heart softens, teaches, and guides in a moment.—*Dickens.*

PRUDENCE.

The prudence of the best heads is often defeated by the tenderness of the best of hearts.
Fielding.

Prudent and active men, who know their strength and use it with limit and circumspection, alone go far in the affairs of the world.—
Goethe.

Be circumspect in your dealings, and let the seed you plant be the offspring of prudence and care; thus fruit follows the fair blossom, as honor follows a good life.—*Hosea Ballou.*

I love prudence very little, if it is not moral.
Joubert.

If the prudence of reserve and decorum dictates silence in some circumstances, in others prudence of a higher order may justify us in speaking our thoughts.—*Burke.*

Prudence is a quality incompatible with vice, and can never be effectively enlisted in its cause.—*Burke.*

The art of living easily as to money is to pitch your scale of living one degree below your means.—*Henry Taylor.*

No other protection is wanting, provided you are under the guidance of prudence.—
Juvenal.

The richest endowments of the mind are temperance, prudence, and fortitude. Prudence is a universal virtue, which enters into the composition of all the rest; and where she is not, fortitude loses its name and nature.—*Voiture.*

It seems as if prudence exhaled a perfume.—
Achilles Poincelot.

Prudence is the virtue of the senses. It is the science of appearances. It is the outmost action of the inward life.—*Emerson.*

Prudence and love are inconsistent; in proportion as the last increases, the other decreases.
Rochefoucauld.

Prudence is a necessary ingredient in all the virtues, without which they degenerate into folly and excess.—*Jeremy Collier.*

Prudence is a duty which we owe ourselves, and if we will be so much our own enemies as to neglect it, we are not to wonder if the world is deficient in discharging their duty to us; for when a man lays the foundation of his own ruin, others too often are apt to build upon it.—
Fielding.

No encomiums are thought too great for prudence; yet cannot prudence insure the least vent.—*Rochefoucauld.*

The great end of prudence is to give cheerfulness to those hours which splendor cannot gild, and acclamation cannot exhilarate.—
Johnson.

Prudence is that virtue by which we discern what is proper to be done under the various circumstances of time and place.—*Milton.*

Spurious prudence, making the senses final, is the god of sots and cowards, and is the subject of all comedy. It is nature's joke, and therefore literature's. True prudence limits this sensualism by admitting the knowledge of an internal and real world.—*Emerson.*

Put armor on thine ears, and on thine eyes.
Shakespeare.

Provision is the foundation of hospitality; and thrift, the fuel of magnificence.—
Sir P. Sidney.

No God is absent where calm Prudence dwells.—*Juvenal.*

PUBLIC.

In a free and republican government, you cannot restrain the voice of the multitude. Every man will speak as he thinks, or more properly, without thinking, and consequently will judge of effects without attending to their causes.—*Washington.*

The public is wiser than the wisest critic.—
Bancroft.

That is, in a great degree, true of all men, which was said of the Athenians, that they were like sheep, of which a flock is more easily driven than a single one.—*Whately.*

I am very anxious to please the public, particularly as it lives and lets live.—*Goethe.*

A thousand wheels of labor are turned by dear affections, and kept in motion by self-sacrificing endurance; and the crowds that pour forth in the morning and return at night are daily processions of love and duty.—*Chapin.*

The public wishes itself to be managed like a woman; one must say nothing to it except what it likes to hear.—*Goethe.*

PUFFING.

Forced to preach the virtues of his pomatum, the charlatan finishes by believing until he has tried himself.—*J. Petit, Senn.*

I would advise those who volunteer the office of puffing, to go the whole length of it. No half-measures will do. Lay it on thick and threefold, or not at all.—*Hazlitt.*

Among the number of much applauded men in the circle of our own friends, we can recollect but few that have heads quite strong enough to bear a loud acclamation of public praise in their favor; among the whole list, we shall scarce find one that has not thus been made, on some side of his character, a coxcomb.
Goldsmith.

PUNCTUALITY.

I could never think well of a man's intellectual or moral character if he was habitually unfaithful to his appointments.—*Emmons.*

I have always been a quarter of an hour before my time, and it has made a man of me.
Lord Nelson.

If I have made an appointment with you, I owe you punctuality; I have no right to throw away your time, if I do my own.—*Cecil.*

I give it as my deliberate and solemn conviction that the individual who is habitually tardy in meeting an appointment, will never be respected or successful in life.—*Rev. W. Fisk.*

Regularity is unity, unity is godlike, only the Devil is changeable.—*Richter.*

Method and punctuality are so little natural to man that where they exist they are commouly the effect of education or discipline.—
W. B. Clulow.

Lost wealth may be replaced by industry, lost knowledge by study, lost health by temperance or medicine; but lost time is gone forever.
Samuel Smiles.

Strict punctuality is perhaps the cheapest virtue which can give force to an otherwise utterly insignificant character.—*J. F. Boyes.*

It is of no use running to set out betimes is the main point.—*La Fontaine.*

PUNISHMENT.

Even legal punishments lose all appearance of justice, when too strictly inflicted on men compelled by the last extremity of distress to incur them.—*Junius.*

That kind of discipline whose pungent severity is in the manifestations of parental love, compassion, and tenderness is the most sure of its object. It so contrives the administration of chastisement as to convince the understanding of those who are exercised by it that reformation is the object aimed at.—*Hosea Ballou.*

There is no greater punishment than that of being abandoned to one's self.—*Pasquier Quesnel.*

If the people be led by laws, and uniformity sought to be given them by punishments, they will try to avoid the punishment, but have no sense of shame.—*Confucius.*

Punishment, that is the justice for the unjust.—*St. Augustine.*

To make punishments efficacious, two things are necessary. They must never be disproportioned to the offence, and they must be certain.—*Simms.*

Gold must be beaten, and a child scourged.—
Ben Sira.

Faults of the head are punished in this world, those of the heart in another; but as most of our vices are compound, so also is their punishment.—*Colton.*

There is no future pang can deal that justice on the self-condemned he deals on his own soul.—*Byron.*

The only effect of public punishment is to show the rabble how bravely it can be borne; and that every one who hath lost a toe-nail hath suffered worse.—*Landor.*

To leave no interval between the sentence and the fulfilment of it doth beseem God only, the Immutable!—*Coleridge.*

Whatever is worthy to be loved for anything is worthy of preservation. A wise and dispassionate legislator, if any such should ever arise among men, will not condemn to death him who has done or is likely to do more service than injury to society. Blocks and gibbets are the nearest objects with legislators, and their business is never with hopes or with virtues.—
Landor.

A variety in punishment is of utility, as well as a proportion.—*Washington.*

Crime and punishment grow out of one stem. Punishment is a fruit that, unsuspected, ripens within the flower of the pleasure that concealed it.—*Emerson.*

There are dreadful punishments enacted against thieves; but it were much better to make such good provisions, by which every man might be put in a method how to live, and so to be preserved from the fatal necessity of stealing and dying for it.—*Moore.*

The punishment of criminals should be of use; when a man is hanged he is good for nothing.—*Voltaire.*

The goodness of God to mankind is no less evinced in the chastisement with which he corrects his children than in the smiles of his providence; for the Lord will not cast off forever, but though he cause grief, yet will he have compassion according to the multitude of his mercies.—*Hosea Ballou.*

It is hard, but it is excellent, to find the right knowledge of when correction is necessary and when grace doth most avail.—*Sir P. Sidney.*

We will not punish a man because he hath offended, but that he may offend no more; nor does punishment ever look to the past, but to the future; for it is not the result of passion, but that the same thing may be guarded against in time to come.—*Seneca.*

We do not correct the man we hang; we correct others by him.—*Montaigne.*

The schoolmaster deserves to be beaten himself who beats nature in a boy for a fault. And I question whether all the whippings in the world can make their parts which are naturally sluggish rise one minute before the hour nature hath appointed.—*Fuller.*

God is on the side of virtue; for whoever dreads punishment suffers it, and whoever deserves it dreads it.—*Colton.*

A sincere acquaintance with ourselves teaches us humility; and from humility springs that benevolence which compassionates the transgressors we condemn, and prevents the punishments we inflict from themselves partaking of crime, in being rather the wreakings of revenge than the chastisements of virtue.—*Jane Porter.*

PUNS.

People that make puns are like wanton boys that put coppers on the railroad tracks. They amuse themselves and other children, but their little trick may upset a freight train of conversation for the sake of a battered witticism.—*Holmes.*

PURITY.

Who has a breast so pure but some uncleanly apprehensions keep lects and law-days and in session sit with meditations lawful?—*Shakespeare.*

Purity is the feminine, truth the masculine, of honor.—*Hare.*

An angel might have stooped to see, and blessed her for her purity.—*Dr. Mackay.*

He that has light within his own clear breast may sit in the centre, and enjoy bright day.—*Milton.*

Blessed are the pure in heart, for they shall see God.—*Bible.*

There dwelleth in the sinlessness of youth a sweet rebuke that vice may not endure.—*Mrs. Embury.*

I pray thee, O God, that I may be beautiful within.—*Socrates.*

The chaste mind, like a polished plane, may admit foul thoughts, without receiving their tincture.—*Sterne.*

Q.

QUACKS.

We affect to laugh at the folly of those who put faith in nostrums, but are willing to see ourselves whether there is any truth in them.—*Hazlitt.*

Heroes have gone out; quacks have come in; the reign of quacks has not ended with the nineteenth century. The sceptre is held with a firmer grasp; the empire has a wider boundary. We are all the slaves of quackery in one shape or another. Indeed, one portion of our being is always playing the successful quack to the other.—*Carlyle.*

" To elevate and surprise " is the great art of quackery and puffing; to raise a lively and exaggerated image in the mind, and take it by surprise before it can recover breath.—*Hazlitt.*

QUARRELS.

Beware of entrance to a quarrel; but, being in, bear it, that the opposer may beware of thee.—*Shakespeare.*

In most quarrels there is a fault on both sides. A quarrel may be compared to a spark, which cannot be produced without a flint, as well as steel. Either of them, may hammer on wood forever; no fire will follow.—*Colton.*

Jars concealed are half reconciled; which, if generally known, it is a double task to stop the breach at home and men's mouths abroad.—*Fuller.*

He that blows the coals in quarrels he has nothing to do with has no right to complain if the sparks fly in his face.—*Franklin.*

Quarrels would never last long if the fault was only on one side.—*Rochefoucauld.*

Whatever mitigates the woes or increases the happiness of others is a just criterion of goodness; and whatever injures society at large, or any individual in it, is a criterion of iniquity. One should not quarrel with a dog without a reason sufficient to vindicate one through all the courts of morality.—*Goldsmith.*

In a false quarrel there is no true valor.— *Shakespeare.*

Two things, well considered, would prevent many quarrels: first, to have it well ascertained whether we are not disputing about terms, rather than things; and, secondly, to examine whether that on which we differ is worth contending about.— *Colton.*

We often quarrel with the unfortunate to get rid of pitying them.— *Vauvenargues.*

We are sure to be losers when we quarrel with ourselves; it is a civil war, and in all such contentions, triumphs are defeats.— *Colton.*

Thou wilt quarrel with a man that hath a hair more or a hair less in his beard than thou hast. Thou wilt quarrel with a man for cracking nuts, having no other reason but because thou hast hazel eyes. Thy head is full of quarrels as an egg is full of meat.—*Shakespeare.*

I consider your very testy and quarrelsome people in the same light as I do a loaded gun, which may, by accident, go off and kill one.— *Shenstone.*

I never love those salamanders that are never well but when they are in the fire of contentions. I will rather suffer a thousand wrongs than offer one. I have always found that to strive with a superior is injurious; with an equal, doubtful; with an inferior, sordid and base; with any, full of unquietness.—*Bishop Hall.*

When worthy men fall out, only one of them may be faulty at the first; but if strife continue long, commonly both become guilty.—*Fuller.*

QUIET.
The grandest operations, both in nature and in grace, are the most silent and imperceptible. The shallow brook babbles in its passage, and is heard by every one; but the coming on of the seasons is silent and unseen. The storm rages and alarms, but its fury is soon exhausted, and its effects are partial and soon remedied; but the dew, though gentle and unheard, is immense in quantity, and the very life of large portions of the earth. And these are pictures of the operations of grace in the church and in the soul.— *Cecil.*

The heart that is to be filled to the brim with holy joy must be held still.—*Bowes.*

Coolness, and absence of heat and haste, indicate fine qualities. A gentleman makes no noise, a lady is serene.—*Emerson.*

Be it mine to draw from wisdom's fount, pure as it flows, that calm of soul which virtue only knows.—*Æschylus.*

Tranquillity consisteth in a steadiness of the mind; and how can that vessel that is beaten upon by contrary waves and winds, and tottereth to either part, be said to keep a steady course? Resolution is the only mother of security.—*Bishop Hall.*

Study to be quiet.—*Bible.*

My notions of life are much the same as they are about travelling; there is a good deal of amusement on the road, but, after all, one wants to be at rest.—*Southey.*

Silken, chaste, and hushed.—*Keats.*

Stillness of person and steadiness of features are signal marks of good-breeding. Vulgar persons can't sit still, or, at least, they must work their limbs or features.—*Holmes.*

I have often said that all the misfortunes of men spring from their not knowing how to live quietly at home, in their own rooms.—*Pascal.*

QUOTATION.
It is almost impossible, after all, for any person who reads much, and reflects a good deal, to be able, upon every occasion, to determine whether a thought was another's or his own. Nay, I declare that I have several times quoted sentences out of my own writings, in aid of my own arguments in conversation, thinking that I was supporting them by some better authority.—*Sterne.*

Full of wise saws and modern instances.— *Shakespeare.*

To appreciate and use correctly a valuable maxim requires a genius, a vital appropriating exercise of mind, closely allied to that which first created it.— *W. R. Alger.*

The Devil can cite Scripture for his purpose. *Shakespeare.*

Abstracts, abridgments, summaries, etc., have the same use with burning glasses, to collect the diffused rays of wit and learning in authors, and make them point with warmth and quickness upon the reader's imagination.— *Swift.*

A great man quotes bravely, and will not draw on his invention when his memory serves him with a word as good. What he quotes he fills with his own voice and humor, and the whole cyclopædia of his table talk is presently believed to be his own.—*Emerson.*

The proverb answers where the sermon fails as a well-charged pistol will do more execution than a whole barrel of gunpowder idly exploded in the air.—*Simms.*

The wise men of old have sent most of their morality down the stream of time in the light skiff of apothegm or epigram.—*Whipple.*

A good thought is a great boon, for which God is to be first thanked, then he who is the first to utter it, and then, in a lesser, but still in a considerable degree, the man who is the first to quote it to us.—*Bovee.*

Have at you with a proverb.—*Shakespeare.*

Why are not more gems from our great authors scattered over the country? Great books are not in everybody's reach; and though it is better to know them thoroughly than to know them only here and there, yet it is a good work to give a little to those who have neither time nor means to get more. Let every book-worm, when in any fragrant, scarce old tome he discovers a sentence, a story, an illustration, that does his heart good, hasten to give it.—*Coleridge.*

A verse may find him who a sermon flies.— *George Herbert.*

He presents me with what is always an acceptable gift who brings me news of a great thought before unknown. He enriches me without impoverishing himself.—*Bovee.*

A thing is never too often repeated which is never sufficiently learned.—*Seneca.*

Particles of science are often very widely scattered, and writers of extensive comprehension have incidental remarks upon topics very remote from the principal subject, which are often more valuable than former treatises, and which are not known because not promised in the title. He that collects these is very laudably employed, as he facilitates the progress of others, and by making that easy of attainment which is already written, may give some adventurous mind leisure for new thoughts and original designs.—*Johnson.*

When we would prepare the mind by a forcible appeal, an opening quotation is a symphony preluding on the chords those tones we are about to harmonize.—*Disraeli.*

I pluck up the goodlisome herbs of sentences by pruning, eat them by reading, digest them by musing, and lay them up at length in the high seat of memory,—by gathering them together; that so, having tasted their sweetness, I may the less perceive the bitterness of life.— *Queen Elizabeth.*

The multiplicity of facts and writings is become so great that everything must soon be reduced to extracts.—*Voltaire.*

Authority, dear boy,—name more, and, sweet my child, let them be men of good repute.— *Shakespeare.*

Whatever we may say against such collections, which present authors in a disjointed form, they nevertheless bring about many excellent results. We are not always so composed, so full of wisdom, that we are able to take in at once the whole scope of a work according to its merits. Do we not mark in a book passages which seem to have a direct reference to ourselves? Young people especially, who have failed in acquiring a complete cultivation of mind, are roused in a praiseworthy way by brilliant passages.—*Goethe.*

With just enough of learning to misquote.— *Byron.*

He that recalls the attention of mankind to any part of learning which time has left behind it may be truly said to advance the literature of his own age.—*Johnson.*

Luminous quotations atone, by their interest, for the dulness of an inferior book, and add to the value of a superior work by the variety which they lend to its style and treatment.— *Bovee.*

I have somewhere seen it observed that we should make the same use of a book that the bee does of a flower; she steals sweets from it, but does not injure it.—*Colton.*

There is no less invention in aptly applying a thought found in a book, than in being the first author of the thought.—*Bayle.*

We ought never to be afraid to repeat an ancient truth, when we feel that we can make it more striking by a neater turn, or bring it alongside of another truth, which may make it clearer, and thereby accumulate evidence. It belongs to the inventive faculty to see clearly the relative state of things, and to be able to place them in connection, but the discoveries of ages gone by belong less to their first authors than to those who make them practically useful to the world.—*Vauvenargues.*

Classical quotation is the parole of literary men all over the world.—*Johnson*

The art of quotation requires more delicacy in the practice than those conceive who can see nothing more in a quotation than an extract.— *Disraeli.*

The adventitious beauty of poetry may be felt in the greater delight which a verse gives in happy quotation than in the poem.—*Emerson.*

This field is so spacious that it were easy for a man to lose himself in it; and if I should spend all my pilgrimage in this walk, my time would sooner end than my way.—*Bishop Hall.*

R.

RAGE.

Oppose not rage while rage is in its force, but give it way awhile and let it waste.— *Shakespeare.*

Rage is mental imbecility.—*Hosea Ballou.*

When one is transported by rage, it is best to observe attentively the effects on those who deliver themselves up to the same passion.— *Plutarch.*

RAIN.

Prelusive drops, let all their moisture flow in large effusion o'er the freshened world.— *Thomson.*

And clouds dissolved the thirsty ground supply.—*Dryden.*

The rain is playing its soft pleasant tune fitfully on the skylight, and the shade of the fast-flying clouds across my book passes with delicate change.—*Willis.*

RAINBOW.

So shines the setting sun on adverse skies, and paints a rainbow on the storm.—*Watts.*

Be thou the rainbow to the storms of life! the evening beam that smiles the clouds away and tints to-morrow with prophetic ray ! — *Byron.*

That gracious thing made up of tears and light.—*Coleridge.*

Look upon the rainbow, and praise Him that made it ; very beautiful it is in the brightness thereof; it compasseth the heaven about with a glorious circle, and the hands of the Most High have bended it.—*Ecclesiasticus.*

RANK.

To be vain of one's rank or place is to disclose that one is below it.—*Stanislaus.*

There are no persons more solicitous about the preservation of rank than those who have no rank at all. Observe the humors of a country christening, and you will find no court in Christendom so ceremonious as the quality of Brentford.—*Shenstone.*

Rank and riches are chains of gold, but still chains.—*Ruffini.*

There is a rabble amongst the gentry, as well as the commonalty ; a sort of plebeian heads, whose fancy moves in the same wheel with the others, — men in the same level with mechanics, though their fortunes do somewhat gild their infirmities, and their purses compound for their follies.—*Sir Thomas Browne.*

Rank is a great beautifier.—*Bulwer Lytton.*

The finest lives, in my opinion, are those who rank in the common model, and with the human race, but without miracle, without extravagance.—*Montaigne.*

RAPTURE.

I spake no word ; inferior joys live but by utterance, rapture is born dumb ! *Henry Neele.*

Rapture is a dream.—*Byron.*

Silence is the ecstatic bliss of souls, that by intelligence converse.—*Otway.*

RARITY.

Rarity gives a charm : thus early fruits are most esteemed ; thus winter roses obtain a higher price ; thus coyness sets off an extravagant mistress ; a door ever open attracts no young suitor.—*Martial.*

RASHNESS.

None are rash when they are not seen by anybody.—*Stanislaus.*

Haste and rashness are storms and tempests, breaking and wrecking business ; but nimbleness is a full, fair wind, blowing it with speed to the haven.—*Fuller.*

Blind fortune treads on the steps of inconsiderate rashness.—*La Fontaine.*

Nothing is more unreasonable than to entangle our spirits in wildness and amazement; like a partridge fluttering in a net, which she breaks not, though she breaks her wings.— *Jeremy Taylor.*

Rashness is the faithful but unhappy parent of misfortune.—*Fuller.*

READING.

Leibnitz has obtained this fruit from his great reading, that he has a mind better exercised for receiving all sorts of ideas, more susceptible of all forms, more accessible to that which is new and even opposed to him, more indulgent to human weakness, more disposed to favorable interpretations, and more industrious to find them.—*Fontenelle.*

We should accustom the mind to keep the best company by introducing it only to the best books.—*Sydney Smith.*

How well he is read, to reason against reading !—*Shakespeare.*

Some read books only with a view to find fault, while others read only to be taught ; the former are like venomous spiders, extracting a poisonous quality, where the latter, like the bees, sip out a sweet and profitable juice.—*L'Estrange.*

I love to lose myself in other men's minds. When I am not walking, I am reading. I cannot sit and think; books think for me. I have no repugnances. Shaftesbury is not too genteel for me, nor Jonathan Wild too low.—*Lamb*.

Sentences are like sharp nails which force truth upon our memory.—*Diderot*.

They that have read about everything are thought to understand everything too; but it is not always so. Reading furnishes the mind only with the materials of knowledge; it is thinking that makes what we read ours. We are of the ruminating kind, and it is not enough to cram ourselves with a great load of collections, — we must chew them over again.—*Channing*.

Read not to contradict and confute, nor to believe and take for granted, nor to find talk and discourse; but to weigh and consider.—
Bacon.

Thou mayest as well expect to grow stronger by always eating, as wiser by always reading. Too much overcharges nature, and turns more into disease than nourishment.—*Fuller*.

When in reading we meet with any maxim that may be of use, we should take it for our own, and make an immediate application of it, as we would of the advice of a friend whom we have purposely consulted.—*Colton*.

It is manifest that all government of action is to be gotten by knowledge, and knowledge, best, by gathering many knowledges, which is reading.—*Sir P. Sidney*.

One of the amusements of idleness is reading without the fatigue of close attention; and the world, therefore, swarms with writers whose wish is not to be studied, but to be read.—
Johnson.

What blockheads are those wise persons who think it necessary that a child should comprehend everything it reads ! —*Southey*.

There are three classes of readers: some enjoy without judgment; others judge without enjoyment; and some there are who judge while they enjoy, and enjoy while they judge. The latter class reproduces the work of art on which it is engaged. Its numbers are very small.—
Goethe.

A good reader is nearly as rare as a good writer. People bring their prejudices, whether friendly or adverse. They are lamp and spectacles, lighting and magnifying the page.—
Willmott.

In science, read, by preference, the newest works; in literature, the oldest. The classic literature is always modern. New books revive and redecorate old ideas; old books suggest and invigorate new ideas.—*Bulwer Lytton*.

The man whose bosom neither riches nor luxury nor grandeur can render happy may, with a book in his hand, forget all his torments under the friendly shade of every tree; and experience pleasures as infinite as they are varied, as pure as they are lasting, as lively as they are unfading, and as compatible with every public duty as they are contributory to private happiness.—*Zimmermann*.

Banqueting with gods on the ambrosia and nectar of the mind.—*W. R. Alger*.

Resolve to edge in a little reading every day, if it is but a single sentence. If you gain fifteen minutes a day, it will make itself felt at the end of the year.—*Horace Mann*.

Digressions incontestably are the sunshine; they are the life, the soul of reading.—*Sterne*.

For general improvement, a man should read whatever his immediate inclination prompts him to; though, to be sure, if a man has a science to learn, he must regularly and resolutely advance. What we read with inclination makes a stronger impression. If we read without inclination, half the mind is employed in fixing the attention, so there is but half to be employed on what we read.—*Johnson*.

I think that a person may as well be asleep, for they can be only said to dream who read anything but with a view of improving their morals or regulating their conduct.—*Sterne*.

From numberless books the fluttering reader, idle and inconstant, bears away the bloom that only clings to the outer leaf; but genius has its nectaries, delicate glands, and secrecies of sweetness, and upon these the thoughtful mind must settle in its labor, before the choice perfume of fancy and wisdom is drawn forth.—
Willmott.

The mind should be accustomed to make wise reflections, and draw curious conclusions as it goes along; the habitude of which made Pliny the Younger affirm that he never read a book so bad but he drew some profit from it.—
Sterne.

To read without reflecting is like eating without digesting.—*Burke*.

Reading furnishes the mind only with materials of knowledge; it is thinking makes what we read ours. So far as we apprehend and see the connection of ideas, so far it is ours; without that it is so much loose matter floating in our brain.—*Locke*.

There is a gentle, but perfectly irresistible coercion in a habit of reading well directed, over the whole tenor of a man's character and conduct, which is not the less effectual because it works insensibly, and because it is really the last thing he dreams of.—*Sir John Herschel*.

Every reader reads himself out of the book that he reads; nay, has he a strong mind, reads himself into the book, and amalgamates his thoughts with the author's.—*Goethe.*

By reading a man does, as it were, antedate his life, and make himself contemporary with past ages.—*Jeremy Collier.*

One must be an inventor to read well. As the proverb says, " He that would bring home the wealth of the Indies must carry out the wealth of the Indies." There is, then, creative reading as well as creative writing. When the mind is braced by labor and invention, the page of whatever book we read becomes luminous with manifold allusion. Every sentence is doubly significant, and the sense of our author is as broad as the world.—*Emerson.*

We are now in want of an art to teach how books are to be read, rather than to read them; such an art is practicable.—*Disraeli.*

By conversing with the mighty dead, we imbibe sentiment with knowledge. We become strongly attached to those who can no longer either hurt or serve us, except through the influence which they exert over the mind. We feel the presence of that power which gives immortality to human thoughts and actions, and catch the flame of enthusiasm from all nations and ages.—*Hazlitt.*

Reading him (Chaucer) is like brushing through the dewy grass at sunrise.—*Lowell.*

Read not books alone, but men, and amongst them chiefly thyself; if thou find anything questionable there, use the commentary of a severe friend, rather than the gloss of a sweet-lipped flatterer: there is more profit in a distasteful truth than deceitful sweetness.—*Quarles.*

I read hard, or not at all; never skimming, never turning aside to merely inviting books; and Plato, Aristotle, Butler, Thucydides, Sterne, Jonathan Edwards, have passed like the iron atoms of the blood into my mental constitution.—*F. W. Robertson.*

A discursive student is almost certain to fall into bad company. Homes of entertainment, scientific and romantic, are always open to a man who is trying to escape from his thoughts. But a shelter from the tempest is dearly bought in the house of the plague. Ten minutes with a French novel or a German rationalist have sent a reader away with a fever for life.—*Willmott.*

When I take up a book I have read before, I know what to expect; the satisfaction is not lessened by being anticipated. I shake hands with, and look our old tried and valued friend in the face, — compare notes and chat the hour away.—*Hazlitt.*

28

People seldom read a book which is given to them; and few are given. The way to spread a work is to sell it at a low price. No man will send to buy a thing that costs even sixpence without an intention to read it.—*Johnson.*

Reading without purpose is sauntering, not exercise. More is got from one book on which the thought settles for a definite end in knowledge, than from libraries skimmed over by a wandering eye. A cottage flower gives honey to the bee, a king's garden none to the butterfly.—*Bulwer Lytton.*

When there is no recreation or business for thee abroad, thou mayest then have a company of honest old fellows, in leathern jackets, in thy study, which may find thee excellent divertisement at home.—*Fuller.*

The first class of readers may be compared to an hour-glass, their reading being as the sand; it runs in and runs out, and leaves not a vestige behind. A second class resembles a sponge, which imbibes everything, and returns it in nearly the same state, only a little dirtier. A third class is like a jelly-bag, which allows all that is pure to pass away, and retains only the refuse and dregs. The fourth class may be compared to the slave of Golconda, who, casting aside all that is worthless, preserves only the pure gems.—*Coleridge.*

Much depends upon when and where you read a book. In the five or six impatient minutes before the dinner is quite ready, who would think of taking up the Faerie Queen for a stopgap, or a volume of Bishop Andrews's Sermons?—*Lamb.*

REALITY.

Reality surpasses imagination; and we see, breathing, brightening, and moving before our eyes sights dearer to our hearts than any we ever beheld in the land of sleep.—*Goethe.*

Things are sullen, and will be as they are, whatever we think them or wish them to be.—*Cudworth.*

REASON.

It is useless to attempt to reason a man out of a thing he was never reasoned into.—*Swift.*

O reason! when will thy long minority expire?—*Hazlitt.*

Philosophers have done wisely when they have told us to cultivate our reason rather than our feelings, for reason reconciles us to the daily things of existence; our feelings teach us to yearn after the far, the difficult, the unseen.—*Bulwer Lytton.*

What can we reason, but from what we know?—*Pope.*

Every sect, as far as reason will help them, gladly use it; when it fails them, they cry out it is a matter of faith, and above reason.—*Locke.*

Men do not often dare to avow, even to themselves, the slow progress reason has made in their minds; but they are ready to follow it if it is presented to them in a lively and striking manner, and forces them to recognize it.—*Condorcet.*

Reason is a very light rider, and easily shook off.—*Swift.*

Reason! how many eyes hast thou to see evils, and how dim, nay, blind, thou art in preventing them.—*Sir P. Sidney*

Reason is a bee, and exists only on what it makes; his usefulness takes the place of beauty.—*Joubert.*

Reasons are the pillars of the fabric of a sermon, but similitudes are the windows which give the best light.—*Fuller.*

Revelation may not need the help of reason, but man does, even when in possession of revelation. Reason may be described as the candle in the man's hand, to which revelation brings the necessary flame.—*Simms.*

Reason cannot show itself more reasonable than to cease reasoning on things abov· reason.—*Sir P. Sidney*

The soul is cured of its maladies by certain incantations; these incantations are beautiful reasons, from which temperance is generated in souls.—*Socrates.*

If reason justly contradicts an article, it is not of the household of faith.—*Jeremy Taylor.*

We are afraid to put men to live and trade each on his own private stock of reason; because we suspect that this stock in each man is small, and that the individuals would do better to avail themselves of the general bank and capital of nations and of ages.—*Burke.*

Reason is the test of ridicule, not ridicule the test of truth.—*Warburton.*

Sound and sufficient reason falls, after all, to the share of but few men, and those few men exert their influence in silence.—*Goethe.*

Polished steel will not shine in the dark; no more can reason, however refined, shine efficaciously, but as it reflects the light of Divine truth, shed from heaven.—*John Foster.*

He that will not reason is a bigot; he that cannot reason is a fool and he that dares not reason is a slave.—*Sir W. Drummond.*

Reason can no more influence the will, and operate as a motive, than the eyes which show a man his road can enable him to move from place to place, or that a ship provided with a compass can sail without a wind.—*Whately.*

When a man has not a good reason for doing a thing, he has one good reason for letting it alone.—*Walter Scott*

Neither great poverty nor great riches will hear reason.—*Fielding.*

Reason is the glory of human nature, and one of the chief eminences whereby we are raised above the beasts, in this lower world.—*. Watts.*

The voice of reason is more to be regarded than the bent of any present inclination; since inclination will at length come over to reason, though we can never force reason to comply with inclination.—*Addison.*

Good reasons must, of force, give place to better.—*Shakespeare.*

As reason is a rebel unto faith, so passion unto reason; as the propositions of faith seem absurd unto reason, so the theories of reason unto passion.—*Sir Thomas Browne.*

Remember always, that man is a creature whose reason is often darkened with error.—*Sir P. Sidney.*

He that follows the advice of reason has a mind that is elevated above the reach of injury; that sits above the clouds, in a calm and quiet ether, and with a brave indifference hears the rolling thunders grumble and burst under his feet.—*Walter Scott.*

There are few things reason can discover with so much certainty and ease as its own insufficiency.—*Jeremy Collier.*

Reason is progressive; instinct, stationary. Five thousand years have added no improvement to the hive of the bee, nor the house of the beaver.—*Colton.*

He is next to the gods whom reason, and not passion, impels.—*Claudian.*

There is, perhaps, something weak and servile in our wishing to rely on or draw assistance from ancient opinions. Reason ought not, like vanity, to adorn herself with old parchments, and the display of a genealogical tree; more dignified in her proceedings, and proud of her immortal nature, she ought to derive everything from herself; she should disregard past times and be, if I may use the phrase, the contemporary of all ages.—*Madame Necker.*

Reason gains all men by compelling none.—*Aaron Hill.*

Reason is like the sun, of which the light is constant, uniform, and lasting; fancy, a meteor of bright, but transitory lustre, irregular in its motion, and delusive in its direction.—*Johnson.*

Wise men are instructed by reason; men of less understanding, by experience; the most ignorant, by necessity; and beasts, by nature.—*Cicero.*

There are those who never reason on what they should do, but what they have done; as if Reason had her eyes behind, and could only see backwards.—*Fielding.*

When my reason is afloat, my faith cannot long remain in suspense, and I believe in God as firmly as in any other truth whatever; in short, a thousand motives draw me to the consolatory side, and add the weight of hope to the equilibrium of reason.—*Rousseau.*

Reason is the director of man's will, discovering in action what is good; for the laws of well-doing are the dictates of right reason.—*Hooker.*

He that speaketh against his own reason speaks against his own conscience, and therefore it is certain no man serves God with a good conscience who serves him against his reason.—*Jeremy Taylor.*

No doubt the testimony of natural reason, on whatever exercised, must, of necessity, stop short of those truths which it is the object of revelation to make known; still it places the existence and personal attributes of the Deity on such grounds as to render doubts absurd and atheism ridiculous.—*Sir John Herschel.*

An idle reason lessens the weight of the good ones you gave before.—*Swift.*

Every man hath a kingdom within himself; reason, as the princess, dwells in the highest and inwardest room; the senses are the guard and attendants on the court, without whose aid nothing is admitted into the presence; the supreme faculties, as will, memory, etc., are the peers; the outward parts and inward affections are the commons; violent passions are rebels, to disturb the common peace.—*Bishop Hall.*

Human reason is like a drunken man on horseback; set it up on one side, and it tumbles over on the other.—*Luther.*

How often do we contradict the right rules of reason in the whole course of our lives! Reason itself is true and just, but the reason of every particular man is weak and wavering, perpetually swayed and turned by his interests, his passions, and his vices.—*Swift.*

Wouldst thou subject all things to thyself? Subject thyself to reason.—*Seneca.*

Sir, you are giving a reason for it; but that will not make it right. You may have a reason why two and two should make five; but they will still make but four.—*Johnson.*

The weakness of human reason appears more evidently in those who know it not than in those who know it.—*Pascal.*

He that takes away reason to make way for revelation puts out the light of both, and does much the same as if he would persuade a man to put out his eyes, the better to receive the remote light of an invisible star by a telescope.—*Locke.*

The total loss of reason is less deplorable than the total deprivation of it.—*Cowley.*

The way to subject all things to thyself is to subject thyself to reason; thou shalt govern many, if reason govern thee. Wouldst thou be crowned the monarch of a little world? command thyself.—*Quarles.*

Reason is an historian, but the passions are actors.—*Rivarol.*

Accurate and just reasoning is the only catholic remedy, fitted for all persons and all dispositions; and is alone able to subvert that abstruse philosophy and metaphysical jargon, which, being mixed up with popular superstition, renders it in a manner impenetrable to careless reasoners, and gives it the air of science and wisdom.—*Hume.*

What is reason now was passion heretofore. *Ovid.*

The authority of reason is far more imperious than that of a master; for he who disobeys the one is unhappy, but he who disobeys the other is a fool.—*Pascal.*

Reason is as it were a light to lighten our steps and guide us through the journey of life. *Cicero.*

REBELLION.
This word, "rebellion," it had froze them up, as fish are in a pond.—*Shakespeare.*

There is little hope of equity where rebellion reigns.—*Sir P. Sidney.*

RECIPROCITY.
Half the misery of human life might be extinguished, would men alleviate the general curse they lie under, by mutual offices of compassion, benevolence, and humanity.—*Addison.*

Life cannot subsist in society but by reciprocal concessions.—*Johnson.*

RECONCILIATION.
To be a finite being is no crime, and to be the Infinite is not to be a creditor. As man was not consulted he does not find himself a party in a bargain, but a child in the household of love. Reconciliation, therefore, is not the consequence of paying a debt, or procuring atonement for an injury, but an organic process of the human life.—*John Weiss.*

RECREATION.

Sweet recreation barred, what doth ensue
but moody and dull melancholy, kinsman to
grim and comfortless despair; and at their
heels, a huge infectious troop of pale distemper-
atures and foes to life.—*Shakespeare.*

For the bow cannot possibly stand always
bent, nor can human nature or human frailty
subsist without some lawful recreation.—
Cervantes.

Men cannot labor on always. They must
have intervals of relaxation. They cannot
sleep through these intervals. What are they
to do? Why, if they do not work or sleep, they
must have recreation. And if they have not
recreation from healthful sources, they will be
very likely to take it from the poisoned fountains
of intemperance. Or, if they have pleasures,
which, though innocent, are forbidden by the
maxims of public morality, their very pleasures
are liable to become poisoned fountains.—
Orville Dewey.

Recreation is intended to the mind as whet-
ting is to the scythe, to sharpen the edge of it,
which otherwise would grow dull and blunt, —
as good no scythe as no edge.—*Bishop Hall.*

REDEMPTION.

Is it not an amazing thing, that men shall
attempt to investigate the mystery of the
redemption, when, at the same time that it is
propounded to us as an article of faith solely,
we are told that "the very angels have desired
to pry into it in vain"?—*Sterne.*

Welcome the hour that may put me where
a man cannot take a dollar in exchange for a
soul!—*John Weiss.*

Upon the present theological computation,
ten souls must be lost for one that is saved. At
which rate of reckoning, heaven can raise but
its cohorts while, hell commands its legions.
From which sad account it would appear, that,
though our Saviour had conquered death by
the resurrection, he had not yet been able to
overcome sin by the redemption.—*Sterne.*

REFINEMENT.

Far better, and more cheerfully, I could
dispense with some part of the downright neces-
saries of life, than with certain circumstances
of elegance and propriety in the daily habits of
using them.—*De Quincey.*

Too great refinement is false delicacy, and
true delicacy is solid refinement.—*Rochefoucauld.*

If refined sense and exalted sense be not so
useful as common sense, their rarity, their
novelty, and the nobleness of their objects
make some compensation, and render them the
admiration of mankind; as gold, though less
serviceable than iron, acquires from its scarcity
a value which is much superior.—*Hume.*

Ages of ignorance and simplicity are thought
to be ages of purity. But the direct contrary I
believe to be the case. Rude periods have that
grossness of manners which is as unfriendly to
virtue as luxury itself. Men are less ashamed
as they are less polished.—*Warton.*

That only can with propriety be styled
refinement which, by strengthening the intellect,
purifies the manners.—*Coleridge.*

To be merely satisfied is not enough. It is
in refinement and elegance that the civilized man
differs from the savage. A great part of our
industry, and all our ingenuity is exercised in
procuring pleasure; and, sir, a hungry man has
not the same pleasure in eating a plain dinner
that a hungry man has in eating a luxurious
dinner. You see I put the case fairly. A
hungry man may have as much, nay, more
pleasure in eating a plain dinner than a man
grown fastidious has in eating a luxurious din-
ner. But I suppose the man who decides
between the two dinners to be equally a hungry
man.—*Johnson.*

REFLECTION.

Reflection is a flower of the mind, giving
out wholesome fragrance; but revery is the
same flower, when rank and running to seed.—
Tupper.

When I look upon the tombs of the great,
every motion of envy dies; when I read the
epitaphs of the beautiful, every inordinate
desire forsakes me; when I meet with the grief
of parents upon a tombstone, my heart melts
with compassion; when I see the tombs of the
parents themselves, I reflect how vain it is to
grieve for those whom we must quickly follow;
when I see kings lying beside those who deposed
them, when I behold rival wits placed side by
side, or the holy men who divided the world
with their contests and disputes, I reflect with
sorrow and astonishment on the frivolous com-
petitions, factions, and debates of mankind.—
Addison.

The advice of a scholar, whose piles of
learning were set on fire by imagination, is
never to be forgotten. Proportion an hour's
reflection to an hour's reading, and so dispirit
the book into the student.—*Willmott.*

Reflection makes men cowards. There is
no object that can be put in competition with
life, unless it is viewed through the medium of
passion, and we are hurried away by the impulse
of the moment.—*Hazlitt.*

REFORM.

Many hope that the tree will be felled who
hope to gather chips by the fall.—*Fuller.*

Charles Fox said that restorations were the
most bloody of all revolutions; and he might
have added that reformations are the best mode
of preventing the necessity of either.—*Colton.*

Each year one vicious habit rooted out, in time might make the worst man good.—*Franklin.*

He that has energy enough in his constitution to root out a vice should go a little further, and try to plant a virtue in its place; otherwise he will have his labor to renew. A strong soil that has produced weeds may be made to produce wheat with far less difficulty than it would cost to make it produce nothing. — *Colton.*

Necessity reforms the poor, and satiety the rich.—*Tacitus.*

Reform, like charity, must begin at home. Once well at home, how will it radiate outwards, irrepressible, into all that we touch and handle, speak and work, — kindling ever new light by incalculable contagion; spreading, in geometric ratio, far and wide; doing good only, wherever it spreads, and not evil.—*Carlyle.*

It is easier to enrich ourselves with a thousand virtues than to correct ourselves of a single fault.—*Bruyère.*

Like bright metal on a sullen ground, my reformation, glittering over my fault, shall show more goodly and attract more eyes than that which hath no foil to set it off.—*Shakespeare.*

He who reforms himself has done more toward reforming the public than a crowd of noisy, impotent patriots.—*Lavater.*

Whatever you dislike in another person take care to correct in yourself by the gentle reproof.—*Sprat.*

RELIGION.

When the rising sun fell on Memnon's statue, it awakened music in the breast of stone. Religion does the same with nature.— *Theodore Parker.*

Religion is the best armor in the world, but the worst cloak.—*Bunyan.*

There is a great deal we never think of calling religion that is still fruit unto God, and garnered by him in the harvest. The fruits of the Spirit are love, joy, peace, long suffering, gentleness, patience, goodness. I affirm that if these fruits are found in any form, whether you show your patience as a woman nursing a fretful child, or as a man attending to the vexing detail of a business, or as a physician following the dark mazes of sickness, or as a mechanic fitting the joints and valves of a locomotive; being honest and true besides, you bring forth truth unto God.—*Robert Collyer.*

Teachers and students of theology get a certain look, certain conventional tones of voice, a clerical gait, a professional neckcloth, and habits of mind as professional as their externals.—*Holmes.*

Educate men without religion, and you make them but clever devils.— *Duke of Wellington.*

The religions of the world are the ejaculations of a few imaginative men.—*Emerson.*

Religion, in its purity, is not so much a pursuit as a temper; or rather it is a temper, leading to the pursuit of all that is high and holy. Its foundation is faith; its action, works; its temper, holiness; its aim, obedience to God in improvement of self, and benevolence to men. **T.** *Edwards.*

Religion converts despair, which destroys, into resignation, which submits.— *Lady Blessington.*

The religious pleasures of a well-disposed mind move gently, and, therefore, constantly. It does not affect by ecstasy and rapture, but is like the pleasure of health, still and sober, yet greater and stronger than when the senses make grosser impressions.—*South.*

Genuine religion is matter of feeling rather than matter of opinion.—*Bovee.*

Religions are not proved, are not demonstrated, are not established, are not overthrown by logic! They are, of all the mysteries of nature and the human mind, the most mysterious and most inexplicable; they are of instinct and not of reason.—*Lamartine.*

Be sure that religion cannot be right that a man is the worse for having.— *William Penn.*

Religion is universal; theology is exclusive, — religion is humanitarian; theology is sectarian, — religion unites mankind; theology divides it, — religion is love, broad and all-comprising as God's love; theology preaches love and practises bigotry. Religion looks to the moral worth of man; theology to his creed and denomination. Religion is light and love, and virtue and peace, unadulterated and immaculate; but theology is the apple of discord, which disunites and estranges one from another. *Dr. M. Lilienthal.*

He who thinks to save anything by his religion, besides his soul, will be a loser in the end.—*Bishop Barlow.*

If we traverse the world, it is possible to find cities without walls, without letters, without kings, without wealth, without coin, without schools and theatres; but a city without a temple, or that practiseth not worship, prayer, and the like, no one ever saw.—*Plutarch.*

If it be the characteristic of a worldly man that he desecrates what is holy, it should be of the Christian to consecrate what is secular, and to recognize a present and presiding Divinity in all things.—*Chalmers.*

The only impregnable citadel of virtue is religion; for there is no bulwark of mere morality, which some temptation may not overtop or undermine, and destroy.—*Jane Porter.*

Religious contention is the Devil's harvest.—
La Fontaine.

The religion of a sinner stands on two pillars; namely, what Christ did for us in the flesh, and what he performs in us by his Spirit. Most errors arise from an attempt to separate these two.—*Cecil.*

True religion and virtue give a cheerful and happy turn to the mind, admit of all true pleasures, and even procure for us the highest.—
Addison.

Most religion-mongers have bated their paradises with a bit of toasted cheese. They have tempted the body with large promises of possessions in their transmortal El Dorado. Sancho Panza will not quit his chimney-corner, but under promise of imaginary islands to govern.—*Lowell.*

No man's religion ever survives his morals.
South.

There are no principles but those of religion to be depended on in cases of real distress; and these are able to encounter the worst emergencies, and to bear us up, under all the changes and chances to which our life is subject.—*Sterne.*

All belief which does not render more happy, more free, more loving, more active, more calm, is, I fear, an erroneous and superstitious belief.—*Lavater.*

I have seen a female religion that wholly dwelt upon the face and tongue; that, like a wanton and an undressed tree, spends all its juice in suckers and irregular branches, in leaves and gum, and, after all such goodly outsides, you should never eat an apple, or be delighted with the beauties or the perfumes of a hopeful blossom.—*Jeremy Taylor.*

Wonderful! that the Christian religion, which seems to have no other object than the felicity of another life, should also constitute the happiness of this.—*Montesquieu.*

Religion in a magistrate strengthens his authority, because it procures veneration, and gains a reputation to it. In all the affairs of this world, so much reputation is in reality so much power.—*Tillotson.*

Religion, richest favor of the skies.—*Cowper.*

Religion cannot change, though we do; and, if we do, we have left God; and whither he can go that goes from God, his own sorrows will soon enough instruct him.—*Jeremy Taylor.*

Test each sect by its best or its worst, as you will, — by its high-water mark of virtue or its low-water mark of vice. But falsehood begins when you measure the ebb of any other religion against the flood-tide of your own.—
T. W. Higginson.

There are a good many pious people who are as careful of their religion as of their best service of china, only using it on holy occasions, for fear it should get chipped or flawed in working-day wear.—*Douglas Jerrold.*

It is a great disgrace to religion, to imagine that it is an enemy to mirth and cheerfulness, and a severe exacter of pensive looks and solemn faces.—*Walter Scott.*

Religion must always be a crab fruit; it cannot be grafted, and keep its wild beauty.—
Emerson.

It has been said that men carry on a kind of coasting trade with religion. In the voyage of life, they profess to be in search of Heaven, but take care not to venture so far in their approximations to it, as entirely to lose sight of the earth; and should their frail vessel be in danger of shipwreck, they will gladly throw their darling vices overboard, as other mariners their treasures, only to fish them up again when the storm is over.—*Colton.*

Measure not men by Sundays, without regarding what they do all the week after.—
Fuller.

See, then, how powerful religion is; it commands the heart, it commands the vitals. Morality, — that comes with a pruning-knife, and cuts off all sproutings, all wild luxuriances; but religion lays the axe to the root of the tree. Morality looks that the skin of the apple be fair; but religion searcheth to the very core.—
Nathaniel Culverwell.

Men will wrangle for religion, write for it, fight for it, die for it; anything but—live for it.—*Colton.*

Never trust anybody not of sound religion, for he that is false to God can never be true to man.—*Lord Burleigh.*

There are those to whom a sense of religion has come in storm and tempest; there are those whom it has summoned amid scenes of revelry and idle vanity; there are those, too, who have heard its "still small voice" amid rural leisure and placid retirement. But perhaps the knowledge which causeth not to err is most frequently impressed upon the mind during the season of affliction.—*Walter Scott.*

My principles in respect of religious interest are two, — one is, that the Church shall not meddle with politics, and the government shall not meddle with religion.—*Kossuth.*

- The main object of the gospel is to establish two principles, — the corruption of nature, and the redemption by Christ Jesus.—*Pascal.*

People of gayety and fashion have occasionally a feeling that a little easy quantity of religion would be a good thing; because, after all, we cannot stay in this world always, and there may be hardish matters to settle in the other place.—*John Foster.*

If men are so wicked with religion, what would they be without it?—*Franklin.*

Man, being not only a religious, but also a social being, requires for the promotion of his rational happiness religious institutions, which, while they give a proper direction to devotion, at the same time make a wise and profitable improvement of his social feelings.—
Hosea Ballou.

A house without family worship has neither foundation nor covering.—*Mason.*

It has been said that true religion will make a man a more thorough gentleman than all the courts in Europe. And it is true; you may see simple laboring men as thorough gentlemen as any duke, simply because they have learned to fear God; and, fearing him, to restrain themselves, which is the very root and essence of all good-breeding.—*Rev. C. Kingsley.*

True religion is the foundation of society. When that is once shaken by contempt, the whole fabric cannot be stable nor lasting.—
Burke.

At bottom every religion is anti-Christian which makes the form, the thing, the letter, the substance. Such a materialistic religion, in order to be at all consistent, ought to maintain a material infallibility.—*Jacobi.*

I am sorry to see how small a piece of religion will make a cloak.—*Sir William Waller.*

True religion, as revealed in the Scriptures, may be compared to a plum on the tree, covered with its bloom. Men gather the plum, and handle it, and turn and twist it about, till it is deprived of all its native bloom and beauty; the fairest hand would as much rob the plum of its bloom, as any other.—*Cecil.*

If we make religion our business, God will make it our blessedness.—*H. G. J. Adam.*

If we subject everything to reason, our religion will have nothing mysterious or supernatural. If we violate the principles of reason, our religion will be absurd and ridiculous.—
Pascal.

An everlasting lodestar, that beams the brighter in the heavens the darker here on earth grows the night.—*Carlyle.*

Religion is as necessary to reason as reason is to religion. The one cannot exist without the other. A reasoning being would lose his reason, in attempting to account for the great phenomena of nature, had he not a Supreme Being to refer to; and well has it been said, that if there had been no God, mankind would have been obliged to imagine one.—*Washington.*

Devotion in distress is born, but vanishes in happiness.—*Dryden.*

Humility and love, whatever obscurities may involve religious tenets, constitute the essence of true religion. The humble is formed to adore; the loving, to associate with eternal love.—*Lavater.*

He that has not religion to govern his morality is not a dram better than my mastiff dog: so long as you stroke him, and please him, and do not pinch him, he will play with you as fine as may be, — he is a very good moral mastiff; but if you hurt him, he will fly in your face, and tear out your throat.—*Selden.*

The pleasure of the religious man is an easy and portable pleasure, such an one as he carries about in his bosom, without alarming either the eye or the envy of the world.—
South.

True religion is the poetry of the heart: it has enchantments useful to our manners; it gives us both happiness and virtue.—*Joubert.*

The religion of one age is the literary entertainment of the next.—*Emerson.*

Whether religion be true or false, it must be necessarily granted to be the only wise principle and safe hypothesis for a man to live and die by.—*Tillotson.*

Nothing exposes religion more to the reproach of its enemies than the worldliness and hard-heartedness of the professors of it.—
Matthew Henry.

Religion is the fear of God, and its demonstration good works; and faith is the root of both: "For without faith we cannot please God"; nor can we fear what we do not believe.
William Penn.

Religion finds the love of happiness and the principles of duty separated in us; and its mission, its masterpiece, is to reunite them.—*Vinet.*

He who possesses religion finds a providence not more truly in the history of the world than in his own family history; the rainbow, which hangs a glistering circle in the heights of heaven, is also formed by the same sun in the dew-drop of a lowly flower.—*Richter.*

Religion is not in want of art; it rests on its own majesty.—*Goethe.*

If there be not a religious element in the relations of men, such relations are miserable, and doomed to ruin.—*Carlyle.*

A prince who loves and fears religion is a lion who stoops to the hand that strokes or to the voice that appeases him. He who fears and hates religion is like the savage beast that growls and bites the chain, which prevents his flying on the passenger. He who has no religion at all is that terrible animal who perceives his liberty only when he tears in pieces, and when he devours.—*Montesquieu.*

We have just enough religion to make us hate, but not enough to make us love, one another.—*Swift.*

Man without religion is a diseased creature, who would persuade himself he is well and needs not a physician; but woman without religion is raging and monstrous.—*Lavater.*

Religion is the only metaphysic that the multitude can understand and adopt.—*Joubert.*

Religion is a necessary, an indispensable element in any great human character. There is no living without it. Religion is the tie that connects man to his Creator, and holds him to his throne.—*Daniel Webster.*

Nothing can be hostile to religion which is agreeable to justice.—*Gladstone.*

A true religious instinct never deprived man of one single joy; mournful faces and a sombre aspect are the conventional affectations of the weak-minded.—*Hosea Ballou.*

It is religion that has formed the Bible, and not the Bible which has formed religion.—*Raphael D' C. Levin.*

You may discover tribes of men without policy, or laws, or cities, or any of the arts of life; but nowhere will you find them without some form of religion.—*Blair.*

Unless we place our religion and our treasure in the same thing, religion will always be sacrificed.—*Epictetus.*

There is something in religion, when rightly apprehended, that is masculine and grand. It removes those little desires which are "the constant hectic of a fool."—*Cecil.*

The faith that does not throw a warmth as of summer around the sympathies and charities of the heart, and drop invigorations like showers upon the conscience and the will, is as false as it is unsatisfying.—*Paul Potter.*

Religion, if it be true, is central truth; and all knowledge which is not gathered round it, and quickened and illuminated by it, is hardly worthy the name.—*Channing.*

The dispute about religion, and the practice of it, seldom go together.—*Young.*

Religion is the final centre of repose; the goal to which all things tend; apart from which man is a shadow, his very existence a riddle, and the stupendous scenes of nature which surround him as unmeaning as the leaves which the sibyl scattered in the wind.—*Robert Hall.*

It is rare to see a rich man religious; for religion preaches restraint, and riches prompt to unlicensed freedom.—*Feltham.*

I have lived long enough to know what I did not at one time believe,—that no society can be upheld in happiness and honor without the sentiment of religion.—*Ld Place.*

There are but two religions,—Christianity and paganism, the worship of God and idolatry. A third between these is not possible. Where idolatry ends, there Christianity begins; and where idolatry begins, there Christianity ends.—*Jacobi.*

Nothing but religion is capable of changing pains into pleasures.—*Stanislaus.*

"When I was young, I was sure of many things; there are only two things of which I am sure now: one is, that I am a miserable sinner; and the other, that Jesus Christ is an all-sufficient Saviour." He is well taught who gets these two lessons.—*Newton.*

Over all the movements of life Religion scatters her favors, but reserves the choicest, her divine blessing, for the last hour.—*Logan.*

When in our days Religion is made a political engine, she exposes herself to having her sacred character forgotten. The most tolerant become intolerant towards her. Believers, who believe something else besides what she teaches, retaliate by attacking her in the very sanctuary itself.—*Béranger.*

The flower of youth never appears more beautiful than when it bends towards the Sun of Righteousness.—*Matthew Henry.*

The religions we call false were once true. They also were affirmations of the conscience correcting the evil customs of their times.—*Emerson.*

Some persons, instead of making a religion for their God, are content to make a god of their religion.—*Helps.*

Let us accept different forms of religion among men, as we accept different languages, wherein there is still but one human nature expressed. Every genius has most power in his own language, and every heart in its own religion.—*Richter.*

I believe in religion against the religious; in the pitifulness of orisons, and in the sublimity of prayer.—*Victor Hugo.*

The external part of religion is doubtless of little value in comparison with the internal, and so is the cask in comparison with the wine contained in it: but if the cask be staved in, the wine must perish.—*Bishop Horne.*

The Word of God proves the truth of religion; the corruption of man, its necessity; government, its advantages.—*Stanislaus.*

True religion teaches us to reverence what is under us, to recognize humility and poverty, and, despite mockery and disgrace, wretchedness, suffering, and death, as things divine.—*Goethe.*

True religion is always mild, propitious, and humble; plays not the tyrant, plants no faith in blood, nor bears destruction on her chariot-wheels; but stoops to polish, succor, and redress, and builds her grandeur on the public good.—*James Miller.*

To what excesses do men rush for the sake of religion, of whose truth they are so little persuaded, and to whose precepts they pay so little regard!—*Bruyère.*

It is a preposterous thing that men can venture their souls where they will not venture their money; for they will take their religion upon trust, but not trust a synod about the goodness of half a crown.—*William Penn.*

Religion intrenches upon some of our privileges, invades none of our pleasures.—*South.*

I extend the circle of real religion very widely. Many men fear God, and love God, and have a sincere desire to serve him, whose views of religious truth are very imperfect, and in some points utterly false. But may not many such persons have a state of heart acceptable before God?—*Cecil.*

To have religion upon authority, and not upon conviction, is like a finger-watch, to be set forwards or backwards, as he pleases that has it in keeping.—*William Penn.*

Religion, like its votaries, while it exists on earth, must have a body as well as a soul. A religion purely spiritual might suit a being as pure, but men are compound animals; and the body too often lords it over the mind.—*Colton.*

The religion of Christ is peace and goodwill,—the religion of Christendom is war and ill-will.—*Landor.*

All the principles which religion teaches, and all the habits which it forms, are favorable to strength of mind. It will be found that whatever purifies fortifies also the heart.—*Blair.*

Where true religion has prevented one crime, false religions have afforded a pretext for a thousand.—*Colton.*

All natural results are spontaneous. The diamond sparkles without effort, and the flowers open impulsively beneath the summer rain. And true religion is a spontaneous thing,—as natural as it is to weep, to love, or to rejoice.—*Chapin.*

Religion is for the man in humble life, and to raise his nature, and to put him in mind of a state in which the privileges of opulence will cease, when he will be equal by nature, and may be more than equal by virtue.—*Burke.*

The call to religion is not a call to be better than your fellows, but to be better than yourself. Religion is relative to the individual.—*Beecher.*

Depend upon it, religion is, in its essence, the most gentlemanly thing in the world. It will alone gentilize, if unmixed with cant; and I know nothing else that will alone.—*Coleridge.*

Religion is like the fashion; one man wears his doublet slashed, another laced, another plain,—but every man has a doublet: so every man has his religion. We differ about trimming.—*Selden.*

It is the property of the religious spirit to be the most refining of all influences. No external advantages, no culture of the tastes, no habit of command, no association with the elegant, or even depth of affection, can bestow that delicacy and that grandeur of bearing which belong only to the mind accustomed to celestial conversation,—all else is but gilt and cosmetics, beside this, as expressed in every look and gesture.—*Emerson.*

In religion as in friendship, they who profess most are ever the least sincere.—*Sheridan.*

Too many people embrace religion from the same motives that they take a companion in wedlock, not from true love of the person, but because of a large dowry.—*Hosea Ballou.*

Religion does what philosophy could never do; it shows the equal dealings of Heaven to the happy and the unhappy, and levels all human enjoyments to nearly the same standard. It gives to both rich and poor the same happiness hereafter, and equal hopes to aspire after it.—*Goldsmith.*

The writers against religion, whilst they oppose every system, are wisely careful never to set up any of their own.—*Burke.*

In all places, and in all times, those religionists who have believed too much have been more inclined to violence and persecution than those who have believed too little.—*Colton.*

Let it not be imagined that the life of a good Christian must necessarily be a life of melancholy and gloominess; for he only resigns some pleasures, to enjoy others infinitely greater.—*Pascal.*

An atheist is but a mad, ridiculous derider of piety; but a hypocrite makes a sober jest of God and religion; he finds it easier to be upon his knee than to rise to a good action.—*Pope.*

REMEMBRANCE.

O, it comes over my memory, as doth the raven over the infected house, boding to all.—
Shakespeare.

Remembrances last longer than present reality, as I have conserved blossoms many years, but never fruits. Yes, there are tender female souls which intoxicate themselves only among the blossoms of the vineyard of joy, as others do only with the berries of the vinehill.—
Richter.

Remembrance wakes with all her busy train.
Goldsmith.

Remembrance is the only paradise out of which we cannot be driven away.—*Richter.*

REMORSE.

To consume an honest soul with remorse is the greatest of all crimes.—*Mademoiselle Clairon.*

I believe that remorse is the least active of all a man's moral senses. We grieve at being found out, and at the sense of shame or punishment, but the mere sense of wrong makes very few people unhappy in Vanity Fair.—
Thackeray.

Remorse is the echo of a lost virtue.—
Bulwer Lytton.

There is a mental fatigue which is a spurious kind of remorse, and has all the anguish of the nobler feeling. It is an utter weariness and prostration of spirit, a sickness of heart and mind, a bitter longing to lie down and die.—
Miss M. E. Braddon.

Remorse is virtue's root; its fair increase are fruits of innocence and blessedness.—*Bryant.*

Remorse is a man's dread prerogative, and is the natural accompaniment of his constitution as a knowing, voluntary agent, left in trust with his own welfare and that of others. Remorse, if we exclude the notion of responsibility, is an enigma in human nature never to be explained.—*Isaac Taylor.*

Remorse, the fatal egg by pleasure laid.—
Cowper.

It is better to be affected with a true penitent sorrow for sin than to be able to resolve the most difficult cases about it.—*Thomas à Kempis.*

I am afraid to think what I have done; look on it again I dare not.—*Shakespeare.*

Sin and hedgehogs are born without spikes; but how they prick and wound after their birth we all know. The most unhappy being is he who feels remorse before the (sinful) deed, and brings forth a sin already furnished with teeth in its birth, the bite of which is soon prolonged into an incurable wound of the conscience.—
Richter.

We can prostrate ourselves in the dust when we have committed a fault, but it is not best to remain there.—*Chateaubriand.*

RENEGADE.

There is no malice like the malice of the renegade.—*Macaulay.*

RENOWN.

It is not possible to be regarded with tenderness, except by a few. That merit which gives greatness and renown diffuses its influence to a wide compass, but acts weakly on every single breast; it is placed at a distance from common spectators, and shines like one of the remote stars, of which the light reaches us, but not the heat.—*Johnson.*

REPARTEE.

Repartee is perfect, when it effects its purpose with a double edge. Repartee is the highest order of wit, as it bespeaks the coolest yet quickest exercise of genius at a moment when the passions are roused.—*Colton.*

I think I never knew an instance of great quickness of parts being joined with great solidity. The most rapid rivers are seldom or never deep.—*Shenstone.*

The artful injury, whose venomed dart scarce wounds the hearing, while it stabs the heart.—*Hannah More.*

REPENTANCE.

Neither angel nor archangel, nor yet even the Lord himself (who alone can say, " I am with you "), can, when we have sinned, release us, unless we bring repentance with us.—
St. Ambrose.

Repentance hath a purifying power, and every tear is of a cleansing virtue; but these penitential clouds must be still kept dropping; one shower will not suffice; for repentance is not one single action, but a course.—*South.*

Late repentance is seldom true, but true repentance is never too late.—*R. Venning.*

O bosom, black as death! O limèd soul; that, struggling to be free, art more engaged. Help, angels, make assay! Bow, stubborn knees! and, heart, with strings of steel, be soft as sinews of the new-born babe; all may be well!—*Shakespeare.*

If thy brother trespass against thee, rebuke him; and if he repent, forgive him.—*Bible.*

Some tears belong to us because we are unfortunate; others, because we are humane; many because we are mortal. But most are caused by our being unwise. It is these last only that of necessity produce more.—
Leigh Hunt.

True repentance consists in the heart being broken for sin, and broken from sin.—*Thornton.*

Once again I do receive thee honest. Who by repentance is not satisfied is nor of heaven nor earth.—*Shakespeare.*

Right actions for the future are the best explanations or apologies for wrong ones in the past; the best evidence of regret for them that we can offer, or the world receive.—*T. Edwards.*

True repentance is to cease from sin.—
St. Ambrose.

Alas! it is not till time with reckless hand has torn out half the leaves from the book of human life, to light the fires of passion with from day to day, that man begins to see that the leaves which remain are few in number, and to remember faintly at first, and then more clearly, that upon the early pages of that book was written a story of happy influence which he would fain read over again.—*Longfellow.*

That golden key that opes the palace of eternity.—*Milton.*

When a man has been guilty of any vice or folly, I think the best atonement he can make for it is to warn others not to fall into the like.
Addison.

Our greatest glory consists not in never falling, but in rising every time we fall.—
Goldsmith.

Let our breasts be altars, and light the flames with sacred love; let our affections be the victims, let those children of our bosom be offered up to God. There is no greater merit in sacrificing a son than in subduing some favorite vice or folly.—*Metastasio.*

He who is sorry for having sinned is almost innocent.—*Seneca.*

True repentance has a double aspect; it looks upon things past with a weeping eye, and upon the future with a watchful eye.—
South.

All of us who are worth anything spend our manhood in unlearning the follies, or expiating the mistakes of our youth.—*Shelley*

The vain regret that steals above the wreck of squandered hours.—*Whittier.*

The severest punishment of any injury is the consciousness of having done it; and no one but the guilty knows the withering pains of repentance.—*Hosea Ballou.*

Before God can deliver us from ourselves, we must undeceive ourselves.—*St. Augustine.*

It is never too late with us, so long as we are still aware of our faults and bear them impatiently, — so long as noble propensities, greedy of conquest, stir within us.—*Jacobi.*

Whatever stress some may lay upon it, a death-bed repentance is but a weak and slender plank to trust our all upon.—*Sterne.*

If hearty sorrow be a sufficient ransom for offence, I tender it here; I do as truly suffer, as ever I did commit.—*Shakespeare.*

If you would be good, first believe that you are bad.—*Epictetus.*

As it is never too soon to be good, so it is never too late to amend; I will, therefore, neither neglect the time present, nor despair of the time past. If I had been sooner good, I might perhaps have been better: if I am longer bad, I shall, I am sure, be worse. That I have stayed long time idle in the market-place deserves reprehension, but if I am late sent into the vineyard I have encouragement to work, — "I will give unto this last, even as unto thee."—
Arthur Warwick.

Repentance clothes in grass and flowers the grave in which the past is laid.—*Sterling.*

He that waits for repentance waits for that which cannot be had as long as it is waited for. It is absurd for a man to wait for that which he himself has to do.—*Nevins.*

Repentance, without amendment, is like continually pumping without mending the leak.
Dilwyn.

The slightest sorrow for sin is sufficient, if it produces amendment; and the greatest is insufficient, if it does not.—*Colton.*

Repentance is accepted remorse.—
Madame Swetchine.

What is past is past. There is a future left to all men, who have the virtue to repent and the energy to atone.—*Bulwer Lytton.*

Repentance is heart's sorrow, and a clear life ensuing.—*Shakespeare.*

Place not thy amendment only in increasing thy devotion, but in bettering thy life. This is the damning hypocrisy of this age; that it slights all good morality, and spends its zeal in matters of ceremony, and a form of godliness without the power of it.—*Fuller.*

He who seeks repentance for the past should woo the angel virtue for the future.— *Bulwer Lytton.*

Repentance is not like the summer fruits, fit to be taken a little and in their own time; it is like bread, the provisions and support of life, the entertainment of every day; but it is the bread of affliction to some, and the bread of carefulness to all; and he that preaches this with the greatest severity, it may be, takes the liberty of an enemy, but he gives the counsel and the assistance of a friend.—*Jeremy Taylor.*

Confess yourself to Heaven; repent what is past; avoid what is to come; and do not spread the compost on the weeds, to make them ranker.—*Shakespeare.*

Virtue is the daughter of Religion; Repentance, her adopted child,—a poor orphan who, without the asylum which she offers, would not know where to hide her sole treasure, her tears! *Madame Swetchine.*

We look to our last sickness for repentance, unmindful that it is during a recovery men repent, not during a sickness.—*Hare.*

A wounded conscience is often inflicted as a punishment for lack of true repentance; gre t is the difference betwixt a man's being frightened at and humbled for his sins.—*Fuller.*

Repentance is not so much remorse for what we have done as the fear of consequences. *Rochefoucauld.*

The effect of every burden laid down is to leave us relieved; and when the soul has laid down that of its faults at the feet of God, it feels as though it had wings.—*Eugénie de Guérin.*

Repentance is nothing else but a renunciation of our will, and a controlling of our fancies, which lead us which way they please.— *Montaigne.*

God hath promised pardon to him that repenteth, but he hath not promised repentance to him that sinneth.—*St. Anselm.*

REPOSE.

Repose without stagnation is the state most favorable to happiness. "The great felicity of life," says Seneca, "is to be without perturbations."—*Bovee.*

Too much rest itself becomes a pain.— *Homer.*

As unity demanded for its expression what at first might have seemed its opposite,—variety; so repose demands for its expression the implied capability of its opposite,—energy. It is the most unfailing test of beauty; nothing can be ignoble that possesses it, nothing right that has it not.—*Ruskin.*

There is no mortal truly wise and restless at once; wisdom is the repose of minds.— *Lavater.*

Have you known how to compose your manners? You have done a great deal more than he who has composed books. Have you known how to take repose? You have done more than he who has taken cities and empires. *Montaigne.*

Repose and cheerfulness are the badge of the gentleman,—repose in energy. The Greek battle pieces are calm; the heroes, in whatever violent actions engaged, retain a serene aspect.— *Emerson.*

REPROACH.

There is an oblique way of reproof which takes off from the sharpness of it.—*Steele.*

I never was fit to say a word to a sinner, except when I had a broken heart myself; when I was subdued and melted into penitence, and felt as though I had just received pardon for my own soul, and when my heart was full of tenderness and pity.—*Payson.*

No reproach is like that we clothe in a smile, and present with a bow.—*Bulwer Lytton.*

Before thou reprehend another, take heed thou art not culpable in what thou goest about to reprehend. He that cleanses a blot with blotted fingers makes a greater blur.—*Quarles.*

Reproof, especially as it relates to children, administered in all gentleness, will render the culprit not afraid, but ashamed to repeat the offence.—*Hosea Ballou.*

Reproach is infinite, and knows no end.— *Homer.*

Too much reproach "o'erleaps itself, and falls on t' other side." Pricked up too sharply, the delinquent, like a goaded bull, grows sullen and savage, and, the persecution continuing, ends in rushing madly on the spear that wounds him.—*Bovee.*

Men are almost always cruel in their neighbors' faults; and make others' overthrow the badge of their own ill-masked virtue.— *Sir P. Sidney.*

REPROOF.

Whenever anything is spoken against you that is not true, do not pass by or despise it because it is false; but forthwith examine yourself, and consider what you have said or done that may administer a just occasion of reproof.— *Plutarch.*

Reprove thy friend privately; commend him publicly.—*Solon.*

Reproof is a medicine like mercury or opium; if it be improperly administered, it will do harm instead of good.—*Horace Mann.*

Some persons take reproof good-humoredly enough, unless you are so unlucky as to hit a sore place. Then they wince and writhe, and start up and knock you down for your impertinence, or wish you good morning.—*Hare.*

Aversion from reproof is not wise. It is a mark of a little mind. A great man can afford to lose; a little insignificant fellow is afraid of being snuffed out.—*Cecil.*

REPUBLIC.

Republics come to an end by luxurious habits; monarchies, by poverty.—*Montesquieu.*

REPUBLICANISM.

Republicanism is not the phantom of a deluded imagination. On the contrary, laws, under no form of government, are better supported, liberty and property better secured, or happiness more effectually dispensed to mankind.— *Washington.*

REPUTATION.

Reputation is a most idle and most false imposition; oft got without merit, and lost without deserving.—*Shakespeare.*

When a man has once forfeited the reputation of his integrity, he is set fast; and nothing will then serve his turn, neither truth nor falsehood.— *Tillotson.*

An honest reputation is within the reach of all men; they obtain it by social virtues, and by doing their duty. This kind of reputation, it is true, is neither brilliant nor startling, but it is often the most useful for happiness.—*Duclos.*

Whatever disgrace we have merited, it is almost always in our power to re-establish our reputation.—*Rochefoucauld.*

A fair reputation is a plant, delicate in its nature, and by no means rapid in its growth. It will not shoot up in a night like the gourd of the prophet; but, like that gourd, it may perish in a night.—*Jeremy Taylor.*

Good-will, like a good name, is got by many actions, and lost by one.—*Jeffrey.*

The reputation of a man is like his shadow, gigantic when it precedes him, and pygmy in its proportions when it follows.—*Talleyrand.*

Reputation is rarely proportioned to virtue. We have seen a thousand people esteemed, either for the merit they had not yet attained or for that they no longer possessed.— *St. Evremond.*

How difficult is it to save the bark of reputation from the rocks of ignorance!—*Petrarch.*

The purest treasure mortal times afford is spotless reputation; that away, men are but gilded loam or painted clay.—*Shakespeare.*

How many people live on the reputation of the reputation they might have made!— *Holmes.*

There are two modes of establishing our reputation,—to be praised by honest men, and to be abused by rogues. It is best, however, to secure the former, because it will be invariably accompanied by the latter.—*Colton.*

" A good name is like precious ointment"; it filleth all round about, and will not easily away; for the odors of ointments are more durable than those of flowers.—*Bacon.*

In all the affairs of this world, so much reputation is in reality so much power.—*Tillotson.*

Nothing so uncertain as general reputation. A man injures me from humor, passion, or interest; hates me because he has injured me; and speaks ill of me because he hates me.— *Henry Home.*

The dark grave, which knows all secrets, can alone reclaim the fatal doubt once cast on woman's name.—*George Herbert.*

He that filches from me my good name robs me of that which not enriches him, but makes me poor indeed.—*Shakespeare.*

He that is respectless in his courses oft sells his reputation at cheap market.—*Ben Jonson.*

A man's reputation is not in his own keeping, but lies at the mercy of the profligacy of others. Calumny requires no proof.—*Hazlitt.*

The world knows the worst of me, and I can say that I am better than my fame.— *Schiller.*

Garments that have once one rent in them are subject to be torn on every nail, and glasses that are once cracked are soon broken; such is man's good name once tainted with just reproach.—*Bishop Hall.*

A good name is properly that reputation of virtue that every man may challenge as his right and due in the opinions of others, till he has made forfeit of it by the viciousness of his actions.—*South.*

The way to gain a good reputation is to endeavor to be what you desire to appear.— *Socrates.*

Some men's reputation seems like seed-wheat, which thrives best when brought from a distance.— *Whately.*

He that tears away a man's good name tears his flesh from his bones, and, by letting him live, gives him only a cruel opportunity of feeling his misery, of burying his better part, and surviving himself.—*South.*

There are few persons of greater worth than their reputation; but how many are there whose worth is far short of their reputation! — *Stanislaus.*

A good name is better than precious ointment.—*Bible.*

Reputation is what men and women think of us. Character is what God and angels know of us.—*Thomas Paine.*

Reputation, reputation, reputation! O, I have lost my reputation! I have lost the immortal part of myself; and what remains is bestial.—*Shakespeare.*

RESENTMENT.

Resentment is a union of sorrow with malignity; a combination of a passion which all endeavor to avoid with a passion which all concur to detest.—*Johnson.*

Resentment is, in every stage of the passion, painful, but it is not disagreeable, unless in excess; pity is always painful, yet always agreeable; vanity, on the contrary, is always pleasant, yet always disagreeable.—*Home.*

There is a spirit of resistance implanted by the Deity in the breast of man, proportioned to the size of the wrongs he is destined to endure.— *C. J. Fox.*

Resentment seems to have been given us by nature for defence, and for defence only; it is the safeguard of justice, and the security of innocence.—*Adam Smith.*

RESERVE.

There is nothing more allied to the barbarous and savage character than sullenness, concealment, and reserve.—*Parke Godwin.*

Reserve is the truest expression of respect towards those who are its objects.—*De Quincey.*

There would not be any absolute necessity for reserve if the world were honest; yet even then it would prove expedient. For, in order to attain any degree of deference, it seems necessary that people should imagine you have more accomplishments than you discover.—*Shenstone.*

Reserve may be pride fortified in ice; dignity is worth reposing on truth.—*W. R. Alger.*

Reserve is no more essentially connected with understanding than a church organ with devotion, or wine with good-nature.—*Shenstone.*

RESIGNATION.

Compose thy mind, and prepare thy soul calmly to obey; such offering will be more acceptable to God than every other sacrifice. He who sheds the blood of a victim offers the blood of another at His throne; he who obeys offers up his own will as his gift.—*Metastasio.*

Like the plants that throw their fragrance from the wounded part, breathe sweetness out of woe.—*Moore.*

It were no virtue to bear calamities if we did not feel them.—*Madame Necker.*

Remember that you are an actor in a drama of such sort as the Author chooses. If short, then in a short one; if long, then in a long one. If it be his pleasure that you should act a poor man, see that you act it well; or a cripple, or a ruler, or a private citizen. For this is your business to act well the given part; but to choose it, belongs to another.—*Epictetus.*

The evil which one suffers patiently as inevitable seems insupportable as soon as he conceives the idea of escaping from it.— *De Tocqueville.*

Our nature is like the sea, which gains by the flow of the tide in one place what it has lost by the ebb in another. A man may acquiesce in the method which God takes to mortify his pride; but he is in danger of growing proud of the mortification.—*Cecil.*

It is a higher exhibition of Christian manliness to be able to bear trouble than to get rid of it.—*Beecher.*

Probably Providence has implanted peevishness and ill-temper in sick and old persons, in compassion to the friends or relations who are to survive; as it must naturally lessen the concern they might otherwise feel for their loss.— *Sterne.*

Sanctified afflictions are an evidence of our adoption: we do not prune dead trees to make them fruitful, nor those which are planted in a desert; but such as belong to the garden, and possess life.—*Arrowsmith.*

We cannot conquer fate and necessity, yet we can yield to them in such a manner as to be greater than if we could.—*Landor.*

Resignation is a daily suicide.—*Balzac.*

There is but one way to tranquillity of mind and happiness; let this, therefore, be always ready at hand with thee, both when thou wakest early in the morning, and all the day long, and when thou goest late to sleep, to account no external things/thine own, but to commit all these to God.—*Epictetus.*

When a misfortune is impending, I cry, "God forbid"; but when it falls upon me, I say, "God be praised."—*Sterne.*

So long as we do not take even the injustice which is done us, and which forces the burning tears from us, — so long as we do not take even this for just and right, we are in the thickest darkness without dawn.—*Rahel.*

What destiny sends, bear! Whoever perseveres will be crowned.—*Herder.*

Pain and pleasure, good and evil, come to us from unexpected sources. It is not there where we have gathered up our brightest hopes, that the dawn of happiness breaks. It is not there where we have glanced our eye with affright, that we find the deadliest gloom. What should this teach us? To bow to the great and only Source of light, and live humbly and with confiding resignation.—*Goethe.*

No cloud can overshadow a true Christian but his faith will discern a rainbow in it.—
Bishop Horne.

Is it reasonable to take it ill, that anybody desires of us that which is their own? All we have is the Almighty's; and shall not God have his own when he calls for it?—*William Penn.*

Misfortunes, in fine, cannot be avoided; but they may be sweetened, if not overcome, and our lives made happy by philosophy.—*Seneca.*

Resignation is, to some extent, spoiled for me by the fact that it is so entirely conformable to the laws of common-sense. I should like just a little more of the supernatural in the practice of my favorite virtue.—
Madame Swetchine.

Suffering becomes beautiful when any one bears great calamities with cheerfulness, not through insensibility, but through greatness of mind.—*Aristotle.*

Nature has made us passive, and to suffer is our lot. While we are in the flesh every man has his chain and his clog; only it is looser and lighter to one man than to another, and he is more at ease who takes it up and carries it than he who drags it.—*Seneca.*

What is resignation? It is putting God between one's self and one's grief.—
Madame Swetchine.

It is resignation and contentment that are best calculated to lead us safely through life. Whoever has not sufficient power to endure privations, and even suffering, can never feel that he is armor proof against painful emotions, — nay, he must attribute to himself, or at least to the morbid sensitiveness of his nature, every disagreeable feeling he may suffer.—
Wilhelm von Humboldt.

Leave to Heaven the measure and the choice.
Johnson.

I have heard a good story of Charles Fox. When his house was on fire, he found all efforts to save it useless, and, being a good draughtsman, he went up to the next hill to make a drawing of the fire, — the best instance of philosophy I ever heard of.—*Southey.*

True resignation, which always brings with it the confidence that unchangeable goodness will make even the disappointment of our hopes and the contradictions of life conducive to some benefit, casts a grave but tranquil light over the prospect of even a toilsome and troubled life.—*Wilhelm von Humboldt.*

The Lord gave and the Lord hath taken away; blessed be the name of the Lord.—*Bible.*

Demand not that events should happen as you wish; but wish them to happen as they do happen, and you will go on well.—*Epictetus.*

RESOLUTION.

If we have need of a strong will in order to do good, it is more necessary still for us in order not to do evil; from which it often results that the most modest life is that where the force of will is most exercised.—*Count Molé.*

A good inclination is but the first rude draught of virtue, but the finishing strokes are from the will; which, if well disposed, will by degrees perfect, — if ill disposed, will by the superinduction of ill habits quickly deface it.—
South.

When desperate ills demand a speedy cure, distrust is cowardice, and prudence folly.—
Johnson.

Be not too slow in the breaking of a sinful custom; a quick, courageous resolution is better than a gradual deliberation; in such a combat he is the bravest soldier that lays about him without fear or wit. Wit pleads, fear disheartens; he that would kill Hydra had better strike off one neck than five heads: fell the tree, and the branches are soon cut off.—*Quarles.*

Experience teacheth us that resolution is a sole help in need.—*Shakespeare.*

I was acquainted once with a gallant soldier who assured me that his only measure of courage was this: upon the first fire, in an engagement, he immediately looked upon himself as a dead man. He then bravely fought out the remainder of the day, perfectly regardless of all manner of danger, as becomes a dead man to be. So that all the life or limbs he carried back again to his tent he reckoned as clear gains, or, as he himself expressed it, so much out of the fire.—*Sterne.*

Sudden resolutions, like the sudden rise of the mercury in the barometer, indicate little else than the changeableness of the weather.—
Hare.

Be stirring as the time, be fire with fire, threaten the threatener, and out-face the brow of bragging horror; so shall inferior eyes, that borrow their behaviors from the great, grow great by your example and put on the dauntless spirit of resolution.—*Shakespeare.*

RESPONSIBILITY.

Every human being has a work to carry on within, duties to perform abroad, influences to exert, which are peculiarly his, and which no conscience but his own can teach.—
Channing.

And how his audit stands who knows, save Heaven ?—*Shakespeare.*

Much misconstruction and bitterness are spared to him who thinks naturally upon what he owes to others, rather than what he ought to expect from them.—*Madame Guizot.*

Every one of us shall give account of himself to God.—*Bible.*

If the master takes no account of his servants, they will make small account of him, and care not what they spend, who are never brought to an audit.—*Fuller.*

Nature holds an immense uncollected debt over every man's head.—*Beecher.*

RESURRECTION.

The diamond which shines in the Saviour's crown shall burn in unquenched beauty at last on the forehead of every human soul.—
Theodore Parker.

Our Lord has written the promise of the resurrection, not in books alone, but in every leaf in spring-time.—*Luther.*

And there, in Abraham's bosom, whatever it be which that bosom signifies, lives my sweet friend. For what other place is there for such a soul ?—*St. Augustine.*

RETIREMENT.

Exert your talents and distinguish yourself, and don't think of retiring from the world until the world will be sorry that you retire. I hate a fellow whom pride or cowardice or laziness drives into a corner, and who does nothing when he is there but sit and growl. Let him come out as I do, and bark.—*Johnson.*

He who lives wisely to himself and his own heart looks at the busy world through the loopholes of retreat, and does not want to mingle in the fray.—*Hazlitt.*

Demean thyself more warily in thy study than in the street. If thy public actions have a hundred witnesses, thy private have a thousand. The multitude looks but upon thy actions ; thy conscience looks into them : the multitude may chance to excuse thee, if not acquit thee ; thy conscience will accuse thee, if not condemn thee.—
Quarles.

Depart from the highway, and transplant thyself in some enclosed ground ; for it is hard for a tree that stands by the wayside to keep her fruit till it be ripe.—*St. Chrysostom.*

He whom God hath gifted with a love of retirement possesses, as it were, an extra sense.—
Bulwer Lytton.

RETRIBUTION.

We must confess that life resembles the banquet of Damocles, — the sword is ever suspended.—
Voltaire.

The essence of justice is mercy. Making a child suffer for wrong-doing is merciful to the child. There is no mercy in letting the child have its own will, plunging headlong to destruction with the bits in its mouth. There is no mercy to society nor to the criminal if the wrong is not repressed and the right vindicated. We injure the culprit who comes up to take his proper doom at the bar of justice, if we do not make him feel that he has done a wrong thing. We may deliver his body from the prison, but not at the expense of justice nor to his own injury.—*Chapin.*

His enemies shall lick the dust.—*Bible.*

Society is like the echoing hills. It gives back to the speaker his words ; groan for groan, song for song. Wouldest thou have thy social scenes to resound with music ? then speak ever in the melodious strains of truth and love. " With what measure ye mete it shall be measured to you again."—*Dr. David Thomas.*

Heaven often regulates effects by their causes, and pays the wicked what they have deserved.
Corneille.

My lord cardinal (Cardinal Richelieu), there is one fact which you seem to have entirely forgotten. God is a sure paymaster. He may not pay at the end of every week or month or year ; but I charge you, remember that he pays in the end.—*Anne of Austria.*

Nemesis is one of God's handmaids.—
W. R. Alger.

Nothing is more common than for great thieves to ride in triumph when small ones are punished. But let wickedness escape as it may, at the law it never fails of doing itself justice ; for every guilty person is his own hangman.—
Seneca.

Whoso diggeth a pit shall fall therein.—
Bible.

Passing too eagerly upon a provocation loses the guard and lays open the body ; calmness and leisure and deliberation do the business much better.—*Jeremy Collier.*

In vain we attempt to clear our conscience by affecting to compensate for fraud or cruelty by acts of strict religious homage towards God.
Blair.

As formerly we suffered from wickedness, so now we suffer from the laws.—*Tacitus.*

Old age seizes upon an ill-spent youth like fire upon a rotten house; it was rotten before, and must have fallen of itself; so that it is no more than one ruin preventing another.—*South.*

The world cannot afford to damn its sinners, nor will it be saved without their help. Humanity is one, and not till Lazarus is cured of his sores will Dives be safe. Whoever will thrust Magdalen into the pit will find that he has dropped with her into the flames the key that should have opened heaven for him, and assuredly shall he remain outside until she, her purification completed, shall take pity on him and bring it thence.—*Celia Burleigh.*

REVENGE.

Revenge, the attribute of gods! they stamped it with their great image on our natures.—
Otway.

Revenge is a common passion; it is the sin of the uninstructed. The savage deems it noble; but Christ's religion, which is the sublime civilizer, emphatically condemns it. Why? Because religion ever seeks to ennoble man; and nothing so debases him as revenge.—
Bulwer Lytton.

Revenge, we find, the abject pleasure of an abject mind.—*Juvenal.*

The best manner of avenging ourselves is by not resembling him who has injured us; and it is hardly possible for one man to be more unlike another than he that forbears to avenge himself of wrong is to him who did the wrong.—
Jane Porter.

If thine enemy hunger, feed him; if he thirst, give him drink: for in so doing thou shalt heap coals of fire on his head.—*Bible.*

He that studieth revenge keepeth his own wounds green.—*Bacon.*

It is through madness that we hate an enemy, and think of revenging ourselves; and it is through indolence that we are appeased, and do not revenge ourselves.—*Bruyère.*

Sweet is revenge, especially to women.—
Byron.

The most tolerable sort of revenge is for those wrongs which there is no law to remedy. But then let a man take heed that the revenge be such as there is no law to punish; else a man's enemy is still beforehand, and is two for one.—*Bacon.*

Revenge, at first though sweet, bitter erelong, back on itself recoils.—*Milton.*

Not to be provoked is best; but if moved, never correct till the fume is spent; for every stroke our fury strikes is sure to hit ourselves at last.—*William Penn.*

Souls made of fire, and children of the sun, with whom revenge is virtue.—*Young.*

Few things are more agreeable to self-love than revenge, and yet no cause so effectually restrains us from revenge as self-love. And this paradox naturally suggests another; that the strength of the community is not unfrequently built upon the weakness of those individuals that compose it.—*Colton.*

Revenge has ears more deaf than adders to the voice of any true decision.—*Shakespeare.*

Revenge commonly hurts both the offerer and sufferer; as we see in a foolish bee, which in her anger invenometh the flesh and loseth her sting, and so lives a drone ever after.—
Bishop Hall.

I will not be revenged, and this I owe to my enemy; but I will remember, and this I owe to myself.—*Colton.*

All the ends of human felicity are secured without revenge, for without it we are permitted to restore ourselves; and therefore it is against natural reason to do an evil that no way co-operates the proper and perfective end of human nature. And he is a miserable person, whose good is the evil of his neighbor; and he that revenges in many cases does worse than he that did the injury; in all cases as bad.—
Jeremy Taylor.

Had all his hairs been lives, my great revenge had stomach for them all.—*Shakespeare.*

If you are affronted, it is better to pass it by in silence, or with a jest, though with some dishonor, than to endeavor revenge. If you can keep reason above passion, that and watchfulness will be your best defendants.—*Newton.*

Revenge is a kind of wild justice, which the more man's nature runs to the more ought law to weed it out.—*Bacon.*

Neither is it safe to count upon the weakness of any man's understanding, who is thoroughly possessed of the spirit of revenge to sharpen his invention.—*Swift.*

On him that takes revenge revenge shall be taken, and by a real evil he shall dearly pay for the goods that are but airy and fantastical; it is like a rolling stone, which, when a man hath forced up a hill, will return upon him with a greater violence, and break those bones whose sinews gave it motion.—*Jeremy Taylor.*

What is revenge, but courage to call in our honor's debts, and wisdom to convert others' self-love into our own protection? — *Young.*

Haste me to know it; that I with wings as swift as meditation, or the thoughts of love, may sweep to my revenge.—*Shakespeare.*

We can more easily avenge an injury than requite a kindness; on this account, because there is less difficulty in getting the better of the wicked than in making one's self equal with the good.—*Cicero.*

Nothing is more ruinous for a man than when he is mighty enough in any part to right himself without right.—*Jacobi.*

Revenge is barren of itself; itself is the dreadful food it feeds on ; its delight is murder, and its satiety, despair.—*Schiller.*

The best sort of revenge is not to be like him who did the injury.—*Marcus Antoninus*

Heat not a furnace for your foe so hot that it doth singe yourself. We may outrun by violent swiftness that which we run at, and lose by overrunning.—*Shakespeare.*

Revenge is an act of passion ; vengeance, of justice : injuries are revenged ; crimes are avenged.—*Johnson.*

In revenge a man is but even with his enemy ; for it is a princely thing to pardon, and Solomon saith it is the glory of a man to pass over a transgression.—*Bacon.*

He that thinks he shows boldness or height of mind by a scurrilous reply to a scurrilous provocation measures himself by a false standard, and acts not the spirit of a man, but the spleen of a wasp.—*South.*

To revenge is no valor, but to bear.— *Shakespeare.*

REVERENCE.

Turks carefully collect every scrap of paper that comes in their way, because the name of God may be written thereon.—*Richter.*

Rather let my head stoop to the block than these knees bow to any save to the God of heaven.—*Shakespeare.*

Some men use no other means to acquire respect than by insisting on it; and it sometimes answers their purpose, as it does a highwayman's in regard to money.—*Shenstone.*

Respect is better procured by exacting than soliciting it.—*Lord Greville.*

In the humblest condition, a power goes forth from a devout and disinterested spirit, calling forth silently moral and religious sentiment, perhaps in a child, or some other friend, and teaching, without the aid of words, the loveliness and peace of sincere and single-hearted virtue.—*Channing.*

I would be like a little bird, which the wind rocks on a branch beneath the mild rays of the sun, and whose voice ascends unceasingly to the blue heaven.—*Rückert.*

Reverence is an ennobling sentiment; it is felt to be degrading only by the vulgar mind, which would escape the sense of its own littleness by elevating itself into an antagonist of what is above it. He that has no pleasure in looking up is not fit so much as to look down. *Washington Allston.*

REVERY.

Revery, which is thought in its nebulous state, borders closely upon the land of sleep, by which it is bounded as by a natural frontier.— *Victor Hugo.*

Sit in revery, and watch the changing color of the waves that break upon the idle sea-shore of the mind.—*Longfellow.*

To lose one's self in revery, one must be either very happy or very unhappy. Revery is the child of extreme.—*Rivarol.*

Revery is when ideas float in our mind without reflection or regard of the understanding.— *Locke.*

REVOLUTION.

We deplore the outrages which accompany revolutions. But the more violent the outrages, the more assured we feel that a revolution was necessary.—*Macaulay.*

It is far more easy to pull down than to build up, and to destroy than to preserve. Revolutions have on this account been falsely supposed to be fertile of great talent; as the dregs rise to the top during a fermentation, and the lightest things are carried highest by the whirlwind.—*Colton.*

The working of revolutions misleads me no more ; it is as necessary to our race as its waves to the stream, that it may not be a stagnant marsh. Ever renewed in its forms, the genius of humanity blossoms.—*Herder.*

Stimulants do not give strength, comets do not give heat, and revolutions do not give liberty.—*Philarète Chasles.*

The best security against revolution is in constant correction of abuses and introduction of needed improvements. It is the neglect of timely repair that makes rebuilding necessary. *Whately.*

Revolutions are like the most noxious dungheaps, which bring into life the noblest vegetables.—*Napoleon.*

Those who give the first shock to a state are naturally the first to be overwhelmed in its ruin. The fruits of public commotion are seldom enjoyed by the man who was the first to set it a going ; he only troubles the water for another's net.—*Montaigne.*

Revolutions are not made, they come. A revolution is as natural a growth as an oak. It comes out of the past. Its foundations are laid far back.—*Wendell Phillips.*

REWARD.

He who wishes to secure the good of others has already secured his own.—*Confucius.*

Every duty brings its peculiar delight, every denial its appropriate compensation, every thought its recompense, every love its elysium, every cross its crown; pay goes with performance as effect with cause. Meanness overreaches itself; vice vitiates whoever indulges in it; the wicked wrong their own souls; generosity greatens; virtue exalts; charity transfigures; and holiness is the essence of angelhood. God does not require us to live on credit; he pays us what we earn as we earn it, good or evil, heaven or hell, according to our choice.— *Charles Mildmay.*

The laurel is cheap to the giver, but precious in his sight who hath won it.—*Tupper.*

He who sows, even with tears, the precious seed of faith, hope, and love shall "doubtless come again with joy and bring his sheaves with him"; because it is in the very nature of that seed to yield, under the kindly influence secured to it, a joyful harvest.—*Cecil.*

A man that fortune's buffets and rewards hast taken with equal thanks.—*Shakespeare.*

It is the amends of a short and troublesome life, that doing good and suffering ill entitles man to one longer and better.—*William Penn.*

RHETORIC.

The two best rules for a system of rhetoric are: first, have something to say; and next, say it.—*George Emmons.*

Rhetoric is nothing but reason well dressed and argument put in order.—*Jeremy Collier.*

Rhetoric in serious discourses is like the flowers in corn; pleasing to those who come only for amusement, but prejudicial to him who would reap profit from it.—*Swift.*

There is a truth and beauty in rhetoric; but it oftener serves ill turns than good ones.— *William Penn.*

Rhetoric is the creature of art, which he who feels least will most excel in; it is the quackery of eloquence, and deals in nostrums, not in cures.—*Colton.*

RICHES.

Man was born to be rich, or inevitably grows rich by the use of his faculties, by the union of thought with nature. Property is an intellectual production The game requires coolness, right reasoning, promptness, and patience in the players. Cultivated labor drives out brute labor.—*Emerson.*

Superfluity comes sooner by white hairs, but Competency lives longer.—*Shakespeare.*

The greatest luxury of riches is that they enable you to escape so much good advice. The rich are always advising the poor; but the poor seldom venture to return the compliment. *Helps.*

He that maketh haste to be rich shall not be innocent.—*Bible.*

An eager pursuit of fortune is inconsistent with a severe devotion to truth. The heart must grow tranquil before the thought can become searching.—*Bovee.*

Riches are apt to betray a man into arrogance.—*Addison.*

Providence has decreed that those common acquisitions — money, gems, plate, noble mansions, and dominion — should be sometimes bestowed on the indolent and unworthy; but those things which constitute our true riches, and which are properly our own, must be procured by our own labor.—*Erasmus.*

In this world, it is not what we take up, but what we give up, that makes us rich.—*Beecher.*

Plenty and indigence depend upon the opinion every one has of them; and riches, no more than glory or health, have no more beauty or pleasure than their possessor is pleased to lend them.—*Montaigne.*

When we see the shameful fortunes amassed in all quarters of the globe, are we not impelled to exclaim that Judas's thirty pieces of silver have fructified across the centuries ? — *Madame Swetchine.*

Everything, virtue, glory, honor, things human and divine, all are slaves to riches.— *Horace.*

If thou art rich, then show the greatness of thy fortune, or what is better, the greatness of thy soul, in the meekness of thy conversation; condescend to men of low estate, support the distressed, and patronize the neglected. Be great.—*Sterne.*

Rich men without wisdom and learning are called sheep with golden fleeces.—*Solon.*

Riches are the pettiest and least worthy gifts which God can give a man. What are they to God's Word ? Yea, to bodily gifts, such as beauty and health; or to the gifts of the mind, such as understanding, skill, wisdom ? Yet men toil for them day and night, and take no rest. Therefore our Lord God commonly gives riches to foolish people to whom he gives nothing else.—*Luther.*

Worldly riches are like nuts; many clothes are torn in getting them, many a tooth broke in cracking them, but never a belly filled with eating them.—*R. Venning.*

We are all of us richer than we think we are; but we are taught to borrow and to beg, and brought up more to make use of what is another's than our own. Man can in nothing fix and conform himself to his mere necessity. Of pleasure, wealth and power he grasps at more than he can hold; his greediness is incapahle of moderation.—*Montaigne.*

A mask of gold hides all deformities.
                                            Decker.

Riches without charity are nothing worth. They are a blessing only to him who makes them a blessing to others.—*Fielding.*

If a man wishes to become rich, he must appear to be rich.—*Goldsmith.*

If I have but enough for myself and family, I am steward only for myself: if I have more, I am but a steward of that abundance for others.
                                            George Herbert.

I cannot call riches better than the baggage of virtue; the Roman word is better, "impedimenta," — for as the baggage is to an army, so is riches to virtue; it cannot be spared nor left behind but it hindereth the march; yea, and the care of it sometimes loseth or disturbeth the victory. Of great riches there is no real use, except it be in the distribution; the rest is but conceit.—*Bacon.*

Much learning shows how little mortals know; much wealth, how little worldlings can enjoy.—*Young.*

Riches are valuable at all times, and to all men, because they always purchase pleasures such as men are accustomed to and desire; nor can anything restrain or regulate the love of money but a sense of honor and virtue, which, if it be not nearly equal at all times, will naturally abound most in ages of knowledge and refinement.—*Hume.*

If thou art rich, thou art poor; for, like an ass, whose back with ingots bows, thou bearest thy heavy riches but a journey, and death unloads thee.—*Shakespeare.*

It has been wisely said, "There be as many miseries beyond riches as on this side of them." I have a rich neighbor who is so busy that he has no leisure to laugh. God knows that the cares, which are the keys that keep those riches, hang often so heavily at the rich man's girdle that they clog him with weary days and restless nights, when others sleep quietly.—
                                            Izaak Walton.

Satiety comes of riches, and contumaciousness of satiety.—*Solon.*

The use we make of our fortune determines its sufficiency. A little is enough if used wisely, and too much if expended foolishly.—*Bovee.*

Misery assails riches, as lightning does the highest towers; or as a tree that is heavy laden with fruit breaks its own boughs, so do riches destroy the virtue of their possessor.—*Burton.*

If all were rich, gold would be penniless.—
                                            Bailey.

Riches, though they may reward virtues, yet they cannot cause them; he is much more noble who deserves a benefit than he who bestows one.—*Feltham.* .

Riches exclude only one inconvenience, — that is, poverty.—*Johnson.*

A man hath riches. Whence came they, and whither go they? for this is the way to form a judgment of the esteem which they and their possessor deserve. If they have been acquired by fraud or violence, if they make him proud and vain, if they minister to luxury and intemperance, if they are avariciously hoarded up and applied to no proper use, the possessor becomes odious and contemptible.—
                                            Bishop Jortin.

Vulgar opulence fills the street from wall to wall of the houses, and begrudges all but the gutter to everybody whose sleeve is a little worn at the elbows.—*John Weiss.*

It was wisely said, by a man of great observation, that there are as many miseries beyond riches as on this side of them.—*Izaak Walton.*

Riches are for the comfort of life, and not life for the accumulation of riches. I asked a holy wise man, "Who is fortunate and who is unfortunate?" He replied: "He was fortunate who ate and sowed, and he was unfortunate who died without having enjoyed."—*Saadi.*

May I deem the wise man rich, and may I have such a portion of gold as none but a prudent man can either bear or employ.—*Plato.*

There is no less merit in keeping what we have got than in first acquiring it. Chance has something to do with the one, while the other will always be the effect of skill.—*Ovid.*

Men leave their riches either to their kindred or their friends, and moderate portions prosper best in both.—*Bacon.*

We see but the outside of a rich man's happiness; few consider him to be like the silkworm, that, when she seems to play, is at the very same time consuming herself.—*Izaak Walton.*

Wealth is not his that has it, but his that enjoys it.—*Franklin.*

"If I was rich," said one, "I—" Illusion! We hold often firmer to the last crown which we have amassed than to the first which we gained.—*J. Petit, Senn.*

He hath riches sufficient who hath enough to be charitable.—*Sir Thomas Browne.*

Riches oftentimes, if nobody takes them away, make to themselves wings and fly away; and truly, many a time the undue sparing of them is but letting their wings grow, which makes them ready to fly away; and the contributing a part of them to do good only clips their wings a little and makes them stay the longer with their owner.—*Leighton.*

He is rich whose income is more than his expenses; and he is poor whose expenses exceed his income.—*Bruyère.*

Wouldst thou multiply thy riches? diminish them wisely; or wouldst thou make thy estate entire? divide it charitably. Seeds that are scattered increase; but, hoarded up, they perish.—*Quarles.*

Riches amassed in haste will diminish; but those collected by hand and little by little will multiply.—*Goethe.*

He who recognizes no higher logic than that of the shilling may become a very rich man, and yet remain all the while an exceedingly poor creature; for riches are no proof whatever of moral worth, and their glitter often serves only to draw attention to the worthlessness of their possessor, as the glow-worm's light reveals the grub.—*Samuel Smiles.*

Ah, if the rich were rich as the poor fancy riches!—*Emerson.*

We are so vain as to set the highest value upon those things to which nature has assigned the lowest place. What can be more coarse and rude in the mine than the precious metals, or more slavish and dirty than the people that dig and work them? And yet they defile our minds more than our bodies, and make the possessor fouler than the artificer of them. Rich men, in fine, are only the greater slaves.—*Seneca.*

Riches do not exhilarate us so much with their possession as they torment us with their loss.—*Gregory.*

Never respect men merely for their riches, but rather for their philanthropy; we do not value the sun for its height, but for its use.—*Bailey.*

No man can tell whether he is rich or poor by turning to his ledger. It is the heart that makes a man rich. He is rich or poor according to what he is, not according to what he has.—*Beecher.*

A wise rich man is like the back or stock of the chimney, and his wealth the fire; he receives it, not for his own need, but to reflect the heat to others' good.—*Seneca.*

The god of this world is riches, pleasure, and pride, wherewith it abuses all the creatures and gifts of God.—*Luther.*

The greatest and the most amiable privilege which the rich enjoy over the poor is that which they exercise the least, — the privilege of making them happy.—*Colton.*

Riches should be admitted into our houses, but not into our hearts; we may take them into our possession, but not into our affections.— *Charron.*

Some of God's noblest sons, I think, will be selected from those that know how to take wealth, with all its temptations, and maintain godliness therewith. It is hard to be a saint standing in a golden niche.—*Beecher.*

Labor not to be rich; . . . . for riches certainly make themselves wings; they fly away as an eagle toward heaven.—*Bible.*

Riches for the most part are hurtful to them that possess them.—*Plutarch.*

However rich or elevated, a nameless something is always wanting to our imperfect fortune.—*Horace.*

Riches, honors, and pleasures are the sweets which destroy the mind's appetite for its heavenly food; poverty, disgrace, and pain are the bitters which restore it.—*Bishop Horne.*

A great fortune is a great slavery.—*Seneca.*

Do we, mad as we all are after riches, hear often enough from the pulpit the spirit of those words in which Dean Swift, in his epitaph on the affluent and profligate Colonel Chartres, announces the small esteem of wealth in the eyes of God, from the fact of his thus lavishing it upon the meanest and basest of his creatures? — *Whipple.*

Great abundance of riches cannot of any man be both gathered and kept without sin.— *Erasmus.*

Every man is rich or poor, according to the proportion between his desires and enjoyments. Any enlargement of riches is therefore equally destructive to happiness with the diminution of possession; and he that teaches another to long for what he shall never obtain is no less an enemy to his quiet than if he had robbed him of part of his patrimony.—*Johnson.*

It is not the greatness of a man's means that makes him independent, so much as the smallness of his wants.—*Cobbett.*

RIDICULE.

How comes it to pass, then, that we appear such cowards in reasoning, and are so afraid to stand the test of ridicule?—*Shaftesbury.*

Ridicule is generally made use of to laugh men out of virtue and good sense, by attacking everything praiseworthy in human life.—
Addison.

The fatal fondness for indulging in a spirit of ridicule, and the injurious and irreparable consequences which sometimes attend the too severe reply, can never be condemned with more asperity than it deserves. Not to offend is the first step towards pleasing. To give pain is as much an offence against humanity as against good-breeding, and surely it is as well to abstain from an action because it is sinful, as because it is unpolite.—*Blair.*

Cervantes smiled Spain's chivalry away.—
Byron.

The raillery which is consistent with good-breeding is a gentle animadversion on some foible, which, while it raises the laugh in the rest of the company, doth not put the person rallied out of countenance, or expose him to shame or contempt. On the contrary, the jest should be so delicate that the object of it should be capable of joining in the mirth it occasions.—
Fielding.

For man learns more readily and remembers more willingly what excites his ridicule than what deserves esteem and respect.—
Horace.

It is easy for a man who sits idle at home, and has nobody to please but himself, to ridicule or censure the common practices of mankind.—*Johnson.*

The talent of turning men into ridicule, and exposing to laughter those one converses with, is the gratification of little minds and ungenerous tempers. A young man with this cast of mind cuts himself off from all manner of improvement.—*Addison.*

Raillery is a mode of speaking in favor of one's wit against one's good-nature.—
Montesquieu.

We can learn to read and write, but we cannot learn raillery; that must be a particular gift of nature; and, to tell the truth, I esteem him happy who does not wish to acquire it. The character of sarcasm is dangerous; although this quality makes those laugh whom it does not wound, it, nevertheless, never procures esteem.—*Oxenstiern.*

Ridicule, which chiefly arises from pride, a selfish passion, is but at best a gross pleasure, too rough an entertainment for those who are highly polished and refined.—
Henry Home.

Ridicule is a weak weapon when levelled at a strong mind; but common men are cowards, and dread an empty laugh.—*Tupper.*

He who brings ridicule to bear against truth finds in his hand a blade without a hilt. The most sparkling and pointed flame of wit flickers and expires against the incombustible walls of her sanctuary.—*Landor.*

Your sayer of smart things has a bad heart.
Pascal.

It is commonly said, and more particularly by Lord Shaftesbury, that ridicule is the best test of truth; for that it will not stick where it is not just. I deny it. A truth learned in a certain light, and attacked in certain words, by men of wit and humor, may, and often doth, become ridiculous, at least so far that the truth is only remembered and repeated for the sake of the ridicule.—*Chesterfield.*

Ridicule is often employed with more power and success than severity.—*Horace.*

Raillery is more insupportable than wrong; because we have a right to resent injuries, but are ridiculous in being angry at a jest.—
Rochefoucauld.

Betray mean terror of ridicule, thou shalt find fools enough to mock thee; but answer thou their language with contempt, and the scoffers will lick thy feet.—*Tupper.*

RIGOR.

Rigor pushed too far is sure to miss its aim, however good, as the bow snaps that is bent too stiffly.—*Schiller.*

RIVALRY.

Two stars keep not their motion in one sphere.—*Shakespeare.*

It is impossible for authors to discover beauties in one another's works : they have eyes only for spots and blemishes.—*Addison.*

Emulation adds its spur.—*Lucan.*

It is the privilege of posterity to set matters right between those antagonists who, by their rivalry for greatness, divided a whole age.—
Addison.

Women do not disapprove their rivals; they hate them.—*James Parton.*

In ambition, as in love, the successful can afford to be indulgent towards their rivals. The prize our own, it is graceful to recognize the merit that vainly aspired to it.—*Bovee.*

ROBBERY.

The robbed that smiles steals something from the thief.—*Shakespeare.*

He that is robbed, not wanting what is stolen, let him not know it, and he is not robbed at all.—*Shakespeare.*

ROGUE.

After long experience of the world, I affirm before God, I never knew a rogue who was not unhappy.—*Junius.*

Make yourself an honest man, and then you may be sure that there is one rascal less in the world.—*Carlyle.*

ROMANCE.

In this commonplace world every one is said to be romantic who either admires a fine thing or does one.—*Pope.*

Romance has been elegantly defined as the offspring of fiction and love.—*Disraeli.*

Romance is the truth of imagination and boyhood. Homer's horses clear the world at a bound. The child's eye needs no horizon to its prospect. The Oriental tale is not too vast. Pearls dropping from trees are only falling leaves in autumn. The palace that grew up in a night merely awakens a wish to live in it. The impossibilities of fifty years are the common-places of five.—*Willmott.*

In the meanest hut is a romance, if you knew the hearts there.—*Varnhagen von Ense.*

What philosopher of the schoolroom, with the mental dowry of four summers, ever questions the power of the wand that opened the dark eyes of the beautiful princess, or subtracts a single inch from the stride of seven leagues?—*Willmott.*

I despair of ever receiving the same degree of pleasure from the most exalted performances of genius which I felt in childhood from pieces which my present judgment regards as trifling and contemptible.—*Burke.*

RUDENESS.

Society is infected with rude, cynical, restless, and frivolous persons who prey upon the rest, and whom no public opinion concentrated into good manners, forms accepted by the sense of all, can reach; the contradictors and railers at public and private tables, who are like terriers, who conceive it the duty of a dog of honor to growl at any passer-by, and do the honors of the house by barking him out of sight.—
Emerson.

RUINS.

The legendary tablets of the past.—
Walter Scott.

The ruins of a house may be repaired; why cannot those of the face?—*La Fontaine.*

Black-letter record of the ages.—*Diderot.*

Tully was not so eloquent as thou, thou nameless column with the buried base.—*Byron.*

Ruins in some countries indicate prosperity; in others, decay. In Egypt, Greece, and Italy they record the decline and fall of great empires; in England, Scotland, and Wales they mark abolition of feudal tyranny, the establishment of popular freedom, and the consolidation of national strength. The lawless power formerly dispersed among petty chiefs is now concentrated in the legal magistrate. The elegant villa has succeeded to the frowning castle. Where the wild deer roamed, the corn now waves; the sound of the hammer has drowned the war-cry of the henchman.—*R. Anderson.*

Mile-stones on the road of time.—*Chamfort.*

As I stand here this pleasant afternoon, looking up at the old chapel (the Mission Dolores), its ragged senility contrasting with the smart spring sunshine, its two gouty pillars with the plaster dropping away like tattered bandages, its rayless windows, its crumbling entrances, the leper spots on its whitewashed wall eating through the dark adobe,—I give the poor old mendicant but a year longer to sit by the highway and ask alms in the names of the blessed saints.—*Bret Harte.*

The broken eggshell of a civilization which time has hatched and devoured.—
Julia Ward Howe.

The monuments of mutability.—*Rivarol.*

RUMOR.

He that easily believes rumors has the principle within him to augment rumors. It is strange to see the ravenous appetite with which some devourers of character and happiness fix upon the sides of the innocent and unfortunate.
Jane Porter.

Stuffing the ears of men with false reports.—
Shakespeare.

How violently do rumors blow the sails of popular judgments! How few there be that can discern between truth and truth-likeness, between shows and substance!—*Sir P. Sidney.*

In every ear it spread, on every tongue it grew.—*Pope.*

The art of spreading rumors may be compared to the art of pin-making. There is usually some truth, which I call the wire; as this passes from hand to hand, one gives it a polish, another a point, others make and put on the head, and at last the pin is completed.—*Newton.*

Rumor is a pipe blown by surmises, jealousies, conjectures; and of so easy and so plain a stop, that the blunt monster with uncounted heads, the still discordant wavering multitude, can play upon it.—*Shakespeare.*

S.

SABBATH.

The green oasis, the little grassy meadow in the wilderness, where, after the week-days' journey, the pilgrim halts for refreshment and repose.—*Dr. Reade.*

On Sunday heaven's gates stand open.—*George Herbert.*

There is a Sunday conscience, as well as a Sunday coat; and those who make religion a secondary concern put the coat and conscience carefully by to put on only once a week.—*Dickens.*

Perpetual memory of the Maker's rest.—*Bishop Mant.*

A world without a Sabbath would be like a man without a smile, like a summer without flowers, and like a homestead without a garden. It is the joyous day of the whole week.—*Beecher.*

Sunday is the golden clasp that binds together the volume of the week.—*Longfellow.*

The Sunday is the core of our civilization, dedicated to thought and reverence. It invites to the noblest solitude and to the noblest society.—*Emerson.*

The Sabbath was made for man, and not man for the Sabbath.—*Bible.*

There are many persons who think Sunday is a sponge with which to wipe out the sins of the week.—*Beecher.*

He that remembers not to keep the Christian Sabbath at the beginning of the week will be in danger to forget before the end of the week that he is a Christian.—*Sir Edmund Turner.*

He who ordained the Sabbath loves the poor.—*Holmes.*

O what a blessing is Sunday, interposed between the waves of worldly business like the divine path of the Israelites through Jordan! There is nothing in which I would advise you to be more strictly conscientious than in keeping the Sabbath day holy. I can truly declare that to me the Sabbath has been invaluable.—*Wilberforce.*

Sunday, that day so tedious to the triflers of earth, so full of beautiful repose, of calmness and strength for the earnest and heavenly-minded.—*Maria M'Intosh.*

SACRIFICE.

Upon such sacrifices the gods themselves throw incense.—*Shakespeare.*

The sacrifices of God are a broken spirit; a broken and a contrite heart, O God, thou wilt not despise.—*Bible.*

Our virtues are dearer to us the more we have had to suffer for them. It is the same with our children. All profound affection admits a sacrifice.—*Vauvenargues.*

We can offer up much in the large, but to make sacrifices in little things is what we are seldom equal to.—*Goethe.*

SADNESS.

It is quite deplorable to see how many rational creatures, or at least who are thought so, mistake suffering for sanctity, and think a sad face and a gloomy habit of mind propitious offerings to that Deity whose works are all light and lustre and harmony and loveliness.—*Lady Morgan.*

A plague of sighing and grief! It blows a man up like a bladder.—*Shakespeare*

SARCASM.

He that cometh to seek after knowledge with a mind to scorn and censure shall be sure to find matter for his humor, but none for his instruction.—*Bacon.*

Sarcasm I now see to be, in general, the language of the Devil; for which reason I have long since as good as renounced it.—*Carlyle.*

At the best, sarcasms, bitter irony, scathing wit, are a sort of sword-play of the mind. You pink your adversary, and he is forthwith dead; and then you deserve to be hung for it.—*Bovee.*

Sarcasm poisons reproof.—*E. Wigglesworth.*

A sneer is the weapon of the weak. Like other devil's weapons, it is always cunningly ready to our hand, and there is more poison in the handle than in the point.—*Lowell.*

SATIETY.

The sweetest honey is loathsome in its own deliciousness, and in the taste confounds the appetite.—*Shakespeare.*

Satiety comes of too frequent repetition; and he who will not give himself leisure to be thirsty can never find the true pleasure of drinking.—*Montaigne.*

With much we surfeit; plenty makes us poor.—*Drayton.*

The fruition of what is unlawful must be followed by remorse. The core sticks in the throat after the apple is eaten, and the sated appetite loathes the interdicted pleasure for which innocence was bartered.—*Jane Porter.*

Some are cursed with the fulness of satiety; and how can they bear the ills of life, when its very pleasures fatigue them ? — *Colton.*

There is no sense of weariness like that which closes in a day of eager and unintermittent pursuit of pleasure. The apple is eaten, but " the core sticks in the throat." Expectation has then given way to ennui, appetite to satiety.— *Bovee.*

The same stale viands, served up over and over, the stomach nauseates.— *R. Wynne.*

The ear is cloyed unto satiety with honeyed strains, that daily from the fount of Helicon flow murmuring.— *William Herbert.*

We grow tired of ourselves, much more of other people. Use may in part reconcile us to our own tediousness, but we do not adopt that of others on the same paternal principle.— *Hazlitt.*

The flower which we do not pluck is the only one which never loses its beauty or its fragrance.— *W. R. Alger.*

The wholesomest meats that are will breed satiety.— *Sir John Harrington.*

The most voluptuous and loose person breathing, were he tied to follow his hawks and his hounds, his dice and his courtships every day, would find it the greatest torment and calamity that could befall him; he would fly to the mines and galleys for his recreation.— *South.*

With pleasure-drugged he almost longed for woe.— *Byron.*

To loathe the taste of sweetness, whereof little more than a little is by much too much.— *Shakespeare.*

Attainment is followed by neglect, possession by disgust; and the malicious remark of the Greek epigrammatist on marriage may be applied to every other course of life, that its two days of happiness are the first and the last.— *Johnson.*

SATIRE.

Satire is a sort of glass wherein beholders generally discover everybody's face but their own; which is the chief reason for that kind of reception it meets with in the world, and that so very few are offended with it.— *Swift.*

Satire is a composition of salt and mercury; and it depends upon the different mixture and preparation of these ingredients, that it comes out a noble medicine or a rank poison.— *Jeffrey.*

Of a bitter satirist — of Swift, for instance — it might be said that the person or thing on which his satire fell shrivelled up as if the Devil had spit on it.— *Hawthorne.*

In the present state of the world it is difficult not to write lampoons.— *Juvenal.*

As men neither fear nor respect what has been made contemptible, all honor to him who makes oppression laughable as well as detestable. Armies cannot protect it then; and walls which have remained impenetrable to cannon have fallen before a roar of laughter or a hiss of contempt.— *Whipple.*

Lampoons and satires, that are written with wit and spirit, are like poisoned darts, which not only inflict a wound, but make it incurable.— *Addison.*

In fashionable circles general satire, which attacks the fault rather than the person, is unwelcome; while that which attacks the person and spares the fault is always acceptable.— *Richter.*

Satire should, like a polished razor keen, wound with a touch that is scarcely felt or seen.— *Mary Wortley Montagu.*

Of satires I think as Epictetus did : " If evil be said of thee, and if it be true, correct thyself; if it be a lie, laugh at it." By dint of time and experience I have learned to be a good posthorse; I go through my appointed daily stage, and I care not for the curs who bark at me along the road.— *Frederick the Great.*

A little wit and a great deal of ill-nature will furnish a man for satire; but the greatest instance of wit is to commend well.— *Tillotson.*

Satires and lampoons on particular people circulate more by giving copies in confidence to the friends of the parties than by printing them.— *Sheridan.*

Let there be gall enough in thy ink; though thou write with a goose-pen, no matter.— *Shakespeare.*

Satirical writers and speakers are not half so clever as they think themselves, nor as they are thought to be. They do winnow the corn, it is true, but it is to feed upon the chaff. I am sorry to add that they who are always speaking ill of others are also very apt to be doing ill to them. It requires some talent and some generosity to find out talent and generosity in others, though nothing but self-conceit and malice are needed to discover or to imagine faults. It is much easier for an ill-natured man than for a good-natured man to be smart and witty.— *Rev. Dr. Sharpe.*

No sword bites so fiercely as an evil tongue.— *Sir P. Sidney.*

A satire should expose nothing but what is corrigible, and should make a due discrimination between those that are and those that are not the proper objects of it.— *Addison.*

We smile at the satire expended upon the follies of others, but we forget to weep at our own.—*Madame Necker.*

Viewed in its happiest form, as a work of art, satire has one defect which seems to be incurable, — its uniformity of censure. Bitterness scarcely admits those fine transitions which make the harmony of a composition. Aquafortis bites a plate all over alike. The satirist is met by the difficulty of the etcher.—*Willmott.*

It is as hard to satirize well a man of distinguished vices as to praise well a man of distinguished virtues.—*Swift.*

But the most annoying of all public reformers is the personal satirist. Though he may be considered by some few as a useful member of society, yet he is only ranked with the hangman, whom we tolerate because he executes the judgment we abhor to do ourselves, and avoid with a natural detestation of his office. The pen of the one and the cord of the other are inseparable in our minds.— *Jane Porter.*

SCANDAL.
Dead scandals form good subjects for dissection.—*Byron.*

Malice may empty her quiver, but cannot wound; the dirt will not stick, the jests will not take. Without the consent of the world, a scandal doth not go deep; it is only a slight stroke upon the injured party, and returneth with the greater force upon those that gave it. *Saville.*

Scandal breeds hatred; hatred begets division; division makes faction, and faction brings ruin.—*Quarles.*

Socrates, when informed of some derogating speeches one had used concerning him behind his back, made only this facetious reply, "Let him beat me too when I am absent."— *La Fontaine.*

The improbability of a malicious story serves but to help forward the currency of it, because it increases the scandal. So that, in such instances, the world is like the pious St. Austin, who said he believed some things because they were absurd and impossible.—*Sterne.*

The tale-bearer and the tale-hearer should be both hanged up, back to back, one by the tongue, the other by the ear.—*South.*

No might nor greatness in mortality can censure escape; back-wounding calumny the whitest virtue strikes; what king so strong, can tie the gall up in the slanderous tongue?— *Shakespeare.*

If there is any person to whom you feel dislike, that is the person of whom you ought never to speak.—*Cecil.*

Many a wretch has rid on a hurdle who has done less mischief than utterers of forged tales, coiners of scandal, and clippers of reputation.— *Sheridan.*

At every word a reputation dies.—*Pope.*

There are a set of malicious, prating, prudent gossips, both male and female, who murder characters to kill time; and will rob a young fellow of his good name before he has years to know the value of it.—*Sheridan.*

Scandal, like a reptile crawling over a bright grass, leaves a trail and a stain.— *Cunningham.*

It generally takes its rise either from an ill-will to mankind, a private inclination to make ourselves esteemed an ostentation of wit, and vanity of being thought in the secrets of the world; or from a desire of gratifying any of these dispositions of mind in those persons with whom we converse.—*Addison.*

Convey a libel in a frown, and wink a reputation down.—*Swift.*

Tears are copiously showered over frailties the discoverer takes a malicious delight in circulating; and thus, all granite on one side of the heart, and all milk on the other, the unsexed scandal-monger hies from house to house, pouring balm from its weeping eyes on the wounds it inflicts with its stabbing tongue. *Whipple.*

If hours did not hang heavy, what would become of scandal?—*Bancroft.*

A tale of scandal is as fatal to the credit of a prudent lady as a fever is generally to those of the strongest constitutions. But there is a sort of puny, sickly reputation, that is always ailing, yet will wither the robuster characters of a hundred prudes.—*Sheridan.*

Scandal is the sport of its authors, the dread of fools, and the contempt of the wise.— *W. B. Clulow.*

SCARS.
The scars of the body, — what are they, compared to the hidden ones of the heart?— *Madame de Maintenon.*

Who has not raised a tombstone, here and there, over buried hopes and dead joys, on the road of life? Like the scars of the heart, they are not to be obliterated.—*Ninon de l'Enclos.*

A scar nobly got is a good livery of honor. *Shakespeare.*

SCENERY.
The morning comes. I don't know a pleasanter feeling than that of walking with the sun shining on objects quite new, and — although you may have made the voyage a dozen times — quite strange.—*Thackeray.*

SCEPTICISM.

I know not any crime so great that a man could contrive to commit as poisoning the sources of eternal truth.—*Johnson.*

I would rather dwell in the dim fog of superstition than in air rarefied to nothing by the air-pump of unbelief; in which the panting breast expires, vainly and convulsively gasping for breath.—*Richter.*

An atheist is more reclaimable than a papist, as ignorance is sooner cured than superstition.—*Sterne.*

Scepticism has never founded empires, established principles, or changed the world's heart. The great doers in history have always been men of faith.—*Chapin.*

Freethinkers are generally those who never think at all.—*Sterne.*

The sceptic, when he plunges into the depths of infidelity, like the miser who leaps from the shipwreck, will find that the treasures which he bears about him will only sink him deeper in the abyss.—*Colton.*

Sceptics are generally ready to believe anything, provided it is only sufficiently improbable; it is at matters of fact that such people stumble.—*Von Knebel.*

SCIENCE.

Let us not fear that the issues of natural science shall be scepticism or anarchy. Through all God's works there runs a beautiful harmony. The remotest truth in his universe is linked to that which lies nearest the Throne.—*Chapin.*

Nothing has tended more to retard the advancement of science than the disposition in vulgar minds to vilify what they cannot comprehend.—*Johnson.*

Science ever has been, and ever must be, the safeguard of religion.—*Sir David Brewster.*

To me there never has been a higher source of earthly honor or distinction than that connected with advances in science. I have not possessed enough of the eagle in my character to make a direct flight to the loftiest altitudes in the social world; and I certainly never endeavored to reach those heights by using the creeping powers of the reptile, who, in ascending, generally chooses the dirtiest path, because it is the easiest.—*Sir H. Davy.*

Science is the natural ally of religion.—
Theodore Parker.

The sciences are of a sociable disposition, and flourish best in the neighborhood of each other; nor is there any branch of learning but may be helped and improved by assistance drawn from other arts.—*Blackstone.*

Science and art are the handmaids of religion.—*François Delsarte.*

The strength of all sciences, which consisteth in their harmony, each supporting the other, is as the strength of the old man's fagot in the band; for were it not better for a man in a fair room to set up one great light, or branching candlestick of lights, than to go about with a small watch-candle into every corner?—
Bacon.

Art and science have their meeting-point in method.—*Bulwer Lytton.*

I have spent much time in the study of the abstract sciences; but the paucity of persons with whom you can communicate on such subjects disgusted me with them. When I began to study man, I saw that these abstract sciences are not suited to him, and that in diving into them, I wandered farther from my real object than those who knew them not, and I forgave them for not having attended to these things. I expected then, however, that I should find some companions in the study of man, since it was so specifically a duty. I was in error. There are fewer students of man than of geometry.—*Pascal.*

Science, when well digested, is nothing but good sense and reason.—*Stanislaus.*

Science confounds everything; it gives to the flowers an animal appetite, and takes away from even the plants their chastity.—*Joubert.*

Science is the topography of ignorance.—
Holmes.

Science corrects the old creeds, sweeps away, with every new perception, our infantile catechisms, and necessitates a faith commensurate with the grander orbits and universal laws which it discloses.—*Emerson.*

Old sciences are unravelled like old stockings, by beginning at the foot.—*Swift.*

Science is, I believe, nothing but trained and organized common-sense, differing from the latter only as a veteran may differ from a raw recruit; and its methods differ from those of common-sense only so far as the guardsman's cut and thrust differ from the manner in which a savage wields his club.—
Professor Huxley.

Learning is the dictionary, but sense the grammar, of science.—*Sterne.*

Science—in other words, knowledge—is not the enemy of religion; for, if so, then religion would mean ignorance. But it is often the antagonist of school-divinity.—*Holmes.*

Science surpasses the old miracles of mythology.—*Emerson.*

It is certain that a serious attention to the sciences and liberal arts softens and humanizes the temper, and cherishes those fine emotions in which true virtue and honor consist. It rarely, very rarely happens that a man of taste and learning is not, at least, an honest man, whatever frailties may attend him.—*Hume.*

When man seized the loadstone of science, the loadstar of superstition vanished in the clouds.—*W. R. Alger.*

The sciences throw an inexpressible grace over our compositions, even where they are not immediately concerned; as their effects are discernible where we least expect to find them. *Pliny.*

Extinguished theologians lie about the cradle of every science, as the strangled snakes beside that of Hercules.—*Professor Huxley.*

Nothing tends so much to the corruption of science as to suffer it to stagnate; these waters must be troubled before they can exert their virtues.—*Burke.*

SCOLDING.
No man was ever scolded out of his sins.—
Cowper.

The utmost that severity can do is to make men hypocrites; it can never make them converts.—*Dr. John Moore.*

SCRIPTURES.
We account the Scriptures of God to be the most sublime philosophy. I find more sure marks of authenticity in the Bible than in any profane history whatever.—*Isaac Newton.*

A stream where alike the elephant may swim, and the lamb may wade.—
Gregory the Great.

I have read it through many times; I now make a practice of going through it once a year. It is a book of all others for lawyers, as well as divines; and I pity the man who cannot find in it a rich supply of thought and rule for conduct. *Daniel Webster.*

The illumined record of celestial truth.—
Hosea Ballou.

Cities fall, empires come to nothing, kingdoms fade away as smoke. Where is Numa, Minos, Lycurgus? Where are their books? and what has become of their laws? But that this book no tyrant should have been able to consume, no tradition to choke, no heretic maliciously to corrupt; that it should stand, unto this day, amid the wreck of all that was human, without the alteration of one sentence so as to change the doctrine taught therein, — surely there is a very singular providence, claiming our attention in a most remarkable manner.—*Bishop Jewell.*

Let others dread and shun the Scriptures in their darkness; I shall wish I may deserve to be reckoned among those who admire and dwell upon them for their clearness. There are no songs comparable to the songs of Zion, no orations equal to those of the prophets, and no politics like those which the Scriptures teach.—
Milton.

I know the Bible is inspired, because it finds me at greater depths of my being than any other book.—*Coleridge.*

A noble book! All men's book! It is our first, oldest statement of the never-ending problem, — man's destiny, and God's ways with him here on earth; and all in such free-flowing outlines, — grand in its sincerity, in its simplicity, in its epic melody, and repose of reconcilement. *Carlyle.*

SEA.
Praise the sea, but keep on land.—
George Herbert.

In the vast archipelago of the east, where Borneo and Java and Sumatra lie, and the Molucca Islands, and the Philippines, the sea is often fanned only by the land and sea breezes, and is like a smooth bed, on which these islands seem to sleep in bliss, — islands in which the spice and perfume gardens of the world are embowered, and where the bird of paradise has its home, and the golden pheasant, and a hundred others of brilliant plumage, whose flight is among thickets so luxuriant, and scenery so picturesque, that European strangers find there the fairy land of their youthful dreams.—
Marryat.

He maketh the deep to boil like a pot.—
Bible.

Surely oak and threefold brass surrounded his heart who first trusted a frail vessel to the merciless ocean.—*Horace.*

He that will learn to pray, let him go to sea.
George Herbert.

The sea has been called deceitful and treacherous, but there lies in this trait only the character of a great natural power, which, to speak according to our own feelings, renews its strength, and, without reference to joy or sorrow, follows eternal laws which are imposed by a higher Power.—*Wilhelm von Humboldt.*

Mystery of waters, — never slumbering sea!
Montgomery

The sea drinks the air and the sun the sea.
Anacreon.

The ocean's surfy, slow, deep, mellow voice, full of mystery and awe, moaning over the dead it holds in its bosom, or lulling them to unbroken slumbers in the chambers of its vasty depths.—*Haliburton.*

The garrulous sea is talking to the shore;
let us go down and hear the graybeard's speech.
Alexander Smith.

There is sorrow on the sea; it cannot be
quiet.—*Bible.*

SEASONS.

The autumn with its fruits provides disorders for us, and the winter's cold turns them
into sharp diseases, and the spring brings
flowers to strew our hearses, and the summer
gives green turf and brambles to bind up our
graves.—*Jeremy Taylor.*

SECRECY.

God preserve us! If men knew what is
done in secret, no one would be free from the
interference of others.—*Saadi.*

Two may keep counsel putting one away!
Shakespeare.

A secret is too little for one, enough for two,
and too much for three.—*Howell.*

Generally he perceived in men of devout
simplicity this opinion: that the secrets of
nature were the secrets of God, — part of that
glory into which man is not to press too boldly.
Bacon.

Fire that is closest kept burns most of all.—
Shakespeare.

Connoisseur says that every secret he tells
to one of the fair sex is a sticking-plaster, which
attaches him to her, and often begets a second
secret.—*Richter.*

When a secret is revealed, it is the fault of
the man who has intrusted it.—*Bruyère.*

You cannot hide any secret. If the artist
succor his flagging spirits by opium or wine,
his work will characterize itself as the effect of
opium or wine. If you make a picture or a
statue, it sets the beholder in that state of mind
you had when you made it. If you spend for
show, on building, or gardening, or on pictures, or on equipages, it will so appear. We
are all physiognomists and penetrators of character, and things themselves are detective.—
Emerson.

Deep in my shut and silent heart.—*Byron.*

Secrecy is best taught by commencing with
ourselves.—*Chamfort.*

Secrecy is for the happy, — misery, hopeless
misery, needs no veil; under a thousand suns it
dares act openly.—*Schiller.*

He that discovers himself, till he hath made
himself master of his desires, lays himself open
to his own ruin, and makes himself prisoner to
his own tongue.—*Quarles.*

Where secrecy or mystery begins, vice or
roguery is not far off.—*Johnson.*

A resolution that is communicated is no
longer within thy power; thy intentions become
now the plaything of chance; he who would
have his commands certainly carried out must
take man by surprise.—*Goethe.*

It is in my memory locked, and you yourself
shall keep the key of it.—*Shakespeare.*

What is mine, even to my life, is hers I
love; but the secret of my friend is not mine!
Sir P. Sidney.

A secret in his mouth is like a wild bird
put into a cage; whose door no sooner opens,
but it is out.—*Ben Jonson.*

Who shall be true to us, when we are so
unsecret to ourselves? —*Shakespeare.*

I will govern my life and my thoughts as if
all the world were to see the one and to read
the other; for what does it signify to make
anything a secret to my neighbor, when to God
all our privacies are open? —*Seneca.*

The truly wise man should have no keeper
of his secret but himself.—*Guizot.*

Nothing is so oppressive as a secret; it is
difficult for ladies to keep it long; and I know
even in this matter a good number of men who
are women.—*La Fontaine.*

If a fool knows a secret, he tells it because
he is a fool; if a knave knows one, he tells it
whenever it is his interest to tell it. But women and young men are very apt to tell whatever
secrets they know, from the vanity of having
been trusted.—*Chesterfield.*

He who trusts a secret to his servant makes
his own man his master.—*Dryden.*

To tell our own secrets is generally folly,
but that folly is without guilt; to communicate
those with which we are intrusted is always
treachery, and treachery for the most part combined with folly.—*Johnson.*

Three may keep a secret, — if two of them
are dead.—*Franklin.*

It is said that he or she who admits the possession of a secret has already half revealed it.
Certainly it is a great deal gained towards the
acquisition of a treasure, to know exactly where
it is.—*Simms.*

Secrecy is the chastity of friendship.—
Jeremy Taylor.

I have played the fool, the gross fool, to
believe the bosom of a friend would hold a secret
mine own could not contain.—*Massinger.*

None are so fond of secrets as those who do not mean to keep them; such persons covet secrets as a spendthrift does money, for the purpose of circulation.—*Colton.*

He deserves small trust who is not privy counsellor to himself.—*Forde.*

He was a wise fellow, and had good diseretion, that, being bid to ask what he would of the king, desired he might know none of his secrets.—*Shakespeare.*

A man is more faithful to the secret of another than to his own; a woman, on the contrary, preserves her own secret better than that of another.—*Bruyère.*

To keep your secret is wisdom; but to expect others to keep it is folly.—*Holmes.*

Secrecy of design, when combined with rapidity of execution, like the column that guided Israel in the deserts, becomes the guardian pillar of light and fire to our friends, a cloud of overwhelming and impenetrable darkness to our enemies.—*Colton.*

We confide our secrets in friendship, but they escape us in love.—*Du Cœur.*

Secrecy has been well termed the soul of all great designs. Perhaps more has been effected by concealing our own intentions than by discovering those of our enemy. But great men succeed in both.—*Colton.*

SELF-CONCEIT.

In one thing men of all ages are alike; they have believed obstinately in themselves.—*Jacobi.*

Self-conceit is a weighty quality, and will sometimes bring down the scale when there is nothing else in it. It magnifies a fault beyond proportion, and swells every omission into an outrage.—*Jeremy Collier.*

Even dress is apt to inflame a man's opinion of himself.—*Henry Home.*

And yet we are very apt to be full of ourselves, instead of Him that made what we so much value, and but for whom we can have no reason to value ourselves. For we have nothing that we can call our own, no, not ourselves; for we are all but tenants, and at will too, of the great Lord of ourselves, and the rest of this great farm, the world that we live upon.
William Penn.

The less a man thinks or knows about his virtues the better we like him.—*Emerson.*

There is no such fop as my young master of his lady-mother's making. She blows him up with self-conceit, and there he stops. She makes a man of him at twelve, and a boy all his life after.—*Henry Home.*

Prize not thyself by what thou hast, but by what thou art; he that values a jewel by her golden frame, or a book by her silver clasps, or a man by his vast estate, errs: if thou art not worth more than the world can make thee, thy Redeemer had a bad pennyworth, or thou an uncurious Redeemer.—*Quarles.*

I have sometimes thought that people are, in a sort, happy, that nothing can put out of countenance with themselves, though they neither have nor merit other people's.—
William Penn.

There is a generation that are pure in their own eyes, and yet is not washed from their filthiness.—*Bible.*

Those who, either from their own engagements and hurry of business, or from indolence, or from conceit and vanity, have neglected looking out of themselves, as far as my experience and observation reach, have from that time not only ceased to advance, and improve in their performances, but have gone backward. They may be compared to men who have lived upon their principal, till they are reduced to beggary, and left without resources.—
Sir Joshua Reynolds.

Many men spend their lives in gazing at their own shadows, and so dwindle away into shadows thereof.—*Hare.*

He that fancies himself very enlightened because he sees the deficiencies of others may be very ignorant, because he has not studied his own.—*Bulwer Lytton.*

In the same degree that we overrate ourselves, we shall underrate others; for injustice allowed at home is not likely to be corrected abroad.—*Washington Allston.*

SELF-CONTROL.

He that ruleth his spirit is better than he that taketh a city.—*Bible.*

The man who could withstand, with his fellow-men in single line, a charge of cavalry may lose all command of himself on the occurrence of a fire in his own house, because of some homely reminiscence unknown to the observing bystander.—*Helps.*

Most powerful is he who has himself in his power.—*Seneca.*

The Romans rightly employed the same word (*virtus*) to designate courage, which is, in a physical sense, what the other is in a moral; the highest virtue of all being victory over ourselves.—*Samuel Smiles.*

Conquer thyself. Till thou hast done that thou art a slave; for it is almost as well for thee to be in subjection to another's appetite as thy own.—*Burton.*

Those who can command themselves command others.—*Hazlitt.*

Who, in the midst of just provocation to anger, instantly finds the fit word which settles all around him in silence is more than wise or just; he is, were he a beggar, of more than royal blood, he is of celestial descent.—*Lavater.*

The constancy of sages is nothing but the art of locking up their agitation in their hearts.
Rochefoucauld.

Over the time thou hast no power; to redeem a world sunk in dishonesty has not been given thee; solely over one man therein thou hast a quite absolute, uncontrollable power; him redeem, him make honest.—*Carlyle.*

No man is free who cannot command himself.—*Pythagoras.*

I think the first virtue is to restrain the tongue; he approaches nearest to the gods who knows how to be silent even though he is in the right.—*Cato.*

What is the best government? That which teaches us to govern ourselves.—*Goethe.*

It is not the man who is beside himself, but he who is cool and collected,—who is master of his countenance, of his voice, of his actions, of his gestures, of every part of his play,—who can work upon others at his pleasure.—
Diderot.

Better conquest never canst thou make than arm thy constant and thy nobler parts against giddy, loose suggestions.—*Shakespeare.*

Who to himself is law no law doth need.—
Chapman.

When Alexander had subdued the world, and wept that none were left to dispute his arms, his tears were an involuntary tribute to a monarchy that he knew not,—man's empire over himself.—*Jane Porter.*

He overcomes a stout enemy that overcomes his own anger.—*Chilo.*

Real glory springs from the silent conquest of ourselves; and without that the conqueror is naught but the first slave.—*Thomson.*

No conflict is so severe as his who labors to subdue himself.—*Thomas à Kempis.*

He who reigns within himself, and rules passions, desires, and fears, is more than a king.—*Milton.*

Do you want to know the man against whom you have most reason to guard yourself? Your looking-glass will give you a very fair likeness of his face.—*Whately.*

SELF-DECEIT.

We deceive and flatter no one by such delicate artifices as we do ourselves.—*Schopenhauer.*

Nothing is so easy as to deceive one's self; for what we wish, that we readily believe; but such expectations are often inconsistent with the real state of things.—*Demosthenes.*

The coward reckons himself cautious, the miser frugal.—*Henry Home.*

Many a man has a kind of a kaleidoscope, where the bits of broken glass are his own merits and fortunes; and they fall into harmonious arrangements, and delight him, often most mischievously and to his ultimate detriment; but they are a present pleasure.—*Helps.*

Every man is his own greatest dupe.—
W. R. Alger.

The greatest of fools is he who imposes on himself, and in his greatest concern thinks certainly he knows that which he has least studied, and of which he is most profoundly ignorant.—
Shaftesbury.

Who has deceived thee so often as thyself?—
Franklin.

From the beginning of the world to this day there was never any great villany acted by men, but it was in the strength of some great fallacy put upon their minds by a false representation of evil for good or good for evil.—*South.*

We cheat ourselves in order to enjoy a calm conscience without possessing virtue.—
St. Lambert.

To be deceived by our enemies or betrayed by our friends is insupportable; yet by ourselves are we often content to be so treated.—
Rochefoucauld.

What man, in his right mind, would conspire his own hurt? Men are beside themselves, when they transgress against their convictions.—*William Penn.*

SELF-DENIAL.

The worst education which teaches self-denial is better than the best which teaches everything else, and not that.—*John Sterling.*

It is certainly much easier wholly to decline a passion than to keep it within just bounds and measures; and that which few can moderate almost anybody may prevent.—*Charron.*

The more a man denies himself the more he shall obtain from God.—*Horace.*

There never did and never will exist anything permanently noble and excellent in a character which was a stranger to the exercise of resolute self-denial.—*Walter Scott.*

Brave conquerors! for so you are, that war against your own affections and the huge army of the world's desires.—*Shakespeare.*

SELF-EXAMINATION.

Never lose sight of this important truth, that no one can be truly great until he has gained a knowledge of himself, a knowledge which can only be acquired by occasional retirement.—*Zimmermann.*

Observe thyself as thy greatest enemy would do ; so shalt thou be thy greatest friend.— *Jeremy Taylor.*

If thou seest anything in thyself which may make thee proud, look a little further and thou shalt find enough to humble thee ; if thou be wise, view the peacock's feathers with his feet, and weigh thy best parts with thy imperfections.—*Quarles.*

I will chide no breather in the world but myself, against whom I know most faults.— *Shakespeare.*

We should every night call ourselves to an account : What infirmity have I mastered to-day ? what passion opposed ? what temptation resisted ? what virtue acquired ? Our vices will abate of themselves if they be brought every day to the shrift.—*Seneca.*

A man has generally the good or ill qualities which he attributes to mankind —*Shenstone.*

When you descant on the faults of others, consider whether you be not guilty of the same. To gain knowledge of ourselves, the best way is to convert the imperfections of others into a mirror for discovering our own.— *Henry Home.*

Whatever you dislike in another person, take care to correct in yourself by the gentle reproof.—*Sprat.*

O that you could turn your eyes towards the napes of your necks, and make but an interior survey of your good selves ! —*Shakespeare.*

In order to judge of the inside of others, study your own ; for men in general are very much alike, and though one has one prevailing passion, and another has another, yet their operations are much the same ; and whatever engages or disgusts, pleases, or offends you in others will, *mutatis mutandis*, engage, disgust, please, or offend others in you.—*Chesterfield.*

I study myself more than any other subject ; it is my metaphysic, it is my physic.— *Montaigne.*

If any speak ill of thee, fly home to thy own conscience and examine thy heart. If thou art guilty, it is a just correction ; if not guilty, it is a fair instruction.—*George Herbert.*

It is greatly wise to talk with our past hours, and ask them what report they bore to heaven, and how they might have borne more welcome news.— *Young.*

It is easy to look down on others ; to look down on ourselves is the difficulty.—*Landor*

Of all literary exercitations, whether designed for the use or entertainment of the world, there are none of so much importance, or so immediately our concern, as those which let us into the knowledge of our own nature. Others may exercise the understanding or amuse the imagination ; but these only can improve the heart and form the human mind to wisdom.—*Bishop Warburton.*

Inspect the neighborhood of thy life ; every shelf, every nook of thy abode ; and, nestling in, quarter thyself in the farthest and most domestic winding of thy snail-house ! —*Richter.*

Never let us be discouraged with ourselves. It is not when we are conscious of our faults that we are the most wicked ; on the contrary, we are less so. We see by a brighter light ; and let us remember for our consolation, that we never perceive our sins till we begin to cure them.—*Fenelon.*

Though not always called upon to condemn ourselves, it is always safe to suspect ourselves. *Whately.*

Go to your bosom, knock there and ask your heart what it doth know that is like my brother's fault ; if it confess a natural guiltiness, such as his is, let it not sound a thought upon your tongue against my brother.—*Shakespeare.*

How shall we learn to know ourselves ? By reflection ? Never ; but only through action. Strive to do thy duty ; then shalt thou know what is in thee.—*Goethe.*

SELFISHNESS.

Selfishness is that detestable vice which no one will forgive in others, and no one is without in himself.—*Beecher.*

All the good maxims which are in the world fail when applied to one's self.—*Pascal.*

How much that the world calls selfishness is only generosity with narrow walls, — a too exclusive solicitude to maintain a wife in luxury, or make one's children rich.— *T. W. Higginson.*

There are persons who regard their friends as victims devoted to their reputation.— *St. Evremond.*

As frost to the bud, and blight to the blossom, even such is self-interest to friendship ; for confidence cannot dwell where selfishness is porter at the gate.—*Tupper.*

The very heart and root of sin is an independent spirit. We erect the idol self; and not only wish others to worship, but worship it ourselves.—*Cecil.*

The fawning courtier and the surly squire often mean the same thing, — each his own interest.—*Bishop Berkeley.*

And, which is yet worse, let every one but dive into his own bosom, and he will find his private wishes spring and his sacred hopes grow up at another's expense. Upon which consideration it comes into my head that Nature does not in this swerve from her general polity; for physicians hold that the birth, nourishment, and increase of everything is the corruption and dissolution of another.—*Montaigne.*

The force of selfishness is as inevitable and as calculable as the force of gravitation.— *Hillard.*

Formerly thy soul was great, ardent, vast; the entire circle of the universe found place in thy heart. O *C*harles, that thou hast become small, that thou hast become miserable, since thou lovest no one but thyself!—*Schiller.*

The selfish man suffers more from his selfishness than he from whom that selfishness withholds some important benefit.—*Emerson.*

The essence of true nobility is neglect of self. Let the thought of self pass in, and the beauty of a great action is gone, like the bloom from a soiled flower.—*Froude.*

A pedant is rarely courageous; the more he esteems himself, the less he exposes himself.— *J. Petit, Senn.*

Aristotle has said that man is by nature a social animal, and he might have added, a selfish one too. Heroism, self-denial, and magnanimity in all instances, where they do not spring from a principle of religion, are but splendid altars on which we sacrifice one kind of self-love to another.—*Colton.*

We wish to constitute all the happiness, or, if that cannot be, the misery of the one we love. *Bruyère.*

Sordid selfishness doth contract and narrow our benevolence, and cause us, like serpents, to infold ourselves within ourselves, and to turn out our stings to all the world besides.— *Walter Scott.*

It is very natural for a young friend and a young lover to think the persons they love have nothing to do but to please them.—*Pope.*

There are some people who think that all the world should share their misfortune, although they do not share in the sufferings of anybody else.—*Achilles Poincelot.*

Selfishness, not love, is the actuating motive of the gallant.—*Madame Roland.*

Milton has carefully marked in his Satan the intense selfishness, the alcohol of egotism, which would rather reign in hell than serve in heaven.—*Coleridge.*

The virtues are lost in self-interest, as rivers are in the sea.—*Rochefoucauld.*

It is not truth, justice, liberty, which men seek ; they seek only themselves. And O that they knew how to seek themselves aright !— *Jacobi.*

That household god, a man's own self.— *Flavel.*

The philosophers have said that every act of virtue or friendship was attended with a secret pleasure; whence they concluded that friendship and virtue could not be disinterested. But the fallacy of this is obvious. The virtuous sentiment or passion produces the pleasure, and does not arise from it. I feel a pleasure in doing good to my friend, because I love him ; but do not love him for the sake of that pleasure.—*Hume.*

For the world is only governed by self-interest.—*Schiller.*

Self-interest, that leprosy of the age, attacks us from infancy, and we are startled to observe little heads calculate before knowing how to reflect.—*Madame de Girardin.*

It is to be doubted whether he will ever find the way to heaven who desires to go thither alone.—*Feltham.*

SELF-LOVE.

By a happy contradiction, no system of philosophy gives such a base view of human nature as that which is founded on self-love. So sure is self-love to degrade whatever it touches.—*Hare.*

Self-love makes as many tyrants, perhaps, as love.—*Imbert.*

The secret of our self-love is just the same as that of our liberality and candor. We prefer ourselves to others, only because we have a more intimate consciousness and confirmed opinion of our own claims and merits than of any other person's.—*Hazlitt.*

In all time self-love has blinded the wisest. *Villefré.*

A man who loves only himself and his pleasures is vain, presumptuous, and wicked even from principle.—*Vauvenargues.*

The most amiable people are those who least wound the self-love of others.—*Bruyère.*

It is this unquiet self-love that renders us so sensitive. The sick man, who sleeps ill, thinks the night long. We exaggerate, from cowardice, all the evils which we encounter; they are great but our sensibility increases them. The true way to bear them is to yield ourselves up with confidence to God.—*Fenelon.*

Our self-love is ever ready to revolt from our better judgment, and join the enemy within.
Steele.

Self-love is an instrument useful but dangerous ; it often wounds the hand which makes use of it, and seldom does good without doing harm.—*Rousseau.*

Self-love is not so vile a sin as self-neglecting.—*Shakespeare.*

The cause of all the blunders committed by man arises from this excessive self-love. For the lover is blinded by the object loved; so that he passes a wrong judgment on what is just, good, and beautiful, thinking that he ought always to honor what belongs to himself in preference to truth. For he who intends to be a great man ought to love neither himself nor his own things, but only what is just, whether it happens to be done by himself, or by another.—*Plato.*

Self-love is the greatest of flatterers.—
Rochefoucauld.

Blind self-love, vanity, lifting aloft her empty head, and indiscretion, prodigal of secrets more transparent than glass, follow close behind.—
Horace.

All other love is extinguished by self-love ; beneficence, humanity, justice, philosophy, sink under it.—*Epicurus.*

Self-love, in a well-regulated breast, is as the steward of the household, superintending the expenditure, and seeing that benevolence herself should be prudential, in order to be permanent, by providing that the reservoir which feeds should also be fed.—*Colton.*

True self-love and social are the same.—
Pope.

Nothing is so capable of diminishing self-love as the observation that we disapprove at one time what we approve at another.—
Rochefoucauld.

Our self-love can be resigned to the sacrifice of everything but itself.—*La Harpe.*

Those who have affirmed self-love to be the basis of all our sentiments and all our actions are much in the right. There is no occasion to demonstrate that men have a face ; as little need is there of proving to them that they are actuated by self-love.—*Voltaire.*

Esteeming others merely for their agreement with us in religion, opinion, and manner of living is only a less offensive kind of self-adoration.—*Rev. T. Adam.*

Reservation is self-love.—*Bettina.*

Self-love exaggerates our faults as well as our virtues.—*Goethe.*

The most notorious swindler has not assumed so many names as self-love, nor is so much ashamed of his own. She calls herself patriotism, when at the same time she is rejoicing at just as much calamity to her native country as will introduce herself into power, and expel her rivals.—*Colton.*

Love thyself last.—*Shakespeare.*

There are wounds of self-love which one does not confess to one's dearest friends.
J. Petit, Senn.

Self-love leads men of narrow minds to measure all mankind by their own capacity.—
Jane Porter.

It is allowed that the cause of most actions, good or bad, may be resolved into the love of ourselves ; but the self-love of some men inclines them to please others, and the self-love of others is wholly employed in pleasing themselves. This makes the great distinction between virtue and vice.—*Swift.*

Offended self-love never forgives.—*Vigée.*

It is falling in love with our own mistaken ideas that makes fools and beggars of half mankind.—*Young.*

Self-love is the most inhibited sin in the canon.—*Shakespeare.*

Self-love is, in almost all men, such an over-weight that they are incredulous of a man's habitual preference of the general good to his own ; but when they see it proved by sacrifices of ease, wealth, rank, and of life itself, there is no limit to their admiration.—*Emerson.*

Self-love, as it happens to be well or ill conducted, constitutes virtue and vice.—
Rochefoucauld.

Cut out the love of self, like an autumn lotus, with thy hand ! --*Buddha.*

Every man, like Narcissus, becomes enamored of the reflection of himself, only choosing a substance instead of a shadow. His love for any particular woman is self-love at second-hand, vanity reflected, compound egotism.
Horace Smith.

Love yourself; and in that love not unconsidered leave your honor.—*Shakespeare.*

Self-love is better than any gilding, to make that seem gorgeous wherein ourselves be parties.—*Sir P. Sidney.*

SELF-PRAISE.

A man's praises have very musical and charming accents in another's mouth, but very flat and untunable in his own.—*Xenophon.*

One seldom speaks of the virtues which one has, but much oftener of that which fails us.— *Lessing.*

SELF-RELIANCE.

Men on all occasions throw themselves upon foreign assistances to spare their own, which are the only certain and sufficient ones with which they can arm themselves.—*Montaigne.*

Help thyself, and God will help thee.— *George Herbert.*

Great is the strength of an individual soul true to its high trust; mighty is it, even to the redemption of a world.—*Mrs. L. M. Child.*

For they can conquer who believe they can.— *Virgil.*

Philosophers have very justly remarked that the only solid instruction is that which the pupil brings from his own depths; that the true instruction is not that which transmits notions wholly formed, but that which renders him capable of forming for himself good opinions. That which they have said in regard to the intellectual faculties applies equally to the moral faculties. There is for the soul a spontaneous culture, on which depends all the real progress in perfection.—*Degerando.*

Let every eye negotiate for itself, and trust no agent.—*Shakespeare.*

Look well into thyself; there is a source which will always spring up if thou wilt always search there.—*Marcus Antoninus.*

Opposition is what we want and must have, to be good for anything. Hardship is the native soil of manhood and self-reliance.— *John Neal.*

It is for little souls, that truckle under the weight of affairs, not to know how clearly to disengage themselves, and not to know how to lay them aside and take them up again.— *Montaigne.*

If you would have a faithful servant, and one that you like, serve yourself.—*Franklin.*

Watch over yourself. Be your own accuser, then your judge; ask yourself grace sometimes, and, if there is need, impose upon yourself some pain.—*Seneca.*

No man should part with his own individuality and become that of another.—*Channing.*

We must calculate not on the weather, nor on fortune, but upon God and ourselves. He may fail us in the gratification of our wishes, but never in the encounter with our exigencies.— *Simms.*

Our remedies oft in ourselves do lie, which we ascribe to Heaven.—*Shakespeare.*

He who thinks he can find within himself the means of doing without others is much mistaken; but he who thinks that others cannot do without him is still more mistaken.— *Rochefoucauld.*

Forget not that the man who cannot enjoy his own natural gifts in silence, and find his reward in the exercise of them, will generally find himself badly off.—*Goethe.*

Time and I against any two.— *Philip the Second.*

Confidence in one's self is the chief nurse of magnanimity, which confidence, notwithstanding, doth not leave the care of necessary furniture for it; and therefore, of all the Grecians, Homer doth ever make Achilles the best armed. *Sir P. Sidney.*

I have ever held it as a maxim never to do that through another which it was possible for me to execute myself.—*Montesquieu.*

Think wrongly, if you please, but in all cases think for yourself.—*Lessing.*

As it is in himself alone that man can find true and enduring happiness, so in himself alone can he find true and efficient consolation in misfortune.—*Babo.*

The basis of good manners is self-reliance.— *Emerson.*

Men seem neither to understand their riches nor their strength, — of the former they believe greater things than they should; of the latter much less. Self-reliance and self-denial will teach a man to drink out of his own cistern, and eat his own sweet bread, and to learn and labor truly to get his living, and carefully to expend the good things committed to his trust.—*Bacon.*

The most difficult thing in life is to know yourself.—*Thales.*

Self-distrust is the cause of most of our failures. In the assurance of strength there is strength, and they are the weakest, however strong, who have no faith in themselves or their powers.—*Bovee.*

It is at the approach of extreme danger when a hollow puppet can accomplish nothing, that power falls into the mighty hands of nature, of the spirit giant-born, who listens only to himself, and knows nothing of compacts.—*Schiller.*

SELF-RESPECT. 468 SELF-SACRIFICE.

Providence has done, and I am persuaded is disposed to do, a great deal for us; but we are not to forget the fable of Jupiter and the countryman.—*Washington.*

Our own opinion of ourselves should be lower than that formed by others, for we have a better chance at our imperfections.—
Thomas à Kempis.

For the man who makes everything that leads to happiness, or near to it, to depend upon himself, and not upon other men, on whose good or evil actions his own doings are compelled to hinge,—such a one, I say, has adopted the very best plan for living happily. This is the man of moderation; this is the man of manly character and of wisdom.—*Plato.*

Welcome evermore to gods and men is the self-helping man.—*Emerson.*

Both poetry and philosophy are prodigal of eulogy over the mind which ransoms itself by its own energy from a captivity to custom, which breaks the common bounds of empire, and cuts a Simplon over mountains of difficulty for its own purposes, whether of good or of evil.—*Horace Mann.*

It is impossible you should take true root but by the fair weather that you make yourself; it is needful that you frame the season for your own harvest.—*Shakespeare.*

The human mind, in proportion as it is deprived of external resources, sedulously labors to find within itself the means of happiness, learns to rely with confidence on its own exertions, and gains with greater certainty the power of being happy.—*Zimmermann.*

In life, as in whist, hope nothing from the way cards may be dealt to you. Play the cards, whatever they be, to the best of your skill.—
Bulwer Lytton.

SELF-RESPECT.
When thou hast profited so much that thou respectest even thyself, thou mayst let go thy tutor.—*Seneca.*

Have not too low thoughts of thyself. The confidence a man hath of his being pleasant in his demeanor is a means whereby he infallibly cometh to be such.—*Burton.*

The pious and just honoring of ourselves may be thought the radical moisture and fountain-head from whence every laudable and worthy enterprise issues forth.—*Milton.*

Who will adhere to him that abandons himself?—*Sir P. Sidney.*

It has been said that self-respect is the gate of heaven, and the most cursory observation shows that a degree of reserve adds vastly to the latent force of character.—*Tuckerman.*

Be noble-minded! Our own heart, and not other men's opinions of us, forms our true honor.—*Schiller.*

It may be no less dangerous to claim, on certain occasions, too little than too much. There is something captivating in spirit and intrepidity, to which we often yield as to a resistless power; nor can he reasonably expect the confidence of others who too apparently distrusts himself.—*Johnson.*

All men are frail, but thou shouldest reckon none so frail as thyself.—*Thomas à Kempis.*

I will have a care of being a slave to myself, for it is a perpetual, a shameful, and the heaviest of all servitudes; and this may be done by moderate desires.—*Seneca.*

To have a respect for ourselves guides our morals; and to have a deference for others governs our manners.—*Sterne.*

Above all things, reverence yourself.—
Pythagoras.

Be and continue poor, young man, while others around you grow rich by fraud and disloyalty; be without place or power, while others beg their way upwards; bear the pain of disappointed hopes, while others gain theirs by flattery; forego the gracious pressure of the hand, for which others cringe and crawl. Wrap yourself in your own virtue, and seek a friend and your daily bread. If you have, in such a course, grown gray with unblenched honor, bless God and die.—*Heinzelmann.*

Self-respect,—that corner-stone of all virtue.—*Sir John Herschel.*

No more important duty can be urged upon those who are entering the great theatre of life than simple loyalty to their best convictions.—*Chapin.*

The truest self-respect is not to think of self.—*Beecher.*

Self-respect is the noblest garment with which a man may clothe himself,—the most elevating feeling with which the mind can be inspired. One of Pythagoras's wisest maxims, in his Golden Verses, is that in which he enjoins the pupil to "reverence himself."—
Samuel Smiles.

I care not so much what I am in the opinion of others as what I am in my own; I would be rich of myself and not by borrowing.—*Montaigne.*

SELF-SACRIFICE.
Happy the man, whom indulgent fortune allows to pay to virtue what he owes to nature, and to make a generous gift of what must otherwise be ravished from him by cruel necessity!—*Hume.*

SELF-SUFFICIENCY.

An obstinate, ungovernable self-sufficiency plainly points out to us that state of imperfect maturity at which the graceful levity of youth is lost and the solidity of experience not yet acquired.—*Junius.*

SELF-WILL.

Self-will is so ardent and active that it will break a world to pieces to make a stool to sit on.—*Cecil.*

———

Weakness has many stages. There is a difference between feebleness by the impotency of the will, of the will to the resolution, of the resolution to the choice of means, of the choice of the means to the application.—
Cardinal de Retz.

———

Lawless are they that make their wills their law.—*Shakespeare.*

SENSIBILITY.

Men's feelings are always purest and most glowing in the hour of meeting and of farewell; like the glaciers, which are transparent and rosy-hued only at sunrise and sunset, but throughout the day gray and cold.—*Richter.*

———

Too much sensibility creates unhappiness, too much insensibility creates crime.—
Talleyrand.

———

Sensibility would be a good portress if she had but one hand; with her right she opens the door to pleasure, but with her left to pain.—
Colton.

———

The wounded limb shrinks even from the gentlest touch, and to the nervous the smallest shadow excites alarm.—*Ovid.*

———

Laughter and tears are meant to turn the wheels of the same machinery of sensibility; one is wind-power, and the other water-power, that is all.—*Holmes.*

———

Where virtue is, sensibility is the ornament and becoming attire of virtue. On certain occasions it may almost be said to become virtue. But sensibility and all the amiable qualities may likewise become, and too often have become, the panders of vice, and the instruments of seduction.—*Coleridge.*

———

The heart that is soonest awake to the flowers is always the first to be touched by the thorns.—*Moore.*

———

Sensibility appears to me to be neither good nor evil in itself, but in its application. Under the influence of Christian principle, it makes saints and martyrs; ill-directed, or uncontrolled, it is a snare, and the source of every temptation; besides, as people cannot get it if it is not given them, to descant on it seems to me as idle as to recommend people to have black eyes or fair complexions.—*Hannah More.*

We care not how many see us in choler, when we rave and bluster, and make as much noise and bustle as we can; but if the kindest and most generous affection comes across us, we suppress every sign of it, and hide ourselves in nooks and coverts.—*Landor.*

———

It is with feeling as with religion; if a man really have any, he will have "none to speak of."—*H. N. Hudson.*

SENSITIVENESS.

Quick sensibility is inseparable from a ready understanding.—*Addison.*

———

Sensitiveness is closely allied to egotism. Indeed, excessive sensibility is only another name for morbid self-consciousness. The cure for tender sensibilities is to make more of our objects and less of ourselves.—*Bovee.*

———

Breasts that beat and cheeks that glow.—
Johnson.

———

The wild-flower wreath of feeling, the sunbeam of the heart.—*Halleck.*

———

How many people there are that are desperate by too quick a sense of a constant infelicity! —
Jeremy Taylor.

———

Mere sensibility is not true taste, but sensibility to real excellence is.—*Hazlitt.*

———

There are moments when petty slights are harder to bear than even a serious injury. Men have died of the festering of a gnat-bite.—
Cecil Danby.

———

Chords that vibrate sweetest pleasure, thrill the deepest notes of woe.—*Burns.*

———

Such war of white and red within her cheeks.—*Shakespeare.*

SENSUALITY.

All sensuality is one, though it takes many forms; all purity is one. It is the same whether a man eat, or drink, or cohabit, or sleep sensually. They are but one appetite, and we only need to see a person do any one of these things to know how great a sensualist he is.—
Thoreau.

———

The body of a sensualist is the coffin of a dead soul.—*Bovee.*

———

Sordid and infamous sensuality, the most dreadful evil that issued from the box of Pandora, corrupts every heart, and eradicates every virtue. Fly! wherefore dost thou linger? Fly, cast not one look behind thee; nor let even thy thought return to the accursed evil for a moment.—*Fenelon.*

———

Ingrateful man with liquorish draughts, and morsels unctuous, greases his pure mind that from it all consideration slips.—*Shakespeare.*

If sensuality be our only happiness we ought to envy the brutes, for instinct is a surer, shorter, safer guide to such happiness than reason.—*Colton.*

If any sensual weakness arise, we are to yield all our sound forces to the overthrowing of so unnatural a rebellion; wherein how can we want courage, since we are to deal against so feeble an adversary, that in itself is nothing but weakness? Nay, we are to resolve that if reason direct it, we must do it; and if we must do it, we will do it; for to say "I cannot" is childish, and "I will not" is womanish.—*Sir P. Sidney.*

A youth of sensuality and intemperance delivers over a worn-out body to old age.—*Cicero.*

Though selfishness hath defiled the whole man, yet sensual pleasure is the chief part of its interest, and therefore by the senses it commonly works, and these are the doors and the windows by which iniquity entereth into the soul.—*Baxter.*

If sensuality were happiness beasts were happier than men; but human felicity is lodged in the soul, not in the flesh.—*Seneca.*

When the cup of any sensual pleasure is drained to the bottom, there is always poison in the dregs. Anacreon himself declares that "the flowers swim at the top of the bowl!"—*Jane Porter.*

For, in the language of Heraclitus, the virtuous soul is pure and unmixed light, springing from the body as a flash of lightning darts from the cloud. But the soul that is carnal and immersed in sense, like a heavy and dank vapor, can with difficulty be kindled, and caused to raise its eyes heavenward—*Plutarch.*

Sin is the mother, and shame the daughter of lewdness.—*Sir P. Sidney.*

I have read of a glass kept in an idol temple in Smyrna, that would make beautiful things appear deformed, and deformed things appear beautiful; carnal sense is such a glass to wicked men, it makes heavenly things which are beautiful to appear deformed, and earthly things which are deformed to appear beautiful.—*R. Venning.*

SENTIMENT.

A general loftiness of sentiment, independence of men, consciousness of good intentions, self-oblivion in great objects, clear views of futurity, thoughts of the blessed companionship of saints and angels, trust in God as the friend of truth and virtue, — these are the states of mind in which I should live.—*Channing.*

Sentiment has a kind of divine alchemy, rendering grief itself the source of tenderest thoughts and far-reaching desires, which the sufferer cherishes as sacred treasures.—*Talfourd.*

A woman should not paint sentiment till she has ceased to inspire it.—*Lady Blessington.*

Sentiment and principle are often mistaken for each other, though, in fact, they widely differ. Sentiment is the virtue of ideas, and principle the virtue of action. Sentiment has its seat in the head; principle, in the heart. Sentiment suggests fine harangues and subtle distinctions; principle conceives just notions, and performs good actions in consequence of them. Sentiment refines away the simplicity of truth, and the plainness of piety; and, as Voltaire, that celebrated wit, has remarked of his no less celebrated contemporary Rousseau, "gives us virtue in words, and vice in deeds." Sentiment may be called the Athenian who knew what was right; and principle, the Lacedemonian who practised it.—*Blair.*

Sentiment is intellectualized emotion; emotion precipitated, as it were, in pretty crystals by the fancy.—*Lowell.*

All sentiment is right; because sentiment has a reference to nothing beyond itself, and is always real wherever a man is conscious of it. But all determinations of the understanding are not right.—*Hume.*

Sentiment is the ripened fruit of fancy.—*Madame Deluzy.*

SENTIMENTALISM.

What we mean by sentimentalism is that state in which a man speaks deep and true, not because he feels them strongly, but because he perceives that they are beautiful, and that it is touching and fine to say them, — things which he fain would feel, and fancies that he does feel.—*F. W. Robertson.*

SEPARATION.

I quit Paris unwillingly, because I must part from my friends; and I quit the country unwillingly, because I must part from myself.—*Joubert.*

When two loving hearts are torn asunder, it is a shade better to be the one that is driven away into action, than the bereaved twin that petrifies at home.—*Charles Reade.*

When loving hearts are separated, not the one which is exhaled to heaven, but the survivor, it is which tastes the sting of death.—*Duchesse de Praslin.*

SERVANTS.

Let thy servants be such as thou mayest command, and entertain none about thee but yeomen, to whom thou givest wages; for those that will serve thee without thy hire will cost thee treble as much as they that know thy fare.—*Sir Walter Raleigh.*

Be not served with kinsman, or friends, or men intreated to stay; for they expect much, and do little; nor with such as are amorous, for their heads are intoxicated; and keep rather too few, than one too many.—*Lord Burleigh.*

SERVITUDE.

Servitude seizes on few, but many seize on her.—*Seneca.*

We become willing servants to the good by the bonds their virtues lay upon us.—
Sir P. Sidney.

I have been formerly so silly as to hope that every servant I had might be made a friend; I am now convinced that the nature of servitude generally bears a contrary tendency. People's characters are to be chiefly collected from their education and' place in life; birth itself does but little.—*Shenstone.*

It is fit and necessary that some persons in the world should be in love with a splendid servitude.—*South.*

SHAKESPEARE.

If we wish to know the force of human genius, we should read Shakespeare. If we wish to see the insignificance of human learning, we may study his commentators.—*Hazlitt.*

Shakespeare, the sage and seer of the human heart.—*Henry Giles.*

Shakespeare must have seemed a dull man at times, he was so flashingly brilliant at others.
Bovee.

Shakespeare was the man who, of all modern and perhaps ancient poets, had the largest and most comprehensive soul. All the images of nature were still present to him, and he drew them not laboriously, but luckily; when he describes anything, you more than see it, you feel it too. Those who accuse him to have wanted learning give him the greater commendation; he was naturally learned; he needed not the spectacles of books to read nature; he looked inward, and found her there.—*Dryden.*

Sweet swan of Avon!—*Ben Jonson.*

Shakespeare stands alone. His want of erudition was a most happy and productive ignorance; it forced him back upon his own resources which were exhaustless.—*Colton.*

Things came to Raffaelle and Shakespeare; Michael Angelo and Milton came to things.—
Fuseli.

Our myriad-minded Shakespeare.—
Coleridge.

Shakespeare knew innumerable things; what men are, and what the world is, and what men aim at there, from the Dame Quickly of modern Eastcheap, to the Cæsar of ancient Rome.—*Carlyle.*

Shakespeare is dangerous to young poets; they cannot but reproduce him, while they fancy that they produce themselves.—*Goethe.*

Shakespeare possesses the power of subordinating nature for the purposes of expression, beyond all poets. His imperial muse tosses the creation like a bauble from hand to hand, and uses it to embody any caprice of thought that is uppermost in his mind. The remotest spaces of nature are visited, and the farthest sundered things are brought together, by a subtile spiritual connection. We are made aware that magnitude of material things is relative, and all objects shrink and expand to serve the passion of the poet.—*Emerson.*

I look on Shakespeare as an intellectual miracle.—*Dr. Chalmers.*

A rib of Shakespeare would have sufficed to produce a Milton, and a rib of Milton all the poets that have succeeded him.—*Landor.*

Never has mind of superior mould, and of lettered tastes, made any advance in comprehension or power, without an increase of admiration for the matchless, resplendent creations of Shakespeare.—*W. B. Clulow.*

Shakespeare is indeed the great conservator of our language. He has imparted to it his own immortality.—*Bovee.*

What has been best done in the world—the works of genius—cost nothing. There is no painful effort, but it is the spontaneous flowing of the thought. Shakespeare made his Hamlet as a bird weaves its nest.—*Emerson.*

I honor his memory, on this side idolatry, as much as any man.—*Ben Jonson.*

The assertion of Bacon, that the most corrected copies of an author are commonly the least correct, may advantageously be stamped as an introductory motto for every copy of Shakespeare.—*Willmott.*

The characteristic of Chaucer is intensity; of Spencer, remoteness; of Milton, elevation; of Shakespeare, everything!—*Hazlitt.*

The conjecture had only a poetical boldness, which supposed that a student might linger over Shakespeare, dwelling upon him line by line, and word by word, until the mind, steeped in brilliancy, would almost scatter light in the dark.—*Willmott.*

He extorts from us the assenting conviction, that if such beings should exist, they would be and do as he represents them.—*Schlegel.*

Admirable as he was in all parts of his art, we must admire him for this, that while he has left us a greater number of striking portraits than all other dramatists put together, he has scarcely left us a single caricature.—*Macaulay.*

He is indeed natural; so profoundly natural as to be beyond the depth of most of us.—*Lamb*

It is not so correct to say that he speaks from nature, as that she speaks through him; his characters are so much nature herself that it seems a sort of injury to call them by so distant a name as imitations of her.—*Pope.*

His genius was like sunlight, which, always taking the precise form and color of the object it shines upon, makes everything else visible, but remains itself unseen.—*H. N. Hudson.*

He does not look at a thing merely, but into it, through it, so that he constructively comprehends it, can take it asunder and put it together again; the thing melts, as it were, into light under his eye, and anew creates itself before him.—*Carlyle.*

SHAME.

Shame is like the weaver's thread; if it breaks in the net, it is wholly imperfect.— *Bulwer Lytton.*

Whilst shame keeps watch, virtue is not wholly extinguished from the heart, nor will moderation be utterly exiled from the mind of tyrants.—*Burke.*

I consider that man to be undone who is insensible to shame.—*Plautus.*

Nothing is truly infamous, but what is wicked; and therefore shame can never disturb an innocent and virtuous mind.—*Sherlock.*

O shame! where is thy blush?— *Shakespeare.*

Shame is a feeling of profanation. Friendship, love, and piety ought to be handled with a sort of mysterious secrecy; they ought to be spoken of only in the rare moments of perfect confidence,— to be mutually understood in silence. Many things are too delicate to be thought, — many more, to be spoken.—*Novalis.*

Those who fear not guilt yet start at shame. *Churchill.*

Of all evils to the generous, shame is the most deadly pang.—*Thomson.*

Shame ever sticks close to the ribs of honor; great men are never sound men after it. It leaves some ache or other in their names still, which their posterity feels at every weather.—*Middleton.*

Shame greatly hurts or greatly helps mankind.—*Homer.*

Be assured that when once a woman begins to be ashamed of what she ought not to be ashamed of, she will not be ashamed of what she ought.—*Livy.*

In shame there is no comfort but to be beyond all bounds of shame.—*Sir P. Sidney.*

I hold him to be dead in whom shame is dead.—*Plautus.*

I know not how to tell thee! Shame rises in my face, and interrupts the story of my tongue!—*Otway.*

Shame may restrain what law does not prohibit.—*Seneca.*

SICKNESS.

When a man is laboring under the pain of any distemper, it is then that he recollects there is a God, and that he himself is but a man. No mortal is then the object of his envy, his admiration, or his contempt; and, having no malice to gratify, the tales of slander excite him not.—*Pliny.*

Sickness is the mother of modesty, as it puts us in mind of our mortality, and while we drive on heedlessly in the full career of worldly pomp and jollity, kindly pulls us by the ear, and brings us to a sense of our duty.— *Burton.*

In sickness let me not so much say, am I getting better of my pain? as am I getting better for it?—*Shakespeare.*

Disease generally begins that equality which death completes; the distinctions which set one man so much above another are very little perceived in the gloom of a sick-chamber, where it will be vain to expect entertainment from the gay, or instruction from the wise; where all human glory is obliterated, the wit is clouded, the reasoner perplexed, and the hero subdued; where the highest and brightest of mortal beings finds nothing left him but the consciousness of innocence.—*Johnson.*

If there be a regal solitude, it is a sick-bed. How the patient lords it there!—*Lamb.*

It is in sickness that we most feel the need of that sympathy which shows how much we are dependent one upon another for our comfort, and even necessities. Thus disease, opening our eyes to the realities of life, is an indirect blessing.—*Hosea Ballou.*

Few spirits are made better by the pain and languor of sickness; as few great pilgrims become eminent saints.—*Thomas à Kempis.*

In sickness the soul begins to dress herself for immortality. And first she unties the strings of vanity that made her upper garments cleave to the world and sit uneasy.— *Jeremy Taylor.*

Of all the know-nothing persons in this world, commend us to the man who has "never known a day's illness." He is a moral dunce, one who has lost the greatest lesson in life; who has skipped the finest lecture in that great school of humanity, the sick-chamber.—*Hood.*

As I see in the body, so I know in the soul; they are oft most desperately sick who are least sensible of their disease; whereas he that fears each light wound for mortal seeks a timely cure, and is healed. I will not reckon it my happiness that I have many sores, but since I have them, I am glad they grieve me. I know the cure is not the more dangerous because my wounds are more grievous; I should be more sick if I complained less.—
Arthur Warwick.

Sickness is a sort of early old age; it teaches us a diffidence in our earthly state.—*Pope.*

The delicate face where thoughtful care already mingled with the winning grace and loveliness of youth, the too bright eye, the spiritual head, the lips that pressed each other with such high resolve and courage of the heart, the slight figure, firm in its bearing and yet so very weak.—*Dickens.*

It is with diseases of the mind as with those of the body; we are half dead before we understand our disorders, and half cured when we do.—*Colton.*

SIGHT.

Sight is by much the noblest of the senses. We receive our notices from the other four, through the organs of sensation only. We hear, we feel, we smell, we taste, by touch. But sight rises infinitely higher. It is refined above matter, and equals the faculty of spirit.—
Sterne.

Our sight is the most perfect and most delightful of all our senses; it fills the mind with the largest variety of ideas, converses with its objects at the greatest distance, and continues the longest in action without being tired or satiated with its proper enjoyments.—*Addison.*

SILENCE.

Silence is a figure of speech, unanswerable, short, cold, but terribly severe.—
Theodore Parker.

Keep thou the door of my lips.—*Bible.*

Looking round on the noisy inanity of the world, words with little meaning, actions with little worth, one loves to reflect on the great empire of silence. The noble silent men, scattered here and there each in his department; silently thinking, silently working; whom no morning newspaper makes mention of!
Carlyle.

Silence never yet betrayed any one!
Rivarol.

The more a man, desirous to pass at a value above his worth, can contrast by dignified silence the garrulity of trivial minds, the more the world will give him credit for the wealth which he does not possess.—*Bulwer Lytton.*

If thou desire to be held wise, be so wise as to hold thy tongue.—*Quarles.*

There is a silence, the child of love, which expresses everything, and proclaims more loudly than the tongue is able to do; there are movements that are involuntary proofs of what the soul feels.—*Alfieri.*

To women silence gives their proper grace.
Sophocles.

True silence is the rest of the mind, and is to the spirit what sleep is to the body, nourishment and refreshment. It is a great virtue; it covers folly, keeps secrets, avoids disputes, and prevents sin.—*William Penn.*

Still as the peaceful walks of ancient night; silent as are the lamps that burn on tombs.—
Shakespeare.

He knows not how to speak who cannot be silent; still less how to act with vigor and decision. Who hastens to the end is silent; loudness is impotence.—*Lavater.*

A person that would secure to himself great deference will, perhaps, gain his point by silence as effectually as by anything he can say.
Shenstone.

Silence is only commendable in a neat's-tongue dried, and a maid not vendible.—
Shakespeare.

Sir, when a woman has the gift of silence she possesses a quality above the vulgar; it is a gift Heaven seldom bestows; without a little miracle it cannot be accomplished; and nature suffers violence when Heaven puts a woman in the humor of observing silence.—*Corneille.*

As we must account for every idle word, so we must for every idle silence.—*Franklin.*

Euripides was wont to say, silence was an answer to a wise man; but we seem to have greater occasion for it in our dealing with fools and unreasonable persons; for men of breeding and sense will be satisfied with reason and fair words.—*Plutarch.*

She half consents who silently denies.—
Ovid.

Nature, which has given us one organ for speaking, has given us two for hearing, that we may learn that it is better to hear than to speak.—*Nabi Effendi.*

By silence, I hear other men's imperfections and conceal my own.—*Zeno.*

I like better for one to say some foolish thing upon important matters than to be silent. That becomes the subject of discussion and dispute, and the truth is discovered.—*Diderot.*

With the wicked, as with a bad dog, silence is more formidable than noise.—*Demophilus.*

Still people are dangerous.—*La Fontaine.*

No one can take less pains than to hold his tongue.' Hear much, and speak little; for the tongue is the instrument of the greatest good and greatest evil that is done in the world.—
Sir Walter Raleigh.

Learn to hold thy tongue. Five words cost Zacharias forty weeks' silence.—*Fuller.*

Silence is one of the great arts of conversation, as allowed by Cicero himself, who says " there is not only an art, but an eloquence in it "; and this opinion is confirmed by a great modern, Lord Bacon. For a well-bred woman may easily and effectually promote the most useful and elegant conversation without speaking a word. The modes of speech are scarcely more variable than the modes of silence.—*Blair.*

Silence is like nightfall; objects are lost in it insensibly.—*Madame Swetchine.*

Not every one who has the gift of speech understands the value of silence.—*Lavater.*

A man's profundity may keep him from opening on a first interview, and his caution on a second; but I should suspect his emptiness, if he carried on his reserve to a third.—*Colton.*

Let us be silent, that we may hear the whispers of the gods.—*Emerson.*

I shall leave the world without regret, for it hardly contains a single good listener.—
Fontenelle.

Silence is the element in which great things fashion themselves together; that at length they may emerge, full-formed and majestic, into the delight of life, which they are thenceforth to rule.—*Carlyle.*

Silence, when nothing need be said, is the eloquence of discretion.—*Bovee.*

Silence is a trick when it imposes. Pedants and scholars, churchmen and physicians, abound in silent pride.—*Zimmermann.*

Be checked for silence, but never taxed for speech.—*Shakespeare.*

The deepest life of nature is silent and obscure; so often the elements that move and mould society are the results of the sister's counsel and the mother's prayer.—*Chapin.*

The temple of our purest thoughts is — silence!—*Mrs. Hale.*

A judicious silence is always better than truth spoken without charity.—*De Sales.*

He who, silent, loves to be with us — he who loves us in our silence — has touched one of the keys that ravish hearts.—*Lavater.*

It is only reason that teaches silence. The heart teaches us to speak.—*Richter.*

They are the strong ones of the earth, the mighty food for good or evil, — those who know how to keep silence when it is a pain and a grief to them; those who give time to their own souls to wax strong against temptation, or to the powers of wrath to stamp upon them their withering passage.—*Emerson.*

Speech is of time, silence is of eternity.—
Carlyle.

If a word be worth one shekel, silence is worth two.—*Rabbi Ben Azai.*

I think the first virtue is to restrain the tongue; he approaches nearest to the gods who knows how to · be silent, even though he is in the right.—*Cato.*

Even a fool, when he holdeth his peace, is counted wise.—*Bible.*

Silence is the understanding of fools and one of the virtues of the wise.—
Bernard de Bonnard.

It is better either to be silent, or to say things of more value than silence. Sooner throw a pearl at hazard than an idle or useless word; and do not say a little in many words, but a great deal in a few.—*Pythagoras.*

None preaches better than the ant, and she says nothing.—*Franklin.*

SIMILE.

A good simile, — as concise as a king's declaration of love.—*Sterne.*

A good simile is the sunshine of wisdom.—
Hosea Ballou.

SIMPLICITY.

Genuine simplicity of heart is a healing and cementing principle.—*Burke.*

The most agreeable of all companions is a simple, frank man, without any high pretensions to an oppressive greatness, — one who loves life, and understands the use of it; obliging alike at all hours; above all, of a golden temper, and steadfast as an anchor. For such an one we gladly exchange the greatest genius, the most brilliant wit, the profoundest thinker.—
Lessing.

Plain living and high thinking.—
Wordsworth.

He alone is a man who can resist the genius of the age, the tone of fashion, with vigorous simplicity and modest courage.—*Lavater.*

When a man is made up wholly of the dove, without the least grain of the serpent in his composition, he becomes ridiculous in many circumstances of life, and very often discredits his best actions.—*Addison.*

Never anything can be amiss when simpleness and duty tender it.—*Shakespeare.*

Purity and simplicity are the two wings with which man soars above the earth and all temporary nature. Simplicity is in the intention, purity in the affection; simplicity turns to God; purity unites with and enjoys him.—
Thomas à Kempis.

In character, in manners, in style, in all things, the supreme excellence is simplicity.—
Longfellow.

The true friend of truth and good loves them under all forms, but he loves them most under the most simple form.—*Lavater.*

Nothing is more simple than greatness; indeed, to be simple is to be great.—*Emerson.*

How desirable is this simplicity! who will give it to me? I will quit all else; it is the pearl of great price.—*Fenelon.*

Simplicity is, of all things, the hardest to be copied.—*Steele.*

I am convinced, both by faith and experience, that to maintain one's self on this earth is not a hardship but a pastime, if we will live simply and wisely; as the pursuits of the simpler nations are still the sports of the more artificial.—*Thoreau.*

An honest tale speeds best, being plainly told.—*Shakespeare.*

Simplicity is the straightforwardness of a soul which refuses itself any reaction with regard to itself or its deeds. This virtue differs from and surpasses sincerity. We see many people who are sincere without being simple. They do not wish to be taken for other than what they are; but they are always fearing lest they should be taken for what they are not.—
Fenelon.

Simplicity is a delicate imposition.—
Rochefoucauld.

When a thought is too weak to be simply expressed, it is a clear proof that it should be rejected.—*Vauvenargues.*

Simplicity is a jewel rarely found.—*Ovid.*

Albert Durer, the famous painter, used to say he had no pleasure in pictures that were painted with many colors, but in those which were painted with a choice simplicity. So it is with me as to sermons.—*Luther.*

A childlike mind in its simplicity practises that science of good to which the wise may be blind.—*Schiller.*

Simplicity of character is the natural result of profound thought.—*Hazlitt.*

The expression of truth is simplicity.—
Seneca.

The greatest truths are the simplest; and so are the greatest men.—*Hare.*

Simplicity is the great friend to nature, and if I would be proud of anything in this silly world, it should be of this honest alliance.—
Sterne.

The feeling heart, simplicity of life and elegance and taste.—*Thomson.*

Simplicity is the character of the spring of life, costliness becomes its autumn; but a neatness and purity, like that of the snow-drop or lily of the valley, is the peculiar fascination of beauty, to which it lends enchantment, and gives a charm even to a plain person, being to the body what amiability is to the mind.—
Longfellow.

The fewer our wants, the nearer we resemble the gods.—*Socrates.*

There are certain occasions when, in art, simplicity is an audacious originality.—
Achilles Poincelot.

SIN.

The worst effect of sin is within, and is manifest not in poverty, and pain, and bodily defacement, but in the discrowned faculties, the unworthy love, the low ideal, the brutalized and enslaved spirit.—*Chapin.*

Sin is essentially a departure from God.—
Luther.

Plate sin with gold, and the strong lance of justice hurtless breaks: arm it in rags, a pygmy's straw doth pierce it.—*Shakespeare.*

Our sins, like to our shadows when our day is in its glory, scarce appeared; towards our evening how great and monstrous they are!—
Suckling.

Sin is a basilisk whose eyes are full of venom. If the eye of thy soul see her first, it reflects her own poison and kills her; if she see thy soul, unseen, or seen too late, with her poison, she kills thee: since therefore thou canst not escape thy sin, let not thy sin escape thy observation.—
Quarles.

Some sins do bear their privilege on earth.—
. *Shakespeare.*

How immense appear to us the sins that we have not committed!—*Madame Necker.*

He that falls into sin is a man, that grieves at it is a saint, that boasteth of it is a devil; yet some glory in that shame, counting the stains of sin the best complexion of their souls.—*Fuller.*

Be not familiar with the idea of wrong, for sin in fancy mothers many an ugly fact.— *Theodore Parker.*

There are some sins which are more justly to be denominated surprises than infidelities. To such the world should be lenient, as, doubtless, Heaven is forgiving.—*Massillon.*

O sin, what hast thou done to this fair earth!—*Dana.*

The whole sum and substance of human history may be reduced to this maxim: that when man departs from the divine means of reaching the divine end, he suffers harm and loss.—*Theodore Parker.*

Pain is the outcome of sin.—*Buddha.*

We are saved from nothing if we are not saved from sin. Little sins are pioneers of hell. The backslider begins with what he foolishly considers trifling with little sins. There are no little sins. There was a time when all the evil that has existed in the world was comprehended in one sinful thought of our first parent; and all the now evil is the numerous and horrid progeny of one little sin. *Howell.*

Few love to hear the sins they love to act.— *Shakespeare.*

If thou wouldst conquer thy weakness, thou must never gratify it. No man is compelled to evil: his consent only makes it his. It is no sin to be tempted, but to be overcome.— *William Penn.*

Sin is ashamed of sin.—*Chapman.*

O sin, how you paint your face! how you flatter us poor mortals on to death! You never appear to the sinner in your true character; you make fair promises, but you never fulfil one; your tongue is smoother than oil, but the poison of asps is under your lip!—*Hosea Ballou.*

He that hath slight thoughts of sin never had great thoughts of God.—*Rev. Dr. Owen.*

Vice is attended with temporary felicity, piety with eternal joy.—*Bayard.*

It is the goodly outside that sin puts on which tempteth to destruction. It has been said that sin is like the bee, with honey in its mouth, but a sting in its tail.—*Hosea Ballou.*

There is a vast difference between sins of infirmity and those of presumption, as vast as between inadvertency and deliberation.—*South.*

God hath yoked to guilt her pale tormentor, misery.—*Bryant.*

Sin is never at a stay; if we do not retract from it, we shall advance in it; and the farther on we go, the more we have to come back.— *Barrow.*

There is no harder work in the world than sin.—*South.*

It should console us for the fact that sin has not totally disappeared from the world, that the saints are not wholly deprived of employment.—*Simms.*

Where is the thief who cannot find bad when he hunts for it?—*St. Augustine.*

Of all the ingenious mistakes into which erring man has fallen, perhaps none have been so pernicious in their consequences, or have brought so many evils into the world, as the popular opinion that the way of the transgressor is pleasant and easy.—*Hosea Ballou.*

Men scanning the surface count the wicked happy; they see not the frightful dreams that crowd a bad man's pillow.—*Tupper.*

Every single gross act of sin is much the same thing to the conscience that a great blow or fall is to the head; it stuns and bereaves it of all use of its senses for a time.—*South.*

If we did not first take great pains to corrupt our nature, our nature would never corrupt us.—*Clarendon.*

Sin first is pleasing, then it grows easy, then delightful, then frequent, then habitual, then confirmed; then the man is impenitent, then he is obstinate, then he is resolved never to repent, and then he is ruined.—*Leighton.*

It is not the back, but the heart, that must bleed for sin.—*South.*

Many afflictions will not cloud and obstruct peace of mind so much as one sin: therefore, if you would walk cheerfully, be most careful to walk holily. All the winds about the earth make not an earthquake, but only that within.— *Leighton.*

Sin is the only thing in the world which never had an infancy, that knew no minority.— *South.*

As sins proceed they ever multiply, and like figures in arithmetic, the last stands for more than all that went before it.—*Sir Thomas Browne.*

To step aside is human!—*Burns.*

Not only commission makes a sin. A man is guilty of all those sins he hateth not. If I cannot avoid all, yet I will hate all.—*Bishop Hall.*

Some voluntary castaways there will always be, whom no fostering kindness and no parental care can preserve from self-destruction; but if any are lost for want of care and culture, there is a sin of omission in the society to which they belong.—*Southey.*

Whatever disunites man from God disunites man from man.—*Burke.*

O, what authority and show of truth can cunning sin cover itself withal! —*Shakespeare.*

Although a man has so well purged his mind that nothing can trouble or deceive him any more, yet he reached his present innocence through sin.—*Seneca.*

I am in process of bringing all my sins to light for the purpose of getting rid of them. We never know how rich we are until we break up housekeeping! —*Hénault.*

Besides the guilt of sin, and the power of sin, there is the stain of sin.—*Nathaniel Culverwell.*

I have learned what a sin is against an infinite imperishable being, such as is the soul of man. *Coleridge.*

Shame is a great restraint upon sinners at first, but that soon falls off; and when men have once lost their innocence, their modesty is not like to be long troublesome to them. For impudence comes on with vice, and grows up with it. Lesser vices do not banish all shame and modesty; but great and abominable crimes harden men's foreheads, and make them shameless.—*Tillotson.*

No man can be stark naught at once. Let us stop the progress of sin in our soul at the first stage, for the farther it goes the faster it will increase.—*Fuller.*

Sin is the fruitful parent of distempers, and ill lives occasion good physicians.—*South.*

Use sin as it will use you; spare it not, for it will not spare you; it is your murderer, and the murderer of the whole world. Use it, therefore, as a murderer should be used; kill it before it kills you; and though it bring you to the grave, as it did your Head, it shall not be able to keep you there. You love not death; love not the cause of death.—*Baxter.*

It is not alone what we do, but also what we do not do, for which we are accountable.— *Molière.*

SINCERITY.
He who is sincere hath the easiest task in the world, for, truth being always consistent with itself, he is put to no trouble about his words and actions; it is like travelling in a plain road, which is sure to bring you to your journey's end better than by-ways in which many lose themselves.—*J. Beaumont.*

Faithfulness and sincerity are the highest things.—*Confucius.*

Now the best way in the world to seem to be anything is really to be what we would seem to be. Besides that it is many times as troublesome to make good the pretence of a good quality as to have it, and if a man have it not it is ten to one but he is discovered to want it, and then all his pains and labor to seem to have it is lost. *Tillotson.*

Sincerity is the indispensable ground of all conscientiousness, and by consequence of all heartfelt religion.—*Kant.*

I remember a passage of one of Queen Elizabeth's great men, as advice to his friend. "The advantage," says he, "I had upon others at court was that I always spoke as I thought; which being not believed by them, I both preserved a good conscience, and suffered no damage from that freedom"; which, as it shows the vice to be older than our times, so does it that gallant man's integrity to be the best way of avoiding it.— *William Penn.*

Her words are trusty heralds to her mind.— *John Ford.*

An inward sincerity will of course influence the outward deportment; but where the one is wanting, there is great reason to suspect the absence of the other.—*Sterne.*

Frank sincerity, though no invited guest, is free to all, and brings his welcome with him.— *Havard.*

Sincerity is an openness of heart; it is found in a very few people, and that which we see commonly is not it, but a subtle dissimulation, to gain the confidence of others.—*Rochefoucauld.*

Sincerity is the face of the soul, as dissimulation is the mask.—*Sanial-Dubay.*

If the show of anything be good for anything I am sure sincerity is better; for why does any man dissemble, or seem to be that which he is not, but because he thinks it good to have such a quality as he pretends to.—*Tillotson.*

I should say sincerity, a deep, great, genuine sincerity, is the first characteristic of all men in any way heroic.— *Carlyle.*

It is with sincere affection or friendship as with ghosts and apparitions, — a thing that everybody talks of, and scarce any hath seen.— *Rochefoucauld.*

Sincerity is the most compendious wisdom, an excellent instrument for the speedy despatch of business. It creates confidence in those we have to deal with, saves the labor of many inquiries, and brings things to an issue in few words.— *Chesterfield.*

SINGULARITY.

Let those who would affect singularity with success first determine to be very virtuous, and they will be sure to be very singular.—*Colton.*

He who would be singular in his apparel had need have something superlative to balance that affectation.—*Feltham.*

SLANDER.

There is no slander in an allowed fool, though he do nothing but rail.—*Shakespeare.*

Slander soaks into the mind as water into low and marshy places, where it becomes stagnant and offensive.—*Confucius.*

Slanderers do not hurt me, because they do not hit me.—*Socrates.*

Life would be a perpetual flea-hunt if a man were obliged to run down all the innuendoes, inveracities, insinuations, and suspicions which are uttered against him.—*Beecher.*

Soft-buzzing slander; silky moths, that eat an honest name.—*Thomson.*

It is a pretty general rule, that the *médisante* is a termagant in her household; and as for our own sex, in nine cases out of ten, the evil tongue belongs to a disappointed man.
Bancroft.

Where it concerns himself, who is angry at a slander makes it true.—*Ben Jonson.*

In all cases of slander currency, whenever the forger of the lie is not to be found, the injured parties should have a right to come on any of the indorsers.—*Sheridan.*

There would not be so many open mouths if there were not so many open ears.—*Bishop Hall.*

The surest method against scandal, is to live it down by perseverance in well-doing, and by prayer to God, that he would cure the distempered mind of those who traduce and injure us.
Boerhaave.

On Rumor's tongue continual slanders ride.
Shakespeare.

How frequently is the honesty and integrity of a man disposed of by a smile or shrug ! How many good and generous actions have been sunk into oblivion by a distrustful look, or stamped with the imputation of proceeding from bad motives, by a mysterious and seasonable whisper ! —*Sterne.*

If slander be a snake, it is a winged one. It flies as well as creeps.—*Douglas Jerrold.*

It is always to be understood, that a lady takes all you detract from the rest of her sex to be a gift to her.—*Addison.*

There is nothing which wings its flight so swiftly as calumny, nothing which is uttered with more ease ; nothing is listened to with more readiness, nothing dispersed more widely.—
Cicero.

Slander is the revenge of a coward, and dissimulation his defence.—*Johnson.*

Curse the tongue whence slanderous rumor, like the adder's drop, distils her venom, withering friendship's faith, turning love's favor.—
James A. Hillhouse.

Set a watch over thy mouth, and keep the door of thy lips, for a tale-bearer is worse than a thief.—*Bible.*

Slander is the solace of malignity.—*Joubert.*

Slander is a poison which extinguishes charity, both in the slanderer and in the person who listens to it; so that a single calumny may prove fatal to an infinite number of souls, since it kills not only those who circulate it, but also all those who do not reject it.—
St. Bernard.

Slander meets no regard from noble minds ; only the base believe what the base only utter.
Beller.

Listen not to a tale-bearer or slanderer, for he tells thee nothing out of good-will ; but as he discovereth of the secrets of others, so he will of thine in turn.—*Socrates.*

The slander of some people is as great a recommendation as the praise of others.—
Fielding.

Believe nothing against another, but on good authority ; nor report what may hurt another, unless it be a greater hurt to another to conceal it.—*William Penn.*

Calumny would soon starve and die of itself if nobody took it in and gave it lodging.—
Leighton.

Any one who is much talked of, must be much maligned. This seems to be a harsh conclusion ; but when you consider how much more given men are to depreciate than to appreciate, you will acknowledge that there is some truth in the saying.—*Helps.*

The worthiest people are the most injured by slander, as we usually find that to be the best fruit which the birds have been pecking at.
Swift.

If any speak ill of thee, flee home to thy own conscience, and examine thy heart : if thou be guilty, it is a just correction ; if not guilty, it is a fair instruction : make use of both ; so shalt thou distil honey out of gall, and out of an open enemy create a secret friend.—*Quarles.*

Slander is a vice that strikes a double blow, wounding both him that commits and him against whom it is committed.—*Saurin.*

Those who, without knowing us, think or speak evil of us, do us no harm; it is not us they attack, but the phantom of their own imagination.—*Bruyère.*

If any one tells you that such a person speaks ill of you, do not make excuse about what is said of you, but answer: "He was ignorant of my other faults, else he would not have mentioned these alone."—*Epictetus.*

Slander, whose edge is sharper than the sword, whose tongue outvenoms all the worms of Nile.—*Shakespeare.*

It is a busy talking world, that with licentious breath blows like the wind as freely on the palace as the cottage.—*Rowe.*

Close thine ear against him that shall open his mouth secretly against another. If thou receivest not his words, they fly back and wound the reporter. If thou dost receive them, they fly forward, and wound the receiver.—*Lavater.*

No sword bites so fiercely as an evil tongue.—*Sir P. Sidney.*

As by flattery a man opens his bosom to his mortal enemy; so by detraction and slander he shuts the same to his best friends.—*South.*

There is nobody so weak of invention that cannot make some little stories to vilify his enemy.—*Addison.*

The best way is to slander Valentine with falsehood, cowardice, and poor descent,—three things that women highly hold in hate.—*Shakespeare.*

The proper way to check slander is to despise it; attempt to overtake and refute it, and it will outrun you.—*Alex. Dumas.*

What indulgence does the world extend to those evil-speakers who, under the mask of friendship, stab indiscriminately with the keen, though rusty blade of slander!—*Madame Roland.*

Have patience awhile; slanders are not long-lived. Truth is the child of Time; erelong she shall appear to vindicate thee.—*Kant.*

Slander is perhaps the only vice which no circumstance can palliate, as well as being one which we are most ingenious in concealing from ourselves.—*Massillon.*

Slander, whose whisper over the world's diameter, as level as the cannon to its blank, transports his poisoned shot.—*Shakespeare.*

When the tongue of slander stings thee, let this be thy comfort,—they are not the worst fruits on which the wasps alight.—*Bürger.*

Remember, when incited to slander, that it is only he among you who is without sin that may cast the first stone.—*Hosea Ballou.*

SLEEP.

Sleep, thou repose of all things; Sleep, thou gentlest of the deities; thou peace of the mind, from which care flies; who dost soothe the hearts of men wearied with the toils of the day, and refittest them for labor.—*Ovid.*

Sleep, the antechamber of the grave.—*Richter.*

There should be hours for necessities, not for delights; times to repair our nature with comforting repose, and not for us to waste these times.—*Shakespeare.*

Sweet nurse of nature, over the senses creep.—*Churchill.*

It is a delicious moment, certainly, that of being well nestled in bed, and feeling that you shall drop gently to sleep. The good is to come, not past; the limbs have just been tired enough to render the remaining in one posture delightful; the labor of the day is gone. A gentle failure of the perceptions creeps over you; the spirit of consciousness disengages itself once more, and with slow and hushing degrees, like a mother detaching her hand from that of a sleeping child, the mind seems to have a balmy lid closing over it, like the eye,—it is closed,—the mysterious spirit has gone to take its airy rounds.—*Leigh Hunt.*

Our foster-nurse of nature is repose.—*Shakespeare.*

Even sleep is characteristic. How charming are children in their lovely innocence! how angel-like their blooming hue! how painful and anxious is the sleep and expression in the countenance of the guilty!—*Wilhelm von Humboldt.*

The timely dew of sleep, now falling, with soft, slumberous weight inclines my eyelids.—*Milton.*

There are many ways of inducing sleep,—the thinking of purling rills, or waving woods; reckoning of numbers; droppings from a wet sponge, fixed over a brass pan, etc. But temperance and exercise answer much better than any of these succedaneums.—*Sterne.*

Sleep, thou most gentle of the deities.—*Ovid.*

Sleep is a god too proud to wait in palaces, and yet so humble too as not to scorn the meanest country cottages.—*Cowley.*

Where, in the sharp lineaments of rigid and unsightly death, is the calm beauty of slumber; telling of rest for the waking hours that are past, and gentle hopes and loves for those which are to come? Lay death and sleep down, side by side, and say who shall find the two akin. Send forth the child and childish man together, and blush for the pride that libels our own old happy state, and gives its title to an ugly and distorted image.—*Dickens.*

One hour's sleep before midnight is worth two after.—*Fielding.*

A captive never wishing to be free!—
Wordsworth.

Alike to the slave and his oppressor cometh night with sweet refreshment, and half of the life of the most wretched is gladdened by the soothings of sleep.—*Tupper.*

Sleep lingers all our lifetime about our eyes, as night hovers all day in the boughs of the fir-tree.—*Emerson.*

One half of life is admitted by us to be passed in sleep, in which, however it may appear otherwise, we have no perception of truth, and all our feelings are delusions; who knows but the other half of life, in which we think we are awake, is a sleep also, but in some respects different from the other, and from which we wake when we, as we call it, sleep. As a man dreams often that he is dreaming, crowding one dreamy delusion on another.—*Pascal.*

Kind sleep affords the only boon the wretched mind can feel; a momentary respite from despair.—*Murphy.*

Thou hast been called, O Sleep, the friend of woe; but it is the happy who have called thee so.—*Southey.*

Downy sleep, death's counterfeit.—
Shakespeare.

Leave your bed upon the first desertion of sleep; it being ill for the eyes to read lying, and worse for the mind to be idle; since the head during that laziness is commonly a cage for unclean thoughts.—*F. Osborn.*

Sleep in peace, and wake in joy.—*Scott.*

How many sleep, who kept the world awake!—*Young.*

Sleep, that knits up the ravelled sleave of care, the death of each day's life, sore labor's bath, balm of hurt minds, great nature's second course, chief nourisher in life's feast.—
Shakespeare.

Put off thy cares with thy clothes; so shall thy rest strengthen thy labor; and so shall thy labor sweeten thy rest.—*Quarles.*

Balm that tames all anguish, saint that evil thoughts and aims takest away, and into souls dost creep, like to a breeze from heaven.
Wordsworth.

Weariness can snore upon the flint, when restive sloth finds the down pillow hard.—
Shakespeare.

Sleep is Death's youngest brother, and so like him, that I never dare trust him without my prayers.—*Sir Thomas Browne.*

To sleep, — there is a drowsy mellifluence in the very word that would almost serve to interpret its meaning, — to shut up the senses and hoodwink the soul; to dismiss the world; to escape from one's self; to be in ignorance of our own existence; to stagnate upon the earth, just breathing out the hours, not living them, — "doing no mischief, only dreaming of it"; neither merry nor melancholy, something between both, and better than either. Best friend of frail humanity, and, like all other friends, it is best estimated in its loss.—*Longfellow.*

Sleep, the type of death, is also, like that which it typifies, restricted to the earth. It flies from hell, and is excluded from heaven.—
Colton.

The long sleep of death closes our scars, and the short sleep of life our wounds. Sleep is the half of time which heals us.—*Richter.*

God gives sleep to the bad, in order that the good may be undisturbed.—*Saadi.*

Blessings light on him that first invented sleep! it covers a man all over, thoughts and all, like a cloak; it is meat for the hungry, drink for the thirsty, heat for the cold, and cold for the hot; in short, money that buys everything, balance and weights that make the shepherd equal to the monarch, and the fool to the wise; there is only one evil in sleep, as I have heard, and it is that it resembles death, since between a dead and sleeping man there is but little difference.—*Cervantes.*

Voluptuous as the first approach of sleep.—
Byron.

In due season he betakes himself to his rest; he (the Christian) presumes not to alter the ordinance of day and night, nor dare confound, where distinctions are made by his Maker.—*Bishop Hall.*

Tired Nature's sweet restorer, balmy sleep!
Young.

Let youth cherish sleep, the happiest of earthly boons, while yet it is at its command; for there cometh the day to all when "neither the voice of the lute nor the birds" shall bring back the sweet slumbers that fell on their young eyes as unbidden as the dews.—*Bulwer Lytton.*

In a sound sleep the soul goes home to recruit her strength, which could not else endure the wear and tear of life.—*Rahel.*

He giveth his beloved sleep.—*Bible.*

Sweet pillows, sweetest bed ; a chamber deaf to noise, and blind to light ; a rosy garland, and a weary head.—*Sir P. Sidney*

Sleep, gentle Sleep, nature's soft nurse, how have I frighted thee, that thou no more wilt weigh my eyelids down, and steep my senses in forgetfulness ?—*Shakespeare.*

SLOTH.
The very soul of the slothful does effectually but lie drowsing in his body, and the whole man is totally given up to his senses.
L'Estrange.

Flee sloth ; for the indolence of the soul is the decay of the body.—*Cato.*

Excess is not the only thing which breaks men in their health, and in the comfortable enjoyment of themselves : but many are brought into a very ill and languishing habit of body by mere sloth ; and sloth is in itself both a great sin, and the cause of many more.—*South.*

Drowsiness shall clothe a man with rags.—
Bible

Sloth is the torpidity of the mental faculties the sluggard is a living insensible.—*Zimmermann*

Yet a little sleep, a little slumber, a little folding of the hands to sleep; so shall thy poverty come as one that travelleth ; and thy want as an armed man.—*Bible.*

Sloth, like rust, consumes faster than labor wears, while the key often used is always bright.
Franklin.

As sloth seldom bringeth actions to good birth ; so hasty rashness always makes them abortive ere well formed.—*Arthur Warwick.*

Many are idly busy. Domitian was busy, but then it was catching flies.—*Jeremy Taylor.*

So fixed are our spirits in slothfulness and cold indifference that we seldom overcome so much as one evil habit.—*Thomas à Kempis.*

Prosperity engenders sloth.—*Livy.*

SMILE.
One may smile, and smile, and be a villain.
Shakespeare.

What a sight there is in that word " smile " ! it changes like a chameleon. There is a vacant smile, a cold smile, a smile of hate, a satiric smile, an affected smile ; but, above all, a smile of love.—*Haliburton.*

There are many kinds of smiles, each having a distinct character. Some announce goodness and sweetness, others betray sarcasm, bitterness, and pride ; some soften the countenance by their languishing tenderness. others brighten by their spiritual vivacity.—*Lavater*

In came Mrs. Fezziwig, one vast substantial smile.—*Dickens.*

What sun is there within us that shoots his rays with so sudden a vigor ! To see the soul flash in the face at this rate one would think would convert an atheist. By the way, we may observe that smiles are much more becoming than frowns. This seems a natural encouragement to good-humor ; as much as to say, if people have a mind to be handsome, they must not be peevish and untoward.—*Jeremy Collier.*

A smile that glowed celestial rosy-red, love's proper hue.—*Milton.*

It is the color which love wears, and cheerfulness, and joy, — these three. It is the light in the window of the face by which the heart signifies to father, husband, or friend that it is at home and waiting.—*Beecher.*

Struck blind with beauty ! shot with a woman's smile.—*Beaumont and Fletcher.*

A beautiful smile is to the female countenance what the sunbeam is to the landscape ; it embellishes an inferior face and redeems an ugly one.—*Lavater.*

The smiles of infants are said to be the first fruits of human reason.—*H. N. Hudson.*

Something of a person's character may be discovered by observing when and how he smiles. Some people never smile ; they merely grin.—
Bovee.

What smiles ! They were the effluence of fine intellect, of true courage ; they lit up her marked lineaments, her thin face, her sunken gray eye, like reflections from the aspect of an angel.—*Charlotte Bronte.*

Softness of smile indicates softness of character.—*Lavater.*

Loud laughter is the mirth of the mob, who are only pleased with silly things ; for true wit or good sense never excited a laugh since the creation of the world. A man of parts and fashion is therefore only seen to smile, but never heard to laugh.—*Chesterfield.*

Loose now and then a scattered smile, and that I will live upon.—*Shakespeare.*

It is a proof of boorishness to confer a favor with a bad grace ; it is the act of giving that is hard and painful. How little does a smile cost !—*Bruyère.*

31

Seldom he smiles, and smiles in such a sort, as if he mocked himself, and scorned his spirit, that could be moved to smile at anything.—
Shakespeare.

The old bridegroom diffused over his face that convulsive smile which with some men resembles the convulsive quiver of the cork when it announces the bite of the fish.—*Richter.*

SOCIABILITY.

We are more sociable, and get on better with people by the heart than the intellect.—
Bruyère.

I cannot be certain not to meet with evil company, but I will be careful not to keep with evil company. I would willingly sort myself with such as should either teach or learn goodness; and if my companion cannot make me better, nor I him good, I will rather leave him ill than he shall make me worse.—
Arthur Warwick.

SOCIETY.

Besides the general infusion of wit to heighten civility, the direct splendor of intellectual power is ever welcome in fine society, as the costliest addition to its rule and its credit.—
Emerson.

There is a sort of economy in Providence that one shall excel where another is defective, in order to make men more useful to each other, and mix them in society.—*Addison.*

Men would not live long in society if they were not the dupes of each other.—
Rochefoucauld.

Society is like a lawn, where every roughness is smoothed, every bramble eradicated, and where the eye is delighted by the smiling verdure of a velvet surface. He, however, who would study nature in its wildness and variety must plunge into the forest, must explore the glen, must stem the torrent, and dare the precipice.— *Washington Irving.*

Society is composed of two great classes, — those who have more dinners than appetite, and those who have more appetite than dinners.
Chamfort.

"It is not safe for man to be alone," nor can all which the cold-hearted pedant stuns our ears with upon the subject ever give one answer of satisfaction to the mind; in the midst of the loudest vauntings of philosophy, Nature will have her yearnings for society and friendship. A good heart wants something to be kind to; and the best parts of our blood, and the purest of our spirits suffer most under the destitution.
Sterne.

Man, in society, is like a flower blown in its native bud. It is there alone his faculties expanded in full bloom shine out, there only reach their proper use.— *Cowper.*

Christian society is like a bundle of sticks laid together, whereof one kindles another. Solitary men have fewest provocations to evil, but, again, fewest incitations to good. So much as doing good is better than not doing evil will I account Christian good-fellowship better than an hermitish and melancholy solitariness.—
Bishop Hall.

Man is a social animal formed to please in society.—*Montesquieu.*

Society, — the only field where the sexes have ever met on terms of equality. the arena where character is formed and studied, the cradle and the realm of public opinion, the crucible of ideas, the world's university, at once a school and a theatre, the spur and the crown of ambition, the tribunal which unmasks pretension and stamps real merit, the power that gives government leave to be, and outruns the lazy Church in fixing the moral sense of the eye.—
Wendell Phillips.

Without good company, all dainties lose their true relish, and, like painted grapes, are only seen, not tasted.—*Massinger.*

There is no security in evil society, where the good are often made worse, the bad seldom better, for it is the peevish industry of wickedness to find or make a fellow. It is like they will be birds of a feather that use to flock together. For such commonly doth their conversation make us as they are with whom we use to converse.—*Arthur Warwick.*

Too elevated qualities often unfit a man for society. We do not go to market with ingots, but with silver and small change.—*Chamfort.*

Unless society can effect by education what Lord Monboddo holds man to have done by willing it, and can get rid of her tail, it will be wisest to let the educated classes keep their natural station at the head.—*Hare.*

Those who have resources within themselves, who can dare to live alone, want friends the least, but, at the same time, best know how to prize them the most. But no company is far preferable to bad, because we are more apt to catch the vices of others than their virtues, as disease is far more contagious than health.—
Colton.

Every man depends on the quantity of sense, wit, or good manners he brings into society for the reception he meets with in it.—
Hazlitt.

An artist should be fit for the best society, and should keep out of it. Society always has a destructive influence upon an artist, — first, by its sympathy with his meanest powers; secondly, by its chilling want of understanding of his greatest; and, thirdly, by its vain occupation of his time and thoughts.—*Ruskin.*

From social intercourse are derived some of the highest enjoyments of life; where there is a free interchange of sentiments, the mind acquires new ideas; and by a frequent exercise of its powers, the understanding gains fresh vigor.—*Addison.*

A man's reception depends upon his coat; his dismissal, upon the wit he shows.—*Beranger.*

In this great society wide lying around us, a critical analysis would find very few spontaneous actions. It is almost all custom and gross sense.—*Emerson.*

Society is no comfort to one not sociable.—
Shakespeare.

We submit to the society of those that can inform us, but we seek the society of those whom we can inform. And men of genius ought not to be chagrined if they see themselves neglected. For when we communicate knowledge, we are raised in our own estimation; but when we receive it, we are lowered.—
Colton.

A man who has tasted with profound enjoyment the pleasure of agreeable society will eat with a greater appetite than he who rode horseback for two hours. An amusing lecture is as useful for health as the exercise of the body.—
Kant.

Society is the atmosphere of souls; and we necessarily imbibe from it something which is either infectious or healthful.—*Bishop Hall.*

It is in the middle classes of society that all the finest feeling, and the most amiable propensities of our nature do principally flourish and abound. For the good opinion of our fellow-men is the strongest, though not the purest motive to virtue. The privations of poverty render us too cold and callous, and the privileges of property too arrogant and consequential, to feel; the first places us beneath the influence of opinion, — the second, above it.—*Colton.*

The upper current of society presents no certain criterion by which we can judge of the direction in which the under current flows.—
Macaulay.

Society will pardon much to genius and special gifts; but, being in its nature conventional, it loves what is conventional, or what belongs to coming together.—*Emerson.*

Society is a long series of uprising ridges, which from the first to the last offer no valley of repose. Wherever you take your stand, you are looked down upon by those above you, and reviled and pelted by those below you. Every creature you see is a farthing Sisyphus, pushing his little stone up some Liliputian mole-hill. This is our world.—*Bulwer Lytton.*

Cursed be the social lies that warp us from the living truth!—*Tennyson.*

Those can most easily dispense with society who are the most calculated to adorn it; they only are dependent on it who possess no mental resources, for though they bring nothing to the general mart, like beggars, they are too poor to stay at home.—*Countess of Blessington.*

It has been said that society is for the happy, the rich; we should rather say the happy have no need of it.—
Madame de Girardin.

It is an aphorism in physic, that unwholesome airs, because perpetually sucked into the lungs, do distemper health more than coarser diet used but at set times. The like may be said of society, which, if good, is a better refiner of the spirits than ordinary books.—*F. Osborn.*

I never mingled with men, but I came home less of a man than I went out.—*Tauler.*

Society everywhere is in conspiracy against the manhood of every one of its members. Society is a joint-stock company, in which the members agree, for the better security of his bread to each shareholder, to surrender the liberty and culture of the eater. The virtue in most request is conformity. Self-reliance is its aversion.—*Emerson.*

We are all a kind of chameleons, taking our hue, the hue of our moral character, from those who are about us.—*Locke.*

The history of any private family, however humble, could it be fully related for five or six generations, would illustrate the state and progress of society better than the most elaborate dissertation.—*Southey.*

SOLITUDE.

Are there no solitudes out of the cave and the desert? or cannot the heart in the midst of crowds feel frightfully alone ? —*Lamb.*

But little do men perceive what solitude is, and how far it extends. For a crowd is no company; men's faces are but like pictures in a gallery, and talk but a tinkling cymbal, where there is no love.—*Bacon.*

In solitude the mind gains strength, and learns to lean upon herself; in the world it seeks or accepts of a few treacherous supports, — the feigned compassion of one, the flattery of a second, the civilities of a third, the friendship of a fourth; — they all deceive, and bring the mind back to retirement, reflection, and books.—*Sterne.*

It had been hard to have put more truth and untruth together in a few words than in that speech, " Whosoever is delighted with solitude is either a wild beast or a god."—*Bacon.*

There is a self-imposed privacy, less easily invaded than convent walls.—*Tuckerman.*

Living a good deal alone will, I believe, correct me of my faults; for a man can do without his own approbation in much society, but he must make great exertions to gain it when he lives alone. Without it I am convinced solitude is not to be endured.—
Sydney Smith.

No doubt solitude is wholesome, but so is abstinence after a surfeit. The true life of man is in society.—*Simms.*

Solitude is a good school, but the world is the best theatre; the institution is best there, but the practice here; the wilderness hath the advantage of discipline, and society opportunities of perfection.—*Jeremy Taylor.*

Those beings only are fit for solitude who like nobody, are like nobody, and are liked by nobody.—*Zimmermann.*

It is solitude should teach us how to die.—
Byron.

Such only can enjoy the country who are capable of thinking when they are there; then they are prepared for solitude, and in that case solitude is prepared for them.—*Dryden.*

If the mind loves solitude, it has thereby acquired a loftier character, and it becomes still more noble when the taste is indulged in.—
Wilhelm von Humboldt.

Leisure and solitude are the best effect of riches, because mother of thought. Both are avoided by most rich men, who seek company and business; which are signs of being weary of themselves.—*Sir W. Temple.*

An entire life of solitude contradicts the purpose of our being, since death itself is scarcely an idea of more terror.—*Burke.*

We must certainly acknowledge that solitude is a fine thing; but it is a pleasure to have some one who can answer, and to whom we can say, from time to time, that solitude is a fine thing.—*Balzac.*

A wise man is never less alone than when he is alone.—*Swift.*

That which happens to the soil when it ceases to be cultivated by the social man happens to man himself when he foolishly forsakes society for solitude; the brambles grow up in his desert heart.—*Rivarol.*

Solitude is not measured by the miles of space that intervene between a man and his fellows. The really diligent student in one of the crowded hives of Cambridge College is as solitary as a dervis in the desert.—*Thoreau.*

Solitude sometimes is best society, and short retirement urges sweet return.—*Milton.*

Birds sing in vain to the ear, flowers bloom in vain to the eye, of mortified vanity and galled ambition. He who would know repose in retirement must carry into retirement his destiny, integral and serene, as the Cæsars transported the statue of Fortune into the chamber they chose for their sleep.—*Bulwer Lytton.*

Solitude bears the same relation to the mind that sleep does to the body. It affords it the necessary opportunities for repose and recovery.—*Simms.*

When we withdraw from human intercourse into solitude, we are more peculiarly committed in the presence of the divinity; yet some men retire into solitude to devise or perpetrate crimes. This is like a man going to meet and brave a lion in his own gloomy desert, in the very precincts of his dread abode.—
John Foster.

Solitude shows us what we should be; society shows us what we are.—*Cecil.*

It is shameful for a man to live as a stranger in his own country, and to be uninformed of her affairs and interests.—*Manilius.*

The love of retirement has in all ages adhered closely to those minds which have been most enlarged by knowledge, or elevated by genius. Those who enjoyed everything generally supposed to confer happiness have been forced to seek it in the shades of privacy.—
Johnson.

They are never alone who are accompanied with noble thoughts.—*Sir P. Sidney.*

How many have found solitude, not only, as Cicero calls it, the pabulum of the mind, but the nurse of their genius! How many of the world's most sacred oracles have been uttered, like those of Dodona, from the silence of deep woods!—*Bulwer Lytton.*

Cease, triflers; would you have me feel remorse? Leave me alone; nor cell nor chain nor dungeons speak to the murderer with the voice of solitude.—*Maturin.*

We ought not to isolate ourselves, for we cannot remain in a state of isolation. Social intercourse makes us the more able to bear with ourselves and with others.—*Goethe.*

He that lives alone lives in danger; society avoids many dangers.—*Marcus Antoninus.*

Solitude can be well applied and sit right upon but very few persons. They must have knowledge enough of the world to see the follies of it; and virtue enough to despise all vanity.—*Cowley.*

Solitude is one of the highest enjoyments of which our nature is susceptible Solitude is also, when too long continued, capable of being made the most severe, indescribable, unendurable source of anguish.—*Deloraine.*

Solitude either develops the mental powers, or renders men dull and vicious.—*Victor Hugo.*

We could not endure solitude were it not for the powerful companionship of hope, or of some unseen one.—*Richter.*

What would a man do if he were compelled to live always in the sultry heat of society, and could never better himself in cool solitude?—*Hawthorne.*

I love to be alone. I never found the companion that was so companionable as solitude. *Thoreau.*

Solitude, the safeguard of mediocrity, is to genius the stern friend, the cold, obscure shelter where moult the wings which will bear it farther than suns and stars. He who would inspire and lead his race must be defended from travelling with the souls of other men, from living, breathing, reading, and writing in the daily time-worn yoke of their opinions.— *Emerson.*

Solitude cherishes great virtues, and destroys little ones.—*Sydney Smith.*

All weighty things are done in solitude, that is, without society. The means of improvement consist not in projects, or in any violent designs, for these cool, and cool very soon, but in patient practising for whole long days, by which I make the thing clear to my highest reason.—*Richter.*

That inward eye which is the bliss of solitude.— *Wordsworth.*

Unsociable humors are contracted in solitude, which will, in the end, not fail of corrupting the understanding as well as the manners, and of utterly disqualifying a man for the satisfactions and duties of life. Men must be taken as they are, and we neither make them or ourselves better by flying from or quarrelling with them.—*Burke.*

In solitude, where we are least alone.— *Byron.*

The love of solitude, when cultivated in the morn of life, elevates the mind to a noble independence, but to acquire the advantages which solitude is capable of affording, the mind must not be impelled to it by melancholy and discontent, but by a real distaste to the idle pleasures of the world, a rational contempt for the deceitful joys of life, and just apprehensions of being corrupted and seduced by its insinuating and destructive gayeties.—*Zimmermann.*

Eagles we see fly alone; and they are but sheep which always herd together.— *Sir P. Sidney.*

The wild bird that flies so lone and far has somewhere its nest and brood. A little fluttering heart of love impels its wings, and points its course. There is nothing so solitary as a solitary man.—*Chapin.*

The great man is he who, in the midst of the crowd, keeps with perfect sweetness the independence of solitude.—*Emerson.*

If solitude deprives of the benefit of advice, it also excludes from the mischief of flattery. But the absence of others' applause is generally supplied by the flattery of one's own breast. *W. B. Clulow.*

The thought, the deadly feel of solitude.— *Keats.*

He who must needs have company must needs have sometimes bad company. Be able to be alone; lose not the advantage of solitude and the society of thyself; nor be only content but delight to be alone and single with Omnipoteney. He who is thus prepared, the day is not uneasy, nor the night black unto him. Darkness may bound his eyes, not his imagination. In his bed he may lie, like Pompey and his sons, in all quarters of the earth; may speculate the universe, and enjoy the whole world in the hermitage of himself.— *Sir Thomas Browne.*

Solitude is the home of the strong; silence, their prayer.—*Ravignan.*

One ought to love society, if he wishes to enjoy solitude. It is a social nature that solitude works upon with the most various power. If one is misanthropic, and betakes himself to loneliness that he may get away from hateful things, solitude is a silent emptiness to him.— *Zimmermann.*

All that poets sing, and grief hath known, of hopes laid waste, knells in that word " alone."—*Bulwer Lytton.*

A certain degree of solitude seems necessary to the full growth and spread of the highest mind; and therefore must a very extensive intercourse with men stifle many a holy germ, and scare away the gods, who shun the restless tumult of noisy companies and the discussion of petty interests.—*Novalis.*

Solitude, the sly enemy that doth separate a man from well-doing.—*Sir P. Sidney*

SONG.

Every pert young fellow that has a moving fancy, and the least jingle of verse in his head, sets up for a writer of songs, and resolves to immortalize his bottle or his mistress.—*Steele.*

A song will outlive all sermons in the memory.—*Henry Giles.*

Vocal portraits of the national mind.—*Lamb.*

It was his nature to blossom into song, as it is a tree's to leaf itself in April.—
Alexander Smith.

Little dew-drops of celestial melody.—
Carlyle.

There is a certain flimsiness of poetry, which seems expedient in a song.—*Shenstone.*

SOPHISTRY.

Sophistry, like poison, is at once detected and nauseated, when presented to us in a concentrated form; but a fallacy which, when stated barely in a few sentences, would not deceive a child, may deceive half the world, if diluted in a quarto volume.—*Whately.*

Some men weave their sophistry till their own reason is entangled.—*Johnson.*

SORROW.

Thou canst not tell how rich a dowry sorrow gives the soul, how firm a faith and eagle sight of God.—*Dean Alford.*

One can never be the judge of another's grief. That which is a sorrow to one, to another is joy. Let us not dispute with any one concerning the reality of his sufferings; it is with sorrows as with countries, — each man has his own.—*Chateaubriand.*

Blessed are they that mourn for they shall be comforted.—*Bible.*

Sorrows, because they are lingering guests, I will entertain but moderately, knowing that the more they are made of, the longer they will continue; and for pleasures, because they stay not, and do but call to drink at my door, I will use them as passengers with slight respect. He is his own best friend that makes least of both of them.—*Bishop Hall.*

The dark in soul see in the universe their own shadow; the shattered spirit can only reflect external beauty, in form as untrue and broken as itself.—*Binney.*

Man alone is born crying, lives complaining, and dies disappointed.—*Sir W. Temple.*

Every Calvary has an Olivet. To every place of crucifixion there is likewise a place of ascension. The sun that was shrouded is unveiled, and heaven opens with hopes eternal to the soul which was nigh unto despair.—
Henry Giles.

Our sorrows are like thunder-clouds, which seem black in the distance, but grow lighter as they approach.—*Richter.*

If there is an evil in this world, it is sorrow and heaviness of heart. The loss of goods, of health, of coronets and mitres, is only evil as they occasion sorrow; take that out, the rest is fancy, and dwelleth only in the head of man.—*Sterne.*

Sorrow breaks seasons and reposing hours, makes the night morning, and the noontide night.—*Shakespeare.*

Out of suffering have emerged the strongest souls; the most massive characters are seamed with scars; martyrs have put on their coronation robes glittering with fire, and through their tears have the sorrowful first seen the gates of heaven.—*Chapin.*

One sorrow never comes, but brings an heir that may succeed as his inheritor.—*Shakespeare.*

No wringing of the hands and knocking the breast, or wishing one's self unborn; all which are but the ceremonies of sorrow, the pomp and ostentation of an effeminate grief, which speak not so much the greatness of the misery as the smallness of the mind.—*South.*

The echo of the nest-life, the voice of our modest, fairer, holier soul, is audible only in a sorrow-darkened bosom, as the nightingales warble when one veils their cage.—*Richter.*

Nature always wears the colors of the spirit. To a man laboring under calamity the heat of his own fire hath sadness in it. Then there is a kind of contempt of the landscape felt by him who has just lost by death a dear friend. The sky is less grand as it shuts down over less worth in the population.—*Emerson.*

Gnarling sorrow hath less power to bite the man that mocks at it, and sets it light.—
Shakespeare.

To love all mankind, from the greatest to the lowest, a cheerful state of being is required; but in order to see into mankind, into life, and still more into ourselves, suffering is requisite.—
Richter.

A sorrow's crown of sorrow is remembering happier things.—*Tennyson.*

Sorrows and disturbances, in some minds, produce the effects of fermentation, leaving that which is wholesome, sound, and clear; in others, those of effervescence, resulting in flatness, vapidity, and inanition.—*J. F. Boyes.*

What signifies sadness, sir; a man grows lean on it.—*Mackenzie.*

As fate is inexorable, and not to be moved either with tears or reproaches, an excess of sorrow is as foolish as profuse laughter; while, on the other hand, not to mourn at all is insensibility.—*Seneca.*

Time will do much for sorrow; pride, perhaps, more.—*Hoffman.*

We fancy that all our afflictions are sent us directly from above; sometimes we think it in piety and contrition, but oftener in moroseness and discontent. It would be well, however, if we attempted to trace the causes of them; we should probably find their origin in some region of the heart which we never had well explored, or in which we had secretly deposited our worst indulgences. The clouds that intercept the heavens from us come not from the heavens, but from the earth.—*Landor.*

He that would soothe sorrow must not argue on the vanity of the most deceitful hopes.
Walter Scott.

Sorrow is sin's echo, and as the echo answers the voice best where there are broken walls and ruined buildings to return it, so is sorrow when reverberated by a broken ruined heart.—
Philip Henry.

The sorrow which calls for help and comfort is not the greatest, nor does it come from the depths of the heart.—*Wilhelm von Humboldt.*

For the external expressions and vent of sorrow, we know that there is a certain pleasure in weeping; it is the discharge of a big and swelling grief, of a full and strangling discontent; and therefore he that never had such a burden upon his heart as to give him opportunity thus to ease it has one pleasure in this world yet to come.—*South.*

Not to sorrow freely is never to open the bosom to the sweets of the sunshine.—*Simms.*

Sorrow is knowledge; they who know thee most must mourn the deepest over the fatal truth, the tree of knowledge is not that of life.—
Byron.

Sorrow is a kind of rust of the soul, which every new idea contributes in its passage to scour away. It is the putrefaction of stagnant life, and is remedied by exercise and motion.—
Johnson.

Every noble crown is, and on earth will ever be, a crown of thorns.—*Carlyle.*

Part of our good consists in the endeavor to do sorrows away, and in the power to sustain them when the endeavor fails, —to bear them nobly, and thus help others to bear them as well.—*Leigh Hunt.*

Light griefs do speak, while sorrow's tongue is bound.—*Seneca.*

A small sorrow distracts, a great one makes us collected; as a bell loses its clear tone when slightly cracked, and recovers it if the fissure is enlarged.—*Richter.*

Even by means of our sorrows we belong to the eternal plan.— *Wilhelm von Humboldt.*

The capacity of sorrow belongs to our grandeur; and the loftiest of our race are those who have had the profoundest grief, because they have had the profoundest sympathies.—
Henry Giles.

Sorrow is Mount Sinai. If one will go up and talk with God, face to face.—*Beecher.*

We may learn from children how large a part of our grievances is imaginary. But the pain is just as real.—*Bovee.*

It is easy in adversity to despise death; real fortitude has he who can dare to be wretched.—
Seneca.

The first pressure of sorrow crushes out from our hearts the best wine; afterwards the constant weight of it brings forth bitterness, the taste and stain from the lees of the vat.—
Longfellow.

Alas! sorrows are oft evolved from good fortune.—*Goethe.*

In the voice of mirth there may be excitement, but in the tones of mourning there is consolation.—*W. G. Clarke.*

When fresh sorrows have caused us to take some steps in the right way, we may not complain. We have invested in a life annuity, but the income remains.—*Madame Swetchine.*

Sorrows remembered sweeten present joy.—
Pollok.

Sorrow, like a heavy hanging bell, once set on ringing, with his own weight goes; then little strength rings out the doleful knell.—
Shakespeare.

The best enjoyment is half disappointment to what we mean, or would have, in this world.
Bailey.

He that hath so many causes of joy, and so great, is very much in love with sorrow and peevishness, who loses all these pleasures, and chooses to sit down on his handful of thorns. Such a person is fit to bear Nero company in his funeral sorrow for the loss of one of Poppea's hairs, or help to mourn for Lesbia's sparrow; and because he loves it he deserves to starve in the midst of plenty, and to want comfort whilst he is encircled with blessings.—
Jeremy Taylor.

There is a joy in sorrow which none but a mourner can know.—*Tupper.*

There is enjoyment even in sadness; and the same souvenirs which have produced long regrets may also soften them.—*De Boufflers.*

The deeper the sorrow, the less tongue hath it.—*Talmud.*

There are sorrows that are not painful, but are of the nature of some acids, and give piquancy and flavor to life.—*Beecher.*

Social sorrow loses half its pain.—*Johnson.*

It would seem that by our sorrows only we are called to a knowledge of the Infinite. Are we happy? The limits of life constrain us on all sides.—*Madame Swetchine.*

Wisely weigh our sorrow with our comfort.
Shakespeare.

The human race are sons of sorrow born; and each must have his portion. Vulgar minds refuse, or crouch beneath their load; the brave bear theirs without repining.—*Mallet.*

If grief is to be mitigated, it must either wear itself out or be shared.—*Madame Swetchine.*

Any mind that is capable of a real sorrow is capable of good.—*Mrs. Stowe.*

Sorrows, as storms, bring down the clouds close to the earth; sorrows bring heaven down close; and they are instruments of cleansing and purifying.—*Beecher.*

Courage! even sorrows, when once they are vanished, quicken the soul, as rain the valley.—
Salis.

Down, thou climbing sorrow! thy element is below.—*Shakespeare.*

Real sorrow is almost as difficult to discover as real poverty. An instinctive delicacy hides the rays of the one and the wounds of the other.
Madame Swetchine.

Sorrow turns the stars into mourners, and every wind of heaven into a dirge.—*Hannay.*

SOUL.
The soul is to the eyes what sight is to the touch; it seizes what escapes all the senses. As, in art, that which is most beautiful is beyond prescription, so, in knowledge, what is most high and most true is beyond experience.
Joubert.

Alas! how seldom is it that the soul is so still that it can hear when God speaks to it!—
Fenelon.

The soul, considered with its Creator, is like one of those mathematical lines that may draw nearer to another for all eternity without a possibility of touching it; and can there be a thought so transporting as to consider ourselves in these perpetual approaches to Him, who is not only the standard of perfection, but of happiness?—*Addison.*

The heart may be broken, and the soul remain unshaken.—*Napoleon.*

I consider the soul of man as the ruin of a glorious pile of buildings; where, amidst great heaps of rubbish, you meet with noble fragments of sculpture, broken pillars and obelisks, and a magnificence in confusion.—*Steele.*

The want of goods is easily repaired, but the poverty of the soul is irreparable.—
Montaigne.

There are some men's souls that are so thin, so almost destitute of what is the true idea of soul, that were not the guardian angels so keen-sighted, they would altogether overlook them.—*Beecher.*

Ah, could the soul, like the body, have a mirror! It has,—a friend.—*W. R. Alger.*

Alas! alas! why, all the souls that were, were forfeit once; and he that might the vantage best have took found out the remedy.—
Shakespeare.

Souls are dangerous things to carry straight through all the spilt saltpetre of this world.—
Mrs. E. B. Browning.

To me the eternal existence of my soul is proved from my idea of activity. If I work incessantly until my death, nature will give me another form of existence when the present can no longer sustain my spirit.—*Goethe.*

In the scenes of moral life the soul is at once actor and spectator.—*Degérando.*

The gods approve the depth, and not the tumult, of the soul.—*Wordsworth.*

After all, let a man take what pains he may to hush it down, a human soul is an awful, ghostly, unquiet possession for a bad man to have. Who knows the metes and bounds of it? Who knows all its awful perhapses,—those shudderings and tremblings, which it can no more live down than it can outlive its own eternity?—*Mrs. Stowe.*

A soul as white as heaven.—
Beaumont and Fletcher.

The action of the soul is oftener in that which is felt and left unsaid than in that which is said in any conversation. It broods over every society, and men unconsciously seek for it in each other.—*Emerson.*

Men possessing small souls are generally the authors of great evils.—*Goethe.*

The human soul is like a bird that is born in a cage. Nothing can deprive it of its natural longings, or obliterate the mysterious remembrance of its heritage.—*Epes Sargent.*

To look upon the soul as going on from strength to strength, to consider that she is to shine forever with new accessions of glory, and brighten to all eternity; that she will be still adding virtue to virtue, and knowledge to knowledge, — carries in it something wonderfully agreeable to that ambition which is natural to the mind of man.—*Addison.*

A man's possessions are just as large as his own soul. If his title-deeds cover more, the surplus acres own him, not he the acres.—
R. F. Hallock.

We may compare the soul to a linen cloth; it must be first washed to take off its native hue and color, and to make it white; and afterwards it must be ever and anon washed to preserve it white.—*South.*

It seems to me as if not only the form, but the soul of man was made to "walk erect, and look upon the stars."—*Bulwer Lytton.*

Embellish the soul with simplicity, with prudence, and everything which is neither virtuous nor vicious. Love all men. Walk according to God; for, as a poet hath said, his laws govern all.—*Marcus Antoninus.*

The wealth of a soul is measured by how much it can feel; its poverty, by how little.—
W. R. Alger.

Where are Shakespeare's imagination, Bacon's learning, Galileo's dream? Where is the sweet fancy of Sidney, the airy spirit of Fletcher, and Milton's thought severe? Methinks such things should not die and dissipate, when a hair can live for centuries, and a brick of Egypt will last three thousand years. I am content to believe that the mind of man survives, somehow or other, his clay.—*Barry Cornwall.*

The soul knows no persons.—*Emerson.*

What is the elevation of the soul? A prompt, delicate, certain feeling for all that is beautiful, all that is grand; a quick resolution to do the greatest good by the smallest means; a great benevolence joined to a great strength and great humility.—*Lavater.*

The body, — that is dust; the soul, — it is a bud of eternity.—*Nathaniel Culverwell.*

I hardly know a sight that raises one's indignation more than that of an enlarged soul joined to a contracted fortune; unless it be that so much more common one, of a contracted soul joined to an enlarged fortune.—
Lord Greville.

The health of the soul is as precarious as that of the body; for when we seem secure from passions, we are no less in danger of their infection than we are of falling ill when we appear to be well.—*Rochefoucauld.*

The soul, immortal as its Sire, shall never die.—*Montgomery.*

The soul may be compared to a field of battle, where the armies are ready every moment to encounter. Not a single vice but has a more powerful opponent, and not one virtue but may be overborne by a combination of vices.
Goldsmith.

Whatever that be which thinks, which understands, which wills, which acts, it is something celestial and divine; and upon that account must necessarily be eternal.—*Cicero.*

It is certain that the soul is either mortal or immortal. The decision of this question must make a total difference in the principles of morals. Yet philosophers have arranged their moral system entirely independent of this. What an extraordinary blindness! —*Pascal.*

Every subject's duty is the king's; but every subject's soul is his own.—*Shakespeare.*

Some men have a Sunday soul, which they screw on in due time, and take off again every Monday morning.—*Robert Hall.*

O, how much greater is the soul of one man than the vicissitudes of the whole globe! Child of heaven, and heir of immortality, how from some star hereafter wilt thou look back on the ant-hill and its commotions, from Clovis to Robespierre, from Noah to the Final Fire! —
Bulwer Lytton.

The soul is cured of its maladies by certain incantations; these incantations are beautiful reasons, from which temperance is generated in souls.—*Socrates.*

If I am mistaken in my opinion that the human soul is immortal, I willingly err; nor would I have this pleasant error extorted from me; and if, as some minute philosophers suppose, death should deprive me of my being, I need not fear the raillery of those pretended philosophers when they are no more.—*Cicero.*

We all dread a bodily paralysis, and would make use of every contrivance to avoid it, but none of us is troubled about a paralysis of the soul.—*Epictetus.*

There are souls which fall from heaven like flowers; but ere the pure and fresh buds can open, they are trodden in the dust of the earth, and lie soiled and crushed under the foul tread of some brutal hoof.—*Richter.*

The soul that lives, ascends frequently, and runs familiarly through the streets of the heavenly Jerusalem, visiting the patriarchs and prophets, saluting the apostles, and admiring the army of martyrs. So do thou lead on thy heart, and bring it to the palace of the Great King.—*Richard Baxter.*

The soul languishing in obscurity contracts a kind of rust, or abandons itself to the chimera of presumption; for it is natural for it to acquire something, even when separated from any one.—*Quintilian.*

Not in the knowledge of things without, but in the perfection of the soul within, lies the empire of man aspiring to be more than man.—
Bulwer Lytton.

We cannot describe the natural history of the soul, but we know that it is divine. All things are known to the soul. It is not to be surprised by any communication. Nothing can be greater than it, let those fear and those fawn who will. The soul is in her native realm; and it is wider than space, older than time, wide as hope, rich as love. Pusillanimity and fear she refuses with a beautiful scorn; they are not for her who putteth on her coronation robes, and goes out through universal love to universal power.—*Emerson.*

The soul has, living apart from its corporeal envelope, a profound habitual meditation which prepares it for a future life.—*Hippel.*

Making one object, in outward or inward nature, more holy to a single heart is reward enough for a life; for the more sympathies we gain or awaken for what is beautiful, by so much deeper will be our sympathy for that which is most beautiful, — the human soul!—
Lowell.

Not all the subtilties of metaphysics can make me doubt a moment of the immortality of the soul, and of a beneficent Providence. I feel it, I believe it, I desire it, I hope it, and will defend it to my last breath.—*Rousseau.*

Memnon's image imparted not its mysterions strains except at the touch of the sunbeams, nor will manner yield its true witchery from any inspiration but that of the soul.—
Tuckerman.

The mind is never right but when it is at peace within itself; the soul is in heaven even while it is in the flesh, if it be purged of its natural corruptions, and taken up with divine thoughts and contemplations.—*Seneca.*

I am fully convinced that the soul is indestructible, and that its activity will continue through eternity. It is like the sun, which, to our eyes, seems to set in night; but it has in reality only gone to diffuse its light elsewhere.
Goethe.

SOUND.

How deep is the magic of sound may be learned by breaking some sweet verses into prose. The operation has been compared to gathering dew-drops, which shine like jewels upon the flower, but run into water in the hand. The elements remain, but the sparkle is gone.—*Willmott.*

SPECIALTY.

A man is like a bit of Labrador spar, which has no lustre as you turn it in your hand, until you come to a particular angle; then it shows deep and beautiful colors. There is no adaptation or universal applicability in men, but each has his special talent, and the mastery of successful men consists in adroitly keeping themselves where and when that turn shall be oftenest to be practised.—*Emerson.*

SPECULATION.

The besetting evil of our age is the temptation to squander and dilute thought on a thousand different lines of inquiry.—
Sir John Herschel.

Conjecture as to things useful is good; but conjecture as to what it would be useless to know, such as whether men went upon all-fours, is very idle.—*Johnson.*

Wise man was he who counselled that speculation should have free course, and look fearlessly towards all the thirty-two points of the compass, whithersoever and howsoever it listed.—*Carlyle.*

SPEECH.

Speech is a faculty given to man to conceal his thoughts.—*Talleyrand.*

Lovers are apt to hear through their eyes, but the safest way is to see through their ears. Who was it that said, "Speak, that I may see you"?—*Sterne.*

Speeches cannot be made long enough for the speakers, nor short enough for the hearers.
Perry.

A sentence well couched takes both the sense and the understanding. I love not those cart-rope speeches that are longer than the memory of man can fathom.—*Feltham.*

A superior man is modest in his speech, but exceeds in his actions.—*Confucius.*

According to Solomon, life and death are in the power of the tongue; and as Euripides truly affirmeth, every unbridled tongue in the end shall find itself unfortunate; for in all that ever I observed in the course of worldly things, I ever found that men's fortunes are oftener made by their tongues than by their virtues, and more men's fortunes overthrown thereby, also, than by their vices.
Sir Walter Raleigh.

It was whispered balm, it was sunshine spoken!—*Moore.*

When speech is given to a soul holy and true, time, and its dome of ages, becomes as a mighty whispering-gallery, round which the imprisoned utterance runs, and reverberates forever.—*James Martineau.*

It was justly said by Themistocles that speech is like tapestry unfolded, where the imagery appears distinct; but thoughts, like tapestry in the bale, where the figures are rolled up together.—*Bacon.*

Speech is as a pump, by which we raise and pour out the water from the great lake of thought, whither it flows back again.—
Sterling.

We seldom repent of speaking little, very often of speaking too much; a vulgar and trite maxim, which all the world knows, but which all the world does not practise.—*Bruyère.*

Such as thy words are, such will thy affections be esteemed; and such will thy deeds as thy affections, and such thy life as thy deeds.—
Socrates.

Speech is too often not, as the Frenchman defined it, the art of concealing thought, but of quite stifling and suspending thought, so that there is none to conceal.—*Carlyle.*

The mouth of a wise man is in his heart; the heart of a fool is in his mouth, because what he knoweth or thinketh he uttereth.—
Bible.

When you speak to any, especially of quality, look them full in the face; other gestures betraying want of breeding, confidence, or honesty; dejected eyes confessing, to most judgments, guilt or folly.—*F. Osborn.*

SPIRE.

Yon towers, whose wanton tops do buss the clouds.—*Shakespeare.*

These pointed spires, that wound the ambient sky.—*Prior.*

Thy best type, desire of the sad heart, — the heaven-ascending spire.—*Bulwer Lytton.*

Magnific walls, and heaven-assaulting spires.
Smart.

How the tall temples, as to meet their God, ascend the skies!—*Young.*

The tapering pyramid, — whose spiky top has wounded the thick cloud.—*Blair.*

SPITE.

Spite is a little word, but it represents as strange a jumble of feelings and compound of discords, as any polysyllable in the language.—
Dickens.

When, to gratify a private appetite, it is once resolved upon that an ignorant and helpless creature shall be sacrificed, it is an easy matter to pick up sticks enough from any thicket where it has strayed, to make a fire to offer it up with.—*Sterne.*

SPORT.

I bear to the wisdom of Sir Philip Sidney, who said that next to hunting he liked hawking worst. However, though he may have fallen into as hyperbolical an extreme, yet who can put too great a scorn upon their folly, that, to bring home a rascal deer, or a few rotten conies, submit their lives to the will or passion of such as may take them under a penalty no less slight than there is discretion shown in exposing them.—*F. Osborn.*

SPRING.

Winter, lingering, chills the lap of May.—
Goldsmith.

Spring is a beautiful piece of work; and not to be in the country to see it done is the not realizing what glorious masters we are, and how cheerfully, minutely, and unflaggingly the fair fingers of the season broider the world for us.—*Willis.*

Winking Maybuds begin to ope their golden eyes.—*Shakespeare.*

Now the bright morning-star, day's harbinger, comes dancing from the east, and leads with her the flowery May, who from her green lap throws the yellow cowslip and the pale primrose.—*Milton.*

When spring unlocks the flowers to paint the laughing soil.—*Heber.*

So then the year is repeating its old story again. We are come once more, thank God! to its most charming chapter. The violets and the Mayflowers are as its inscriptions or vignettes. It always makes a pleasant impression on us, when we open again at these pages of the book of life.—*Goethe.*

The boyhood of the year.—*Tennyson.*

When the measured dance of the hours brings back the happy smile of spring, the buried dead is born again in the life-glance of the sun. The germs which perished to the eye within the cold breast of the earth spring up with joy in the bright realm of day.—*Schiller.*

Fresh as the lovely form of youthful May, when nymphs and graces in the dance unite.—
Wieland.

Most gladly would I give the blood-stained laurel for the first violet which March brings us, the fragrant pledge of the new-fledged year.—
Schiller.

Let us fill urns with rose-leaves in our May, and hive the thrifty sweetness for December!
Bulwer Lytton.

Stately spring! whose robe-folds are valleys, whose breast-bouquet is gardens, and whose blush is a vernal evening.—*Richter.*

Under this sycamore-tree, with the sound of the clear river Dove in our ears, with the odor of Mayflowers freshly around us after this gentle shower, and in the sight of these meadows, gold and silver, the overflowing of nature for the delectation of all quiet and contemplative anglers, we do well sigh that our life is so much in walls and so little here.—*Izaak Walton.*

But when shall spring visit the mouldering urn ? O, when shall it dawn on the night of the grave ? —*Beattie.*

Spring hangs her infant blossoms on the trees.—*Cowper.*

If spring came but once in a century, instead of once a year, or burst forth with the sound of an earthquake, and not in silence, what wonder and expectation there would be in all hearts to behold the miraculous change ! But now the silent succession suggests nothing but necessity. To most men only the cessation of the miracle would be miraculous, and the perpetual exercise of God's power seems less wonderful than its withdrawal would be.—*Longfellow.*

Sweet spring, full of sweet days and roses, a box where sweets compacted lie.— *George Herbert.*

Spring, the Raphael of the northern earth, stood already out of doors, and covered all apartments of our Vatican with his pictures.— *Richter.*

When well-apparelled April on the heel of limping winter treads.—*Shakespeare.*

It is not merely the multiplicity of tints, the gladness of tone, or the balminess of the air which delight in the spring; it is the still consecrated spirit of hope, the prophecy of happy days yet to come; the endless variety of nature, with presentiments of eternal flowers which never shall fade, and sympathy with the blessedness of the ever-developing world.—*Novalis.*

Come, gentle spring! ethereal mildness! come.—*Thomson.*

The golden line is drawn between winter and summer. Behind all is blackness and darkness and dissolution. Before is hope, and soft airs, and the flowers, and the sweet season of hay ; and people will cross the fields, reading or walking with one another ; and instead of the rain that soaks death into the heart of green things, will be the rain which they drink with delight; and there will be sleep on the grass at midday, and early rising in the morning, and long moonlight evenings.— *Leigh Hunt.*

Rough winds do shake the darling buds of May.—*Shakespeare.*

For lo, the winter is past, the rain is over and gone ; the flowers appear on the earth ; the time of the singing of birds is come, and the voice of the turtle is heard in our land.—*Bible.*

When every brake hath found its note, and sunshine smiles in every flower.— *Edward Everett.*

What child has a heart to sing in this capricious clime of ours, when spring comes sailing in from the sea, with wet and heavy cloud-sails and the misty pennon of the east-wind nailed to the mast.—*Longfellow.*

In the spring a young man's fancy lightly turns to thoughts of love.—*Tennyson.*

STARS.

The innumerable stars shining in order, like a living hymn written in light.—*Willis.*

Canst thou bind the sweet influences of Pleiades, or loose the bands of Orion ? —*Bible.*

When I gaze into the stars, they look down upon me with pity from their serene and silent spaces, like eyes glistening with tears over the little lot of man. Thousands of generations, all as noisy as our own, have been swallowed up by time, and there remains no record of them any more. Yet Arcturus and Orion, Sirius and Pleiades, are still shining in their courses, clear and young, as when the shepherd first noted them in the plain of Shinar ! — *Carlyle.*

Ye stars ! which are the poetry of heaven.— *Byron*

It is a gentle and affectionate thought, that in immeasurable height above us, at our first birth, the wreath of love was woven with sparkling stars for flowers.—*Coleridge.*

What are ye orbs? The words of God ? the Scriptures of the skies ? —*Bailey.*

If the stars should appear one night in a thousand years, how would men believe and adore ; and preserve for many generations the remembrance of the city of God which had been shown ! But every night come out these envoys of beauty, and light the universe with their admonishing smile.—*Emerson.*

The gems of heaven, that gild night's sable throne.—*Dryden.*

And lo, the star, which they saw in the east, went before them, till it came and stood over where the young child was.—*Bible.*

This majestical roof, fretted with golden fire.—*Shakespeare.*

Blossomed the lovely stars, the forget-me-nots of the angels.—*Longfellow.*

A single star is rising in the east, and from afar sheds a most tremulous lustre; silent Night doth wear it like a jewel on her brow.—
Barry Cornwall.

It is a truly sublime spectacle when in the stillness of the night, in an unclouded sky, the stars, like the world's choir, rise and set, and as it were divide existence into two portions,— the one, belonging to the earthly, is silent in the perfect stillness of night; whilst the other alone comes forth in sublimity, pomp, and majesty. Viewed in this light, the starry heavens truly exercise a moral influence over us; and who can readily stray into the paths of immorality if he has been accustomed to live amidst such thoughts and feelings, and frequently to dwell upon them? How are we entranced by the simple splendors of this wonderful drama of nature!—
Wilhelm von Humboldt.

Clad in the beauty of a thousand stars.—
Marlowe.

O powers illimitable! it is but the outer hem of God's great mantle our poor stars do gem.—*Ruskin.*

The sentinel stars set their watch in the sky.—*Campbell.*

On the wide-stretching plains of Western Asia, in the warm cloudless Assyrian night, with the lamps of heaven flashing out their radiance in uninterrupted splendor from the centre to the boundless horizon, it was no wonder that students and sages should have accepted for deities those distant worlds of fire on which eyes, brain, hopes, thoughts, and aspirations were nightly fixed.—
G. J. W. Melville.

Shrines to burn earth's incense on, the altar-fires of heaven!—*Whittier.*

Those gold candles fixed in heaven's air.—
Shakespeare.

All these stupendous objects are daily around us; but because they are constantly exposed to our view, they never affect our minds, so natural is it for us to admire new, rather than grand objects. Therefore the vast multitude of stars which diversify the beauty of this immense body does not call the people together; but when any change happens therein, the eyes of all are fixed upon the heavens.—
St. Basil.

The stars hang bright above, silent, as if they watched the sleeping earth.—*Coleridge.*

STATESMAN.

I look upon an able statesman out of business like a huge whale, that will endeavor to overturn the ship unless he has an empty cask to play with.—*Steele.*

True statesmanship is the art of changing a nation from what it is into what it ought to be.—
W. R. Alger.

It is curious that we pay statesmen for what they say, not for what they do; and judge of them from what they do, not from what they say. Hence they have one code of maxims for profession and another for practice, and make up their consciences as the Neapolitans do their beds, with one set of furniture for show and another for use.—*Colton.*

STATION.

Our distinctions do not lie in the places which we occupy, but in the grace and dignity with which we fill them.—*Simms.*

There is a kind of elevation which does not depend on fortune. It is a certain air which distinguishes us, and seems to destine us for great things; it is a price which we imperceptibly set on ourselves. By this quality we usurp the deference of other men; and it puts us, in general, more above them than birth, dignity, or even merit itself.—
Rochefoucauld.-

Lord Bacon has compared those who move in higher spheres to those heavenly bodies in the firmament, which have much admiration, but little rest; and it is not necessary to invest a wise man with power, to convince him that it is a garment bedizened with gold, which dazzles the beholder by its splendor, but oppresses the wearer by its weight.—
Colton.

They that stand high have many blasts to shake them.—*Shakespeare.*

Men and statues that are admired in an elevated situation have a very different effect upon us when we approach them; the first appear less than we imagined them, the last bigger.—*Lord Greville.*

Eminent stations make great men more great, and little ones less.—*Bruyère.*

How happy the station which every minute furnishes opportunities of doing good to thousands! how dangerous that which every moment exposes to the injuring of millions!—
Bruyère.

Whatever our place, allotted to us by Providence, that for us is the post of honor and duty. God estimates us not by the position we are in, but by the way in which we fill it.—
T. Edwards.

Whatever poets may write, or fools believe, of rural innocence and truth, and of the perfidy of courts, this is most undoubtedly true,—that shepherds and ministers are both men; their natures and passions the same, the modes of them only different.—*Chesterfield.*

He who thinks his place below him will certainly be below his place.—*Saville.*

The crowns of kings do not prevent those who wear them from being tormented sometimes by violent headaches.—*Plutarch.*

True dignity is never gained by place, and never lost when honors are withdrawn.—
Massinger.

Whom the grandeur of his office elevates over other men will soon find that the first hour of his new dignity is the last of his independence.—*Chancellor D'Aguesseau.*

I shall show that the place does not honor the man, but the man the place.—*Agesilaus.*

If any man is rich and powerful, he comes under the law of God by which the higher branches must take the burnings of the sun, and shade those that are lower; by which the tall trees must protect the weak plants beneath them.—*Beecher.*

A true man never frets about his place in the world, but just slides into it by the gravitation of his nature, and swings there as easily as a star.—*Chapin.*

Men in great places are thrice servants; servants of the sovereign or state, servants of fame, and servants of business; so as they have no freedom, neither in their persons nor in their actions nor in their times.—*Bacon.*

Every man whom chance alone has, by some accident, made a public character, hardly ever fails of becoming, in a short time, a ridiculous private one.—*Cardinal de Retz.*

STRANGER.
A stranger, if just, is not only to be preferred before a countryman, but a kinsman.—
Pythagoras.

Stranger is a holy name.—*Walter Scott.*

STRENGTH.
The exhibition of real strength is never grotesque. Distortion is the agony of weakness. It is the dislocated mind whose movements are spasmodic.—*Willmott.*

We deceive ourselves when we fancy that only weakness needs support. Strength needs it far more. A straw or a feather sustains itself long in the air—*Madame Swetchine.*

The virtue of Paganism was strength; the virtue of Christianity is obedience.—*Hare*

Although men are accused for not knowing their own weakness, yet perhaps as few know their own strength. It is in men as in soils, where sometimes there is a vein of gold which the owner knows not of.—*Swift.*

Strength, wanting judgment and policy to rule, overturneth itself.—*Horace.*

The ideal of morality has no more dangerous rival than the ideal of highest strength, of most powerful life. It is the maximum of the savage.—*Novalis.*

Strength is born in the deep silence of long-suffering hearts; not amidst joy.—
Mrs. Hemans.

Strength alone knows conflict; weakness is below even defeat, and is born vanquished.
Madame Swetchine.

Men mighty-thewed as Samson was, dark-browed as kings in iron cast, broad-breasted as twin gates of brass.—*Joaquin Miller.*

STUBBORNNESS.
A stubborn mind conduces as little to wisdom or even to knowledge, as a stubborn temper to happiness.—*Southey.*

STUDY.
A few books, well studied, and thoroughly digested, nourish the understanding more than hundreds but gargled in the mouth, as ordinary students use.—*F. Osborn.*

You are to come to your study as to the table, with a sharp appetite, whereby that which you read may the better digest. He that has no stomach to his book will very hardly thrive upon it.—*Earl of Bedford.*

There are more men ennobled by study than by nature.—*Cicero.*

Mankind have a great aversion to intellectual labor, but, even supposing knowledge to be easily attainable, more people would be content to be ignorant than would take even a little trouble to acquire it.—*Johnson.*

As land is improved by sowing it with various seeds, so is the mind by exercising it with different studies.—*Melmoth.*

How our delight in any particular study, art, or science rises and improves in proportion to the application which we bestow upon it. Thus, what was at first an exercise becomes at length an entertainment.—*Addison.*

Examples teach us that in military affairs, and all others of a like nature, study is apt to enervate and relax the courage of man, rather than to give strength and energy to the mind.—
Montaigne.

Dr. Johnson held that "impatience of study was the mental disease of the present generation"; and the remark is still applicable. We may not believe that there is a royal road to learning, but we seem to believe very firmly in a "popular" one.—*Samuel Smiles.*

As turning the logs will make a dull fire burn, so change of studies a dull brain.—
Longfellow.

A boy will learn more true wisdom in a public school in a year than by a private education in five. It is not from masters, but from their equals, that youth learn a knowledge of the world.—*Goldsmith.*

Studies teach not their own use; but that is a wisdom without them, and above them, won by observation.—*Bacon.*

The ancient practice of allowing land to remain fallow for a season is now exploded, and a succession of different crops found preferable. The case is similar with regard to the understanding, which is more relieved by change of study than by total inactivity.—
W. B. Clulow.

Study is the bane of boyhood, the aliment of youth, the indulgence of manhood, and the restorative of age.—*Landor.*

He that studies only men will get the body of knowledge without the soul; and he that studies only books, the soul without the body.
Colton.

I study much, and the more I study, the oftener I go back to those first principles which are so simple that childhood itself can lisp them.
Madame Swetchine.

He has his Rome, his Florence, his whole glowing Italy, within the four walls of his library. He has in his books the ruins of an antique world, and the glories of a modern one.
Longfellow.

If you devote your time to study, you will avoid all the irksomeness of this life; nor will you long for the approach of night, being tired of the day; nor will you be a burden to yourself, nor your society insupportable to others.—
Seneca.

STUPIDITY.

For of a truth, stupidity is strong, most strong, as the poet Schiller sings,— "Against stupidity the very gods fight unvictorious." There is in it a placid inexhaustibility, a calm, viscous infinitude, which will baffle even the gods, which will say calmly, "Try all your lightnings here, see whether I cannot quench them!"
Carlyle.

STYLE.

Whatever is pure is also simple. It does not keep the eye on itself. The observer forgets the window in the landscape it displays. A fine style gives the view of fancy — its figures, its trees, or its palaces, — without a spot.
Willmott.

The least degree of ambiguity which leaves the mind in suspense as to the meaning ought to be avoided with the greatest care.—*Blair.*

With many readers brilliancy of style passes for affluence of thought; they mistake buttercups in the grass for immeasurable mines of gold under ground.—*Longfellow.*

A chaste and lucid style is indicative of the same personal traits in the author.—
Hosea Ballou.

Gentleness in the gait is what simplicity is in the dress. Violent gesture or quick movement inspires involuntary disrespect. One looks for a moment at a cascade; but one sits for hours, lost in thought, and gazing upon the still water of a lake. A deliberate gait, gentle manners, and a gracious tone of voice — all of which may be acquired — give a mediocre man an immense advantage over those vastly superior to him. To be bodily tranquil, to speak little, and to digest without effort are absolutely necessary to grandeur of mind or of presence, or to proper development of genius.—
Balzac.

A good style fits like a good costume.—
Alcott.

A copious manner of expression gives strength and weight to our ideas, which frequently make impression upon the mind, as iron does upon solid bodies, rather by repeated strokes than by a single blow.—*Melmoth.*

Men who make money rarely saunter; men who save money rarely swagger.—
Bulwer Lytton.

He who thinks much says but little in proportion to his thoughts. He selects that language which will convey his ideas in the most explicit and direct manner. He tries to compress as much thought as possible into a few words. On the contrary, the man who talks everlastingly and promiscuously, who seems to have an exhaustless magazine of sound, crowds so many words into his thoughts that he always obscures, and very frequently conceals them.—*Washington Irving.*

A pure style in writing results from the rejection of everything superfluous.
Madame Necker.

Style is the physiognomy of the mind. It is more infallible than that of the body. To imitate the style of another is said to be wearing a mask. However beautiful it may be, it is through its lifelessness insipid and intolerable, so that even the most ugly living face is more engaging.—*Schopenhauer.*

Every style formed elaborately on any model must be affected and straight-laced.—
Whipple.

Unconsciousness is one of the most important conditions of a good style in speaking or in writing.—*Richard Grant White.*

The unaffected of every country nearly resemble each other, and a page of our Confucius and your Tillotson have scarce any material difference. Paltry affectation, strained allusions, and disgusting finery are easily attained by those who choose to wear them; they are but too frequently the badges of ignorance or of stupidity, whenever it would endeavor to please.—*Goldsmith.*

In composing, think much more of your matter than your manner. To be sure, spirit, grace, and dignity of manner are of great importance, both to the speaker and writer; but of infinitely more importance is the weight and worth of matter.—*Wirt.*

It is difficult to descend with grace without seeming to fall.—*Blair.*

An era is fast approaching when no writer will be read by the majority, save and except those than can effect that for bales of manuscript that the hydrostatic screw performs for bales of cotton, by condensing that matter into a period that before occupied a page.—*Cottar.*

Digressions in a book are like foreign troops in a state, which argue the nation to want a heart and hands of its own; and often either subdue the natives, or drive them into the most unfruitful corners.—*Swift.*

Some authors write nonsense in a clear style, and others sense in an obscure one; some can reason without being able to persuade, others can persuade without being able to reason; some dive so deep that they descend into darkness, and others soar so high that they give us no light; and some, in a vain attempt to be cutting and dry, give us only that which is cut and dried. We should labor, therefore, to treat with ease of things that are difficult; with familiarity, of things that are novel; and with perspicuity, of things that are profound.—*Colton.*

Whoever wishes to attain an English style, familiar but not coarse, and elegant but not ostentatious, must give his days and nights to the volumes of Addison.—*Johnson.*

Proper words in proper places make the true definition of a style.—*Swift.*

Those who make antitheses by forcing the sense are like men who make false windows for the sake of symmetry. Their rule is not to speak justly, but to make accurate figures.—*Pascal.*

The truly sublime is always easy, and always natural.—*Burke.*

It is far more difficult to be simple than to be complicated; far more difficult to sacrifice skill and cease exertion in the proper place, than to expend both indiscriminately.—*Ruskin.*

Style supposes the reunion and the exercise of all the intellectual faculties. The style is the man.—*Buffon.*

Harmony of period and melody of style have greater weight than is generally imagined in the judgment we pass upon writing and writers. As a proof of this, let us reflect what texts of scripture, what lines in poetry, or what periods we most remember and quote, either in verse or prose, and we shall find them to be only musical ones.—*Shenstone.*

The way to elegancy of style is to employ your pen upon every errand; and the more trivial and dry it is, the more brains must be allowed for sauce.—*F. Osborn.*

A great writer possesses, so to speak, an individual and unchangeable style, which does not permit him easily to preserve the anonymous.—*Voltaire.*

If I were to choose the people with whom I would spend my hours of conversation, they should be certainly such as labored no further than to make themselves readily and clearly apprehended, and would have patience and curiosity to understand me. To have good sense and ability to express it are the most essential and necessary qualities in companions. When thoughts rise in us fit to utter among familiar friends, there needs but very little care in clothing them.—*Steele.*

Submit your sentiments with diffidence. A dictatorial style, though it may carry conviction, is always accompanied with disgust.—*Washington.*

Propriety of thought and propriety of diction are commonly found together. Obscurity and affectation are the two greatest faults of style.—*Macaulay.*

Generally speaking, an author's style is a faithful copy of his mind. If you would write a lucid style, let there first be light in your own mind; and if you would write a grand style, you ought to have a grand character.—*Goethe.*

Long sentences in a short composition are like large rooms in a little house.—*Shenstone.*

The words in prose ought to express the intended meaning; if they attract attention to themselves, it is a fault; in the very best styles, as Southey's, you read page after page without noticing the medium.—*Coleridge.*

A good writer does not write as people write, but as he writes.—*Montesquieu.*

He who would reproach an author for obscurity should look into his own mind to see whether it is quite clear there. In the dusk the plainest writing is illegible.—*Goethe.*

When you doubt between words, use the plainest, the commonest, the most idiomatic. Eschew fine words as you would rouge, love simple ones as you would native roses on your cheek.—*Hare.*

Young people are dazzled by the brilliancy of antithesis, and employ it. Matter-of-fact men, and those who like precision, naturally fall into comparisons and metaphor. Sprightly natures, full of fire, and whom a boundless imagination carries beyond all rules, and even what is reasonable, cannot rest satisfied even with hyperbole. As for the sublime, it is only great geniuses and those of the very highest order that are able to rise to its height.—*Bruyère.*

Every good writer has much idiom; it is the life and spirit of language.—*Landor.*

The want of a more copious diction, to borrow a figure from Locke, is caused by our supposing that the mind is like Fortunatus's purse, and will always supply our wants, without our ever putting anything into it.—*Bovee.*

You know that in everything women write there are always a thousand faults of grammar, but, with your permission, a harmony which is rare in the writings of men.—*Madame de Maintenon.*

In some exquisite critical hints on "Eurythmy," Goethe remarks, "that the best composition in pictures is that which, observing the most delicate laws of harmony, so arranges the objects that they by their position tell their own story." And the rule thus applied to composition in painting applies no less to composition in literature.—*Bulwer Lytton.*

I look upon paradoxes as the impotent efforts of men who, not having capacity to draw attention and celebrity from good sense, fly to eccentricities to make themselves noted.—*Horace Walpole.*

The style of writing required in the great world is distinguished by a free and daring grace, a careless security, a fine and sharp polish, a delicate and perfect taste; while that fitted for the people is characterized by a vigorous natural fulness, a profound depth of feeling, and an engaging naïveté.—*Goethe.*

Grace was in all her steps, heaven in her eye, in every gesture dignity and love.—*Milton.*

The censure of frequent and long parentheses has led writers into the preposterous expedient of leaving out the marks by which they are indicated. It is no cure to a lame man to take away his crutches.—*Whately.*

When we meet with a natural style, we are surprised and delighted, for we expected to find an author, and we have found a man.—*Pascal.*

The old prose writers wrote as if they were speaking to an audience; while, among us, prose is invariably written for the eye alone.—*Niebuhr.*

Nothing is so difficult as the apparent ease of a clear and flowing style; those graces which from their presumed facility encourage all to attempt an imitation of them are usually the most inimitable.—*Colton.*

I hate a style, as I do a garden, that is wholly flat and regular; that slides along like an eel, and never rises to what one can call an inequality.—*Shenstone.*

Any one may mouth out a passage with a theatrical cadence, or get upon stilts to tell his thoughts; but to write or speak with propriety and simplicity is a more difficult task. Thus it is easy to affect a pompous style, to use a word twice as big as the thing you want to express; it is not so easy to pitch upon the very word that exactly fits it.—*Hazlitt.*

Justness of thought and style, refinement in manners, good-breeding and politeness of every kind, can come only from the trial and experience of what is best.—*Duncan.*

Miss Edgeworth and Madame de Staël have proved that there is no sex in style; and Madame la Roche Jacqueline, and the Duchesse d'Angouleme have proved that there is no sex in courage.—*Colton.*

A sentence, well couched, takes both the sense and the understanding.—*Feltham.*

Style! style! why, all writers will tell you that it is the very thing which can least of all be changed. A man's style is nearly as much a part of him as his physiognomy, his figure, the throbbing of his pulse,—in short, as any part of his being which is at least subjected to the action of the will.—*Fenelon.*

Antithesis may be the blossom of wit, but it will never arrive at maturity unless sound sense be the trunk, and truth the root.—*Colton.*

To write a genuine familiar or truly English style is to write as any one would speak in common conversation, who had a thorough command and choice of words, or who could discourse with ease, force, and perspicuity, setting aside all pedantic and oratorical flourishes.—*Hazlitt.*

The way to acquire lasting esteem is not by the fewness of a writer's faults, but the greatness of his beauties, and our noblest works are generally most replete with both.—*Goldsmith.*

Persons are oftentimes misled in regard to their choice of dress by attending to the beauty of colors, rather than selecting such colors as may increase their own beauty.—*Shenstone.*

32

It is equally true of the pen as the pencil, that what is drawn from life and the heart alone bears the impress of immortality.—
Tuckerman.

Style is only the frame to hold our thoughts. It is like the sash of a window; if heavy, it will obscure the light. The object is to have as little sash as will hold the light, that we may not think of the former, but have the latter.—
Emmons.

One tires of a page of which every sentence sparkles with points, of a sentimentalist who is always pumping the tears from his eyes or your own.—*Thackeray.*

Style is the dress of thoughts; and let them be ever so just, if your style is homely, coarse, and vulgar, they will appear to as much disadvantage, and be as ill received, as your person, though ever so well proportioned, would if dressed in rags, dirt, and tatters.—*Chesterfield.*

Style may be defined, — proper words in proper places.—*Swift.*

A composition which dazzles at first sight by gaudy ephithets, or brilliant turns of expression, or glittering trains of imagery, may fade gradually from the mind, leaving no enduring impression; but words which flow fresh and warm from a full heart, and which are instinct with the life and breath of human feeling, pass into household memories, and partake of the immortality of the affections from which they spring.—*Whipple.*

Obscurity in writing is commonly an argument of darkness in the mind. The greatest learning is to be seen in the greatest plainness.
Wilkins.

If you would be pungent, be brief, for it is with words as with sunbeams, the more they are condensed, the deeper they burn.—*Saxe.*

We know much of a writer by his style. An open and imperious disposition is shown in short sentences, direct and energetic. A secretive and proud mind is cold and obscure in style. An affectionate and imaginative nature pours out luxuriantly, and blossoms all over with ornament.—*Beecher.*

SUBLIMITY.
The sublime and the ridiculous are often so nearly related that it is difficult to class them separately. One step above the sublime makes the ridiculous, and one step above the ridiculous makes the sublime again.—*Thomas Paine.*

Sublimity is Hebrew by birth.—*Coleridge.*

Stupidity has its sublime as well as genius, and he who carries that quality to absurdity has reached it, which is always a source of pleasure to sensible people.—*Wieland.*

How sublime is the audacious tautology of Mohammed, God is God!—*W. R. Alger.*

The sublime, when it is introduced at a seasonable moment, has often carried all before it with the rapidity of lightning, and shown at a glance the mighty power of genius.—
Longinus.

One source of the sublime is infinity.—
Burke.

The sublime is the temple-step of religion, as the stars are of immeasurable space. When what is mighty appears in nature, — a storm, thunder, the starry firmament, death, — then utter the word "God" before the child. A great misfortune, a great blessing, a great crime, a noble action, are building-sites for a child's church.—*Richter.*

From the sublime to the ridiculous there is but one step.—*Napoleon.*

"The sublime," says *Longinus, ."*is often nothing but the echo or image of magnanimity"; and where this quality appears in any one, even though a syllable be not uttered, it excites our applause and admiration.—*Hume.*

Nothing so effectually deadens the taste of the sublime as that which is light and radiant.
Burke.

SUBORDINATION.
I am a friend to subordination, as most conducive to the happiness of society. There is a reciprocal pleasure in governing and being governed.—*Johnson.*

SUBTLETY.
Subtlety will sometimes give safety, no less than strength; and minuteness has sometimes escaped, where magnitude would have been crushed. The little animal that kills the boa is formidable chiefly from its insignificance, which is incompressible by the folds of its antagonist.—*Colton.*

Subtlety may deceive you; integrity never will.—*Cromwell.*

It is said that Windham, when he came to the end of a speech, often found himself so perplexed by his own subtilty that he hardly knew which way he was going to give his vote. This is a good illustration of the fallaciousness of reasoning, and of the uncertainties which attend its practical application.—*Hare.*

SUCCESS.
Success serves men as a pedestal; it makes them look larger, if reflection does not measure them.—*Joubert.*

Had I miscarried, I had been a villain; for men judge actions always by events; but when we manage by a just foresight, success is prudence, and possession right.—*Higgons.*

Both as to high and low indifferently, men are prepossessed, charmed, fascinated by success; successful crimes are praised very much like virtue itself, and good fortune is not far from occupying the place of the whole cycle of virtues. It must be an atrocious act, a base and hateful deed, which success would not be able to justify.—*Bruyère.*

Success has a great tendency to conceal and throw a veil over the evil deeds of men.—*Demosthenes.*

Julius Cæsar owed two millions when he risked the experiment of being general in Gaul. If Julius Cæsar had not lived to cross the Rubicon, and pay off his debts, what would his creditors have called Julius Cæsar ? —*Bulwer Lytton.*

The earnest desire of succeeding is almost always a prognostic of success.—*Stanislaus.*

He that would relish success to a good purpose should keep his passions cool, and his expectations low; and then it is possible that his fortune might exceed his fancy; for an advantage always rises by surprise, and is almost always doubled by being unlooked for.—*Jeremy Collier.*

Let them call it mischief; when it is past and prospered, it will be virtue.—*Ben Jonson.*

Success produces confidence, confidence relaxes industry, and negligence ruins that reputation which accuracy had raised.—*Johnson.*

That which turns out well is better than any law.—*Menander.*

The rude reproaches of the rascal herd, who, for the self-same actions, if successful, would be as grossly lavish in their praise.—*Thomson.*

Who shall tax successful villany, or call the rising traitor to account ? —*Havard.*

The surest hindrance to success is to have too high a standard of refinement in our own minds, or too high an opinion of the judgment of the public. He who is determined not to be satisfied with anything short of perfection will never do anything at all either to please himself or others.—*Hazlitt.*

In everything the ends well defined are the secret of durable success.—*Cousin.*

It is not in mortals to command success, but we will do more, Sempronius; we will deserve it.—*Addison.*

Constant success shows us but one side of the world; for, as it surrounds us with friends, who will tell us only our merits, so it silences those enemies from whom alone we can learn our defects.—*Colton.*

The man who is always fortunate cannot easily have a great reverence for virtue.—*Cicero.*

Few things are impracticable in themselves; and it is for want of application, rather than of means, that men fail of success.—*Rochefoucauld.*

Nothing succeeds so well as success.—*Talleyrand.*

Success is full of promise till men get it; and then it is a last year's nest, from which the bird has flown.—*Beecher.*

Success often costs more than it is worth.—*E. Wigglesworth.*

To know a man, observe how he wins his object, rather than how he loses it; for when we fail, our pride supports us, — when we succeed, it betrays us.—*Colton.*

It is success that colors all in life; success makes fools admired, makes villains honest.—*Thomson.*

There is nothing so sure of succeeding as not to be over brilliant, as to be entirely wrapped up in one's self, and endowed with a perseverance which, in spite of all the rebuffs it may meet with, never relaxes in the pursuit of its object. It is incredible what may be done by dint of importunity alone; and where shall we find the man of real talents who knows how to be importunate enough!—*Baron de Grimm.*

Not that which men do worthily, but that which they do successfully, is what history makes haste to record.—*Beecher.*

What succeeds we keep, and it becomes the habit of mankind.—*Theodore Parker.*

The great highroad of human welfare lies along the old highway of steadfast well-doing; and they who are the most persistent, and work in the truest spirit, will invariably be the most successful; success treads on the heels of every right effort.—*Samuel Smiles.*

The surest way not to fail is to determine to succeed.—*Sheridan.*

We tell our triumphs to the crowd, but our own hearts are the sole confidants of our sorrows.—*Bulwer Lytton.*

There is a glare about worldly success, which is very apt to dazzle men's eyes.—*Hare.*

If you wish success in life, make perseverance your bosom friend, experience your wise counsellor, caution your elder brother, and hope your guardian genius.—*Addison.*

Had I succeeded well, I had been reckoned amongst the wise; our minds are so disposed to judge from the event.—*Euripides.*

"I confess," says a thoughtful writer, "that increasing years bring with them an increasing respect for men who do not succeed in life, as those words are commonly used." Ill success sometimes arises from a conscience too sensitive, a taste too fastidious, a self-forgetfulness too romantic, a modesty too retiring.—*G. A. Sala.*

Success consecrates the foulest crimes.— *Seneca.*

One line, a line fraught with instruction, includes the secret of Lord Kenyon's final success, — he was prudent, he was patient, and he persevered.—*G. Townsend.*

Successful minds work like a gimlet, — to a single point.—*Bovee.*

The talent of success is nothing more than doing what you can do well, and doing well whatever you do without a thought of fame. If it comes at all it will come because it is deserved, not because it is sought after.—*Longfellow.*

Success makes success, as money makes money.—*Chamfort.*

The thinking part of mankind do not form their judgment from events; and their equity will ever attach equal glory to those actions which deserve success, and those which have been crowned with it.—*Washington.*

Didst thou never hear that things ill got had ever bad success ? —*Shakespeare.*

The path of success in business is invariably the path of common-sense. Notwithstanding all that is said about "lucky hits," the best kind of success in every man's life is not that which comes by accident. The only "good time coming" we are justified in hoping for is that which we are capable of making for ourselves.—*Samuel Smiles.*

Success! to thee, as to a God, men bend the knee.—*Æschylus.*

Popularity disarms envy in well-disposed minds. Those are ever the most ready to do justice to others who feel that the world has done them justice. When success has not this effect in opening the mind it is a sign that it has been ill-deserved.—*Hazlitt.*

Near or far off, well won is still well shot.— *Shakespeare.*

It is possible to indulge too great contempt for mere success, which is frequently attended with all the practical advantages of merit itself, and with several advantages that merit alone can never command.—*W. B. Clulow.*

SUICIDE.

We must not pluck death from the Maker's hand.—*Bailey.*

Against self-slaughter there is a prohibition so divine, that cravens my weak hand.— *Shakespeare.*

Our pious ancestors enacted a law that suicides should be buried where four roads meet, and that a cart-load of stones should be thrown upon the body. Yet when gentlemen or ladies commit suicide, not by cord or steel, but by turtle-soup or lobster-salad, they may be buried in consecrated ground, and under the auspices of the Church ; and the public are not ashamed to read an epitaph on their tombstones false enough to make the marble blush. Were the barbarous old law now in force that punished the body of the suicide for the offence of his soul, we should find many a Mount Auburn at the cross-roads.—*Horace Mann.*

God has appointed us captains of these our bodily forts, which, without treason to that majesty, are never to be delivered over till they are demanded.—*Sir P. Sidney.*

Suicide is not to fear death, but yet to be afraid of life. It is a brave act of valor to contemn death ; but where life is more terrible than death, it is then the truest valor to dare to live ; and herein religion hath taught us a noble example, for all the valiant acts of Curtius, Scævola, or Codrus do not parallel or match that one of Job.—*Sir Thomas Browne.*

Why, he that cuts off twenty years of life cuts off so many years of fearing death.— *Shakespeare.*

Suicide sometimes proceeds from cowardice, but not always ; for cowardice sometimes prevents it ; since as many live because they are afraid to die, as die because they are afraid to live.—*Colton.*

He is not valiant that dares die ; but he that boldly bears calamity.—*Massinger.*

Suicide is a crime the most revolting to the feelings ; nor does any reason suggest itself to our understanding by which it can be justified. It certainly originates in that species of fear which we denominate poltroonery. For what claim can that man have to courage who trembles at the frowns of fortune ? True heroism consists in being superior to the ills of life in whatever shape they may challenge him to combat.—*Napoleon.*

When affliction thunders over our roofs, to hide our heads, and run into our graves, shows us no men, but makes us fortune's slaves.— *Ben Jonson.*

Men would not be so hasty to abandon the world either as monks or as suicides, did they but see the jewels of wisdom and faith which are scattered so plentifully along its paths ; and lacking which no soul can come again from beyond the grave to gather.—*Mountford.*

We ought not to quit our post without the permission of Him who commands; the post of man is life.—*Pythagoras.*

Suicides pay the world a bad compliment. Indeed, it may so happen that the world has been beforehand with them in incivility. Granted. Even then the retaliation is at their own expense.—*Zimmermann.*

The coward sneaks to death; the brave live on.—*Dr. George Sewell.*

The dread of something after death, that un discovered country, from whose bourne no traveller returns, puzzles the will, and makes us rather bear the ills we have, than fly to others that we know not of. – *Shakespeare.*

What poetical suicides and sublime despair might have been prevented by a timely dose of blue pill, or the offer of a *loge aux Italiens!* — *Sir Charles Morgan.*

Fool! I mean not that poor-souled piece of heroism, self-slaughter; O no! the miserablest day we live there is many a better thing to do than die.—*George Darley.*

SUN.

The weary sun hath made a golden set; and, by the bright track of his fiery car, gives token of a goodly day to-morrow.— *Shakespeare.*

More joyful eyes look at the setting than at the rising sun. Burdens are laid down by the poor, whom the sun consoles more than the rich. No star and no moon announce the rising sun; and does not the setting sun, like a lover, leave behind his image in the moon? I yearn towards him when he sets, not when he rises.—*Richter.*

High in his chariot glowed the lamp of day. *Falconer.*

The sun, which is as a bridegroom coming out of his chamber, and rejoiceth as a strong man to run a race. His going forth is from the end of the heaven, and his circuit unto the ends of it. And there is nothing hid from the heat thereof.—*Bible.*

The self-same sun that shines upon his court hides not his visage from our cottage, but looks on alike.—*Shakespeare.*

Suns are sunflowers of a higher light.— *Richter.*

The sun, if he could avoid it, would not shine upon a dunghill; but his rays are so pure and celestial, I never heard that they were polluted by it.—*Sterne.*

The very dead creation from thy touch assumes a mimic life.—*Thomson.*

O sun! of this great world both eye and soul.—*Milton.*

That orbed continent, the fire that severs day from night.—*Shakespeare.*

The glorious sun, — the centre and soul of our system, the lamp that lights it, the fire that heats it, the magnet that guides and controls it; the fountain of color which gives its azure to the sky, its verdure to the fields, its rainbow hues to the gay world of flowers, and the purple light of love to the marble cheek of youth and beauty.— *Sir David Brewster.*

The sun, God's crest upon his azure shield, the heavens.—*Bailey.*

But yonder comes the powerful king of day rejoicing in the east.—*Thomson.*

The sun, reflecting upon the mud of strands and shores, is unpolluted in his beam.— *Jeremy Taylor.*

SUNSET.

Sunsets in themselves are generally superior to sunrises; but with the sunset we appreciate images drawn from departed peace and faded glory.—*Hillard.*

Gilding pale streams with heavenly alchemy. *Shakespeare.*

SUPERFLUITIES.

What man in his right senses, that has wherewithal to live free, would make himself a slave for superfluities? What does that man want who has enough? Or what is he the better for abundance that can never be satisfied? *L'Estrange.*

It is impossible to diminish poverty by the multiplication of effects, for, manage as we may, misery and suffering will always cleave to the border of superfluity.—*Jacobi.*

Were the superfluities of a nation valued, and made a perpetual tax or benevolence, there would be more almshouses than poor, schools than scholars, and enough to spare for government besides.— *William Penn.*

SUPERSTITION.

Superstition always inspires littleness, religion grandeur of mind; the superstitious raises beings inferior to himself to deities.—*Lavater.*

It were better to have no opinion of God at all than such an opinion as is unworthy of him; for the one is unbelief, and the other is contumely; and certainly superstition is the reproach of the Deity.—*Bacon.*

Superstition changes a man to a beast, fanatacism makes him a wild beast, and despotism a beast of burden.—*La Harpe.*

Superstition is a senseless fear of God; religion, the pious worship of God.—*Cicero.*

Weakness, fear, melancholy, together with ignorance, are the true sources of superstition. Hope, pride, presumption, a warm indignation, together with ignorance, are the true sources of enthusiasm.—*Hume.*

Superstition renders a man a fool, and scepticism makes him mad.—*Fielding.*

Death approaches, which is always impending over us like the stone over Tantalus; then comes superstition, with which he who is racked can never find peace of mind.—*Cicero.*

Look how the world's poor people are amazed at apparitions, signs, and prodigies!—*Shakespeare.*

Superstition without a veil is a deformed thing; there is also a superstition in avoiding superstition, when men think they do best if they go farthest from the superstition,—by which means they often take away the good as well as the bad.—*Bacon.*

The greatest burden in the world is superstition, not only of ceremonies in the Church, but of imaginary and scarecrow sins at home.—*Milton.*

Superstition! that horrid incubus which dwelt in darkness, shunning the light, with all its racks, and poison chalices, and foul sleeping draughts, is passing away without return. Religion cannot pass away. The burning of a little straw may hide the stars of the sky; but the stars are there, and will reappear.—*Carlyle.*

Heart-chilling superstition! thou canst glaze even Pity's eye with her own frozen tear.—*Coleridge.*

Superstition is the poetry of life. It is inherent in man's nature; and when we think it is wholly eradicated, it takes refuge in the strangest holes and corners, whence it peeps out all at once, as soon as it can do it with safety.—*Goethe.*

I think we cannot too strongly attack superstition, which is the disturber of society; nor too highly respect genuine religion, which is the support of it.—*Rousseau.*

*L*iberal minds are open to conviction. Liberal doctrines are capable of improvement. There are proselytes from atheism; but none from superstition.—*Junius.*

As it addeth deformity to an ape to be so like a man, so the similitude of superstition to religion makes it the more deformed.—*Bacon.*

That the corruption of the best thing produces the worst, is grown into a maxim, and is commonly proved, among other instances, by the pernicious effects of superstition and enthusiasm, the corruptions of true religion.—*Hume.*

Superstition is but the fear of belief, religion is the confidence.—*Lady Blessington.*

Superstition is not, as has been defined, an excess of religious feeling, but a misdirection of it, an exhausting of it on vanities of man's devising.—*Whately.*

Superstition is the poesy of practical life; hence, a poet is none the worse for being superstitious.—*Goethe.*

They that are against superstition oftentimes run into it of the wrong side. If I wear all colors but black, then I am superstitious in not wearing black.—*Selden.*

SUSPICION.

Suspicion is no less an enemy to virtue than to happiness. He that is already corrupt is naturally suspicious, and he that becomes suspicious will quickly be corrupt.—*Colton.*

The virtue of a coward is suspicion.
George Herbert.

He that lives in perpetual suspicion lives the life of a sentinel,—of a sentinel never relieved, whose business it is to look out for and expect an enemy, which is an evil not very far short of perishing by him.—*Young.*

Ignorance is the mother of suspicion.—*W. R. Alger.*

Suspicion is far more apt to be wrong than right; oftener unjust than just. It is no friend to virtue, and always an enemy to happiness.—*Hosea Ballou.*

Suspicion always haunts the guilty mind.—*Shakespeare.*

Surmise is the gossamer that malice blows on fair reputations, the corroding dew that destroys the choice blossom. Surmise is primarily the squint of suspicion, and suspicion is established before it is confirmed.—*Zimmermann.*

Suspicion is a heavy armor, and with its own weight impedes more than protects.—*Byron.*

Better is the mass of men, suspicion, than thy fears; purer than thy judgments, ascetic tongue of censure; in all things worthier to love, if not also wiser to esteem.—*Tupper.*

Suspicion is ever strong on the suffering side.—*Publius Syrus.*

Never put much confidence in such as put no confidence in others. A man prone to suspect evil is mostly looking in his neighbor for what he sees in himself. As to the pure all things are pure, even so to the impure all things are impure.—*Hare.*

A dull head thinks of no better way to show himself wise, than by suspecting everything in his way.—*Sir P. Sidney.*

Any base heart can devise means of vileness, and affix the ugly shapings of its own fancy to the actions of those around him; but it requires loftiness of mind, and the heaven-born spirit of virtue, to imagine greatness where it is not, and to deck the sordid objects of nature in the beautiful robes of loveliness and light.—*Jane Porter.*

Whose own hard dealings teach them, suspect the thoughts of others!—*Shakespeare.*

There is nothing makes a man suspect much, more than to know little; and therefore men should remedy suspicion by procuring to know more, and not to keep their suspicions in smother.—*Bacon.*

Suspicion shall be all stuck full of eyes.— *Shakespeare.*

Suspicions among thoughts are like bats amongst birds, they ever fly to twilight; they are to be repressed, or, at least, well guarded, for they cloud the mind.—*Bacon.*

Open suspecting of others comes of secretly condemning ourselves.—*Sir P. Sidney.*

SURETY.
Beware of suretyship for thy best friend. He that payeth another man's debt seeketh his own decay. But if thou canst not otherwise choose, rather lend thy money thyself upon good bonds, although thou borrow it; so shalt thou secure thyself, and pleasure thy friend.— *Lord Burleigh.*

If any friend desire thee to be his surety, give him a part of what thou hast to spare; if he press thee further, he is not thy friend at all, for friendship rather chooseth harm to itself than offereth it. If thou be bound for a stranger, thou art a fool; if for a merchant, thou puttest thy estate to learn to swim.— *Sir Walter Raleigh.*

Such as are betrayed by their easy nature to be ordinary security for their friends leave so little to themselves, as their liberty remains ever after arbitrary at the will of others; experience having recorded many, whom their fathers had left elbow-room enough, that by suretyship have expired in a dungeon.— *F. Osborn.*

SWORD.
The sword is but a hideous flash in the darkness, right is an eternal ray.—*Victor Hugo.*

SYMPATHY.
Every man rejoices twice when he has a partner of his joy; a friend shares my sorrow and makes it but a moiety, but he swells my joy and makes it double.—*Jeremy Taylor.*

Sympathy is the first great lesson which man should learn. It will be ill for him if he proceeds no farther; if his emotions are but excited to roll back on his heart, and to be fostered in luxurious quiet. But unless he learns to feel for things in which he has no personal interest, he can achieve nothing generous or noble.—*Talfourd.*

A crowd always thinks with its sympathy, never with its reason.—*W. R. Alger.*

Let us cherish sympathy. By attention and exercise it may be improved in every man. It prepares the mind for receiving the impressions of virtue; and without it there can be no true politeness. Nothing is more odious than that insensibility which wraps a man up in himself and his own concerns, and prevents his being moved with either the joys or the sorrows of another.—*Beattie.*

All sympathy not consistent with acknowledged virtue is but disguised selfishness.— *Coleridge.*

It is by sympathy we enter into the concerns of others, that we are moved as they are moved, and are never suffered to be indifferent spectators of almost anything which men can do or suffer. For sympathy may be considered as a sort of substitution, by which we are put into the place of another man, and affected in many respects as he is affected.—*Burke.*

And share the inward fragrance of each other's heart.—*Keats.*

Every human feeling is greater and larger than the exciting cause,—a proof, I think, that man is designed for a higher state of existence, and this is deeply implied in music, in which there is always something more and beyond the immediate expression.—*Coleridge.*

It is a lively spark of nobleness to descend in most favor to one when he is lowest in affliction.—*Sir P. Sidney.*

A helping word to one in trouble is often like a switch on a railroad-track,—but one inch between wreck and smooth-rolling prosperity.—*Beecher.*

Public feeling now is apt to side with the persecuted, and our modern martyr is full as likely to be smothered with roses as with coals. *Chapin.*

It may, indeed, be said that sympathy exists in all minds, as Faraday has discovered that magnetism exists in all metals; but a certain temperature is required to develop the hidden property, whether in the metal or the mind.— *Bulwer Lytton.*

Not being untutored in suffering, I learn to pity those in affliction.—*Virgil.*

The man who melts with social sympathy, though not allied, is than a thousand kinsmen of more worth.—*Euripides.*

Graceful, particularly in youth, is the tear of sympathy, and the heart that melts at the tale of woe; we should not permit ease and indulgence to contract our affections, and wrap us up in a selfish enjoyment. But we should accustom ourselves to think of the distresses of human life, of the solitary cottage, the dying parent, and the weeping orphan. Nor ought we ever to sport with pain and distress in any of our amusements, or treat even the meanest insect with wanton cruelty.—*Blair.*

The greatest pleasures of which the human mind is susceptible are the pleasures of consciousness and sympathy.—*Parke Godwin.*

Sympathy wanting, all is wanting; its personal magnetism is the conductor of the sacred spark that lights our atoms, puts us in human communion, and gives us to company, conversation, and ourselves.—*Alcott*

All powerful souls have kindred with each other.—*Coleridge.*

There is naught in this bad world like sympathy; it is so becoming to the soul and face, sets to soft music the harmonious sigh, and robes sweet friendship in a Brussels lace.— *Byron.*

We are governed by sympathy; and the extent of our sympathy is determined by that of our sensibility.—*Hazlitt.*

We are accustomed to see men deride what they do not understand, and snarl at the good and beautiful because it lies beyond their sympathies.—*Goethe.*

It is an eternal truth in the political as well as the mystical body, that " where one member suffers, all the members suffer with it."—*Junius*

The individual soul should seek for an intimate union with the soul of the universe — *Novalis.*

Man is one; and he hath one great heart. It is thus we feel, with a gigantic throb athwart the sea, each other's rights and wrongs; thus are we men.—*Bailey.*

The Devil himself would be but a contemptible adversary, were he not sure of a correspondent, and a party that held intelligence with him in our own breasts. All the blowing of a fire put under a caldron could never make it boil over, were there not a fulness of water within it.—*South.*

One of the greatest of all mental pleasures is to have our thoughts often divined; ever entered into with sympathy.—*Miss L. E. Landon.*

Kindred weaknesses induce friendships as often as kindred virtues.—*Bovee.*

Nature always wears the colors of the spirit. To a man laboring under calamity the heat of his own fire hath sadness in it. Then there is a kind of contempt of the landscape felt by him who has just lost by death a dear friend. The sky is less grand as it shuts down over less worth in the population.—*Emerson.*

It is certain my belief gains quite infinitely the very moment I can convince another mind thereof.—*Novalis.*

Helpless mortal! Thine arm can destroy thousands at once, but cannot enclose even two of thy fellow-creatures at once in the embrace of love and sympathy!—*Richter.*

The making one object, in outward or inward nature, more holy to a single heart, is reward enough for a life; for the more sympathies we gain or awaken for what is beautiful, by so much deeper will be our sympathy for that which is most beautiful, the human soul.— *Lowell.*

When a man can look upon the simple wild-rose, and feel no pleasure, his taste has been corrupted.—*Beecher.*

The capacity of sorrow belongs to our grandeur, and the loftiest of our race are those who have had the profoundest sympathies, because they have had the profoundest sorrows.— *Henry Giles.*

Happy is the man who has that in his soul which acts upon the dejected as April airs upon violet roots. Gifts from the hand are silver and gold, but the heart gives that which neither silver nor gold can buy. To be full of goodness, full of cheerfulness, full of sympathy, full of helpful hope, causes a man to carry blessings of which he is himself as unconscious as a lamp is of its own shining. Such a one moves on human life as stars move on dark seas to bewildered mariners; as the sun wheels, bringing all the seasons with him from the south.—*Beecher.*

To rejoice in another's prosperity is to give content to your own lot; to mitigate another's grief is to alleviate or dispel your own.— *T. Edwards.*

To commiserate is sometimes more than to give; for money is external to a man's self, but he who bestows compassion communicates his own soul.—*Mountford.*

There are eyes which need only to look up, to touch every chord of a breast choked by the stifling atmosphere of stiff and stagnant society, and to call forth tones which might become the accompanying music of a life. This gentle transfusion of mind into mind is the secret of sympathy.—*Richter.*

The world has no sympathy with any but positive griefs. It will pity you for what you lose; never for what you lack.—
Madame Swetchine.

Nothing precludes sympathy so much as a perfect indifference to it.—*Hazlitt.*

Conversation augments pleasure and diminishes pain by our having shares in either; for silent woes are greatest, as silent satisfaction least; since sometimes our pleasure would be none but for telling of it, and our grief insupportable but for participation.—*Wycherley.*

One common calamity makes men extremely affect each other, though they differ in every other particular.—*Steele.*

The most reserved of men, that will not exchange two syllables together in an English coffee-house, should they meet at Ispahan, would drink sherbert and eat a mess of rice together.—*Shenstone.*

Far better one unpurchased heart than glory's proudest name.—*Tuckerman.*

No man can force the harp of his own individuality into the people's heart; but every man may play upon the chords of the people's heart, who draws his inspiration from the people's instinct.—*Kossuth.*

Truth is the root, but human sympathy is the flower of practical life.—*Chapin.*

He that sympathizes in all the happiness of others perhaps himself enjoys the safest happiness, and he that is warned by all the folly of others has perhaps attained the soundest wisdom.—*Colton.*

SYSTEM.
Nothing truly precious swims helplessly in the great wake of God's clear method, but every part of the man can be, and therefore strives to be, abreast of the other. The mountains follow the earth, the air has clasped the mountains, and daylight and starlight stream forward entangled in the air. Clutching for dear life to each other, all solid and tenuous things describe the great invariable motion, and God is in the manifoldness, drenching it with uniformity.—*John Weiss.*

T.

TABLE-TALK.
Conversation should be pleasant without scurrility, witty without affectation, free without indecency, learned without conceitedness, novel without falsehood.—*Shakespeare.*

TACT.
I have known some men possessed of good qualities, which were very serviceable to others, but useless to themselves; like a sundial on the front of a house, to inform the neighbors and passengers, but not the owner within.—
Swift.

Tact is one of the first of mental virtues, the absence of which is frequently fatal to the best of talents. Without denying that it is a talent of itself, it will suffice if we admit that it supplies the place of many talents.—*Simms.*

Grant graciously what you cannot refuse safely, and conciliate those you cannot conquer.
Colton.

Talent is something, but tact is everything. Talent is serious, sober, grave, and respectable; tact is all that, and more too. It is not a seventh sense, but is the life of all the five. It is the open eye, the quick ear, the judging taste, the keen smell, and the lively touch; it is the interpreter of all riddles, the surmounter of all difficulties, the remover of all obstacles.
W. P. Scargill.

TALENT.
Great talents have some admirers, but few friends.—*Niebuhr.*

Talent is some one faculty unusually developed; genius commands all the faculties.—
F. H. Hedge.

Talents give a man a superiority far more agreeable than that which proceeds from riches, birth, or employments, which are all external. Talents constitute our very essence.—*Rollin.*

Now this is how I define talent; it is a gift God has given us in secret, which we reveal without knowing it.—*Montesquieu.*

The true eye for talent presupposes the true reverence for it.—*Carlyle.*

The world is always ready to receive talent with open arms. Very often it does not know what to do with genius. Talent is a docile creature. It bows its head meekly while the world slips the collar over it. It backs into the shafts like a lamb.—*Holmes.*

Talents are best nurtured in solitude; character is best formed in the stormy billows of the world.—*Goethe.*

It is an uncontrolled truth that no man ever made an ill figure who understood his own talents, nor a good one who mistook them.—
Swift.

Talents angel-bright, if wanting worth, are shining instruments in false ambition's hand, to finish faults illustrious, and give infamy renown.—*Young.*

A man with great talents, but void of discretion, is like Polyphemus in the fable, strong and blind, endued with an irresistible force, which for want of sight is of no use to him.—*Addison.*

Talent, like beauty, to be pardoned, must be obscure and unostentatious.—*Lady Blessington.*

Talents, to strike the eye of posterity, should be concentrated. Rays, powerless while they are scattered, burn in a point.—*Willmott.*

Talent is a cistern; genius, a fountain.—*Whipple.*

Talent for talents' sake is a bauble and a show. Talent working with joy in the cause of universal truth lifts the possessor to new power as a benefactor.—*Emerson.*

TALKING.

We speak little if not egged on by vanity.—*Rochefoucauld.*

Talkers and futile persons are commonly vain and credulous withal, for he that talketh what he knoweth will also talk what he knoweth not; therefore set it down that a habit of secrecy is both politic and moral: and in this part it is good, that a man's face gives his tongue leave to speak; for the discovery of a man's self by the tracts of his countenance is a great weakness, and betraying by how much it is many times more marked and believed than a man's words.—*Bacon.*

Talking and eloquence are not the same; to speak, and to speak well are two things.—*Ben Jonson.*

There is such a torture, happily unknown to ancient tyranny, as talking a man to death. Marcus Aurelius advises to assent readily to great talkers, — in hopes, I suppose, to put an end to the argument.—*Sterne.*

You cram these words into mine ears, against the stomach of my sense.—*Shakespeare.*

Writing or printing is like shooting with a rifle; you may hit your reader's mind, or miss it; — but talking is like playing at a mark with the pipe of an engine; if it is within reach, and you have time enough, you can't help hitting it.—*Holmes.*

Those who have few affairs to attend to are great speakers. The less men think, the more they talk.—*Montesquieu.*

Brisk talkers are usually slow thinkers. There is, indeed, no wild beast more to be dreaded than a communicative man having nothing to communicate. If you are civil to the voluble they will abuse your patience; if brusque, your character.—*Swift.*

The talkative listen to no one, for they are ever speaking. And the first evil that attends those who know not to be silent is that they hear nothing.—*Plutarch.*

I prefer the wisdom of the unlearned to the folly of the loquacious.—*Cicero.*

It has been said in praise of some men, that they could talk whole hours together upon anything; but it must be owned to the honor of the other sex, that there are many among them who can talk whole hours together upon nothing. I have known a woman branch out into a long extempore dissertation on the edging of a petticoat, and chide her servant for breaking a china cup, in all the figures of rhetoric.—*Addison.*

Every absurdity has a champion to defend it; for error is always talkative.—*Goldsmith.*

There is the same difference between their tongues as between the hour and the minute-hand; one goes ten times as fast, and the other signifies ten times as much.—*Sydney Smith.*

Those whose tongues are gentlemen ushers to their wit, and still go before it.—*Ben Jonson.*

Depend upon it, if a man talks of his misfortunes, there is something in them that is not disagreeable to him; for where there is nothing but pure misery, there never is any recourse to the mention of it.—*Johnson.*

There are many who talk on from ignorance rather than from knowledge, and who find the former an inexhaustible fund of conversation.—*Hazlitt.*

Talk without truth is the hollow brass; talk without love is like the tinkling cymbal, and when it does not tinkle it jingles, and when it does not jingle, it jars.—*Mrs. Jameson.*

Speaking much is a sign of vanity; for he that is lavish in words is a niggard in deed.—*Sir Walter Raleigh.*

The common fluency of speech in many men, and most women, is owing to a scarcity of matter and a scarcity of words, for whoever is a master of language and has a mind full of ideas will be apt in speaking to hesitate upon the choice of both; whereas common speakers have only one set of ideas, and one set of words to clothe them in, and these are always ready at the mouth; so people come faster out of a church when it is almost empty, than when a crowd is at the door.—*Swift.*

This I always religiously observed, as a rule, never to chide my husband before company nor to prattle abroad of miscarriages at home. What passes between two people is much easier made up than when once it has taken air.—*Erasmus.*

If any man think it a small matter, or of mean concernment, to bridle his tongue, he is much mistaken; for it is a point to be silent when occasion requires, and better than to speak, though never so well.—*Plutarch.*

It has been well observed that the tongue discovers the state of the mind no less than that of the body; but in either case, before the philosopher or the physician can judge, the patient must open his mouth.—*Colton.*

If thy words be too luxuriant, confine them, lest they confine thee; he that thinks he never can speak enough may easily speak too much. A full tongue and an empty brain are seldom parted.—*Quarles.*

We oftener say things because we can say them well than because they are sound and reasonable.—*Landor.*

Cautiously avoid talking of the domestic affairs either of yourself or of other people. Yours are nothing to them but tedious gossip; theirs are nothing to you.—*Chesterfield.*

What a spendthrift he is of his tongue!—*Shakespeare.*

Great knowledge, if it be without vanity, is the most severe bridle of the tongue. For so have I heard that all the noises and prating of the pool, the croaking of frogs and toads, is hushed and appeased upon the instant of bringing upon them the light of a candle or torch. Every beam of reason and ray of knowledge checks the dissolutions of the tongue.—*Jeremy Taylor.*

One learns taciturnity best among those people who have none, and loquacity among the taciturn.—*Richter.*

The man who talks everlastingly and promiscuously, who seems to have an exhaustless magazine of sound, crowds so many words into his thoughts that he always obscures, and very frequently conceals them.—*Washington Irving.*

Let your words be few and digested; it is a shame for the tongue to cry the heart mercy, much more to cast itself upon the uncertain pardon of others' ears.—*Bishop Hall.*

TASTE.

A good taste in art feels the presence or the absence of merit; a just taste discriminates the degree,—the *poco più* and the *poco meno.* A good taste rejects faults; a just taste selects excellences. A good taste is often unconscious; a just taste is always conscious. A good taste may be lowered or spoilt; a just taste can only go on refining more and more.—*Mrs. Jameson.*

Taste is, so to speak, the microscope of judgment.—*Rousseau.*

A man loves the meat in his youth that he cannot endure in his age.—*Shakespeare.*

True taste is forever growing, learning, reading, worshipping, laying its hand upon its mouth because it is astonished, casting its shoes from off its feet because it finds all ground holy.—*Ruskin.*

Good taste is the flower of good sense.—*Achilles Poincelot.*

We imperatively require a perception of and a homage to beauty in our companions. Other virtues are in request in the field and workyard, but a certain degree of taste is not to be spared in those we sit with.—*Emerson.*

Taste consists in the power of judging; genius, in the power of executing.—*Blair.*

Taste, when once obtained, may be said to be no acquiring faculty, and must remain stationary; but knowledge is of perpetual growth and has infinite demands. Taste, like an artificial canal, winds through a beautiful country, but its borders are confined and its term is limited. Knowledge navigates the ocean, and is perpetually on voyages of discovery.—*Disraeli.*

Bad taste is a species of bad morals.—*Bovee.*

May not taste be compared to that exquisite sense of the bee, which instantly discovers and extracts the quintessence of every flower, and disregards all the rest of it?—*Lord Greville.*

Men more easily renounce their interests than their tastes.—*Rochefoucauld.*

It is for the most part in our skill in manners, and in the observances of time and place and of decency in general, that what is called taste by way of distinction consists; and which is in reality no other than a more refined judgment.—*Burke.*

It seems with wit and good-nature, *Utrum horum mavis accipe.* Taste and good-nature are universally connected.—*Shenstone.*

A truly elegant taste is generally accompanied with an excellency of heart.—*Fielding.*

Taste and elegance, though they are reckoned only among the smaller and secondary morals, yet are of no mean importance in the regulation of life. A moral taste is not of force to turn vice into virtue; but it recommends virtue with something like the blandishments of pleasure.—*Burke.*

Taste depends upon those finer emotions which make the organization of the soul.—*Sir J. Reynolds.*

Taste is pursued at a less expense than fashion.—*Shenstone.*

Taste is, in general, considered as that faculty of the human mind by which we perceive and enjoy whatever is beautiful or sublime in the works of nature or art.—
Sir A. Alison.

Talk what you will of taste, my friend, you will find two of a face as soon as of a mind.—
Pope.

Taste is not stationary. It grows every day, and is improved by cultivation, as a good temper is refined by religion. In its most advanced state it takes the title of judgment. Hume quotes Fontenelle's ingenious distinction between the common watch that tells the hours, and the delicately constructed one that marks the seconds and smallest differences of time.—
Willmott.

Good taste comes more from the judgment than from the mind.—*Rochefoucauld.*

Taste is often one of the aspects of fashion. Folly borrows its mask, and walks out with Wisdom arm in arm. Like virtues of greater dignity, it is assumed.—*Willmott.*

Taste is the mind's tact.—*De Boufflers.*

A fastidious taste is like a squeamish appetite; the one has its origin in some disease of the mind, as the other has in some ailment of the stomach.—*Southey.*

True purity of taste is a quality of the mind; it is a feeling which can, with little difficulty, be acquired by the refinement of intelligence; whereas purity of manners is the result of wise habits, in which all the interests of the soul are mingled and in harmony with the progress of intelligence. That is why the harmony of good taste and of good manners is more common than the existence of taste without manners, or of manners without taste.—
Rœderer.

I think I may define it to be that faculty of the soul which discerns the beauties of an author with pleasure, and the imperfections with dislike.—*Addison.*

Taste is the next gift to genius.—*Lowell.*

It is that faculty by which we discover and enjoy the beautiful, the picturesque, and the sublime in literature, art, and nature; which recognizes a noble thought, as a virtuous mind welcomes a pure sentiment, by an involuntary glow of satisfaction. But while the principle of perception is inherent in the soul, it requires a certain amount of knowledge to draw out and direct it.—*Willmott.*

A lady of genius will give a genteel air to her whole dress by a well-fancied suit of knots, as a judicious writer gives a spirit to a whole sentence by a single expression.—*Gay.*

A delicacy of taste is favorable to love and friendship, by confining our choice to few people, and making us indifferent to the company and conversation of the greater part of men.—
Hume.

Taste, if it mean anything but a paltry connoisseurship, must mean a general susceptibility to truth and nobleness; a sense to discern, and a heart to love and reverence, all beauty, order, goodness, wheresoever and in whatsoever forms and accomplishments they are to be seen.—*Carlyle.*

Delicacy of taste has the same effect as delicacy of passion; it enlarges the sphere both of our happiness and misery, and makes us sensible to pain as well as pleasures, which escape the rest of mankind.—*Hume.*

TATTLING.

Fire and sword are but slow engines of destruction in comparison with the babbler.—
Steele.

Be careful that you believe not hastily strange news and strange stories; and be much more careful that you do not report them, though at the second hand; for if it prove an untruth (as commonly strange stories prove so), it brings an imputation of levity upon him that reports it, and possibly some disadvantage to others.—*Sir Matthew Hale.*

Talkers are no good-doers.—*Shakespeare.*

Yet have I ever heard it said that spies and tale-bearers have done more mischief in this world than poisoned bowl or the assassin's dagger.—*Schiller.*

Merrily and wittily said Plautus, who was one of the merry wits of his time, "I would," said he, "by my will have tale-bearers and tale-hearers punished,—the one hanging by the tongue, the other by the ears. Were his will a law in force with us, many a tattling gossip would have her vowels turned to mutes, and be justly tongue-tied, that desires to be tied by the teeth at your table."—
Arthur Warwick.

The tongue is the worst part of a bad servant.—*Juvenal.*

We acknowledge that we should not talk of our wives; but we seem not to know that we should talk still less of ourselves.—
Rochefoucauld.

I will be silent and barren of discourse when I chance to hear a tale, rather than go with child therewith, till another's ears be my midwife, to deliver me of such a deformed monster. I may hear a tale of delight, and perhaps smile at an innocent jest; I will not jest nor joy at a tale disgracing an innocent person.—*Arthur Warwick.*

The excessive pleasure we feel in talking of ourselves ought to make us apprehensive that we afford little to our auditors.—*Rochefoucauld.*

TAVERN.

There is nothing which has yet been contrived by man, by which so much happiness is produced as by a good tavern or inn.—*Johnson.*

A tavern is the throne of human felicity.—*Johnson.*

TAXES.

The taxes are indeed very heavy, and if those laid on by the government were the only ones we had to pay, we might more easily discharge them; but we have many others, and much more grievous to some of us. We are taxed twice as much by our idleness, three times as much by our pride, and four times as much by our folly; and from these taxes the commissioners cannot ease or deliver us, by allowing an abatement.—*Franklin.*

The repose of nations cannot be secure without arms, armies cannot be maintained without pay, nor can the pay be produced except by taxes.—*Tacitus.*

Taxing is an easy business. Any projector can contrive new impositions, any bungler can add to the old; but is it altogether wise to have no other bounds to your impositions than the patience of those who are to bear them?—*Burke.*

Kings ought to shear, not skin their sheep.—*Herrick.*

What a benefit would the American government, not yet relieved of its extreme need, render to itself, and to every city, village, and hamlet in the States, if it would tax whiskey and rum almost to the point of prohibition! Was it Bonaparte who said that he found vices very good patriots? "He got five millions from the love of brandy, and he should be glad to know which of the virtues would pay him as much." Tobacco and opium have broad backs, and will cheerfully carry the load of armies, if you choose to make them pay high for such joy as they give and such harm as they do.—*Emerson.*

We have always considered taxes to be the sinews of the state.—*Cicero.*

The general rule always holds good. In constitutional states liberty is a compensation for the heaviness of taxation. In despotic states the equivalent for liberty is the lightness of taxation.—*Montesquieu.*

TEACHING.

Delightful task! to rear the tender thought, to teach the young idea how to shoot, to pour the fresh instruction over the mind, to breathe the enlivening spirit, and to fix the generous purpose in the glowing breast.—*Thomson.*

Put a man into a factory, as ignorant how to prepare fabrics as some teachers are to watch the growth of juvenile minds, and what havoc would be made of the raw material!—*Horace Mann.*

If ever I am an instructress, it will be to learn more than to teach.—*Madame Deluzy.*

There is nothing more frightful than for a teacher to know only what his scholars are intended to know.—*Goethe.*

The teacher is like the candle which lights others in consuming itself.—*Ruffini.*

It is the duty of a man of honor to teach others the good which he has not been able to do himself because of the malignity of the times, that this good finally can be done by another more loved in heaven.—*Machiavelli.*

To sentence a man of true genius to the drudgery of a school is to put a race-horse in a mill.—*Colton.*

Teachers should be held in the highest honor. They are the allies of legislators; they have agency in the prevention of crime; they aid in regulating the atmosphere, whose incessant action and pressure cause the life-blood to circulate, and to return pure and healthful to the heart of the nation.—*Mrs. Sigourney.*

The one exclusive sign of a thorough knowledge is the power of teaching.—*Aristotle.*

Education of youth is not a bow for every man to shoot in that counts himself a teacher; but will require sinews almost equal to those which Homer gave to Ulysses.—*Milton.*

If, in instructing a child, you are vexed with it for a want of adroitness, try, if you have never tried before, to write with your left hand, and then remember that a child is all left hand.—*J. F. Boyes.*

A teacher who is attempting to teach without inspiring the pupil with a desire to learn is hammering on cold iron.—*Horace Mann.*

Do not, then, train boys to learning by force and harshness; but direct them to it by what amuses their minds, so that you may be the better able to discover with accuracy the peculiar bent of the genius of each.—*Plato.*

Whetstones are not themselves able to cut, but make iron sharp and capable of cutting.—*Isocrates.*

For my part, I am convinced that the method of teaching which approaches most nearly to the method of investigation is incomparably the best; since, not content with serving up a few barren and lifeless truths, it leads to the stock on which they grew.—*Burke.*

In the education of children there is nothing like alluring the appetites and affection; otherwise you make so many asses laden with books.—*Montaigne.*

Improvement depends far less upon length of tasks and hours of application than is supposed. Children can take in but a little each day; they are like vases with a narrow neck; you. may pour little or pour much, but much will not enter at a time.—*Michelet.*

The temper of the pedagogue suits not with the age; and the world, however it may be taught, will not be tutored.—*Shaftesbury.*

A tutor should not be continually thundering instruction into the ears of his pupil, as if he were pouring it through a funnel, but, after having put the lad, like a young horse, on a trot, before him, to observe his paces, and see what he is able to perform, should, according to the extent of his capacity, induce him to taste, to distinguish, and to find out things for himself; sometimes opening the way, at other times leaving it for him to open; and by abating or increasing his own pace, accommodate his precepts to the capacity of his pupil.—
Montaigne.

It would be a great advantage to some schoolmasters if they would steal two hours a day from their pupils and give their own minds the benefit of the robbery.—*J. F. Boyes.*

A good schoolmaster minces his precepts for children to swallow, hanging clogs on the nimbleness of his own soul, that his scholars may go along with him.—*Fuller.*

Do not allow your daughters to be taught letters by a man, though he be a St. Paul or St. Francis of Assissium. The saints are in Heaven.—*Bishop Liguori.*

Men must be taught as though you taught them not.—*Pope.*

Those who educate children well are more to be honored than they who produce them; for these only gave them life, those the art of living well.—*Aristotle.*

Be understood in thy teaching, and instruct to the measure of capacity; precepts and rules are repulsive to a child, but happy illustration winneth him.—*Tupper.*

TEARS.

There is something so moving in the very image of weeping beauty.—*Steele.*

A smile is ever the most bright and beautiful with a tear upon it. What is the dawn without its dew? The tear is rendered by the smile precious above the smile itself.—*Landor.*

Tearless grief bleeds inwardly.—*Bovee.*

The tears live in an onion that should water this sorrow.—*Shakespeare.*

Tears, idle tears, I know not what they mean,—tears from the depth of some divine despair rise in the heart, and gather in the eyes, in looking on the happy autumn fields, and thinking of the days that are no more.—
Tennyson.

O, let not woman's weapons, water-drops, stain my man's cheeks!—*Shakespeare.*

They that sow in tears shall reap in joy.—
Bible.

The cloudy weather melts at length into beauty, and the brightest smiles of the heart are born of its tears.—*Hosea Ballou.*

Like Niobe, all tears.—*Shakespeare.*

It is delightful to kiss the eyelashes of the beloved,—is it not? But never so delightful as when fresh tears are on them.—*Landor.*

Weep for love, but not for anger; a cold rain will never bring flowers.—*Duncan.*

Nature confesses that she has bestowed on the human race hearts of softest mould, in that she has given us tears.—*Juvenal.*

Tears such as angels weep.—*Milton.*

I would hardly change the sorrowful words of the poets for their glad ones. Tears dampen the strings of the lyre, but they grow the tenser for it, and ring even the clearer and more ravishingly.—*Lowell.*

Love is loveliest when embalmed in tears.—
Walter Scott.

Astronomers have built telescopes which can show myriads of stars unseen before; but when a man looks through a tear in his own eye, that is a lens which opens reaches in the unknown, and reveals orbs which no telescope, however skilfully constructed, could do; nay, which brings to view even the throne of God, and pierces that nebulous distance where are those eternal verities in which true life consists.—
Beecher.

Nature's tears are reason's merriment.—
Shakespeare.

There is a certain pleasure in weeping; grief finds in tears both a satisfaction and a cure.—*Ovid.*

O, banish the tears of children! Continual rains upon the blossoms are hurtful.—*Richter.*

Easy-crying widows take new husbands soonest; there is nothing like wet weather for transplanting.—*Holmes.*

Believe these tears, which from my wounded heart bleed at my eyes.—*Dryden.*

Tears, except as a private demonstration, are an ill-disguised expression of self-consciousness and vanity, which is inadmissible in good society.—*Holmes.*

The tears of penitents are the wine of angels.
St. Bernard.

There appears much joy in him, even so much that joy could not show itself modest enough without a badge of bitterness. A kind overflow of kindness, — there are no faces truer than those that are so washed.—*Shakespeare.*

Tears of joy, like summer rain-drops, are pierced by sunbeams.—*Hosea Ballou.*

So looks the lily after a shower, while drops of rain run gently down its silken leaves, and gather sweetness as they pass.—*Fielding.*

Sad, unhelpful tears.—*Shakespeare.*

Sooner mayest thou trust thy pocket to a pickpocket than give loyal friendship to the man who boasts of eyes to which the heart never mounts in dew! Only when man weeps he should be alone, not because tears are weak, but they should be secret. Tears are akin to prayer, — Pharisees parade prayers, impostors parade tears.—*Bulwer Lytton.*

After his blood, that which a man can next give out of himself is a tear.—*Lamartine.*

How many a holy and obsequious tear hath dear religious love stolen from mine eye, as interest of the dead! —*Shakespeare.*

Hide not thy tears; weep boldly, and be proud to give the flowing virtue manly way; it is nature's mark to know an honest heart by.
Aaron Hill.

We often shed tears which deceive ourselves after having deceived others.—
Rochefoucauld.

Hide thy tears, — I do not bid thee not to shed them, — it were easier to stop Euphrates at its source than one tear of a true and tender heart.—*Byron.*

Tears harden lust, though marble wear with raining.—*Shakespeare.*

As Rubens by one stroke converted a laughing into a crying child, so nature frequently makes this stroke in the original; a child's eye, like the sun, never draws water so readily as in the hot temperature of pleasure.—
Richter.

The safety-valves of the heart, when too much pressure is laid on.—*Albert Smith.*

Friends, I owe more tears to this dead man than you shall see me pay.—*Shakespeare.*

Those tender tears that humanize the soul.
Thomson.

There is a sacredness in tears. They are not the mark of weakness, but of power. They speak more eloquently than ten thousand tongues. They are the messengers of overwhelming grief, of deep contrition, and of unspeakable love.— *Washington Irving*

Tears are due to human misery.—*Virgil.*

How sometimes nature will betray its folly, its tenderness, and make itself a pastime to harder bosoms! —*Shakespeare.*

The graceful tear that streams for others' woes.—*Akenside.*

· God made both tears and laughter, and both for kind purposes; for as laughter enables mirth and surprise to breathe freely, so tears enable sorrow to vent itself patiently. Tears hinder sorrow from becoming despair and madness; and laughter is one of the very privileges of reason, being confined to the human species.
Leigh Hunt.

All the rarest hues of human life take radiance and are rainbowed out in tears.—*Massey.*

Scorn the proud man that is ashamed to weep.— *Young.*

What is the matter, that this distempered messenger of wet, the many-colored Iris, rounds thine eye? —*Shakespeare.*

Tears are the noble language of the eye.—
Herrick.

Pride dries the tears of anger and vexation; humility, those of grief. The one is indignant that we should suffer; the other calms us by the reminder that we deserve nothing else.—
.   *Madame Swetchine.*

The tear of joy is a pearl of the first water; the mourning tear, only of the second.—*Richter.*

The April is in her eyes; it is love's spring, and these the showers to bring it on.—
Shakespeare.

Man is the weeping animal born to govern all the rest.—*Pliny.*

And that same dew, which some time on the buds was wont to swell like round and orient pearls, stood now within the pretty floweret's eyes, like tears that did their own disgrace bewail.—*Shakespeare.*

Every tear of sorrow sown by the righteous springs up a pearl.—*Matthew Henry.*

How much better is it to weep at joy than to joy at weeping!—*Jane Porter.*

Tears are the tribute of humanity to its destiny.—*W. R. Alger.*

Tears,—it is the best brine a maiden can season her praise in.—*Shakespeare.*

Tears are the natural penalties of pleasure. It is a law that we should pay for all that we enjoy.—*Simms.*

My eyes are dim with childish tears.— *Wordsworth.*

Of all the portions of life it is in the two twilights, childhood and age, that tears fall with the most frequency; like the dew at dawn and eve.—*W. R. Alger.*

I can approve of those only who seek in tears for happiness.—*Pascal.*

The good widow's sorrow is no storm, but a still rain; commonly it comes to pass that that grief is quickly emptied that streameth out at so large a vent, whilst their tears that but drop will hold running a long time.— *Fuller.*

See, see, what showers arise, blown with the windy tempest of my heart.—*Shakespeare.*

Heaven and God are best discerned through tears; scarcely perhaps are discerned at all without them. The constant association of prayer with the hour of bereavement and the scenes of death suffice to show this.— *James Martineau.*

Sweet tears! the awful language eloquent of infinite affection, far too big for words.— *Pollok.*

Tears of joy are the dew in which the sun of righteousness is mirrored.—*Richter.*

Tears are nature's lotion for the eyes. The eyes see better for being washed with them.— *Bovee.*

A man is seldom more manly than when he is what you call unmanned,—the source of his emotion is championship, pity, and courage; the instinctive desire to cherish those who are innocent and unhappy, and defend those who are tender and weak.—*Thackeray.*

For beauty's tears are lovelier than her smile.—*Campbell.*

Tears are the softening showers which cause the seed of heaven to spring up in the human heart.—*Walter Scott.*

What a hell of witchcraft lies in the small orb of one particular tear!—*Shakespeare.*

The sweet dew that lingered in her eye for pity's sake was—like an exhalation in the sun—dried and absorbed by love.—*Barry Cornwall.*

Ope the sacred source of sympathetic tears. *Gray.*

The waiting tears stood ready for command, and now they flow to varnish the false tale.— *Rowe.*

See yonder rock from which the fountain gushes; is it less compact of adamant, though waters flow from it? Firm hearts have moister eyes.—*Walter Scott.*

Let me wipe off this honorable dew, that silverly doth progress on thy cheeks.— *Shakespeare.*

Down she bent her head upon an arm so white that tears seemed but the natural melting of its snow, touched by the flushed cheek's crimson.—*Miss L. E. Landon.*

Trust not those cunning waters of his eyes, for villany is not without such rheum.— *Shakespeare.*

Shame on those breasts of stone that cannot melt in soft adoption of another's sorrow.— *Aaron Hill.*

Tears may soothe the wounds they cannot heal.—*Thomas Paine.*

TEMPER.

It is an unhappy, and yet I fear a true reflection, that they who have uncommon easiness and softness of temper have seldom very noble and nice sensations of soul.— *Lord Greville.*

The happiness and misery of men depend no less on temper than fortune.— *Rochefoucauld.*

Through certain humors or passions, and from temper merely, a man may be completely miserable, let his outward circumstances be ever so fortunate.—*Lord Shaftesbury.*

Too many have no idea of the subjection of their temper to the influence of religion, and yet what is changed, if the temper is not? If a man is passionate, malicious, resentful, sullen, moody, or morose after his conversion as before it, what is he converted from or to?— *John Angell James.*

Courtesy of temper, when it is used to veil churlishness of deed, is but a knight's girdle around the breast of a base clown.— *Walter Scott.*

Those who are surly and imperious to their inferiors are generally humble, flattering, and cringing to their superiors.—*Fuller.*

Unsociable tempers are contracted in solitude, which will in the end not fail of corrupting the understanding as well as the manners, and of utterly disqualifying a man for the satisfactions and duties of life. Men must be taken as they are, and we neither make them nor ourselves better by flying from or quarrelling with them.—*Burke.*

TEMPERANCE.

Though I look old, yet I am strong and lusty, for in my youth I never did apply hot and rebellious liquors in my blood.—
Shakespeare.

Drinking water neither makes a man sick, nor in debt, nor his wife a widow.—*John Neal.*

Temperance is a tree which has for a root very little contentment, and for fruit, calm and peace.—*Buddha.*

The receipts of cookery are swelled to a volume, but a good stomach excels them all; to which nothing contributes more than industry and temperance.—*William Penn.*

In temperance there is ever cleanliness and elegance.—*Joubert.*

Every moderate drinker could abandon the intoxicating cup if he would; every inebriate would if he could.—*J. B. Gough.*

Except thou desire to hasten thine end, take this for a general rule, that thou never add any artificial heat to thy body by wine or spice, until thou find that time hath decayed thy natural heat, and the sooner thou beginnest to help nature, the sooner she will forsake thee, and trust altogether to art.—*Sir Walter Raleigh.*

Great men should drink with harness on their throats.—*Shakespeare.*

The first draught serveth for health, the second for pleasure, the third for shame, and the fourth for madness.—*Anacharsis.*

There is no difference between knowledge and temperance; for he who knows what is good and embraces it, who knows what is bad and avoids it, is learned and temperate.—
Socrates.

Above all, let the poor hang up the amulet of temperance in their homes.—*Horace Mann.*

Temperance keeps the senses clear and unembarrassed, and makes them seize the object with more keenness and satisfaction. It appears with life in the face, and decorum in the person; it gives you the command of your head, secures your health, and preserves you in a condition for business.—*Jeremy Collier.*

Every inordinate cup is unblessed, and the ingredient is a devil.—*Shakespeare.*

Temperance, indeed, is a bridle of gold; and he who uses it rightly is more like a god than a man.—*Burton.*

Men live best on moderate means; nature has dispensed to all men wherewithal to be happy, if mankind did but understand how to use her gifts.—*Claudian.*

Temperance is a virtue which casts the truest lustre upon the person it is lodged in, and has the most general influence upon all other particular virtues of any that the soul of man is capable of; indeed so general, that there is hardly any noble quality or endowment of the mind but must own temperance either for its parent or its nurse; it is the greatest strengthener and clearer of reason, and the best preparer of it for religion, the sister of prudence, and the handmaid to devotion.—
South.

Temperance is corporeal piety; it is the preservation of divine order in the body.—
Theodore Parker.

If it is a small sacrifice to discontinue the use of wine, do it for the sake of others; if it is a great sacrifice, do it for your own.—
Samuel J. May.

O temperance, thou fortune without envy; thou universal medicine of life, that clears the head and cleanses the blood, eases the stomach, strengthens the nerves, and perfects digestion.—
Sir W. Temple.

Temperance is reason's girdle and passion's bridle, the strength of the soul and the foundation of virtue.—*Jeremy Taylor.*

We ought to love temperance for itself, and in obedience to God who has commanded it and chastity; but what I am forced to by catarrhs, or owe to the stone, is neither chastity nor temperance.—*Montaigne.*

The smaller the drink, the clearer the head, and the cooler the blood; which are great benefits in temper and business.—*William Penn.*

TEMPTATION.

The Devil has a great advantage against us, inasmuch as he has a strong bastion and bulwark against us in our own flesh and blood.—
Luther.

When a man resists sin on human motives only, he will not hold out long.—
Bishop Wilson.

It has been wisely said, "that well may thy guardian angel suffer thee to lose thy locks, when thou darest wilfully to lay thy head in the lap of temptation!" Was it not easier for the hero of Judæa to avoid the touch of the fair Philistine, than to elude her power when held in her arms?—*Jane Porter.*

33

Few men have virtue to withstand the highest bidder.—*Washington.*

Shut the door of that house of pleasure which you hear resounding with the loud voice of a woman.—*Saadi.*

When the flesh presents thee with delights, then present thyself with dangers; where the world possesses thee with vain hopes, there possess thyself with true fear; when the devil brings thee oil, bring thou vinegar. The way to be safe is never to be secure.—*Quarles.*

It is the bright day that brings forth the adder, and that craves wary walking.—
Shakespeare.

We like slipping, but not falling; our real desire is to be tempted enough.—*Hare.*

St. Augustine teaches us that there is in each man a Serpent, an Eve, and an Adam. Our senses and natural propensities are the Serpent; the excitable desire is the Eve; and reason is the Adam. Our nature tempts us perpetually; criminal desire is often excited; but sin is not completed till reason consents.—
Pascal.

God is better served in resisting a temptation to evil than in many formal prayers.—
William Penn.

To attempt to resist temptation, to abandon our bad habits, and to control our dominant passions in our own unaided strength, is like attempting to check by a spider's thread the progress of a ship of the first rate, borne along before wind and tide.—*Rev. Dr. Waugh.*

Do not give dalliance too much the rein; the strongest oaths are straw to the fire in the blood.—*Shakespeare.*

Temptations are a file which rub off much of the rust of self-confidence.—*Fenelon.*

A vacant mind invites dangerous inmates, as a deserted mansion tempts wandering outcasts to enter and take up their abode in its desolate apartments.—*Hillard.*

How oft the sight of means to do ill deeds makes deeds ill done!—*Shakespeare.*

We are surrounded by abysses, but the greatest of all depths is in our own heart, and an irresistible leaning leads us there. Draw thyself from thyself!—*Goethe.*

If you take temptations into account, who is to say that he is better than his neighbor?—
Thackeray.

Sometimes we are devils ourselves, when we will tempt the frailty of our powers, presuming on their changeful potency.—*Shakespeare.*

One does not require nor think of a fire often in spring or autumn; yet I don't know how it is, but when we have happened by chance to pass near one, the sensation it communicates is so pleasant that we feel rather inclined to indulge it. This is analogous to temptation,—and the moral is, "keep away from the fire."—*Sterne.*

Most dangerous is that temptation that doth goad us on to sin in loving virtue.—
Shakespeare.

A beautiful woman, if poor, should use double circumspection; for her beauty will tempt others, her poverty herself.—*Colton.*

St. James says, "Count it all joy, when you fall into divers temptations."—*Sterne.*

No place, no company, no age, no person is temptation-free; let no man boast that he was never tempted, let him not be high-minded, but fear, for he may be surprised in that very instant wherein he boasteth that he was never tempted at all.—*Spencer.*

Might shake the saintship of an anchorite.
Byron.

The difference between those whom the world esteems as good and those whom it condemns as bad, is in many cases little else than that the former have been better sheltered from temptation.—*Hare.*

He who has no mind to trade with the Devil should be so wise as to keep from his shop.—
South.

When I cannot be forced, I am fooled out of my integrity. He cannot constrain if I do not consent. If I do but keep possession, all the posse of hell cannot violently eject me; but I cowardly surrender to his summons. Thus there needs no more to be my undoing but myself.—*Fuller.*

It is one thing to be tempted, another thing to fall.—*Shakespeare.*

The time for reasoning is before we have approached near enough to the forbidden fruit to look at it and admire.—*Margaret Percival.*

Watch and pray, that ye enter not into temptation.—*Bible.*

The temptation is not here, where you are reading about it or praying about it. It is down in your shop, among bales and boxes, ten-penny nails, and sand-paper.—*Chapin.*

TENDERNESS.

Tenderness, without a capacity of relieving, only makes the man who feels it more wretched than the object which sues for assistance.—
Goldsmith.

The less tenderness a man has in his nature, the more he requires from others.—*Rahel.*

The quiet tenderness of Chaucer, where you almost seem to hear the hot tears falling, and the simple choking words sobbed out.—*Lowell.*

Tenderness is the infancy of love.—*Rivarol.*

A tender-hearted and compassionate disposition, which inclines men to pity and feel the misfortunes of others, and which is, even for its own sake, incapable of involving any man in ruin and misery, is of all tempers of mind the most amiable; and though it seldom receives much honor, is worthy of the highest.— *Fielding.*

Tenderness is the repose of passion.— *Joubert.*

TERROR.

Terror itself, when once grown trancendental, becomes a kind of courage; as frost sufficiently intense, according to the poet Milton, will burn.—*Carlyle.*

The most terrible of all things is terror.— *W. R. Alger.*

Most terrors are but spectral illusions. Only have the courage of the man who could walk up to his spectre seated in the chair before him, and sit down upon it; the horrid thing will not partake the chair with you.—*Helps.*

By the apostle Paul, shadows to-night have struck more terror to the soul of Richard than can the substance of ten thousand soldiers.— *Shakespeare.*

TESTIMONY.

Testimony is like an arrow shot from a long bow; the force of it depends on the strength of the hand that draws it. Argument is like an arrow from a cross-bow, which has equal force though shot by a child.—*Johnson.*

THANKS.

Evermore thanks, the exchequer of the poor. *Shakespeare.*

Thanks, oftenest obtrusive.—*Shenstone.*

THEFT.

O theft most base, that we have stolen what we do fear to keep! —*Shakespeare.*

Virtuosi have been long remarked to have little conscience in their favorite pursuits. A man will steal a rarity who would cut off his hand rather than take the money it is worth. Yet, in fact, the crime is the same.—*Horace Walpole.*

Suspicion always haunts the guilty mind; the thief still fears each bush an officer.— *Shakespeare.*

What is dishonestly got vanishes in profligacy.—*Cicero.*

I will example you with thievery : the sun is a thief, and with his great attraction robs the vast sea ; the moon is an arrant thief, and her pale fire she snatches from the sun ; the sea is a thief, whose liquid surge resolves the moon into salt tears ; the earth is a thief, that feeds and breeds by a composture stolen from general excrement ; — each thing is a thief.—*Shakespeare.*

THEOLOGY.

A theology at war with the laws of physical nature would be a battle of no doubtful issue. The laws of our spiritual nature give still less chance of success to the system which would thwart or stay them.—*Channing.*

Theology is but a science of mind applied to God. As schools change, theology must necessarily change. Truth is everlasting, but our ideas of truth are not. Theology is but our ideas of truth classified and arranged.— *Beecher.*

He that seeks perfection upon earth leaves nothing new for the saints to find in heaven ; for whilst men teach, there will be mistakes in divinity, and as long as no other govern, errors in the state.—*F. Osborn.*

THEORIES.

To despise theory is to have the excessively vain pretension to do without knowing what one does, and to speak without knowing what one says.—*Fontenelle.*

The human mind feels restless and dissatisfied under the anxieties of ignorance. It longs for the repose of conviction ; and to gain this repose it will often rather precipitate its conclusions than wait for the tardy lights of observation and experiment. There is such a thing, too, as the love of simplicity and system, — a prejudice of the understanding which disposes it to include all the phenomena of nature under a few sweeping generalities, — an indolence which loves to repose on the beauties of a theory rather than encounter the fatiguing detail of its evidences.—*Chalmers.*

The theory that can absorb the greatest number of facts, and persist in doing so, generation after generation, through all changes of opinion and of detail, is the one that must rule all observation.—*John Weiss.*

THOUGHT.

A thought is often original, though you have uttered it a hundred times. It has come to you over a new route, by a new and express train of association.—*Holmes.*

The value of a thought cannot be told.— *Bailey.*

By virtue of the Deity thought renews itself inexhaustibly every day, and the thing whereon it shines, though it were dust and sand, is a new subject with countless relations.—*Emerson.*

Thought is the wind, knowledge the sail, and mankind the vessel.—*Hare.*

I can readily conceive of a man without hands or feet; and I could conceive of him without a head, if experience had not taught me that by this he thinks. Thought, then, is the essence of man, and without this we cannot conceive of him.—*Pascal.*

Every day a little life, a blank to be inscribed with gentle thoughts.—*Rogers.*

Love's heralds should be thoughts, which ten times faster glide than the sunbeams, driving back shadows over lowering hills.—
Shakespeare.

Thought discovered is the more possessed.—
Young.

I imagine that thinking is the great desideratum of the present age; and the cause of whatever is done amiss may justly be reckoned the general neglect of education in those who need it most, the people of fashion. What can be expected where those who have the most influence have the least sense, and those who are sure to be followed set the worst examples? —
Bishop Berkeley.

The rich are too indolent, the poor too weak, to bear the insupportable fatigue of thinking.—
Cowper.

A thinking man is the worst enemy the Prince of Darkness can have; every time such a one announces himself, I doubt not there runs a shudder through the nether empire; and new emissaries are trained with new tactics, to, if possible, entrap him, and hoodwink and handcuff him.—*Carlyle.*

Our thoughts are ours, their ends none of our own.—*Shakespeare.*

Thoughts come into our minds by avenues which we never left open, and thoughts go out of our minds through avenues which we never voluntarily opened.—*Emerson.*

Thoughts that do often lie too deep for tears.—*Wordsworth.*

All that a man does outwardly is but the expression and completion of his inward thought. To work effectually, he must think clearly; to act nobly, he must think nobly. Intellectual force is a principal element of the soul's life, and should be proposed by every man as the principal end of his being.—*Channing.*

The greatest events of an age are its best thoughts. It is the nature of thought to find its way into action.—*Bovee.*

Speech is external thought, and thought internal speech.—*Rivarol.*

The walls of rude minds are scrawled all over with facts, with thoughts. They shall one day bring a lantern and read the inscriptions.—
Emerson.

Great thoughts proceed from the heart.—
Vauvenargues.

The more we examine the mechanism of thought, the more we shall see that the automatic, unconscious action of the mind enters largely into all its processes. Our definite ideas are stepping-stones; how we get from one to the other, we do not know; something carries us; we do not take the step.—*Holmes.*

Speech is the vestment of thought, and expression its armor.—*Rivarol.*

Thought is the slave of life, and life time's fool; and time, that takes survey of all the world, must have a stop.—*Shakespeare.*

Before men we stand as opaque bee-hives. They can see the thoughts go in and out of us; but what work they do inside of a man they cannot tell. Before God we are as glass bee-hives, and all that our thoughts are doing within us he perfectly sees and understands.—
Beecher.

Learning without thought is labor lost; thought without learning is perilous.—*Confucius.*

Thinkers are scarce as gold; but he whose thoughts embrace all his subject, pursues it uninterruptedly and fearless of consequences, is a diamond of enormous size.—*Lavater.*

A thought came like a full-blown rose, flushing his brow.—*Keats.*

Liberty of thinking, and of expressing our thoughts, is always fatal to priestly power, and to those pious frauds on which it is commonly founded.—*Hume.*

Orthodoxy is the Bourbon of the world of thought. It learns not, neither can it forget.—
Professor Huxley.

It is curious to note the old sea-margins of human thought! Each subsiding century reveals some new mystery; we build where monsters used to hide themselves.—*Longfellow.*

Thoughts are winged.—*Shakespeare.*

When the great God lets loose a thinker on this planet, then all things are at risk. There is not a piece of science, but its flank may be turned to-morrow; there is not any literary reputation, nor the so-called eternal names of fame, that may not be revised and condemned.—
Emerson.

Nurture your mind with great thoughts. To believe in the heroic makes heroes.—*Disraeli.*

, Thought precedes the will to think, and error lives ere reason can be born.—*Congreve.*

Many of the finest and most interesting emotions perish forever, because too complex and fugitive for expression. Of all things relating to man, his feelings are perhaps the most evanescent, the greater part dying in the moment of their birth. But while emotions perish, thought blended in diction is immortal.
．　　　　　　　　　　*W. B. Clulow.*

In that sweet mood when pleasant thoughts bring sad thoughts to the mind. — *Wordsworth.*

It is because we underrate thought, because we do not see what a great element it is in religious life, that there is so little of practical and consistent religion among us.—*Chapin.*

The power of thought, the magic of the mind.—*Byron.*

A very sea of thought; neither calm nor clear, if you will, yet wherein the toughest pearl-diver may dive to his utmost depth, and return not only with sea-wreck but with true orients.—
　　　　　　　　　　　　　Carlyle.

It is the hardest thing in the world to be a good thinker without being a good self-examiner.—*Shaftesbury.*

Thought is the seed of action ; but action is as much its second form as thought is its first. It rises in thought, to the end that it may be uttered and acted. The more profound the thought, the more burdensome. Always in proportion to the depth of its sense does it knock importunately at the gates of the soul, to be spoken, to be done.—*Emerson.*

There is nothing either good or bad, but thinking makes it so.—*Shakespeare.*

Only those thoughts which the most pro-found earnestness has produced and perfected take a cheerful form.—*Jacobi.*

All that we are is the result of what we have thought; it is founded on our thoughts, it is made up of our thoughts. If a man speaks or acts with an evil thought, pains follows him, as the wheel follows the foot of him who draws the carriage.—*Buddha.*

Thinking nurseth thinking.—*Sir P. Sidney.*

With thought, with the ideal, is immortal hilarity, the rose of joy. Round it all the muses sing.—*Emerson.*

The power of thought, the magic of the mind.—*Byron.*

Thought means life, since those who do not think do not live in any high or real sense. Thinking makes the man.—*Alcott.*

The key to every man is his thought. Sturdy and defying though he look, he has a helm which he obeys, which is the idea after which all his facts are classified. He can only be reformed by showing him a new idea which commands his own.—*Emerson.*

Thoughts are but dreams till their effects be tried.—*Shakespeare.*

The happiness of your life depends upon the quality of your thoughts; therefore guard accordingly, and take care that you entertain no notions unsuitable to virtue and reasonable nature.—*Marcus Antoninus.*

Our thoughts are heard in heaven ! —*Young.*

The habit of reflecting gives an inner life, which all that we see animates and embellishes. In this disposition of the soul everything becomes an object of thought. If the young botanist trembles with joy at the sight of a new plant, the moral botanist joys no less to see germinate around him truths with a much superior prize to that of an unknown flower.—*Bonstetten.*

Thought is free.—*Shakespeare.*

There are few who have at once thought and capacity for action. Thought expands, but lames ; action animates, but narrows.—
　　　　　　　　　　　　　Goethe.

A moment's thought is passion's passing knell.—*Keats.*

As he thinketh in his heart, so is he.—*Bible.*

Thoughts come maimed and plucked of plumage from the lips, which, from the pen, in the silence of your own leisure and study, would be born with far more beauty.
　　　　　　　　　　Lady Blessington.

A thought often makes us hotter than a fire.
　　　　　　　　　　　　Longfellow.

We should round every day of stirring action with an evening of thought. We learn nothing of our experience except we muse upon it.—*Bovee.*

His bold brow bears but the scars of mind, the thoughts of years, not their decrepitude.—
　　　　　　　　　　　　　Byron.

· There is no thought in any mind, but it quickly tends to convert itself into a power, and organizes a huge instrumentality of means.—
　　　　　　　　　　　　　Emerson.

The busiest of living agents are certain dead men's thoughts.—*Bovee.*

Those recesses of the inner life, which the God who made us keeps from every eye but his own.— *Mrs. Jameson.*

Unless a man can link his written thoughts with the everlasting wants of men, so that they shall draw from them as from wells, there is no more immortality to the thoughts and feelings of the soul than to the muscles and the bones.— *Beecher.*

A thought embodied and embrained in fit words walks the earth a living being.— *Whipple.*

Thoughts shut up want air, and spoil, like bales unopened to the sun.—*Young.*

It is by thought that has aroused my intellect from its slumbers, which has "given lustre to virtue, and dignity to truth," or by those examples which have inflamed my soul with the love of goodness, and not by means of sculptured marble, that I hold communion with Shakespeare and Milton, with Johnson and Burke, with Howard and Wilberforce.— *Wayland.*

O guard thy roving thoughts with jealous care, for speech is but the dial-plate of thought; and every fool reads plainly in thy words what is the hour of thy thought.—*Tennyson.*

Flowing water is at once a picture and a music, which causes to flow at the same time from my brain, like a limpid and murmuring rivulet, sweet thoughts, charming reveries, and melancholy remembrances.—*Alphonse Karr.*

In matters of conscience first thoughts are best; in matters of prudence last thoughts are best.—*Robert Hall.*

Thought engenders thought. *P*lace one idea on paper, another will follow it, and still another, until you have written a page; you cannot fathom your mind. There is a well of thought there which has no bottom; the more you draw from it, the more clear and fruitful it will be.—*G. A. Sala.*

Constant thought will overflow in words unconsciously.—*Byron.*

It may be said that it is with our thoughts as with our flowers. Those whose expression is simple carry their seed with them; those that are double by their richness and pomp charm the mind, but produce nothing.—*Joubert.*

Man is a thinking being, whether he will or no; all he can do is to turn his thoughts the best way.—*Sir W. Temple.*

Every great originating mind produces in some way a change in society; every great originating mind, whose exercise is controlled by duty, effects a beneficial change. This effect may be immediate, may be remote. A nation may be in a tumult to-day for a thought which the timid Erasmus placidly penned in his study more than two centuries ago.— *Whipple.*

The thinker requires exactly the same light as the painter, clear, without direct sunshine, or blinding reflection, and, where possible, from above.—*Schlegel.*

A man would do well to carry a pencil in his pocket, and write down the thoughts of the moment. Those that come unsought for are commonly the most valuable, and should be secured, because they seldom return.—*Bacon.*

High erected thoughts seated in the heart of courtesy.—*Sir P. Sidney.*

Thinking leads man to knowledge. He may see and hear, and read and learn, whatever he pleases, and as much as he pleases; he will never know anything of it, except that which he has thought over, that which by thinking he has made the property of his mind. Is it then saying too much, if I say that man, by thinking only, becomes truly man? Take away thought from man's life, and what remains?— *Pestalozzi.*

Alas, we make a ladder of our thoughts, where angels step, but sleep ourselves at the foot; our high resolves look down upon our slumbering acts.—*Miss L. E. Landon.*

There is a thread in our thoughts, as there is a pulse in our feelings; he who can hold the one knows how to think, and he who can move the other knows how to feel.—*Disraeli.*

It is only by labor that thought can be made healthy, and only by thought that labor can be made happy; and the two cannot be separated with impunity.—*Ruskin.*

Thoughts perhaps, which, like field-mice of the soul, leap under the feet and stick like adders.—*Richter.*

Nothing is comparable to the pleasure of an active and prevailing thought, — a thought prevailing over the difficulty and obscurity of the object, and refreshing the soul with new discoveries and images of things; and thereby extending the bounds of apprehension, and as it were enlarging the territories of reason.— *South.*

THOUGHTLESSNESS.

Some people pass through life soberly and religiously enough, without knowing why, or reasoning about it, but, from force of habit merely, go to heaven like fools.—*Sterne.*

Ah, how unjust to nature and himself is thoughtless, thankless, inconsistent man!— *Young.*

THREATS.

I consider it a mark of great prudence in a man to abstain from threats or any contemptuous expressions, for neither of these weaken the enemy, but threats make him more cautious, and the other excites his hatred, and a desire to revenge himself.—*Machiavelli.*

If I had a thunderbolt in my eye, I can tell who should down.—*Shakespeare.*

THUNDER.

The herald, earth-accredited, of heaven,— which when men hear, they think upon beaven's king, and run the items over of the account to which he is sure to call them.—
Sheridan Knowles.

TIME.

As every thread of gold is valuable, so is every minute of time.—*Rev. John Mason.*

To-day, to-morrow, every day, to thousands the end of the world is close at hand. And why should we fear it ? We walk here, as it were, in the crypts of life ; at times, from the great cathedral above us, we can hear the organ and the chanting choir ; we see the light stream through the open door, when some friend goes up before us ; and shall we fear to mount the narrow staircase of the grave that leads us out of this uncertain twilight into life eternal ? —
Longfellow.

If you have time don't wait for time.—
Franklin.

Time has been given only for us to exchange each year of our life with the remembrance of truth.—*St. Martin.*

It is only necessary to give to each thing the time which it claims.—*Angelo Pandolfini.*

Time, the cradle of hope, but the grave of ambition, is the stern corrector of fools, but the salutary counsellor of the wise, bringing all they dread to the one, and all they desire to the other ; but, like Cassandra, it warns us with a voice that even the sagest discredit too long, and the silliest believe too late. Wisdom walks before it, opportunity with it, and repentance behind it ; he that has made it his friend will have little to fear from his enemies, but he that has made it his enemy will have little to hope from his friends.—*Colton.*

Time well employed is Satan's deadliest foe ; it leaves no opening for the lurking fiend.—
Wilcox.

Time is but a stream I go a fishing in. I drink at it ; but while I drink I see the sandy bottom, and detect how shallow it is. Its thin current slides away, but eternity remains. I would drink deeper, fish in the sky, whose bottom is pebbly with stars.—*Thoreau.*

We take no note of time but from its loss.—
Young.

Who shall contend with time,—unvanquished time, the conqueror of conquerors and lord of desolation ?—*H. K. White.*

Time destroys the speculations of man, but it confirms the judgment of nature.—*Cicero.*

Be avaricious of time ; do not give any moment without receiving it in value ; only allow the hours to go from you with as much regret as you give to your gold ; do not allow a single day to pass without increasing the treasure of your knowledge and virtue. The use of time is a debt we contract from birth, and it should only be paid with the interest that our life has accumulated.—*Letourneur.*

The velocity with which time flies is infinite, as is most apparent to those who look back.—
Seneca.

They that drive away time spur a free horse.
Robert Mason.

Lost, yesterday, somewhere between sunrise and sunset, two golden hours, each set with sixty diamond minutes. No reward is offered, for they are gone forever !—*Horace Mann.*

Time antiquates antiquities, and hath an art to make dust of all things.—
Sir Thomas Browne.

We all sorely complain of the shortness of time, and y et have much more than we know what to do with. Our lives are either spent in doing nothing at all, or in doing nothing to the purpose, or in doing nothing that we ought to do. We are always complaining that our days are few, and acting as though there would be no end of them.—*Seneca.*

Time is the old justice that examines all offenders.—*Shakespeare.*

Time is painted with a lock before, and bald behind, signifying thereby, that we must take time (as we say) by the forelock, for when it is once passed there is no recalling it.—*Swift.*

The great rule of moral conduct is, next to God, to respect time.—*Lavater.*

How silent, how spacious, what room for all, yet without place to insert an atom,—in graceful succession, in equal fulness, in balanced beauty, the dance of the hours goes forward still. Like an odor of incense, like a strain of music, like a sleep, it is inexact and boundless. It will not be dissected, nor unravelled, nor shown.—*Emerson.*

Time, with all its celerity, moves slowly on to him whose whole employment is to watch its flight.—*Johnson.*

One always has time enough, if one will apply it well.—*Goethe.*

Time is the greatest of all tyrants. As we go on towards age, he taxes our health, limbs, faculties, strength, and features.—*John Foster.*

Time travels in divers paces with divers persons.—*Shakespeare.*

As nothing truly valuable can be attained without industry, so there can be no persevering industry without a deep sense of the value of time.—*Mrs. Sigourney.*

Time is the king of men ; he is both their parent, and he is their grave, and gives them what he will, not what they crave.—*Shakespeare.*

Time,—that black and narrow isthmus between two eternities.—*Colton.*

There are no fragments so precious as those of time, and none are so heedlessly lost by people who cannot make a moment, and yet can waste years.—*Montgomery.*

Time is the nurser and breeder of all good.
Shakespeare.

Nothing lies on our hands with such uneasiness as time. Wretched and thoughtless creatures ! In the only place where covetousness were a virtue we turn prodigals.—*Addison.*

As if you could kill time without injuring eternity.—*Thoreau.*

Time is the most undefinable yet paradoxical of things ; the past is gone, the future is not come, and the present becomes the past, even while we attempt to define it, and, like the flash of the lightning, at once exists and expires.—*Colton.*

The inaudible and noiseless foot of time.—
Shakespeare.

If time, like money, could be laid by while one was not using it, there might be some excuse for the idleness of half the world, but yet not a full one. For even this would be such an economy as the living on a principal sum, without making it purchase interest.—*Sterne.*

Time has only a relative existence.—*Carlyle.*

Our acts of kindness we reserve for our friends, our bounties for our dependants, our riches for our children and relations, our praises for those who appear worthy of them, our time we give all to the world ; we expose it, I may say, a prey to all mankind.—*Massillon.*

Time is the greatest of innovators.—*Bacon.*

God, who is liberal in all his other gifts, shows us, by the wise economy of his providence, how circumspect we ought to be in the management of our time, for he never gives us two moments together.—*Fenelon.*

Thou shoreless flood, which in thy ebb and flow claspest the limits of mortality.—*Shelley.*

Time is like a river, in which metals and solid substances are sunk, while chaff and straws swim upon the surface.—*Bacon.*

When young, our years are ages ; in mature life, they are three hundred and sixty-five days ; in old age, they have dwindled to a few weeks. Time is, indeed, the messenger with wings at his feet. Yesterday he took my wife ; to-day, my son ; to-morrow he will take me.—
Madame de Gasparin.

O time ! whose verdicts mock our own, the only righteous judge art thou !—*T. W. Parsons.*

Time knows not the weight of sleep or weariness, and night's deep darkness has no chain to bind his rushing pinion.—*George D. Prentice.*

Time doth transfix the flourish set on youth, and delves the parallels in beauty's brow.—
Shakespeare.

Observe a method in the distribution of your time. Every hour will then know its proper employment, and no time will be lost. Idleness will be shut out at every avenue, and with her that numerous body of vices that make up her train.—*Bishop Horne.*

Time is an herb that cures all diseases.—
Franklin.

Time destroys the groundless conceits of man, but confirms that which is founded on nature and reality.—*Cicero.*

I wasted time, and now doth time waste me.
Shakespeare.

The wheel track in which we roll on towards eternity, conducting us to the Incomprehensible. In its progress there is a ripening power, and it ripens us the more and the more powerfully when we duly estimate it, listen to its voice, do not waste it, but regard it as the highest finite good, in which all finite things are resolved.
Wilhelm von Humboldt.

Whatever passes away is too vile to be the price of time, which is itself the price of eternity.
Massillon.

Make use of time, if thou valuest eternity. Yesterday cannot be recalled ; to-morrow cannot be assured ; to-day only is thine, which, if thou procrastinatest, thou losest ; which loss is lost forever.—*Jeremy Taylor.*

Remorseless time ! fierce spirit of the glass and scythe,—what power can stay him in his silent course, or melt his iron heart with pity ! —
George D. Prentice.

Man seems to be deficient in nothing so much as he is in time.—*Zeno.*

Time is like a ship which never anchors ; while I am on board, I had better do those things that may profit me at my landing, than practise such as shall cause my commitment when I come ashore.—*Feltham.*

Opinions, theories, and systems pass by turns over the grindstone of time, which at first gives them brilliancy and sharpness, but finally wears them out.—*Rivarol.*

Time is the chrysalis of eternity.—*Richter.*

That great mystery of time, were there no other; the illimitable, silent, never-resting thing called "time," rolling, rushing on, swift, silent, like an all-embracing ocean-tide, on which we and all the universe swim like exhalations, like apparitions which are and then are not. This is forever very literally a miracle, — a thing to strike us dumb; for we have no word to speak about it.— *Carlyle.*

The strong hours conquer us.—*Schiller.*

Since time is not a person we can overtake when he is past, let us honor him with mirth and cheerfulness of heart while he is passing.—*Goethe.*

He who runs against time has an antagonist not liable to casualties.—*Johnson.*

What is time ? — the shadow on the dial, the striking of the clock, the running of the sand, day and night, summer and winter, months, years, centuries, — these are but arbitrary and outward signs, — the measure of time, not time itself. Time is the life of the soul. If not this, then tell me what is time ?—*Longfellow.*

Man has here two and a half minutes, — one to smile, one to sigh, and half an one to love ; for in the midst of this minute he dies.—*Richter.*

We sleep, but the loom of life never stops; and the pattern which was weaving when the sun went down is weaving when it comes up to-morrow.—*Beecher.*

Time sadly overcometh all things, and is now dominant, and sitteth upon a sphinx, and looketh unto Memphis and old Thebes, while his sister Oblivion reclineth semi-somnons on a pyramid, gloriously triumphing, making puzzles of Titanian erections, and turning old glories into dreams.—*Sir Thomas Browne.*

Think with terror on the slow, the quiet power of time.—*Schiller.*

There is nothing of which we are apt to be so lavish as of time, and about which we ought to be more solicitous, since without it we can do nothing in this world. Time is what we want most, but what, alas ! we use worst.—*William Penn.*

Time sheds a softness on remote objects or events, as local distance imparts to the landscape a smoothness and mellowness which disappear on a nearer approach.— *W. B. Clulow.*

The past and future are veiled ; but the past wears the widow's veil, the future the virgin's.—*Richter.*

There is nothing that we can properly call our own but our time, and yet everybody fools us out of it who has a mind to do it. If a man borrows a paltry sum of money, there must be bonds and securities, and every common civility is presently charged upon account. But he who has my time he owes me nothing for it, though it be a debt that gratitude itself can never repay.—*Seneca.*

Time never bears such moments on his wing as when he flies too swiftly to be marked.—*Joanna Baillie.*

Imitate time ; it destroys everything slowly; it undermines, it wears away, it detaches, it does not wrench.—*Joubert.*

Time is the herald of truth.— *Cicero.*

Beauty, wit, high birth, vigor of bone, desert in service, love, friendship, charity, are subjects all to envious and calumniating time.—*Shakespeare.*

Time wasted is existence; used, is life.—*Young.*

Time is never more misspent than while we declaim against the want of it ; all our actions are then tinctured with peevishness. The yoke of life is certainly the least oppressive when we carry it with good-humor ; and in the shades of rural retirement, when we have once acquired a resolution to pass our hours with economy, sorrowful lamentations on the subject of time misspent and business neglected never torture the mind.—*Zimmermann.*

Those that dare lose a day are dangerously prodigal ; those that dare misspend it, desperate.—*Bishop Hall.*

Time will bring to light whatever is hidden ; it will conceal and cover up what is now shining with the greatest splendor.—*Horace.*

The use of time is fate.— *Chapman.*

The greatest loss of time is delay and expectation, which depends upon the future. We let go the present, which we have in our power, and look forward to that which depends upon chance, — and so relinquish a certainty for an uncertainty.—*Seneca.*

Time is a continual over-dropping of moments, which fall down one upon the other and evaporate.—*Richter.*

A year! A life! What are they ? The telling of a tale, the passing of a meteor, a dim speck seen for a moment on time's horizon dropping into eternity.—*Thomason.*

Time travels like a ship in the wide ocean, which hath no bounding shore to mark its progress.—*Joanna Baillie.*

Like an inundation of the Indus is the course of time. We look for the homes of our childhood, they are gone; for the friends of our childhood, they are gone. The loves and animosities of youth, where are they ? Swept away like the camps that had been pitched in the sandy bed of the river.—*Longfellow.*

We should count time by heart throbs.— *James Martineau.*

Time will discover everything to posterity; it is a babbler, and speaks even when no question is put.—*Euripides.*

Therefore conceal nothing; for time, that sees and hears all things, discovers everything. *Sophocles.*

A man's time, when well husbanded, is like a cultivated field, of which a few acres produces more of what is useful to life, than extensive provinces, even of the richest soil, when overrun with weeds and brambles.—*Hume.*

Here is a day now before me; a day is a fortune and an estate; who loses a day loses life.—*Emerson.*

No preacher is listened to but time; which gives us the same train and turn of thought that elder people have tried in vain to put into our heads.—*Swift.*

TIMIDITY.

That mute eloquence which passeth speech. *Rogers.*

One with more of soul in his face than words on his tongue.—*Wordsworth.*

Silent when glad; affectionate, though shy. *Beattie.*

Presumption will be easily corrected; but timidity is a disease of the mind more obstinate and fatal.—*Johnson.*

Looks that asked, yet dared not hope relief. *Rogers.*

A woman is seldom merciful to the man who is timid.—*Bulwer Lytton.*

TITLE.

Titles, the servile courtier's lean reward.— *Rowe.*

Title and ancestry render a good man more illustrious, but an ill one more contemptible. Vice is infamous, though in a prince; and virtue honorable, though in a peasant.—*Addison.*

Virtue is the first title of nobility.—*Molière.*

Titles of honor are like the impressions on coin, which add no value to gold and silver, but only render brass current.—*Sterne.*

Some people are all quality; you would think they were made up of nothing but title and genealogy. The stamp of dignity defaces in them. the very character of humanity, and transports them to such a degree of haughtiness that they reckon it below themselves to exercise either good-nature or good manners.— *L'Estrange.*

For it is not titles that reflect honor on men, but men on their titles.—*Machiavelli.*

Of the king's creation you may be; but he who makes a count never made a man.— *Southern.*

Titles and mottoes to books are like escutcheons and dignities in the hands of a king. The wise sometimes condescend to accept of them; but none but a fool would imagine them of any real importance. We ought to depend upon intrinsic merit, and not the slender helps of the title.—*Goldsmith.*

Titles of honor add not to his worth, who is himself an honor to his title.—*John Ford.*

Kings do with men as with pieces of money; they give them what value they please, and we are obliged to receive them at their current and not at their real value.—*Rochefoucauld.*

Titles are of no value to posterity; the name of a man who has achieved great deeds imposes more respect than any or all epithets. *Voltaire.*

Titles, indeed, may be purchased; but virtue is the only coin that makes the bargain valid.—*Burton.*

TOIL.

Toil to some is happiness, and rest to others. This man can only breathe in crowds, and that man only in solitudes.—*Bulwer Lytton.*

Bodily labor alleviates the pain of the mind; whence arises the happiness of the poor. *Rochefoucauld.*

Toil and pleasure, in their natures opposite, are yet linked together in a kind of necessary connection.—*Livy.*

TOLERATION.

Be thankful that your lot has fallen on times when, though there may be many evil tongues and exasperated spirits, there are none who have fire and fagot at command.— *Southey.*

May they who celebrate thy name by waxlight at noonday tolerate such as are content with the light of the sun ! — *Voltaire.*

I would recommend a free commerce both of matter and mind. I would let men enter their own churches with the same freedom as their own houses ; and I would do it without a homily or graciousness or favor, for tyranny itself is to me a word less odious than toleration.—*Landor.*

They who boast of their tolerance merely give others leave to be as careless about religion as they are themselves. A walrus might as well pride itself on its endurance of cold.—*Hare.*

Let us not take offence at men because of their rudeness, ingratitude, injustice, arrogance, love of self, and forgetfulness of others ; they are so formed, such is their nature; to be annoyed with them for such conduct is the same as to exclaim against a stone falling or a fire burning.—*Bruyère.* •

No one, judging from his own feelings and powers, can be aware of the kind or degree of temptation or terror, or the seeming incapacity to resist them, which may induce others to deviate.—*Abernethy.*

Whenever we cease to hate, to despise, and to persecute those who think differently from ourselves, whenever we look on them calmly, we find among them men of pure hearts and unbiased judgments, who, reasoning on the same data with ourselves, have arrived at different conclusions on the subject of the spiritual world.—*Sismondi.*

TOMB.

The house appointed for all living.—*Bible.*

By an unfaltering trust, approach thy grave, like one that wraps the drapery of his couch about him, and lies down to pleasant dreams.—
Bryant.

A tomb is a monument placed on the limits of two worlds.—*Bernardin de St. Pierre.*

I would rather sleep in the southern corner of a little country churchyard than in the tomb of the Capulets.—*Burke.*

The Earth, that is Nature's mother, is her tomb.—*Shakespeare.*

It is a harsh world in which affection knows no place to treasure up its loved and lost but the lone grave.— *Willis.*

All that tread the globe are but a handful to the tribes that slumber in its bosom.—*Bryant.*

TO-MORROW.

To-morrow, do thy worst, for I have lived to-day.—*Dryden.*

To-morrow thou wilt live, didst thou say, Posthumus? to-day is too late; he is the wise man who lived yesterday.—*Martial.*

To-morrow, and to-morrow, and to-morrow creeps in this petty pace from day to day, to the last syllable of recorded time ; and all our yesterdays have lighted fools the way to dusty death.—*Shakespeare.*

To-morrow to fresh woods, and pastures new.—*Milton.*

To-morrow may never come to us. We do not live in to-morrow. We cannot find it in any of our title-deeds. The man who owns whole blocks of real estate, and great ships on the sea, does not own a single minute of to-morrow. To-morrow! It is a mysterious possibility, not yet born. It lies under the seal of midnight, behind the veil of glittering constellations.—*Chapin.*

To-morrow is a satire on to-day, and shows its weakness.—*Young.*

TONGUE.

The tongue should not be suffered to outrun the mind.—*Chilo.*

It is observed in the course of worldly things, that men's fortunes are oftener made by their tongues than by their virtues ; and more men's fortunes overthrown thereby than by vices.—*Sir W. Raleigh.*

The tongue of the wise useth knowledge aright, and is as choice silver.—*Bible.*

A wound from a tongue is worse than a wound from the sword; the latter affects only the body, — the former, the spirit, the soul.—
Pythagoras.

Give not thy tongue too great a liberty, lest it take thee prisoner. A word unspoken is like the sword in the scabbard, thine; if vented, thy sword is in another's hand. If thou desire to be held wise, be so wise as to hold thy tongue.—*Quarles.*

Woman's tongue is her sword, which she never lets rust.—*Madame Necker.*

The tongue is, at the same time, the best part of man and his worst; with good government, none is more useful, and without it, none is more mischievous.—*Anacharsis.*

The chameleon, who is said to feed upon nothing but air, has of all animals the nimblest tongue.—*Swift.*

Death and life are in the power of the tongue.—*Bible.*

By examining the tongue of a patient, physicians find out the diseases of the body, and philosophers the diseases of the mind.—*Justin.*

A fool's heart is in his tongue ; but a wise man's tongue is in his heart.—*Quarles.*

A tart temper never mellows with age; and a sharp tongue is the only edge-tool that grows keener with constant use.—*Washington Irving.*

The heart's attorney.—*Shakespeare.*

Since I cannot govern my own tongue, though within my own teeth, how can I hope to govern the tongue of others ? —*Franklin.*

Give your tongue more holiday than your hands or eyes.—*Rabbi Ben-Azai.*

In the use of the tongue God hath distinguished us from beasts, and by the well or ill using it we are distinguished from one another; and therefore, though silence be innocent as death, harmless as a rose's breath to a distant passenger, yet it is rather the state of death than life.—*Jeremy Taylor.*

The tongue of a fool is the key of his counsel, which in a wise man wisdom hath in keeping.—*Socrates.*

TRADE.
He that hath a trade hath an estate; and he that hath a calling hath a place of profit and honor. A ploughman on his legs is higher than a gentleman on his knees.—*Franklin.*

There is nothing so useful to man in general, nor so beneficial to particular societies and individuals, as trade. This is that *alma mater,* at whose plentiful breast all mankind are nourished.—*Fielding.*

There is a Spanish proverb, that a lapidary who would grow rich must buy of those who go to be executed, as not caring how cheap they sell; and sell to those who go to be married, as not caring how dear they buy.—*Fuller.*

TRADITION.
What an enormous " camera-obscura ", magnifier is tradition ! How a thing grows in the human memory, in the human imagination, when love, worship, and all that lies in the human heart, is there to encourage it; and in the darkness, in the entire ignorance, without date or document, no book, no Arundel marble, only here and there some dull monumental cairn ! —*Carlyle.*

TRAGEDY.
Tragedy has the great moral defect of giving too much importance to life and death.—*Chamfort.*

Tragedy warms the soul, elevates the heart, can and ought to create heroes. In this sense, perhaps, France owes a part of her great actions to Corneille.—*Napoleon.*

The pleasure arising from an extraordinary agitation of the mind is frequently so great as to stifle humanity; hence arises the entertainment of the common people at executions, and of the better sort at tragedies.—*L'Abbé du Bois.*

TRAVEL.
All travel has its advantages. If the passenger visits better countries, he may learn to improve his own ; and if fortune carries him to worse, he may learn to enjoy his own.—*Johnson.*

Travel is the frivolous part of serious lives, and the serious part of frivolous ones.—
Madame Swetchine.

There are two things necessary for a traveller, to bring him to the end of his journey, — a knowledge of his way, a perseverance in his walk. If he walk in a wrong way, the faster he goes the farther he is from home ; if he sit still in the right way, he may know his home, but never come to it : discreet stays make speedy journeys. I will first then know my way, ere I begin my walk ; the knowledge of my way is a good part of my journey.—*Arthur Warwick.*

Travellers must be content.—*Shakespeare.*

One telling Socrates that such a one was nothing improved by his travels, " I very well believe it," said he, " for he took himself along with him."—*Montaigne.*

I think it not fit that every man should travel. It makes a wise man better, and a fool worse.—*Feltham.*

Those who visit foreign nations, but who associate only with their own countrymen, change their climate, but not their customs ; they see new meridians, but the same men ; and with heads as empty as their pockets, return home with travelled bodies, but untravelled minds.—
Colton.

Travellers never did lie, though fools at home condemn them.—*Shakespeare.*

To be a good traveller argues one no ordinary philosopher. A sweet landscape must sometimes be allowed to atone for an indifferent supper, and an interesting ruin charm away the remembrance of a hard bed.—*Tuckerman.*

Men may change their climate, but they cannot change their nature. A man that goes out a fool cannot ride or sail himself into commonsense.—*Addison.*

Usually speaking, the worst-bred person in company is a young traveller just returned from abroad.—*Swift.*

As the Spanish proverb says, " He who would bring home the wealth of the Indies must carry the wealth of the Indies with him," so it is in travelling ; a man must carry knowledge with him if he would bring home knowledge.—
Johnson.

Travel gives a character of experience to our knowledge, and brings the figures upon the tablet of memory into strong relief.—*Tuckerman.*

Travellers find virtue in a seeming minority in all other countries, and forget that they have left it in a minority at home.—
T. W. Higginson.

Peregrination charms our senses with such unspeakable and sweet variety, that some count him unhappy that never travelled, — a kind of prisoner, and pity his case; that, from his cradle to his old age, he beholds the same still, — still, still, the same, the same.—*Burton.*

He travels safe, and not unpleasantly, who is guarded by poverty and guided by love.—
Sir P. Sidney.

The proper means of increasing the love we bear our native country is to reside some time in a foreign one.—*Shenstone.*

A pilgrimage is an admirable remedy for over-fastidiousness and sickly refinement.—
Tuckerman.

A traveller! By my faith, you have great reason to be sad. I fear you have sold your own lands, to see other men's; then to have seen much, and to have nothing, is to have rich eyes and poor hands.—*Shakespeare.*

A traveller without observation is a bird without wings.—*Saadi.*

They, and they only, advantage themselves by travel, who, well fraught with the experience of what their own country affords, carry ever with them large and thriving talents.
F. Osborn.

He who never leaves his country is full of prejudices.—*Carlo Goldoni.*

The world is a great book, of which they that never stir from home read only a page.—
St. Augustine.

Railway travelling is not travelling at all; it is merely being sent to a place, and very little different from becoming a parcel.—*Ruskin.*

TREACHERY.
It is time to fear when tyrants seem to kiss.
Shakespeare.

There is no traitor like him whose domestic treason plants the poniard within the breast which trusted to his truth.—*Byron.*

In general, treachery, though at first sufficiently cautious, yet in the end betrays itself.—
Livy.

Though those that are betrayed do feel the treason sharply, yet the traitor stands in worse case of woe.—*Shakespeare.*

Men are oftener treacherous through weakness than design.—*Rochefoucauld.*

Deliberate treachery entails punishment upon the traitor. There is no possibility of escaping it, even in the highest rank to which the consent of society can exalt the meanest and worst of men.—*Junius.*

TREASON.
Cæsar had his Brutus; Charles the First, his Cromwell; and George the Third — ("Treason!" cried the Speaker) — may profit by their example. If this be treason, make the most of it.—*Patrick Henry.*

Treason is like diamonds; there is nothing to be made by the small trader.—
Douglas Jerrold.

In the clear mind of virtue treason can find no hiding-place.—*Sir P. Sidney.*

Is there not some chosen curse, some hidden thunder in the stores of heaven, red with uncommon wrath, to blast the man who owes his greatness to his country's ruin!—*Addison.*

Treason doth never prosper; what is the reason? Why, if it prosper, none dare call it treason.—*Sir John Harrington.*

Smooth runs the water where the brook is deep; and in his simple show he harbors treason. The fox barks not, when he would steal the lamb.—*Shakespeare.*

Fellowship in treason is a bad ground of confidence.—*Burke.*

It is the just decree of Heaven that a traitor never sees his danger till his ruin is at hand.—
Metastasio.

Treason is but trusted like the fox, who, never so tame, so cherished, and locked up, will have a wild trick of his ancestors.—*Shakespeare.*

TREES.
A large, branching, aged oak is perhaps the most venerable of all inanimate objects.—
Shenstone.

Mouldering and moss-grown, through the lapse of years, in motionless beauty stands the giant oak; whilst those that saw its green and flourishing youth are gone and are forgotten.—
Longfellow.

The groves were God's first temples.—
Bryant.

The works of a person that builds begin immediately to decay, while those of him who plants begin directly to improve. In this, planting promises a more lasting pleasure than building; which, were it to remain in equal perfection, would at best begin to moulder and want repairs in imagination. Now trees have a circumstance that suits our taste, and that is annual variety.—*Shenstone.*

Trees the most lovingly shelter and shade us when, like the willow, the higher soar their summits the lowlier droop their boughs.—
Bulwer Lytton.

Trees have about them something beautiful and attractive even to the fancy, since they cannot change their places, are witnesses of all the changes that take place around them; and as some reach a great age, they become, as it were, historical monuments,.and like ourselves they have a life, growing and passing away,—not being inanimate and unvarying like the fields and rivers. One sees them passing through various stages, and at last step by step approaching death, which makes them look still more like ourselves.—
Wilhelm von Humboldt.

A brotherhood of venerable trees.—
Wordsworth.

The willow is a sad tree, whereof such who have lost their love make their mourning garlands, and we know what exiles hung up their harps upon such doleful supporters. The twigs are physic to drive out the folly of children.—*Fuller.*

TRIALS.

A virtuous and well-disposed person is like good metal, — the more he is fired, the more he is fined; the more he is opposed, the more he is approved. Wrongs may well try him, and touch him but they cannot imprint on him any false stamp.—*Richelieu.*

Reckon any matter of trial to thee among thy gains.—*Rev. T. Adam.*

Trials are medicines which our gracious and wise Physician prescribes, because we need them; and he proportions the frequency and the weight of them to what the case requires. Let us trust in his skill, and thank him for his prescription.—*Newton.*

God hath many sharp-cutting instruments and rough files for the polishing of his jewels; and those he especially loves, and means to make the most resplendent, he hath oftenest his tools upon.—*Leighton.*

Prosperity tries the fortunate, adversity the great.—*Pliny the Younger.*

If we would know whether a staff be strong, or a rotten, broken reed, we must observe it when it is leaned on, and weight is borne upon it. If we would weigh ourselves justly, we must weigh ourselves in God's scales, that he makes use of to weigh us.—*Jonathan Edwards.*

God often lays the sum of his amazing providences in very dismal afflictions; as the limner first puts on the dusky colors, on which he intends to draw the portraiture of some illustrions beauty.—*Charnock.*

As the musician straineth his strings, and yet he breaketh none of them, but maketh thereby a sweeter melody and better concord; so God, through affliction, makes his own better unto the fruition and enjoying of the life to come.—*Daniel Cawdrey.*

Every man will have his own criterion in forming his judgment of others. I depend very much on the effect of affliction. I consider how a man comes out of the furnace; gold will lie for a month in the furnace without losing a grain.—*Cecil.*

TRIFLES.

Trifles make perfection, but perfection itself is no trifle.—*Michael Angelo.*

A fly is a very light burden; but if it were perpetually to return and settle on one's nôse, it might weary us of our very lives.—
Fredrika Bremer.

Trifles lighter than straws are levers in the building up of character.—*Tupper.*

Trifles we should not let plague us only, but also gratify us; we should seize not their poison-bags only, but their honey-bags also.—
Richter.

A little thing consoles us, because a little thing afflicts us.—*Pascal.*

Whoever shall review his life, will find that the whole tenor of his conduct has been determined by some accident of no apparent moment.—*Johnson.*

The smallest hair throws its shadow.—
Goethe.

To pursue trifles is the lot of humanity; and whether we bustle in a pantomime or strut at a coronation, whether we shout at a bonfire or harangue in a senate-house, — whatever objeet we follow, it will at last surely conduct us to futility and disappointment. The wise bustle and laugh as they walk in the pageant, but fools bustle and are important; and this, probably, is all the difference between them.—
Goldsmith.

There is nothing too little for so little a creature as man. It is by studying little things that we attain the great art of having as little misery and as much happiness as possible.—
Johnson.

There some trifles well habited, as there are some fools well clothed.—*Chamfort.*

A spark is a molecule of matter, yet may it kindle the world; vast is the mighty ocean, but drops have made it vast. Despise not thou small things, either for evil or for good; for a look may work thy ruin, or a word create thy wealth.—*Tupper.*

There is a vigilance and judgment about trifles which men only get by living in a crowd; and those are the trifles of detail, on which the success of execution depends.—
Horner.

The great moments of life are but moments like the others. Your doom is spoken in a word or two. A single look from the eyes, a mere pressure of the hand, may decide it; or of the lips though they cannot speak.—
Thackeray.

The power of duly appreciating little things belongs to a great mind; a narrow-minded man has it not, for to him they are great things.—
Whately.

A slight answer to an intricate and useless question is a fit cover to such a dish, — a cabbage-leaf is good enough to cover a dish of mushrooms.—*Jeremy Taylor.*

Those who place their affections at first on trifles for amusement, will find these trifles become at last their most serious concerns.—
Goldsmith.

Contentions for trifles can get but a trifling victory.—*Sir P. Sidney.*

In mortals there is a care for trifles which proceeds from love and conscience, and is most holy; and a care for trifles which comes of idleness and frivolity, and is most base. And so, also, there is a gravity proceeding from thought, which is most noble; and a gravity proceeding from dulness and mere incapability of enjoyment, which is most base.—*Ruskin.*

It has been well observed that the misery of man proceeds not from any single crush of overwhelming evil, but from small vexations continually repeated.—*Johnson.*

The calm or agitation of our temper does not depend so much on the important events of life, as on an agreeable or disagreeable adjustment of little things which happen every day.—*Rochefoucauld.*

A snapper up of unconsidered trifles.—
Shakespeare.

Trifles discover a character more than actions of importance. In regard to the former, a person is off his guard, and thinks it not material to use disguise. It is, to me, no imperfect hint towards the discovery of a man's character, to say he looks as though you might be certain of finding a pin upon his sleeve.—
Shenstone.

There is no real elevation of mind in a contempt of little things; it is, on the contrary, from too narrow views that we consider those things of little importance which have in fact such extensive consequences.—*Fenelon.*

A stray hair, by its continued irritation, may give more annoyance than a smart blow.
Lowell.

As small letters hurt the sight, so do small matters him that is too much intent upon them; they vex and stir up anger, which begets an evil habit in him in reference to greater affairs.—*Plutarch.*

There is nothing insignificant, nothing!—
Coleridge.

Those who bestow too much application on trifling things become generally incapable of great ones.—*Rochefoucauld.*

What mighty contests rise from trivial things!—*Pope.*

Great merit, or great failings will make you respected or despised; but trifles, little attentions, mere nothings, either done or neglected, will make you either liked or disliked, in the general run of the world. Examine yourself, why you like such and such people and dislike such and such others; and you will find that those different sentiments proceed from very slight causes.—*Chesterfield.*

Petty vexations may at times be petty, but still they are vexations. The smallest and most inconsiderable annoyances are the most piercing.—*Montaigne.*

The pathetic almost always consists in the detail of little circumstances.—*Gibbon.*

Trifles themselves are elegant in him.—
Pope.

When I see the elaborate study and ingennity displayed by woman in the pursuit of trifles, I feel no doubt of their capacity for the most herculean undertakings.—
Julia Ward Howe.

These little things are great to little man.—
Goldsmith.

Frivolous curiosity about trifles, and laborious attentions to little objects which neither require nor deserve a moment's thought, lower a man, who from thence is thought (and not unjustly) incapable of greater matters. Cardinal de Retz very sagaciously marked out Cardinal Chigi for a little mind, from the moment he told him that he had wrote three years with the same pen, and that it was an excellent good one still.—*Chesterfield.*

Each particle of matter is an immensity, each leaf a world, each insect an inexplicable compendium.—*Lavater.*

A grain of sand leads to the fall of a mountain when the moment has come for the mountain to fall.—*Ernest Renan.*

The gay motes that people the sunbeams.—
Milton.

It is curious to observe the triumph of slight incidents over the mind ; and what incredible weight they have in forming and governing our opinions, both of men and things, that trifles light as air shall waft a belief into the soul, and plant it so immovable within it, that Euclid's demonstrations, could they be brought to batter it in breach, should not all have power to overthrow it ! —*Sterne.*

The earth hath bubbles, as the water has, and these are of them.—*Shakespeare.*

There is not one grain in the universe, either too much or too little, nothing to be added, nothing to be spared ; nor so much as any one particle of it, that mankind may not be either the better or the worse for, according as it is applied.—*L'Estrange.*

Men are led by trifles.—*Napoleon.*

The mind of the greatest man on earth is not so independent of circumstances as not to feel inconvenienced by the merest buzzing noise about him ; it does not need the report of a cannon to disturb his thoughts. The creaking of a vane or a pully is quite enough. Do not wonder that he reasons ill just now ; a fly is buzzing by his ear ; it is quite enough to unfit him for giving good counsel.—*Pascal.*

The creation of a thousand forests is in one acorn.—*Emerson.*

A little, and a little, collected together become a great deal ; the heap in the barn consists of single grains, and drop and drop form an inundation.—*Saadi.*

TRIUMPH.
Triumph is the finest thing in the world, — the "long live the king !" the hats in the air at the point of the bayonets ; the compliments of the master to his warriors ; the visits of the intrenchments, the villages, and redoubts ; the joy, the glory, the tenderness. But the foundation of all that is human blood and shreds of human flesh.—*D. Argenson.*

TROUBLES.
If you tell your troubles to God, you put them into the grave ; they will never rise again when you have committed them to him. If you roll your burden anywhere else, it will roll back again, like the stone of Sisyphus.—
Spurgeon.

The true way of softening one's troubles is to solace those of others.—
Madame de Maintenon.

In adverse hours the friendship of the good shines most ; each prosperous day commands its friends.—*Euripides.*

Men's happiness springs mainly from moderate troubles, which afford the mind a healthful stimulus, and are followed by a reaction which produces a cheerful flow of spirits.—
E. Wigglesworth.

Men are born to trouble at first, and exercised in it all their days. There is a cry at the beginning of life, and a groan at its close.—
Rev. W. Arnot.

Troubles are usually the brooms and shovels that smooth the road to a good man's fortune; of which he little dreams ; and many a man curses the rain that falls upon his head, and knows not that it brings abundance to drive away hunger.—*Basil.*

Tribulation will not hurt you unless it does —what, alas ! it too often does—unless it hardens you, and makes you sour and narrow and sceptical.—*Chapin.*

You can imagine thistle-down so light that when you run after it your running motion would drive it away from you, and that the more you tried to catch it the faster it would fly from your grasp. And it should be with every man, that, when he is chased by troubles, they, chasing, shall raise him higher and higher.—*Beecher.*

Outward attacks and troubles rather fix than unsettle the Christian, as tempests from without only serve to root the oak faster ; whilst an inward canker will gradually rot and decay it.—*Hannah More.*

TRUST.
Take special care that thou never trust any friend or servant with any matter that may endanger thine estate ; for so shalt thou make thyself a bond-slave to him that thou trustest, and leave thyself always to his mercy.—
Sir Walter Raleigh.

The soul and spirit that animates and keeps up society is mutual trust.—*South.*

I think that we may safely trust a good deal more than we do. We may waive just so much care of ourselves as we honestly bestow elsewhere.—*Thoreau.*

The ordinary saying is, Count money after your father ; so the same prudence adviseth to measure the ends of all counsels, though uttered by never so intimate a friend.—
F. Osborn.

There is none deceived but he that trusts.—
Franklin.

Trust not any man with thy life, credit, or estate. For it is mere folly for a man to enthrall himself to his friend, as though, occasion being offered, he should not dare to become an enemy.—*Lord Burleigh.*

If thou be subject to any great vanity or ill (from which I hope God will bless thee), then therein trust no man; for every man's folly ought to be his greatest secret.—
Sir Walter Raleigh.

I can forgive a foe, but not a mistress and a friend; treason is there in its most horrid shape, where trust is greatest!—*Dryden.*

Let not the titles of consanguinity betray you into a prejudicial trust; no blood being apter to raise a fever, or cause a consumption sooner in your poor estate, than that which is nearest your own.—*F. Osborn.*

TRUTH.

Truth is as impossible to be soiled by any outward touch as the sunbeam.—*Milton.*

O man, little hast thou learnt of truth in things most true, and how therefore shall thy blindness wot of truth in things most fallen?—
Tupper.

Truth is only developed in the hour of need; time, and not man, discovers it.—*Bonald.*

As it has been finely expressed, " Principle is a passion for truth." And as an earlier and homelier writer hath it, " The truths we believe in are the pillars of our world."—*Bulwer Lytton.*

It is strange, but true; for truth is always strange, stranger than fiction.—*Byron.*

There are some faults slight in the sight of love, some errors slight in the estimate of wisdom; but truth forgives no insult, and endures no stain.—*Ruskin.*

Truth is too simple for us; we do not like those who unmask our illusions.—*Emerson.*

Truth, like the Venus de Medici, will pass down in thirty fragments to posterity; but posterity will collect and recompose them into a goddess.—*Richter.*

All truth contains an echo of sadness—
F. W. Trafford.

There are those who hold the opinion that truth is only safe when diluted, — about one fifth to four fifths lies, — as the oxygen of the air is with its nitrogen. Else it would burn us all up.—*Holmes.*

Truth is the shortest and nearest way to our end, carrying us thither in a straight line.—
Tillotson.

A writer who builds his arguments upon facts is not easily to be confuted. He is not to be answered by general assertions or general reproaches. He may want eloquence to amuse and persuade; but, speaking truth, he must always convince.—*Junius.*

Nothing is really beautiful but truth, and truth alone is lovely.—*Boileau.*

I am inclined to think that there is nothing more flattering than a naked truth, boldly uttered; but, all the same, those who can bear it are the rare exceptions in human nature.—
Madame Swetchine.

He who seeks the truth should be of no country.—*Voltaire.*

Truth is the band of union and the basis of human happiness. Without this virtue there is no reliance upon language, no confidence in friendship, no security in promises and oaths.—
Jeremy Collier.

The expression of truth is simplicity.—
Seneca.

Truth does not consist in minute accuracy of detail, but in conveying a right impression; and there are vague ways of speaking that are truer than strict facts would be. When the Psalmist said, " Rivers of water run down mine eyes, because men keep not thy law," he did not state the fact, but he stated a truth deeper than fact and truer.—*Dean Alford.*

There are few persons to whom truth is not a sort of insult.—*Ségur.*

Truth has no gradations; nothing which admits of increase can be so much what it is, as truth is truth. There may be a strange thing, and a thing more strange. But if a proposition be true, there can be none more true.—*Johnson.*

Truth is a queen who has her eternal throne in heaven, and her seat of empire in the heart of God.—*Bossuet.*

Truth is tough. It will not break, like a bubble, at a touch; nay, you may kick it about all day, like a football, and it will be round and full at evening. Does not Mr. Bryant say that Truth gets well if she is run over by a locomotive, while Error dies of lockjaw if she scratches her finger?—*Holmes.*

The greatest truths are commonly the simplest.—*Malesherbes.*

When the truth offends no one it should come from our lips as naturally as the air we breathe.—*Stanislaus.*

Abstract truth is the eye of reason.—
Rousseau.

In all new truths, or renovation of old truths, it must be as in the ark between the destroyed and the about-to-be-renovated world. The raven must be sent out before the dove, and ominous controversy must precede peace and the olive-wreath.—*Coleridge.*

34

He that speaks the truth will find himself in sufficiently dramatic situations.—
Professor Wilson.

Some people look upon truth as an invalid, who can only take the air in a close carriage, with a gentleman in a black coat on the box.—
Holmes.

Truths are first clouds, then rain, then harvest and food.—*Beecher.*

Every newly discovered truth judges the world, separates the good from the evil, and calls on faithful souls to make sure of their election.—*Julia Ward Howe.*

No pleasure is comparable to the standing upon the vantage-ground of truth.—*Bacon.*

If you can but give to the fainting soul at your door a cup of water from the wells of truth, it shall flash back on you the radiance of God. As you save, so shall you be saved.—
Conway.

I will be mindful of the truth, so long as I shall be able. Mayest thou grant me the truth, tell me the best to be done.—*Zend Avesta.*

Receiving a new truth is adding a new sense.—*Liebig.*

. After all, the most natural beauty in the world is honesty and moral truth; for all beauty is truth. True features make the beauty of a face, and true proportions the beauty of architecture, as true measures that of harmony and music. In poetry, which is all fable, truth still is the perfection.—*Shaftesbury.*

General abstract truth is the most precious of all blessings; without it, man is blind; it is the eye of reason.—*Rousseau.*

Truth is the ground of science, the centre wherein all things repose, and is the type of eternity.—*Sir P. Sidney.*

Truth is a gem that is found at a great depth; whilst on the surface of this world all things are weighed by the false scale of custom.
Byron.

"Truth," I cried, "though the heavens crush me for following her; no falsehood, though a whole celestial Lubberland were the price of apostasy!"—*Carlyle.*

Seven years of silent inquiry are needful for a man to learn the truth, but fourteen in order to learn how to make it known to his fellowmen.—*Plato.*

Of all the duties, the love of truth, with faith and constancy in it, ranks first and highest. Truth is God. To love God and to love truth are one and the same.—*Silvio Pellico.*

All men wish to have truth on their side; but few to be on the side of truth.—*Whately.*

Weigh not so much what men say, as what they prove; remembering that truth is simple and naked, and needs not invective to apparel her comeliness.—*Sir P. Sidney.*

Truth, whether in or out of fashion, is the measure of knowledge, and the business of the understanding; whatever is besides that, however authorized by consent, or recommended by rarity, is nothing but ignorance, or something worse.—*Locke.*

Truth may be stretched, but cannot be broken, and always gets above falsehood, as oil does above water.—*Cervantes.*

Truth, like the juice of the poppy, in small quantities, calms men; in larger, heats and irritates them, and is attended by fatal consequences in its excess.—*Landor.*

Truth is truth, though from an enemy, and spoken in malice.—*G. Lillo.*

Certainly, truth should be strenuous and bold; but the strongest things are not always the noisiest, as any one may see who compares scolding with logic.—*Chapin.*

Blessed be the God's voice; for it is true, and falsehoods have to cease before it!—
Carlyle.

According to Democritus, truth lies at the bottom of a well, the depth of which, alas! gives but little hope of release. To be sure, one advantage is derived from this, that the water serves for a mirror, in which truth may be reflected. I have heard, however, that some philosophers, in seeking for truth, to pay homage to her, have seen their own image and adored it instead.—*Richter.*

Truth comes home to the mind so naturally that when we learn it for the first time, it seems as though we did no more than recall it to our memory.—*Fontenelle.*

For all the practical purposes of life, truth might as well be in a prison as in the folio of a schoolman; and those who release her from the cobwebbed shelf, and teach her to live with men, have the merit of liberating, if not of discovering her.—*Colton.*

It is commonly said that truth is often eclipsed, but never extinguished.—*Livy.*

Truth and justice are the immutable laws of social order. Far from us be the dangerous maxim, that it is sometimes useful to mislead, to enslave, and to deceive mankind, to insure their happiness. Cruel experience has at all times proved that with impunity these sacred laws can never be injured.—*Laplace.*

Argument may be overcome by stronger argument, and force by greater force; but truth and force have no relation, — nothing in common, nothing by which the one can act upon the other. They dwell apart, and will continue to do so till the end of time.—*Pascal.*

Truth has not such an urgent air.—*Boileau.*

Truth is a good dog; but beware of barking too close to the heels of an error, lest you get your brains kicked out.—*Coleridge.*

The language of truth is simple.—*Euripides.*

Truth lies in a small compass! The Aristotelians say, all truth is contained in Aristotle, in one place or another. Galileo makes Simplicius say so, but shows the absurdity of that speech by answering, all truth is contained in a lesser compass, namely, in the alphabet.— *Zimmermann.*

What we have in us of the image of God is the love of truth and justice.—*Demosthenes.*

Truth is the object of our understanding, as good is of our will; and the understanding can no more be delighted with a lie than the will can choose an apparent evil.—*Dryden.*

Endless is the search of truth.—*Sterne.*

He that opposes his own judgment against the consent of the times ought to be backed with unanswerable truths; and he that has truth on his side is a fool, as well as a coward, if he is afraid to own it because of the currency or multitude of other men's opinions.—*De Foe.*

Truth is truth to the end of reckoning.— *Shakespeare.*

Truth makes on the ocean of nature no one track of light; every eye, looking on, finds its own.—*Bulwer Lytton.*

Truth is always straightforward.—*Sophocles.*

Truth is the most powerful thing in the world, since even fiction itself must be governed by it, and can only please by its resemblance. The appearance of reality is necessary to make any passion agreeably represented, and to be able to move others we must be moved ourselves, or at least seem to be so, upon some probable grounds.—*Shaftesbury.*

Truth needs no color; beauty, no pencil.— *Shakespeare.*

Truth, like medicine, must be qualified for the weak and infantine.—*Zimmermann.*

Some men are more beholden to their bitterest enemies than to friends who appear to be sweetness itself. The former frequently tell the truth, but the latter never.—*Cato.*

The usefullest truths are plainest; and while we keep to them, our differences cannot rise high.—*William Penn.*

Pure truth, like pure gold, has been found unfit for circulation, because men have discovered that it is far more convenient to adulterate the truth than to refine themselves. They will not advance their minds to the standard, therefore they lower the standard to their minds.—*Colton.*

Truth, though it always lies between two extremes, does not always lie in the middle.— *Niebuhr.*

The triumphs of truth are the most glorious, chiefly because they are the most bloodless of all victories, deriving their highest lustre from the number of the saved, not of the slain. *Colton.*

The smallest pebble in the well of truth has its peculiar meaning, and will stand when man's best monuments have passed away.— *Willis.*

It is dangerous to follow Truth too near, lest she should kick out our teeth! — *Sir Walter Raleigh.*

You need not tell all the truth, unless to those who have a right to know it all. But let all you tell be truth.—*Horace Mann.*

Don't be "consistent," but be simply true. *Holmes.*

The greatest truths are wronged if not linked with beauty, and they win their way most surely and deeply into the soul, when arranged in this their natural and fit attire.— *Channing.*

The golden beams of truth and the silken cords of love, twisted together, will draw men on with a sweet violence whether they will or no.—*Cudworth.*

The confusion and undesigned inaccuracy so often to be observed in conversation, especially in that of uneducated persons, proves that truth needs to be cultivated as a talent, as well as recommended as a virtue.—*Mrs. Fry.*

Truth needs no flowers of speech.—*Pope.*

Liars act like the salt miners; they undermine the truth, but leave just so much standing as is necessary to support the edifice.—*Richter.*

Truth is always consistent with itself, and needs nothing to help it out. It is always near at hand, and sits upon our lips, and is ready to drop out before we are aware; whereas a lie is troublesome, and set a man's invention upon the rack; and one trick needs a great many more to make it good.—*Tillotson.*

Truth and reason are common to every one, and are no more his who spake them first than his who speaks them after.—*Montaigne.*

One of the sublimest things in the world is plain truth.—*Bulwer Lytton.*

Theory is continually the precursor of truth; we must pass through the twilight and its shade, to arrive at the full and perfect day.—
James Douglas.

The dignity of truth is lost with much protesting.—*Ben Jonson.*

The love of truth is the stimulus to all noble conversation. This is the root of all the charities. The tree which springs from it may have a thousand branches, but they will all bear a golden and generous fruitage.—*Orville Dewey.*

Truth irritates those only whom it enlightens, but does not convert.—*Pasquier Quesnel.*

A man has no more right to utter untruths to his own disparagement than to his own praise. Truth is absolute. It is obligatory under all circumstances, and in all relations.—
Dr. Kitto.

Nature loves truth so well, that it hardly ever admits of flourishing.—*Pope.*

Truths of all others the most awful and interesting are too often considered as so true that they lose all the power of truth, and lie bed-ridden in the dormitory of the soul, side by side with the most despised and exploded errors.—*Coleridge.*

The face of Truth is not less fair and beautiful for all the counterfeit visors which have been put upon her.—*Shaftesbury.*

We want such an access of truth that the general mind can be fed with a worthier conception of God, which will make every thought of him inspiring as the dawn of the morning, and will banish the superstition that this life is the final state of probation as an insult to his plan of eternal education and a chimera of a barbarous age.—*Thomas Starr King.*

Truth itself shall lose its credit, if delivered by a person that has none.—*South.*

Love of truth will bless the lover all his days; yet when he brings her home, his fair-faced-bride, she comes empty-handed to his door, herself her only dower.—*Theodore Parker.*

If an offence come out of the truth, better is it that the offence come, than the truth be concealed.—*St. Jerome.*

Some modern zealots appear to have no better knowledge of truth, nor better manner of judging it, than by counting noses.—*Swift.*

Truth can hardly be expected to adapt herself to the crooked policy and wily sinuosities of worldly affairs; for truth, like light, travels only in straight lines.—*Colton.*

Truth is so great a perfection, that if God would render himself visible to men, he would choose light for his body and truth for his soul.
Pythagoras.

It is not enough that we swallow truth; we must feed upon it, as insects do on the leaf, till the whole heart be colored by its qualities, and show its food in every fibre.—*Coleridge.*

Truth is a torch, but a terrific one; therefore we all try to reach it with closed eyes, lest we should be scorched.—*Goethe.*

A truth which one has never heard causes the soul surprise at first, which touches it keenly; but when it is accustomed to it, it becomes very insensible there.—*Nicole.*

Truth hath a quiet breast.—*Shakespeare.*

The man who loves with his whole heart truth will love still more he who suffers for truth.—*Lavater.*

In all nations truth is the most sublime, the most simple, the most difficult, and yet the most natural thing.—*Madame de Sévigné.*

The jealous keys of truth's eternal doors. —
Shelley.

Truth is a naked and open daylight, that doth not show the masks and mummeries of the world half so stately and daintily as candle-lights.—*Bacon.*

Truth, like the sun, submits to be obscured, but only for a time.—*Bovee.*

Each truth sparkles with a light of its own, yet it always reflects some light upon another; a truth, while lighting another, springs from one, in order to penetrate another. The first truth is an abundant sense, from which all others are colored, and each particular truth, in its turn, resembles a great river that divides into an infinite number of rivulets.—*Scheuchzer.*

Truth is born with us; and we must do violence to nature, to shake off our veracity —
St. Evremond.

There is small chance of truth at the goal, where there is not childlike humility at the starting-post.—*Coleridge.*

Truth will be uppermost one time or another, like cork, though kept down in the water.—
Sir W. Temple.

Truly, I see he that will but stand to the truth, it will carry him out.—*George Fox.*

Avoid situations which put our duties in opposition with our interests, and which show us our good in the misfortunes of others ; sure that in such situations, whatever sincere love of virtue we have, we weaken sooner or later, without perceiving it, and we become unjust and deceitful in deed, without having ceased to be just and good in the soul.—*Rousseau.*

Truth hath better deeds than words to grace it.—*Shakespeare.*

As any one may bring himself to believe almost anything that he is inclined to believe, it makes all the difference whether we begin or end with the inquiry, What is truth ? — *Whately.*

Truth, like roses, often blossoms upon a thorny stem.—*Hafiz.*

Ah, if we would but pledge ourselves to truth as heartily as we do to a real or imaginary mistress, and think life too short only because it abridges our time of service, what a new world we should have ! —*Lowell.*

There is no right faith in believing what is true, unless we believe it because it is true.— *Whately.*

If new-got gold is said to burn the pockets till it be cast forth into circulation, much more may new truth.— *Carlyle.*

TWILIGHT.

As twilight melts beneath the moon away. *Byron.*

What heart has not acknowledged the influence of this hour, the sweet and soothing hour of twilight, the hour of love, the hour of adoration, the hour of rest, when we think of those we love only to regret that we have not loved them more dearly, when we remember our enemies only to forgive them.—*Longfellow.*

Hail, twilight ! sovereign of one peaceful hour ! — *Wordsworth.*

A tender sadness drops upon my soul, like the soft twilight dropping on the world.— *Alexander Smith.*

The curfew tolls the knell of parting day.— *Gray.*

How beautiful the silent hour, when morning and evening thus sit together, hand in hand, beneath the starless sky of midnight ! — *Longfellow.*

It was the time that wakes desire, and melts the heart of voyagers, when they have that day bid farewell to their dear friends, and that thrills the pilgrim newly on his way with love, if he from far hears the vesper-bell, that seems to mourn the dying day.—*Dante.*

How dear to my soul is the mild twilight hour ! —*Moore.*

Twilight hour ! whose mantle is the drapery of dreams, and who hast ever been in poetry life's holy time ; thou who wert wont to steal upon us, as thy sandals were of dew ! how sadly comes the rustle of thy step, in the decaying seasons of the year ! — *Willis.*

Nature hath appointed the twilight as a bridge to pass us out of night into day.—*Fuller.*

TYPE.

I like the click of the type in the composing-stick of the compositor better than the click of the musket in the hands of the soldier. It bears a leaden messenger of deadlier power, of sublimer force, and of a surer aim, which will hit its mark, though it is a thousand years ahead ! — *Chapin.*

TYRANNY.

Tyranny and anarchy are never far asunder. *Bentham.*

An extreme rigor is sure to arm everything against it, and at length to relax into a supine neglect.—*Burke.*

I have heard politicians and coffee-house wiseacres talking over the newspaper and railing at the tyranny of the emperor, and wondered how these, who are monarchs too in their way, govern their own dominions at home, where each man rules absolute. When the annals of each little reign are shown the Supreme Master under whom we hold sovereignty, histories will be laid bare of household tyrants cruel as Amurath, savage as Nero, and reckless and dissolute as Charles.—*Thackeray.*

Hardness ever of hardness is mother.— *Shakespeare.*

The lust of dominion innovates so imperceptibly that we become complete despots before our wanton abuse of power is perceived ; the tyranny first exercised in the nursery is exhibited in various shapes and degrees in every stage of our existence.—*Zimmermann.*

A great deal of the furniture of ancient tyranny is torn to rags ; the rest is entirely out of fashion.—*Burke.*

The framers of preventive laws, no less than private tutors and schoolmasters, should remember that the readiest way to make either mind or body grow awry is by lacing it too tight.— *Coleridge.*

He who strikes terror into others is himself in continual fear.— *Claudian.*

Every wanton and causeless restraint of the will of the subject, whether practised by a monarch, a nobility, or a popular assembly, is a degree of tyranny.—*Blackstone.*

Free governments have committed more flagrant acts of tyranny than the most perfect despotic governments which we have ever known.
Burke.

Tyranny, in a word, is a farce got up for the entertainment of poor human nature; and it might pass very well if it did not so often turn into a tragedy.—*Hazlitt.*

Power exercised with violence has seldom been of long duration, but temper and moderation generally produce permanence in all things.
Seneca.

Power, unless managed with gentleness and discretion, does but make a man the more hated. No intervals of good-humor, no starts of bounty, will atone for tyranny and oppression.—
Jeremy Collier.

Hateful is the power, and pitiable is the life, of those who wish to be feared rather than to be loved.—*Cornelius Nepos.*

It is strange to see the unmanlike cruelty of mankind, who, not content with their tyrannous ambition to have brought the others' virtuous patience under them, think their masterhood nothing without doing injury to them.—
Sir P. Sidney.

It is a wicked and cowardly thing to attempt to rule the spirit by the flesh.—
F. W. Robertson.

There is a natural and necessary progression, from the extreme of anarchy to the extreme of tyranny; and arbitrary power is most easily established on the ruins of liberty abused to licentiousness.—*Washington.*

Tyranny sways, not as it hath power, but as it is suffered.—*Shakespeare.*

It is worthy of observation that the most imperious masters over their own servants are at the same time the most abject slaves to the servants of other masters.—*Seneca.*

U.

UGLINESS.

Absolute ugliness is admitted as rarely as perfect beauty; but degrees of it, more or less distinct, are associated with whatever has the nature of death and sin, just as beauty is associated with what has the nature of virtue and of life.—*Ruskin.*

Ugliness without tact is horrible. It ought to be lawful to extirpate such wretches.—
Hawthorne.

UNBELIEF.

How deeply rooted must unbelief be in our hearts, when we are surprised to find our prayers answered, instead of feeling sure that they will be so, if they are only offered up in faith, and accord with the will of God!—*Hare.*

There is but one thing without honor, smitten with eternal barrenness, inability to do or to be, — insincerity, unbelief. He who believes nothing, who believes only the shows of things, is not in relation with nature and fact at all.—
Carlyle.

UNCERTAINTY.

All that lies betwixt the cradle and the grave is uncertain.—*Seneca.*

Delude not yourself with the notion that you may be untrue and uncertain in trifles and in important things the contrary. Trifles make up existence, and give the observer the measure by which to try us; and the fearful power of habit, after a time, suffers not the best will to ripen into action.—*C. M. von Weber.*

Uncertainty! fell demon of our fears! The human soul, that can support despair, supports not thee.—*Mallet.*

UNCOUTHNESS.

To reject wisdom because the person who communicates it is uncouth and his manners are inelegant, what is it but to throw away a pine-apple, and assign for a reason the roughness of its coat?—*Bishop Horne.*

UNDERSTANDING.

I know no evil so great as the abuse of the understanding, and yet there is no one vice more common.—*Steele.*

The defects of the understanding, like those of the face, grow worse as we grow old.—
Rochefoucauld.

It is not the eye, that sees the beauty of the heaven, nor the ear, that hears the sweetness of music or the glad tidings of a prosperous accident, but the soul, that perceives all the relishes of sensual and intellectual perfections; and the more noble and excellent the soul is, the greater and more savory are its perceptions.—
Jeremy Taylor.

The light of the understanding, humility kindleth and pride covereth.—*Quarles.*

It is the same with understanding as with eyes; to a certain size and make, just so much light is necessary, and no more. Whatever is beyond brings darkness and confusion.—
Shaftesbury.

He who calls in the aid of an equal understanding doubles his own; and he who profits of a superior understanding raises his powers to a level with the height of the superior understanding he unites with.—*Burke.*

It is not proper to understand the intelligible with vehemence, but if you incline your mind, you will apprehend it; not too earnestly, but bringing a pure and inquiring eye. You will not understand it as when understanding some particular thing, but with the flower of the mind. Things divine are not attainable by mortals who understand sensual things, but only the light-armed arrive at the summit.—
Zoroaster.

The improvement of the understanding is for two ends : first, our own increase of knowledge ; secondly, to enable us to deliver and make out that knowledge to others.—*Locke.*

UNDERTAKING.

Whatever situation in life you ever wish or propose for yourself, acquire a clear and lucid idea of the inconveniences attending it.—
Shenstone.

UNEASINESS.

Men tire themselves in pursuit of rest.—
Sterne.

Generally we are occupied either with the miseries which now we feel, or with those which threaten ; and even when we see ourselves sufficiently secure from the approach of either, still fretfulness, though unwarranted by either present or expected affliction, fails not to spring up from the deep recesses of the heart, where its roots naturally grow, and to fill the soul with its poison.—*Pascal.*

Is it not astonishing that the love of repose keeps us in continual agitation ? —*Stanislaus.*

UNFAITHFULNESS.

There is not so agonizing a feeling in the whole catalogue of human suffering ·as the first conviction that the heart of the being whom we most tenderly love is estranged from us.—
Bulwer Lytton.

Such an act takes off the rose from the fair forehead of an innocent love, and sets a blister there.—*Shakespeare.*

The unfaithful woman, if she is known for such by the person concerned, is only unfaithful. If she is thought faithful, she is perfidious.
Bruyère.

There is no trust, no faith, no honesty in men ; all perjured, all forsworn, all naught, all dissemblers.—*Shakespeare.*

UNFORTUNATE.

It is not becoming to turn from friends in adversity, but then it is for those who have basked in the sunshine of their prosperity to adhere to them. No one was ever so foolish as to select the unfortunate for a friend.—*Lucan.*

The brave unfortunate are our best acquaintance.—*Francis.*

UNGRATEFULNESS.

Ungratefulness is the very poison of manhood.—*Sir P. Sidney.*

UNHAPPINESS.

When men are unhappy, they do not imagine they can ever cease to be so ; and when some calamity has fallen on them, they do not see how they can get rid of it. Nevertheless, both arrive ; and the gods have ordered it so, in the end men seek it from the gods.—*Epictetus.*

The most unhappy of all men is he who believes himself to be so.—*Henry Home.*

Let us think sometimes upon unhappiness as we think of the character of persons with whom we find ourselves obliged to associate for a day. Reflection gives an anticipated experience ; it gives unhappiness the air of novelty which renders it appalling.—*Droz.*

But a perverse temper and fretful disposition will, wherever they prevail, render any state of life whatsoever unhappy.—*Cicero.*

Man's unhappiness, as I construe, comes of his greatness ; it is because there is an infinite in him, which with all his cunning he cannot quite bury under the finite.—*Carlyle.*

UNION.

The multitude which does not reduce itself to unity is confusion ; the unity which does not depend upon the multitude is tyranny.—
Pascal.

I know that there is one God in heaven, the Father of all humanity, and heaven is therefore one. I know that there is one sun in the sky, which gives light to all the world. As there is unity in God, and unity in the light, so is there unity in the principles of freedom. Wherever it is broken, wherever a shadow is cast upon the sunny rays of the sun of liberty, there is always danger to free principles everywhere in the world.—*Kossuth.*

Men's hearts ought not to be set against one another, but set with one another, and all against the evil thing only.—*Carlyle.*

When all move together, nothing moves in appearance, as in a vessel. When everything tends to disorder, nothing seems to get out of place. He who stops to remark upon the conduct of others is like a fixed point.—*Pascal.*

Union does everything when it is perfect ; it satisfies desires, it simplifies needs, it foresees the wishes of the imagination ; it is an aisle always open, and becomes a constant fortune.—
De Sénancour.

I do not want the walls of separation between different orders of Christians to be destroyed, but only lowered, that we may shake hands a little easier over them.—*Rowland Hill.*

UNKINDNESS.

More hearts pine away in secret anguish for unkindness from those who should be their comforters than for any other calamity in life.
Young.

As "unkindness has no remedy at law," let its avoidance be with you a point of honor.—
Hosea Ballou.

He who has once stood beside the grave, to look back upon the companionship which has been forever closed, feeling how impotent there are the wild love, or the keen sorrow, to give one instant's pleasure to the pulseless heart, or atone in the lowest measure to the departed spirit for the hour of unkindness, will scarcely for the future incur that debt to the heart which can only be discharged to the dust.—*Ruskin.*

She hath tied sharp-toothed unkindness, like a vulture here.—*Shakespeare.*

Unkind language is sure to produce the fruits of unkindness,—that is, suffering in the bosom of others.—*Bentham.*

UNSEASONABLENESS.

Uttered out of time, or concealed in its season, good savoreth of evil.—*Tupper.*

USE.

Use almost can change the stamp of nature.
Shakespeare.

Use is the judge, the law and rule of speech.
Roscommon.

USEFULNESS.

A cock, having found a pearl, said that a grain of corn would be of more value to him.—
Fierre Leroux.

Have I done anything for society? I have then done more for myself. Let that truth be always present to thy mind, and work without cessation.—*Simms.*

Thousands of men breathe, move, and live; pass off the stage of life and are heard of no more. Why? They did not a particle of good in the world; and none were blest by them, none could point to them as the instrument of their redemption; not a line they wrote, not a word they spoke, could be recalled, and so they perished,—their light went out in darkness, and they were not remembered more than the insects of yesterday. Will you thus live and die, O man immortal? Live for something.—
Chalmers.

The useful and the beautiful are never separated.—*Periander.*

We live in a world which is full of misery and ignorance, and the plain duty of each and all of us is to try to make the little corner he can influence somewhat less miserable and somewhat less ignorant than it was before he entered it. To do this effectually, it is necessary to be fully possessed of only two beliefs: the first, that the order of nature is ascertainable by our faculties to an extent which is practically unlimited; the second, that our volition counts for something as a condition of the course of events.—
Professor Huxley.

USURER.

A money-lender,—he serves you in the present tense; he lends you in the conditional mood; keeps you in the subjunctive; and ruins you in the future!—*Addison.*

Go not to a covetous old man with any request too soon in the morning, before he hath taken his day's prey; for his covetousness is up before him, and he before thee, and he is in ill-humor; but stay till the afternoon, till he be satiated upon some borrower.—*Fuller.*

UTILITY.

Of all parts of wisdom, the practice is the best. Socrates was esteemed the wisest man of his time because he turned his acquired knowledge into morality, and aimed at goodness more than greatness.—*Tillotson.*

V.

VAGRANT.

Beware of those who are homeless by choice! You have no hold on a human being whose affections are without a tap-root!—*Southey.*

VAIN-GLORY.

Some intermixture of vain-glorious tempers puts life into business, and makes a fit composition in grand enterprises and hazardous undertakings. For men of solid and sober natures have more of the ballast than the sail.—*Bacon.*

The vain-glory of this world is a deceitful sweetness, a fruitless labor, a perpetual fear, a dangerous honor; her beginning is without Providence, and her end not without repentance.—*Quarles.*

VALOR.

Fear to do base, unworthy things is valor; if they be done to us, to suffer them is valor too.
Ben Jonson.

No man can answer for his own valor or courage, till he has been in danger.—
Rochefoucauld.

I love the man that is modestly valiant; that stirs not till he most needs, and then to purpose. A continued patience I commend not.—*Feltham.*

There is no love-broker in the world can more prevail in man's commendation with woman than report of valor.—*Shakespeare.*

The truly valiant dare everything, but doing any other body an injury.—*Sir P. Sidney.*

The love of glory, the fear of shame, the design of making a fortune, the desire of rendering life easy and agreeable, and the humor of pulling down other people, are often the causes of that valor so celebrated among men.
—*Rochefoucauld.*

Valor is the contempt of death and pain.—*Tacitus.*

The mean of true valor lies between the extremes of cowardice and rashness.—*Cervantes.*

Whatever comes out of despair cannot bear the title of valor, which should be lifted up to such a height, that holding all things under itself, it should be able to maintain its greatness, even in the midst of miseries.—*Sir P. Sidney.*

Perfect valor is to do unwitnessed what we should be capable of doing before all the world.
—*Rochefoucauld.*

It is held that valor is the chiefest virtue, and most dignifies the haver.—*Shakespeare.*

It is said of untrue valors that some men's valors are in the eyes of them that look on.—*Bacon.*

Valor is abased by too much loftiness.—*Sir P. Sidney.*

Valor hath its bounds, as well as other virtues, which once transgressed, the next step is into the territories of vice, so that, by having too large a proportion of this heroic virtue, unless a man be very perfect in its limits, which upon the confines are very hard to discern, he may unawares run into temerity, obstinacy, and folly.—*Montaigne.*

Valor would cease to be a virtue, if there were no injustice.—*Agesilaus.*

VANITY.

Vanity indeed is a venial error; for it usually carries its own punishment with it.—*Junius.*

Every man's vanity ought to be his greatest shame; and every man's folly ought to be his greatest secret.—*Quarles.*

It was prettily devised of Æsop, the fly sat upon the axletree of the chariot-wheel, and said, "What a dust do I raise!" So are there some vain persons that, whatsoever goeth alone or moveth upon greater means, if they have never so little hand in it, they think it is they that carry it.—*Bacon.*

Alas, for human nature that the wounds of vanity should smart and bleed so much longer than the wounds of affection!—*Macaulay.*

Vanity is so anchored in the heart of man that a soldier, suttler, cook, street porter, vapor and wish to have their admirers; and philosophers even wish the same. And those who write against it wish to have the glory of having written well; and those who read it wish to have the glory of having read well; and I, who write this, have perhaps this desire; and perhaps those who will read this.—*Pascal.*

O, how true it is there can be no *tête-à-tête* where vanity reigns!—*Madame de Girardin:*

Vanity is the foundation of the most ridiculous and contemptible vices, — the vices of affectation and common lying!—*Adam Smith.*

The soul of this man is in his clothes.—*Shakespeare.*

We are so presumptuous that we wish to be known to all the world, even to those who come after us; and we are so vain that the esteem of five or six persons immediately around us is enough to amuse and satisfy us.—*Pascal.*

What fervent love of herself would Virtue excite if she could be seen!—*Cicero.*

Here Vanity assumes her pert grimace.—*Goldsmith.*

Vanity bids all her sons be brave, and all her daughters chaste and courteous. But why do we need her instructions? Ask the comedian who is taught a part which he does not feel.
—*Sterne.*

Vanity is never at its full growth, till it spreadeth into affectation; and then it is complete.—*Saville.*

Vanity calculates but poorly on the vanity of others; what a virtue we should distil from frailty, what a world of pain we should save our brethren, if we would suffer our own weakness to be the measure of theirs.—*Bulwer Lytton.*

It is difficult to divest one's self of vanity, because impossible to divest one's self of self-love.—*Horace Walpole.*

To be vain is rather a mark of humility than pride.—*Swift.*

O vanity, how little is thy force acknowledged or thy operations discerned! How wantonly dost thou deceive mankind under different disguises! Sometimes thou dost wear the face of pity; sometimes of generosity; nay, thou hast the assurance to put on those glorious ornaments which belong only to heroic virtue.—*Fielding.*

Vanity, indeed, is the very antidote to conceit; for while the former makes us all nerve to the opinion of others, the latter is perfectly satisfied with its opinion of itself.—*Bulwer Lytton.*

I give vanity fair quarter, wherever I meet with it, being persuaded that it is often productive of good to the possessor, and to others who are within his sphere of action ; and therefore, in many cases, it would not be altogether absurd if a man were to thank God for his vanity, among the other comforts of life.—*Franklin.*

Vain is the world, but only to the vain.—
Young.

When we are conscious of the least comparative merit in ourselves, we should take as much care to conceal the value we set upon it, as if it were a real defect ; to be elated or vain upon it is showing your money before people in want.—
Colley Cibber.

Every present occasion will catch the senses of the vain man ; and with that bridle and saddle you may ride him.—*Sir P. Sidney.*

Vanity keeps persons in favor with themselves, who are out of favor with all others.—
Shakespeare.

Charms which, like flowers, lie on the surface and always glitter easily produce vanity ; hence women, wits, players, soldiers, are vain, owing to their presence, figure, and dress. On the contrary, other excellences, which lie down like gold, and are discovered with difficulty, — strength, profoundness of intellect, morality, — leave their possessors modest and proud.—
Richter.

Every man has just as much vanity as he wants understanding.—*Pope.*

A weakness natural to superior and to little men, when they have committed a fault, is to wish to make it pass as a work of genius, a vast combination which the vulgar cannot comprehend. Pride says these things and folly credits them.—*Chateaubriand.*

A golden mind stoops not to shows of dross.
Shakespeare.

People who are very vain are usually equally susceptible ; and they who feel one thing acutely, will so feel another.—*Bulwer Lytton.*

Virtue would not go far, if vanity did not keep it company.—*Rochefoucauld.*

Pride is never more offensive than when it condescends to be civil ; whereas vanity, whenever it forgets itself, naturally assumes good-humor.—*Cumberland.*

Thy pride is but the prologue of thy shame ; where vain-glory commands, there folly counsels ; where pride rides, there shame lackeys.—
Quarles.

Our vanity is the constant enemy of our dignity.—*Madame Swetchine.*

Scarcely have I ever heard or read the introductory phrase, "I may say without vanity," but some striking and characteristic instance of vanity has immediately followed.—*Franklin.*

Not a vanity is given in vain.—*Pope.*

Tell me not of the pain of falsehood to the slandered ! There is nothing so agonizing to the fine skin of vanity as the application of a rough truth.—*Bulwer Lytton.*

Vanity makes men ridiculous, pride odious, and ambition terrible.—*Steele.*

Vanity may be likened to the smooth-skinned and velvet-footed mouse, nibbling about forever in expectation of a crumb ; while self-esteem is too apt to take the likeness of the huge butcher's dog, who carries off your steaks, and growls at you as he goes.—*Simms.*

To be a man's own fool is bad enough ; but the vain man is everybody's.—
William Penn.

Vanity is a strong temptation to lying ; it makes people magnify their merit, over flourish their family, and tell strange stories of their interest and acquaintance.—*Jeremy Collier.*

There is much money given to be laughed at, though the purchasers don't know it ; witness A.'s fine horse, and B.'s fine house.—
Franklin.

Every one at the bottom of his heart cherishes vanity ; even the toad thinks himself good-looking, — "rather tawny perhaps, but look at his eye ! "—*Wilson.*

There is more jealousy between rival wits than rival beauties, for vanity has no sex. But in both cases there must be pretensions, or there will be no jealousy.—*Colton.*

Vanity of vanities, saith the preacher, vanity of vanities ; all is vanity.—*Bible.*

Does not vanity itself cease to be blamable, is it not even ennobled, when it is directed to laudable objects, when it confines itself to prompting us to great and generous actions ? —
Diderot.

Verily every man at his best state is altogether vanity.—*Bible.*

Extinguish vanity in the mind, and you naturally retrench the little superfluities of garniture and equipage. The blossoms will fall of themselves when the root that nourishes them is destroyed.—*Steele.*

There is no vice or folly that requires so much nicety and skill to manage as vanity ; nor any which by ill management makes so contemptible a figure.—*Swift.*

There is no folly of which a man who is not a fool cannot get rid except vanity; of this nothing cures a man except experience of its bad consequences, if indeed anything can cure it.— *Rousseau.*

A vain man can never be altogether rude. Desirous as he is of pleasing, he fashions his manners after those of others.— *Goethe.*

When men will not be reasoned out of a vanity, they must be ridiculed out of it.— *L'Estrange.*

Vanity is the natural weakness of an ambitious man, which exposes him to the secret scorn and derision of those he converses with, and ruins the character he is so industrious to advance by it.— *Addison.*

The vanity of human life is like a river, constantly passing away, and yet constantly coming on.— *Pope.*

· Vanity finds in self-love so powerful an ally that it storms, as it were, by a *coup de main*, the citadel of our heads, where, having blinded the two watchmen, it readily descends into the heart.— *Colton.·*

Vanity is omnivorous.— *Burke.*

If you cannot inspire a woman with love of you, fill her above the brim with love of herself; all that runs over will be yours.— *Colton*

If most married women possessed as much prudence as they do vanity, we should find many husbands far happier.— *Belknap.*

It is our own vanity that makes the vanity of others intolerable to us.— *Rochefoucauld.*

The general cry is against ingratitude, but sure the complaint is misplaced, it should be against vanity. None but direct villains are capable of wilful ingratitude; but almost everybody is capable of thinking he hath done more than another deserves, while the other thinks he hath received less than he deserves.— *Pope.*

In a vain man, the smallest spark may kindle into the greatest flame, because the materials are always prepared for it.— *Hume.*

When a man has no longer any conception of excellence above his own, his voyage is done, he is dead, — dead in trespasses and sin of bleareyed vanity.— *Beecher.*

She neglects her heart who studies her glass. *Lavater.*

The youth who, like a woman, loves to adorn his person, has renounced all claim to wisdom and to glory; glory is due to those only who dare to associate with pain, and have trampled pleasure under their feet.— *Fenelon.*

Vanity and pride of nations; vanity is as advantageous to a government as pride is dangerous.— *Montesquieu.*

Men speak but little when vanity does not induce them to speak.— *Rochefoucauld.*

Ladies of fashion starve their happiness to feed their vanity, and their love to feed their pride.— *Colton.*

Vanity is so constantly solicitous of self, that, even where its own claims are not interested, it indirectly seeks the aliment which it loves, by showing how little is deserved by others.— *Simms.*

There is no restraining men's tongues or pens when charged with a little vanity.— *Washington.*

I would much rather fight pride than vanity, because pride has a stand-up way of fighting. You know where it is. It throws its black shadow on you, and you are not at a loss where to strike. But vanity is that delusive, that insectiferous, that multiplied feeling, and men that fight vanities are like men that fight midges and butterflies. It is easier to chase them than to hit them.— *Beecher.*

Never expect justice from a vain man; if he has the negative magnanimity not to disparage you, it is the most you can expect.— *Washington Allston.*

Vanity is so closely allied to virtue, and to love the fame of laudable actions approaches so near the love of laudable actions for their own sake, that these passions are more capable of mixture than any other kinds of affection; and it is almost impossible to have the latter without some degree of the former.— *Hume.*

If vanity does not entirely overthrow the virtues, at least it makes them all totter.— *Rochefoucauld.*

Extreme vanity sometimes hides under the garb of ultra modesty.— *Mrs. Jameson.*

VARIETY.

As land is improved by sowing it with various seeds, so is the mind by exercising it with different studies.— *Pliny.*

Variety is the very spice of life.— *Cowper.*

The most delightful pleasures cloy without variety.— *Publius Syrus.*

How nature delights and amuses us by varying even the character of insects; the illnature of the wasp, the sluggishness of the drone, the volatility of the butterfly, the slyness of the bug! — *Sydney Smith.*

I take it to be a principal rule of life, not to be too much addicted to any one thing.— *Terence.*

VEGETATION.

Every green thing loves to die in bright colors. The vegetable cohorts march glowing out of the year in flaming dresses, as if to leave this earth were a triumph and not a sadness. It is never nature that is sad, but only we, that dare not look back on the past, and that have not its prophecy of the future in our bosoms.—*Beecher.*

Every green herb, from the lotus to the darnel, is rich with delicate aids to help incurious man.—*Tupper.*

The earth is a machine which yields almost gratuitous service to every application of intellect. Every plant is a manufacturer of soil. In the stomach of the plant development begins. The tree can draw on the whole air, the whole earth, on all the rolling main. The plant is all suction-pipe, — imbibing from the ground by its root, from the air by its leaves, with all its might.—*Emerson.*

VENGEANCE.

Is it to be thought unreasonable that the people, in atonement for the wrongs of a century, demand the vengeance of a single day ?—*Robespierre.*

Vengeance has no foresight.—*Napoleon.*

If you have committed iniquity, you must expect to suffer ; for vengeance with its sacred light shines upon you.—*Sophocles.*

I shall see the wingèd vengeance overtake such children.—*Shakespeare.*

Vengeance comes not openly, either upon you or any wicked man, but steals silently and imperceptibly, placing its foot on the bad.—*Euripides.*

Deep vengeance is the daughter of deep silence.—*Alfieri.*

VICE.

Sloth has prevented as many vices in some minds, as virtues in others. Idleness is the grand Pacific Ocean of life, and in that stagnant abyss, the most salutary things produce no good, the most noxious no evil. Vice indeed, abstractedly considered, may be and often is engendered in idleness, but the moment it becomes efficiently vice, it must quit its cradle and cease to be idle.—*Colton.*

The vicious obey their passions, as slaves do their masters.—*Diogenes.*

Virtue seems to be nothing more than a motion consonant to the system of things ; were a planet to fly from its orbit, it would represent a vicious man.—*Shenstone.*

Many a man's vices have at first been nothing worse than good qualities run wild.—*Hare.*

I never heard yet that any of these bolder vices wanted less impudence to gainsay what they did, than to perform it first.—*Shakespeare.*

Vice stings us even in our pleasures, but virtue consoles us even in our pains.—*Cowper.*

What we call vice in our neighbor may be nothing less than a crude virtue. To him who knows nothing more of precious stones than he can learn from a daily contemplation of his breastpin, a diamond in the mine must be a very uncompromising sort of stone.—*Simms.*

What maintains one vice would bring up two children.—*Franklin.*

If people had no vices but their own, few would have so many as they have. For my own part, I would sooner wear other people's clothes than their vices ; and they would sit upon me just as well. I hope you will have none ; but, if ever you have, I beg at least, they may be all your own. Vices of adoption are, of all others, the most disgraceful and unpardonable.—*Chesterfield.*

No one is born without vices, and he is the best man who is encumbered with the least.—*Horace.*

When our vices have left us, we flatter ourselves that we have left them.—*Rochefoucauld.*

The martyrs to vice far exceed the martyrs to virtue, both in endurance and in number. So blinded are we by our passions, that we suffer more to be damned than to be saved.—*Colton.*

No man ever arrived suddenly at the summit of vice.—*Juvenal.*

Why is there no man who confesses his vices ? It is because he has not yet laid them aside. It is a waking man only who can tell his dreams.—*Seneca.*

Vice is but a nurse of agonies.—*Sir P. Sidney.*

Vices and frailties correct each other, like acids and alkalies. If each vicious man had but one vice, I do not know how the world could go on.—*Whately.*

A few vices are sufficient to darken many virtues.—*Plutarch.*

People do not persist in their vices because they are not weary of them, but because they cannot leave them off. It is the nature of vice to leave us no resource but in itself.—*Hazlitt.*

Vices are seldom single.—*Bishop Hall.*

Crimes sometimes shock us too much ; vices almost always too little.—*Hare.*

Vice, — that digs her own voluptuous tomb!
Byron.

It is but a step from companionship to slavery when one associates with vice.—
Hosea Ballou.

Say everything for vice which you can say, magnify any pleasure as much as you please, but don't believe you have any secret for sending on quicker the sluggish blood, and for refreshing the faded nerve.—*Sydney Smith.*

To attack vices in the abstract, without touching persons, may be safe fighting indeed, but it is fighting with shadows.—*Junius.*

What once were vices are now the manners of the day.—*Seneca.*

There will be nothing more that posterity can add to our immoral habits; our descendants must have the same desires and act the same follies as their sires. Every vice has reached its zenith.—*Juvenal.*

Vices are as well contrary to themselves as to virtue.—*Fuller.*

What often prevents our abandoning ourselves to a single vice is, our having more than one.—*Rochefoucauld.*

Vice itself lost half its evil, by losing all its grossness.—*Burke.*

The vices enter into the composition of the virtues, as poisons into that of medicines. Prudence collects and arranges them, and uses them beneficially against the ills of life.—
Rochefoucauld.

Vices that are familiar we pardon, and only new ones reprehend.—*Publius Syrus.*

It may be said that the vices await us in the journey of life like hosts with whom we must successively lodge; and I doubt whether experience would make us avoid them if we were to travel the same road a second time.—
Rochefoucauld.

There is no vice so simple, but assumes some mark of virtue on its outward parts.—
Shakespeare.

Though a man cannot abstain from being weak, he may from being vicious.—*Addison.*

A full mind is the true pantheism, *plena jovis.* It is only in some corner of the brain which we leave empty that Vice can obtain a lodging. When she knocks at your door, be able to say, "No room for your ladyship, — pass on."—*Bulwer Lytton.*

Vice is contagious, and there is no trusting the sound and the sick together.—*Seneca.*

Vice, like disease, floats in the atmosphere.
Hazlitt.

Vice gets more in this vicious world than piety.—*Fletcher.*

Vice is the greatest of all Jacobins, the arch-leveller.—*Hare.*

The vices operate like age, — bring on disease before its time, and in the prime of youth, leave the character broken and exhausted.—
Junius.

Our pleasant vices make instruments to scourge us.—*Shakespeare.*

Let thy vices die before thee.—*Franklin.*

There are vices which have no hold upon us, but in connection with others; and which, when you cut down the trunk, fall like the branches.—*Pascal.*

Vice leaves repentance in the soul, like an ulcer in the flesh, which is always scratching and lacerating itself; for reason effaces all other griefs and sorrows, but it begets that of repentance, which is so much the more grievous, by reason it springs within, as the cold and hot of fevers are more sharp than those that only strike upon the outward skin.—*Montaigne.*

Vices are often habits rather than passions.
Rivarol.

Long careers of vice, that prosper even in their epitaphs, make cemeteries seem ridiculous, and death anything but a leveller.—*John Weiss.*

The vices of some men are magnificent.—
Lamb.

VICISSITUDES.

Misfortune does not always wait on vice; nor is success the constant guest of virtue.
Hazard.

Such are the vicissitudes of the world, through all its parts, that day and night, labor and rest, hurry and retirement, endear each other. Such are the changes that keep the mind in action; we desire, we pursue, we obtain, we are satiated; we desire something else, and begin a new pursuit.—*Johnson.*

Sometimes ha'th the brightest day a cloud; and after summer evermore succeeds barren winter, with his wrathful nipping cold; so cares and joys abound, as seasons fleet.—*Shakespeare.*

The most affluent may be stripped of all, and find his worldly comforts like so many withered leaves dropping from him.—*Sterne.*

Happy the man who can endure the highest and the lowest fortune. He who has endured such vicissitudes with equanimity has deprived misfortune of its power.—*Seneca.*

VICTORY.

Victory, with advantage, is rather robbed than purchased.—*Sir P. Sidney.*

The smile of God is victory.—*Whittier.*

Victories that are cheap are cheap. Those only are worth having which come as the result of hard fighting.—*Beecher.*

How beautiful is victory, but how dear!—
De Boufflers.

Pursue not a victory too far. He hath conquered well that hath made his enemy fly; thou mayest beat him to a desperate resistance, which may ruin thee.—*George Herbert.*

In victory, the hero seeks the glory, not the prey.—*Sir P. Sidney.*

I love victory, but I love not triumph.
Madame Swetchine.

It is the contest that delights us, not the victory. We are pleased with the combat of animals, but not with the victor tearing the vanquished. What is sought for but the crisis of victory? and the instant it comes, it brings satiety.—*Pascal.*

A victory is twice itself, when the achiever brings home full numbers.—*Shakespeare.*

VIGILANCE.

"Who will guard the guards?" says a Latin verse,—"*Quis custodiet ipsos custodes?*" I answer, "The enemy." It is the enemy who keeps the sentinel watchful.—
Madame Swetchine.

VILLANY.

The most stormy ebullitions of passion, from blasphemy to murder, are less terrific than one single act of cool villany; a still rabies is more dangerous than the paroxysms of a fever. Fear the boisterous savage of passion less than the sedately grinning villain.—*Lavater.*

VINDICTIVENESS.

No reasonable man would be eager to possess himself of the invidious power of inflicting punishment, if he were not predetermined to make use of it.—*Junius.*

VIOLENCE.

Violent fires soon burn out themselves, small showers last long, but sudden storms are short; he tires betimes that spurs too fast betimes.—*Shakespeare.*

Violence ever defeats its own ends. Where you cannot drive you can always persuade. A gentle word, a kind look, a good-natured smile can work wonders and accomplish miracles. There is a secret pride in every human heart that revolts at tyranny. You may order and drive an individual, but you cannot make him respect you.—*Hazlitt.*

The violence done us by others is often less painful than that which we do to ourselves.—
Rochefoucauld.

Nothing violent, oft have I heard tell, can be permanent.—*Marlowe.*

VIRTUE.

Virtue with some is nothing but successful temerity.—*Seneca.*

What we take for virtues is often nothing but an assemblage of different actions, and of different interests, that fortune or our industry know how to arrange; and it is not always from valor and from chastity that men are valiant, and that women are chaste.—
Rochefoucauld.

Virtue maketh men on the earth famous, in their graves illustrious, in the heavens immortal.
Chilo.

Virtue may be said to steal, like a guilty thing, into the secret haunts of vice and infamy; it clings to their devoted victim, and will not be driven quite away. Nothing can destroy the human heart.—*Hazlitt.*

Virtue has many preachers, but few martyrs.
Helvetius.

Do not be troubled because you have not great virtues. God made a million spears of grass where he made one tree. The earth is fringed and carpeted, not with forests, but with grasses. Only have enough of little virtues and common fidelities, and you need not mourn because you are neither a hero nor a saint.—
Beecher.

Some, by admiring other men's virtues, become enemies to their own vices.—*Bias.*

The height and value of true virtue consists in the facility, utility, and pleasure of its exercise; so far from difficulty, that boys, as well as men, and the innocent as well as the subtle, may make it their own; and it is by order and good conduct, and not by force, that it is to be acquired.—*Montaigne.*

Our virtues are commonly disguised vices.—
Rochefoucauld.

No virtue can be real that has not been tried. The gold in the crucible alone is perfect; the loadstone tests the steel, and the diamond is tried by the diamond, while metals gleam the brighter in the furnace.—*Calderon.*

The virtues, like the Muses, are always seen in groups. A good principle was never found solitary in any breast.—*Jane Porter.*

The virtue of a man ought to be measured not by his extraordinary exertions, but by his every-day conduct.—*Pascal.*

Virtue is more to man than either water or fire. I have seen men die from treading on water and fire, but I have never seen a man die from treading the course of virtue.—
Confucius.

Assume a virtue, if you have it not.—
Shakespeare.

I have known persons without a friend,— never any one without some virtue. The virtues of the former conspired with their vices to make the whole world their enemies.—
Hazlitt.

If you can be well without health, you can be happy without virtue.—*Burke.*

Though Virtue give a ragged livery, she gives a golden cognizance; if her service make thee poor, blush not. Thy poverty may disadvantage thee, but not dishonor thee.—
Quarles.

Virtue is everywhere the same, because it comes from God, while everything else is of men.—*Voltaire.*

Content not thyself that thou art virtuous in the general; for one link being wanting, the chain is defective. Perhaps thou art rather innocent than virtuous, and owest more to thy constitution than to thy religion.—
William Penn.

Virtue, the more it is exposed, like purest linen, laid in open air, will bleach the more, and whiten to the view.—*Dryden.*

It is the edge and temper of the blade that make a good sword, not the richness of the scabbard, and so it is not money or possessions that make men considerable, but virtue.—
Seneca.

Virtue is health, vice is sickness.—*Petrarch.*

If our virtues did not go forth of us, it were all alike as if we had them not.—*Shakespeare.*

Guilt, though it may attain temporal splendor, can never confer real happiness; the evil consequences of our crimes long survive their commission, and, like the ghosts of the murdered, forever haunt the steps of the malefactor; while the paths of virtue, though seldom those of worldly greatness, are always those of pleasantness and peace.—*Walter Scott.*

Virtue alone is true nobility.—*Gifford.*

There is no community or commonwealth of virtue; every man must study his own economy, and erect these rules unto the figure of himself.—*Sir Thomas Browne.*

Virtue consisteth of three parts,—temperance, fortitude, and justice.—*Epicurus.*

Let this great maxim be my virtue's guide,— in part she is to blame that has been tried; he comes too near that comes too near that comes to be denied.—
Mary Wortley Montagu.

Virtue is that which must tip the preacher's tongue and the ruler's sceptre with authority.—
South.

We must not love virtue for the bare sake of reputation and human esteem. To do good, purely to be gazed at and talked of and applauded, this was the character of the Pharisees, whose vices were real, and whose virtues were imaginary; but had their virtues been as real as their vices, this poor view and narrow purpose would have spoilt them all; and they could only expect their reward where they sought it, that is, from men.—*Jortin.*

It is only virtue which no one can misuse; because it would not be virtue if a bad use were made of it.—*Bossuet.*

I would be virtuous for my own sake, though nobody were to know it; as I would be clean for my own sake, though nobody were to see me.—*Shaftesbury.*

In the truly great, virtue governs with the sceptre of knowledge.—*Sir P. Sidney.*

Virtue is the nursing-mother of all human pleasures, who, in rendering them just, renders them also pure and permanent; in moderating them, keeps them in breath and appetite; in interdicting those which she herself refuses, whets our desires to those that she allows; and, like a kind and liberal mother, abundantly allows all that nature requires, even to satiety, if not to lassitude.—*Socrates.*

Virtue by calculation is the virtue of vice.—
Joubert.

When men grow virtuous in their old age, they are merely making a sacrifice to God of the Devil's leavings.—*Swift.*

Virtue is the beauty, and vice the deformity, of the soul.—*Socrates.*

The recognition of virtue is not less valuable from the lips of the man who hates it, since truth forces him to acknowledge it; and though he may be unwilling to take it into his inmost soul, he at least decks himself out in its trappings.—*Montaigne.*

Virtues, like essences, lose their fragrance when exposed. They are sensitive plants, which will not bear too familiar approaches.—
Shenstone.

True Virtue, when she errs, needs not the eyes of men to excite her blushes; she is confounded at her own presence, and covered with confusion of face.—*Jane Porter.*

There have been men who could play delightful music on one string of the violin, but there never was a man who could produce the harmonies of heaven in his soul by a one-stringed virtue.—*Chapin.*

Virtue, without talent, is a coat of mail without a sword; it may indeed defend the wearer, but will not enable him to protect his friend.—
Colton.

Virtue will catch as well as vice by contact; and the public stock of honest manly principle will daily accumulate. We are not too nicely to scrutinize motives as long as action is irreproachable. It is enough (and for a worthy man perhaps too much) to deal out its infamy to convicted guilt and declared apostasy.—
Burke.

What is virtue but a medicine, and vice but a wound?—*Hooker.*

Virtue, like fire, turns all things into itself; our actions and our friendships are tinctured with it, and whatever it touches becomes amiable.—*Seneca.*

There are odious virtues; such as inflexible severity, and an integrity that accepts of no favor.—*Tacitus.*

No man is born wise; but wisdom and virtue require a tutor; though we can easily learn to be vicious without a master.—*Seneca.*

A virtuous and well-disposed person, like a good metal, the more he is fired, the more he is fined; the more he is opposed, the more he is approved: wrongs may well try him, and touch him, but cannot imprint in him any false stamp.—
Richelieu.

The more tickets you have in a lottery, the worse your chance. And it is the same of virtues, in the lottery of life.—*Sterne.*

Virtue is not to be considered in the light of mere innocence, or abstaining from harm; but as the exertion of our faculties in doing good.—
Bishop Butler.

A man that hath no virtue in himself ever envieth virtue in others; for men's minds will either feed upon their own good or upon others' evil; and who wanteth the one will prey upon the other.—*Bacon.*

Most people are so constituted that they can only be virtuous in a certain routine; an irregular course of life demoralizes them.—
Hawthorne.

Virtue is shut out from no one; she is open to all, accepts all, invites all, gentlemen, freedmen, slaves, kings, and exiles; she selects neither house nor fortune; she is satisfied with a human being without adjuncts.—*Seneca.*

As they suspect a man in the city who is ostentatious of his riches, so should the woman be who makes the most noise of her virtue.—
Fielding.

The soul's calm sunshine, and the heartfelt joy, is virtue's prize.—*Pope.*

There is no virtue which does not rejoice a well-descended nature; there is a kind of I know not what congratulation in well-doing, that gives us an inward satisfaction, and a certain generous boldness that accompanies a good conscience.—
Montaigne.

Virtue and vice are both prophets; the first, of certain good; the second, of pain or else of penitence.—*R. Venning.*

They who disbelieve in virtue because man has never been found perfect, might as reasonably deny the sun because it is not always noon.
Hare.

Some virtuous women are too liberal in their insults to a frail sister; but virtue can support itself without borrowing any assistance from the vices of other women.—*Fielding.*

Our virtues would be proud if our faults whipped them not; and our crimes would despair if they were not cherished by our virtues.
Shakespeare.

An effort made with ourselves for the good of others, with the intention of pleasing God alone.—*Bernardin de St. Pierre.*

Virtue has resources buried in itself, we know not of till the invading hour calls them from their retreat. Surrounded by foes without, and when Nature itself turns traitor, and is its most deadly enemy within, it assumes a new and superhuman power, which is greater than nature itself. Whatever be its sect, from whatever segment of the globe its orisons rise, virtue is God's empire, and from his throne of thrones he will defend it.—*Bulwer Lytton.*

Virtue, though in rags, may challenge more than vice set off with all the trim of greatness.
Massinger.

The advantage to be derived from virtue is so evident that the wicked practise it from interested motives.—*Vauvenargues.*

Virtue is like a rich stone, best plain set.—
Bacon.

Many new years you may see, but happy ones you cannot see without deserving them. These virtue, honor, and knowledge alone can merit, alone can produce.—*Chesterfield.*

All virtue lies in individual action, in inward energy, in self-determination. The best books have most beauty.—*Channing.*

Virtue itself turns vice, being misapplied, and vice sometimes by action dignified.—
Shakespeare.

Determine with yourself to employ a certain stated time, in order to acquire the virtue to which you are least disposed.—*Richter.*

Nothing is more easy than irreproachable conduct.—*Madame de Maintenon.*

Virtue that transgresses is but patched with sin; and sin that amends is but patched with virtue.—*Shakespeare.*

Virtue alone outbuilds the pyramids; her monuments shall last, when Egypt's fall.—
Young.

I cannot worship the abstractions of Virtue; she only charms me when she addresses herself to my heart, speaks through the love from which she springs.—*Niebuhr.*

Virtue in distress, and vice in triumph, make atheists of mankind.—*Dryden.*

Virtue is despotic; life, reputation, every earthly good, must be surrendered at her voice. The law may seem hard, but it is the guardian of what it commands; and is the only sure defence of happiness.—*Jane Porter.*

Virtue often trips and falls on the sharp-edged rock of poverty.—*Eugene Sue.*

Virtues go ever in troops; they go so thick, that sometimes some are hid in the crowd; which yet are, but appear not.—*Bishop Hall.*

Virtue, vain word, futile shadow, slave of chance! Alas! I believe in thee!—*Brutus.*

Virtue's office never breaks men's troth.—
Shakespeare.

If the most virtuous are those who pretend to have been strongly enticed by their vices before submitting, we could better say that the soldier, who suffered all the agony of terror, and finally fled before the enemy, is more worthy of esteem than the soldier who, without fear and without resistance, remained firm at his post. The bravest is he who does not hesitate before danger; the most upright, he who does not hesitate to do that which is right. How then, in other circumstances, the most virtuous would be he who has struggled before succumbing, and not he who remained pure?—
V. Guichard.

The only amaranthine flower on earth is virtue.—*Cowper.*

Certainly, virtue is like precious odors, most fragrant when they are incensed or crushed; for prosperity doth best discover vice, but adversity doth best discover virtue.—*Bacon.*

35

Live virtuously, my lord, and you cannot die too soon, nor live too long.—
Lady Rachel Russell.

Blessed is the memory of those who have kept themselves unspotted from the world! Yet more blessed and more dear the memory of those who have kept themselves unspotted in the world!—*Mrs. Jameson.*

Virtue is a state of war, and to live in it we have always to combat with ourselves.—
Rousseau.

The most virtuous of all men is he that contents himself with being virtuous without seeking to appear so.—*Plato.*

I am no herald to inquire of men's pedigrees; it sufficeth me, if I know their virtues.—
Sir P. Sidney.

Recommend to your children virtue; that alone can make happy, not gold.—*Beethoven.*

Virtue is nothing but an act of loving that which is to be beloved, and that act is prudence, from whence not to be removed by constraint is fortitude; not to be allured by enticements is temperance; not to be diverted by pride is justice.—*Quarles.*

A heart unspotted is not easily daunted.—
Shakespeare.

Virtue is that perfect good, which is the compliment of a happy life; the only immortal thing that belongs to mortality.—*Seneca.*

There are some persons on whom virtue sits almost as ungraciously as vice.—
Bouhours.

Virtue consists in doing our duty in the several relations we sustain, in respect to ourselves, to our fellow-men, and to God, as known from reason, conscience, and revelation.—
Alexander.

It is difficult to persuade mankind that the love of virtue is the love of themselves.—*Cicero.*

As many as are the difficulties which Virtue has to encounter in this world, her force is yet superior.—*Shaftesbury.*

Parley and surrender signify the same thing where virtue is concerned.—
Madame de Maintenon.

Where is the reward of virtue? and what recompense has nature provided for such important sacrifices as those of life and fortune, which we must often make to it? O sons of earth! Are ye ignorant of the value of this celestial mistress? And do ye meanly inquire for her portion, when ye observe her genuine beauty?—*Hume.*

Is any one able for one day to apply his strength to virtue? I have not seen the case in which his strength would be sufficient.—
Confucius.

Such as have virtue always in their mouths, and neglect it in practice, are like a harp, which emits a sound pleasing to others, while itself is insensible of the music.—*Diogenes.*

Virtue is beauty.—*Shakespeare.*

No virtue fades out of mankind. Not over-hopeful by inborn temperament, cautious by long experience, I yet never despair of human virtue.—*Theodore Parker.*

I cannot praise a fugitive and cloistered virtue unexercised and unbreathed, that never sallies out and seeks her adversary, but slinks out of the race, where that immortal garland is to be run for, not without dust and heat.—
Milton.

VISITS.

Visits are for the most part neither more nor less than inventions for discharging upon our neighbors somewhat of our own unendurable weight.—*Nicole.*

Fish and visitors smell in three days.—
Franklin.

Visits are unsatiable devourers of time, and fit only for those who, if they did not visit, would do nothing.—*Cowper.*

VITUPERATION.

Scurrility has no object in view but incivility; if it is uttered from feelings of petulance, it is mere abuse; if it is spoken in a joking manner, it may be considered raillery.—*Cicero.*

VIVACITY.

The vivacity which augments with years is not far from folly.—*Rochefoucauld.*

VOCATION.

The highest excellence is seldom attained in more than one vocation. The roads leading to distinction in separate pursuits diverge, and the nearer we approach the one, the farther we recede from the other.—*Bovee.*

VOICE.

How wonderful is the human voice! It is indeed the organ of the soul! The intellect of man sits enthroned visibly upon his forehead and in his eye; and the heart of man is written upon his countenance. But the soul reveals itself in the voice only, as God revealed himself to the prophet of old, in "the still, small voice," and in a voice from the burning bush. The soul of man is audible, not visible. A sound alone betrays the flowing of the eternal fountain, invisible to man!—*Longfellow.*

The tones of human voices mightier than strings or brass to move the soul.—*Klopstock.*

Her voice was ever soft, gentle, and low; an excellent thing in woman.—*Shakespeare.*

The music of the heart.—*Akenside.*

To a nice ear, the quality of a voice is singularly affecting. Its depth seems to be allied to feeling; at least, the contralto notes alone give an adequate sense of pathos. They are born near the heart.—*Tuckerman.*

The voice is the flower of beauty.—*Zeno.*

The influence of temper upon tone deserves much consideration. Habits of querulousness or ill-nature will communicate a cat-like quality to the singing, as infallibly as they give a quality to the speaking voice. That there really exist amiable tones is not an unfounded opinion. In the voice there is no deception; it is to many the index of the mind, denoting moral qualities; and it may be remarked that the low, soft tones of gentle and amiable beings, whatever their musical endowments may be, seldom fail to please; besides which, the singing of ladies indicates the cultivation of their taste generally, and the embellishment of their mind.—*Mordaunt.*

The warder of the mind.—*Rousseau.*

There is in the voice of a menaced man, who calls you, something imperions, which subdues and commands.—*M. de Martignac.*

Reader, when that which thou lovedst has long vanished from the earth or from thy fancy, then will nevertheless the beloved voice come back, and bring with it all thy old tears, and the disconsolate heart which has shed them. –
Richter.

A lovely countenance is the fairest of all sights, and the sweetest harmony is the sound of the voice of her whom we love.—*Bruyère.*

Her voice is soft; not shrill and like the lark's, but tenderer, graver, almost hoarse at times! As though the earnestness of love prevailed and quelled all shriller music.—
Barry Cornwall.

How often you are irresistibly drawn to a plain, unassuming woman, whose soft silvery tones render her positively attractive! In the social circle, how pleasant it is to hear a woman talk in that low key which always characterizes the true lady. In the sanctuary of home, how such a voice soothes the fretful child and cheers the weary husband!—*Lamb.*

VOLITION.

A man with a half-volition goes backwards and forwards, and makes no way on the smoothest road; a man with a whole volition advances on the roughest, and will reach his purpose, if there be even a little wisdom in it.—
Carlyle.

VOLUPTUOUSNESS.

Voluptuousness, like justice, is blind; but that is the only resemblance between them.—*Pascal.*

The rich and luxurious may claim an exclusive right to those pleasures which are capable of being purchased by pelf, in which the mind has no enjoyment, and which only afford a temporary relief to languor by steeping the senses in forgetfulness; but in the precious pleasures of the intellect, so easily accessible by all mankind, the great have no exclusive privilege; for such enjoyments are only to be procured by our own industry.—*Zimmermann.*

VOWS.

Men's vows are women's traitors.—*Shakespeare.*

Make no vows to perform this or that; it shows no great strength, and makes thee ride behind thyself.—*Fuller.*

The vows that woman makes to her fond lover are only fit to be written on air or on the swiftly passing stream.—*Catullus.*

Those mouth-made vows, which break themselves in swearing.—*Shakespeare.*

Hasty resolutions are of the nature of vows; and to be equally avoided.—*William Penn.*

The gods are deaf to hot and peevish vows; they are polluted offerings, more abhorred than spotted livers in the sacrifice.—*Shakespeare*

VULGARITY.

To endeavor to work upon the vulgar with fine sense is like attempting to hew blocks with a razor.—*Pope.*

Flourishing vulgarity is more unconscious than wicked; a destitute refinement is a great deal more capable of bearing malice.—*John Weiss.*

Vulgarity is setting store by the things which are seen.—*Lady Morgan.*

Disorder in a drawing-room is vulgar; in an antiquary's study, not; the black battle-stain on a soldier's face is not vulgar, but the dirty face of a housemaid is.—*Ruskin.*

W.

WALKING.

The art of walking is at once suggestive of the dignity of man. Progressive motion alone implies power, but in almost every other instance it seems a power gained at the expense of self-possession.—*Tuckerman.*

The sum of the whole is this: walk and be happy, walk and be healthy. "The best of all ways to lengthen our days" is not, as Mr. Thomas Moore has it, "to steal a few hours from night, my love"; but, with leave be it spoken, to walk steadily and with a purpose. The wandering man knows of certain ancients, far gone in years, who have staved off infirmities and dissolution by earnest walking, — hale fellows close upon eighty and ninety, but brisk as boys.—*Dickens.*

If you are for a merry jaunt, I will try for once who can foot it farthest.—*Dryden.*

WANTS.

Wants awaken intellect. To gratify them disciplines intellect. The keener the want the lustier the growth.—*Wendell Phillips.*

The fewer our wants, the nearer we resemble the gods.—*Socrates.*

It is not from nature, but from education and habits, that our wants are chiefly derived.—*Fielding.*

He can feel no little wants who is in pursuit of grandeur.—*Lavater.*

Great wants proceed from great wealth; but they are undutiful children, for they sink wealth down to poverty.—*Henry Home.*

The relief that is afforded to mere want, as want, tends to increase that want.—*Whately.*

Nature has provided for the exigency of privation, by putting the measure of our necessities far below the measure of our wants. Our necessities are to our wants as Falstaff's pennyworth of bread to his any quantity of sack.—*Bovee.*

Constantly choose rather to want less, than to have more.—*Thomas à Kempis.*

We should wish for few things with eagerness, if we perfectly knew the nature of that which was the object of our desire.—*Rochefoucauld.*

Human life is a constant want, and ought to be a constant prayer.—*S. Osgood.*

Every one is the poorer in proportion as he has more wants, and counts not what he has, but wishes only what he has not.—*Manilius.*

The stoical scheme of supplying our wants by lopping off our desires is like cutting off our feet when we want shoes.—*Swift.*

WAR.

Rash, fruitless war, from wanton glory waged, is only splendid murder.—*Thomson.*

If war has its chivalry and its pageantry, it has also its hideousness and its demoniac woe. *Bullets respect not beauty.* They tear out the eye, and shatter the jaw, and rend the cheek.—*Abbott.*

The warrior who cultivates his mind polishes his arms.—*De Boufflers.*

War kills men, and men deplore the loss; but war also crushes bad principles and tyrants, and so saves societies.—*Colton.*

Of all the evils to public liberty, war is perhaps the most to be dreaded, because it comprises and develops the genius of every other. War is the parent of armies; from these proceed debt and taxes. And armies and debts and taxes are the known instruments for bringing the many under the dominion of the few.—*Madison.*

There are few die well that die in a battle.—*Shakespeare.*

War suspends the rules of moral obligation, and what is long suspended is in danger of being totally abrogated. *Civil wars strike deepest of all into the manners of the people.—Burke.*

Grim-visaged War hath smoothed his wrinkled front.—*Shakespeare.*

It is only necessary to make war with five things: with the maladies of the body, the ignorances of the mind, with the passions of the body, with the seditions of the city, and the discords of families.—*Pythagoras.*

War! that mad game the world so loves to play.—*Swift.*

Among arms, said the Roman author, laws are silent. Among arms, we may add, the temples of prayer are voiceless.—*Bartol.*

Let the gulled fool the toils of war pursue, where bleed the many to enrich the few.—*Shenstone.*

Wars are to the body politic, what drams are to the individual. There are times when they may prevent a sudden death, but if frequently resorted to, or long persisted in, they heighten the energies only to hasten the dissolution.—*Colton.*

War is the sink of all injustice.—*Fielding.*

A wise minister would rather preserve peace than gain a victory; because he knows that even the most successful war leaves nations generally more poor, always more profligate, than it found them. There are real evils that cannot be brought into a list of indemnities, and the demoralizing influence of war is not amongst the least of them.—*Colton.*

Great warriors, like great earthquakes, are principally remembered for the mischief they have done.—*Bovee.*

He who makes war his profession cannot be otherwise than vicious. War makes thieves, and peace brings them to the gallows.—*Machiavelli.*

There never was a good war or a bad peace.—*Franklin.*

"War," says Machiavelli, "ought to be the only study of a prince"; and, by a prince, he means every sort of state, however constituted. "He ought," says this great political doctor, "to consider peace only as a breathing-time, which gives him leisure to contrive, and furnishes ability to execute military plans." A meditation on the conduct of political societies made old Hobbes imagine that war was the state of nature.—*Burke.*

War ought never to be accepted, until it is offered by the hand of necessity.—*Sir P. Sidney.*

If the cause and end of war be justifiable, all the means that appear necessary to the end are justifiable also.—*Paley.*

Every war involves a greater or less relapse into barbarism. War, indeed, in its details, is the essence of inhumanity. It dehumanizes. It may save the state, but it destroys the citizen.—*Bovee.*

Even in a righteous cause force is a fearful thing; God only helps when men can help no more.—*Schiller.*

Cannon and firearms are cruel and damnable machines. I believe them to have been the direct suggestion of the Devil. Against the flying ball no valor avails; the soldier is dead ere he sees the means of his destruction. If Adam had seen in a vision the horrible instruments his children were to invent, he would have died of grief.—*Luther.*

Cruelty in war buyeth conquest at the dearest price.—*Sir P. Sidney.*

The gospel has but a forced alliance with war. Its doctrine of human brotherhood would ring strangely between the opposed ranks. The bellowing speech of cannon and the baptism of blood mock its liturgies and sacraments. Its gentle beatitudes would hardly serve as mottoes for defiant banners, nor its list of graces as names for ships-of-the-line.—*Chapin.*

The king who makes war on his enemies tenderly distresses his subjects most cruelly.—*Johnson.*

I hear the hoarse-voiced cannon roar, the red-mouthed orators of war.—*Joaquin Miller.*

Kings play at war unfairly with republics; they can only lose some earth, and some creatures they value as little, while republics lose in every soldier a part of themselves.—*Landor*.

War is a game, which, were their subjects wise, kings should not play at.—*Cowper*.

Use makes a better soldier than the most urgent considerations of duty, — familiarity with danger enabling him to estimate the danger. He sees how much is the risk, and is not afflicted with imagination; knows practically Marshal Saxe's rule, that every soldier killed costs the enemy his weight in lead.—*Emerson*.

More soluble is this knot, like almost all the rest, if men were wise, by gentleness than war.
Tennyson.

What a fine-looking thing is war! Yet, dress it as we may, dress and feather it, daub it with gold, huzza it, and sing swaggering songs about it, — what is it, nine times out of ten, but murder in uniform!—*Douglas Jerrold*.

Some general officers should pay a stricter regard to truth than to call the depopulating other countries the service of their own.—
Fielding.

Laws are commanded to hold their tongues among arms; and tribunals fall to the ground with the peace they are no longer able to uphold.—*Burke*.

That men should kill one another for want of somewhat else to do, which is the case of all volunteers in war, seems to be so horrible to humanity that there needs no divinity to control it.—*Clarendon*.

All things that are made for our general uses are at war, — even we among ourselves.
John Fletcher.

Here avarice and cruelty know no bounds; barbarities are authorized by decrees of the senate and votes of the people; and enormities, forbidden in private persons, are ordered and sanctioned by legislators. Things which, if a man had done in his private capacity, they would have paid for with their lives, the very same things we extol to the skies, when they do them with their regimentals on their backs.
Seneca.

The natural principle of war is to do the most harm to our enemy with the least harm to ourselves; and this of course, is to be effected by stratagem.—*Washington Irving*.

Cry "Havoc!" and let slip the dogs of war.—*Shakespeare*.

War, — the trade of barbarians, and the art of bringing the greatest physical force to bear on a single point.—*Napoleon*.

He who has made no mistakes in war has never made war.—*Turenne*.

What I thought at fifteen years I still think; — war, which society draws upon itself, is but an organized barbarism, and an inheritance of the savage state, however disguised or ornamented.—*Louis Bonaparte*.

Success in war, like charity in religion, covers a multitude of sins.—*Napier*.

War mends but few, and spoils multitudes; it legitimates rapine and authorizes murder; and these crimes must be ministered to by their lesser relatives, by coveteousness and anger and pride and revenge, and heats of blood, and wilder liberty, and all the evil that can be supposed to come from or run to such cursed causes of mischief.—*Jeremy Taylor*.

The worse the man, the better the soldier; if soldiers be not corrupt, they ought to be made so.—*Napoleon*.

I abominate war as unchristian. I hold it the greatest of human crimes. I deem it to involve all others, — violence, blood, rapine, fraud; everything that can deform the character, alter the nature, and debase the name of man.—*Lord Brougham*.

There is strength and a fierce instinct, even in common souls, to bear up manhood with a stormy joy when red swords meet in lightning.
Mrs. Hemans.

War, even in the best state of an army, with all the alleviations of courtesy and honor, with all the correctives of morality and religion, is nevertheless so great an evil, that to engage in it without a clear necessity is a crime of the blackest dye. When the necessity is clear, it then becomes a crime to shrink from it.—
Southey.

Peace is the happy, natural state of man; war his corruption, his disgrace.—*Thomson*.

War and economy are things not easily reconciled, and the attempt of leaning towards parsimony in such a state may be the worst economy in the world.—*Burke*.

The measure of civilization in a people is to be found in its just appreciation of the wrongfulness of war.—*Helps*.

WASTE.

Waste cannot be accurately told, though we are sensible how destructive it is. Economy, on the one hand, by which a certain income is made to maintain a man genteelly; and waste, on the other, by which on the same income another man lives shabbily, cannot be defined. It is a very nice thing; as one man wears his coat out much sooner than another, we cannot tell how.—*Johnson*.

More water glideth by the mill than wots the miller of.—*Shakespeare.*

Time elaborately thrown away.—*Young.*

WEAKNESS.

There are some weaknesses that are peculiar and distinctive to generous characters, as freckles are to a fair skin.—*Bovee.*

More men are guilty of treason through weakness than any studied design to betray.
Rochefoucauld.

The more weakness, the more falsehood; strength goes straight; every cannon-ball that has in it hollows and holes goes crooked. Weaklings must lie.—*Richter.*

Weakness is the only fault that is incorrigible.—*Rochefoucauld.*

Weakness has its hidden resources, as well as strength. There is a degree of folly and meanness which we cannot calculate upon, and by which we are as much liable to be foiled as by the greatest ability or courage.—*Hazlitt.*

The weak may be joked out of anything but their weakness.—*Zimmermann.*

Men are in general so tricky, so envious, and so cruel that when we find one who is only weak, we are too happy.—*Voltaire.*

Delusion and weakness produce not one mischief the less, because they are universal.—
Burke.

Weakness is more opposite to virtue than is vice itself.—*Rochefoucauld.*

Weakness to be wroth with weakness.—
Tennyson.

Every one has a besetting sin to which he returns.—*La Fontaine.*

Some of our weaknesses are born in us, others are the result of education; it is a question which of the two gives us most trouble.—
Goethe.

Weaknesses, so called, are nothing more nor less than vice in disguise !—*Lavater.*

WEALTH.

He that will not permit his wealth to do any good to others while he is living prevents it from doing any good to himself when he is dead; and by an egotism that is suicidal and has a double edge, cuts himself off from the truest pleasure here, and the highest happiness hereafter.—*Colton.*

Seek not proud wealth; but such as thou mayst get justly, use soberly, distribute cheerfully, and love contentedly.—*Bacon.*

Property is like snow; if it falleth level to-day, it will be blown into drifts to-morrow. —
Sinclair.

People who are arrogant on account of their wealth are about equal to our Laplanders, who measure a man's worth by the number of his reindeer.—*Fredrika Bremer.*

The million covet wealth, but how few dream of its perils ! —*John Neal.*

Many in hot pursuit have hasted to the goal of wealth, but have lost, as they ran, those apples of gold, the mind and the power to enjoy it.—*Tupper.*

Riches are gotten with pain, kept with care, and lost with grief. The cares of riches lie heavier upon a good man than the inconveniences of an honest poverty.—*L'Estrange.*

Wealth, after all, is a relative thing, since he that has little, and wants less, is richer than he that has much, but wants more.—*Colton.*

That plenty should produce either covetousness or prodigality is a perversion of providence; and yet the generality of men are the worse for their riches.—*William Penn.*

It is far more easy to acquire a fortune like a knave than to expend it like a gentleman.—
Colton.

Money and time are the heaviest burdens of life, and the unhappiest of all mortals are those who have more of either than they know how to use.—*Johnson.*

Our wealth is often a snare to ourselves, and always a temptation to others.—*Colton.*

Many a beggar at the cross way, or gray-haired shepherd on the plain, hath more of the end of all wealth than hundreds who multiply the means.—*Tupper.*

As riches and favor forsake a man, we discover him to be a fool, but nobody could find it out in his prosperity.—*Bruyère.*

What real good does an addition to a fortune, already sufficient, procure ? Not any. Could the great man, by having his fortune increased, increase also his appetites, then precedence might be attended with real amusement.
Goldsmith.

There is no society, however free and democratic, where wealth will not create an aristocracy.—*Bulwer Lytton.*

Worldly wealth is the Devil's bait; and those whose minds feed upon riches recede, in general, from real happiness, in proportion as their stores increase; as the moon, when she is fullest, is farthest from the sun —*Burton.*

Gross and vulgar minds will always pay a higher respect to wealth than to talent; for wealth, although it be a far less efficient source of power than talent, happens to be far more intelligible.—*Colton.*

The most brilliant fortunes are often not worth the littleness required to gain them.—*Rochefoucauld.*

Whosoever shall look heedfully upon those who are eminent for their riches will not think their condition such as that he should hazard his quiet, and much less his virtue, to obtain it, for all that great wealth generally gives above a moderate fortune is more room for the freaks of caprice, and more privilege for ignorance and vice, a quicker succession of flatteries, and a larger circle of voluptuousness.—*Johnson.*

Wealth is not his that has it, but his that enjoys it.—*Franklin.*

Wherever there is excessive wealth, there is also in the train of it excessive poverty; as where the sun is brightest the shade is deepest.—*Landor.*

There is a burden of care in getting riches, fear in keeping them, temptation in using them, guilt in abusing them, sorrow in losing them, and a burden of account at last to be given up concerning them.—*Matthew Henry.*

The way to wealth is as plain as the road to market. It depends chiefly on two words, — industry and frugality.—*Franklin.*

The pulpit and the press have many commonplaces denouncing the thirst for wealth, but if men should take these moralists at their word, and leave off aiming to be rich, the moralists would rush to rekindle at all hazards this love of power in the people, lest civilization should be undone.—*Emerson.*

Wealth is a weak anchor, and glory cannot support a man; this is the law of God, that virtue only is firm, and cannot be shaken by a tempest.—*Pythagoras.*

If thou desire to purchase honor with thy wealth, consider first how that wealth became thine: if thy labor got it, let thy wisdom keep it; if oppression found it, let repentance restore it; if thy parent left it, let thy virtues deserve it: so shall thy honor be safer, better, and cheaper.—*Quarles.*

What a man does with his wealth depends upon his idea of happiness Those who draw prizes in life are apt to spend tastelessly, if not viciously; not knowing that it requires as much talent to spend as to make.—*Whipple.*

Wealth hath never given happiness, but often hastened misery; enough hath never caused misery but often quickened happiness.—*Tupper.*

What money creates, money preserves : if thy wealth decays, thy honor dies; it is but a slippery happiness which fortunes can give, and frowns can take; and not worth the owning which a night's fire can melt, or a rough sea can drown.—*Quarles.*

Without a rich heart wealth is an ugly beggar.—*Emerson.*

Wealth is not acquired, as many persons suppose, by fortunate speculations and splendid enterprises, but by the daily practice of industry, frugality, and economy. He who relies upon these means will rarely be found destitute, and he who relies upon any other will generally become bankrupt.—*Wayland.*

Less coin, less care ; to know how to dispense with wealth is to possess it.—*Reynard.*

What does competency in the long run mean? It means, to all reasonable beings, cleanliness of person, decency of dress, courtesy of manners, opportunities for education, the delights of leisure, and the bliss of giving.—*Whipple.*

It requires a great deal of boldness and a great deal of caution to make a great fortune; and when you have got it, it requires ten times as much wit to keep it.—*Rothschild.*

One cause of the insufficiency of riches (to produce happiness) is, that they very seldom make their owner rich.—*Johnson.*

Leisure and solitude are the best effect of riches, because mother of thought. Both are avoided by most rich men, who seek company and business, which are signs of being weary of themselves.—*Sir W. Temple.*

A great fortune is a great servitude.—*Seneca.*

It hath been observed by wise and considering men, that wealth hath seldom been the portion, and never the mark to discover good people; but that Almighty God, who disposeth all things wisely, hath of his abundant goodness denied it (he only knows why) to many, whose minds he hath enriched with the great blessings of knowledge and virtue, as the fairer testimonies of his love to mankind.—*Izaak Walton.*

Many men want wealth, — not a competence alone, but a five-story competence. Everything subserves this; and religion they would like as a sort of lightning-rod to their houses, to ward off by and by the bolts of Divine wrath.—*Beecher.*

WEARINESS.

Weariness can snore upon the flint, when resty sloth finds the down pillow hard.—*Shakespeare.*

O Christ! for the eloquent quiet, for the final folding of hands.—*Joaquin Miller.*

WELCOME.

Small cheer and great welcome makes a merry feast.—*Shakespeare.*

How beautiful upon the mountains are the feet of him that bringeth glad tidings! —*Bible.*

Welcome as happy tidings after fears.— *Otway.*

Welcome as kindly showers to long-parched earth.—*Dryden.*

The appurtenance of welcome is fashion and ceremony.—*Shakespeare.*

WELL-DOING.

Let no man be sorry he has done good, because others concerned with him have done evil! If a man has acted right, he has done well, though alone; if wrong, the sanction of all mankind will not justify him.—*Fielding.*

The Hebrews have a saying that God is more delighted in adverbs than in nouns; it is not so much the matter that is done, but the matter how it is done, that God minds. Not how much, but how well! It is the well-doing that meets with a well-done. Let us therefore serve God, not nominally or verbally, but adverbially.—*R. Venning.*

WICKEDNESS.

The disposition to do a bad deed is the most terrible punishment of the deed it does.— *Charles Mildmay.*

It is a man's own dishonesty, his crimes, his wickedness, and barefaced assurance, that takes away from him soundness of mind; these are the furies, these the flames and firebrands, of the wicked.—*Cicero.*

To see and listen to the wicked is already the beginning of wickedness.—*Confucius.*

There is no man suddenly either excellently good or extremely wicked; but grows so, either as he holds himself up in virtue, or lets himself slide to viciousness.—*Sir P. Sidney.*

They that plough iniquity and sow wickedness reap the same.—*Bible.*

Wickedness may well be compared to a bottomless pit, into which it is easier to keep one's self from falling, than, being fallen, to give one's self any stay from falling infinitely.— *Sir P. Sidney.*

I never wonder to see men wicked, but I often wonder to see them not ashamed.—*Swift.*

Combinations of wickedness would overwhelm the world, by the advantage which licentious principles afford, did not those who have long practised perfidy grow faithless to each other.—*Johnson.*

There is a method in man's wickedness; it grows up by degrees.— *Beaumont and Fletcher.*

If the wicked flourish, and thou suffer, be not discouraged; they are fatted for destruction, thou art dicted for health.—*Fuller.*

The sure way to wickedness is always through wickedness.—*Seneca.*

In the wicked there are not materials to form a great man. Dilate upon the wisdom of his views and designs, admire his conduct, exaggerate as you may his ability to find the most fit and direct means to reach the ends at which he aims: if these ends be base, forethought can have no part in them; and when forethought is wanting, find greatness if you can. *Bruyère.*

Wickedness resides in the very hesitation about an act, even though it be not perpetrated. *Cicero.*

No wickedness proceeds on any ground of reason.—*Livy.*

Great God, have pity on the wicked, for thou didst everything for the good, when thou madest them good!—*Saadi.*

WIFE.

It very seldom happens that a man is slow enough in assuming the character of a husband, or a woman quick enough in condescending to that of a wife.—*Addison.*

First get an absolute conquest over thyself, and then thou wilt easily govern thy wife.— *Fuller.*

A good wife is Heaven's last, best gift to man,—his gem of many virtues, his casket of jewels; her voice is sweet music, her smiles his brightest day, her kiss the guardian of his innocence, her arms the pale of his safety, her industry his surest wealth, her economy his safest steward, her lips his faithful counsellors, her bosom the softest pillow of his cares.— *Jeremy Taylor.*

A light wife doth make a heavy husband.— *Shakespeare.*

The death of a man's wife is like cutting down an ancient oak that has long shaded the family mansion. Henceforth the glare of the world, with its cares and vicissitudes, falls upon the old widower's heart, and there is nothing to break their force, or shield him from the full weight of misfortune. It is as if his right hand were withered; as if one wing of his angel was broken, and every movement that he made brought him to the ground.— *Lamartine.*

She commandeth her husband, in any equal matter, by constant obeying him.—*Fuller.*

The good wife is none of our dainty dames, who love to appear in a variety of suits every day new; as if a good gown, like a stratagem in war, were to be used but once. But our good wife sets up a sail according to the keel of her husband's estate; and if of high parentage, she doth not so remember what she was by birth, that she forgets what she is by match.
Fuller.

You are my true and honorable wife; as dear to me as are the ruddy drops that visit my sad heart.—*Shakespeare.*

Nothing can be more touching than to behold a soft and tender female, who had been all weakness and dependence, and alive to every trivial roughness while treading the prosperous paths of life, suddenly rising in mental force to be the comforter and supporter of her husband under misfortune, and abiding with unshrinking firmness the bitterest blast of adversity.—
Washington Irving.

WILFULNESS.

Self-will is so ardent and active that it will break a world to pieces to make a stool to sit upon.—*Cecil.*

To wilful men the injuries that they themselves procure must be their schoolmasters.—
Shakespeare.

WILL.

God takes men's hearty desires and will, instead of the deed, where they have not power to fulfil it; but he never took the bare deed instead of the will.—*Richard Baxter.*

There is nothing good or evil save in the will.—*Epictetus.*

Our bodies are our gardens, to the which our wills are gardeners; so that if we will plant nettles or sow lettuce, set hyssop and weed up thyme, supply it with one gender of herbs or distract it with many, either to have it sterile with idleness or manured with industry, — why, the power and corrigible authority of this lies in our wills.—*Shakespeare.*

No one is a slave whose will is free.—
Tyrius Maximus.

In the moral world there is nothing impossible if we can bring a thorough will to it. Man can do everything with himself, but he must not attempt to do too much with others.
Wilhelm von Humboldt.

Whatever the will commands, the whole man must do; the empire of the will over all the faculties being absolutely overruling and despotic.—*South.*

Calmness of will is a sign of grandeur. The vulgar, far from hiding their will, blab their wishes. A single spark of occasion discharges the child of passions into a thousand crackers of desire.—*Lavater.*

He who is firm in will moulds the world to himself.—*Goethe.*

No action will be considered as blameless, unless the will was so; for by the will the act was dictated.—*Seneca.*

The saddest failures in life are those that come from the not putting forth of power and will to succeed.—*Whipple.*

Every man stamps his value on himself. The price we challenge for ourselves is given us. There does not live on earth the man, be his station what it may, that I despise myself compared with him. Man is made great or little by his own will.—*Schiller.*

It is the will that makes the action good or ill.—*Herrick.*

We cannot be held to what is beyond our strength and means; for at times the accomplishment and execution may not be in our power, and indeed there is nothing really in our own power except the will; on this are necessarily based and founded all the principles that regulate the duty of man.—*Montaigne.*

Will is deaf, and bears no heedful friends.—
Shakespeare.

A good inclination is but the first rude draught of virtue; but the finishing strokes are from the will, which, if well disposed, will by degrees perfect; if ill-disposed, will by the superinduction of ill habits quickly deface it.—*South.*

People do not lack strength; they lack will.
Victor Hugo.

The despotism of will in ideas is styled plan, project, character, obstinacy; its despotism in desires is called passion.—*Rivarol.*

The general of a large army may be defeated, but you cannot defeat the determined mind of a peasant.—*Confucius.*

If the will, which is the law of our nature, were withdrawn from our memory, fancy, understanding, and reason, no other hell could equal, for a spiritual being, what we should then feel from the anarchy of our powers. It would be conscious madness, — a horrid thought!—
Milton.

He wants wit that wants resolved will.—
Shakespeare.

WILLING.

A willing heart adds feather to the heel, and makes the clown a wingèd Mercury.—
Joanna Baillie.

WILLS.

You will give me nothing during your life; you say that you will give me something after your death: if you are not a fool, you know what I wish for.—*Martial.*

What you leave at your death, let it be without controversy, else the lawyers will be your heirs.—*F. Osborn.*

What thou givest after thy death, remember that thou givest it to a stranger, and most times to an enemy; for he that shall marry thy wife will despise thee, thy memory, and thine, and shall possess the quiet of thy labors, the fruit which thou hast planted, enjoy thy love, and spend with joy and ease what thou hast spared and gotten with care and travail.—
Sir Walter Raleigh.

WIND.

A wailing, rushing sound, which shook the walls as though a giant's hand were on them; then a hoarse roar, as if the sea had risen; then such a whirl and tumult, that the air seemed mad; and then, with a lengthened howl, the waves of wind swept on.—*Dickens.*

The wind, a sightless laborer, whistles at his task.—*Wordsworth.*

Seas are the fields of combat for the winds; but when they sweep along some flowery coast, their wings move mildly, and their rage is lost.
Dryden.

WINE.

Good wine is a good familiar creature, if it be well used.—*Shakespeare.*

Wine heightens indifference into love, love into jealousy, and jealousy into madness. It often turns the good-natured man into an idiot, and the choleric into an assassin. It gives bitterness to resentment, it makes vanity insupportable, and displays every little spot of the soul in its utmost deformity.—*Addison.*

Wine and youth are fire upon fire.—
Fielding.

Look not thou upon the wine when it is red, when it giveth his color in the cup, when it moveth itself aright; at the last it biteth like a serpent, and stingeth like an adder.—*Bible.*

There is a devil in every berry of the grape.
Koran.

That is a treacherous friend against whom you must always be on your guard. Such a friend is wine.—*Bovee.*

Wine that maketh glad the heart of man.—
Bible.

As the most fermenting in a vessel works up to the top whatever it has in the bottom, so wine, in those who have drunk beyond the measure, vents the most inward secrets.—*Montaigne.*

The gentle apple's winy juice.—*Cowley.*

The first glass for myself, the second for my friends, the third for good-humor, and the fourth for mine enemies.—*Sir W. Temple.*

Polished brass is the mirror of the body and wine of the mind.—*Æschylus.*

What stores of sentiment in that butt of raciest Sherry! What a fund of pensive thought! What suggestions for delicious remembrance! What "aids to reflection" in that Hock of a century old! What sparkling fancies, whirling and foaming, from a stout body of thought in that full and ripe champagne! What mild and serene philosophy in that Burgundy, ready to shed "its sunset glow" on society and nature!—*Talfourd.*

Wine invents nothing; it only tattles —
Schiller.

Wine is a turncoat; first a friend, and then an enemy.—*Fielding.*

O thou invisible spirit of wine, if thou hast no name to be known by, let us call thee — Devil!
Shakespeare.

Poor wine at the table of a rich host is an insult without an apology. Urbanity ushers in water that needs no apology, and gives a zest to the worst vintage.—*Zimmermann.*

Some men are like musical glasses; to produce their finest tones you must keep them wet.
Coleridge.

The conscious water saw its God, and blushed.—*Crashaw.*

Old Port wine is more ancient to the imagination than any other, though in fact it may have been known fewer years; as a broken Gothic arch has more of the spirit of antiquity about it than a Grecian temple. Port reminds us of the obscure Middle Ages; but Hock, like the classical mythology, is always young.—
Talfourd.

From wine what sudden friendship springs!
Gay.

Wine is a noble, generous liquor, and we should be humbly thankful for it; but, as I remember, water was made before it.—.
John Eliot.

Wine maketh the hand quivering, the eye watery, the night unquiet, lewd dreams, a stinking breath in the morning, and an utter forgetfulness of all things.—*Pliny.*

Wine has drowned more than the sea.
Publius Syrus.

From a time-changed bottle, tenderly drawn from a crypt, protected by huge primeval cobwebs, you may taste antiquity and feel the olden time on your palate!—*Talfourd.*

This is the great fault in wine; it first trips up the feet, it is a cunning wrestler.—*Plautus.*

WINTER.

Winter is the night of vegetation. The plants sleep through it, as reptiles and insects do.—*Bovee.*

Stern winter loves a dirge-like sound.—
Wordsworth.

The frost performs its secret ministry unhelped by any wind.—*Coleridge.*

O wind, if winter comes, can spring be far behind? —*Shelley.*

WISDOM.

Wisdom is like electricity. There is no permanently wise man, but men capable of wisdom, who, being put into certain company, or other favorable conditions, become wise for a short time, as glasses rubbed acquire electric power for a while.—*Emerson.*

Wisdom is to the mind what health is to the body.—*Rochefoucauld.*

There is not a man in the world but desires to be, or to be thought to be, a wise man; and yet, if he considered how little he contributes himself thereunto, he might wonder to find himself in any tolerable degree of understanding.—*Clarendon.*

He who learns the rules of wisdom, without conforming to them in his life, is like a man who labored in his fields, but did not sow.—
Saadi.

The god, O men, seems to me to be really wise; and by his oracle to mean this, that the wisdom of this world is foolishness, and of none effect.—*Plato.*

True wisdom is to know what is best worth knowing, and to do what is best worth doing.—
Humphreys.

Wisdom is a fox who, after long hunting, will at last cost you the pains to dig out; it is a cheese, which, by how much the richer, has the thicker, the homelier, and the coarser coat; and whereof to a judicious palate, the maggots are best. It is a sack posset, wherein the deeper you go, you'll find it the sweeter. Wisdom is a hen, whose cackling we must value and consider, because it is attended with an egg. But lastly, it is a nut, which, unless you choose with judgment, may cost you a tooth, and pay you with nothing but a worm.—*Swift.*

A man must become wise at his own expense.—*Montaigne.*

Much of this world's wisdom is still acquired by necromancy, — by consulting the oracular dead.—*Hare.*

A man's wisdom is his best friend; folly, his worst enemy.—*Sir W. Temple.*

Wisdom may be the ultimate arbiter, but is seldom the immediate agent in human affairs.
Sir J. Stephen.

The fool is willing to pay for anything but wisdom. No man buys that of which he supposes himself to have an abundance already.—
Simms.

No man is the wiser for his learning; it may administer matter to work in, or objects to work upon; but wit and wisdom are born with a man.—*Selden.*

Wisdom adorns riches, and shadows poverty.
Socrates.

Wisdom and understanding are synonymous words; they consist of two propositions, which are not distinct in sense, but one and the same thing variously expressed.—*Tillotson.*

Wisdom sits with children round her knees.
Wordsworth.

Lessons of wisdom have never such power over us as when they are wrought into the heart through the groundwork of a story which engages the passions; is it that we are like iron, and must first be heated before we can be wrought upon? or is the heart so in love with deceit that where a true report will not reach it, we must cheat it with a fable, in order to come at the truth? —*Sterne.*

The wisdom of one generation will be folly in the next.—*Priestley.*

Every moment instructs, and every object; for wisdom is infused into every form. It has been poured into us as blood; it convulsed us as pain; it slid into us as pleasure, it enveloped us in dull, melancholy days, or in days of cheerful labor: we did not guess its essence until after long time.—*Emerson.*

To one it is the mighty heavenly goddess; to another it is an excellent cow that furnishes him with milk.—*Schiller.*

Knowledge is proud that he has learned so much; wisdom is humble that he knows no more.—*Cowper.*

A wise man doubteth; a fool rageth, and is confident; the novice saith, I am sure that it is so; the better learned answers, Peradventure it may be so, but I prithee inquire. Some men are drunk with fancy, and mad with opinion. It is a little learning, and but a little, which makes men conclude hastily. Experience and humility teach modesty and fear.—
Jeremy Taylor.

The sea does not contain all the pearls, the earth does not enclose all the treasures, and the flint-stone does not enclose all the diamonds, since the head of man encloses wisdom.—*Saadi.*

The clouds may drop down titles and estates, wealth may seek us; but wisdom must be sought.—*Young.*

Wisdom and goodness to the vile seem vile.
Shakespeare.

True wisdom is a thing very extraordinary. Happy are they that have it: and next to them, not those many that think they have it, but those few that are sensible of their own defects and imperfections, and know that they have it not.—*Tillotson.*

We ought not to judge of men's merits by their qualifications, but by the use they make of them.—*Charron.*

Our wisdom is no less at fortune's mercy than our wealth.—*Rochefoucauld.*

The price of wisdom is above rubies.—*Bible.*

There is this difference between happiness and wisdom: he that thinks himself the happiest man is really so; but he that thinks himself the wisest is generally the greatest fool.
Bacon.

Wisdom no more consists in science than happiness in wealth.—*De Boufflers.*

If wisdom were conferred with this proviso, that I must keep it to myself and not communicate it to others, I would have none of it.—
Seneca.

Man's chief wisdom consists in being sensible of his follies.—*Rochefoucauld.*

Wisdom for a man's self is, in many branches thereof, a depraved thing; it is the wisdom of rats, that will be sure to leave a house somewhat before it fall; it is the wisdom of the fox, that thrusts out the badger who digged and made room for him; it is the wisdom of crocodiles, that shed tears when they would devour.
Bacon.

Her ways are ways of pleasantness, and all her paths are peace.—*Bible.*

Look about, my son, and see how little wisdom it takes to govern the world.—
Oxenstiern.

Whoever is wise is apt to suspect and be diffident of himself, and upon that account is willing to "hearken unto counsel"; whereas the foolish man, being in proportion to his folly full of himself, and swallowed up in conceit, will seldom take any counsel but his own, and for that very reason, because it is his own.
Balguy.

Wisdom is the olive that springeth from the heart, bloometh on the tongue, and beareth fruit in the actions.—*Grymestone.*

The wisest man is generally he who thinks himself the least so.—*Boileau.*

If thou kiss Wisdom's cheek and make her thine, she will breathe into thy lips divinity, and thou, like Phœbus, shalt speak oracle.—*Decker.*

He is wise that is wise to himself.—
Euripides.

Man falls much more short of perfect wisdom, and even of his own ideas of perfect wisdom, than animals do of man; yet the latter difference is so considerable, that nothing but a comparison with the former can make it appear of little moment.—*Hume.*

Give tribute, but not oblation, to human wisdom.—*Sir P. Sidney.*

Were wisdom to be sold, she would give no price; every man is satisfied with the share he has from nature.—*Henry Home.*

The temple of wisdom is seated on a rock, above the rage of the fighting elements, and inaccessible to all the malice of man. The rolling thunder breaks below; and those more terrible instruments of human fury reach not to so sublime a height.—*Hume.*

Be wisely worldly, but not worldly wise.—
Quarles.

Call him wise whose actions, words, and steps are all a clear because to a clear why.—
Lavater.

The glory and increase of wisdom stands in exercising it.—*Sir P. Sidney.*

When a man seems to be wise, it is merely that his follies are proportionate to his age and fortune.—*Rochefoucauld.*

The weak have remedies, the wise have joys; superior wisdom is superior bliss.—
Young.

The first point of wisdom is to discern that which is false; the second, to know that which is true.—*Lactantius.*

Wisdom is ofttimes nearer when we stoop than when we soar.—*Wordsworth.*

The sublimity of wisdom is to do those things living which are to be desired when dying.—*Jeremy Taylor.*

Wisdom is the talent of buying virtuous pleasures at the cheapest rate.—*Fielding.*

Wisdom does not show itself so much in precept as in life,—in a firmness of mind and a mastery of appetite. It teaches us to do, as well as to talk; and to make our words and actions all of a color.—*Seneca.*

As whole caravans may light their lamps from one candle without exhausting it, so myriads of tribes may gain wisdom from the great *B*ook without impoverishing it.—
Rabbi Ben-Azai.

*F*ull oft we see cold wisdom waiting on superfluous folly.—*Shakespeare.*

The wise man is but a clever infant spelling letters from a hierographical prophetic book, the lexicon of which lies in eternity.—*Carlyle.*

The only medicine for suffering, crime, and all the other woes of mankind is wisdom. Teach a man to read and write, and you have put into his hands the great keys of the wisdom box. But it is quite another matter whether he ever opens the box or not. And he is as likely to poison as to cure himself, if, without guidance, he swallows the first drug that comes to hand.—*Professor Huxley.*

In seeking wisdom, thou art wise; in imagining that thou hast attained it, thou art a fool.—*Rabbi Ben-Azai.*

I would have you wise unto that which is good, and simple concerning evil.—*Bible.*

The end of wisdom is consultation and deliberation.—*Demosthenes.*

WISHES.

I respect the man who knows distinctly what he wishes. The greater part of all the mischief in the world arises from the fact that men do not sufficiently understand their own aims. They have undertaken to build a tower, and spend no more labor on the foundation than would be necessary to erect a hut.—*Goethe.*

We are poor, indeed, when we have no half-wishes left us. The heart and the imagination close the shutters the instant they are gone.—
Landor.

Like our shadows, our wishes lengthen as our sun declines.—*Young.*

I could write down twenty cases, wherein I wished God had done otherwise than he did; but which I now see, had I had my own will, would have led to extensive mischief. The life of a *C*hristian is a life of paradoxes.—*Cecil.*

WIT.

Wit, to be well defined, must be defined by wit itself; then it will be worth listening to.—
Zimmermann.

When we seek after wit, we discover only foolishness.—*Montesquieu.*

Some wits, like oracles, deal in ambiguities, but not with equal success; for though ambiguities are the first excellence of an impostor, they are the last of a wit.—*Young.*

Self-wit is so ardent and active that it will break a sword to pieces to make a stool to sit on.—*Cecil.*

Let your wit rather serve you for a buckler to defend yourself, by a handsome reply, than the sword to wound others, though with ever so facetious reproach; remembering that a word cuts deeper than a sharper weapon, and the wound it makes is longer curing.—
F. Osborn.

To place wit before good sense is to place the superfluous before the necessary.—
M. de Montlosier.

Wit does not take the place of knowledge.—
Vauvenargues.

Wit is not levelled so much at the muscles as at the heart; and the latter will sometimes smile when there is not a single wrinkle on the cheek.—*Lord Lyttelton.*

Wit will never make a man rich, but there are places where riches will always make a wit.
Johnson.

Wit gives to life one of its best flavors; common-sense leads to immediate action, and gives society its daily motion; large and comprehensive views, its annual rotation; ridicule chastises folly and imprudence, and keeps men in their proper sphere; subtlety seizes hold of the fine threads of truth; analogy darts away in the most sublime discoveries; feeling paints all the exquisite passions of man's soul, and rewards him by a thousand inward visitations for the sorrows that come from without.—
Sydney Smith.

There are some men who are witty when they are in a bad humor, and others only when they are sad.—*Joubert.*

There is many a man hath more hair than wit.—*Shakespeare.*

We find ourselves less witty in remembering what we have said than in dreaming of what we would have said.—*J. Petit, Senn.*

It is inconceivable how much wit it requires to avoid being ridiculous.—*Chamfort.*

Less judgment than wit is more sail than ballast. Yet it must be confessed that wit gives an edge to sense, and recommends it extremely.—*William Penn.*

Men are contented to be laughed at for their wit, but not for their folly.—*Swift.*

That which we call wit consists much in quickness and tricks, and is so full of lightness that it seldom goes with judgment and solidity; but when they do meet, it is commonly in an honest man.—*King James I.*

There are heads sometimes so little, that there is no room for wit, sometimes so long that there is no wit for so much room.—*Fuller.*

Wit is the god of moments, but genius is the god of ages.—*Bruyère.*

False wit is a fatiguing search after cunning traits, an affectation of saying in enigmas what others have already said naturally, to hang together ideas which are incompatible, to divide that which ought to be united, of seizing false relations.—*Voltaire.*

The character of false wit is that of appearing to depend only upon reason.
Vauvenargues.

There is no quality of the mind or of the body that so instantaneously and irresistibly captivates, as wit. An elegant writer has observed that wit may do very well for a mistress, but that he should prefer reason for a wife.—*Colton.*

It is often a sign of wit not to show it, and not to see that others want it.—*Madame Necker.*

Though wit be very useful, yet unless a wise man has the keeping of it, that knows when, where, and how to apply it, it is like wild-fire, that flies at rovers, runs hissing about, and blows up everything that comes in its way, without any respect or discrimination.—*Walter Scott.*

If satire charms, strike faults, but spare the man.—*Young.*

Wit should exalt an appetite, not provoke disgust. Wit, without wisdom, is salt without meat; and that is but a comfortless dish to set a hungry man down to.—*Bishop Horne.*

Wit is the refractory pupil of judgment.—*Shenstone.*

From Lucifer to Jerry Sneak there is not an aspect of evil, imperfection, and littleness which can elude the lights of humor or the lightning of wit.—*Whipple.*

Wit generally succeeds more from being happily addressed than from its native poignancy. A jest, calculated to spread at a gaming-table, may be received with perfect indifference should it happen to drop in a mackerel-boat.—*Goldsmith.*

Wit is the flower of the imagination; judgment is its fruit.—*Livy.*

Nature and society are so replete with startling contrasts that wit often consists in the mere statement and comparison of facts, as when Hume says that the ancient Muscovites wedded their wives with a whip instead of a ring.—*Whipple.*

Wit is an unruly engine, wildly striking sometimes a friend, sometimes the engineer.—*George Herbert.*

Genuine witticisms surprise those who say them as much as those who listen to them; they arise in us in spite of us, or, at least, without our participation,—like everything inspired.—*Joubert.*

Wit is a dangerous weapon, even to the possessor, if he knows not how to use it discreetly.—*Montaigne.*

Wit, like hunger, will be with great difficulty restrained from falling on vice and ignorance, where there is great plenty and variety of food.
Fielding.

The triumphs of wit should rather be compared to the inroads of the Parthians, splendid, but transient; a victory succeeded by surprise, and indebted more to the sharpness of the arrow than the strength of the arm, and to the rapidity of an evolution rather than the solidity of a phalanx.—*Colton.*

I cannot imagine why we should be at the expense to furnish wit for succeeding ages, when the former have made no sort of provision for ours.—*Swift.*

Don't put too fine a point to your wit, for fear it should get blunted.—*Cervantes.*

The essence of the ludicrous consists in surprise,—in unexpected terms of feeling and explosions of thought,—often bringing dissimilar things together with a shock; as when some wit called Boyle, the celebrated philosopher, the father of chemistry and brother of the Earl of Cork.—*Whipple.*

The most brilliant flashes of wit come from a clouded mind, as lightning leaps only from an obscure firmament.—*Bovee.*

Wit in women is a jewel, which, unlike all others, borrows lustre from its setting, rather than bestows it; since nothing is so easy as to fancy a very beautiful woman extremely witty.—*Colton.*

The best thing next to wit is a consciousness that it is not in us; without wit, a man might then know how to behave himself, so as not to appear to be a fool or a coxcomb.—*Bruyère.*

It is by vivacity and wit that man shines in company; but trite jokes and loud laughter reduce him to a buffoon.—*Chesterfield.*

There is just the same sort of difference between the flow of false wit and of true as between buffo music, like that of Mozart and Rossini, and the melancholy merriment of a fiddle-scraper in the street.—*Leigh Hunt.*

Antithesis may be the blossom of wit, but it will never arrive at maturity unless sound sense be the trunk, and truth the root.—*Colton.*

Wit is brushwood, judgment timber; the one gives the greatest flame, the other yields the durablest heat; and both meeting make the best fire.—*Sir Thomas Overbury.*

Wit, — the pupil of the soul's clear eye.—*Sir John Davies.*

Wit, bright, rapid, and blasting as the lightning, flashes, strikes, and vanishes, in an instant; humor, warm and all-embracing as the sunshine, bathes its object in a genial and abiding light.—*Whipple.*

I love a teeming wit as I love my nourishment.—*Ben Jonson.*

Many species of wit are quite mechanical; these are the favorites of witlings, whose fame in words scarce outlives the remembrance of their funeral ceremonies.—*Zimmermann.*

Wit and wisdom differ; wit is upon the sudden turn, wisdom is bringing about ends.—*Selden.*

Wit must be without effort. Wit is play, not work; a nimbleness of the fancy, not a laborious effort of the will; a license, a holiday, a carnival of thought and feeling, not a trifling with speech, a constraint upon language, a duress upon words.—*Bovee.*

It is having in some measure a sort of wit, to know how to use the wit of others.—*Stanislaus.*

Man could direct his ways by plain reason, and support his life by tasteless food; but God has given us wit and flavor and brightness and laughter and perfumes, to enliven the days of man's pilgrimage, and to "charm his pained steps over the burning marle."—*Sydney Smith.*

Wit should be wit, but never satire.—*Madame La Rochejaquelein.*

The essence of every species of wit is surprise; which, *vi termini*, must be sudden; and the sensations which wit has a tendency to excite are impaired or destroyed as often as they are mingled with much thought or passion.—*Sydney Smith.*

That is not wit which consists not with wisdom.—*South.*

Sharpness cuts slight things best; solid, nothing cuts through but weight and strength; the same in the use of intellectuals.—*Sir W. Temple.*

Wit is of the true Pierian spring, that can make anything of anything.—*Chapman.*

Perpetual aiming at wit is a very bad part of conversation. It is done to support a character: it generally fails; it is a sort of insult on the company, and a restraint upon the speaker.—*Swift.*

Truth, when witty, is the wittiest of all things.—*Hare.*

With the latitude of unbounded scurrility, it is easy enough to attain the character of a wit, especially when it is considered how wonderfully pleasant it is to the generality of the public to see the folly of their acquaintance exposed by a third person.—*Fielding.*

Sharp wits, like sharp knives, do often cut their owner's fingers.—*Arrowsmith.*

Superiority in wit is more frequently the cause of vanity than superiority of judgment; as the person that wears an ornamental sword, is ever more vain than he that wears a useful one.—*Shenstone.*

Wit is the rarest quality to be met with among people of education, and the most common among the uneducated.—*Hazlitt.*

Wit and humor belong to genius alone.—*Cervantes.*

I give you full credit for your elegant diction, well-turned periods, and Attic wit; but wit is oftentimes false, though it may appear brilliant; which is exactly the case of your whole performance.—*Junius.*

In cheerful souls there is no wit. Wit shows a disturbance of the equipoise.—*Novalis.*

Wit consists in assembling, and putting together with quickness, ideas in which can be found resemblance and congruity, by which to make up pleasant pictures and agreeable visions in the fancy.—*Locke.*

The wit of men compared to that of women is like rouge compared to the rose.—*Saint Foix.*

Locke says that wit and judgment rarely meet in the same person; because that their talents are directly opposite, — the first collecting together all ideas which are any way alike, and the latter employed in separating those which in any particular differ. Methinks there is more wit than judgment in this remark, for the same quickness which can form an assemblage is as nimble at distinguishing. The proverb is not applicable here, "Those who hide can find."—*Sterne.*

The impromptu reply is precisely the touchstone of the man of wit.—*Molière.*

It is no great advantage to possess a quick wit, if it is not correct; the perfection is not speed, but uniformity.—*Vauvenargues.*

It is with wits as with razors, which are never so apt to cut those they are employed upon as when they have lost their edge.—*Swift.*

Wit, like every other power, has its boundaries. Its success depends on the aptitude of others to receive impressions; and that as some bodies, indissoluble by heat, can set the furnace and crucible at defiance, there are minds upon which the rays of fancy may be pointed without effect, and which no fire of sentiment can agitate or exalt.—*Johnson.*

It is a certain rule that wit and passion are entirely incompatible. When the affections are moved, there is no place for the imagination.—*Hume.*

There are as many and innumerable degrees of wit, as there are cubits between this and heaven.—*Montaigne.*

I have seen many so prone to quip and gird, as they would rather lose their friend than their jest. And if perchance their boiling brain yield a quaint scoff, they will travail to be delivered of it, as a woman with child. These nimble fancies are but the froth of wit.—
Lord Burleigh.

Wit spares neither friend nor foe, says L'Estrange, for there is as much intemperance in wit as in wine.—*Colton.*

WOE.

As in a picture, which receives greater life by the darkness of shadows than by glittering colors, so the shape of loveliness is perceived more perfect in woe than in joyfulness.—
Sir P. Sidney.

One woe doth tread upon another's heel, so fast they follow.—*Shakespeare.*

So many great, illustrious spirits have conversed with woe, have in her school been taught, as are enough to consecrate distress, and make ambition even wish the frown beyond the smile of fortune.—*Thomson.*

WOMAN.

Next to God we are indebted to women, first for life itself, and then for making it worth having.—*Bovee.*

I have often had occasion to remark the fortitude with which women sustain the most overwhelming reverses of fortune. Those disasters which break down the spirit of a man and prostrate him in the dust seem to call forth all the energies of the softer sex, and give such intrepidity and elevation to their character, that at times it approaches to sublimity.—
Washington Irving.

The purer the golden vessel the more readily is it bent; the higher worth of women is sooner lost than that of men.—*Richter.*

Honor women! They strew celestial roses on the pathway of our terrestrial life.—*Boiste.*

Nature sent women into the world with this bridal dower of love, not, as men often think, that they altogether and entirely love them from the crown of their head to the sole of their feet, but for this reason, that they might be, what their destination is, mothers, and love children, to whom sacrifices must ever be offered, and from whom none are to be obtained.—*Richter.*

It is against womanhood to be forward in their own wishes.—*Sir P. Sidney.*

There is one in the world who feels for him who is sad a keener pang than he feels for himself; there is one to whom reflected joy is better than that which comes direct; there is one who rejoices in another's honor more than in any which is one's own; there is one on whom another's transcendent excellence sheds no beam but that of delight; there is one who hides another's infirmities more faithfully than one's own; there is one who loses all sense of self in the sentiment of kindness, tenderness, and devotion to another;—that one is woman.—*Washington Irving.*

Women commiserate the brave, and men the beautiful.—*Landor.*

They govern the world,—these sweet-lipped women,—because beauty is the index of a larger fact than wisdom.—*Holmes.*

Kindness in woman, not their beauteous looks, shall win my love.—*Shakespeare.*

If we were to form an image of dignity in a man we should give him wisdom and valor, as being essential to the character of manhood. In the like manner, if you describe a right woman in a laudable sense, she should have gentle softness, tender fear, and all those parts of life which distinguish her from the other sex; with some subordination to it, but such an inferiority that makes her still more lovely.—*Steele.*

They are the books, the arts, the academies, that show, contain, and nourish all the world.
Shakespeare.

Women that are the least bashful are not unfrequently the most modest; and we are never more deceived than when we would infer any laxity of principle from that freedom of demeanor which often arises from a total ignorance of vice.—*Colton.*

Woman is like the reed which bends to every breeze, but breaks not in the tempest.—
Whately.

Pleasure is to women what the sun is to the flower; if moderately enjoyed, it beautifies, it refreshes, and it improves; if immoderately, it withers, deteriorates, and destroys.—*Colton.*

Women, like princes, find few real friends.—
Lord Lyttelton.

Women are the poetry of the world, in the same sense as the stars are the poetry of heaven. Clear, light-giving, harmonious, they are the terrestrial planets that rule the destinies of mankind.—*Hargrave.*

O woman! in ordinary cases so mere a mortal, how, in the great and rare events of life, dost thou swell into the angel!—
Bulwer Lytton.

They are not easily kept in the path of duty by harshness; distrust, bolts, and iron grating do not produce virtue in women and girls. It is honor which must keep them to their duty, and not severity.—*Molière.*

Every woman is at heart a rake.—*Pope.*

How little do lovely women know what awful beings they are in the eyes of inexperienced youth! Young men brought up in the fashionable circles of our cities will smile at this. Accustomed to mingle incessantly in female society, and to have the romance of the heart deadened by a thousand frivolous flirtatious, women are nothing but women in their eyes; but to a susceptible youth like myself, brought up in the country, they are perfect divinities.—*Washington Irving.*

The Hand that hath made you fair hath made you good; the goodness that is cheap in beauty makes beauty brief in goodness; but grace, being the soul of it your complexion, should keep the body of it ever fair.—
Shakespeare.

Women are engaged to men by the favors they grant them; men are disengaged by the same favors.—*Bruyère.*

The world is the book of women. Whatever knowledge they may possess is more commonly acquired by observation than by reading.
Rousseau.

The modest virgin, the prudent wife, or the careful matron are much more serviceable in life than petticoated philosophers, blustering heroines, or virago queens. She who makes her husband and her children happy, who reclaims the one from vice, and trains up the other to virtue, is a much greater character than ladies described in romance, whose whole occupation is to murder mankind with shafts from their quiver or their eyes.—*Goldsmith.*

Woman, once made equal to man, becometh his superior.—*Socrates.*

Teach him to live unto God and unto thee; and he will discover that women, like the plants in woods, derive their softness and tenderness from the shade.—*Landor.*

It is a great mistake to suppose that a woman with no heart will be an easy creditor in the exchange of affection. There is not on earth a more merciless exacter of love from others than a thoroughly selfish woman; and the more unlovely she grows, the more jealously and scrupulously she exacts love to the uttermost farthing.—*Mrs. Stowe.*

The society of women is the element of good manners.—*Goethe.*

O, if the loving, closed heart of a good woman should open before a man, how much controlled tenderness, how many veiled sacrifices and dumb virtues, would he see reposing therein!—*Richter.*

The foundation of domestic happiness is faith in the virtue of woman.—*Landor.*

Honor to women! they twine and weave the roses of heaven into the life of man; it is they that unite us in the fascinating bonds of love; and, concealed in the modest veil of the graces, they cherish carefully the external fire of delicate feeling with holy hands.—*Schiller*

For silence and a chaste reserve is woman's genuine praise, and to remain quiet within the house.—*Euripides.*

A woman's noblest station is retreat.—
Lord Lyttelton.

Man is the creature of interest and ambition. His nature leads him forth into the struggle and bustle of the world. Love is but the embellishment of his early life, or a song piped in the intervals of his acts. But a woman's whole life is a history of the affections. The heart is her world; it is there her ambition strives for empire; it is there her avarice seeks for hidden treasures. She sends forth her sympathies on adventure, she embarks her whole soul in the traffic of affection; and, if shipwrecked, her case is hopeless, for it is a bankruptcy of the heart.—*Washington Irving.*

Woman's power is over the affections. A beautiful dominion is hers, but she risks its forfeiture when she seeks to extend it.—*Bovee.*

When women sue, they sue to be denied.—
Young.

The prevailing manners of an age depend, more than we are aware of, or are willing to allow, on the conduct of the women; this is one of the principal things on which the great machine of human society turns. Those who allow the influence which female graces have in contributing to polish the manners of men would do well to reflect how great an influence female morals must also have on their conduct.—*Blair.*

Women are a new race, recreated since the world received Christianity.—*Beecher.*

36

The brain women never interest us like the heart women; white roses please less than red.—*Holmes.*

She hath a natural wise sincerity, a simple truthfulness, and these have lent her a dignity as moveless as the centre.—*Lowell.*

Women will suggest a thousand excuses to themselves for the folly of those they like; besides, it requires a penetrating eye, in the generality of women, to discern a fool through the disguises of gayety and good breeding.—*Fielding.*

All a woman has to do in this world is contained within the duties of a daughter, a sister, a wife, and a mother.—*Steele.*

This I set down as a positive truth. A woman with fair opportunities, and without an absolute hump, may marry whom she likes. Only let us be thankful that the darlings are like the beasts of the field, and don't know their own power.—*Thackeray.*

A woman moved is like a fountain troubled, muddy, ill-seeming, thick, bereft of beauty.—*Shakespeare.*

The wisest woman you talk with is ignorant of something that you know, but an elegant woman never forgets her elegance.—*Holmes.*

O woman! woman! thou shouldest have few sins of thine own to answer for! Thou art the author of such a book of follies in a man that it would need the tears of all the angels to blot the record out.—*Bulwer Lytton.*

Nothing does so much honor to a woman as her patience, and nothing does her so little as the patience of her husband.—*Joubert.*

To a man who is uncorrupt and properly constituted, woman remains always something of a mystery and a romance. He never interprets her quite literally. She, on her part, is always striving to remain a poem, and is never weary of bringing out new editions of herself in novel bindings.—*James Parton.*

The woman that deliberates is lost.—*Addison.*

A woman too often reasons from her heart; hence two thirds of her mistakes and her troubles.—*Bulwer Lytton.*

A woman who has never been pretty has never been young.—*Madame Swetchine.*

An inconstant woman is one who is no longer in love; a false woman is one who is already in love with another person; a fickle woman is she who neither knows whom she loves nor whether she loves or not; and the indifferent woman, one who does not love at all.—*Bruyère.*

But what is woman? Only one of nature's agreeable blunders.—*Cowley.*

Woman is at best a contradiction still.—*Pope.*

How many women are born too finely organized in sense and soul for the highway they must walk with feet unshod! Life is adjusted to the wants of the stronger sex. There are plenty of torrents to be crossed in its journey; but their stepping-stones are measured by the stride of men, and not of women.—*Holmes.*

Women see through Claude Lorraines.—*Emerson.*

It is beauty, that doth oft make women proud; it is virtue, that doth make them most admired; it is modesty, that makes them seem divine.—*Shakespeare.*

Woman's honor is nice as ermine, will not bear a soil.—*Dryden.*

If thou wouldest please the ladies, thou must endeavor to make them pleased with themselves.—*Fuller.*

No amount of preaching, exhortation, sympathy, benevolence, will render the condition of our working-women what it should be so long as the kitchen and the needle are substantially their only resources.—*Horace Greeley.*

Women do act their part when they do make their ordered houses know them.—*Sheridan Knowles.*

I have often thought that the nature of women was inferior to that of men in general, but superior in particular.—*Lord Greville.*

Woman has this in common with angels, that suffering beings belong especially to her.—*Balzac.*

By her we first were taught the wheedling arts.—*Gay.*

It is wise, I suppose, that we should attach ourselves to things which are transient; else it seems to be a perilous trust when a man ties his hopes to so frail a thing as woman. They are so gentle, so affectionate, so true in sorrow, so untired and untiring; but the leaf withers not sooner, the tropic lights fade not more abruptly into darkness.—*Barry Cornwall.*

To feel, to love, to suffer, to devote herself will always be the text of the life of woman.—*Balzac.*

Most men like in women what is most opposite their own characters.—*Fielding.*

Women can less easily surmount their coquetry than their passions.—*Rochefoucauld.*

Make the doors upon a woman's wit, and it will out at the casement; shut that, and it will out at the key-hole; stop that, it will fly with the smoke out at the chimney.—*Shakespeare.*

She is not made to be the admiration of everybody, but the happiness of one.—*Burke.*

Win her and wear if you can. She is the most delightful of God's creatures, — Heaven's best gift, — man's joy and pride in prosperity, man's support and comforter in affliction.—
Shelley.

Who is it can read a woman?—*Shakespeare*

There is nothing by which I have, through life, more profited than by the just observations, the good opinion, and the sincere and gentle encouragement of amiable and sensible women.
. *Romilly.*

A woman's fitness comes by fits.—
Shakespeare.

Even the most refined and polished of men seldom conceal any of the sacrifices they make, or what it costs to make them. This is reserved for women, and is one of the many proofs they give of their superiority in all matters of affection and delicacy.—*Willmott.*

To the disgrace of men it is seen that there are women both more wise to judge what evil is expected, and more constant to bear it when it is happened.—*Sir P. Sidney.*

She certainly is no true woman for whom every man may not find it in his heart to have a certain gracious and holy and honorable love; she is not a woman who returns no love, and asks no protection.—*Bartol.*

Most of their faults women owe to us, whilst we are indebted to them for most of our better qualities.—*Charles Lemesle.*

Women are never stronger than when they arm themselves with their weakness.—
Madame du Deffand.

Her passions are made of nothing but the finest part of pure love. We cannot call her winds and waters, sighs and tears; they are greater storms and tempests than almanacs can report. This cannot be cunning in her. If it be, she makes a shower of rain as well as Jove.
Shakespeare.

The pearl is the image of purity, but woman is purer than the pearl.—*Bourdon.*

A man gets into another world, strange to him as the orb of Sirius, if he can transport himself into the centre of a woman's heart, and see the life there, so wholly unlike our own. Things of moment to us, to it so trivial; things trifling to us, to it so vast!—*Bulwer Lytton.*

To describe women, the pen should be dipped in the humid colors of the rainbow, and the paper dried with the dust gathered from the wings of a butterfly.—*Diderot.*

The errors of women spring almost always from her faith in the good or her confidence in the true.—*Balzac.*

A good woman is the loveliest flower that blooms under heaven; and we look with love and wonder upon its silent grace, its pure fragrance, its delicate bloom of beauty. Sweet and beautiful! the fairest and the most spotless! is it not pity to see them bowed down or devoured by grief or death inexorable, wasting in disease, pining with long pain, or cut off by sudden fate in their prime? We may deserve grief, but why should these be unhappy? — except that we know that Heaven chastens those whom it loves best; being pleased, by repeated trials, to make these pure spirits more pure.—*Thackeray.*

A woman may be ugly, ill-shaped, wicked, ignorant, silly, and stupid, but hardly ever ridiculous.—*Louis Desnoyers.*

Let men say what they will; according to the experience I have learned, I require in married women the economical virtue above all other virtues.—*Fuller.*

A virtuous mind in a fair body is indeed a fine picture in a good light, and therefore it is no wonder that it makes the beautiful sex all over charms.—*Addison.*

Woman, last at the cross, and earliest at the grave.—*E. S. Barrett.*

Sing of the nature of women, and then the song shall be surely full of variety, old crotchets, and most sweet closes. It shall be humorous, grave, fantastic, amorous, melancholy, sprightly, one in all and all in one.—*John Marston.*

The empire of woman is an empire of softness, of address, of complacency. Her commands are caresses, her menaces are tears.—
Rousseau.

Nature has given women two painful but heavenly gifts, which distinguish them, and often raise them above human nature, — compassion and enthusiasm. By compassion, they devote themselves; by enthusiasm they exalt themselves.—*Lamartine.*

Woman is a flower that breathes its perfume in the shade only.—*Lamennais.*

Some are so uncharitable as to think all women bad, and others are so credulous as to believe they are all good. All will grant her corporeal frame more wonderful and more beautiful than man's. And can we think God would put a worse soul into a better body?—*Feltham.*

Women have more heart and more imagination than men.—*Lamartine.*

Women's thoughts are ever turned upon appearing amiable to the other sex; they talk and move and smile with a design upon us; every feature of their faces, every part of their dress, is filled with snares and allurements. There would be no such animals as prudes or coquettes in the world, were there not such an animal as man.—*Addison.*

I have always said it, — nature meant to make woman as its masterpiece.—*Lessing.*

O woman! lovely woman! Nature made thee to temper man; we had been brutes without you. Angels are painted fair, to look like you; there is in you all that we believe of beaven, — amazing brightness, purity, and truth, eternal joy, and everlasting love.—*Otway.*

Women are extreme in all points. They are better or worse than men.—*Bruyère.*

Women will find their place, and it will neither be that in which they have been held, nor that to which some of them aspire. Nature's old Salic law will not be repealed, and no change of dynasty will be effected.— *Professor Huxley.*

Women are as roses; whose fair flower, being once displayed, doth fall that very hour. *Shakespeare.*

Most females will forgive a liberty, rather than a slight; and if any woman were to hang a man for stealing her picture, although it were set in gold, it would be a new case in law; but if he carried off the setting, and left the portrait, I would not answer for his safety.—*Colton.*

Women have more strength in their looks than we have in our laws, and more power by their tears, than we have by our arguments.— *Saville.*

Women govern us; let us render them perfeet: the more they are enlightened, so much the more shall we be. On the cultivation of the mind of women depends the wisdom of men. It is by women that nature writes on the hearts of men.—*Sheridan.*

A woman's heart is just like a lithographer's stone, — what is once written upon it cannot be rubbed out.—*Thackeray.*

The majority of women have no principles of their own; they are guided by the heart, and depend, for their own conduct, upon that of the men they love.—*Bruyère.*

Women never truly command till they have given their promise to obey; and they are never in more danger of being made slaves than when the men are at their feet.—*Farquhar.*

Women do not transgress the bounds of decorum so often as men; but when they do, they go greater lengths.—*Colton.*

All the reasonings of men are not worth one sentiment of women.—*Voltaire.*

A handsome woman who has the qualities of an agreeable man is the most delicious society in the world. She unites the merit of both sexes. Caprice is in women the antidote to beauty.—*Bruyère.*

WONDER.

In wonder all philosophy began, in wonder it ends, and admiration fills up the interspace; but the first wonder is the offspring of ignorance, the last is the parent of adoration.— *Coleridge.*

It was through the feeling of wonder that men now and at first began to philosophize.— *Aristotle.*

Numbers of people are always standing with open mouths in a silly wonderment, enveloped in an obscurity, to which they bow with respect. They admire nature only because they believe it to be a kind of magic, which nobody understands; and we may be sure that a thing loses its value in their eyes as soon as it can be explained.—*Fontenelle.*

All wonder is the effect of novelty upon ignorance.—*Johnson.*

The man who cannot wonder, who does not habitually wonder and worship, were he president of innumerable royal societies, is but a pair of spectacles behind which there is no eye. *Carlyle.*

Wonder is involuntary praise.— *Young.*

Wonder, connected with a principle of rational curiosity, is the source of all knowledge and discovery, and it is a principle even of piety; but wonder which ends in wonder, and is satisfied with wonder, is the quality of an idiot.—*Horsley.*

A wonder lasts but nine days, and then the puppy's eyes are open.—*Fielding.*

WOODS.

In the woods, too, a man casts off his years, as the snake his slough, and, at what period soever of life, is always a child. In the woods is perpetual youth. Within these plantations of God a decorum and sanctity reign, a perennial festival is dressed, and the guest sees not how he should tire of them in a thousand years. In the woods we return to reason and faith.— *Emerson.*

The nunneries of silent nooks, the murmured longing of the wood.—*Lowell.*

WORDS.

Men suppose that their reason has command over their words; still, it happens that words, in return, exercise authority on reason.—*Bacon.*

Cast forth thy act, thy word, into the ever-living, ever-working universe. It is a seed-grain that cannot die; unnoticed to-day, it will be found flourishing as a banyan grove, perhaps, alas, as a hemlock forest, after a thousand years.—*Carlyle.*

Few words to fair faith.—*Shakespeare.*

Words ought to carry their sense and signification, and they ought never to be obscure. Word is a habit which we give imagination, in order to clothe thought, and make it better known by the color by which it is painted; but it is a cloak which ought not to conceal it; it is a head-dress, not a mask; it ought to set it off, and serve as an adornment, and not hide it from the eyes and envelope it in a disguise.—*La Pretieuse.*

Words may be said to be the echoes of the heart.—*Hosea Ballou.*

What you keep by you you may change and mend; but words once spoken can never be recalled.—*Roscommon.*

Learn the value of a man's words and expressions, and you know him. Each man has a measure of his own for everything; this he offers you inadvertently in his words. He who has a superlative for everything wants a measure for the great or small.—*Lavater.*

Nothing is rarer than the use of a word in its exact meaning.—*Whipple.*

I hate anything that occupies more space than it is worth. I hate to see a load of band-boxes go along the street, and I hate to see a parcel of big words without anything in them.—*Hazlitt.*

A soft answer turneth away wrath; but grievous words stir up anger.—*Bible.*

I conceive that words are like money, not the worse for being common, but that it is the stamp of custom alone that gives them circulation or value. I am fastidious in this respect, and would almost as soon coin the currency of the realm as counterfeit the King's English.—*Hazlitt.*

There is a relation to be observed between the words and the mouth which pronounces them.—*Bruyère.*

In their intercourse with the world people should not take words as so much genuine coin of standard metal, but merely as counters that people play with.—*Douglas Jerrold.*

Such as thy words are, such will thy affections be esteemed; and such will thy deeds as thy affections, and such thy life as thy deeds.—*Socrates.*

It is with a word as with an arrow: the arrow once loosed does not return to the bow; nor a word to the lips.—*Abd-el-Kader.*

Words before blows.—*Shakespeare.*

"Words, words, words!" says Hamlet, disparagingly. But God preserve us from the destructive power of words! There are words which can separate hearts sooner than sharp swords. There are words whose sting can remain through a whole life!—*Mary Howitt.*

If you do not wish a man to do a thing, you had better get him to talk about it; for the more men talk, the more likely they are to do nothing else.—*Carlyle.*

Volatility of words is carelessness in actions; words are the wings of actions.—*Lavater.*

Words should be employed as the means, not as the end; language is the instrument, conviction is the work.—*Sir J. Reynolds.*

A word fitly spoken is like apples of gold in pictures of silver.—*Bible.*

Syllables govern the world.—*Coke.*

A winged word hath struck ineradicably in a million hearts, and envenomed every hour throughout their hard pulsation. On a winged word hath hung the destiny of nations. On a winged word hath human wisdom been willing to cast the immortal soul, and to leave it dependent for all its future happiness.—*Landor.*

It is a kind of good deed to say well; and yet words are no deeds.—*Shakespeare.*

Words are things; and a small drop of ink, falling like dew upon a thought, produces that which makes thousands, perhaps millions, think.—*Byron.*

Words are the soul's ambassadors.—*Howell.*

I am not so lost in lexicography as to forget that words are the daughters of earth, and that things are the sons of heaven.—*Johnson.*

Cold words that hide the envious thought.—*Willis.*

Words become luminous when the finger of the poet touches them with his phosphorus.—*Joubert.*

Words have a separate effect on the mind abstracted from their signification and their imitative power; they are more or less agreeable to the ear by the fulness.—*Henry Home.*

There are words which are worth as much as the best actions, for they contain the germ of them all.—*Madame Swetchine.*

How forcible are right words!—*Bible.*

Words, " those fickle daughters of the earth," are the creation of a being that is finite, and when applied to explain that which is infinite, they fail; for that which is made surpasses not the maker; nor can that which is immeasurable by our thoughts be measured by our tongues.
Colton.

Words are women, deeds are men.—
George Herbert.

For words are wise men's counters, they do but reckon by them; but they are the money of fools.—*Thomas Hobbes.*

Words are but lackeys to sense, and will dance attendance without wages or compulsion.
Swift.

A man may be concise and utter much at the same time, especially in writing; for in conversation a great talker and a sayer of nothing do generally signify but one and the same thing.—*Coste.*

A word spoken in season, at the right moment, is the mother of ages.—*Carlyle.*

A word spoken in due season, how good it is!—*Bible.*

Moral life is no creation of moral phrases. The words that are truly vital powers for good or evil are only those which, as Pindar says, " the tongue draws up from the deep heart."—
Whipple.

Words are but pictures of our thoughts.—
Dryden.

The words of a language resemble the strings of a musical instrument, which yield only uninteresting tones when struck by an ordinary hand, but from which a skilful performer draws forth the soul of harmony, awakening and captivating the passions of the mind.—
W. B. Clulow.

Words are as they are taken, and things are as they are used. There are even cursed blessings.—*Bishop Hall.*

A blemish may be taken out of a diamond by careful polishing, but if your words have the least blemish there is no way to efface it.—
Confucius.

Words are the wings of actions.—*Lavater.*

The word that once escapes the tongue cannot be recalled; the arrow cannot be detained which has once sped from the bow.—*Metastasio.*

He that hath knowledge spareth his words.
Bible.

They have been at a great feast of languages, and stolen the scraps. They have lived long in the alms-basket of words!
Shakespeare.

The words in prose ought to express the intended meaning; if they attract attention to themselves, it is a fault; in the very best styles, as Southey's, you read page after page without noticing the medium.—*Coleridge.*

Pleasant words are as an honeycomb, sweet to the soul, and health to the bones.—*Bible.*

It is as easy to draw back a stone thrown with force from the hand, as to recall a word once spoken.—*Menander.*

The world is satisfied with words; few care to dive beneath the surface.—*Pascal.*

Mankind in general are so little in the habit of looking steadily at their own meaning, or of weighing the words by which they express it, that the writer who is careful to do both, will sometimes mislead his readers through the very excellence which qualifies him to be their instructor.—*Coleridge.*

We should be as careful of our words as of our actions, and as far from speaking ill as from doing ill.—*Cicero.*

Words have not their import from the natural power of particular combinations of characters, or from the real efficacy of certain sounds, but from the consent of those who use them, and arbitrarily annex certain ideas to them, which might have been signified with equal propriety by any other.—*Oliver Cromwell.*

Words are the voice of the heart.—
Confucius.

High air-castles are cunningly built of words, the words well bedded also in good logic mortar; wherein, however, no knowledge will come to lodge. "The whole is greater than the part," — how exceedingly true! "Nature abhors a vacuum,"—how exceedingly false and calumnious!—*Carlyle.*

Rich in fit epithets, blest in the lovely marriage of pure words.—*Anthony Brewer.*

WORK.

I protest against the unfair distribution of the world's work, which can only be well done when every man and woman is fitted to work, left free to choose the field in which to work, and condemned by public opinion if they refuse to work.—*Celia Burleigh.*

Get work! Be sure it is better than what you work to get.—*Mrs. E. B. Browning.*

It is not work that kills men; it is worry. Work is healthy; you can hardly put more upon a man than he can bear. Worry is rust upon the blade. It is not the revolution that destroys the machinery, but the friction.—
Beecher.

The modern majesty consists in work. What a man can do is his greatest ornament, and he always consults his dignity by doing it.
Carlyle.

We enjoy ourselves only in our work, our doing; and our best doing is our best enjoyment.—*Jacobi.*

Work is of a religious nature, — work is of a brave nature, which it is the aim of all religion to be. "All work of man is as the swimmer's." A waste ocean threatens to devour him; if he front it not bravely, it will keep its word. By incessant wise defiance of it, lusty rebuke and buffet of it, behold how it loyally supports him, — bears him as its conqueror along! "It is so," says Goethe, "with all things that man undertakes in this world."
Carlyle.

Work is the only universal currency which God accepts. A nation's welfare will depend on its ability to master the world; that, on power of work; that, on its power of thought.—
Theodore Parker.

Work, according to my feeling, is as much of a necessity to man as eating and sleeping. Even those who do nothing which to a sensible man can be called work, still imagine that they are doing something. The world possesses not a man who is an idler in his own eyes.—
Wilhelm von Humboldt.

All men, if they work not as in a great taskmaster's eye, will work wrong, work unhappily for themselves and you.—*Carlyle.*

God is a worker. He has thickly strewn infinity with grandeur. God is love; he yet shall wipe away Creation's tears, and all the worlds shall summer in his smile. Why work I not? the veriest mote that sports its one-day life within the sunny beam has its stern duties.
Alexander Smith.

The true epic of our times is, not arms and the man, but tools and the man, — an infinitely wider kind of epic.—*Carlyle.*

WORLD.

Whoever has seen the masked at a ball dance amicably together, and take hold of hands without knowing each other, leaving the next moment to meet no more, can form an idea of the world.—*Vauvenargues.*

The world is deceitful; her end is doubtful, her conclusion is horrible, her judge is terrible, and her judgment is intolerable.—*Quarles.*

The only fence against the world is a thorough knowledge of it.—*Locke.*

He that knows a little of the world will admire it enough to fall down and worship it; but he that knows it most will most despise it.
Colton.

The judgment of the world stands upon matter of fortune.—*Sir P. Sidney.*

Delusive ideas are the motives of the greatest part of mankind, and a heated imagination the power by which their actions are incited; the world in the eye of a philosopher may be said to be a large madhouse.—*Mackenzie.*

We may despise the world, but we cannot do without it.—*Baron Wessenberg.*

God, we are told, looked upon the world after he had created it and pronounced it good; but ascetic pietists, in their wisdom, cast their eyes over it, and substantially pronounce it a dead failure, a miserable production, a poor concern.—*Bovee.*

What is this world? Thy school, O misery! Our only lesson is to learn to suffer.—*Young.*

He who imagines he can do without the world deceives himself much; but he who fancies the world cannot do without him is still more mistaken.—*Rochefoucauld.*

The world is an excellent judge in general, but a very bad one in particular.—
Lord Greville.

The world is a country which nobody ever yet knew by description; one must travel through it one's self to be acquainted with it. The scholar, who in the dust of his closet talks or writes of the world, knows no more of it than that orator did of war, who judiciously endeavored to instruct Hannibal in it.—
Chesterfield.

Trust not the world, for it never payeth that it promiseth.—*St. Augustine.*

A good man and a wise man may at times be angry with the world, at times grieved for it; but be sure no man was ever discontented with the world who did his duty in it.—*Southey.*

The world is all title-page without contents.
Young.

Once kick the world, and the world and you live together at a reasonable good understanding.—*Swift.*

The great see the world at one end by flattery, the little at the other end by neglect; the meanness which both discover is the same; but how different, alas! are the mediums through which it is seen!—*Lord Greville.*

The world is his who can see through its pretension. What deafness, what stone-blind custom, what overgrown error you behold, is there only by sufferance, by your sufferance. See it to be a lie, and you have already dealt it its mortal blow.—*Emerson.*

For the fashion of this world passeth away.
Bible.

We did not make the world, but we may mend it, and must live in it. We shall find that it abounds with fools who are too dull to be employed, and knaves who are too sharp. The compound character is most common, and is that with which we shall have the most to do.
Colton.

The world is but a large prison, out of which some are daily selected for execution.—
Sir Walter Raleigh.

We may be pretty certain that persons whom all the world treats ill deserve entirely the treatment they get. The world is a looking-glass, and gives back to every man the reflection of his own face. Frown at it, and it will in turn look sourly upon you ; laugh at it and with it, and it is a jolly, kind companion ; and so let all young persons take their choice.—
Thackeray.

Count the world not an inn, but an hospital ; and a place not to live in, but to die in.—
Colton.

I am not at all uneasy that I came into, and have so far passed my course in this world ; because I have so lived in it that I have reason to believe I have been of some use to it ; and when the close comes, I shall quit life as I would an inn, and not as a real home. For nature appears to me to have ordained this station here for us, as a place of sojournment, a transitory abode only, and not as a fixed settlement or permanent habitation.—*Cicero.*

I hold the world but as the world, Gratiano ; a stage, where every man must play a part, and mine a sad one.—*Shakespeare.*

We are to avoid the danger, rather than to oppose it. This is a great doctrine of Scripture. An active force against the world is not so much inculcated as a retreating, declining spirit. Keep thyself unspotted from the world.
Cecil.

WORLDLINESS.
It has been well said that there is a sin of other-worldliness no less than a sin of worldliness, and Christendom has had a large measure of the former sin as well as of the latter. People have been taught so much about preparing for beaven that they have sometimes become very indifferent workers on earth, and in anticipating the joys of the future world have overlooked the infinite possibilities for good in the world that now is.—*W. J. Potter.*

As the love of the heavens makes us heavenly, the love of virtue virtuous, so doth the love of the world make one become worldly.—
Sir P. Sidney.

It is not the "flesh," nor the "eye" nor "life," which are forbidden, but it is the lust of the flesh, and the lust of the eye, and the pride of life. It is not this earth, nor the men who inhabit it, nor the sphere of our legitimate activity, that we may not love ; but the way in which the love is given, which constitutes worldliness.—*F. W. Robertson.*

The beauty of all worldly things is but as a fair picture drawn upon the ice, that melts away with it. The fashion of this world passeth away.—*Jeremiah Burroughs.* .

WORSHIP.
It is for the sake of man, not of God, that worship and prayers are required ;. not that God may be rendered more glorious, but that man may be made better, — that he may be confirmed in a proper sense of his dependent state, and acquire those pious and virtuous dispositions in which his highest improvement consists.—*Blair.*

The dullest observer must be sensible of the order and serenity prevalent in those households where the occasional exercise of a beautiful form of worship in the morning gives, as it were, the key-note to every temper for the day, and attunes every spirit to harmony.—
Washington Irving.

If my soul is not engaged in my worship it is even as though I worshipped not.—
Confucius.

In Sophocles, Jocasta prays to the Lycian Apollo, and says "that she came to his temple because it was the nearest." This was but a sorry compliment to his godship. It is the same, however, that people generally pay to religion, who abide by the doctrines and faith they have been bred up in, merely to save themselves the trouble of seeking farther.—*Sterne.*

The act of divine worship is the inestimable privilege of man, the only created being who bows in humility and adoration.—
Hosea Ballou.

The act of worship is among all creation indigenous and peculiar to man. As he alone stands erect and raises his front without effort toward heaven, so he bends the knee in reasoning adoration, neither cowering down with his head in the dust, nor grovelling on his belly like other creatures, in abject fear ; but, wanton, unstable, and extravagant even in his noblest aspirations, this viceroy of earth has been ever prone to waver in his allegiance, eager to amplify his worship of the one true God into a thousand false religions, more or less beautiful, poetical, and absurd.—*G. J. W. Melville.*

WORTH.

Worth begets in base minds envy ; in great souls, emulation.—*Fielding.*

True worth is as inevitably discovered by the facial expression, as its opposite is sure to be clearly represented there. The human face is nature's tablet, the truth is certainly written thereon.—*Lavater.*

Worth makes the man, and want of it the fellow.—*Pope.*

Real worth requires no interpreter; its every-day deeds form its blazonry.—*Chamfort.*

WRITING.

If you would write to any purpose, you must be perfectly free from within. Give yourself the natural rein ; think on no pattern, no patron, no paper, no press, no public; think on nothing, but follow your impulses. Give yourself as you are, — what you are, and how you see it. Every man sees with his own eyes, or does not see at all. This is incontrovertibly true. *Bring* out what you have. If you have nothing, be an honest beggar, rather than a respectable thief.—*Emerson.*

Look, then, into thine heart and write! — *Longfellow.*

The difference betwixt a witty writer and a writer of taste is chiefly this : the former is negligent what ideas he introduces, so he joins them surprisingly ; the latter is principally careful what images he introduces, and studies simplicity rather than surprise in his manner of introduction.—*Shenstone.*

Every great and original writer, in proportion as he is great or original, must himself create the taste by which he is to be relished.— *Wordsworth.*

Devise, wit! write,   ! for I am for whole volumes in folio.—*Shakespeare.*

If you would learn to write, it is in the street you must learn it. Both for the vehicle and for the aims of fine arts, you must frequent the public square. The people, and not the college, is the writer's home. A scholar is a candle which the love and desire of all men will light.—*Emerson.*

Whatever may be our natural talents, the art of writing is not acquired all at once.— *Rousseau.*

Fine writing, according to Mr. Addison, consists of sentiments which are natural, without being obvious. There cannot be a juster and more concise definition of fine writing.—*Hume.*

A successful author is equally in danger of the diminution of his fame, whether he continnes or ceases to write.—*Johnson.*

An incurable itch of scribbling clings to many, and grows inveterate in their distempered breast.—*Juvenal.*

Writing grows a habit, like a woman's gallantry ; there are women who have had no intrigue, but few who have had but one only ; so there are millions of men who have never written a book, but few who have written only one. *Byron.*

Writings may be compared to wine. Sense is the strength, but wit the flavor.—*Sterne.*

The small reckoning I have seen made, especially in their lifetime, of excellent wits bids me advise that, if you find any delight in writing, to go on ; but, in hope to please or satisfy others, I would not black the end of a quill. Long experience has taught me that builders always, and writers for the most part, spend their money and time in the purchase of reproof and censure from envious contemporaries or self-conceited posterity.—*F. Osborn.*

The mind conceives with pain, but it brings forth with delight.—*Joubert.*

A man who writes well writes not as others write, but as he himself writes ; it is often in speaking badly that he speaks well. *Montesquieu.*

WRONG.

Wrong is wrong ; no fallacy can hide it, no subterfuge cover it so shrewdly but that the All-Seeing One will discover and punish it.— *Rivarol.*

There is no God dare wrong a worm.— *Emerson.*

To revenge a wrong is easy, usual, and natural, and, as the world thinks, savors of nobleness of mind ; but religion teaches the contrary, and tells us it is better to neglect than to requite it.—*J. Beaumont.*

He who commits a wrong will himself inevitably see the writing on the wall, though the world may not count him guilty.—*Tupper.*

Wrong is but falsehood put in practice.— *Landor.*

There are few people who are more often in the wrong than those who cannot endure to be so.—*Rochefoucauld.*

We make ourselves more injuries than are offered to us ; they many times pass for wrongs in our own thoughts, that were never meant so by the heart of him that speaketh. The apprehension of wrong hurts more than the sharpest part of the wrong done.—*Feltham.*

It is vain to trust in wrong ; as much of evil, so much of loss, is the formula of human history.—*Theodore Parker.*

Y.

YEARNINGS.

Ere yet we yearn for what is out of our reach, we are still in the cradle. When wearied out with our yearnings, desire again falls asleep, — we are on the death-bed.—*Bulwer Lytton.*

YOUTH.

Youth, enthusiasm, and tenderness are like the days of spring. Instead of complaining, O my heart, of their brief duration, try to enjoy them.—*Rückert.*

As I approve of a youth that has something of the old man in him, so I am no less pleased with an old man that has something of the youth. He that follows this rule may be old in body, but can never be so in mind.—*Cicero.*

Youth is beautiful. Its friendship is precious. The intercourse with it is a purifying release from the worn and stained harness of older life.—*Willis.*

Youthful rashness skips like a hare over the meshes of good counsel.—*Shakespeare.*

He who cares only for himself in youth will be a very niggard in manhood, and a wretched miser in old age.—*J. Hawes.*

Youth is the gay and pleasant spring of life, when joy is stirring in the dancing blood, and Nature calls us with a thousand songs to share her general feast.—*Ridgway.*

Life's enchanted cup but sparkles near the brim ! —*Byron.*

In the morning of our days, when the senses are unworn and tender, when the whole man is awake in every part, and the gloss of novelty fresh upon all the objects that surround us, how lively at that time are our sensations, but how false and inaccurate the judgments we form of things ! —*Burke.*

Youth is a continual intoxication ; it is the fever of reason.—*Rochefoucauld.*

Every period of life has its peculiar temptations and dangers. But youth is the time when we are the most likely to be ensnared. This, pre-eminently, is the forming, fixing period, the spring season of disposition and habit ; and it is during this season, more than any other, that the character assumes its permanent shape and color, and the young are wont to take their course for time and for eternity.—*J. Hawes.*

Keep true to the dreams of thy youth.—
Schiller.

Treasures are not for youth ; at twenty years one does not know how to be rich, or to be loved.—*Madame de Girardin.*

Unless a tree has borne blossoms in spring, you will vainly look for fruit on it in autumn.
Hare.

In the species with which we are best acquainted, namely, our own, I am far, even as an observer of human life, from thinking that youth is its happiest season, much less the only happy one.—*Paley.*

My salad days, when I was green in judgment.—*Shakespeare.*

I love the acquaintance of young people ; because, in the first place, I do not like to think myself growing old. In the next place, young acquaintances must last longest, if they do last ; and then, sir, young men have more virtue than old men ; they have more generous sentiments in every respect.—*Johnson.*

Remember now thy Creator in the days of thy youth.—*Bible.*

Young people, at their entrance upon the world, should be either bashful or giddy ; a composed self-sufficiency generally turns to impertinence.—*Rochefoucauld.*

Youth should be a savings-bank.—
Madame Swetchine.

The best rules to form a young man are, to talk little, to hear much, to reflect alone upon what has passed in company, to distrust one's own opinions, and value others' that deserve it.
Sir W. Temple.

Youth, when thought is speech and speech is truth.—*Walter Scott.*

At almost every step in life we meet with young men from whom we anticipate wonderful things, but of whom, after careful inquiry, we never hear another word. Like certain chintzes, calicoes, and ginghams, they show finely on their first newness, but cannot stand the sun and rain, and assume a very sober aspect after washing-day.—*Hawthorne.*

The golden age never leaves the world ; it exists still, and shall exist, till love, health, poetry, are no more, — but only for the young.
Bulwer Lytton.

It is a truth but too well known, that rashness attends youth, as prudence does old age.—
Cicero.

It is not easy to surround life with any circumstances in which youth will not be delightful ; and I am afraid that, whether married or unmarried, we shall find the vesture of terrestrial existence more heavy and cumbrous the longer it is worn.—*Steele.*

Youth is not the age of pleasure; we then expect too much, and we are therefore exposed to daily disappointments and mortifications. When we are a little older, and have brought down our wishes to our experience, then we become calm and begin to enjoy ourselves.—
Lord Liverpool.

Like virgin parchment, capable of any inscription.—*Massinger.*

O the joy of young ideas painted on the mind, in the warm, glowing colors fancy spreads on objects not yet known, when all is new and all is lovely!—*Hannah More.*

The fairest flower in the garden of creation is a young mind, offering and unfolding itself to the influence of Divine Wisdom, as the heliotrope turns its sweet blossoms to the sun.—
Sir J. E. Smith.

He felt, with indescribable strength and sweetness, that the lovely time of youth is our Italy and Greece, full of gods, temples, and bliss; and which, alas! so often Goths and Vandals stalk through, and strip with their talons.
Richter.

Youth will never live to age, without they keep themselves in breath with exercise, and in heart with joyfulness. Too much thinking doth consume the spirits; and oft it falls out, that while one thinks too much of doing, he leaves to do the effect of his thinking.—
Sir P. Sidney.

Girls we love for what they are; young men for what they promise to be.— *Goethe.*

For the short-lived bloom and contracted span of brief and wretched life is fast fleeting away! While we are drinking and calling for garlands, ointments, and women, old age steals swiftly on with noiseless step.—*Juvenal.*

Youth no less becomes the light and careless livery that it wears, than settled age his sables and his weeds, importing health and graveness.
Shakespeare.

It is with youth as with plants; from the first fruits they bear we learn what may be expected in future.—*Demophilus.*

Let youth cherish the happiest of earthly boons while yet it is at its command; for there cometh a day to all " when neither the voice of the lute nor the birds " shall bring back the sweet slumbers that fall on their young eyes as unbidden as the dews.—*Bulwer Lytton.*

Youth holds no society with grief.—
Euripides.

The camomile, the more it is trodden, the faster it grows; yet youth, the more it is wasted, the sooner it wears.—*Shakespeare.*

Youth is like Adam's early walk in the Garden. In the beautiful words of Burke, " The senses are unworn and tender, and the whole frame is awake in every part." The dew lies upon the grass. No smoke of busy life has darkened or stained the morning of our day. The pure light shines about us. If any little mist happen to rise, the sunbeam of hope catches and paints it.—*Willmott.*

The morning of life is like the dawn of day, full of purity, of imagery, and harmony.—
Chateaubriand.

Which of us that is thirty years old has not had his Pompeii? Deep under ashes lies the life of youth, — the careless sport, the pleasure and passion, the darling joy.—*Thackeray.*

Hard are life's early steps; and but that youth is buoyant, confident, and strong in hope, men would behold its threshold and despair.
Miss L. E. Landon.

He wears the rose of youth upon him.—
Shakespeare

Death is dreadful, but in the first springtide of youth, to be snatched forcibly from the banquet to which the individual has but just sat down is peculiarly appalling.—
Walter Scott.

Youth ever thinks that good whose goodness or evil he sees not.—*Sir P. Sidney.*

Youth is not rich in time; it may be, poor; part with it, as with money, sparing; pay no moment but in purchase of its worth; and what its worth ask death-beds, they can tell.—
Young.

Young men are apt to think themselves wise enough, as drunken men are to think themselves sober enough.—*Chesterfield.*

Youth is ever confiding; and we can almost forgive its disinclination to follow the counsels of age, for the sake of the generous disdain with which it rejects suspicion.— *W. H. Harrison.*

The destiny of any nation at any given time depends on the opinions of its young men under five-and-twenty.— *Goethe.*

How charming the young would be to talk to, with their freshness, fearlessness, and truthfulness, if only — to take a metaphor from painting — they would make more use of grays and other neutral tints, instead of dabbing on so ruthlessly the strongest positives in color!—
Helps.

There is no funeral so sad to follow as the funeral of our own youth, which we have been pampering with fond desires, ambitious hopes, and all the bright berries that hang in poisonous clusters over the path of life.—*Landor.*

The self-conceit of the young is the great source of those dangers to which they are exposed.—*Blair.*

Youth is ever apt to judge in haste, and lose the medium in the wild extreme.— *Aaron Hill.*

Use thy youth so that thou mayest have comfort to remember it when it hath forsaken thee, and not sigh and grieve at the account thereof. Use it as the springtime which soon departeth, and wherein thou oughtest to plant and sow all provisions for a long and happy life. *Sir Walter Raleigh.*

The youth of the soul is everlasting and eternity is youth.—*Richter.*

Deal mildly with his youth; for young hot colts, being raged, do rage the more.— *Shakespeare.*

Among all the accomplishments of youth there is none preferable to a decent and agreeable behavior among men, a modest freedom of speech, a soft and elegant manner of address, a graceful and lovely deportment, a cheerful gravity and good-humor, with a mind appearing ever serene under the ruffling accidents of human life.—*Watts.*

Self-flattered, unexperienced, high in hope, when young, with sanguine cheer and streamers gay, we cut our cable, launch into the world, and fondly dream each wind and star our friend.—*Young.*

Z.

ZEAL.

Zeal is very blind, or badly regulated, when it encroaches upon the rights of others.— *Pasquier Quesnel.*

The good which bloodshed could not gain your peaceful zeal shall find.—*Whittier.*

If we had the whole history of zeal, from the days of Cain to our times, we should see it filled with so many scenes of slaughter and bloodshed as would make a wise man very careful not to suffer himself to be actuated by such a principle, when it regards matters of opinion and speculation.—*Addison.*

The zeal which begins with hypocrisy must conclude in treachery; at first it deceives, at last it betrays.—*Bacon.*

The worst of madmen is a saint run mad.— *Pope.*

Whether zeal or moderation be the point we aim at, let us keep fire out of the one, and frost out of the other.—*Addison.*

Zealous men are ever displaying to you the strength of their belief, while judicious men are showing you the grounds of it.—*Shenstone.*

True zeal is an *ignis lambeus,* a soft and gentle flame, that will not scorch one's hand.— *Cudworth.*

On such a theme it were impious to be calm; passion is reason, transport, temper, here!—*Young.*

Whoever regards the early history of Christianity will perceive how necessary to its triumph was that fierce spirit of zeal, which, fearing no danger, accepting no compromise, inspired its champions and sustained its martyrs.—*Bulwer Lytton.*

Old zeal is only to be cozened by young hypocrisy.—*Farquhar.*

Zeal without knowledge is like expedition to a man in the dark.—*Newton.*

Zeal for the public good is the characteristic of a man of honor and a gentleman, and must take the place of pleasures, profits, and all other private gratifications. Whoever wants this motive is an open enemy or an inglorious neuter to mankind, in proportion to the misapplied advantages with which nature and fortune have blessed him.—*Steele.*

Zeal and duty are not slow, but on occasion's forelock watchful wait.—*Milton.*

Thou knowest that in the ardor of pursuit men soon forget the all from which they started. *Schiller.*

It is a zealot's faith that blasts the shrines of the false god, but builds no temple to the true.—*Sydney Dobell.*

We do that in our zeal our calmer moments are afraid to answer.—*Walter Scott.*

There is a holy mistaken zeal in politics as well as religion. By persuading others, we convince ourselves.—*Junius.*

There is no zeal blinder than that which is inspired with a love of justice against offenders. *Fielding.*

Never let your zeal outrun your charity. The former is but human, the latter is divine.— *Hosea Ballou.*

There is a boldness, a spirit of daring, in religious reformers, not to be measured by the general rules which control men's purposes and actions.—*Daniel Webster.*

Perfectly truthful men of very vivid imagination and great force of sentiment often feel so warmly, and express themselves so strongly, as to give to what they say and write a disagreeable air of exaggeration, and almost of falsehood.—*J. F. Boyes.*

Zeal is fit for wise men, but flourishes chiefly among fools.—*Tillotson.*

A just cause and a zealous defender make an imperious resolution cut off the tediousness of cautious discussions.—*Sir P. Sidney.*

Through zeal knowledge is gotten, through lack of zeal knowledge is lost; let a man who knows this double path of gain and loss thus place himself that knowledge may grow.—
Buddha.

Some things will not bear much zeal; and the more earnest we are about them, the less we recommend ourselves to the approbation of sober and considerate men.—*Tillotson.*

It is a coal from God's altar must kindle our fire; and without fire, true fire, no acceptable sacrifice.—*William Penn.*

It is admirably remarked, by a most excellent writer, that zeal can no more hurry a man to act in direct opposition to itself, than a rapid stream can carry a boat against its own current.
Fielding.

Zeal ever follows an appearance of truth, and the assured are too apt to be warm; but it is their weak side in argument; zeal being better shown against sin than persons, or their mistakes.—*William Penn.*

The eloquent man is he who is no eloquent speaker, but who is inwardly drunk with a certain belief.—*Emerson.*

Let us take heed we do not sometimes call that zeal for God and his gospel which is nothing else but our own tempestuous and stormy passion. True zeal is a sweet, heavenly, and gentle flame, which maketh us active for God, but always within the sphere of love. It never calls for fire from heaven to consume those that differ a little from us in their apprehensions. It is like that kind of lightning, which philosophers speak of, that melts the sword within, but singeth not the scabbard; it strives to save the soul, but hurteth not the body.—*Cudworth.*

Zeal without humility is like a ship without a rudder, liable to be stranded at any moment.
Feltham.

Any zeal is proper for religion but the zeal of the sword and the zeal of anger; this is the bitterness of zeal, and it is a certain temptation to every man against his duty.—
Jeremy Taylor.

To be furious in religion is to be irreligiously religious.—*William Penn.*

Zeal for uniformity attests the latent distrusts, not the firm convictions, of the zealot. In proportion to the strength of our self-reliance, is our indifference to the multiplication of suffrages in favor of our own judgment.—
Sir J. Stephen.

He that does a base thing in zeal for his friend burns the golden thread that ties their hearts together.—*Jeremy Taylor.*

INDEX OF AUTHORS.

THE END.